McGRAW-HILL SERIES IN POLITICAL SCIENCE

Joseph P. Harris, CONSULTING EDITOR

THE AMERICAN FEDERAL GOVERNMENT

McGRAW-HILL SERIES IN POLITICAL SCIENCE

Joseph P. Harris, CONSULTING EDITOR

BONE: *American Politics and the Party System*

FERGUSON AND McHENRY: *The American Federal Government*

FERGUSON AND McHENRY: *The American System of Government*

FERGUSON AND McHENRY: *Elements of American Government*

REED: *Municipal Management*

STRAUSZ-HUPÉ AND POSSONY: *International Relations*

WILSON: *The American Political Mind*

THE AMERICAN FEDERAL GOVERNMENT

by John H. Ferguson

PROFESSOR OF POLITICAL SCIENCE
THE PENNSYLVANIA STATE COLLEGE

and Dean E. McHenry

ASSOCIATE PROFESSOR OF POLITICAL SCIENCE
UNIVERSITY OF CALIFORNIA, LOS ANGELES

SECOND EDITION

McGRAW-HILL BOOK COMPANY, INC.

New York Toronto London

1950

THE AMERICAN FEDERAL GOVERNMENT

PREFACE

To a world ravished by war, pestilence, hunger, and disillusionment, the institutions of a nation as secure and prosperous as the United States are certain to be the objects of envy and emulation by less fortunate peoples. An introspective American, examining the causes of the political stability and high standard of living he enjoys, will concede that these blessings flow more from favorable circumstances than from inherent national superiority. Without the great natural resources of North America our poverty might have retarded the growth of democratic political institutions. Our physical separation from Europe and Asia provided us with an important margin of security that helped make possible a civil rather than a military government.

On the other hand, man has played a large part in molding political institutions that suit our circumstances. Despite its many faults, American government has maintained a delicate balance between order and freedom. The Constitution has proved to be a remarkably adaptable instrument, changing both by formal amendment and by reinterpretation to meet altered conditions and problems. The United States has pioneered and made distinctive contributions to the art of government through its written constitution, federal system, protection of civil liberties, and judicial review.

Mature college students, for whom this book is intended, should be prepared to examine the shortcomings as well as the virtues of American government. Accordingly, not only do we refuse to gloss over faults, but we conceive it to be one of our tasks to expose and document them. None of these faults disturbs us more than civic inertia, disregard of public affairs, and even contempt for public officials. We believe that freedom and responsibility are bracketed together, and that the former cannot long endure without accepting the latter.

In preparing the second edition we have been impressed with the large number of important changes that have occurred in American government since this book first appeared in 1947. The congressional reorganization has gone into effect and can be subjected to preliminary appraisal. An historic controversy has raged over civil rights. The Taft-Hartley law has drastically changed the labor scene. There has been much ferment in the fields of social insurance, health, education, housing, agriculture, utilities, and public ownership. The Hoover Commission has completed and published the most comprehensive study ever conducted of the executive branch of the federal government, and many of its recommendations have already been adopted.

The United Nations is approaching its fifth birthday, and we now see that collective security is far from achieved. The "cold war" moves rapidly from phase to phase, and external military and economic aid programs require description and evaluation. Separate armed services have moved through federation to unification. These and other significant developments require many additions and revisions of the first edition in order to bring it up to date.

We have continued the pattern of organization used in the first edition. The initial section deals with historical background, general principles and other essentials. The second part includes a discussion of Congress, the presidency, the courts, and federal powers. A third group of chapters is concerned with the administrative organization and functions of the Federal government.

For those who wish a book embracing all levels of American government —national, state, and local—we suggest *The American System of Government*, the second edition of which will be published simultaneously with this volume. *The American System of Government* contains all of the chapters herein plus an additional part comprising chapters on state and local governments.

To meet the demand for a briefer coverage of the whole compass of American government, the authors have prepared a new book entitled *Elements of American Government*. The scope of the *Elements* book is similar to that of the *American System*, but the former is considerably more compact and has been made simpler both through elimination of complicated materials and substitution of less advanced terminology.

In all these volumes the authors have striven for maximum clarity and simplicity of presentation. As a further aid, the publisher and authors have prepared a series of ten silent filmstrips to accompany these textbooks. In the books themselves numerous charts, summaries, maps, and other illustrations have been included and a list of visual materials appears as an appendix. As in the previous edition, four basic documents are included in the appendixes. The authors have also tried to sift the important from the mass of minutiae and thereby bring into focus major facts and problems of public policy. Many controversial subjects are introduced, but in doing so an attempt has been made to present fairly various points of view and to introduce readers to additional sources. The lists of references at the ends of chapters have been screened and brought up to date with sufficient attention given to bibliographical detail to facilitate library work.

Colleagues and librarians of The Pennsylvania State College and the University of California, Los Angeles, have aided us with criticisms, suggestions, and bibliography. Dr. Max Kampleman, on leave from Bennington College, has given invaluable assistance in bringing organizational charts up to date. We are especially indebted to Professors Richard W. Van Wagenen of Duke University, Spencer D. Albright of the University of Richmond, Elton Atwater of American University, and Guy Fox of Michigan State College, who kindly gave us the benefit of extended comments on the first edition.

John H. Ferguson
Dean E. McHenry

State College, Pa.
Los Angeles, Calif.
April, 1950

TEXT-FILMS

The following is a list of the McGraw-Hill Text-Films, all 35mm silent filmstrips, available for use with this book. A brief description of each of these is given at the end of the chapter or chapters with which it is correlated.

The Constitution—Principles and Methods of Change
The Federal System—Part I
The Federal System—Part II
Political Parties and Elections
Congress: Organization and Procedures
The President: Office and Powers
Federal Courts and Law Enforcement
Public Administration and Civil Service
Federal Finance
Foreign Relations

TEXT-FILMS

The following is a list of the McGraw-Hill Text-Films correlated [illegible] available for use with this book. A brief description of each of these is given at [illegible] chapter or chapters with which it is correlated.

The Constitution: Its Structure and Methods of [illegible]
The Federal System: Part I
The Federal System: Part II
Political Parties and Elections
Congress: Organization and Procedures
The Presidency: Powers and Duties
Federal Courts and Law Enforcement
Public Administration and Civil Service
Federal Finance
Foreign Relations

CONTENTS

Appendixes

Chapter 1

GOVERNMENT AND MODERN SOCIETY

I believe, first, that the technological future is far less dreadful and frightening than many of us have been led to believe, and that the hopeful aspects of modern applied science outweigh by a heavy margin its threat to our civilization. I believe, second, that the democratic process is itself an asset with which, if we can find the enthusiasm and the skill to use it and the faith to make it strong, we can build a world in which all men can live in prosperity and peace.

Vannevar Bush, *Modern Arms and Free Men.*[1]

America has failed again and again in her effort to create a free society; yet the thing that impresses me most about America today is her will to return to that lost fight. . . . We may never stop calling ourselves a democracy; the Romans, after all, called themselves a free Republic under Nero. But the time may be at hand when we must either create the reality or lose our chance to create it.

Herbert Agar, *Pursuit of Happiness; the Story of American Democracy.*[2]

The present population of the world is about two billion. These people live on six continents and on islands of the seven seas. Virtually all of them are subject to some sort of political control. Political institutions vary widely, their nature and form being determined by such factors as geography, climate, history and tradition, observation, and experimentation. Examples of these influences are numerous. Geographic separation from the continent of Europe permitted in Britain the development of civil government and liberties that were not possible in less secure European countries. Likewise the American physical endowment shaped our institutions and practices, the frontier inducing the adoption of home rule and proclivity for experimentation. As for the factor of climate, there is a good deal of evidence that man is more vigorous in temperate zones and that inhabitants of such areas achieve the greatest economic and political advancement.[3] Political forms also are evolved and passed along to later generations; for example, the kingship in many lands is so firmly connected with the national tradition that it could not easily be abandoned, even though it long since has lost governmental power. Nations also develop political institutions through observation and experimentation; the British

[1] (New York, Simon and Schuster, 1949.)

[2] (Boston: Houghton Mifflin, 1938), pp. 356–357.

[3] For the physiological basis of this contention, see Clarence A. Mills, *Climate Makes the Man* (New York: Harper, 1942).

parliamentary system has been emulated in two-thirds of the existing national states; American federalism has been copied lock and stock, but not always barrel, by several countries.

Origin of the Modern State.—No man can say with certainty precisely how the modern state came into being. Many of the theories of state origin are well grounded in anthropological and historical fact; others are based upon rationalizations, superstitions, and fictional legends.

The *instinctive* theory was expounded by Aristotle in his *Politics*. It was based upon the premise that "man is by nature a political animal." Human impulses, such as sex, gregariousness, hunger, and the like, created a demand common to men which led to the establishment of political organization and a willingness to abide by laws.

The *force* theory was expounded by many political philosophers. In general, this school of thought claims that the state grew out of the triumph of those interests and individuals who possessed superior strength, and that the state is the embodiment of that force which it is justified in using to enforce and accomplish its will.

According to the *divine-right* theory, the state is a creation of supernatural forces, and men, unable to govern themselves, turned to some leader divinely appointed or inspired to rule. Even in recent times emperors and kings have claimed to be the chosen instruments of heaven for the governing of their subjects.

The *contract* theory, which greatly influenced the American founding fathers through the writings of Hobbes, Locke, and Rousseau, held that men emerged from the state of nature by entering into a contract to submit to a common external authority. Some difference of opinion occurs among proponents of this view on whether man in the state of nature was perfect or wicked and whether the contract once made could be dissolved.

Popularized largely through the writings of Karl Marx and his disciples, the *economic* theory claims that men are motivated chiefly by economic necessity. Some men came to possess more of the world's goods than others, and political authority was established by those who had, in order to safeguard their possessions and further exploit those who had not. Proponents of this theory argue that the modern state continues this tradition by providing a vehicle for exploitation by the capitalist class.

The more fruitful approach is to avoid seeking a single explanation of the origin of the state, and to examine the gradual development of political institutions from such records of early times as are available. The basic group of primitive man was the family or kinship group. The family group grew in size, and clans and tribes were formed. Tribes were united by commerce, conquest, and alliance, and the early kingdoms made their appearance. Then the city-state emerged as the major political unit of the Mediterranean world. After a period dominated by the Roman Empire, Europe entered the feudal era, in which political authority was fragmented into many pieces. Feudalism ended gradually with the merger of principalities and city-states into larger and larger kingdoms, thus launching the modern national state system.

In the process of this development, covering thirty or more centuries, all the theories of state origin mentioned above played some part. Instinct certainly drew the family group together and caused its expansion as the necessity for protection grew. Force operated at nearly all stages, causing consolidation of smaller units into bigger ones through the imposition of the will of the stronger upon the weaker. By claiming divine sponsorship or birth, priests and kings have extended their sway and gathered new subjects. While it is unlikely that savages gathered in a forest clearing and resolved to form a government, conferences and constituent assemblies and constitutional conventions have led to the formation of political institutions among men. Although the economic theory is not acceptable as the primary explanation of the origin of the state, economic motives have unquestionably been important in the development of government.

POLITICAL UNITS OF THE WORLD

National States.—Out of the welter of the Second World War, it now appears that about seventy national states will emerge. A state may be defined as "a permanent association of people, politically organized upon a definite territory and habitually obeying the same autonomous government."[1] Thus, for a state to exist, the following elements must be present: (1) population, (2) territory that is more or less permanent, (3) political organization or government, (4) sovereignty, and (5) unity sufficient to bind the community together for sustained collective action.

The state may have a large or small *population.* China has over 450,000,000 people, whereas Iceland has only 134,000. Yet both are national states, with membership in the United Nations and diplomatic representation abroad. Population of a state may be divided into citizens, aliens, stateless, wards, and (now, happily, almost obsolete) slaves.

Whether a state exists does not depend upon the amount of *territory* to which it claims title. Luxembourg, with 999 square miles, is a member of the family of nations along with the Union of Soviet Socialist Republics, which has nearly 8,500,000 square miles within its territorial limits.

The *political organization* of a state may take any form, but it must be powerful and stable enough to command the obedience of the people and to fulfill the international obligations of the state.

[1] Amos S. Hershey, *The Essentials of International Public Law and Organization* (New York: Macmillan, rev. ed., 1929), p. 158.

Major Political Units of the World

(Status as of Jan. 1, 1950)

National States (By Population)*

UN US	China	UN US	Burma	UN US AS	Bolivia
UN US CN	India	UN US	Czechoslovakia	UN US AS	Guatemala
UN US	Russia (USSR)	UN US	Afghanistan	UN US	Yemen
UN AS	United States	UN US CN	Canada	UN US AS	Ecuador
(Occ.)	Japan	UN US CN	U. of So. Africa	UN US AS	Haiti
(Occ.)	Germany	UN US AS	Colombia	US	Hungary
US	Indonesia (USI)	UN US	Netherlands	UN US	Norway
UN US CN	Pakistan	UN US	Belgium	UN US	Syria
UN US CN	United Kingdom	US	Portugal	US	Eire (Ireland)
UN US AS	Brazil	UN US CN	Australia	UN US AS	Uruguay
US	Italy	UN US	Greece	UN US AS	Dominican Rep.
UN US	France	US	Bulgaria	UN US AS	Salvador
US	Spain	UN US AS	Peru	UN US	Israel
US	Korea	US CN	Ceylon	UN US CN	New Zealand
UN US	Poland	US	Austria	UN US	Liberia
UN US AS	Mexico	UN US	Sweden	UN US AS	Honduras
UN US	Philippines	UN US	Saudi Arabia	UN US AS	Paraguay
UN US	Turkey	UN US AS	Chile	UN US AS	Nicaragua
UN US	Egypt	UN US AS	Cuba	UN US	Lebanon
UN US	Thailand (Siam)		Nepal		Albania
UN US	Iran (Persia)	UN US	Iraq	UN US AS	Costa Rica
UN US AS	Argentina	US	Switzerland	UN US AS	Panama
US	Rumania	UN US AS	Venezuela	US	Transjordan
UN US	Ethiopia	UN US	Denmark	UN US	Luxembourg
UN US	Yugoslavia	US	Finland	UN US	Iceland

*UN = member United Nations
US = recognized by United States
CN = member (British) Commonwealth of Nations
AS = member Organization of American States

United Nations Trust Territories (By Trustee)

Australia:
- New Guinea

Belgium:
- Ruanda-Urundi

France:
- Cameroons
- Togoland

New Zealand:
- Western Samoa

United Kingdom:
- Tanganyika
- Cameroons
- Togoland

United States:
- Caroline Islands
- Marianas
- Marshall Islands

Australia, New Zealand, and United Kingdom:
- Nauru

Italy:
- Somaliland

United Nations:
- Libya

Major Colonies and Protectorates (By Controlling Power)

Belgium:
- Belgian Congo

France:
- French Indo-China
- French West Africa
- Algeria
- Morocco
- Madagascar
- French Equatorial Africa
- Tunis

Netherlands:
- Indies

United Kingdom:
- Nigeria
- Anglo-Egyptian Sudan
- Uganda
- Gold Coast
- Kenya
- Malaya
- Nyasaland
- Sierra Leone
- No. Rhodesia
- So. Rhodesia
- Jamaica
- Basutoland
- Aden
- Somaliland
- Trinidad

United States:
- Puerto Rico

The most provocative of these elements is *sovereignty*. It means simply supreme temporal power, and it must exist before a community can be treated as a state. Where it shall rest and by whom it shall be exercised are among the most controversial of all subjects. It may repose in an emperor or monarch, as in the days of Caesar or Henry VIII. Or it may be held by a church, feudal lords, the people, a parliament, the proletarian class, or the state itself conceived as an ideal person, as in Fascist Italy. Where it is located, there is the situs of power.

Of all these elements, *unity* is the most basic. Its absence, total or partial, explains many historical phenomena. Lack of a full measure of unity was one of several difficulties encountered in molding thirteen American colonies into an effective single nation. It helps to explain why peoples of India, China, and parts of Africa have been slow about developing over-all political institutions. It also accounts for many of the difficulties encountered by those who would create a united states of Europe or a world federation or world government. Before these heroic goals can be achieved, a consciousness of identity and unity with other states must exist.

States decide among themselves whether a given unit possesses the attributes of statehood. While unanimity is unnecessary, "recognition" by the more powerful states usually is indispensable. Recognition is followed by exchange of diplomats and negotiation of treaties. Thenceforth the newcomer is considered an international personality with all the rights, privileges, and immunities of international law. Since the First World War, the admission of a state to a general international organization (League of Nations or United Nations) has been considered a signal for general recognition of national statehood.

Dominions.—A dominion is a territory having autonomy in the conduct of its internal and external affairs, but maintaining a degree of affiliation with a mother country. The idea of dominion status grew out of British experience in granting larger and larger powers of self-government to Canada and other former colonies. Today the British dominions—Canada, Australia, New Zealand, Union of South Africa, India, Pakistan, and Ceylon—are independent national states that have chosen, for a variety of reasons, to remain associated with the United Kingdom and with each other through the Commonwealth of Nations.[1]

Protectorates.—A protectorate is a territory with a measure of autonomy but having by treaty made itself dependent upon a foreign state for assistance, such as financial, commercial, or military. Tunisia and Morocco

[1] Professor F. R. Scott correctly argues, in "The End of Dominion Status," *Canadian Bar Review*, vol. 23 (December, 1945), pp. 724–749, that dominion status has evolved into complete national independence and therefore the term is now obsolete. The standard work on dominion status is Kenneth C. Wheare, *The Statute of Westminster and Dominion Status* (New York: Oxford, 3d ed., 1947).

are French protectorates in North Africa; Tonga in the Pacific, Uganda in Africa, and some of the Malay States in Asia are British protectorates. Although the United States acknowledges no formal protectorates, her influence over Haiti, Santo Domingo, Panama, and Cuba at times resembles that relationship.

Trust Territories.—The mandate system was devised after the First World War as a means of administering territories taken from the defeated Central Powers by the victorious Allies. Under this arrangement, responsibility for control of such areas was given to the League of Nations, which in turn made some "advanced" state guardian of each area on behalf of the League.

The United Nations Charter created a new system of international supervision of dependent areas. Supervised by the Trusteeship Council, the new plan operates somewhat like the mandate system. The Charter placed no specific territories under trust, but left that to subsequent negotiations between the UN and the powers in possession of dependent areas. Australia, Belgium, France, New Zealand, and the United Kingdom received UN approval of trust agreements they submitted for territories formerly held by them under League mandate. The Union of South Africa refused to submit a trust plan for South West Africa, which it hopes to annex. The United States has been given trusteeship control over the former Japanese mandates of the North Pacific—the Caroline, Mariana, and Marshall Islands. After much disagreement the former Italian colonies in North Africa were placed under direct UN administration; Italy was assigned a trusteeship over its former colony Somaliland. The trusteeship chapters of the Charter also laid down principles that should govern the administration of all colonial peoples, whether within the trust system or not.

Colonies.—Colonies are territories in which sovereignty is exercised by a parent national state. Most colonies are geographically separated from the country administering sovereignty; European powers hold the greatest share of colonial possessions, which are located mainly on the continents of Africa and Asia and on islands. Actually, most colonies have been granted some degree of self-government, ranging from nearly complete internal autonomy to meager participation in local affairs. The United States has refrained from using the term "colony," and persists in calling its dependent areas "territories." Nevertheless, the status of the Virgin Islands and of Puerto Rico is not unlike that of British colonies like Jamaica and the Bahamas, or French colonies like New Caledonia and Martinique.[1]

Nationalism.—In order to understand the attitude of peoples toward their political units, their behavior and aspirations, it is necessary to

[1] For a fuller discussion of territories of the United States, see Chap. 26.

probe what Frederick L. Schuman calls "the cult of the nation-state."[1] The spirit of nationalism drives national states to glorify their own race, culture, institutions, ideals, and purposes. In its harmless form nationalism leads to commemoration of heroes and history in storybook, song, and dance. In its dangerous form it leads to jingoism, economic autarchy, violation of the rights of neighbors, and so to war. Persistence of extreme nationalist spirit constitutes a formidable barrier to international cooperation.

Nationalism operates also as a separatist influence within national states. In the 1930's, Sudeten German propaganda was a grave threat to Czechoslovakian unity. Between wars Yugoslavia was weakened by Croat nationalist aspirations for autonomy or a separate national state. The boundaries of a national state can rarely be drawn so perfectly as to include only persons of a common linguistic, cultural, ethnic, and religious background. The presence of any minority may lead to separatist agitation.

The nationalist spirit also motivates colonial peoples to revolt against their imperial masters. It drives Egyptian students to demonstrate against British "protection." It induces Indonesians to fight to the death against Netherlands forces. It whets the will of the Annamese to expel their French overlords from Indo-China. It has led the Irish to demand and receive complete independence, despite the economic and other advantages of the British connection. A rising nationalist spirit has played a large part in the achievement, during the postwar period, of national statehood by India, Pakistan, Burma, and Transjordan.

One of the great tasks of the present age is to reconcile nationalist aspirations with the preeminent fact that this is an interdependent world. Nationalism can be tolerated, even encouraged, up to the point where its exercise invades the rights and security of other peoples. For China or India a new nationalism may serve to unite diverse elements and thereby promote social and economic progress. For the major nations there is needed a new patriotism—a devotion to internationalism, a conviction that all peoples of the earth can live together in peace and security.

FORMS OF GOVERNMENT

Government is an essential element of a state, for it is the agency through which the state expresses and enforces its will. The state is the principal from which government, the agent, derives its authority and in whose name it acts. Governmental systems vary widely, but it is possible to classify them according to their principal features.

[1] See Frederick L. Schuman, *International Politics; the Destiny of the Western State System* (New York: McGraw-Hill, 4th ed., 1948), pp. 422–510.

Classification According to Distribution of Powers.—A government is *unitary* when the powers of government are concentrated in a single central government, with legal omnipotence over all territory within the state. Local governments may and usually do exist, but they are creatures of the central government and act as its administrative agents. Most of the national states of the world have a unitary form of government. Examples are Cuba and Colombia, Belgium and Czechoslovakia, Great Britain and France, Afghanistan and Siam, and within each of our forty-eight states.

A government is *federal* if political authority is divided between self-governing parts and the central whole, each operating within its sphere of action as defined in fundamental law. Although the idea of federalism is old, the adoption of the federal system by the American Constitutional Convention of 1787 gave impetus to extensive adoptions of the plan by modern states. Examples are the United States, Canada, Australia, Mexico, Brazil, and Switzerland. A weak federation is often called a "confederation," which is a sort of association or league of sovereign states. Under a confederation the central organ is of limited power. Examples are the American states under the Articles of Confederation and the Confederate States of America during the Civil War. Some look upon the League of Nations and the United Nations as weak confederations.

Classification by Type of Executive.—In the *parliamentary* form, executive powers are exercised by a prime minister and his cabinet. They are usually members of the parliament and continue to hold ministerial office only so long as their policies are supported by a majority of parliament. Thus parliament is the supreme branch of government, with authority over other branches. Among the characteristics of this form is a weak titular executive like the British king or the president of France under the Third Republic (1875–1940). In recent years the parliamentary form often is designated the "cabinet" form. The latter name properly emphasizes the fact that although parliament is the ultimate master, in Britain party discipline has grown so rigid that a cabinet can rarely be overthrown except when no one party has a majority. The parliamentary form is also used in most of the countries of Europe and the British Commonwealth.

In the *presidential* form there is a separation of powers among the principal branches of government, usually executive, legislative, and judicial. The separation is usually set forth in a written constitution. The chief executive generally is elected, and he continues in office to the expiration of his term, regardless of the support given him by the legislative branch. The legislature, executive, and the judiciary are coordinate branches, and each in its own field has its own constitutional authority. Although much criticized in recent years for its proclivity for stalemate, the presidential form has been continued in most of the countries that have adopted it.

The form is found in the United States, the forty-eight states, and most of the Latin-American republics.

Classification as to Number Participating.—An *autocratic* or dictatorial form is one with political authority exercised by a single individual. The existence of a dictatorship is ascertained more by a study of inner functioning than by a look at formal institutions. An autocrat may capture control of a government regardless of whether it is unitary or federal, parliamentary or presidential, monarchy or republic. The tyrants of ancient Greece and Rome, the absolute monarchs of the Middle Ages, and the dictators of modern authoritarian states are examples.

An *oligarchic* or aristocratic form may be said to exist if political authority is exercised by a few individuals in the interests of a class or minority. Where the form exists, a few rule who have become dominant through privileged birth, wealth, military prowess, influence with a royal family, or position in a priestly hierarchy. The form prevailed in city-states of ancient Greece and Rome, in the medieval cities of western Europe, and in some of the authoritarian regimes of modern times. The survival of a titled aristocracy in a country like Great Britain is not evidence of an oligarchic system; the peerage is a vestige of the past, but often has been adapted and enlarged to fill the needs of the present day.

A *democratic* form of government exists where a considerable number of the adult population participate in the formation of public policy, the selection of officials, and the control of administration and law enforcement. A distinction is made between "direct" or "pure" democracy and "representative" democracy. In the former, the body of citizens assemble periodically and perform the functions usually assigned to legislatures. Examples are found in ancient Greece and Rome, the *Landesgemeinde* of Swiss cantons, and the New England town meetings.[1]

This custom is practicable only in small units, where the population is sparse and homogeneous, and where the issues are fairly simple. It is not practiced in modern national, state, and municipal governments, although modifications are found in the form of the initiative, referendum, and recall. In a representative democracy, the voters wield influence through officials selected to express and enforce their will. This system appears to have originated in the medieval states of western Europe, it was perfected in Britain, and it is now widely practiced throughout the world.

Other Classifications.—Even after the three classifications given above are mastered, other problems persist. A few generations ago the distinction between monarchical and republican forms was hotly debated in the United States. The monarchy is headed by a ruler, real or titular, who usually attains his position through heredity, and who serves for life. In a repub-

[1] See p. 20.

lic sovereign power rests in representatives chosen by the people. Absolute monarchs, unrestrained by legislatures and popular controls, were common in bygone days but are today found only in a few remote places like Saudi Arabia and Afghanistan. Constitutional monarchs, whose power is very limited, still sit on thrones of Great Britain, Netherlands, Sweden, Norway, Denmark, and other countries. The controversy between monarchists and republicans in a given country is meaningful mainly in terms of the other issues involved.

What of communism and fascism? These are not forms of government. In political ideology the significant classification is that based on number participating. Both communism and fascism, as practiced at present, use the dictatorship form and should be grouped with other autocratic regimes. In the field of economic thought, there are significant differences which will be considered in the next section. Russian communism professes devotion to true democracy, but many of the democratic principles set forth in the 1936 constitution of the Soviet Union have not been applied. In discussing ideologies the student must use great caution not to confuse political and economic doctrines.

stress

Careful classification is a prerequisite to useful discussion of forms of government. Nearly all governments can be classified under one of the headings in each category. For example:

United States is federal, presidential, democratic, and republican.
Great Britain is unitary, parliamentary, democratic, and monarchical.
Canada is federal, parliamentary, democratic, and monarchical.
Nazi Germany was unitary, parliamentary, autocratic, and republican.
Prewar Japan was unitary, parliamentary, autocratic, and monarchical.
Brazil under Vargas was federal, presidential, autocratic, and republican.

FUNCTIONS OF GOVERNMENT

Although the role of government is highly controversial, there is general agreement over certain essential, or minimum, functions. All agree that only government should be permitted to enact laws and back them with sufficient force to compel acceptance and obedience. It is also generally agreed that governments should provide courts for the settlement of private controversies, protect life and property, defend the community from attack, conduct foreign relations, provide a medium of exchange and a postal system, and restrain individual, group, and commercial excesses. If government would confine itself to these, its role would be largely that of lawgiver, judge, policeman, and soldier. But few modern governments stop at this point. Instead, they have become gigantic regulatory and service institutions. This transition has been accompanied by diverse ideologies and vehement controversy.

Anarchists and Syndicalists.—*Anarchism* is a school of thought that seeks the complete elimination of the state, and its replacement by a free and spontaneous cooperation among individuals and groups. Anarchists regard the state as an instrument of domination and exploitation. Most of them expect that the new society will come into being as a result of revolutionary action, but no new government or coercive system will replace the old. Anarchism has never become the gospel of a mass movement, but its proponents often touch a responsive chord in people concerned over the expanding authority of modern government.[1]

Syndicalism holds somewhat similar views concerning the role of the state. Using the general strike as a method of seizing power, the syndicalist would establish in place of the state a series of industries managed by the workers. These industries would be federated together on a functional basis; most syndicalists would permit this federation to exercise some coercive powers, particularly in the transitional period.

Communism, as laid down by Karl Marx, viewed the state as an instrument through which the capitalist class dominates and exploits the masses. The orthodox Marxist expected the state to wither away after the masses gained power, its place being taken by self-governing industries and cooperative endeavor. To this extent the communists envisage the same objective as the anarchists do. The communist regime in Russia, however, has so expanded the functions of government that it must be regarded as state socialist in its view of the role of the state. Russian communists persist in regarding state socialism as a transitional phase, but it is difficult for an outside observer to see how the existing Soviet totalitarian state can wither away.

Individualism.—The laissez-faire individualist regards the state as a necessary evil. He would have the state perform only the minimum or essential functions, leaving promotion and regulation of the economic order to private enterprise and to natural economic forces. That government is best, says a modern individualist, which governs least. To him government in recent years has constantly threatened individual freedom and private initiative. Economic *laissez faire*, once the creed of radicals, has become the doctrine of conservatism or even of reaction.

In order to be consistent, advocates of *laissez faire* must accept the withdrawal of nearly all forms of government support and paternalism. He who wants natural economic laws to govern production, distribution, and exchange must give up the protective tariff, governmental subsidy, marketing aids, and other services to business and agriculture. He must be prepared for the inequality that will result from unregulated operation of a "survival of the fittest" plan.

[1] A good survey of anarchist thought is Paul Eltzbacher, *Anarchism* (New York: Tucker, 1908).

Individualism has a tremendous appeal to many Americans. It played a great part in the development of the country, in the early settlement of the east coast, in pushing back the frontiers to the west. It has been allied in many ways to opposition to state interference in individual opinions and conduct. Like many slogans, "free enterprise" is both appealing and vague, and its full implications are rarely examined.[1]

Progressivism.—A middle way between individualist and collectivist views on governmental functions is advocated by a diverse group known by such designations as "progressives," "liberals," "new dealers," and proponents of the "welfare state." In one sense they seek to revive the utilitarian ideals of the greatest good to the greatest number. Supporters of this social-welfare point of view do not advocate socialism, although they are critical of the abuses of private enterprise and the profit motive. Seeking to correct and strengthen the existing economic order, they extend piecemeal the functions of government. In addition to the minimum functions, they would have government regulate, stimulate, coordinate, plan, and supervise the national economy; some utilities would come under public ownership and operation, and government would accept responsibility for providing full employment, social security, and housing. They also favor expanded public-health, education, and nutrition programs. As a means to achieving social justice, they often encourage nonbusiness groups, especially labor, farmers, and consumers. This will be recognized as the "New Deal" and "Fair Deal" programs that have won wide acceptance in the United States during the last two decades.[2]

Collectivism.—The state socialist advocates the public ownership of the principal means of production, exchange, and distribution. There are many varieties of socialist thought. Some derive their doctrine from the writings of Marx and Engels; some stem from other sources. Socialists condemn the capitalist system for concentrating wealth in the hands of the few and producing recurring economic crises. Having won power through the ballot box, most socialists anticipate a gradual transformation of the economic system from capitalist to socialist. Revolutionary socialists expect to win power only by violence, and hence predict a rapid transition to the new society.

Although socialist philosophy has made great headway in many countries of the world, it has never been adopted by a major political movement in the United States. The Labor parties of Great Britain, Australia, and

[1] One of the ablest of recent tracts for economic *laissez faire* is Friedrich A. Hayek, *The Road to Serfdom* (Chicago: University of Chicago Press, 1944). The best answer to Hayek is Herman Finer, *Road to Reaction* (Boston: Little, Brown, 1946).

[2] An interesting recent study of positivism in action is Thomas P. Jenkin, *Reactions of Major Groups to Positive Government in the United States, 1930–1940* (Berkeley and Los Angeles: University of California Press, 1945).

New Zealand profess a mild socialist doctrine and have been able to place into force much of their programs. Social Democratic and Socialist parties of European countries have played a major part in continental politics for decades. The lack of headway made by the socialists in the United States may be explained in terms of the relatively high standard of living and the frequency with which the old parties borrow planks from socialist platforms in order to solve a persistent problem.

Under a state socialist scheme, as envisaged by socialists of British and western European countries, the government would nationalize credit and banking, transportation and communication, and the principal production industries. There would be central planning of the economic life of the country, and such private enterprise as was permitted to continue would be required to conform to the central plan. In their practice to date, the Russian communists have behaved much like state socialists, except that they have been more revolutionary in methods and more total in application. Instead of withering away, the state has reached a new high in the functions performed and the obedience exacted.

Fascism is even more difficult to classify in respect to functions of government. As practiced in Italy and Germany, private property was permitted to remain, but all the rights of individuals, groups, and parties were subordinated to state interests. The state demanded and received total control, loyalty, and obedience—hence the term "totalitarian." Generally the fascist dictators found it unnecessary to socialize industry, for their control was complete and effective with private ownership. The fascist economic system may be described as a government-dominated capitalist one.

THE CHANGING AMERICAN SCENE

Changes since 1789.—While the American constitutional framework remains about the same as in 1789, governmental forms and functions have changed greatly. The nation now commands the patriotism once pledged to the respective states. The negative individualism of old has been replaced by a new attachment to positive government—the social-welfare state. Governments at all levels, but especially the federal, have grown to undreamed-of proportions. The electorate has expanded until it includes virtually all adults, both men and women. Political parties have come to be indispensable adjuncts of government. Pressure groups have become nationally organized, vocal, and very powerful in determining governmental policy. The electoral college has withered to uselessness. The presidency has attained a commanding position.

Big government requires huge budgets, revenues, and expenditures. It also requires millions of employees, skilled administrators, and the newest administrative techniques and equipment. Government has accepted responsibility for providing countless services, for regulating many segments of the economy, and for a degree of central planning unthinkable in the nineteenth century. At the same time, government has been given responsibility for fighting wars in all parts of the world, for governing an overseas empire, and for playing a decisive role in international politics.

Factors Producing Change.—Many decry current trends, view with alarm, and demand return to a simpler society, but the problems multiply and government rises to solve them. How can this be explained? An important factor has been the tremendous growth in population. Others have been an absence of an old, rigid social structure with inhibiting cultural patterns; an abundance of natural resources; scientific discoveries that have revolutionized production, transportation, and communication; the growth of large-scale business enterprise; and, finally, depressions and wars. These are dynamic forces that are bound to produce change. As long as they persist, governments will be compelled to adapt to them.

The twentieth-century American can ill afford to spend his time yearning for the simple society that prevailed long ago. The task ahead is one of devising institutions and policies that will expand the area of human liberty and opportunity and yet be competent to deal with the problems that arise in the one complex world in which we find ourselves.

References

Bryce, James: *Modern Democracies* (New York: Macmillan, 2 vols., 1921).

Chaplin, Ralph: *Wobbly; the Rough-and-tumble Story of an American Radical* (Chicago: University of Chicago Press, 1948).

Coker, Francis W.: *Recent Political Thought* (New York: Appleton-Century-Crofts, 1934).

Ebenstein, William: *Fascist Italy* (New York: American Book, 1939).

——— *Man and the State* (New York: Rinehart, 1947).

Finer, Herman: *The Theory and Practice of Modern Government* (New York: Henry Holt, 2d ed., 1949).

Gettell, Raymond G.: *Political Science* (Boston: Ginn, rev. ed., 1949).

Hall, H. Duncan: *Mandates, Dependencies and Trusteeships* (Washington, D.C.: Carnegie Endowment, 1948).

Hayes, Carlton J. H.: *The Historical Evolution of Modern Nationalism* (New York: Macmillan, 1948).

Jessup, Philip C.: *A Modern Law of Nations—An Introduction* (New York: Macmillan, 1948).

MacIver, Robert M.: *The Web of Government* (New York: Macmillan, 1947).

Mises, Ludwig von: *Human Action: A Treatise on Economics* (New Haven: Yale University Press, 1949).

Rossiter, Clinton L.: *Constitutional Dictatorship; Crisis Government in Modern Democracies* (Princeton, N.J.: Princeton University Press, 1948).

Sait, Edward M.: *Political Institutions: A Preface* (New York: Appleton-Century-Crofts, 1938).

Sweezy, Paul M.: *Socialism* (New York: McGraw-Hill, 1949).

Wilson, Francis G.: *The American Political Mind; A Textbook in Political Theory* (New York: McGraw-Hill, 1949).

Chapter 2

COLONIZATION, INDEPENDENCE, AND CONFEDERATION

We hold these truths to be self-evident, that all men are created equal, that they are endowed by their Creator with certain unalienable Rights, that among these are Life, Liberty, and the pursuit of Happiness.

The Declaration of Independence.

American institutions, like those of other nations, have their origin deeply embedded in the past. The development of political institutions divides itself naturally into four important periods: the Colonial, the Revolutionary, the Confederate, and the Constitutional. A brief historical review of government during the first three is essential to an understanding of the constitutional period which is the subject of succeeding chapters. Such a review ought not merely to engender respect for the past and an understanding of the present, but it should also contribute to the adventurous criticism and thinking so badly needed in modern times.

COLONIZATION

Basis of England's Title to America.—Columbus discovered the West Indian Islands in 1492, but it remained for John Cabot, an Italian in the service of England, to explore what is now the eastern coastline of the United States. Although unwilling to assist Columbus, King Henry VII of England quickly realized the importance of his discovery and in 1496 commissioned Cabot to "seek out, discover and find whatsoever isles, countries, regions or provinces of the heathen and infidels whatsoever they be, and in what part of the world soever they be, which before this time have been unknown to all Christians" and "to set up our banners and ensigns in every village, town, castle, isle, or mainland of them newly found." Cabot made two voyages and by 1498 had discovered Newfoundland and St. Johns and sailed southward along the eastern coast of America[1] to what is now the Maryland-Virginia border. England's title in the New World was thus based upon the law of discovery and conquest. By a similar process, Spanish explorers established the title of their country to what is

[1] The word "America" was deliberately invented in 1507 by Martin Waldseemüller, an obscure German professor in a French university, otherwise known as Hylacomylus. "America" is the latinized and feminized first name of Amerigo Vespucci, a Florentine naval astronomer, who claimed to have been the first to see the mainland of what is now the United States. For an interesting account of how this took place, see Stephan Zweig, *Amerigo, a Comedy of Errors in History* (New York: Viking, 1942).

now Florida, the southwest and western parts of America; French explorers planted the flag of France in the regions of Nova Scotia, the St. Lawrence River, Great Lakes, and the Mississippi Valley to the Gulf of Mexico; while Dutchmen established claims in the valleys of the Hudson and Delaware rivers.

Rights of the Indians.—Wherever the early explorers traveled, they found Indians living in the tribal stage. Contrary to popular impression, the Indians were not nomadic but occupied well-defined areas. For example, tribes belonging to the Iroquois family inhabited the St. Lawrence and Great Lakes region, those belonging to the Muskhogean family lived in the southeastern section, while those belonging to the Sioux family occupied the north-central territory. European nations claimed the right of *dominion* over lands held by Indian tribes in consequence of discovery but accorded the Indians the right of *occupancy*. This meant that European states claimed the right to colonize and manage external affairs, while the Indians retained ownership and possession of their lands with complete authority over internal tribal matters. This arrangement led the colonists to treat with the Indian tribes as "nations" and call their chiefs or sachems "kings." Although the Indians were brutally treated and ruthlessly exploited by the whites, land was seldom taken from them by conquest; rather, it appears that the colonists paid for most of the land taken, transfers being conveyed by solemn treaties.[1]

Elimination by England of Other European Powers East of Mississippi.—Following the discovery of America, many attempts at colonization were made, but it was not until 1607 that the first permanent settlement was

[1] This understanding and procedure was followed by the United States until 1871. Of it the Supreme Court said in an early decision: "It has never been contended that the Indian title amounted to nothing. Their right to possession has never been questioned." Johnson *v.* McIntosh, 8 Wheaton 543 (1823). While an act of Congress adopted in March, 1793, stated that no purchase or grant of lands should have any validity "unless the same be made by a treaty or convention entered into pursuant to the constitution." Accordingly, between the formation of the United States and 1871, the American government concluded 371 treaties with the Indians. In only two instances were Indian titles extinguished by conquest—one in the case of the Creeks at the close of the Creek War in 1814; the other in the case of the Sioux in Minnesota after an outburst in 1862. Even in those cases the Indians were provided with other reservations and were subsequently paid the net proceeds arising from the sale of land vacated. An act of Mar. 3, 1871, brought Indians under direct control of Congress and substituted simple agreements for solemn treaties. Today, nearly all land titles formerly belonging to Indians have been acquired by the United States, the Indians having been allotted in exchange certain reservations on which they may continue to live. Frederick W. Hodge (ed.), *Handbook of American Indians* (Washington: Government Printing Office, 2 vols., 1907–1910), vol. I, pp. 803–805; George Dewey Harmon, *Sixty Years of Indian Affairs* (Chapel Hill: The University of North Carolina Press, 1941), Chap. VI; United States Department of Interior, *Handbook of Federal Indian Law* (Washington: Government Printing Office, 1942).

established at Jamestown, Va. The Pilgrim Fathers established the second settlement at Plymouth, Mass., in 1620. Then followed a series of settlements along the Atlantic seaboard until in 1732 the thirteenth colony, Georgia, was established. The British, Dutch, Swedes, French, and Spaniards all played a part in colonizing America, but the British soon acquired a controlling influence. By 1664, in which year Holland's colonies (New Netherlands) were conquered, England had acquired dominion over all the Atlantic seaboard south of the Gulf of St. Lawrence to Florida. At the end of the French and Indian War, in 1763, England had eliminated Spanish control over Florida and French control over all her possessions in North America east of the Mississippi River. Thus, on the eve of the American Revolution, England had control over all the present United States east of the Mississippi River.

Three Types of Colonies.—Before colonies could be established in America, it was necessary to have legal authorization to do so. This was granted by the king in charters, issued in some instances to trading companies, in others to individuals, and in still others to groups of colonists. The charters authorized three types of colonial governments: royal (often called "crown"), proprietary, and charter (sometimes called "corporate").

Royal Colonies.—Royal colonies were the most numerous, including New Hampshire, New York, New Jersey, Virginia, North Carolina, South Carolina, Georgia, and Massachusetts (after 1691). The charters granted to those establishing these colonies were subsequently canceled[1] or withdrawn, after which time the king exercised control directly through commissions and instructions issued to governors. The commissions were very much alike. They appointed a governor as the king's representative or deputy who was to be governed by instructions. They also provided for a council composed of men appointed by the Crown or governor who would serve as an upper house of the legislature and assist the governor in discharging his duties. The governor was given power to suspend members of council from office, and in case of vacancies, to appoint others, subject, of course, to the Crown's approval. The commissions also authorized a general assembly of representatives to be chosen by the voters and a system of courts the judges of which were to be appointed by the governor with the advice of the council. Laws enacted by the legislature required the approval of the Crown and appeals could be taken from the highest colonial court to the King in Council. The royal colonies, mentioned above, were governed in this manner from shortly after their establishment until 1775.

Proprietary Colonies.—At the time of the Revolution, there were three proprietary colonies: Maryland, Delaware, and Pennsylvania. Upon Lord

[1] Massachusetts, however, restored her charter as an instrument of government in 1775.

Baltimore and William Penn, proprietors of these three colonies,[1] and their heirs was conferred absolute proprietorship of the territory. Their charters authorized them (the proprietors) to appoint governors and other officers,

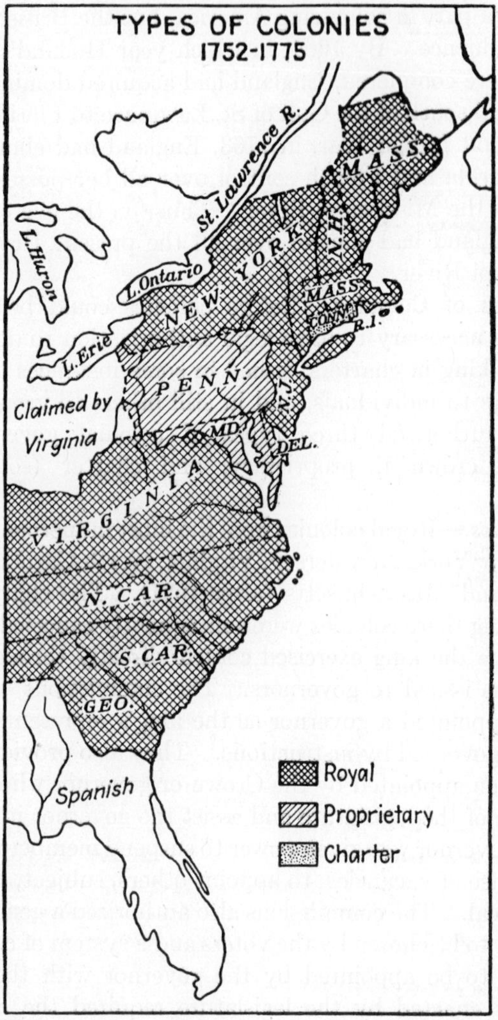

establish legislatures, create courts and appoint judges thereto, create local governments, and exercise the usual prerogatives that in royal colonies belonged to the Crown. In Delaware and Maryland, the legislature was

[1] Penn was given title to Pennsylvania in 1681 and in 1682 he was given a supplemental deed by the Duke of York which included the area that became the state of Delaware in 1776.

Colonial Governments

Name	Founder	Date	Status in 1775	Government
Rhode Island.	Roger Williams	1636	Charter (Self-governing)	*Charter* granted directly to colonists. *Governors* chosen by freemen for 1-year term. *Legislature* bicameral: both houses elected by freemen for 1-year terms. *Judges* appointed by governor in council. *Crown* could not veto laws, but cases could be appealed from highest colonial court to King in Council.
Connecticut. .	Emigrants from Massachusetts	1636	Charter (Self-governing)	
Maryland. . . .	Lord Baltimore	1634	Proprietary	*Proprietor* owned colony but acknowledged sovereignty of King of England. *Governor* appointed by proprietor. *Legislature* bicameral (except in Pennsylvania). Upper house appointed by proprietor. Lower house elected by freemen. Laws (except those of Maryland) were subject to approval and veto by Crown. *Judges* appointed by governor and council. Appeals could be taken to King in Council.
Delaware	Swedes	1638	Proprietary	
Pennsylvania.	William Penn	1681	Proprietary	
Virginia.	London Company	1607	Royal	*Crown* controlled directly by commissions and instructions to colonial government. *Governor* appointed by Crown and acted as king's deputy. *Legislature* bicameral (except in Georgia). Upper house appointed by king, lower house elected by freemen. Upper house acted as governor's council. All laws subject to approval and veto by Crown. *Judges* appointed by governor. Appeals could be taken to King in Council.
Massachusetts.	Puritans of the Mass. Bay Colony	1628	Royal	
North Carolina	Eight nobles	1663	Royal	
South Carolina	Eight nobles	1663	Royal	
New York. . . .	Duke of York	1664	Royal	
New Hampshire.	John Mason	1629	Royal	
New Jersey. . .	Berkeley and Carteret	1664	Royal	
Georgia.	James Oglethorpe	1732	Royal	

bicameral, consisting of an upper house called a "council" whose members were appointed by the proprietor, and a lower house made up of representatives elected by freemen. In Pennsylvania the legislature was unicameral; the council had no legislative powers but served merely as an advisory body to the governor. Laws were subject to veto by the Crown, except in Maryland, and appeals could be taken from the highest colonial court to the King in Council.

Charter Colonies.—Charter colonies were Rhode Island and Connecticut. These differed in that charters were granted to the colonists as a group after they had already settled and there was no point at which the British government had authority to interfere with administration of the colonies. They were organized altogether upon popular and democratic principles: governors were elected annually by the freemen of the colony, and while they were supposed to be acceptable to the Crown, approval was seldom sought. Members of both branches of the legislature were likewise chosen annually by the freemen. Acts of the legislature were not subject to the governor's veto, nor was it necessary for them to be sent to England for approval. Judges and all other officers were appointed by the legislature, although appeals could be taken from the highest colonial courts to the King in Council.

Inhabitants of these colonies cherished the charters whose provisions left them almost complete autonomy and spared them many of the excesses of royal governors suffered by neighboring colonists. A story familiar to New England illustrates the extent to which charters were treasured. In 1685, King James issued an order for the repeal of the charter of Connecticut. The colony offered its submission and in 1687, Sir Edward Andros went to Hartford, and in the name of the Crown declared the government dissolved. The charter was not surrendered, however, but secreted in an oak tree which is still venerated and displayed to sight-seers. Immediately after the revolution of 1688, the people resumed the exercise of all its powers. Succeeding monarchs silently permitted them to retain it without any struggle or resistance. Unlike most of the colonies that adopted new constitutions after the Declaration of Independence, Connecticut retained her charter as a fundamental law until 1818 and Rhode Island hers until Dorr's Rebellion in 1842. Indeed, it has been said that had all the colonies been allowed so much autonomy and independence, the Revolution would never have occurred.

New England Towns and Their Government.—In the New England colonies the principal unit of local government was the town (elsewhere called "township"). Counties existed but played a minor role, handling chiefly such matters as the administration of justice and the militia. The predominance of town government resulted from the fact that the first colonists came not as individuals but as church congregations or groups seeking religious freedom. Once here, the rugged soil, rigorous climate, the presence of hostile Indians and wild animals encouraged small-scale farming, manufacturing, trading, fishing, and residence in compact communities. The town was sometimes wholly rural, sometimes wholly urban, and sometimes partly rural and urban. The towns were incorporated and their boundaries defined by the colonial legislature. They were then left to govern themselves, provided, of course, they did nothing contrary to the laws of the colony.

Governmentally, the towns were pure or direct democracies. Town meetings, which were advertised meetings of voters, convened at least once a year (ordinarily in March) but many times oftener. In the early days nonattendance was punishable by fine. At these gatherings such laws were enacted and officials chosen as seemed necessary to manage local business. For the management of affairs between town meetings a board of selectmen consisting of from three to thirteen members was elected. Besides these, the principal officers were a town clerk and constable. Other officers were treasurer, assessor, surveyor of highways; the tithingman, a kind of Sunday constable who saw that people came to church and with foxtail wand kept them awake during sermons; the fence viewer, who supervised erection of boundary fences between adjoining properties; the hog reeve, who saw that rings were kept in noses of swine running at large; the field driver, who impounded stray cattle; the pound keeper, who caught and attended stray dogs; overseers of the poor, town criers, and many others. The town served as an electoral district for representation in the colonial legislature and representatives thereto were chosen by the town meeting. These gatherings of voters were social as well as political events and became deeply rooted in the affections of the people, resulting in a society as democratic as the world has ever seen. Of them Thomas Jefferson once said, "They have proved themselves the wisest invention ever devised by the wit of man for the perfect exercise of self government and for its preservation." Today in the more rural parts of New England, the old machinery of town government functions much as it always did, but in more thickly populated sections, where the population is likely to be heterogeneous, many modifications have occurred.

Southern Counties and Their Government.—In the Southern colonies town government never took root; instead, the county was the primary unit of local government and administration. These colonies were settled more by individual entrepreneurs than by dissenting congregations; wild animals were scarce and there were comparatively few hostile Indians but, more important, the land and climate were suitable for large-scale agriculture, particularly the growing of tobacco, cotton, indigo, and rice. Instead of homogeneous, compact communities, the plantation system developed, necessitating a unit of local government larger than in the North. At first many local matters were attended to by the plantation owners.

Later, parishes were established which served as both ecclesiastical and civil districts. These were governed by a vestry, consisting usually of several "selected men" chosen at first by the parishioners (though later the practice of cooptation became established), the minister, and church-wardens. A strong system of local government failed to develop and before long the parish was overshadowed by the county.

Southern counties were less democratic than Northern towns. There was no popular assembly; rather the principal officers were usually lieutenant, sheriff, justices of the peace, and coroners. These officers were appointed by the governor of the colony commonly upon the recommendation of the justices of peace. The justices, ordinarily a self-perpetuating body of aristocratic planters, dominated county governments. Thus controlled, the county became the unit of representation in the colonial assembly, and the unit of military, judicial, highway, and fiscal administration.

Local Government in the Middle Colonies.—In the middle colonies, both towns and counties exercised important functions. In New York and New Jersey the towns, resembling those of New England, played a larger role than the county, whereas in Pennsylvania and Delaware the county predominated. It was in these colonies that the practice of electing county officers, particularly governing boards, similar to those found in counties at the present time, originated.

Cities and Their Government during the Colonial Period.—Within themselves the colonies were unitary. Large cities did not exist; in fact, as late as the Revolution, only about 3 per cent of the population lived in boroughs (or cities), of which there were only twenty-four. These were established by charters issued by colonial governors and included New York, the oldest, Albany, Philadelphia, Annapolis, Norfolk, and smaller places mainly in Pennsylvania and New Jersey. In New England urban areas, such as Boston, the town-meeting system of rural areas proved sufficiently elastic for municipal purposes.

The principal governing authority in most of the boroughs was the common council composed of a mayor and recorder, both appointed by the governor, a small number of aldermen, and a somewhat larger number of councilmen elected by the voters. These acted as a single body, a quorum requiring the attendance of the mayor and a specified number of both aldermen and councilmen. The common council had control over all matters of administration, while the mayor and aldermen had certain judicial functions in addition to their duties as part of the common council. Three of the boroughs—Philadelphia, Annapolis, and Norfolk—were governed as "close corporations." There, the aldermen and councilmen held their positions for life, while the mayor and recorder were chosen by the common council from among the aldermen. When vacancies occurred among the aldermen, they were appointed by the common council, and vacancies for councilmen were filled by the mayor, recorder, and aldermen. These governing bodies were thus self-perpetuating and lacking in the democratic features obtaining in other colonial boroughs and present-day municipal governments.

Advantages and Disadvantages of Colonial Status.—Certain advantages flowed from colonial status. There was, in general, a common tradition, culture, and language. Since most white inhabitants were British subjects, there was a common citizenship. Every colonist had a right to inhabit, if he pleased, any other colony; and he was capable of inheriting land in every other colony. The common law, with its invaluable guarantees of personal liberty, was the birthright and inheritance of all. Since appeals from local courts could be, and frequently were, taken to the King in Council, the law in the colonies was uniform as far as fundamental principles were concerned. England afforded protection from attacks by foreigners and pirates, handled foreign relations for the colonies, helped the colonists defend themselves against the Indians, counseled on questions of internal policy, and assisted with the administration of local laws. Moreover, England retained control over commerce among the colonies and with foreign nations, and while this was often irritating, it did prevent the erection of intercolonial trade barriers. Likewise, centralized control over monetary matters provided a uniform currency advantageous to all.

The most serious disadvantages arising from colonial status were that the colonies followed the fate of England in war or peace and were frequently embroiled in war whether they liked it or not;[1] the colonies were subject to the arbitrary whims and caprice of British kings and their agents; and, being distantly removed and without representation, there was always the danger that Parliament would enact legislation detrimental to the best interests of the colonists.

INDEPENDENCE

Disputes with England.—Between the founding of Jamestown and the Declaration of Independence, 169 years elapsed. During this time, incessant disputes arose between the colonists and representatives of the British government, particularly the royal governors who were, for the most part, noblemen broken in fortune, frequently corrupt, and nearly always of weak character. Many of the disputes were local and personal, involving such matters as the taxation of proprietaries' lands, the extension of the franchise, the importation of convicts, the raising of troops, the issue of paper money, the organization of banks on insecure foundations, and the establishment of courts of law.

[1] For example, the war with France and her allies which lasted for over 50 years (1690–1748).

More serious quarrels arose when England enacted legislation monopolizing trade with the colonies, restricting the production and exportation of certain commodities (such as wool, wool products, and iron manufactures) in order to provide protection to manufacturers in England, and taxing colonists for the general support of colonial administration. In addition to outright disobedience to obnoxious laws and orders, the colonial legislatures frequently withheld appropriations for salaries for officials and soldiers until their demands were complied with, or addressed petitions to the home government. When, after the ascension of King George III to the throne in 1760, Britain decided to deal firmly with her high-spirited and recalcitrant subjects in the American colonies, resentment was fanned to revolutionary fervor. All attempts at conciliation having failed by 1776, the colonists were faced with the alternatives of submission or rebellion, and, as we know, they chose the latter.

Committees of Correspondence.—On the eve of the Revolution the colonists were faced with a determined government in England and governmental machinery in all the colonies, except Rhode Island and Connecticut, over which they could not hope to obtain control inasmuch as the governors, councils, and judges were, for the most part, loyalists beholden to the king and obliged to obey his commands. Revolutionary activity being treasonable and punishable by death, the only alternative was to persuade fellow colonists to form a "united front." This was done through a system of committees of correspondence.

The first of such committees was organized by Samuel Adams in Boston in 1772. Thereby was hatched what has been called by a bitter critic the "foulest, subtlest, and most venomous serpent ever issued from the egg of sedition."[1] Within a year almost every town in Massachusetts had formed similar committees and, encouraged by such events as the Boston Tea Party, they quickly spread to other colonies. By the end of 1773 a complete network of committees had been established, organized somewhat like modern political parties and performing many of the same functions. They not only exchanged ideas and information but took over the management of township, county, and colonial affairs. Later, they elected the Continental Congress and provided an agency through which the decisions of that body were enforced. Thus, although the regularly constituted British-controlled governmental machinery still remained, an extralegal system grew up beside it which sapped the old of its authority. A Tory later said that the work of the committees was "the source of the rebellion" and a recent writer[2] has said:

[1] John E. Miller, *Sam Adams, Pioneer of Propaganda* (Boston: Little, 1936), p. 264. Quoted by permission of Little, Brown & Company and Atlantic Monthly.

[2] *Ibid.*, pp. 271–272. Quoted by permission of Little, Brown & Company and Atlantic Monthly.

The committees of correspondence that made the American Revolution possible were the town committees dominated by local "Sam Adamses" who were in close touch with Boston and other centers of radicalism. . . . Without their aid it is doubtful if the first Continental Congress would have been held in 1774 and the revolutionary movement in the colonies brought to its fruition in the Declaration of Independence. They made possible the domination of a great part of British America by cliques of radical patriots who looked to Sam Adams for leadership against the mother country. . . . After 1774, the colonies fairly bristled with hot-tempered Liberty Boys, who, instead of calling themselves Sons of Liberty [as those who had previously resisted the Stamp Act called themselves], were now known as the committees of correspondence. But under whatever name these patriots worked, their purpose remained the same: to defend colonial liberty with arms rather than submit to British "tyranny."

The First Continental Congress.—Attempts on the part of Great Britain to punish the people of Massachusetts, who were more rebellious than others, united the colonies. On June 17, 1774, Massachusetts issued a call proposing that each of the colonies appoint delegates to attend a conference to consider relations with England. In response, delegates from every colony except Georgia met in Philadelphia on Sept. 5, 1774. The assemblage, which included the ablest men in the colonies, called itself the First Continental Congress. Whence came the delegates? Certainly they could not have been appointed by the regularly established colonial governments still under the domination of Britain. Rather, the delegations were appointed or elected by local committees, state conventions called by the local committees, or by state legislatures in which the revolutionary elements were dominant. The delegates styled themselves "the delegates appointed by the good people of these colonies."

The Congress adopted an impressive Declaration of Rights, agreed to stop the importation and consumption of British goods, and established a Continental Association to oversee the enforcement of the boycott. The association was to consist of a system of committees elected in towns, cities, and counties throughout the country and supervised by colonial committees of correspondence, for the purpose of detecting and blacklisting parties caught violating the boycott. Before adjourning on Oct. 26, it was agreed that Congress should convene again in May, 1775, unless their grievances had been redressed before that time.

The Second Continental Congress.—Britain was not in a mood to be conciliatory, but, rather, replied with more repressive measures. Massachusetts prepared for war and before the time appointed for another congress to convene, blood had been shed at Concord and Lexington. The Second Continental Congress, which convened in Carpenter's Hall in Philadelphia on May 10, 1775, was a unicameral body comprised of practically the same men who had met earlier. Georgia, which had not sent delegates to the earlier congress, did so during the middle of July. As formerly, the delegates were chosen by popular conventions of the people of the various states or by the popular branch of the state legislatures, although after the Declaration of Independence and the establishment of new state governments the delegates were appointed by the legislatures of the states. The Second Continental Congress served as the official organ of government for the united colonies until March, 1781, when the Articles of Confederation became effective. It was, thus, America's first national government.

The Declaration of Independence.—When the Congress met in May, 1775, there were few who desired or advocated independence. Washington, who had been appointed Commander in Chief of the colonial forces in July, 1775, said a year later: "When I took command of the army, I abhorred the idea of independence; now, I am convinced, nothing else will save us." Others had reached the same conclusion. Accordingly, Congress, on June 11, 1776, approved the appointment of a committee of five, with Thomas Jefferson as chairman, to draft a declaration of independence. A resolution to declare independence, introduced by Richard Henry Lee of Virginia, was approved by unanimous vote of Congress on July 2, and the entire declaration was approved two days later. It became the "birth certificate of the American nation."

Creation by Declaration of a Nation with de facto Status.—Two important questions of constitutional law were raised by the Declaration. The document declared "That these United Colonies are . . . absolved from all allegiance to the British Crown, and that all political connection between them and the state of Great Britain, is and ought to be totally dissolved. . . ." Did this destroy British sovereignty, as it announced, or did the colonies remain merely in a state of rebellion until the end of the war? The American view has been that the Declaration made them independent and sovereign both internally and externally; hence all steps taken by Congress after that date had the sanction of law. This view was pointedly stated by Justice Story:

> The Declaration of Independence has . . . always been treated as an act of paramount and sovereign authority, complete and perfect *per se*, and *ipso facto* working an entire dissolution of all political connection with, and allegiance to, Great Britain. And this, not merely as a practical fact, but in a legal and constitutional view of the matter by the courts of justice.[1]

From the standpoint of international law, however, the better view appears to be that since foreign governments, with the exception of France and the Netherlands, refused to recognize the United Colonies and receive their

[1] Joseph Story, *Commentaries on the Constitution of the United States* (Boston: Little, Brown, 2 vols., 1873), vol., I, pp. 149–150.

ministers, they remained in a *de facto* status until 1783, after which their status became *de jure*. This meant that although Britain's sovereignty was doubtful, the United States was, nevertheless, not entitled to all the rights and privileges of nationhood until after the rebellion had terminated in its favor.

Creation by Declaration of One Nation—Not Thirteen.—The second question of constitutional law raised was whether one nation or thirteen of them was brought into existence by the Declaration. If one, then only the central government had authority to levy war, send and receive ambassadors, ministers, and consuls, and make treaties. If thirteen, then all were competent to do these things. The words of the Declaration are so ambiguous as to permit two interpretations. States' rights advocates called attention to these words: "these United Colonies are, and of right ought to be *free and independent states* . . . and that as *free and independent states* . . . *they* have full power to levy war, conclude peace, and contract alliances, establish commerce, and do all other acts and things which independent states may of right do." On the other hand, nationalists stressed the statement that the Declaration was made "in the name and by the authority of the good people of these colonies" by "the representatives of the United States of America, in general Congress assembled." To quote Justice Story again:

> It [the Declaration of Independence] was not an act done by the State governments then organized, nor by persons chosen by them. It was emphatically the act of the whole *people* of the united colonies, by the instrumentality of their representatives, chosen for that among other purposes. . . . It was an act of original, inherent sovereignty by the people themselves, resulting from their right to change the form of government, and to institute a new one, whenever necessary for their safety and happiness. . . . It was, therefore, the achievement of the whole for the benefit of the whole.[1]

Provincialism was strong; the newly created states were as jealous of each other as of Britain; the Congress was weak and at the mercy of the states; and many of the states proceeded as if they were sovereign. Nevertheless, in American law the theory has prevailed that a nation was created by the Declaration and the states remained sovereign only in the sense that in matters of a local nature they were self-governing. Of this the Supreme Court said in a recent decision:

> As a result of the separation from Great Britain by the colonies, acting as a unit, the powers of external sovereignty passed from the Crown not to the colonies severally, but to the colonies in their collective and corporate capacity as the United States of America. Even before the Declaration, the colonies were a unit in foreign affairs, acting through a common agency—namely, the Continental Congress,

[1] *Ibid.*, p. 149.

composed of delegates from the thirteen colonies. That agency exercised the powers of war and peace, raised an army, created a navy, and finally adopted the Declaration of Independence. Rulers come and go; governments end and forms of government change; but sovereignty survives. A political society cannot endure without a supreme will somewhere. Sovereignty is never held in suspense. When, therefore, the external sovereignty of Great Britain in respect of the colonies ceased, it immediately passed to the Union. . . .[1]

Overhauling of State Governments.—As events moved toward a showdown in 1775, crisis developed in the internal affairs of the colonies, requiring them to reorganize their governments. The flight of most of the royal governors and other British officials left the people in the royal colonies without any official government, while in other instances, as in Massachusetts, resistance to British authorities made new arrangements necessary. Turning to Congress for advice, that body recommended that the states adopt "such governments as shall, in the opinion of the representatives of the people, best conduce to the happiness and safety of their constituents." Since no machinery existed with which to make the transition, Congress recommended that new governments be established by "assemblies or conventions" in the respective states. Most of the states did so in 1775 and 1776; Massachusetts slipped back to her charter of 1691 until a new constitution was adopted in 1780 which has remained in effect to the present; while Rhode Island and Connecticut kept their colonial charters with scarcely any changes at all. For the first time in the history of the world a large group of communities had begun the formation of their own governments under written constitutions. As they did so, they referred to themselves as "states" rather than "colonies" as theretofore.

Provisions of the New State Constitutions.—These new constitutions followed the main outlines of the colonial governments and established the governmental framework of our present states. Seven of them contained bills of rights. All of them severely restricted the suffrage. All established three branches of government each supposedly independent of the other, but in practice the legislative branch became supreme. Reflecting the colonies' dislike of governors, the new constitutions deprived executives of many powers held during the colonial period. Executives were elected by the people in four states—by the legislature in the others—and customarily for terms of 1 year. In Pennsylvania and Georgia the legislature was unicameral, but in the other states the colonial custom of having two houses was followed. The lower house, variously called "house of burgesses," "house of commons," or "house of representatives," was almost exactly like that of colonial times; members were elected by the voters and served for 1-year terms. The upper house, called "legislative council" in New Jersey and Delaware and "senate" or "council"

[1] United States *v.* Curtiss-Wright Export Corp., 299 U.S. 304 (1936).

elsewhere, was, as a rule, elected by the voters or the lower house for terms varying from 1 to 5 years. The senate was a smaller body than the house, its members were chosen for longer terms, and the qualifications of its members were more exacting. The senate came to be recognized as representing propertied interests, while the house represented the people of the state.

The judicial systems of the colonies were incorporated in the new state governments with only a few changes. First, there were local peace magistrates and local inferior courts for the trial of petty civil cases and offenses. Above these stood a central court (analogous to our county or district courts of common pleas, quarter session, oyer and terminer, etc.) with civil and criminal jurisdiction over more serious cases. At the top stood a supreme court of review. In some states justices of peace and judges were appointed by the governor alone or with the advice and consent of the upper house, while in others they were chosen by the legislature. Georgia alone provided for popular election—the method now followed by all but a few of the states. Appointment was commonly for short terms and judges were usually subject to removal by the legislatures.

CONFEDERATION

Adoption of Articles of Confederation.—Both the First and Second Continental Congresses met and functioned without constitutions. They were created to meet an emergency and were looked upon merely as temporary agencies. When war appeared imminent and independence desirable, steps were taken to place the central government on a firm and permanent basis. On June 12, 1776, the day after a committee was appointed to prepare a declaration of independence, Congress appointed another committee consisting of one member from each colony "to prepare and digest the form of a confederation to be entered into between these colonies." The committee reported a month later and the plan was debated off and on until approved by Congress on Nov. 17, 1777. As approved, the Articles required ratification by the legislatures of all the states. All but Delaware and Maryland ratified in 1778. Holding out for assurances over the proper distribution and control of the territories west of the Allegheny Mountains, Delaware ratified in 1779, while Maryland delayed until Mar. 1, 1781, on which date the Articles went into effect. They were the first constitution of the United States of America.

Nature of the Union Created by the Articles.—It has been observed that, from a legal point of view, one nation, rather than thirteen, was created by the Declaration of Independence and suggested that in practice Congress was almost completely at the mercy of the states. The Articles removed all pretense about the nature of the new government. They were adopted by "delegates of the states," and Article III stated that the "states . . . severally enter into a firm league of friendship with each other." This was not, therefore, a union of all the people of the colonies considered as a whole, but a league of states. While binding themselves together "for their common defense, the security of their liberties, and their mutual general welfare," each retained "its sovereignty, freedom and independence, and every power, jurisdiction and right, which is [was] not expressly delegated to the United States, in Congress assembled."

Government Established by the Articles.—The governmental machinery authorized by the Articles was meager indeed. Congress, which continued to be called the Second Continental Congress, was the sole organ of government. There was no executive branch, but Congress was authorized to appoint such committees and "civil officers" as its executive business might require, and these were to perform their duties under its direction. Nor was there a separate judicial branch such as exists today. Federal courts were authorized only "for the trial of piracies and felonies committed on the high seas," for "reviewing and determining finally appeals in all cases of captures," and for the settlement of disputes between the states.

The Congress was unicameral and comprised of not less than two or more than seven delegates from each state appointed annually by the state legislatures. No person could be a delegate for more than 3 years in any term of 6 years. The delegates were paid by the states, if at all; they voted by states, with each state having one vote, and delegates could be recalled at any time and replaced by others.

Delegation of Powers to Congress by the Articles.—In constructing the Articles, the central government was given many of the powers wielded by the British government during the colonial period. No implied powers were granted; rather, Congress had only powers "expressly delegated." Specifically, some of those were: to declare war and conclude peace; conduct foreign relations, including the sending of ambassadors and making treaties; requisition revenue from the states in proportion to the value of land within each state; requisition soldiers in proportion to the number of white inhabitants in each state; borrow money, emit bills of credit, and coin money; build and equip a navy; settle disputes between the states; establish a postal system; regulate weights and measures; create courts for limited purposes; and appoint committees and officers. The most important of these, including the addition of amendments, could be exercised only with the concurrence of all the states, while the others required the approval of at least nine state delegations.

Obligations of States under the Articles.—On their part, the states pledged themselves to observe their obligations and the orders of Congress; extend full rights to one another's citizens; give full faith and credit to the records, acts, and judicial proceedings of every other state; deliver up fugitives from justice to each other; submit their disputes to Congress for settlement, and allow open intercourse and commerce between the states.

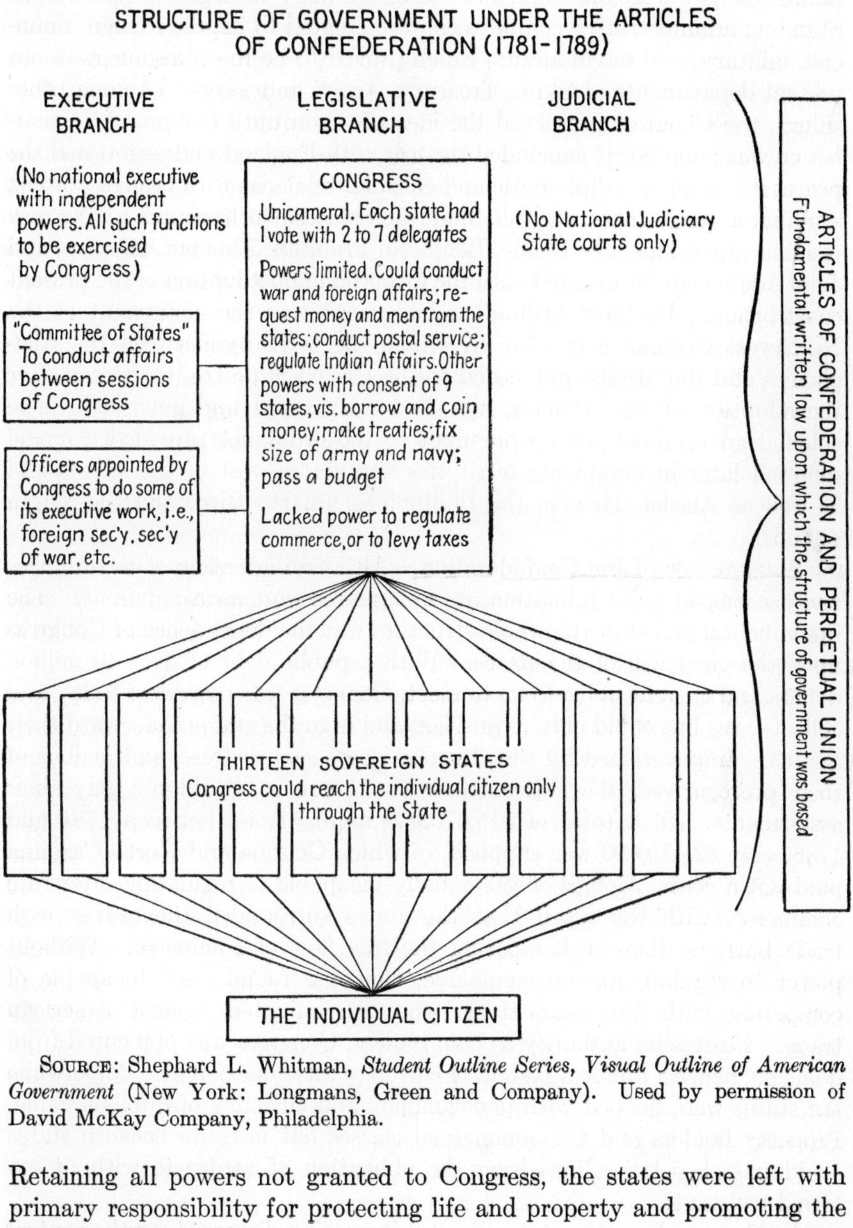
STRUCTURE OF GOVERNMENT UNDER THE ARTICLES OF CONFEDERATION (1781-1789)
EXECUTIVE BRANCH
LEGISLATIVE BRANCH
JUDICIAL BRANCH
(No national executive with independent powers. All such functions to be exercised by Congress)
CONGRESS
Unicameral. Each state had 1 vote with 2 to 7 delegates
Powers limited. Could conduct war and foreign affairs; request money and men from the states; conduct postal service; regulate Indian Affairs. Other powers with consent of 9 states, vis. borrow and coin money; make treaties; fix size of army and navy; pass a budget
Lacked power to regulate commerce, or to levy taxes
(No National Judiciary State courts only)
"Committee of States" To conduct affairs between sessions of Congress
Officers appointed by Congress to do some of its executive work, i.e., foreign sec'y, sec'y of war, etc.
THIRTEEN SOVEREIGN STATES
Congress could reach the individual citizen only through the State
THE INDIVIDUAL CITIZEN
ARTICLES OF CONFEDERATION AND PERPETUAL UNION
Fundamental written law upon which the structure of government was based

SOURCE: Shephard L. Whitman, *Student Outline Series, Visual Outline of American Government* (New York: Longmans, Green and Company). Used by permission of David McKay Company, Philadelphia.

Retaining all powers not granted to Congress, the states were left with primary responsibility for protecting life and property and promoting the general welfare.

Achievements of the Confederation.—Congress met annually in Philadelphia or other cities. Although entitled to ninety-one members, sessions were seldom attended by one-third that number and the rules adopted permitted as few as one-eighth of the entire body to negative resolutions. Standing administrative committees were created to handle foreign, financial, military, and naval affairs, which proved to be the forerunners of our present departments of State, Treasury, Army, and Navy. Among other things, the Congress preserved the idea of union until our present constitution was adopted; it concluded the war with England and negotiated the peace; it established diplomatic and consular relations with foreign powers, sending, among others, such distinguished statesmen to represent the new republic abroad as Silas Deane, Benjamin Franklin, Thomas Jefferson, and John Adams; and it assisted with the formation and adoption of the present constitution. Its most brilliant achievement was the enactment of the Northwest Ordinance in 1787 by which the territory between the Alleghenies and the Mississippi, ceded to the United States by the states after the adoption of the Articles, was to be organized and governed. The colonial government set up pursuant to the ordinance provided a model followed later in organizing territories and states west of the Mississippi as well as Alaska, Hawaii, the Philippines, Puerto Rico, and the Virgin Islands.

Weaknesses of the Confederation.—Although adoption of the Articles had occasioned great jubilation, its weaknesses were soon apparent. The fundamental defect of the whole structure was the dependence of Congress upon the good will of the states. With a public debt of over 40 million dollars and current obligations to meet, Congress was powerless to lay and collect taxes but could only requisition and urge the states to forward their quotas. Impoverished by war, harassed by social distress, and jealous of their prerogatives, the states either could not or would not pay their assessments. Of a total of $15,670,000 requisitioned between 1781 and 1786, only $2,419,000 was supplied, of which Georgia and North Carolina paid not a cent. Congress was equally incapable of regulating interstate commerce, with the result that the states surrounded themselves with trade barriers, thereby hampering the free flow of commerce. Without power to regulate foreign commerce, Congress found itself incapable of competing with European rivals who discriminated against American trade. Possessing authority to coin money, Congress was prevented from doing so; hence a uniform system of currency was nonexistent. Meanwhile the states were flooded with paper money and currency of dubious value. Property holders and the commercial classes felt insecure because states could pass legislation impairing the obligation of contracts without external restraint.

As time went on, the states showed increasing disregard for the central government. Knowing that they were usurping powers of Congress, some of the states insisted on regulating relations with the Indians. Others sent agents abroad for the negotiation of agreements and treaties as if they were sovereign nations. Most states organized their own navy and army and some conducted war outside their jurisdiction without the consent of Congress. Without larger powers, and without an independent executive and judiciary, the confederate congress became increasingly helpless. Two amendments which would have authorized Congress to levy tariff duties on imports failed of ratification by only one state—Rhode Island on the first occasion, New York on the other. All other attempts to improve the Articles having failed, the states were on the verge of civil war by the end of 1786. How serious affairs were was illustrated by Shays' Rebellion (1786) during which a multitude of angry debtors attempted to prevent the collection of debts and taxes by preventing judges from holding court in several parts of Massachusetts. At one time it looked as if the state government might be overwhelmed. Although suppressed, the incident frightened the leaders and conservative elements within the population to the point that they were willing to take steps to improve the framework of government.

The Conference at Alexandria.—Ignoring Congress, Maryland and Virginia, who had had incessant disputes over tariffs and navigation on the Potomac and adjoining waters, agreed to confer about those problems. Both appointed commissioners who met first at Alexandria, Va., then at Washington's home at Mount Vernon, in March, 1785. The commissioners formed a plan which contemplated uniform import duties and regulation of commerce and currency in the two states. Realizing that other states might also be interested in these problems, they recommended that invitations be sent to them to meet at some future time.

The Annapolis Convention.—Upon receipt of its commissioners' report, the Virginia legislature proposed that commissioners from all the states should meet at Annapolis for the purpose of considering the trade and commerce of the United States as a whole. Representatives of only five states appeared at the opening of the convention in September, 1786, but others had been appointed. When, after three weeks, the others did not appear, the delegates passed a resolution proposing that in 1787 another convention be called to meet in Philadelphia for the purpose of considering the state of the union. Congress was slow in approving the plan. Meanwhile, six states appointed delegates to the proposed Philadelphia convention. Finally, on Feb. 21, 1787, Congress recommended that the convention be held, in terms that ignored the Annapolis movement, but set the same place and date. Thereupon, all the other states, save Rhode Island, appointed delegates to attend the convention which formulated the present constitution.

REFERENCES

ADAMS, RANDOLPH G.: *Political Ideas of the American Revolution* (New York: Facsimile Library, 1939).

ANDREWS, CHARLES M.: *The Colonial Background of the American Revolution* (New Haven: Yale University Press, 1924).

BEARD, CHARLES A., and MARY R. BEARD: *The Rise of American Civilization* (New York: Macmillan, rev. and enl. ed., 4 vols., 1927–1942).

BECKER, CARL: *The Declaration of Independence* (New York: Harcourt Brace, 1922).

BLOOM, SOL (ed.): *History of Formation of the Union under the Constitution . . .* (Washington: Government Printing Office, 1941).

BRIDENBAUGH, CARL: *Cities in the Wilderness* (New York: Ronald, 1938).

BRYCE, JAMES: *The American Commonwealth* (New York: Macmillan, rev. ed., 2 vols., 1914).

BURDICK, CHARLES K.: *The Law of the American Constitution; Its Origin and Development* (New York: Putnam, 1922).

BURNETT, EDMUND C.: *The Continental Congress* (New York: Macmillan, 1941).

CHANNING, EDWARD: *Town and County Government in the English Colonies of North America* (Baltimore: Johns Hopkins Press, 1884).

DICKERSON, OLIVER M.: *American Colonial Governments* (Cleveland: Clark, 1912).

FISKE, JOHN: *The Critical Period of American History* (Boston: Houghton Mifflin, 1916).

HOCKETT, HOMER C.: *The Constitutional History of the United States, 1776–1826* (New York: Macmillan, 2 vols., 1939).

JENSEN, MERRILL: *The Articles of Confederation* (Madison: University of Wisconsin Press, 1940).

KENT, JAMES (ed. by W. M. Lacy): *Commentaries on American Law* (Philadelphia: Blakiston, 4 vols., 1889).

NEVINS, ALLAN: *The American States during and after the Revolution* (New York: Macmillan, 1924).

OSGOOD, HERBERT L.: *The American Colonies in the 17th Century* (New York: Columbia University Press, 1930).

——— *The American Colonies in the 18th Century* (New York: Columbia University Press, 4 vols., 1924–1925).

SAUNDERS, JENNINGS B.: *Evolution of the Executive Departments of the Continental Congress, 1774–1789* (Chapel Hill: The University of North Carolina Press, 1935).

SMITH, JOSEPH H.: *Appeals to the Privy Council from the American Plantations* (New York: Columbia University Press, 1949).

STORY, JOSEPH: *Commentaries on the Constitution of the United States* (Boston: Little, Brown, 4th ed., 2 vols., 1873).

THORPE, FRANCIS N.: *The Federal and State Constitutions, Colonial Charters, and Other Organic Laws of the States, Territories, and Colonies . . .*, House Doc. 357, 59th Cong., 2d Sess. (Washington: Government Printing Office, 7 vols., 1909).

UNITED STATES DEPARTMENT OF INTERIOR: *Handbook of Federal Indian Law* (Washington: Government Printing Office, 1942).

WISSLER, CLARK: *Indians of the United States; Four Centuries of Their History and Culture* (New York: Doubleday, 1940).

Chapter 3

FRAMING AND ADOPTING THE CONSTITUTION

The fabric of American empire ought to rest on the solid basis of *the consent of the people.* The streams of national power ought to flow immediately from that pure, original fountain of all legitimate authority.

Alexander Hamilton, *The Federalist.*[1]

THE CONSTITUTIONAL CONVENTION

Calling the Convention.—Acting upon the recommendation of the Annapolis Convention and in response to pressure from several states that had already appointed delegates, Congress adopted a resolution on Feb. 21, 1787, calling upon the states to send delegates to Philadelphia to meet on the second Monday in May

> . . . for the sole and express purpose of revising the Articles of Confederation and reporting to Congress and the several legislatures such alterations and provisions therein as shall when agreed to in Congress and confirmed by the states render the federal constitution adequate to the exigencies of Government & the preservation of the Union.

Delegates were promptly appointed in eleven of the states either by legislatures or by governors. New Hampshire was favorably disposed, but owing to local conditions failed to act before the convention was well under way. Rhode Island, where "radicals" who feared further centralization of power were in control, refused to send delegates. Credentials given the delegates authorized them to proceed to Philadelphia and there join with others in "devising, deliberating on, and discussing," to quote from credentials given the Pennsylvania delegation, "all such alterations and further Provisions, as may be necessary to render the federal Constitution fully adequate to the exigencies of the Union. . . ."[2]

Personnel of the Convention.—In all, seventy-four delegates were appointed; fifty-five put in an appearance at some time or other; an average of thirty were present at the sessions; and, at the close, thirty-nine signed the completed document. Thomas Jefferson and John Adams were in Europe on diplomatic missions or they surely would have been appointed.

[1] (New York: Modern Library, 1937), No. 22, p. 141.

[2] Copies of credentials furnished several delegations are printed in Arthur T. Prescott, *Drafting the Federal Constitution* (Baton Rouge: Louisiana State University Press, 1941), pp. 11–23. Others may be found in Charles C. Tansill (ed.), *Documents Illustrative of the Formation of the Union of the American States,* House Doc. 398, 69th Cong., 1st Sess. (Washington: Government Printing Office, 1927), pp. 55–84.

Patrick Henry "smelt a rat"[1] and declined appointment. Richard Henry Lee, then attending the sessions of Congress in New York, also declined, explaining that because he was a member of Congress he ought not to participate in the convention. John Jay was asked to be a delegate but declined. Samuel Adams and John Hancock were not appointed, while Thomas Paine had gone to Europe. Otherwise, nearly all the important leaders of the country were designated to attend the convention. The most distinguished figure was George Washington, who was still "first in the hearts of his countrymen." Others of prominence were James Madison, Edmund Randolph, and George Mason, of Virginia; Benjamin Franklin, Robert Morris, James Wilson, and Gouverneur Morris, of Pennsylvania; John Rutledge and Charles Pinckney, of South Carolina; Oliver Ellsworth, William Samuel Johnson, and John Sherman, of Connecticut; Rufus King, of Massachusetts; Alexander Hamilton, of New York; William Paterson, of New Jersey; and John Dickinson, of Delaware.

Qualifications of the Delegates.—The delegates were, on the whole, young men. Franklin, the oldest, was eighty-one; Dayton (New Jersey), the youngest, was twenty-six; fourteen were fifty or over; twenty-one were less than forty. The average was forty-two.[2] Most of them came from the educated and professional classes. Twenty-five were college men and thirty-three were lawyers or had studied law. Most outstanding of all was their wide experience in public affairs. Forty-six had served in the colonial or state legislatures; ten had attended state constitutional conventions; seven had been state governors. In national affairs, forty-two had been delegates to the Continental Congress; eight were signers of the Declaration of Independence; six were signers of the Articles of Confederation; seven had attended the Annapolis Convention; and three had been executive officers under the Continental Congress.[3]

From an economic point of view, the delegates belonged to the class described as "the rich, the well born, and the able." Charles A. Beard, after exhaustive research, has pointed out that:

1. All the delegates belonged to the professional and propertied classes—none represented in his personal economic interests the small-farming or mechanic class.

[1] The "rat" apparently was a suspicion that the nationalists intended doing more than revise the Articles. More particularly, his opposition to the movement for revision was based upon a fear that Northern statesmen would carry out a project begun by John Jay whereby navigation rights on the Mississippi would be sacrificed to Spain to the detriment of the South. Moses C. Tyler, *Patrick Henry* (Boston and New York: Houghton, 1915), pp. 298–312.

[2] Sol Bloom (ed.), *History of the Formation of the Union under the Constitution* . . . (Washington: Government Printing Office, 1935), p. 16.

[3] *Ibid.;* Max Farrand, *The Framing of the Constitution of the United States* (New Haven: Yale University Press, 1940 printing), pp. 38–39.

2. Most of the members came from towns on or near the coast, hence the hinterland with its small farmers, merchants, traders, and poorer classes generally was unrepresented.

3. Forty of the delegates had dealt extensively in public securities.

4. At least twenty-four delegates had engaged in lending money for interest.

5. Fourteen had invested in public lands for speculative purposes.

6. Eleven were personally interested in mercantile, manufacturing, and shipping enterprises.

7. At least fifteen were slaveholders.[1]

It is apparent, therefore, that the men who wrote the Constitution were practical men of affairs and that most of them had business and financial interests that stood to benefit by a revision of the Articles.

This is not to say that the men who wrote the Constitution were motivated solely, or even primarily, by personal and selfish considerations. Like all human beings, their thoughts were shaped by a multitude of factors. Fundamentally, it cannot be gainsaid, the Constitution reflects what in their judgment was necessary and adequate to protect and promote the economic interests of the "upper" classes of which they were a part.[2] If the document seems unduly cautious and conservative, one must remember that it provided for a more popular style of government than existed at that time in any other important country of the world. One must remember, also, that it contained provisions guaranteeing not only property rights but civil and political liberties as well. What is more significant, their handiwork has proved sufficiently flexible to permit control to pass from a small, wealthy, and conservative class to the masses without bloodshed or violence.

Estimates of the Delegates.—Much praise has been heaped upon those who attended the convention and wrote the Constitution. Jefferson, writing from Paris, characterized them as "an assembly of demi-gods." A French chargé, writing to his government, said "if all the delegates named for this Philadelphia Convention are present, one will never have seen, even in Europe, an assembly more respectable for talents, knowledge,

[1] *An Economic Interpretation of the Constitution of the United States* (New York: Macmillan, 1939 ed.), pp. 149–151. Used by permission of The Macmillan Company, publishers.

[2] Beard concludes: "The members of the Philadelphia Convention which drafted the Constitution were, with a few exceptions, immediately, directly, and personally interested in, and derived economic advantages from, the establishment of the new system." Also, that "The Constitution was essentially an economic document based upon the concept that the fundamental private rights of property are anterior to government and morally beyond the reach of popular majorities." *Ibid.*, p. 324. Quoted by permission of The Macmillan Company, publishers. Cf. Charles Warren, *Congress, the Constitution and the Supreme Court* (Boston: Little, Brown, 1925), p. 78.

disinterestedness and patriotism than those who will compose it."[1] Charles A. Beard has written:

It was a truly remarkable assembly of men that gathered in Philadelphia on May 14, 1787, to undertake the work of reconstructing the American system of government. It is not merely patriotic pride that compels one to assert that never in the history of assemblies has there been a convention of men richer in political experience and in practical knowledge, or endowed with a profounder insight into the springs of human action and the intimate essence of government. It is indeed an astonishing fact that at one time so many men skilled in statecraft could be found on the very frontiers of civilization among a population numbering about four million whites. It is no less a cause for admiration that their instrument of government should have survived the trials and crisis of a century that saw the wreck of more than a score of paper constitutions.[2]

Perhaps Professor Farrand, a distinguished historian of the Constitution, is near the truth when he concludes:

Great men there were, it is true, but the convention as a whole was composed of men such as would be appointed to a similar gathering at the present time: professional men, business men, and gentlemen of leisure; patriotic statesmen and clever, scheming politicians; some trained by experience and study for the task before them, and others utterly unfit. It was essentially a representative body, taking possibly a somewhat higher tone from the social conditions of the time, the seriousness of the crisis, and the character of the leaders.[3]

Organization of the Convention.—The second Monday in May, 1787, fell on the fourteenth, and on that day delegates from several of the states gathered in Independence Hall in Philadelphia where Congress had sat and the Declaration of Independence had been adopted. Because representatives from a majority of states failed to appear, the delegates met daily only to adjourn, until finally, on May 25, a quorum was present.

The convention organized immediately. Their first act was to choose a president. Franklin was a logical choice because of his age and reputation and also because he was then president of the state in whose capital the convention was being held. He withdrew, however, whereupon the Pennsylvania delegation placed Washington's name in nomination and he was promptly chosen by a unanimous vote. Major William Jackson, a former assistant secretary of war, who had actively sought the position, was then chosen secretary and other minor officers were appointed. Steps were then taken to have rules formulated. Among others, those adopted provided that each state delegation should have one vote, that a majority of

[1] Quoted in Homer C. Hockett, *The Constitutional History of the United States, 1776–1826* (New York: Macmillan, 2 vols., 1939), vol. 1, p. 206.

[2] *The Supreme Court and the Constitution* (New York: Macmillan, 1912), pp. 86–87. Quoted by permission of The Macmillan Company, publishers.

[3] Farrand, *op. cit.*, pp. 40–41.

states should constitute a quorum, and that the proceedings should be kept secret.[1]

Records of the Convention.—Jackson's minutes consist of the formal journal of the convention, the journal of the Committee of the Whole House, and records of votes cast.[2] The minutes consist of little more than a bare record of events and reveal little of what was said during the debates. Besides being meager, they were kept in an untidy manner and historians have found them frequently in error. Before the convention adjourned, the secretary was directed to leave his papers with Washington, who was instructed to keep them until further directed by Congress. Washington deposited them with the Department of State in 1796, where they remained untouched until 1818 when Congress ordered them to be printed.[3] Fortunately for posterity, notes were kept by several of the delegates, the most complete and reliable of which were those kept by the indefatigable Madison. These were purchased by Congress after Madison's death in 1836 and published in 1840 under the title of *The Papers of James Madison*.[4] Immediately they became the most authoritative source of information about the convention. One should note that no official records of the convention were available to those who construed the Constitution for 30 years prior to 1819. One should also note that Madison's illuminating notes were unavailable for more than half a century.

The Virginia Plan.—Preliminaries were over by May 29, whereupon the convention resolved itself into a committee of the whole for the purpose of hearing and giving preliminary consideration to various plans and proposals. The first and most important question presented to the committee was whether merely to revise the Articles or to construct a truly national government. The committee promptly decided in favor of a national government. Thereupon Governor Edmund Randolph of Virginia pre-

[1] In their anxiety for secrecy the delegates took every precaution against "leaks." Sentries were placed at the door to prevent eavesdropping. According to the Beards ". . . they even had a discreet colleague accompany the aged Franklin to his convivial dinners with a view to checking that amiable gentleman whenever, in unguarded moments, he threatened to divulge secrets of state." Charles A. and Mary R. Beard, *The Rise of American Civilization* (New York: Macmillan, 4 vols., 1927–1942), vol. I, p. 312. Quoted by permission of The Macmillan Company, publishers. In spite of their precautions, the pledge to secrecy appears not to have been faithfully kept by some of the members. Max Farrand (ed.), *The Records of the Federal Convention of 1787* (New Haven: Yale University Press, 3 vols., 1911), vol. I, p. 15.

[2] The originals of these may be found at present in the Bureau of Rolls and Library of the Department of State in Washington. Farrand, *Records . . .*, vol. I, pp. xi–xii.

[3] They may be consulted in almost any good library under the title of *Journal, Acts and Proceedings of the Convention, . . . which formed the Constitution of the United States* (Boston: T. B. Wait, 1819).

[4] The most pertinent documents, including Madison's Notes, may be found in *Documents Illustrative of the Formation of the Union of the American States*, previously cited.

sented a plan prepared under the leadership of Madison. The Virginia plan, as it was called, represented the large-state group and those favoring a strong central government and contemplated a complete overhauling of the Articles. Details of this and other plans presented are suggested and compared in the accompanying chart.

Presented on May 29, the Virginia plan was discussed for 2 weeks during which time serious objections were raised. Critics contended that it contemplated too great a departure from the Articles and placed the small states in a position of inequality. Had the plan been adopted as proposed, Virginia, for example, would have had fifteen or sixteen representatives in Congress while Georgia, Delaware, or Rhode Island would each have had only two or three. Besides giving the large states complete control over the legislature, adoption of the plan would have given them complete control over the executive and judicial branches as well.

The New Jersey and Other Plans.—Objections such as these led to counterproposals. Chief of these were the New Jersey, Pinckney, and Hamilton plans. Of these, the New Jersey plan, presented on June 15 by William Paterson, received most consideration. It contemplated a less radical departure from the Articles than the Virginia plan and won the support of confederationists and small-state delegations. After 4 days of debate the committee of the whole voted seven to five to reject it in favor of something more akin to the proposals made by Governor Randolph of Virginia.

Plans before the Constitutional Convention[1]

	Randolph (5/29/87), *Virginia*	Paterson (6/15/87), *New Jersey*	Pinckney (5/29/87), *South Carolina*	Hamilton (6/18/87), *New York*
Legislative	Bicameral One house popularly elected. Other chosen by first, from nominees of state legislatures.	Unicameral Delegates to be chosen by state legislatures.	Bicameral House of Delegates with one delegate for each 1,000 inhabitants (3/5 Negroes included). Senate elected by House of Delegates from four districts. Each state to have a number proportional to population.	Bicameral Assembly elected by people on basis of population. Terms, 3 years. Senate elected for life terms by electors chosen by people. States to have number set forth in constitution.

[1] For texts of these plans see Farrand, *Records* . . ., vol. III, pp. 593–631.

PLANS BEFORE THE CONSTITUTIONAL CONVENTION[1]—(*Continued*)

	Randolph (5/29/87), *Virginia*	Paterson (6/15/87), *New Jersey*	Pinckney (5/29/87), *South Carolina*	Hamilton (6/18/87), *New York*
Legislative	Bicameral Voting based on money contributions or free population or both.	Unicameral Each state one vote.	Bicameral Each delegate and senator to have one vote.	Bicameral
	Powers of Congress broad.	Powers of Congress enlarged. States to collect taxes but Congress to act if states default.	Powers of Congress broad.	Congress to have power to pass all laws deemed necessary to common defense and general welfare of Union. Senate alone to declare war, approve treaties and appointments.
Executive	Single executive chosen by Congress for one term only.	Plural executive chosen by Congress for one term only.	President elected by Congress annually.	President elected for life term by electors chosen by people within each state.
	Authority to execute laws.	Authority to execute laws, appoint, direct military operations.		Powers include: veto, execution of laws, war, treaties, appointments, pardons.
	Executive and "a convenient number" of the judiciary to form a Council of Revision to exercise a suspensive veto over acts of the national and state legislatures.			

[1] For texts of these plans see Farrand, *Records* . . ., vol. III, pp. 593–631.

PLANS BEFORE THE CONSTITUTIONAL CONVENTION[1]—(*Continued*)

	Randolph (5/29/87), *Virginia*	Paterson (6/15/87), *New Jersey*	Pinckney (5/29/87), *South Carolina*	Hamilton (6/18/87), *New York*
Judicial	Supreme and inferior courts. Judges appointed by Congress for life.	Supreme court only. Judges appointed by plural executive for life.	A federal court. Admiralty courts might be established by Congress in each state. Judges appointed for life.	Supreme court appointed by president with consent of Senate for life terms. Legislature given power to institute courts in each state. A special court provided to hear controversies over territories arising between United States and particular states.
Federal-State Relations	Federal government to admit new states and guarantee republican form of government. Federal government to negative state laws incompatible with the Union; also to use force against any state failing to fulfill its duty.	Acts of Congress and treaties "Supreme law of the respective states." Conflicting state laws forbidden. Federal executive to use force against noncooperative states.	Federal government to admit new states. States prohibited from keeping troops of war, entering into compacts etc. State laws to be approved by federal legislature before becoming effective.	State laws contrary to Constitution are void. Governors of states appointed by federal government and have veto over state legislation.

[1] For texts of these plans see Farrand, *Records* . . ., vol. III, pp. 593–631.

The Critical Period.—After endorsing the Virginia plan, the convention reconstituted itself (on June 18) to hear and consider the report of the committee of the whole. The next 5 weeks (until July 26) was the crucial period. On several occasions the convention appeared ready to go on the rocks. Martin of Maryland reported, on June 28, that it was on the verge of dissolution, "scarce held together by the strength of a hair," and Franklin proposed that the convention henceforth open its sessions with prayers. To this suggestion Hamilton and others thought that to start at that late date would bring on "some disagreeable animadversions" and lead the public to believe that the convention was split with dissension. Another delegate observed that the true cause was that the convention had no funds with which to hire a preacher. Whatever the reason, the suggestion was not followed, but the delegates nevertheless found ways of compromising their differences.

The Connecticut Compromise.—The Constitution has been referred to as a "bundle of compromises." This is true, although some of the compromises were of more importance than others. The crucial question was, How could a government strong enough to meet the exigencies of the hour be erected which would not "swallow up" the states nor place the small ones at the mercy of the larger? The nationalists argued that since state sovereignty had been the fundamental weakness of the Articles, a new government to be strong must derive its authority directly from the people. Accordingly, they pleaded for representation proportionate in both houses to population or tax contribution or both. Small-state delegates, on the other hand, made it clear that they would never enter a union in which their identity and equality would be impaired. Said John Dickinson of Delaware, "We would sooner submit to a foreign power, than to submit to be deprived of an equality of suffrage, in both branches of the legislature, and thereby thrown under the dominion of the larger states."[1] The solution of this impasse was an absolute prerequisite to further progress.

Day after day the issue was debated until finally, as hope ebbed, Dr. Johnson of Connecticut renewed a suggestion previously made which led to a solution. Said he:

> The controversy must be endless whilst Gentlemen differ in the grounds of their arguments; Those on one side considering the States as districts of people composing one political Society; those on the other considering them as so many political societies. . . . On the whole . . . in some respects the States are to be considered in their political capacity, and in others as districts of individual citizens, the two ideas embraced on different sides, instead of being opposed to each other, ought to be combined; that in *one* branch the *people,* ought to be represented; in the *other,* the *States.*[2]

Several days later a committee of eleven, one from each state represented, was appointed to effect a compromise along the lines suggested by Dr. Johnson. They reported on July 5, and after 10 days more of bitter debate (on July 16) the convention agreed to representation in proportion

[1] Farrand, *Records* . . ., vol. I, p. 242.

[2] *Ibid.*, vol. I, pp. 461–462. This was Madison's rendition of Dr. Johnson's remarks.

to population in the House of Representatives and equal representation of the states in the Senate with the proviso that all revenue bills must originate in the most popular house. Before giving full assent, however, the small-state delegations insisted on receiving some guarantee that once the new government was established, their equality in the Senate would not be changed. Accordingly, a provision was inserted in the amendment article (Article V) stating that no amendment might ever be made to the constitution which deprived any state of equal representation in the Senate without its consent. This became the only unamendable provision of the Constitution.

The Three-fifths Compromise.—No less fundamental than the dispute between large and small states was one involving the economic interests of the sections. Underlying debate was a deep-seated conflict between the planting interests of the South founded on slave labor, and the commercial and industrial interests of the North. Having leaped the hurdle of representation, the question arose of whether slaves should be counted in determining the number of representatives each state should have and for apportioning direct taxes. There were six slave states, which for obvious reasons wanted the slaves counted for representation but not for determining their share of direct taxes. Northern delegates contended that it was unfair to include them for representation inasmuch as slaves were not in law and fact equal with freemen. Moreover, to count them equally would make it possible for Southern states to increase their representation by the mere expedient of importing more slaves. Naturally Northern delegates wanted slaves counted when allocating quotas for direct taxes. In the end, Southern delegates agreed to a provision whereby three-fifths of all slaves would be counted in apportioning representatives provided they would be counted similarly when apportioning direct taxes.[1]

Commerce and Slave-trade Compromise.—Sectionalism showed itself on still another question of importance. Delegates from New England and the middle states where manufacturing, trade, and shipping interests were dominant came to the convention determined to see that the central government was given adequate powers to regulate interstate and foreign

[1] The Fourteenth Amendment, adopted after the Civil War (1868), modified this compromise provision by requiring that all persons, Negroes as well as white, should be counted when determining the number of representatives to which each state was entitled. While the Fourteenth Amendment said nothing about changing the basis for apportioning direct taxes, the three-fifths ratio was rendered meaningless by the Thirteenth Amendment which abolished slavery.

There is reason to suspect that this compromise proved more advantageous to the North than to the South inasmuch as Southern states had their representation diminished by the provision for a period extending from 1789 to 1860, whereas direct taxes were levied only four times prior to the Civil War and on each occasion they remained in effect for only a short time. See p. 365.

commerce. The planters of the South, however, were afraid that a government with those powers would prohibit the importation of slaves and enter into commercial agreements with foreign states which would adversely affect their interests. Ultimately, Congress was given plenary power "to regulate commerce with foreign nations and among the several states," and the President was empowered to negotiate treaties. The South was placated by two provisions: one declaring that the slave trade could not be prohibited for 20 years; the other requiring that treaties receive the approval of two-thirds of the Senate before becoming effective. Although not a part of the compromise, insertion of the provision forbidding the taxation of exports helped to allay the fears of Southern delegates.

Conclusion by the Convention of Its Labor.—By July 26 the larger issues had been agreed upon and the substance of the future Constitution formulated into twenty-six resolutions. On the date mentioned, these were referred to a Committee of Detail consisting of five men. After the appointment of this committee the convention recessed until Aug. 6 when it reassembled to receive the committee's report. For the next 5 weeks the convention labored day after day for 5 or 6 hours daily, discussing article by article, section by section. Finally, on Sept. 8, a Committee on Style was appointed to "revise the style of and arrange the articles which had been agreed to by the house." The committee arranged the document in its present form (excepting the amendments) and on Sept. 13 reported its handiwork written in the handwriting of its chairman, Gouverneur Morris. The Constitution was formally adopted on the fifteenth and 2 days later the signatures of thirty-nine of the delegates present—all but Gerry, Mason, and Randolph[1]—were attached whereupon the convention adjourned.

Sources of the Constitution.—For a long time there was a tendency in the United States to regard the Constitution as a new invention in political science. This impression was conveyed by the famous remark of the great English statesman William Gladstone when he observed that "as the British Constitution is the most subtle organism which has proceeded from progressive history, so the American Constitution is the most wonderful work ever struck off at a given time by the brain and purpose of man." Instead of having been "struck off at a given time," it had its roots deep in the past and, while containing some novel features, it is the embodiment of many antecedents.

In fact, there was little in the Constitution that was new. The men who wrote the document were familiar with the governments of antiquity, the English Constitution, and the governments of western Europe. They

[1] These men were in agreement with most of the Constitution but believed provision should have been made for a second convention to discuss criticisms and suggestions made during the process of ratification.

were also familiar with the political writings of the period, the most outstanding of which were Blackstone's *Commentaries on the Laws of England*, John Locke's *Two Treatises on Government*, Montesquieu's *Spirit of Laws*, and Rousseau's *Social Contract*. Moreover, they were saturated with the revolutionary literature that some of their contemporaries, including some of those in attendance at the convention, helped to write and disseminate.

Of more immediate importance, however, were the records and experiences of the Continental Congress, the Articles of Confederation, the state constitutions adopted after 1775, and the colonial charters and governments. Indeed, several students have found words and phrases in American colonial and revolutionary documents that are identical with or similar to virtually every provision of the Constitution.[1] It is instructive to compare these phrases from the Articles of Confederation and the Constitution:

Articles	*Constitution*
Congress shall have the power of "making rules for the government and regulation of the said land and naval forces. . . ."	Congress shall have power "to make rules for the government and regulation of the land and naval forces."
Congress shall have the power of "fixing the standard of weights and measures throughout the United States."	Congress shall have power to "fix the standard of weights and measures."
"Nor shall any person holding any office of profit or trust under the United States, or any of them, accept of any present, emolument, office or title of any kind whatsoever from any king, prince, or foreign state; nor shall the United States in Congress assembled, or any of them, grant any title of nobility."	"No title of nobility shall be granted by the United States; and no person holding any office of profit or trust under them shall, without the consent of the Congress, accept of any present, emolument, office, or title, of any kind whatever, from any king, prince, or foreign state."

Compare also certain provisions in the constitution of Massachusetts with those of the Constitution:[2]

[1] See especially, Breckinridge Long, *Genesis of the Constitution of the United States of America* (New York: Macmillan, 1926), pp. 223*ff;* Sydney G. Fisher, *The Evolution of the Constitution of the United States* (Philadelphia: Lippincott, 1897), *passim;* Charles E. Stevens, *Sources of the Constitution of the United States* (New York: Macmillan, new ed., 1894), *passim;* Warren, *op. cit.*, pp. 31–32; Robert L. Schuyler, *The Constitution of the United States: An Historical Survey of Its Formation* (New York: Macmillan, 1923), pp. 153–161.

[2] Warren, *op. cit.*, pp. 31–32.

Massachusetts	*Constitution*
"We . . . the people of Massachusetts . . . do . . . ordain and establish the following . . . as the Constitution of the Commonwealth of Massachusetts."	"We, the people of the United States . . . do ordain and establish this Constitution for the United States of America."
"Judgment shall not extend further than to removal from office and disqualification to hold or enjoy any place of honor, trust, or profit under this Commonwealth; but the party so convicted shall be, nevertheless, liable to indictment, trial, judgment and punishment, according to the laws of the land."	"Judgment . . . shall not extend further than to removal from office and disqualification to hold and enjoy any office of honor, trust or profit under the United States; but the party convicted shall, nevertheless, be liable and subject to indictment, trial, judgment and punishment according to law."
"All money bills shall originate in the House of Representatives; but the Senate may propose or concur with amendments as on other bills."[1]	"All bills for raising revenue shall originate in the House of Representatives; but the Senate may propose or concur with amendments as on other bills."

The Constitution was not, therefore, "solely the product" of the "creative wisdom" of the founding Fathers. Rather, it is more accurate to say the Constitution was a digest of the most approved principles and provisions of the charters of government with which the authors of the Constitution were intimately acquainted.

THE CAMPAIGN FOR RATIFICATION

Overcoming of Weaknesses of Articles.—Since the sole purpose for which the convention was called was for revising and improving the Articles, and the Constitution begins by referring to a "more perfect union," one might inquire as to how weaknesses of the Articles were overcome. The weaknesses and changes are made clearer by setting them forth in parallel columns.

Weaknesses of the Articles	*How Overcome by Constitution*
1. States were sovereign.	1. People of the whole nation were made sovereign. A federal union was created from which secession was impossible and the Federal Constitution and laws were made the supreme law of the land.

[1] The constitutions of seven other states contained the same statement. *Ibid.*

Weaknesses of the Articles	*How Overcome by Constitution*
2. No independent executive.	2. Article II provides for president chosen indirectly by the voters. President is given "the executive power"; he is made Commander in Chief of the Army and Navy, and may take all steps necessary to see that laws are faithfully executed.
3. No federal courts. Federal laws enforced by state courts.	3. Separate system of federal courts provided by Article III with authority to enforce federal laws and annul state laws inconsistent with Federal Constitution or laws.
4. No power to collect taxes.	4. Article I, Section VIII, empowers Congress to "*lay* and *collect* taxes, duties, imposts and excises."
5. No power over interstate and foreign commerce.	5. Article I, Section VIII, gives Congress power to regulate commerce with foreign nations, among the several states and with Indian tribes.
6. Congress an assembly of *delegates* chosen by state legislatures who were expected to vote as instructed and could be recalled.	6. Congress composed of *representatives* who have definite tenure and can act in any manner they choose. House of Representatives chosen by direct vote of people, Senate by state legislatures (now direct popular vote).
7. Articles could be amended only by consent of all the states.	7. Can be amended with approval of three-fourths of states.
8. Congress had only specifically delegated powers.	8. Congress given implied powers as well as delegated.
9. Central government could not act directly upon people.	9. Central government exercises its powers directly upon the people and concurrently with state governments.

Ratification Procedure.—The convention had been called to consider and suggest amendments to the Articles. Had the Articles been followed, it would have been necessary for Congress to consider and approve all the changes contained in the new Constitution and then refer them to the states to be approved by the legislature of *every* state before going into effect. Rather than follow this procedure the convention recommended one that was without legal sanction. It placed in the body of the Constitution itself (Article VII) a provision declaring that ratifications by conventions of the people of nine states should be sufficient for the establishment of the Constitution. The document was then sent to the Confederate Congress with the advice that the Congress should approve it, then refer it to the state legislatures which, in turn, should pass it along to conventions of the people in each state. It was also suggested that when nine conventions had approved, Congress should take steps to put the new government into operation and then go out of existence.[1] Of this action on the part of the convention Professor Burgess wrote:

> What they [the convention] actually did, stripped of all fiction and verbiage, was to assume constituent powers, ordain a Constitution of government and of liberty, and demand the *plébiscite* thereon, over the heads of all existing legally organized powers. Had Julius or Napoleon committed these acts, they would have been pronounced *coups d'état*. Looked at from the side of the people exercising the *plébiscite*, we term the movement revolution.[2]

Several considerations prompted this presumptuousness on the part of the convention. The nationalists had triumphed at the convention and they wanted to eliminate as many obstacles to acceptance as possible. Their greatest fear was that one or two state delegations in the discredited Congress would stymie action there or that one or two state legislatures would obstruct ratification. That this was a real danger is evident when it is recalled that Rhode Island had not been represented at the convention, most of the New York delegation had left the convention partly as a protest against its proceedings, and a number of delegates had spoken in opposition to the Constitution itself and the proposed method of ratification. Accordingly, the only chance of success was to hope that Congress would obediently refer the new Constitution to the states and that at least nine of them would provide for conventions. Besides improving the possibility of adoption, reference to conventions elected by the voters especially for the purpose of considering the Constitution would give greater validity to the words "We the people . . . do ordain and establish this constitution." It would also serve to emphasize the outstanding difference between the Constitution and the Articles, *viz.*, that this was a union of the people and not of the states. The gravity of the emergency, they believed, justified circumvention of the Articles.

[1] Beard, *The Supreme Court and the Constitution*, pp. 99–100; John W. Burgess, *Political Science and Comparative Constitutional Law* (Boston: Ginn, 2 vols., 1902), vol. I, p. 105.

[2] *Ibid.*

Federalists and Antifederalists.—The contest over adoption of the Constitution split leaders and the populace into two factions: the Federalists, who favored ratification, and the Antifederalists, those who opposed it. The contest was intense and bitter. For the most part, the campaign for ratification was led by those who had attended the convention. Popular support came largely from the more populous sections along the seaboard and from groups interested in finance, manufacturing, trade, and shipping. The Federalists had talent, wealth, and professional abilities on their side and they spent freely to educate the public and influence convention delegates.[1]

Conspicuous among the leaders of the Antifederalists were some of the "Old Patriots" of the Revolution including Patrick Henry, Richard Henry Lee, Samuel Adams, George Mason, and Elbridge Gerry. Their followers were chiefly back-country pioneers and small farmers who distrusted the "upper" classes and had few resources with which to support a campaign. Generally speaking, Dr. Beard writes, they "could do nothing but gnash their teeth."[2] They were further weakened by property-holding and tax-paying qualifications for voting. Moreover, they labored under the difficulty of getting country voters out in late fall and winter to vote in town or county elections.

Criticisms of the Proposed Constitution.—The Federalists dwelt upon the weaknesses of the Articles and labored to convince the people that the choice before them was the proposed Constitution or anarchy, chaos, and possibly civil war. Meanwhile, complaints were heard concerning almost every provision of the proposed document. The pious complained that the Constitution nowhere recognized the existence of God. Many who otherwise favored a stronger government strenuously objected to the fact that they were being asked to accept or reject the document with no opportunity of amending it prior to taking final action. Others opposed because the convention had exceeded its instructions and recommended adoption contrary to the method required by the Articles. Many contended that the President would become a monarch since he could serve for an indefinite number of terms.

Patriots like Patrick Henry, Richard Henry Lee, and others, noting that the document contained no bill of rights, dwelt upon dangers to liberty. The courts, it was feared, would usurp the powers and functions of state judiciaries. Paper money advocates feared the central government would upset the gains they had made through their state governments. Southerners were afraid the commercial interests of the North might dominate the Congress and use the treaty, tax, and commerce

[1] Beard, *An Economic Interpretation of the Constitution of the United States*, pp. 251–252.

[2] Beard, *The Supreme Court and the Constitution*, p. 102.

powers in a manner detrimental to their sectional interests. Northerners made a moral issue out of concessions made to the slave trade; while residents of larger states argued that too much had been conceded the small states. In general, the most persistent theme was that the states would be destroyed and the central government would become a tyrannical overlord. To offset these objections the Federalists yielded to the extent of promising the addition of a bill of rights as soon as the new government was organized. Without this concession the Constitution could never have been adopted.[1]

Ratification Completed.—Immediately upon the adjournment of the convention on Sept. 15, the document was sent to Congress, which was then meeting in New York City. There it was received without enthusiasm. After all, it was expecting a great deal to ask Congress "to light its own funeral pyre," as Bancroft has said. Nevertheless, Congress obediently (on Sept. 28, 1787) adopted a resolution transmitting it to the state legislatures to be submitted by them to state conventions. One state after another then enacted legislation authorizing the election of delegates to attend the conventions.

Voters in most of the states went to the polls to choose delegates during the fall and winter of 1787–1788. The number of delegates attending the state conventions varied from about 30 in Delaware to about 355 in Massachusetts. Delaware, one of the small states that had been appeased by the Connecticut Compromise, was the first to ratify. Others ratified in the following order and by the division of votes mentioned:

1. Delaware, Dec. 7, 1787; unanimous.
2. Pennsylvania, Dec. 12, 1787; 46–23.
3. New Jersey, Dec. 19, 1787; unanimous.
4. Georgia, Jan. 2, 1788; unanimous.
5. Connecticut, Jan. 9, 1788; 128–40.
6. Massachusetts, Feb. 6, 1788; 187–168.
7. Maryland, Apr. 28, 1788; 63–11.
8. South Carolina, May 23, 1788; 149–73.
9. New Hampshire, June 21, 1788; 57–46.
10. Virginia, June 25, 1788; 89–79.
11. New York, July 26, 1788; 30–27.
12. North Carolina, Nov. 21, 1789; 184–77.
13. Rhode Island, May 29, 1790; 34–32.

The Campaign for Ratification in Virginia and New York.—Note that nine states, sufficient to make the Constitution effective, had ratified by

[1] For further discussion of the Bill of Rights see Chap. 7. The most important source dealing with discussion of the proposed constitution is Jonathan Elliot, *Debates in the Several State Conventions on the Adoption of the Federal Constitution* (Washington: printed by the editor, 5 vols., 2d ed., 1836–1845).

the middle of June, 1788, but two of the largest states, Virginia and New York, were not among them. Everyone recognized the necessity of their adherence if the new union was to be successful; hence all eyes were upon the conventions in those states. The debate in the Virginia convention was one of the most celebrated in our history. Patrick Henry led the opposition, exclaiming and expostulating "in a turbulent stream of rhetoric."[1] He was supported in the convention by such celebrities as George Mason, William Grayson, and James Monroe; while outside, Richard Henry Lee worked sedulously against adoption. It was no easy task to engage such a brilliant orator as Patrick Henry in forensic combat, but Madison did so and once more distinguished himself. Of him during this contest Professor McLaughlin has written:

> Madison was the active leader of the Federalist forces, and he led them well; his temper was never ruffled nor his reason clouded. A careful study of Henry's brilliant oratory leaves one in wonder that day after day his fervid exclamations were answered with imperturbable calmness and placid good sense. Madison had none of the graces of oratory; he was small and unimpressive; his manner seemed at times to betoken irresolution; when he rose to speak, his voice was low, and he stood hat in hand as if he had just come in to give a passing word of counsel. But he knew what he was talking about, he was prepared to speak, and he did not envelop his thought in ornamental rhetorical wrappings.[2]

Madison was ably supported by John Marshall, then a young man of thirty-two, and Edmund Randolph. Although the latter was one of the three who had refused to sign the Constitution, he had since been won over to the Federalist cause. Washington was not a delegate, but his influence was great. The Federalists prevailed by a majority of ten votes but not without promising the addition of a bill of rights.

Likewise, in New York the campaign was intense and bitter and the outcome doubtful. When the Constitution was published the opposition was at first overwhelming. To overcome this opposition Alexander Hamilton induced James Madison and John Jay to unite with him in publishing a series of anonymous essays defending the new instrument and urging the necessity of its adoption. Gouverneur Morris was asked to join, but declined. During the winter of 1787–1788—before the convention met in Albany—seventy-seven essays appeared in the New York press entitled "The Federalist" and signed first "a Citizen of New York," then "Publius." These, together with eight others (making a total of eighty-five), were later published in book form under the same title.[3] These

[1] Andrew C. McLaughlin, *The Confederation and the Constitution, 1783–1789* (New York: Harper, 1905), p. 300.

[2] *Ibid.*

[3] *The Federalist* has appeared in more than thirty editions. The best for present use are those by Henry C. Lodge (New York: Putnam, 1888), and Paul L. Ford (New York:

essays did much to win support for the Constitution in New York and have since been considered the ablest exposition of the principles underlying the Constitution as well as one of the world's greatest treatises on government. After 5 weeks of acrimonious debate, the New York Convention ratified the Constitution by the narrow margin of three votes, and then only upon condition that a bill of rights be added at the earliest possible moment.

Extent of Popular Participation in Adoption of the Constitution.—The Constitution begins by saying "We, the people . . . do ordain and establish this Constitution. . . ." and much has been said about popular sovereignty. While this is undoubtedly true in a juristic or legal sense, it is nevertheless an exaggeration of what actually occurred. Actually, comparatively few people participated directly in the adoption of the Constitution. The suggestion of calling a constitutional convention was not submitted to popular vote. Delegates to the Philadelphia Convention were not elected by the voters but, rather, appointed by the legislatures and governors. Finally, the Constitution was not submitted to the voters for popular approval. The only point at which the voters were allowed to participate directly was in choosing delegates to attend the state conventions which ratified the Constitution.

Even so, only a few people—estimated at 160,000—participated in the choice of delegates. Of these probably not more than 100,000 favored adoption. Indeed, historians are inclined to believe that the Constitution would have failed of adoption had it been submitted to popular referendum.[1]

THE "MORE PERFECT" UNION

Organization of National Government.—The addition of Virginia and New York brought eleven states under the "new roof," whereupon the old Congress took steps looking toward the establishment of the new government.[2] On Sept. 13, 1788, Congress chose New York as the capital city and designated the first Wednesday in January as the day for the choice of presidential electors by the states,[3] the first Wednesday in Feb-

Holt, 1898). A popular inexpensive edition was published by Random House, Inc., New York, in the Modern Library Series, 1937.

[1] Beard, *An Economic Interpretation of the Constitution of the United States*, pp. 249–252.

[2] The formal organization of the old Congress was maintained until May 2, 1789, but for lack of a quorum it transacted no official business after the preceding October.

[3] Electors were chosen in two of the states, Virginia and Maryland, by direct vote of the people as is done now. Massachusetts selected two electors at large by direct vote and added eight more chosen by the legislature from twenty-four names sent up by the eight congressional districts. In seven other states selections were made by the legislatures. Three states named no electors: Rhode Island and North Carolina because of their failure to ratify the Constitution, and New York because of the inability of its legislature to come to an agreement. Asa E. Martin, *History of the United States* (Boston: Ginn, 2 vols., 1928), vol. I, p. 85.

ruary as the day upon which electors would meet in their respective states and vote for President, and the first Wednesday in March for the inauguration of the new government. Electors were appointed and met accordingly, twenty-two senators and fifty-nine representatives were duly elected, and the first Congress assembled on Mar. 4, 1789, in Federal Hall on Wall Street. Because a quorum was lacking, no business was transacted until Apr. 6. Then the electoral votes were counted by the president of the Senate before a joint session of Congress. George Washington was found to have been elected President by unanimous vote and John Adams Vice-President by a substantial majority. After a historic trip from his home at Mount Vernon to the new capital, Washington was inaugurated on Apr. 30. Immediately the new Congress proceeded to the task of creating and defining the powers, duties, and jurisdiction of the administrative and judicial branches of government, while the new president concerned himself with the selection of persons to fill the numerous offices. The promised bill of rights was proposed on Sept. 25, 1789. North Carolina ratified the Constitution in November, and Rhode Island did likewise in the following May after Congress had threatened to deprive her of the privilege of trading with the Union and secession had been threatened by several counties in which Federalist sentiment was strong.

References

Beard, Charles A.: *The Supreme Court and the Constitution* (New York: Macmillan, 1912).

——— *An Economic Interpretation of the Constitution of the United States* (New York: Macmillan, 1913).

Brant, Irving: *James Madison, the Nationalist, 1780–1787* (Indianapolis: Bobbs-Merrill, 1948).

Bryce, James: *The American Commonwealth* (New York: Macmillan, new ed., compl. rev., 2 vols., 1922–1923).

Burgess, John W.: *Political Science and Comparative Constitutional Law* (Boston: Ginn, 2 vols., 1902).

Butzner, Jane: *Constitutional Chaff; Rejected Suggestions of the Constitutional Convention of 1787* (New York: Columbia University Press, 1941).

Elliot, Jonathan (ed.): *Debates in the Several State Conventions on the Adoption of the Federal Constitution* (Washington: printed by the editor, 2d ed., 5 vols., 1836–1845).

Farrand, Max: *The Framing of the Constitution of the United States* (New Haven: Yale University Press, 1940 printing).

——— (ed.): *The Records of the Federal Convention of 1787* (New Haven: Yale University Press, 3 vols., 1911).

Fisher, Sydney G.: *The Evolution of the Constitution of the United States* (Philadelphia: Lippincott, 1897).

Hamilton, Alexander, *et al.* (ed. by Paul L. Ford): *The Federalist* (New York: Holt, 1898).

Harding, Samuel B.: *The Contest over the Ratification of the Federal Constitution in the State of Massachusetts* (New York: Longmans, 1896).

Long, Breckinridge: *Genesis of the Constitution of the United States of America* (New York: Macmillan, 1926).

McLaughlin, Andrew C.: *The Confederation and the Constitution, 1783–1789* (New York: Harper, 1905).

Miner, Clarence E.: *The Ratification of the Constitution by the State of New York* (New York: Columbia University Press, 1921).

Prescott, Arthur T. (comp.): *Drafting the Federal Constitution* (Baton Rouge: Louisiana State University Press, 1941).

Schuyler, Robert L.: *The Constitution of the United States: an Historical Survey of Its Formation* (New York: Macmillan, 1923).

Stevens, Charles E.: *Sources of the Constitution of the United States* (New York: Macmillan, 1894).

Stone, Frederick D., and John B. McMaster: *Pennsylvania and the Federal Constitution, 1787–1788* (Lancaster: Inquirer Printing and Publishing Co., for Historical Society of Pennsylvania, 1888).

Story, Joseph: *Commentaries on the Constitution of the United States* (Boston: Little, Brown, 4th ed., 2 vols., 1873).

Tansill, Charles C. (ed.): *Documents Illustrative of the Formation of the Union of the American States*, House Doc. 398, 69th Cong., 1st Sess. (Washington: Government Printing Office, 1927).

Umbreit, Kenneth B.: *Founding Fathers; Men Who Shaped Our Tradition* (New York: Harper, 1941).

Van Doren, Carl: *The Great Rehearsal; The Story of the Making and Ratifying of the Constitution of the United States* (New York: Viking, 1948).

White, Leonard D.: *The Federalists* (New York: Macmillan, 1948).

Chapter 4

CONSTITUTIONAL PRINCIPLES AND METHODS OF CHANGE

> The constitutional fathers, fresh from a revolution, did not forge a political strait-jacket for the generations to come.
>
> Justice Murphy in Schneiderman *v.* United States.[1]

The Constitution was not a revolutionary document but was designed to establish what was regarded then as a strong central government. The document itself is brief and contains little detail as compared with state constitutions. Its provisions are built around several fundamental principles deemed of crucial importance to those responsible for its drafting and adoption. Although the principles remain, the Constitution has been by no means static. This chapter reviews fundamental features and methods by which the Constitution has been adapted to changing conditions.

PRINCIPLES

Popular Sovereignty.—Sovereignty, or the authority and power to command and coerce all others, resides somewhere in every fully developed national state. During the Colonial period, the King and Parliament of England were sovereign; during the Revolution, Britain's sovereignty was suspended, the colonists claiming that they themselves were supreme; under the Articles of Confederation, ultimate authority was reposed in each of the thirteen states. But adoption of the Constitution transferred sovereignty to the people of the country. The preamble declares that "We the People of the United States . . . do ordain and establish this Constitution for the United States of America," and the presumption of popular sovereignty runs throughout the document. Accordingly, when a sufficient number of qualified voters act in unison, there is no legal limit to their power. They reign in the American political world, said De Tocqueville, "as the Deity does in the Universe."

Sovereignty in the People of the Whole Nation.—Although the principle itself is clear enough, several controversies have arisen over its application. The first and most troublesome arose between the advocates of States' rights and the nationalists. Admitting that the people were sovereign, the advocates of States' rights, of whom John C. Calhoun was the foremost and most capable spokesman, insisted that it was the people in each state who had ultimate legal authority. This meant, for example, that if the

[1] 320 U.S. 118 (1942).

people of a particular state wished to withdraw from the Union, they had the legal right to do so. The nationalists, on the other hand, claimed that it was the people of the whole nation irrespective of state lines who were sovereign. If this theory prevailed, the people of a particular state did not have final authority over their affairs; but, rather, their will was but a small segment of the whole and as such was subject to control by all the people of the nation. The Civil War settled the argument in favor of the nationalists. In consequence, sovereignty rests in the people of the several states, taken collectively.

Sovereignty in Only Some of the People. — Another controversy revolves around the nature of the franchise. The people are sovereign, yes. But which people, and how many of them? The courts have held that the word "people" as used in the preamble is synonymous with "citizens";[1] hence, aliens and nationals do not share sovereignty. But how many citizens exercise the rights of sovereignty? In practice, only those who vote or, at most, all those who are eligible to vote. But suppose that only a few are eligible to vote, as was the case during the formative years of the nation. Is the minority that holds political power obliged to extend the suffrage to the masses? The answer to this question is that at any given time sovereignty legally resides in that body of qualified voters who are competent to participate in amending the Constitution; voting is a privilege to be extended at the discretion of those who presently exercise power; the unenfranchised have no legal right to vote. Thus, youths under twenty-one, Negroes before the Civil War, women before they were enfranchised, and millions of others who fail to qualify for voting are not among the "people" in whom sovereignty resides.[2]

Popular Sovereignty and the Right to Revolt.—A third controversy, which is still heard, revolves around the question of whether the people have a legal right to revolt. Logically, if the voters are sovereign, it would seem that they can do anything they please whether by peaceful means or otherwise. Being reasonable and peace-loving people, they will normally use existing political machinery to express their will. But suppose only a few possess the franchise and will not enact legislation to enfranchise the masses. Or suppose that the Administration in power acts dictatorially, suppressing liberties, and otherwise ignoring the Constitution. What then? Have the people, or groups of them, the right to revolt?

Opinion is sharply divided on this thorny question. During the early

[1] United States Senate, *The Constitution of the United States of America* (annotated), Sen. Doc. 232, 74th Cong., 2d Sess. (Washington: Government Printing Office, 1938), p. 75.

[2] Edward M. Sait, *Political Institutions, A Preface* (New York: Appleton-Century, 1938), p. 143; Thomas M. Cooley, *A Treatise on the Constitutional Limitations Which Rest upon the Legislative Power of the States of the American Union* (Boston: Little, 6th ed., 1890), pp. 39–40.

years of the republic, the right of revolution was staunchly defended, doubtless in justification of the revolt from England, but also because it accorded with the democratic theory that pervaded the political atmosphere of the time. Typical of the expressions were the words of the Declaration of Independence which ran:

> We hold these truths to be self-evident. . . . That whenever any Form of Government becomes destructive of these ends, it is the Right of the People to alter or to abolish it, and to institute new Government, laying its foundation on such principles and organizing its powers in such form as to them shall seem most likely to effect their Safety and Happiness.

As memory of the Revolution dimmed, however, less emphasis came to be placed upon the right of revolution and more upon the right of existing governments to maintain law and order. In one of the few pronouncements upon the subject, the Supreme Court took the position that a state was justified in using as much military force as was necessary to put down an armed insurrection too strong to be controlled by the civil authority.[1] Another learned authority has said that, though the people are sovereign and may change or abolish their governments, yet this control "must be exercised in the legitimate mode previously agreed upon."[2] According to him, any attempt on the part of any group, "to interfere with the regular working of the agencies of government at any other time or in any other mode than as allowed by existing law . . . would be revolutionary in character, and must be resisted by the officers who, for the time being, represent legitimate government."[3] This view, though at variance with theory and the utterances of early American statesmen, is undoubtedly the one that would be acted upon by the Federal, state, and local governments if any sought to express their supposed right of revolution.[4]

A Federal System.—As noted on page 8, a state may be organized on a unitary basis, or as a confederation, or as a federal union. The circumstances existing in 1787 precluded consideration of a unitary system; the only choice lay between continuing and strengthening the confederation or building a federal union. By heroic efforts, a plan was devised which retained the states as integral units while welding the entire population into a powerful unit for dealing with matters of national concern.

Though there was much doubt in the minds of people living at the time

[1] Luther *v.* Borden, 7 Howard 1 (1849). This case grew out of Dorr's Rebellion in Rhode Island in 1842. The rebellion occurred as a result of the unwillingness of the established government to extend the suffrage to a greater number of people.

[2] Cooley, *op. cit.*, p. 747.

[3] *Ibid.*

[4] For a fuller discussion see William F. Willoughby, *The Government of Modern States* (New York: Appleton-Century, rev. and enl. ed., 1936), pp. 274–279; Edwin Mims, Jr., *The Majority of the People* (New York: Modern Age, 1941), Chaps. I and II.

of the adoption of the Constitution about the practicability of a federal union, their fears were ill-founded. The American federal union, though severely strained by the Civil War, has stood the test of over a century and a half. It stands today as the oldest federal union in existence. So successful has it been that many other countries have followed the American model, and a number of people now visualize a postwar world organized on a federal basis.[1]

Federal Supremacy.—In a federal system, jurisdictional conflicts are bound to arise between the central and regional governments. Experience demonstrates that when such conflicts arise federal law must be paramount or the interests of the people of the nation will be at the mercy of the inhabitants of individual states. Realizing this, the founding Fathers never doubted the necessity of subordinating state laws to those of the Federal government if and when the two came into conflict. Accordingly, they stipulated that the Federal Constitution, acts of Congress, and treaties were the "supreme law of the land."[2] When a conflict exists between federal and state law the matter is decided by federal courts.

A Representative System.—The Constitution established a representative democracy. Town meetings are still held in a few New England communities, and the referendum, initiative, and recall are used in a number of states. But, on the whole, American governmental institutions are run by representatives chosen directly or indirectly by the voters. This is especially true of the Federal government. As things stand, voters cannot initiate federal laws as they can in a number of states and cities. Nor can laws be enacted by referendums, although Congress can stipulate that referendums may be used to help determine when certain legislative provisions will become effective.[3] Nor are voters permitted to vote to recall federal officers as may be done in some of the states. Indeed, on only three occasions does the electorate participate directly in federal affairs: *viz.*, when voting for representatives, when choosing United States senators, and when voting for electors to choose the President and Vice-President. When these are chosen, all matters of government are left in their hands.

Three proposals have been made in recent years for allowing more direct participation in policy formation. One contemplates the direct election

[1] This subject is fully discussed in Chap. 25.

[2] See also p. 88.

[3] This is provided in the Agricultural Adjustment Act wherein farmers must vote and approve by a two-thirds majority before marketing quotas become effective. See p. 788. This arrangement has been held by the Supreme Court not to be an illegal delegation of powers given to Congress. Currin *v.* Wallace, 306 U.S. 1 (1939); United States *v.* Rock Royal Cooperative, 307 U.S. 533 (1939). Advisory referendums are also apparently constitutional. Where these are used the legislature merely submits a proposal to the voters to determine public sentiment. After the referendums the legislature is free to use its discretion about passing or rejecting the proposals voted upon.

of a President and Vice-President rather than election by the electoral college as at present. Another would require that constitutional amendments be submitted to popular referendum for ratification rather than to state legislatures or conventions as is now the case. The third proposes that the Constitution be amended to require a referendum vote before Congress can declare war except where the United States or a country in the Western Hemisphere is attacked. While there has been considerable sentiment in favor of each of these, none has been able to muster sufficient votes to pass the Congress. Whether the demand for more direct participation in the determination of governmental policies will become more urgent will, doubtless, depend upon the degree of confidence the public continues to have in those whom they elect.

Limited Government.—Government is admittedly a necessity, but it implies coercion and restraint. How to get enough governmental authority without creating an agency that will become abusive of liberty is a problem as old as human society. Those who wrote and ratified the Constitution thought they had found an answer to the paradoxical question. (1) They assumed that the people were sovereign. (2) The organization and powers of their governments were set forth in written documents in language as plain as could be commanded. (3) After carefully stating what powers they wished the Federal government to exercise, they left all residual powers to the states or to the people. (4) The three branches of government were separated and made to operate with elaborate checks and balances. (5) Both the Federal and state governments were specifically forbidden to perform certain acts. (6) Individual and personal rights were protected against invasion by either the Federal or state governments. (7) Powers could be exercised only by elected officers or those duly appointed by officials who had been chosen by the voters. And (8) it was provided that amendments could not be added to the Constitution unless desired by an overwhelming majority of the voters.

American governments, the states in particular, have frequently ignored injustices perpetrated by groups of citizens against races and minorities, and they themselves have occasionally been guilty of violating human liberties. On the whole, however, the record is a good one.[1]

Recent years have witnessed a decline in emphasis upon keeping government limited in favor of sentiment for bigger and stronger governments. The industrial revolution, wars, and depressions have created conditions that lead many to fear their consequences more than they do strong government. To these people government has become the champion and protector of the common man. Although insisting upon governmental respect for personal rights, many of the new schools look with impatience upon other traditional restraints that impede prompt enactment of welfare

[1] See also Chap. 7.

programs. This poses the crucial question of whether American governments can continue to meet recurring crises, provide the manifold services expected of them, and still avoid becoming dictatorial and tyrannical. British and American experience suggests that this can be done, although even there prolonged emergencies tend to weaken the bulwarks of personal liberty and democratic control.

Separation of Powers.—The three powers (or branches) of government may be united or separated. Where the parliamentary form exists, parliament is the central agency; the real executive, which is the prime minister and his cabinet, is selected by parliament from its own membership; and the courts are subordinate to the will of the legislature. Where dictatorships exist, powers are either united in the executive branch or, although technically separated, they are completely subordinate to the executive. Where powers are separated, each branch has its own powers and prerogatives the exercise of which serves to restrain the other branches, thus creating a check-and-balance system. The latter has long been considered a safeguard against tyranny.

Colonial statesmen had read about the separation of powers in writings of the Englishman John Locke and the Frenchman Montesquieu,[1] and their experience with autocratic British kings and colonial governors made them receptive to the theory. Consequently, it was incorporated into every one of the state constitutions adopted during the Revolution. A classic expression of the doctrine is found in the constitution of Massachusetts:

> In the government of this commonwealth, the legislative department shall never exercise the executive and judicial powers, or either of them: the executive shall never exercise the legislative and judicial powers, or either of them: the judicial shall never exercise the legislative and executive powers, or either of them: to the end that it may be a government of laws, and not of men.[2]

In view of the widespread distrust of political power generally and of a national government in particular, it was inevitable that powers should be separated in the new Constitution.

Constitutional Basis of Separation of Powers.—Unlike the constitution of Massachusetts, quoted above, the Federal Constitution does not state categorically that the powers are and must remain separated. That they are separated is because of language used in creating the three branches: Article I begins by saying, "*All* legislative powers herein granted shall be vested in a Congress." Article II begins with the statement that "*The* executive power shall be vested in a President." And Article III states

[1] P. 46.

[2] The Constitution of 1780 as reprinted in *The Constitution of the Several States of the Union and the United States* (New York: Barnes), p. 89.

that "*The* judicial power . . . shall be vested in one Supreme Court, and in such inferior courts as Congress may from time to time ordain and establish."[1] This inclusive and exclusive language, coupled with the fact that the powers are set forth in three different articles, provides the constitutional basis for their separation.

Checks and Balances.—Separation of powers is implemented by an elaborate system of checks and balances. To mention only a few: Congress is checked by the requirement that laws must receive the approval of both houses, by the President's veto, and by the power of judicial review of the courts. The President is checked by the fact that he cannot enact laws, that no money may be spent except in accordance with appropriations made by law, that Congress can override his veto, that he can be impeached, that treaties must be approved and appointments confirmed by the Senate, and by judicial review. The judicial branch is checked by the power retained by the people to amend the Constitution, by the power of the President with the advice and consent of the Senate to appoint judges, by the fact that judges can be impeached, and by the fact that Congress can determine the size of courts and limit the appellate jurisdiction of both the Supreme Court and inferior courts.

Criticisms of Separation of Powers.—While the doctrine of separation of powers has many apologists, it also has its critics. Some think that in spite of their formal separation there are too many ways whereby one or more of the branches acquires too much influence. Thus, the complaint is heard that the President by use of the radio, movie, press conference, patronage, and a widespread bureaucracy has acquired the ability to dominate Congress, to administer justice by the substitution of administrative adjudication, or by the exercise of undue influence over judicial decisions. Others complain because of legislative interference with administration. Still others think the courts have usurped authority which properly belongs to Congress and the President. Although there is some truth in each of these contentions, and certain corrections might well be made,[2] the fact is that it would be impossible to devise a workable governmental system without a considerable number of interrelationships between the three branches. Moreover, existing checks and balances do tend to restrain, with the result that over a period of time each of the three branches tends to "hold its own" in relation to the others.

Another group of critics decries separation of powers because it tends toward frustration of leadership and produces stalemates. They point to the British system where the three branches are united under Parliament with responsibility for leadership resting in the prime minister and cabinet who are at all times accountable to Parliament. The opposite is true under

[1] Italics are the authors'.
[2] See, for example, pp. 328, 454.

the American system, where the President may be of one political persuasion and Congress of another, with the result that little may be accomplished. Even where the Presidential and congressional majorities are of the same party, leadership is difficult. Members of Congress are likely to be prejudiced against executive initiative because the President is not one of them. The President and his cabinet cannot defend their policies on floors of the House and Senate. The executive may outline a budgetary plan only to see it emasculated by Congress. The President may negotiate treaties but a minority of the Senate can prevent their ratification. The President is charged with responsibility for effective administration but Congress can intervene and obstruct by withholding appropriations, by attaching riders to bills, by failing to confirm presidential appointments, or by insisting upon rewarding the friends and districts of congressmen. At the same time, critics insist, the courts may construe the Constitution so narrowly as to frustrate both the President and Congress.

These possibilities do exist. At the same time there are factors that tend to unify powers. Most important is the political party. Another is the fact that the President may initiate legislation, send messages to Congress, defend measures before committees, appeal and maneuver for public support, labor with individual congressmen, and threaten to withhold patronage. Meanwhile, if both the President and Congress persist, the courts can be brought to a more accommodating point of view, or if not, constitutional amendments can be sought.

In spite of these unifying devices, comparison with the British form leads to the conclusion that effective leadership is less likely to exist in the United States, except possibly during emergencies. In the past, however, Americans have not been conspicuously desirous of executive leadership. Various proposals have been made to ensure greater presidential leadership but early enactment of any of them seems unlikely. But if the emphasis upon a positive governmental program that existed during the depression and war persists, the situation may change and bring with it modifications in the traditional patterns of checks and balances.

Judicial Review.—The Constitution is silent on the important question of what would happen if the President, Congress, or the courts violated the Constitution. The President can, and often has, vetoed acts of Congress because he considered them in conflict with the Constitution. Likewise, Congress can retaliate in many ways against a President who violates the Constitution. Both the President and Congress have ways of reprimanding federal courts whose conduct and decisions they consider contrary to the Constitution. These checks operate continuously, and usually without great publicity or discussion. But early in American history the courts undertook to declare acts of Congress unconstitutional and this has occasioned violent controversy. Acceptance of the principle of judicial review has made the Supreme Court the most powerful judicial agency in the world. Several other countries have emulated American practice, but in none of them have the courts come to play such an important role as in the United States.

Judicial Review Intended.—Because the Constitution does not specifically grant the power of judicial review and the courts by their decisions have often irritated Congress, the President, and large sectors of the public, there has been much dispute over the courts' right to exercise the prerogative. The controversy has caused intensive historical research to discover the origin of the practice and the intent of those who wrote the Constitution. The evidence reveals that judicial review as we know it emerged with the adoption of written constitutions by the American states after their break with England in 1776.[1] The evidence also reveals that a majority of those who attended the Constitutional Convention favored judicial review.[2] Why, then, was specific provision not made for it? The answer seems to be that the framers of the Constitution believed the power to be clearly enough implied from language used.

Constitutional Basis for Judicial Review.—One of the pertinent provisions is found in Article VI which reads, in part, "This *Constitution*, and the *Laws* of the United States *which shall be made in Pursuance thereof;* and all Treaties made, or which shall be made, under the Authority of the United States, shall be the supreme Law of the Land. . . ."[3] Another relevant provision is Article III, Section 2, which says, "The judicial Power shall extend to all Cases, in Law and Equity, arising under this Constitution, the Laws of the United States, and Treaties made, or which shall be made, under their Authority. . . ."

With these as background, the Supreme Court faced the issue for the first time in Marbury *v.* Madison.[4] Briefly, the facts were that Congress had provided in the Judiciary Act of 1789 that requests for writs of mandamus[5] might originate in the Supreme Court. On the night of Mar. 3, 1801, Marbury had been appointed justice of peace for the District of Columbia by President Adams, whose term expired before the commission was delivered. The incoming President, Jefferson, and his Secretary of State, Madison, refused to deliver the commission to Marbury who imme-

[1] Westel W. Willoughby, *The Constitutional Law of the United States* (New York: Baker, Voorhis, 2d ed., 3 vols., 1929), in vol. I, p. 66; Charles G. Haines, *The American Doctrine of Judicial Supremacy* (Berkeley and Los Angeles: University of California Press, 2d ed., 1932), Chaps. III, IV, and V.

[2] *Ibid.*, Chap. VIII; Charles A. Beard, *The Supreme Court and the Constitution* (New York: Macmillan, 1912), *passim.*

[3] Italics are the authors'.

[4] 1 Cranch 137 (1803).

[5] Judicial orders commanding government officials to perform duties required by law.

diately petitioned the Supreme Court for a writ of mandamus as he was permitted to do by the Judiciary Act of 1789. Chief Justice Marshall wrote the opinion for the Court. After first saying that he thought Marbury was entitled to the commission, he went on to declare that the Supreme Court was without authority to grant a writ compelling delivery. This was because the Judiciary Act of 1789 had enlarged the original jurisdiction of the Supreme Court as prescribed by the Constitution, hence was in violation of the Constitution and therefore null and void.

Chief Justice Marshall's justification is based upon the following assumptions: (1) that the Constitution is a written document that clearly defines and limits the powers of government; (2) that the Constitution is a fundamental law and superior to ordinary legislative enactments; (3) that an act of the legislature that is contrary to the fundamental law is void and therefore cannot bind the courts; (4) that the judicial power together with oaths to uphold the Constitution that judges take requires that the courts declare when they believe acts of Congress violative of the Constitution. Although Marshall's reasoning has had many critics and his facts may have been of doubtful accuracy,[1] the principle of judicial review was firmly embedded in the American system of government.

Experience with Judicial Review.—To date there have been seventy-eight or more cases in which federal statutes have been declared unconstitutional by the Supreme Court. After the Marbury decision, 54 years elapsed before another statute was invalidated by the famous Dred Scott Case.[2] In that instance, a divided court declared the Missouri Compromise of 1820 unconstitutional and by doing so intensified the situation that later erupted in Civil War. The timetable of instances of judicial review is

	Number of Laws Declared Unconstitutional in Whole or in Part		Number of Laws Declared Unconstitutional in Whole or in Part
1790–1800	0	1880–1890	5
1800–1810	1	1890–1900	5
1810–1820	0	1900–1910	9
1820–1830	0	1910–1920	7
1830–1840	0	1920–1930	19
1840–1850	0	1930–1940	16
1850–1860	1	1940–1950	2[3]
1860–1870	4	Total	78
1870–1880	9		

[1] Haines, *op. cit.*, pp. 193–203.

[2] Dred Scott *v.* Standford, 19 Howard 393 (1857).

[3] One of these was Tot *v.* United States, 319 U.S. 463 (1943). This decision held invalid a provision of the Federal Firearms Act of 1938 that established the presumption that an accused criminal who had a prior crime record had obtained his firearm through the channels of interstate commerce and subsequent to the effective date of the statute—July 30, 1938. Establishment of the presumption shifted burden of proof from the

shown one page 65.[1] Review of the cases discloses two that have led to adoption of constitutional amendments;[2] only a few involving large questions of public policy, like the one arising from the NIRA,[3] where the Court was unanimous or nearly so; a few dealing with civil rights; several dealing with questions of a technical character; and a considerable number[4] of important, closely divided opinions many of which have been reversed by later courts.

Many who have reviewed American experience with judicial review contend that the Supreme Court has expanded its authority to such an extent that it has become a nonelective superlegislature. It is also insisted that the Court has shown undue partiality for property rights and excessive dependence upon legal formulas with the result that it has seriously retarded social progress. As evidence, critics offer the number of cases wherein the courts have declared welfare legislation unconstitutional only later to reverse their decisions in response to popular insistence.

While there is validity to these criticisms, there are few in the United States who advocate complete abandonment of judicial review. Various reforms have been suggested[5] but none has evoked popular enthusiasm. Experience in the United States and elsewhere suggests that while the courts may check political departments temporarily, they are likely to accommodate eventually if pressures are intense and persistent. Accordingly, whether important change is made in the practice of judicial review is likely to depend upon the degree of judicial restraint and the intensity and duration of future crises.

METHODS OF CHANGE

The American Constitution is the world's classic example of a written constitution. Nevertheless, it takes only cursory examination to discover

---

government to the accused. This, the Supreme Court ruled, violated due process of law guaranteed by the Fifth Amendment. The second case was United States *v.* Lovett, 328 U.S. 303 (1946). See p. 151.

[1] This tabulation to 1936 is based upon a study made by Wilfred C. Gilbert, of the Legislative Reference Service, entitled *Provisions of Federal Laws Held Unconstitutional by the Supreme Court of the United States* (Washington: Government Printing Office, 1936). Cf. Robert H. Jackson, *The Struggle for Judicial Supremacy* (New York: Knopf, 1941), p. 40. Information subsequent to 1936 was obtained from court decisions and the Administrative Office of the United States Courts.

[2] The Dred Scott decision led to the Thirteenth and Fourteenth Amendments, while the decision in Pollock *v.* Farmers' Loan and Trust Co. (158 U.S. 601, 1895) led to the Sixteenth Amendment.

[3] See p. 382.

[4] Like those dealing with the questions of legal tender, child labor, minimum wages for women, federal taxation of state instrumentalities, and regulation of large-scale productive enterprises.

[5] See, for example, p. 348.

that it has many unwritten features. Upon becoming acquainted with the document for the first time, one is likely to be astonished at finding that many of the most conspicuous features of the American system of government have no apparent constitutional foundation—features that have been added over the years by interpretation, custom, and usage.

Amendment.—The most obvious manner by which the Constitution may be changed is by the addition of amendments.[1] The method by which this is to be done is set forth in Article V which reads:

> The Congress, whenever two thirds of both Houses shall deem it necessary, shall propose Amendments to this Constitution, or, on the Application of the Legislatures of two thirds of the several States, shall call a Convention for proposing Amendments, which, in either Case, shall be valid to all Intents and Purposes, as Part of this Constitution, when ratified by the Legislatures of three fourths of the several States, or by Conventions in three fourths thereof, as the one or the other Mode of Ratification may be proposed by the Congress; Provided that no Amendment which may be made prior to the Year One thousand eight hundred and eight shall in any Manner affect the first and fourth Clauses in the Ninth Section of the first Article; and that no State, without its Consent, shall be deprived of its equal Suffrage in the Senate.

Before proceeding to a discussion of the procedure set forth in this article, two observations of a general character may be made. One is that the proposal and ratification of amendments is solely a legislative function—the President need not sign proposed amendments before they are sent to the states, nor do the state governors need to sign instruments of ratification. The second observation is that, except for the provision that a state's equality of representation cannot be diminished without its consent, any provision whatsoever can be legally altered by amendment.[2]

Proposal of Amendments.—Article V provides two methods by which amendments may be proposed; *viz.*, by a two-thirds[3] vote of both houses of Congress, and by a constitutional convention called after receiving petitions from legislatures in two-thirds of the states. Thus far, out of

[1] The discussion that follows is based largely upon the following sources: Denys P. Myers, *The Process of Constitutional Amendment*, Sen. Doc. 314, 76th Cong., 3d Sess. (Washington: Government Printing Office, 1940); Department of State Publication 573, *Ratification of the Twenty-first Amendment to the Constitution of the United States* (Washington: Government Printing Office, 1934); and *The Constitution of the United States* (annotated), cited above, pp. 555–558.

[2] Observe, however, that prior to 1808 amendments could not be made to the first and fourth clauses in the ninth section of Article I, which clauses permitted the slave trade for a period of 20 years after the adoption of the Constitution and stipulated that direct taxes must be apportioned among the states on the basis of population. These exceptions are no longer of importance.

[3] Two-thirds of the members present, assuming the presence of a quorum—not necessarily two-thirds of the total membership.

thousands of resolutions introduced in Congress,[1] only twenty-seven have mustered the necessary two-thirds vote of both houses.[2] None has been proposed by the alternate method of constitutional convention.

AMENDMENT PROCEDURE

Method of Proposal	*Methods of Ratification*
(Either may be used.)	(States may select either method unless Congress specifies which should be followed.)
1. By two-thirds vote of both houses of Congress (method used to propose all 27 amendments)	Legislatures in three-fourths (36) of the states (method used to ratify first 20 amendments); or Conventions in three-fourths (36) of the states (method used to ratify 1 Amendment—the 21st).
2. By constitutional convention called by Congress when petitioned to do so by two-thirds (32) of the states (method unused to date)	Legislatures in three-fourths (36) of the states; or Conventions in three-fourths (36) of the states.

If Congress is unwilling to submit amendments to the states, the legislatures thereof may force action by petitioning Congress to call a constitutional convention for the purpose. By 1940, petitions had been addressed to Congress on at least eighty-three occasions.[3] Some of these have been general in character, asking only that a convention be called. Others have urged calling a convention to consider specific matters such as the outlawing of polygamy, the direct election of the President and Vice-President, the control of trusts, and the direct election of senators. Petitions have never been received concerning any one subject from as many as two-thirds of the states, but enough were submitted urging the direct election of senators to play an important, if not decisive, role in forcing the submission of the Seventeenth Amendment.[4] If two-thirds of the states were to petition, Congress would be under obligation to call a convention.

Ratification.—Two methods of ratification are also provided by Article V; *viz*., by legislatures in three-fourths of the states or by conventions in a

[1] For a compilation of these from 1789 to 1889 see Herman V. Ames, *The Proposed Amendments to the Constitution of the United States during the First Century of Its History* (American Historical Association, Annual Report, 1896, II, published as House Doc. 353, pt. 2, 54th Cong., 2d Sess.). For those introduced between 1889 and 1928 see Michael A. Musmanno, *Proposed Amendments to the Constitution* . . . House Doc. 551, 70th Cong., 2d Sess. (Washington: Government Printing Office, 1929).

[2] For those proposed but unratified see p. 831.

[3] John M. Mathews and Clarence A. Berdahl, *Documents and Readings in American Government* (New York: Macmillan, rev. ed., 1940), pp. 48–50.

[4] *Ibid*., p. 48.

similar number of the states. Congress may indicate which method of ratification is to be followed, as it did in proposing that the twenty-first be considered in conventions, but failure to express preference leaves the states free to choose either one. States must use either legislatures or conventions—something else cannot be substituted—and the decision to ratify is irrevocable.[1] A rejection, however, does not preclude reconsideration of the proposal either by the same legislature or convention or by subsequent ones. The usual procedure is for the governor of the state, upon receipt of copy of a joint resolution of Congress, to refer the matter to the state legislature. If the resolution calls for the use of conventions, the state legislature will usually enact the necessary authorization, stating where and when the convention will be held, the number of delegates, etc. If conventions are not called for, the legislature may consider the amendment at any time it wishes. Ratification is legally consummated the minute the requisite three-fourths of the states ratify.

Thus far, all but the last of the twenty-one amendments have been approved by state legislatures. This method is simpler and less expensive inasmuch as legislatures are or will be in session anyway. The convention method may be somewhat faster due to the fact that those who attend do so for the single purpose of considering an amendment, whereas legislatures may be precariously divided along party lines and have many other matters to deal with. The convention method is also more likely to reflect clearly public opinion because the delegates are chosen after a campaign in which those who favor and those who oppose have done everything possible to elect a majority favorable to their point of view. The principal reason that impelled Congress to require that the Twenty-first Amendment be ratified by conventions seems to have been the desire for speedy action at a time when public opinion, as expressed in the election of a Democratic President and Congress in 1932, was known to be sympathetic to repeal of prohibition.

Time Necessary for Completing Ratification.—Ratification of an amendment may take place within a few minutes or many years after its proposal. Congress placed a time limit of 7 years in the Eighteenth, Twentieth, and Twenty-first Amendments. This action encouraged the belief that amendments "died of old age" unless a time limit were included or, as the Supreme Court said, unless ratification were completed "within some reasonable time after proposal."[2] But in 1939, the Supreme Court took a different view.[3] Holding that the child-labor amendment was still "alive" after 15 years, the Supreme Court said that the question as to whether there should be a time limit is a political one. Being such, Congress, and not the courts,

[1] Hawke *v.* Smith, 253 U.S. 221, 231 (1920).
[2] Dillon *v.* Gloss, 256 U.S. 368 (1921).
[3] Coleman *et al. v.* Miller *et al.*, 307 U.S. 433 (1939).

must decide what is a reasonable period. If Congress wishes to limit the period for ratification to 7 or any other number of years, it may do so; otherwise, proposed amendments are before the states indefinitely. Apparently, then, a state could still ratify any of the six amendments that have been proposed and remain unratified by the requisite number of states. On one occasion Ohio ratified an amendment submitted 80 years earlier. Connecticut, Georgia, and Massachusetts, somewhat embarrassed upon finding that they had never done so, ratified the first ten amendments as recently as 1939.[1] On the whole, the time required for ratification has been rather short, varying between 3 years and 7 months for the Sixteenth Amendment and only 7 months for the Twelfth. The average for the twenty-one amendments is 21 months.[2]

The First Twelve Amendments.—The first ten amendments, the famous Bill of Rights, were proposed by the first Congress in fulfillment of the pledge made by the Federalists in order to ensure the adoption of the Constitution. These, it should be noted, restrict the national government; they do not pertain to the states.[3] The Eleventh was added after the states had been incensed by a decision of the Supreme Court in which it held that Article III of the Constitution permitted states to be sued in federal courts.[4] The amendment was intended to guarantee that a "sovereign" state would never again be summoned before the federal judiciary as Georgia had been in the case cited. The Twelfth Amendment grew out of the election of 1800 during which Jefferson and Burr defeated Adams and Pinkney. When the electoral college met to cast their ballots, they discovered that by voting for the President and Vice-President on the same ballot, as Article II required, Jefferson and Burr had exactly the same number of votes. Although everyone understood Jefferson to have been the candidate for President and Burr the candidate for Vice-President, a tie existed which necessitated putting the election up to the House of Representatives. To ensure that this would never happen again, the Twelfth Amendment was proposed and promptly ratified.

The Civil War Amendments.—The next three amendments grew out of the Civil War. The Thirteenth prohibited slavery; the Fourteenth defined citizenship, forbade states to deprive persons of life, liberty, and property without due process of law, forbade states to deny anyone equal protection of the law, and provided a method by which states were to be punished for denying the right to vote to adult male citizens. The Fifteenth went still further by specifically forbidding either the Federal government or the states to deny people the right to vote because of race, color, or previous

[1] Myers, *op. cit.*, pp. 10–20.

[2] *Ibid.*, p. 29.

[3] Barron *v.* Baltimore, 7 Peters 243 (1833). For a fuller discussion see pp. 130.

[4] Chisholm *v.* Georgia, 2 Dallas 419 (1793).

condition of servitude. These three amendments were added only by resort to questionable methods. Approval of the Thirteenth was obtained with the help of West Virginia, whose secession from Virginia was of dubious legality, and with the aid of carpetbagger legislatures in several Southern states. Sufficient ratifications to the Fourteenth and Fifteenth were obtained only by making their approval a prerequisite for readmission of Southern states to full rights in the Union. Although the Fourteenth provides that states shall be punished for denying adult males the right to vote by having their representation in Congress diminished, Congress has never enforced the provision and is not likely to do so. The late Senator Borah sponsored an amendment that would have repealed this unenforced section of the Fourteenth Amendment. Though stymied, there is still some sentiment for the proposal.

Sixteenth to Nineteenth Amendments.—Forty-three years elapsed before additional amendments were added, during which time many people had become convinced that the Constitution could never again be changed by the amendment procedure. The next one overcame a decision of the Supreme Court wherein it was held that income taxes were direct taxes and as such must be apportioned among the states on the basis of population.[1] Since this precluded graduated income taxes based upon the capacity of people to pay, the Sixteenth Amendment was added. The Seventeenth was added shortly thereafter in order to transfer the election of United States senators from the state legislatures to the voters themselves. The Eighteenth was proposed after America had entered the First World War and ratified 2 months after the armistice. Its primary purpose was to add federal power to that of the states for the purpose of more effectually eliminating the evils of the liquor traffic. The Nineteenth resulted from years of agitation on the part of feminist leaders and organizations who clamored for legal recognition of woman's right to vote. Although many states had already granted women the privilege of voting, an amendment was necessary to ensure universal recognition of the privilege throughout the nation.

Recent Amendments.—The Twentieth Amendment added three procedural changes. Formerly, Congress convened regularly on the first Monday in December and remained in session as long as it pleased, passing up the first Mar. 4 that came along. This was the "long session." But when it convened the following December, Congress could remain in session only until Mar. 4, at which time the 2-year term for which representatives were chosen and the term of one-third of the senators expired. This was the "short session." Meanwhile, in the November that preceded the commencement of the short session, the entire membership of the House of Representatives and one-third of the Senate had stood for reelec-

[1] Pollock *v.* Farmers' Loan and Trust Company, 157 U.S. 429 (1895).

tion. Although some were defeated in November, they nevertheless convened with the rest in December and continued to serve throughout the short session, *i.e.*, until the following March 4. The fact that they could continue to serve for 4 months after having been defeated caused them to be dubbed "lame ducks." Meanwhile, while the lame ducks served throughout the short session, the new members chosen in the preceding November remained out of office. Since their terms began on Mar. 4, they could be called into special session at any time after that date, but if the President did not see fit to call a special session, they regularly convened in the following December—13 months after election. The Twentieth Amendment ended this by terminating all terms on Jan. 3 and providing that Congress would convene regularly on the same date. This means that both sessions of a Congress can be "long" and that only 2 months elapse between election and the commencement of duties. The second provision of the amendment moved the President's inauguration from Mar. 4 to Jan. 20. A third empowered Congress to provide for choosing a President and Vice-President in the event that something happened to prevent those elected in November of an election year from being inaugurated on the following Jan. 20. This was intended to overcome embarrassment such as occurred in the famous Hayes-Tilden contest of 1876 wherein controversy developed over which one was elected and the outcome remained uncertain until within a few hours of the date of inauguration.

Prohibition imposed gigantic responsibilities upon the national, state, and local governments, leading to endless controversy over the wisdom and desirability of attempting to interfere with personal liberty to the extent of forbidding the manufacture, transportation, and sale of intoxicating beverages. The depression which followed the stock market crash of 1929 brought with it an economic and social revolution which, in turn, brought into positions of power and influence the critics of prohibition. The result was the Twenty-first Amendment which repealed the Eighteenth and, significantly, empowered the states to control interstate shipments of intoxicating liquors.

Amendments Few and Hard to Obtain.—Looking over the twenty-one amendments, one is impressed by the infrequency with which they have been added. Omitting the first ten, which were adopted within a short time after the Constitution became effective, an amendment has been adopted on an average of one about every 15 years. But this is too favorable a picture. The Thirteenth, Fourteenth, and Fifteenth were ratified under questionable circumstances. If these are omitted, the record is one amendment added approximately every 20 years. While amendments can be speedily proposed and ratified, as was illustrated by the Twelfth, opinion must be overwhelmingly in favor of a proposal before this can happen. Proponents must marshal a two-thirds vote in both houses, or a total of 290 votes in the lower house and 64 votes in the Senate if the total membership is present. Opponents, on the other hand, need muster but one-third of the membership in only *one* of the houses (145 votes in the House or 32 in the Senate) to block a proposal. The situation is, if anything, worse when it comes to ratification. Proponents must obtain affirmative action in both houses of state legislatures in thirty-six states,[1]

TIMETABLE OF AMENDMENTS

Period	Number of years	Amendment ratified
1789–1792	4	I–X
1792–1798	6	None
1798–1804	6	XI, XII
1804–1865	61	None
1865–1870	5	XIII, XIV, XV
1870–1913	43	None
1913–1920	7	XVI, XVII, XVIII, XIX
1920–1933	13	None
1933–1934	1	XX, XXI
1934–1950	16	None

Average: For the twenty-one, one about every 8 years.
Omitting the first ten, one about every 15 years.

or a total of seventy-two separate legislative bodies. While opponents need to induce only *one* house in thirteen different states, or thirteen separate legislative bodies, to block ratification. These facts suggest that a small minority, estimated by some to be as low as 5 per cent of the population, can permanently defeat an amendment desired by a considerable majority of the people. This is particularly true where the amendment is likely to affect the economic interests of some geographic section of the country adversely.

The magnitude of the effort involved has undoubtedly deterred more frequent use of the amending procedure. Where no structural or procedural change is sought, but merely a different interpretation of a general phrase, those interested in seeing the Constitution altered are likely to seek their objective by putting pressure upon the courts rather than by resort to the amendment procedure. This was conspicuously the case during the controversy over slavery, legal tender, child labor, and the program of the New Deal.

Proposals to Change Amendment Procedure.—This situation has led many to advocate simplification of the amending procedure. The suggestions most frequently made are that the proposal of amendments be modified

[1] Except in the state of Nebraska where the legislature is unicameral.

to require only a majority vote in both houses of Congress, and ratification be changed to require the approval of two-thirds (rather than three-fourths) of the states, a simple majority of states, or a majority of the people voting by referendum in a majority of the states. Thus far it has been impossible to evoke enthusiasm for any of these suggestions. In any case, a determined minority, anticipating certain amendments that would be sure to follow, would probably resist simplifying the amendment procedure as strenuously as it would oppose specific amendments themselves.

Other Suggested Amendments.—Each year sees a number of resolutions proposing amendments introduced in Congress where they are referred to the judiciary committees of the respective houses and seldom given serious consideration. Each year also sees memorials adopted by one or more state legislatures calling upon Congress to call a convention for the consideration of suggested amendments. These, too, are referred to the judiciary committees and usually straightway forgotten. Something may come of them in the future if public opinion becomes sufficiently aroused. Among those currently active are suggestions for abolishing the electoral college; requiring that treaties be ratified by a majority vote of both houses of Congress rather than two-thirds of the Senate; limiting the number of terms a President may serve to two;[1] giving Congress power to outlaw child labor;[2] compelling recognition of equal rights for women; giving Congress power to abolish the poll tax as a prerequisite for voting; giving Congress power to act when state officials fail to prevent lynchings; and limiting the power of Congress to tax incomes, estates, and gifts to a maximum rate of 25 per cent.

Judicial Interpretation.—As already intimated, a constitution also grows and changes by judicial interpretation. This is particularly true of the American Federal Constitution, because it is written in concise, general words and phrases which often admit of varying interpretations. Almost every clause of the Constitution has been before the courts and it is chiefly from their decisions that an understanding of the document must be derived. Former Chief Justice Hughes epitomized the situation when he said, "We are under the Constitution, but the Constitution is what the judges say it is." A few illustrations make his meaning clear. The preamble, the courts have held, does not convey a grant of power; it is merely a declaration of purpose. A tax on incomes is a direct tax rather than an indirect one. Congress can create corporations, such as banks, to carry out its delegated powers. The Constitution does not follow the flag into

[1] This proposal mustered the necessary two-thirds approval of both houses of Congress and had been ratified by twenty-one states as of Jan. 1, 1949. For a discussion of the proposed amendment, see p. 300. For a copy of its text, see p. 831.

[2] The proposal passed Congress in 1924 and has been ratified by twenty-eight state legislatures. See copy of text, p. 831.

newly acquired territories. The first ten amendments apply to the national government only. The courts have authority to declare acts of Congress unconstitutional. A federal petit jury must consist of twelve persons.

Ordinarily, in deciding cases that come before them, the courts follow the rule of *stare decisis; i.e.*, they decide as they did in previous cases unless there is some compelling reason for them not to do so. This practice permits the formation of a body of "judge-made law." But judges may depart from precedents and these changes of opinion have the same effect, at least temporarily, as if formal amendments were enacted. American history is strewed with conspicuous instances of court reversals. In 1932 Justice Brandeis listed forty important instances wherein the Supreme Court had reversed itself or drastically modified its decisions.[1] Since his listing, more reversals have occurred than during any previous period of equal length. Careful study reveals that since 1936 the Supreme Court has reversed or greatly modified its interpretations of at least four of the most controversial provisions of the Constitution—the tax power, the commerce power, the Fifth and the Fourteenth Amendments. Indeed, constitutional lawyers of only a decade ago would scarcely recognize the Constitution of today. Then, Congress could not regulate manufacturing, mining, the generation of electric power, and agricultural production because they had no direct effect upon interstate commerce. Now, these are admitted to have sufficient effect upon interstate commerce to permit federal control. Then, Congress could not tax state instrumentalities and their employees, nor could states tax federal employees. Now, most of these intergovernmental immunities are gone. Then, states deprived liberty without due process of law by fixing minimum wages for women. Today, they do not. Then, a primary was not an election; now it is. If one were forced to decide which has had the greater influence in shaping American institutions, the amendment article or judicial interpretation, a strong case could be made for the latter.

Legislative Elaboration.—The Constitution is also what Congress says it is. Simple, general phrases may be elaborated by statutes in such a way as to give them unexpected meaning. Where this occurs, the effect is often as significant as if amendments were formally enacted. The principal basis for congressional elaboration has been the implied power that authorizes the enactment of all laws that are "necessary and proper" for carrying delegated powers into effect. Illustrations of the use of this power are legion. Executive departments are anticipated by three casual references in the Constitution but no direct authority to create them is given. Believing them necessary and proper for effective administration, Congress has not hesitated to legislate them into existence. Nowhere does the Constitution prescribe the precise manner by which inferior

[1] Burnet *v.* Coronado Oil and Gas Company, 285 U.S. 393 (1932).

officers of the government are to be selected. Article II, Section 2, merely states that their appointment may be vested in the President alone, in the courts of law, or in the heads of departments. Nevertheless, Congress many years ago enacted a civil service law which provided, among other things, for the creation of a Civil Service Commission and the recruitment of thousands of employees on the basis of ratings made in competitive examinations. The Constitution anticipates that the circumstance might arise when both the President and Vice-President might be removed from office and authorizes Congress to provide for the choice of a Chief Executive if such a contingency should arise. The provision was elaborated by the Presidential Succession Act of 1886 and more recently the Act of July 18, 1947 wherein it was provided that first the Speaker, then the President pro tempore of the Senate, then cabinet heads should become President in the order in which the departments were established. By broadly interpreting its powers, Congress has established and implemented a huge defense establishment, created dozens of administrative boards and bureaus, annexed a far-flung empire, entered into the business of education, banking, insurance, construction, transportation, generating electric power, and found authority to regulate the economic and social life of a highly industrialized and complicated nation.

Executive Interpretation.—The courts and Congress do not have a monopoly on the right to construe the Constitution. Over the years Presidents have insisted that the document meant what they said it did and their views have frequently prevailed. Jefferson, while admitting that his power to do so was doubtful, acquired Louisiana without prior authorization by Congress. Lincoln insisted that the Southern states had never been out of the Union. Johnson, Wilson, and Franklin D. Roosevelt contended that Congress could not restrict the removal of executive employees. Cleveland asserted the right to use federal troops within a state to enforce federal law or protect federal property. Theodore Roosevelt maintained that he could agree to supervise collection of Santo Domingo customs by executive agreement rather than by treaty as many in Congress preferred. Wilson asserted the right to arm merchantmen in spite of congressional opposition. Coolidge defended his refusal to send troops into a state to maintain order merely because a state legislature or governor asked him to do so. Various presidents have insisted that they were justified in sending armed forces anywhere in the world to protect American lives and property without obtaining legislative approval. Franklin D. Roosevelt successfully contended that the Constitution was broad enough to justify a far-reaching program of recovery and reform. Illustrations could be multiplied, but enough have been given to suggest that the Chief Executive has played a significant role in modifying and expanding the Constitution.

Custom and Usage.—Many of the unwritten provisions of the Constitution have been added simply by custom and usage. Political parties are not mentioned in the Constitution but long ago they became indispensable institutions. The electoral college, though looked upon as a brilliant invention by the framers of the Constitution, ceased functioning as originally intended as early as 1796. The President's cabinet is almost entirely the product of custom. Legislative committees are not authorized in the Constitution, but custom and usage have made them as permanent as if they were. Custom decrees that members of the House of Representatives must be residents of the districts from which they are chosen, et cetera.

The Constitution a Living Document.—Originally only a skeletal framework of government, the Constitution became a "living" document. Though written and unfrequently amended, it has kept pace with the American people, allowing them a maximum of freedom while providing machinery through which order might be maintained, domestic problems resolved with a minimum of violence, and national aspirations realized. Occasionally a voice is raised calling for a complete revision of the famous document.[1] Frequently, also, dissatisfied minorities clamor for drastic alterations. The latter may get their wish if revolutionary conditions prevail for a prolonged period of time. If such conditions can be avoided, total revision seems improbable. Amendments may be added occasionally but, as in the past, the Constitution is more likely to be adapted to changing needs and conditions by interpretation, custom, and usage.

References

AMES, HERMAN V.: "The Proposed Amendments to the Constitution . . . during the First Century of Its History" in *Annual Report of the American Historical Association for the Year 1896* (Washington: 1897), vol. II.

BEARD, CHARLES A.: *The Supreme Court and the Constitution* (New York: Macmillan, 1912).

BROWN, EVERETT S.: *Ratification of the Twenty-first Amendment to the Constitution of the United States; State Convention Records and Laws* (Ann Arbor: University of Michigan Press, 1938).

BURDICK, CHARLES K.: *The Law of the American Constitution: Its Origin and Development* (New York: Putnam, 1922).

CARR, ROBERT K.: *The Supreme Court and Judicial Review* (New York: Rinehart, 1942).

COOLEY, THOMAS M.: *A Treatise on Constitutional Limitations . . .* (Boston: Little, Brown, 6th ed., 1890).

CORWIN, EDWARD S.: *Court over Constitution; a Study of Judicial Review as an Instrument of Popular Government* (Princeton, N.J.: Princeton University Press, 1938).

——— *The Twilight of the Supreme Court* (New Haven: Yale University Press, 1934).

[1] See especially William Y. Elliott, *The Need for Constitutional Reform . . .* (New York: McGraw-Hill, 1935).

ELLIOTT, WILLIAM Y.: *The Need for Constitutional Reform; a Program for National Security* (New York: McGraw-Hill, 1935).

FENN, PERCY T.: *The Development of the Constitution* (New York: Appleton-Century-Crofts, 1948).

HAINES, CHARLES G.: *The American Doctrine of Judicial Supremacy* (Berkeley and Los Angeles: University of California Press, 2d ed., 1932).

——— *The Role of the Supreme Court in American Government* and *Politics, 1789–1835* (Berkeley and Los Angeles: University of California Press, 1944).

HAZLITT, HENRY: *A New Constitution Now* (New York: Whittlesey, 1942).

HEHMEYER, ALEXANDER: *Time for a Change; A Proposal for a Second Constitutional Convention* (New York: Rinehart, 1943).

HORWILL, HERBERT W.: *Usages of the American Constitution* (London: Oxford, 1925).

McBAIN, HOWARD L.: *The Living Constitution; a Consideration of the Realities and Legends of Our Fundamental Law* (New York: Macmillan, 1934).

McLAUGHLIN, ANDREW C.: *A Constitutional History of the United States* (New York: Appleton-Century-Crofts, 1935).

MERRIAM, CHARLES E.: *The Written Constitution and the Unwritten Attitude* (New York: Richard R. Smith, 1931).

MUNRO, WILLIAM B.: *The Makers of the Unwritten Constitution* (New York: Macmillan, 1930).

MUSMANNO, MICHAEL A.: *Proposed Amendments to the Constitution* . . ., House Doc. 551, 70th Cong., 2d Sess. (Washington: Government Printing Office, 1929).

MYERS, DENYS P.: *The Process of Constitutional Amendment*, Sen. Doc. 314, 76th Cong., 3d Sess. (Washington: Government Printing Office, 1941).

ORFIELD, LESTER B.: *Amending the Federal Constitution* (Chicago: Callaghan, 1942).

STORY, JOSEPH: *Commentaries on the Constitution of the United States* (Boston: Little, Brown, 4th ed., 2 vols., 1873).

SWISHER, CARL B.: *American Constitutional Development* (Boston: Houghton Mifflin, 1943).

——— *The Growth of Constitutional Power in the United States* (Chicago: University of Chicago Press, 1946).

TANSILL, CHARLES C. (ed.): *Proposed Amendments to the Constitution Introduced in Congress, December 4, 1899–July 2, 1926*, Sen. Doc. 93, 69th Cong., 1st Sess. (Washington: Government Printing Office, 1926).

WARREN, CHARLES: *Congress, the Constitution, and the Supreme Court* (Boston: Little, Brown, 1925).

WILLOUGHBY, WESTEL W.: *The Constitutional Law of the United States* (New York: Baker, Voorhis, 2d ed., 3 vols., 1929).

WRIGHT, BENJAMIN F.: *The Growth of American Constitutional Law* (New York: Reynal & Hitchcock, 1942).

TEXT-FILM

The following McGraw-Hill 35mm silent filmstrip is recommended for use with Chaps. 3 and 4:

The Constitution—Principles and Methods of Change. The underlying philosophy and the seven basic principles of the Constitution are outlined. Methods of change are explained. Protection of individual rights is included briefly.

Chapter 5

THE FEDERAL SYSTEM

All Americans have long been agreed that the only possible form of government for their country is a Federal one. All have perceived that a centralized system would be inexpedient, if not unworkable, over so large an area. . . .

James Bryce, *The American Commonwealth.*[1]

FEDERALISM IN THEORY AND PRACTICE

The Federal State.—The federal state is one in which authority is divided between self-governing parts and the central whole, each part operating in its sphere of action as defined in fundamental law.[2] Among federal states of the modern world are the United States of America, Switzerland, Canada, and the Commonwealth of Australia. The unitary state concentrates power in a single central government, which has legal omnipotence over all territory within the state. Examples of unitary states in recent times include France, Great Britain, and most of the smaller nations of the world.

Under the federal scheme, matters that are considered of primary importance to the country as a whole are assigned to the national government. Usually these services include foreign relations, defense, foreign commerce, and monetary matters. Functions deemed principally of local interest are given to provincial (in United States, state) governments. Local affairs include such matters as regulation of local commerce, public education, roads and highways. In all federal systems a basic difficulty is the impossibility of distributing powers between central and local governments on a permanently satisfactory basis. With changing conditions, alteration in distribution of powers is necessary; hence, there is a recurrence of constitutional crises in countries using the federal plan.

History of Federalism.—Federalism has been practiced since ancient times. Greek city-states united into leagues for common worship and

[1] (London: Macmillan, 2 vols., 1889), vol. I, p. 334. Used by permission of the publishers.

[2] See p. 8. The leading sources on the general aspects of federalism are: Sobei Mogi, *The Problem of Federalism* (London: Allen & Unwin, 1931); Carl J. Friedrich, *Constitutional Government and Democracy* (Boston: Little, 1941), Chap. XV; Herman Finer, *The Theory and Practice of Modern Government* (New York: Holt, rev. ed., 1949), Chaps. 10 and 11; Brij M. Sharma, *Federal Polity* (Lucknow: Upper India Publishing House, 1931); Dattatraya G. Karve, *Federations, a Study in Comparative Politics* (New York: Oxford, 1932); and Kenneth C. Wheare, *Federal Government* (New York: Oxford, 1947).

for the resistance of common enemies. In medieval times three notable confederations were established. The Lombard League was formed by northern Italian cities to resist the Hohenstaufens. In northern Germany the Hanseatic League achieved considerable commercial and political strength. The Netherlands Confederation bound the northern lowland provinces through the years of Spanish oppression.

Modern federations had a forerunner in the old Swiss Confederation, to which the authors of *The Federalist* allude frequently. It was, however, the launching of the United States that drew the attention of the modern world to the possibilities of federalism. The founding Fathers found little in historical precedent that would guide them in building the first modern truly federal constitution and in solving the difficult problems of distribution of powers between national and state governments. It is remarkable therefore, that they succeeded in framing a fundamental law that, with few amendments, has proved adaptable through a century and a half of revolutionary change.

Reasons for Adoption of Federalism.—A careful examination of a world map reveals a striking geographic fact about nations with the federal form of government. Nearly all countries very large in area have adopted the federal principle. Among these far-flung nations utilizing federalism in one form or another may be listed the Soviet Union, United States, Canada, Australia, Argentina, Brazil, and Mexico. In addition, most plans for governing free China and independent India involve federation, as do many proposals for world organization.

In virtually all the modern federal systems, historical or ethnic factors have made the formation of a unitary government impossible. A federal union was the natural solution for the American states, which sought effective unity on common problems yet wished to preserve individuality in local affairs. Switzerland is a trilingual country, with strong traditions of cantonal self-government. The First Reich (1871–1918) and Second Reich (1918–1933) eras in Germany found federation an appropriate device in transition from individual principalities to the centralized, totalitarian state. Both Canada and Australia were made up of former colonies of Great Britain; in each the welding of these territories together under unitary form was ruled out because of both geographic extent and historical separation. In Canada the French problem made federation even more necessary. Although the Bolshevik program of reform required close coordination, the polyglot population and scattered lands of Russia dictated federal form, if not spirit.

In two of the four Latin-American federations, Mexico and Venezuela, the adoption of federalism was due in large part to the desire to imitate the liberal institutions of the United States. Although strong reasons existed for the use of the federal plan in Argentina and Brazil, these coun-

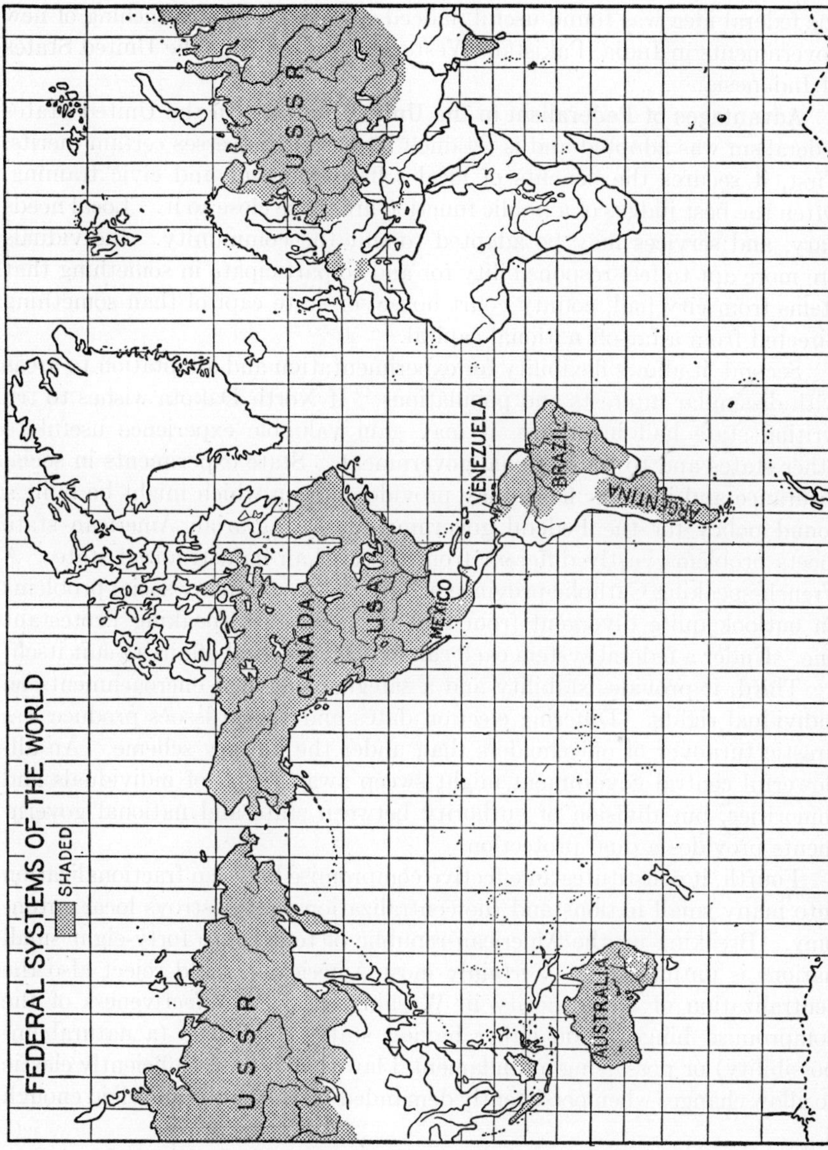
FEDERAL SYSTEMS OF THE WORLD
SHADED
U S S R
CANADA
U S A
MEXICO
VENEZUELA
BRAZIL
ARGENTINA
AUSTRALIA
U S S R

tries in recent years have all but abandoned federalism through constant national intervention in state affairs.[1] Following the Second World War the federal idea was found useful, indeed essential, in the launching of new governments in India, Pakistan, Western Germany, and the United States of Indonesia.

Advantages of Federalism in the United States.—In the United States federalism was adopted and is retained because it possesses certain merits. First, it secures the benefits of local self-government and civic training. Often the best judges of a public function are those close to it. Local needs vary, and services may be adapted to suit the community. Individuals are more apt to feel responsibility for and to participate in something that stems from city hall, county court house, or state capitol than something directed from a far-off national capital.

Second, it allows flexibility for experimentation and adaptation to areas with dissimilar interests and populations. If North Dakota wishes to try writing state hail insurance, it may gain valuable experience useful to other states and to the national government. State experiments in social insurance and in other fields may provide data on which might be built a sound policy for the Federal government. An agrarian American state meets problems vastly different from those of an industrialized state. A French-speaking Catholic province of Canada has on many social problems an outlook quite divergent from that of an English-speaking Protestant one. Under a federal system each can manage its local affairs to suit itself.

Third, it provides stability and a safeguard against encroachments on individual rights. Differing election dates and varied issues produce less drastic turnover of officeholders than under the unitary scheme. An all-powerful central government might sweep away rights of individuals and minorities, but division of authority between state and national governments provides a dual protection.

Fourth, it constitutes an effective compromise between fractionalization into many small nations and the centralization that destroys local autonomy. Breaking up the American republic of today into forty-eight small nations is unthinkable. Certainly most Americans would reject also the centralization of all authority in Washington. The effectiveness of the compromise hinges upon either having static conditions (a natural impossibility) or possessing a fundamental law that is both sufficiently elastic to allow changes when persistently demanded by the public and rigid enough

[1] Russell H. Fitzgibbon, "Constitutional Development in Latin America: A Synthesis," *American Political Science Review*, vol. 39 (June, 1945), pp. 511–522. For further information on Latin-American federations see Karl Loewenstein, *Brazil under Vargas* (New York: Macmillan, 1942), pp. 59–75; also articles by Clarence H. Haring, Percy A. Martin, and J. Lloyd Mecham in Conyers Read (ed.) *The Constitution Reconsidered* (New York: Columbia University Press, 1938), pp. 341–384.

to resist momentary gusts of passion. Viewed over a long-time period, the American federal system has proved adaptable to the needs of a growing people and a dynamic society.

Shortcomings of American Federalism.—No useful purpose is served, however, by heaping unstinted praise upon federalism and closing eyes to its several shortcomings. First, and most important, distribution of powers between two levels of government on a permanently satisfactory basis is impossible. Technological developments, economic conditions, wars, social changes—these alter the problems of government and may necessitate reallocation of responsibilities for particular public services. If the constitution in which powers are assigned is precise and inflexible, dissatisfaction over the resulting social lag may be very great. At several critical periods in American history problems that had become clearly national in scope were held not subject to federal legislation. Three federal attempts to curb the evils of child labor were declared unconstitutional before the wages-and-hours law of 1938 finally was found valid.[1] In the United States the national and state powers were defined in very general terms. Federal authority has been expanded mainly through liberalized interpretations of national powers by the Supreme Court.

Second, diffusion of authority leads to delay and deadlock in critical times. In war and economic depression the country has found its parts divided against themselves and lacking the unity necessary to solve the great issues at hand. The sense of corporate unity that has enveloped the nation during its major wars and the broad nature of the war powers have caused less embarrassment than have some domestic crises. During the depression of the early 1930's many cases of inactivity were the result of this disunity.

Third, confusion arises under the federal plan from the lack of uniformity in laws, and extra expense is incurred through the maintenance of two levels of government. While some progress has been made toward securing uniform state legislation in certain fields, the diversity of state law is enormous, to the great dismay of the individual and to the added expense of those doing business. Often it is said that two levels of government are more expensive than one; the statement may be true, probably more true than not, but the scope of the problem makes the question highly speculative.

The present trend appears to be away from federalism. Several states that formerly utilized federalism have lost its form or spirit as they have become dictatorships. Germany, Austria, and other onetime federal states fell into this category. Other federal states, like the United States, have been altered profoundly in the last two decades, chiefly in the direction of expanding central authority at the expense of local autonomy.

[1] Cf. p. 737.

The Balance Sheet of Federalism[1]

Merits of Well-conceived Local Control

1. Promotes local unity, sense of neighborhood responsibility, spirit of self-reliance and capacity for group action.
2. Secures close adaptation of public services to local needs.
3. Promotes and safeguards freedom, democracy, and responsible government.
4. Promotes socially beneficial intercommunity competition.
5. Permits safe experimentation with new forms and methods of government, thus fostering a gradual improvement in government throughout the country.
6. Promotes political stability.
7. Promotes national unity and national security.
8. Relieves the national government of congestion of business.

Shortcomings of Excessive Decentralization

1. Results in an inefficient and an uneconomic management of local affairs.
2. Fosters local autocratic rule by petty officials and powerful minority groups.
3. Breeds narrow parochialism and produces national and regional disunity and disorganization.
4. Results in extreme inequality in the standards of public service and protection of civil rights throughout the country or the region.
5. Produces inertia and extreme rigidity in the organization and operation of the government.
6. Lessens national security.

Merits of Well-conceived Central Control

1. Unifies the nation.
2. Provides for the common or national needs of the population and for a coordinated development of the nation's resources.
3. Safeguards the nation's independence.
4. Safeguards the liberties of the people in a democratic country and provides for an equality of social, economic, and educational opportunities in the various sections of the country.
5. Responds quickly to changed national situations and takes care of national emergencies.
6. Is more efficient and economical in many respects than are local governments.
7. Gives common direction to local governments, impels them to maintain minimum standards of public service, and helps them to operate more efficiently.

Dangers of Excessive Centralization of Government

1. Promotes a rule of an irresponsible national bureaucracy and destroys democracy.
2. Results in a neglect of local needs.
3. Destroys local civic interest, initiative, and responsibility, individual freedom and self-reliance.
4. Results in the instability of governmental policies, and of the government itself.
5. Results in inefficiency and waste.
6. Produces a congestion of business, industry, arts, and culture in the capital and the economic and cultural decay of the rest of the country.
7. Weakens national unity and national security.

[1] Condensed from Paul Studenski and Paul R. Mort, *Centralized vs. Decentralized Government in Relation to Democracy* (New York: Teachers College, Columbia University, 1941).

Read, will help

DISTRIBUTION OF POWERS

Delegated Powers of the National Government.—The American national government possesses only those powers specifically delegated to it, or reasonably to be inferred from the Constitution. The Tenth Amendment declares: "The powers not delegated to the United States by the Constitution, nor prohibited by it to the States, are reserved to the States respectively, or to the people."

The major federal powers are enumerated as powers of Congress in Article I, Section 8. They are shown on the accompanying chart.[1] Other federal powers are provided for in other parts of the Constitution.

That the national government today appears to possess powers not exercised in the years following 1789 does not disprove the fact that the United States has a central government of enumerated powers only. Some of the federal powers, especially tax and commerce, have grown tremendously in scope; the Constitution has shown great capacity for adaptation to changed conditions. Nevertheless, every activity of the national government must be justified under one or more of the specifically delegated powers. Congress lacks a general welfare power, under which it might do anything required by the public interest. Each act of Congress must be hung upon a constitutional "hook"—commerce, tax, monetary, or other. If no constitutional delegation can be found, or if one is improperly used, the legislation may be attacked as unconstitutional. The fact that Congress possesses only powers specifically delegated to it is one of the outstanding features of American government and must be understood as a prerequisite to further progress.

Implied Powers.—After the list of powers of Congress given in Article I, Section 8, the Constitution grants Congress authority to: "make all Laws which shall be necessary and proper for carrying into Execution the foregoing Powers, and all other Powers vested by this Constitution in the Government of the United States, or in any Department or Officer thereof." This "elastic" or "necessary and proper" clause has given rise to extended controversy over the breadth of national authority.

The "strict constructionalist" versus "broad constructionalist" conflict over this point has raged at several periods of national history. What unspecified powers reasonably might be implied from those specifically delegated? Hamilton and his followers claimed that Congress possessed authority to do many things in addition to the powers explicitly stated. Jefferson and his supporters insisted that federal powers should be interpreted by the letter of the Constitution and that no authority could be exercised unless specifically delegated.

[1] Each of these is discussed in detail in later chapters.

Under John Marshall, Chief Justice from 1801 to 1835, the Supreme Court rendered many decisions that supported broad interpretation. The most celebrated case was McCulloch *v.* Maryland (1819).[1] Maryland had levied a tax upon notes issued by the Baltimore branch of the second United

Examples of Federal Powers

Delegated

1. To tax.
2. To borrow and coin money.
3. To establish post offices and post roads.
4. To grant patents and copyrights.
5. To regulate interstate and foreign commerce.
6. To establish inferior courts.
7. To declare war, grant letters of marque and reprisal.
8. To raise and support an army.
9. To maintain a navy.
10. To provide for militia.
11. To govern territories and property.
12. To define and punish piracies and felonies on the high seas.
13. To fix standards of weights and measures.
14. To conduct foreign relations.

Implied

1. To establish banks or other corporations implied from delegated powers to tax, borrow, and to regulate commerce.
2. To spend money for roads, schools, health, insurance, etc., implied from powers to establish post roads, to tax to provide for general welfare and national defense, and to regulate commerce.
3. To create military and naval academies implied from powers to raise and support army and navy.
4. To generate electricity and sell surplus, implied from power to dispose of government property, commerce, and war powers.
5. To assist and regulate agriculture implied from power to tax and spend for general welfare and regulate commerce.

Reserved to States

1. To regulate intrastate commerce.
2. To establish local governments.
3. To protect health, safety, and morals.
4. To protect life and property and maintain order.
5. To propose and ratify amendments.
6. To conduct elections.
7. To change state constitutions and governments.

Concurrent

1. Both Congress and states may tax.
2. Both may borrow money.
3. Both may charter banks and other corporations.
4. Both may establish and maintain courts.
5. Both may make and enforce laws.
6. Both may take property for public purposes.
7. Both may spend money to provide for general welfare.

Prohibitions upon Congress

1. No tax on exports.
2. Direct taxes must be proportionate to population of states.
3. Indirect taxes must be uniform.
4. Guarantees contained in Bill of Rights not to be abridged.
5. Preference may not be given to one state over another in matters of commerce.
6. State boundaries cannot be changed without consent of states involved.
7. Newly admitted states cannot be placed on plane of inequality with original states.
8. May not permit slavery.
9. May not grant titles of nobility.

Prohibitions on States

1. May not coin money, keep troops or ships of war in time of peace.
2. May not enter into treaties.
3. May not pass laws impairing obligation of contract.
4. May not deny persons equal protection of the laws.
5. May not violate Federal Constitution or obstruct federal laws.
6. May not prevent persons from voting because of race, color, or sex.
7. May not tax imports.
8. May not tax exports.
9. May not permit slavery.
10. May not grant titles of nobility.

States Bank. The cashier refused to pay the tax. Two principal questions were posed. First, may the United States charter such a bank? The Court answered that it might do so under the congressional power to coin money and to regulate the value thereof. Marshall argued:

[1] 4 Wheaton 316.

We admit, as all must admit, that the powers of the government are limited, and that its limits are not to be transcended. But we think the sound construction of the Constitution must allow to the national legislature that discretion, with respect to the means by which the powers it confers are to be carried into execution, which will enable that body to perform the high duties assigned to it, in the manner most beneficial to the people. Let the end be legitimate, let it be within the scope of the Constitution, and all means which are appropriate, which are plainly adapted to that end, which are not prohibited, but consist with the letter and spirit of the Constitution, are constitutional. . . .

Another question involved the power of the state to tax the issue of the bank. The court denied to the state authority to tax a federal instrumentality on the ground that the "power to tax involves the power to destroy."

The ultimate decision regarding the validity of invoking implied power in a given instance is rendered by the federal Supreme Court. In its decisions regarding the scope of national power the Court has been far from consistent. Very great latitude has been permitted by the Court in some lines and at certain periods. In other fields and at other times the Congress has been held to the letter of the fundamental law. Over a century and a half the Court has built up lines of legal precedent on both sides of many such issues before the Court. Therefore, the judge who is predisposed for or against expansion of the scope of federal power may easily find important cases to support his decision. The judge wanting to interpret national power narrowly cites as authority cases from the Taney or Taft eras in the Court. The broad construction of federal authority is justified by citing from Marshall and Stone epochs.

Powers of the States.—The state governments possess an indefinite grant of the remaining powers that are not given to the Federal government nor prohibited to the states.[1] The sweeping nature of this authority is indicated in the language of the Tenth Amendment. This authority does not mean, however, that the states have unlimited power, for they specifically are forbidden to do many things, especially in Article I, Section 10. There the states are forbidden to make treaties, emit bills of credit, make other than gold and silver legal tender, pass a bill of attainder, pass an ex post facto law, impair the obligation of contracts, grant titles of nobility, tax imports or exports, lay tonnage taxes, keep troops or warships in peacetime, make compacts without congressional approval.

Being residual in nature, state powers are broader than those of the Federal government. States are assumed to have authority to do anything that is not prohibited in federal or state constitutions. The principal state power, the police power, gives the state sanction to provide for the health, morals, safety, and welfare of its people.

[1] See p. 360.

All governmental power, however, cannot be classified exclusively into federal or state categories. Inevitably, some powers are shared by the two levels of government; these are usually called "concurrent powers." For example, both state and Federal governments set standards of weights and measures, tax and borrow, and enact bankruptcy laws.

The Supreme Law of the Land.—The supremacy of the Federal Constitution, and of national law within its sphere, is assured by Article VI, Clause 2, which provides:

> This Constitution, and the Laws of the United States which shall be made in Pursuance thereof; and all Treaties made, or which shall be made, under the Authority of the United States, shall be the supreme Law of the Land; and the Judges in every State shall be bound thereby, any Thing in the Constitution or Laws of any State to the Contrary notwithstanding.

Perhaps more than any other portion of the Constitution, this clause expresses the spirit of the Union. The Federal Constitution is paramount over all other forms of law, state or national. Federal law, if validly enacted under the Constitution, ranks above state law. State laws that conflict with valid federal laws or treaties may be adjudged unconstitutional on such grounds. The final verdict in a dispute between national and state jurisdiction or law is given by the federal judiciary.

In event of conflict between federal and state laws either an officer of the Federal government or a private citizen can institute a suit in federal court. If the court finds the state law in conflict, the law is unenforceable. Failure of a state to respect the decision would justify the use of military force by the Federal government. The first occasion upon which a state law was declared unconstitutional by the United States Supreme Court was that of Fletcher *v.* Peck[1] wherein an act of Georgia was at issue. Since then nearly five hundred state laws have failed to meet the test of constitutionality. Happily, the Federal government has seldom found it necessary to resort to the use of force.

UNITS OF AMERICAN GOVERNMENT

Number and Diversity of Units.—One attribute of the American federal system that proves most confusing is the multiplicity of units of government and the diversity in their names, powers, and duties. Thus far only the two major levels of government, federal and state, have been mentioned. Legally the state possesses all the power exercised by both state and local governments; in practice, however, it delegates both powers and functions to a multiplicity of political subdivisions. The full list of these local units is astonishing and causes the average citizen to despair of finding the

[1] 6 Cranch 87 (1810).

precise governmental unit charged with the service concerning which he seeks information. The Bureau of the Census has enumerated, as of 1942, the following units of government:[1]

Units of government	Number	Per cent of all units
United States government	1	*
States (four officially use "Commonwealth")	48	*
Counties (Louisiana uses "parishes")	3,050	2.0
Townships or towns (22 states)	18,919	12.2
Municipalities (incorporated places)	16,220	10.4
School districts	108,579	70.0
Special districts	8,299	5.4
Total	155,116	100.0

* Less than 0.05 of 1 per cent.

It has been pointed out already that the United States proper, without territories, contains more than 3,000,000 square miles; the 1940 census recorded a population in that area of 131,669,275, and it is expected that the 1950 census will show over 150,000,000.

The States.—The states vary greatly in area, in population, and in wealth. Their equality in the Union is like the dictum that all men are created equal: politically it is so in one sense, but each individual is endowed differently in physique, in abilities, and in his share of the world's goods. In area the states vary from Rhode Island, with 1,214 square miles, to Texas, with 267,339 square miles. In population (estimated as of July 1, 1947, by the Bureau of the Census) they ranged from Nevada, with 139,000, to New York, with 14,165,000. In wealth some far outstrip others in resources, access to markets, and industrial facilities. Pressure for federal aid often is most intense from the poorer states, and the use of federal grants helps to correct some of the inequalities between states.

Local Governments.—Units of local government will be dealt with in detail in subsequent chapters, but some introductory comments are in place here. All but Rhode Island use counties (Louisiana parishes are similar), although the importance of the county varies considerably. In the South, West, and Middle Atlantic areas counties are the major units of local government; in New England they have a minimum of functions and exist largely for administrative convenience. The New England town,

[1] United States Department of Commerce, Bureau of the Census, *Governmental Units in the United States, 1942* (Washington: Government Printing Office, 1944), p. 1. The total number of units in 1942 was about 10,000 less than reported as of January, 1941, by William Anderson in *The Units of Government in the United States* (Chicago: Public Administration Service, 1942), p. 17. Almost the entire reduction was in the number of school districts.

embracing rural and urban territories, has broad governmental functions. The Middle Western township is a distant cousin, but is primarily rural and is assigned less important powers and duties. School districts and other special districts usually have the power to tax and constitute an important category of governmental units.

ADMISSION OF STATES TO THE UNION

The thirteen states existing at the time of the federal Constitutional Convention were given an opportunity to be blanketed in as charter members of the Union. The new government was declared in operation after eleven states had ratified the Constitution. North Carolina and Rhode Island finally ratified in 1789 and 1790, respectively. The union of thirteen states lasted only 1 year, however, for the flow of new states continued with never a decade's interruption until the last contiguous continental territories (Arizona and New Mexico) became states in 1912.

Order of Admission of States to the Union

(Original thirteen states listed in order of ratification)

State	Date	State	Date
Delaware	1787	Arkansas	1836
Pennsylvania	1787	Michigan	1837
New Jersey	1787	Florida	1845
Georgia	1788	Texas	1845
Connecticut	1788	Iowa	1846
Massachusetts	1788	Wisconsin	1848
Maryland	1788	California	1850
South Carolina	1788	Minnesota	1858
New Hampshire	1788	Oregon	1859
Virginia	1788	Kansas	1861
New York	1788	West Virginia	1863
North Carolina	1789	Nevada	1864
Rhode Island	1790	Nebraska	1867
Vermont	1791	Colorado	1876
Kentucky	1792	North Dakota	1889
Tennessee	1796	South Dakota	1889
Ohio	1803	Montana	1889
Louisiana	1812	Washington	1889
Indiana	1816	Idaho	1890
Mississippi	1817	Wyoming	1890
Illinois	1818	Utah	1896
Alabama	1819	Oklahoma	1907
Maine	1820	New Mexico	1912
Missouri	1821	Arizona	1912

Admission Procedure.—Procedure for the admission of new states is well established. Congress, under Article IV, Section 3, has the sole power of admitting new states. The major restriction upon the authority of Congress is the requirement that territory of existing states may not be taken without their consent.

The admission process normally has involved five steps: (1) A territorial government is organized. (2) The territory applies to Congress for admission to the Union. (3) Congress enacts an "enabling act" outlining procedure for framing the constitution. (4) The territory frames a constitution. (5) Congress passes a resolution of admission.

Can Congress Impose Conditions for Admission?—Congress can and has withheld admission from would-be states until certain conditions were met. If, however, these conditions pertain to internal matters, they cannot be enforced after the admission of the state. Once admitted, the state achieves a condition of equality with all other states, and may not be bound by prior commitments.[1] On the other hand, conditions imposed regarding disposition of federal lands ceded to states and other matters under federal jurisdiction are fully enforceable in law.

The imposition of conditions on new states began in 1802 with the admission of Ohio. Although acts of admission usually described the status of each new state as "on an equal footing with the original states," Congress repeatedly placed detailed conditions on new members of the Union. Utah, on admission in 1896, was required to forbid polygamy and to assure nonsectarian public schools. Oklahoma, as a condition of admission in 1907, promised not to move its capital from Guthrie for a period of years. Four years later the state voted removal of the capital to Oklahoma City. When the case was appealed to the United States Supreme Court, this restriction on the state was declared invalid on the ground that all states are politically equal and have full control over their internal affairs. The enabling act to admit Arizona was vetoed by President Taft in 1911 because of his objection to a provision for recall of the judiciary. An amended act was passed eliminating recall of judges; after admission in 1912, Arizona promptly restored judicial recall provisions.[2]

Statehood for Hawaii and Alaska.—More than three decades after the last contiguous territories of continental United States became states, serious consideration is now being given to the admission of Hawaii and Alaska.[3] Their important roles and loyalty during the Second World War have added much weight to their claims to statehood. The future of Puerto Rico is very much in doubt, for sentiment there appears to be divided sharply between those who wish independence and those who desire statehood.

[1] The leading case in this field is Coyle *v.* Smith, 221 U.S. 559 (1911).

[2] Frederick L. Bird and Frances M. Ryan, *The Recall of Public Officers* (New York: Macmillan, 1930), p. 6.

[3] See also p. 581.

RESTRICTIONS ON THE STATES

Some prohibitions against state action were necessary in order to protect the Federal government against state encroachments and to ensure national supremacy in national matters. Others were deemed necessary to assure individual rights against attack by the states. Powers denied to the states include those listed in Article I, Section 10. While the most sweeping prohibitions are contained in the Fourteenth Amendment, states are also restrained by the Fifteenth Amendment from withholding suffrage rights because of race, color, or previous condition of servitude, and by the Nineteenth because of sex.

Treaties and Compacts.—Two provisions in Article I, Section 10, protect the Union by forbidding American states to enter into special arrangements with foreign nations, and by ensuring federal control over interstate agreements. No state may enter into a treaty, alliance, or confederation. This is an unconditional prohibition, and helps to make exclusive federal control over foreign relations. This clause was used frequently during and after the Civil War to sustain the Northern contention that states have no right to secede from the Union. It prevents New York from making a treaty with Canada with respect to the St. Lawrence waterway. It forbids Texas to join a league of nations or a Pan-American union. It makes impossible the adherence of the New England states to a new world union of the democracies.

The restriction against entering an agreement or compact with another state or foreign power is less drastic, for Congress may permit such action. Although informal "gentlemen's agreements" between state governors and foreign governments are not unknown, they are extremely rare. On the other hand, many interstate compacts have been negotiated and approved by Congress. A very lively interest in this device has developed during the past decade. It will be evaluated in the next chapter.

Denial of Monetary Powers.—No money may be coined by states, nothing but gold and silver coin made legal tender for payment of debts, and no bills of credit emitted. The courts have held that money means gold, silver, and copper coin and also that coinage involves molding a metallic substance of intrinsic value.[1] During the Revolution and Confederation the variety of moneys and the disparity of values were so great that stress was placed on the necessity of a uniform medium of exchange, with value controlled by the national government. States have been inclined not to interfere in this field; some discussion arose when states first began to issue sales-tax tokens, but it is now generally agreed that such do not constitute coin.

[1] Griswold *v.* Hepburn, 63 Ky. 20 (1865). For a fuller discussion of federal fiscal power, see Chap. 17 below.

Since the Constitution forbids states to make other than gold and silver coin legal tender in payment of debts, state experimentation in monetary reform is curbed effectively. Notes issued by state banks have continued to circulate, but no state can force their acceptance. Congress alone retains the authority to establish other forms of legal tender. Thus a "United States note" may be inscribed "This note is legal tender at its face value for all debts, public and private" without any mention of gold or silver. But if its government fell into the hands of monetary reformers who sought to issue "prosperity certificates," a state could not compel the acceptance of such scrip.

Indeed, the issuance of such scrip probably is forbidden by the constitutional provision that no state shall emit bills of credit. A bill of credit is a paper medium issued by a state and intended to circulate as money. State bank notes were not prohibited by this clause; they continued to circulate until taxed out of existence by the Federal government in the 1860's. The dated stamp scrip or warrants proposed under the "Retirement Life Payments" scheme which the California electorate defeated in 1938, 1939, and 1942 very likely would have been deemed bills of credit by the courts. The Canadian province of Alberta, under its "social credit" administration, in 1936 paid road workers with "prosperity certificates"; certainly these would have been called a violation of the bills of credit prohibition if an American state had issued them. In placing this provision in the Constitution, its framers showed appreciation for the principle, known as Gresham's law, that a cheaper medium of exchange tends to displace the dearer when the two are permitted to circulate side by side.

Limitation of State War Powers.—Three points among the list of restrictions touch upon the authority of the states in relation to war. States are forbidden to issue letters of marque and reprisal; Article I, Section 8, of the Constitution authorizes Congress to grant such documents. A letter of marque and reprisal empowers the holder to privateer and prey upon the commerce of another nation. Because such approval of privateering is likely to involve a country in war, the power wisely was reserved for the level of government with control over foreign relations.

States also are denied the right to keep troops or ships of war without the consent of Congress. This denial does not prevent the maintenance of a state militia that may be deemed necessary to put down armed insurrection too strong for civil authority to curb. Since the First World War, the state militias have been organized as units of the National Guard, under joint federal-state auspices. The purpose of the restriction was to prevent the development of state armies and navies, and to ensure federal supremacy in the defense field. During the Second World War, Congress authorized states to form militia and guard units outside the National Guard organization.

The final restraint, forbidding a state to engage in war unless actually invaded, is of little practical importance today but may have constituted some deterrent on provocative incidents precipitated by state officers. Congress has the sole power to declare war, and it is fitting that the states should not compromise the position of the Federal government by rash actions on their international boundaries.

Limitations on State Tax Power.—The authors of the Constitution were careful to forbid Congress to discriminate between states and ports in matters of regulation and taxation.[1] It was fitting, therefore, that they should prohibit unfair uses of state tax powers. States were denied the right to tax imports or exports. Goods might be taxed by a state before shipment to another state or after arrival from another state. Long controversy has ensued over what constitutes arrival. The courts developed an "original-package" doctrine under which a commodity leaves the channel of trade only when the original box, bale, or carton in which it was shipped is opened. Only then is it taxable by the state. Reasonable state inspection fees on exported or imported goods may properly be collected. It is well established that states may not burden interstate commerce through taxation.

State tonnage duties on ships are prohibited except with the consent of Congress. This tax is charged on the basis of tonnage capacity of a vessel, for entering or leaving a port. It should be distinguished from a wharfage charge or fee, which validly may be collected from a ship for wharfage services.

The implied restriction, derived from the very nature of the federal system, that states cannot tax federal instrumentalities and the Federal government cannot tax states is of very great importance. It was stated in McCulloch *v.* Maryland (1819) in terms of "power to tax involves the power to destroy." The list of exemptions from state taxation expanded greatly through the years, including not only federal property, but also federal salaries, gasoline used by federal agencies, and income from federal bonds. Finally, in 1939 the Supreme Court began to narrow the field of reciprocal immunity.[2]

The Fourteenth Amendment, Section 4, forbids states to assume or pay any debt or obligation incurred in aid of insurrection or rebellion against the United States. Such debts are declared illegal and void.

Protection of Personal and Property Rights.—As is noted in a later chapter,[3] states are prevented from violating personal and property rights. They may not pass ex post facto laws, bills of attainder, or laws impairing the obligation of contract. Nor may they deny due process of

[1] See Chap. 17.

[2] For fuller discussion of reciprocal immunity, see p. 370.

[3] Chap. 7.

law, deprive persons of equal protection under the law, or abridge the privileges and immunities of American citizens. When states violate liberties, a federal question arises that justifies resort to federal courts. While this provides only a legal remedy, experience has demonstrated the wisdom of subjecting member units of the federal union to constitutional limitations enforceable by the central government.

Suffrage Restrictions.—The Constitution in its original form gave to the states virtually the whole responsibility for determining who might vote in both federal and state elections. The electorate for federal officers was declared to be the same in each state as that for the most numerous branch of the state legislature. This situation was altered, however, by both the Fifteenth and Nineteenth Amendments; and Section 2 of the Fourteenth contained a penalty which might be invoked against states disfranchising a proportion of the male population.[1]

The Fifteenth Amendment declares simply: "The right of citizens of the United States to vote shall not be denied or abridged by the United States or by any State on account of race, color, or previous condition of servitude." Congress is given authority to enforce this provision by appropriate legislation. The meaning is clear, and the amendment has been used to sweep away several attempts to restrain Negro participation in elections. A number of indirect ways have been developed, however, to bar colored people on grounds of illiteracy, nonpayment of poll taxes, and similar devices. Acts by private individuals and bodies are not included in this prohibition.

The Nineteenth Amendment banning discrimination on account of sex effectively ended all state denial of woman suffrage. As the amendment refers only to the right to vote, several states continued to ban women from jury duty.

The penalty contained in Amendment XIV, providing that a state's representation in the House of Representatives may be reduced in the proportion to which adult (twenty-one years) citizens are denied the right to vote, has never been invoked by Congress.

FEDERAL OBLIGATIONS TO THE STATES

The number of federal guarantees to the states is not large, but taken together they are of considerable importance. The Federal government is bound to respect the territorial integrity of existing states in admitting new states; it must guarantee a republican form of government to the states; it is bound to protect states against domestic violence and foreign invasions; it is forbidden to alter the constitutional grant of two senators for each state; it cannot permit states to be sued by individuals in the federal courts.

[1] For a more complete discussion of suffrage, see Chap. 11.

Territorial Integrity of the States.—Under the terms of Article IV, Section 3, Clause 1:

New States may be admitted by the Congress into this Union; but no new State shall be formed or erected within the Jurisdiction of any other State; nor any State be formed by the Junction of two or more States, or Parts of States, without the Consent of the Legislatures of the States concerned as well as of the Congress.

The admission process, which has been described earlier, is prescribed by Congress. Congress has great powers in this regard, but it cannot impose conditions upon purely state matters, nor can it carve up existing states without their consent. The territorial integrity of states was much discussed in the Constitutional Convention before the final language was agreed upon. It has been interpreted to mean that the territory of no state may be taken without its own consent. Actually several states, formed from parts of others, have been admitted. Kentucky, formerly a part of Virginia, secured that state's approval, and Congress admitted it as a separate state in 1792. Tennessee was formed in 1796 after North Carolina ceded the territory to the United States. Vermont was admitted to the Union in 1791, in spite of claims by New York to her territory. Massachusetts agreed to Maine's separation in advance of that state's admission in 1820. West Virginia's separation from Virginia was authorized by a "rump" or irregular legislature of Virginia during the Civil War.

Although continental territory of the United States (except that in the District of Columbia and Alaska) is fully organized into states, occasionally proposals are made for creating a new state out of a portion of one or two existing states. During 1941–1942 an amusing plan was advanced for the formation of a forty-ninth state called "Jefferson" out of the counties of southern Oregon and northern California. Frequently schemes for creating city-states of Chicago or New York are put forward. Before Congress could admit any such new state, however, the consent of the existing states concerned would have to be obtained.

A Republican Form of Government.—"The United States shall guarantee to every State in this Union a Republican Form of Government. . . ." This statement appears in Article IV, Section 4. Various theories have been advanced to explain what the founding Fathers meant by this provision. Some say it means representative government; others, the form used in 1789; still others declare it means democratic government with broad suffrage rights. The fact of the matter is that no one knows or is likely soon to secure a precise answer. The courts regard the question as political in nature and, therefore, decline to rule whether or not a given state government meets the requirements imposed by the Constitution. Instead, the matter is left for the Congress and the President to determine.

The President may indicate his choice between two rival regimes by using troops to protect or restore order, as in Dorr's Rebellion of Rhode Island.[1] Congress may announce its acceptance or rejection of a particular state regime by seating or refusing to seat senators and representatives from the state concerned, as it often did in the reconstruction era. Several times during the era of Huey Long's predominance over Louisiana, efforts were made to persuade Congress to refuse seats to Louisiana legislators on the ground that they came from a state without republican form of government, but no action was taken.

Arguing that "republican form" meant representative government, a corporation operating in Oregon once sought to prove in the courts that the state government had lost its lawful authority through the adoption of the initiative and referendum. The Supreme Court indicated the political character of the question and declared that determination rested with the Congress through admission or rejection of senators and representatives.[2]

Defense against Invasion and Violence.—The latter part of Article IV, Section 4 requires that the United States ". . . shall protect each of them against Invasion; and on Application of the Legislature, or of the Executive (when the Legislature cannot be convened) against domestic violence." This restatement of the federal obligation to protect against foreign enemies is the logical companion to the prohibition of state armies and navies and properly derives from the federal war power.

Much difficulty is encountered in determining when domestic violence reaches the point requiring federal intervention. The President makes this decision. Normally he sends in federal troops only after a request for help has come from the governor or legislature of the state concerned or when federal law or federal property is violated. President Cleveland broke the Chicago Pullman strike of 1894 with troops that he sent in over the protest of Governor J. P. Altgeld of Illinois. Cleveland used the grounds of protecting the mails and freeing interstate commerce of obstructions. President Roosevelt in 1941 used the Army to break up a strike in a California aircraft factory without any formal request from the governor.

Equal Representation in the Senate.—No state may be denied equal representation in the United States Senate without its own consent. Since no state is likely to agree to reduction of Senate representation, the two-member-per-state basis is likely to remain indefinitely. The Constitution states that this portion of the fundamental law cannot be changed by amendment.

State Immunity from Suit.—The original Constitution assigned the national judiciary jurisdiction over suits between a state and citizens of

[1] Luther *v.* Borden, 7 Howard 1 (1849).

[2] Pacific States Telephone and Telegraph Co. *v.* Oregon, 223 U.S. 118 (1912).

another state. After the decision of the Supreme Court in Chisholm *v.* Georgia,[1] upholding a citizen's suit against the state, a great storm of disapproval arose. The Eleventh Amendment, outlawing such suits, was ratified finally in 1798. Under this amendment, a state may not be sued in federal courts by an individual without its own consent. Lacking such consent, the individual may seek remedy through legislative action on a "claim" bill.

STATE OBLIGATIONS TO THE UNION

Elections of Federal Officials.—No separate federal election machinery is comprehended in the Constitution. Instead the states are obliged to conduct elections for federal officials. Presidential electors are chosen in each state in whatever manner the state legislature directs. All states now use the direct election method. Members of the House of Representatives are elected by the people, in most cases from single-member districts. Senators, under the Seventeenth Amendment, are elected at large in each state. For all three offices the suffrage requirements for voters are identical to those for the most numerous branch of the state legislature. Each state decides for itself the method of nominating, if any, that shall be employed. Congress has used its power to set a common election date for federal officers, but Maine, which has an earlier date set in its constitution, is permitted to continue its own general election date.

Participation in Amending Process.—States also are obliged to participate in the federal constitutional amending process. One of the methods of proposing amendments (federal constitutional convention) and both schemes of ratification (state legislatures and state conventions) require the participation of the several states.

References

ANDERSON, WILLIAM: *Federalism and Intergovernmental Relations* (Chicago: Public Administration Service, 1946).

——— *The Units of Government in the United States* (Chicago: Public Administration Service, 2d ed., 1942).

BRYCE, JAMES: *The American Commonwealth* (New York: Macmillan, rev. ed., 2 vols., 1889).

FINER, HERMAN: *The Theory and Practice of Modern Government* (New York: Holt, rev. ed., 1949).

FREEMAN, EDWARD A.: *A History of Federal Government from Foundation of the Achaian League to the Disruption of the United States* (London: Macmillan & Co., Ltd., 1863).

——— *A History of Federal Government in Greece and Italy* (London: Macmillan & Co., Ltd., 2d ed., 1893).

[1] 2 Dallas 419 (1793).

GRAVES, W. BROOKE (ed.): "Intergovernmental Relations in the United States," *Annals of the American Academy of Political and Social Science*, vol. 207 (January, 1940).

HAINES, CHARLES G.: "James Bryce and American Constitutional Federalism," in Robert C. Brooks (ed.), *Bryce's American Commonwealth, Fiftieth Anniversary* (New York: Macmillan, 1939).

KARVE, DATTATRAYA G.: *Federations, a Study in Comparative Politics* (New York: Oxford University Press, 1932).

MAXWELL, JAMES A.: *The Fiscal Impact of Federalism in the United States* (Cambridge, Mass.: Harvard University Press, 1946).

MOGI, SOBEI: *The Problem of Federalism* (London: G. Allen, 2 vols., 1931).

POUND, ROSCOE, and OTHERS: *Federalism as a Democratic Process* (New Brunswick, N.J.: Rutgers University Press, 1942).

POWELL, ALDEN L.: *National Taxation of State Instrumentalities* (Urbana: University of Illinois Press, 1936).

STUDENSKI, PAUL, and PAUL R. MORT: *Centralized and Decentralized Government in Relation to Democracy* (New York: Teachers College, Columbia University, 1941).

TOCQUEVILLE, ALEXIS DE: *Democracy in America* (New York: Knopf, 2 vols., 1945).

WHEARE, KENNETH C.: *Federal Government* (New York: Oxford, 1947).

TEXT–FILM

The following McGraw-Hill 35mm silent filmstrip is recommended for use with Chap. 5 of this text.

The Federal System—Part I. Federalism in theory and practice; distribution of powers between the Federal government and the states. Restrictions on the states, and federal obligations to them.

Chapter 6

INTERSTATE AND FEDERAL-STATE RELATIONS

> An ideal federal system in our modern era contemplates a group of semi-independent democracies held together by a constitution and a common tradition, and functioning smoothly through a statecraft that includes a large factor of cooperation. This cooperation must be partly in the field of interstate and partly in that of Federal-State relations. The true spirit of the Federal system is sustained by efficient *voluntary* relationships, which make the compulsions of the unitary state unnecessary.
>
> United States Treasury Department, Committee on Intergovernmental Fiscal Relations, *Federal, State, and Local Fiscal Relations . . . a Report . . .*[1]

INTERSTATE RELATIONS

Constitutional Interstate Obligations.—The Constitution imposes upon each state certain obligations to all other states. The principal interstate duties are enumerated in Article IV, which is devoted to states' relations. In each case the responsibility of the state is outlined in general form only, and it has remained for the courts to expound the meaning of the particular obligation in specific terms.

Full Faith and Credit.—The first among these interstate obligations is contained in Article IV, Section 1, which reads:

> Full Faith and Credit shall be given in each State to the public Acts, Records, and judicial Proceedings of every other State. And the Congress may by general Laws prescribe the Manner in which such Acts, Records, and Proceedings shall be proved, and the Effect thereof.

In 1804 Congress extended coverage of this clause to acts, records, and proceedings of territories of the United States. The clause does not include foreign governmental acts and proceedings. Federal courts, also, are bound to give state court decisions full faith and credit.

In general, full faith and credit means that every state must accept another state's statutes, charters, deeds, vital records, judicial decisions, and court records. For example, an ordinary civil judgment of Iowa courts ordering Smith to pay Brown $1,000 will be enforced by Kansas courts without an examination of the case on its merits, but merely after a determination of the authenticity of the original judgment. A Massa-

[1] Sen. Doc. 69, 78th Cong., 1st Sess. (Washington: Government Printing Office, 1943), p. 37.

chusetts marriage license is accepted as proof of wedded status in Pennsylvania. A Texas birth certificate may be used in Oregon to establish date of birth. A will properly drawn in Idaho is binding in the courts of Wyoming.

Two notable exceptions to full faith and credit exist. First, the clause does not cover state proceedings under criminal law. A person convicted of a crime in Alabama is not punished for it in Kentucky. Such cases are handled through extradition, under which the state to which a fugitive from justice has fled delivers him up to the state where the crime was committed. Second, divorce decrees granted by courts of a state in which neither party has a bona fide residence sometimes are not accepted by the courts of other states. Mr. and Mrs. A, who have lived together in New York, separate. Mr. A proceeds to Nevada where, after a few weeks, he is granted a divorce, without summons to Mrs. A. Returning to New York, Mr. A remarries. The second Mrs. A bears two children. Ten years later Mr. A dies suddenly. The first Mrs. A demands and is granted the whole of Mr. A's estate on the ground that their marriage was never legally dissolved under the laws of New York. The late Mr. A is adjudged a bigamist, his children and their mother are left penniless, and the children have the stigma of illegitimacy. Divorces granted in the state in which a couple has been domiciled are valid; even those issued by a state in which one of the parties has actual residence generally are accepted.[1]

Privileges and Immunities.—Further protection against interstate discrimination was secured through the provision that the citizens of each state are guaranteed the privileges and immunities of citizens of the several states.[2] This clause, it will be seen, assures the citizen of one state the right to be protected, to travel, to reside, to secure habeas corpus, to sue in courts, to make contracts, to marry, to hold property, to enjoy tax equality, and to engage in trade or business in any other state.

Such guarantees are of great importance in making this one nation instead of many nations. The courts have ruled invalid several attempts by states to give their own citizens rights denied to citizens of other states. During the 1930's a number of proposals were made in states of the Pacific Southwest to curb the influx of migrants from drought and dust-bowl areas. It is quite valid for states to require of a citizen residence for a given period before achieving the right of suffrage, or securing eligibility to poor relief.

[1] The status of Nevada divorces has been much controverted in recent years. In Williams *v.* North Carolina, 317 U.S. 287 (1942) the Supreme Court ruled that the full-faith-and-credit clause required the acceptance of two Nevada divorces obtained after 6 weeks of residence. The case was reheard by the court in Williams *v.* North Carolina, 325 U.S. 226 (1945) and the Court held that North Carolina had power to determine the validity of domicile. The conviction of bigamy was upheld and the state court sentence was sustained.

[2] See p. 157.

No state, however, can directly forbid by law indigent migrants to enter. Local authorities plagued the migrants with vagrancy ordinances, and private individuals and groups conspired to frighten them away. California forbade by law the transportation of indigent persons into the state, but the statute was declared unconstitutional.[1]

The rights of resident citizens and of citizens of other states are not, however, precisely equal. States have been permitted three major exceptions and a number of minor ones to the application of the privileges-and-immunities clause.

First, corporations are not considered citizens under this clause, and, therefore, out-of-state concerns may be burdened with discriminatory legislation. States are subject to restraint in this field, nevertheless, under the due-process clause of the Fourteenth Amendment.

Second, the right to engage in certain professions or businesses may be restricted by state law to citizens who have resided in the state for a given number of months or years. By admission to the bar or to the practice of medicine in one state one does not thereby secure the right to practice in all states.[2]

Third, the privileges of sharing in the property or proprietary functions of a state may be denied to a nonresident, or offered to him on a very different basis. A state university may require payment of a tuition fee by a nonresident, although none is collected from residents. For example, the University of California charges $150 per semester tuition for out-of-state students and no tuition fee for Californians. States customarily charge much higher fees for fish and game licenses to nonresidents than to residents. It is valid for Idaho to charge local sportsmen $2 per season for a permit covering all fish and game, and to charge an out-of-state person $50 for the same privilege.

Extradition of Fugitives.—The process of extradition is explained clearly in the second clause of Article IV, Section 2:

> A person charged in any State with Treason, Felony, or other Crime, who shall flee from Justice, and be found in another State, shall on Demand of the executive Authority of the State from which he fled, be delivered up, to be removed to the State having Jurisdiction of the Crime.

It is similar to international extradition, but rendition between nations is carried out under treaty; among the American states no treaty is necessary, for the Constitution provides a direct and uniform rule. Any violation of state law, whether felony or misdemeanor, may be the basis for a request

[1] Edwards *v.* California, 314 U.S. 160 (1941). The majority opinion rejected the law on grounds of obstruction of interstate commerce.

[2] For details see United States Department of Commerce, Marketing Laws Survey, *State Occupational Legislation*, March, 1943.

for rendition. Any person charged with a crime who leaves the state in which the alleged crime was committed may be extradited, whether he deliberately fled or not. Federal law extends extradition to territories.

Ordinarily the process works smoothly. Congress has directed by law that the governor of a state or territory has the duty of detaining the fugitive for whom extradition is asked. The governor of the state from which he fled is notified when the accused person is located. The formal request for rendition then follows. Usually the governor delivers up the fugitive without question. Occasionally, however, governors examine the facts behind a requested extradition and refuse to hand over fugitives. This refusal may occur when an executive distrusts the system of justice used in the state making the request, as was the situation in *I am a Fugitive from a Chain Gang*. Or it may be due to humanitarian considerations, such as a long record of reformed living. No court or officer has power to force a governor to render up a person if the governor refuses the request of extradition.

Interstate Cooperation. *Compacts.*—The Constitution provides for interstate relations largely in negative, prohibitory terms. Even the provision for interstate compacts in Article I, Section 10 is in the form of a prohibition: "No State shall, without the Consent of Congress . . . enter into any Agreement or Compact with another state. . . ." Normally a compact is negotiated between representatives of state executives, ratified by the states concerned, and submitted to Congress for consent, which is given by law. Increasingly in recent years Congress has consented in advance to a compact or an idea for a compact; sometimes no compact or state ratification has followed. Up to 1948 approximately eighty-five compacts had been authorized by Congress; over fifty of these became effective through state ratification.[1] Most interstate compacts deal with relatively minor matters, especially with boundary lines, rivers, harbors, waterways, bridges, and the like. During the last 10 years several compacts have been made on pressing economic and governmental problems.

Best known among interstate compacts, the New York Port Authority is scarcely typical. It was negotiated between New York and New Jersey in 1920 and approved by Congress in 1921. The original plan was to provide an agency for the coordinated development of the metropolitan port facilities of American's leading harbor. The authority has been unable to make much progress in getting railroads, shipping lines, and others to

[1] In December, 1935, the National Resources Committee reported in its *Regional Factors in National Planning and Development* (Washington: Government Printing Office, 1935), p. 36, that fifty-seven compacts had been authorized by Congress but that only thirty-four were finally ratified by the states and went into effect. The latest figures may be obtained by adding the compacts authorized and ratified since that date. *The Book of the States* lists compacts on which action has been taken during the last decade.

cooperate in its comprehensive plan but has been a conspicuous success in building and maintaining bridge and tunnel facilities across the Hudson River. The authority is directed by twelve commissioners, six from each state. The commissioners are unsalaried; they place responsibility for the operation of the vast enterprise on well-paid career officials. Authority power is not great. Each major construction project requires the statutory approval of New York and New Jersey; and the governors of the two states have been given veto power over acts of the authority. In spite of these restrictions, the authority has made a remarkable record of successfully operating a huge public enterprise.[1]

The Interstate Oil Compact is an outstanding attempt to stabilize a chaotic industry by interstate action. It was negotiated by representatives of Texas, Oklahoma, California, Kansas, and New Mexico in early 1935; the compact was ratified by Texas, Oklahoma, Kansas, New Mexico, Illinois, and Colorado; it was consented to by Congress later in 1935 and renewed in 1937, 1939, 1941, and 1943. Michigan, Arkansas, Louisiana, Kentucky, New York, Ohio, Pennsylvania, Montana, Florida, West Virginia, Georgia, and Indiana came in subsequently. The purpose of the compact was declared to be prevention of oil and gas waste. The text of the compact does not mention control of production directly, but the primary work of the commission (one commissioner from each state) appears to be the approval of production quotas. The oil compact has suffered in effectiveness due to California's unwillingness to ratify. For an industry as competitive as petroleum it may be regarded as a modest success.[2]

Most widely accepted of all is the Crime Compact of 1934, for which blanket approval was given by Congress the same year. Forty-one states by 1948 had ratified this agreement for interstate supervision of parolees and probationers. The reform of released convicts inevitably is complicated by the notoriety an ex-criminal achieves in his home community. Previously it has been difficult or impossible to provide proper parole facilities in other states. Now an ex-convict may have a chance to start anew under favorable circumstances and proper supervision in the state of his choice.

Evaluation of the Compact Method.—While the compact method is a useful device through which regional problems may be attacked, it is likely to succeed mainly in restricted areas and in noncontroversial fields.

[1] See Port of New York Authority, *The Port of New York* (New York: The Authority, 1941); "Port of New York Authority," *Fortune*, vol. 8 (September, 1933), pp. 22–31; see also Frederick L. Bird, *A study of the Port of New York Authority . . .* (New York: Dun & Bradstreet, 1949), *passim*.

[2] See Interstate Oil Compact Commission, *The Interstate Compact to Conserve Oil and Gas; a Summary of Its Organization, Purposes and Functions* (Oklahoma City, 1942); and Wilfred D. Webb, "The Interstate Oil Compact—Theory and Practice," *Southwestern Social Science Quarterly*, vol. 21 (March, 1941), pp. 293–301.

The compact is inflexible and difficult to amend. Commissions created by compacts are given little discretionary authority and rarely have any power of enforcement. If one state involved in the subject covered by the compact refuses to ratify, the whole project may fail because of limited adherence. Like a confederation requiring unanimous consent before acting, the compact scheme may be foredoomed to failure because the minority, however small, may veto the effectiveness of the majority will. Even when the necessary states do ratify, Congress may withhold consent, as it has from the New England flood-control compacts. If enforcement action is required, enforcement may be nonuniform in the participating states.

Granting these objections, however, the government recognizes that the compact still has a useful role in solving problems that fall between federal and single-state jurisdiction and competence. It is no cure-all, no panacea for all ills, but it may serve as a method through which states with common problems may work together on a modest cooperative basis.

Many interstate agreements are made effective without any congressional action. Executive arrangements, more informal than compacts, often suffice to ensure parallel action between two or more states. Usually these are mere agreements to follow the principles of reciprocity, to give assurances that each will treat the other with fairness and equality.

Uniform State Laws.—Uniform state action is another road to interstate cooperation. Founded in 1892, the National Conference of Commissioners on Uniform State Laws is the leading organization promoting action in this field. Over the years conference subcommittees have drawn up with great care, and the general body has ratified, more than ninety acts. In addition, several other national groups have prepared proposed laws that have had wide acceptance among the states. The conference is composed of representatives from each state, appointed by the governor; it is financed by the American Bar Association, state appropriations, and by other bodies.

One law, the Negotiable Instruments Act, has been adopted by all forty-eight states and by five territories, but the average act on the conference list has been adopted by only 25 per cent of the states.[1] The advantages of uniform laws are obvious. Uniformity in state law simplifies greatly the task of doing business across state lines. Unfortunately, however, state legislatures do not always adopt proposed acts without amendment. A drastically amended uniform law is little more advantageous than one of homespun origin. Moreover, despite a clause declaring for uniform inter-

[1] Rodney L. Mott, "Uniform Legislation in the United States," *Annals of the American Academy*, vol. 207 (January, 1940), pp. 79–92. Progress in this field may be followed in National Conference of Commissioners on Uniform State Laws, *Handbook of the . . . and Proceedings of the Annual Conference . . .*, published annually.

pretation, the courts of the various states may give diverse interpretations to uniform laws. Prof. J. A. Clifford Grant has suggested that truer uniformity may be obtained from state adoption of federal laws, in order that a common system of interpretation may prevail.[1]

The Council of State Governments.—In view of the large number of interstate problems needing solution, it is surprising that the first general continuing interstate organization was established only in 1925. The parent organization was called the American Legislators' Association; in 1935, it fostered the establishment of the Council of State Governments, with broad functions.[2] The council provides the secretariat for the Governors' Conference, the American Legislators' Association, the National Association of Attorneys General, and the National Association of Secretaries of State. It cooperates with the National Conference of Commissioners on Uniform State Laws and many other bodies of public officials. It publishes a monthly magazine, *State Government*, the only journal devoted exclusively to this field.

The council is governed by a board of managers, to which each state contributing to its support is entitled to appoint one member; associated groups also are represented. Every 2 years, the council holds a meeting of its general assembly, to which each participating state sends one senator, one representative, and one administrator. Here state and national problems of the broadest character may be considered. In 1948, all forty-eight states were participating in the work of the council. This participation is directed in each state by a state commission on interstate cooperation, usually established by state law and composed of members of the legislature and representatives of the executive branch.

These commissions on interstate cooperation keep the states in touch with the work of the council and with interstate problems generally; they provide a mechanism through which the states may be represented at national and regional conferences on particular interstate problems. The most important work in recent years has centered around the problem of state trade barriers. After national and regional conferences on trade walls, state representatives returned home and helped to repeal some existing barriers and to accomplish the defeat of proposed new ones. Much good work has been done in securing interstate action dealing with relief, crime, fisheries, water pollution, conservation of natural resources, and other problems. The Council of State Governments provides a much-needed agency through which the states may approach the solution of common problems. In 15 years of existence it has secured participation

[1] J. A. Clifford Grant, "The Search for Uniformity of Law," *American Political Science Review*, vol. 32 (December, 1938), pp. 1082–1098.

[2] For history and functions of the council, see the current issue of *The Book of the States*, published biennially in Chicago.

of all of the states, has focused national attention on the gravity of interstate problems, and has provided machinery through which the solution of many problems may be approached.

Interstate Discrimination. *State Trade Barriers.*—One of the primary motives in the formation of the Union was the elimination of state tariff barriers. It was recognized that the country could enjoy neither prosperity nor unity with walls built around each state. The founding Fathers drew with great care the sections of the Constitution prohibiting state duties on imports and exports and assuring the Federal government of paramount power over interstate and foreign commerce. In spite of these constitutional provisions, the states over the years have managed to build up a large number of trade walls. The condition became particularly alarming during the 1930's, when discriminatory and counterdiscriminatory legislation reached state statute books with regularity.[1]

A state trade barrier may be defined as a statute, regulation, or practice that operates unfairly or tends to operate to the disadvantage of persons, products, or services coming from sister states to the advantage of local residents.[2] Examples are plentiful. Under the guise of protecting the health, morals, safety, and welfare of its people, a state law will require inspection and quarantine of plant and animal life. This requirement sounds legitimate, but it may be enforced in such a way that out-of-state nurserymen or stock raisers virtually are denied access to the state market. For example, New York state, seeking to curb Bang's disease, imposed a very rigid inspection on cattle being shipped into the state, even though it did little to clean up infected herds at home.[3] If New York inspectors reject Louisiana cattle, then Louisiana's retaliatory quarantine embargo may be placed into effect, and all movement of plant and animal life from New York to Louisiana be banned.

State laws governing motor vehicles, especially trucks, establish standards so diverse from those of other states that truckers of neighboring states cannot meet the requirements without excessive cost. State taxes and fees in other fields often are arranged so that out-of-state competition is stymied effectively. This practice is most common in the alcoholic-beverage field, over which states have a special power stemming from the Twenty-first Amendment. Differentials to favor local manufacturers or products are established through high license fees for importation or for

[1] The pioneer work in the trade-barrier field is F. Eugene Melder, *State and Local Barriers to Interstate Commerce* (Orono: University of Maine Press, 1937). The same author wrote *State Trade Walls* (New York: Public Affairs Committee, 1939).

[2] Paul F. Truitt, "An Outline of Certain Factors Involved in the Study of the Interstate Trade Barriers Question," United States Department of Commerce, December, 1941, mimeographed.

[3] George R. Taylor, Edgar L. Burtis, and Frederick V. Baugh, *Barriers to Internal Trade in Farm Products* (Washington: Government Printing Office, 1939), p. 93.

the privilege of selling in the state.[1] Discrimination against out-of-state wine is carried on by having two excise taxes: a high one for imported and a low one for native-produced beverage. In addition, most states have general laws giving resident producers and vendors an advantage when the state seeks to purchase goods for its own use.

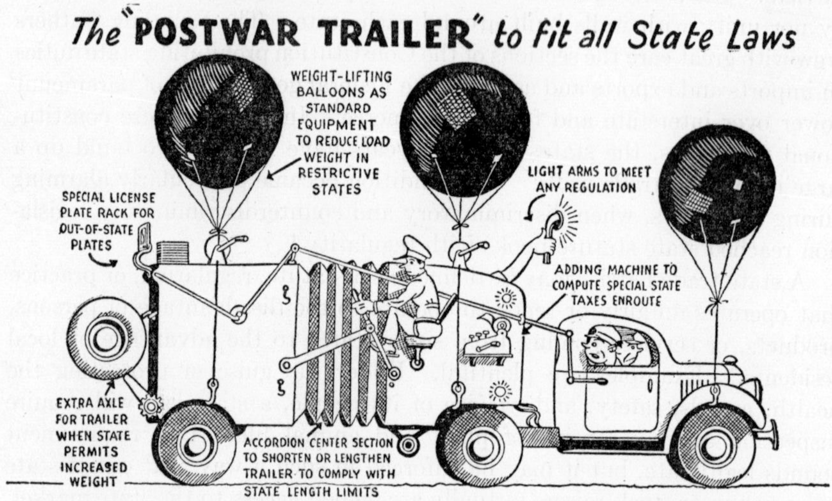

Ike Doodleschmalz M.E. DDS.—Independent industrial engineer deluxe, has submitted this design to the Fruehauf Trailer Company as the answer to some of the conflicting state laws and trade barriers which prevent motor transport from properly serving the public. Maybe he has something.

Among the economic interests adversely affected by state trade barriers is the trucking industry. SOURCE: The Fruehauf Trailer Company.

Removal of trade barriers requires action by the states themselves. The Federal government can assist in several ways. The Council of State Governments, a federal interdepartmental committee, and other bodies have worked hard to prevent new trade walls and to break down existing ones. Much progress has been made in this direction. After a careful analysis of the legal situation, Mr. Justice Jackson, who at that time was the Solicitor General, turned to the possibility of congressional action with these words:

> We must not forget that while the commerce clause of itself will not keep open the channels of interstate trade, the Congress has a wide choice of means to use the grant of power effectively to achieve that end.[2]

[1] These data are drawn from Thomas S. Green, Jr., *Liquor Trade Barriers* (Chicago: Public Administration Service, 1939), pp. 12–19.

[2] Robert H. Jackson, "The Supreme Court and Interstate Barriers," *Annals of the American Academy*, vol. 207 (January, 1940), pp. 70–79, at p. 78.

He pointed out that while the more obvious discriminations by states might be curbed through litigation in the federal courts, Congress must provide a statutory basis for a more general and positive attack. A careful study of federal legislation was made in 1940 to ascertain how it might be used to curb state and local trade barriers.[1] The most promising lines of action enumerated were: (1) cooperative action by federal agencies and the Council of State Governments in persuading states to defeat and repeal offensive legislation, (2) federal court action against trade barriers through injunctions, antitrust prosecutions, and intervention as *amicus curiae* (friend of the court), (3) uniform state laws, drafted by federal agencies and enacted by the states, (4) standardization of name, quality, and containers for foods under the powers granted in the federal Food, Drug and Cosmetic Act, (5) pressure on states to relax barriers through federal grants-in-aid devices. The dangerous trend toward "Balkanization" of the country by the erection of trade barriers, which gained much support during the depression period, has been successfully halted and even reversed. Nevertheless, there still exists much state legislation of a restrictive character.

Tax Competition.—Closely connected with the general trade-barrier problem are the tax discriminations used by some states against other states and out-of-state producers, and the tax factors by which residents and producers are aided.[2] State laws often provide for tax exemption of businesses in order to induce them to move to or remain in the state. Florida once made a bid for rich and aged persons by providing in her constitution that no inheritance tax could be enacted.[3] Taxes that retaliate against other states by levies on insurance premiums, liquor, and other things are common. Conflicts often arise between states over the share of a large estate taxable by each. While the state in which the deceased person has been domiciled generally has the best claim, other states in which portions of the estate are located may claim the right to tax them.

The state sales tax has come into general use during the last decade. Many people make large purchases out of state in order to avoid payment of sales taxes. To plug this loophole, several states have levied "use" taxes,

[1] United States Department of Commerce, Interdepartmental Committee on Interstate Trade Barriers, *A Summarized Report of the Legal Subcommittee* (Washington: Government Printing Office, December, 1940).

[2] For a general survey of this problem see James W. Martin, "Tax Competition between States," *Annals of the American Academy*, vol. 207 (January, 1940), pp. 62–69. Certain aspects, especially margarine taxation, are treated in Taylor, Burtis, and Baugh, *op. cit.* The fullest coverage of this field is Tax Institute, *Tax Barriers to Trade* (Philadelphia: Tax Institute, 1941).

[3] Eventually Florida was induced to abandon this form of tax competition by a federal law setting up a credit for state taxation. See discussion of tax offset device, p. 118.

requiring payment of the equivalent of the sales tax before an article may be used in the state. If a citizen of California buys an automobile in Detroit, California requires that he pay either the California sales tax or use tax before it can be brought into the state. Exceptionally heavy taxes may be charged against out-of-state corporations. Dairying states widely use taxes on oleomargarine to discourage consumption of vegetable fats and to promote the sale of butter fats. States also have engaged in open warfare through alcoholic-beverage taxes, which have favored home-produced liquors and applied heavy and retaliatory taxes on liquors from out of state.

FEDERAL-STATE RELATIONS

The term "centralization" refers to the relationship between different levels of government. The process of centralization involves assumption by the higher level of government of both activities and authority from the lower level.

Federal centralization is the tendency for the national government to assume influence or control over functions and fields formerly considered under state jurisdiction. State centralization is used to describe the process of state assumption of authority over former local activities.

It was inevitable that the relations between nation and state would not have remained static over 150 years. Changing social and economic conditions require the reallocation of responsibilities; virtually all these changes have strengthened the national government at the expense of the state. It is true, of course, that the states also have new and expanded functions, sometimes taken over from local governments. The over-all general tendency, however, has been in the direction of greater federal centralization. The purpose of this section is to examine some of the devices and avenues through which federal authority over the states and over former state functions has developed and to appraise some of the expedients to which the states have resorted to correct their own inadequacies.

Federal Grants-in-Aid.—In a recent study by a committee of the Council of State Governments, federal grants-in-aid were defined as:

> payments made by the national government to state and local governments, subject to certain conditions, for the support of activities administered by the states and their political subdivisions.[1]

The term includes both regular grants, which are "permanent" or recurring, and emergency grants, which are temporary and extraordinary. The term

[1] Council of State Governments, *Federal Grants-in-Aid* (Chicago: The Council, 1949), p. 29.

grants-in-aid does *not* include the following payments: (1) shared revenues, collected by the Federal government and paid in whole or in part to state or local governments; (2) payments in lieu of taxes, through which the nation reimburses the states and localities for services for which they cannot tax federal property; (3) payments for contractual services performed by the United States government; (4) payments of cash loans; (5) payments to individuals within states, as in the National Guard; and (6) payments in kind, such as farm commodities or war surpluses.

Nature of Subsidy System.—Although the earliest grants to states were in land or money, without the imposition of conditions on their use, present-day grants are almost wholly *conditional*. This means that grants are made for specified purposes and subject to conditions stipulated by Congress or the administering agency. Other federal nations, such as Australia and Canada, make extensive use of "unconditional" grants to states or provinces; this type of grant is for general purposes and is accompanied by no detailed specifications as to use.

The constitutional justification for federal grants is found both in the power of Congress to dispose of territory and other property, and in its power to tax and spend.[1] The former no longer looms large on the grants front, now that most grants are in cash rather than in kind. In 1923 the Supreme Court had before it for the first time cases involving a modern conditional grant, the maternal and child health program. The act was challenged as invading state power and as burdening disproportionately the taxpayers of the several states. Although the court did not provide direct answers to the issues, it did refuse to declare the aid program void, and it made virtually impossible the challenge by state or taxpayer of the validity of such an expenditure.[2] Subsequent cases have resulted in similar verdicts. The constitutionality of using the power to tax and spend for federal grants appears to be fully assured.

Today there are some twenty-five aided functions, and several proposals for new federal grants are pending. Arguments for and against grants-in-aid will be considered in a subsequent section of this chapter, but a general explanation of why the Federal government has made such extensive use of this device is in place here. Perhaps the greatest impetus comes from a desire to finance more and improved services by taxing on the broad base of the whole nation and spending in the areas of greatest need. The grant-in-aid offers a middle ground between direct federal assumption of certain state and local functions and their continuation under exclusive state and local financing, with haphazard coverage and diverse standards. It makes possible the achievement of national minimum standards, yet retains most of the benefits of administration close to the people.

[1] For fuller consideration of powers aspect, see p. 373.

[2] Massachusetts *v.* Mellon and Frothington *v.* Mellon, 262 U.S. 447 (1923).

Services Aided by Federal Grants.—For the year 1947–1948 the largest regular federal grants-in-aid (excluding shared revenues, emergency grants, and payments to individuals within states) were for the following purposes and in the following amounts:[1]

Old-age assistance	$562,373,583
Highways	303,065,504
Aid to dependent children	139,584,402
Unemployment compensation	67,721,807
Public employment offices	65,888,465
School lunch program	65,094,232
Vocational education	26,387,207
Agricultural extension work	26,205,864

Lesser grants were made for agricultural experiment stations, forest-fire cooperation, airport program, wildlife conservation, agricultural colleges, venereal disease control, tuberculosis control, general health assistance, maternal and child health, aid to crippled children, child-welfare services, aid to the blind, vocational rehabilitation, and some minor functions. There has been a tremendous increase in the use of grants-in-aid. In 1911–1912 the total federal grants scarcely exceeded $5,000,000; for 1947–1948 they were over $1,400,000,000 for regular, permanent functions. All forms of federal grants, including grants-in-aid, shared revenues, emergency grants, and payments to individuals within states, aggregated $5,551,054,046 in 1947–1948.[2]

Conditions Attached to Federal Grants.—The basis of allocation, the state contribution, and the extent of federal control depend upon the nature of the service aided and the temper of Congress when the grant is authorized. Basis of allocation may be equal among the states, according to need, number aided, rural population, total population, or some other formula or combination. Generally Congress requires that a state must match the federal contribution with a state contribution. The state appropriation often is required on a dollar-for-dollar basis, but sometimes it must be more or may be less; occasionally no matching is required. Apportionment and matching features of various grant programs are tabulated in the table on the opposite page.

Federal administrative controls vary greatly. Sweeping supervisory powers are exercised by federal road officials over the construction of federally aided state highways. The amount of control by federal authorities over educational services and agricultural experiment stations is almost nil.

[1] United States Department of the Treasury, *Annual Report for Fiscal Year Ended June 30, 1948* (Washington: Government Printing Office, 1949), pp. 507–512.

[2] About $3,500,000,000 of this was for veterans' readjustment benefits. *Ibid.*, p. 622.

Apportionment and Matching of Federal Grants-in-Aid*

Program	Basis of allocation	Matching required
Old age	Amount state spends	US pays ½ to ¾
Highways	Population, area, and RFD mileage	Largely $ for $
Dependent children	Amount state spends	US pays ½ to ¾
Unemployment compensation	Amount necessary for efficient operation	None
Employment offices	Amount necessary for efficient operation	None
School lunches	Population and financial need	Wealthier states, $ for $; others, less
Vocational education	Population	$ for $
Agricultural extension	Uniform by states and population	Most, none; small part, $ for $
Vocational rehabilitation	Amount state spends	Largely $ for $
Venereal diseases	Need for aid and per capita income	S $1 for US $2
General health	Population, need for aid, and financial need	S $1 for US $2
Maternal and child health	Number of live births, financial need, and uniform	½ requires none; ½ $ for $
Forest fire	"Fair and equitable"	$ for $
Crippled children	Need for aid and uniform by states	½ requires none; ½ $ for $
Agricultural experiment	Population and uniform by states	First $90,000, none; thereafter, $ for $
Tuberculosis	Need for aid and financial need	S $1 for US $2
Agricultural colleges	Population and uniform by states	None
Airports	Population, need for aid, and area	Largely $ for $
Child welfare	Population and uniform by states	None
Wildlife restoration	Area and hunting license holders	S $1 for US $3
Hospital construction	Population and per capita income	S $2 for US $1

*Compiled from Council of State Governments, *Federal Grants-in-Aid* (Chicago: The Council, 1949), pp. 51–67. Aided programs are listed in order of amounts received.

It would be poor policy, indeed, for the Federal government to hand out money without some method of checking the stewardship of the states in its expenditure. On the other hand, petty and detailed checking is not likely to produce other than resentment. Constant federal pressure has done much to keep the spoils system out of state unemployment-insurance administration, and from state welfare agencies. Under the second Hatch

Act, Congress attempted to keep state and local employees in federally aided functions out of politics. The law was so sweeping in its coverage, however, that it is regarded by many as invasive on civil rights.

Equalization through Variable Grants.—All the grants that deviate from apportionment of equal amounts for each state and a standard matching formula might be considered variable. Such adjustments are made mainly to take into account need, both for financial aid and for the services being provided. When the results of existing apportionment and matching rules are studied, however, many programs are found deficient so far as equalizing tendencies are concerned. The new hospital construction grants, for example, require $2 from the state for each $1 from the Federal government, although apportionment favors states with low per capita income. The "open end" method of allocating public assistance grants, under which there is no top limit of the amount of federal aid to each state and the Federal government is committed to pay a fixed proportion of the total state expenditures for this purpose, has led to far larger grants to the wealthier states. This fault has been only partially corrected by the rule under which the Federal government pays three-fourths of the lowest monthly payments, and one half of the payments above this amount.

When per capita grants are compared with per capita income it is found that some of the richest states, such as Nevada, Montana, Wyoming, North Dakota, Colorado, California, and Washington, are among the largest recipients of federal subsidies in proportion to population. On the other hand, some of the states with lowest per capita income, such as Virginia, North Carolina, Kentucky, and Mississippi, are near the bottom in federal aid received.[1] Even when allowance is made for the highway and airport programs that favor the sparsely populated areas of the West, federal aid as at present constituted does not appear to aid the neediest states as much as its proponents desire. This condition arises in part from inability of states with the least resources to raise matching funds. In their efforts to secure such funds, there is grave danger that states may neglect unaided functions.

Because of these considerations, much attention has been devoted to constructing variable grant formulas in education, health, and assistance fields. Of necessity, these formulas are complex, and no attempt will be made to describe them here. Among the problems encountered, according to the Council of State Governments' report, is that of measuring the states with reference to fiscal capacity and tax effort expended to raise their own funds. Perhaps the simplest and most acceptable of the ways to judge fiscal capacity is to use per capita income, with some adjustments for goods produced for home use and tax payments. Tax effort is harder to estimate, for there is considerable variation in state tax structures and rates.

[1] Council of State Governments, *op. cit.*, p. 85.

The danger that states may withdraw their support for functions which receive federal aid, thus shifting the cost to the Federal government, may be avoided by requiring maintenance of support at the same level reached in earlier years or, as contained in the aid-to-general-education bill passed by the Senate in the Eightieth Congress, by specifying a definite percentage of aggregate income that must be spent for the function. Such controls might tempt states to starve unaided functions and spend extravagantly on aided ones. This might be curbed by establishing a ratio between state collections and state fiscal capacity and requiring a state to tax up to a minimum standard in order to be eligible for federal aid, but such a requirement is highly unlikely.

Many other questions regarding equalization among states remain. Should a maximum federal contribution for an aided function be set? Should the grant-in-aid formula be set in the law or left to the discretion of the administrator? These and other questions regarding variable grants require answers before the present haphazard grants-in-aid programs can achieve the goal of equalization.[1]

Appraisal of Federal Grants.—Conditional grants-in-aid have both coercive and cooperative aspects. The bait of money is so attractive that rarely does a state resist the impulse to accept grants. Actually, however, the upper layer of government is only offering to provide something the lower might not be able to afford. The clear alternative to federal grants, if services are to be standardized at a high level, is direct federal assumption of the many functions. The grant system postpones or renders unnecessary that more drastic step toward centralization. It implies that there is a virtue in local administration, but it insists upon uniform minimum standards. Paradoxical as it seems, federal grants to states are both a step toward centralization and a substitute for centralization.

Many unsolved problems concerning grants-in-aid remain. Prof. Joseph P. Harris once called attention to deficiencies in the present system of distributing grants.[2] State and local budgets have been distorted badly; unaided services have suffered seriously, particularly in the poorer states; vocational education is expanded abnormally, while in the poorer states general elementary education is allowed to languish; old-age assistance booms, while general relief in many states has been neglected or curtailed. The methods of allocating federal aid to the states, though different for each form of federal aid, are in most instances reasonably satisfactory and well designed to accomplish the purposes of Congress in

[1] For further reading, see especially Byron L. Johnson, *The Principle of Equalization Applied to the Allocation of Grants-in-Aid*, Bureau of Research and Statistics Memorandum No. 66 (Washington: Social Security Administration, 1947).

[2] Joseph P. Harris, "The Future of Grants-in-Aid," *Annals of the American Academy*, vol. 207 (January, 1940), pp. 14–26.

making the grant. Federal aid for old-age assistance, however, has been severely criticized because the provision for matching, without limitation as to the amount which may be allocated to individual states, has resulted in far greater aid to the wealthier than to the poorer states. Distribution is in proportion to wealth instead of need. Many proposals have been made to revise the formula to take into account the financial needs of the several states, and thus enable the poorer states to raise their standards.

The next great step in the federal-grant program probably will be toward aid for general education. In 1936 President Roosevelt appointed an Advisory Committee on Education to study federal aid to education. It issued a series of staff studies and made its own report in 1938. To equalize in part the great inequalities of educational opportunity in the several states, it recommended that federal aid for general education be instituted, beginning with 72 million dollars in the first year, and expanding to 202 million dollars in the sixth.[1] This federal-aid program was not accepted by Congress before entrance into the Second World War. It was revived after the war in the form of a bill that would have provided 300 million dollars annually under a formula which would have given the poorer states the largest share.[2]

Arguments on Federal Grants-in-Aid*

For	Against
1. Is useful device to join levels of government in common enterprise.	1. Permits Federal government to enter fields denied to it by Constitution.
2. Provides way to finance key services beyond capacity of states and local governments.	2. Is spent for local, not national, purposes, thus leading to sectional jealousies and jockeying for benefits.
3. Helps redistribute income and promotes progressive taxation.	3. Places unfair tax burden on some states to support services in others.
4. Improves state and local standards of administration.	4. Leads to extravagant spending both by Federal government and by states.
5. Provides substitute for direct national assumption of functions.	5. Distorts state budgets and tends to destroy budgetary control.
6. Induces state and local governments to enter neglected fields.	6. Violates doctrine that government which spends moneys should collect.
7. Involves two levels of government in checking upon extravagance.	7. Brings federal control of local activities and builds bureaucracy.
8. Insures a national minimum of services and performance level.	8. Will lead to federal monopoly of tax power, destroy local independence.

* Condensed from Council of State Governments, *Federal Grants-in-Aid* (Chicago: The Council, 1949), pp. 41–42.

The federal-subsidy system is now so well established that it seems as though we are harking back to a far-off age in reading the attack written by the late James M. Beck, former Solicitor General and congressman, in 1932:

[1] United States Advisory Committee on Education, *Report of the Committee* (Washington: Government Printing Office, 1938), p. 195.

[2] Such a bill passed the Senate in both the Eightieth and Eighty-first Congresses.

> . . . the great incentive and principal cause of these subsidies is the persistent desire of the smaller agricultural states of the South and West, with their wholly disproportionate representation in the Senate, to milk for the benefit of these sections the larger and wealthier industrial states.[1]

In spite of such attacks, however, the grant system has grown and flourished. It has done much to raise the standards of essential services in the states and has provided an effective substitute for drastic centralization.

Other Federal-State Financial Arrangements.—In addition to grants-in-aid, there are several other varieties of federal aid to the states. These include shared revenues, in lieu payments, contractual arrangements, loans, payments to individuals within states, and a few others.

Most of the existing shared-revenue arrangements were made because the Federal government acknowledged an obligation to make a contribution to a state or local government. Federal revenues from national forests, mineral leases on the public domain, hunters of migratory birds, leases on flood-control lands, leases of federally owned power sites—all these are shared with state or local governments. Since most federal agencies do not pay state or local taxes, it is extremely important that some contribution be made to compensate for the loss of revenue. In some counties of Western states more than 90 per cent of the land area is owned by federal agencies; in 1937 the percentage of federally owned land areas was 82.67 of Nevada, 63.05 of Arizona, 60.45 of Utah, 58.07 of Idaho, 46.29 of Oregon, 42.72 of Wyoming, and 39.46 of California.[2] The laws permitting in lieu payments and shared revenues are so diverse that many cases of rank injustice can easily be found. The armed forces, for example, make no in lieu payments, so cities, counties, and states acquiring large military reservations may be called upon for expanded services at the very time when their tax bases are being reduced through federal land purchases. The problem is likely to get worse before it gets better, for the Supreme Court's verdict in United States *v.* California[3] gives the Federal government clear title to coastal tidelands. Representatives of the states are alarmed lest Congress assert federal control not only over coastal tidelands, but over all submerged lands and previously submerged lands under inland waterways as well. Such an interpretation would affect every state in the Union and might cast doubt upon the ownership of much land and many improve-

[1] James M. Beck, *Our Wonderland of Bureaucracy* (New York: Macmillan, 1932), p. 225. Used by permission of the Macmillan Company, Publishers. According to John W. Hanes, Chairman, Citizens National Committee, federal grants-in-aid represent an "effort to achieve social goals by means that adversely affect the democratic process and individual responsibility." *The New York Times*, Jan. 15, 1944.

[2] United States Federal Real Estate Board, *Federal Ownership of Real Estate and Its Bearing on State and Local Taxation . . .*, House Doc. 111, 76th Cong., 1st Sess. (Washington: Government Printing Office, 1939), Appendix B.

[3] 332 U.S. 19 (1947).

ments. The states are still seeking passage of legislation in Congress to return title of disputed lands to the states.

Strictly speaking, a contractual arrangement under which a federal agency makes payments to a state agency for certain services is not federal aid. Examples are not hard to find. In 1946 Congress provided for remuneration of states for apprenticeship training furnished by state and local agencies. The GI Bill authorized veterans' unemployment allowances, administered under contract with state employment departments; the same legislation provides for educational benefits for veterans, which, if obtained in state colleges and universities, involve federal payments to states.

The National Guard is in a class by itself. Once grouped with federally aided state services, it now is so fully under federal control that at most it could be called a cooperative activity. Federal funds are paid out directly to individuals, not through the states. States have certain powers over their units of the National Guard and certain obligations to provide facilities.

Federal Credits for State Taxation.—The Federal government can encourage states to take action along desired lines through still another use of the tax power, known as "tax offset," or federal credits for state taxation. This practice involves levying a federal tax but provides that the United States will yield and collect only a portion of the original rate if the state levies a similar tax for an approved purpose.

The device was employed first in the federal estate tax of 1924 which gave credit up to 80 per cent to taxpayers who paid a state inheritance tax. Its operation is best shown by example. Suppose Mr. A. M. Welloff died in Illinois, leaving to his daughter, Miss Welloff, a large estate on which the federal inheritance tax was calculated to be $10,000. If Illinois collected as much as $8,000 in state inheritance taxes, then the United States waived that amount and collected only $2,000 on the estate. Prior to the federal law, several states did not tax inheritances; Florida even advertised for the rich to retire there and escape the burden of estate taxation. Had Welloff died in Florida after 1924 and before Florida finally adopted an inheritance-tax law, the amount of tax paid on his estate would have been $10,000, but all would have gone to the Federal government. Naturally states hastened to enact laws to take advantage of this offset, and soon no taxless paradise was available for the rich.

The Unemployment Insurance Offset.—Another decade passed before the tax offset was used again. During the prolonged discussions that preceded the enactment of the Social Security Act, the idea of utilizing the sanction of tax offset in order to ensure state cooperation was proposed. The plan was adopted with respect to unemployment insurance, the administration of which was left to the states but subjected to extensive federal controls through a grant-in-aid for administrative purposes.

The Social Security Act of 1935 levied a federal tax on the pay rolls of employers of eight or more persons. This tax (which began at 1 per cent and ultimately increased to 3 per cent) is collected in full from employers doing business in states that have no "approved" system of unemployment compensation; in states with an insurance scheme approved by the Social Security Board, the Federal government waives 90 per cent of its tax and collects only 10 per cent. For example, the Nuform Bustle Company of Des Moines would have to pay 3 per cent on its pay roll to the United States Treasury if Iowa had no approved unemployment-insurance scheme, and the employees would receive no benefits if they became unemployed. Since Iowa adopted a proper unemployment-compensation plan, however, the company pays only $^{3}/_{10}$ of 1 per cent to the Federal government, plus whatever state pay-roll tax may be levied, and has the satisfaction of seeing its employees protected in lay-off seasons. Naturally, all states promptly enacted unemployment-compensation laws in order to take advantage of the provisions of the federal law.

Evaluation of the Tax Offset.—After the Supreme Court approved this exercise of the tax power,[1] renewed attention was directed toward the potentialities of this device. In the two instances it was employed, the tax offset proved so powerful that it virtually forced uniformity of action by the states. There were compelling reasons for the adoption of this coercive device in both cases. States with inheritance taxes were seriously threatened by the open bid of Florida for wealthy persons to establish residence there. Although unemployment-insurance laws could have been enacted by the states before 1935, actually interstate competition for business and industry was so keen that only Wisconsin enacted the necessary pay-roll tax and got its system under way. The federal law acted as an umbrella, permitting all states to enact unemployment-compensation laws without fear of driving industries to other states.

Congress is likely to use sparingly a weapon so powerful as the tax-credit device. Important as they are, federal grants-in-aid and other methods of inducing states to take desired action are less compelling, because the application of federal credits for state taxation has the sanction of forfeiture of tax revenues by an unyielding state.

Federal Cooperation and Expansion. *Restricting Lanes of Interstate Commerce.*—By the exercise of its power over commerce, Congress may help states to control some problems over which they otherwise could not make their control effective. The United States either refuses to allow passage, in or out of a state, of a certain commodity that the state seeks to prohibit or makes the commodity subject to the laws of the state immediately upon arrival.

[1] Steward Machine Co. *v.* Davis, 301 U.S. 548 (1937). The Court held the tax was an excise tax, the classification of employers was reasonable, and the state did not surrender any powers essential to sovereignty.

The earliest experience with this form of cooperative effort was in the field of liquor. After the court ruled in 1890 that a state prohibition law could not apply to liquor in interstate commerce,[1] Congress enacted the Wilson Act subjecting liquor shipments into states to state regulation from the time of their arrival. This act was upheld in the courts.[2] The method of "divestment" used in the Wilson Act was later used in subjecting to state regulation game birds and animals (1900), oleomargarine (1902), misbranded gold and silver (1906), plant life under quarantine (1926), convict-made goods (1929), and prize-fight films (1940).[3]

A stronger type of divestment occurs when the Federal government prohibits the movement of goods into a state in violation of state law. The Webb-Kenyon Act of 1913 forbade transportation of liquor into states forbidding its use.[4] Dormant during nation-wide prohibition, the same principle was written into the Twenty-first Amendment, Section 2, which provides:

> The transportation or importation into any State, Territory, or possession of the United States for delivery or use therein of intoxicating liquors, in violation of the laws thereof, is hereby prohibited.

The Webb-Kenyon method was also used in the Ashurst-Sumners Act of 1935,[5] which banned the transportation of prison-made goods in violation of state law. After the Supreme Court held this law valid,[6] much hope was aroused that Congress might be able to ban the products of child labor from states prohibiting their sale. Instead, Congress chose to regulate child labor directly and uniformly through the Wages and Hours Law. In 1940 a second Ashurst-Sumners Act placed an absolute prohibition on all shipment of prison-made goods in interstate commerce.

A third type of federal restriction is imposed in order to prohibit the movement of goods and persons from a state in violation of that state's law. This variety of control has been extended to automobile theft (1919), other stolen property (1934), kidnaped persons (1932), fugitive felons (1934).[7] After the oil-control features of the National Recovery Act of 1933 were declared unconstitutional,[8] Congress forbade shipments

[1] Leisy & Co. *v.* Hardin, 135 U.S. 100 (1890).

[2] *In re* Rahrer, 140 U.S. 545 (1891).

[3] Joseph E. Kallenbach, *Federal Cooperation with the States under the Commerce Clause* (Ann Arbor: University of Michigan Press, 1942), pp. 112–199.

[4] 37 Stat. 699.

[5] 49 Stat. 494.

[6] Kentucky Whip and Collar Co. *v.* Illinois Central, 299 U.S. 334 (1937).

[7] See Kallenbach, *op. cit.*, pp. 315–331.

[8] Panama Refining Co. *v.* Ryan, 293 U.S. 388 (1935). The grounds were excessive delegation of legislative authority to the President.

of petroleum in interstate commerce in excess of quotas set by state law.[1] This legislation helps oil-producing states to enforce their laws relating to the production of petroleum under the terms of the Interstate Oil Compact of 1935.

The cooperative nature of this device has been demonstrated in the various examples of its use. In most cases it makes possible more effective state control, instead of displacing state with federal authority. As a consequence, the states have generally looked with favor upon this device.

Cooperative and Reciprocal Arrangements.—A number of other voluntary, cooperative arrangements have been made between state and Federal governments. Cooperation may be mere consultation between federal and state officials in order to exchange information and to plan together common or interrelated functions. State departments of agriculture usually act in close harmony with the United States Department of Agriculture. The federal Department of Labor holds an annual conference to which are invited state labor officials, who are encouraged to interchange ideas.

Relying upon its power to spend money, Congress has established many research and informational services which may induce states to undertake programs of action or raise standards of performance for existing activities. This is what Jane Perry Clark has called "informational inducement."[2]

Another little-noticed field of cooperation is reciprocal use of officials by Federal and state governments. Many state constitutions forbid state officers (to be distinguished from employees) from holding federal posts, but a considerable development has occurred in spite of this limitation. Federal use of state employees and agencies is the more extensive. During the First World War and the Second World War, conscription was federally supervised but locally administered by officials who were appointed by the states. State prohibition-enforcement agents, during the era of the Eighteenth Amendment, often were made part-time federal officers. Less direct state use of federal officials is found, although federal forest rangers may enforce state fish and game laws, and Federal Bureau of Investigation agents frequently apprehend violators of state criminal laws. The county agent or farm adviser performs functions for three levels of government—national, state, and county.

Federal-local Relations.—Previous to 1933 contacts between the Federal government, cities, and counties were largely informal. Federal marshals and district attorneys worked with sheriffs, police chiefs, and prosecutors; the Office of Education issued publications and otherwise served local

[1] The Connally Act of 1935, 49 Stat. 30, was renewed in 1937, 1939, and made permanent in 1942, 56 Stat. 381.

[2] Jane Perry Clark, *The Rise of a New Federalism* (New York: Columbia University Press, 1938).

school districts; cities and counties helped enforce federally fixed standards of weights and measures; but the relationship was seldom direct and formal.

Since 1933 the picture has changed. Contacts have increased a hundred-fold and have become direct and formal. The Works Projects Administration paid the relief labor costs for locally sponsored work-relief projects. The Public Works Administration made grants and loans to local bodies for major construction jobs and then helped supervise the work. Recent legislation permits the use of federal aid in building highways within cities. The United States Housing Authority makes grants to municipal and county housing authorities for the construction of locally owned and managed housing projects.[1] Indeed, federal-local contacts have become so numerous as seriously to disturb those who fear federal domination.

Direct Federal Expansion of Activities.—Perhaps more than all others combined, broadened interpretation of federal powers has been the avenue of federal encroachment on what were formerly state functions. An astounding expansion of federal governmental activities has taken place during the last 30 years. How this expansion has been accomplished and justified may best be studied in connection with the federal powers concerned. Classified by powers, the major expansion may be sketched in summary form.

The commerce power now extends federal control not only to every sort of transportation and communication, but also to manufacturing, mining, and other businesses that affect interstate commerce.[2] In the decade of 1930 to 1940 alone, Congress has validly employed the commerce power to regulate labor relations, control radio broadcasting, provide retirement system for railroad employees, fix minimum wages and maximum hours, regulate interstate bus and truck lines, control small streams even of doubtful navigability, regulate stock exchanges, forbid transportation of strikebreakers, punish extorters, kidnapers, and vehicle thieves. The most monumental of court decisions involving the commerce power were in the NLRB cases and in the Wages and Hours Case.[3]

Next in importance comes the tax power, and its implied companion, the spending power. Not only does the tax power justify the grant-in-aid, the tax offset, and expenditures for research and informational services, but it is used for regulatory purposes as well. Between the Civil War and the First World War, broad interpretation of the tax power permitted use of the power to tax state bank notes out of circulation, colored oleomargarine out of existence, phosphorus matches off the market, and to bring dealers of narcotics under federal control. Then the trend was reversed,

[1] For fuller discussion of public works and housing see Chap. 29.

[2] See p. 383.

[3] National Labor Relations Board *v.* Jones and Laughlin Steel Corporation, 301 U.S. 1 (1937), and United States *v.* Darby Lumber Co., 312 U.S. 100 (1941).

and the court struck down as void several attempts to regulate through the tax power. This line of decisions was arrested in the Social Security cases[1] and the tax power now appears available for regulatory purposes.[2]

Through its monetary power, the Federal government validly has extended its activities into such diverse fields as incorporating credit unions, insuring bank deposits, chartering and regulating savings and loan associations, and participating in international stabilization funds. Congress

Can state boundaries be redrawn to conform to physical and economic factors?

SOURCE: United States National Resources Planning Board, *Regional Factors in National Planning and Development* (Washington: Government Printing Office, 1935).

has used the war power to justify in part the great regional-planning scheme of the Tennessee Valley Authority, to authorize the broad wartime controls covering production, transportation, distribution, conscription, and nearly every aspect of economic and social life in the country. Even the treaty power has been used as the basis of federal expansion of authority.

Proposed Reform of the Federal System. *State Lines and Administrative Areas.*—State boundaries of today are products of historical factors, early transportation limits, and other forces, many of which are no longer

[1] Steward Machine Co. *v.* Davis, 301 U.S. 548 (1937), validated the unemployment insurance tax offset, and Helvering *v.* Davis, 301 U.S. 619 (1937), approved the old-age insurance scheme.

[2] See also p. 366.

valid. Criminals and diseases, plagues of man, do not respect state lines. They may be dealt with effectively either through cooperative effort of two or more states, or they may be handled through federal action. Some students of federal problems feel that the answer to many interstate difficulties may be the drawing of state lines so that a smaller number of regional states might coincide with economic and physiographic lines. One form of regional action is secured through interstate compact or informal agreement of neighboring states, who agree to a common program for a common problem, as is the case with the Colorado River Compact or some of the recent river-pollution compacts.

The Federal government sets up various administrative areas to aid in the execution of national law; most of these groupings respect state lines but combine several states for administrative convenience. An independent federal agency like the Tennessee Valley Authority has broad planning powers over an area including portions of several states, and may be a forerunner of other regional projects under federal auspices. This practice is open to the objection, as in all federal plans, that the people of the area have no direct voice in the management of the scheme. Some advantages might accrue from standardizing all federal administrative areas, but standardization would represent no particular contribution toward helping the states to settle interstate regional problems. The task of getting small states to consolidate with others appears virtually impossible, given the constitutional inviolability of the territory of a state without its own consent.

Alterations in the Federal System.—Various proposals have been made for recasting the balance between nation and states. Some have urged that the Federal government be given full general police power—to provide for the health, morals, safety, and welfare of the people. This scheme would require a constitutional amendment, the ratification of which would be exceedingly difficult to secure. It should be recognized that assigning such a sweeping power to the Federal government would transform our system into a unitary one for all practical purposes.

A second school of thought, which has prevailed during the New Deal era, argues that the language of the Constitution confers sufficient authority upon the Federal government to deal with national problems. It maintains that the courts were in error between 1933 and 1936 in narrowly construing federal powers, but that this mistake has since been corrected through broad construction. Therefore, the constitutional crisis is over, for the times and the new court personnel have combined to produce liberalized decisions. This policy comprehends no sudden changes in existing forms but calls for the remodeling of practices and rejuvenation within the old framework.

Finally, there are the vigilant States' righters, and the decentralists who see the virtues of local self-government slipping away in the face of growing state and federal centralization. The more rabid expend their energies shouting invectives at the federal octopus. The more thoughtful concentrate on improvements in state administration and legislation. As shown above, significant progress has been made in the direction of interstate organization and cooperation.

Amount of Centralization.—Those who favor greater centralization raise many valid objections to the federal system as we have it. It does produce indefensible inequality in an essential public service like education. It provides an outlet for narrow sectional feelings, as evidenced by state trade barriers. It makes difficult the prompt solution of national problems on a national basis. One of the most brilliant political scientists of our time, Harold J. Laski of the University of London, condemned our "obsolescent federalism" in these terms:

> But a contracting capitalism cannot afford the luxury of federalism. It is insufficiently positive in character; it does not provide for sufficient rapidity of action; it inhibits the emergence of necessary standards of uniformity; it relies upon compacts and compromises which take insufficient account of the urgent category of time; it leaves the backward areas a restraint, at once parasitic and poisonous, on those which seek to move forward; not least, its psychological results, especially in an age of crisis, are depressing to a democracy that needs the drama of positive achievement to retain its faith.[1]

On the other hand, the dangers from excessive centralization appear as bad or worse. In a country huge both in area and in population a distant national bureaucracy is not likely to understand local needs. Civic interest and participation in government may be reduced in proportion to the size of the political unit and the distance from the seat of power. Alexis de Tocqueville, the first foreign observer of this new republic, wrote more than a hundred years ago one of the strongest arguments for decentralization:

> But I am of the opinion that a central administration is fit only to enervate the nations in which it exists, by incessantly diminishing their local spirit. Although such an administration can bring together, on a given point, all the disposable resources of a people, it injures the renewal of those resources. It may insure a victory in the hour of strife, but it gradually relaxes the sinews of strength. It may help admirably the transient greatness of a man, but not the durable prosperity of a nation.[2]

[1] Harold J. Laski, "The Obsolescence of Federalism," *New Republic*, vol. 98 (May 3, 1939), pp. 367–369.

[2] Alexis de Tocqueville, *Democracy in America* (New York: Knopf, 2 vols., 1945), vol. I, p. 87.

The answer for America probably lies in the middle ground. Federal centralization will continue to reduce the relative importance of the states, as national control over insurance, public utilities, agriculture, social services, and general business increases. Grants-in-aid may expand to general education and other fields, reemphasizing that although federal financing and control over policy are mounting, the state and its local subdivisions may still play an important role in administering functions close to the people served.

References

BALL, VAUGHN C., and OTHERS: "The Uniform Laws Movement: Symposium," *Ohio State Law Journal*, vol. 9 (Autumn, 1948), pp. 551–688.

BARD, ERWIN W.: *The Port of New York Authority* (New York: Columbia University Press, 1942).

BENSON, GEORGE C. S.: *The New Centralization* (New York: Rinehart, 1941).

BIRD, FREDERICK L.: *A Study of the Port of New York Authority; Its Purpose—Its Accomplishments—Its Plans for the Future* (New York: Dun & Bradstreet, 1949).

BITTERMAN, HENRY J.: *State and Federal Grants-in-Aid* (Chicago: Mentzer, 1938).

CLARK, JANE PERRY: *The Rise of a New Federalism* (New York: Columbia University Press, 1938).

COUNCIL OF STATE GOVERNMENTS: *The Book of the States* (Chicago: The Council, biennial).

——— *Federal Grants-in-Aid, Report of the Committee on . . .* (Chicago: The Council, 1949).

——— *Trade Barriers among the States* (Chicago: The Council, 1939).

——— *State Government* (Chicago: The Council, monthly).

EISNER, MARK, and OTHERS: *Tax Barriers to Trade* (Philadelphia: Tax Institute, 1941).

GRAVES, W. BROOKE: *Uniform State Action* (Chapel Hill: The University of North Carolina Press, 1934).

GREEN, THOMAS S., JR.: *Liquor Trade Barriers* (Chicago: Public Administration Service, 1940).

HEINBERG, JOHN G.: *Manual on Federal-State Relations . . .*, Missouri Constitutional Convention Report No. 3 (Columbia: University of Missouri, 1943).

JOHNSON, BYRON L.: *The Principle of Equalization Applied to the Allocation of Grants-in-Aid*, Bureau of Research and Statistics Memorandum No. 66 (Washington: Social Security Administration, 1947).

KALLENBACH, JOSEPH E.: *Federal Cooperation with the States, under the Commerce Clause* (Ann Arbor: University of Michigan Press, 1942).

KEY, VLADIMIR O.: *The Administration of Federal Grants to States* (Chicago: Public Administration Service, 1937).

MACDONALD, AUSTIN F.: *Federal Aid: A Study of the American Subsidy System* (New York: Crowell, 1928).

MELDER, F. EUGENE: *State and Local Barriers to Interstate Commerce in the United States* (Orono: University of Maine Press, 1937).

NOTZ, REBECCA L.: *Acts of Congress Providing for Grants-in-Aid to States*, Public Affairs Bulletin No. 70 (Washington: Library of Congress, 1949).

TAYLOR, GEORGE R., and OTHERS: *Barriers to Internal Trade in Farm Products* (Washington: Government Printing Office, 1939).

UNITED STATES ADVISORY COMMITTEE ON EDUCATION: *Report of the Committee* (Washington: Government Printing Office, 1938).

UNITED STATES DEPARTMENT OF COMMERCE, MARKETING LAWS SURVEY: *Bibliography of Barriers to Trade between States* (Washington: Bureau of Foreign and Domestic Commerce, 1942).

UNITED STATES DEPARTMENT OF COMMERCE: *A Summarized Report of the Legal Subcommittee of the Interdepartmental Committee on Interstate Trade Barriers* (Washington: Department of Commerce, 1940).

UNITED STATES NATIONAL RESOURCES COMMITTEE: *Regional Factors in National Planning and Development* (Washington: Government Printing Office, 1935).

TEXT-FILM

The following McGraw-Hill 35mm silent filmstrip is recommended for use with Chap. 6 of this text.

The Federal System—Part II. Relations between the states and problems of interstate competition and of centralization.

Chapter 7

INDIVIDUAL RIGHTS

The Constitution expresses more than the conviction of the people that democratic processes must be preserved at all costs. It is also an expression of faith and a command that freedom of the mind and spirit must be preserved, which government must obey, if it is to adhere to that justice and moderation without which no free government can exist.

Mr. Justice Stone dissenting in Minersville School District *v.* Gobitis.[1]

The period during which North America was colonized was one of absolutism. Monarchs of Europe imbued with the notion that their authority was derived directly from God claimed and exercised unlimited authority, often with a heartless indifference toward the liberties of their subjects. Absolutism did not go unchallenged. In the contest, often interspersed with bloody civil wars, the challengers came to believe themselves endowed by the law of nature with a set of "natural" and "inalienable" rights that could not be abridged by government authorities. Such was the opinion of those who framed the Declaration of Independence. When independence had been won, Americans recognized the necessity of government but still remained fearful of arbitrary political power. To protect themselves they carefully drafted state constitutions including within them bills of rights. The confederation was too weak to be greatly feared, but the proposal to establish a strong central government again raised the specter of tyranny. Accordingly, the Constitution as it came from the hands of the framers provided for a limited government, and before ratification could be completed it became necessary to promise the inclusion of a bill of rights.

GENERAL CONSIDERATIONS

Rights Relative—Not Absolute.—The Declaration of Independence speaks of "natural" or "unalienable" rights, and the language of the Constitution suggests that rights are absolute. If this were true governments could under no circumstances legislate on matters proscribed. But this is not the case. Over the years many laws have been passed restricting vulgarity, profanity, slander, libel, and the like, even though in doing so freedom of speech was curtailed. The power to govern coexists with personal rights and the two must be reconciled. Power cannot be exercised

[1] 310 U.S. 586 (1940).

without regard to constitutionally protected rights and the latter cannot be enjoyed without regard for other individuals and the community. This being the case, it becomes necessary to strike a balance, to draw boundary lines. This is done by legislatures, executives, and especially the courts, all of which are influenced by public opinion. While admitting

PROTECTIONS OF AND DANGERS TO CIVIL LIBERTIES

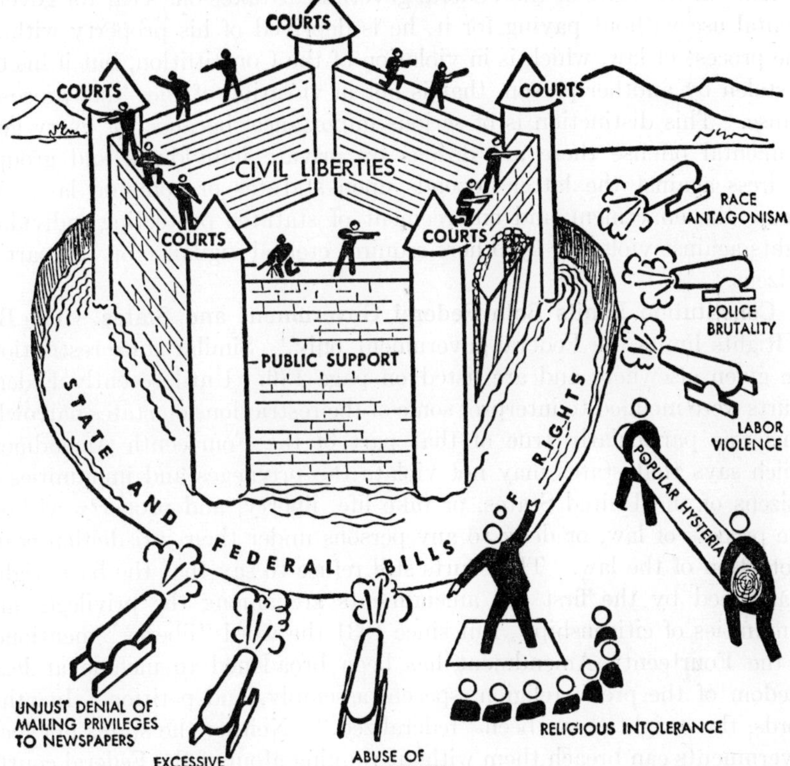

SOURCE: Robert E. Cushman, *Our Constitutional Freedoms* (National Foundation For Education in American Citizenship and Public Affairs Committee, Inc., 1944).

that rights are relative, there is danger, especially in periods of emergency or hysteria, that they may be emasculated. The Bill of Rights, it should be remembered, is as much a part of the Constitution as those sections delegating powers to Congress, including those granting the power to declare and prosecute war.

The Bill of Rights Limits Governments—Not Individuals.—The rights clauses of the Constitution protect people from the actions of governments, not from one another. Sometimes the words are "Congress shall make no law . . .," or "No state shall . . .," but where such words are omitted they should be inferred. Thus, if a mayor suppresses free speech, the Constitution is violated. But if a gang of hoodlums breaks up a meeting, the action is probably illegal but does not violate the Bill of Rights. The Constitution is violated if a state or the national government denies an accused person a fair trial, but a lynching mob can seize and destroy a suspect in complete disregard for his rights without violating the Constitution. If the state or the Federal government takes one's car for governmental use without paying for it, he is deprived of his property without due process of law, which is in violation of the Constitution, but if his car is stolen by another person, that is not in violation of the "due process" clause. This distinction is of serious importance, because for every governmental offense there are dozens by private individuals and groups. Redress against the latter depends upon statutes or common law. To secure the enactment and enforcement of statutes protecting individual rights against violation by others requires eternal vigilance on the part of citizens.

Constitution Limits Both Federal Government and States.—The Bill of Rights limits the Federal government only.[1] Similar state restrictions are given elsewhere and are listed on page 136. Until recently Federal courts were inclined to interpret some of the restrictions on states narrowly. This was particularly true of that part of the Fourteenth Amendment which says that states may not violate the privileges and immunities of citizens of the United States, or take life, liberty, and property without due process of law, or deny to any persons under their jurisdiction equal protection of the law. The courts still refuse to say that the basic rights guaranteed by the first ten amendments are among the privileges and immunities of citizenship. But since 1931 the word "liberty" mentioned in the Fourteenth Amendment has been broadened to include at least freedom of the press, religion, speech, assembly, and petition. In other words, these rights have been "federalized." Neither the states nor local governments can breach them without running afoul of the Federal courts. This protection is of great value in view of opportunities and temptations that forty-eight states and thousands of cities and other local governments have to abridge liberties. Indeed, by far the most civil-rights cases reaching Federal courts challenge state and local action, not federal.

Rights of Aliens and Nationals Also Guaranteed.—Rights are guaranteed to all "persons." This being the case, aliens and nationals are entitled to the same personal and property rights as citizens. They do not, however, enjoy certain "privileges and immunities" that are pledged to citizens only.[2]

[1] Barron *v.* Baltimore, 7 Peters 243 (1823); Twining *v.* New Jersey, 211 U.S. 78 (1908).

[2] See p. 157.

Limited Ability of Federal Government to Safeguard Rights.—When Federal and state governments trespass upon civil liberties, the usual procedure is for the injured party to appeal to Federal courts. On occasions like these the courts play a negative role. Damage has already been done, and the victim may be unable to make protest or may have to wait years for adequate redress. Moreover, as indicated above, for offenses by private individuals and groups the Bill of Rights provides no legal remedy. A number of states have enacted antidiscrimination statutes; a few have created fair employment practices commissions to work constantly at the task of preventing employers from discriminating because of race, color, creed, or national origin. Nevertheless, much dissatisfaction has been expressed in recent years over the alleged inadequacy of state law. The time has come, critics say, for the Federal government to play an affirmative role as well as a negative one.[1]

Among other things, critics argue, this requires legislation strengthening federal enforcement machinery and imposing penalties upon state and local officials and private parties who violate civil rights. In times past Congress has attempted to do just this. Soon after passage of the Thirteenth Amendment the worst forms of slavery were successfully outlawed. Passage of the Fourteenth Amendment was followed by a series of civil rights acts intended to outlaw the most serious forms of discrimination against Negroes. One of the acts (that of 1875) went so far as to make it a federal crime to deny service on equal terms in hotels, public conveyances, and theaters and other places of amusement. Those responsible for these measures assumed that the Civil War amendments, each of which contained clauses saying Congress had power to take appropriate steps to see that its provisions were enforced, justified affirmative action. These champions were, however, doomed to disappointment. In less than thirty years the program ended in failure. The Supreme Court led the way in a series of decisions that drastically narrowed the scope of federal authority.[2] Congress followed by repealing most of the statutes. After these events, administrative officers were reluctant to proceed at the risk of meeting further rebuffs. That this hesitation was justified is illustrated by the case of Screws *v.* United States.[3] Here the Department of Justice tried to enforce a remaining provision of the Civil Rights Act of 1866. Screws, a county sheriff in Georgia, was tried and convicted by federal officers for brutally beating and killing a Negro prisoner whom he held in custody. Although Screws was undoubtedly guilty, a majority of

[1] See especially the excellent study by Robert K. Carr, *Federal Protection of Civil Rights: Quest for a Sword* (Ithaca, N.Y., Cornell University Press, 1947).

[2] See especially the Civil Rights Cases, 109 U.S. 3 (1883); the Slaughter House Cases, 16 Wallace 36 (1873); and United States *v.* Cruikshank, 92 U.S. 542 (1876).

[3] 325 U.S. 91 (1945).

the Supreme Court interpreted the federal statute so technically and narrowly as to reverse the conviction and order a new trial.

To Secure These Rights.—Recent years have witnessed a renewal of interest. Private organizations, like the American Civil Liberties Union, have for many years called attention to public and private violations of rights. A Senate Committee headed by Senator Robert F. La Follette dramatically focused attention in the mid-1930's on outrages by employers and sympathizers committed against labor leaders and other "radicals." John Steinbeck dramatized in *The Grapes of Wrath* the indignities suffered during drought and depression years by destitute sharecroppers and itinerant workers. In 1939, upon the initiative of Attorney General Frank Murphy, later associate justice of the Supreme Court, the President created a Civil Rights Division in the Department of Justice to investigate violations of liberties and prosecute wherever possible. During the recent war, the President established by executive order a Fair Employment Practices Commission for the purpose of discouraging discrimination in employment because of race, color, or national origin. Shortly after the war, in 1946, President Truman appointed a committee of distinguished citizens, known as the President's Committee on Civil Rights, to explore the entire subject and make recommendations. The committee issued a notable report entitled *To Secure These Rights*[1] that precipitated a bitter controversy in and out of Congress and led a group of Southern states to break with the President in his 1948 campaign for reelection. Whether one agrees with the report or not, it deserves careful study.

The Committee Report.—The committee called attention to lynching and to the fact that the culprits are seldom discovered or punished. It discovered numerous instances of police brutality in various parts of the nation. Indeed, it quoted testimony given by J. Edgar Hoover, Director of the FBI, to the effect that at a particular jail "it was seldom that a Negro man or woman was incarcerated who was not given a severe beating, which started off with a pistol whipping and ended with a rubber hose."[2] The committee reported that Negroes, Mexicans, Indians, and other minorities often find it impossible to obtain justice, partly because of their poverty, partly because of the "complete absence of people of their own kind from jury lists," partly because of the fee system in many communities which "sometimes stimulates arbitrary arrests and encourages unjust convictions," and partly because in certain states "the white population can threaten and do violence to the minority members with little or no fear of legal reprisals."

[1] The report was published as a government document in 1947 and may be obtained from the Government Printing Office, Washington. It was also published under the same title by Simon and Schuster (New York, 1947).

[2] *Ibid.*, p. 26.

The committee also found some involuntary servitude among the poor, arising from state peonage laws imposing penalties for nonfulfillment of contracts to perform labor. It criticized the wartime treatment of Japanese-Americans along the West coast with resultant curtailment of liberty, forced removal to detention and relocation centers, and financial hardship. The committee discovered many instances of discrimination against aliens and even American nationals like the natives of Guam, Samoa, Puerto Rico, and the Panama Canal Zone. The committee noted that because of restrictions on the right to vote in some states, particularly the poll tax requirement in seven Southern states, comparatively few people went to the polls in these states. It found numerous violations of freedom of speech, press, religion, and assembly. It pointed out the dangers of "Red hunting" among civil servants by congressional committees and loyalty boards. It found an abundance of evidence indicating discrimination against Negroes in the armed forces, civil service, District of Columbia, American territories, by state and local governments, landlords, private employers, and in professional and service occupations. The committee was especially severe in its condemnation of racial segregation, declaring that the "separate but equal" doctrine allowed by the Supreme Court since 1896 has been a failure. This doctrine, said the committee,

> . . . stands convicted on three grounds. It contravenes the equalitarian sprit of the American heritage. It has failed to operate, for history shows that inequality of service has been the omnipresent consequence of separation. It has institutionalized segregation and kept groups apart despite indisputable evidence that normal contacts among these groups tend to promote social harmony.[1]

Proposed Remedies.—After reviewing the American scene and finding conditions that were heartening as well as disappointing, the President's Committee on Civil Rights made numerous proposals. Most important of all, the committee said, is the necessity of having an informed and alert public that is both tolerant and aggressive in defense of rights for all, especially minorities and advocates of unpopular causes. More specific suggestions included: (1) reorganization and strengthening of the Civil Rights Section of the Department of Justice; (2) creation by the states of divisions similar to the federal Civil Rights Section; (3) special training for federal and state police in the handling of cases involving civil rights; (4) establishment of federal and state permanent commissions on civil rights to maintain constant surveillance; (5) clarification and strengthening of federal statutes to make it unmistakably clear what conduct is and what is not a federal crime; (6) federal legislation outlawing police brutality, lynching, and all forms of peonage; (7) federal legislation outlawing the poll tax and other serious impediments to voting in primaries and elections; (8) self-govern-

[1] *Ibid.*, p. 87.

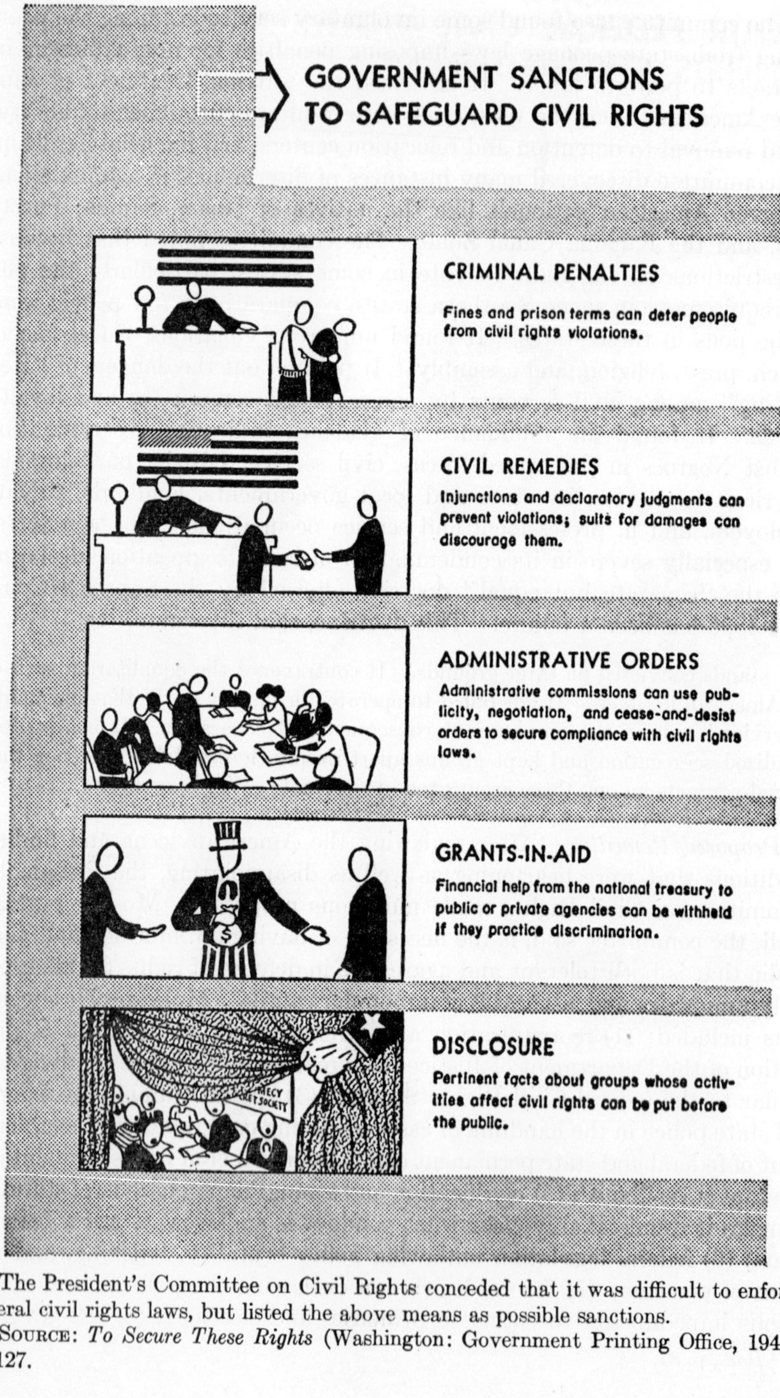

GOVERNMENT SANCTIONS
TO SAFEGUARD CIVIL RIGHTS
CRIMINAL PENALTIES
Fines and prison terms can deter people from civil rights violations.
CIVIL REMEDIES
Injunctions and declaratory judgments can prevent violations; suits for damages can discourage them.
ADMINISTRATIVE ORDERS
Administrative commissions can use publicity, negotiation, and cease-and-desist orders to secure compliance with civil rights laws.
GRANTS-IN-AID
Financial help from the national treasury to public or private agencies can be withheld if they practice discrimination.
DISCLOSURE
Pertinent facts about groups whose activities affect civil rights can be put before the public.

The President's Committee on Civil Rights conceded that it was difficult to enforce federal civil rights laws, but listed the above means as possible sanctions.

SOURCE: *To Secure These Rights* (Washington: Government Printing Office, 1947), p. 127.

OUR FEDERAL CIVIL RIGHTS MACHINERY NEEDS STRENGTHENING

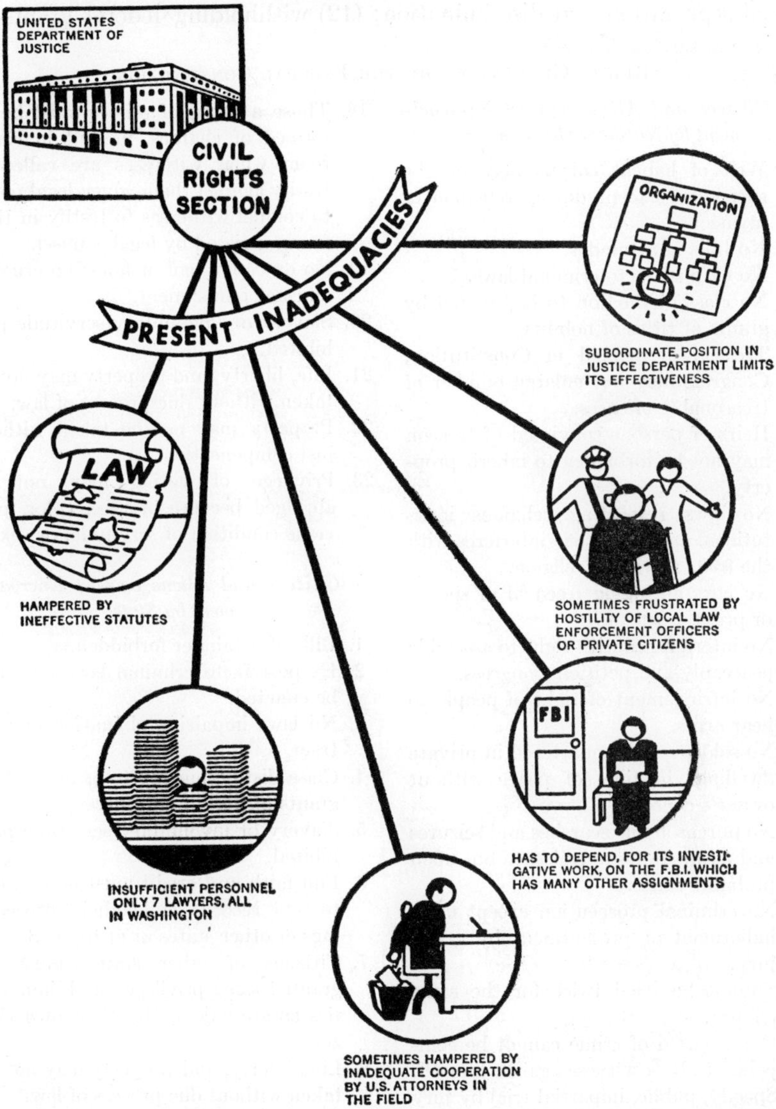

UNITED STATES DEPARTMENT OF JUSTICE
CIVIL RIGHTS SECTION
PRESENT INADEQUACIES
ORGANIZATION
SUBORDINATE POSITION IN JUSTICE DEPARTMENT LIMITS ITS EFFECTIVENESS
LAW
HAMPERED BY INEFFECTIVE STATUTES
SOMETIMES FRUSTRATED BY HOSTILITY OF LOCAL LAW ENFORCEMENT OFFICERS OR PRIVATE CITIZENS
FBI
HAS TO DEPEND, FOR ITS INVESTIGATIVE WORK, ON THE F.B.I. WHICH HAS MANY OTHER ASSIGNMENTS
INSUFFICIENT PERSONNEL ONLY 7 LAWYERS, ALL IN WASHINGTON
SOMETIMES HAMPERED BY INADEQUATE COOPERATION BY U.S. ATTORNEYS IN THE FIELD

Despite the many handicaps pictured above, the Civil Rights Section, since its creation in 1939, has made a good record. To overcome these difficulties, the President's Committee recommended the establishment of regional offices, increased appropriation and staff, more investigation, and other organizational and procedural improvements.

Source: *To Secure These Rights* (Washington: Government Printing Office, 1947), p. 115.

ment for the District of Columbia; (9) citizenship for the people of Guam and Samoa; (10) repeal of state laws discriminating against aliens; (11) federal and state laws ending "Jim Crow" laws and other serious forms of racial segregation and discrimination; (12) withholding federal grants-in-

Rights Guaranteed by the Federal Constitution

To Citizens and Aliens against Encroachment by National Government

1. Writ of habeas corpus may not be suspended except during rebellion or invasion.
2. No bills of attainder.
3. No ex post facto criminal laws.
4. No class distinction to be created by grants of titles of nobility.
5. Treason is defined in Constitution; Congress may not enlarge number of treasonable offenses.
6. Heirs of persons convicted of treason may not be forbidden to inherit property.
7. No laws respecting religious institutions, and none that interferes with the free exercise of religion.
8. No laws abridging freedom of speech or press.
9. No interference with right to assemble peaceably and petition Congress.
10. No infringement of right of people to bear arms.
11. No soldiers to be quartered in private dwellings in time of peace without owner's consent.
12. No unreasonable searches and seizures and no warrants to be issued but upon probable cause.
13. No criminal prosecution except upon indictment or presentment by grand jury.
14. Cannot be tried twice for the same offense.
15. One accused of crime cannot be compelled to be a witness against himself.
16. Speedy, public, impartial trial by jury of 12 persons whose verdict of guilt must be unanimous.
17. Trial by jury in civil suits involving a sum of more than $20.
18. Those accused of crimes must be informed of charges, present in courtroom when witnesses are called to testify against them, given legal power to compel witnesses to testify in their favor, assisted by legal counsel.
19. No excessive bail or fines; no cruel or unusual punishment.
20. Slavery or involuntary servitude prohibited.
21. Life, liberty, and property may not be taken without due process of law.
22. Property may not be taken without just compensation.
23. Privilege of voting may not be abridged because of race, color, previous condition of servitude, or sex.

To Citizens and Aliens against Encroachment by State

1. Bills of attainder forbidden.
2. Ex post facto criminal laws may not be enacted.
3. No laws impairing obligation of contract.
4. Class distinction not to be created by grants of title of nobility.
5. Slavery or involuntary servitude prohibited.
6. Full faith and credit must be granted to acts, records, and judicial proceedings of other states or of the U.S.
7. Citizens of other states must be granted same privileges and immunities as are enjoyed by their own citizens.
8. Life, liberty, and property may not be taken without due process of law.*
9. Equal protection of the laws may not be denied.
10. Privileges of voting may not be denied because of race, color, previous condition of servitude, or sex.

* This has been interpreted to include guarantees of freedom of speech, press, religion, and assembly.

aid from public and private agencies that practice discrimination and segregation.

The Fight in Congress.—It was to be expected that drastic and comprehensive proposals like these would provoke bitter controversy. Some progress has been made by executive order toward ending segregation and discrimination in the armed forces and federal civil service. At the same time, the screening of civil servants for disloyalty has been made less arbitrary. But in Congress the fight rages. Chief attention has focused upon bills making it illegal for state officers to conspire or otherwise cooperate with lynchers, bills making it illegal to require payment of poll taxes as a condition for voting for federal officers, and bills establishing a federal Fair Employment Practices Commission with authority to end discrimination in employment on government contracts and in interstate commerce.

These and other measures suggested by the President's Committee raise fundamental questions. One is whether the Federal government has constitutional authority to do as suggested. This is at least debatable for many of the proposals. The issues are difficult and extremely confused. Doubts could be removed by constitutional amendment, but this is probably impossible of attainment in view of certain opposition from the Southern bloc. Some champions of civil liberties admit having doubts but suggest federal action as a means of having the disputed issues brought to the courts for clarification.

Another serious issue raised by proposed federal legislation is whether in a system like ours it is better to attempt correction of the evils by federal legislation or to wait for relief by enlightened public opinion and state action. Proponents of federal intervention contend that the states have had ample time to correct the evils complained of, that continuance of present practices makes a mockery of democracy, and that federal legislation can be more effective than state because federal officers are further removed from local prejudices and pressures. Opponents protest bitterly. To impose federal penalties upon state governments and agents would, they claim, vitiate state sovereignty and rights. They insist that the evils are exaggerated, that the states are aware of their problems and have made great strides toward their improvement, and that state legislation is much preferable because it is enacted and enforced by those most familiar with conditions and problems.

RIGHTS GUARANTEED TO PERSONS AND PROPERTY

Life, Liberty, and Property.—In general, all rights pertain either to life, liberty, or property. The term "life" includes not merely animal existence, but the retention of limbs and organs by which life is enjoyed. The word "liberty" embraces all our liberties—personal, civil, and political.

This includes, among other things, freedom to move about, to think, to engage in some useful occupation, to make choices, to marry and establish a home, to participate in political activities, to speak, write, and worship. The word "property" includes the right to enter an occupation and engage in business, to acquire property, to hold and possess valuable objects, to enjoy the rewards of ownership, and to dispose of property by loan, lease, gift, or sale. These are the great liberties that the Constitution seeks to ensure "to ourselves and our posterity." In general, they can be regulated and restricted if due process of law is followed, although, as we shall see, there are certain practices that the Constitution proscribes altogether.

Prohibition of Slavery.—The Thirteenth Amendment provides that "neither slavery nor involuntary servitude, except as a punishment for crime whereof the party shall have been duly convicted, shall exist within the United States or any place subject to their jurisdiction." The terms "slavery" and "involuntary servitude" are nearly synonymous, although the latter has a somewhat broader meaning. The obvious purpose of this language was to forbid all shades and conditions of slavery. Though intended to free the Negro, the guarantee extends to people of other races as well.

Several interesting questions have arisen from the amendment. One of the first inquired whether the amendment applied to an uncivilized tribe of Alaskan Indians whose custom it had long been to practice slavery. The Supreme Court held that the amendment applied.[1] On another occasion, the question arose whether slavery was also outlawed within Indian tribes inasmuch as the Indians had long retained the right to govern their internal affairs. Again the amendment was held applicable.[2] It is now assumed that slavery cannot exist either within the forty-eight states or any American territory, either incorporated or unincorporated.

On various occasions the amendment has been held to forbid attempts on the part of shipping companies to force seamen to work on board vessels without having previously voluntarily contracted to do so,[3] the farming out of vagrants for hire, attempting to force people to work under threat of conviction for vagrancy, and state peonage laws that attempt to force laborers, renters, and sharecroppers to fulfill contracts that they may have made for labor.[4]

On the other hand, the amendment does not forbid certain acts of compulsion that require involuntary labor. On one occasion it was contended

[1] *In re* Sah Quah (D.C. Alaska, 1886) 31 F. 327.

[2] United States *v.* Choctaw Nation, 38 Ct. Cl. 668, 566 (1903).

[3] If valid contracts have been entered into, however, performance probably could be enforced. See Robertson *v.* Baldwin discussed on p. 406.

[4] Such persons may, of course, be sued for damage on grounds of fraud or breach of contract.

that a Florida law requiring all able-bodied men to perform work upon roads and bridges for 6 days each year or provide a substitute amounted to involuntary servitude. Distinguishing between a "duty" or "obligation" and a "servitude," the Supreme Court upheld the Florida statute, saying that the Thirteenth Amendment "certainly was not intended to interdict enforcement of those duties which individuals owe to the State, such as service in the army, militia, on the jury, etc."[1] A similar decision was reached when it was contended that the military draft law of 1917 required involuntary servitude.[2] The courts have also permitted states and municipalities to compel criminals to work out their fines on the streets or public works. They have also upheld a state law compelling physicians to report contagious diseases without compensation. They have also upheld a state law making it a misdemeanor for landlords intentionally to fail to furnish utility and other services promised in a lease.

Due Process of Law.—The Fifth Amendment forbids Congress to deprive any person of "life, liberty, or property, without due process of law," and the Fourteenth Amendment imposes the same limitation upon the states. This is one of the most important, as well as controversial, of all guarantees. The protection extends to both natural persons, *i.e.*, ordinary human beings, and to artificial persons such as corporations. At common law "due process" required that persons suspected of violating the law should be tried in accordance with "the law of the land." The requirement was met if an accused person was given "his day in court" according to the *procedures* known to common law. This was undoubtedly the meaning intended when the words were written into the Fifth Amendment, and the federal courts so held until about 1890. Beginning in the early 1850's[3] state courts began to interpret the due-process clauses of state constitutions in such a manner as to require not only that the proper procedures be followed, but that the law itself should be reasonable. Cautiously at first, then boldly, the federal courts accepted the doctrine, with the result that they claimed competence to scrutinize the *substance* or *content* of federal and state laws. Having the power of judicial review, this meant that the courts became a sort of superlegislature, or "third House," with authority to set aside any law which they deemed "unreasonable, arbitrary, or capricious." Accordingly, due process came to have both a procedural and substantive meaning. In other words, the courts came to concern themselves not only with *how* the government proceeds, but also with *what* it is attempting to do.

Procedural Due Process.—Procedural due process means that in dealing with people governments must proceed according to "settled usages and

[1] Butler *v.* Perry, 240 U.S. 328, 333 (1916).

[2] Arver *v.* United States, 245 U.S. 366, 390 (1918). See p. 404.

[3] The first case appears to have been that of Wynehamer *v.* New York, 13 N.Y. 378.

modes of procedure." The standards are fairly definite. The Constitution specifically mentions certain steps that must not be omitted, and others have crystallized from experience dating back to the days of Magna Charta. Among other things, proper procedure requires that (1) the government, or subordinate agency, have jurisdiction over the person or object with which it seeks to interfere; (2) the legislation or order be properly enacted or prepared and published; (3) crimes must be clearly defined; (4) those accused must be properly apprehended and notified of the nature of the accusation and the time and place of the hearing; (5) opportunity must be given for the accused to prepare and present his defense; and (6) the tribunal before which the trial or hearing is to be conducted must be so constituted as to ensure an honest and impartial decision.

Just Compensation for Property Taken for Public Use.—Both the Federal and state governments have the power of eminent domain. That is, they may compel private owners to transfer property to them if deemed necessary for the public welfare. Governments not only may exercise the prerogative themselves but they can also permit its use by quasi-public agencies such as public-utility companies. Such great authority is susceptible of abuse. Accordingly, the Fifth Amendment states that Congress shall not take private property for public use without just compensation, and states have a similar limitation placed upon them by the Fourteenth Amendment and their own constitutions. Note that the government is obliged to pay only for private property taken for "public use." This would not prevent the government from taking one's property as punishment for crime or for failure to pay taxes. It would prevent taking a person's farm for use as a military camp without paying for it, or taking private property in order to build a road. What compensation is "just" must be settled by negotiations between interested parties or, in case of disagreement, by an appropriate court.

Forbidding of Impairment of Contracts.—Almost everyone enters into several contracts daily. We may contract for a newspaper at the newsstand, a meal at the restaurant, a ride upon the trolley car, a job, an automobile, a room or house—necessities of all kinds. Contracts may be oral, written, or merely implied. They may be for small amounts or large. The right to enter into such agreements and to have the assistance of government, if necessary, in obtaining their fulfillment is indispensable to group life. Those who wrote the Constitution were particularly conscious of the importance of ensuring the sanctity of contracts because a number of states had just enacted laws the effect of which was to benefit debtors at the expense of those to whom they were indebted. Accordingly, the Constitution expressly provides that states may not impair the "obligation of contracts," and a similar limitation is placed upon Congress by the due-process-of-law clause of the Fifth Amendment.

These guarantees have proved to be highly contentious. An early case was one involving Dartmouth College.[1] There the court had before it an attempt on the part of the legislature of New Hampshire to reorganize the college contrary to provisions of a charter issued by the British Crown in 1769. The court declared the charter a valid contract and the legislature's action illegal. Because this meant that charters and franchises issued by governments to private corporations were contracts, the decision led governments to be cautious about entering into such long-term agreements. It also caused them to insert clauses reserving the right to repeal and amend. Later decisions have determined that a state cannot contract away its police power or its power of eminent domain (the condemning of property for public use).

Like others, the right of contract is not absolute. This was illustrated in the Minnesota Moratorium Case which grew out of the depression.[2] The state mortgage moratorium law provided that debtors could go to court and obtain as much as two years' deferment on foreclosure by creditors. This law was attacked by a creditor who claimed that the obligation of contract was being impaired, and, also, that he suffered both deprivation of property without due process of law and denial of equal protection. Chief Justice Hughes, speaking for the court, found that the moratorium law was a reasonable exercise of the state's police power to protect the interests of society during an economic depression, and that it did not violate the contract clause of the Constitution.

Titles of Nobility.—Although those who adopted the Constitution were not democrats in the modern sense of the word, they did fear the emergence of a class system under which certain groups might obtain special status. To ensure equality the Constitution declared that neither the national nor state governments might grant titles of nobility. Note that this does not prohibit the acceptance of foreign titles by American citizens.[3] Rather, the provision forbids the issuance of titles by American governments.

As a further precaution, the Constitution provides that "no Person holding any Office of Profit or Trust under them, [the United States] shall, without the consent of the Congress, accept of any present, Emolument, Office, or Title of any kind whatever, from any King, Prince, or foreign State." Thus an officer of the national government (but not of a state) is prevented from accepting such things as medals, portraits, books, honorary positions, titles of rank, and almost everything else offered by a foreign government unless Congress first gives consent. Congress has assented on

[1] Trustees of Dartmouth College *v.* Woodward, 4 Wheaton 518 (1819).

[2] Home Building and Loan Association *v.* Blaisdell, 290 U.S. 398 (1934). See also p. 424.

[3] This was the object of an amendment proposed in 1810—the third amendment proposed but not ratified. See p. 831.

many occasions where heads of states wished to decorate American military and naval officers or reward American diplomats. A common practice is for some near relative to receive the gift or for the donor to await the recipient's retirement from public office.

Equal Protection of the Laws.—States are forbidden to "deny to any person within their jurisdiction the equal protection of the laws," but a similar restraint against the Federal government is unmentioned. Gross denial of equal protection by the Federal government would, however, undoubtedly be held to violate the due-process clause of the Fifth Amendment. Although the provision was inserted in the Fourteenth Amendment for the protection of Negroes, it stands also as a guarantee to others, including corporations. The guarantee of equal protection does not require that persons be treated exactly alike: tariffs on uncut diamonds may be lower than on polished; races may be segregated by requiring them to attend separate schools or ride in separate cars; minimum-wage laws may be enacted for women without also including men or children; maximum hours may be established for men in hazardous employments without also including nonhazardous industries; aliens may be forbidden to practice medicine, law, or other professions; taxes may be imposed upon retailers of certain products, like liquors, and not others; chain stores may be taxed more heavily than independents; the rich may be taxed at higher rates than the poor; etc. In cases like these, people, objects, or businesses are classified. The test is whether the classification is reasonable and appropriate. If it is, then everyone within each group must be treated alike.

On the other hand, equal protection would be denied if a law were so administered as to discriminate against Chinese launderers in favor of American;[1] if Negroes, women, or wage-earners were systematically excluded from grand and petit juries;[2] if employers were denied the right to obtain injunctions while permitting them to employees;[3] if Negro barbers were forbidden to serve white children;[4] if Negro, Chinese, Japanese, and Indian students were prevented from attending state-supported schools when equally good facilities were not also provided for them by the state;[5] if state law required Negroes entering the state riding in first-class Pullman cars to move into "Jim Crow" cars when to do so would necessitate continuing the journey in cars with unequal comforts and conveniences;[6] or

1 Yick Wo *v.* Hopkins, 118 U.S. 356 (1886).

2 Norris *v.* Alabama, 294 U.S. 587 (1935); Smith *v.* Texas, 311 U.S. 128 (1940); Patton *v.* Missouri, 322 U.S. 443 (1947).

3 Truax *v.* Corrigan, 257 U.S. 312 (1921).

4 Chaires *v.* City of Atlanta (1927) 139 S.E. 559, 164 Ga. 755.

5 Missouri *ex rel.* Gaines *v.* Canada, 305 U.S. 337 (1938); Sipuel *v.* Board of Regents of the University of Oklahoma, 322 U.S. 631 (1948).

6 Mitchell *v.* United States, 313 U.S. 80 (1940).

if state courts enforce restrictive covenants barring the sale or transfer of real estate to Negroes and other non-Aryans.[1]

Religious Faith and Practice.—As the Constitution came from the Constitutional Convention, it said nothing about the church or religious liberty, implying that the situation as it existed in the states would remain undisturbed. To confirm this understanding, the First Amendment provided that "Congress shall make no law respecting an establishment of religion, or prohibiting the free exercise thereof." Thus, so far as the Federal Constitution was concerned, states remained free to deal with the subject of religion as they saw fit, subject of course to limits in their own constitutions. This was the situation until recently. Present decisions of the Supreme Court construe the Fourteenth Amendment to include the same guarantees of religious liberty as those contained in the First Amendment. Accordingly, the Constitution now prohibits both Federal and state governments from interfering with the church or religious liberty.

Forbidding of a State Church.—Note that the First Amendment proscribes laws respecting an *establishment* of religion. This means that Congress, and probably the states, cannot either directly or indirectly establish a state church or state religion nor show partiality for any religious sect, organization, or mode of worship. It does not mean that religious faith and practice may not be encouraged by law, nor that cognizance cannot be taken of religious principles of sects and individuals. Congress employs chaplains to open its sessions with prayer, it supports chaplains in the Army and Navy, it has exempted ministers of religion and theological students from military draft, it has exempted religious institutions from payment of taxes and from provisions of the Social Security Act, during prohibition it made wine available for religious rites, and it has exempted conscientious objectors from strict military service. Such acts as these have been held not to violate the First Amendment.

Recently this provision has provoked considerable controversy, especially at the state level. Essence of the argument is whether the amendment was intended to erect a wall of separation between church and state or merely to prevent the showing of governmental preference toward particular faiths, churches, or sects. In a recent decision the Supreme Court had this to say:[2]

The "establishment of religion" clause of the First Amendment means at least this: Neither a state nor the Federal Government can set up a church. Neither can pass laws which aid one religion, aid all religions, or prefer one religion over another. Neither can force nor influence a person to go to or to remain away from church against his will or force him to profess a belief or disbelief in any religion. No person can be punished for entertaining or professing religious beliefs or disbeliefs, for

[1] Shelley *v.* Kraemer, 334 U.S. 1 (1948).

[2] Everson *v.* Board of Education, 330 U.S. 15–16 (1946).

church attendance or non-attendance. No tax in any amount, large or small, can be levied to support any religious activities or institutions, whatever they may be called, or whatever form they may adopt to teach or practice religion. Neither a state nor the Federal Government can, openly or secretly, participate in the affairs of any religious organizations or groups and vice versa. In the words of Jefferson, the clause against establishment of religion by law was intended to erect a "wall of separation between church and state."

Nevertheless, by a 5-to-4 vote, the Court upheld a New Jersey law whereby patrons of Catholic schools were reimbursed with tax funds for bus fares paid going to and returning from school. School transportation, the court majority argued, was in the same category as police and fire protection and other public services. To withhold these, or any of them, from Catholics, would discriminate against them and thereby interfere with their free exercise of religion.

A short time later the Supreme Court ruled on an arrangement whereby the public schools of Champaign, Ill., released time to local religious groups for instruction. Only pupils whose parents gave written consent were required to attend religious classes. Protest was made by one of the parents who claimed that the Fourteenth Amendment was violated. The Supreme Court agreed,[1] saying the use of a tax-supported school system with its machinery for compulsory school attendance for religious instruction was unconstitutional support of an establishment of religion. This decision is difficult for the layman to reconcile with the Everson case mentioned above. It had widespread repercussions, affecting as it did similar arrangements in some 2,200 communities in forty-six states.[2]

Guarantee of Free Exercise of Religion.—Also forbidden are laws prohibiting the *free exercise* of religion. Opinion differs so widely on the subject of what conduct is religiously motivated that distinctions are frequently close and hard to make. According to court decisions, the guarantee is not violated if Congress outlaws bigamous and polygamous marriages even though Mormons thought these essential to their faith.[3] Nor is it violated if religious objectors are required to take military training as a condition for attendance at a state university.[4] Religious objectors may be drafted for military service[5] and a state may deny them licenses to practice law.[6]

On the other hand, the free exercise of religion is abridged if children of religious sects like that of Jehovah's Witnesses are compelled to salute

[1] McCullum *v.* Board of Education, 333 U.S. 203 (1948).

[2] For critical analyses of the Everson and McCullum cases see articles by Edward S. Corwin and Milton R. Konvitz in *Law and Contemporary Problems*, vol. XIV (Winter, 1949).

[3] Reynolds *v.* United States, 98 U.S. 145 (1878); Davis *v.* Beason, 133 U.S. 333 (1890).

[4] Hamilton *v.* Regents of the University of California, 293 U.S. 245 (1934).

[5] Arver *v.* United States, 245 United States 366 (1918). See also p. 404.

[6] *In re* Summers, 325 U.S. 538 (1945). The court divided 5 to 4 in this decision.

and pledge allegiance to the flag;[1] or if attendance at private religious schools is forbidden through the device of making attendance at public schools compulsory.[2] The free exercise of religion is also abridged if a municipal ordinance makes it illegal to distribute religious tracts without an official permit;[3] or if a state law requires those soliciting funds for religious purposes first to secure approval of a local public official.[4] The same is true if a municipal ordinance imposes a flat tax on those who make a livelihood by distributing religious tracts.[5]

Freedom of Speech and Press.—The First Amendment also provides that "Congress shall make no law . . . abridging the freedom of speech, or of the press." Here, again, is a restriction that applied to Congress only until the courts' recent expansion of the Fourteenth Amendment. Now, the same restrictions apply to both Federal and state governments. In general, the intent of the provisions is to secure the unrestricted discussion of public affairs. Inasmuch as majorities need no special protection, the guarantees have meaning only insofar as they afford protection to minorities that propagate unpopular, even loathsome, ideas.

Since rights are not absolute, most people readily agree that the guarantees do not forbid laws holding people responsible for utterances that are libelous, slanderous, indecent, or obscene. The controversy begins when governmental officials attempt to censor or punish minorities for utterances about public affairs with which they disagree.

Interpretations.—Looking over past experience,[6] one is likely to feel

[1] In Minersville School District *v.* Gobitis, 310 U.S. 586, decided in 1940, the Supreme Court ruled by an 8 to 1 verdict that a state law compelling school children to salute the flag was not an unconstitutional infringement of the free exercise of religion. Two years later three of the justices took occasion to say that they had changed their minds (Jones *v.* City of Opelika, 316 U.S. 584, 1942) and shortly thereafter the Gobitis decision was overruled by a 5 to 3 vote (West Virginia State Board of Education *v.* Barnette, 319 U.S. 324, 1942).

[2] Pierce *v.* Society of the Sisters, 268 U.S. 510 (1925).

[3] Coleman *v.* City of Griffin, 303 U.S. 404 (1938).

[4] Cantwell *v.* Connecticut, 310 U.S. 296 (1940).

[5] Follett *v.* McCormick, 321 U.S. 565 (1943).

[6] By far the best discussion of this subject is found in Zechariah Chafee Jr., *Free Speech in the United States* (Cambridge: Harvard University Press, 1941). See also Robert E. Cushman, *Leading Constitutional Decisions* (New York: Crofts, 7th ed., 1940), pp. 79–106; Leon Whipple, *Our Ancient Liberties* (New York: Wilson, 1927), pp. 79–107; Charles K. Burdick, *The Law of the American Constitution; Its Origin and Development* (New York: Putnam, 1922), pp. 342–375; Morris L. Ernst and Alexander Lindey, *The Censor Marches On* (New York: Doubleday, 1940); George Seldes, *Freedom of the Press* (Indianapolis: Bobbs-Merrill, 1935); Charles H. Maxson, *Citizenship* (New York: Oxford, 1930); New York State Constitutional Convention Committee, *Problems Relating to Bill of Rights and General Welfare* (Albany: The Committee, 1938), vol. VI, Chap. XII; and Mauritz Hallgren, *Landscape of Freedom* (New York: Howell, Soskin, 1941), pp. 354 *ff.*

that the guarantee of freedom of speech and press are meaningless, especially in time of war. In 1798 Congress passed the Alien and Sedition Acts providing severe punishment for anyone found publishing false, scandalous, and malicious criticism of the President or members of Congress.[1] During the Civil War opposition was suppressed by placing large zones under martial law, whether or not actual military operations were in progress within the area. Under the Espionage Act of 1917 and amendments of the following year, popularly known as the Sedition Act, dozens of pacifist, pro-German, Socialist, and radical publications were excluded from the mails,[2] while hundreds were imprisoned for alleged subversive criticism and agitation against the war policies of the government.[3] America's entry into war in 1941 brought about a repetition of some of the experiences of the First World War,[4] although after the attack on Pearl Harbor the absence of a large organized opposition resulted in fewer violations of civil liberties, except possibly in the case of American citizens of Japanese origin.[5]

In spite of this dark picture, the constitutional guarantees of free speech and press are not without significance. The notorious Minnesota "gag law," which empowered the courts to suppress publication of printed matter deemed to be scandalous, malicious, defamatory, or obscene,[6] was declared invalid. Later, a Louisiana statute imposing a tax upon large newspapers most of which were hostile to the late Huey Long was declared unconstitutional.[7] In a more recent case, the Supreme Court upheld the solicitation of members for the Communist party if in doing so forceful resistance to or overthrow of the government was not advocated.[8] More recently, the Court upheld attendance and participation in Communist meetings where no unlawful conduct or utterances occurred.[9] The Court has also

[1] Although these measures never reached the Supreme Court, they were generally approved by the lower courts. The acts expired in 1801, President Jefferson pardoned all who had been imprisoned, and many years later Congress refunded all fines collected.

[2] Including the now respectable *Nation* magazine.

[3] The most prominent of these was Eugene V. Debs, Socialist leader and five times candidate for President. Debs started serving a 10-year sentence in April, 1919, and was pardoned by President Harding on Christmas Day, 1921. While in prison Debs polled nearly a million votes for President in the election of 1920.

[4] For current reports on civil liberty violations see the publications of the Civil Liberties Union, 170 Fifth Avenue, New York City, and *The Bill of Rights Review* published quarterly by the Bill of Rights Committee of the American Bar Association, 31 Nassau Street, New York City.

[5] For a discussion of the treatment of this group see p. 408.

[6] Near *v.* Minnesota, 283 U.S. 697 (1931).

[7] Grosjean *v.* American Press Company, 297 U.S. 233 (1936).

[8] Herndon *v.* Lowry, 301 U.S. 242 (1937).

[9] DeJonge *v.* Oregon, 299 U.S. 353 (1937).

set aside state laws forbidding the display of banners and placards in aid of picketing in labor disputes;[1] it has declared a state law invalid that required labor organizers to register before soliciting members;[2] while the courts have reprimanded the Postmaster General for denying the magazine *Esquire* second-class mailing privileges because he thought its contents obscene.

"Bad Tendency" vs. "Clear and Present Danger" Tests.—Since it is difficult to draw the line between permissible restraint and freedom, attempts have been made to find a satisfactory formula upon which to base decisions. In general, it is agreed that there should not be *previous restraint.*[3] That is, people should not be required, under threat of penalty, to obtain censors' approval prior to publication. The general belief is that it is enough that the law hold people responsible for what is actually said or written.

Beyond this there is deep cleavage of opinion. One school contends that utterances are illegal if they have a "bad tendency," while the more tolerant school insists that the rule should be "clear and present danger." Under the former, it is sufficient that persons merely utter revolutionary doctrines whether or not their remarks are taken seriously by anyone. Under the latter, one is judged guilty only if revolutionary doctrines are uttered under circumstances that are likely to lead clearly and immediately to force or violence. The "bad-tendency" rule has prevailed throughout most of our national life, but in recent years the more tolerant view has met with greater judicial favor.[4]

The practical difference between the two doctrines is illustrated by two cases. One, decided in 1925, involved Benjamin Gitlow,[5] indicted by New York state for publishing a socialist manifesto pleading for organization of industrial workers, mass strikes, destruction of the bourgeois state, and substitution of a new regime dominated by the proletariat. The publication emphasized, however, that

> It is not a problem of immediate revolution. It is a problem of immediate revolutionary struggle. The revolutionary epoch of the final struggle may last for years and tens of years. . . . The old order is in decay. Civilization is in collapse. The proletarian revolution and the communist reconstruction of society—the struggle for these—is now indispensable.

[1] Thornhill *v.* Alabama, 310 U.S. 88 (1940); Carlson *v.* California, 310 U.S. (1940).

[2] Thomas *v.* Collins, 323 U.S. 516 (1944).

[3] Near *v.* Minnesota, 283 U.S. 697 (1931). There are exceptions to this, however, especially in the case of censorship of motion pictures.

[4] For an excellent review of the manner in which these two rules have been applied by the courts see New York State Constitutional Convention Committee, *op. cit.*, vol. VI, pp. 163–176.

[5] Gitlow *v.* New York, 268 U.S. 652 (1924).

Although no unlawful action had resulted from the appeal, and none was particularly imminent, a majority of the Supreme Court considered the publication of sufficient threat to justify restricting freedom of speech and press. Here the threat, rather than clear and present danger of illegal action, was the controlling consideration.

A second case was decided in 1949.[1] Terminiello, a Catholic priest and follower of Gerald K. Smith, addressed a Chicago meeting. The hall was so heavily picketed that police escort was required to enter the building. Outside, the crowd yelled epithets, threw bricks and ice picks, broke windows, and generally attempted to force entry and break up the meeting. Inside, Terminiello fanatically lashed his critics, praised General Franco, and condemned Jews, Communists, Mrs. Roosevelt, Henry Wallace, and others with whom he disagreed. At the close of the speech Terminiello was arrested for violating a Chicago ordinance making it illegal to make, aid, countenance, or assist in making any improper noise, riot, disturbance, breach of peace, or diversion tending to breach the peace. He was convicted and the verdict was upheld by the higher courts of Illinois. But the United States Supreme Court, by a 5-to-4 vote, supported Terminiello, saying:

> . . . A function of free speech under our system of government is to invite dispute. It may indeed best serve its high purpose when it induces a condition of unrest, creates dissatisfaction with conditions as they are, or even stirs people to anger. Speech is often provocative and challenging. It may strike at prejudices and preconceptions and leave profound unsettling effects as it presses for acceptance of an idea.

Terminiello had not pleaded for violence, and there was no clear and present danger to the community great enough to justify restricting freedom of speech.

Freedom of Assembly and Petition.—Where freedom of speech and press exists, it is essential that people be permitted to gather in groups to discuss mutual problems and, if they desire, make their opinions known to governmental authorities. These rights are guaranteed by the First and Fourteenth Amendments. These guarantees require, however, that the assembly be peaceful and that the petitioners ask only for objects that are lawful and not a menace to public safety. The right of petition carries with it no power to compel consideration. Thousands of memorials are received that are given no consideration whatever. When addressed to Congress or state legislatures, they are generally referred to committees where they are promptly pigeonholed and forgotten. When received in sufficient number on a particular subject, however, they are bound to impress individual legislators and sometimes the entire Congress. The

[1] Terminiello *v.* City of Chicago, 337 U.S. 1 (1948).

right of petition has seldom been violated, but because the right of assembly is closely connected with speech and press it has been the subject of considerable litigation. One recent case occurred when Mayor Hague, long-time boss of Jersey City, N.J., refused permission to persons whom he considered radicals to use public parks, halls, and streets as meeting places. His action was held to be a denial of the right of assembly as well as a denial of freedom of speech and press.[1]

Right to Bear Arms.—The Second Amendment states that "A well regulated Militia being necessary to the security of a free State, the right of the people to bear Arms shall not be infringed." The Constitution forbids states to keep standing armies but permits them to maintain militias composed of armed civilians. The amendment quoted above prevents the Federal government from destroying state militias by the device of making it a federal crime for their inhabitants to bear arms. Congress can forbid the carrying of concealed weapons in the District of Columbia and other territories.[2] Congress can also tax the manufacture and sale of arms and munitions and regulate the shipment of arms in foreign and interstate commerce. Moreover, Congress can disarm violators of federal laws and enemy aliens. But Congress could not go so far as to forbid the possession of arms to rank-and-file citizens. States may, of course, regulate or entirely forbid the possession and use of firearms and other weapons.

Quartering of Soldiers.—One of the worst indignities that can be imposed upon civilians is that of being compelled to give board and room to soldiers, especially in time of peace. The colonists had enough of that during the Revolution when they were frequently ordered to quarter British troops. Accordingly, the Fourth Amendment says "No soldier shall, in time of peace be quartered in any house, without the consent of the owner, nor in time of war, but in a manner prescribed by law." The full meaning of this provision is unknown inasmuch as no instance has come before the Supreme Court where its violation was alleged.

SAFEGUARDS FOR THOSE ACCUSED OF CRIMES

Definition of Treason.—Treason is generally considered one of the highest crimes that can be committed in society, since its aim is an overthrow of the government. History is filled with instances where in times of excitement those in power have sought to destroy their critics and enemies by arbitrarily declaring their conduct treasonable. Because of this experience, the Constitution includes a definition of treason; no acts other than those contained within the definition can be declared to constitute the offense. Congress can neither extend, nor restrict, nor define the

[1] Hague *v.* C.I.O., 307 U.S. 496 (1939).
[2] See p. 575.

crime. Its power is limited to prescribing the punishment. According to that definition, only two things are treasonable: (1) levying of war against the United States, and (2) adhering to enemies of the United States or giving them aid or comfort while the United States is at war. In so defining the term, the Constitution adopted the very words of the statute of treason enacted during the reign of Edward III. Thus, by implication, the Constitution recognizes the well-settled interpretation of these phrases which has prevailed for ages.

Besides defining what constitutes treason, the Constitution declares that "no Person shall be convicted of Treason unless on the Testimony of two Witnesses to the same overt Act, or on Confession in open Court." This is to guarantee that no one can be convicted except for some overt act and then never upon the testimony of a single person, however high. It is also a guarantee that those in authority will not obtain confessions behind closed doors where the temptation to promise favor or use third-degree methods is always present. Instead, if there is to be a confession it must be made in open court.

Still further, the Constitution declares that while Congress may declare what punishment is to be meted out to those convicted of treason, "no Attainder of Treason shall work Corruption of Blood, or Forfeiture except during the Life of the Person attainted." This means that as part of the punishment, the children or heirs of traitors may not be forbidden to inherit property. This is to ensure that innocent children will not suffer because of an offense of an ancestor.

What has been said above pertains to the Federal government only. Besides being a traitor under federal law, one can also commit treason against a state. Accordingly, most of the state constitutions in defining treason use language nearly identical with that contained in the Federal Constitution. Death is nearly always the penalty for treason under state law. The famous case of John Brown at Harper's Ferry, Va., is thought to be the only instance on record where the extreme penalty has been inflicted for treason against a state.[1]

Habeas Corpus.—The national Constitution forbids the Federal government, but not the states, to suspend the privilege of the writ of habeas corpus "unless when in cases of rebellion or invasion the public safety may require it." Such a writ is a command on the part of a judicial officer to have the body of someone being held in custody produced for the purpose of determining the legality of his detention. Without it, military and police officers could take people into custody, keeping them there indefinitely without hearing or trial. When the Bastille was stormed during the French Revolution, men were loosed who had been imprisoned for

[1] W. Brooke Graves, *American State Government* (New York: Heath, rev. ed., 1941), p. 564.

years without ever having been given trial. Under dictatorial regimes people are not infrequently spirited away by secret police to be put to death or confined in concentration camps without ever being heard of again. The privilege of the writ of habeas corpus is a protection against such restraints and it has been rightfully esteemed one of the great bulwarks of liberty. When the writ is issued, the police must produce a prisoner and show adequate cause for his detention. If the judge is unconvinced, the prisoner must be set at liberty. The privilege of the writ can be suspended only in the event of rebellion or invasion, and then only when "the public safety may require it."[1] The only occasion since the Civil War when the writ has been suspended occurred in Hawaii during the Second World War. After its suspension, civilian laws were displaced by military orders, and civilians were tried by military tribunals without benefit of jury trial and other normal procedures. Although this system continued throughout most of the war, it was later declared illegal by the Supreme Court.[2] Congress had not intended, the Court said, the Hawaiian Organic Act to authorize such drastic subordination of civilian life to the military.

Bill of Attainder.—A bill of attainder is a legislative act that inflicts punishment without judicial trial. In times of rebellion or political excitement it was not uncommon for Parliament to punish minorities by enacting special bills declaring them guilty of treason or felony. Punishment was often inflicted without allowing the accused party an opportunity to answer the charges, or even without the formality of proof. Indeed, in England it was not uncommon for Parliament to attaint a man after he was dead. To guarantee that such things would not happen, the Constitution forbids both the Federal and state governments from enacting bills of attainder. Accordingly, legislatures enact laws defining crimes, but the courts must be the judge of innocence or guilt. A few attempts to violate the guarantee have occurred, the most notable being in 1865 when Congress passed the Test Oath Act. That law provided that no one might be admitted to practice before the federal courts who could not swear that he had never voluntarily participated in rebellion against the United States. This, the Supreme Court said, was a bill of attainder since it imposed the penalty of exclusion from legal practice without judicial trial.

A more recent case involved three federal employees[3] accused by the Dies Committee of having associated with groups engaged in un-American activities. Because the men had been duly appointed and served meritoriously, the President refused to dismiss them, whereupon Congress in-

[1] For discussion of the wartime suspension of the writ see p. 413.

[2] Duncan *v.* Kahanamoku, 327 U.S. 304 (1945).

[3] Prof. Robert Morss Lovett, Goodwin B. Watson, and William E. Dodd, Jr.

serted a provision in a deficiency appropriation bill forbidding payment of their salaries and debarring them from future employment with the Federal government. This had the appearance of being legislative punishment without judicial trial. The gentlemen in question continued in office for a brief time, then brought suit for salary, claiming that their constitutional rights had been violated. The Court of Claims, before which the case originated, refused to pass on the larger question of constitutionality but ruled that the men were entitled to unpaid salary. Three judges went further and expressed their belief that Congress had violated the constitutional provision forbidding bills of attainder,[1] and with this view the Supreme Court later agreed by a unanimous decision.[2]

Ex Post Facto Legislation.—Both the Federal and state governments are forbidden by the Federal Constitution to enact ex post facto legislation. Literally, ex post facto means "subsequent to the act." Accordingly, an ex post facto law is one that renders an act punishable in a manner in which it was not punishable when it was committed. Such laws have been held to include: (1) those that make acts criminal which were innocent when done; (2) those that aggravate a crime or make it greater than it was when committed; (3) those that alter the rules of evidence, permitting less or different evidence to convict a person of an offense committed prior to their passage; (4) those that operate in any way to the disadvantage of one accused of a crime committed prior to the enactment of the law.[3] Although the term "ex post facto" would appear to include any act operating upon a previous fact, the courts have always given the words their common-law meaning, holding that the prohibition applies only to criminal legislation and not civil also.

Searches and Seizures.—In medieval England the king's officers frequently searched people and their property without warrants and seized whatsoever they wanted for use as evidence to prove one's guilt. A measure of protection was found in the common-law maxim that a man's house is his castle and this guarantee was written into our Constitution. The Fourth Amendment states, "The right of the people to be secure in their persons, houses, papers, and effects, against unreasonable searches and seizures, shall not be violated, and no Warrants shall issue, but upon probable cause, supported by Oath or affirmation, and particularly describing the place to be searched, and the persons or things to be seized."

Several things should be noted about this provision. First, people are

[1] The cases were decided by the Court of Claims of the United States on Nov. 5, 1945, and are referred to as Nos. 46026, 46027, and 46028.

[2] United States *v.* Lovett, 328 U.S. 303 (1946).

[3] It should be noted, however, that laws that mitigate the character or punishment of a crime already committed may not violate the prohibition inasmuch as they are in favor of the accused party.

to be secure in their "persons, houses, papers, and effects." This includes outbuildings, including barn and garage, office, shop, factory, or warehouse. It also prevents the tapping of telephone wires.[1] It also includes letters, books, accounts, and packages.[2] It does not include an open field, where, for example, an illicit still might be kept. Second, only "unreasonable" searches and seizures are forbidden. To be reasonable they must be made by authority of search warrant except in a few instances where circumstances will not allow or justify the delay.[3] Third, before a search warrant can be issued, the place to be searched and the person or things to be seized must be described under oath before a judicial officer having jurisdiction. In doing so, sufficient evidence must be presented to convince the judicial officer that there is reason to believe that a violation of the law has occurred.

Indictment by Grand Jury.—The Fifth Amendment provides, among other things, that no one, except persons employed in the armed forces, may be held "for a capital, or otherwise infamous crime, unless on a presentment or indictment of a Grand Jury." A "capital" crime is one punishable by death. An "infamous" one has never been clearly defined but is known to include offenses that are punishable by imprisonment, hard labor, or the loss of civil or political privileges. If such a crime is committed, a grand jury composed of from sixteen to twenty-three persons must (unless waived by the defendant) be assembled for the purpose of deciding whether there is sufficient evidence to proceed with trial. The accused cannot insist that he be permitted to appear before the grand jury, but permission to do so is sometimes given. If twelve or more grand jurors believe the evidence sufficiently incriminating to justify trial, a "true bill" is reported to the judge. If not, the accused must be promptly released until convincing evidence is produced. The form of the indictment is very important inasmuch as the accused can be tried only for offenses mentioned in it.

[1] Nardone *v.* United States, 302 U.S. 379 (1937). See, however, Olmstead *v.* United States, 277 U.S. 438 (1928).

[2] This provision explains why postal authorities cannot open letters and packages without warrants unless the sender gives them permission to do so by writing some such words as "may be opened for postal inspection if necessary." Ex parte Jackson, 96 U.S. 727 (1877).

[3] Federal courts now permit searches and seizures without warrant in the following types of cases, but then only where there are reasonable grounds for suspicion: (1) a house may be entered to arrest for felony or breach of peace a person known to be therein; (2) search may be made as an incident to a lawful arrest; (3) where a business is conducted under license, agents may enter without warrant to see if the terms of the license are being kept; (4) boats, automobiles, and other vehicles may be searched if there is reason to believe they are carrying illegal commodities; (5) where officers have visible evidence of commission of a crime. Frank A. Magruder and Guy S. Claire, *The Constitution* (New York: McGraw-Hill, 1933), pp. 249–250.

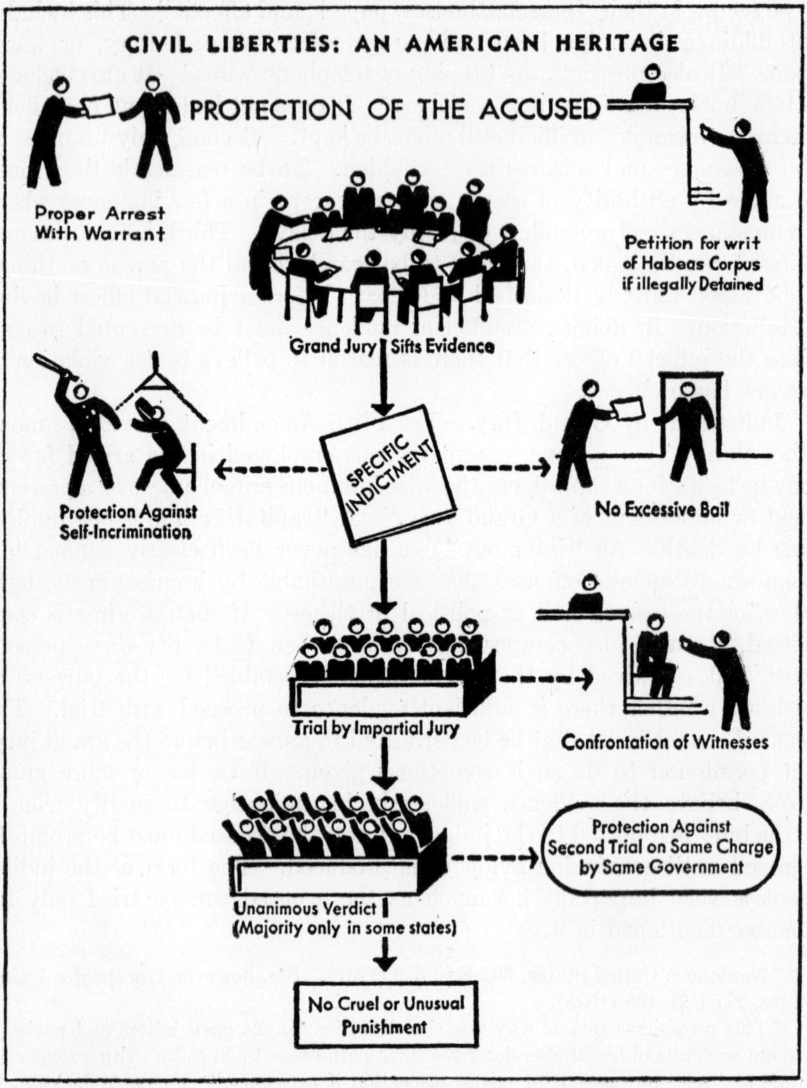

SOURCE: Robert E. Cushman, *Our Constitutional Freedoms* (National Foundation for Education in American Citizenship and Public Affairs Committee, Inc., 1944), p. 19.

The grand jury has been the subject of much criticism on the ground that it is clumsy and ill suited to modern conditions, especially in cities. England, the country of its origin, has almost completely discarded the device and many of our states now permit trial upon "information," *i.e.*, a simple affidavit by a prosecuting officer. The federal courts, however, insist that the grand jury be used in capital and felonous cases.

Trial by Jury.—Trial by jury in *criminal* cases is guaranteed both by provisions in the body of the Constitution[1] and by the Sixth Amendment. From these provisions and court decisions we find that: (1) every person accused of a criminal offense against federal law is entitled to jury trial, except public officials who are subject to impeachment; (2) jury trial may be waived by the defendant with court approval; (3) federal juries must be composed of twelve persons,[2] either men or women, or both; (4) trials must be "speedy," *i.e.*, reasonably prompt; (5) trials must be "public" in order that friends of the accused may see that injustice is not done; (6) the jury must be "impartial" and to this end attorneys for both parties are permitted to question and challenge prospective jurors and cross-examine witnesses; (7) members of juries must be drawn from the district wherein the crime was committed and the district must have been defined prior to the trial; (8) the verdict must be unanimous;[3] (9) the trial must be in the presence of a judge having power to instruct the jury both as to law and facts; (1) the verdict of a jury is final unless upon appeal by the defendant a new trial is awarded because a mistake was made in law or procedure.

Self-incrimination.—No one accused of committing a criminal act may be compelled to bear witness against himself. This means (1) that one cannot be made to testify at his own trial or before a grand jury that is considering indicting him; (2) that one may not be compelled to produce documentary evidence that might tend to show that he himself committed a crime; and (3) that confidants such as doctors, priests, ministers, and intimate members of one's family cannot be compelled to testify when to do so would be a breach of confidence against an accused person. This right may be waived by the accused, in which case he may be put on the witness stand and cross-examined like any other witness. Accused persons are sometimes given "immunity baths," *i.e.*, they are promised immunity from prosecution if they will become witnesses for the state, thus helping to solve a crime and perhaps convict others more important in the case. The introduction of evidence of fingerprints, photographs, and measurements is always permissible, although there is some doubt about tests of lie detectors if objection is made by the defendant.

Miscellaneous Rights.—Besides trial by jury, the Sixth Amendment also requires that one accused of a criminal offense shall be (1) informed of the charges for which he is to be tried; (2) present in the courtroom when witnesses are called to testify against him; (3) given legal power to compel witnesses to testify; and (4) assisted by legal counsel if he so desires.

[1] Article III, Section 2.

[2] State juries, however, may be abolished altogether or consist of fewer or more than twelve.

[3] Here, again, federal practice differs from that of some states. The latter may, if they wish, permit convictions by less than a unanimous vote.

Bail and Punishment.—The Eighth Amendment states that "Excessive bail shall not be required, nor excessive fines imposed, nor cruel and unusual punishments inflicted." This does not require that all offenders be released on bail, but simply that the amount of bail must not be excessive. What is "excessive" has never been fixed by the courts; the amount necessarily varies with circumstances and the gravity of the offense.

The provision that cruel or unusual punishments shall not be administered was directed mainly at the barbarity of early English law. It now prohibits punishments that are "so palpably excessive and disproportionate as to shock the sense of justice of all reasonable people."

A recent case is one of the very few that have arisen under this provision. It involved a young Negro, Willie Francis, sentenced to death in Louisiana. The electric chair accidentally failed to work when current was first applied, and a second attempt was threatened. The defendant appealed to the courts, contending in part that it was cruel and unusual punishment to force him to suffer the ordeal again. Rejecting his appeal by a 5-to-4 decision, the majority said: "The cruelty against which the Constitution protects a convicted man is cruelty inherent in the method of punishment, not the necessary suffering involved in any method employed to extinguish life humanely."[1]

Double Jeopardy.—According to the Fifth Amendment, an accused person may not be "subject for the same offense to be twice put in jeopardy of life or limb." This was included to prevent persons from being tried over and over for the same offense. One is put in jeopardy "when he is put on trial, before a court of competent jurisdiction upon an indictment or information which is sufficient in form and substance to sustain a conviction and a jury has been charged with his deliverance."[2] One is not in jeopardy when the case is merely before a grand jury; hence the same evidence may be presented more than once for the purpose of obtaining an indictment. One may be tried a second time if the indictment was defective, if the jury cannot come to a decision, if the jury is discharged for some good reason such as illness of a juror, or if the term of court as fixed by law comes to an end before the trial is finished. However, once a case is started, a prosecutor may not drop it in the hope of improving his chances of winning by discontinuing the case until a later time. Once trial has begun, the defendant is entitled to a verdict. When a decision has been reached, the prisoner is forever free from another trial for the same offense.

It is interesting to note that a person may by a single act violate both Federal and state law. If this happens, he may be tried in both federal

[1] Louisiana *v.* Resweber, 329 U.S. 459 (1947).

[2] Thomas M. Cooley, *Constitutional Limitations* . . . (Boston: Little, 6th ed., 1890), p. 399.

and state courts, acquitted in one, but found guilty in the other. Here, although there was but one act, two offenses were committed; hence the offender was not put in jeopardy twice for the *same* offense. A number of such instances have arisen, especially during prohibition when the Federal and state governments were concurrently responsible for the enforcement of liquor laws.

PRIVILEGES AND IMMUNITIES OF CITIZENS

In addition to guaranteeing certain "rights," the Constitution also mentions "privileges" or "immunities" that are derived from national citizenship. The actual words are: "No State shall make or enforce any law which shall abridge the privileges or immunities of citizens of the United States. . . ."[1] The rights previously discussed in this chapter are guaranteed to *all persons*, but privileges or immunities are guaranteed only to *citizens* of the United States. The difference between rights and privileges or immunities is not altogether clear, nor has any complete list of the latter ever been made. The guarantee is important, however, inasmuch as states are expressly forbidden to violate them.

The Fourteenth Amendment made Negroes citizens and the privilege-and-immunity clause was undoubtedly included to prevent the states from depriving the new citizens of rights guaranteed by the first eight amendments. Nevertheless, in early decisions[2] the Supreme Court narrowed the meaning of the words, saying that a right was to be distinguished from a privilege or immunity. The former included those mentioned in the Bill of Rights, but the latter included something additional.

While no complete list of privileges and immunities has been or can be made, experience suggests that they include the right to governmental protection while on the high seas or in foreign countries; freedom to expatriate (except when the nation is at war); the right to have access to ports of the United States, to navigable waters, and agencies of the Federal government, including courts of law; freedom to run for federal office and vote for federal officers;[3] freedom to enjoy all rights and advantages secured by treaties; freedom to assemble peaceably and petition for redress of grievances; the right to petition for writ of habeas corpus; freedom to enter the country and to prove citizenship if questioned; and liberty to inform the Federal government of violations of its laws.[4] These the

[1] Amendment 14, Section 1. See also p. 101.

[2] See especially, Slaughter House Cases, 16 Wallace 36 (1873).

[3] But not for state officers and offices. These are privileges of state citizenship rather than federal. Snowden *v.* Hughes, 321 U.S. 1 (1943).

[4] Whether freedom of moving from one state to another is a privilege of national citizenship was discussed at length in the recent case of Edwards *v.* People of the State of California, 314 U.S. 160 (1941). Four of the justices insisted that interstate travel

states may not violate. Aliens may enjoy some of them as a matter of grace, but they cannot demand them as a matter of right as citizens can. Neither are corporations protected by the privileges-and-immunities clause inasmuch as they are not citizens within the meaning of the Fourteenth Amendment.

References

BALDWIN, ROGER N.: *Civil Liberties and Industrial Conflict* (Cambridge, Mass.: Harvard University Press, 1938).

BECKER, CARL L.: *Freedom and Responsibility in the American Way of Life* (New York: Knopf, 1945).

——— *New Liberties for Old* (New Haven: Yale University Press, 1941).

——— and OTHERS: *Safeguarding Civil Liberty Today* (Ithaca, N.Y.: Cornell University Press, 1945).

BURDICK, CHARLES K.: *The Law of the American Constitution; Its Origin and Development* (New York: Putnam, 1922).

CARR, ROBERT K.: *Federal Protection of Civil Rights: Quest for a Sword* (Ithaca, N.Y.: Cornell University Press, 1947).

CHAFEE, ZECHARIAH: *Free Speech in the United States* (Cambridge, Mass.: Harvard University Press, 1941).

——— *Government and Mass Communications*, a report from the Commission on Freedom of the Press (Chicago: University of Chicago Press, 2 vols., 1947).

——— *The Inquiring Mind* (New York: Harcourt Brace, 1928).

CORWIN, EDWARD S.: *Liberty against Government* (Baton Rouge: Louisiana State University Press, 1948).

DAWSON, JOSEPH M.: *Separation of Church and State Now* (New York: Richard R. Smith, 1948).

DAY, EDMUND E.: *The Defense of Freedom* (Ithaca, N.Y.: Cornell University Press, 1941).

DE HAAS, ELSA: *Antiquities of Bail; Origin and Historical Development in Criminal Cases to the Year 1275* (New York: Columbia University Press, 1940).

DOWELL, E. FOSTER: *History of Criminal Syndicalism Legislation in the United States* (Baltimore: Johns Hopkins Press, 1939).

GERALD, J. EDWARD: *The Press and the Constitution, 1931–47* (Minneapolis: University of Minnesota Press, 1948).

GRAVES, W. BROOKE: *Anti-discrimination Legislation in the American States*, Public Affairs Bulletin No. 65 (Washington: Library of Congress, 1948).

HALLGREN, MAURITZ A.: *Landscape of Freedom; A Story of American Liberty and Bigotry* (New York: Howell, Soskin, 1941).

HOCKING, WILLIAM E.: *Freedom of the Press; A Framework of Principle* (Chicago: University of Chicago Press, 1947).

HOLCOMBE, ARTHUR N.: *Human Rights in the Modern World* (New York: New York University Press, 1948).

JOHNSON, ALVIN W., and FRANK H. YOST: *Separation of Church and State in the United States* (Minneapolis: University of Minnesota Press, 1948).

KESSELMAN, LOUIS C.: *The Social Politics of the FEPC; a Study in Reform Pressure Movements* (Chapel Hill: The University of North Carolina Press, 1948).

---

was a privilege guaranteed by the Constitution but the majority refused to base their decision on that ground and proceeded to declare the law an invalid obstruction of interstate commerce.

Konvitz, Milton R.: *The Constitution and Civil Rights* (New York: Columbia University Press, 1947).

Lauterbach, Albert T.: *Economic Security and Individual Freedom: Can We Have Both?* (Ithaca, N.Y.: Cornell University Press, 1948).

Lien, Arnold J.: *Privileges and Immunities of Citizens of the United States* (New York: Columbia University Press, 1913).

Meiklejohn, Alexander: *Free Speech and Its Relation to Self-government* (New York: Harper, 1948).

Mott, Rodney L.: *Due Process of Law* (Indianapolis: Bobbs-Merrill, 1926).

New York State Constitutional Convention Committee: *Problems Relating to the Bills of Rights and General Welfare* (Albany: The Committee, 1938), vol. VI.

Orfield, Lester B.: *Criminal Procedure from Arrest to Appeal* (New York: New York University Press, 1947).

Patterson, Giles J.: *Free Speech and a Free Press* (Boston: Little, Brown, 1939).

Rankin, Robert S.: *When Civil Law Fails* (Durham, N.C.: Duke University Press, 1939).

Torpey, William G.: *Judicial Doctrines of Religious Rights in America* (Chapel Hill: University of North Carolina Press, 1948).

United Nations: *Yearbook of Human Rights* (Lake Success: United Nations, annual).

United States President's Committee on Civil Rights: *To Secure These Rights* (Washington: Government Printing Office, 1947; also New York: Simon and Schuster, 1947).

United States Senate Committee on Education and Labor: *Violations of Free Speech and Rights of Labor; Hearings . . .*, 75th Cong., 3d Sess., pursuant to S. Res. 266 (Washington: Government Printing Office, 55 vols. bound in 14, 1936).

Warsoff, Louis A.: *Equality and the Law* (New York: Liveright, 1938).

Weintraub, Ruth G.: *How Secure These Rights* (New York: Doubleday, 1949).

Whipple, Leon: *The Story of Civil Liberty in the United States* (New York: Vanguard, 1927).

Wright, Benjamin: *The Contract Clause of the Constitution* (Cambridge, Mass.: Harvard University Press, 1938).

Chapter 8

POPULATION, IMMIGRATION, ALIENS, AND CITIZENSHIP

For it is safe to assert that nowhere in the world today is the right of citizenship of greater worth to an individual than it is in this country. It would be difficult to exaggerate its value and importance. By many it is regarded as the highest hope of civilized man.

Justice Murphy in Schneiderman *v.* United States.[1]

POPULATION

Population Growth.—From the days of colonial settlement to the time of the Civil War the population of the United States grew more rapidly than in any other country of the world. This rapid growth is considered one of the outstanding phenomena of world history. From 2½ million souls in 1776 the numbers increased by leaps and bounds until the First World War, since which time the rate of increase has been slower. In 1940 the population of continental United States was nearly 132 million.[2] The population of the United States by decades and the decennial rates of increase are shown in the following table:[3]

POPULATION OF THE UNITED STATES, 1790-1940

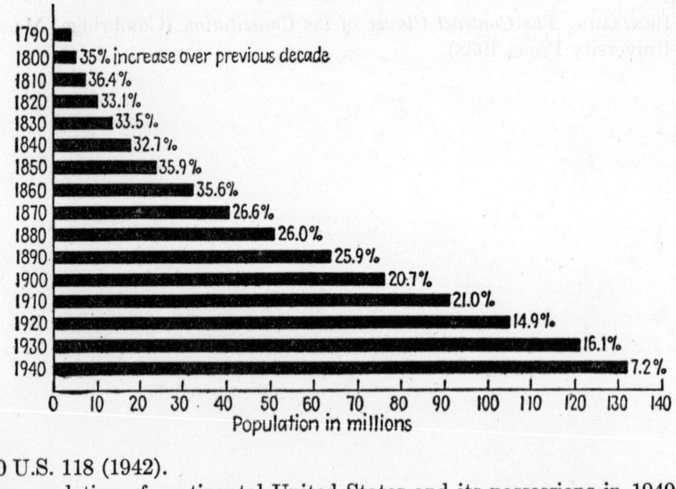

[1] 320 U.S. 118 (1942).

[2] The population of continental United States and its possessions in 1940 was approximately 150,621,231, or 8.8 per cent more than the 1930 population of 138,439,069. United States Department of Commerce, *Statistical Abstract of the United States*, 1943 (Washington: Government Printing Office, 1944), p. 2.

[3] *Ibid.*

It is apparent that while the growth has been continuous, the decennial rate of increase has been declining since about 1860, and startlingly so during the period following 1930. This was due to a declining birth rate and diminishing immigration. Population experts predict that the population will continue to increase, albeit at an ever slower rate, until it reaches approximately 165 million by about 1990, after which it is expected to decline.[1]

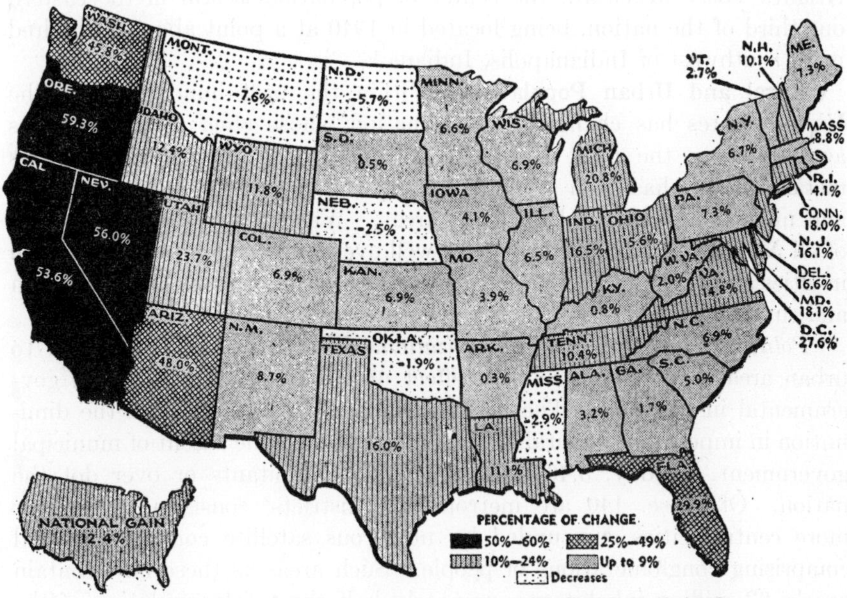

United States Population Changes, State by State, 1940–1949

Population Distribution.—Of all the countries of the world only China, India, and Russia contain more people than the United States. Though large, the density of population is comparatively sparse, amounting to an average of only 44.2 per square mile as compared with 848 per square mile in the United Kingdom, 382 in the German Reich, 469 in Japan proper, and 197 in France. The most densely populated subdivision of the United States is the District of Columbia, while others in which there is greatest

[1] For these and other predictions see Warren S. Thompson and Pascal K. Whelpton, Chap. I, in *Recent Social Trends in the United States* (New York: McGraw-Hill, 1 vol. ed., 1933). For a more detailed discussion of the same topic by the same authors see *Population Trends in the United States* (New York: McGraw-Hill, 1933). See also United States National Resources Committee, *The Problem of a Changing Population* (Washington: Government Printing Office, 1938), pp. 20–27; and United States Department of Commerce, Bureau of the Census, *Population, Estimated Future Population by Age and Sex: 1945–1980* (Series P–3, No. 15, July 23, 1941) and *Forecasts of the Population of the United States 1945–1975* (Washington: Government Printing Office, 1947).

concentration of people are the Atlantic seaboard states of Rhode Island, New Jersey, Massachusetts, Connecticut, Maryland, and the agricultural-industrial states of New York, Pennsylvania, Ohio, and Illinois. The most sparsely populated state is Nevada, with an average of only 1 inhabitant for each square mile. Wyoming, Montana, New Mexico, Arizona, Idaho, and Utah follow in the order named. Although the trend of migration within the United States has been predominantly from the Atlantic coast westward, the center of population is still in the eastern one-third of the nation, being located in 1940 at a point about a hundred miles southwest of Indianapolis, Indiana.[1]

Rural and Urban Population.—Within the past hundred years the United States has changed from a nation whose chief occupation was agriculture to the most highly industrialized one in the world. This metamorphosis has been accompanied by the growth of towns and cities and migration from rural to urban areas. Whereas in 1790, 95 per cent of all Americans lived in rural areas, well over half the population now live in cities and towns. This trend is shown by decades in the chart of urban and rural population.[2]

Political Significance of Urbanization.—The migration from rural to urban areas has had a profound effect upon American politics and governmental institutions. The most conspicuous result has been the diminution in importance of rural local government and the ascent of municipal government. Today, 3,464 cities of 2,500 inhabitants or over dot the nation. Of these, 140 are metropolitan districts[3] consisting of one or more central cities surrounded by numerous satellite communities and comprising conglomerations of people. Such areas as these now contain nearly 63 million inhabitants, or nearly half the total population of the nation. Obviously, the forms and functions of governments in modern cities must differ from those considered adequate for a horse-and-buggy era.[4]

Equally significant has been the gradual diminution of political influence in state and national politics of rural voters in favor of a new urban

[1] Precisely, 2 miles southeast by east of Carlisle, Sullivan County, Indiana.

[2] Urban population comprises, in general, all persons living in incorporated places, such as cities, towns, villages, and boroughs, having a population of 2,500 or more; while the rural population is made up of persons living outside such places.

[3] A metropolitan district is defined by the Census Bureau as a central city having a population of 50,000 or more, with its adjacent and contiguous minor civil divisions or incorporated places having a population of 150 or more per square mile. For a list of the areas together with relevant statistics see Bureau of the Census, *Population, Estimated Future Population by Age and Sex: 1945–1980*, pp. 58–65.

[4] For excellent discussions of this subject see two reports by the Urbanism Committee to the National Resources Committee entitled *Our Cities, Their Role in the National Economy* (Washington: Government Printing Office, 1937), and *Urban Government* (Washington: Government Printing Office, 1939). See also Don J. Bogue, *The Structure of the Metropolitan Community* (Ann Arbor: University of Michigan Press, 1949).

middle class of voters.[1] Because members of state legislatures and the federal Congress are chosen from electoral districts that follow arbitrary geographic lines, and not necessarily population concentration, rural elements continue to be overrepresented. But when it comes to choosing candidates at large, as in the case of state governors and the President, urban elements can be dominant. As things now stand, so far as the

URBAN AND RURAL POPULATION OF THE UNITED STATES:

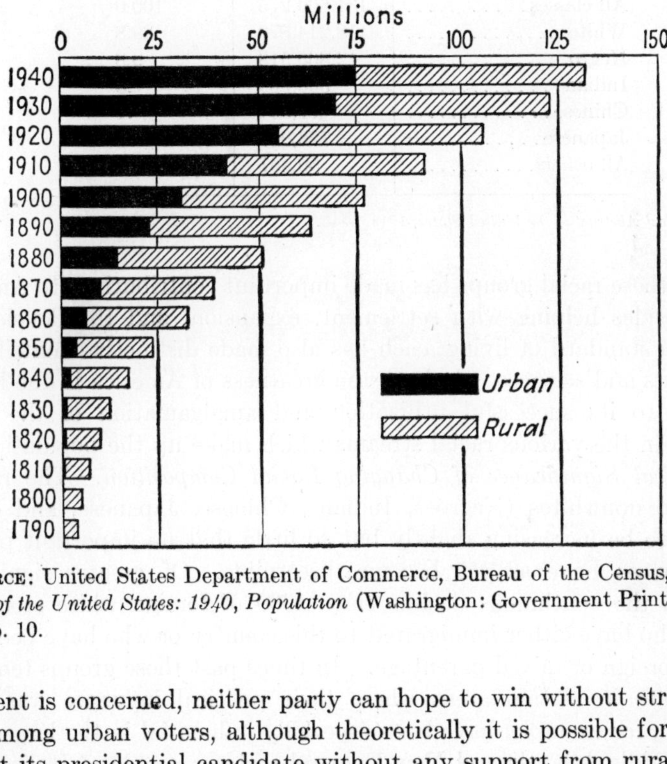

SOURCE: United States Department of Commerce, Bureau of the Census, *Sixteenth Census of the United States: 1940, Population* (Washington: Government Printing Office, 1942), p. 10.

President is concerned, neither party can hope to win without strong support among urban voters, although theoretically it is possible for a party to elect its presidential candidate without any support from rural voters. Professor Holcombe has said that "This dominating position of the urban population in presidential elections marks a revolution in American politics" and he predicts that "The new urban class politics will increasingly dominate the national political scene."[2]

[1] Arthur N. Holcombe, *The New Party Politics* (New York: Norton, 1933), and *The Middle Classes in American Politics* (Cambridge: Harvard University Press, 1940); David O. Walter, "Reapportionment and Urban Representation," *The Annals of the American Academy of Political and Social Science*, vol. 195 (January, 1938), p. 13.

[2] *The New Party Politics*, pp. 34–35; see also Holcombe's contribution in *The American Political Scene*, ed. by Edward B. Logan (New York: Harper, rev. ed., 1938).

Racial Characteristics.—Racially, the population of the United States is extremely heterogeneous, comprising people of all races and nationalities. The distribution according to the 1940 census was as follows:

POPULATION, CONTINENTAL UNITED STATES, 1940*

Race or nativity	Population	Per cent of total
All classes	131,669,275	100.0
White	118,214,870	89.8
Negro	12,865,518	9.8
Indian	333,969	.3
Chinese	77,504	.1
Japanese	126,947	.1
All others	50,467	Less than .1

* *Statistical Abstract of the United States*, 1943, p. 15.

Each of these racial groups has made important contributions to American life. Besides helping with settlement, expansion, and the development of a high standard of living, each has also made distinctive contributions to the arts and sciences. Indeed, the greatness of America is due in large measure to its successful utilization and amalgamation of the genius inherent in the various racial streams which make up the population.

Political Significance of Changing Racial Composition.—The ratio of whites to nonwhites (Negroes, Indians, Chinese, Japanese, and others) appears to be increasing slightly but so little that no important political consequences have as yet become discernible. Of greater significance has been the continuous decline since 1900 of foreign white stock, *i.e.*, whites who have either immigrated to this country or who have been born here of foreign or mixed parentage. In times past these groups tended to concentrate in certain areas where their political influence was great. The Irish, for example, have been especially influential in the larger cities of the Middle Atlantic and New England regions; people of Italian, Austrian, Russian, Polish, and Hungarian stock have wielded considerable influence in the Middle Atlantic region; folks of Scandinavian origin have been politically dominant in rural sections of the North Central region; while those of English stock have had considerable influence in the Middle Atlantic, East North Central, and New England areas. While their influence is still far from being negligible, it is certain to diminish if the present trend continues. At the same time there should be less need for Americanization programs such as there have been in the past, the number of naturalizations should diminish, and the population should become more homogeneous and "American."

IMMIGRATION

Colonial and State Control of Immigration.—Except for Indians[1] every person in the United States is either an immigrant himself or the descendant of ancestors who immigrated to this country. Attempts to select immigrants date back to the Colonial period when legislation was enacted to prevent the entrance of paupers, criminals, and certain religious sects

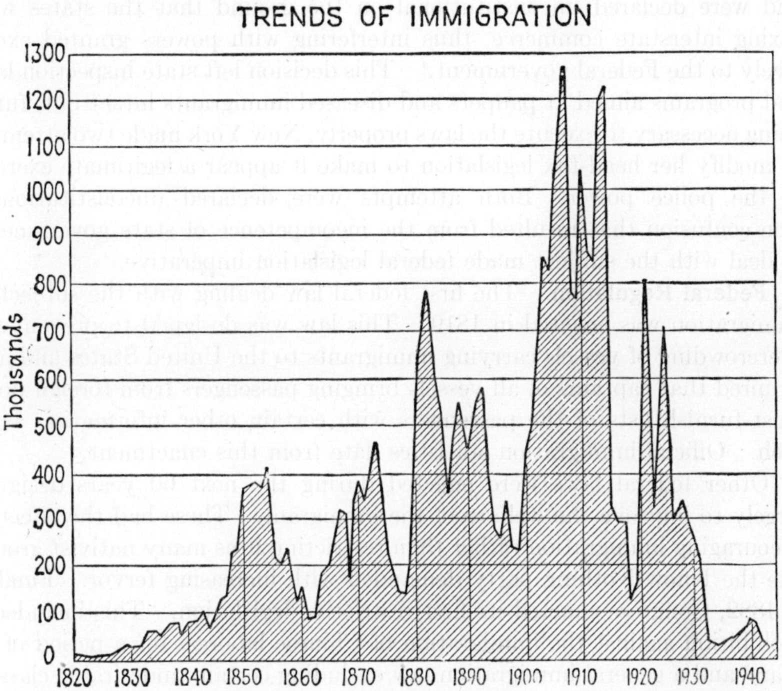

SOURCE: Maurice R. Davie, *What Shall We Do about Immigration?* Public Affairs Pamphlet No. 115 (Public Affairs Committee, Inc., 1946). No official records were kept of immigration prior to 1820. It is estimated that about 250,000 immigrants entered the country from the close of the Revolutionary War up to 1829. *The World Almanac*, 1941, p. 524.

like Catholics and Quakers. After the Revolution the states fell heir to the task but, in general, few restrictions were added prior to 1830. After that date the arrival of increasingly large numbers gave rise to new social problems which led to a clamor for more stringent control. The states undertook the job and, except for a few federal laws enacted during the period, carried the brunt of the burden until 1882. State control was never entirely satisfactory inasmuch as the states were in competition

[1] And most Negroes who came to the United States prior to the Civil War. Being slaves, they were chattels rather than immigrants.

with each other for desirable immigrants and they lacked power to regulate foreign commerce.

State Regulation Unconstitutional.—In order to strengthen their control, several states enacted laws requiring the bonding of captains of ships as a guarantee that immigrants would not become public charges and requiring the payment of a head tax for every immigrant. The laws of New York and Massachusetts came before the Supreme Court in the Passenger Cases and were declared unconstitutional on the ground that the states were taxing interstate commerce, thus interfering with powers granted exclusively to the Federal government.[1] This decision left state inspection laws and programs aimed at paupers and diseased immigrants intact but, funds being necessary to execute the laws properly, New York made two attempts to modify her head-tax legislation to make it appear a legitimate exercise of the police power. Both attempts were declared unconstitutional.[2] The confusion that resulted from the incompetence of state governments to deal with the subject made federal legislation imperative.

Federal Regulation.—The first federal law dealing with the subject of immigration was enacted in 1819. This law was designed to prevent the overcrowding of vessels carrying immigrants to the United States and also required that captains of all vessels bringing passengers from foreign ports must furnish lists of the passengers with certain other information as to each. Official immigration statistics date from this enactment.

Other federal laws were enacted during the next 60 years designed largely to improve the welfare of the immigrant. These had the effect of encouraging immigration rather than restricting it as many nativist groups like the Know-Nothing party demanded with increasing fervor. Finally, in 1882, Congress enacted its first restrictive legislation. This included a prohibition against the immigration of Chinese laborers for a period of 10 years[3] and a general immigration law excluding certain undesirable classes. In response to antialien agitation on the part of nativist groups, organized labor, and others, one restriction after another was added after 1882 until by the time of the First World War there were more than thirty excluded classes. Careful selection, coupled with the policy of numerical restriction adopted in the 1920's, has greatly curtailed immigration. Indeed, the tide has been almost completely reversed; during the years 1931 to 1936 inclusive more people left the country than entered. The trend of immigration is shown in the graph on page 165.

[1] 7 Howard 283 (1849).

[2] Henderson *v.* Mayor of New York, 92 U.S. 25 9(1875); People *v.* Compagnie Générale Transatlantique, 107 U.S. 59 (1883).

[3] For a good discussion of laws of the United States dealing with Orientals, see Charles P. Howland (ed.), *Survey of American Foreign Relations* (New Haven: Yale University Press, 1929), pp. 492*ff;* and Maurice R. Davies, *World Immigration* (New York: Macmillan, 1936), Chap. 7.

After the Second World War, Congress was swamped with demands to aid Europe's displaced millions. The Displaced Persons Act of 1948 was the result. This permitted an additional 202,000 qualified persons to immigrate annually for the following 2 years. Among other things, the law established preference groups with farmers receiving special consideration; it required guarantees of employment, support, housing, and character; it prescribed the filing of reports by newly admitted displaced persons; and it established a commission to administer the act. Many complained that too few were permitted in view of the great need, that the law discriminated against Jews, that it was too partial to farmers, and in general that it was so cautious and complicated as to defeat its purpose. The measure became an issue in the 1948 presidential campaign, but by the end of 1949 efforts to liberalize the legislation had failed.

Excluded Classes.—Among those now generally excluded from entering the United States are those ineligible to citizenship, mental and physical defectives, paupers or vagrants, persons with loathsome or dangerous contagious diseases, persons having committed crimes involving moral turpitude,[1] polygamists, prostitutes and procurers, contract laborers,[2] persons likely to become a public charge, persons who have been deported by formal procedure, natives of the "barred zone" (which includes, roughly, the area surrounding the East Indian Islands), wartime draft evaders, those over sixteen years of age who are unable to read the English language or some other language or dialect,[3] Japanese, anarchists, and certain others who believe in or advocate revolution or violence.[4] An interesting exception was made by the Central Intelligence Agency Act of 1949 as a means of encouraging aliens to betray secrets to American intelligence officers.[5] The provision reads:

[1] That is, those who have committed an act that in itself is one of baseness, vileness, and depravity as distinguished from one that is wrong merely because prohibited by law.

[2] An exception is made for professional actors, artists, lecturers, singers, nurses, ministers of religion, college professors, persons belonging to a recognized learned profession, and domestic servants. With permission of the Secretary of Labor, skilled labor may be brought in if labor of like kind is not unemployed and available in the United States. Exhibitors or holders of concessions may also import employees necessary to install or conduct their businesses at fairs and expositions that have been authorized by Congress.

[3] The test is simple. Each alien may designate the particular language or dialect in which he desires the examination to be made. Between thirty or forty common words are printed (or typed) on slips of paper in the language of the immigrant. These must be read and understood sufficiently well to convince consular officers that the immigrant is literate.

[4] For a more detailed summary of the law relating to excluded classes, see United States Department of State, *Admission of Aliens into the United States* (Washington: Government Printing Office, 1935), pp. 81*ff*.

[5] Public Law 110, 81st Cong., 1st Sess., Section 8.

Whenever the Director [of the Central Intelligence Agency], the Attorney General, and the Commissioner of Immigration shall determine that the entry of a particular alien into the United States for permanent residence is in the interest of national security or essential to the furtherance of the national intelligence mission, such alien and his immediate family shall be given entry into the United States for permanent residence without regard to their inadmissibility under the immigration or any other laws and regulations, or to the failure to comply with such laws and regulations applying to admissibility; Provided, That the number of aliens and members of their immediate families entering the United States under the authority of this section shall in no case exceed one hundred persons in any one fiscal year.

The Quota System.—At the close of the First World War there was prospect of an immediate rush of immigrants from European countries. This led Congress to enact emergency legislation in 1921 inaugurating a policy of allowing only a certain number of aliens of each nationality to enter each year and granting preference to immigrants from countries in northern and western Europe. Permanent legislation was enacted in 1924 but the method of determining quotas that is now followed went into effect on July 1, 1929.

The present law provides that:

The annual quota of any nationality . . . for each fiscal year . . . shall be a number which bears the same ratio to 150,000 as the number of inhabitants in continental United States in 1920 having that national origin . . . bears to the number of inhabitants in continental United States in 1920, but the minimum quota of any nationality shall be 100.[1]

This means that a maximum of 150,000 quota immigrants might enter the United States each year.[2] This total is then divided among the various nationalities of the world in proportion to the ratio between their numbers in 1920 and the total population of the United States in that year with the following exceptions: No nationality has a quota of fewer than 100; natives of most countries in the Western Hemisphere may enter without quota restrictions provided they are otherwise qualified; natives of countries in the "barred zone" and Japanese, although entitled to more by application of the national-origins principle, are given quotas of only 100 each and these may be filled only by people belonging to the professional classes; and, as noted above, up to 100 may be admitted as a reward for aiding American intelligence officers.

[1] *United States Code Annotated* (Washington: Government Printing Office, 1942), Title 8, p. 417.

[2] Because of the provision that no nationality shall have a quota of fewer than 100 the total amounts to slightly more than 150,000, to be exact, 153,774. For the original calculations see United States Senate, *Immigration Quotas on the Basis of National Origins*, Sen. Doc. 259, 70th Cong., 2nd Sess. (Washington: Government Printing Office, 1929).

Repeal of Chinese Exclusion Act.—The influx of large numbers of Orientals following the middle of last century led a number of states, especially those along the West coast, to enact discriminatory legislation of various types. The Federal government, in turn, began a policy of excluding Chinese laborers in 1882. Later, Congress yielded to the pressure of anti-Oriental elements by lumping most countries of the Orient in the barred zone and by adopting the Oriental Exclusion Act of 1924 which denied the Chinese and Japanese quotas calculated on the same basis as those of other countries. This action was deeply resented by all Orientals and accounts in no small measure for the tension that led to war between the United States and Japan in 1941. Under the Exclusion Act, China and Japan became entitled to only the minimum quota of 100, whereas, had their quotas been calculated on the same basis as others, they would have been entitled to 105 and 185, respectively. When the recent war found China and the United States allied, steps were taken to correct the long-standing insult to China. Accordingly, in 1943 Congress placed Chinese immigration on the same basis as that of others, with the result that their quota was raised from 100 to 105. In 1946 the bars against Indians were lifted and they too were placed on the same quota basis as others. Filipinos, who had previously had a quota of 50, were also placed on the same basis as others following achievement of complete independence in 1946.[1] For other Orientals, however, the law remained unchanged.

Quota Control.—Nationality is determined by country of birth and not necessarily country of residence. Thus, if a native of France makes application to immigrate at a consulate in Russia, the alien must enter under the French quota and not the Russian. This necessitates having a point of clearance for each nationality, and for this purpose certain consulates are designated "quota control offices" by the Department of State. All quota numbers for Frenchmen, for example, are issued by the consulate general at Paris whether the prospective immigrant is located in France or some other country; quota numbers for Italians are issued by the consulate general at Naples; and so on.

Selection of Immigrants and Nonimmigrants.—Prior to 1924 the American government exercised no control over immigrants at the point of embarkation other than that exercised indirectly through shipping companies and their agents. This meant that thousands came to American ports only to be denied admission. The trials and tribulations encountered by countless numbers who arrived at Ellis Island and other ports of entry only to be sent back is one of the most heart-rending chapters in American history. Most of this was changed by the act of 1924 which charged

[1] More important were provisions adopted in 1943 for Chinese and 1946 for Indians and Filipinos permitting them to naturalize. See below, p. 178.

American consuls stationed in foreign countries with primary responsibility for the selection of immigrants.[1]

People wishing to come to the United States are classified as either immigrants or nonimmigrants. If the former, they intend taking up permanent residence; if nonimmigrants, they wish only to pay a temporary visit, discuss official business, or travel across the United States en route somewhere else. Whether immigrant or nonimmigrant, a visa must be obtained from an American consul before embarkation. A passport and other documents must be submitted at the time application is made. After careful examination and inquiry, the consul determines whether an alien is admissible. His refusals are final but not necessarily his approvals, because an alien may become ineligible for admission between the time when the visa is granted and arrival at an American port. As vessels approach ports of entry, immigrants are inspected by representatives of the United States Public Health Service, traveling documents are scrutinized by immigration officials attached to the Immigration and Naturalization Service, and travelers' possessions are evaluated by customs officials. If all is in order, aliens are admitted without further hindrance; if irregularities are discovered, they may be detained until the matter is satisfactorily adjusted or debarred from entrance. Appeal may be taken from the decisions of immigration officials (but not those of consuls) to the Board of Immigration Appeals in the Department of Justice.

Deportations.—In general, aliens are deportable if subsequent to entry they are found to have entered the country illegally or have since entry become members of excluded classes. Deportations are made by the Immigration and Naturalization Service in the Department of Justice. Aliens found deportable on other than criminal, immoral, or subversive grounds, or because of mental or physical defects, who are willing and able to leave the country without expense to the United States, are often permitted to do so. Deportation warrants are not executed for these and they may reenter the country at some future time if their disqualifications are removed.[2] Other deportable aliens are arrested and ejected by warrant

[1] For a good description of consuls at work on immigration problems, see Graham H. Stuart, *American Diplomatic and Consular Practice* (New York: Appleton-Century, 1936), pp. 417–428; see also United States Department of State, *The Immigration Work of the Department of State and Its Consular Officers* (Washington: Government Printing Office, 1939), and *Admission of Aliens into the United States, passim.*

[2] Legislation enacted in 1940 eases the situation of certain aliens whose deportation would result in serious economic detriment to a resident spouse, parent, or minor child. In this event, the Department of Justice may suspend deportation if the immigrant in question is not ineligible for naturalization or if the alien has resided in the United States for 7 continuous years. Such suspension orders are valid only in the event Congress does not cancel them by concurrent resolution. *United States Code Annotated,* Title 8, Cumulative Supplement for 1948, p. 31.

and may never reenter the country. Of those deported by warrant, the principal offenses are usually entry without valid visa and violation of criminal statutes. By far the greatest number are normally returned to Mexico and Canada because of the fact that the long land frontiers make illegal entry much easier than at maritime ports.

If deported within 5 years after entry and the steamship trip to this country can be verified, an alien must be returned at the expense of the steamship company. Otherwise, the entire expense is borne by the American government except where aliens subject to deportation voluntarily depart. Deportations are usually made to the country from which the immigrant came or to the port from which he embarked. Before expulsions can be made, passports must be obtained from the country of which the deportee is a citizen and in the past most nations have, as a general rule, accepted the return of their own citizens. Owing to unsettled conditions abroad since 1939, however, it has been increasingly difficult to effectuate deportations.

ALIENS

Aliens, Nationals, and Citizens.—The people now living within the jurisdiction of the United States may be divided into three classes—aliens, nationals, and citizens. An alien is one who though living in the United States owes permanent allegiance to a foreign country. Broadly construed, nationals include both citizens and noncitizens who owe permanent allegiance to the United States, although the word "national" is commonly used to refer only to noncitizens such as natives of Guam and Samoa. All nationals, whether citizens or not, are entitled to the protection of the American government wherever they may be. Citizens are nationals who enjoy a special status and upon whom rests the primary responsibility of organizing and controlling the nation.

The Number of Aliens.—The first complete census of aliens in the United States resulted from compulsory registration required by the Alien Registration Act of 1940. In January, 1941, there were 4,741,971 aliens in continental United States. Of the forty-eight states, fourteen were accountable for 87.68 per cent of the total; each of the remaining states had less than 1 per cent of the total. The fourteen states with the heaviest alien registration are shown on the next page.[1]

The Status of Aliens.—Generally speaking, aliens owe a temporary allegiance to the country in which they may be located and are, therefore, obliged to obey local laws. They must pay all taxes that are not discrim-

[1] United States Department of Justice, *Annual Report*, 1941 (Washington: Government Printing Office, 1942), p. 259; *Monthly Labor Review*, vol. 52 (March, 1941), pp. 666–667.

State	Number	Per cent of total
New York	1,212,622	25.7
California	526,937	11.1
Pennsylvania	361,475	7.6
Massachusetts	356,028	7.5
Illinois	319,385	6.7
Michigan	290,730	6.1
New Jersey	270,973	5.7
Texas	204,450	4.3
Ohio	196,214	4.1
Connecticut	152,664	3.2
Washington	82,644	1.7
Wisconsin	72,928	1.5
Minnesota	58,584	1.2
Rhode Island	52,339	1.1

inatory or confiscatory. They are exempt from military and jury services, although during times of domestic disorder they may be compelled to render police or militia service.[1] They are, with a few exceptions, permitted to own property and engage in business, to sue and be sued in American courts, and to attend public schools and enjoy other public facilities. The civil rights guaranteed to citizens by the Constitution extend to them also and the equal-protection clause of the Fourteenth Amendment presumes to guarantee them from discriminatory treatment by the forty-eight states.

State and Local Discrimination.—Nevertheless, aliens suffer discriminations of many sorts within the United States. They may not vote in any state, they are ineligible to hold most public offices, and most of the states require that only citizens may engage in certain occupations and professions. The Supreme Court has upheld a Pennsylvania law that forbids aliens to own rifles and shotguns;[2] an ordinance of an Ohio city forbidding aliens to obtain licenses to operate pool halls;[3] and statutes of several Western states forbidding aliens to acquire title to real estate.[4]

[1] This is a general rule supported by international law. The Selective Training and Service Act of 1940 required all resident male aliens in the United States to register; it made alien registrants eligible for military training and service if they had declared their intention of becoming citizens; but otherwise aliens were exempt from the draft. Refusal of declarant aliens to be inducted under the act resulted in cancellation of the declaration of intention and debarment from citizenship in the future.

[2] Patsone *v.* Pennsylvania, 232 U.S. 139 (1914).

[3] Ohio *v.* Deckebach, 274 U.S. 392 (1927).

[4] Terrace *v.* Thompson, 263 U.S. 197 (1923); Porter *v.* Webb, 263 U.S. 255 (1923); Webb *v.* O'Brien, 263 U.S. 313 (1923); Frick *v.* Webb, 263 U.S. 326 (1923); see also Samuel F. Bemis, *A Diplomatic History of the United States* (New York: Holt, 1936), pp. 670–671.

Aliens are frequently denied relief, pensions, workmen's compensation benefits, and employment on public works.[1] Aliens have occasionally been the victims of race prejudice and even race riots leading to diplomatic intervention by their governments. Recently, Pennsylvania, fearing "fifth columnist" activity, went so far as to require aliens within the state to register and report periodically to public officers, but this came to an abrupt end when the Supreme Court ruled that the state had exercised a power that belonged exclusively to the Federal government.[2]

Federal Discrimination and Registration.—The Federal government has been somewhat more reticent than the states in enacting legislation discriminating against aliens although fear of radicals and fifth columnists has prompted considerable legislation of this kind in recent years. Aliens may not hold positions with the Federal government; they are forbidden employment in certain special defense occupations, and they were excluded from all relief and work projects under the Works Project Administration and the National Youth Administration.[3] In June, 1940, Congress enacted the Alien Registration Act charging the Department of Justice with the responsibility of registering and fingerprinting all aliens over fourteen years of age. Registration took place at post offices and other public places throughout continental America, Alaska, Hawaii, Puerto Rico, and the Virgin Islands. Henceforth aliens entering the country will be registered and fingerprinted at American consulates before leaving for the United States.

Enemy Aliens.—"Enemy aliens," *i.e.*, nationals of states with whom a country is at war, present a difficult problem. Prior to the First World War it was the general practice among nations to permit such aliens to remain during good behavior unless their expulsion was required by military considerations. But at the outbreak of the war most belligerent nations either ordered enemy aliens to leave or placed them in concentration camps. At the same time steps were taken by the belligerents to liquidate the commercial and property interests of enemy aliens found within their borders.[4] In the United States resident enemy aliens are entitled to the right of protection of person and property as long as they conduct themselves properly, although the courts have held that the guarantees of the Fifth and Sixth Amendments are inapplicable to them.[5]

During the First World War enemy aliens were not expelled, but several states enacted legislation requiring them to register, while the Federal

[1] Heim *v.* McCall, 239 U.S. 175 (1915); Crane *v.* New York, 239 U.S. 195 (1915).

[2] Hines *v.* Davidowitz, 312 U.S. 52 (1941).

[3] "Alien Employment Laws," *Monthly Labor Review*, vol. 52 (March, 1941), pp. 652–653.

[4] Amos S. Hershey, *The Essentials of International Public Law and Organization* (New York: Macmillan, 1929), p. 565.

[5] *United States Code Annotated*, Title 50, p. 12.

government required registration, fixed zones within which they could not reside or enter, and otherwise drastically curtailed their utterances and activities. Although the property of resident enemy aliens was not itself confiscated, the financial and commercial interests of many were seriously injured by legislation creating an Alien Property Custodian with authority to seize properties that were owned or controlled by enemy countries or persons residing within those countries to prevent them from exercising any control over or deriving any profit from the use of property situated within the United States. Altogether, hundreds of millions of dollars' worth of property was sequestered which was subsequently held as a kind of pledge for the repayment by Germany of the war claims of American citizens. The settlement of these claims was a constant source of friction after the war and 20 years later approximately 20 per cent of the property had not yet been returned or compensated.[1] Although disapproved by accepted rules of international law, the Supreme Court has upheld the confiscation of private property believed to be enemy owned if adequate provision is made for return in case of mistake.[2]

America's entrance into war in December, 1941, was followed by acts similar to those taken during the preceding World War. Enemy aliens over fourteen years of age were required to register and carry certificates of identification with them at all times. Travel was restricted, jobs could not be changed without advance notice, the possession of articles like firearms and cameras was forbidden, those with dubious records were arrested, given hearings, and then released, paroled, or interned. Alien Japanese and American citizens of Japanese descent living on the West coast were ordered to relocation camps where, after long delay, many of the loyal were separated and permitted to relocate in other parts of the country. Although upheld by the Supreme Court, this treatment of natural-born citizens has been widely criticized as being both unnecessary and unjust.[3] As during the last war, billions of dollars' worth of enemy-owned property was sequestered for the duration and placed under the custody of the Alien Property Custodian.

[1] Edwin M. Borchard and William P. Lage, *Neutrality for the United States* (New Haven: Yale University Press, 2d ed., 1940), pp. 278–279.

[2] Brown *v.* United States, 8 Cranch 110 (1814); United States *v.* Chemical Foundation, Inc., 272 U.S. 1 (1926); Hershey, *op. cit.*, p. 567; Borchard and Lage, *loc. cit.*

[3] Facts surrounding the handling of evacuees may be found in reports of the House Select Committee Investigating National Defense Migration. See especially, the committee's fourth interim report entitled *National Defense Migration* which contains findings and recommendations. This was House Report No. 2124, 77th. Cong., 2d. Sess. (Washington: Government Printing Office, 1942). Criticisms of the program may be found in annual reports of the American Civil Liberties Union while the best defense is contained in the majority opinions of the United States Supreme Court. These cases are discussed and cited on p. 408.

CITIZENSHIP

General Rules for Determining Citizenship.—Two general principles are employed by modern states for the determination of citizenship: *jus soli* and *jus sanguinis*. Where *jus soli* is followed, citizenship is determined by place of birth; where *jus sanguinis* is used it is the nationality of one's parents and ancestors that determines citizenship. There is frequently conflict between the two, in which case a person is said to possess dual or multiple nationality. Thus, for example, one born in England of Italian parents is English by *jus soli* and Italian by *jus sanguinis*. Controversies arising out of conflicting claims are commonly settled by treaty, but in the absence of treaty the effective law is that of the country in which the person may be located. In practice, states seldom adhere strictly to one principle but employ both. Such is the case in the United States.

Citizenship Prior to 1868.—All the colonial charters save that given to William Penn contained a provision stating that the inhabitants of the colonies and their children shall be deemed British subjects.[1] English citizenship was terminated by the Declaration of Independence and passed immediately to the individual colonies. Since the states were admittedly sovereign under the Articles of Confederation, there was no national citizenship; rather, the inhabitants and their descendants were merely citizens of their respective states.[2] When the Constitution was adopted, persons recognized as citizens in the several states became also citizens of the United States. While recognizing a dual citizenship, the Constitution did not state whether state citizenship depended on United States citizenship or vice versa, but prior to 1868 the generally accepted view was that United States citizenship, except in cases of naturalization, was subordinate to and derived from state citizenship.

Citizenship Defined.—In the famous Dred Scott Case, decided in 1857, the Supreme Court ruled that neither a state nor the Federal government could confer federal citizenship upon native-born Negroes, whether slave or free.[3] This, followed by the Civil War, led to the adoption of the Fourteenth Amendment which, among other things, defined citizenship, saying: "All persons born or naturalized in the United States, and subject to the jurisdiction thereof are citizens of the United States and of the State in which they reside."

Several things should be observed about the above definition. (1) It incorporated into the Constitution as the basic rule to be followed in determining citizenship the principle of *jus soli* which had been followed since

[1] Joseph Story, *Commentaries on the Constitution of the United States* (Boston: Little, 2 vols., 1873), vol. I, p. 84.

[2] Charles K. Burdick, *The Law of the American Constitution* . . . (New York: Putnam, 1922), p. 318.

[3] Dred Scott *v.* Sandford, 19 Howard 393 (1857).

colonial days. (2) Two methods of acquiring citizenship were acknowledged: by birth and by naturalization. (3) Only those who are subject to the jurisdiction of the United States at the time of birth or naturalization are citizens. (4) Children born anywhere in the United States and subject to the jurisdiction of the Federal government are citizens regardless of the laws of any particular state.[1] (5) American citizens are also citizens of the state in which they reside.[2]

Rules Relating to Citizenship by Birth.[3]—Three things must be kept in mind throughout the discussion of rules that follows. One is that the courts have never decided under what circumstances one is a "natural-born" citizen. Another is that some people are citizens at birth because of the Fourteenth Amendment, while others are citizens at birth as a result of legislation enacted by Congress. A third is that in legislating upon the subject Congress has made some people citizens by birth *jus sanguinis*. From the new Nationality Act and innumerable court decisions the following rules may be noted:

1. While artificial creatures like corporations are "persons" within the meaning of some provisions of the Constitution, they are not "persons" within the meaning of the citizenship clause of the Fourteenth Amendment. Hence, only human beings ("natural persons") are citizens and entitled to the privileges and immunities of citizens of the United States.
2. One is born "in the United States" if born (1) within one of the forty-eight states, (2) the District of Columbia, (3) the territories of Hawaii, Alaska, Puerto Rico, the Virgin Islands, Indian, Eskimo, Aleutian, or other aboriginal tribes, (4) American territorial waters, (5) American embassies and legations abroad, and (6) American public vessels wherever they may be (but not private vessels flying the American flag on the high seas or in foreign territorial waters). Hence, children born within these places are American citizens provided they are subject to the jurisdiction of the United States at the time of birth.

[1] The immediate effect of this was to make native-born Negroes citizens of the United States, thereby entitling them to privileges and immunities that could not be impaired by the states.

[2] Residence is usually defined by state law and if native-born persons cannot prove legal residence they can claim federal citizenship only.

[3] Before 1940 the law of the United States pertaining to citizenship was contained in a number of statutes dating back to the early days of the Republic. In 1933, President Roosevelt appointed a committee consisting of the Secretary of State, the Attorney General, and the Secretary of Labor to study the law of citizenship and make recommendations. The committee reported in 1938, suggesting that the nationality laws be revised and brought together in a single statute. These recommendations were transmitted to Congress and from them emerged the Nationality Act of 1940. For the report of the President's committee see *Codification of the Nationality Laws of the United States* (Washington: Government Printing Office, 3 vols., 1939). The act itself may be found in *United States Code Annotated*, Title 8, p. 593.

3. The following are not American citizens by birth because though born within the United States they are not "subject to the jurisdiction thereof": (1) children born of foreign sovereigns and diplomatic officers,[1] (2) children born on foreign public ships in American territorial waters, (3) children born of enemies in hostile occupation. Otherwise, children born within the United States of alien parents are American citizens. This is true even though the parents are within the United States for a temporary stay only.[2]
4. Children born abroad of parents, both of whom are American citizens or one of whom is an American citizen and the other a national, are American citizens if one parent has resided within the United States or one of its outlying possessions prior to the birth of their children.[3]
5. Children born abroad of parents, one of whom is an American citizen and the other an alien are citizens provided: (1) their citizen parent has had 10 years' residence in the United States or outlying possessions, 5 of which were after attaining the age of sixteen,[4] (2) the children come to the United States and reside for a total of 5 years between the ages of thirteen and twenty-one.

Citizenship of Women.—Prior to Sept. 22, 1922, American women who married aliens expatriated themselves. On the other hand, alien women, if eligible for naturalization, acquired citizenship by marrying American citizens. Passage of the Cable Act on the date mentioned reversed these provisions and now American women do not lose citizenship by marriage nor do alien women acquire citizenship by marriage to Americans. Women who lost citizenship prior to 1922 and alien women who marry Americans may, if eligible for naturalization, be naturalized by a simplified procedure.

Naturalization.—The term "naturalization" means the grant of a new nationality to a natural person after birth.[5] Before the adoption of the Constitution most of the thirteen colonies had naturalization laws, but

[1] But children born of foreign consular officers in the United States are citizens inasmuch as consuls are subject to the civil and criminal jurisdiction of the courts of the country in which they reside. United States *v.* Wong Kim Ark, 169 U.S. 649, 678 (1898).

[2] *Ibid.*

[3] Prior to 1940, children born abroad of American parents at least one of whom had resided in the United States were required to register at an American consulate at the age of eighteen and swear allegiance at the age of twenty-one in order to retain the right of protection. This, apparently, is no longer necessary, such children being American citizens and entitled to protection as long as they do not expatriate themselves in one of the ways discussed below.

[4] An amendment adopted in 1946 to accommodate American soldiers who were drafted in their teens, hence often prevented from living in the country the required period of time, provides that children born to them and alien wives are citizens if the father lived in the United States 5 years after age twelve. The children must, of course, come to the United States and live 5 years between the ages of thirteen and twenty-one.

[5] The term is not ordinarily applied to the conferring of nationality *jus sanguinis* at birth upon a child born abroad.

they varied widely. Since uniformity is obviously desirable, those who wrote the Constitution inserted a clause giving Congress power "to establish an uniform Rule of Naturalization through the United States."[1] The power was first asserted in 1790, since which time naturalization has been controlled exclusively by the Federal government. Naturalization laws are administered by the Immigration and Naturalization Service in the Department of Justice, although certificates of naturalization are issued by the federal district courts and state courts "having a seal, a clerk, and jurisdiction in actions of law or equity or law and equity, in which the amount in controversy is unlimited." Persons may be naturalized singly by their own action, or collectively by act of Congress.

Qualifications for Individual Naturalization.—Only members of certain races may be naturalized. The law, as amended in 1943 and 1946, provides that only white persons, persons of African nativity or descent, descendants of races indigenous to the continents of North and South America or adjacent islands, Filipinos or persons of Filipino descent, Chinese or persons of Chinese descent,[2] and persons of races indigenous to India might naturalize.

Besides racial qualifications, applicants must be able to speak English; they must be of good moral character; they must not be anarchists; they must not have been convicted of desertion from the military and naval forces or draft evasion while the United States was at war; they must not be citizens of countries with which the United States is at war; they must be willing to declare their intention to reside permanently in the United States, renounce allegiance to "any foreign prince, potentate, state, or sovereignty," to state that they are "attached to the principles of the Constitution of the United States and well disposed to the good order and happiness of the United States," and to take an oath to "support and defend the Constitution and laws of the United States against all enemies, foreign and domestic." Moreover, before the process of naturalization can be completed, the alien must be at least twenty-one years of age and have resided in the United States continuously for the 5 previous years and the state in which his petition is filed for at least 6 months.

Refusal of Naturalization to Religious Pacifists.—The oath of allegiance contains, among others, the following words: "I hereby declare . . . that I will support and defend the Constitution and laws of the United States of America against all enemies, foreign and domestic; that I will bear true faith and allegiance to the same; and that I take this obligation freely without any mental reservation or purpose of evasion. . . ." Do these words require willingness to bear arms?

[1] Article I, Section 8.

[2] Previously, as noted above, Chinese and those of Chinese descent were denied the right to naturalize. The same was true of Filipinos and Indians.

In 1929 the Supreme Court had before it a case involving Mme. Rosika Schwimmer, a Hungarian woman forty-nine years of age, a linguist, lecturer, and writer, who testified that she had "no sense of nationalism, only a cosmic consciousness of belonging to the human family," and would for conscientious reasons be unable to take up arms in defense of the country if ordered to do so.[1] A second case concerned Douglas C. Macintosh, a native of Canada who at the time was a professor of religion at the Divinity School of Yale University. In applying for citizenship he was willing to promise in advance to bear arms in defense only if he believed the war to be morally justified.[2] A third case involved a World War nurse of Canadian origin named Marie Bland. She was willing to take the oath with the understanding that she would defend the United States so far as her conscience as a Christian would allow.[3] In all three instances the Supreme Court ruled that the words to "support and defend" implied the necessity of bearing arms. Unwillingness to take up arms whenever Congress ordered, the Court said, demonstrated a lack of attachment to the principles of the Constitution.

This doctrine drew vigorous dissent within the Supreme Court itself and considerable public criticism. In the meantime, Congress codified and revised the laws of citizenship in the Nationality Act of 1940 but in so doing said nothing about which view conformed with congressional intent. The act merely embodied the oath of allegiance, which had previously been prescribed by administrative regulation, in the statute itself but without changing its terminology.

The issue was reconsidered in 1946 in a case involving James L. Girouard, a member of the Seventh Day Adventist Church and a native of Canada. He was willing to perform noncombatant service in the Army but would not promise to bear arms. This time the Supreme Court split five to three in favor of Girouard, stating that the Court had not stated the "correct rule of law" in its previous decisions. According to the majority, Congress had never (not even in the Nationality Act of 1940) affirmatively indicated its intention of barring pacifists from naturalization. Noting that there were other ways of upholding and defending the Constitution than by bearing arms, the majority felt that in the absence of clear language requiring a promise to bear arms even though contrary to religious scruples, the Court ought not to imply such a prerequisite. The minority disagreed, saying that whatever may have been congressional intent prior to 1940, the act of that year should be construed as reaffirming earlier decisions of the Supreme Court. In consequence of this reversal, pacifist aliens may now naturalize if otherwise qualified.

[1] United States *v.* Schwimmer, 279 U.S. 644 (1929).
[2] United States *v.* Macintosh, 283 U.S. 605 (1931).
[3] United States *v.* Bland, 283 U.S. 636 (1931).

Procedure for Naturalizing Individual Aliens.—The first step to be taken by an alien qualified to become a citizen is to make a *declaration of intention.* This may be done at any time after reaching the age of eighteen but must be done at least 2 years before being admitted to citizenship. Blanks may be obtained from the Immigration and Naturalization Service in Washington or from a court having authority to naturalize. Ordinarily, the declaration will be made before the clerk of a court having jurisdiction over the district in which the alien resides.

The second step is to *file a petition.* This may be done after 5 years of continuous residence in the United States, but not less than 2 nor more than 10 years after the declaration of intention. The petition must be verified by two witnesses and accompanied by proof of legal entry into the country. After stating further facts about oneself, family, arrival, residence, and occupation, the petitioner renews the pledges previously made in the declaration. After the petition is filed, an exhaustive investigation is made by naturalization examiners attached to the Immigration and Naturalization Service who, upon completing their investigation, report to the appropriate court.

Upon receipt of this report, but not before 30 days after the petition is filed and never within 60 days preceding a general election within the territorial jurisdiction of the court, the third step is taken. The alien appears, with his two witnesses unless they are told by the examiner that it is unnecessary for them to attend, for a *hearing in open court.* This may be a real hearing in which the prospective citizen is examined by the judge or representatives of the government, and witnesses are called upon to testify. Usually, however, the examination is perfunctory, the judge merely following the recommendations of the officers who conducted the preliminary investigation. If the judge is satisfied that the petitioner is eligible for naturalization, the oath is taken, a certificate of naturalization is issued, and the erstwhile alien becomes a full-fledged citizen. Total fees vary from a minimum of $10 upward.

Collective Naturalization.—At various times large groups of people have been made American citizens by a single legislative enactment. When the Constitution was adopted, all persons who were citizens of the original states became citizens of the United States. The treaties of acquisition conveyed citizenship to the inhabitants of the territories of Louisiana, Florida, Mexico, and Alaska. In the joint resolution admitting Texas to the Union, American citizenship was substituted for Texan. By special acts Congress collectively naturalized the inhabitants of Hawaii in 1900, of Puerto Rico in 1917, of Indian tribes in 1924, and the Virgin Islands in 1927.

Distinctions between Natural-born and Naturalized Citizens.—For the most part naturalized and natural-born citizens are entitled to the same rights and privileges. There are a few differences, however. Only a natural-born citizen may become President or Vice-President, although naturalized citizens may hold any other federal office. Natural-born citizens may live or travel abroad without impairing their status; naturalized citizens may lose citizenship if they take up residence abroad after being admitted to citizenship. Natural-born citizens are entitled to full protection by the American government wherever they may be, but because of claims arising out of dual citizenship the American government may, in the absence of treaty guarantees, find it inexpedient to afford full protection to those who return to their countries of origin. With these exceptions, naturalized citizens are on a plane of equality with those who are natural-born.

Loss of Citizenship.—Contrary to a general impression, federal and state laws do not deprive persons of citizenship for the commission of ordinary felonies. State laws frequently deny criminals certain privileges without depriving them of citizenship. Indeed, states could not take away federal citizenship if they wanted to. In federal law, nationality is forfeited only upon conviction of treason, attempting by force to overthrow the American government, bearing arms against the United States, desertion from the armed and naval forces, or draft dodging while the United States is at war.

Citizenship may be lost, however, for reasons other than the commission of crimes. It may be lost by (1) naturalization to a foreign state, taking an oath of allegiance to a foreign state, or by formally renouncing American citizenship before an officer designated by the Attorney General or an American diplomatic or consular officer in a foreign state; (2) voluntary renunciation during wartime if approved by the Attorney General; (3) entering, or serving in, the armed forces of a foreign state if to do so causes one to acquire the nationality of that state; (4) accepting, or performing the duties of, any office, post, or employment under the government of a foreign state or political subdivision thereof for which only nationals of such state are eligible; (5) voting in a political election in a foreign state or participating in an election or plebiscite to determine the sovereignty over foreign territory; (6) if a child, by the naturalization of a parent to a foreign state; (7) if a naturalized citizen, by returning to the country of origin and residing for 2 or more years or by going to any other foreign country and residing continuously for 5 years; and, finally, if naturalized, citizenship can be annulled if it is subsequently proved that naturalization was obtained by fraudulent or other illegal means.[1]

[1] In 1942 the United States Supreme Court had before it the important question of whether membership and active participation in the Communist party prior to and at the time of naturalization indicated lack of attachment to constitutional principles and therefore justified cancellation of naturalization. The Court ruled that membership

References

ALEXANDER, NORMAN: *The Rights of Aliens under the Federal Constitution* (Montpelier, Vt.: Capital City Press, 1931).

BEARD, ANNIE E. S.: *Our Foreign-born Citizens; What They Have Done for America* (New York: Crowell, rev. ed., 1939).

BOGUE, DON J.: *The Structure of the Metropolitan Community* (Ann Arbor: University of Michigan Press, 1949).

BORCHARD, EDWIN M.: *The Diplomatic Protection of Citizens Abroad* (New York: Banks Law Publishing Co., rev. ed., 1927).

BRINKMAN, CARL: *Recent Theories of Citizenship in Its Relation to Government* (New Haven: Yale University Press, 1927).

CLARK, JANE PERRY: *The Deportation of Aliens from the United States to Europe* (New York: Columbia University Press, 1931).

DAVIES, MAURICE R.: *World Immigration* (New York: Macmillan, rev. ed., 1936).

GETTYS, CORA LUELLA: *The Law of Citizenship in the United States* (Chicago: University of Chicago Press, 1934).

HANSEN, MARCUS: *The Immigrant in American History* (Cambridge, Mass.: Harvard University Press, 1940).

HARTMAN, EDWARD G.: *The Movement to Americanize the Immigrant* (New York: Columbia University Press, 1948).

HOLCOMBE, ARTHUR N.: *The Middle Class in American Politics* (Cambridge, Mass.: Harvard University Press, 1940).

——— *The New Party Politics* (New York: Norton, 1933).

KANSAS, SIDNEY: *U.S. Immigration, Exclusion and Deportation, and Citizenship* (Albany: Bender, rev. ed., 1940).

KOHLER, MAX J.: *Immigration and Aliens in the United States* (New York: Bloch, 1936).

KONVITZ, MILTON R.: *The Alien and the Asiatic in American Law* (Ithaca, N.Y.: Cornell University Press, 1946).

MCKENZIE, RODERICK D.: *Oriental Exclusion* (Chicago: University of Chicago Press, 1928).

MOORE, JOHN B.: *A Digest of International Law*, House Doc. 551, 56th Cong., 2d Sess. (Washington: Government Printing Office, 8 vols., 1906).

MYRDAL, GUNNAR: *Population, a Problem for Democracy* (Cambridge, Mass.: Harvard University Press, 1940).

SECKLER-HUDSON, CATHERYN: *Statelessness: with Special Reference to the United States* (Washington: Digest Press, 1934).

SILVING, HELEN: *Immigration Laws of the United States* (New York: Oceana Publishers, 1948).

THOMPSON, WARREN S., and PASCAL K. WHELPTON: *Population Trends in the United States* (New York: McGraw-Hill, 1933).

UNITED STATES DEPARTMENT OF COMMERCE, BUREAU OF THE CENSUS: *Forecasts of the Population of the United States 1945–1975* (Washington: Government Printing Office, 1947).

UNITED STATES DEPARTMENT OF LABOR: *Annual Reports*, prior to 1940. Since that time see Attorney General, *Annual Reports*.

---

in the party, in the absence of overt acts that present a clear and present danger to the existing order, does not justify cancellation of naturalization. Schneiderman *v.* United States, 320 U.S. 118 (1942).

UNITED STATES DEPARTMENT OF STATE: *Admission of Aliens into the United States* (Washington: Government Printing Office, 1936).

UNITED STATES NATIONAL RESOURCES COMMITTEE: *The Problem of a Changing Population* (Washington: Government Printing Office, 1938).

VAN VLECK, WILLIAM C.: *The Administrative Control of Aliens; a Study in Administrative Law and Procedure* (New York: Commonwealth Fund, 1932).

WOOFTER, THOMAS J.: *Races and Ethnic Groups in American Life* (New York: McGraw-Hill, 1933).

Chapter 9

PUBLIC OPINION AND PRESSURE GROUPS

The obvious weakness of government by opinion is the difficulty of ascertaining it.

James Bryce, *The American Commonwealth.*[1]

Americans of all ages, all conditions, and all dispositions constantly form associations.

Alexis de Tocqueville, *Democracy in America.*[2]

In its broadest sense the term "politics" means the relationship of the governor and the governed in every type of situation and institution involving people, not only in the state, but also in industry, a lodge, a club, a church, or a union.[3] For the student of government, however, the politics of the state is the major concern. He seeks data on how groups and individuals attempt to control offices and policies of government. He is only incidentally concerned with how Reverend Brethren was selected moderator of the presbytery or with how John L. Lewis managed to rule the United Mine Workers so long. If the church starts a campaign to prohibit pinball games in taverns or if the union contributes $100,000 to a political fund, then the political scientist wants to know what they do and how they do it.

Even within the field of political science, the word "politics" has two meanings. Sometimes it is used to designate the entire art and science of government and is nearly synonymous with political science.[4] More commonly, however, the term is used to indicate a subdivision of political science that includes public opinion, pressure groups, political parties, nominations and elections, legislation, and kindred matters. The other great division of political science comparable to politics is administration. Politics is policy formation; administration is policy execution. In teaching, however, political science is further subdivided into the fields of politics, political theory, comparative government, international relations, public administration, and public law. The loose and popular usage of

[1] (New York: Macmillan, 2 vols., 1889), vol. 2, p. 345. Used by permission of the publishers.

[2] (New York: Knopf, 2 vols., 1945), vol. 2, p. 106.

[3] Harold D. Lasswell in his *Politics, Who Gets What, When, How* (New York: Whittlesey, 1936), p. 1 declared: "The study of politics is the study of influence and the influential."

[4] See Lindsay Rogers, "Politics," *Encyclopedia of the Social Sciences*, vol. 12, pp. 224–227.

"politics" to imply invidious manipulation and selfish spoils-seeking debases a word of lofty origin, a word that should be reserved for describing the citizen's role in the making of public policy.

As employed in the next three chapters, then, "politics" embraces all phases of the process of making public policy. Around the turn of the century, attention was directed toward the importance of political parties and their operation. In the 1920's came a fad of emphasizing the pressure group in the role of policy maker. In the last decade students of politics have been intrigued with a new field, "public opinion," which includes some social psychology, propaganda and censorship, opinion measurement, and channels of communication. Each of these aspects will be dealt with in succeeding sections.

PUBLIC OPINION

The Democratic Political Process.—The process of public policy making in free countries involves several distinct steps. In the first place, one must begin with individual opinion. Si Perkins's opinion on the tariff is determined by many factors, including emotions, environment, and reason.

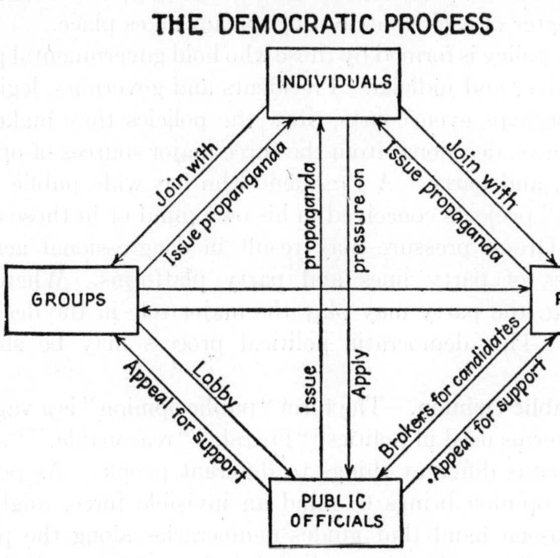

Emotions or impulses are classified variously by different psychologists, but lists of driving human forces normally include fear, sex, gregariousness, acquisitiveness, self-preservation, and others. Environment influences mightily the formation of the individual opinion; especially important are economic status, social standing, family situation, religious connections, and the like. The individual reasons within the framework of his impulses, his environment, and his mental abilities. Groups and persons with preconceived notions press the individual to accept their point of view on the subject.

Next, individuals of similar opinions unite to promote and to defend their interests. The groups they form—leagues, unions, associations, clubs, institutes, chambers—disseminate propaganda about their cause to influence individuals, other groups, political parties, and public officials. Groups also employ all the techniques of pressure commonly called "lobbying."

Third, there is the role of the political party. Parties make up their policy declarations, or platforms, from the opinions of individuals, often as crystallized by groups. In a two-party system party platforms are of necessity somewhat general in nature, for they represent compromises between diverse points of view. The American parties rarely place a plank in their platforms until the policy represented by it is well worn and widely accepted. Parties act in the field of public policy formation as canalizers; taking the lesser streams of group opinion, they merge them into a mighty river. In that river as it flows to sea are the waters of thousands of tributaries, great and small. Naturally, much dilution of the original character of each contributing stream takes place.

Finally, public policy is formed by those who hold governmental power—executive, legislative, and judicial. Presidents and governors, legislatures and congresses, perhaps even courts, draw the policies they make public (through orders, laws, decisions) from the three major sources of opinion—individual, group, and party. A President who has wide public support may initiate "pet" projects conceived in his own mind or in those of influential advisers. Group pressure may result in congressional action for benefits regardless of party lines and party platforms. Where party discipline is strong, the party may play the major role in the declaration of public policy. This democratic political process may be shown in the diagram.

Meaning of Public Opinion.—The term "public opinion" is a vague one. Like many other terms used in politics ("liberal," "reasonable," "sound," "efficient"), it means different things to different people. As popularly employed, public opinion brings to mind an invisible force, mighty and mysterious, an unseen hand that guides democracies along the paths of righteousness. Used here, it means a belief, judgment or conclusion on a particular issue shared by a considerable majority of the community. One of the pioneer public relations counselors has called it ". . . an ill-defined, mercurial and changeable group of individual judgments."[1] Public opinion is, then, an aggregate of individual beliefs.

[1] Edward L. Bernays, *Crystallizing Public Opinion* (New York: Boni & Liveright, 1923), p. 61.

What of the inclusiveness of the word "public"? Does it mean the whole population? Does it mean only qualified voters? Rarely, if ever, could the whole population be considered as participating in public policy making. For practical purposes it means that sector of the population which can make a decision on the subject at hand on public questions.[1]

Manifestations of Public Opinion.—On hardly any issue can one say with finality that public opinion is "thus and so." There are several indexes of value, but no one is perfect, and each usually is capable of more than one interpretation. By a careful study of two or more, it may be possible for a student to draw valid conclusions regarding an issue.

First, election returns seldom show public sentiment on a single issue but rather on an aggregate of issues and candidates. A successful candidate will look upon his election as a mandate to follow a certain policy in respect to public problem No. 1, but his personality, stand on other issues, or party affiliation might have been quite as influential in determining election results. Rarely does one issue loom so large in a campaign that the verdict can be looked upon as a referendum on that question.

Second, public referendums and plebiscites may provide good evidence of the popular will on a given subject. Referendums are used in states permitting direct legislation and popular ratification of state constitutional amendments; they are also common in local governmental affairs. Their shortcomings arise from the fact that they are not very widely used and from the lack of intelligent participation by the voters. The latter weakness may be attributed to inertia or incapacity of the voters and to the complicated nature of many propositions.

Third, lobbying and pressure sometimes are mistaken for expressions of public opinion. All legislators and many administrators are under pressure by individuals and groups that pull and haul over every issue of importance. Of course, public officials take into consideration such pressure when deciding questions of policy. The pressure may, and often does, come from a very small minority. The legislator who determines his stand by counting the telegrams and letters he receives on a question and follows the advice of the greatest number often finds himself with the minority so far as real public opinion is concerned. With lobbying and pressure should be classed newspaper editorials and other types of private opinion, publicly expressed. No editor, however gifted or conceited, can claim unerringly to express the true voice of the people.

Fourth, straw votes, based on scientific sampling of a cross section of the

[1] For a fuller consideration of the nature of public opinion, see A. Lawrence Lowell, *Public Opinion and Popular Government* (New York: Longmans, 1921), pp. 3–54; William Albig, *Public Opinion* (New York: McGraw-Hill, 1939), pp. 1–25; Harold D. Lasswell, *Democracy through Public Opinion* (Menasha, Wis.: Banta, 1941); Leonard W. Doob, *Public Opinion and Propaganda* (New York: Holt, 1948).

population, have emerged as a reasonably accurate instrument of opinion measurement. Although perhaps too much has been claimed for the public-opinion polls, they do serve a useful purpose in indicating which way the winds of public sentiment are blowing.

Public-opinion Polls.—The sampling of public opinion has been attempted for nearly 50 years.[1] The earliest straw votes were conducted by newspapers. Because many polls involved the printing of ballots in the sponsoring journals or the handing out of ballots on a very free basis, the results were likely to be highly inaccurate. Later other publications, notably the *Literary Digest*, undertook nation-wide polls of popular sentiment through mail ballots. Although this method proved more accurate than the ballot in the paper scheme, it was not possible to ensure a representative sample or cross section of the people.

During the 1930's "scientific" sampling was developed. This method requires a personal interview and great care to ensure the representativeness of the sample. In order to secure an accurate cross section of the population, the poll taker must obtain the proper proportion of persons from each state, sex, age group, income class, political party, and occupation. If a thoroughly representative sample is obtained, then the total number interviewed may be a very small fraction of the whole population. No matter how carefully controlled the poll taking is, however, there is margin for error because of the natural tendency of the interviewer to approach the most available and articulate among the groups and categories assigned.[2]

The two polls best known to the public are the American Institute of Public Opinion, headed by Dr. George Gallup, and the *Fortune* Quarterly Survey, conducted by Elmo Roper. Both were founded in 1935. The Gallup poll is conducted by a central staff in Princeton, N.J., and by several hundred part-time field workers throughout the country. Results are sold to subscribing newspapers. Gallup uses a somewhat larger sample than does Roper and is able to conduct a poll on a given question in less than one week. The Roper poll is conducted from a New York headquarters through a rather small number of field interviewers. *Fortune* publishes survey results four times a year. Because Mr. Roper conducts an extensive business as a market analyst, his commercial surveys help him keep his field staff rather active through the year. Other polls, less well known to the public but doing important work on the frontiers of

[1] Claude E. Robinson, *Straw Votes, a Study in Political Prediction* (New York: Columbia University Press, 1932), pp. 47–52.

[2] The method used by Gallup is described in George Gallup and Saul F. Rae, *The Pulse of Democracy* (New York: Simon and Schuster, 1940), pp. 3–121. The most complete study of polling techniques is Hadley Cantril, *Gauging Public Opinion* (Princeton, N.J.: Princeton University Press, 1944). Current developments in opinion measurement may be followed in the *Public Opinion Quarterly*.

opinion research are the Princeton Office of Public Opinion Research, directed by Hadley Cantril, the National Opinion Research Center of the University of Chicago, headed by Clyde W. Hart, and the Crossley poll, headed by Archibald M. Crossley.

By far the most dramatic of the tests applied to public-opinion polls is that of predicting election results. The *Literary Digest* poll flourished under the spell of its success in calling the elections of the 1920's and perished after its colossal failure in the 1936 election. Examination of the figures given below will indicate how badly the *Literary Digest* poll miscarried in 1936; its failure was due mainly to the reliance placed upon securing expressions of opinion by mail from automobile owners and telephone subscribers.

A comparison of presidential election predictions and votes follows:

DEMOCRATIC PERCENTAGE OF MAJOR PARTY VOTE

Source	Year	Actual vote, per cent	*Literary Digest*, per cent	Gallup AIPO, per cent	Roper *Fortune*, per cent	Crossley poll, per cent
(1)	1936	60.7	40.9	53.8	61.7	53.8
(2)	1940	55.0	.....	52.0	55.2	
(3)	1944	53.8	.....	53.3	53.6	52.2
(4)	1948	52.3	.....	47.3	41.5	47.3

(1) Daniel Katz and Hadley Cantril, "Public Opinion Polls," *Sociometry*, vol. 1 (July–October, 1937), pp. 155–179.

(2) Daniel Katz, "The Public Opinion Polls and the 1940 Election," *Public Opinion Quarterly*, vol. 5 (March, 1941), pp. 52–78.

(3) Daniel Katz, "The Polls and the 1944 Election," *Public Opinion Quarterly*, vol. 8 (Winter, 1944–45), pp. 468–482.

(4) *The World Almanac, 1949*. The polls estimated the 1948 election results in percentages of popular vote for each of four candidates for President. Gallup's forecast was 44.5 per cent of the popular votes for Truman; Roper's, 37.5; Crossley's, 45. To make them comparable with figures for early years, the 1948 forecasts have been adjusted to Democratic percentage of major party vote.

Until 1948 Roper appeared to demonstrate an uncanny ability to predict popular votes in national elections, but in the 1948 presidential election he underestimated the Truman vote by well over 10 per cent. Gallup underrated the Democratic vote at all four elections, actually missing by a wider margin in 1936 than in 1948. Crossley, who was nearest the actual vote in 1948, announced that he would abandon election forecasting.

Dozens of reasons have been offered to explain the 1948 debacle of the pollsters. Critics declare that the polls consistently have misjudged the opinions of lower-income groups, because such people are tense, insecure, and suspicious of college-trained interviewers. Most of the polls completed their sampling weeks before the election and therefore could not take into account last-minute changes in opinion. After the 1948 election Gallup and Roper looked back over their records and found an unusually high proportion of their interviewees had answered "undecided." In the future it may be expected that the polls will send into the field better trained interviewers and will interpret their results with more caution.

The significance of the opinion poll is still being debated hotly. Some enthusiasts predict that the poll has opened up a new era of democracy in which the masses become articulate and representatives hear the authentic voice of the people. Enemies of straw voting claim that polling in advance of an election has a band-wagon effect on voters who drop their own convictions and vote on what they believe to be the winning side. Critics have expressed fear that the polls might be rigged to show desired results but have been answered effectively with the argument that a successful business concern or journal will not risk its reputation lightly. Students of opinion measurement have been very active during the last decade in working out new techniques and in rectifying errors. In general, they conclude that the modern opinion poll is a useful device of democracy, but is neither panacea nor taps for our institutions.

Propaganda.—In a broad sense, propaganda is the "technique of influencing human action by manipulation of representations."[1] It is effort directed at securing public support for an opinion or a policy. Broadly, it is special pleading or arguing for one's own convictions. Usage in English has added to the word an invidious connotation, narrowing the scope of its meaning. Now it means special pleading that is rigged in some respect, that conceals something or that states the case in overdrawn terms. In practice, Americans use propaganda to describe the arguments of opponents, but refer to their own pleadings as merely stating the case or as presenting the facts. Since few, if any, proponents of an idea ever present their arguments in a wholly impartial manner, it is well to adhere to a broad definition of the term. Therefore, the terms "propaganda," "special pleading," and "publicity" will be used as meaning much the same thing.

Over a 4-year period, 1937 through 1941, the endowed Institute for Propaganda Analysis issued regular bulletins reviewing various aspects of the propaganda question. A prerequisite of these studies was a classification of propaganda devices that appeared in one of the initial issues.[2] Seven common propaganda devices were isolated: (1) name calling, (2) glittering generalities, (3) transfer, (4) testimonial, (5) plain folks, (6) card stacking, and (7) band wagon. Name calling is used as a substitute for

[1] Harold D. Lasswell, "Propaganda," *Encyclopedia of the Social Sciences*, vol. 12, p. 521.

[2] *Propaganda Analysis*, vol. 1, no. 2 (November, 1937).

arguing; bad names like red or fascist are assigned to opponents and the core of a controversy need never be reached. To employ glittering generalities or prove a point with a single instance, you devour an adversary with a sweeping generalization, such as: "John is a trade unionist and a socialist; therefore all unionists are socialists." Transfer means that an existing confidence in something is carried over to the propagandist's cause; thus every political movement calls itself 100 per cent American. The use of testimonials is common both in advertising and in politics; the opinion of a person is used to give prestige to a commodity or a candidate. Plain-folks appeal aims to win confidence by plain, homey doings; for example, the office seeker poses with his family or dons overalls and tries to act like a farmer. Card stacking includes any sort of fact juggling or falsification. A band-wagon appeal is an appeal to join the crowd, for "everyone's doing it."

The institute's classification is interesting and useful, but it is not complete, nor is each device mutually exclusive. It leaves out repetition, often called a leading weapon in word warfare. Hitler, in *Mein Kampf*, said:

> The masses, however, with their inertia, always need a certain time before they are ready even to notice a thing and they will lend their memories only to the thousandfold repetition of the most simple ideas.[1]

The necessity for simplicity is stressed over and over in Hitler's writings; simple ideas must be repeated until the least intelligent can understand or will believe. The appeal, therefore, is mainly on the emotional plane. Other rules of propaganda include never admitting virtue on the other side, using the spectacular to attract attention, avoiding arguments.[2]

Censorship.—Propaganda may be made more effective by the simultaneous use of censorship. Censorship is the suppression of facts or opinions that might undermine the existing order or authorities. In peacetime we have a mild form of censorship, in that lewd and immoral publications are denied transit and sale, and that some states make criminal the utterance of revolutionary sentiments advocating the overthrow of government by force.

[1] Adolf Hitler, *Mein Kampf* (New York: Reynal, 1940), p. 239. The latest edition is one by Ralph Manheim published by Houghton Mifflin Company (1943).

[2] For further reading on general propaganda, see Edward L. Bernays, *Propaganda* (New York: Liveright, 1928); Leonard W. Doob, *Propaganda—Its Psychology and Technique* (New York: Holt, 1935); Frederick E. Lumley, *The Propaganda Menace* (New York: Century, 1933); Frederick C. Bartlett, *Political Propaganda* (London: Cambridge, 1940). Among the leading sources on war propaganda are George Creel, *How We Advertised America* (New York: Harper, 1920); Harold D. Lasswell, *Propaganda Technique in the World War* (New York: Knopf, 1927); James R. Mock and Cedric Larson, *Words That Won the War* (Princeton, N.J.: Princeton University Press, 1939).

In wartime censorship is more extensive; in general, it forbids the publication of any matter that may aid the enemy or handicap the nation's war effort. This is a very broad control, and specific regulation comes from agencies set up for the purpose. In the First World War both propaganda and censorship were handled by George Creel's Committee on Public Information.[1] In the Second World War, after some preliminary organizing and reorganizing, power over censorship was assigned to the office of Censorship, headed by Byron Price.[2] The Office of War Information, directed by Elmer Davis, handled the affirmative publicity task.

Even in wartime, censorship in the United States has been largely of the so-called "voluntary" type. Newspapers and radio stations were given lists of what were regarded as matters best left unpublicized. If there was a question about whether or not a certain event should be hushed up, it might be referred to the appropriate governmental agency for a reply.

Censorship at the source is one of the most potent methods known. If the Army or Navy refuses to give out data on some military action of importance, newsmen have no alternative but to wait until a communiqué is issued. Many foreign governments close up sources of information and leave correspondents with no news to report. American reporters abroad have developed ingenious methods of evading censorship imposed by foreign governments. Despite censorship at the source, they often manage to eke out information from reluctant officials. If one mode of communication is censored and another is not, then the free channel is used; in the 1930's stories were telephoned out of Germany with little restraint, while the same information was forbidden by telegraph and radio. American press and radio network correspondents frequently are withdrawn from censorship countries and assigned to free ones in order to write a series of articles on what goes on inside the censored country.[3]

An intelligent student of public affairs can keep himself rather well informed regardless of censorship. In respect to news originating in this country, he must bear in mind that while libel laws deter the publication or broadcast of some stories, they eliminate chiefly those of doubtful validity or those concerning which there is no conclusive factual proof. Although the circulation of some books and magazines is interfered with occasionally by local authorities and by the Post Office Department, the cases of injustice are few. The reader or the listener must not forget to

[1] See James R. Mock, *Censorship—1917* (Princeton, N.J.: Princeton University Press, 1941).

[2] For a description of organization and policies, see Byron Price, "Governmental Censorship in Wartime," *American Political Science Review*, vol. 36 (October, 1942), pp. 837–849.

[3] Examples of censorship evasion are found in Eugene J. Young, *Looking behind the Censorships* (New York: Lippincott, 1938).

note the sources of his information and the nature of the channel through which he receives it. His suspicions should be aroused by a sensational story about one country date-lined from another country. The regular press services, especially Associated Press and United Press, have good reputations, and credence in their dispatches is justified, but some other services and "special correspondents" frequently slant the news to fit the prejudices of their owners and masters. Radio stations are licensed by the Federal Communications Commission and are restrained by the necessity of securing renewal of licenses every year.

Channels of Communication.—Public opinion is influenced actively through the dissemination of information—called "propaganda" or "education," depending on one's prejudices—and by a great number of other forces as well. The mediums through which opinion is influenced are varied. Nearly all social institutions, such as the family, the school, the church, and the club, influence the thinking of people on public questions. All of us acquire opinions from friends and associates, teachers, preachers, lecturers, debaters, novelists, and playwrights. The average person daily adopts points of view or information from newspapers, radio, motion pictures, magazines, pamphlets, and other instruments of distributing intelligence.

The Newspaper.—The newspaper often is designated as the most potent molder of public opinion in the mass. Newspapers of some sort reach a majority of homes in the United States regularly. In 1949 there were 12,814 newspapers published in the United States. Of these, 2,014 were dailies, with an aggregate circulation of 52,097,872; Sunday circulation totaled 45,367,607.[1]

Since newspapers are widely read and, in some cases at least, highly influential, their ownership and policies are matters of vital public interest. Most newspapers are money-making enterprises, conducted mainly for the profit of their owners. To make a profit, a newspaper must build up a circulation, and, intimately connected with that, get advertising. Although the greater income derives from advertising, the newspaper must maintain its circulation at a high level in order to attract advertisers. With a few exceptions, the political policy of a newspaper is determined by the opinions of the owner or owners. It must be borne in mind, however, that a paper's policy may be influenced by the beliefs and sentiments of both readers and advertisers. The former, reader censorship, is often underestimated; newspaper buyers effectively modify policies by going on strike—refusing to buy or to resubscribe because of a disagreement with editorial policy. The latter, pressure by advertisers, frequently is overstressed; it is likely to be a subtle force operating as a restraining or ac-

[1] *Directory of Newspapers and Periodicals, 1949* (Philadelphia: N. W. Ayer, 1949), p. 11.

celerating force, but unlikely to manifest itself in the form of direct threats by advertisers.

Many of the evils of the newspaper world are blamed on the tendency to multiple ownership. It is true, of course, that some danger is involved in concentrating the power of the press in the hands of a few great lords. News tends to be standardized; the editorial prejudices of one man may be presented to millions daily; in a crisis extra power is concentrated in the hands of those who control chains of newspapers. The outstanding example of multiple newspaper control in America is found in the vast interests of William Randolph Hearst. Hearst at one time controlled twenty-nine daily newspapers in eighteen large cities; in three cities Hearst papers had more than one-half of all daily circulation; in three others his papers approached one-half.[1] In order to survive a severe financial crisis in 1938–1939, Hearst interests liquidated some less profitable holdings. By 1948 only twelve dailies remained in the chain, but control was retained over news and feature services in others. In national influence the Hearst group is being pressed by the Scripps-Howard papers, which numbered nineteen in 1940.[2] The entrance and exit of Marshall Field as a champion of the liberal press has served to remind us how close to impossible it is to launch a new daily newspaper in a large metropolitan area even if great financial resources are available. The McCormick-Patterson papers of Chicago, New York, and Washington now constitute the third most influential group.

In general, the observing newspaper reader will find that a large proportion of the nonlocal dispatches in the average newspaper come from one of the great wire services. Few newspapers can afford to keep a staff of reporters at the diverse spots in the world from which news is likely to originate. Therefore, nearly all dailies and many papers issued less frequently subscribe to one or more of the great news services. The Associated Press, designated AP, is a cooperative news-gathering agency owned by the newspapers it serves; it maintains bureaus in strategic points throughout the world but relies mainly on member newspapers for local news. The United Press is a private agency that sells its services on contract with newspapers, especially afternoon publications; its own staff collects news and wires it to subscribing newspapers. Both AP and UP present the news in an objective manner; a paper's local news may be colored and its editorial page may exhibit bias, but the reader desiring impartial treatment of the news may be reasonably certain of the accuracy of AP or UP news stories. The headlines, however, are composed in the

[1] Oliver Carlson and Ernest S. Bates, *Hearst, Lord of San Simeon* (New York: Viking Press, 1937), pp. 301–303.

[2] Moody's *Manual of Investments—Industrial Securities, 1940* (New York: Moody's Investors Service, 1940).

newspaper office and may reflect the bias of the owner or staff; this factor is particularly important because many people scan newspapers superficially, scarcely reading beyond the heads.

Newspapers are not obliged to print all the news stories that the wire services send to them; obviously they could not, for space is limited and a great bulk of news stories is available. In choosing which dispatches are to be used and which are to be thrown away, the editor must exercise much discretion which may be highly effective in influencing public opinion. An editor, under orders from his owner-publisher, may throw away stories that place a certain political leader in a favorable or neutral light and print only those that show him unfavorably. Or, perhaps more deadly still, newspapers may decline to publish anything about a political enemy; many politicians feel that being ignored by the press is one of the worst things that can happen to them.

The Radio and Television.—A second important medium in influencing public opinion is the radio. Although it is a comparatively recent development, advertisers, politicians, and government have not overlooked its importance as a means of conditioning the thinking of people. The number of receiving sets of all sorts was estimated by the Federal Communications Commission in 1948 at 75,000,000.[1] This is enough for two sets in every home; it is believed that over 90 per cent of American homes have receivers, a coverage considerably more complete than that of newspapers. In the same year there were the following major broadcasting facilities: 2,034 AM (amplitude modulation) standard-band stations, 1,020 FM (frequency modulation) short-wave stations, and 109 TV (television) stations.

The early development of the broadcasting business was chaotic and haphazard. The Department of Commerce attempted to exercise some control under the authority of a weak act of 1912 governing ship-to-shore communications. The Federal Radio Act of 1927 and the Federal Communications Act of 1934 granted extensive powers over broadcasters to a regulatory commission. The system of control that the United States has evolved differs materially from that found in most other countries; here private initiative is given greater play, while abroad broadcasting is often a government monopoly in whole or in part, with radio advertising curtailed or forbidden.

The extent of governmental control bears upon the question of public opinion in several ways. Private owners cannot use radio stations for the dissemination of their own particular ideas. They are, in addition, subject to the limitation imposed by law which requires that all candidates for public office shall have equal opportunities to rent time on the air. More-

[1] United States Federal Communications Commission, *Annual Report . . . 1948* (Washington: Government Printing Office, 1949).

over, the radio audience is a fleeting thing; because listeners may tune out easily, the broadcaster's propaganda must be at once discreet and entertaining. The broadcaster must also bear in mind that he is engaged in a business vested with public interest, and if his record shows an overload of political propaganda on one side, he may be refused when he applies to the FCC for the renewal of his annual license to operate.

Because the radio is sold for commercial advertising, political groups wishing broadcasting facilities for a desirable evening hour must pay large sums of money for the privilege or ask for "sustaining" (free) time. If a national audience is desired, then it is necessary to negotiate with one of the four great broadcasting systems—the National Broadcasting Company, the Columbia Broadcasting System, the Mutual Broadcasting System, or the American Broadcasting Company, or with some of the regional networks. These great chains own some stations and make contracts with others that are individually owned. The national networks exercise a fairly rigid supervision—called "editorial discretion" by them and "censorship" by their opponents—which operates to curtail what the broadcasting companies regard as "poor taste" or "propaganda." Until 1945 both NBC and CBS followed the general rule of refusing to sell time for the discussion of public issues, except in the period between the national party conventions and the general election in November every 4 years. All networks give some time free of charge to opposing sides of important public questions. News broadcasts constitute a second great means of influencing the public mind. The terse news reports over the radio give a minimum of information on current events, and rarely give any suggestion of editorialization. Many of the news commentators, however, are clearly expressing opinions, and may have a considerable influence in determining public reactions to given situations.

It is now generally understood that the number of standard broadcast channels is limited by physical laws. The number available is also restricted by international agreement, which assigns to the United States 93 standard channels of the 106 total with 10 kilocycles width. The need for regulation is obvious to most people; the chaos of the 1926 period sufficed to convince even the most doubting that governmental assignment of frequencies was essential. As radio developed, it was inevitable that stations would unite to present common programs of regional and national interest. In 1948, over 1,100 AM stations were affiliated with one of the four national networks. After a 3-year study of chain broadcasting, the FCC in 1941 ordered stations not to make exclusive contracts with networks, to limit station contracts with networks to one year, and to cease affiliation with any chain owning more than one network. The latter provision forced NBC to dispose of its Blue Network to the ABC. Both CBS and NBC protested vigorously against the FCC order and challenged its validity in the courts. Mutual favored the report. The courts upheld the FCC order and it is now in effect.[1]

It appears unlikely that American radio will follow the broadcasting systems of most other countries in establishing a publicly owned monopoly. For better or for worse, this country may be expected to continue with the existing plan of regulated private enterprise. The principal controversy is likely to concern the extent of FCC control. Naturally, the established interests wish to retain their favorable position under a minimum of regulation, and the outsiders desire rules and orders that will permit them to become established. Serious questions of public policy emerge.

In 1946 the FCC issued a "blue book" entitled *Public Service Responsibility of Broadcast Licensees* which laid down the following standards that will be taken into account in granting or renewing licenses: (1) a reasonable number of sustaining programs, (2) some local "live" programs, (3) adequate time for discussion of public issues and balanced treatment of controversies, and (4) elimination of advertising excesses. The National Association of Broadcasters protested violently that these rules would mean censorship and loss of freedom of speech.

The ownership pattern in broadcasting also has been regulated by FCC rules, which now limit a single owner to seven stations in each category: AM, FM, and TV. The commission also has an order forbidding multiple ownership of AM stations in overlapping primary coverage areas. The regulatory body has sought in vain legislation which would permit it to control the transfer of station ownership. Stations are being sold for sums far in excess of their physical value. Since the number of standard-band frequencies available is strictly limited, the FCC grants what is in effect a monopolistic privilege. Other public utilities are forced to accept rate regulation, control of earnings, and checking on the quality of their service. Why should broadcast licensees be exempt? In 1949 the FCC further intervened in the program content field by banning "giveaway" programs; some of the networks will fight the prohibition in court.

Grave issues concerning the freedom of the air remain. The law requires a station permitting one candidate to speak to grant the same privilege to an opposing candidate. This has not assured true equality of access to the air to persons of diverse political and economic philosophies. Perhaps the greatest hope for fuller freedom of the air lies in the development of the FM field. Some authorities estimate that about 5,000 FM broadcasting stations may be possible in the United States. Such an expansion could open the air waves to nearly all opinion groups of the country. The development of FM, however, appears to have been stunted by the rapid rise of television. Instead of purchasing FM sets after the

[1] United States Federal Communications Commission, *Report on Chain Broadcasting* (Washington: Government Printing Office, 1941).

war, people in and near metropolitan areas have moved into television. The video version of the radio medium is so attractive and absorbing that it has already cut heavily into AM listening and motion-picture attendance. The large investment required for a television station and the prospect for months or years of operating losses probably will tend to concentrate ownership in the hands of large economic interests. The FCC and the public have a great stake in seeing that maximum freedom is retained in television, which has so much potentiality for revolutionizing educational and entertainment practices.

The Motion Picture.—The motion picture is also a powerful molder of opinions and attitudes. It is difficult to believe the statistics on the products of filmland. In 1939–1940 between 52 million and 55 million Americans attended motion pictures weekly; the industry had a capital investment of around 2 billion dollars; the United States supplied about 65 per cent of world films.[1] The ownership pattern of production, distribution, and exhibition facilities is similar to that of newspaper and radio chains. Eight major corporations dominate the industry: Metro-Goldwyn-Mayer, Twentieth Century-Fox, Warner Brothers, Paramount, United Artists, Radio-Keith-Orpheum, Universal, and Columbia. Some producers of note are independent, but many have working agreements with one of the major studios.

Regular feature films are more likely to shape attitudes than opinion. There is a strong proclivity to glorify wealth, elaborate homes, and well-dressed people. Producers find it safer and more profitable to stress sex appeal rather than social problems. Crime is a favorite subject, but the Motion Picture Producers and Distributors of America (Johnston Office) requires that criminals be punished in the film. In the last decade of crisis and war, feature films have dealt increasingly with real political and economic problems. *Blockade* appealed to the conscience of the world during the Spanish civil war. *Grapes of Wrath* told the story of the migrant family. *Wilson* helped people to see the issues of 1944 through portrayal of the events of 1919. During both world wars extensive use was made of the feature film to arouse loyalty to the country and hatred of the enemy.

Newsreels are second to the feature films in commercial importance. Generally about 10 minutes in length, they are almost invariably shown, even with double-feature programs. The five principal producers are Movietone, Universal, RKO-Pathé, Paramount, and MGM News of the Day. Each one does a fairly objective job of reporting.[2] *The March of*

[1] Leo C. Rosten, *Hollywood, the Movie Colony, the Movie Makers* (New York: Harcourt, 1941), pp. 3–4.

[2] One notorious case of misrepresentation was in the California campaign of 1934 when much of the industry turned its guns on Upton Sinclair, Democratic candidate

Time is a hybrid newsreel-documentary; it has succeeded in presenting vital problems to audiences in interesting form. The documentary is a "film of reality" offering nonfiction on the screen. Many of the best of these pictures were made for the Federal government, beginning in 1935 with *The Plow That Broke the Plains* and in 1937 *The River*. During the Second World War, the British government's *Desert Victory* and the Army Air Forces' *Memphis Belle* won top laurels and indicate the great potentialities of the documentary.

A related field is that of educational and commercial films. They are made for and financed by organized groups, business concerns, and other bodies. Some second-grade movie houses will show advertising pictures if a fee is paid. Most of these pictures, however, are shown in schools, churches, clubs, and other groups. Sometimes a rental fee is charged, but usually the film is free except for carriage charges. Highly popular in the commercial field are animated cartoons, especially those of the Disney variety. During the war Disney shifted over to educational films to a considerable extent and made a very ambitious series for the Coordinator of Inter-American Affairs on disease, nutrition, and like subjects. One Hollywood firm made *Hell Bent for Election*, a flashy animated, for the United Automobile Workers during the 1944 campaign.

Governments restrain the motion-picture industry comparatively little. Like other corporations, movie concerns must submit to securities control by the Securities and Exchange Commission (SEC). A few states have established boards of censorship; occasionally a film is banned by some local authority. Most of the regulation of the industry either is self-imposed or comes from private associations. The Eric Johnston Office, headed by a former president of the United States Chamber of Commerce, enforces the industry's own code. During the 1930's moral standards in films were alleged to have declined, and Catholics formed the Legion of Decency, which did much to raise the tone of pictures. A large number of other groups are given preview privileges and their ratings help producers prejudge audience reactions to new films.

Sporadically, proposals are made in Congress for legislation to break up the centralization of the production-distribution industry. Some are aimed at the device of "block-booking" and "blind-selling." These terms mean that an exhibitor buys a year's supply of films consisting largely of unknowns; if he declines to book blind, the distributor may refuse to supply him with any films, or may make the price impossibly high. Although no bill has yet been enacted by Congress, five of the companies, when threatened with antitrust prosecution, agreed to curb the worst abuses.

---

for governor. For Sinclair's reaction, see his "The Movies and Political Propaganda," in William J. Perlman, *The Movies on Trial* (New York: Macmillan, 1936), pp. 189–195.

During 1948 and 1949 some of the companies finally reorganized in order to separate their producing and exhibiting functions.

PRESSURE GROUPS

Reason for Pressure Groups.—Recognizing that "in unity there is strength," individuals with common interests and like points of view join together into a mass of associations, clubs, unions, and leagues. These groups, together with business companies, corporations, and partnerships, may have interests that they wish to promote or defend through governmental action or inaction. Increasingly organized groups and business interests are finding contracts with government essential to their welfare. Therefore, they set up headquarters in Washington and in the state capitals and bring pressure to bear upon both legislators and executives. This activity, popularly known as "lobbying," is usually quite a legitimate exercise of the right to petition for redress of grievances; normally it operates under the guarantees of freedom of speech and press.

The necessity for group representation arises in part from the impossibility of representing perfectly all the diverse elements of society through the regular elective and appointive officials. In this country nearly all legislatures are elected from single-member geographical districts, a situation that notoriously magnifies the strength of a majority or a plurality and minimizes the influence of minorities. Denied direct representation in legislative bodies, or achieving only a small measure of it, or frustrated in attempts to make parties take their policies, organizations have resorted to extralegal means of making their influence felt. Elective officials are constantly concerned that their actions harmonize with that phantom, public opinion. Pressure groups provide a real service in directing and stimulating expressions of opinion by their membership and other interested persons.

Special-interest groups are both numerous and varied. Several students have indicated that the number of significant pressure bodies operating on a national scale is around 500. Some of the groups have large numbers of dues-paying members, such as the great farm groups and labor unions; others lack a definite membership but are effective because they have money to spend and advocate a cause in which many people are vitally interested, like the public-utility companies. Lobbying organizations may also be classified according to their aims: most are interested in the welfare of a special sector of society; some, however, like the moral groups, have programs that are "uplift" in nature, designed to help the other fellow.[1]

[1] Pioneer studies of pressure groups are Peter H. Odegard, *Pressure Politics, the Story of the Anti-saloon League* (New York: Columbia University Press, 1928); E. Pendleton Herring, *Group Representation before Congress* (Baltimore: The Johns Hopkins

Farm Groups in Politics.—The leading agrarian organizations on the national scene are the American Farm Bureau Federation and the National Grange; the Farmers' Union and groups set up on commodity lines, often producers' cooperatives, play a lesser but important role. The Farm Bureau is much younger than the Grange, but it has achieved a strength in Congress not enjoyed by its rival. It has a large dues-paying membership, a budget of commensurate size, and a staff of well-paid and qualified employees and officers. Nationally, the Farm Bureau has a reputation for being considerably to the left of the Grange; it has been a persistent advocate of farm relief, of "parity," of "McNary-Haugenism," of the AAA. The Farm Bureau was launched as a national organization in 1920. Its remarkable growth is due in no small part to the early connection between the bureau and the agricultural extension services, cosponsored by the state universities and the federal Department of Agriculture. The farm advisers or county agents sought means of reaching farmers in groups, and their connections with local Farm Bureau centers followed. Although there is no uniform pattern over the country, the county agent is the active promoter and organizer of the Farm Bureau in many states.[1] Before Congress, the Farm Bureau is vigorous, emphatic, and demanding. Geographically, the Farm Bureau is strongest in the Middle West.

The Grange has a rich historical background; after a modest beginning in the 1860's, it swept to great strength in the next two decades as the spearhead of agrarian revolt. While still retaining the trappings of old—the fraternal order form, the ritual, the glorification of farm life—the modern Grange has become the conservative among national farm groups. Its stand on present-day issues reflects the conservatism of the Northeastern farmers, who constitute the most influential section of membership. The Grange lobbies in Congress less actively than does its rival. It has been hostile to many New Deal proposals and unenthusiastic about others. The Farmers' Union is influential on the western side of the Mississippi Valley and is devoted to a program of cooperative endeavor. Representing less prosperous farmers, it takes a somewhat more left-wing view on issues than does either the Grange or the Farm Bureau. Some of the organizations, in particular commodity fields, such as dairymen, peanut

---

Press, 1929); and Harwood L. Childs, *Labor and Capital in National Politics* (Columbus: Ohio State University Press, 1930). More recent studies of national pressure politics are Elmer E. Schattschneider, *Politics, Pressures and the Tariff* (New York: Prentice-Hall, 1935), and Donald C. Blaisdell, *Economic Power and Political Pressures*, Monograph no. 26, Temporary National Economic Committee (Washington: Government Printing Office, 1941).

[1] The role of the county agent is traced thoroughly in Gladys Baker, *The County Agent* (Chicago: University of Chicago Press, 1939). Two recent books on farm organizations are Wesley McCune, *The Farm Bloc* (New York: Doubleday, 1943), and Orville M. Kile, *The Farm Bureau through Three Decades* (Baltimore: Waverly Press, 1948).

growers, and others, exert very great influence upon legislation and administrative policy that concerns them.[1]

Organized Labor.—Leading the field of labor organizations in the United States are the American Federation of Labor and the Congress of Industrial Organizations; unaffiliated with either but powerful in their own right are the railroad brotherhoods and other independent unions. The American Federation of Labor was organized in 1886, after previous experimentation with earlier adaptations of the British Trades Union Congress model. From the beginning the AFL engaged in both economic and political activities. Since the primary work on the economic front was done by the individual unions that belonged to the federation, the AFL and the state federations of labor tended to emphasize political activities. Samuel Gompers, founder of the AFL, opposed direct participation in politics and sponsored a policy of rewarding friends and defeating enemies. The AFL lobbies vigorously for its objectives in the political field but does not affiliate with any party. It prefers to support proved friends and to defeat opponents regardless of party label.

In the early thirties conflict within the AFL over organizing policies reached an acute stage. Some of the strongest member unions, which were organized on an industrial, as opposed to a craft, basis, sought to spur organization of the unorganized on an industrial basis. They formed a Committee for Industrial Organization in 1935; the next year the AFL council ordered these unions to quit the CIO or be suspended from the AFL. Conflicts of personalities over organizing zeal and other factors not directly connected with the industrial versus craft controversy were important in the split. Most of the union originally connected with the CIO withdrew from the AFL.

In its new role of rival body, the CIO, led by John L. Lewis of the United Mine Workers, put organizers into the field in mass-production industries—steel, automobile, rubber, and others—and aroused a pitch of enthusiasm for unionism scarcely before known in the country. Soon the CIO unions claimed an aggregate membership above that of the AFL. Eventually the CIO was put on a more permanent basis and its name was changed to Congress of Industrial Organizations. On the political front, the CIO unions led in the formation of labor's Nonpartisan League, which entered the campaigns of 1936 and 1938 with slashing aggressiveness but with only modest success. By 1940 Mr. Lewis became angry with President Roosevelt over alleged lack of "postelection good faith," and in the election of that year he bolted the Democratic party and declared his support for Wendell Willkie, Republican candidate. Lewis's declaration that he would

[1] For further information on farm groups, see William B. Bizzell, *The Green Rising* (New York: Macmillan, 1926); Orville M. Kile, *The Farm Bureau Movement* (New York: Macmillan, 1921); and Arthur Capper, *The Agricultural Bloc* (New York: Harcourt, 1922).

resign as CIO head if Roosevelt were reelected was carried out after the election. Lewis was replaced by Philip Murray, a former lieutenant, who then was denounced by Lewis and expelled from the miners' union. Lewis took his huge union out of the CIO, and later, back to the AFL. The prospects for getting the rival factions of organized labor together appear dim at the moment.

The independent unions, especially the powerful railroad brotherhoods, maintain separate lobbyists in the national and state capitals, but in common matters they cooperate closely with both AFL and CIO representatives. Although beset with family quarreling and jurisdictional disputes, American organized labor often is substantially united in its general legislative goals and methods. Lobbying of the direct and blunt type is employed widely. Through endorsements of candidates and campaign activities the unions seek to help friends and defeat enemies. Their success in the last decade in securing favorable legislation, like the National Labor Relations Act and the wages-and-hours law, is eloquent testimony as to the effectiveness of these methods. Many observers feel, however, that American labor someday will follow the lead of other labor movements in forming or joining a third party devoted to the interests of labor, perhaps attempting to serve farmers as well.[1]

In November, 1943, the CIO undertook political action on a scale and with a consistency previously unequaled in the American labor movement. The CIO Political Action Committee, headed by Sidney Hillman, was directed to conduct a broad campaign to mobilize organized labor for action on the progressive political front.[2] The CIOPAC collected its initial funds of more than $600,000 from the unions; it spent more than one-half this amount up to July 23 (the day Mr. Roosevelt was nominated), when it decided to freeze its funds from union sources and to raise money by individual contributions of $1. In mid-1944 it was decided to launch a companion organization, the National Citizens Political Action Committee, in order to include people not affiliated with CIO unions. Both committees continued in existence after the 1944 election. It is generally conceded that the PAC was partly responsible for the heavy vote in the 1944 election and for the defeat of a number of alleged antilabor and reactionary members of the Senate and House.

In 1946 the labor groups relaxed, the vote was low, and labor-endorsed candidates were defeated in many areas. Enactment of the Taft-Hartley

[1] Valuable background material will be found in Mollie Ray Carroll, *Labor and Politics* (Boston: Houghton, 1923); Lewis L. Lorwin, *The American Federation of Labor* (Washington: Brookings, 1933); Rowland H. Harvey, *Samuel Gompers, Champion of the Toiling Masses* (Stanford: Stanford University Press, 1935).

[2] Joseph Gaer, *The First Round, The Story of the CIO Political Action Committee* (New York: Duell, Sloan & Pearce, 1944), pp. 60–63. This book presents the inside story of the CIOPAC from the CIO point of view. Attacks on the CIOPAC are found in a variety of newspapers and magazines, especially during the 1944 campaign.

Read

Act by the Eightieth Congress followed. Enraged, the unions plunged into political activity with renewed vigor. The AFL put money and effort into the work of its Labor's League for Political Education. The CIOPAC continued to serve as the political spearhead of the industrial unions. With some exceptions, the labor leadership supported Mr. Truman; his victory, and that of the Democrats in both House and Senate, may be attributed in part to labor's political activity. Many former NCPAC leaders supported the Wallace third-party movement in 1948.

Business Interests.—Unlike farm and labor elements, business interests have no membership in the millions. Nor is there so much unity in the organization of business as exists among farmers and workers. Business, however, does have the power of money to a degree unmatched by the other two great elements in society. As America becomes more and more industrialized, commercial interests gain in relative importance. The Chamber of Commerce of the United States and the National Association of Manufacturers are the mightiest of business groups; behind them rank hundreds of trade associations in every conceivable industry.

The national Chamber of Commerce since 1912 has been the outstanding business group of this country. Its total affiliated membership has almost reached the one-million mark in good times, and it has connections with state and local bodies and branches. The Chamber of Commerce slogan "Less government in business and more business in government" was discredited considerably in the recent great depression, but that policy is still adhered to by many. Most proposals for social reform or protective labor legislation have received opposition. One feature of Chamber of Commerce procedure differs from that of the average pressure group. The stand of Chamber lobbyists on pending national legislation sometimes is determined through a referendum, in which member organizations indicate their opinions by questionnaire answers. The Chamber of Commerce of the United States is reasonably representative of the various business interests of the country.

The National Association of Manufacturers was established in 1895. It is more vigorously antilabor and hostile toward social legislation than the Chamber. Besides lobbying in Congress, the NAM engages extensively in propaganda work, through motion pictures, the radio, and the press.

During and since the Second World War, forward-looking business interests have joined together to form the Committee for Economic Development, which has issued a number of basic economic studies.

Trade associations numbered approximately 8,000 in 1940, of which 2,000 were national in scope.[1] Each one exists for the purpose of defending

[1] United States Congress, Temporary National Economic Committee, *Final Report of the Executive Secretary*, 77th Cong., 1st Sess., Senate Committee Print (Washington: Government Printing Office, 1941), p. 85.

or promoting interests of those who participate in the industry. Although they sometimes engage in price fixing and other practices of doubtful legality, it is quite proper for them to seek special representation for their industry or line. These groups, great and small, cover such diverse industries as brewing, tombstones, sugar refining, baking, and liquor distilling. While they are substantially united on labor and tax issues, they may fight each other over tariff schedules and other matters.

Other Groups.—Through professional societies the physician, the attorney, the teacher, the dentist, the architect, achieve special representation for their professions. Women's groups of influence—the National League of Women Voters, the Federation of Women's Clubs, the Business and Professional Women's Clubs—are interested in a vast range of governmental matters, some affecting women and children, but some general in nature. Efforts of a number of women's groups are coordinated through a Women's Joint Congressional Committee.

Reformers of all shades also secure a voice in Washington through organized groups, such as antiliquor, antivice, anti-spoils-system associations; religious groups often indulge in special pleading for reforms. Various veterans' organizations do battle with one another and with the peace groups, which are far from united on the issues. Public employees form organizations or unions to promote their interests; some are AFL, some CIO, but most are unaffiliated and independent.

Pressure Group Techniques.—The men and women who represent organized groups before the legislative and executive branches of government are known as legislative agents, advocates, counsels, lobbyists, or executive secretaries. Popularly they are known as lobbyists. Many come to this work after serving as members of Congress or as attachés or as holders of other public offices; a large proportion come from practicing law, which combines easily with the work of a legislative agent. Nearly all groups and their representatives are bipartisan in their approach, seeking support from all public officers, regardless of party affiliation.

Techniques of interest groups and lobbyists vary considerably, but most legislative pressure techniques can be classed under one of four headings: informational, social, propaganda, and campaign. Informational services may begin with the preparation of proposed legislation by attorneys for the interest group. After a legislator who will introduce the bill has been found, he is furnished with information about the matter. Group proponents present arguments for their side of the question when the bill is before committee, then present to all legislators literature and data in support of it. It must be borne in mind that special-interest groups oppose more measures than they support.

The social front is cared for by cultivating the personal acquaintance of as many legislators as possible, particularly of those strategically placed on the committees with which the lobbyist is most likely to deal. This cultivation may involve any sort of entertainment such as dinners, parties, and the like. Propaganda activities call for many kinds of publicity to influence public opinion, through mail appeals, radio talks, newspaper stories, and advertisements. The purpose often is to stimulate interested persons or group members to bring pressure to bear upon a legislator whose support is needed. The individual may be encouraged to telegraph, or write, or call upon the legislator, in an endeavor to win him over to the group's point of view.

Behind the other activities often lie a number of campaign activities. Groups in politics on other than a sporadic basis commonly find it advisable to survey the legislative field before the need of support becomes pressing. The legislator wants help at election time. The campaign period is the logical one in which to sound out the candidates and get them committed to a favorable point of view if possible. This sounding out may be done in writing, as in the answers to a questionnaire, or it may be done through a verbal promise, preferably given in a public meeting. If the candidate is favorable, the organization may endorse him openly, or it may prefer to send the word along to membership under cover. In any case, financial support of the candidate may reinforce the memory of the would-be official, and a campaign contribution from the group or from individuals connected with the group is valuable for this purpose. Some groups contribute to more than one candidate for an office, in order to ensure that they will have influence with the winner, whoever he may be.[1]

Although strict regulation of the lobby has been demanded repeatedly, Congress imposed no general controls until the Congressional Reform Act of 1946, which requires lobbyists to register and file statements of expenditures made to influence legislation.[2] Registration laws are unlikely to be very effective, but they do, if enforced, bring pressure groups out into the open, a convenience to the legislators and the press. With campaign expenditures, however, the most effective restriction is an occasional legislative investigation.

Pressure Politics and Democracy.—Pressure politics constitutes a very important element in American government. The power of pressure groups is demonstrated not only before Congress and state legislatures, but also in administrative agencies and in the several mediums of mass communication that have so much role in the formation of public opinion.

[1] In addition to the works previously cited (Herring, Odegard, Childs, Blaisdell, Schattschneider), techniques of lobbyists are dealt with in Belle Zeller, *Pressure Politics in New York* (New York: Prentice-Hall, 1937), and Dayton D. McKean, *Pressures on the Legislature of New Jersey* (New York: Columbia University Press, 1938).

[2] For an excellent study of the 1946 act and experience under it during the initial months of operation, see Belle Zeller, "The Federal Regulation of Lobbying Act," *American Political Science Review*, vol. 42 (April, 1948), pp. 239–271.

On the whole, the activities of special-interest groups probably do more good than harm. Group representation provides a valuable supplement to the usual form of legislative representation and makes possible direct expression of points of view by those most directly affected by a proposed line of action.

On the other hand, serious abuses have developed. Some of these can be corrected by carefully drawn and enforced corrupt-practices legislation, but others pose such complex problems that only general solutions can be proposed. The most serious consequence of pressure-group preponderance is that general or national interests of the great masses of people are subordinated to the special interests of articulate and well-organized minorities. The consumer, for example, often has a completely inadequate voice in the determination of public policy because he has no powerful organization that can compete with farm, labor, and business groups. All Americans are consumers, but their interests as producers often outweigh consumer interests. An individual's own immediate selfish interests may appear to be served by a 50 per cent price increase in the product he is making, yet that price increase may be disadvantageous to users of that product all over the country. Since the consumers have no effective organization, their protests may not be heard at all.

General or national interests, as opposed to special-group interests, may receive support through (1) coalitions of groups, in opposition to the selfish demands of one group, (2) restoration of party responsibility and discipline in national affairs, and (3) development of a strong consumers' cooperative movement. The first method operates occasionally when labor and agriculture team up to forestall a tax policy demanded by business, or labor and business work together to defeat a farm subsidy plan, or business and agriculture jointly oppose wage demands by labor. The other methods will be discussed in subsequent chapters.

References

PUBLIC OPINION, POLLS, PROPAGANDA, AND CENSORSHIP

Albig, William: *Public Opinion* (New York: McGraw-Hill, 1939).

Bean, Louis H.: *How to Predict Elections* (New York: Knopf, 1948).

Cantril, Hadley: *Gauging Public Opinion* (Princeton, N.J.: Princeton University Press, 1944).

——— *Psychology of Social Movements* (New York: Wiley, 1941).

Childs, Harwood L.: *An Introduction to Public Opinion* (New York: Wiley, 1940).

Doob, Leonard W.: *Propaganda—Its Psychology and Technique* (New York: Holt, 1935).

——— *Public Opinion and Propaganda* (New York: Holt, 1948).

Gallup, George: *A Guide to Public Opinion Polls* (Princeton, N.J.: Princeton University Press, 2d ed., 1948).

——— and Saul F. Rae: *The Pulse of Democracy* (New York: Simon and Schuster, 1940).

KOOP, THEODORE F.: *The Weapon of Silence* (Chicago: University of Chicago Press, 1946).

LASSWELL, HAROLD D.: *Democracy through Public Opinion* (Menasha, Wis.: Banta, 1941).

——— *Propaganda Technique in the World War* (New York: Knopf, 1927).

LAZARSFELD, PAUL F., and OTHERS: *The People's Choice: How the Voter Makes Up His Mind in a Presidential Campaign* (New York: Columbia University Press, 2d ed., 1948).

LINEBARGER, PAUL M. A.: *Psychological Warfare* (Washington: Infantry Journal Press, 1948).

LUMLEY, FREDERICK E.: The Propaganda Menace (New York: Appleton-Century-Crofts, 1933).

MOCK, JAMES R.: *Censorship, 1917* (Princeton, N.J.: Princeton University Press, 1941).

——— and CEDRIC LARSON: *Words That Won the War* (Princeton, N.J.: Princeton University Press, 1939).

Public Opinion Quarterly. Issued by Princeton University Press since 1937.

ROBINSON, CLAUDE E.: *Straw Votes, a Study in Political Prediction* (New York: Columbia University Press, 1932).

ROGERS, LINDSAY: *The Pollsters* (New York: Knopf, 1949).

CHANNELS OF COMMUNICATION

ALLPORT, GORDON W., and HADLEY CANTRIL: *Psychology of Radio* (New York: Richard R. Smith, 2d ed., 1941).

BRYSON, LYMAN: *Time for Reason about Radio* (New York: Stewart, 1948).

CHAFEE, J. ZECHARIAH: *Government and Mass Communications* (Chicago: University of Chicago Press, 2 vols., 1947).

CHARTERS, WERRETT W. (chairman): *Motion Pictures and Youth; a Summary* (New York: Macmillan, 1933). A summary of twelve Payne Fund studies on the influence of motion pictures on children.

COMMISSION ON FREEDOM OF THE PRESS: *A Free and Responsible Press; a General Report on Mass Communication* (Chicago: University of Chicago Press, 1947).

DALE, EDGAR: *How to Appreciate Motion Pictures* (New York: Macmillan, 1933).

FIELD, MARSHALL: *Freedom Is More than a Word* (Chicago: University of Chicago Press, 1945).

FROST, S. E., JR.: *Is American Radio Democratic?* (Chicago: University of Chicago Press, 1937).

HETTINGER, HERMAN S. (ed.): "New Horizons in Radio," *Annals of the American Academy of Political and Social Science*, vol. 213 (January, 1941).

HUETTIG, MAE D.: *Economic Control of the Motion Picture Industry* (Philadelphia: University of Pennsylvania Press, 1944).

ICKES, HAROLD L. (ed.): *Freedom of the Press Today* (New York: Vanguard, 1941).

LAZARSFELD, PAUL F.: *Radio and the Printed Page* (New York: Duell, Sloan & Pearce, 1940).

LEE, ALFRED M.: *The Daily Newspaper in America; the Evolution of a Social Instrument* (New York: Macmillan, 1937).

PERLMAN, WILLIAM J. (ed.): *The Movies on Trial* (New York: Macmillan, 1936).

ROBINSON, THOMAS P.: *Radio Networks and the Federal Government* (New York: Columbia University Press, 1943).

ROSE, CORNELIA B., JR.: *National Policy for Radio Broadcasting* (New York: Harper, 1940).

Rosten, Leo C.: *Hollywood, the Movie Colony, the Movie Makers* (New York: Harcourt Brace, 1941).
Siepmann, Charles A.: *Radio's Second Chance* (Boston: Little, Brown, 1946).
Thorp, Margaret: *America at the Movies* (New Haven: Yale University Press, 1939).
United States Federal Communications Commission: *An Economic Study of Standard Broadcasting* (Washington: Government Printing Office, 1947).
——— *Public Service Responsibility of Broadcast Licensees* (Washington: Government Printing Office, 1946).
——— *Report on Chain Broadcasting* (Washington: Government Printing Office, 1941).
Waples, Douglas (ed.): *Print, Radio, and Film in a Democracy* (Chicago: University of Chicago Press, 1942).
Watkins, Gordon S. (ed.): "The Motion Picture Industry," *Annals of the American Academy of Political and Social Science*, vol. 254 (November, 1947).
White, Llewellyn, and Robert D. Leigh: *Peoples Speaking to Peoples* (Chicago: University of Chicago Press, 1946).
Willey, Malcolm, and Ralph D. Casey (eds.): "The Press in the Contemporary Scene," *Annals of the American Academy of Political and Social Science*, vol. 219 (January, 1942).

PRESSURE GROUPS

Blaisdell, Donald C.: *Economic Power and Political Pressures*, Temporary National Economic Committee, Monograph 26 (Washington: Government Printing Office, 1941).
Chase, Stuart: *Democracy under Pressure: Special Interests vs the Public Welfare* (New York: Twentieth Century Fund, 1945).
Childs, Harwood L.: *Labor and Capital in National Politics* (Columbus, Ohio: The Ohio State University Press, 1930).
Garceau, Oliver: *Political Life of the American Medical Association* (Cambridge. Mass.: Harvard University Press, 1941).
Herring, E. Pendleton: *Group Representation before Congress* (Baltimore: Johns Hopkins Press, 1929).
Kile, Orville M.: *The Farm Bureau through Three Decades* (Baltimore: Waverly Press, 1948).
McCune, Wesley: *The Farm Bloc* (New York: Doubleday, 1943).
McKean, Dayton D.: *Pressures on the Legislature of New Jersey* (New York: Columbia University Press, 1938).
Odegard, Peter H.: *Pressure Politics, the Story of the Anti-saloon League* (New York: Columbia University Press, 1928).
Rutherford, Mary L.: *The Influence of the American Bar Association on Public Opinion and Legislation* (Chicago: Foundation Press, 1937).
Schattschneider, Elmer E.: *Politics, Pressures and the Tariff* (New York: Prentice-Hall, 1935).
Zeller, Belle: *Pressure Politics in New York* (New York: Prentice-Hall, 1937).

Chapter 10

POLITICAL PARTIES

I often think it's comical—Fal, lal, la!
How Nature always does contrive—Fal, lal, la!
That every boy and every gal
That's born into the world alive
Is either a little Liberal
Or else a little Conservative!
Fal, lal, la!

Gilbert and Sullivan, *Iolanthe.*

There is no essential difference between the Republican and Democratic parties as regards principles. They are like two hogs, one a large fellow with both feet in the trough, the other a lean, restless brute doing his best to get an opening for himself. The trough represents the ultimate consumer.

David Starr Jordan, "Taking Politics Out of Politics."[1]

GENERAL ASPECTS

Nature of the Political Party.—A political party is an organization of voters adhering to common principles and seeking power to control the government. In the United States, the Republican and Democratic parties frequently appear to support similar principles. Over much of American history the two major parties have resembled each other to an unusual extent, the resemblance forcing people to the conclusion that our parties were rival vote-catching arrangements manipulated by professional politicians seeking the spoils of office. Certainly under the two-party system parties have platforms and principles that are extremely general in nature, for an enormous amount of compromising must be done in framing them.

People encounter much difficulty in distinguishing between a political party and a pressure group. A vast organization like the Townsend movement of the 1930's appears at first blush to have all the characteristics of a political party. Indeed, a Townsend party appeared in several states, but the group proper has confined its political efforts to lobbying and to the support of or opposition to candidates of the regular parties. The primary difference between party and pressure groups is found in the essential aim: parties seek largely to capture offices; pressure groups aim mainly to influence policies.

Neither major American party has a definite membership. Persons may be considered members of a political party because they register as

[1] An address to a Stanford University assembly, Apr. 20, 1910, quoted in San Francisco *Bulletin*, Apr. 21, 1910.

members, think themselves to be members, or contribute money and hold a membership card. The first two are the most common forms of affiliation; the last is limited to small parties of the "left wing."

Factors in Party Allegiance.—It is interesting to speculate on how an individual's party affiliation is determined, how one chooses sides in the game of party politics. Exact data on this subject are scarce, but some surveys that have been made shed light on certain of its aspects. The first, and perhaps the most important, determinant is family tradition. Roughly 75 per cent of all voters take the party of their parents.[1] This political ancestor worship is evidenced by the common expression, "My family is a Republican family," or "We have been Democrats for a hundred years." Because many other factors are influenced by family—economic status, religion, section of residence—this factor assumes an extraordinary importance.

Economic position ranks second in influence on party bias. No general rule applies to all periods, but recently there has been an increasing tendency for the well-to-do to vote Republican and for the less fortunate to vote Democratic. National origin plays a role too, for descendants of northern Europeans tend to the Republican party, while those of southern and eastern Europeans prefer the Democratic party. This choice is probably connected with the economic role of each. Religious connections appear to play little part in pushing adherents into one party rather than the other, but it is an interesting fact that the Republican party is much more strongly Protestant than is the Democratic. Sectionalism, or geographic influence, is decisive in many cases and in certain parts of the country. In the South nearly everyone is Democratic; in Maine and Vermont the Republican majority is large.

The Two-party System.—The two-party system exists in the United States, Great Britain, and some of the British dominions. Various explanations for it have been offered. First, some say that the peoples of the English-speaking countries are less doctrinaire and more inclined to compromise. Second, fewer problems of race, nationality, and religion factionalize the people than in the countries of continental Europe. Third, the early English two-party system was transplanted in the Colonial era and has been perpetuated. Fourth, the two-party plan is produced by the operation of the American voting systems, especially the electoral college and the single-member district plan of electing legislative representatives. This fourth point requires elaboration. The importance of the presidency is so great that a third party secures adherents only with greatest difficulty,

[1] Charles E. Merriam and Harold F. Gosnell, *The American Party System* (New York: Macmillan, 4th ed., 1949), p. 141, declared the number of hereditary voters runs from 65 to 85 per cent, averaging about 75 per cent. This figure was confirmed in a study made during 1938–1939 in the Middle Atlantic states. The full results are in the possession of Dr. McHenry.

for "band-wagon" sentiment argues against "losing your vote" by supporting other than one of the two major parties. It is also true that the electoral-college method of electing the President would be very undemocratic if a strong third party should emerge. If no majority is won in the electoral college, the election of the Chief Executive is thrown to the House of Representatives, which must select from the highest three, each state casting one vote.

The single-member district scheme of electing legislative representatives also discourages the development of minor parties. It tends to magnify the strength of the leading party, yielding a proportion of legislative seats far above the proportion of popular votes received. For example, a party polling 52 per cent of the popular vote cast for representatives in Congress may receive 75 per cent of the seats, not only depriving the major opposition party of representation strictly proportionate to its voting strength, but usually eliminating minor parties almost completely.[1]

The consequences of the two-party system are extremely important. First, it usually produces a situation in which one party actually has the power to govern. Under the parliamentary plan, the two-party scheme nearly always provides one party with a mandate from the electorate and a majority in the legislative body strong enough to carry out the mandate. Under the presidential plan, the separation of powers occasionally may lead to deadlock between executive and legislative branches, but normally it results in a situation where the President has a congressional majority of his own party. In spite of the theoretical advantages of proportional representation (PR),[2] support has declined in the years of crisis, because of a new recognition that producing the power to govern through a roughly democratic means is superior to representing all the elements in the body politic exactly in proportion to their strength in the electorate.

Second, major parties under the two-party system become moderate, compromising bodies, highly irritating to those who demand sharp definitions of party policy. Each party is faced with the task of attracting to the party standards an aggregation of interests strong enough to win power. Because each major party is at all times either the government or the opposition (alternative government), it is held close to realities and can ill afford to make irresponsible policy declarations.

Although there are some who would exchange the two-party plan for a multiparty scheme, the disadvantages of having many parties of strength would be very great under our form of government. The multiparty

[1] Elmer E. Schattschneider, *Party Government* (New York: Rinehart, 1942), pp. 77–78, compiled the United States House of Representatives membership by parties over 40 years and found that minor parties elected slightly more than 1 per cent of the membership.

[2] See p. 246.

system produces instability, confuses the electorate with a multitude of alternatives, represents local groups and factions on a national scale, diffuses responsibility for action and inaction; it would make continued functioning of the electoral college virtually impossible.[1]

Third Parties.—Third parties have come and gone, but over a period of 150 years none except the Republican party has ever gained sufficient strength to displace an existing major party. Several times minor party candidates for the presidency have polled sufficient votes to hold the balance of power between the two majors, but they have been unable to keep their separate identity or strength for long. Since the Civil War third parties have made respectable showings on six occasions.[2] The Populists polled over one million votes in 1892; so did both Wallace, Progressive, and Thurmond, States' Rights, in 1948. Eugene Debs, Socialist candidate for the presidency, secured nearly a million votes both in 1912 and in 1920. With Theodore Roosevelt as a standard-bearer, the Progressives of 1912 polled over 4 million votes, exceeding the vote for President Taft, the official Republican candidate. The most recent great revolt came in 1924 when Robert M. La Follette, Progressive candidate, polled 4½ million votes for the presidency.

Third parties in American politics have played the role of innovators of policy, not of holders of office. The old parties have not hesitated to take plank after plank from Populists, Greenbackers, Socialists, and Progressives and install them in their own platforms. Much of what the left-wing parties advocated two or three decades ago may be found in the Democratic and Republican platforms of today. Those who participate in third-party movements may themselves never enjoy the fruits of office, but they may see the policies for which they worked become law of the land under old-party auspices. Yet the similarity of the two old parties is so great that many persons argue that a recasting of the party system is needed. One party, they say, should become a genuine conservative

[1] The case against the two-party system is stated in William MacDonald, *A New Constitution for a New America* (New York: Huebsch, 1921), p. 145, who declares: "The two-party system, by its inevitable tendency to eliminate all grounds of difference save one, and that not necessarily the most vital, forces public opinion into a characterless mold of composite compromise, and by repressing dissent represses also the growth of intelligent opinion and strengthens the power of the political machine." An earlier critic was Josephus N. Larned, "Criticism of Two-party Politics," *Atlantic Monthly*, vol. 107 (1911), pp. 289–300, who found both parties controlled by "irresistible leagues" of self-seekers and office seekers.

[2] Leading sources on third parties are Nathan Fine, *Labor and Farmer Parties in the United States, 1828–1928* (New York: Rand School, 1928); Fred E. Haynes, *Third Party Movements since the Civil War* (Iowa City: State Historical Society of Iowa, 1916), and *Social Politics in the United States* (Boston: Houghton, 1924); John D. Hicks, *The Populist Revolt* (Minneapolis: University of Minnesota Press, 1931); William Hesseltine, *The Rise and Fall of Third Parties . . .* (Washington: Public Affairs Press, 1948).

party, and the other the party of progressive reform. Fifteen years ago it was thought that the Democratic party might die, and a farmer-labor or progressive party arise to replace it. Since the New Deal era, however, much attention has been given to the tendency for progressives to concentrate in the Democratic party, and for the Republican party to become the organ of conservatism. This division will be far from sharp, however, until the "solid South" is broken up and divides along natural party lines, and progressive elements of the Republican party are enticed or smoked out. At the moment there appears to be little evidence of either of these developments.

History of American Parties.—The Democratic party is a venerable body, nearly a century and a half old. It took form during Washington's administration, under the leadership of Jefferson, who was an exponent of strict construction. Known under various names, including Antifederalist, Republican, Democratic Republican, and Democratic, the party has shown enormous ability to survive under the most difficult of circumstances. Early in history it took a stand against high tariffs and enlisted the support of small farmers of the West and of urban workers of the East. After the extinction of the Federalist party around 1816, the party enjoyed a period of noncompetition in the political field. Substantial opposition generated in the Jacksonian era, however, and the party, now labeled Democratic, soon faced a formidable Whig opponent. Although the Civil War made of the Democratic party a minority group for decades, the party rebounded with vigor in Congress and captured the presidency twice with Cleveland, twice with Wilson, and four times with Franklin D. Roosevelt.

The Republican party of today is the successor of two earlier major parties. The Federalist party, led by Hamilton, emerged during Washington's administration as the champion of strong national government. It expired after making tactical errors during the War of 1812. When opposition crystallized against Jackson, it called itself National Republican, then Whig. In 1856 a new party, calling itself Republican, strode upon the scene, nominated John C. Frèmont as presidential candidate, and took a strong stand on the slavery issue. Its victory in 1860 with Lincoln precipitated the Civil War, the results of which secured Republican predominance in national politics for the greater part of the period since then. Over the years it has stood for high tariffs, strong national government, "hard" money, and conservatism; yet it has had room for trust busting and Theodore Roosevelt progressivism.[1]

[1] There are many histories of American parties, including Charles A. Beard, *American Party Battle* (New York: Macmillan, 1913); Wilfred E. Binkley, *Political Parties: Their Natural History* (New York: Knopf, 1942); Frank R. Kent, *The Democratic Party, a History* (New York: Century, 1928); William S. Myers, *The Republican Party* (New York: Century, 1928); Edgar E. Robinson, *Evolution of American Political Parties* (New York: Harcourt, 1924).

HISTORY OF AMERICAN PARTIES

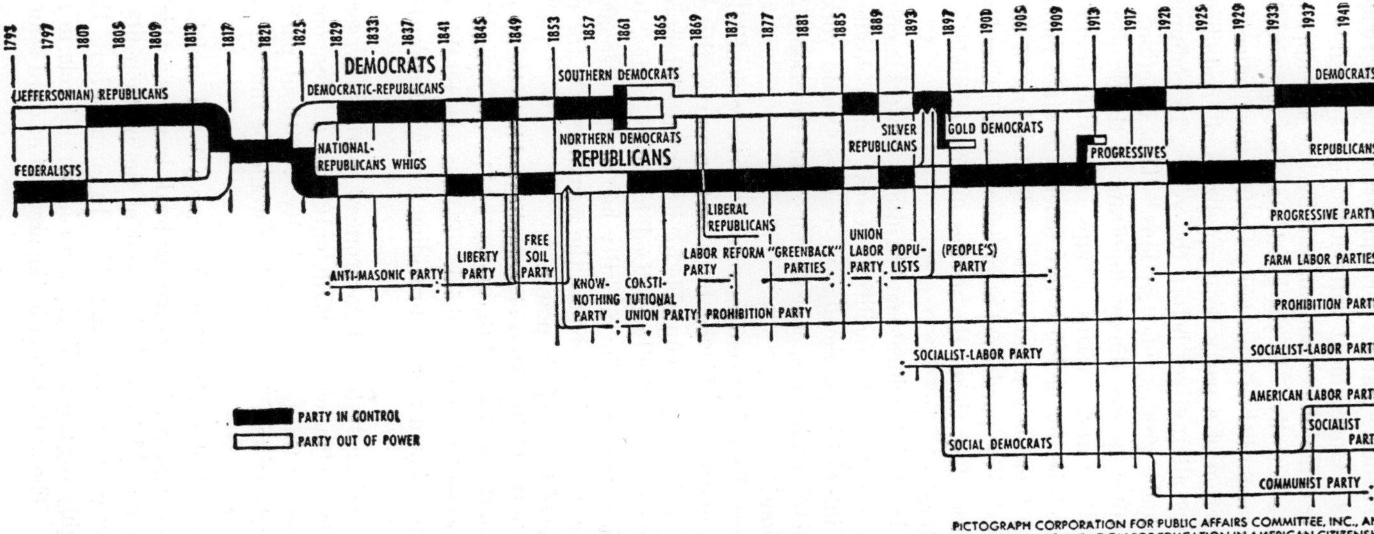

SOURCE: From Franklin L. Burdette, *Political Parties: An American Way* (Indianapolis and New York: National Foundation for Education in American Citizenship and the Public Affairs Committee, Inc., 1946), pp. 16–17.

Functions of Parties.—Parties perform certain necessary services in the governing process. Government without parties is possible, a number of states have made some offices nonpartisan by law and appear to conduct public affairs satisfactorily. In the great majority of cases, however, the political party is regarded as a necessity for free government.

The first function of a party is to canalize and crystallize opinion, to narrow the policy alternatives before the voters, to compromise diverse views of individuals, groups, and sections. This function, as shown in the previous chapter, is exceedingly important to the democratic political process. Individuals and pressure groups ordinarily cannot reduce the number of possibilities for action before federal or state public officers in such a way that there is general public understanding of the issues. A second service is similar; parties act as brokers of candidates for office. By selecting and promoting them, the parties narrow candidate alternatives before the electorate.

Parties also do much to educate and to interest voters in politics. They maintain elaborate publicity facilities. Great party leaders stimulate enthusiasm and interest in public affairs. Parties also do work in the field of naturalization of immigrants, once an important function of great urban party organizations.

Another group of services centers around party responsibility. If the control of government is achieved by a certain party, the electorate is entitled to hold that party accountable for its stewardship in office. This responsibility is very imperfectly realized in many states, but a rough measure of justice is done. The minority has no less responsibility than the majority, for the task is to expose the weaknesses of the majority, to furnish criticisms of the party in power.

Government in the United States is complicated both by the distribution of powers between the nation and the states, and by the separation of power into legislative, executive, and judicial. Parties correct this diffusion of governmental authority in part by providing somewhat compatible groups of officeholders.

Under the American system of government, parties also serve to make the electoral-college plan work. With only two parties, one candidate nearly always secures the necessary majority. Without parties, or even with the multiparty system, most elections would be thrown to the House of Representatives.

Finally, the political party often performs a social and humanitarian function. Parties and their auxiliaries hold bazaars, whists, dances, picnics; such events add to the enjoyment of the participants and to the political consciousness of a community. In areas where the political party is thoroughly organized, it plays an important role in humanizing big government. The party leader in the precinct or ward is an interpreter of the individual's needs and desires to public officials and, vice versa, the policies and structure of government are explained to the citizen by his local party leader. Although such services sometimes extend into the field of special favors granted to the faithful and withheld from others, a great deal of legitimate aid may be rendered by a party.

PARTY ORGANIZATION

Party organization has two distinct parts, but interconnections are frequent and one is hard to describe without the other. The permanent organization includes the tiers of party committees that reach from bottom to top of the party hierarchy. The periodic organization consists of party

PERMANENT PARTY ORGANIZATION IN U.S.A.

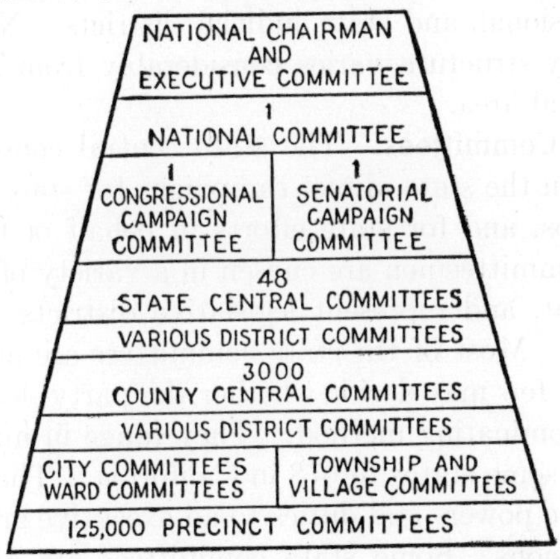

primaries and conventions, meeting annually or less frequently and deciding highly important questions concerning party structure. The periodic organization will be dealt with in some detail in the next chapter. Primary emphasis here will be placed upon the permanent organization, but brief references will be made to conventions and primaries.

Local Organization.—The precinct, or polling district, is the basic unit in party organization. Its size depends upon population density and number of voters election officials can handle conveniently. Between 100 and 500 voters are included in the average precinct. Around 125,000 precincts exist in the United States; of these perhaps 100,000 have definite party organizations active in them. The chairman or executive of the party precinct unit is responsible for the party's direct contacts with voters in their home districts and provides the personal services in exchange for which people of the precinct may be willing to cast their ballots.

The ward committee is usually the next level of party organization in an urban community. A ward is a district from which city councilmen are elected. This party committee coordinates the work of precinct units and deals with local political problems, especially with municipal-council politics. A city committee oversees the ward and precinct levels and gives particular attention to municipal problems and offices. Township or village committees exist in rural areas to bring together precinct representatives and to plan party activities in relation to local governments.

County Committees.—County central committees coordinate the work of all lesser bodies, act on matters affecting county government, and deal in important matters with state central committees. There are over 3,000 counties in the country, and virtually all are organized by one or both parties.

District party organizations in considerable number stand between the state and local levels. They are set up in state senatorial, state representative, congressional, and state judicial districts. Naturally, their position in the party structure varies considerably from state to state and from urban to rural area.

State Central Committees.—The state central committees oversee all party machinery in the state, direct campaigns for state offices, for United States senatorships, and for state efforts in behalf of the national party tickets. State committeemen are chosen in a variety of ways, by election or by appointment, and represent legislative districts, counties, or some other subdivision. Most of the state committees are not assigned significant powers, but a few may decide whether the party shall use the convention or primary nominating method. They range in number of members from a handful in some states to 678 in California. The large committees in practice delegate powers and duties to an executive group, which makes the effective decisions. Some state committees are given authority to fill vacancies that occur after convention or primary among the party nominees for offices. Occasionally the chairman of the state central committee is a political figure of importance; perhaps more commonly he is front for a stronger man or group in the background.

The National Committee.—The national committee stands at the head of permanent party organization in the country. It is composed of one man and one woman from each state and territory; a total of the members, over one hundred for each party, most commonly are chosen by state delegations to national party conventions, but some states require that they be selected in state convention or committee, or elected in direct primary elections. Nominally, the power of the national committee is great, but increasingly in recent years it has confined its work to ratifying the presidential nominee's choice for chairman, to electing other officers, and to planning the national convention. There is little significant difference between the Republican and Democratic practice in this regard.

By long usage the national chairman is selected by the presidential nominee and formally elected by the committee. He becomes party campaign manager and directs national headquarters. An executive committee, chosen by the chairman, is delegated most of the committee's authority for the 3 years between national campaign periods. Under the control of the national chairman, the central office is manned with workers doing research, advertising, publicity, money raising; others do "stratified electioneering," appealing to special groups of voters, such as women, veterans, Negroes, farmers, laborers, and foreign-born. Both parties keep some bureaus, especially publicity, open year in and year out. The effective work of Charles Michelson, Democratic publicity chief, is credited with contributing largely to public hostility toward the Hoover administration between 1930 and 1932.

In each state the national committeeman and committeewoman handle liaison work with the state organization and help to direct patronage matters when their party holds the presidency.

Campaign Committees.—The Senatorial Campaign Committee and the Congressional Campaign Committee are maintained by each party to direct campaign efforts in behalf of party aspirants for national legislative posts. Separate bodies were established to prevent campaigning from falling wholly into executive hands. The Republicans originated the plan, forming a joint body in 1866 during the struggle between President Johnson and the congressional leaders. Subsequently the body split into separate groups for Senate and House. The Republican Senatorial Campaign Committee of today is composed of seven members chosen for 2-year terms by the Republican caucus of the Senate. The Republican Congressional Campaign Committee is composed of one Representative from each state having a Republican in the House; selection is made by the state congressional delegation. The Democratic arrangements are nearly the same.

These campaign committees function chiefly during campaigns. The task of each is to secure the reelection of old and the election of new party members to House and Senate. Each group attempts to maintain a small staff on a permanent basis. Since none has demonstrated much independent money-raising ability, each has relied for support mainly upon the party national committee. They compile the voting records of sitting members, analyze political possibilities in the various states and districts, and do other things to prepare for congressional elections.

Party Finances.—Money is of key importance in American politics. An enormous amount must be spent to reach the largest participating democratic electorate in the world. Public inertia is high, and it takes much to break it down and secure political activity. The general use of the direct primary doubles the number of elections that must be fought. Elective offices are very numerous. Terms of public officers are relatively short.

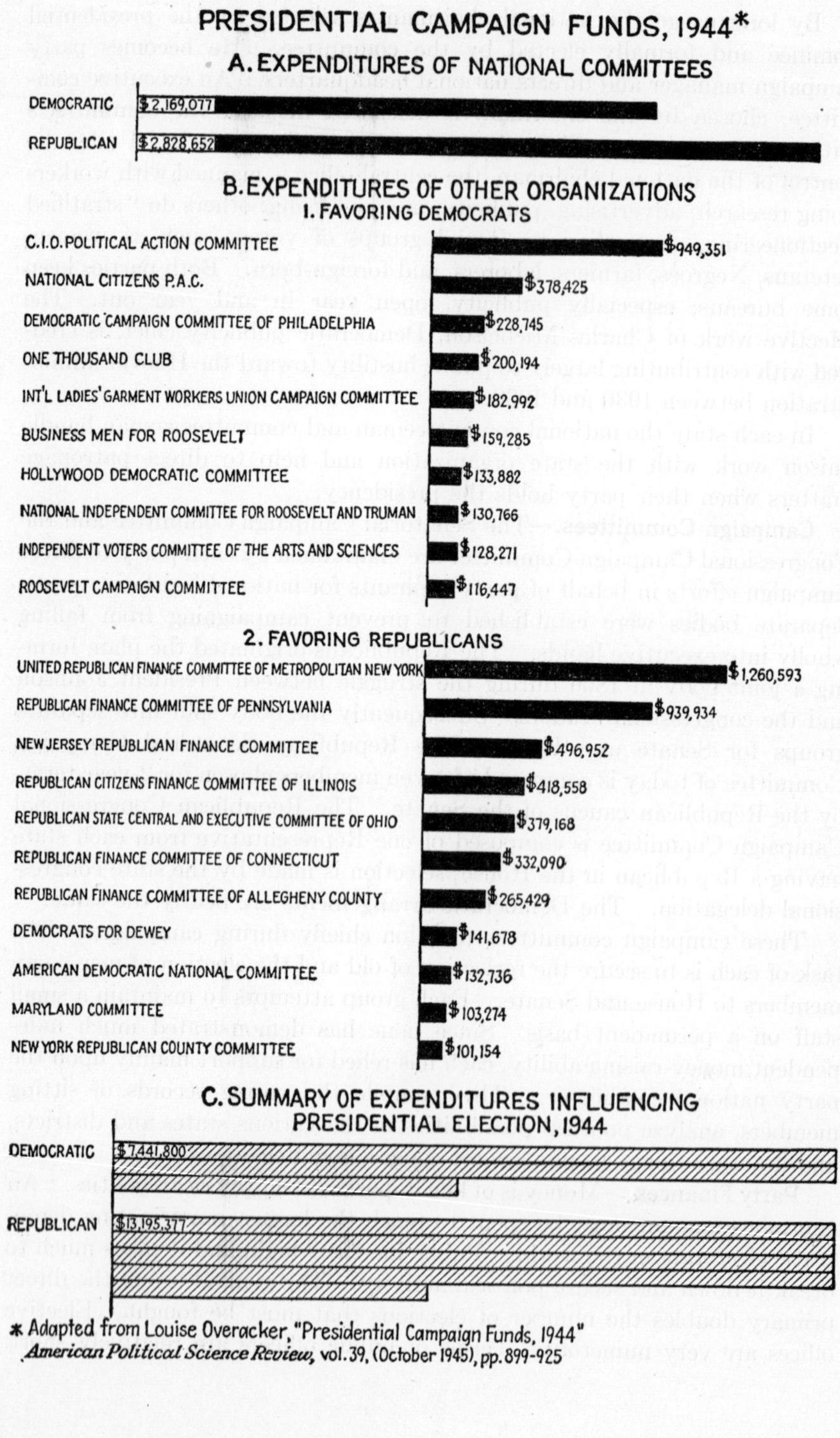
PRESIDENTIAL CAMPAIGN FUNDS, 1944*
A. EXPENDITURES OF NATIONAL COMMITTEES
DEMOCRATIC
$2,169,077
REPUBLICAN
$2,828,652
B. EXPENDITURES OF OTHER ORGANIZATIONS
1. FAVORING DEMOCRATS
C.I.O. POLITICAL ACTION COMMITTEE
$949,351
NATIONAL CITIZENS P.A.C.
$378,425
DEMOCRATIC CAMPAIGN COMMITTEE OF PHILADELPHIA
$228,745
ONE THOUSAND CLUB
$200,194
INT'L LADIES' GARMENT WORKERS UNION CAMPAIGN COMMITTEE
$182,992
BUSINESS MEN FOR ROOSEVELT
$159,285
HOLLYWOOD DEMOCRATIC COMMITTEE
$133,882
NATIONAL INDEPENDENT COMMITTEE FOR ROOSEVELT AND TRUMAN
$130,766
INDEPENDENT VOTERS COMMITTEE OF THE ARTS AND SCIENCES
$128,271
ROOSEVELT CAMPAIGN COMMITTEE
$116,447
2. FAVORING REPUBLICANS
UNITED REPUBLICAN FINANCE COMMITTEE OF METROPOLITAN NEW YORK
$1,260,593
REPUBLICAN FINANCE COMMITTEE OF PENNSYLVANIA
$939,934
NEW JERSEY REPUBLICAN FINANCE COMMITTEE
$496,952
REPUBLICAN CITIZENS FINANCE COMMITTEE OF ILLINOIS
$418,558
REPUBLICAN STATE CENTRAL AND EXECUTIVE COMMITTEE OF OHIO
$379,168
REPUBLICAN FINANCE COMMITTEE OF CONNECTICUT
$332,090
REPUBLICAN FINANCE COMMITTEE OF ALLEGHENY COUNTY
$265,429
DEMOCRATS FOR DEWEY
$141,678
AMERICAN DEMOCRATIC NATIONAL COMMITTEE
$132,736
MARYLAND COMMITTEE
$103,274
NEW YORK REPUBLICAN COUNTY COMMITTEE
$101,154
C. SUMMARY OF EXPENDITURES INFLUENCING PRESIDENTIAL ELECTION, 1944
DEMOCRATIC
$7,441,800
REPUBLICAN
$13,195,377

* Adapted from Louise Overacker, "Presidential Campaign Funds, 1944" *American Political Science Review*, vol. 39, (October 1945), pp. 899-925

It is necessary to buy the means of reaching the voters; radio time, newspaper space, and literature printing cost much money. There are no really accurate figures on total campaign costs, for no adequate system of reporting expenditures has been devised. In 1936 the two national committees reported spending amounts that totaled more than 14 million dollars; of this over 5 million was Democratic and nearly 9 million Republican. This was the largest expenditure on record, but nearly as much was spent in 1928. The 1940 amendments to the Hatch Act of 1939 forbid any party committee to spend more than 3 million dollars in one campaign, but this law was evaded by assigning excess expenditures to state and auxiliary bodies.[1] Official reports showed that both Republican and Democratic national committees spent between $2,000,000 and $2,800,000 in the 1940, 1944, and 1948 campaigns. After expenditures from other national and state groups and parties were added, the Republican 1940 total was nearly $15,000,000 and the Democratic was over $5,850,000. In 1944 the Republicans spent over $13,000,000 and Democrats nearly $7,500,000.

Political funds come from various sources. Perhaps the most meaningful classification places on one side the contributions of well-wishers genuinely interested in the cause; on the other, the donations of those who want something in return. Neither major party has succeeded in getting more than a small proportion of its revenues through small donations (1 to 10 dollars) from individuals; the Democrats made real progress in this direction in 1936 and 1940. Revenues other than individual contributions have loomed larger in recent years. Losing out on big donations, the Democrats after 1932 secured much money through high-priced "Jackson Day" dinners, book sales, and trade-union contributions. Corporations are forbidden by federal law and by most state laws to make campaign contributions. The Public Utility Holding Company Act of 1935 forbids contributions to political campaigns. Therefore, gifts from corporate and utility sources are made by officers of such concerns, who may be compensated through bonuses or expense accounts. Officeholders are always a mainstay of financial support for the party in power. The Hatch Act and civil service rules prevent the taking of forced contributions from federal officers and from state and local employees who engage in federally aided work. Occasionally a wealthy candidate is able to make a sizable contribution himself; those who are chosen for this purpose are called "fat cats."

[1] The matter of party funds is best handled by Prof. Louise Overacker in her *Money in Elections* (New York: Macmillan, 1932). Figures and analysis for 1936 and 1940 are given in her articles, "Campaign Funds in the Presidential Election of 1936," *American Political Science Review*, vol. 31 (June, 1937), pp. 473–498; "Campaign Finance in the Presidential Election of 1940," *ibid.*, vol. 35 (August, 1941), pp. 701–727; "Presidential Campaign Funds, 1944," *ibid.*, vol. 39 (October, 1945), pp. 899–925.

The principal federal law governing money in elections is the Corrupt Practices Act of 1925, as amended subsequently. One purpose of the law is to give publicity to campaign funds. Financial statements must be filed with the clerk of the House of Representatives by political committees and by candidates for federal offices. The law also sets an alternative

ECONOMIC INTERESTS OF CONTRIBUTORS TO CAMPAIGN FUNDS*

(In amounts contributed to National Committees, One Thousand Club, and United Republican Finance Committee of Metropolitan New York, 1944)

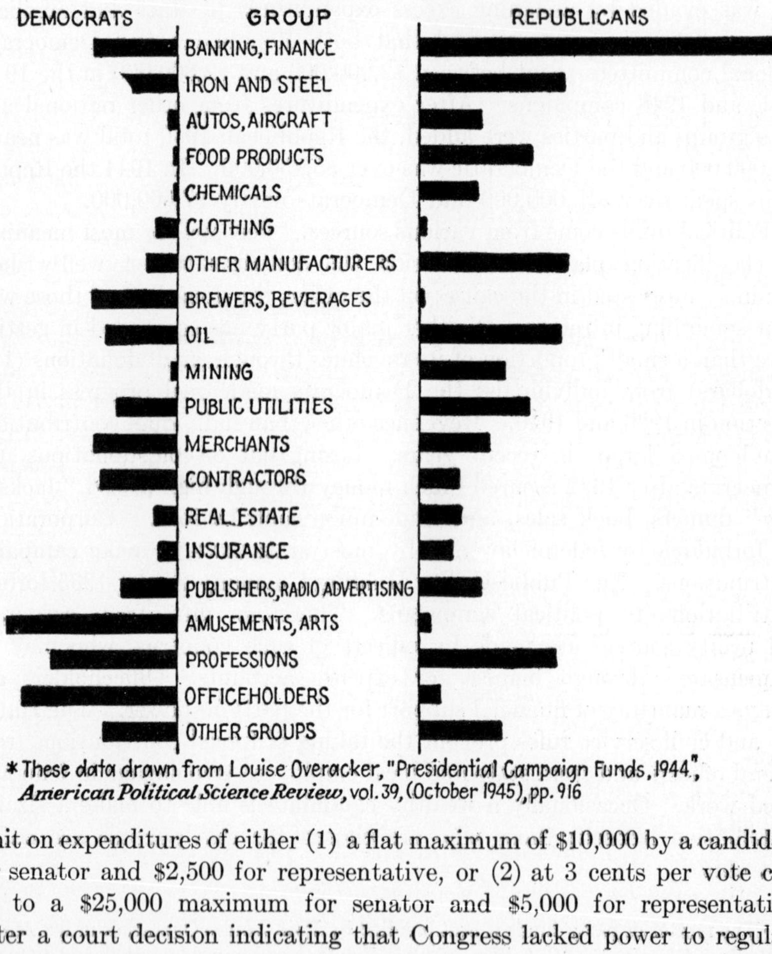

* These data drawn from Louise Overacker, "Presidential Campaign Funds, 1944", *American Political Science Review*, vol. 39, (October 1945), pp. 916

limit on expenditures of either (1) a flat maximum of $10,000 by a candidate for senator and $2,500 for representative, or (2) at 3 cents per vote cast up to a $25,000 maximum for senator and $5,000 for representative. After a court decision indicating that Congress lacked power to regulate primaries, Congress gave up all control over the nominating process, but a recent court decision appears to permit primary regulation.[1] The Hatch

[1] Newberry *v.* United States, 256 U.S. 232 (1921), was the adverse decision; United States *v.* Classic, 313 U.S. 299 (1941), was the favorable one.

Act changes of 1940 limited individual contributions to a maximum of $5,000 and limited party committee expenditure to 3 million dollars in a single campaign. Corrupt-practices laws, federal and state, are disregarded and evaded very generally. Reports filed are often put in such form that the public cannot secure desired information; many groups and candidates do not file reports at all. The limitations on expenditures by senatorial candidates are ridiculous in the large states, where $25,000 would not buy a penny post card for each voter. In many sections the real contest for office is the primary election; since federal law does not cover the primary election, there is little use in attempting to regulate an uncontested final election. The outstanding weakness of American corrupt-practices laws is not difficult to find; responsibility for spending has not been fixed. There is little use in defining either objects for which money may be spent or who may contribute or how much may be spent, when it is not determined who can spend for political purposes. American laws were copied from the British law, but the drafter here neglected the first essential of British law: no person except the candidate or the agent appointed by him may spend to further his campaign.

Machines and Bosses.—Although political parties appear essential to the proper functioning of democratic politics on a national scale, parties themselves are often controlled by a single autocrat or a group. Political parties in a big democracy are huge leviathans that must be manned and fed and directed. In parties and in areas where the civic spirit and interest are high, party affairs may be conducted on a democratic basis. Examples of democratic parties are the labor parties of Great Britain, Australia, and New Zealand, and the Cooperative Commonwealth Federation of Canada.[1] More commonly, however, party machinery in democratic countries falls under the control of a small group or an individual. A student of continental European politics has called this the "oligarchical tendency," in which control passes from the masses to professional leadership.[2]

The boss is a political leader who maintains power through corruption, spoils, and patronage. The machine is the organization through which the dominant group or individual rules. Political machines and bosses have flourished in American urban communities, utilizing legendary methods: bribery, patronage, special favors, rigged elections. During the past 20 years, however, the number of prominent bosses has declined to almost nil.

[1] See Dean E. McHenry, *The Labour Party in Transition, 1931–1938* (London: Routledge, 1938), *His Majesty's Opposition* (Berkeley and Los Angeles: University of California Press, 1940), and *The Third Force in Canada, the Cooperative Commonwealth Federation, 1932–1948* (Berkeley and Los Angeles: University of California Press, 1950).

[2] Robert Michels, *Political Parties, a Sociological Study of the Oligarchical Tendencies of Modern Democracy* (New York: Hearst's International Library Co., 1915), pp. 54*ff*.

Nonpartisanship.—Shortly after the turn of the century, criticisms of political parties were so violent that one of the progressive reforms proposed in many states was the outright abolition of parties. It was argued that, especially in local government, the issues had little relation to national party alignment, and that there was no Republican or Democratic way to pave a street. This was answered with the assertion that the vital local problems are connected with state and national issues, and that the political party performs functions without which a big democracy cannot exist.

In practice, the elimination of parties from state and local affairs by legislation has produced disappointing results. In some instances the parties have continued to exist without recognition on the ballot, as in the Minnesota legislature. In most cases, however, parties cut out of local affairs have withered on what was left of the vine; they have been so weakened by the severance of roots from local politics that they have had to live from year to year on the plasma of national-election activity. Denied the leadership of his party, the urban voter in a nonpartisan election is often completely at sea and without knowledge on the stands of candidates on public issues. Politics degenerates into irresponsibility, with interests, groups, and individuals striving for power and influence.

Seeking to rid themselves of the evils of the party system, reformers abolished the system itself, expecting to see the evils expire too. Actually, however, spoils and corruption continued, and the voter no longer had a clear alternative to accepting the officeholders in control. Instead, he was forced to grope through the long ballot, searching, often in vain, for a clue on how to vote. Deploring the trend toward nonpartisanship in local government, the late Edward M. Sait declared:

> Very soon there would be no parties anywhere in the United States, if they were left floating in the air without any local base. National organization depends ultimately upon precinct organization. The conduct of national campaigns depends upon continuous experience in fighting local campaigns. Democracy cannot live without parties and parties cannot live in the stratosphere.[1]

On the other hand, most authorities on local government favor nonpartisanship for municipal and county elections. Since most local jurisdictions that have abolished party designations are unlikely to return to partisanship, the party organization must be strengthened by other means. While the detailed steps toward restoring parties will vary from state to state, attention might be given to election of precinct leaders, to preprimary conferences, and to rigid party affiliation tests for candidates for state and congressional offices.

[1] Edward M. Sait, *American Parties and Elections* (New York: Appleton-Century, 1942), p. 242. Copyrighted by the publisher; quoted by permission.

References

Beard, Charles A.: *The American Party Battle* (New York: Macmillan, 1928).

Brooks, Robert C.: *Political Parties and Electoral Problems* (New York: Harper, 3d ed., 1933).

Bruce, Harold R.: *American Parties and Politics* (New York: Holt, 3d ed., 1936).

Douglas, Paul H.: *The Coming of a New Party* (New York: Whittlesey, 1932).

Fine, Nathan: *Labor and Farmer Parties, 1828–1928* (New York: Rand School, 1928).

Fisher, Margaret J.: *Parties and Politics in the Local Community* (Washington: National Council for the Social Studies, 1945).

Forthal, Sonya: *Cogwheels of Democracy, a Study of the Precinct Captain* (New York: William-Frederick Press, 1946).

Gosnell, Harold F.: *Grassroots Politics* (Washington: American Council on Public Affairs, 1942).

——— *Machine Politics: Chicago Model* (Chicago: University of Chicago Press, 1937).

Herring, E. Pendleton: *The Politics of Democracy* (New York: Norton, 1940).

Hesseltine, William B.: *The Rise and Fall of Third Parties . . .* (Washington: Public Affairs Press, 1948).

Hicks, John D.: *The Populist Revolt* (Minneapolis: University of Minnesota Press, 1931).

Holcombe, Arthur N.: *The Middle Classes in American Politics* (Cambridge, Mass.: Harvard University Press, 1940).

Kent, Frank R.: *The Democratic Party, a History* (New York: Appleton-Century-Crofts, 1928).

Key, Vladimir O.: *Politics, Parties, and Pressure Groups* (New York: Crowell, 2d ed., 1947).

McKean, Dayton D.: *The Boss: the Hague Machine in Action* (Boston: Houghton Mifflin, 1940).

——— *Party and Pressure Politics* (Boston: Houghton Mifflin, 1949).

Merriam, Charles E.: *Chicago: a More Intimate View of Urban Politics* (New York: Macmillan, 1929).

——— and Harold F. Gosnell: *The American Party System* (New York: Macmillan, 4th ed., 1949).

Minault, Sylvain S.: *Corrupt Practices Legislation in the 48 States* (Chicago: Council of State Governments, 1942).

Morse, Anson D.: *Parties and Party Leaders* (Boston: Marshall Jones, 1923).

Myers, William S.: *The Republican Party, A History* (New York: Appleton-Century-Crofts, 2d ed., 1931).

Odegard, Peter H., and E. Allen Helms: *American Politics, A Study in Political Dynamics* (New York: Harper, 2d ed., 1947).

Ostrogorski, M.: *Democracy and the Party System in the United States* (New York: Macmillan, 1910).

Overacker, Louise: *Money in Elections* (New York: Macmillan, 1932).

——— *Presidential Campaign Funds* (Boston: Boston University Press, 1946).

Peel, Roy V.: *The Political Clubs of New York City* (New York: Putnam, 1935).

Pollock, James K.: *Party Campaign Funds* (New York: Knopf, 1926).

Robinson, Edgar E.: *Evolution of American Political Parties* (New York: Harcourt Brace, 1924).

Rohlfing, Charles C., and James C. Charlesworth (eds.): "Parties and Politics: 1948," *Annals of the American Academy of Political and Social Science*, vol. 259 (September, 1948).

REDDIG, WILLIAM M.: *Tom's Town: Kansas City and the Pendergast Legend* (Philadelphia: Lippincott, 1947).

SAIT, EDWARD M. (revised by Howard R. Penniman): *American Parties and Elections* (New York: Appleton-Century-Crofts, 4th ed., 1947).

SCHATTSCHNEIDER, ELMER E.: *Party Government* (New York: Rinehart, 1942).

ZINK, HAROLD: *City Bosses in the United States* (Durham. N. C.: Duke University Press, 1930).

TEXT-FILM

The following McGraw-Hill 35mm silent filmstrip is recommended for use with Chaps. 10 and 11 of this text.

Political Parties and Elections. The role of the individual, political party, and public opinion in nominations and elections. The right to vote; various forms of the ballot.

Chapter 11

SUFFRAGE, NOMINATIONS, AND ELECTIONS

Independently of all these considerations, it is a personal injustice to withhold from any one, unless for the prevention of greater evils, the ordinary privilege of having his voice reckoned in the disposal of affairs in which he has the same interest as other people. If he is compelled to pay, if he may be compelled to fight, if he is required implicitly to obey, he should be legally entitled to be told what for; to have his consent asked, and his opinion counted at its worth, though not at more than its worth.

John Stuart Mill, *Utilitarianism, Liberty and Representative Government.*[1]

THE RIGHT TO VOTE

Federal Requirements.—Matters pertaining to suffrage are regulated chiefly by the states. Four federal requirements are set forth in the Constitution. (1) Those people permitted to vote for the most numerous branch of the state legislature are allowed in each state to participate also in elections of federal officers. (2) The Fourteenth Amendment establishes a penalty (reduction of congressional representation) that might be invoked by Congress against any state that disfranchised a proportion of its adult male population, but this penalty has never been applied. (3) The Fifteenth Amendment forbids states to deny or to abridge the right to vote on account of race, color, or previous condition of servitude. (4) The Nineteenth Amendment prohibits discrimination because of sex. By these three amendments the amount of state discretion in suffrage matters has been reduced over the years, and the original reliance upon state definition of who might vote has been altered.

State Prerequisites for Voting.[2]—1. One universal requirement for voting is citizenship. All states now insist that a person must be a full-fledged citizen of the United States before exercising the franchise. Several states formerly permitted aliens to vote if they had declared their intention to become citizens.

2. A minimum voting age of twenty-one long prevailed in all states, but in 1944 Georgia reduced its voting age to eighteen. During the Second World War the paradox involved in drafting young men of eighteen to fight for their country, yet denying them the vote until they were twenty-one

[1] (New York: Dutton, 1910), p. 279. First published in 1861.

[2] Factual data are drawn from *The Book of the States, 1948–1949*, pp. 96–97. See current issue for latest information.

inspired a campaign in several states to reduce the voting age. Although only Georgia responded to the "vote at eighteen" movement, the return of decorated veterans of the war, including many officers, who are still too young to vote may stimulate action in other states. It has been argued that the eighteen to twenty-one group is as alert and as able to understand political issues as the age group seventy-five years and over, yet no one has suggested seriously that a maximum age for voting be established. If enfranchised in all states, the eighteen to twenty-one group would add approximately 8 million new voters to the American electorate.

3. Another qualification imposed in all states is a requisite period of residence. Most states require that a person must have lived in the state for 1 year, but several of the North and East demand only 6 months' residence, and a handful of states in the deep South insist upon 2 years. There are also requirements of residence in counties and in precincts; the median is about 90 days in the county and 30 days in the polling district.

4. Registration is almost uniformly required; only two states have no registration plans in operation, but several require only urban voters to sign up in advance. The purpose of registration is to prevent fraudulent voting.[1] It requires that voters be enrolled in advance of an election, and permits the inspection of the rolls by interested persons. A majority of the states have now adopted the permanent type of registration, under which a voter, once enrolled, remains on the rolls until he dies, moves, fails to vote in an important election, or otherwise disqualifies himself. A few states still retain the periodic system, which calls for a complete reregistration every year, 2 years, 4 years, or 6 years. Because periodic registration is more expensive and more trouble for the public, it is generally considered inferior to permanent registration.

5. The literacy test is employed in some form in nineteen states. In some states this test of ability to read and write is carefully administered; it represents a defense against an uninformed electorate and a proper barrier against fraud, for the votes of illiterates might be bought and delivered in the presence of their assisters. On the other hand, it is frequently used unfairly to disfranchise political enemies or Negroes.

6. Many states disqualify various groups of persons from voting because of insanity, idiocy, feeble-mindedness, or conviction of a felony.

7. Evidence of tax payment is still required in several states. In the early days of the republic, the right to vote was reserved carefully for those who held property. As the spirit of democracy spread, property qualifications were lessened and repealed. Today only a few vestigial property qualifications remain, usually as alternatives for other requirements. Seven states, however, have retained poll taxes as prerequisites to voting.

[1] Joseph P. Harris, *Registration of Voters in the United States* (Washington: Brookings, 1929) is the standard work on registration.

Because the poll tax has become one of the most controversial of questions concerning the right to vote, fuller examination is required.

Poll Taxes under Fire.—Bitter controversy has been aroused by recent attempts to eliminate state poll taxes as prerequisites to voting in Alabama, Arkansas, Mississippi, South Carolina, Tennessee, Texas, and Virginia. They are head taxes of from one to two dollars on each adult (or each male) within specified age groups. In order to discourage poll-tax payment, usually no bills are sent out and little effort is made to collect; payments are often due far in advance of elections. Alabama has a cumulative tax; before a person can vote he must pay up delinquent taxes for each year missed between the ages of twenty-one and forty-five, a maximum of $36.

The effect of the poll tax has been to disfranchise poor people, both white and Negro, in the poll-tax states. Partly because of the poll tax, participation in elections is very low in the states using this device. In 1940 the eight states with poll taxes accounted for less than 6 per cent of the major party vote for presidential electors, although they had more than 18 per cent of the nation's population. Critics of the poll tax have stressed the corrupting influence of this requirement for voting. The participating electorate is so small that vested interests or political machines may control elections by buying poll-tax receipts for a few hundred persons. The basic argument against the poll tax is that voting is a right that should not be abridged through lack of capacity to pay.

Organizations[1] seeking the elimination of the poll tax have concentrated their attack on three principal fronts. First, they have sought congressional legislation to abolish the poll tax in federal elections. First introduced in the House of Representatives in 1940, the bill would have outlawed poll taxes as fostering pernicious political activities, under the power of Congress to control the "manner" of electing senators and representatives. In various forms it was reintroduced in the Seventy-seventh, Seventy-eighth, Seventy-ninth, Eightieth, and Eighty-first Congresses, and passed by the House of Representatives each time but it was obstructed in the Senate through filibuster and threat of filibuster. Opponents of the legislation charge that the bill is unconstitutional and invasive of state rights. Proponents cite eminent legal authorities who assert that the Federal government has adequate power to keep the states from denying the franchise to citizens on grounds of nonpayment of the poll tax, which is not a true "qualification."[2]

[1] The leading ones are the National Committee to Abolish the Poll Tax, Washington, D.C.; the Southern Electoral Reform League, with headquarters in Atlanta, Ga.; and the Southern Conference Educational Fund, with offices in New Orleans, La. The last-mentioned publishes a monthly journal, *The Southern Patriot*.

[2] The question of constitutionality is discussed at length in Senate Hearings. See United States Senate, Committee in the Judiciary, *Hearings . . . on S. 1280*, 77th Cong.,

SUFFRAGE IN POLL TAX STATES

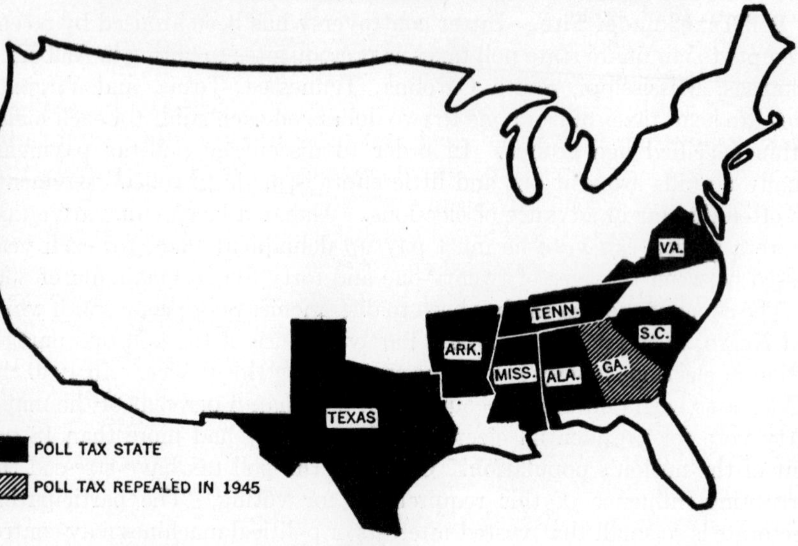

POTENTIAL VOTERS WHO VOTED IN THE 1944 PRESIDENTIAL ELECTIONS

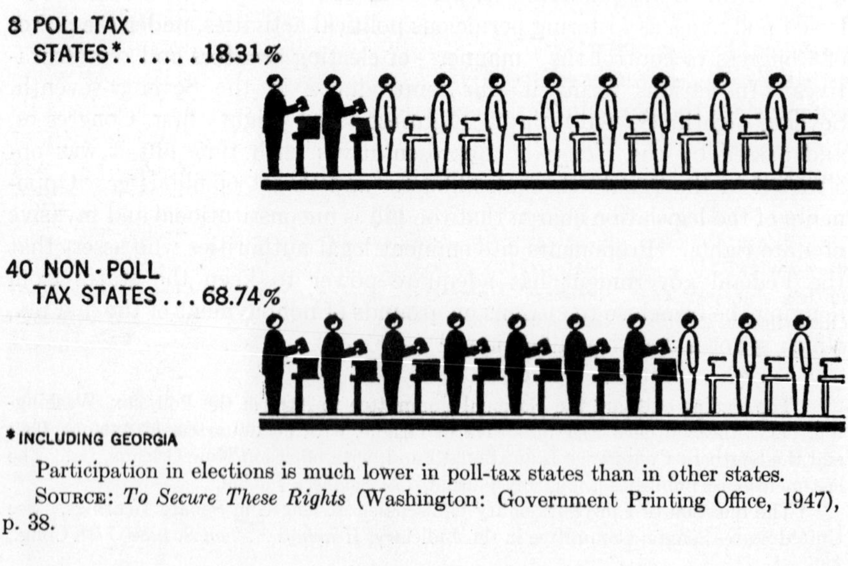

*INCLUDING GEORGIA

Participation in elections is much lower in poll-tax states than in other states.

Source: *To Secure These Rights* (Washington: Government Printing Office, 1947), p. 38.

Second, Southern states are being urged to repeal their poll-tax laws. Four of them have removed the poll tax since the First World War: North Carolina in 1920, Louisiana in 1934, Florida in 1937, and Georgia in 1945. A fifth state, Tennessee, in 1943 repealed its poll-tax law by legislative action, but the state Supreme Court declared the repeal void because the law was "constitutionally mandatory."[1] The Georgia legislature, strongly urged by Governor Ellis Arnall, abolished the poll tax of that state in 1945, but it will require a constitutional amendment in each of the remaining poll-tax states to accomplish repeal.

Third, court proceedings are being instituted to test the constitutionality of poll taxes in both state and federal courts.

The White Primary.—The most recent and effective device developed by the Southern states to disfranchise colored people is the white primary. Since the Democratic party enjoys an almost unbroken supremacy in the states of the deep South, voting in the Democratic primary is far more important than voting in the general election. The earliest barriers to Negro participation in Democratic party affairs were erected by party rule. In 1923, however, the Texas legislature enacted a law forbidding Negro participation in Democratic primary elections. An El Paso Negro physician, denied the right to vote in the 1924 Democratic primary, brought suit in the courts and secured a decision from the United States Supreme Court declaring the Texas law a violation of the equal-protection clause of the Fourteenth Amendment.[2] Then the Texas legislature repealed the voided statute and substituted a provision that the executive committee of each party might prescribe the qualifications for party membership. After the Democratic party banned Negro participation by party rule, the validity of the delegation of this authority was tested in the courts. The Supreme Court again ruled that equal protection had been denied.[3] Subsequently the state convention of the party limited the primary to white voters; since the party in Texas is a private association which conducts its own primaries, the Court held that it could exclude colored people without violation of equal protection.[4] Finally, this decision was reversed in 1944

2d Sess. (Washington: Government Printing Office, 1942); and *Hearings* . . . on *HR 7*, 78th Cong., 1st Sess. (Washington: Government Printing Office, 1943). The issues were reviewed in United States House of Representatives, House Administration Committee, *Anti-poll Tax Legislation, Hearings* . . ., 80th Cong., 1st Sess. (Washington: Government Printing Office, 1947), and Senate Committee on Rules and Administration, *Poll Tax, Hearings* . . ., 80th Cong., 2nd Sess. (Washington: Government Printing Office, 1948).

[1] Biggs *v.* Beeler, 173 S.W.2d 144, 946 (1943). On general problem see Henry N. Williams, "The Poll Tax and Constitutional Problems Involved in Its Repeal," *University of Chicago Law Review*, vol. 11 (February, 1944), pp. 177–183.

[2] Nixon *v.* Herndon, 273 U.S. 536 (1927).

[3] Nixon *v.* Condon, 286 U.S. 73 (1932).

[4] Grovey *v.* Townsend, 295 U.S. 45 (1935).

when the Supreme Court declared invalid the same rules of the Texas Democratic party that forbade Negro voting, on the ground that the Classic case fused general and primary elections into a single instrumentality.[1] Despite this ruling, which voided all or virtually all the white primaries in the Southern states, few Negroes were permitted to vote in the 1944 primaries of the South. South Carolina immediately undertook to repeal all statutory references to primaries, hoping thus to establish the wholly private character of the political party and its primary. The indications are that the white primary is far from abandoned.

METHODS OF NOMINATING CANDIDATES

Early Presidential Nominations.—No nominating methods were necessary in the first three presidential elections. Members of the electoral college considered themselves free agents but managed to agree without difficulty upon Washington twice and Adams once. The emergence of political parties by 1800 brought with it the necessity of some machinery for making the party's choice.

The congressional caucus emerged quite naturally to fill the need. Composed of the party's senators and representatives in Congress, it was easy to convene and reasonably representative of party sentiment. The chief weakness of this scheme of nominating, however, was that it denied representation to states that had no congressmen of a particular party. In 1824, after the Federalist party had expired, the Democratic-Republicans in congressional caucus chose Crawford of Georgia; three other aspirants of the same party, Jackson, John Quincy Adams, and Clay, entered their candidacies. The election was thrown to the House of Representatives, which chose Adams, and the congressional caucus was badly discredited.

The national convention, composed of delegates from the various states, replaced the congressional caucus as a nominating body for the election of 1832. The Antimasonic party first employed the device in 1831; both the new National Republicans and Jackson's Democrats adopted this method which has been used since that time.

National Party Conventions.—The national conventions have never been governed by federal law. For 20 years, between 1921 and 1941, the Supreme Court decision, Newberry *v.* United States, stood as a barrier to congressional attempts to regulate the nominating process.[2] A recent decision, United States *v.* Classic, appears to mark a reversal of the court's attitude.[3] No attempt, however, has yet been made by Congress to utilize

[1] Smith *v.* Allwright, 321 U.S. 649 (1944).

[2] 256 U.S. 232 (1921). Congress ceased attempting to legislate regarding spending in primary campaigns after this adverse decision.

[3] 313 U.S. 299 (1941). The Classic case concerned prosecution for frauds perpetrated in a primary election.

this renewed power. The only legal control is exercised by the states, which by law may establish methods of selecting delegates as well as rules governing their conduct.

When a convention will be held is determined largely by custom. Republicans meet around the middle of June, and Democrats about two weeks later. The precise date is set by the national committee.

Where the convention will meet is decided by the national committee, but the decision rests upon several factors:

1. Financial inducement is offered by various cities; in recent years around $200,000 has been paid by business people of the successful city to secure a major party convention.

2. Strategic location of a city in a pivotal state or section is highly important, for each party hopes to arouse support in the region of the convention city.

3. Facilities and accessibility, including hotel, restaurant, and transportation services on an adequate scale and a mammoth meeting hall are necessary.

Convention Representation and Delegates.—The basis of representation in national conventions traditionally has been two delegates for each senator and representative from each state.[1] Since 1916 the Republicans have reduced the representation of Southern states. At present this plan gives one district delegate from each congressional district that polls at least 1,000 votes for a Republican candidate at the last election, plus one additional delegate if the district gave the Republican candidate 10,000 or more votes, and four delegates (two for each senator) at large plus three additional delegates for each state that went Republican in the last presidential election or elected a Republican senator 2 years later. (Congressmen at large, if any, entitle the state to two more delegates.) For example, Michigan's representation in the 1948 Republican convention was figured as follows:

17	One for each congressional district (all polled 1,000 or more Republican votes)
17	Additional because each district gave Republican candidates 10,000 votes or more in 1944 or 1946
4	At large (two for each senator)
3	Additional because Michigan elected a Republican senator in 1946
41	Total

[1] As used here, delegate means vote in convention. In order to honor party bigwigs, the state organizations often send huge delegations to national conventions, each individual casting only a fraction of one vote. In the Democratic convention of 1940, one district in Mississippi sent 54 delegates to cast its two votes; each delegate had 1/27 of a vote. That same convention adopted a rule, effective in 1944, that no delegate may have less than one-half vote.

In 1948 the Republican convention had a total voting strength of 1,094 and in 1944, 1,058. In 1940 the Democrats yielded to Southern pressure and provided a modest bonus for states showing Democratic voting strength. Each state that goes Democratic in a presidential election is given two extra votes at large in the national convention 4 years later. This new scheme

THE PRESIDENTIAL PRIMARY
SHORT BALLOT FOR DELEGATES INDICATING PREFERENCE: CALIFORNIA

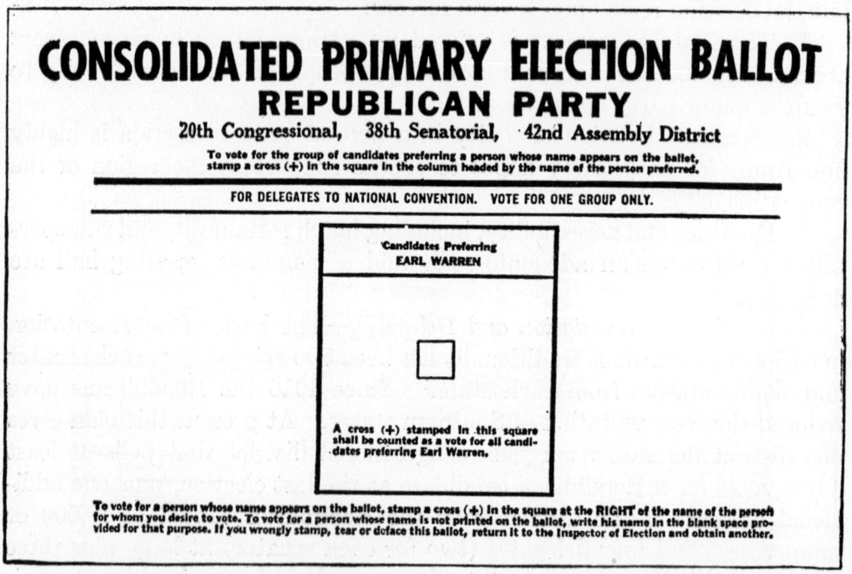

CONSOLIDATED PRIMARY ELECTION BALLOT
REPUBLICAN PARTY
20th Congressional, 38th Senatorial, 42nd Assembly District

To vote for the group of candidates preferring a person whose name appears on the ballot, stamp a cross (+) in the square in the column headed by the name of the person preferred.

FOR DELEGATES TO NATIONAL CONVENTION. VOTE FOR ONE GROUP ONLY.

Candidates Preferring
EARL WARREN

A cross (+) stamped in this square shall be counted as a vote for all candidates preferring Earl Warren.

To vote for a person whose name appears on the ballot, stamp a cross (+) in the square at the RIGHT of the name of the person for whom you desire to vote. To vote for a person whose name is not printed on the ballot, write his name in the blank space provided for that purpose. If you wrongly stamp, tear or deface this ballot, return it to the Inspector of Election and obtain another.

California has long elected delegates to the party national conventions on an at-large basis. In the 1944 presidential primary the state eliminated from the ballot the names of the individual candidates for delegate and adopted a presidential primary "short ballot." As shown above, only the names of the presidential aspirants appear on the ballot.

went into effect for the 1944 convention and increased the total number of votes from 1,094 in 1940 to 1,176 in 1944 and to 1,234 in 1948. The state of Washington, for example, had its votes in the 1948 Democratic convention computed as follows:

12	Two for each congressional district
4	At large (two for each senator)
4	Bonus because state went Democratic in 1944
20	Total

Delegates are selected in two ways:[1] (1) state and district conventions or party committees, used in about three-fourths of the states, utilize state and

[1] A convenient compilation is that of Edwin A. Halsey, *Manner of Selecting Delegates to National Political Conventions with Information on States Holding Presidential Primaries* (Washington: Government Printing Office, 1944). He reports that thirty-two states provided for the party convention method of selecting delegates, thirteen had presidential primaries, and three used a combination of the two.

congressional-district machinery to choose delegates and often to direct how they shall vote; (2) presidential primaries, used in approximately one-fourth of the states, involve choice directly by the electorate. The first method is regaining favor, largely because it is flexible and provides maximum bargaining power for state interests. Two states use a combination of the two. Two main forms of the presidential primary are these: (1) election of delegates, who may be pledged or unpledged, and (2) popular

THE PRESIDENTIAL PRIMARY
LONG BALLOT FOR DELEGATES INDICATING PREFERENCE: OHIO

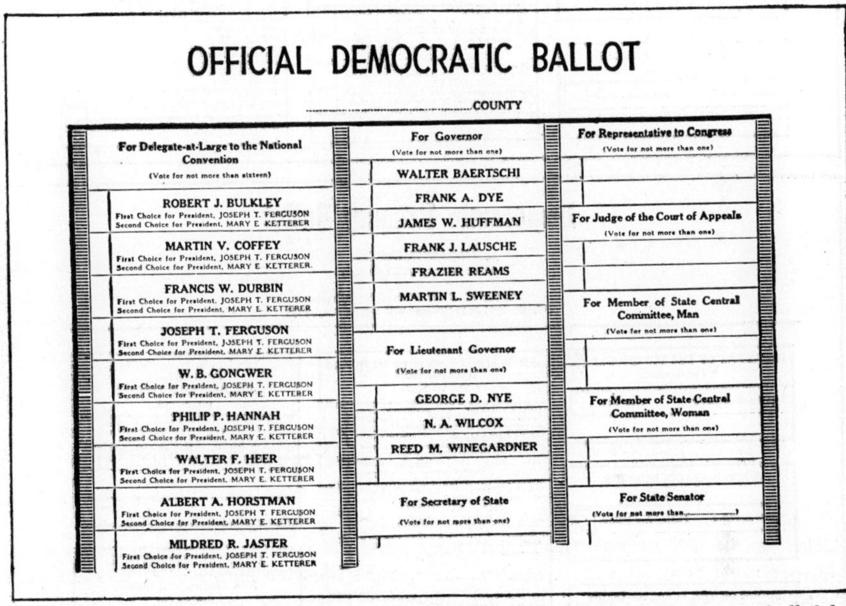
OFFICIAL DEMOCRATIC BALLOT

................................COUNTY

For Delegate-at-Large to the National Convention
(Vote for not more than sixteen)

ROBERT J. BULKLEY
First Choice for President, JOSEPH T. FERGUSON
Second Choice for President, MARY E. KETTERER

MARTIN V. COFFEY
First Choice for President, JOSEPH T. FERGUSON
Second Choice for President, MARY E. KETTERER

FRANCIS W. DURBIN
First Choice for President, JOSEPH T. FERGUSON
Second Choice for President, MARY E. KETTERER

JOSEPH T. FERGUSON
First Choice for President, JOSEPH T. FERGUSON
Second Choice for President, MARY E. KETTERER

W. B. GONGWER
First Choice for President, JOSEPH T. FERGUSON
Second Choice for President, MARY E. KETTERER

PHILIP P. HANNAH
First Choice for President, JOSEPH T. FERGUSON
Second Choice for President, MARY E. KETTERER

WALTER F. HEER
First Choice for President, JOSEPH T. FERGUSON
Second Choice for President, MARY E. KETTERER

ALBERT A. HORSTMAN
First Choice for President, JOSEPH T. FERGUSON
Second Choice for President, MARY E. KETTERER

MILDRED R. JASTER
First Choice for President, JOSEPH T. FERGUSON
Second Choice for President, MARY E. KETTERER

For Governor
(Vote for not more than one)

WALTER BAERTSCHI
FRANK A. DYE
JAMES W. HUFFMAN
FRANK J. LAUSCHE
FRAZIER REAMS
MARTIN L. SWEENEY

For Lieutenant Governor
(Vote for not more than one)

GEORGE D. NYE
N. A. WILCOX
REED M. WINEGARDNER

For Secretary of State
(Vote for not more than one)

For Representative to Congress
(Vote for not more than one)

For Judge of the Court of Appeals
(Vote for not more than one)

For Member of State Central Committee, Man
(Vote for not more than one)

For Member of State Central Committee, Woman
(Vote for not more than one)

For State Senator
(Vote for not more than..................)

Ohio has retained the long presidential primary ballot, listing the names of all delegates, together with the first and second choices for President of each. Almost invariably Ohio delegates to national conventions are pledged to "favorite sons" who are not serious contenders for the presidential nomination. With the delegation pledged to an obscure "favorite son," the best possible deal is made with one of the leading aspirants for the nomination at the convention.

expression of preference among presidential aspirants. A few states provide for both. The presidential primary is losing favor. Even in its heyday (1924 with 24 states) it was not a decisive force. Leading candidates ignore the primaries (as did Landon in 1936) or fail utterly in them (as did Hoover in 1928), yet secure the nomination without difficulty. A strong tendency is noted for states using the presidential primary to select delegates pledged to a "favorite son," some man from the home state. Sometimes this tactic is employed in a serious attempt to call the country's attention to his talents, but more often it is a subterfuge through which

THE PRESIDENTIAL PRIMARY

Preference Vote and Election of Delegates: Pennsylvania

Republican Primary Ballot

First Election District, Second Ward
CITY OF PITTSBURGH

County of Allegheny, State of Pennsylvania
Primary Held on the Twenty-fifth Day of April, 1944

PRESIDENT OF THE UNITED STATES Vote for One

UNITED STATES SENATOR Vote for One	
James J. Davis	Allegheny County

DELEGATE-AT-LARGE TO NATIONAL CONVENTION Vote for Four	
Edward Martin (Does not promise to support popular choice of party in the State for President)	Washington County
G. Mason Owlett (Does not promise to support popular choice of party in the State for President)	Tioga County
M. Harvey Taylor (Does not promise to support popular choice of party in the State for President)	Dauphin County
Marion Margery Scranton (Does not promise to support popular choice of party in the State for President)	Lackawanna County

DELEGATE TO NATIONAL CONVENTION 32nd Congressional District Vote for Two	
Harry A. Estep (Does not promise to support popular choice of party in the 32nd District for President)	18th Ward, Pittsburgh
James F. Malone, Jr. (Does not promise to support popular choice of party in the 32nd District for President)	5th Ward, Pittsburgh
George F. Otto (Does not promise to support popular choice of party in the 32nd District for President)	2nd Ward, Pittsburgh
Paul F. Hanzel (Does not promise to support popular choice of party in the 32nd District for President)	23rd Ward, Pittsburgh

Democratic Primary Ballot

Third Election District
BOROUGH OF ASPINWALL

County of Allegheny, State of Pennsylvania
Primary Held on the Twenty-fifth Day of April, 1944

PRESIDENT OF THE UNITED STATES Vote for One	
Franklin D. Roosevelt	New York

UNITED STATES SENATOR Vote for One	
Francis J. Myers	Philadelphia County

JUDGE OF THE SUPREME COURT Vote for One	
Charles Alvin Jones	Allegheny County

DELEGATE-AT-LARGE TO NATIONAL CONVENTION Vote for Twelve	
Joseph F. Guffey (Promises to support popular choice of party in the State for President)	Allegheny County
Emma Guffey Miller (Promises to support popular choice of party in the State for President)	Butler County
John J. Kane (Promises to support popular choice of party in the State for President)	Allegheny County
Frank C. Walker (Promises to support popular choice of party in the State for President)	Lackawanna County
Philip H. Murray (Promises to support popular choice of party in the State for President)	Allegheny County
Matthew H. McCloskey, Jr. (Promises to support popular choice of party in the State for President)	Montgomery Co.
Francis Biddle (Promises to support popular choice of party in the State for President)	Philadelphia County
Allen K. Grim (Promises to support popular choice of party in the State for President)	Berks County
A. P. Barnum (Promises to support popular choice of party in the State for President)	Washington County
David L. Lawrence (Promises to support popular choice of party in the State for President)	Allegheny County
Meredith Meyers (Promises to support popular choice of party in the State for President)	Mifflin County
William C. Bullitt (Promises to support popular choice of party in the State for President)	Philadelphia County

DELEGATE TO NATIONAL CONVENTION 30th Congressional District Vote for Two	
Irwin D. Wolf (Promises to support popular choice of party in the 30th District for President)	Fox Chapel Borough
Robert C. Malcolm (Promises to support popular choice of party in the 30th District for President)	West Deer Township

ALTERNATE DELEGATE TO NATIONAL CONVENTION 30th Congressional District Vote for Two	
Nellie Chillcott (Promises to support popular choice of party in the 30th District for President)	21st Ward, Pittsburgh
Edward D. Johnson (Promises to support popular choice of party in the 30th District for President)	27th Ward, Pittsburgh

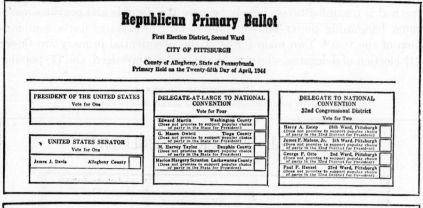

These portions of 1944 Pennsylvania primary ballots illustrate several points regarding presidential primaries: (1) The voter is given an opportunity to vote for *both* his presidential preferences and his delegates to the convention. (2) Leading aspirants for the presidential nominations are reluctant to enter presidential primaries. Note especially the absence from the Republican ballot of Willkie, Dewey, Bricker, and Stassen—all of whom had their "hats in the ring" at the time. (3) The delegates-at-large are mainly persons of national prominence, especially those on the Democratic ballot.

a state delegation may remain quite free to shift to a likely candidate who gives assurances that he will reward the state properly.

National Convention Procedure.—The order of business is much the same in both party gatherings. The national chairman calls the meeting to order. A temporary convention chairman is chosen and he gives the "keynote" address. Committees of the convention are set up with one delegate from every state and territory on each committee. The credentials committee determines which are the official delegates for the final roll call; occasionally there is a contest over the authenticity of a delegation's credentials, and control of this committee may affect the choice of candidate for the presidency. The committee on permanent organization brings in the slate of convention officers; its rejection may forecast a revolt against a leading presidential aspirant. A rules-and-order-of-business

THE PRESIDENTIAL PRIMARY, 1944*

A. MANDATORY PRIMARY STATES

State	Date of primary	Type of primary
California..........	May 16	Delegates elected; may be pledged.
Illinois.............	Apr. 11	District delegates elected; preference vote; at-large chosen by convention.
Maryland..........	May 1	Preference vote.
Massachusetts......	Apr. 25	Delegates elected; may be pledged.
Nebraska..........	Apr. 11	Delegates elected; preference vote.
New Hampshire.....	Mar. 14	Delegates elected; may be pledged.
New Jersey........	May 16	Delegates elected; may be pledged.
New York..........	Mar. 28	District delegates elected; at-large chosen by convention.
Ohio...............	May 9	Delegates elected; preference vote.
Oregon............	May 19	Delegates elected; preference vote.
Pennsylvania.......	Apr. 25	Delegates elected; preference vote.
South Dakota......	May 2	Delegates elected; pledged.
West Virginia......	May 9	Delegates elected; preference vote.
Wisconsin..........	Apr. 4	Delegates elected; preference vote.

B. OPTIONAL PRIMARY OR CONVENTION STATES

State	Date of primary	Type of primary
Alabama..........	May 2	Delegates elected.
Arkansas..........	Two months before conventions.	Preference vote.
Florida............	May 2	Delegates elected; preference vote.
Georgia...........	July 4	Preference vote.

* Adapted from United States Department of Commerce, Bureau of the Census, *Elections Calendar for 1944* (Washington: Bureau of the Census, 1944), pp. 6–22.

committee proposes rules of procedure usually identical with those of previous conventions. Finally, the platform-and-resolutions committee drafts the party declaration of principles and policies. The report on the platform is often hotly debated, but usually the majority report is adopted.

Choosing candidates for President and Vice-President comes as the final important action. The roll is called by states, and delegations place in nomination the favored aspirants; this place on the agenda is occasion for elaborate oratory by nominators and seconders. When all contenders for the nomination are before the convention, the first polling begins by states in alphabetical order. Often, especially in Republican conventions, some candidate secures the requisite majority on the first ballot. Sometimes conventions deadlock and many votes are required; the Democrats took 103 ballots in 1924 before the warring Smith and McAdoo factions could agree on John W. Davis as a compromise candidate.

Voting is done by states, but in Republican conventions delegates may be polled individually. The Democrats have a unit rule under which a majority of a state delegation may cast the full vote of a state (unless forbidden by that state's law). In 1936 the Democrats abolished the companion two-thirds rule, though Southern Democrats clung to it as vital to the protection of the minority and as an assurance against party splits. Its repeal, and the retention of the unit rule, makes likely in future Democratic conventions quick victories for aspirants with plurality support.

The vice-presidential contest may be decided by a number of considerations. The successful presidential aspirant may have traded support with another who receives the vice-presidential nomination (Garner in 1932). Or balance will be sought for the ticket by nominating one who contrasts with the presidential nominee in section, religion, personality, policy, and other attributes (Robinson in 1928).

Reform of the National Convention.—The national convention is one of our most criticized political institutions. To make the all-important choices of who shall be major party nominees for the presidency, we have two aggregations of a thousand or more delegates, chosen by miscellaneous means unlikely to produce majority choice, and meeting in an atmosphere of colossal clowning and high-pressure methods, wholly unregulated by federal law. Woodrow Wilson, in his first annual message to the Congress in 1913, urged the enactment of legislation to provide primary elections so that voters could select nominees for the presidency without the intervention of nominating conventions.[1] He suggested that platforms be made by a new type of party convention composed of nominees for the Senate and House, national committeemen, and the presidential nominee.

[1] James D. Richardson (ed.), *Messages and Papers of the Presidents* (New York: Bureau of National Literature, 20 vols., 1897–1916), vol. 18, p. 7910.

Although the Congress took no action, the states moved rapidly to legislate regarding the selection of delegates and the expression of preferences by the electorate. After the Newberry decision it was assumed for 20 years that Congress lacked power to regulate the nominating process. During this interim, presidential primary enthusiasm waned, and the old-fashioned national convention with state and district convention-selected delegates has returned to favor. Professor Overacker classifies proposals for a national presidential primary into three: (1) combine primary with existing conventions; (2) have existing convention propose nominees but submit to primary for ratification; (3) eliminate the convention and provide for direct nation-wide primary.[1] After examining the difficulties connected with each proposal, Overacker concludes that no plan is very promising.

More drastic proposals are likely to attract the attention necessary to secure reform on a national basis. Restoration of the congressional caucus (perhaps with nominees for Senate and House instead of sitting members) would help bring the legislative and executive branches closer together and assure greater deliberation and dignity. The whole question of nominating method may best be dealt with in connection with reform of the mode of election of the President. Of the several plans proposed, that of Wilson for a nation-wide direct primary might be most satisfactory, but it would require a preferential voting plan to assure majority choice.

Nominations for Congressional and State Offices.—The development of nominating methods may be indicated chronologically. Self-announcement and selection by informal caucus was used in the early days. This gave way in turn to the legislative caucus, which was composed of partisans in legislative bodies. Criticisms of the unrepresentative character of the legislative caucus led to a modification called the "mixed" (mongrel) caucus, composed of legislators and some outside representatives. Gradually this form was superseded by the delegate convention, set up especially to make nominations. The convention system later was denounced as unrepresentative and controlled by corrupt interests. It was replaced by the direct primary, in which party voters participate directly in the nominating process.

The Convention System.—After 1910 the convention was replaced largely by the direct primary. Now the older method is in exclusive use in only one state, Connecticut, but it is in partial or optional operation in several others. Important use is made of the convention plan of nominating for some state-wide congressional and state offices in Indiana and New York. It is optional with the parties in several Southern states. Subordinate employment is made of conventions for framing party platforms in many other states. The usual pattern of the delegate convention calls for the

[1] Charles E. Merriam and Louise Overacker, *Primary Elections* (Chicago: University of Chicago Press, 1928), p. 191.

election of delegates by voters affiliated with the party, or by party groups and committees. The delegates meet in convention under a procedure not unlike that of a national convention.

The state and local convention method of nominating party candidates, discredited during the reform movement of the first two decades of the century, is being restored to favor in the thinking of many students of government. The direct primary has not brought all the improvements predicted by those who claimed it to be a panacea for many ills. The direct primary, particularly the open form of it, makes possible the sudden capture of a party's nomination by a maverick group or colorful individual with no previous responsibility in the party. Far from removing the control over the nominating process from bosses and machines, adoption of the primary in many states induced a sinister alliance of vested interests with newspapers. This combination succeeds in primaries because of public disinterest, disciplined machine vote, and blind following of newspaper endorsements. Restoration of the convention system for making nominations of candidates for state-wide offices may produce abler and more responsible leadership. A major party in New York, for example, can offer a nomination to a leading citizen, whereas an Illinois party rarely can avoid a wide-open primary fight that drives men of reputation from consideration.

The Direct Primary.—The direct primary is the most widely adopted of all nominating schemes. It is now mandatory or optional with the parties in forty-seven states. Only Connecticut has no provision for this nominating method. Party voters indicate on a direct-primary ballot which aspirants they prefer to have as their party's nominees for public office. Usually this is done through a publicly conducted poll with all the safeguards of a general election. Most of the states use the "closed primary," which means that each voter may participate only in the nomination of candidates for the party with which he is registered or affiliated. The other type, "open primary," is employed in nine states.[1] It allows the voter to decide at the voting place in which party's primary he wishes to vote.

These who seek party nominations usually are required to file petitions signed by a certain number or percentage of voters. Some states require payment of a filing fee. In most states the individual obtaining the largest vote, even though no majority, receives the nomination of his party for office. Ten states, all Southern or border except Utah, seek to ensure a majority choice by holding a subsequent "run-off" primary, in which the two leading contestants for each nomination vie for a majority vote. A

[1] The open primary is sometimes called the "Wisconsin type." It is used also in Idaho, Illinois, Indiana, Minnesota, Montana, South Dakota, Utah, and Vermont. Spencer D. Albright, *The American Ballot* (Washington: American Council on Public Affairs, 1942), p. 119, and *The Book of the States, 1948–1949*, p. 92.

PRIMARY ELECTION BALLOTS

The Open Primary: Wisconsin

OFFICIAL PRIMARY BALLOT
GENERAL ELECTION
SOCIALIST PARTY

To vote for a person whose name is printed on the ballot, mark a cross (X) in the square at the RIGHT of the name of the person for whom you desire to vote. To vote for a person whose name is not printed on the ballot write his name in the blank space provided for that purpose.

STATE
Governor — Vote for one
GEORGE A. NELSON
Lieutenant Governor — Vote for one
GEORGE E. HELBERG

LEGISLATIVE
State Senator — Vote for one
JOHN SIKKEMA
Member of Assembly 1st District — Vote for one
SAMUEL MINTZ

OFFICIAL PRIMARY BALLOT
GENERAL ELECTION
PROGRESSIVE PARTY

To vote for a person whose name is printed on the ballot, mark a cross (X) in the square at the RIGHT of the name of the person for whom you desire to vote. To vote for a person whose name is not printed on the ballot write his name in the blank space provided for that purpose.

STATE
Governor — Vote for one
RALPH F. AMOTH
ALEXANDER O. BENZ
JOHN H. KAISER
LEO E. VAUDREUIL

LEGISLATIVE
State Senator — Vote for one
FRED RISSER
Member of Assembly 1st District — Vote for one
LYALL T. BEGGS

OFFICIAL PRIMARY BALLOT
GENERAL ELECTION
REPUBLICAN PARTY

To vote for a person whose name is printed on the ballot, mark a cross (X) in the square at the RIGHT of the name of the person for whom you desire to vote. To vote for a person whose name is not printed on the ballot write his name in the blank space provided for that purpose.

STATE
Governor — Vote for one
WALTER S. GOODLAND
ROLAND E. KANNENBERG
DELBERT J. KENNY
MILTON T. MURRAY
CHRISTIAN J. OTJEN
Lieutenant Governor — Vote for one

LEGISLATIVE
State Senator — Vote for one
ANTHONY J. FIORE
Member of Assembly 1st District — Vote for one
CYRIL E. MARKS
STUART H. BECKER
COUNTY

OFFICIAL PRIMARY BALLOT
GENERAL ELECTION
DEMOCRAT PARTY

To vote for a person whose name is printed on the ballot, mark a cross (X) in the square at the RIGHT of the name of the person for whom you desire to vote. To vote for a person whose name is not printed on the ballot write his name in the blank space provided for that purpose.

STATE
Governor — Vote for one
DANIEL W. HOAN
JOHN N. ZIMMERMANN
Lieutenant Governor — Vote for one
MARSHALL WHALING
Secretary of State — Vote for one

LEGISLATIVE
State Senator — Vote for one
GEORGE McD. SCHLOTTHAUER
Member of Assembly 1st District — Vote for one
COUNTY
County Clerk — Vote for one

Under Wisconsin's open primary scheme, each voter receives all ballots. In 1944 these four ballots were stapled together. The voter took all four to the polling booth, marked the one of his choice. Both marked and unmarked ballots are deposited in ballot boxes in order to assure secrecy.

The Closed Primary: New Jersey

OFFICIAL REPUBLICAN PARTY PRIMARY BALLOT
City of Trenton, County of Mercer, Ward No. 14, District No. 1, May 16, 1944.

For United States Senator to Fill a Vacancy. — *Vote for One.*
☐ H. ALEXANDER SMITH — Regular Organization Republican
☐ ANDREW O. WITTREICH — Republican - - - Against Executive Dictatorship
☐

For Member of House of Representatives. — *Vote for One.*
☐ D. LANE POWERS — Regular Republican
☐

For Members of the General Assembly. — *Vote for Three.*

OFFICIAL DEMOCRATIC PARTY PRIMARY BALLOT
City of Trenton, County of Mercer, Ward No. 14, District No. 1, May 16, 1944

For United States Senator to Fill a Vacancy. — *Vote for One.*
☐ ELMER H. WENE — Regular Organization Democrat
☐

For Member of House of Representatives. — *Vote for One.*
☐ DON GUINNESS — "Regular Democrat"
☐

For Members of the General Assembly. — *Vote for Three.*
☐ KENNETH W. O'DELL — "Regular Democrat"

In New Jersey, as in other closed primary states, the voter is permitted to participate only in primary of the party with which he is registered or affiliated. Although in most northern and western states primary elections are conducted by public election officials, Republicans are given only Republican ballots and Democrats only Democratic.

few states, notably California, permit an aspirant to enter the primaries of more than one party. This is called "cross" or "double" filing. California makes the winning of his own party primary a prerequisite to a candidate's holding another party nomination.

Combination schemes to blend convention and primary plans have been worked out in some states. A preprimary convention or assembly may be used to recommend candidates to the voters, as in Colorado, Nebraska, and Utah. Or, as in Iowa and South Dakota, a postprimary convention may make a final choice between contenders for the nomination if none gets a minimum percentage of the vote.

The nonpartisan primary, used for certain local and state offices in some states, is in reality a preliminary election rather than a primary in the usual sense. Under this plan, candidates enter their names for the nonpartisan office by filing petitions or paying fees or both. If any candidate for the office secures a majority in the first election, he is declared elected. If there is no majority, the two highest candidates engage in a "run-off" contest at general election time. No party designations of any kind are permitted on the ballot. Mechanically the nonpartisan "primary" and election plan is usually superior to the partisan, for the chance of minority winners nearly always is eliminated.

CAMPAIGNS AND ELECTIONS

Methods of Campaigning.—As a first step in a political campaign, regular party machinery is manned with full force. In a presidential contest the national chairman is in command; in a state-wide campaign, the state chairman or a comparable official is in charge. Headquarters agencies are placed on an active basis.

The strategy employed depends upon office sought, personality of the candidate, and circumstances. Candidates for the presidency increasingly take the "swing around the circle," making personal appearances in most sections. An incumbent President sometimes conducts a "front porch" campaign and makes few speeches; this is especially effective if the country is in a prosperous condition. Issues largely are determined by circumstances.

Voters are reached as individuals in a variety of ways: (1) Canvass by direct personal contact of party workers with voters. It may be a systematic house-to-house canvass, or an informal contact at a place where voters gather. (2) Appeals by mail are less effective than personal canvass but are often easier to make. Such approaches are expensive and require much care in the drafting but make possible stratified electioneering among individuals of different racial, occupational, or other groups.

Voters are reached in the mass through the following: (1) Meetings of all kinds are held indoors and outdoors with single speakers and joint debates, sometimes impromptu and occasionally elaborately planned. (2) Radio broadcasts of candidates and other party speakers have grown of great importance in the last few campaigns. (3) Printed literature is prepared and distributed, including newspaper advertisements and articles, pamphlets, leaflets, posters, and others. (4) Motion pictures and recordings are used at meetings and have proved an effective campaign medium.

Authority over Elections.—The states are required by the Constitution to provide for the election of members of both houses of Congress. "The Times, Places, and Manner of holding Elections for Senators and Representatives shall be prescribed in each State by the Legislature thereof; but the Congress may at any time by Law make or alter such Regulations. . . ."[1]

In 1872 Congress set as election day for federal officers the Tuesday after the first Monday of November in even-numbered years. Now all states except Maine, which has a constitutional provision requiring a September election, adhere to the congressional date. The manner of holding elections is regulated by Congress in several respects: (1) In 1842 Congress enacted that representatives be elected by districts. (2) Thirty years later districts were required to be of equal population and contiguous territory. (3) A 1911 act added the word "compact." (4) Congress has also ruled out oral voting in the election of representatives. Both items (2) and (3) were omitted in the 1929 act.

Otherwise, the states have wide authority over elections. As stated before, in providing who shall vote for the most numerous branch of the state legislature, states decide who shall vote for federal officers. But state voting requirements tend to uniformity, with citizenship, an age of twenty-one years, residence, and registration on the required list in virtually all states. Constitutional amendments restrict the authority of the state to discriminate because of race, color, previous condition of servitude, or sex.

Election Administration.—In most states elections are supervised by a state election board or the secretary of state. Counties and cities place in charge of election administration either regular officials with other tasks (as county clerk) or create special officers (registrars or commissioners). Precincts are the essential cell units in elections. The number of officials in each depends upon the size of the precinct, the length of the ballot, the equipment, and the skill of the officers themselves.

The Australian ballot is in general use in this country; it is printed at public expense, secret, all-inclusive, available only on election day, and its use is protected by numerous safeguards. American ballots fall into two general types: (1) the office-block form (Massachusetts) on which candidates are listed by the office they seek, and (2) the party column type (Indiana) on which all candidates of a particular party are listed together.

[1] Article I, Section 4.

GENERAL ELECTION BALLOT FORMS

PARTY COLUMN: INDIANA

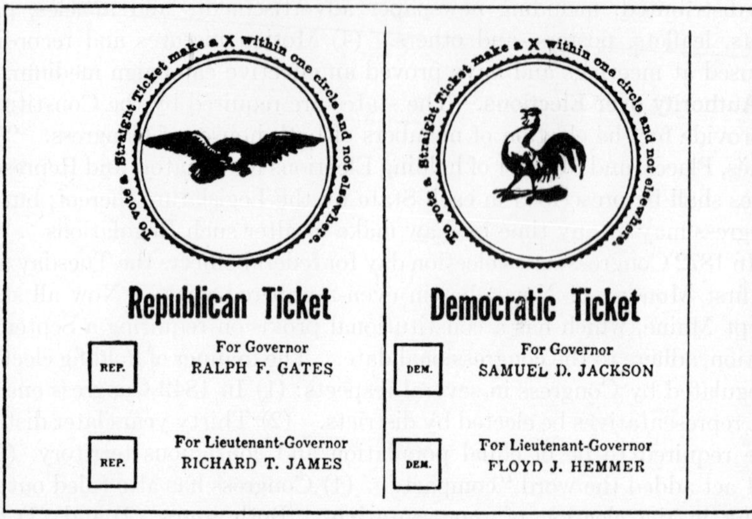

This portion of Indiana's state ballot for the November 1944 election illustrates the straight-ticket party column form. Twenty-seven states use this form. Three additional states have party column ballots but no straight-ticket voting.

OFFICE BLOCK: MASSACHUSETTS

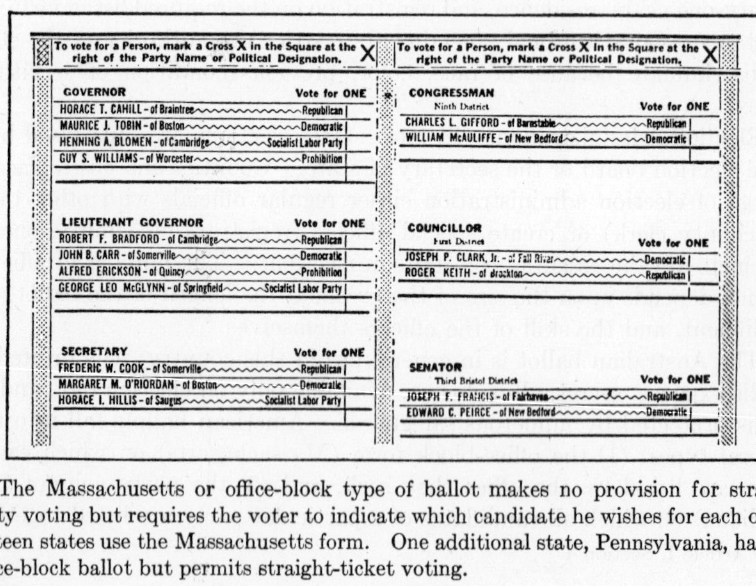
To vote for a Person, mark a Cross X in the Square at the right of the Party Name or Political Designation. X

GOVERNOR — Vote for ONE

HORACE T. CAHILL – of Braintree	Republican	
MAURICE J. TOBIN – of Boston	Democratic	
HENNING A. BLOMEN – of Cambridge	Socialist Labor Party	
GUY S. WILLIAMS – of Worcester	Prohibition	

LIEUTENANT GOVERNOR — Vote for ONE

ROBERT F. BRADFORD – of Cambridge	Republican	
JOHN B. CARR – of Somerville	Democratic	
ALFRED ERICKSON – of Quincy	Prohibition	
GEORGE LEO McGLYNN – of Springfield	Socialist Labor Party	

SECRETARY — Vote for ONE

FREDERIC W. COOK – of Somerville	Republican	
MARGARET M. O'RIORDAN – of Boston	Democratic	
HORACE I. HILLIS – of Saugus	Socialist Labor Party	

To vote for a Person, mark a Cross X in the Square at the right of the Party Name or Political Designation. X

CONGRESSMAN — Ninth District — Vote for ONE

CHARLES L. GIFFORD – of Barnstable	Republican	
WILLIAM McAULIFFE – of New Bedford	Democratic	

COUNCILLOR — First District — Vote for ONE

JOSEPH P. CLARK, Jr. – of Fall River	Democratic	
ROGER KEITH – of Brockton	Republican	

SENATOR — Third Bristol District — Vote for ONE

JOSEPH F. FRANCIS – of Fairhaven	Republican	
EDWARD C. PEIRCE – of New Bedford	Democratic	

The Massachusetts or office-block type of ballot makes no provision for straight party voting but requires the voter to indicate which candidate he wishes for each office. Sixteen states use the Massachusetts form. One additional state, Pennsylvania, has the office-block ballot but permits straight-ticket voting.

The voting machine is a mechanical adaptation of the Australian ballot. It has the obvious advantages of speed, accuracy, and simplicity, but it is expensive, fragile, and sometimes discourages split voting.

The method of electing the President is examined in some detail in a subsequent chapter. It must be explained here, however, that the voter does not vote directly for his choice for the presidency, but for the electors who go through the formality of casting their ballots for the candidates to whom they have been pledged. Every state now elects presidential electors on a state-wide basis, with each voter able to vote for the whole number of electors to which his state is entitled. In recent years twenty states have adopted the "presidential short ballot," which eliminates the names of the individual electors from the ballot and permits the voter to mark his ballot for the whole slate of electors pledged to the presidential and vice-presidential candidates of his choice. Three other states in effect have the presidential short ballot through their general use of voting machines.

Absentee Voting.—Absentee voting was originated for military personnel during the Civil War and expanded greatly during the Second World War. It was extended to civilians gradually during the past 40 years. All states now permit absentee voting by persons in the armed services. During the Second World War, especially just before the 1944 election, nearly every state extended its provisions for military voting, mainly in the direction of liberalizing registration rules and application forms and in extending the time for returning the ballots. The state absentee plans were supplemented by federal application forms and federal war ballots; the latter were honored by twenty states.

Absentee voting, as its name implies, permits a qualified person who is away from his legal residence or confined for some reason on election day to cast his ballot by mail or in advance of the election. Although state laws have a considerable variety of provisions, there are features common to most states.[1] (1) Application is made within the time limits set by law. (2) The ballot is mailed by election officials. (3) The absent voter fills out the ballot in the presence of a notary public or public official. (4) The ballot is returned to the election official by mail. (5) Absentee ballots are counted either in a central election office or sent to the precincts for counting. A few states permit a voter to cast his ballot in person a few days early in case he expects to be away on election day. Approximately one-half of the states provide for absentee registration, so that a person who is away at registration time can enter his name on the roll. This is of particular value to people who work in Washington, D.C., but maintain legal addresses in their home states and to those from states that require frequent reregistration.

[1] The best recent source of information on absentee voting is George F. Miller, *Absentee Voters and Suffrage Laws* (Washington: Daylion Co., 1949).

Proportional Representation.—Proportional representation (PR) is a system of voting that yields to each party or group the approximate strength to which its vote entitles it. PR is applied to the selection of legislative bodies and is designed to correct the absurd disproportion produced by the single-member district plurality plan. Several methods of PR are in use in different parts of the world, but the Hare plan of single transferable vote is the most common in the United States. Under the Hare system, several representatives are elected from a single district. The voter indicates his choice of candidates by writing numbers—1, 2, 3, 4, etc. opposite the candidates of his choice. The ballots are collected and counted centrally.

The first step in counting PR ballots is to establish the "quota." This is done by dividing the number of valid ballots by the number of candidates to be elected plus one. If nine seats in a city council are to be filled, and the number of votes cast is 100,000, then the quota is 10,001. It is figured:

$$\text{9 councilors} + 1 = 10\overline{)100{,}000}^{\;10{,}000\; +\; 1\; =\; 10{,}001 \text{ quota}}$$

The ballots are sorted by first choices, and all candidates with more than the quota are declared elected. Their surplus beyond the quota is distributed to second choices on the ballots concerned. Finally, candidates with the lowest number of votes are eliminated and their ballots distributed by second choices until all seats are filled.

Proposed only occasionally for use in selecting members of Congress and of state legislatures, PR has been used successfully in several cities including New York and Cincinnati. Proponents maintain that it (1) ensures minority representation, (2) reduces power of small organized machines, (3) makes legislative bodies truly representative.[1] The case against PR, once the preserve of bosses and others inconvenienced by it, recently has been argued forcefully by competent students of government. The disadvantages are that it (1) increases the number of groups and parties; (2) reduces the chances of one group securing the power to govern; (3) is too complicated for the voter to understand.[2]

After observing the instability of governments in continental European countries under the multiparty system, Americans have become increasingly cautious over PR lest adoption of the reform would eliminate the likelihood of a clear majority in legislative bodies. PR is unlikely to be adopted by

[1] See George H. Hallett, Jr., *Proportional Representation—The Key to Democracy* (Washington: The National Home Library Foundation, 1937), pp. 58–74.

[2] Ferdinand A. Hermens, *Democracy or Anarchy? A Study of Proportional Representation* (Notre Dame: Review of Politics, University of Notre Dame, 1941); and *P.R.: Democracy and Good Government* (Notre Dame: Review of Politics, University of Notre Dame, 1943).

the Federal government in the United States. It will be proposed seriously as a panacea for some of the ills of state legislatures and might conceivably prove a good remedy. In local affairs, where fewer great policy decisions are made and the work of government is mainly administration, PR provides a fair method of representation. Even in municipal government, however, PR has been losing ground and its prospects for the future appear dim.[1]

Initiative, Referendum, Recall.—Although not employed in Federal politics in the United States, the initiative, referendum, and recall play an important part in the government of many states and their subdivisions.

The initiative is an electoral device through which an individual or group may propose statutory legislation or constitutional amendments by securing the signatures of the requisite number of voters and may place the measure before the electorate for adoption or rejection. The drafting of such measures normally is done by interested groups or their attorneys. The number or proportion of signatures required is set by law or constitution. Some states require that initiative propositions be submitted to the legislature before they are placed before the people, but if the legislature takes adverse or no action, then the matter is taken up by the electorate. If a majority of the voters favor an initiative measure or a part of the constitution, it becomes law; frequently statutes thus adopted have a privileged status and may not be repealed by the legislature.[2]

The referendum is a scheme through which voters may, by petition, force submission to the whole electorate of a bill passed by the legislature. The number or proportion of voters' signatures required usually is less than that of the initiative. Emergency measures commonly are excluded from referendum action. If the voters disapprove of the act as passed by the legislature, it becomes null and void. The referendum is used by more states than is the initiative, and it has been proposed seriously for inclusion in the Federal Constitution in connection with a congressional declaration of war.[3] The most common reasons given for adopting the initiative and

[1] Its demise in New York is traced in Belle Zeller and Hugh A. Bone, "The Repeal of P.R. in New York City—Ten Years in Retrospect," *American Political Science Review*, vol. 42 (December, 1948), pp. 1127–1148.

[2] The constitutional and statutory initiative is in use in Arizona, Arkansas, California, Colorado, Massachusetts, Michigan, Missouri, Nebraska, Nevada, North Dakota, Ohio, Oklahoma, and Oregon. The initiative for ordinary laws only is in use in Idaho, Maine, Montana, South Dakota, Utah, and Washington. The two most complete studies are Vladimir O. Key, Jr. and Winston W. Crouch, *The Initiative and Referendum in California* (Berkeley: University of California Press, 1939), and James K. Pollock, *The Initiative and Referendum in Michigan* (Ann Arbor: University of Michigan, Bureau of Government, 1940).

[3] See also p. 74. In addition to the states with the initiative, two others, Montana and New Mexico, utilize the referendum.

referendum are that they (1) provide a check on corrupt and inert legislatures; and (2) provide a useful device for the education of voters. Those who oppose direct legislation often argue that these devices (1) place an additional burden on an already overburdened electorate, and (2) modify representative government by destroying legislative responsibility.

The recall is an instrument through which voters may, by signing petitions, require a special election to determine whether or not an official shall be superseded before his term expires. The number or proportion of signatures required varies considerably. If the majority of votes are for the recall of an official, the office is then declared vacant. A successor may be chosen on the same ballot, elected at a subsequent election, or appointed by some official or body. Various restrictions are placed upon the use of the recall to prevent attempts to recall just after election to office, or repeated attempts. The recall has been adopted in some form in eleven states and a thousand municipalities. Despite the lack of constitutional authority, two states have attempted to inaugurate the recall of federal officials. Arizona and North Dakota sought to apply their recall to federal judges, senators, and representatives. Candidates for Congress were requested to state in advance their willingness to abide by a recall vote on their removal; federal judges serving in the state would be asked to resign in case of an adverse vote in a recall election. The indirect or advisory recall never functioned and it obviously lacked any real sanction.[1]

The case for the recall is that it (1) provides a continuous control by the electorate over public officials, and (2) removes single officials from the shelter of a ticket and forces them to stand on their own merits. Against the recall are the arguments that it (1) gives a powerful weapon to minorities and factions which may be used for petty personal and partisan purposes, and (2) weakens official courage and independence by rendering the officer vulnerable to momentary fits of public indignation.

The Overburdened Voter.—Even a casual examination of American ballots and election returns gives ample evidence of the impression that the voter is assigned more work than he can or will perform satisfactorily. In simple and small communities a large amount of direct democracy may be successful. The town meeting of New England and the *Landesgemeinde* retained in a few Swiss cantons are examples of government that functions very close to the people. Of course direct democracy can have only very limited application in modern America, where the communities are too large and the problems of government too technical for use of the mass-meeting technique. The other possibility is representative government, in which voters choose representatives who devote such time as is necessary to public affairs. A hundred years and more ago there arose a mistaken

[1] Frederick L. Bird and Frances M. Ryan, *The Recall of Public Officers* (New York: Macmillan, 1930), pp. 16–17. This is the best general source on the recall.

idea that the more offices made elective, the more democratic a government was. The mania for popular election swept through the states and local governments and dozens of minor officials were given their own pedestals and made elective by the people. Although a few states and local governments have experienced reorganizations that reduced the number of elective offices, most of them today elect too many officials. Not only does this seriously diffuse executive power, but it places a burden of impossible proportions on the voter. Unable to secure easily information concerning the stewardship in office of a particular obscure incumbent, he either relies on the recommendation of a newspaper or the party label or some other unreliable index.

A generation ago critics of the long ballot were well organized and articulate. They sought:

1. That only those offices should be elective which are important enough to attract (and deserve) public examination; and
2. That very few offices should be filled by election at any one time, so as to permit adequate and unconfused public examination of the candidates.[1]

The short-ballot movement made some headway, but its work remained only partially done when the reform tide had ebbed. The Federal government has few elective officers and a rather short ballot—including candidates only for presidential elector, senator, and representative. With the presidential short ballot, eliminating candidates for elector from the ballot, the remaining federal elective offices certainly qualify as important enough to attract public attention. Most states, counties, and municipalities, however, continue to burden the voter with the task of selecting officers—ranging from tax commissioner to dogcatcher—who should be appointed by a chief executive. Several states have general-election ballots that include the names of candidates for thirty or more offices plus complicated initiative-and-referendum propositions numbering twenty and over.

The number of elections in the United States is staggering. In 1943, according to the Bureau of the Census, 137,661 were held, and in 1944, 126,840.[2] In 1944, on 151 days out of 364 elections were held somewhere in the country. It appears that the second short-ballot principle had been more honored than the first, in that elective offices are filled at scattered times. These minor elections for school and special districts and for local governments often fail to attract any considerable proportion of the eligible voters. In the average Northern and Western state, 50 to 80 per cent

[1] Richard S. Childs, *Short Ballot Principles* (Boston: Houghton, 1911), p. vii.

[2] United States Department of Commerce, Bureau of the Census, *Elections Calendar for 1944* (Washington: Bureau of the Census, 1944), p. 3. These figures include primaries: 6,586 in 1943 and 6,861 in 1944.

participation in state and federal elections is common, while local elections often attract less than 25 per cent of the eligibles.

It is easy to say that the American voter must be made more alert to his civic responsibilities, but it is difficult to make him so. Certainly all efforts to stimulate interest in and discussion of public affairs are to be encouraged. Compulsory voting has been suggested as a remedy for nonvoting. It has been used with some success in Australia, Belgium, Czechoslovákia, Holland, and other countries. The usual form is to impose a fine upon those who fail to participate in elections; in some cases the nonvoter is disfranchised as well. Proposed repeatedly in the United States, compulsory voting has not been applied by any state.

Cannot the task of the voter be made easier? It can by reducing the number of elective offices and the number of elections. Contrary to uninformed opinion, neither of these steps reduces the measure of democracy; actually moderate reform along these lines will make more, not less, democracy. If the elective offices are reduced to a reasonable number, the remaining officers can be given the responsibility over a larger sphere of activity and can be empowered to appoint the necessary subordinates to carry out the work. In the end, the governor or mayor assigned additional authority following the abolition of executive offices, such as controller and commissioner of works, is likely to be more truly responsible to the public than those officers were when they were elective. The electorate can judge the general conduct of a mayor or governor but is unable even to name the incumbents of other elective executive officers, much less judge the quality of their work. Although there are some good arguments against mixing national and local affairs, the multiplicity of elections has been carried too far. Not only is the expense of conducting elections greater than necessary, but the participation in local elections is so small that consolidation of elections is urgently needed.

References

ALBRIGHT, SPENCER D.: *The American Ballot* (Washington: American Council on Public Affairs, 1942).

BEAN, LOUIS H.: *Ballot Behavior* (Washington: American Council on Public Affairs, 1940).

BONTECOU, ELEANOR: *The Poll Tax* (Washington: American Association of University Women, 1942).

COUNCIL OF STATE GOVERNMENTS: *Book of the States* (Chicago: The Council, biennial).

FARLEY, JAMES A.: *Behind the Ballots* (New York: Harcourt Brace, 1938).

HALLETT, GEORGE H., JR.: *Proportional Representation, the Key to Democracy* (Washington: National Home Library Foundation, 1937).

HARRIS, JOSEPH P.: *Registration of Voters in the United States* (Washington: Brookings, 1929).

——— *Election Administration in the United States* (Washington: Brookings, 1934).

HERMENS, FERDINAND A.: *Democracy or Anarchy? A Study of Proportional Representation* (Notre Dame: Review of Politics, University of Notre Dame, 1941).

MERRIAM, CHARLES E., and LOUISE OVERACKER: *Primary Elections* (Chicago: University of Chicago Press, 1928).

MILLER, GEORGE F.: *Absentee Voters and Suffrage Laws* (Washington: Daylion Co., 1949).

PEEL, ROY V., and THOMAS C. DONNELLY: *The 1932 Campaign* (New York: Farrar, Straus, 1935).

PORTER, KIRK H.: *A History of Suffrage in the United States* (Chicago: University of Chicago Press, 1918).

ROBINSON, EDGAR E.: *The Presidential Vote, 1896–1932* (Stanford University, Calif.: Stanford University Press, 1934).

——— *They Voted for Roosevelt; The Presidential Vote, 1932–1944* (Stanford University, Calif.: Stanford University Press, 1947).

TITUS, CHARLES H.: *Voting Behavior in the United States, A Statistical Study* (Berkeley and Los Angeles: University of California Press, 1935).

Chapter 12

CONGRESS: ORGANIZATION AND POLITICS

> This conflict between the Executive and Congress is the most significant fact about the American government today. Unless something is done to cure it, it may prove to be a tragic fact. The difficulty is that the conflict is fundamentally imbedded in our system. The power of the popular leader is snatched from institutions which were intended to deny power. The President can put over his policies only by subordinating Congress.
>
> Thomas K. Finletter, *Can Representative Government Do the Job?*[1]

STRUCTURE AND HISTORY

The first article of the Federal Constitution provides for the legislative branch of government, the "Congress of the United States." Although but recently separated from England, the new country took from the mother country the general outline of its legislative institutions. Several other examples and forerunners, together with the necessity of compromising large and small state demands, played a part in the molding of Congress, 1787 model.

The English Parliament.—The Parliament of the mother country, directly and indirectly, was the most influential factor affecting the thinking of the founding Fathers in respect to the legislature. English parliamentary institutions had developed from the Witenagemot of the Saxon kings, through the despotic rule of the Normans.[2] The "model parliament" of 1295 had representation of clergy, barons, and commoners. The lords spiritual and lords temporal came to meet together, while the commoners met apart; from this flows the two-house tradition. Gradually, although with notable interruptions, Parliament gained power to legislate by bill, to levy taxes, to choose and depose kings. Both tradition and form were transplanted from the British Parliament to the American colonies. Parliamentary supremacy was becoming well established by the time of the American Revolution. The House of Lords, spiritual and temporal, and the House of Commons were separately organized to represent distinct elements in society. The American constitutional convention delegates, of course, had not the advantage of British experience

[1] (New York: Reynal, 1945), p. 17.

[2] See Sir Courtenay Ilbert, *Parliament, Its History, Constitution and Practice* (New York: Holt, 1911), pp. 7–31.

with broadened franchise, gained in the Reform Acts of 1832 and 1867, or with the operation of "classical" parliamentary government, as developed in the Disraeli-Gladstone era.

American Legislatures.—American colonial legislatures, as shown in a previous chapter, followed a pattern that had general rather than detailed similarity. Each colony had a legislative assembly, usually a two-house organization. The upper chamber, or "governor's council," often had legislative, executive, and judicial powers. In the royal colonies, as is commonly the case in the British crown colonies of today, members of the council were appointed by the Crown on recommendation of the governor. In proprietary colonies, appointment came from the proprietor. The two charter colonies, Connecticut and Rhode Island, elected the councilors. Pennsylvania had no governor's council and was thereby the only colony with a single-house legislature.

Intended as a popular body, the lower house was elected by the colonial subjects who could meet the property qualifications required for voting. The members—called "burgesses," "representatives," or "commoners"—represented the people who lived in the districts from which they were selected.

Revolutionary Assemblies.—After an initial period of chaotic rule by "rump" legislatures, eleven of the newly independent states reformed their legislatures in the new constitutions adopted between 1775 and 1780; only Rhode Island and Connecticut kept their old constitutions. In all thirteen states the state legislatures were given broad powers. Eleven of the states continued with bicameral legislatures. Pennsylvania retained its single-house plan until 1790; Georgia experimented with unicameralism from 1777 to 1789. The two-house states kept the lower house much as before the Revolution. The upper house, soon to be termed "senate" generally, was made elective by districts, but its members were assigned longer terms than were lower-house members.

Early National Legislatures.—The First Continental Congress, assembled in Philadelphia in 1774, was more like a convention than a national legislature but must be regarded as a stone-age ancestor of the Congress of today. The Second Continental Congress, which provided such national government as the country had during the Revolutionary War, may be compared with a modern European constituent assembly, for it both governed the emerging nation and framed the Articles of Confederation. This was a unicameral body, to which each state sent its delegates.

Under the Articles of Confederation, this country was governed principally by the Congress. It was a one-house body with a rather fluid membership of delegates from the states. Each state had one vote, which might be cast by the two to seven delegates from that state. States could appoint and recall delegates as they saw fit.

Other Considerations.—More telling as determinant of congressional structure in the Constitution than the precedents cited above, however, was the necessity of compromising the differences between large and small states. Under the terms of the "great compromise," each state was represented equally in the Senate. The seats in the House of Representatives were to be apportioned among the states according to their populations.

Little serious consideration is given today to departure from the two-house plan for Congress. The national utilization of the bicameral plan, however, has led states to imitate. Both Pennsylvania and Georgia promptly abandoned the single-chamber plan after Congress was made a two-house body. Vermont, admitted in 1791, used unicameralism until 1836. The bicameral stereotype prevailed in all states for a hundred years, until Nebraska adopted her single-house plan in 1934 and put it into effect in 1937.

BASIS OF REPRESENTATION

The House of Representatives was intended as the popular branch of Congress and therefore was made larger and more responsible to the public will than was the upper chamber. The Senate, the deliberative house of Congress, was made a smaller body and removed from popular passions and pressures.

Constitutional Provisions.—As provided in the Constitution, seats in the United States House of Representatives are apportioned among the states according to population, determined by the census each 10 years. Members are elected by the people, and the electorate is the same as that for the most numerous branch of the state legislature. The Fifteenth Amendment forbids states to deny the vote to any person because of race, color, or previous condition of servitude. The Nineteenth prohibits discrimination on account of sex. Although the Fourteenth Amendment provides for penalty against states that deny the vote to adult male citizens, by reducing proportionately representation in the House, the penalty has never been invoked and may be regarded as a dead letter.

In its original form the Senate was composed of two senators from each state, chosen by the state legislature. The rising tide of democracy swept aside the old method of selection and imposed the new, as contained in the Seventeenth Amendment. It provided that the people of each state should elect senators directly. The electorate is the same as that for the House.

Methods of Apportionment.—The apportioning of House seats among the states has given rise to periodic controversies. The original sixty-five members of the House were allocated in the Constitution. Thereafter assignments were made by Congress after each census, ranging from the basis of 1 representative for each 30,000 (1792) to 1 for 300,000 (1941).

Only after the 1920 census did Congress deadlock and fail to carry out the constitutional mandate to reapportion each 10 years. The Reapportionment Act of 1929 set the "permanent" number of House members at 435 and provided for automatic reapportionment in case Congress fails to act. The law provided that after each census the President shall report to

VOTING STRENGTH OF THE STATES IN THE HOUSE OF REPRESENTATIVES

HOW THE STATES WOULD LOOK IF THEIR AREA WERE PROPORTIONAL TO THE POPULATION, 1940 CENSUS

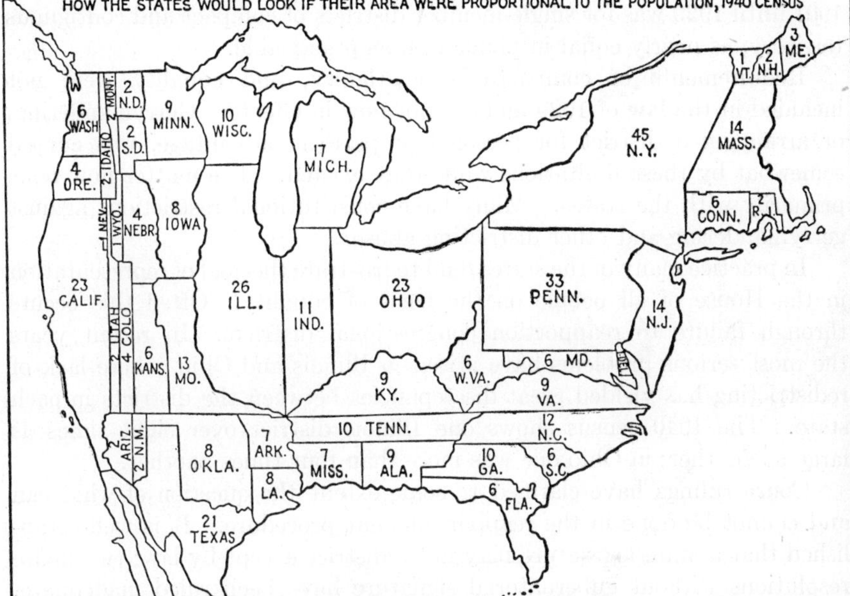

SOURCE: National Opinion Research Center.

Congress the population and the number of representatives to which each state shall be entitled according to two complex mathematical formulas: (1) equal proportions, and (2) major fractions. Should Congress fail to act within 60 days, the reapportionment goes into effect automatically, utilizing the formula employed in the last reapportionment. In 1931 Congress took no action, and the presidential plan based on major fractions was deemed in force. In 1941, however, after the 60-day period had elapsed, the 1929 act was amended to require that the equal-proportions method be used beginning with the Seventy-eighth Congress (1942–1943).[1] The present rule, therefore, requires the President to figure apportionment of House seats only by equal proportions.

[1] 55 Stat. 762, adopted Nov. 15, 1941. In 1931 the allocation of seats was identical under both formulas, so Congress permitted the major-fractions plan, used in 1911, to prevail. In 1941 the two methods showed only one difference: under major fractions Arkansas lost one seat and Michigan gained one; under equal proportions Arkansas kept its seat and Michigan gained none. Democratic elements pushed through a bill to substitute equal proportions for major fractions.

Read - understand

Apportionment within States.—No provision requiring election of representatives by district appears in the Constitution. It was imposed by law in 1842, however, and has prevailed ever since that time. The original law required that each district should elect one representative and that the district must be composed of contiguous territory. In 1872 another rule was added requiring districts of substantially equal population. In 1901 the feature of compactness was added. Thus the requirement from 1901 until 1929 was for single-member districts of compact and contiguous territory, as nearly equal in population as practicable.

Requirements of compactness, contiguity, and equality were not included in the law of 1929 and are not now in effect.[1] Gerrymandering, or arranging a district for personal or partisan advantage, was curbed somewhat by these limitations while they existed. The matter now rests primarily with the states. Many have constitutional restrictions against gerrymandering and other districting abuses.[2]

In practice many of the states tend to frustrate the goal of representation in the House of all people on the basis of equality. Often this occurs through failure to reapportion congressional districts. In recent years the most serious problems have arisen in Illinois and Ohio, where lack of redistricting has yielded great discrepancies between the districts in each state. The 1940 census shows one Illinois district over eight times as large as another; in Ohio one was more than four times another.

Court rulings have clarified to some extent the question of what can and cannot be done in the reapportionment procedure. It is well established that a state legislature may not redistrict except by law; two-house resolutions without gubernatorial signature have been ruled inadequate. If a state is allocated new seats in the House and does not redistrict, the new members are elected at large.[3]

Congress should hasten the modernization of congressional districts by

[1] Wood *v.* Broom, 287 U.S. 1 (1932).

[2] By far the most thorough study of apportionment problems is Laurence F. Schmeckebier, *Congressional Apportionment* (Washington: Brookings, 1941).

[3] Minnesota's legislature in 1931 attempted to place into operation a reapportionment despite a veto by the governor. It was declared invalid in Smiley *v.* Holm, 285 U.S. 361 (1932). The New York legislature tried in 1931 to reapportion by concurrent resolution, not submitted to the governor. It, too, was declared void, in Koenig *v.* Flynn, 285 U.S. 379 (1932). Missouri, also with a vetoed reapportionment bill, went through similar court proceedings with similar results. Minnesota, having lost one representative, was forced in 1932 to elect all nine on an at-large basis. New York, having gained two, was able to use the old districts and fill the new seats by an at-large election. In 1941 Congress provided by law for the contingency that a state might not redistrict after a national reapportionment. It followed the same rules already established in the courts. A state gaining seats in the House may elect the new members at large. A state losing seats and not redistricting must elect all members at large. 55 Stat. 761.

CONGRESSIONAL DISTRICTS IN COOK COUNTY

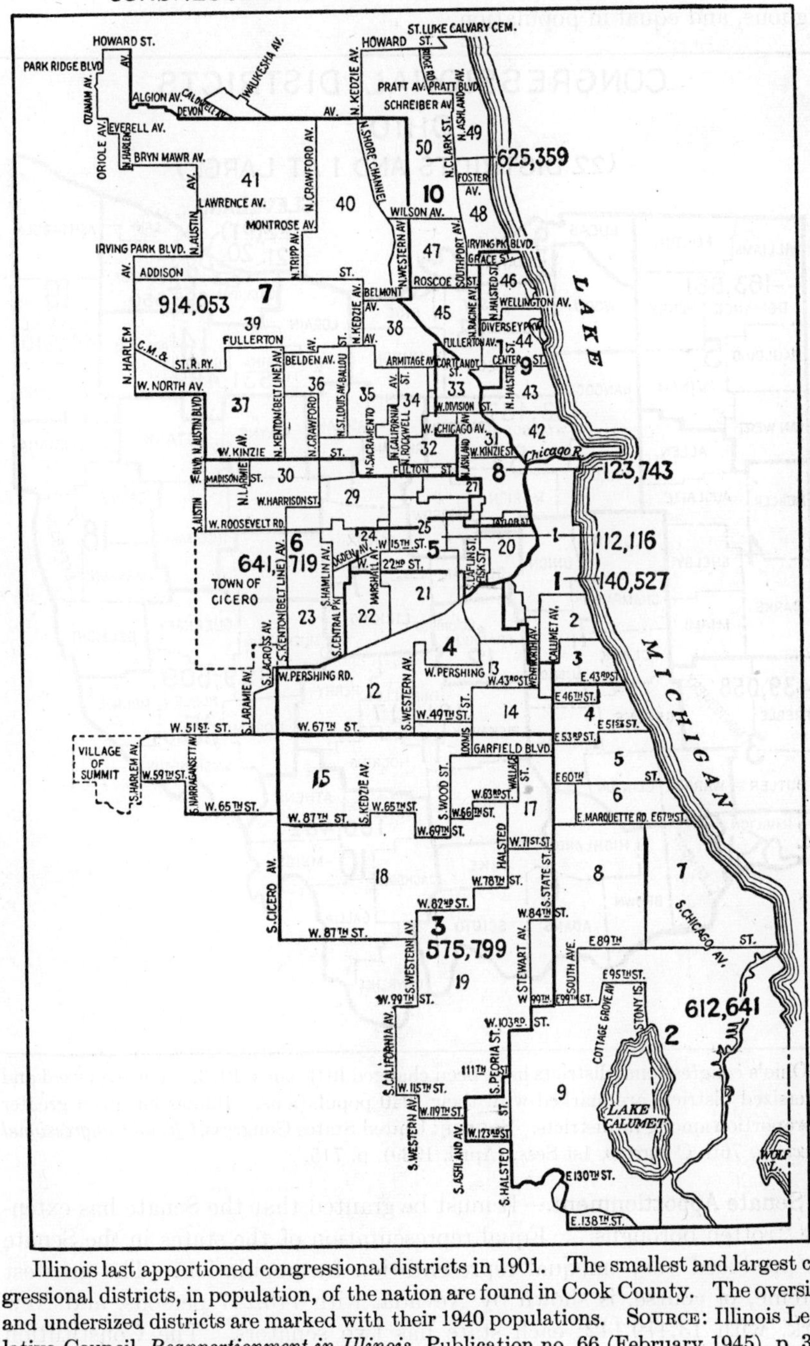

Illinois last apportioned congressional districts in 1901. The smallest and largest congressional districts, in population, of the nation are found in Cook County. The oversized and undersized districts are marked with their 1940 populations. SOURCE: Illinois Legislative Council, *Reapportionment in Illinois*, Publication no. 66 (February 1945), p. 35.

restoring to the law the requirement that districts must be compact, contiguous, and equal in population.

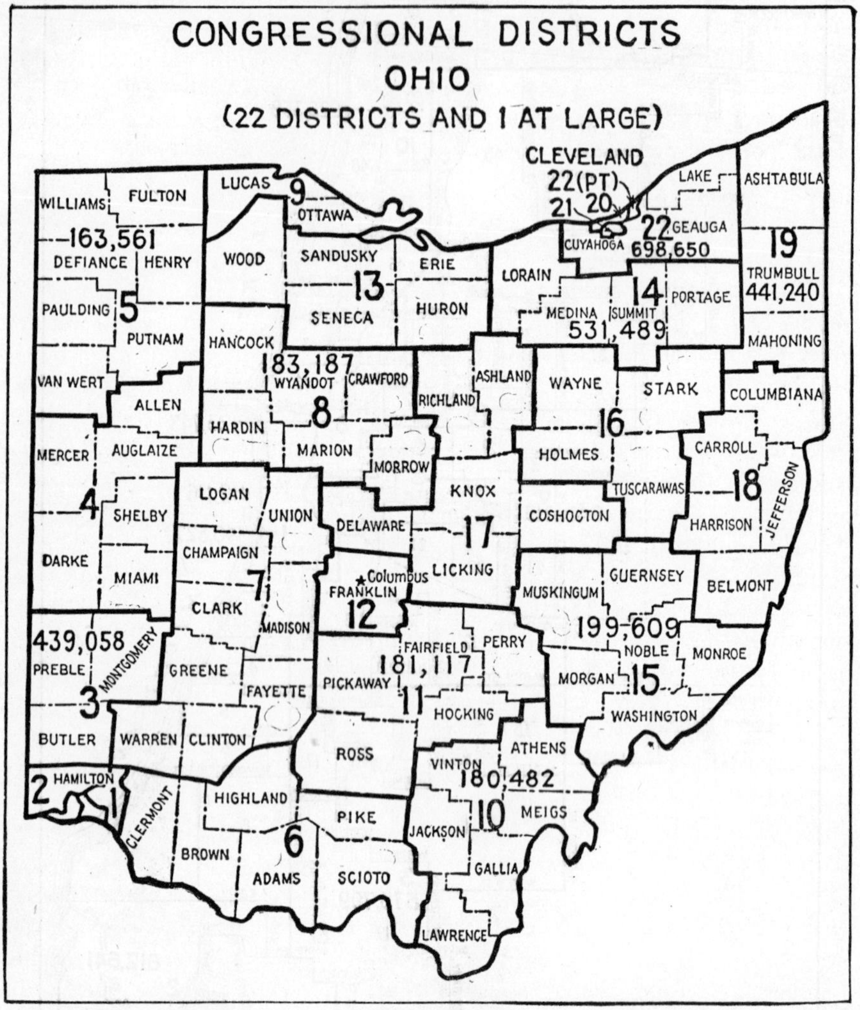

Ohio's congressional districts have been changed little since 1913. The oversized and undersized districts are marked with their 1940 populations. Illinois has even greater disproportion among its districts. SOURCE: United States Congress, *Official Congressional Directory*, 76th Congress, 1st Sess. (April, 1939), p. 715.

Senate Apportionment.—It must be granted that the Senate has extensive "rotten boroughs." Equal representation of the states in the Senate has produced very unequal representation by population. The greatest extreme, of course, is shown by Nevada, with 110,247 persons, and New York, with 13,479,142; each state has two senators. The Constitution provides, however, that no state may be deprived of equal representation in the Senate without its own consent. As a practical matter, changing the basis of representation in the Senate appears out of the question, short of a great upheaval or general alteration of our federal system. The disproportionate influence of small states is especially noticeable in treaty and constitutional amendment proceedings, in which, because a two-thirds majority is required, a minority representing a minute fraction of the nation's population can frustrate the will of the majority.

CONGRESSIONAL PERSONNEL

Qualifications.—The House of Representatives has a short term (2 years) and a low age requirement (twenty-five). Each representative must be a resident of the state from which he is elected, and he must have been a citizen of the United States for at least 7 years. Custom decrees that a representative must reside in the district that he represents, but there have been exceptions. The Constitution provides that each house is judge of "the elections, returns, and qualifications" of its own members. Under such authority, the House has barred regularly elected members for their beliefs, faith, and practices. The House has refused admission to a polygamist and to a socialist who had been convicted of sedition. Denial of the right to take a seat requires only a simple majority vote. Expulsion of a sitting member of the House requires a two-thirds vote. Vacancies in the House normally are filled by special election called by the executive authority of the state concerned.

United States senators serve long terms (6 years) and have a higher age requirement (thirty years). Like the representative, a senator must be a resident of the state he represents. Nine years of citizenship are required in the upper house. Power to judge its own membership extends to the Senate, too, and is employed even more vigorously than in the House. The Senate refused to admit two duly elected members (Frank L. Smith of Illinois and William S. Vare of Pennsylvania) because of huge expenditures in primary elections of 1926.[1] Thus, although since the Newberry decision Congress has not attempted to regulate money in primaries, the Senate may bar offenders from the seats that they win.

[1] Smith, then head of the Illinois utilities commission, accepted contributions from Samuel Insull, whose operating companies he was supposed to regulate. It is estimated that Smith and his opponent spent over $1,000,000 seeking the Republican nomination for senator. See Carroll H. Woody, *The Case of Frank L. Smith* (Chicago: University of Chicago Press, 1931). Vare and Pepper, his opponent, spent over $2,000,000 in the Pennsylvania Republican primary. Newberry, who spent $190,000 in the Michigan Republican primary of 1918, was seated after long delay. Spencer Irwin, *Henry Ford vs. Truman H. Newberry* (New York: Richard R. Smith, 1935).

Since the adoption of the Seventeenth Amendment, Senate vacancies may be filled by appointment of a governor if state law authorizes it.

Previous Experience of Congressmen.—No method exists for a full evaluation of those who serve the country in Senate and House. It is possible to tabulate data on various external attributes but impossible to delve into all the inner springs. It is well known that about 60 per cent of the members of the two houses are attorneys. The second largest occupational group is composed of persons in the various branches of business enterprise. Teachers, farmers, and newspapermen follow next in order. Getting a start in American politics commonly requires either wealth or an occupation that can combine with the erratic periods of service involved. Once successfully established in a safe seat, the representative or senator may abandon his normal occupational pursuits and live on his congressional salary. Certainly membership in Congress constitutes a full-time job, and the salary has been made somewhat commensurate with it. For the lawyer the field of state and local politics has more than the usual glamour; he receives a form of advertising which usually helps his law practice, and he may work himself into line for a judicial post. Or he may win a seat in Congress.

A review of the personnel of the Seventy-seventh Congress revealed that the average age of senators was fifty-eight, while that of representatives was fifty-two. Nearly all had previous public experience before election to congressional office. A large majority of them had attended college or professional schools.[1]

Privileges and Compensation.—Privileges of senators and representatives include certain immunity from arrest and extraordinary freedom of speech. The constitutional provision that national legislators are immune from arrest except for treason, felony, and breach of peace has been interpreted by the courts to prohibit only arrests in civil suits. In criminal cases members are as liable to arrest as any other citizens. The same clause declares that "for any speech or debate in either house, they shall not be questioned in any other place." This means that senators and representatives may speak and act freely without fear of criminal prosecutions or civil suits. Of course, the House and Senate have full power to determine their own rules, to discipline members for excesses, and, in extreme cases, to expel a member. For mild offenses and indiscretions a member is called to order. Occasionally a house will censure a member; expulsion is very rare.

Compensation and perquisites of office include salary, mileage, stationery, clerk hire, and the postal frank. The salary of senators and repre-

[1] A detailed analysis may be found in Madge M. McKinney, "The Personnel of the Seventy-seventh Congress," *American Political Science Review*, vol. 36 (February, 1942), pp. 67–75.

sentatives is now $12,500 per year, and each has an additiona expense allowance of $2,500 yearly. The Speaker of the House president of the Senate draw $30,000 each per year and $10,00 tax-free expense allowance. These salaries are determined by may be altered by Congress. Each member is allowed 20 cents per mile traveling expense to and from sessions. An allowance for clerk hire is made for each member; this sometimes is used to employ members of his family or political supporters. Official mail may be sent under postal frank free of charge to the sender. This privilege is often used for the dissemination of political and partisan speeches and "extensions of remarks" from the *Congressional Record*.

The public reacts unfavorably to proposals for increases in congressional compensation. In 1873 there was a great storm over a "salary grab." In early 1942 there was a controversy over the adoption of congressional pensions, and the legislators were attacked viciously for enacting the new perquisites of office. The law was repealed promptly. The Seventy-eighth congress voted an expense account of $2,500 per year for representatives, but the senators received none. President Truman, former Representative Maury Maverick, and others have urged salary increases for both senators and representatives, ranging from $15,000 to $25,000. The Congressional Reform Act of 1946 raised the basic salary to $12,500 and applied the $2,500 expense allowance to both senators and representatives.

Sessions and Congresses.—A Congress has a life of 2 years, coinciding with the term of office of representatives. Each Congress since the first (1789–1790) has been numbered consecutively; the Congress elected in 1946 and serving 1947–1948 was the Eightieth; that elected in 1948 and serving 1949–1950 was the Eighty-first.

A regular session occurs once each year. Since the Twentieth Amendment was adopted, each regular session begins on Jan. 3, unless another date is provided by law. Adjournment is decided by the two houses. In even-numbered years during normal times adjournment comes in early summer in order to leave time for campaigning. In odd years Congress holds forth until middle or late summer. The President has power to call special sessions. Within each 2-year Congress, sessions are numbered consecutively, whether regular or special, beginning with "first" for each Congress.

The original constitutional provision regarding sessions called for the assembling of Congress on the first Monday of December of each year. The first regular session met 13 months after election. The second regular session convened in December after a new Congress had been elected but with the old personnel. This became known as the "lame-duck" session; for many defeated members of Congress continued to function for 3 months after their rejection by the electorate. The Twentieth Amendment, fathered by Senator Norris and adopted in 1933, abolished the lame-duck session and provided that a new Congress, fresh from the elections of November, begins active legislative work early in January.

PARTY GOVERNMENT

Party lines are rather strictly drawn in the House and Senate. Like the houses of the British Parliament, organization and procedure are linked to partisanship. There is not, however, in the American Congress the strict discipline imposed in the House of Commons. Groups, sectional and economic, often claim a greater share of a congressman's loyalty than does his party. On the other hand, the parties in Congress play a far larger role than do the parties in many state legislatures, especially in the Western states.

The Caucus or Conference.—In the House virtually all members elected as Democrats affiliate with the Democratic caucus, while the Republicans join the Republican conference. These are the partisan groups from which partisan officers in the House draw their authority, and in the name of which the majority and minority perform their important functions in the House. In tangible form, the caucus or conference is a meeting of all representatives elected to the House under the label of a particular party. Meeting on the eve of a new Congress, the party group elects its own officers and nominates its candidates for the House offices. Each group has its chairman and secretary.

One of the most crucial matters determined in caucus or conference is the binding of members to vote on the House floor according to the caucus decision. Both parties, upon occasion, attempt to bind their members, but there is often much insurgency. The Democratic rule permits the caucus to set the party "line" if two-thirds of those voting approve. No member is bound, however, on questions of constitutional construction, or on matters on which he has made contrary pledges to his constituents. The Republicans get along without formal rules in their conference but take such actions as are deemed necessary by majority vote. A Democratic caucus rule provides that violators of group regulations automatically cease to be members of the caucus. Since the fall of Cannon in 1910 the Republicans have generally been tolerant of independence, but in 1925 thirteen Republicans who supported Senator La Follette for President were not invited to the conference and were read out of the party. Both parties limit caucus attendance to their partisan members of the House.[1]

[1] The most recent description of party government in Congress is in Floyd M. Riddick, *The United States Congress, Organization and Procedures* (Manassas, Va.: National Capitol Publishers, 1949), pp. 42–57. See also his *Congressional Procedure* (Boston: Chapman & Grimes, Inc., 1941), pp. 29–40. To the latter he appends the

The Senate party caucuses play less important roles than do the House groups. As in the House, however, the majority caucus nominates officers for the Senate and determines committee assignments for the majority. Binding caucus decisions are exceedingly rare. The minority caucus provides a list of committee posts for the minority.

Party Leadership.—The post in the House most sought after is the speakership, and it is within the gift of the majority party. Intraparty differences are ironed out in caucus, and the candidate of the party is agreed upon before each new Congress opens. Second most desirable is the majority floor leadership. Often a greater contest for this post develops than for the speakership, for the floor leader in recent years commonly has inherited the speakership when vacated. The majority floor leader is chief spokesman and strategist of his party on the floor. The minority caucus goes through the motions of nominating a candidate for the speakership, too. After he is defeated for election on the floor of the House, he becomes minority floor leader, generalissimo of the opposition forces. Both majority and minority floor leaders keep in touch with members on the floor through whips, who canvass party membership in the House and inform representatives of forthcoming business and of the position of the party on it. Both party groups in the House have steering committees, which are executive committees of the party caucuses. The job of the steering committee is to keep in touch with the business of the house and to advise the floor leader on matters of policy and tactics.

Party organization on the Senate side follows much the same pattern. Assigned a constitutional presiding officer, the Senate selects its next highest officer, the president pro tempore. The nominee of the majority-party caucus is formally elected on the floor of the Senate. Majority and minority floor leaders are chosen by the respective caucuses. The Democratic party in the Senate has a steering committee.

Party Role in Committees.—Until 1911 the Speaker of the House appointed all committees of that body. The principal reform that followed the successful revolt against arbitrary rule by Speaker Cannon in March, 1910, was the election of standing committees by the House. Each party is given representation on each standing committee of the House somewhat in proportion to its strength in the whole house. For example, if the Republicans hold two-thirds of the House seats, they would take about two-thirds of the places on each committee. Actually each major party chooses its own representatives for standing committee assignments. Minor parties secure committee posts through one of the major parties.

The Republican conference uses a Committee on Committees for selection of committee personnel. This committee is composed of one rep-

---

Democratic rules and sample minutes of both Democratic caucus and Republican conference, pp. 352–365. See also Paul D. Hasbrouck, *Party Government in the House of Representatives* (New York: Macmillan, 1927).

resentative from each state having Republican members of the House. Members are selected by the Republican state delegations and ratified by the conference. The Committee on Committees meets and draws up a slate of Republican members for the standing committees of the House; it also recommends personnel for the party steering committee. In voting within the Republican Committee on Committees, members cast the number of votes their state has in Republican representatives in Congress.

The Democratic caucus first elects its members of the House Ways and Means Committee; these then determine, sometimes in consultation with the party steering committee, standing-committee assignments for Democratic representatives. After approval by the party caucus, party slates are reported on the floor of the House and are accepted quickly and without difficulty.

Senate selection of committee personnel is similar to that of the House. Standing committees are elected, but the nominating process within the parties is the crucial matter. The Republicans use the Committee on Committees device. The Democrats in the Senate employ their steering committee as a Committee on Committees. In the Republican party, appointment to the committee-selecting body is made by the caucus chairman; in the Democratic, appointment is by the floor leader. Considerations of seniority are influential in both. The slates of the two parties are accepted almost automatically on the floor of the Senate.

Campaign Committees.—Not satisfied that the proper attention would be given by national party organizations to the campaigns of congressional candidates, a joint congressional campaign committee was organized by the Republicans for the campaign of 1866. The Democrats followed suit. In 1916 the senatorial element split off the Republican committee, and formed a separate group. The Democrats did likewise in 1918. Today there are four such campaign committees: Republican congressional campaign committee, Democratic congressional campaign committee, Republican senatorial campaign committee, and Democratic senatorial campaign committee. In recent years they have been quite active. Each party's House campaign group is composed of one representative from each state having representation of the party. The membership of both Republican and Democratic senatorial campaign committees is appointed by the appropriate caucus chairman.

ORGANIZATION AND LEADERSHIP

Speaker of the House.—The House of Representatives chooses its own Speaker. The nominee of the majority party invariably is elected by the House. This election takes place at the beginning of each new Congress. The Constitution does not require it, but every Speaker has been at the

Reed

time of his selection a member of the House. Seniority is an important consideration in choosing a Speaker, but personal popularity and political backing are also prerequisites. The tradition is now well established that Speakers are reelected in subsequent Congresses if their party maintains a majority.

Unlike the impartial and judicious Speaker of the British House of Commons, the American House presiding officer acts as a party leader and uses the powers of his office to promote his party's program. Like the presidency, the speakership can be an office of great magnitude or one of only modest influence. It depends upon the incumbent and the circumstances in his party, in Congress, and in the country. The most powerful Speakers, like Reed, Cannon, and Longworth, built up the authority and prestige of the office to a high level. Others have been content to deal with the House as merely its presiding officer.

Nominal powers of the Speaker include appointment of select and conference committees, signature of documents in behalf of the House, reference of bills to committees, and general conduct of parliamentary business, which includes recognition of members who wish to have the floor. Since the loss in 1911 of the power to appoint standing committees, the greater authority of the Speaker has flowed from his work in presiding. Speaker Reed established that members present but refusing to answer to their names could be counted for purposes of securing a quorum. He also refused to put motions that were dilatory or intended to obstruct the business of the House. The power over recognition, as developed by Speaker Gillette and others, permits the presiding officer to use his discretion as to who is entitled to the floor. The Speaker may ignore entirely the attempt of a member to claim the floor, unless he has explained his purpose in an interview. More bluntly, the Speaker may turn to one who seeks the floor and ask: "For what purpose does the gentleman rise?" If the purpose is not regarded as proper, the Speaker may reply: "The Chair cannot recognize the gentleman for that purpose." The Speaker rules on all points of order, and his decisions rarely are overruled on appeal to the House. It is possible for the Speaker to vote if he chooses; he may speak to a question if he wishes.[1]

House Floor Leaders.—The majority and minority floor leaders, selected by their respective party caucuses, fill posts that have developed into their present form since the turn of the century. The majority leader, when of the same party as the President, often is the Administration spokesman. Each floor leader is manager of his party's program on the floor

[1] The best sources of information on the development of the speakership include: Mary P. Follett, *The Speaker of the House of Representatives* (New York: Longmans, 1896); Chang-wei Chiu, *The Speaker of the House of Representatives since 1896* (New York: Columbia University Press, 1928).

and has effective control, through cooperation with the Speaker, over important aspects of procedure.

House Rules Committee.—Over a period of more than a century the House Rules Committee has built up authority over the procedure of the House until now it has virtual life-and-death power over legislation in the lower house. Each Congress is deluged with such a mass of proposed legislation (10,000 to 33,000 bills introduced each 2 years) that full consideration cannot be given to all. Even the committees of the House do insufficient culling to permit the body to concentrate on major bills. One of the main methods of achieving this end has been through Rules Committee special rules or special orders. The number adopted is not large, but the device usually applies to bills of high importance to the majority group. Direct control of the Rules Committee by the Speaker was broken in 1910, and now the chairman of the committee is regarded as a considerable power in the House, third only after Speaker and majority floor leader.

Senate Leaders.—The Vice-President of the United States, as president of the Senate, conducts himself as a rather impartial presiding officer. He votes only in case of a tie. His appointive power is slight. A president pro tempore is elected by the Senate after nomination by the majority-party caucus. He presides over the upper house in the absence of the president, and succeeds to the presidency of the United States in the event of the death or disability of President, Vice-President, and Speaker of the House.

COMMITTEE SYSTEMS

House Standing Committees.—The methods of the party groups in selecting standing-committee personnel have been described already. Standing committees are by far the most important class of committees, for they constitute the screen through which the great mass of proposed legislation is sifted. After the party groups have completed their slates of committee assignments, they are put together in resolution form and adopted by the House. Few new members are given committee posts of great importance. The majority committeeman who is senior in point of service generally is made chairman. When the Democrats are in the majority, this means that the principal chairmanships are held by Southerners. In the Eighty-first Congress, for example, ten standing committees (out of nineteen) were headed by representatives from the South, and the speakership was held by Sam Rayburn of Texas.

The nineteen House standing committees range in number of members from nine to forty-five, averaging around twenty-five. With few exceptions, members are now limited to a single standing-committee assignment. Before the enactment of the Legislative Reorganization Act of 1946, there were many more committees. In the Seventy-ninth Congress, the number

Mead

of regular House committees was forty-seven, and members were permitted to serve on two or more of all but the most important committees.

Public bills are referred to committees by the Speaker, who sometimes exercises considerable discretion but is ultimately subject to the will of the House. Once assigned, it is difficult to secure rereference of a bill. Traditionally, standing-committee chairmen wield great power over the meeting, procedure, and action of their committees.

Committees of the House hold their meetings and conduct hearings during the morning hours. About one-half have regular meeting days; the remainder meet on call of the chairman. Most committee meetings are open to the public, but some are closed. On important bills extended hearings may be held by committees or subcommittees, with witnesses from various parts of the country testifying. When consideration of a bill is completed by a committee, it may vote to report the bill out to the House with a favorable recommendation, or it may defeat the bill and "pigeon-hole" it. The most influential of the House committees, after Rules, are Ways and Means, Appropriations, Commerce, Banking and Currency, Agriculture, Armed Services, and Foreign Affairs.

Other House Committees.—House select committees are established for various purposes. Their personnel is appointed by the Speaker. They are created by simple resolution. Usually a select committee is given the task of studying some problem for a definite period of time. The best known select committees are investigating committees. Such committees generally are given power to meet even after Congress has adjourned, to administer oaths, to subpoena persons and records, and the like.[1]

Senate Committees.—Senate standing committees are "elected" by the Senate, but this process is more properly described as ratification of the slates selected by the two major party groups. The majority party receives all chairmanships. The rule of seniority is highly important in the Senate also, but the longer term and the greater tendency to reelect senators makes overwhelming sectional domination less likely. In the Eighty-first Congress, only five of the fifteen standing committees were headed by senators from the deep South. Some of the most important committees, however, are led by men of advanced age—in their seventies and eighties. All except one of the standing committees had thirteen members; the Appropriations Committee alone had twenty-one. Each senator is limited to two committees. Before the 1946 reform law, the number of Senate committees had ranged from thirty-three to seventy-three in recent congresses.

[1] Three works of importance deal with congressional investigating committees: Marshall E. Dimock, *Congressional Investigating Committees* (Baltimore: The Johns Hopkins Press, 1929); Ernest J. Eberling, *Congressional Investigations* (New York: Columbia University Press, 1928); M. Nelson McGeary, *The Development of Congressional Investigative Power* (New York: Columbia University Press, 1940).

At the time of introduction, bills are referred by the presiding officer to the committee which is to consider the proposed measure. The committee may consider the bill, hold hearings if it chooses, and report or not report back to the Senate. The Appropriations Committee alone meets on call of the chairman; all others have regular meetings.

Investigating committees of the Senate are even better known than those of the House. The power of the Senate to conduct investigations between sessions was fully assured in McGrain *v.* Daugherty,[1] and the Senate has used its power with vigor. Among well-known Senate inquiries were Teapot Dome, munitions, and the Truman committee investigating war expenditures. Members of Senate select committees are appointed by the president of the Senate.

Joint Committees.—Frequently the House and Senate have business in common which requires the forming of joint committees for its solution. Some of these are set up to plan memorials, monuments, or commemoration celebrations. Some deal with common facilities like capital buildings and grounds, printing, library, and other problems.

More important are the joint investigating committees occasionally established by two-house resolution or by statute. A recent example is the Joint Committee on the Organization of Congress. The Temporary National Economic Committee, which reported in 1941, contained members of both houses and representatives of several federal executive agencies.

The most common joint committees are conference committees. These bodies are established on a temporary basis to compromise the differences between Senate and House versions of the same bill. House conferees are appointed by the Speaker and those of the Senate by the Vice-President of the United States. Most important pieces of legislation are amended in some form or other in the second house. Then the amended bill is sent back to the first house for acceptance. If the first house declines to accept the amendments, this house may ask the second to recede from the amendments. If it will not, then a conference is arranged. Normally three representatives and three senators constitute such a committee, though many are larger. If the conferees can agree on a compromise, then the results are reported to each house. Should the House and Senate both agree to accept the conference committee recommendation, then the bill is deemed passed in the form the conference committee has proposed. If, on the other hand, one or both houses refuse to accept, then the bill dies or another conference must be arranged.

References

(See also works listed after next chapter.)

ALEXANDER, DE ALVA S.: *History and Procedure of the House of Representatives* (Boston: Houghton Mifflin, 1916).

[1] 273 U.S. 135 (1927).

BROWN, GEORGE R.: *The Leadership of Congress* (Indianapolis: Bobbs-Merrill, 1922).

CHAMBERLAIN, JOSEPH P.: *Legislative Processes: National and State* (New York: Appleton-Century-Crofts, 1936).

CHIU, CHANG-WEI: *The Speaker of the House of Representatives since 1896* (New York: Columbia University Press, 1928).

DENNISON, ELEANOR E.: *The Senate Foreign Relations Committee* (Stanford University, Calif.: Stanford University Press, 1942).

DIMOCK, MARSHALL E.: *Congressional Investigating Committees* (Baltimore: Johns Hopkins Press, 1929).

EBERLING, ERNEST J.: *Congressional Investigation* (New York: Columbia University Press, 1928).

ERWIN, SPENCER: *Henry Ford vs. Truman H. Newberry; A Study in American Politics, Legislation and Justice* (New York: Richard R. Smith, 1935).

EWING, CORTEZ A.: *Congressional Elections, 1896–1944* (Norman: University of Oklahoma Press, 1947).

FOLLETT, MARY P.: *The Speaker of the House of Representatives* (New York: Longmans, 1896).

HASBROUCK, PAUL D.: *Party Government in the House of Representatives* (New York: Macmillan, 1927).

HAYNES, GEORGE H.: *The Senate of the United States; Its History and Practice* (Boston: Houghton Mifflin, 2 vols., 1938).

LUCE, ROBERT: *Congress—an Explanation* (Cambridge, Mass.: Harvard University Press, 1926).

——— *Legislative Assemblies* (Boston: Houghton Mifflin, 1924).

——— *Legislative Principles* (Boston: Houghton Mifflin, 1930).

MCGEARY, M. NELSON: *The Development of Congressional Investigative Power* (New York: Columbia University Press, 1940).

RIDDICK, FLOYD M.: *Congressional Procedure* (Boston: Chapman & Grimes, Inc., 1941).

——— *The United States Congress Organization and Procedure* (Manassas, Va.: National Capitol Publishers, 1949).

ROGERS, LINDSAY: *The American Senate* (New York: Knopf, 1926).

SCHMECKEBIER, LAURENCE F.: *Congressional Apportionment* (Washington: Brookings, 1941).

TORREY, VOLTA: *You and Your Congress* (New York: Morrow, 1944).

WESTPHAL, ALBERT C. F.: *The House Committee on Foreign Affairs* (New York: Columbia University Press, 1942).

WILSON, WOODROW: *Congressional Government* (Boston: Houghton Mifflin, 1885).

WOODDY, CARROLL H.: *The Case of Frank L. Smith; A Study in Representative Government* (Chicago: University of Chicago Press, 1931).

YOUNG, ROLAND: *This Is Congress* (New York: Knopf, 1943).

TEXT-FILM

The following McGraw-Hill 35mm silent filmstrip is recommended for use with Chaps. 12 and 13 of this text.

Congress: Organization and Procedure. Organization and membership of Congress; party government and leadership. Detailed steps by which a bill becomes a law; consideration of suggestions for strengthening Congress.

Chapter 13

CONGRESS: PROCEDURE AND PROBLEMS

> With the increasing specialization in administration, with the government extending the scope of its power, it is imperative that some institution correlate and control the myriad governmental activities. This Congress can do, and I believe that the future of Congress lies in organizing itself toward that end.
>
> Roland Young, *This Is Congress.*[1]

PROCEDURE IN THE HOUSE

Introduction of Bills.—A bill is introduced in the House of Representatives merely by sending it to the clerk's desk. A member must appear as its sponsor. Before formal introduction, however, a great deal of planning and drafting must be done. Actually the two main sources of bills are executive agencies and private pressure groups, not the legislators themselves. An idea for legislation may be taken to private attorneys for drafting, or it may be whipped into the form of a bill or resolution by the staff of the Legislative Counsel.

Simple bills are designated "HR" or "S" depending upon the house of origin and are numbered consecutively during a Congress. Joint resolutions, marked "H.J. Res." and "S.J. Res." differ from ordinary bills only in that they are intended for temporary situations. Neither concurrent resolutions, which deal with matters pertaining to the legislative branch, or simple resolutions, which concern internal matter in one house only, are submitted to the President for signature.[2]

No limit is imposed on the number of bills a member may introduce. Each Congress in the last 20 years has faced an average of about 14,000 bills introduced; slightly less than 1,000 were enacted in an average Congress. All bills not enacted are wiped off the records at the close of a

[1] (New York: Knopf, 1943), p. xii.

[2] In recent years Congress has been encroaching on the President's veto power by using the concurrent resolution to nullify executive acts and terminate delegated powers. Both the Reorganization Act of 1939 and the Lend-Lease Act of 1941 contained provisions for nullification or termination by concurrent resolution. The problem is discussed in Howard White, "The Concurrent Resolution in Congress," *American Political Science Review*, vol. 35 (October, 1941), pp. 886–889; and John D. Millett and Lindsay Rogers, "The Legislative Veto and the Reorganization Act of 1939," *Public Administration Review*, vol. 1 (Winter, 1941), pp. 176–189. The Administrative Reorganization Act of 1949 provided that either house could nullify a reorganization plan proposed by the President.

Congress. In order to secure consideration in the next 2-year period, it is necessary to reintroduce the proposed legislation.[1]

Committee Stage.—Reference to committee is the next step in the legislative process. In committee, bills are given a preliminary examination. Most of them are buried as meriting no further consideration. The more important pieces of legislation are studied in detail, public hearings are held, and the testimony of interested persons is heard. The committee arrives at its verdict. If it is favorable, the proposed legislation, often in amended form, is forwarded to the floor of the House. On important matters the committee report may be extensive and exhaustive; on minor matters it may convey little more than a simple affirmative. In general, bills that secure favorable committee action are in a strong position to secure passage in the House; conversely, committee rejection of a measure makes passage extremely unlikely.

Although committee action is often taken in executive (closed) session, the vote of individual committeemen usually is available to the public. Hearings of the major committees on important legislation are published, some in the "documents" series of Congress. Minority reports also may be filed.

Calendars.—Each bill reported out of committee to the floor of the House is placed on one of three principal calendars. Bills raising revenue, appropriating money or property, directly or indirectly, are placed on the "Union" calendar. All other public bills, not fiscal in nature, go to the "House" calendar. All bills of a private character are assigned to the "Private" calendar. Noncontroversial bills may be transferred from either Union or House calendar to the Consent calendar, provided request is filed. Bills withdrawn from committee by petition are placed before the House on the Discharge Calendar. Members keep track of bills mainly through the daily issue of *Calendars of the United States House of Representatives and History of Legislation.* Listed in this publication are the special orders of the day, unfinished business, bills in conference, the four calendars mentioned, with all bills on them, a history of active bills, and a summary table on status of fifteen or twenty major bills.

A rule of the House requires that bills be taken up in their calendar order, but numerous exceptions are made in order that action may be secured on the more important measures.

Selection for Consideration.—At appropriate times bills may be taken up out of calendar order through several devices. (1) A motion may be

[1] Procedure is covered most adequately in Floyd M. Riddick, *Congressional Procedure* (Boston: Chapman & Grimes, Inc., 1941) and *The United States Congress, Organization and Procedure* (Manassas, Va.: National Capitol Publishers, 1949). Current developments in congressional procedure are covered in the reviews of each session of Congress, contained in *The American Political Science Review.* During the last two decades they have been written by E. Pendleton Herring, by Orman R. Altman, and by Floyd M. Riddick.

HOUSE DEVICES USED TO SELECT BILLS FOR CONSIDERATION

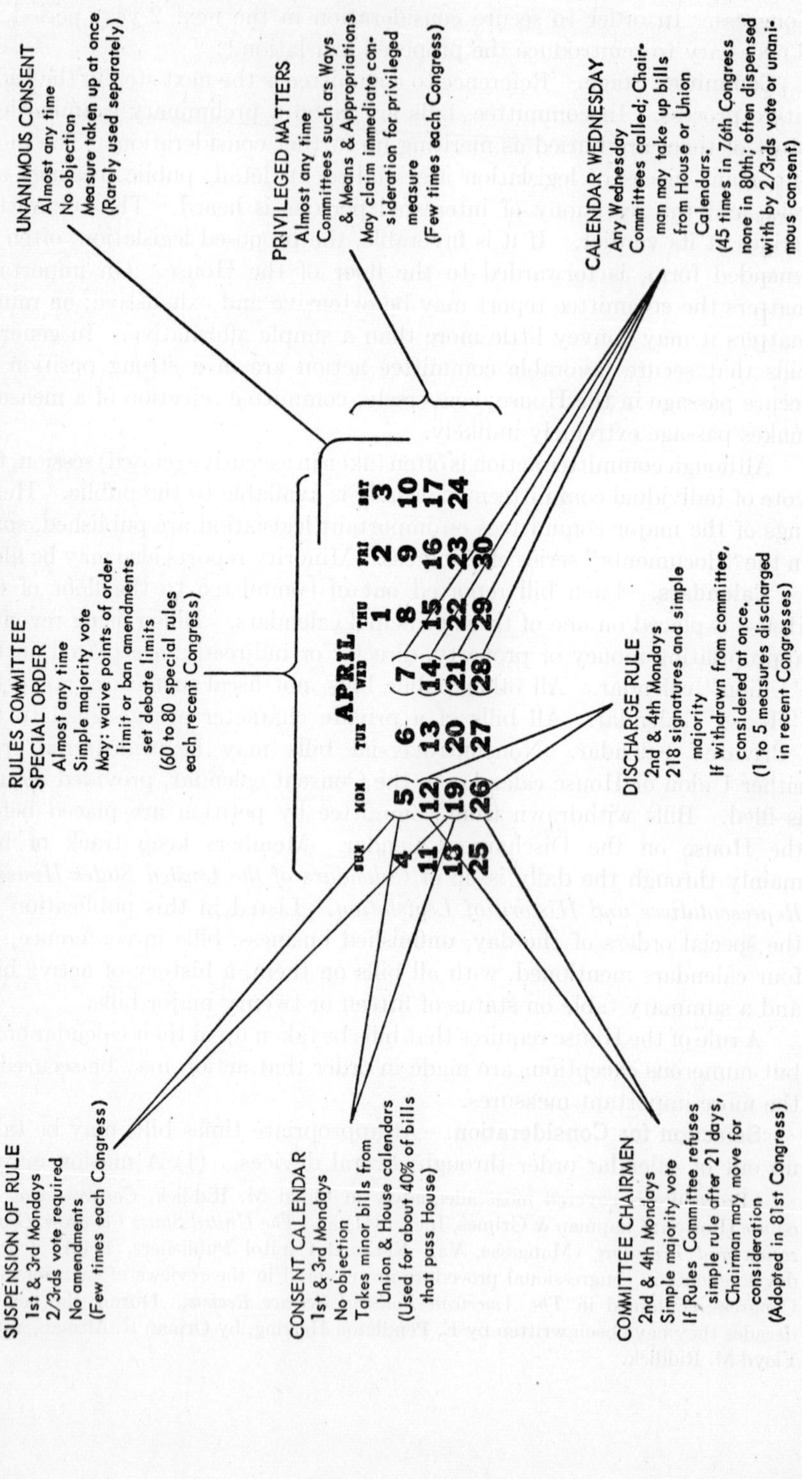
UNANIMOUS CONSENT
Almost any time
No objection
Measure taken up at once
(Rarely used separately)
PRIVILEGED MATTERS
Almost any time
Committees such as Ways & Means & Appropriations
May claim immediate consideration for privileged measure
(Few times each Congress)
CALENDAR WEDNESDAY
Any Wednesday
Committees called; Chairman may take up bills from House or Union Calendars.
(45 times in 76th Congress none in 80th; often dispensed with by 2/3rds vote or unanimous consent)
RULES COMMITTEE SPECIAL ORDER
Almost any time
Simple majority vote
May: waive points of order
limit or ban amendments
set debate limits
(60 to 80 special rules each recent Congress)
APRIL
SUN MON TUE WED THU FRI SAT
1 2 3
4 5 6 7 8 9 10
11 12 13 14 15 16 17
18 19 20 21 22 23 24
25 26 27 28 29 30
DISCHARGE RULE
2nd & 4th Mondays
218 signatures and simple majority
If withdrawn from committee, considered at once.
(1 to 5 measures discharged in recent Congresses)
SUSPENSION OF RULE
1st & 3rd Mondays
2/3rds vote required
No amendments
(Few times each Congress)
CONSENT CALENDAR
1st & 3rd Mondays
No objection
Takes minor bills from Union & House calendars
(Used for about 40% of bills that pass House)
COMMITTEE CHAIRMEN
2nd & 4th Mondays
Simple majority vote
If Rules Committee refuses simple rule after 21 days, Chairman may move for consideration
(Adopted in 81st Congress)

made to suspend the rules (on first and third Mondays and during last six days of session) and must receive a two-thirds vote. (2) Some committees may bring up privileged matters (especially revenue and appropriation bills). (3) Special orders or rules are highly privileged and may be brought in at any time by the Rules Committee. They are adopted by a majority vote. (4) Bills may be brought by unanimous consent from the Consent Calendar (on first and third Mondays) for immediate consideration. (5) Committees may call up for passage some of their own bills, otherwise unprivileged, from House or Union calendars (on Wednesdays except during the last two weeks of a session). (6) Members may secure unanimous consent for immediate consideration of a measure. (7) Chairmen of committees, since 1949, may move for immediate consideration of bills (on second and fourth Mondays) for which the Rules Committee refuses, after 21 days, to report a special rule.

Committee of the Whole.—The House, sitting in a more informal capacity, handles all Union Calendar bills as the "Committee of the Whole House on the State of the Union." Private Calendar bills are discussed as in "Committee of the Whole." The House resolves itself into such a status on passage of a motion directing this action. The Speaker appoints a member to act as chairman, and himself retires. Sometimes the length of debate on a particular bill is set in the motion to resolve; usually this is divided into one-half for those opposing, one-half for those supporting. Procedure in Committee of the Whole is freer than in the House. Attendance of 100 members suffices for a quorum, in place of the usual majority. No record roll-call votes are taken. A bill is read section by section, and amendments may be offered to appropriate sections. When the work at hand is completed, the Committee of the Whole rises and reports back to the House the action that has been taken. Its recommendations may be accepted or rejected by the House.

Consideration on the Floor.—When at last the House turns its attention to a certain bill, debate on the merits of the proposed legislation is in order. Three readings of each bill are required by House rules. The first reading requirement is satisfied by printing the title in the *Record* and *Journal* at the time of introduction. The second reading, the only one in full, occurs at the time the bill is taken up for consideration in the House or in Committee of the Whole. General debate precedes second reading. Amendments may be offered as the appropriate sections are read. Some amendments are general, "considered" amendments, seriously intended as alterations in the bill at hand. Others are *pro forma*, involving the striking out of the last word or two of a section; in the short debate that may ensue a member may make some point he otherwise could not have made.

In the conduct of debate on a particular bill, management of the pro side is in the hands of the chairman or other ranking members of the committee

Read - important

that recommended the measure. Ranking minority members of the same committee may be recognized as in charge of the cons. Time for debate generally is predetermined in the House, and the time is divided equally between sponsors and opponents. The members in control grant time to those who wish to speak. It is very common for members to ask the one who has the floor if he will yield. If the member who holds recognition wishes to step aside for a moment, a question or brief statement may be interposed.

At the conclusion of consideration, the Speaker states: "The question is on the engrossment and third reading of the bill." If adopted, the bill is ordered engrossed and read a third time. Then: "The question is upon the final passage of the bill." After the bill is passed, it is sent to the Senate.

House Closure.—In a body the size of the House of Representatives, the necessity of curbing debate is obvious. Debate is cut off formally by the adoption of a motion calling for the previous question. Such a motion may serve to close debate upon either passage of a bill or upon amendments to a bill. Should the previous question be carried before any debate takes place, each side is given 20 minutes to present its case.

Other methods of controlling the time expended in debate are used. Special orders brought in by the Rules Committee often limit debate. Speakers of the House have built up authority to refuse to put dilatory motions. House rules prevent speeches of more than 1 hour, unless unanimous consent be given. Informal agreements on the allocation of time increasingly are made between majority and minority leaders and have proved highly satisfactory in curbing excessive verbosity.

Voting in the House.—Four methods of voting are used by the House. (1) Usually the first attempted is viva voce, or voice vote. If this is indecisive, or one-fifth of a quorum requests, another method may be used. (2) Division means standing vote, counted by the Speaker. (3) Voting with tellers involves the members' filing past a given point to be counted for or against a bill. (4) Yeas and nays voting requires a call of the roll by the clerk, each member's vote being recorded. The first three methods are rapid, but provide no record roll call through which a citizen may examine the voting record of his representative. The fourth method takes a great amount of House time, for the names of 435 members must be called orally, and those who did not respond the first time are called again. This process often takes a half hour or more.

On one spectacular occasion, in 1935, the Scripps-Howard newspapers recorded the votes of representatives participating in a teller vote. The vote was upon the so-called "death sentence" on utility holding companies. The press gallery was filled with staff members who knew congressional personnel; they simply put down the names of the members of the House who filed by with the "aye" group, and those who appeared with the "no" group. Ordinarily, however, the public is left in the dark concerning the votes of individual congressmen, unless the yeas and nays are recorded by full roll call.

Several state legislative bodies have solved the problem of making record roll-call votes in brief time by installing an electric recording device. The names of the legislators appear on an illuminated board on the front wall of the chamber. Each legislator's desk is fitted with a panel containing "yes" and "no" buttons. When buttons are pushed, the great scoreboard shows how each legislator votes. Vast amounts of time have been saved in the states where used, but Congress has not seen fit to adopt such a scheme.

Laymen often are confused by the pairing of House members for record votes. Pairs are personal contracts between two members; usually they are of opposite points of view and different parties. If one is absent, the other does not vote; the pairing is announced after a roll call.

Discharge Rule.—Withdrawal of a bill on which a House committee refuses to report may be obtained under the discharge rule. The rule was first adopted in 1910 and, in several different forms, has persisted since that time. The present rule, adopted in 1935, provides that when signatures of 218 members of the House are obtained on a petition to withdraw a bill, a sponsor may move to discharge the committee from further consideration. The matter is placed on a "Discharge Calendar" for "seven days of grace." The motion may be taken up only on the second and fourth Mondays and requires a simple majority to carry.

Much controversy has ensued over the merits of the discharge rule. Majority party leaders have been inclined to debunk it as an obstacle to proper handling of House business. Independent and minority elements have praised the device as an essential weapon of the forces of democracy in the struggle against domination. Each major party, depending upon its situation in the House, has been friend and then foe of the rule. After the Democrats secured a slight majority in the House, the liberal discharge rule of 1931 was adopted. This permitted a petition to be filed with only 145 signatures. When, however, the Democrats secured a great majority, the 1935 amendment was added, requiring 218 signatures. In practice many attempts to discharge are made, but only a handful receive sufficient signatures, and only very few bills actually are withdrawn from committee.[1]

[1] In the 78th Congress twenty-one discharge motions were filed, but only three bills actually were discharged; in the 79th, thirty-five motions led to one discharge; in the 80th, twenty produced one.

SENATE PROCEDURE

General Aspects.—Introduction of a Senate bill is accomplished by the announcement by a senator that he introduces it. The title of the bill is read, constituting first reading. Second reading is considered completed if there is no objection, and the bill is sent to the committee requested by the author. The Senate committee system already has been described; it does not differ in important respects from that of the House. After a standing committee reports favorably on a bill, it is placed on the Senate calendar for at least one day before being taken up. A rather simple calendar is sufficient to serve the needs of the Senate, and the smaller size of the upper house makes unnecessary the elaborate selective and restrictive devices employed in the House of Representatives.

The Senate normally meets at high noon. During the first hour or more of the day the Senate disposes of prayer, communications, committee reports, introduction of bills and resolutions. After this is completed, the Senate turns to the calendar of bills and takes up those unobjected to in the order listed on the calendar. This is called the "morning hour" and ends at 2 P.M. Thereafter the Senate proceeds to the consideration of other legislation. Voting is by voice vote, standing vote, or roll-call vote. The Senate does not use the teller plan. Roll-call voting takes rather little time and is used very commonly. Pairing is frequent.[1]

Filibustering and Closure.—The reluctance of the Senate to impose restrictions on debate is widely known, for the filibuster is the most spectacular of American legislative exploits. Senators have intense pride in the Senate's reputation as a forum of free discussion. Occasionally senators representing a minority point of view obstruct and frustrate the will of the majority through a filibuster. During the filibuster senators hold the floor for hours, delivering relevant and irrelevant remarks, aimed primarily at obstruction until some concessions are obtained. The longest filibuster on record is that of Robert M. La Follette, Sr., who in 1908 spoke for 18 hours against a currency bill.

The closure rule of the Senate, adopted in 1917, requires a petition to end debate signed by one-sixth (sixteen) of the senators. On the second day after this is filed, the Senate must vote by a two-thirds majority to bring debate to a close. After adoption of a closure motion, no senator may speak more than one hour to the question, and other delaying parliamentary tactics are greatly restricted. Closure has been invoked in the Senate only four times between 1917 and 1949, but threat of its use has been sufficient to head off or terminate several filibusters. A mild form of closure, capable of stopping spur-of-the-moment filibusters, is found in

[1] The procedure of the Senate is dealt with exhaustively in George H. Haynes, *The Senate of the United States* (Boston: Houghton, 2 vols., 1938).

the unanimous consent agreements by which the debate on particular measures is limited in advance.[1]

In 1949, after a filibuster on civil rights legislation, the Senate adopted a revised closure rule by which any matter under Senate proceedings (except change of rules) is subject to closure, and a two-thirds vote of the total membership of the Senate (64 members) is required to carry closure, rather than the old requirement of two-thirds of those present. The net result of these changes is to make closure more difficult to use, but to extend the possibility of its use to procedural matters.

Amendments and Riders.—Senate rules governing amendments to bills are not so strict as those in the House. This is especially true in respect to the requirement that an amendment be "germane," which means pertinent or in close relationship. Except to general appropriation bills, the Senate is free to add unrelated amendments to bills. Sometimes a whole bill of subsidiary interest will be amended onto a bill of great importance. This is called a "rider." The government of Cuba was provided for under the "Platt Amendment," a rider to an Army appropriation bill in 1901; this continued on the statute books, highly offensive to Cuban pride, until the inauguration of the "good-neighbor policy" after 1933. Presidential authority to reduce the gold content of the dollar was granted in a Senate rider to the Agricultural Adjustment Act of 1933. The President has no item veto, and therefore must sign or veto the whole bill presented to him.

Appointments and Treaties.—By the Constitution the Senate is given special powers over appointments and treaties. The President nominates and the Senate confirms officers of the United States by simple majority. The fundamental law speaks of "advice and consent" by the upper house. The development of "senatorial courtesy" and the political contacts of President and senators will be treated subsequently. The procedure of the Senate on appointments is to receive the nominations of the President and to refer them to appropriate committees. After these committees report, action on the confirmation takes place on the floor.

Treaty ratification requires a two-thirds vote on the floor. A treaty is received from the President and referred to the Committee on Foreign Relations. Upon its report the Senate usually resolves itself into the "Committee of the Whole" for the consideration of the treaty. This is the only remaining use of the Committee of the Whole in the upper house. The Committee considers and reports its recommendation back to the Senate. There is strong agitation to modify the power of Senate minori-

[1] Franklin L. Burdette, *Filibustering in the Senate* (Princeton, N.J.: Princeton University Press, 1940) tells the interesting story of Senate filibuster and closure. Lindsay Rogers, *The American Senate* (New York: Knopf, 1926), presents a convincing case for the freedom of debate of the Senate.

ties over treaties by assigning responsibility for ratification to a simple majority either of the Senate or of the two houses.[1]

MATTERS OF JOINT CONCERN

Conference Committees.—If both houses pass identical versions of the same bill, it is enrolled, signed, and sent to the President. In case different versions of the same bill have been passed and neither house will recede, then the bill is sent to a conference committee. These committees, usually consisting of three or more members from each house, meet to thrash out their differences. Each house may choose to instruct its conferees, but normally they are left free to negotiate for themselves. After agreement is reached, each set of conferees reports back to its house. The report may be accepted, or rejected and further negotiation ordered. Conference committees, as the late Senator Norris frequently pointed out, have become a sort of third house of our legislative bodies. They are often criticized because proceedings are secret, bills may be rewritten arbitrarily, and their reports seldom are considered carefully.[2]

The Legislative Reform Act of 1946 confines the reports of conference committees to legislative controversies submitted and stipulates that where the rule is violated the conference report shall be subject to a point of order.

Records and Laws.—Records of debates and proceedings in the Senate and House are printed in the *Congressional Record*, which has been the public and official record since 1873. The *Record* is substantially a stenographic report of the debates and proceedings. It is well known that a great many speeches that appear in the *Record* were not delivered orally but are "extensions of remarks" included by unanimous consent. In addition to the *Record*, each house keeps a journal of its proceedings and acts. The journal of the previous day is read, usually in part only, at the opening of the session each day. Once enacted and signed by the President, measures become laws and may be found in the *Statutes at Large of the United States* for the particular session. From time to time statutes are codified in *The Code of the laws of the United States of a General and Permanent Character* . . . , commonly called "U. S. Code."

Impeachment.—Constitutional authority to impeach is vested solely in the House; power to try impeachment cases rests with the Senate alone.

[1] For further consideration of the treaty power of the Senate, see Kenneth Colegrove, *The American Senate and World Peace* (New York: Vanguard, 1944); Royden J. Dangerfield, *In Defense of the Senate; a Study in Treaty-making* (Norman: University of Oklahoma Press, 1933); Denna F. Fleming, *The Treaty Veto of the American Senate* (New York: Putnam, 1930). See also p. 73.

[2] The standard work on this subject is Ada C. McCown, *The Congressional Conference Committee* (New York: Columbia University Press, 1927).

The House usually refers a motion proposing impeachment of an officer to the appropriate standing committee or to a specially created investigating committee. If an impeachment motion is adopted by the House, a committee may be set up to draft articles of impeachment. After their adoption, managers are chosen in whatever manner the House directs. The Senate, upon being informed of House action, sets up a committee to prepare for the trial.

The House managers appear in the Senate at the appointed time and commence their prosecution of the case. If the President is impeached, the Chief Justice of the Supreme Court presides over the Senate trial. The accused officer has a right to appear and to testify in his own behalf. A two-thirds vote of the Senate is necessary for conviction. The Senate has sat as a court of impeachment on only twelve occasions in the country's history. Nine cases involved judges, of whom four were convicted and removed, four were acquitted, and one resigned under fire. The first officer ever impeached was a senator in 1798, but the Senate dismissed that case for want of jurisdiction. Two reconstruction-era cases were the only ones involving executive officers: President Andrew Johnson was acquitted in 1868; Grant's Secretary of War was acquitted in 1876.

Selection of President and Vice-President.—It has been more than one hundred years since the House of Representatives was called upon to elect a President. This responsibility falls upon it when no candidate secures a majority in the electoral college. The Constitution provides that if no candidate for President secures a majority of the electoral votes, the House shall choose from among the three highest. In selecting a President, the House votes by states, each state having one vote. The successful candidate must secure the votes of a majority of the states. The House elected Thomas Jefferson President, following the indecisive election of 1800, and John Quincy Adams after that of 1824.

Should no candidate secure a majority of the electoral votes for Vice-President, the Twelfth Amendment provides that the Senate shall choose from among the two highest candidates. A majority of the total membership of the Senate is necessary to elect. The electoral vote was inconclusive only in 1836; in that case the Senate chose Richard M. Johnson as Vice-President during the Van Buren administration.

CONGRESSIONAL PROBLEMS

General Appraisal.—Among national legislatures and parliaments of the world, the American Congress stands out as one of the most successful. It has endured over a century and a half. On the whole it has proved reasonably representative of the national will. The Senate is unquestionably the outstanding second chamber among national parliamentary bodies.

The House and Senate provide one of the few remaining examples of the two-house plan operating on a substantially coordinate basis. Although its time and energy have often been frittered away upon unimportant issues chosen because of excessive localism, narrow partisanship, and desire for meddling, when great national issues have emerged upon the scene, the Congress has rarely, if ever, failed to serve the country loyally. The men and women who have served in Congress have been of surprisingly high type, when one considers how ill informed the electorate is, and how prevalent is the contemptuous attitude of many people toward Congress.

External Control.—The founding Fathers incorporated in the Constitution the principle of the separation of powers. If the plan operated in pure form, it would involve the leadership of Congress from within. Strong internal leaders have developed in both House and Senate at various periods of history. For the last half century and more, however, leadership and direction have come increasingly from outside of Congress, especially from the President acting as leader of his party. Outstanding congressional leaders—Cannon, Longworth, Cummins, and Robinson—have considered themselves servants of their parties and party leaders. This condition gives rise to the charge that Congress is subject to outside dictation.

A related accusation is made to the effect that Congress is under the control of pressure groups and defers somewhat willingly to their beck and call. There is some evidence of deference to organized groups, although the picture is much overdrawn by some critics. On the other hand, as shown in an earlier chapter, the special-interest group has an important role in the legislative process. Congress plays the role of compromiser and conciliator, seeking a workable solution by composing the differences of warring factions. The road to reform for the abuses that arise from excessive demands of pressure groups is for the citizenry to join up in counterpressure groups. The most striking need is for adequate consumer representation.

Localism and Sectionalism.—A great amount of localism persists in congressional politics. Senators and representatives commonly regard themselves as "ambassadors of locality," rather than delegates of the whole nation. This is demonstrated many times over in every session, but especially in the scramble over the "pork barrel" of rivers and harbors appropriations, and in the "logrolling" over economic issues like the tariff and farm relief. The electorate of a district or state then is informed of the glorious service of its legislator, often through an extension of remarks from the *Record* such as: "What Blanton's Twelve Counties, Seventeenth District (Texas), have Received from Government since 1933." Yet, in another sense, the representative should serve his district; for he is elected by it and is to some extent at least expected to represent its views on public questions.

The interests of the country as a whole occasionally may be served through the alliances and counteralliances made by various economic, sectional, and partisan groups. A few congressmen, and especially senators, enjoy such prestige in their home states that on most issues they are left free to serve the country with detachment and distinction. In the recent past, Senators Borah of Idaho, Norris of Nebraska, Cutting of New Mexico, and others enjoyed such popularity in their states that they were able to devote themselves largely to national interests as they saw them, without the distortion of localism.

Local interests gain exaggerated importance in this country through the tradition that a representative must live in his district. The custom is so well established that it would be very difficult to change. The advantages of the British system, under which the member of Parliament need not be, and usually is not, a resident of his district, should not be overlooked.

Read!

Petty Matters.—Even a cursory observer of Congress is impressed with the amount of legislative time wasted on relatively minor issues, and the hasty fashion (especially in the House) in which matters of great importance are dealt with. A large proportion of the bills on the calendars of the two houses concern petty matters that might more properly be handled by delegating rule-making authority to administrative agencies. The most extreme proposal along this line is one made with reference to the British Parliament. Some years ago Sir Stafford Cripps urged that the "mother of parliaments" confine its lawmaking solely to one omnibus appropriation and planning bill per session. The American Congress certainly would not be willing to abdicate to this extent, but it might well provide for the settlement of private claims through courts or administrative tribunals, and for reduction in the number of minor public bills by the delegation of legislative authority (with appropriate standards) to the executive. Some progress has already been made through the flexible tariff, executive trade agreements, blanket appropriation measures, and the like. In time of war Congress appropriates billions of dollars to the military establishments with a minimum of restrictions on where or how the money shall be spent. In peacetime, the small-town post office, a veterans' hospital, a port dredging job, all must be authorized according to the political formula worked out in detail by Congress.

The congressman also is expected to serve his constituents as an "errand boy," in varied fields quite divorced from legislation. One representative estimated that three-fourths of a member's time is taken up by contacting executive agencies, dealing with District of Columbia matters, handling claims against the government, finding jobs for constituents, and other petty functions. Such work is so time consuming that few members find it possible to study legislation adequately.[1]

STRENGTHENING THE CONGRESS

Relations with the Executive.—Considered broadly, the over-all leadership of Congress is most likely to come from the executive. The President is the representative of the nation, the generalissimo of the Administration, the people's choice. The nation, and its Congress, quite properly look to

PARTY COMPLEXION OF CONGRESS

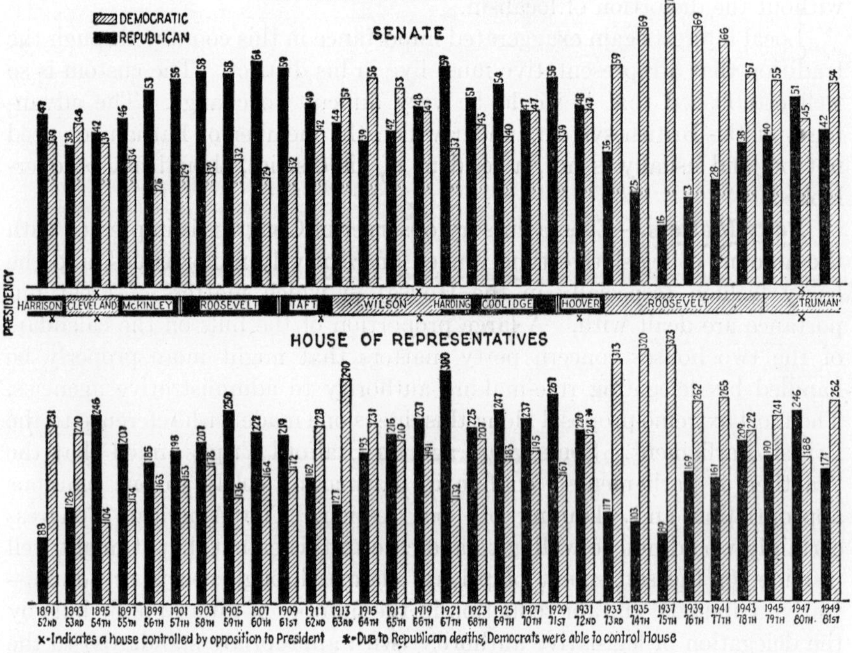

him for leadership. The presidential system has great weaknesses not present in the parliamentary scheme. If a new start were being made, the latter, with executive responsible to the legislative, might well be favored. But the tradition of separation is established in this republic, and means must be improvised to make the system work. Presidential leadership should not mean, however, servile acceptance of every executive proposal to the Congress. Congress should exercise its own independent judgment upon every recommendation of the executive. Experience has

[1] Testimony of Estes Kefauver, United States Congress, Joint Committee on the Organization of Congress, *Hearings*, part 1 (Washington: Government Printing Office. 1945), pp. 66–71.

shown that the American system works best with the President accepting and actively playing the role of chief legislator. Executive-legislative relations might be improved and made more direct if the two houses would amend their rules to permit cabinet members to be questioned in person on the floor of the House and Senate.[1]

Other proposals for improved relations with the executive call for a joint legislative-executive cabinet composed of legislators and executive heads in approximately equal number. Nearly all reform plans include some provision for regular consultation between congressional leaders and the President. Several favor careful coordination of legislative committees with the corresponding executive departments.

Leadership and Committees.—If Congress is not to be dominated by the executive, internal reforms are necessary to provide an alternative leadership. Proposals for strengthening congressional leadership are so intertwined with those for committee revision, the two must be considered together. Students of Congress generally agree that the Senate and House had too many committees, resulting in diffused authority, overlapping jurisdiction, and conflicting committee meetings for many members. Some attack selection of chairmen by seniority; perhaps election by party caucus would prove most satisfactory. The solution offered by many critics of the committee system is to reduce the number of committees in each house to about ten, but the reductions accomplished in the 1946 reorganization to fifteen in the Senate and nineteen in the House have improved the situation greatly.

After the reorganization of the committees is completed, it is often proposed that the chairmen of the committees, all members of the majority party, constitute a sort of "legislative cabinet," or "legislative policy committee," similar to the legislative council scheme now used by several states. This cabinet would become the body through which the business of Congress is planned, the work of the committees is coordinated, and contacts with executive heads are maintained.

The objections to these proposals come mainly from the Congress itself. Reduction in the number of committees will mean the abolition of dozens of chairmanships now existing, together with their small patronage and prestige value. Some legislative matters might not get the attention they deserve from a large committee. The "legislative-cabinet" idea often is feared by the rank-and-file legislator because he feels that some of the prerogatives of the membership will be assumed by the leadership.

[1] This proposal is generally known as the "Kefauver Plan" after its chief sponsor, who is now senator from Tennessee. See Estes Kefauver, "The Need for Better Executive-legislative Teamwork in the National Government," *American Political Science Review*, vol. 38 (April, 1944), pp. 317–325. In the 79th Congress, the proposal was introduced as House Resolution 31 (Kefauver) and Senate Resolution 8 (Fulbright).

FOUR PLANS FOR CONGRESSIONAL REFORM AND THE REORGANIZATION ACT

Features	National Planning Association[1]	American Political Science Association[2]	Joint Committee of Congress[3]	Legislative Reorganization Act[4]
Leadership	Majority and minority policy committees, each house.	Legislative council to plan majority program in Congress.	Majority and minority policy committees, each house.	No provision; Senate policy group added.
Relations with President	Majority policy committees consult with President.	Legislative council to promote liaison and cooperation.	Joint council of executive and policy committees.	No provision.
Question period	Experiment with department heads.	No recommendation.	No jurisdiction.	No provision.
Liaison with departments	....	Committees parallel departments and work with them.	Committees review agencies within their jurisdiction.	No provision.
Control over administration	Broader appropriation bills; control through Accounting Office.	House committee on appropriations oversees administrative performance.	Service audits by Comptroller General; no more indefinite appropriations.	Service audits; definite appropriations.
Members' offices	Adequate personal staffs.	Substantial clerk hire increase.	An administrative assistant for each.	No provision; Senate got later.
Library of Congress	Expansion of reference service.	More funds and better facilities.	Increased funds and services.	Increased funds and services.
Legislative counsel	....	More appropriations and services.	Expanded funds and personnel.	Expanded funds and personnel.
Number of committees	15 each house.	Eliminate inactive.	Senate 16; House 18.	Senate 15; House 19.
Committee jurisdiction	Equivalent in Senate and House.	Parallel committees in the two houses.	Clearly defined jurisdiction.	Clearly defined jurisdiction.
Committee staffs	Adequate staffs.	Independent qualified experts.	Four added experts per committee.	Four added experts per committee.
Committee chairmen	Find substitute for seniority.	Six-year tenure *or* party group choose; curb chairman's power.	No agreement.	No provision.
Retirement	Annuity at 55.	Contributory plan like civil service.	Contributory plan.	Contributory plan.
Salaries	$25,000.	$15,000.	$15,000, taxable as businessman's.	$12,500 plus $2,500 expenses.
Reduction of work load	Reduce or reallocate.	Home rule for D.C.; delegate claims; cut private bills.	Home rule for D.C.; delegate claims; digest bills.	Delegate small claims; allows suits vs. U.S.
Lobbyist control	No provision.	Groups register; reveal membership and finances.	Groups register; list expenditures.	Groups register; list expenditures.

[1] Robert Heller, *Strengthening the Congress* (Washington, D.C.: National Planning Association, 1945).

[2] George Galloway and Others, *The Reorganization of Congress* (Washington: Public Affairs press, 1945).

[3] *Report of the Joint Committee on the Organization of Congress* (Washington: Government printing office 1946).

[4] 60 Stat. 831.

Aids for Congress.—Congress is attempting to perform its important work without proper help. Legislative costs are unbelievably low. Only a few committees are adequately staffed. The Legislative Reference Service of the Library of Congress has never been assigned the importance of comparable bodies in the states. The Offices of the Legislative Counsel have been badly financed and supported. Individual legislators, even with the additional clerk hire provided in 1944, often cannot keep abreast of their correspondence and routine duties.

Most of these difficulties can be overcome by making Congress more generous with itself. The Legislative Counsels and the Library of Congress should have the appropriations necessary for them to do the job. Allocation of a well-paid executive assistant to each member of the House and Senate would provide a welcome relief from humdrum office work and would release members to spend more time on legislation. It is highly important, however, that additional employees authorized for members' offices and committees be qualified persons, chosen for other than political qualifications. This might be controlled in part by making most of the appointments in the Library of Congress and assigning them to work with particular members or committees according to the type of legislation at hand. Expansion of congressional bill-drafting facilities could release the legislative branch from excessive reliance upon measures prepared in executive departments and by private agencies.

Congress and the Public.—That Congress has done a poor job in public relations is generally agreed. The executive branch has great advantages of prestige and concentrated responsibility. The Congress is large and unwieldy, fettered by tradition and handicapped by the lack of leadership from within. A number of proposals have been made for improving public understanding of Congress and its problems. First, the House and Senate might reduce the amount of time spent in session, concentrating into one or two days a week the important legislative business that must be conducted on the floor. Second, these sessions could be broadcast directly over the radio to the whole country and ought to command more attention from the newspapers. Third, public attention should be focused on committee proceedings, where detailed work is done on legislation; this would be made easier by reducing the number of committees and making provision for public attendance at committee hearings. Fourth, recesses should be taken at appropriate intervals so that legislators could return to their districts and report in person to their constituents.

From public understanding of Congress and the issues before it might come appreciation for congressional needs and problems. Often hostile to proposals for increasing the perquisites of legislative office, public opinion, when properly informed, might recognize that congressional salaries ought to be increased to $20,000 or more. Moreover, Congress ought to be encouraged to cease being so stingy with itself regarding staff assistance. With the federal budget running into many billions of dollars, even a slight saving in administrative expenditures would more than justify Congress in spending ten times as much as formerly on investigators, technical staff, legislative draftsmen, and research assistance. Another reform, dear to the hearts of many Congressmen, is the longer term of office. Representatives would like very much to have terms of 4 years, and there is much to be said for the change. Besides relieving members of the House from the insistent pressure of repairing political fences for reelection, the 4-year term would reduce considerably the possibility of a deadlock with a President of one party and the House majority of another. The 4-year term for House would introduce problems in connection with the Senate term, for the present scheme used in the Senate requires election of one-third of the membership each 2 years. Extending the Senate term to 8 years with one-half of the senators elected each 4 years is one possibility, but it might lead to deadlock between President and Senate majority. The Senate term might be reduced to 4 years; although this would virtually eliminate the possibility of deadlock, with all representatives and senators and the President elected at the same time, it is not likely to prove popular with the Senate, two-thirds of which must vote affirmatively in order to submit the necessary constitutional amendment.[1]

The reform of Congress, long discussed sporadically in academic and congressional circles, became a major item on the agenda of American democracy in 1945 and 1946. Urged for several years by a committee on Congress of the American Political Science Association and by many individual critics, the Seventy-ninth Congress established a joint committee to study its organization. After extended hearings, the committee filed its report on Mar. 4, 1946.[2] The committee, headed by Senator Robert M. La Follette, managed to reach agreement on most of the acute organizational problems facing Congress. As shown in tabular form on an earlier page, the report called for the creation of majority- and minority-party committees in each house, a joint legislative-executive council composed of congressional and executive leaders, a fairly drastic reorgan-

[1] For further reading on the reform of Congress, the following are especially recommended: Young, *op. cit.;* George B. Galloway, *Congress on Trial* (New York: Crowell, 1946); Thomas K. Finletter, *Can Representative Government Do the Job?* (New York: Reynal & Hitchcock, Inc., 1945); Robert Heller, *Strengthening the Congress* (Washington, D.C.: National Planning Association, 1945); James M. Burns, *Congress on Trial* (New York: Harper, 1949); and Estes Kefauver and Jack Levin, *A Twentieth Century Congress* (New York: Duell, Sloan & Pearce, 1947).

[2] United States Congress, Joint Committee on the Organization of Congress *Hearings*, parts 1–4 (Washington: Government Printing Office, 1945), and *Organization of the Congress*, Report of the . . . pursuant to House Con. Res. 18, 79th Cong., 2d Sess., Senate Report No. 1011 (Washington: Government Printing Office, 1946).

ization of committee systems of the Senate and House, great increases in aids to the Congress, reduction of petty duties that take congressional time, and more adequate compensation of members. The committee could not reach agreement on reform of the seniority system or of House Rules Committee powers. It considered the proposal of a question hour and of Senate filibusters as outside the scope of its powers.

1946 Reform.—In July, 1946, during the closing rush of the second session of the Seventy-ninth Congress, the Legislative Reorganization Act of 1946 was enacted.[1] The principal features of the legislation may be summarized as follows:

Standing Committees.—The Senate was reduced from thirty-three to fifteen committees; the House, from forty-seven to nineteen.

Compensation.—The salary was increased from $10,000 to $12,500 and tax-free expense account extended to both senators and representatives.

Retirement.—The scheme requires members to contribute 6 per cent of basic salaries; on retirement at the age of sixty-two or later, after 6 or more years of service, an annuity will be paid at the rate of 2½ per cent of basic salary for the years of service, but not in excess of three-fourths of the closing salary.

Aids.—Each committee employs the services of four experts at $5,000 to $8,000 per year. Both the Legislative Reference Service and the Offices of the Legislative Counsel will be allowed more staff and larger appropriations.

Lobbying.—Groups must report their contributions and expenditures for lobbying, including the names and addresses of those who contribute $500 and more. Paid lobbyists must register with the Clerk of the House and the Secretary of the Senate, listing their names, addresses, employers, salaries, expenses, time employed, and the like. This information will be published in the *Congressional Record.*

Claims.—Claims of $1,000 and less may be settled by the heads of the federal agency concerned. Suits against the Federal government are authorized in the district courts, with the right of appeal.

Further Reorganization Needed.—The Legislative Reorganization Act has been in operation long enough to disclose both the improvements it effected and its shortcomings. Some of the weaknesses resulted from House amendments to the bill; several beneficial points were not included either in the report of the reorganization committee or in the bill.

While the committee system has been improved by the reduction in number of committees, the seniority method of choosing chairmen remains. The "life-and-death" powers of the House Rules Committee are little diminished. The number and jurisdiction of House and Senate committees

[1] 60 Stat. 831. The Senate passed the bill on June 10, 1946, by a vote of 48 to 16. The House adopted the measure July 25, 1946, by a vote of 229 to 61.

are not in harmony, nor are they properly coordinated with executive departments. Some special investigating committees are still being created to conduct probes that might more effectively be handled by subgroups of standing committees. Staffing of committees and of senators' offices has been made more adequate, but members of the House still need administrative assistants, and many committees still cannot match in expertness the executive and special-interest representatives who come to testify.

Petty demands on congressional time have been reduced but far from eliminated. Home rule for the District of Columbia not only would give self-government to residents of the District, but would unburden Congress and leave more time for national matters. Some claim bills and various appointment matters still plague individual legislators.

Legislative-executive relationships were not directly improved by the 1946 act. For more than a decade, except during the Eightieth Congress, informal weekly conferences have been taking place at the White House between the President and majority party congressional leaders. There remains a need for some formal council in which the President and cabinet members might meet regularly with congressional leaders. Such a council was proposed in all the leading reorganization plans, but was left out of the Reorganization Act. The "question period" proposal of Senator Kefauver, while less widely supported, suggests another way in which executive-legislative misunderstandings might be minimized. The Senate has moved to further develop its own leadership through the creation of majority and minority policy committees, but the House has taken no comparable action.[1]

References

(See also works listed after preceding chapter.)

ALEXANDER, DE ALVA S.: *History and Procedure of the House of Representatives* (Boston: Houghton Mifflin, 1916).

BURDETTE, FRANKLIN L.: *Filibustering in the Senate* (Princeton, N.J.: Princeton University Press, 1940).

BURNS, JAMES M.: *Congress on Trial; The Politics of Modern Lawmaking* (New York: Harper, 1949).

CHAMBERLAIN, JOSEPH P.: *Legislative Processes: National and State* (New York: Appleton-Century-Crofts, 1936).

COLEGROVE, KENNETH: *The American Senate and World Peace* (New York: Vanguard, 1944).

DANGERFIELD, ROYDEN J.: *In Defense of the Senate; A Study in Treaty-making* (Norman, Okla.: University of Oklahoma Press, 1933).

[1] Professor George E. Outland, scholarly ex-congressman, summarizes the case for further reforms in "Congress Still Needs Reorganization," *Western Political Quarterly*, vol. 1 (June, 1948), pp. 154–164.

FINLETTER, THOMAS K.: *Can Representative Government Do the Job?* (New York: Reynal & Hitchcock, Inc., 1945).

FLEMING, DENNA F.: *The Treaty Veto of the American Senate* (New York: Putnam, 1930).

GALLOWAY, GEORGE: *Limitation of Debate in the United States Senate*, Public Affairs Bulletin No. 64 (Washington: Library of Congress, 1948).

——— *Congress at the Crossroads* (New York: Crowell, 1946).

——— *et al.: The Reorganization of Congress* (Washington: Public Affairs Press, 1945). A report of the Committee on Congress of the American Political Science Association.

HELLER, ROBERT: *Strengthening the Congress* (Washington: National Planning Association, 1945).

KEFAUVER, ESTES, and JACK LEVIN: *A Twentieth Century Congress* (New York: Duell, Sloan & Pearce, 1947).

LUCE, ROBERT: *Legislative Problems* (Boston: Houghton Mifflin, 1935).

——— *Legislative Procedure* (Boston: Houghton Mifflin, 1922).

MCCOWN, ADA C.: *The Congressional Conference Committee* (New York: Columbia University Press, 1927).

RIDDICK, FLOYD M.: *Congressional Procedure* (Boston: Chapman & Grimes, Inc., 1941).

——— *The United States Congress Organization and Procedure* (Manassas, Va.: National Capitol Publishers, 1949).

——— and GEORGE H. SMITH: *Congress in Action* (Manassas, Va.: National Capitol Publishers, 1948).

ROGERS, LINDSAY: *The American Senate* (New York: Knopf, 1926).

TORREY, VOLTA: *You and Your Congress* (New York: Morrow, 1944).

UNITED STATES CONGRESS: *Official Congressional Directory.* Issued for each session of each Congress.

——— *Congressional Record.* Issued daily when House or Senate meet. Bound volumes available after close of each session.

UNITED STATES CONGRESS JOINT COMMITTEE ON THE ORGANIZATION OF CONGRESS: *Hearings*, parts 1–4, 79th Cong., 1st Sess. (Washington: Government Printing Office, 1945).

——— *Report of the Joint Committee on the Organization of Congress . . .* pursuant to H. Con. Res. 18, Senate Report No. 1011 (Washington: Government Printing Office, 1946).

UNITED STATES HOUSE OF REPRESENTATIVES: *Cannon's Procedure in the House of Representatives*, House Doc. 731, 80th Cong. (Washington: Government Printing Office, 1948).

WALKER, HARVEY: *The Legislative Process* (New York: Ronald, 1948).

YOUNG, ROLAND: *This Is Congress* (New York: Knopf, 1943).

Chapter 14

PRESIDENT: THE OFFICE

When foreign affairs play a prominent part in the politics and policy of a nation, its Executive must of necessity be its guide: must utter every initial judgment, take every first step of action, supply the information upon which it is to act, suggest and in large measure control its conduct.

Woodrow Wilson, *Congressional Government.*[1]

STRUCTURE AND ROLE

Question of a Separate Executive Branch.—When the Constitutional Convention of 1787 came to discuss the execution of laws, it was necessary to justify the establishment of a separate executive branch. Under the Articles of Confederation no separate executive existed; Congress exercised all executive authority through committees and special agents, but in general this plan had worked rather badly. The office of governor, found in all the states, was also a possible model. Although authority, terms, and modes of election varied, all were separately organized and all were single executives. The separation of authority between Crown and Parliament, then undergoing change in Britain, was cited by those who desired an independent executive. Those who wanted no separate executive argued that the tyranny of George III gave ample support to their view. Montesquieu and Locke were quoted on their advocacy of the separation of powers by proponents of the separate executive. In the Convention of 1787, however, little controversy arose over the necessity of national executive. Madison's notes contain no record of a delegate having spoken against an executive branch, although some delegates wanted an executive "absolutely dependent" on the legislative branch.[2]

Form of the Executive.—If a separate executive were to be established, should it be single or plural? Some proposed vesting the executive authority in a group or council, like the two consuls of Rome. This plural type of executive has the obvious disadvantage of dividing authority, which can so easily lead to irresponsibility. The convention's decision for a single executive was made by a vote of seven states to two.[3] Even after the single

[1] (Boston: Houghton, 1913), xi–xii. First published in 1885.

[2] Charles C. Tansill (ed.), *Documents Illustrative of the Formation of the Union of the American States*, House Doc. 398, 69th Cong., 1st Sess. (Washington: Government Printing Office, 1927), pp. 131–134. Hereafter cited as *Documents*.

[3] *Documents*, p. 146. The vote was taken on June 4, 1787. It was phrased: "Shall the blank for the number of the executive be filled with a single person?" *Ibid.*, p. 145.

executive was agreed upon, many argued for making executive actions subject to a council of advisers, a device already used to curb the powers of many governors. Diffusion of authority was charged against this plan, too, and eventually the convention was won over to a single chief magistrate, styled "President," with no advisory council.

The desire to make the President subject to some advisory body did lead to giving the Senate power to advise and consent to appointments and treaties proposed by the executive. On the whole, however, the President was left free to set up his own advisory services. The cabinet, without a constitutional or statutory status and completely under executive control, is the leading formal agency for consultation. Each chief executive may choose in addition such other advisers as he deems fit.

Scope of Executive Authority.—The question of powers of the separate, single executive was most perplexing and most crucial. The heritage of colonial and revolutionary days directed that a weak executive, if any, be established. Years of struggle with royal and proprietary governors taught American colonists to distrust executive power. The aversion of the people to monarchy, particularly to George III, strengthened the position of those who desired a weak executive.

On the other hand, the breakdown of central government under the Articles of Confederation led some to demand an energetic executive. It was argued that if the separation of powers were desirable, it was logical to have three coordinate branches, with no one predominant over the others. The convention finally decided to vest in the President most, but not all, of the executive power. Power to confirm appointments and to ratify treaties was reserved for the Senate. The President was given important legislative and some judicial authority. Sections 2 and 3 of Article II of the Constitution were devoted to an enumeration of presidential powers. The President was made commander-in-chief of the Army and Navy, was given power to appoint, to make treaties, to receive ambassadors and ministers, to grant reprieves and pardons, to enforce laws, and to perform certain duties in connection with the Congress. The legislative, executive, and judicial functions of the President will be examined in the next chapter.

Much of the President's authority accrues to him by virtue of factors beyond the formal powers. His prestige as chief representative of the American people, and as leader of his political party, plays a large part in making him a strong leader if he chooses the role and has the personal qualities to fill it.

THE SELECTION PROCESS

Constitutional Provisions.—Direct election of the President was considered a practical impossibility by most of the framers of the Constitution, even though direct election of the governor had been successful in New

York and Massachusetts.[1] Selection by Congress was most widely supported in the convention; this selection method was included in both Virginia and New Jersey plans, and was adopted unanimously at one point in the convention's proceedings.

The electoral-college mode of selection eventually chosen was a compromise, combining, its craftsmen felt, the virtues of independence from the legislative branch with indirect popular participation. Each state chooses, in any way its legislature specifies, electors equal in number to the representatives and senators from that state. All states now use popular election on a state-wide basis. The electors meet in their own states and cast ballots for presidential and vice-presidential candidates. The results in each state are sent to the national capital and opened in the presence of Congress. Under the original plan each elector voted for two persons; the candidate receiving a majority of electoral votes became President, and the second highest became Vice-President.

This scheme caused a tie between Jefferson and Burr in 1800. Although the electors clearly intended that Jefferson should be President and Burr Vice-President, under the terms of the Constitution each had exactly seventy-three votes, and election was thrown to the House of Representatives. In the House some federalists supported Burr, but eventually Jefferson was elected. It was clear that the mode of election was defective and must be amended. The Twelfth Amendment corrected this by providing for separate voting for President and Vice-President. If no presidential candidate secures a majority of electoral votes, the House of Representatives chooses from the three highest, with each state casting one vote. Only two presidential elections have been thrown to the House: the 1800 Jefferson-Burr mix-up and the 1824 contest among Clay, John Quincy Adams, Jackson, and Crawford. If no vice-presidential candidate secures a majority, the Senate chooses from the two highest. Great confusion can arise over the counting of electoral votes. In 1876 Samuel J. Tilden led Rutherford B. Hayes by 184 to 165 electoral votes, but Congress, with Democratic House and Republican Senate, disagreed over the acceptance of conflicting returns from certain states. Eventually, in 1877 Congress created by statute an Electoral Commission composed of five members of the House, five senators, and five Supreme Court justices. The verdict of the commission, rendered on a strictly partisan basis, awarded the twenty disputed votes to Hayes, which gave the presidency to him. A law of 1887 declares that each state shall determine the authenticity of its selection of electors.

Procedure in the States.—Within this constitutional framework, a standardized state procedure has developed, under which electors are elected

[1] James Wilson of Pennsylvania favored direct election. Madison records Wilson as saying that while apprehensive that he might be regarded as visonary, "'. . . in theory he was for an election by the people." *Ibid.*, p. 134.

popularly on a general-ticket basis. With few exceptions, this scheme has been followed throughout the country for over a hundred years. Since each state has a number of electoral votes equal to its total of United States senators and representatives, each voter casts his ballot for a considerable group. This ranges from forty-seven in New York, thirty-five in Pennsylvania, twenty-eight in Illinois to three in Nevada, Delaware, Wyoming, and Vermont. The list of electors is made up by the official party organization in each state.

The threat, in 1944 and 1948, of some Southern electors elected under the Democratic label to bolt their party and vote for a third-party presidential candidate has served to focus extraordinary interest on the law and tradition governing the selection and pledging of electors. Professor Silva found twenty-seven states in which electors were nominated by state party conventions; ten, by other party bodies; seven, in party primaries; three, in optional primary or convention; in Pennsylvania alone the presidential nominee selects his party's candidates for elector.[1] While nearly one-half of the states now use the presidential short ballot, which includes only the names of candidates for the presidency and vice-presidency, five states, all small or Southern, go to the opposite extreme and print only the names of candidates for presidential electors, omitting the names of presidential standard-bearers.

Although most state laws concerning electors appear to be based on the assumption that electors will vote automatically for their party's nominees, only California and Oregon require it directly. States have power, if they choose to exercise it, to require pledges of candidates for elector, or to direct electors concerning their conduct in case their party's presidential or vice-presidential candidate dies before the meetings of the electoral college.[2]

At one time the states followed a uniform practice of printing the names of all would-be electors on the ballots, but this was expensive in the large states and virtually impossible when a voting machine was used. Consequently, by 1948 twenty states, including most of the largest ones, had adopted the "presidential short ballot," on which the names of individual electors do not appear, but a phrase such as "Twenty-five Electors pledged to vote for Harry S. Truman for President and Alben Barkley for Vice-President."[3] The electors selected then assemble in the state capital and go through the formality of casting their ballots; a 1934 federal law requires

[1] Ruth C. Silva, "State Law on the Nomination, Election, and Instruction of Presidential Electors," *American Political Science Review*, vol. 42 (June, 1948), pp. 523–524.

[2] *Ibid.*, p. 529.

[3] The states using the presidential short ballot are California, Colorado, Connecticut, Delaware, Illinois, Indiana, Iowa, Kentucky, Maryland, Massachusetts, Michigan, Missouri, Nebraska, New Hampshire, North Carolina, Ohio, Pennsylvania, Texas, Washington, and Wisconsin. In addition New Jersey, New York, and Rhode Island have, in effect, adopted the short ballot through general use of the voting machine.

OFFICIAL NATIONAL
PARTY COLUMN BALLOT
A vote for the Candidates for President and Vice President shall be a vote for the electors of such party, the names of whom are on file with the Secretary of State.
USE X ONLY IN MARKING BALLOT
FOR A STRAIGHT TICKET MARK WITHIN THIS CIRCLE
REPUBLICAN TICKET
For President
THOMAS E. DEWEY
For Vice President
JOHN W. BRICKER
FOR A STRAIGHT TICKET MARK WITHIN THIS CIRCLE
DEMOCRATIC TICKET
For President
FRANKLIN D. ROOSEVELT
For Vice President
HARRY S. TRUMAN

Twenty states in 1948 utilized the presidential short ballot. Three others in effect had the short ballot because voting machines were used generally. The names of candidates for elector are eliminated from the ballot, and only the names of the party's nominees for President and Vice-President appear.

THE LONG BALLOT

OFFICIAL BALLOT

DEMOCRATIC PARTY	REPUBLICAN PARTY	TEXAS REGULARS PARTY	SOCIALIST PARTY
For Electors for President and Vice President:	For Electors for President and Vice President:	For Electors for President and Vice President:	For Electors for President and Vice President:
R. D. SANDERS	O. SAM CUMMINGS	T. J. HOLBROOK	A. B. ROSENTHAL
JIM STRONG	FRANK PUTNAM	E. B. GERMANY	P. E. SIMMONS
G. C. HARRIS	H. G. WHEAT	T. G. TILFORD	ROY FRIDDELL
GEO. W. EDDY	S. I. DUNN	ERNEST A. BOSL	C. V. MULLER
F. L. HENDERSON	J. B. MILLER	ARCH H. ROWAN	CHARLES M. ALBRECHT
W. N. FOSTER	FLOYD HARRY	JOHN WHEELER	A. E. CAY
PAT N. FAHEY	W. P. LUSE	JOHN H. CROOKER	F. E. LEONARD
E. HAWES, JR.	BEN BALLARD	MRS. F. R. CARLTON	W. A. THOMAS
W. L. CROSTHWAIT	CHAS. F. ADAMS	J. HARRY BURKE	J. T. SANDERS
H. P. JOHNSON	MRS. W. F. JONES	OLIN P. McWHIRTER	MOLLIE WILSON
W. W. DOWD	R. R. WELLS	W. EDWARD LEE	MARCUS ANDERSON
MRS. DALLAS SCARBOROUGH	FLOYD MOONEY	E. R. SPENCER	JACK WALLACE
ROBERT LEE BOBBITT	W. R. PHILLIPS	FRED BROWN	G. W. M. TAYLOR
H. G. LUCAS	H. H. MORSE	H. J. MOSSER	
MRS. CLARA DRISCOLL	W. C. WITCHER	MRS. CECIL SMITH	
J. W. PHILLIPS	ROY T. OSBORNE	RICHARD S. BROOKS	
J. E. WHEAT	JESSE DENNETT	E. L. KLETT	
HARRY STARR	JOE SUNDERLAND	RAYMOND ROBBINS	
T. S. JONES	E. G. HAMPTON	T. J. McMAHON	
HOMER PHARR	S. E. FISH	MRS. ORVILLE TUNSTILL	
THOS. J. PITTS	A. E. QUEST	DONLEY SUDDATH	
TOM NELSON	ROBERT V. MAVERICK	CLYDE WARWICK	
FRED H. MINOR	BEN ROBEY	HORACE BLALOCK	

The presidential long ballot, which includes the names of candidates for elector, serves little useful purpose because the splitting of votes is both rare and impractical. It is also wasteful of paper and of the time of both voter and election board. Texas adopted a presidential short-ballot law in 1932, but it has not been applied because of vagueness of construction. In 1945 a valid presidential short ballot was adopted.

that the electors meet on the first Monday after the second Wednesday in December. No general official meeting of all electors in the country is held, though in recent years attempts have been made to assemble as many as possible in Washington for unofficial celebrations.

Under the terms of the Twentieth Amendment, the two houses of Congress meet in joint session on Jan. 6 following a presidential election. The electoral votes are counted and the results are announced. Inauguration takes place on Jan. 20.

Electoral-college Shortcomings.—It is not difficult to find fault with the electoral-college system of choosing the President. Under the original plan it was expected that the leading citizens chosen as electors would be free agents and would select as President the outstanding American who met the formal requirements. After the emergence of the party system, electors were more and more bound to vote for the candidates adopted by their party. Sentiment for popular election of electors grew rapidly during the Jacksonian era, and by 1832 all states but one dropped election by legislature and adopted popular election. After the Civil War popular election was universal. Likewise, all states came to adhere to the plan of at-large election, with all candidates for elector running on a state-wide ticket.

Election at large seriously distorts the presidential vote of each state. If the Republican electoral list in Ohio receives 1,500,000 votes and the Democratic 1,500,001, all of Ohio's twenty-five electoral votes go to the Democratic candidate for the presidency. It is a sort of "unit rule," under which the winner of a plurality in each state takes all, and the national total of popular votes counts for nothing officially. This distortion within each state would not be a serious matter if the result were fair and equitable nationally. Of course, it is not. Good luck has produced a majority winner in nearly every presidential campaign, but a streak of bad luck may bring repeated minority winners. The charts on page 297 show how the popular and electoral votes were related in past elections. In two crucial elections, of Wilson in 1912 and of Lincoln in 1860, an electoral majority was secured without a popular majority, but in each case there was a popular plurality. Hayes in 1876 and Harrison in 1888 were elected with a majority of electoral votes, but with a minority of popular votes.

Reform in Presidential Selection.—The most obvious and most drastic change in method of choosing the President is to provide for outright popular election. This is simple and direct; it is in keeping with democratic tradition; it assures a majority or plurality choice. Objections to direct election come from the smaller states and from the South. The smaller states would lose their advantage of a certain minimum of three electoral votes and its consequent multiplication of their influence in presidential elections. The Southern states would suffer for their virtual exclusion of the Negro from elections. Since Southern participation in voting is low, influence in presidential elections would drop accordingly. Opposition from these two sources makes proposal of the necessary constitutional amendment by a two-thirds vote in each house of Congress a

Popular Vote For Presidential Electors, 1896-1948

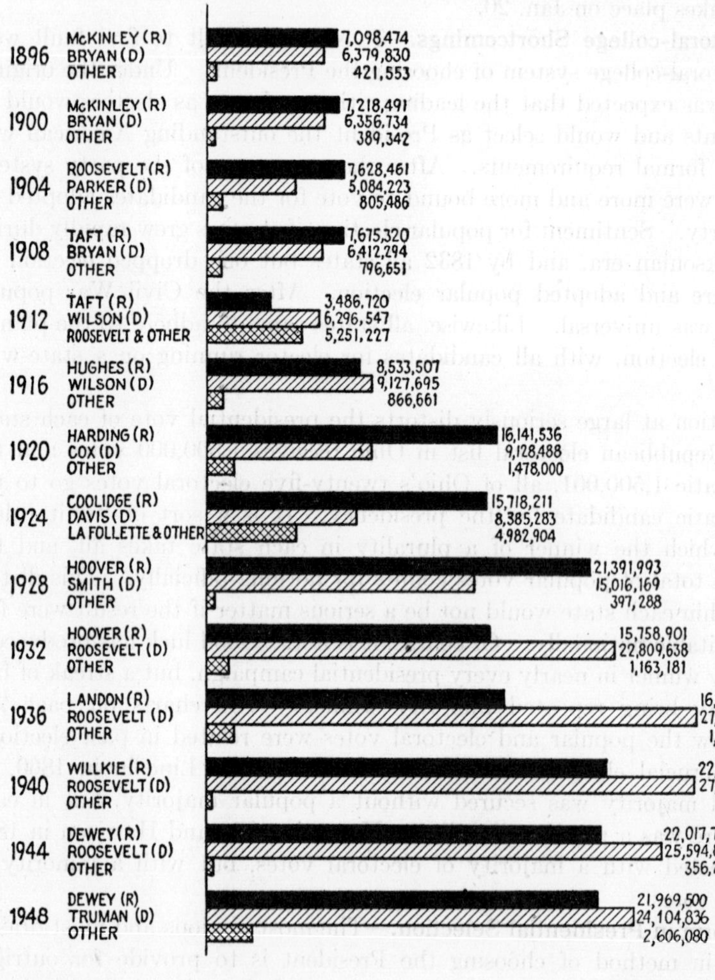

practical impossibility. Ratification by three-fourths of the states also could not be obtained.

A middle way for reforming presidential selection is to persuade the states to change their methods of choosing presidential electors from election at large to election by districts. In 1891 the Michigan legislature took

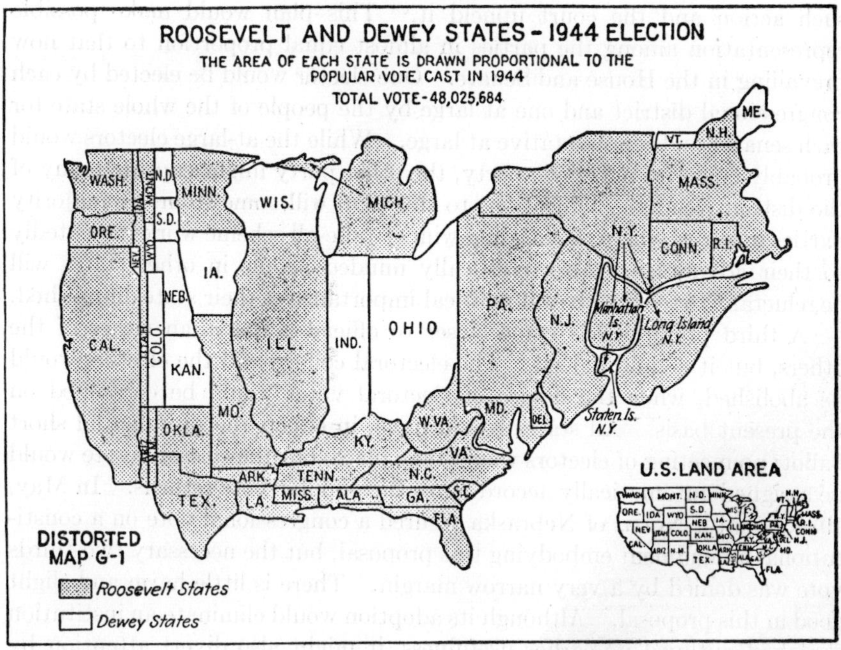

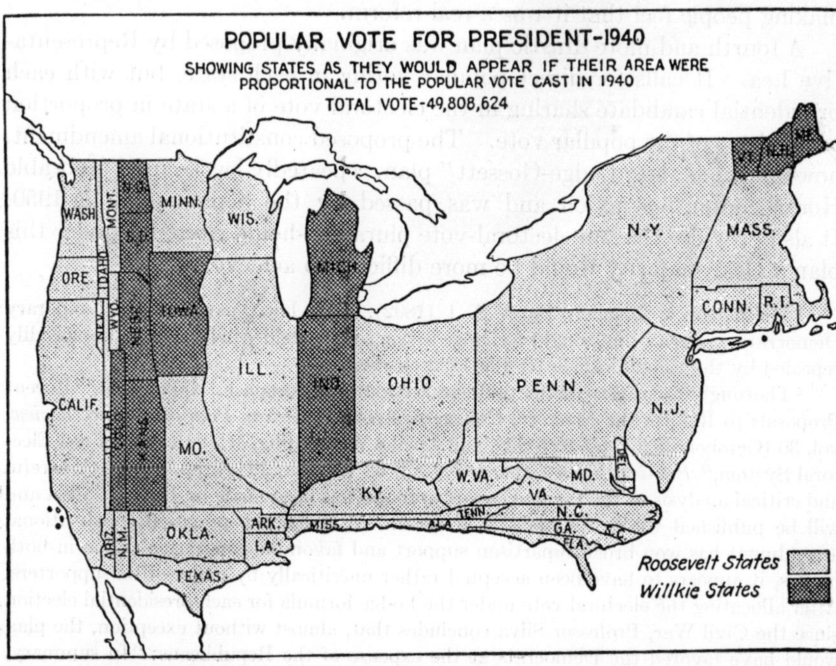

SOURCE: National Opinion Research Center, University of Denver.

such action and the court upheld it.[1] This plan would make possible representation among the parties in almost equal proportion to that now prevailing in the House and Senate. One elector would be elected by each congressional district and one at large by the people of the whole state for each senator and representative at large. While the at-large electors would probably come from a single party, the other party might capture many of the district electors. Objections to this plan will come from the majority parties in states where the existing winner-take-all scheme works repeatedly to their advantage. Also, politically minded people in other states will be reluctant to see the pivotal political importance of their state diminished.

A third proposal has come closer to official action than either of the others, but it is mild indeed. The electoral college and the electors would be abolished, while the device of electoral votes would be continued on the present basis. All states would have, in effect, the presidential short ballot; no meeting of electors would take place, but the electoral vote would be assigned automatically according to the popular-vote returns. In May, 1934, Senator Norris of Nebraska secured a congressional vote on a constitutional amendment embodying this proposal, but the necessary two-thirds vote was denied by a very narrow margin. There is little harm and slight good in this proposal. Although its adoption would eliminate an institution that had outlived its earlier usefulness, it might also divert attention by making people feel that it was a real reform.

A fourth and more drastic plan was originally proposed by Representative Lea. It calls for direct popular voting in each state, but with each presidential candidate sharing in the electoral vote of a state in proportion to his share of the popular vote. The proposed constitutional amendment, now known as the "Lodge-Gossett" plan, repeatedly has secured favorable House committee action and was passed by the Senate early in 1950. It also provides that an electoral-vote plurality should elect; for under this plan a clear majority would be more difficult to achieve.[2]

[1] McPherson *v.* Blacker, 146 U.S. 1 (1892). The law, enacted by a temporary Democratic majority that sought a chance to win some presidential electors, was speedily repealed by the Republicans after the 1892 election.

[2] Thorough discussions of the problem are found in Joseph E. Kallenbach, "Recent Proposals to Reform the Electoral College System," *American Political Science Review*, vol. 30 (October, 1936), pp. 924–929, and Lucius Wilmerding, Jr., "Reform of the Electoral System," *Political Science Quarterly*, vol. 64 (March, 1949), pp. 1–23. A careful and critical analysis of the Lodge-Gossett proposal has been made by Ruth C. Silva and will be published while this book is in press. Although the proposed constitutional amendment has won broad bipartisan support and favorable committee action in both houses, it appears to have been accepted rather uncritically by many of its supporters. After allocating the electoral vote under the Lodge formula for each presidential election since the Civil War, Professor Silva concludes that, almost without exception, the plan would have favored the Democrats at the expense of the Republicans: "In summary, the Lodge formula would reduce the possibility of a Republican's reaching the Presi-

Read

PREREQUISITES AND PERQUISITES

Presidential Term of Office.—In the Constitutional Convention sharp controversy arose over the length of a presidential term. Alexander Hamilton once expressed himself as favoring a life term for the executive. The two alternatives considered most carefully, however, were (1) 6 or 7 years without reeligibility, or (2) 4 years with the possibility of reelection.[1]

Arguments for the longer term have been given in most effective form by William H. Taft, between his single term in the presidency and his chief-justiceship. A 7-year term without reeligibility, Taft once declared, would give the President "courage and independence" and relieve the federal employee from the "absorbing and diverting" interest in securing his reelection.[2] Against the long term, perhaps the strongest point is that during 6 or 7 years the popular will may change greatly and the views of the executive may become quite out of harmony with public sentiment.

The Federalist, numbers 71 and 72, probably written by Hamilton, are devoted to the defense of the 4-year term with reeligibility. This plan was adopted, he asserted, because it offers inducement for a President to do well, it gives the public the value of an executive's experience, and it secures a stability of policy. A 2-year term would be too short to obtain the "desired firmness and independence."

After Washington declined to serve a third term, there grew up a tradition that the limit of two terms should apply to all who served as President. When Grant was proposed for a third term, a storm of disapproval arose. Theodore Roosevelt, who reached the office through the vice-presidency and served only one full term, was sharply criticized for seeking election in 1912. Although the Republican forces made anti-third term a major issue in the 1940 campaign, the tradition was broken with the reelection of Franklin D. Roosevelt. Those who oppose the third term on principle fear that a man who serves so long in the presidency may build up a machine that will dominate the government and control the people. This is the consideration that prompted several states and some of the Latin-American republics to forbid even a second term to their governors and presidents. Proponents of the third term argue that a President should serve as long as he is willing and able and the people wish to reelect him. They maintain that popular controls through elections, legislative controls through Con-

---

dency with a popular plurality, but would enable a Democrat to salvage victory from popular defeat." Only in the unlikely event of emergence of close Democratic-Republican rivalry in the South would the Lodge plan produce satisfactory results and majority winners. The authors are grateful to Professor Silva for a preview of her article.

[1] The 7-year term was adopted first (*Documents*, p. 135). Then a 6-year term was substituted (*ibid.*, p. 415). Finally the 4-year plan was agreed upon (*ibid.*, p. 676).

[2] William H. Taft, *The Presidency* (New York: Scribner, 1916), p. 4.

gress, and judicial controls through the courts are adequate to prevent the rise of dictatorship in the country.

The Eightieth Congress submitted to the state legislatures a proposed constitutional amendment which declared: "No person shall be elected . . . more than twice . . ." or more than once if he succeeded to the presidency and served more than two years of the term of another.[1] By the end of 1949 it appeared unlikely that this proposed Twenty-second Amendment would receive the necessary thirty-six ratifications.

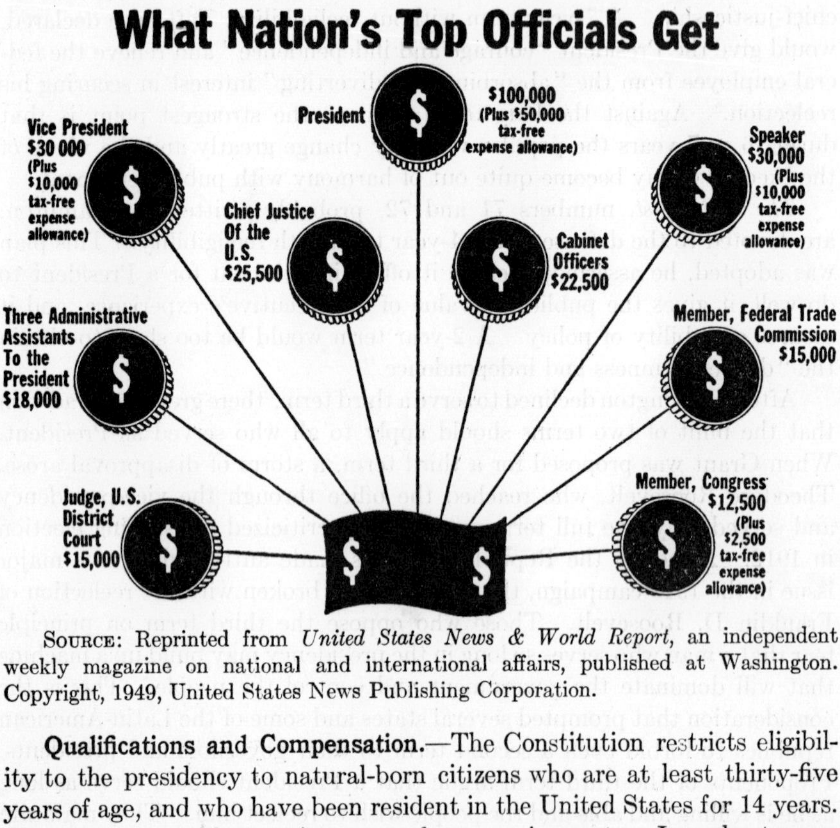

SOURCE: Reprinted from *United States News & World Report*, an independent weekly magazine on national and international affairs, published at Washington. Copyright, 1949, United States News Publishing Corporation.

Qualifications and Compensation.—The Constitution restricts eligibility to the presidency to natural-born citizens who are at least thirty-five years of age, and who have been resident in the United States for 14 years. Few controversies have arisen over these requirements. In order to provide for those who were born before the United States existed, persons who were citizens at the time of the adoption of the Constitution were made eligible. It is possible that a person born abroad of American parents

[1] A similar proposal was the subject of extended hearings in 1940: United States Senate, Committee on the Judiciary, *Third Term for President of the United States, Hearings . . .*, 76th Cong., 3d Sess. (Washington: Government Printing Office, 1940). See also Charles W. Stein, *The Third Term Tradition* (New York: Columbia University Press, 1942). The full text of the Amendment is given on p. 831.

might be regarded as "natural-born." Few complaints have been voiced over the age requirement. Theodore Roosevelt reached the presidency at forty-two; only five others reached it in their forties. The question of residence in the United States was raised in connection with Herbert Hoover, who had lived abroad for many years, but interpretation of this clause as requiring residence of 14 years continuously and immediately preceding election appears unwarranted.

The compensation of the President is fixed by Congress,[1] but it may not be diminished or increased during his term of office. From 1909 to 1949 it was $75,000 per year; in January, 1949, it was raised to $100,000 and an additional $50,000 tax-free expense allowance was provided. Travel, official entertaining, and White House are supported out of separate budget items. Even when all presidential perquisites are considered, however, the chief executive receives less compensation than hundreds of people in business and entertainment.

Succession.—According to the Constitution, if the President vacates his office, the Vice-President succeeds; if both offices fall vacant, Congress determines by law ". . . what officer shall then act as President. . . ."[2] In a statute enacted in 1886, Congress provided that the heads of the executive departments should succeed in the following order: State, Treasury, War, Justice, Post Office, Navy, and Interior.[3] The Twentieth Amendment provides that if no President is chosen by the beginning of the next term, the Vice-President-elect shall serve as President until such time as a President qualifies. If neither President-elect nor Vice-President-elect has qualified, Congress may declare who shall act as President.

Prior to the time Harry S. Truman was sworn in following the death of Franklin D. Roosevelt in April, 1945, six Vice-Presidents had succeeded to the presidency, all because of the deaths of the Presidents. William H. Harrison died in April, 1841, one month after his inauguration, and was succeeded by Tyler. General Zachary Taylor, who died in 1850, was followed by Fillmore. The assassination of Lincoln in 1865 left the presidency for Andrew Johnson. President James A. Garfield, who died from an assassin's bullet in 1881, was followed by Chester A. Arthur. McKinley's assassination in 1901 opened the way for the brilliant career of Theodore Roosevelt. Warren G. Harding's death in 1923 left the presidency to Calvin Coolidge. Only the last two managed to secure election for another term in the presidency. No provision is made in the law or Constitution

[1] Benjamin Franklin argued in the constitutional convention against any salary for the President. Madison recorded concerning this suggestion: "It was treated with great respect, but rather for the author of it, than from any apparent conviction of its expediency or practicability." *Documents*, p. 141.

[2] Article II, Section 1, Clause 5.

[3] 24 Stat. 7. The other cabinet posts did not then exist.

for succession in the case the President becomes disabled. Both Garfield and Wilson had considerable periods of incapacity but no method of removing the executive exists unless it be impeachment.

The death of Franklin D. Roosevelt in April, 1945, just at the end of the war in Europe and on the eve of the San Francisco Conference, focused the attention of the country on presidential succession law. President Truman soon recommended to Congress that a new succession law be enacted, replacing the heads of the executive departments with the Speaker of the House and the president pro tempore of the Senate. At the time, President Truman's sentiments were believed to be motivated largely by the fact that Secretary of State Edward R. Stettinius, Jr., was almost wholly lacking in political experience. The President repeated his recommendation in his State of the Union message of January, 1946.

In 1947 a new act was passed, providing that should both the President and Vice-President become unable to discharge the powers and duties of the presidency, the succession should be: Speaker of the House, president pro tempore of the Senate, and heads of the executive departments in order of the 1886 act except that the posts of Agriculture, Commerce, and Labor were added to the end.[1] The new act has been criticized severely for its failure to define "disability" and for the debatable unconstitutionality both of classifying the Speaker and the president pro tempore as "officers of the United States," as the Constitution requires for succession, and of declaring that he who succeeds becomes President and is entitled to serve out the remainder of the full term.[2]

It is difficult to see how the Speaker of the House and the president pro tempore of the Senate would be better material for the presidency than the heads of the executive departments. While the speakership normally is filled by a person of long experience in legislative matters, proved executive ability is rare in that office. The president pro tempore of the Senate seldom is a man of distinction and sometimes is a party wheel horse of indifferent qualification except that of long seniority. On the other hand, the Secretary of State and the Secretary of the Treasury are often experienced in both administration and politics.

[1] Public Law 199, 80th Cong., 1st Sess. Subsequently, under the National Security Act of 1947, the Secretary of Defense displaced the Secretary of War, and the Secretary of Navy was eliminated.

[2] See Ruth C. Silva, "The Presidential Succession Act of 1947," *Michigan Law Review*, vol. 47 (February, 1949), pp. 451–476; Everett S. Brown and Ruth C. Silva, "Presidential Succession and Inability," *Journal of Politics*, vol. 11 (February, 1949), pp. 236–256; Joseph E. Kallenbach, "The New Presidential Succession Act," *American Political Science Review*, vol. 41 (October, 1947), pp. 931–941.

THE PRESIDENT AND HIS COLLEAGUES

The Cabinet.—After the proposal for a council of advisers was eliminated by the Constitutional Convention, many assumed that the Senate would attempt to fill this role. But the first Senate was reluctant to advise directly with President Washington. Therefore, formal preconsultation, even on appointments and treaties, was dropped, never to be revived.

President Washington began to call department heads into consultation, and these early meetings were soon known as "cabinet" meetings. The cabinet has remained as it began, an informal group without legal sanction, its personnel determined by custom and by the will of the President. The cabinet meets only at the request of the President, it exercises only such authority as he chooses to vest in it, and it may be dissolved if the executive wishes. In practice, the cabinet plays an important part in the determination of executive policy and in coordinating administrative work. Reemphasis must be given to the fact that the cabinet is the creature of the President. No votes are taken, unless the President asks for one; as Lincoln once said, the only vote that counts is the President's own.

Traditionally the cabinet has been composed of the heads of executive departments. Sometimes the Vice-President is included as a member. In cabinet personnel, as in other cabinet matters, the President is the master. This was illustrated in the long struggle over administrative reorganization during 1937 to 1939. Congress, in the Reorganization Act of 1939, denied to the President the authority to create any new departments. President Roosevelt promptly created three new "agencies"; in September, 1939, he invited their heads—the Federal Security Administrator, the Federal Works Administrator, and the Federal Loan Administrator—to attend cabinet meetings.

Mr. Vice-President.—Vice-Presidents are the forgotten men in American history. The office is one of importance, and yet it is the butt of endless jokes. Almost the only Vice-Presidents remembered from one generation to another are those who succeeded to the presidency. The Vice-President presides over the Senate, and he becomes President when that office falls vacant. These duties alone should make the office one of the most coveted in the gift of the people. In practice, however, it is looked upon as a political graveyard to be avoided by politicians of promise.

The reasons for the discrepancy between the potentialities of the office and its reputation are to be found principally in the method of nominating for the office. Each party, as seen earlier, uses the vice-presidency to balance the ticket, or to appease or reward some element. Thus the proper running mate for Alfred E. Smith, Catholic and Eastern, was Joseph T. Robinson, Protestant and Southern; for Wendell Willkie, a novice in politics and identified with Eastern corporate interests, Charles McNary, veteran senator and champion of farm and progressive interests. While in both these cases the vice-presidential candidates were able men, the method often produces candidates of questionable qualifications.

Second, the immediate responsibilities of office are not great. The Senate is a body with customs and traditions that the presiding officer must respect and accept. As president of the Senate, he fills a correct and impartial role, voting only in case of a tie. Vice-President Dawes, who tried to modernize the Senate, found the upper chamber unwilling to accept his proposals, or even to listen patiently. A vigorous man gets restive under such conditions; his frustration is noticed and the prestige of the office degenerates accordingly.

The possibilities of the office were demonstrated when Henry A. Wallace was Vice-President. President Roosevelt was strong enough to choose his running mate without the usual trading of votes and appeasing of factions. After his election, the President gave Wallace many responsibilities. Although less close to Mr. Roosevelt in outlook, Mr. Truman as Vice-President was able to help the President with congressional problems. Alben Barkley filled the office with dignity and was especially valuable in liaison work with party and Congress.

Since 1949 the Vice-President has been paid a salary of $30,000 per year and has received $10,000 annual tax-free expense allowance.

HEADQUARTERS STAFF

The Chief Administrator.—The Constitution vests in the President the "executive power" of the United States. In fact, however, the President has less sweeping authority over administration than might be assumed from the language of the fundamental law. Congress frequently determines the structure and authority of administrative agencies; it decides what functions require new agencies or remodeled ones, determines powers and duties, and controls in many other ways the framework within which administration operates. Many bureaus, however, have been established by executive order rather than an act of Congress and consequently may have to be reorganized or even abolished and their functions assigned elsewhere by similar executive act. Presidential authority over the Administration has been weakened during the last half century by several developments, but the factors operating to strengthen the hand of the President have outweighed them.

Since the turn of the century, especially during the administrations of Theodore Roosevelt, Woodrow Wilson, and Franklin Roosevelt, presidential authority over administration has increased markedly. The power to appoint and remove executive officers gives the President a commanding position in the field of personnel. Increasingly complex international situations have dictated more executive discretion in foreign affairs, trade, and defense matters. Economic depression intensified the tendency to delegate more authority in the fields of relief and business regulation.

The emergency nature of many governmental responsibilities is especially important in explaining augmented presidential power over administration. Whereas Congress once was able to stipulate in great detail the precise form, duties, and procedure of administrative agencies, now such variable factors as business conditions, foreign tariff rates, and droughts in farm regions require flexibility and loose construction of statutes. The trend is toward a situation under which Congress lays down broad principles and standards in legislation, leaving to the President and other executive officers the responsibility for details. Such details often include the whole structure and personnel of administrative agencies and the allocation of funds for specific purposes.

The Presidential Secretariat.—Viewed from the standpoint of the President, the first essential in fulfilling his responsibilities as chief administrator is an able core of attachés to aid him in keeping abreast of administrative work. For the early Presidents this was no great task, requiring only a small secretariat. To keep informed concerning the administrative leviathan of today requires most careful organization and planning. The administrative picture may be visualized with the President in the center, surrounded by concentric circles. Within the first are the President's secretaries and the White House staff that functions under them, a total of over 200 employees in the White House Office.

The President's office now contains three principal executive secretaries. The number and duties vary considerably from President to President and from time to time. Usually one is assigned to public relations and the control of information going out of the White House. A second handles visitors of the President, sifting the important from the unimportant and keeping the executive appointment calendar. The third may be given miscellaneous duties. In addition, each President has personal secretaries and clerks.

A recent development is the authorization of "administrative assistants" to the President, in addition to the executive secretaries. The President's Committee on Administrative Management urged that the lack of staff assistance to the President be remedied by the appointment of six administrative assistants who ". . . should be possessed of high competence, great physical vigor, and a passion for anonymity."[1] The Administrative Reorganization Act of 1939 provided for six administrative assistants to the President. By the end of 1944, five had been appointed. The early incumbents of the office have followed the plan outline by the President's

[1] United States President's Committee on Administrative Management, *Report . . . with Studies . . .* (Washington: Government Printing Office, 1937), p. 5.

committee: they have carried out the assignments of the President unobtrusively, collecting data, conferring with public officials, American and foreign, multiplying the eyes and ears of the President in effective fashion.

In addition to the three secretaries and six administrative assistants, the chief executive's personal staff includes an assistant to the President, a special counsel to the President, an executive clerk, and Army, Navy, and Air Force aides. The Commission on Organization of the Executive Branch of the Government, headed by Herbert Hoover, recommended that the executive office should add a staff secretary, who would keep the President informed on the status of work undertaken by various parts of the President's office and cabinet and other committees.[1]

The Staff Services.—Another method of presidential control over the administrative machinery is through the agencies that provide essential services for the various operating functions of government. These "staff" services are housekeeping in nature. They might include such matters as personnel, budgeting, planning, purchasing, reporting, and other services that may be provided centrally for operating agencies engaged in such "line" functions as public health, welfare, conservation, business regulation, and defense.

Federal agencies performing essentially staff functions and now under direct presidential control include the Bureau of the Budget and the Liaison Office for Personnel Management.[2] Through agencies of this kind the President is able to exert a degree of control over the Administration which would not otherwise be possible. One of the most telling presidential weapons is the budget, which is prepared by the Bureau of the Budget under executive direction and sent to Congress with his stamp of approval.

Well-developed staff agencies, working in close cooperation with the White House, give to the Chief Executive a strategic position in the cockpit of control, with appropriate instruments and levers governing the essential services for each of the operating agencies under his jurisdiction. The Administrative Reorganization Act of 1939 gave to the President power to shuffle many agencies by executive order. President Roosevelt brought into his executive office the National Resources Planning Board (since abolished), the Bureau of the Budget, and the Office of Government Reports.

[1] United States Commission on Organization of the Executive Branch of the Government, *General Management of the Executive Branch* (Washington: Government Printing Office, 1949), pp. 22–23. Hereafter the Commission will be cited as "Hoover Commission."

[2] The agencies in the Executive Office of the President were discussed by their directors in a series of papers under the general heading "The Executive Office of the President" in *Public Administration Review*, vol. 1 (Winter, 1941), pp. 101–140.

The terms of the act would not permit him to change the independent status of the Civil Service Commission or of the General Accounting Office and the Comptroller General. Some authorities favor the extension of presidential control over staff agencies, far beyond that granted under the 1939 act. The purse-string controls of accounting and auditing remain under the control of the Comptroller General, who is appointed for a 15-year term by the President but is removable only by Congress. Responsibility for government personnel is shared by the President with the Civil Service Commission, which is independent of the executive. The Commission does not appoint directly any except its own employees. It certifies qualified persons for appointment to the department or agency, which still retains responsibility for appointment and removal. Since 1938 the Council of Personnel Administration has served to coordinate federal personnel work. Composed of the personnel officers of the major operating services, it advises both President and Commission on merit-system matters. Before the wartime inflation of the public service, somewhat more than two-thirds of federal civil employees were under the classified service, for which the Commission certified eligibility. The remainder of the officeholders are beyond the protection of the formal merit system. The President enjoys great influence over most positions, and the influence may be used to keep administrative action within the policies of his regime.

The Hoover Commission recommended the creation, within the President's office, of an Office of Personnel, headed by the chairman of the Civil Service Commission. This new office would provide the President with staff advice and assistance regarding federal personnel problems. The proposal would provide the President with a means of keeping in touch with the offices of personnel that are scattered through the departments and agencies and of giving him an over-all picture of conditions in the federal service. Acting under the Reorganization Act of 1949, President Truman, in his reorganization plan 5, made the changes recommended by the Hoover Commission.

The Commission also proposed the strengthening of the Bureau of the Budget, particularly with respect to its secondary duties such as advising the President on improvements in governmental management, developing administrative reorganization plans, clearing departmental proposals for legislative enactments, and coordinating services, such as statistics and publications, that are used by many agencies.[1]

In order to organize properly federal supply, records management, and building operation and maintenance, the Hoover Commission proposed that these activities be grouped in a new agency, the Office of General

[1] Hoover Commission, *General Management of the Executive Branch*, pp. 25–27, and *Budgeting and Accounting*, pp. 21–31.

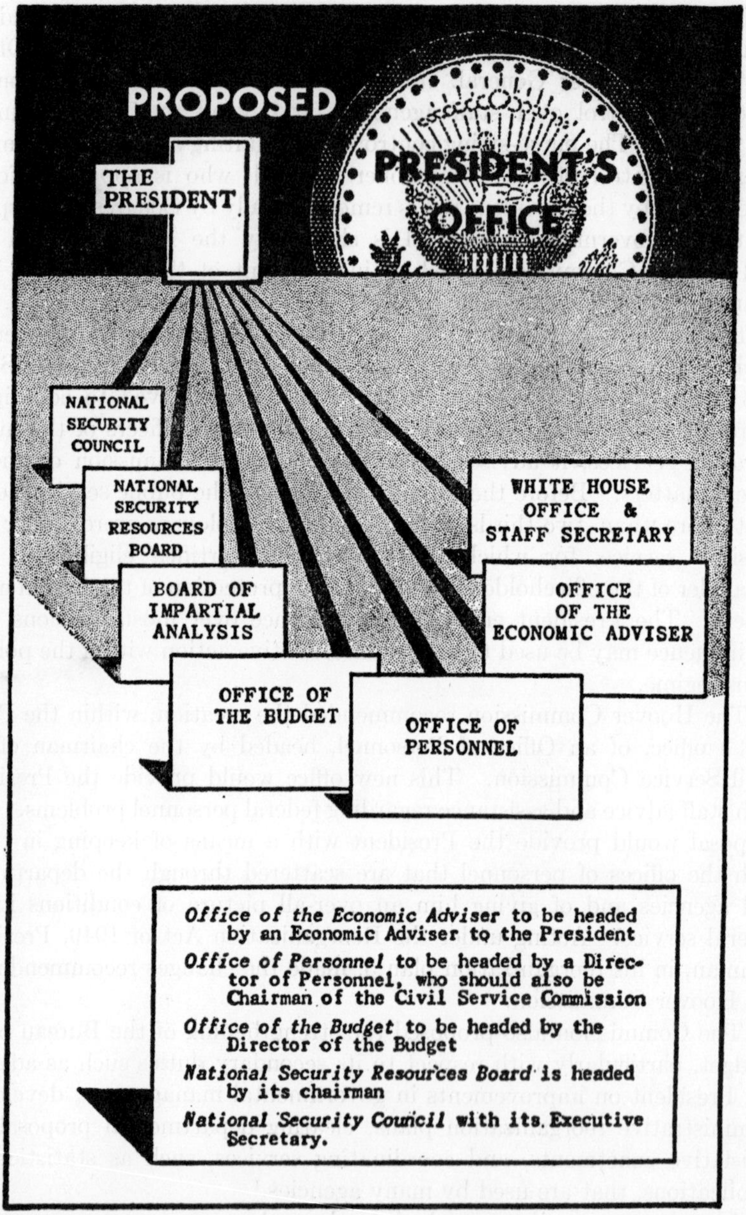
PROPOSED
PRESIDENT'S OFFICE
THE PRESIDENT
NATIONAL SECURITY COUNCIL
NATIONAL SECURITY RESOURCES BOARD
BOARD OF IMPARTIAL ANALYSIS
OFFICE OF THE BUDGET
OFFICE OF PERSONNEL
WHITE HOUSE OFFICE & STAFF SECRETARY
OFFICE OF THE ECONOMIC ADVISER
Office of the Economic Adviser to be headed by an Economic Adviser to the President
Office of Personnel to be headed by a Director of Personnel, who should also be Chairman of the Civil Service Commission
Office of the Budget to be headed by the Director of the Budget
National Security Resources Board is headed by its chairman
National Security Council with its Executive Secretary.

The organization proposed by the Hoover Commission for the President's office was largely achieved within six months of the date of the report. Only the Board of Impartial Analysis, a body to review and report on development projects, did not exist. The Council of Economic Advisers remained a plural body instead of becoming a single-headed one. SOURCE: Hoover Commission, *Concluding Report*, p. 52.

Services.[1] The administrator of the office would report directly to the President.

The General Services Administration was created by statute in 1949 and to the new office were transferred the Bureau of Supply of the Department of the Treasury, the National Archives, and the Federal Works Agency, but not the Public Roads Administration, which the President transferred to the Department of Commerce under his 1949 reorganization plan 7. The Hoover recommendation that General Services be made the liaison agency between some District of Columbia agencies and the President has not yet been put into force.

Recent legislation added to the number of agencies attached closely to the Executive Office of the President. The Employment Act of 1946 created the Council of Economic Advisers.[2] The three economists who constitute the Council help the President prepare his annual economic report to Congress, study economic trends, and recommend to the President appropriate policies. Perhaps anticipating something like the public disagreement that has developed among Council members, the Hoover Commission recommended that the body be displaced by a single-headed Office of Economic Adviser.

From time to time the President seeks advice by setting up committees of the cabinet on particular problems of policy or administration. Two of these committees, the National Security Council and the National Security Resources Board, were established by law in the National Security Act of 1947.[3] The Hoover Commission favored making both the Council and the Board formally a part of the President's office and urged that the President be given discretionary authority to alter their membership and assignments. President Truman transferred both committees to the Executive Office of the President in reorganization plan 4 (1949).

Calling attention to the useful work of special advisory commissions and of individual consultants appointed by the President, the Hoover Commission recommended that he be given adequate funds to operate freely in this sphere. The Hoover group also felt strongly that the President should have power to organize and reorganize his own office without the approval of Congress and to appoint his own staff (except the Civil Service Commission) without confirmation by the Senate.

LINE ORGANIZATION

The Executive Departments.—Most important among the line functions are the regular executive departments of the Federal government, now ten

[1] Hoover Commission, *Office of General Services*, pp. 1–50.

[2] 60 Stat. 24.

[3] 61 Stat. 499.

in number. According to custom, the heads of the departments are considered members of the President's cabinet by virtue of their offices. These departments were established by Congress in the following order:

State (originally Foreign Affairs) 1789
War 1789 (lost cabinet status 1947)
Treasury 1789
Navy 1798 (lost cabinet status 1947)
Interior (originally Home) 1849
Agriculture 1862 (elevated to full membership status 1889)
Justice (Attorney General 1789) 1870
Post Office (Postmaster General 1789) 1872
Commerce (originally Commerce and Labor) 1903
Labor 1913
Defense (National Defense Establishment 1947)

The theory underlying the organization of departments is that similar functions should be grouped for convenience and efficiency into a relatively small number of departments, the heads of which should coordinate the endeavors of the operating services and be responsible to the Chief Executive. While this is the theory, several federal departments possess functions that are not related to their major functions. Interior, for example, has served as a catchall for miscellaneous agencies that failed to fit elsewhere. At the same time, several activities—like public health, transportation, public works, and conservation—are divided among half a dozen departments.

Each executive department is headed by a secretary, appointed by the President with the advice and consent of the Senate. The department head usually is chosen for political qualifications: political prominence, campaign support, factional affiliation, sectional considerations. It is not surprising, therefore, that his main contribution often proves to be his conduct of departmental external relationships—with President, with Congress, with press, and with public. Usually he is not prepared to manage the detailed operation of his department; that is better left to the permanent career officials, operating under the supervision of the secretary and his political aides. He has important duties in determining departmental policy, appointing and removing officers, and settling disputes and appeals.

The Reorganization Act of 1939 banned new departments but gave the President considerable power to reshuffle bureaus and agencies. President Roosevelt promptly created three new "agencies" which are much like departments in fact but not in name. The "administrator" of each was invited to sit with the President's cabinet. In the beginning these agencies were the Federal Security Agency, Federal Works Agency, and Federal

Loan Agency. Reorganized many times during and after the war, by the time the Hoover Commission reported in 1949 the first two still existed under their original names. The Housing and Home Finance Agency, created in 1947, contained some of the activities originally vested in the Loan Agency, which was abolished.

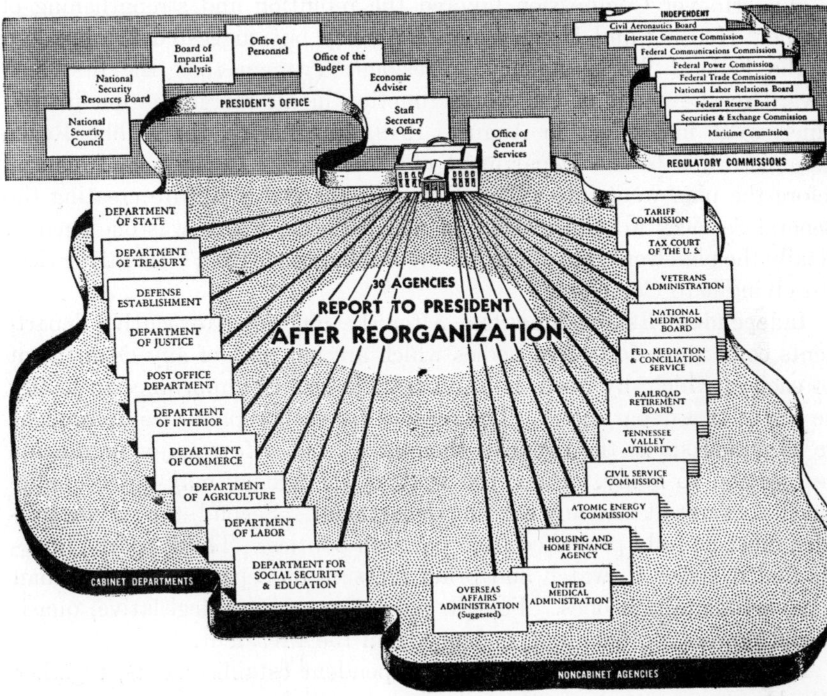

This is the Hoover Commission's "before and after" diagram, which shows the total number of agencies reporting to the President reduced from 52 to 30. Many of the recommended steps have been taken already, but one major proposal of the President, creation of a Department of Welfare, was defeated in the Senate in 1949. Diagram from Hoover Commission, *Concluding Report*, facing p. 1.

The Hoover Commission recommended that a new department be created in the welfare-education field. Several existing functions of the Federal Security Agency, notably the Public Health Service, Food and Drug Administration, and Bureau of Employment Security, would be transferred to other departments. The new Department for Social Security and Education would embrace the remaining social security services, education, vocational rehabilitation, Indian affairs, and certain lesser activities that are related.[1] President Truman, in his 1949 reorganization plan 1, proposed instead to transform the present Federal Security Agency into a Department of Welfare, headed by a Secretary of Welfare, and continu-

[1] Hoover Commission, *Social Security and Education; Indian Affairs*, pp. 3–12.

ing to perform all of the services of the existing Agency except employment and unemployment compensation, which were sent to the Department of Labor. Of all the seven plans submitted to Congress in June, 1949, the one providing for a Department of Welfare alone was nullified by adverse congressional action.

The Hoover Commission favored the retention and strengthening of the new Housing and Home Finance Agency but suggested the breakup of the Federal Works Agency. President Truman took the first step toward reassignment of the works function in his reorganization plan 7, which went into effect in August, 1949, transferring the Public Roads Administration to the Department of Commerce. In the meantime and before the plan went into effect, Congress enacted a statute creating the General Services Administration, of which Public Roads was one agency. Finally the plan went into effect, taking Public Roads from General Services and giving it to Commerce.

Independent Establishments.—After the nine great executive departments come some forty-five bodies which are not part of any department yet each of which, by itself, is insufficient in size or importance to justify the status of a department. The reasons for their separate establishment are as numerous as the agencies themselves, but a few major arguments are common to many. First, the work of the agency may be so unique that it does not fit into any existing department. Second, the service provided must be fully protected from partisan politics. Third, special interests find it easier to watch and bring pressure on separate agencies than on departmentalized ones. Fourth, possession of quasi-legislative, quasi-judicial powers requires independence from the President.

The more important of existing independent establishments, together with the years created, are the following:

Civil Service Commission 1883
Interstate Commerce Commission 1887
Federal Trade Commission 1914
Tariff Commission 1916
Federal Power Commission 1920
General Accounting Office 1921
Veterans' Administration 1930
Tennessee Valley Authority 1933
Securities and Exchange Commission 1934
Federal Communications Commission 1935
National Labor Relations Board 1935
Maritime Commission 1936
Civil Aeronautics Board 1940
Atomic Energy Commission 1946

Nearly one-half of those listed are regulatory commissions with varying responsibilities for supervising commercial activities.

Congress has seen fit to assign much responsibility for the execution of laws to such independent bodies. To some extent this represents a diffusion of the executive power, which the Constitution vests in the President both directly and by its charge that he take care that the laws be executed faithfully. In virtually every case, the independent agency is governed by a board or commission, appointed by the President for terms sufficiently long for a President to be unable to secure control in one term. This has the advantage of insulating a board or commission from the political whim of the executive, but the disadvantage of continuing in office those whose policies long since have been repudiated at the polls. When a change of administration involves a transformation in policy, as in 1933, the disparity between presidential and commission views on public questions may be a very critical matter. It is now settled that Congress may in the law creating agencies regulate and limit the power of the President to remove members of regulatory commissions.

The status of independent agencies has brought condemnation upon them as "a headless fourth branch of government," "miniature independent governments," and "irresponsible commissions." Under President Roosevelt's reorganization orders of 1939 some progress was made in incorporating independent agencies into the departmental system, but a large number of the establishments were exempted from any change. The 1939 act withheld from the President the power to alter the status of most of the regulatory commissions. One proposal insistently urged by the President's Committee on Administrative Management was that the administrative functions of regulatory commissions should be separated from judicial functions. Administrative work would be coordinated into an appropriate regular department; semilegislative and semijudicial work would continue independent of presidential control.[1]

The Hoover Commission suggested that some commissions be divested of their administrative duties but that the remaining ones should transfer all administrative responsibility to their chairmen.[2] President Truman took the first steps toward the latter end in his initial plans under the Reorganization Act of 1949. Plan 5 fixed administrative authority on the chairman of the Civil Service Commission; plan 6 did likewise for the chairman of the Maritime Commission.

[1] Robert E. Cushman, "The Problem of the Independent Regulatory Commission," in United States President's Committee on Administrative Management, *op. cit.*, pp. 207–243. See also the same author's book entitled *The Independent Regulatory Commissions* (New York: Oxford, 1941).

[2] Hoover Commission, *The Independent Regulatory Commissions*, pp. 5–6.

REFERENCES

(See also works listed after next chapter)

AGAR, HERBERT: *The People's Choice* (Boston: Houghton Mifflin, 1933).

BEAN, LOUIS H.: *Ballot Behavior, A Study of Presidential Elections* (Washington: American Council on Public Affairs, 1940).

CORWIN, EDWARD S.: *The President: Office and Powers* (New York: New York University Press, rev. ed., 1948).

EWING, CORTEZ A. M.: *Presidential Elections, from Abraham Lincoln to Franklin D. Roosevelt* (Norman, Okla.: University of Oklahoma Press, 1940).

HART, JAMES: *The American Presidency in Action 1789* (New York: Macmillan, 1948).

HATCH, LOUIS C.: *A History of the Vice-Presidency of the United States* (New York: American Historical Society, 1934).

HURD, CHARLES: *The White House; the Story of the House, Its Occupants, Its Place in American History* (New York: Harper, 1940).

LASKI, HAROLD J.: *The American Presidency* (New York: Harper, 1940).

LEARNED, HENRY B.: *The President's Cabinet* (New Haven: Yale University Press, 1912).

LEVIN, PETER: *Seven by Chance, The Accidental Presidents* (New York: Farrar, Straus, 1948).

MACMAHON, ARTHUR W., and JOHN D. MILLETT: *Federal Administrators; a Biographical Approach to the Problem of Departmental Management* (New York: Columbia University Press, 1939).

MARCY, CARL: *Presidential Commissions* (New York: Columbia University Press, 1945).

MERIAM, LEWIS, and LAURENCE F. SCHMECKEBIER: *Reorganization of the National Government, What Does It Involve?* (Washington: Brookings, 1939).

PATTERSON, CALEB P.: *Presidential Government in the United States* (Chapel Hill: The University of North Carolina Press, 1947).

POLLARD, JAMES E.: *The Presidents and the Press* (New York: Macmillan, 1947).

REYNOLDS, MARY T.: *Interdepartmental Committees in the National Administration* (New York: Columbia University Press, 1939).

SHORT, LLOYD M.: *Development of National Administrative Organization in the United States* (Baltimore: Johns Hopkins Press, 1923).

STANWOOD, EDWARD: *A History of the Presidency* (Boston: Houghton Mifflin, 2 vols., 1916). Vol. 1 covers 1788–1897, and vol. 2 1897–1916.

STEIN, CHARLES W.: *The Third Term Tradition* (New York: Columbia University Press, 1942).

STODDARD, HENRY L.: *Presidential Sweepstakes: The Story of Political Conventions and Campaigns* (New York: Putnam, 1948).

TAFT, WILLIAM H.: *The Presidency* (New York: Scribner, 1916).

THACH, CHARLES C.: *The Creation of the Presidency, a Study in Constitutional History* (Baltimore: Johns Hopkins Press, 1922).

UNITED STATES COMMISSION ON ORGANIZATION OF THE EXECUTIVE BRANCH OF THE GOVERNMENT ("Hoover Commission"): *Report* . . . (Washington: Government Printing Office, 19 vols., 1949). In addition, 19 task force reports were published. The *reports*, without dissents and separate opinions, are available in *The Hoover Commission Report on the Organization of the Executive Branch of the Government* (New York: McGraw Hill, 1949).

UNITED STATES CONGRESS: *Documents Illustrative of the Formation of the Union of the American States*, House Doc. 398, 69th Cong., 1st Sess. (Washington: Government Printing Office, 1927).

UNITED STATES CONGRESS: *The Electoral College*, Sen. Doc. 243, 78th Cong., 2d Sess. (Washington: Government Printing Office, 1944).

UNITED STATES HOUSE OF REPRESENTATIVES: *Amend the Constitution with Respect to Election of President and Vice-President . . . Hearings . . . .* 81st Cong., 1st Sess. (Washington: Government Printing Office, 1949). Briefer hearings were held by the same committee in 1947.

UNITED STATES NATIONAL ARCHIVES ESTABLISHMENT: *United States Government Organization Manual* (Washington: Government Printing Office, issued annually).

UNITED STATES PRESIDENT'S COMMITTEE ON ADMINISTRATIVE MANAGEMENT: *Report . . . with Studies of Administrative Management in the Federal Government* (Washington: Government Printing Office, 1937).

UNITED STATES SENATE: *Presidential Succession . . . Hearings . . . .* 80th Cong., 1st Sess. (Washington: Government Printing Office, 1947).

WALLACE, SCHUYLER C.: *Federal Departmentalization, a Critique of Theories of Organization* (New York: Columbia University Press, 1941).

TEXT-FILM

The following McGraw-Hill 35mm silent filmstrip is recommended for use with Chaps. 14 and 15 of this text.

The President: Office and Powers. Structure and role of the executive branch. The selection of the President and various individuals and agencies that help him to administer the government. Powers of the President are examined in detail.

Chapter 15

POWERS OF THE PRESIDENT

> The Constitution does give the President wide discretion and great power, and it ought to do so. It calls from him activity and energy to see that within his proper sphere he does what his great responsibilities and opportunities require.
>
> William H. Taft, *The Presidency.*[1]

APPOINTMENT AND REMOVAL

Scope of the Appointing Power.—The power to appoint is one of the most far-reaching in the list of presidential powers. Through it the President commands the allegiance of a great number of federal officers and secures the support of many national legislators for his program.

In Article II, Section 2, the President is given power to "nominate, and by and with the advice and consent of the Senate, shall appoint Ambassadors, other public Ministers and Consuls, judges of the Supreme Court, and all other officers of the United States which shall be established by law; . . ." The article goes on to provide that Congress may vest appointment of "inferior officers" in the President alone, in the courts, or in department heads. Thus, appointments to the federal services fall into two general groups: those that require senatorial confirmation, called "officers," and those that do not, called "inferior officers." There is no logical line of demarcation between the two. Included in the "officers" category are diplomats, judges, department heads, regulatory commissioners, marshals, and collectors of customs. Often Congress seeks to enlarge this group in order to broaden the possibilities of patronage. Some bureau chiefs and virtually all subordinate employees fall within the "inferior officers" group.

Senatorial Confirmation.—The Senate has interpreted "advice and consent" as justification for withholding confirmation from proposed officers on grounds that sometimes appear petty or personal. It rarely interferes with the President's selection of his own cabinet; a notable exception was Charles B. Warren, nominated by President Coolidge as Attorney General and rejected in 1925 by the Senate. Appointments to the diplomatic corps normally secure the Senate's approval without difficulty, but the Senate's rejection of Martin Van Buren as Minister to Britain will be remembered from the Jackson administration. Supreme Court justiceships may be filled by the President without much interference, yet the Senate

[1] (New York: Scribner, 1916), p. 141.

refused to consent to President Hoover's appointment of Circuit Judge John J. Parker in 1930 largely because of Negro and labor opposition.

Other appointments, especially those of a local nature, are subject to a custom called "senatorial courtesy." This is an unwritten rule which requires that the President confer with and secure the consent of the senator or senators of his party from the state in which an appointment is made. Almost invariably the Senate will reject a presidential appointment if a strenuous objection is raised by a senator of the President's party from the state involved. One of the best examples of the operation of senatorial courtesy was the Floyd H. Roberts case of 1938–1939. President Roosevelt appointed Roberts, a Virginia jurist, as judge of the federal District Court for western Virginia. The appointment was objectionable to the two Virginia senators, Carter Glass and Harry Byrd, both anti-Roosevelt Democrats, but was favored by Governor Price, a New Deal Democrat. When the candidate's name reached the Senate for confirmation, Glass and Byrd announced that the appointment was "personally obnoxious" to them; the Senate committee reported adversely, and the Senate rejected the appointment by a vote of seventy-two to nine.[1]

Sometimes when senators who are unpopular with their colleagues attempt to obstruct confirmation of an appointment, the Senate will approve in spite of their protests. Only a few rejections occur during each session of Congress; these may be attributed mainly to the fact that the President accepts suggestions from senators and appoints those whom they recommend.

Suppose the Senate has confirmed fully an appointment of the President, can the upper house subsequently call the matter back for reconsideration? In a case arising from the desire of the Senate to reconsider confirmation of several appointees of President Hoover to the Federal Power Commission,[2] the Supreme Court declared that it could not. Shortly after taking office, these appointees had reversed the policies of the commission and dismissed several employees. Under the rules of the Senate, the matter might be brought up for reconsideration, but the Court ruled that once the consent was given and the officers had been fully installed, it was not possible for the Senate to withdraw confirmation.

Presidents may fill vacancies that occur during recess of the Senate, but such commissions expire at the end of the next session. Existing law prohibits the payment of a salary to an officer appointed to fill a vacancy that existed when the Senate was in session. Usually a President will

[1] President Roosevelt reviewed his side of this case in a letter to Judge Roberts, appearing in *The New York Times*, Feb. 8, 1939. Senator Thomas of Utah gave a carefully reasoned defense of senatorial courtesy and Senator Byrd stated his view in the same paper, Feb. 10, 1939.

[2] United States *v.* Smith, 186 U.S. 6 (1932).

not give a recess appointment to a person previously rejected by the Senate.

Power to Remove.—Although it takes the President and the Senate to appoint officers, the first Congress declared by law that the President alone might remove all officers appointed by him except judges. In the reconstruction controversies between President Johnson and Congress, the executive was forbidden by law to remove officers without the consent of the Senate. This was repealed about 20 years later. In the meantime, however, an act of 1876 provided that first-, second-, and third-class postmasters might be removed only with the consent of the Senate. In spite of the act, President Wilson removed one Myers from his office of postmaster of Portland, Ore. A legal suit arose over Myers's claim for back salary, and he alleged that his removal was illegal under the 1876 law. The statute was declared unconstitutional by the Supreme Court; the power to remove, said the Court, was implied not only from the power to appoint, but also from the general authority of the executive to see that the laws are executed faithfully.[1]

After the Myers verdict, the President's removal power appeared limited only in respect to judges. Then, in the early stages of the New Deal came a decision that modified this conception. Humphrey, a Federal Trade Commissioner, was removed by President Roosevelt because the Commissioner's philosophy of business regulation differed widely from Mr. Roosevelt's. Under the law the President was empowered to remove for "inefficiency, neglect of duty, or malfeasance in office," but he gave no such reason. The Court took notice that a regulatory commission's powers are quasi-legislative and quasi-judicial in nature and ruled that the President's removal authority could be limited in respect to officers exercising such powers.[2] Apparently the present rule is that the President may remove executive officers at will, but that regulatory commissioners with part judicial and part legislative powers may be protected by statutory limitations on the removal power.

WAR AND DIPLOMATIC POWERS

The War Powers.—As commander in chief of the armed forces, the President has extensive authority over both military and foreign policy of the country. The executive shares power over the military establishments with Congress, which may make rules, appropriate money, and declare war; the Senate confirms appointments of military officers. Presidential control of the militia is limited to periods when it is called into the service of the United States. By his actions, nevertheless, the Presi-

[1] Myers *v.* United States, 272 U.S. 52, 164 (1926).

[2] Humphrey's Executor (Rathbun) *v.* United States, 295 U.S. 602 (1935).

dent virtually may force Congress to appropriate money, as when Theodore Roosevelt ordered the fleet around the world despite congressional disapproval. Likewise, a President by belligerent use of the armed forces may involve the country in a state of war, leaving Congress with no alternative but to declare it. Without consulting Congress, Presidents have often ordered marines to land in Central American and Caribbean countries to protect American property and lives.

In time of war the powers of the President as commander in chief are even greater. He directs the armed forces on land and sea. He governs conquered territory until Congress provides by law for its civil government. Without much statutory authority Lincoln suppressed civil rights, seized enemy property. Wilson exercised vast powers, largely conferred upon him by act of Congress. In the Second World War, President Franklin Roosevelt could rely upon a great mass of specific legislation, granting to the executive additional emergency and war powers. His control of radio was assured under the Federal Communications Act of 1934. Congress provided for calling the National Guard into federal service more than a year before it declared war. Discretion was given the executive in the execution of the selective service law of 1940. A series of laws, beginning not long after war broke out in Europe, step by step gave the President very great authority over the industrial facilities of the country, over matters of production, priorities, conditions, and contracts. After war was declared, power over foreign communications, war functions and agencies, alien property, and other matters was added by congressional action.[1]

Foreign Affairs.—As in military affairs, the President dominates the field of foreign affairs. The Constitution gives him authority to make treaties (with the consent of two-thirds of the Senate), to appoint diplomats and consuls (subject to ratification by a Senate majority), and to receive foreign diplomatic and consular representatives.

Most treaties are negotiated through the usual diplomatic channels, utilizing the regular diplomatic agents of the countries involved. A projected treaty to govern international extradition between the United States and Brazil would be negotiated by the State Department and the Brazilian ambassador in Washington, or by the Brazilian foreign ministry and the American ambassador in Rio de Janeiro. For a convention or treaty of extraordinary importance or of a multilateral nature, the Secretary of State or some special agent or commission may negotiate it. President

[1] A convenient compilation of war powers previous to the Second World War is contained in the appendix of E. Pendleton Herring, *Presidential Leadership, the Political Relations of Congress and the Chief Executive* (New York: Farrar, 1940). For powers during the last war, see Margaret Fennell, *Acts of Congress Applicable in Time of Emergency,* Public Affairs Bulletin No. 35 (Washington: Library of Congress, 1945).

Wilson himself went to Europe to participate in framing the Treaty of Versailles. When negotiation is completed, the Chief Executive sends the treaty to the Senate for its approval. Individual senators are consulted frequently in advance of and during negotiation stages. The Senate Foreign Relations Committee plays the key role in the ratification process. It holds hearings, at which State Department officials may be called to testify. A two-thirds majority on the floor of the Senate is required to approve a treaty.

The scope of the treaty-making power is not known precisely. Apparently the power may not be used to accomplish something specifically forbidden to the Federal government by the Constitution. But the treaty power has been used to achieve federal control in spheres where no other authority existed. In 1916, after adverse lower-court decisions voided attempts under the commerce clause to regulate and protect migratory birds, a treaty was negotiated and ratified with Great Britain, acting for Canada, providing that each country should protect such wild fowl. After the treaty came into force, Congress implemented it by enacting a law providing for the protection of migratory birds. The treaty and act were found constitutional in Missouri *v.* Holland.[1] As a result of this case, the power of Congress to enact laws in support of treaties obviously becomes broader than its ordinary statute-making authority, but the precise limits of such power are as yet unsettled.

The President may also make international arrangements without senatorial participation. "Executive agreements" are pledges of certain action by executives of two countries. For example, the President will exchange letters with the prime minister of Canada, in which each agrees to permit citizens of the other country to travel without passports. A famous example from history is the "gentlemen's agreement" between President Theodore Roosevelt and the Emperor of Japan, under which Roosevelt agreed to try to persuade Congress to kill exclusion legislation and the Japanese agreed to forbid the emigration of coolies.

During the last 15 years the "trade agreement" has come into prominence. It is neither treaty nor executive agreement but deserves a special category created by the Trade Agreements Act of 1934 and the subsequent renewals. Recognizing its inability to reduce tariff rates due to the pressure of affected groups, Congress vested in the President authority to adjust tariff barriers by negotiation and allowed him to proclaim in effect special trade agreements with individual foreign countries. These reciprocal trade agreements are not submitted to the Senate for confirmation but are fully enforceable in the courts.

Another highly important power of the President in foreign affairs is his authority to recognize countries and governments. This is done simply by receiving diplomatic representatives of the nation or regime, or it may

[1] 252 U.S. 416 (1920)

be accomplished by altering the assignments or instructions of our agents abroad. For example, after the Italians completed the conquest of Ethiopia in 1936, the American legation in Addis Ababa was reduced to a consulate. Likewise the President may indicate dissatisfaction with a nation's representative by dismissing or asking the recall of a diplomat or consul to the United States. A more extreme form of indicating displeasure with a country involves closing its consulates, as were those of Germany in 1940.

Recognition may be used as an instrument in foreign policy, for it has often been withheld to show disapproval of a government. From the time of the Bolshevik revolution of 1917 until 1933, this country indicated distaste for the Communist regime by maintaining no official contact with the Soviet government. When President Roosevelt decided to open diplomatic relations, he cabled directly to the President of the Council of Soviets. The Russian government sent M. Litvinov, its foreign commissar, to discuss Soviet-American problems. After the talks had concluded, the two nations exchanged ambassadors. The extinction of the independence of a nation is recognized by the United States through the closing of a legation or embassy. Recognition by the United States often is a most crucial matter for a new regime in a Latin-American republic; by withholding recognition, as from the Grau San Martin government in Cuba in 1933, this country may cause the downfall of one and the rise of another regime.

Although the question of the delegation of legislative authority by Congress to the President requires more detailed attention in another place, this delegation in the field of foreign affairs has been given a special status. A case arose over the President's action in placing into effect an arms embargo, banning shipments to Bolivia and Paraguay which were then at war over the Gran Chaco. Congress had provided for the arms embargo to be proclaimed in force by the President whenever he found that a condition of war existed. President Roosevelt's order was attacked by an aircraft concern that was prevented from exporting planes to the belligerents. The Supreme Court upheld the constitutionality of the legislation and the proclamation on the ground that the President had a very special responsibility over foreign affairs.[1] The neutrality laws of the late 1930's employed the arms embargo as a prominent feature, and their constitutionality was regarded as certain after the Curtiss-Wright case.

Occasionally treaties and laws conflict, and the courts are faced with the question of which to enforce. They have equal standing; so the courts enforce the latest expression of policy, whether law or treaty.

[1] United States *v.* Curtiss-Wright Export Corporation, 299 U.S. 304 (1936). For a good discussion of the foreign affairs power, see Foster H. Sherwood, "Foreign Relations and the Constitution," *Western Political Quarterly*, vol. 1 (December, 1948), pp. 386–399.

JUDICIAL AND ADMINISTRATIVE POWERS

Pardons and Reprieves.—The President's power to grant pardons and reprieves is judicial in nature, and it is exclusive. A pardon is a release from liability for punishment. If the pardon is absolute, it wipes out all charges and restores the condition that existed before the alleged crime was committed. If it is conditional, it may leave certain disabilities or obligations on the offender. A reprieve, also issued by the executive, postpones the execution of a penalty; its use may be dictated by humanitarian considerations, or by the expectation of new evidence. An amnesty is a group pardon, issued by the President to a class of offenders. A good example of amnesty is Jefferson's freeing of all convicted under the Sedition Act of 1798.

In general, Congress cannot restrict the President in the exercise of his pardoning power. A congressional attempt to avoid by statute the full effect of President Johnson's proclamation of amnesty for Confederates convicted of treason was declared unconstitutional on the ground that it interfered with the pardoning power.[1] A nice problem in the separation of powers is raised with the question of whether the President may pardon a person found guilty of contempt of a federal court or one of the houses of Congress. It appears that the President may pardon for any offense except those convicted by impeachment. President Roosevelt issued a last-minute pardon to Dr. Francis E. Townsend, old-age-pension advocate, who was held in contempt of a House of Representatives investigating committee; no contest arose, however, for the leading sponsor of the pardon was the chairman of the House committee. Even earlier a presidential pardon for contempt of court was upheld in the Supreme Court.[2]

Execution of the Laws.—The constitutional provision that the President ". . . shall take Care that the Laws be faithfully executed . . ." and that section requiring his oath to preserve, protect, and defend the Constitution give the executive very broad responsibilities. In practice, Congress confers upon subordinate officials and upon independent agencies law-enforcement duties. It is the President's role to oversee execution of the laws. This general responsibility is carried out through the various powers of the President—appointment, war, foreign affairs, legislative—and through an indefinite authority that flows from his oath and the execution of the laws clause.

A striking illustration of this extra authority is found in what is one of the most dramatic cases in American constitutional law, *in re* Neagle.[3]

[1] *Ex parte* Garland, 4 Wallace 333 (1867).

[2] *Ex parte* Grossman, 267 U.S. 87, 122 (1925).

[3] 135 U.S. 1 (1890). The background of the case is described in interesting fashion by Carl B. Swisher, *Stephen J. Field, Craftsman of the Law* (Washington: Brookings, 1930), pp. 321–361.

Because of an adverse court decision, David S. Terry and his adventuress wife threatened bodily harm to Mr. Justice Field of the Supreme Court. Acting under no specific law, a deputy marshal was assigned to protect Field while riding circuit in California. Meeting Field in a railroad-station restaurant, Terry attacked him, and the marshal shot and killed Terry. The marshal, Neagle, was charged with murder in the state court. The federal court issued a writ of habeas corpus directing his release, and it was upheld in the Supreme Court. The highest tribunal declared that the executive possessed authority implied by the nature of government under the Constitution. It follows, therefore, that the President may use as much force as necessary or expedient to execute the laws and protect federal property and agents.[1]

In enforcing the law the President has very great discretion. First he must interpret the law, a process that touches upon both legislative and judicial sides. After interpretation, the President decides which laws to enforce vigorously, slightly, or not at all. The laws on the statute books are so extensive that the President and his subordinates must pick and choose those that are to be singled out for particular attention.

LEGISLATIVE POWERS

The Veto Power.—The founding Fathers also departed from strict separation of powers by giving the President power to recommend and to veto legislation. Bills passed by both houses of Congress must be submitted to the President before becoming law. If he approves, he signs a measure. If he disapproves, he returns it to the house of origin with his objections. The proposed legislation is then dead unless each house votes by a two-thirds majority to pass it over his veto, in which case it becomes law without presidential approval. If the President does not return the bill within 10 days, excluding Sundays, it becomes law without his signature. But if Congress adjourns before the 10 days have elapsed, the President may kill the bill simply by failing to act upon it; this is a "pocket veto,"[2] and it is absolute. The President may approve legislation within the 10-day limit even when Congress has finally adjourned.[3]

All bills and joint resolutions except constitutional amendments are sent to the President for approval. Concurrent resolutions, in which both houses join in a declaration of principles or opinion, and simple resolu-

[1] For circumstances under which the President might intervene with force to help states maintain law and order, see p. 97.

[2] Okanogan Indians *v.* United States, 279 U.S. 655 (1929). An attack on the pocket veto was made in the 79th Congress through House Res. 98, which would change the rules of the House to make delivery to the clerk delivery to the House during interim periods between sessions of the same Congress.

[3] Edwards *v.* United States, 286 U.S. 482 (1932).

tions, which deal with internal affairs of one house, need not be sent to the President because neither has the effect of law.

Governors in thirty-seven states are empowered to exercise the "item veto" in respect to appropriation bills, but the President does not possess this power. The item veto gives the executive power to strike out specific sections or parts yet sign the remaining portion of the bill. During the decade of the thirties, after Congress showed an inability to resist group pressure for higher and higher appropriations, a proposal to give the President an item veto arose. A general item-veto power could not be conferred without a constitutional amendment, and dozens have been proposed in the House and Senate. Although a considerable amount of support for this scheme has been evident at times, no action has yet been taken. Interest then shifted to the possibility of inserting a clause into each appropriation bill, bestowing on the President the power to strike out items. Competent attorneys have maintained that this power may be given by Congress without constitutional amendment. In favor of giving the President an item veto are the arguments that it will help reduce extravagance, eliminate pork-barrel legislation, and assure executive responsibility for fiscal affairs. Against it, it is argued that legislative responsibility will be weakened and presidential power increased to an unwarranted extent.[1]

Power to Recommend Legislation.—Presidential authority to recommend legislation and call special sessions of Congress is found in Article II, Section 3:

> He shall from time to time give to the Congress Information of the State of the Union, and recommend to their Consideration such Measures as he shall judge necessary and expedient; he may, on extraordinary Occasions, convene both Houses, or either of them, and in Case of Disagreement, between them, with Respect to the Time of Adjournment, he may adjourn them to such Time as he shall think proper; . . .

The President's major annual message, roughly comparable to the Speech from the Throne in British countries, is called the State of the Union message. Both Washington and Adams delivered their important messages in person and orally. Jefferson declined to appear before Congress, preferring to send written messages. Wilson revived the practice of appearing personally, and it has been continued since that time. Lesser messages may be sent in considerable number; they are read by a clerk, often inaudibly, and printed in the *Congressional Record*. The personal appearance of a President before a joint session calls public and congres-

[1] See Bryant Putney, "Extension of the Veto Power," *Editorial Research Reports*, vol. 2, no. 24 (Dec. 28, 1937). A Gallup poll released Nov. 16, 1945, showed strong public support for giving the item veto to the President by constitutional amendment.

sional attention to his message, which now invariably is heard by tens of millions over the radio and heard and seen by additional millions through television and newsreel. The annual and special messages of the Presidents recommend the enactment of certain bills or the adoption of certain policies. Most Presidents also attempt to secure the passage of their proposals through appeals to public opinion and by pressure on Congress.

Congress may be called into special session by the President, but the federal executive lacks the power, possessed by many state governors, to stipulate the exact purpose of the special session. Once assembled, Congress may proceed with any matter within its competence, even the impeachment of the President. Although the President can convene either house separately, this privilege has been used very little. Since the two houses rarely have serious disagreement over the date of adjournment, the President's power in this regard is of little practical importance.

Delegation of Legislative Authority to President.—Congress often delegates discretionary authority to the President. When this presidential discretion involves actual policy making by the executive, it may be called "delegation of legislative authority." On two occasions in recent years the courts ruled that Congress made unconstitutional delegations of legislative authority to the executive. Both of these cases arose out of the National Recovery Act of 1933. The first concerned a provision in the law giving the President discretion to bar from interstate commerce oil produced in excess of state quotas. Here the Court ruled that Congress failed to establish sufficient standards or policy to guide the executive.[1] The second case arose over the general NRA code-making authority which the Court found delegated lawmaking to an even greater extent and was therefore even more unconstitutional.[2]

Other instances of delegation have received approval in the courts, or have not been tested. The flexible tariff, under which the President may alter duties on imports as much as 50 per cent, was found constitutional.[3] The special responsibility of the President for foreign affairs has been treated already; congressional delegation of power to proclaim when a state of war exists between other countries was declared valid in the Curtiss-Wright case. No one has successfully challenged the validity of vesting in the executive the authority to alter the gold content of the dollar.

It is difficult to draw the line between invalid delegation and valid delegation. The general rule is that Congress must fix primary standards.

[1] Panama Refining Co. *v.* Ryan, 293 U.S. 388 (1935). For a fuller discussion, see p. 447.

[2] Schechter Poultry Corp. *v.* United States, 295 U.S. 495 (1935). See also p. 659.

[3] Hampton & Co. *v.* United States, 276 U.S. 394 (1928). The constitutionality of reciprocal trade agreements appears assured from an earlier decision on the 1890 law giving the President power to suspend the free list on articles of any country discriminating against the United States. See Marshall Field & Co. *v.* Clark, 143 U.S. 649 (1892).

After these are fixed, power to fill in details may be conferred upon the executive. The Court has not, however, been consistent, and the line of demarcation between proper and improper delegation can only be guessed, after careful reading of the cases cited and judging the contemporary temper of the Court.

Emergency Powers.—Congress has conferred upon the President by law many powers that the executive may exercise only during an "emergency." The existence of such powers was brought forcibly to the attention of the nation when the newly inaugurated President, Franklin Roosevelt, proclaimed a bank holiday and prohibited gold and silver exports and foreign exchange transactions. This action was taken under the "Trading with the Enemy Act" of 1917; doubt whether the act was still in force existed, but the President's proclamation was validated three days later by the emergency banking act, and the President was given control over gold during a "national emergency."

After this beginning followed a decade of controversy over emergency powers. Congress repeatedly added to this category of presidential authority, although not without strong opposition. In point of fact, however, much of the heat was over delegation of discretionary authority to the President without limitation as to emergency periods. The definition of an emergency is left to the President, but it is clear that either periods of foreign danger or economic depression or both are implied in the various statutes. President Roosevelt announced the existence of an "emergency" at the beginning of war in Europe in September, 1939, and proclaimed a "limited emergency" in mid-1941. Existing statutes then permitted the executive to suspend sugar quotas, terminate charters of government-owned ships, requisition privately owned ships, restrict foreign travel, control radio and other communications, and take additional steps.[1] After the United States entered the global war in December, 1941, numerous other wartime and postwar emergency statutes were placed on the books, granting to the President vast powers over the resources, industrial plants, and man power of the country.

THE CHIEF MAGISTRATE

The People's Choice.—James Bryce, one of the greatest foreign students of American institutions, entitled a short chapter in his *American Commonwealth* "Why Great Men Are Not Chosen Presidents."[2] He gave three reasons: (1) a small proportion of first-rate Americans enter politics;

[1] For a list of discretionary and emergency powers as of Jan. 1, 1940, see Edward S. Corwin, *The President: Office and Powers* (New York: New York University Press, 1940), pp. 369–373.

[2] (New York: Macmillan, 2 vols., 1889), vol. 1, pp. 71–80.

(2) American politics offers few opportunities for individual distinction; and (3) prominent men make more enemies than "safe" men. Bryce was impressed with the excess of party loyalty and the power of party organization; he blamed party managers for choosing undistinguished candidates rather than risking loss of an election with a prominent one. Looking back over American history, one may see that Bryce was troubled especially by the fact that between Jackson and Lincoln a number of inconspicuous politicians and soldiers served as Presidents, and that Clay, Calhoun, and Webster, the leading men of the time, never reached the chief executive office. If Bryce could have reviewed 150 years of the American presidency, instead of two-thirds of that, he certainly would have been impressed with men who came later. There is evidence in his own subsequent writings that he modified the views previously expressed.[1]

The nominating method affects the quality of presidential timber greatly. The candidate must be reasonably prominent in the country. Some record in public office is almost indispensable—usually as a governor or a federal department head, seldom as a senator or representative. His own policy convictions and beliefs are important in relation to conditions in the country and sentiment in the party. Personal factors, like religion and personality, are taken into consideration. The aspirant for the presidency normally must have some solid political support, especially in his own state. Presidential hopefuls are most likely to be successful in getting a major party nomination if they reside in a large and pivotal state. A state ranking below twelfth or fifteenth in population is quite unlikely to produce a serious candidate. Moreover, if the state is sure to go for one party, neither party, under normal conditions, will choose a candidate from that state. The party naturally takes for granted a state that it wins regularly; the party with a hopeless position in a given state will gain nothing from seeking a candidate there.

The successful candidate for the presidency may be the active leader of his party if he has the personal qualities and can command the backing. Theodore Roosevelt, Woodrow Wilson, and Franklin D. Roosevelt all made vigorous party leaders. William H. Taft, Warren Harding, and Calvin Coolidge made no real effort to dominate party affairs. Under favorable political conditions and with the requisite personal qualities, the President can be a strong executive. He is elected by the whole people; he can take swift, decisive action.

Able men increasingly are elected President. When the two parties are evenly balanced, the candidates put forward by each tend to be outstanding. When one party enjoys a considerable majority over the other,

[1] See especially James Bryce, *Modern Democracies* (New York: Macmillan, 2 vols., 1921), vol. II, pp. 66–76.

the minority party appears to find the stronger candidates, as with Cleveland, Wilson, and Franklin D. Roosevelt by the Democrats.

Future of Executive Power.—Although sentiment against additional authority for the President had reached a high pitch by the end of the Second World War, it was obvious that any halt in the expansion of executive powers was likely to be temporary rather than permanent. Under the American system of government, leadership must come, if there is to be any, from the President. Even if the Congress should reorganize itself by concentrating authority in the hands of its own leaders, this action would be unlikely to upset the trend toward placing more and more responsibility on the Chief Executive. Strengthening the Congress is essential. The House and Senate should do more of their own thinking and planning and drafting. The Union will still look to the President, however, for broad national leadership, and Congress will continue to get most of its proposed bills from the executive agencies that are doing the day-to-day job of administering existing law.

Actually, further expansion of executive power may be expected. The conditions of the modern world are so critical, both in war and in peace, that speedy and positive action is necessary. The President alone can provide this kind of leadership. Congress can investigate, criticize, revise, and do certain other things well, but the legislative branch is unable to act swiftly enough to beat an aggressor to the punch some Sunday morning at 8 A.M. E.S.T. Therefore, contingents of United States armed forces might be ordered to meet an invasion of Norway without a declaration of war by Congress. Congress has found itself unable to resist pressure groups sufficiently to reduce tariffs or to reorganize administrative agencies. Finally, the job is delegated to the President. Many Americans demand strong executive leadership; others decry the trend.

References

(See also works listed at end of preceding chapter)

BERDAHL, CLARENCE A.: *The War Powers of the Executive in the United States* (Urbana: University of Illinois Press, 1921).

BINKLEY, WILFRED E.: *The Powers of the President* (New York: Doubleday, 1937).

——— *President and Congress* (New York: Knopf, 1947).

CHAMBERLAIN, LAWRENCE H.: *The President, Congress, and Legislation* (New York: Columbia University Press, 1946).

CORWIN, EDWARD S.: *The President's Control of Foreign Relations* (Princeton, N.J.: Princeton University Press, 1917).

HART, JAMES: *The Ordinance-making Powers of the President of the United States* (Baltimore: The Johns Hopkins Press, 1925).

——— *Tenure of Office under the Constitution* (Baltimore: The Johns Hopkins Press, 1930).

HERRING, E. PENDLETON: *Presidential Leadership, the Political Relations of Congress and the Chief Executive* (New York: Farrar, 1940).

Holt, William S.: *Treaties Defeated by the Senate; a Study of the Struggle between President and Senate over the Conduct of Foreign Relations* (Baltimore: The Johns Hopkins Press, 1933).

Humbert, William H.: *The Pardoning Power of the President* (Washington: American Council on Public Affairs, 1941).

Larkin, John D.: *The President's Control over the Tariff* (Cambridge, Mass.: Harvard University Press, 1936).

McClure, Wallace M.: *International Executive Agreements; Democratic Procedure under the Constitution of the United States* (New York: Columbia University Press, 1941).

Milton, George F., *The Use of Presidential Power, 1789–1943* (Boston: Little, 1944).

Morganston, C. E.: *The Appointing and Removal Power of the President of the United States*, Sen. Doc. 172, 70th Cong., 2d Sess. (Washington: Government Printing Office, 1929).

Rich, Bennett M.: *The Presidents and Civil Disorder* (Washington: Brookings, 1941).

Small, Norman J.: *Some Presidential Interpretations of the Presidency* (Baltimore: The Johns Hopkins Press, 1932).

Taft, William H.: *Our Chief Magistrate and His Powers* (New York: Columbia University Press, 1916).

Chapter 16

FEDERAL COURTS AND LAW ENFORCEMENT

Yet trial-court fact-finding is the toughest part of the judicial function. It is there that court-house government is least satisfactory. It is there that most of the very considerable amount of judicial injustice occurs. It is there that reform is most needed.

Judge Jerome Frank, *Courts on Trial.*[1]

A Dual System.—Where a federal form of government exists, either the Federal government may enforce all law, state as well as national; or the states may enforce all law; or each may assume responsibility for enforcing its own. Under the Articles of Confederation, the states undertook the enforcement of enactments of Congress but this proved so unsatisfactory that the Constitution authorized the Federal government to enforce its own laws, leaving the states to do likewise. Accordingly, the President, acting through various administrative agencies, is charged with the responsibility of detecting and prosecuting violations of federal laws while a federal judiciary is responsible for the trial of cases involving federal matters. At the same time, each state has a law-enforcement and judicial system of its own. Care must be taken not to confuse the two.

Types of Federal Courts.—There are two general types of federal courts: constitutional and legislative. Constitutional are those established by authority of Article III to exercise "the judicial power of the United States." They consist of the Supreme Court, circuit courts of appeal, and district courts. Legislative courts do not exercise the judicial power but are special courts created to aid with the administration of laws enacted pursuant to powers delegated to Congress. The difference is not in method of procedure; nor is one created by the Constitution and the other by the legislature. Both are authorized by the Constitution and both are created and organized by Congress. The difference lies in the source of their authority and the nature of the cases over which they have jurisdiction. Article III mentions the types of cases and controversies to which the judicial power extends and these must all come before constitutional courts. But legislative courts are created as necessary and proper instruments to carry into execution such powers as those of regulating interstate commerce, spending public funds, laying and collecting import duties, and governing the territories. Legislative courts are described later in this chapter.[2]

[1] (Princeton, N.J.: Princeton University Press, 1949), p. 4.

[2] For an excellent discussion and description of legislative courts, see Robert J. Harris, *The Judicial Power of the United States* (Baton Rouge: Louisiana State University Press, 1940), Chap. IV.

Federal Law.—Federal law consists of the Constitution, statutes, treaties, international law, and orders of executive and administrative bodies. There is no federal common law. Common law, brought to American shores from Britain during the Colonial period, is a body of legal precepts founded on reason as applied in past judicial decisions. It obtains in all American states except Louisiana. In the absence of statutes, the common law is likely to be controlling, and even where legislation exists the courts are greatly influenced by common-law principles. Federal judges are similarly affected, but the fact that the national government is based on delegated powers precludes judicial application of the common law itself.

Types of Cases.—Because of the absence of federal common law, all cases and controversies reaching Federal courts arise from one of the types of law mentioned above. In character, cases may be criminal, civil, admiralty and maritime, those involving international law, or cases in equity.

A *criminal* case ordinarily is one in which it is alleged that a federal law imposing penalties has been violated and agents of the government conduct the prosecution, seeking to prove someone guilty. In general, federal offenses consist of felonies, the most serious offenses known to law, and misdemeanors, less serious offenses.

A *civil* case is ordinarily a suit between two or more private parties. The government may be, and frequently is, a party to a civil suit, but if so it will not appear as a prosecutor but in the capacity of a private citizen either as plaintiff or defendant. Settlement is usually made by payment of money damages. Since nonpayment of debt is no longer punishable by imprisonment, one who loses a civil suit seldom goes to jail.

Admiralty and *maritime* cases are either criminal or civil cases arising on the high seas or navigable waters or in connection with matters closely pertaining thereto. *International law* is recognized as a part of federal law and consists of rules drawn from international agreements, treaties, practices, and other sources. It might be applied by the courts in cases involving foreign governments, their representatives, or their citizens or subjects. Piracy, violations of neutrality, violence or insult to a public minister, counterfeiting of foreign money, and the slave trade are examples of offenses to which the rules of international, as well as national, law might be applied. All cases of the several types mentioned above are adjudicated by the same federal courts and judges, but the rules and procedures vary with the nature of the case.

Equity is a branch of civil law that may be applied by the courts to provide "substantial justice" when a remedy "at law" is not readily available. A case in equity is, then, one in which relief cannot be obtained either by criminal prosecution or an ordinary civil suit. Thus, if one believes an act of Congress unconstitutional, the only way relief can be obtained, since the government cannot be prosecuted or sued, is by asking a federal court for an injunction to prevent further enforcement of the objectionable statute. This would be a case in equity. To illustrate further, a federal court might mistakenly have sentenced a man to 10 years' imprisonment when the maximum allowed by the law was 5 years. A request for correction would be a case in equity.

CONSTITUTIONAL COURTS

Jurisdiction.—Article III of the Constitution extends "the judicial power of the United States" to nine classes of "cases" and "controversies"[1] depending upon the nature of the subject matter and the character or citizenship of parties in dispute. Those that may be brought because some *federal question* is involved are (1) cases arising under the Constitution, (2) cases arising under federal laws and treaties, and (3) admiralty and maritime cases. Those that may be brought because of the *character or citizenship of the parties* involved include (1) cases affecting ambassadors, other public ministers, and foreign consuls, (2) controversies to which the United States is a party, (3) controversies between two or more states, (4) controversies between citizens of different states (diverse citizenship), (5) controversies between citizens of the same state claiming lands under grants of different states, and (6) controversies between a state, or its citizens, and a foreign state, or its citizens or subjects. This last has been qualified by the Eleventh Amendment, Congress, and the courts in accordance with the precept that a sovereign cannot be sued without his consent. Accordingly, states now may be sued in federal courts without their consent only by another state in the Union or a foreign state. If an alien, citizen of another state, or citizen of the same state wishes to sue a state, he can do so only with the consent of the latter, and then only in state courts. States may, however, initiate suits in federal courts against aliens, citizens of other states, and foreign governments, although it is customary for disputes with the latter to be settled by diplomatic negotiation. Nothing has happened to prevent citizens of a state from suing or being sued by citizens of another state in federal courts.

[1] Because the judicial power extends only to "cases" and "controversies," the Supreme Court has long taken the position that it cannot give advisory opinions (*i.e.*, opinions for the benefit of the President or Congress on the probable constitutionality of contemplated measures) but must wait until real cases arise. The supreme courts of many states issue advisory opinions and many feel that the United States Supreme Court could do likewise without seriously distorting the Constitution. Federal courts advance the same reason for refusing to issue declaratory judgments (*i.e.*, judgments in which the courts simply declare the rights of the parties or express an opinion on a question of law, without ordering anything), except where real cases are before it for consideration.

Jurisdiction Not Exclusive.—Although the cases mentioned above may come before federal courts, the Constitution does not insist that they be brought there. Congress is free to distribute jurisdiction over them as it pleases. Indeed, Congress may completely divest federal courts of jurisdiction in certain instances. As matters stand, federal courts are given *exclusive* jurisdiction over some of them, *concurrent* jurisdiction over others, and totally *denied* consideration of still others. Among those that must come before Federal courts are (1) civil actions in which states are parties (subject to the exceptions noted above); (2) all suits and proceedings brought against (but not necessarily all those initiated by) ambassadors, others possessing diplomatic immunity, and foreign consuls; (3) all cases involving federal criminal laws; (4) all admiralty, maritime, patent-right, copyright, and bankruptcy cases; and (5) all civil cases against the Federal government where consent to sue has been granted. Jurisdiction is shared with state courts in cases, which of necessity are always civil, involving amounts of $3,000 or more. Because it is to the plaintiff's advantage to begin suit in either a state or federal court, the defendant in such cases has been given the privilege of having the case removed to a federal court, provided the request is made before the state court has reached a decision. Cases involving parties with diverse citizenship that may not come before federal courts at all are civil disputes involving less than $3,000. These cases must be tried in state courts if at all.

Supreme Court. *Organization.*—Article III states that "The judicial power of the United States shall be vested in one Supreme Court, and in such inferior Courts as Congress may from time to time ordain and establish." Only a Supreme Court is specifically mentioned, its creation being mandatory. Others are "inferior courts" which may be created or abolished by Congress at will.

The Supreme Court was created by the Judiciary Act of 1789. The Court held its first two terms on Wall Street in New York City, but in neither term were there any cases. Its next two terms were held in Philadelphia, thereafter it met in Washington. As first constituted it consisted of a Chief Justice and five associate justices. Its membership was reduced to five in 1801; increased to seven in 1807; increased to nine in 1837 and ten in 1863; reduced to seven in 1866; and in 1869 it was fixed at nine where it has remained ever since.[1]

Justices are appointed by the President by and with the advice and consent of the Senate. No qualifications are stated in the Constitution;

[1] An attempt was made under the leadership of President Franklin D. Roosevelt in 1937 to have the membership of the Court vary between nine and fifteen depending upon whether justices resigned at the age of seventy and the President's willingness to appoint another judge to assist the elderly one. The attempt failed of enactment. See below, p. 348.

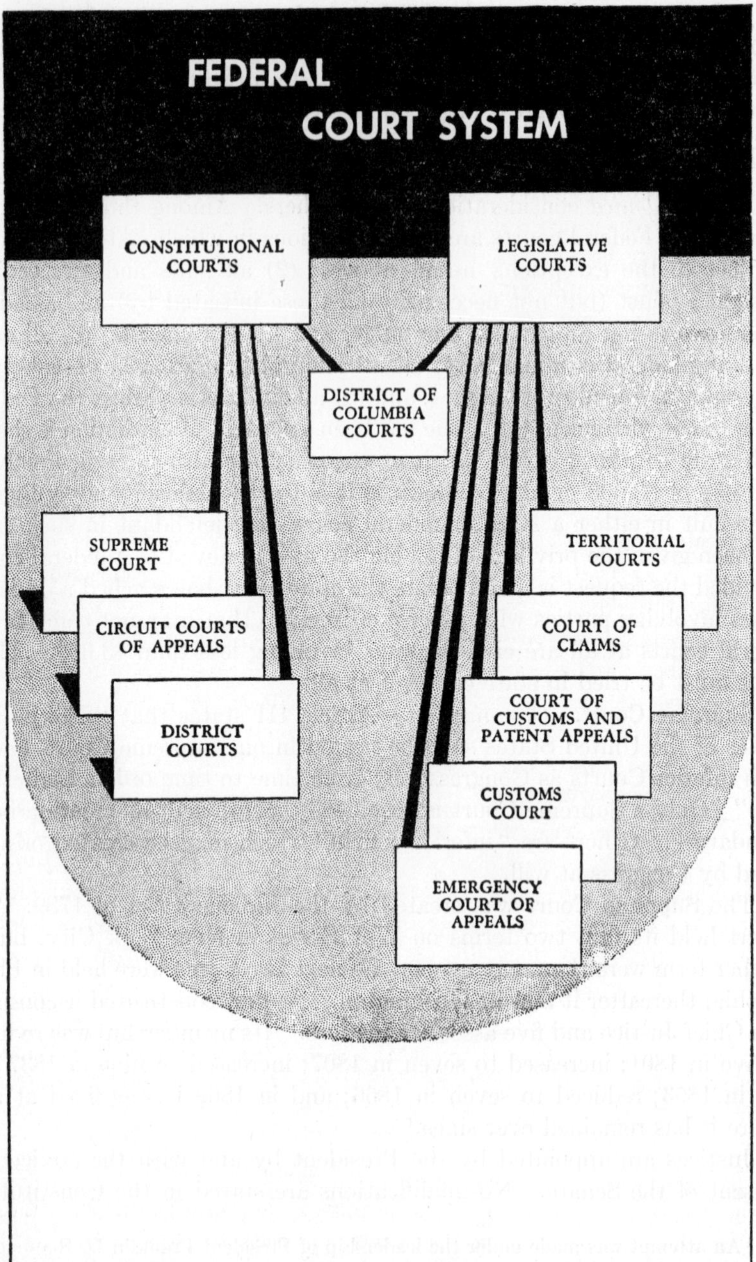
FEDERAL
COURT SYSTEM
CONSTITUTIONAL COURTS
LEGISLATIVE COURTS
DISTRICT OF COLUMBIA COURTS
SUPREME COURT
CIRCUIT COURTS OF APPEALS
DISTRICT COURTS
TERRITORIAL COURTS
COURT OF CLAIMS
COURT OF CUSTOMS AND PATENT APPEALS
CUSTOMS COURT
EMERGENCY COURT OF APPEALS

hence the President is free to appoint anyone for whom senatorial confirmation can be obtained. Terms of federal judges are for good behavior and they are removable by impeachment only.[1] After reaching the age of seventy judges may "resign" or "retire" and receive full salary as long as they live, provided they have served as federal judges, for 10 years or more.[2] If they retire (but not if they resign), they are still federal judges and eligible for service upon assignment in the lower courts. The Chief Justice's salary is $25,500, the association justices' $25,000. These are fixed by Congress and while they can be raised at any time, they cannot be diminished[3] during the tenure of any particular judge.

Characteristics of the Justices.—Although the Constitution does not require it, every chief and associate justice has been a lawyer. All have been men. As lawyers, many of them have had large corporations or men of wealth for their clients, others have been professors of law, while still others have spent most of their years in politics or as consultants to administrative agencies. Some have been men of wealth, but most have been moderately well-to-do. Their average age at the time of appointment has been well over fifty, while the average age of those sitting at particular times has varied from about forty-nine to seventy-two years, the latter being as recently as 1937.[4] Most of the judges have been prominent members of the same political party as the President who appointed them. Most of them have had previous political or judicial experience, a number having served on state supreme courts and in Congress. Practically all have come from the Eastern part of the nation, Massachusetts and New York accounting for nearly one-fourth of the total. In 1937, twenty-one states had never been represented on the Court. Most of the justices have been college trained, more having attended Harvard, Yale, and Princeton than any other particular college or university.[5] Some of the justices have been brilliant, more have been of average ability, while a few have been decidedly mediocre. In spite of their robes, justices

[1] To date (1950) nine judges of constitutional courts have been impeached. Of these only four were convicted. Samuel Chase, who was acquitted in 1805, was the only member of the Supreme Court in this group. The number would undoubtedly have been greater had not other judges of minor federal courts resigned when threatened with impeachment. On the removal of judges see William S. Carpenter, *Judicial Tenure in the United States* (New Haven: Yale University Press, 1918).

[2] Below, p. 349.

[3] Below, p. 372.

[4] Justice Story, appointed at the age of thirty-two by President Madison, was the youngest ever to sit on the court. For data concerning the ages of Supreme Court justices, see United States Senate Committee on the Judiciary, *Hearings on S. 1392, a Bill to Reorganize the Judicial Branch of the Government*, 75th Cong., 1st Sess. (Washington: Government Printing Office, 6 parts, 1937), part 1. Also see Morris L. Ernst, *The Ultimate Power* (New York: Doubleday, 1937), Chap. XXV.

[5] *Ibid.*, p. 296.

are human and influenced by the same considerations as other members of the human race.[1]

Jurisdiction.—The Supreme Court has original and appellate jurisdiction. Its original jurisdiction extends to two types of cases: (1) those affecting ambassadors, other public ministers, and consuls; and (2) those in which states are parties. Congress cannot increase the number of cases that may originate before the Supreme Court.[2] In all cases other than those involving states and representatives of foreign governments, the Supreme Court has appellate jurisdiction, both as to law and facts "with such exceptions, and under such regulations as Congress shall make." In accordance with this provision, Congress has defined in detail the appellate jurisdiction of the Court.

Comparatively few cases commence in the Supreme Court and, while juries may be used, they have been in only a few cases. The great majority of cases that reach the Supreme Court are started elsewhere. At present, cases come to it from state courts, circuit courts of appeals, and, in a few instances, federal district courts. Cases reach the Court either by appeal or by writ of certiorari.[3] The expectation is that only questions involving constitutionality and those of great national importance will reach the highest court in the land.

Sessions and Conferences.—The Supreme Court begins its term annually on the first Monday in October and usually ends early in the following June. Special sessions may be called by the Chief Justice when the Court is adjourned, but the occasion must be of unusual importance and urgency.[4]

[1] For an interesting account of the lives of the Chief Justices up to and including Chief Justice Charles E. Hughes, see Kenneth B. Umbreit, *Our Eleven Chief Justices* (New York: Harper, 1938).

[2] Marbury *v.* Madison, 1 Cranch 137 (1803).

[3] On appeal, cases are removed to a superior court for the purpose of subjecting the entire cause—the facts as well as the law—to review and revisal. A *writ of certiorari* is a command issued by a superior court directing an inferior court (state or federal) to send up the record and proceedings in a cause before verdict, with its certificate to the correctness and completeness of the record, for review or retrial. Formerly many cases reached the Supreme Court by *writ of error*. This was a common-law writ by which the record was removed after final judgment to a superior court for the purpose of obtaining a review of the law (not the facts also) to ascertain whether errors of law were made by a lower court. Congress abolished the writ in 1928, substituting appeal as a method of obtaining relief.

[4] In 1942 the Court held its first special session since 1920 when the justices were called to meet on July 29 to consider a petition for writ of habeas corpus which would have transferred the trial of seven German saboteurs from the special military tribunal, before which they were then being tried, to the regular courts. The motion was promptly dismissed, the military tribunal resumed its proceedings and shortly thereafter found the defendants guilty. Five were promptly put to death while the other two were sentenced to life imprisonment at hard labor.

All sessions are held in the Court's beautiful and spacious white marble building located across from the capitol building in Washington.

The Chief Justice is the executive officer of the Court; he presides at all sessions and conferences, and announces its orders. Legally, however, his decisions have no greater weight than those of other justices. The associate justices have precedence according to the date of appointment, or, if two happen to have been appointed at the same time, then according to their age. In the absence of the Chief Justice, the associate justice first in precedence performs his duties. The Court divides its time about equally between the hearing of cases and intervening recesses. That is, the Court holds sessions daily, except Saturday and Sunday, for about 2 weeks and then recesses for 2 weeks during which time the justices study and write opinions.

By the time oral argument is finished the justices have usually made up their minds.[1] Following an examination of records and briefs, the justices compare their views and register their votes at a Saturday's conference. The Chief Justice usually states his opinion first but votes last. After a decision has been reached, the Chief Justice either assigns the opinion to be written to one of those who voted as he did or agrees to write the opinion himself. If he voted with the minority, the senior associate justice in the majority assigns the case to one with whom he agreed. Every judge goes to conference with the knowledge that he may have the responsibility of writing the opinion that will accord with his vote. This means that every justice must be keenly attentive to every case. It also means that every justice must organize his own thoughts inasmuch as he is required to vote before listening to plausible and convincing opinions written by his colleagues. If a majority cannot reach an agreement, the case may be reargued one or more times.

Decisions and Opinions.—Several hundred cases reach the Supreme Court each year. A large number of appeals and petitions for writs of certiorari are disposed of without serious consideration for want of jurisdiction or merit. Many petitions for certiorari are merely granted or denied upon comparatively short briefs without oral argument. Others involving rather well settled points of law about which the Court can come to a decision without oral hearings are disposed of in *per curiam* decisions. The remainder are cases of considerable importance and are disposed of only after oral hearing and then in written opinions. A decision may be

[1] These remarks are based upon the account given by the former Chief Justice Charles E. Hughes, in an account written after he had been an associate justice but retired to become the Republican presidential candidate in 1916 and before he reentered the Court in 1929. See his account in *The Supreme Court of the United States* (New York: Columbia University Press, 1928), pp. 56–65.

unanimous or divided. If divided, both a majority and dissenting opinion are usually written. Again, one or more justices might agree with the conclusion reached in the majority or dissenting opinions but for different reasons. In that event, concurring opinions may be written. Thus, in a case involving complicated and controversial issues, there may be as many as four written opinions: the majority opinion, one dissenting, one concurring with the majority, and another concurring with the minority. Six justices constitute a quorum and at least a majority must concur before a decision is made. If a majority cannot agree, even though the case may be reargued, the decision of the lower court is allowed to stand. Opinions, as well as information about the disposition of other cases, are published and may be found in any good library in volumes known, since 1882, as *United States Reports*.[1]

Circuit Courts of Appeal.—Immediately below the Supreme Court stand the Circuit Courts of Appeal, created in 1891 to facilitate the disposition of cases and ease the burden upon the Supreme Court. The courts operate in the District of Columbia and ten circuits, or regions, into which the country and its territories have been divided. Each court comprises from three to six circuit judges, two of whom constitute a quorum. The justices of the Supreme Court may also sit as judges, each within a circuit to which he has been assigned.[2] Time, however, prevents justices of the high court from "riding circuit" as they did in the early days of the republic. District judges may also be assigned to serve on the circuit courts, although in no case may they sit in judgment of cases in which they may have participated as district judges. In some circuits, court is always held in the same city; in others, it may be held in two or more designated cities. The courts sit at regular intervals in buildings owned or leased by the Federal government. Circuit judges are appointed by the President with the advice and consent of the Senate. Their term is for good behavior, and their salary $17,500.

The circuit courts have only slight original jurisdiction. They are primarily appellate courts. With few exceptions, cases decided in the district courts, legislative courts, and quasi-judicial boards and commissions go next to the circuit courts. Their decisions are final in all criminal cases not involving questions of constitutionality. Their decisions may be reviewed only by the Supreme Court.

[1] Prior to 1882 these volumes were published under the name of the court reporter who prepared them for publication. Their titles, the number of volumes, and dates of issue are Dallas, 4 vols., 1790–1800; Cranch, 9 vols., 1801–1815; Wheaton, 12 vols., 1816–1827; Peters, 16 vols., 1828–1842; Howard, 24 vols., 1843–1860; Black, 2 vols., 1861–1862; Wallace, 23 vols., 1863–1874; and Otto, 17 vols., 1875–1882.

[2] Since there are ten circuits and only nine Supreme Court justices, one justice is assigned two circuits. In 1950 Justice Clark was assigned to both the eighth and tenth circuits, while the Chief Justice presided over the court of appeals for the District of Columbia as well as the fourth circuit.

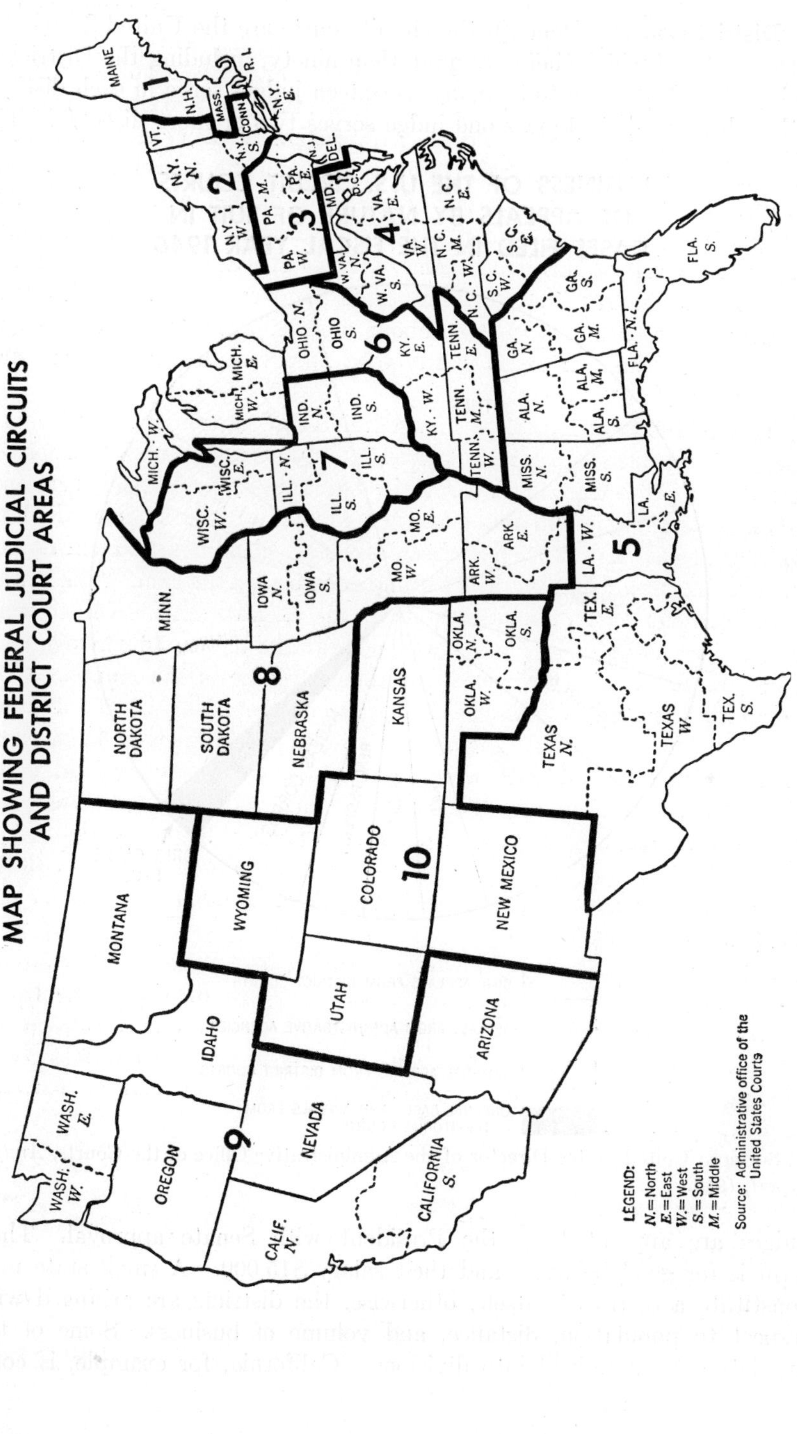
MAP SHOWING FEDERAL JUDICIAL CIRCUITS AND DISTRICT COURT AREAS
MAINE
N.H.
VT.
MASS.
CONN.
R.I.
N.Y. E.
N.Y. S.
N.Y. N.
N.Y. W.
N.J.
DEL.
PA. E.
PA. M.
PA. W.
MD.
D.C.
VA. E.
VA. W.
W. VA. N.
W. VA. S.
N.C. E.
N.C. M.
N.C. W.
S.C. E.
S.C. W.
GA. N.
GA. M.
GA. S.
FLA. N.
FLA. S.
ALA. N.
ALA. M.
ALA. S.
MISS. N.
MISS. S.
LA. E.
LA. W.
TENN. E.
TENN. M.
TENN. W.
KY. E.
KY. W.
OHIO N.
OHIO S.
MICH. E.
MICH. W.
IND. N.
IND. S.
ILL. N.
ILL. E.
ILL. S.
WISC. E.
WISC. W.
MINN.
IOWA N.
IOWA S.
MO. E.
MO. W.
ARK. E.
ARK. W.
OKLA. N.
OKLA. E.
OKLA. W.
TEX. E.
TEXAS N.
TEXAS W.
TEX. S.
NORTH DAKOTA
SOUTH DAKOTA
NEBRASKA
KANSAS
MONTANA
WYOMING
COLORADO
NEW MEXICO
IDAHO
UTAH
ARIZONA
WASH. E.
WASH. W.
OREGON
NEVADA
CALIF. N.
CALIFORNIA S.
1
2
3
4
5
6
7
8
9
10
LEGEND:
N. = North
E. = East
W. = West
S. = South
M. = Middle
Source: Administrative office of the United States Courts

District Courts.—Beneath the circuit courts are the United States district courts, of which there are more than ninety, including the District of Columbia. From one to as many as sixteen judges serve in each district, although in a few instances one judge serves two or more districts. The

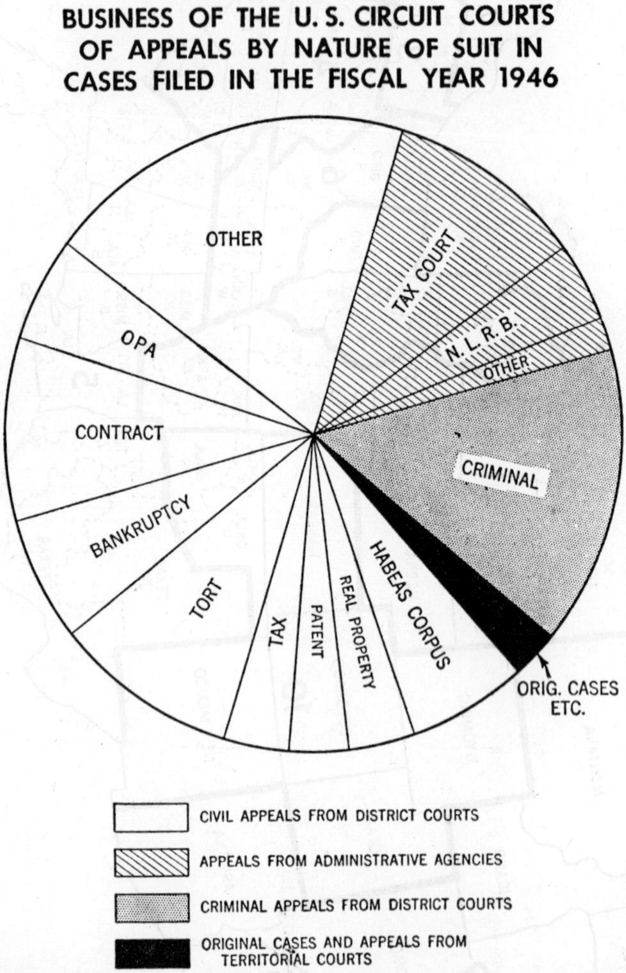

Source: United States Director of the Administrative Office of the Courts, *Annual Report, 1948*.

judges are appointed by the President with Senate approval. Their term is for good behavior and their salary $15,000. A small state may constitute a district in itself; otherwise, the districts are arranged with respect to population, distance, and volume of business. Some of the districts are subdivided into divisions. California, for example, is com-

CIVIL CASES COMMENCED IN UNITED STATES DISTRICT COURTS FROM 1905 TO 1948

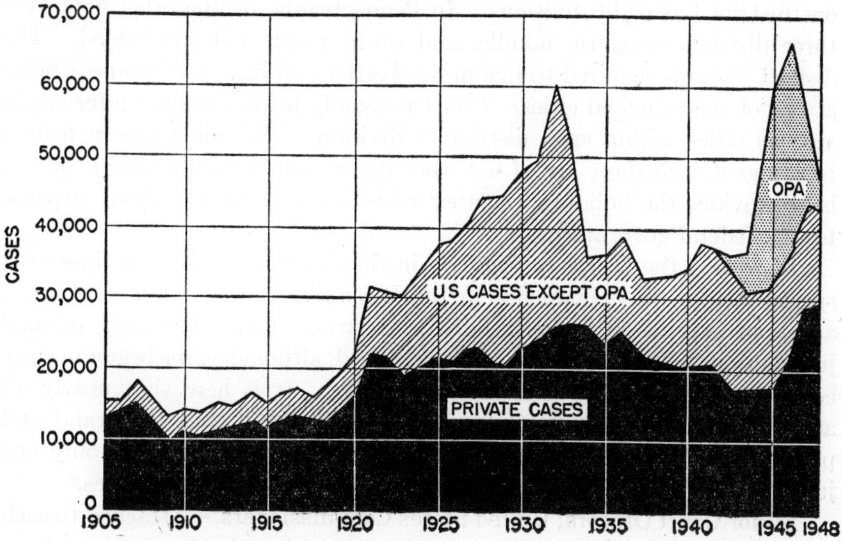

CRIMINAL CASES COMMENCED IN UNITED STATES DISTRICT COURTS FROM 1905 TO 1948

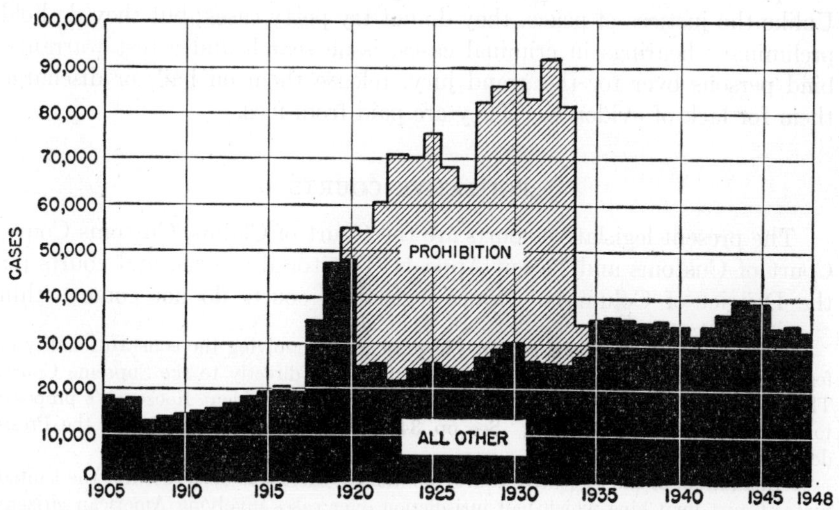

SOURCE: United States Director of the Administrative Office of the Courts, *Annual Report, 1948* (Washington, Government Printing Office, 1948).

prised of two districts—northern and southern—but each district is subdivided into a northern and southern division. In Nebraska there is only one district but eight divisions. In Pennsylvania, on the other hand, the three districts—eastern, middle, and western—are not subdivided. The district judge is required to live in his district and have a permanent office at one of the principal cities. Court is usually held at regular intervals in various cities within each district or division. The court sits in federal buildings if such there are; if not, the city or county within which court is held provides the building, together with light and heat, without expense to the Federal government.

Excepting the few that originate in the Supreme Court and those of a special nature that commence in the legislative courts, most other cases and controversies start before district courts. Theirs is chiefly original jurisdiction; no cases come to them on appeal, although cases begun in state courts are occasionally transferred to them. It is here that nearly all accused of committing federal crimes are tried and that the grand and petit juries are used if at all. Ordinarily, cases are tried with only one judge presiding, but three judges must sit in certain types of cases.[1]

Minor Court Officers; United States Commissioners.—Attached to each district court are the usual clerks, a reporter (since 1945), stenographers, bailiffs, and other attendants. These are all appointed by the court and responsible to it. Referees in bankruptcy are also appointed by the courts. In addition, each court appoints one or more commissioners who serve for terms of 4 years. These are usually part-time quasi-judicial officers who perform about the same functions as do justices of peace in the states. Unlike the justices of peace, they do not try petty cases; but they do hold preliminary hearings in criminal cases, issue search and arrest warrants, bind persons over for the grand jury, release them on bail, or discharge them for lack of evidence. They are paid from fees.

LEGISLATIVE COURTS

The present legislative courts are the Court of Claims, Customs Court, Court of Customs and Patent Appeals, Territorial Courts, and courts for the District of Columbia.[2] Since legislative courts do not come within

[1] Since 1937 this has been required in most cases involving the constitutionality of federal statutes. Appeal may be taken in such cases directly to the Supreme Court. This, it will be recognized, was part of the outcome of President Roosevelt's proposal to reorganize the federal courts. See pp. 348–350 for further discussion of the President's proposal.

[2] In addition to the legislative courts mentioned, there was until recently the United States Court for China which had jurisdiction over cases involving American citizens in China. It was abolished on May 20, 1943, when the United States entered into treaty abandoning extraterritorial rights in the Chinese republic.

the scope of the Judicial Article (Art. III), their judges need not serve for terms of life or good behavior and they may be removed by methods other than impeachment. Moreover, they have only such jurisdiction as Congress wishes to give them.

Court of Claims.—Since governments cannot be sued without their consent, there are two methods by which one might obtain satisfaction for injury done. One is for the legislature to enact general or special legislation whenever necessary, and this was the practice until 1855 and still remains so in special instances. The other is for the government to consent to be sued. The former results in the introduction of a multitude of bills which are time consuming and frequently petty in nature. To avoid this the Court of Claims was established in 1855 with authority to adjudicate all claims arising out of the Constitution, acts of Congress, regulations of the executive departments, or out of contracts entered into by the Federal government or its agents. Claims are forever barred, however, unless brought within 6 years. The court consists of a chief justice and four associate justices who are appointed by the President with Senate approval for terms of good behavior. Their salary is $17,500. The court sits in Washington, beginning on the first Monday in December each year.

United States Customs Court.—When goods enter the country, they are met by customs officers who place valuations upon them and collect tariff duties. Controversies inevitably arise and to adjudicate these the Customs Court was established. It is composed of nine judges appointed by the President with Senate approval for good behavior. Not more than five may be from the same political party, and the judges receive $15,000 a year. The office of the court is located in New York City and most of its business is conducted there, although sessions are held in other cities, including San Juan, Puerto Rico.

United States Court of Customs and Patent Appeals.—Created in 1910, this court is composed of five members appointed for terms of good behavior. Their salary is $17,500 a year. The court is in continuous session, and although it usually sits in Washington, it may convene in any judicial circuit at any time. The court hears appeals from the decisions of the Customs Court and the United States Patent Office, and its judgments and decrees are final with the exception that they may be reviewed upon certiorari by the Supreme Court.

Territorial Courts.—These are courts set up pursuant to the power given to Congress to make all needful rules and regulations respecting American territories.[1] The most important are located in Hawaii, Alaska, Puerto Rico, the Virgin Islands, and the Panama Canal Zone. These differ from district courts in that they have jurisdiction over all matters, local as well

[1] Article IV, Section 3.

as all federal, which Congress may assign directly, or indirectly through the territorial government. Within each territory there is usually a court resembling a district court with general jurisdiction over the entire area and, in addition, a system of local courts similar to those found in the American states.[1] Judges of the general courts of the territories are usually appointed for terms of 4 years, although in Hawaii the term is 6 years and in Puerto Rico there is no fixed term.

Courts of the District of Columbia.—Although similar, the Supreme Court draws a distinction between territorial courts and courts of the District of Columbia. Because the District of Columbia is permanent, and not transitory like other territories, the "judicial power" of the United States as defined in Article III operates within it. Accordingly, its courts are constitutional and parallel with other "inferior courts." Nevertheless, the same courts are also legislative inasmuch as Congress is given full authority to govern the district which constitutes the seat of government. Within the District two courts have been established, a Court of Appeals and a District Court. The former has jurisdiction over appeals emanating from the District Court as well as over all matters that Circuit Courts of Appeal are competent to handle. The latter deals with local matters and cases and controversies similar to those that come before constitutional district courts.

JUDICIAL ADMINISTRATION

The Congress and President must establish courts, appoint the judges, raise and appropriate money to operate the courts, and lay down the broad outlines of jurisdiction and procedure. Moreover, the President is charged with primary responsibility for law enforcement. Nevertheless, the courts perform many tasks of an administrative character.

Administrative Functions of the Courts.—In the first place, the courts have many appointments to make that require the examination and selection of applicants. These include clerks, commissioners, messengers, stenographers, and other aides. Second, each court must superintend civil and criminal procedure. This involves such duties as the issuance of writs and warrants, taking of bail, the appointment of grand and petit juries, the admission of attorneys to practice, the assessment and collection of fees, the admission of evidence, and court procedures in general. Third, the courts handle noncontentious cases, *i.e.*, those in which parties are not in dispute. These include administering estates, appointing receivers in bankruptcy, issuing licenses, performing marriages, and naturalizing aliens. Fourth, the courts must enforce their orders. This is usually done through

[1] For courts in the respective territories, see Chap. 26.

the issuance of writs,[1] disrespect for which is punishable as contempt of court.[2]

Administrative Office of the Courts.—Until recently, administration was divided between the Department of Justice and the courts. Criticism of the inefficient manner in which the judiciary operated led, in 1922, to the establishment of an annual conference of senior circuit judges under the chairmanship of the Chief Justice. Although many beneficial reforms resulted, responsibility for administration still remained divided. Attention was focused upon the question in 1937 when the President proposed the creation of a "proctor" under the supervision of the Supreme Court with responsibility for administrative matters pertaining to the judicial system, but the proposal was lost sight of in the heat of controversy over the President's alleged attempt to "pack" the courts. Two years later, however, Congress established the Administrative Office of the United States Courts. The office is subordinate to the annual conference of senior circuit judges and the Supreme Court. It is conducted by a director and assistant director appointed by the Supreme Court for as long as their services are satisfactory.

Centralization of Judicial Administration.—By the creation of the Administrative Office, a clear distinction was made between judicial administration and law enforcement. The Department of Justice still retains full responsibility for the latter, while the task of over-all administration of the judicial system was centralized in the hands of the Administrative Office. The office is divided into four main divisions. One, called the Division of Business Administration, provides the courts with quarters, supplies, and clerical and administrative service, including the payment of salaries and expenses. The second, called the Division of Procedural Studies and Statistics, is designed to furnish information about the state of judicial business throughout the country and to make recommendations whereby justice may be given with greater dispatch and economy. The third, the Probation Division, exercises a general supervision over the federal probation system, which was previously conducted by the Bureau

[1] The most common are *warrants*, which are commands for appearance, arrest, search or seizure; *summonses*, which direct plaintiffs in civil suits to appear and make answer to complaints; *subpoenas*, which compel the appearance of witnesses or the production of evidence; *writs of execution*, which direct defendants to satisfy judgments awarded in civil suits; *writs of ejectment*, which eject defendants from real estate held by them which the court has found belongs to plaintiffs; *injunctions*, which restrain from threatened damage to property; *mandamuses*, which order public officials to perform some act required of them by law; and *certiorari*, which order public officials, especially inferior judicial tribunals, to send up records for review.

[2] Persons may be fined or imprisoned for contempt of court. Trial is usually without jury if the contempt is committed in the presence of the court but otherwise with jury if the defendant insists.

of Prisons in the Department of Justice. The fourth, the Bankruptcy Division, keeps in touch with bankruptcy proceedings pending before federal courts. One interesting result of the work of the office has been the inauguration of periodic conferences in the various circuits, attended by both federal and state judges and attorneys.

RECENT CONTROVERSY OVER COURT REORGANIZATION

With the three branches of government separated, disputes will inevitably arise between them. Those between the executive and Congress are likely to be short-lived inasmuch as frequent elections permit their differences to be resolved by the voters. The situation is different, however, in the event of controversy between the political branches and the courts. Judges appointed for life and having the power of judicial review can stymie legislative action for rather long periods of time. When they do so, criticism, whether just or unjust, is inevitable. It is generally agreed that the courts must have sufficient independence to resist popular clamor, and yet self-restraint on the part of the courts is essential if they are not to negate powers granted to the other branches. The chief criticism in recent years has been that the courts have been so partial to large corporate, business, and property interests as to render the state and Federal governments incapable of enacting socially desirable legislation. Resentment that had been accumulating since the reconstruction period following the Civil War reached a climax in 1937.

Checks upon the Courts.—In spite of their great authority and independence, the courts are not invulnerable. Judges are human and sensitive to criticism and therefore are not likely to resist the persistent pressure of public opinion. If they grossly misbehave, judges can be impeached. Their decisions can be overridden by constitutional amendment, although this is a slow and none too hopeful solution.[1] Of course, judges die, retire, and resign, providing opportunities for the appointment of younger men. As a last resort, Congress could refuse to appropriate money for judicial salaries and expenses, increase the number of judges, abolish the inferior courts, or amend the jurisdiction of the courts to prevent certain types of cases from ever reaching either the lower courts or the Supreme Court.[2]

[1] See pp. 72–74.

[2] On several occasions the latter has been done. One of the most conspicuous occasions occurred in 1868 when Congress took away the appellate jurisdiction of the Supreme Court under the Habeas Corpus Act of 1867 at a time when the constitutionality of the measure had already been argued. The Court was forced to admit that Congress had acted within its province. *Ex parte* McCardle, 7 Wallace 506 (1869). For a discussion of this event see Charles Warren, *The Supreme Court in United States History* (Boston: Little, 3 vols., 1922), vol. II, 22*ff.*; and Hughes, *op. cit.*, p. 26. At least three other instances have occurred: one when Congress provided that the deci-

Indeed, in many respects the judiciary is the weakest of the three branches. It possesses the power neither of purse nor sword.

New Deal Legislation Unconstitutional.—President Hoover left office in March, 1933, in the midst of the great depression. On the same date President Roosevelt entered upon his duties promising a "New Deal." He and Congress moved quickly, passing legislation of far-reaching proportions in record-breaking time. Haste was justified by the emergency.

Between 1933 and 1937 the Supreme Court consisted of nine justices, all of whom had been appointed prior to 1933 and all but two of whom (McReynolds and Brandeis) had been appointed by Republican presidents. Their average age was seventy-two (in 1937), the highest in Supreme Court history, and it so happened that four (McReynolds, Sutherland, Butler, and Van Devanter) of the six who were over seventy were "conservatives," while the fifth (Hughes) was a "middle-of-the-roader" and only the sixth (Brandeis) a "liberal." In 3 years this court declared New Deal statutes, or provisions thereof, unconstitutional in twelve instances, five of them during the court term beginning in October, 1935. On most of the measures the Court was sharply divided into "conservative" and "liberal" blocs, as is shown in the following table:

Affiliation of Supreme Court Justices with Majority and Minority Groups[1]
(On basis of 27 important cases decided between 1933 and 1937)

Justice	By whom appointed	Age 1937	Voted for constitutionality (No. of cases)	Voted against constitutionality (No. of cases)	Per cent favorable to New Deal	
Brandeis....	Wilson '16	81	19	8	0.704	"Liberals"
Stone.......	Coolidge '25	65	20	7	0.741	
Cardozo.....	Hoover '32	67	20	7	0.741	
Roberts.....	Hoover '32	62	15	12	0.555	Held balance of power
Hughes.....	Hoover '30	75	17	10	0.626	
Van Devanter	Taft '10	78	6	21	0.222	"Conservative"
Sutherland..	Harding '22	75	6	21	0.222	
Butler.......	Harding '22	71	5	22	0.185	
McReynolds.	Wilson '14	75	4	23	0.148	

[1] For a similar chart based upon a smaller sampling of cases, see H. Arthur Steiner, *Significant Supreme Court Decisions, 1934–1937* (New York: Wiley, 2d ed., 1937), p. 6.

sions of the Circuit Courts of Appeal should be final in all criminal cases except where constitutional issues were involved; another in 1932 when the courts were forbidden by provisions of the Norris-LaGuardia Act from enforcing "yellow-dog" contracts; and the third in 1935 when Congress withdrew the right of suit on claims arising from processing taxes under the AAA where these taxes had been passed on by the processor to the consumer.

It is apparent that Justice Hughes and Roberts held the balance of power. This meant that in five-to-four decisions, of which there were ten during the 4-year period, either Hughes or Roberts cast the deciding vote, and in all probability it was the latter oftener than the Chief Justice.

Situation in 1937 Unprecedented.—The situation as it existed during President Roosevelt's first term was unprecedented in several ways. First, the economic crisis was of major proportions, an emergency psychology was present, and the President was one of such character as to act boldly, even rashly as many insist. Second, the justices were older than at any other period. Third, no vacancies occurred during the 4-year period. Fourth, seldom, if ever, had the Supreme Court been so rigidly and evenly divided into blocs. Fifth, never had the courts been called upon to pass judgment upon so many measures involving extremely controversial points of constitutional law in a similarly short period of time, and in no similar period had they declared so many statutes unconstitutional.

The President's Proposals.—Flushed with victory in the election of November, 1936,[1] the President decided upon a showdown with the courts. Less than 3 weeks after inauguration, on Feb. 4, he sent a message to Congress which prompted one of the most exciting debates in American history.

The immediate target of the President's proposals was the aged justices on the Supreme and lower courts.[2] Age undoubtedly has its effect upon judicial decisions and there have been many, including the then Chief Justice,[3] who have advocated retirement at seventy-five or earlier. To compel retirement, however, required a constitutional amendment, and the President was unwilling to brook the delays and difficulties which this would certainly encounter. Accordingly, he proposed to "rejuvenate" the courts by making it possible to appoint a new judge for every federal judge who had served 10 years and who remained on the bench after reaching the age of seventy, provided the Supreme Court should never exceed fifteen and not more than fifty new judges should be added to the lower courts. This would tend to embarrass older judges into retiring or resigning, but if they chose to remain it was with knowledge that younger judges might be appointed to "assist" and perhaps counterbalance their conservatism. Since there were at the time six justices on the Supreme Court over seventy, had they not retired the President might have appointed

[1] Nothing was said, however, in the platform of the Democratic party or by the President during the campaign which foreshadowed the drastic proposals that the President later submitted.

[2] Besides the six on the Supreme Court, a total of twenty-four judges who were seventy or over sitting on lower courts were affected by the President's bill. *Adverse Report on Reorganization of the Federal Judiciary*, Sen. Rep. 711, 75th Cong., 1st Sess. (Washington: Government Printing Office, 1937), p. 33.

[3] Hughes, *op. cit.*, pp. 73–77.

six additional judges, raising the membership of the Court to the maximum of fifteen. As things then stood, the addition of six "liberals" to the three already on the Court would have ensured more favorable consideration of "New Deal" legislation.[1]

Three additional proposals were less controversial. One was that the Chief Justice be empowered to assign circuit and district judges to serve temporarily in districts other than their own. Another, that the Supreme Court be authorized to appoint a "proctor" who would be a business manager for the judicial system with the expectation that delays and inefficiencies might be eliminated. The third was that when the constitutionality of a federal law was challenged in a private suit before a lower court, the Attorney General should be notified and given opportunity of defending the law. Moreover, it was suggested that such cases should be decided only by courts consisting of three judges. Furthermore, if the lower court should declare the law unconstitutional, either the Attorney General or one of the private parties might take an appeal directly to the Supreme Court. This, it was hoped, would eliminate the situation where private parties could rush to district courts and obtain injunctions from a single judge which would render the enforcement of an act of Congress impossible for several months or years while the measure was running the gamut of legal procedures en route to the Supreme Court where final judgment would be rendered.

Adoption of Proposals.—The proposal that new justices be authorized for those who failed to retire or resign was defeated in its entirety. Out of it, however, came a measure permitting Supreme Court justices with 10 years of service to retire at seventy with full pay.[2] Otherwise, all the President's recommendations were adopted at the time or have been since, either in whole or in part. By an act dated Aug. 24, 1937,[3] district judges may be transferred from one district to another within the same judicial circuit by the senior circuit judge, or from within one circuit to another by the Chief Justice. By the same act, the Attorney General must be given notice of proceedings involving the constitutionality of federal statutes. Moreover, all such proceedings must be conducted before courts consisting of three judges, one of whom must be a circuit judge.[4] Still further, if the decision is against the constitutionality of a statute, the case may be appealed by either party directly to the Supreme Court where the matter must be heard "at the earliest possible time and shall take precedence over

[1] Above, p. 347.

[2] Public no. 10, Mar. 1, 1937, *United States Statutes at Large* (Washington: Government Printing Office, 1937), vol. 50, p. 24.

[3] *Ibid.*, pp. 751–753.

[4] Temporary restraining orders may still be issued by a single judge when delay would cause irreparable damage.

all other matters not of a like character." The proposal to create a business manager for the courts was defeated at the time but adopted 2 years later with the establishment of the Administrative Office of the Courts.[1]

Other Results of the Controversy.—Although failure to enact the principal feature of his program was a serious political defeat, it has been said that the President "lost his battle but won his war." There is truth in the statement. Shortly after the controversy, vacancies occurred by resignation, retirement, or death, permitting the appointment of younger men. By the fall of 1937 the "liberals" were clearly in the majority and by September, 1942, only two of the men who constituted the Supreme Court during the President's first term (Stone and Roberts) remained, while the President had appointed 38 out of the 55 sitting on the Circuit Courts of Appeals and 138 of the 230 judges sitting on district and other United States courts. It is safe to say that all of these appointees held views acceptable to the President at the time of appointment.[2]

Even before any changes were made in the personnel of the Supreme Court, the Court manifested a change of mind by (1) reversing its previous attitude toward state minimum-wage laws for women; (2) redefining the commerce clause to include manufacturing; (3) upholding the tax provisions of the Social Security Act; and (4) upholding the Railway Labor Act. Although still not without reverberations, the President's reelection for a third term in 1940 and the outbreak of war in 1941 silenced criticism. Meanwhile, the country adjusted itself to an interpretation of the Constitution that greatly broadened the powers of both the Federal government and the states.

LAW ENFORCEMENT

No Centralized Federal Police Force.—In the past there has been no unified federal police force operating over the nation. Detection of violations has been left to various administrative agencies, most of which perform civil and administrative as well as criminal duties. While probably every administrative agency makes investigations of some sort or another, a few have been more conspicuous than others. Among these are the Secret Service Division (charged with detection of counterfeiting, forgery, and protecting the President), the Bureau of Customs, the Alcohol Tax Unit, and the Intelligence Unit of the Bureau of Internal Revenue (charged with detecting income-tax evasion) in the Treasury Department; the Coast Guard; the inspectors of the Post Office Department; the Division of Investigations in the Department of Interior (charged with discovering violations of federal laws pertaining to lands, public works, conservation);

[1] Above, p. 345.

[2] *The New York Times*, Sept. 27, 1942.

the Legal Investigating Division of the Federal Trade Commission; the Bureau of Inquiry of the Interstate Commerce Commission; the Federal Bureau of Investigation, the Antitrust Division, the Immigration and Naturalization Service of the Department of Justice; and many others.[1]

The Federal Bureau of Investigation (FBI).—Out of the First World War and the necessity of enforcing prohibition arose a conviction that a permanent body of trained agents was required to investigate violations of federal laws. The conviction also grew that in order to ensure the closest cooperation with district attorneys, marshals, and the courts, these should be under the Department of Justice. Aided by a wave of kidnaping, racketeering, and gangsterism which swept over the country, the Federal Bureau of Investigation was reorganized in 1934. Under the direction of J. Edgar Hoover, several hundred agents, popularly known as "G men," have been specially recruited and trained, and almost every device known to modern science has been adopted for use in detecting violators. The bureau is charged with the investigation of all violations of federal laws except those specifically assigned to other agencies such as counterfeiting and postal violations. While its fingerprint files, laboratory, and advisory services are available to state and local enforcement officers, the FBI usually does not take the initiative in local cases, except where federal laws, agents, or properties are involved.

Common Federal Criminal Offenses.—Within recent years the number of federal violations has increased by leaps and bounds in step with the rapid expansion of federal activities. Thousands are apprehended and prosecuted each year. Although the various offenses cannot be detailed here, some idea of their character is shown by the following list:

Counterfeiting and forgery
Customs Act violations
Embezzlement and fraud
Escape, flight, mutiny, etc.
Extortion and racketeering
Immigration Act violations
Internal Revenue Act violations
Interstate Commerce Act violations
Juvenile delinquency
Kidnaping
Larceny and theft
Liquor law violations
Narcotic Drug Act violations
National Bank and Federal Reserve Act violations
National bank robbery
National Bankruptcy Act violations
National Firearms violations
Postal law violations
Selective Service Act violations
White Slave Traffic Act violations

[1] For a review of the development and work of these so-called "police agencies," see Arthur C. Millspaugh, *Crime Control by the National Government* (Washington: Brookings, 1937). See also Bruce Smith, *Police Systems in the United States* (New York: Harper, 1940).

Liquor law violations ordinarily greatly exceed all others. Postal law violations are usually the next most numerous, followed by violations of the Interstate Commerce, Narcotic, and Immigration Acts.

Supervision of Prosecutions by Department of Justice.—Many violations of federal laws are dealt with by executive and administrative procedures,[1] but a larger number must be dealt with before federal courts. General supervision over all prosecutions is exercised by the Department of Justice. The department, upon receipt of evidence from one of the "police" agencies, turns the matter over to one of the United States district attorneys who prepares the case with the assistance of specialists from either the Department of Justice or other administrative agencies. There is always one attorney in each judicial district and usually several assistants. They are appointed by the President with Senate approval for terms of 4 years. Upon them falls the primary responsibility of proving guilt in the courts.

Execution of Federal Laws.—Within each judicial district is also a United States marshal with perhaps several deputies. Marshals are appointed by the President with Senate approval for terms of 4 years. They are to the federal courts what sheriffs are to states and counties. It is their duty to make arrests, take charge of prisoners, and execute court orders. They have authority to command all necessary assistance and on occasion have appointed deputies—otherwise known as *posse comitatus*—by tens, hundreds, or thousands. Marshals are, to quote a former Attorney General, "the first line of federal defense on occasions of domestic disturbance."[2]

Federal Prisons and Correctional Institutions.—As in the states, violators of federal laws include men, women, boys, girls, those who are physically and mentally normal, and an unfortunate group who are physically and mentally sick. Institutions, staffs, and regimen must be adapted to the prisoners' conditions.

There are no federal "jails," except in the territories; only "prisons" and correctional institutions. Nearly all of these are under the supervision of the Bureau of Prisons in the Department of Justice.[3] A considerable number of federal offenders are kept in state, county, and city jails. If possible, these jails must measure up to federal specifications, to determine which inspections are made by the Bureau of Prisons. Of more than 3,000 jails reported in 1944, only 448 are approved, and 334 were approved

[1] See Chap. 21.

[2] Homer Cummings and Carl McFarland, *Federal Justice* (New York: Macmillan, 1937), p. 544.

[3] For reports of the bureau see its annual report entitled *Federal Offenders* prior to 1942 and *Federal Prisons* since, published by the Federal Prisons Industries, Inc. Press, Leavenworth, Kansas. A briefer summary is always included in the *Annual Report of the Attorney General.*

UNITED STATES PRISON SYSTEM

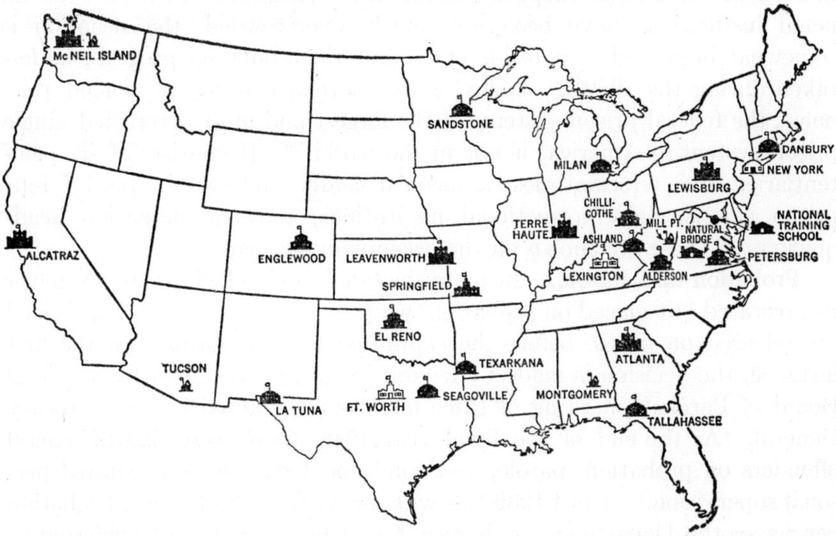

SOURCE: *Federal Prisons, 1948.*

Penitentiaries
- Alcatraz Island, Calif.
- Atlanta, Ga.
- Leavenworth, Kans.
- Lewisburg, Pa.
- McNeil Island, Wash.
- Terre Haute, Ind.

Reformatories
- Chillicothe, Ohio
- El Reno, Okla.
- Englewood, Colo.
- Petersburg, Va.

Reformatories for women
- Alderson, W. Va.

Medical center
- Springfield, Mo.

Correctional institutions
- Ashland, Ky.
- Danbury, Conn.
- La Tuna, Texas
- Milan, Mich.
- Sandstone, Minn.
- Seagoville, Texas
- Tallahassee, Fla.
- Texarkana, Texas

Institutions for juveniles
- National Training Schools for Boys, Washington, D. C.
- Natural Bridge, Va.

Prison Camps
- McNeil Island, Wash.
- Mill Point, W. Va.
- Montgomery, Ala.
- Tucson, Ariz.

Detention headquarters
- New York, N. Y.

Public health service hospitals
- Fort Worth, Texas
- Lexington, Ky.

for emergency use only by federal prisoners.[1] Those who are not detained in state institutions are kept in federal ones. Although in the past federal penal institutions have been notoriously overcrowded, the situation is somewhat improved as a result of an ambitious building program undertaken during the 1930's. Today, with a normal capacity of 20,000 prisoners, the federal prison system is "the largest and most diversified single prison system in America, if not in the world."[2] It consists of six penitentiaries, five reformatories, a medical center and two hospitals,[3] four prison camps, eight correctional institutions, and one detention headquarters. These are shown on the accompanying map.

Probation and Parole.—In many instances federal violators are never incarcerated but placed on probation, while in other cases those imprisoned are released on parole before the expiration of their terms. In the first instance, the decision is made by federal judges; in the latter by a federal Board of Parole, consisting of three members appointed by the Attorney General. At the end of the fiscal year 1948, there were 32,613 federal offenders on probation, parole, and conditional release who required personal supervision.[4] Until 1939 this was the work of the Federal Probation Service of the Department of Justice, but it has since been transferred to the Administrative Office of the Courts. Positions in the Probation Service were long looked upon as patronage "plums" by the President and Congress, but in 1937 the service was placed on a career basis. Now employees are recruited through regular civil service examinations. Even so, inadequately qualified personnel are often appointed, and salaries are still below those paid by leading states like New York and New Jersey and even below those paid investigators in other agencies of the Federal government.[5]

References

Alfange, Dean: *The Supreme Court and the National Will* (New York: Doubleday, 1937).

Aumann, Francis R.: *The Changing American Legal System* (Columbus: The Ohio State University Press, 1940).

[1] Ratings are made on the basis of personnel, administration and discipline, building and equipment, food, cleanliness, personal hygiene, employment and industries, medical service, hospital facilities, education and recreation, rehabilitation, and religious instruction. Of 563 jails inspected in 1944, 44.9 per cent rated under 50 per cent. Only a few were rated "good." See *Federal Offenders*, 1940, p. 15, and *Federal Prisons*, 1944, p. 28.

[2] *Federal Offenders*, 1940, p. 1.

[3] These three are under the supervision not of the Bureau of Prisons but of the United States Public Health Service. See p. 759.

[4] United States Director of the Administrative Office of the Courts, *Annual Report, 1945* (Washington: Government Printing Office, 1945), p. 18.

[5] Henry P. Chandler, "Probation in the Federal System of Criminal Justice," *Federal Probation*, vol. IX (January-March, 1945), No. 1, pp. 3–7. See also Mr. Chandler's remarks in United States Director of the Administrative Office of the Courts, *Annual Report, 1948*, p. 70.

BOUDIN, LOUIS B.: *Government by Judiciary* (New York: Godwin, 1932).

CALLENDER, CLARENCE N.: *American Courts, Their Organization and Procedure* (New York: McGraw-Hill, 1927).

CARDOZO, BENJAMIN N.: *The Nature of the Judicial Process* (New Haven: Yale University Press, 1921).

CARPENTER, WILLIAM S.: *Judicial Tenure in the United States* (New Haven: Yale University Press, 1918).

CARR, ROBERT K.: *Democracy and the Supreme Court* (Norman, Okla.: University of Oklahoma Press, 1936).

——— *The Supreme Court and Judicial Review* (New York: Farrar, Straus, 1942).

——— *Federal Protection of Civil Rights: Quest for a Sword* (Ithaca, N.Y.: Cornell University Press, 1947).

COLLINS, FREDERICK L.: *FBI in Peace and War* (New York: Putnam, 1943).

CORWIN, EDWARD S.: *Court over Constitution* (Princeton, N.J.: Princeton University Press, 1938).

CUMMINGS, HOMER, and CARL MCFARLAND: *Federal Justice* (New York: Macmillan, 1937).

CURTIS, CHARLES P.: *Lions under the Throne; A Study of the Supreme Court of the United States* (Boston: Houghton Mifflin, 1947).

CUSHMAN, ROBERT E. (ed.): "Ten Years of the Supreme Court: 1937–1947," *American Political Science Review*, vol. XLII (February, 1948), pp. 32–67.

DODGE, ARTHUR J.: *Origin and Development of the Office of Attorney-General*, House Doc. 510, 70th Cong., 2d Sess. (Washington: Government Printing Office, 1929).

EWING, CORTEZ: *The Judges of the Supreme Court, 1789–1937* (Minneapolis: University of Minnesota Press, 1938).

FIELD, OLIVER P.: *The Effect of an Unconstitutional Statute* (Minneapolis: University of Minnesota Press, 1935).

FLOHERTY, JOHN J.: *Inside the FBI* (Philadelphia: Lippincott, 1943).

FRANK, JEROME: *Courts on Trial* (Princeton, N.J.: Princeton University Press, 1949).

FRANKFURTER, FELIX, and JAMES LANDIS: *The Business of the Supreme Court* (New York: Macmillan, 1927).

GILBERT, WILFRED C.: *Provisions of Federal Law Held Unconstitutional by the Supreme Court of the United States* (Washington: Government Printing Office, 1936).

HAINES, CHARLES G.: *The American Doctrine of Judicial Supremacy* (Berkeley and Los Angeles: University of California Press, 2d ed., 1932).

——— *The Role of the Supreme Court in American Government and Politics, 1789–1835* (Berkeley and Los Angeles: University of California Press, 1944).

HARRIS, ROBERT J.: *The Judicial Power of the United States* (Baton Rouge, La.: Louisiana State University Press, 1940).

HUGHES, CHARLES E.: *The Supreme Court of the United States* (New York: Columbia University Press, 1928).

LANGELUTTIG, ALBERT G.: *The Department of Justice of the United States* (Baltimore: Johns Hopkins Press, 1927).

MILLSPAUGH, ARTHUR C.: *Crime Control by the National Government* (Washington: Brookings, 1937).

POUND, ROSCOE: *Organization of Courts* (Boston: Little, Brown, 1940).

PRICHETT, CHARLES HERMAN: *The Roosevelt Court: A Study in Judicial Politics and Values, 1937–1947* (New York: Macmillan, 1948).

SMITH, BRUCE: *Police Systems in the United States* (New York: Harper, 1940).

SUNDERLAND, EDSON R.: *Judicial Administration* (Chicago: Callaghan, 2d ed., 1948).

UMBREIT, KENNETH B.: *Our Eleven Chief Justices, A History of the Supreme Court in Terms of Their Personalities* (New York: Harper, 1938).

United States Bureau of Prisons: *Federal Offenders* (Leavenworth: Federal Prisons Industries, Inc., Press, published annually).

United States Department of Justice: *Annual Report* (Washington: Government Printing Office).

United States Director of the Administrative Office of the Courts: *Annual Report* (Washington: Government Printing Office).

United States Senate, Committee on the Judiciary: *Adverse Report on Reorganization of the Federal Judiciary*, Sen. Rep. 711, 75th Cong., 1st Sess. (Washington: Government Printing Office, 1937).

——— *Hearings on S. 1392, a Bill to Reorganize the Judicial Branch of the Government*, 75th Cong., 1st Sess. (Washington: Government Printing Office, 6 parts, 1937).

Warren, Charles: *The Supreme Court in United States History* (Boston: Little, 3 vols., 1922).

Wendell, Mitchell: *The Relations between Federal and State Courts* (New York: Columbia University Press, 1949).

Willoughby, William F.: *Principles of Judicial Administration* (Washington: Brookings, 1929).

TEXT-FILM

The following McGraw-Hill 35mm silent filmstrip is recommended for use with Chap. 16 of this text.

Federal Courts and Law Enforcements. The structure of federal judiciary system—its powers, duties, and relationship to other branches of government. Law enforcement agencies considered.

Chapter 17

FEDERAL POWERS— GENERAL ASPECTS, TAXATION, AND MONETARY

All legislative Powers herein granted shall be vested in a Congress of the United States. . . .

The Constitution, Article I, Section 1.

The Constitution grants powers to each of the three branches of government. Those given to the President and the courts have been discussed; there remain to be treated the great grants made to Congress.

While the President and courts have broad powers, Congress, the only branch chosen directly by the people, stands at the base of the pyramid. The President can initiate, suggest, and recommend; the courts can interpret narrowly or broadly; but both must look to Congress for enabling legislation and funds. Upon Congress rests the primary responsibility for establishing and controlling the entire government as well as for translating the popular will into law. The powers given to Congress are fundamental; they constitute the heart of the Federal government.

GENERAL ASPECTS

Nonlegislative Powers.—In addition to making laws, Congress performs several other important tasks. A distinction is made, therefore, between legislative powers upon which general laws are based, and nonlegislative powers from which Congress gets authority for its other functions. Nonlegislative powers may be classified as (1) constituent, (2) electoral, (3) executive, (4) directory and supervisory, (5) inquisitorial, and (6) judicial.

Constituent are those that relate to changing the Constitution, including authority to propose amendments either by the concurrence of two-thirds of both houses, or by calling a convention for the purpose when petitioned to do so by two-thirds of the states. Herein is also included authority to decide what method of ratification shall be followed by the states and whether a time limit shall accompany the amendment.

Electoral are those relating to the election of President and Vice-President. The electoral votes must be counted in the presence of both houses, and in the event of a tie or lack of a majority, election of the President devolves upon the House and that of the Vice-President upon the Senate. Moreover, Congress must provide for settling disputes if certain electoral votes are contested and also provide a method of choosing the President and

Vice-President upon the death or disqualification of both of these officers either before or after their inauguration.

Executive powers are those used when performing functions that are essentially executive in character. The appointment of officers is generally an executive prerogative; thus, when the House and Senate appoint their own officers and committees it may properly be said that they are exercising executive powers. The same is true when the Senate confirms presidential appointees and gives advice and consent to the ratification of treaties.

Closely related are powers which for convenience are called *directory* and *supervisory*. Although the President is usually thought to be the chief administrator, Congress exercises considerable control and supervision over the administrative branch. It is Congress that decides whether there is to be a department, commission, board, or other agency. After creating them, Congress may expand the agencies, consolidate them, or abolish them altogether. Congress defines their powers and duties, appropriates all funds without which they cannot operate, authorizes the employment of personnel, and subjects them to periodic investigation and review. Indeed, work of this kind absorbs far more of the energy and time of Congress than any other.

Direction and review go on constantly. They may result from complaints received by congressmen from constituents back home, from newspaper articles and editorials, from a congressman's own experience and thinking, or from mere rumor. Inquiry takes a variety of forms. Almost all agencies are required to make annual reports to Congress. Irregularities may be discovered and disclosed by the Bureau of the Budget or General Accounting Office. Congressmen often write to administrators for information and explanations or they may call upon them personally. Agencies may be excoriated in Congressional debate, or special investigations may be undertaken by congressional committees. Senatorial confirmation of an appointment or approval of a treaty may occasion widespread inquiry. Normally, the most thorough review occurs when representatives of the various agencies appear before committees to defend budgetary estimates for the following year.

Administrators often complain that they are unduly hampered and harassed by congressmen. Not infrequently an administrative agency charged with carrying out a controversial program is required to defend itself before a dozen or more different committees. Congressmen frequently speak and vote from personal prejudice and whimsy; laws may be drafted with so much rigid detail as to hamper effective administration; appropriations may be inadequate; or congressmen may insist that appointments be made from among persons whose names they suggest. There is substance to these criticisms. The reorganization of congressional procedure discussed in a previous chapter[1] would eliminate some of them, but in the end a government with powers separated can function properly only if there is considerable self-restraint on the part of each of the branches.

Inquisitorial is a term used to describe congressional authority to conduct investigations.[2] These may be conducted by the House and Senate as a body or, as is commonly the case, by standing or special committees. The Senate, because it is smaller in size and its members have longer terms, has conducted by far the largest number of investigations. The power to make investigations may be, and frequently is, delegated to permanent departments, commissions, and legislative courts, or to commissions composed of individuals who have no official connection with the government. Congress itself, or its instrumentalities, may issue subpoenas to summon witnesses and compel the production of books and papers. Warrants of arrest may also be issued. Failure to obey congressional writs and orders may be punished by Congress itself. Contemptuous conduct arises most frequently from refusal of witnesses to appear and give testimony before congressional committees. Instead of meting out punishment directly for conduct of this sort, Congress has made the offense a misdemeanor punishable by the courts in the usual manner.

Judicial powers are those that enable Congress to pass judgment upon certain parties. Each house of Congress is the sole judge of the qualifications of its own members and each house can expel its members provided two-thirds of them agree. Impeachment and contempt proceedings are also judicial in nature.[3]

Legislative Powers of Congress.—Legislative powers may be classified into six groups: (1) delegated, (2) implied, (3) inherent, (4) concurrent, (5) prohibited, and (6) reserved. Since these have been commented upon earlier[4] they will be dealt with briefly here.

Delegated powers are those specifically enumerated in the Constitution, most of them in Article I, Section 8. These have been given by the sovereign people to the central government at Washington. *Implied* powers are those that may reasonably be deduced from delegated powers, or, to use the language of the Constitution, those that are "necessary and proper" for carrying delegated powers into execution. The fact that the Federal government has implied powers does not mean that anything can be done that may seem necessary and proper. If that were true, the system would be unitary rather than federal. Rather, implications can be made only

[1] Chap. 13.

[2] For an excellent review of the subject of congressional investigation see M. Nelson McGeary, *The Development of Congressional Investigative Power* (New York: Columbia University Press, 1940).

[3] The impeachment process is fully explained on p. 278.

[4] Pp. 357–358.

from some specifically delegated power. In the field of international relations the Federal government has powers that are said to be *inherent, i.e.*, powers that arise from the fact that the United States is a sovereign state and because of that may do what other national states may do.

Reserved powers are those that have not been delegated to the Federal government. Some are retained by the states while certain ones that states have been prohibited from exercising have been reserved to the people. Powers that may be exercised by both the national and state governments are known as *concurrent*. The term also refers to powers, like bankruptcy, which may be exercised by the states until such time as Congress decides to assert its authority. Some powers, referred to as *prohibited*, are denied to both the Federal and state governments, others to the Federal only, while still others only to the states.

Some Powers Mandatory, Others Permissive.—Although Congress possesses broad powers, the Constitution, for the most part, leaves Congress free to use them at its discretion. Only a few are made mandatory: Congress is obliged to order a census every 10 years and reapportion seats in the House of Representatives after each census; Congress was required to create a Supreme Court and regulate its appellate jurisdiction; and Congress is expected to call a constitutional convention for the purpose of proposing amendments if petitioned to do so by two-thirds of the states. Interestingly enough, though these are mandatory, there is no way, either by appeal to the executive or the judiciary, by which Congress can legally be compelled to perform them. This was illustrated when after the 1920 census Congress failed for 10 years to provide a means of reapportioning membership in the House of Representatives and no effective method was available to force earlier action. Except for the powers mentioned, all others are permissive and may or may not be used as seems desirable.

No Emergency Powers.—It cannot be emphasized too often that in dealing with domestic affairs the Federal government has only such powers as are granted to it by the Constitution. In periods of stress it has been claimed, sometimes by Congress but oftener by the President, that the national government is endowed with powers that are neither delegated nor implied but that arise from the fact that the government speaks for a sovereign nation. This is true only in the field of international relations. In the Legal Tender Cases,[1] the Supreme Court came near saying that inherent powers existed for dealing with internal domestic affairs but failed to do so and has since generally repudiated the idea. Later, during the First World War, Congress passed the Adamson Act temporarily limiting hours and wages in order to avert a threatened strike on the part of railroad labor. A majority of the Supreme Court upheld the legislation as a reasonable exercise of the power to regulate interstate

[1] 12 Wallace 457 (1871).

commerce, taking cognizance of the threatened emergency in doing so.[1] About the same time, the Supreme Court upheld emergency rent legislation enacted under the police power in the District of Columbia and the state of New York.[2]

Recalling these precedents, President Roosevelt and Congress enacted sweeping legislation following 1933, arguing as partial justification for their constitutionality that emergency conditions demanded the steps taken. The Supreme Court acknowledged that extraordinary conditions might afford a reason for an extraordinary use of existing powers but insisted that critical circumstances could not enlarge the scope of constitutional authority. "Emergency does not create power. Emergency does not increase granted power or diminish the restrictions imposed upon power granted or reserved," said the court in 1934.[3] A year later a unanimous court voided the NIRA, saying, among other things, "extraordinary conditions do not create or enlarge constitutional powers."[4] Thus, in emergencies Congress must rely upon some delegated power. If none can be found, the Constitution requires that the matter be left to the states or that an amendment be sought.

No "Police Power" in Congress.—Unitary governments ordinarily have authority to take whatever steps are necessary to protect and preserve the health, safety, morals, and convenience of the people. This is commonly referred to as the "police power." In the United States this power is one reserved to the states; it is not possessed by the national government, except within the District of Columbia and other territories. State and local governments undertake to regulate physicians and contagious diseases, to dispose of garbage and sewage, to provide hospitals and schools, to ensure pure food and water supply, and to do a host of other things simply because the welfare of the population demands them. The Federal government, however, may do such things only to the extent that they are reasonably required to regulate interstate and foreign commerce properly, conduct a postal system, raise and support an army and navy, or exercise some other power delegated by the Constitution.

Denied Power to Do Something Specifically Forbidden.—As noted above, the Constitution mentions certain things that Congress is forbidden to do. The delegated powers may not, therefore, be exercised in such a manner as to do things expressly forbidden. Congress may not, for example, tax exports, pass ex post facto laws, grant titles of nobility, nor impair the liberties guaranteed by the Bill of Rights.

[1] Wilson *v.* New, 243 U.S. 332 (1917).

[2] Block *v* Hirsh, 256 U.S. 135 (1921); Marcus Brown *v.* Feldman, 256 U.S. 170 (1921); Levy Leasing Co. *v.* Siegel, 258 U.S. 242 (1922).

[3] Home Building and Loan Association *v.* Blaisdell, 290 U.S. 398 (1934).

[4] Schechter *v.* United States, 295 U.S. 495 (1935). See also p. 382.

Powers to Be Clearly Granted.—As noted above, Congress has implied power, but it is frequently difficult to decide what is and what is not a "necessary and proper" use of a delegated power. Although permitting a liberal construction of the phrase, the courts insist that there must be some clear and direct relationship between a delegated power and the object sought by its exercise. The power to coin money and regulate its value justifies the creation of national banks; the power to coin money justifies the printing of paper notes; the power to regulate interstate commerce justifies the fixing of passenger and freight rates for interstate carriers, and also the regulation of intrastate commerce that directly affects interstate commerce; the power to tax to promote the general welfare justifies the establishment of land-grant colleges, a retirement system for aged employees, and the subsidization of farmers. In these instances the courts have found a clear and direct relationship between some delegated power and the object or purpose of the enactments. But when Congress required railroads to establish a retirement system for superannuated employees, the court construed the act to be "an attempt for social ends" which had nothing to do with interstate commerce.[1] A revised measure based upon the taxing and spending powers was passed later and has been generally thought to be constitutional. Likewise, in the NIRA decision, the Supreme Court considered the burden upon interstate commerce caused by depressed local businesses so indirect as to be beyond the scope of the commerce power.[2]

Powers Not to Be Delegated to the Executive.—One of the fundamental principles of the Constitution is that the legislative, executive, and judicial branches are separate and independent of each other.[3] Many laws are passed embodying general principles and authorizing administrative officers to fill in details, but too much cannot be left to the administrators. Congress must clearly declare its will and establish primary standards. If this is not done but left to the executive, the courts will hold that Congress has illegally delegated powers granted solely to itself. The first case in which it was held that legislative powers had been delegated arose from a section of the NIRA.[4] In that case the Supreme Court ruled that in authorizing the President to make regulations governing interstate shipments of "hot oil"[5] too much discretion had been allowed. Later, major portions of the NIRA were declared unconstitutional chiefly because Congress had allowed too much discretion to the President and code authorities.

[1] Railroad Retirement Board *v.* Alton R. Co., 295 U.S. 330 (1935).

[2] Schechter *v.* United States, 295 U.S. 495 (1935).

[3] Above, p. 61.

[4] Panama Refining Company *v.* Ryan, 293 U.S. 388 (1935).

[5] That is, oil produced in excess of quotas established by state law.

Powers Not to Be Delegated by Congress to the States.—Likewise, powers granted to Congress cannot be delegated to the states. This means that Congress cannot authorize states to regulate interstate commerce, coin money, declare war, or exercise any other power conferred exclusively upon it by the Constitution. When in 1918 Congress passed legislation providing that longshoremen injured during the course of employment were entitled to the rights and remedies of the state wherein the injury occurred, the Supreme Court held that Congress had transferred its authority to the states.[1] Thereupon, Congress reenacted the measure providing a uniform system of federally administered insurance for maritime workers injured on board vessels.[2] Sometimes there is overlapping between state and federal jurisdiction, in which case a state might proceed to perform an act pursuant to a reserved power which Congress is also competent to do by a delegated power. This often happens. When it does, and the matter does not require uniform treatment throughout the country, the state law is allowed to stand until Congress acts, after which the state law must yield.[3]

Powers Not to Be Delegated by Congress to the People.—Many states have provisions that permit the use of the initiative and referendum. The initiative is a device whereby a law may be proposed by a petition circulated and signed by a predetermined number of qualified voters. The referendum permits laws to become effective upon the favorable vote of a certain number of voters. There is no provision in the Federal Constitution for the use of these devices. All federal laws must originate in and be approved by Congress,[4] otherwise there would be an illegal delegation of powers.

Congress Denied the Right to Usurp Powers Reserved to the States.—Just as the states may not invade the domain of Congress, so may Congress not usurp powers reserved to the states. Finding the demarcation line is extremely difficult, with the result that political and judicial opinion shifts from time to time. Thus, prior to 1937 the Supreme Court was inclined to halt federal power in favor of state. While this temper lasted, federal laws were declared unconstitutional which taxed the salaries of state judges and state instrumentalities, regulated the employment of children, induced farmers to contract to curtail production, regulated manufacturing, mining, and local businesses, and permitted local governments to reorganize their indebtedness under federal laws. More recently, however, most of these decisions have been reversed. Even so, it is clear that there are still areas where the Federal government may

[1] Knickerbocker Ice Co. *v.* Stewart, 253 U.S. 149 (1920).

[2] See p. 773.

[3] For a fuller discussion see p. 392.

[4] They can be suggested, of course, by the President or anyone else. See also p. 270.

not trespass. It is certain, for example, that state powers would be usurped if Congress were to regulate commerce that is very local and isolated, or to tax with intent to burden or destroy state and local governments and their activities.

Congress Required to Respect Spheres of Other Branches.—Just as all legislative powers belong to Congress, the executive power is given solely to the President and the judicial power entirely to the courts. Congress is precluded, therefore, from usurping executive and judicial powers. A few instances have arisen from which illustrations may be drawn. In 1876 Congress provided that postmasters could be removed by the President only with the concurrence of the Senate. President Wilson resisted the statute, contending that the power of removal belonged to the executive. The Supreme Court agreed with the President, saying that the statute was an unwarranted infringement of the executive power.[1] Likewise with the courts. An example occurred when in 1792 Congress directed federal circuit judges to investigate claims and report their findings to the War Department for final action. The courts objected and in Hayburn's Case[2] ruled that the legislature had imposed a nonjudicial duty upon them inasmuch as executive officials were permitted to review and possibly modify or reverse decisions made by the judges.

TAXATION AND FISCAL POWERS

The Tax Clause.—The most serious weakness of the Articles of Confederation was that Congress could assess the states but lacked authority to lay and collect taxes directly from the people. In view of this, it is not surprising that authority to tax stands first on the list of powers delegated to Congress. The first paragraph of Article I, Section 8, provides:

> The Congress shall have Power to Lay and collect Taxes, Duties, Imposts and Excises, to pay the Debts and provide for the common Defence and general Welfare of the United States; but all Duties, Imposts and Excises shall be uniform throughout the United States.

This brief clause, pregnant with meaning itself, but more so when read with the knowledge that Congress has power to do whatever is necessary and proper to carry it into effect, is authority for nearly all federal taxation.

Four Types of Levies.—Note that Congress may lay and collect levies of four types: (1) taxes, (2) duties, (3) imposts, and (4) excises. A tax is an exaction for the support of government. The word "taxes," as used in the tax clause, refers to direct taxes and was probably intended to include only property and capitation (poll) taxes, although in 1895 the Supreme Court ruled that a tax on income from property was also a direct

[1] Myers *v.* United States, 272 U.S. 52 (1926). See also p. 318.
[2] 2 Dallas 409 (1792).

tax.[1] Direct taxes (other than income) have been levied only five times since 1789, the last to help finance the Civil War. If income taxes are excluded, no federal revenues are today collected from direct taxes. "Duties," "imposts," and "excises," include all indirect taxes. "Duties" and "imposts" are nearly synonymous terms referring to tariffs. An "excise" is an internal tax generally imposed upon manufactures but sometimes upon consumption and retail sales. In 1949, income taxes accounted for the largest amount of federal revenue, then followed excises, taxes, and tariffs (duties and imposts), in the order mentioned.[2]

Controversy over Income Taxes.—As noted elsewhere,[3] the Constitution requires that all direct taxes be apportioned among the states on the basis of population. Toward the end of the last century the question arose as to whether a tax upon incomes was a direct or indirect tax. If direct, then income taxes must be apportioned among the states on the basis of population; if indirect, the Constitution would be satisfied if taxes were graduated but uniform within all classifications throughout the country. The controversy arose from a graduated federal income-tax law enacted in 1894 that did not provide for apportionment among the states. One Pollock, a stockholder in the Farmers Loan and Trust Company of New York, brought suit to enjoin his company from paying the tax upon its income derived from real-estate, state, and local government bonds. The Supreme Court had considerable difficulty in reaching a decision. A similar law, enacted in 1861 but which had expired in 1872, had been upheld by a unanimous court,[4] but in the cases at hand[5] the Supreme Court ruled that taxes upon incomes were direct, hence unconstitutional, because they were not apportioned among the states.

These decisions precluded the enactment of future income-tax legislation inasmuch as administration would be difficult if apportionment were undertaken and, what was worse, it would be impossible to devise a tax schedule that would fall upon people in proportion to their ability to pay. Though from an economic point of view the Court was undoubtedly correct in saying that a tax on income was a direct tax,[6] there could be no

[1] See also p. 44.

[2] For the amounts, see p. 506.

[3] P. 44.

[4] Springer *v.* United States, 102 U.S. 586 (1881).

[5] Pollock *v.* Farmers' Loan and Trust Co., 157 U.S. 429 (1895), 158 U.S. 601 (1895).

[6] Economists generally agree that a tax upon incomes is a direct tax in the sense that it cannot readily be passed on to someone other than the person from whom collection is made. But the courts had previously held that not only income taxes but certain others which economists agree are direct were indirect within the meaning of the Constitution. For example, the Supreme Court had held federal taxes on carriages, on corporations' earnings, and inheritances to be indirect, although most economists would classify them as direct. Edwin R. A. Seligman, *The Income Tax* (New York: Macmillan, 1911), pp. 533–534.

doubt that their decision was a clear reversal of previous precedents. The Court's decisions were the subject of much controversy and have been roundly condemned by many.[1] The decisions stood, nevertheless, although rendered insignificant by adoption of the Sixteenth Amendment.

The Income-tax Amendment.—Years of agitation, particularly in the West and South, led to the adoption of the Sixteenth Amendment in 1913. It reads:

> The Congress shall have power to lay and collect taxes on incomes, from whatever source derived, without apportionment among the several States, and without regard to any census or enumeration.

Note that the amendment does not settle the argument of whether a tax upon incomes is direct or indirect. It merely obviates the necessity of apportionment.

Shortly after the adoption of the income-tax amendment a dispute arose over what the words "from whatever source derived" were intended to mean. Some argued that the phrase was not intended to enlarge the list of what might be taxed but merely to reverse the Pollock decisions rendering it unnecessary to apportion income taxes. Others interpreted the phrase literally saying "from whatever source derived" meant just that. If this opinion prevailed, there would be no doubt but that Congress could tax incomes of state employees, or income derived from federal, state, and local bonds. The argument was temporarily settled in 1916 when the Supreme Court restricted the amendment to its narrowest construction.[2] The decision was reaffirmed in 1928 when the Court held that Congress was forbidden to tax interest on state and local government bonds even in an indirect way.[3] However, in 1938, the Supreme Court endorsed federal taxation of income paid employees by state governments[4] and by doing so created the distinct impression of favoring the broader, more literal interpretation of the Sixteenth Amendment. If this impression is correct, legal obstacles to federal taxation of income from state and local government securities have probably been removed.

Purposes for Which Congress May Tax.—The primary purpose for which taxes should be levied is to obtain revenue, but Congress often has other purposes in mind. Tariff laws have always sought to protect American industry as well as to raise revenue, and their constitutionality has never

[1] See especially, Edward S. Corwin, *Court over Constitution* (Princeton, N.J.: Princeton University Press, 1938), pp. 194–201; Charles E. Hughes, *The Supreme Court of the United States* (New York: Columbia University Press, 1928), p. 54; Charles Warren, *The Supreme Court in United States History* (Boston: Little, 3 vols., 1923), vol. III, pp. 421–422; and Seligman, *op. cit.*

[2] Brushaber *v.* Union P. R. Co., 240 U.S. 1 (1916).

[3] National Life Insurance Co. *v.* United States, 277 U.S. 508 (1928).

[4] See p. 371.

seriously been contested. In 1866 Congress levied a tax of 10 per cent on notes issued by state banks for the purpose of driving them out of existence, and the measure was upheld.[1] In 1882 Congress imposed a head tax upon immigrants, the proceeds being earmarked for temporary care of the immigrants and not for the general support of government, and the Supreme Court sustained the legislation.[2] In 1902 Congress imposed a tax of 10 cents a pound on colored oleomargarine in order to discourage its consumption in favor of butter, and the law was upheld.[3] In 1912 a tax of 2 cents a hundred was laid upon matches made with poisonous phosphorus for the purpose of protecting workmen from the horrid occupational disease known as "phossie jaw." Although the law completely destroyed the white phosphorus industry, it was never challenged. Again, in 1914 and 1919 Congress required dealers in narcotics to pay a tax and submit to regulation, and the legislation was upheld.[4]

In all the above cases which reached the Supreme Court, the court refused to look behind the face of tax legislation into the motives that prompted its enactment. A halt was called, however, in 1922. In two cases coming before it in that year, the Court distinguished between a "true" tax intended to raise revenue and tax measures intended to penalize or regulate matters reserved for state control. In the first case, the Supreme Court had before it the child labor law of 1919.[5] That measure levied a tax of 10 per cent upon the net profits of all establishments employing children in violation of standards set up in the act. The Drexel Furniture Company, doing business in North Carolina, permitted a boy under the age of fourteen years to work in its factory during the taxable year 1919. Whereupon Bailey, the United States collector of internal revenue, notified the company that it was obliged to pay 10 per cent of its net profits for the year, or $6,312.79. Upon appeal to the Supreme Court, the law was declared unconstitutional. The tax, the Court said, was not a true one but a penalty intended to regulate business, a matter reserved to the states. The second case[6] involved a federal law enacted in 1921 intended to abolish dealings in futures upon the grain markets by imposing a tax of 20 cents a bushel upon all contracts for future delivery and subjecting boards of trade to detailed regulations. Hill, representing the Board of Trade of the City of Chicago, brought suit against Wallace, the Secretary of Agriculture, seeking to enjoin collection of the tax and enforcement of the law. The Court declared the law unconstitutional,

[1] Veazie Bank *v.* Fenno, 8 Wallace 533 (1869).
[2] Head Money Cases, 112 U.S. 580 (1884).
[3] McCray *v.* United States, 195 U.S. 27 (1904).
[4] United States *v.* Doremus, 249 U.S. 86 (1919).
[5] Bailey *v.* Drexel Furniture Company, 259 U.S. 20 (1922). See also p. 738.
[6] Hill *v.* Wallace, 259 U.S. 44 (1922).

saying the tax was a penalty enacted to regulate a subject reserved to the states.

The same reasoning has been followed since (at least until 1937), and may be illustrated by several decisions. The Revenue Act of 1926 imposed a special excise tax of $1,000 upon retail liquor dealers who carried on business within a state contrary to state and local laws. Tested in 1935, the Supreme Court held the exaction to be not a tax but a penalty for the violation of state laws, the effect of which was to usurp the police powers of the states.[1] A case arose in the following year from the first Guffey Coal Act wherein the bituminous coal industry was brought under federal control. The act levied a tax of 15 per cent upon all bituminous coal producers, 90 per cent of which was rebated to those who agreed to comply with a code established for the industry. This tax, the Court ruled, was not a true tax but a penalty designed to accomplish results beyond the reach of federal powers.[2]

A case decided in 1937[3] has raised some doubt about what the attitude of the Court may be in the future. The Court had before it the National Firearms Act of 1934, which in addition to requiring dealers in firearms to obtain an annual license of $200, required the payment of a tax of $200 on each transfer of sawed-off shotguns, other firearms capable of being concealed (except revolvers and pistols), machine guns, and mufflers or silencers for any firearms. Although expected to produce some revenue, the principal purpose of the legislation was probably the suppression of traffic in such weapons. Mr. Justice Stone stated:

> Every tax is in some measure regulatory. To some extent it interposes an economic impediment to the activity taxed as compared with others not taxed. But a tax is not any the less a tax because it has a regulatory effect . . . and it has long been established that an Act of Congress which on its face purports to be an exercise of the taxing power is not any the less so because the tax is burdensome or tends to restrict or suppress the thing taxed.

Moreover, continued the learned justice:

> Inquiry into the hidden motives which may move Congress to exercise a power constitutionally conferred upon it is beyond the competency of the courts. . . .
>
> Here the annual tax of $200 is productive of some revenue. We are not free to speculate as to the motives which led Congress to impose it, or as to the extent to which it may operate to restrict the activities taxed. As it is not attended by an offensive regulation, and since it operates as a tax, it is within the national taxing power.

[1] United States *v.* Constantine, 296 U.S. 287 (1935).
[2] Carter *v.* Carter Coal Co., 298 U.S. 238 (1936).
[3] Sonzinsky *v.* United States, 300 U.S. 506.

In other words, a tax may be a penalty and the courts are incompetent to inquire into the motives that led to its enactment. This comes close to returning to the position adhered to prior to 1922. What regulation the Court might consider "offensive" and what levy might not operate as a tax must await future decisions.

Expressed Limitations upon the Tax Power.—The Constitution now specifically imposes one absolute prohibition upon the power to tax and three restrictions upon the manner in which taxes are to be levied.

No Taxes upon Exports.—The single prohibition is that Congress may not place any tax or duty on articles "exported from any state." This provision was added upon the insistence of Southern states who feared that their exports, particularly of cotton, might be discriminated against. "Exports" refers to goods shipped from any state to a foreign country and not to articles shipped from one state to another. A tax upon the production of articles even though applied to that portion which is intended for export is not considered an export tax. The provision would be violated, however, if a tax were laid on articles in the process of exportation, or if bills of lading and insurance policies for articles being exported were taxed.

Direct Taxes to Be Apportioned.—The first restriction is that direct taxes (other than income) must be laid in proportion to the population of each state. In levying direct taxes, Congress must first decide exactly how much money it wishes to raise and then allot to each state that proportion of this sum which the population of the state bears to the total population of the country. This provision makes administration clumsy and results in taxation that bears no relation to peoples' ability to pay. Hence, the infrequent resort to direct taxes throughout our history.[1]

Indirect Taxes to Be Uniform.—A second restriction is that indirect taxes must be "uniform throughout the United States." This does not mean that they must be the same for everything and everybody; it is geographic uniformity that is required. Congress is free to make classifications for the purpose of taxation, but once having done so, the tax cannot be more nor less for objects within the same class at any point within the United States. The tariff on men's shoes, for example, may be higher than the tariff on women's, but the rate on men's cannot be less at the port of New Orleans than at New York. Employers of fewer than eight persons are exempt from paying a pay-roll tax to the Federal government from which to pay unemployed workmen, but all employers of eight or more must be taxed at the same rate whether they live in Maine or California. Large corporations may be required to pay at higher rates than smaller ones, but all of the same class and size must pay at the same rate whether they operate in Kansas or Ohio. Since only incorporated

[1] Above, p. 44.

territories—Hawaii and Alaska—are integral parts of the "United States" the uniformity clause also applies to them.[1] It does not apply, however, to unincorporated territories. This means that people or objects in such territories as Puerto Rico and Samoa might be taxed at rates either higher or lower than those charged within the forty-eight states, Hawaii, and Alaska.

Taxes Not to Discriminate between Ports.—The third restriction is that Congress may not levy any tax that gives preference "to the ports of one state over those of another." While federal levies must be uniform at all ports, Congress is not required to treat all ports alike in *every* respect. Congress has, for example, established ports of entry, erected lighthouses, improved rivers and harbors at some ports without doing the same for all.

Implied Restrictions upon the Taxing Power.—In addition to the general limitations, expressed and implied, mentioned above, several others pertaining particularly to the use of the taxing power should be noticed.

State and Federal Governments Not to Burden One Another.—In a federal system, especially where the power to tax is shared concurrently by the national government and states, one government is likely to tax the other either deliberately or otherwise. This happened early in our history when Maryland and several other states imposed taxes upon bank paper issued by the National Bank for the purpose of impeding the operations of the bank. This action led to the famous case of McCulloch *v.* Maryland[2] wherein the Supreme Court held that the Federal government, its agents and instrumentalities could not be taxed by the states saying that "the power to tax involves the power to destroy." While observing that a federal tax upon the states would be more justifiable than a state tax upon the Federal government, the Court nevertheless pointed out that federal taxes that burdened the states would not be permitted.

Following this doctrine of intergovernmental immunity, the Supreme Court held federal salaries immune from state taxation[3] and state salaries free from federal taxation.[4] Likewise, federal securities were declared free from state taxation,[5] and the securities of state and local governments, and the interest on them, immune from federal taxation.[6] Later the immunity was extended to cover sales of goods to the government. Thus, a state tax on the sale of gasoline to the Federal government was held

[1] See p. 574.

[2] 4 Wheaton 316 (1819).

[3] Dobbins *v.* Commissioners of Erie County, 16 Peters 345 (1842).

[4] Collector *v.* Day, 11 Wallace 113 (1871).

[5] Weston *v.* Charleston, 2 Peters 449 (1829).

[6] Mercantile Bank *v.* New York, 121 U.S. 138 (1887); Pollock *v.* Farmers' Loan and Trust Company, 158 U.S. 601 (1895).

invalid,[1] while a federal tax on the sale of motorcycles to a municipal police department was held void.[2]

The doctrine of intergovernmental immunity has always had its critics, but not until 1902 were any modifications made. In that year the Court distinguished between functions that were strictly governmental and others that were commercial or proprietary in nature. The former were still immune from taxation but the latter were not. This meant that the national government might tax liquor monopolies,[3] the salaries of persons employed in the management of municipally owned railways and other utilities,[4] or the proceeds from the sale of athletic tickets by state universities.[5] Whether the reverse would be true, *i.e.*, that states might tax federal instrumentalities engaged in proprietary operations, has never been judicially determined. In the case of the TVA the states have not attempted to tax its operations, but the Federal government has expressly authorized the Authority to pay the states in which its projects are located an amount equivalent to the taxes that would be collected from a similar private enterprise.[6]

Within recent years the courts have gone even further in breaking down the doctrine of intergovernmental immunities. The first significant break with the past occurred in 1938 when it was held that the salaries of officers of the Port of New York Authority were subject to federal taxation.[7] The Supreme Court went still further a year later, holding that the states might tax the salaries of federal employees and the Federal government might tax the incomes of employees of state and local governments.[8] A tax on income, said the Court, is neither economically nor legally a tax upon the source. Hence, there is no basis for the assumption that a tax upon the salary of employees by one government is tantamount to an interference by one government with the other in the performance of its functions.

As far as the Federal government is concerned, the test in the future is to be, apparently, whether its taxation imposes a burden so direct as to impede the operations of a state or local agency engaged in a strictly governmental function. The same is probably true for the states, although the Court made it clear that the states would not be permitted to tax federal employees or instrumentalities if Congress declares its intention

[1] Panhandle Oil Co. *v.* Mississippi, 277 U.S. 218 (1928).

[2] Indian Motocycle Co. *v.* United States, 283 U.S. 570 (1931).

[3] South Carolina *v.* United States, 199 U.S. 437 (1905).

[4] Metcalf and Eddy *v.* Mitchell 269, U.S. 514 (1926); Helvering *v.* Power, 239 U.S. 214 (1934).

[5] Allen *v.* Regents of University of Georgia, 304 U.S. 439 (1938).

[6] See p. 719.

[7] Helvering *v.* Gearhardt, 304 U.S. 405 (1938).

[8] Graves *v.* *ex rel.* O'Keefe, 306 U.S. 466 (1939).

that they should be immune. Since these recent decisions, all state and local government employees have become subject to federal taxation while at least forty states have imposed taxes upon the incomes of federal employees living within their jurisdiction.

Taxation of Judges' Salaries.—To ensure judicial independence, the Constitution provides that federal judges[1] shall be paid compensation which "shall not be diminished during their continuance in office." From this provision controversy has arisen over whether judges might be required to pay taxes upon that portion of their income received from salaries. The issue of immunity from taxation first arose when Congress abolished fees charged by justices of peace in the District of Columbia. This was declared unconstitutional insofar as it applied to incumbent justices.[2] Later, during the Civil War, Congress taxed salaries of federal judges and, although never judicially tested, the legislation was generally thought to be unconstitutional and the money was later refunded. In 1919 Congress enacted a revenue law which did not exempt judges' salaries but when tested it was declared unconstitutional.[3] A later law imposed a tax upon the salaries of only those judges appointed subsequent to enactment of the legislation, but this, too, proved unacceptable.[4] In this instance the Supreme Court said that the Constitution imposed upon Congress the duty "definitely to declare what sum shall be received by each judge out of the public funds." Less than this amounted to an unconstitutional threat to judicial independence.

This doctrine prevailed until 1938 when it was overruled.[5] This case grew out of the revenue acts of 1932 and 1936, which taxed the salaries of judges appointed subsequently. A circuit judge named Woodrough, appointed in 1933, paid under protest a tax of more than $600 and then brought suit to recover the amount and prevent future collections. The district court, following precedents mentioned above, held the acts of Congress violative of the Constitution; but the Supreme Court by vote of seven to one[6] upheld the tax measures. The majority concluded that judicial independence was not threatened by subjecting judicial salaries to a general, nondiscriminatory tax. Rather, said the Court, "To subject them [judges] to a general tax is merely to recognize that judges are also citizens, and that their particular function in government does not generate an immunity from sharing with their fellow citizens the material burden

[1] And, incidentally, the President. What is said here about federal judges would probably apply to the President as well.

[2] United States *v.* More, 3 Cranch 159 (1805).

[3] Evans *v.* Gore, 253 U.S. 245 (1920).

[4] Miles *v.* Graham, 268 U.S. 501 (1925).

[5] O'Malley *v.* Woodrough, 307 U.S. 277 (1938).

[6] One justice, McReynolds, did not participate. Justice Butler registered the sole dissent.

of the government whose Constitution and laws they are charged with administering." Although the measures here in question applied only to judges appointed after passage of the tax laws, Congress later (in 1939) extended the law to those appointed prior to 1932.

The Spending Power.—According to the tax clause quoted above, after revenue is raised it may be spent for three purposes: (1) to pay the debts, (2) to provide for the common defense, and (3) to provide for the general welfare. Since little controversy has arisen over expenditures for the first two, attention will be given to the third only.

Money may be spent to provide for the "general welfare." The word "general" refers to that which is designed to benefit a considerable number of people as contrasted with something which is local or private. But may Congress spend money for any and all "public" purposes? One school, led by James Madison, which interprets the Constitution narrowly, insists that Congress can spend money only to carry out the delegated powers mentioned in the Constitution. Others, led by Alexander Hamilton and Joseph Story, insist that the taxing-and-spending clause is complete in itself and not limited to the fulfillment of other enumerated powers. The latter interpretation would authorize Congress to tax and spend for *any* purpose as long as it provides for the *general* welfare.

The Supreme Court had never met the issue squarely until 1935, when it affirmed the broader view.[1] Accordingly, the spending power is one of the most important and most frequently used by Congress. It is authority for expenditures for relief, public works, old-age insurance, unemployment compensation, soil conservation, most federal educational programs, and many other activities. In carrying out such measures as these the theory is that Congress has taxed to raise money to be spent to provide for the general welfare.

Spending Clause Not a Grant of Plenary Power to Provide for the General Welfare.—Although the courts have interpreted the spending power broadly, they have not said that Congress possesses a broad, plenary authority to do whatever is necessary to provide for the general welfare. Recall the tax clause which says that "Congress shall have power to lay and collect taxes, duties, imposts and excises, to pay the debts, provide for the common defense and the general welfare of the United States." Some historians[2] contend that a semicolon, rather than a comma, should appear between the word "excises," and the phrase "to pay the debts." With a

[1] United States *v.* Butler, 297 U.S. 1 (1936). Although affirming the broader view, this decision nevertheless found the Agricultural Adjustment Act unconstitutional. See p. 787.

[2] See especially, Charles A. Beard, *Public Policy and the General Welfare* (New York: Farrar, 1941), Chaps. 6 and 7; and Edward S. Corwin, *The Twilight of the Supreme Court* (New Haven: Yale University Press, 1934), pp. 152–154. See also Charles Warren, *The Making of the Constitution* (Boston: Little, 1937), pp. 464–479.

semicolon, the sentence would be divided into two parallel parts giving Congress not only the power to lay and collect taxes, but also the power to proceed to do whatever it deemed necessary to pay the debts, provide for the common defense and the general welfare. Thus, Congress would possess a general police power. With a comma, the sentence means that taxes may be laid *in order to* pay the debts, provide for the common defense and the general welfare. So far as the history of the clause is concerned, the draft of the Constitution reported by the Committee on Style did contain a semicolon, but the semicolon was displaced by a comma in the final draft. Some contend that the copyist took unwarranted liberty with the document. Be that as it may, the courts have always held that Congress does not have a general-welfare power. As matters stand, Congress has no separate power to provide for the general welfare but may spend money to obtain such ends. This accounts for the resort to taxation, subsidies to the state and local governments, and federal spending rather than to more direct methods of providing for the public welfare.

Restrictions on the Spending Power.—The spending power is subject to two specific restrictions in addition to the general limitations discussed earlier in this chapter. An appropriation may not be made for "armies" for a period of longer than 2 years;[1] and no money may be spent unless appropriated by Congress.

MONETARY POWERS

The Borrowing Power.—If tax revenues are insufficient to meet current expenditures, governments, like individuals, may borrow to meet their obligations. Article I, Section 8, Clause 2, gives Congress authority "To borrow Money on the credit of the United States." Congress may authorize the borrowing of money from any source, foreign or domestic, and up to any amount. The only collateral required, at least so far as the Constitution is concerned, is "the credit of the United States." The power to borrow, together with the power to coin and regulate the value of money, implies authority to issue paper money and compel its acceptance as legal tender.[2] The power also justifies the creation of national banks to buy and sell government bonds.[3] The Federal government may exempt its securities and the income derived from them from future federal taxes, although since 1939 it has not done so. States and local governments, as noted above, may not tax federal securities nor the income derived from them unless Congress gives its consent at the time securities are issued. When Congress borrows money, it pledges repay-

[1] Article I, Section 8, Clause 12. Appropriations may, however, be made for the Navy and other branches of the government for longer than 2 years.

[2] See p. 376.

[3] See p. 517.

ment in currency the value of which Congress itself has power to determine. In this lies the danger that future circumstances might lead to debt repudiation through the expedient of changing the value of the dollar, in which case it would be difficult to find any legal remedy except for injured parties to plead that property had been taken without due process of law.

The Power to Coin Money.—In order to provide money with a fixed and uniform standard of value throughout the country, Congress was authorized "To Coin money, regulate the Value thereof, and of foreign coin. . . ."[1] Congress authorized the first mint and laid the foundation of our monetary system in 1792.

The words of the Constitution authorize Congress to "coin money" and during our early history this was thought to include authority to make either metallic coins or print paper notes. Proceeding upon this assumption, Congress authorized the First and Second National Banks (created in 1791 and 1816, respectively) to issue paper notes and their constitutionality was never questioned. During the Civil War, however, when Congress issued 450 million dollars' worth of treasury notes ("greenbacks") and made them legal tender, the courts were called to pass upon their constitutionality. The decision was awaited with considerable anxiety inasmuch as it was bound to have a tremendous effect not only upon the credit of the national government but upon the banking and credit system of the country as well. The Court announced its decision in the famous case of Hepburn *v.* Griswold.[2] "Money" was defined to mean gold, copper, and silver coins; while coinage was defined as "the conversion of metal into money by governmental direction and authority . . . to mold into form a metallic substance of intrinsic value and stamp on it its legal value." Accordingly, said the Court, only metallic coins could be manufactured by the Federal government and made legal tender in payment of debts between private parties created before enactment of the law. The law was, therefore, unconstitutional; it exceeded the powers delegated to Congress, violated the spirit of the Constitution, and deprived creditors of property without due process of law.

The decision in Hepburn *v.* Griswold was reached by a four-to-three vote, there being two vacancies. On the day the decision was announced, President Grant sent to the Senate the names of two men to fill the vacancies existing on the Court. Four days later, by a five-to-four vote, with the two new justices joining the three who had dissented in the previous case to make the majority, the Court voted to reconsider the issues involved.[3] Less than 15 months after the first decision, the Court reversed

[1] Article I, Section 8.

[2] 8 Wallace 603 (1870).

[3] President Grant was accused of "packing" the Court, but the evidence seems to suggest that no understanding was reached between the President and the two new

itself,[1] this time saying that the power to issue paper notes in wartime and make it legal tender was implied from the power to coin money and fight a war. Authority to make paper money legal tender in time of peace was upheld 13 years later.[2]

The Power to Regulate the Value of Money.—Closely related to the coinage power is the authorization to regulate the value of domestic and foreign money in the United States. This enables Congress to establish and maintain a uniform monetary standard throughout the country and to raise or lower the value of money whenever it sees fit. Since money is the lifeblood of the economic system of the nation, the use of this power is certain to have a tremendous effect, for good or for ill, not only upon domestic affairs but international as well. The authorization enables Congress to determine whether the monetary system shall be based on a standard of gold, silver, or something else. It enables Congress to prescribe the relationship that shall exist between precious metals, as, for example, 15 grains of gold to 1 of silver, or as William J. Bryan advocated, 16 to 1. The authorization also permits Congress to compel the surrender of money of a particular type, as it did gold and gold certificates in 1933. Moreover, Congress may abrogate gold clauses in private contracts[3] although it may not abrogate promises to pay in gold or its equivalent contained in contracts between the national government and other parties.[4] Finally, this power, along with the borrowing, taxing, and spending powers, is authority for the establishment and regulation of the banking and credit system of the nation.

The Power to Punish Counterfeiting.—Article I, Section 8, also empowers Congress "To provide for the Punishment of counterfeiting the Securities and current Coin of the United States." The inclusion of this clause was probably unnecessary, since had it not been expressly granted it would have been implied from the power to coin money. The power is a concurrent one—the states as well as the national government may punish for counterfeiting, although most states leave detection and punishment to the Federal government.

---

jurists to the effect that they would act as they subsequently did. The incident was unfortunate, nevertheless, and greatly diminished the prestige of the court. See Robert E. Cushman, *Leading Constitutional Decisions* (New York: Crofts, 7th ed., 1940), pp. 222–223; Hughes, *op. cit.*, pp. 51–53; Warren, *The Supreme Court in United States History* Vol. III, pp. 220–254.

[1] Legal Tender Cases, 12 Wallace 457 (1871).

[2] Julliard *v.* Greenman, 110 U.S. 421 (1884).

[3] Norman *v.* Baltimore and O. R. Co., 294 U.S. 240 (1935).

[4] Perry *v.* United States, 294 U.S. 330 (1935). Although in this case it was said that Congress had exceeded its powers by abrogating gold clauses in its own obligation, the Court added that one must show actual loss or damage before being entitled to recovery.

States Denied Authority over Money.—Besides granting Congress authority to coin money and regulate its value, the Constitution expressly forbids the states to "coin Money; emit Bills of Credit; [and] make any Thing but gold and silver Coin a Tender in Payment of Debts. . . ."[1] Since states are forbidden to "coin money," there are no state mints where coins are made. Several states have recently enacted sales taxes authorizing the issuance and circulation of tokens of various sorts with which to pay taxes when purchases are made. These, it was contended, were "money" "coined" by the states. The Supreme Court upheld their use, however, inasmuch as the tokens were not to pass currently as coins but were to be used only as evidence that tax was paid.[2]

The states are also forbidden to "emit" bills of credit. These refer to paper money issued on the credit of a state government with the intention that it will circulate as a common medium of exchange. Although state governments cannot themselves issue paper money, they may authorize state incorporated banks to do so. In this event the notes are issued on the credit of the banks and not on that of the state; hence, according to definition, they are not legally "bills of credit."[3] Prior to the Civil War state banks issued bank notes in large amounts. Issued only upon the credit of the banks, their value was ofttimes uncertain; moreover, since the states lacked authority to make them legal tender, many people objected to their use for that reason. In consequence, shortly after the Civil War Congress undertook to force them out of existence by imposing a tax of 10 per cent upon them at the time of issuance. When challenged in the courts, the measure was upheld as a constitutional exercise of the power to tax, coin money, and regulate the value thereof.[4] The tax accomplished its purpose, with the result that state bank notes have been nonexistent for many years.

The states are also forbidden to "make anything but gold and silver coin a tender in payment of debts." When something is made legal tender, it must be accepted by creditors when offered in payment of debt. Since the only thing that the states can make legal tender is gold and silver coin, which must all be manufactured by the United States, the practical result is that Congress is solely responsible for the determination of what shall be legal tender.

[1] Article I, Section 10.

[2] Morrow *v.* Henneford, 182 Wash. 625 (1935).

[3] There is a long list of cases dealing with this subject. They are cited in United States Senate, *Constitution of the United States of America* (annotated), Sen. Doc. 232, 74th Cong., 2d Sess. (Washington: Government Printing Office, 1938), pp. 208–209.

[4] Veazie Bank *v.* Fenno, 8 Wallace 533, 552 (1889). See p. 367.

References

BURDICK, CHARLES K.: *The Law of the Constitution; Its Origin and Development* (New York: Putnam, 1922).

CORWIN, EDWARD S.: *Court over Constitution* (Princeton, N. J.: Princeton University Press, 1938).

——— *The Twilight of the Supreme Court* (New Haven: Yale University Press, 1934).

CUSHMAN, ROBERT E.: *Leading Constitutional Decisions* (New York: Crofts, 7th ed., 1940).

DYKSTRA, GERALD O., and L. G. DYKSTRA: *Selected Cases on Government and Business* (Chicago: Callaghan, 1937).

KOONTZ, HAROLD A.: *Government Control of Business* (Boston: Houghton Mifflin, 1941).

LARKIN, JOHN D.: *The President's Control over the Tariff* (Cambridge, Mass.: Harvard University Press, 1936).

LAWSON, J. L.: *The General Welfare Clause; a Study of the Power of Congress under the Constitution* (Falls Church, Va.: The Author, 2d printing, 1934).

MCGEARY, M. NELSON: *The Development of Congressional Investigative Power* (New York: Columbia University Press, 1940).

MAGRUDER, FRANK A., and GUY S. CLAIRE: *The Constitution* (New York: McGraw-Hill, 1st ed., 1933).

MATHEWS, JOHN M.: *The American Constitutional System* (New York: McGraw-Hill, 2d ed., 1940).

ORTH, SAMUEL P., and ROBERT E. CUSHMAN: *American National Government* (New York: Crofts, 1931).

SELIGMAN, EDWIN R. A.: *The Income Tax* (New York: Macmillan, 1911).

STORY, JOSEPH: *Commentaries on the Constitution of the United States* (Boston: Little, 4th ed., 2 vols., 1873).

UNITED STATES SENATE: *The Constitution of the United States of America* (annotated), Sen. Doc. 232, 74th Cong., 2d Sess. (Washington: Government Printing Office, 1938).

WARREN, CHARLES: *The Supreme Court in United States History* (Boston: Little, 3 vols., 1923).

——— *The Making of the Constitution* (Boston: Little, 1937).

WILLOUGHBY, WESTEL W.: *The Constitutional Law of the United States* (New York: Baker, Voorhis, 2d ed., 3 vols., 1929).

WILMERDING, LUCIUS: *Spending Power; A History of the Efforts of Congress to Control Expenditures* (New Haven: Yale University Press, 1943).

WRIGHT, BENJAMIN F.: *Contract Clause of the Constitution* (Cambridge, Mass.: Harvard University Press, 1938).

Chapter 18

FEDERAL POWERS—INTERSTATE COMMERCE[1]

Here is a word [Commerce] reputable, imposing, elegant, even romantic.
Walton H. Hamilton and Douglass Adair, *The Power to Govern.*[2]

One of the most serious defects of the Articles of Confederation was the inability of Congress to regulate interstate and foreign commerce. Each state erected tariff and other barriers to trade while foreign nations played one state off against another for their own commercial advantage. Even while the Constitutional Convention was sitting in Philadelphia, New Jersey passed a law taxing the lighthouse at Sandy Hook, owned by New York but situated on New Jersey land, in retaliation for the enactment of a law by New York imposing entrance and clearance fees for vessels leaving New York ports bound to Connecticut and New Jersey.[3] The situation had become well-nigh intolerable to the shippers, traders, financiers, and business classes generally, causing them to demand a central government capable of putting an end to commercial obstructions. Indeed, said Chief Justice Marshall, "It may be doubted whether any of the evils proceeding from the feebleness of the Federal Government [under the Articles] contributed more to that great revolution which introduced the present system, than the deep and general conviction that commerce ought to be regulated by Congress."[4] Though this conviction was general, many in the Southern states were afraid Northern representatives in control of Congress might exploit a broad grant of power to regulate commerce to their own sectional advantage. This led to the commerce and slave-trade compromise discussed earlier.[5]

The Commerce Clause.—After conflicting views had been compromised, the convention approved the following clause without a dissenting voice: "Congress shall have power . . . to regulate Commerce with foreign Nations, among the several States, and with the Indian Tribes."[6] The word "regulate" is one of the broadest that could have been used. It has been construed to grant authority not merely to direct the flow of commerce, but

[1] Because the rules governing foreign commerce and commerce with Indian tribes are similar to those pertaining to interstate commerce, they are not discussed separately in this chapter.

[2] (New York: Norton, 1937), p. 59.

[3] Charles Warren, *The Making of the Constitution* (Boston: Little, 1937), p. 567.

[4] Brown *v.* Maryland, 12 Wheaton 419 (1827).

[5] See p. 44.

[6] Article I, Section VIII, paragraph 3.

also to foster, protect, control, restrain, and even prohibit commerce in certain instances, as by forbidding the interstate transportation of impure food, drugs, products made by child labor, and women for immoral purposes. The word "commerce" was likewise chosen with care. Other words such as "business," "industry," "traffic," or "trade" might have been used, but none of these fully revealed what was intended.[1] The authors of the Constitution desired a clause that would grant to the national government unquestioned authority to control all forms of intercourse affecting two or more states, foreign nations, and the Indian tribes, while at the same time leaving to the states authority over the multiplicity of affairs that concern only localities.

Importance of the Commerce Power.—Next to the power to tax, the commerce clause has become one of the most important grants of authority contained in the Constitution. Turning to the *United States Code*,[2] which contains the acts of Congress presently effective, one finds innumerable statutes based upon the commerce power. One discovers, for example, statutes enacting tariffs and embargoes; admitting and excluding immigrants; regulating the marketing of agricultural products, the buying and selling of articles for export and shipment among the states, canals, rivers, harbors, ships at sea, railroads, airways, radio broadcasting, buses, trucks, bridges and ferries, pipe lines, transmission of electric energy, telephone, telegraph, monopolies, unfair trade practices; regulating the interstate transportation of foods and drugs, firearms, women for immoral purposes, stolen automobiles, kidnaped persons, intoxicating beverages; regulating minimum wages and maximum hours; guaranteeing the right of employees to join unions and bargain collectively, and a host of others. Indeed, the commerce power is authority for most of the distinctly regulatory activities of the Federal government. It, more than any other power, has been the means whereby the national government has assumed ever-increasing authority over matters affecting the daily lives of the American people.

Distinction between Intrastate and Interstate Commerce.—Before the Civil War when society was predominantly rural and businesses were small, the line of demarcation between intrastate and interstate commerce could be drawn with comparative ease. Today the situation is different. The transformation from a simple agrarian society to a gigantic industrial nation has caused all economic activity to become commingled. As the ripples of a pool radiate to the farthest extremity, so every business transaction may affect the economic life of the nation to some degree. Economically, then, no clear-cut division can be made between commerce that is interstate and that that is local.

[1] For an interesting discussion of the etymology of these words, see Hamilton and Adair, *op. cit.*, pp. 59–63, 112–121.

[2] (Washington: Government Printing Office, 1941), Title 15.

Nevertheless, the Constitution requires that a distinction be made. While permitting a broad interpretation, the Supreme Court has recently said that federal authority may not be pushed to such an extent as to destroy the distinction that the commerce clause establishes between commerce among the states and the internal concerns of the state.[1] Where the line shall be drawn cannot be determined in advance but must await specific situations. The review of cases which follows suggests that the pendulum has swung from a broad to a narrow construction and has now swung back to a broader interpretation than was hitherto imaginable. Chief Justice Waite spoke prophetically when he said the commerce power is "not confined to the instrumentalities . . . known or in use when the Constitution was adopted," but "keeps pace with the progress of the country" and adapts itself "to the new developments of time and circumstances."[2]

INTRASTATE COMMERCE

Control over intrastate commerce is reserved to the states. In general, intrastate commerce embraces all intercourse within a single state that does not seriously affect intercourse with other states. Various words have been used to indicate when local matters become interstate. First the courts said the effect must be "close," "substantial," or "material"; later "direct" as opposed to "indirect" and "remote," but in recent years the use of such words has been discontinued.[3] Now the mechanical application of legal formulas is unfeasible; hence facts are allowed to speak for themselves in every instance that arises. Ordinarily the President and Congress must first decide when the effect is serious enough to concern other states, but their decisions must later be approved by the federal courts.

The Original Package Doctrine.—As early as 1827[4] the Supreme Court evolved a formula which has helped determine where interstate commerce starts and ends. According to that formula, known since as the "original package doctrine," intrastate commerce ends and interstate commerce begins as soon as the original package has been delivered to and accepted by a carrier for shipment across one or more state lines or to a foreign country. Interstate commerce continues as long as the article shipped remains in the original package unopened, unused, or unsold. State jurisdiction begins when the original package is opened and the article becomes mingled in the general mass of property within the state. Thus, taxicabs, local buses, and streetcars carrying passengers (original pack-

[1] National Labor Relations Board *v.* Jones and Laughlin Steel Corporation, 299 U.S. 534 (1937).

[2] Pensacola Tel. Co. *v.* Western Union Tel. Co., 96 U.S. 1, 9 (1877).

[3] Wickard *v.* Filburn, 317 U.S. 111 (1942).

[4] Brown *v.* Maryland, 12 Wheaton 419 (1827).

ages) to a depot are not engaged in interstate commerce even though the passengers later journey to other states. Interstate commerce begins when the passengers board the train and ends when they leave the carrier and mingle with the crowds. Logs (original packages) stored on a river bank awaiting spring freshets to float them to another state are not interstate commerce; but once floated, they become commerce and remain so until they are sold and delivered for processing. Logs frozen in a river while being floated from state to state are interstate commerce—although they have temporarily come to "rest," they remain in the original packages and have not become mingled with the mass of state property. Before prohibition "dry" states were forbidden to seize or confiscate liquor shipped into their states until the original package was sold or opened.[1] This led to importations on consignment, C.O.D., and by other devices whereby someone from out of state retained ownership until the articles were safely delivered, thus making seizure next to impossible. A small laundry would not be engaged in interstate commerce, but if it shipped a few finished shirts across state lines, the shirts would become interstate commerce when presented for shipment and would remain so until they reached their destination and remained unopened. A paper package of cigarettes 3 inches long and 1½ inches wide, containing ten cigarettes, is not an original package, but a pine box containing the same number of cigarettes may be the original package. Natural gas transported through pipe lines is an original package, but it may lose its interstate character by entering intermediate lines and the pipes of individual consumers.

Local Businesses.—All businesses are local in the sense that they, or parts of them, are situated within one of the states. Some of them, like the peanut vender, the bakery, barbershop, and hardware store are probably very small; others, like the Ford Motor Company, are very large; while still others range somewhere in between. In this field it is harder than in almost any other to draw the line between intra- and interstate commerce. Since the National Industrial Recovery Act, enacted in 1933, went further in regulating businesses, both large and small, than any law previously or subsequently enacted, reference to the case in which its constitutionality was considered may help to make a distinction.

NIRA Unconstitutional.—Among other things, the NIRA authorized the formation of codes of fair competition, several hundred of which were put into effect. The groups that formed the codes wrote into them regulations governing wages, hours, fair trade practices, prices, etc.[2] Among the businesses affected were barbershops, local retail stores, small mines and factories, and many other businesses heretofore understood to be engaged in local commerce, hence not subject to federal control. After

[1] Leisy *v.* Hardin, 135 U.S. 100 (1890).

[2] For a fuller discussion see p. 659.

several months of operation the law was challenged by the Schechter Brothers,[1] who operated slaughterhouses in New York City for the purpose of killing poultry purchased from near-by New Jersey and Pennsylvania and sold to retail poultry dealers and butchers within New York City, who, in turn, sold directly to consumers. Though nearly all the poultry handled by the Schechter Brothers originated outside the state of New York, they sold all of it within the state; hence there was no flow from one state through New York and thence into another. The Supreme Court was unanimous in saying that the Schechter Brothers, and inferentially many others governed by the codes, were not engaged in interstate commerce. Their business, the Court said, had only an indirect effect upon interstate commerce, hence could not be regulated by Congress.

Although, as will be seen, the Court has since greatly expanded the commerce clause, it still insists that local commerce must intimately affect interstate before coming under the jurisdiction of Congress. This means, therefore, that such businesses as locally owned restaurants, hotels, barbershops, retail stores, bakeries, agricultural production (but not marketing), very small mines, factories, and utilities are generally still considered to be intrastate commerce.

Size Not the Controlling Factor.—Size itself is not the controlling factor, however. Federal agencies may assert jurisdiction whenever an enterprise produces, buys, or sells in appreciable quantities outside a single state, or where local businesses may have some intimate corporate or functional relationship with firms about whose interstate character there can be no doubt. Thus, a wheat farmer may be penalized for growing more than his quota even though the excess is fed to livestock on the farm on the theory that home consumption would ultimately disrupt marketing and price control.[2] Stockyards are subject to federal control because livestock produced locally commence a "flow" which, after going through the hands of slaughterers, packers, wholesalers, and retailers, ultimately reaches customers miles away.[3] Congress may regulate safety appliances on railway cars whether moving intrastate or interstate, because the cars might readily become commingled.[4] The Interstate Commerce Commission may fix rates for a railroad operating entirely within a state if it competes with an interstate carrier.[5] A labor dispute, minimum wages, hours, child labor, and working conditions in small subsidiaries of large corporations could doubtless be subject to federal control. Enough illustrations have been given to make it clear that in every case the test is not size but

[1] Schechter Poultry Corp. *v.* United States, 295 U.S. 495 (1935).

[2] Wickard *v.* Filburn, 317 U.S. 111 (1942).

[3] Stafford *v.* Wallace, 258 U.S. 495 (1922).

[4] Southern Railway Co. *v.* United States, 222 U.S. 20 (1911).

[5] The Shreveport Case, 234 U.S. 342 (1914).

the degree of relationship to commerce carried on among the states; or, as it was recently expressed by Chief Justice Stone: "It is the effect upon the interstate commerce or its regulation, regardless of the particular form which the competition may take, which is the test of federal power."[1]

Amusements.—Millions of dollars are spent annually by the American people for amusements such as movies, vaudeville, theaters, athletic contests, circuses, carnivals, and the like. Like other businesses, many companies providing such entertainments have become big, offering performances in several states and transporting large quantities of materials and supplies in doing so. From these circumstances the question arose of whether amusements were subject to federal or state control. The question was considered at length by the Supreme Court in 1922.[2] In that case, the Federal Baseball Club, with headquarters at Baltimore, brought suit against the National League claiming that the latter had conspired to monopolize the baseball business, thus violating the Sherman Antitrust Act, a federal law. Overlooking the question of whether the National League had in fact conspired to monopolize, the court ruled that it did not come within the scope of the Sherman Act because its primary purpose was that of providing a local exhibition. The interstate transportation of players and supplies, while in themselves subject to congressional control, were in this instance merely incidental to the principal purpose of providing local entertainment. Thus, amusements are not interstate commerce.

Congress can forbid the interstate shipment of objectionable films, and it may break up a monopoly in the sale and distribution of motion-picture films.[3] It could not, however, require that a pool hall, a movie, ball club, or circus obtain a license to perform locally; nor could it forbid immoral exhibitions; nor fix minimum wages and maximum hours and guarantee collective bargaining in businesses whose principal purpose is that of providing amusement. Jurisdiction over matters such as these is reserved to the states.

Fish and Game.—All the states have enacted laws designed to protect wild life, and no one has seriously contended that in doing so states were exceeding their authority. A number of states have, however, enacted laws discriminating against nonresidents and forbidding the shipment of fish and game outside the state. Pennsylvania, for example, charges nonresidents over three times more for fishing licenses than residents and forbids the taking or shipping of deer killed within the state beyond its borders. From laws such as these, cases have reached the courts in which it was alleged that the states were burdening interstate commerce.

[1] United States *v.* Wrightwood Dairy Co., 315 U.S. 110 (1941).

[2] Federal Baseball Club of Baltimore *v.* National Baseball League, 259 U.S. 200 (1922).

[3] Interstate Circuit *v.* United States, 306 U.S. 208 (1939).

The leading case is Geer *v.* Connecticut.[1] Connecticut had made it a crime for anyone to transport certain types of game killed within the state to places outside the state. A person named Geer was convicted of violating the law and the matter ultimately reached the United States Supreme Court. The principal issue was whether forbidding the interstate transportation of game was a burden upon interstate commerce and hence a subject that only Congress could control. In an interesting opinion in which the Court went back to ancient Greece and Rome for illustrations, the Court upheld the Connecticut statute. Game is, said the Court, the common property of the people of a state. Since it is the people's property, they retain complete control over its use. A state government, acting as the people's trustee, cannot only regulate the circumstances under which hunting might be done but also prevent the interstate shipment of game killed within the state. The same reasoning applies to fish and fishing.

The full import of this construction was shown when a short time afterwards Congress, asserting the commerce power, enacted legislation regulating the hunting of migratory birds. The measure was promptly challenged on the ground that Congress had invaded powers reserved to the states. The contention was upheld in the lower federal courts[2] and because it was thought that the decisions correctly reflected the attitude of the higher courts, appeal was never taken. In consequence of the above decisions, Congress cannot, under the commerce power, regulate the killing of fish and game even though they be migratory or swim in or upon navigable rivers and territorial waters.

Power of Congress to Regulate Fish and Game by Treaty Power.—This does not mean that Congress is entirely powerless in the matter. Congress can, and has, forbidden the interstate *shipment* of game killed in violation of state laws and the legislation has been upheld.[3] Moreover, following the attempt at control by use of the commerce power, mentioned above, the Federal government concluded treaties with Canada and Mexico by which the signatories undertook to protect migratory birds. Thereupon Congress enacted legislation similar to that which had been based upon the commerce power but declared unconstitutional. When challenged by the state of Missouri,[4] the Supreme Court upheld federal control inasmuch as the legislation was based upon the treaty power—not the power to regulate interstate commerce. Today, then, Congress uses the interstate-commerce power to regulate the interstate shipment of fish and game, the treaty power to regulate migratory birds, but it leaves

[1] 161 U.S. 519 (1896).

[2] United States *v.* Shauver, 214 Fed. 154; United States *v.* McCullough, 221 Fed. 288.

[3] Rupert *v.* United States, 181 Fed. 87 (1910).

[4] Missouri *v.* Holland, 252 U.S. 416 (1920).

to the states the regulation of fishing and the hunting of nonmigratory birds and animals within the forty-eight states.[1]

Professional Occupations.—A considerable number of people are professional workers such as doctors, dentists, lawyers, accountants, and architects. Because their activities are usually confined to the localities they serve, it has always been assumed that they were not engaged in interstate commerce. In recent years, however, professional groups, like most others, have formed associations for their mutual advantage and through these have in certain instances attained a high degree of control over the entire profession. This gives rise to the question of whether a professional service is a "trade" and if so when it becomes interstate commerce.

These issues have not been definitively settled by the courts.[2] There is reason to believe, however, that professional workers are engaged in trade or commerce. Normally their activities are sufficiently localized to be considered only intrastate in character, but it is not inconceivable that they would be considered within the purview of the interstate-commerce clause if they organize on a large scale and act collectively to promote their professional interests.

INTERSTATE COMMERCE

Definition of Interstate Commerce.—Because the term "interstate commerce" is nowhere defined in the Constitution, its meaning must be sought elsewhere, especially in court decisions. The famous Steamboat Case[3] was the first in which the Court had occasion to construe the power. The New York legislature had given Robert R. Livingston and Robert Fulton an exclusive right to navigate steamboats on the waters of the state. Ogden secured a license for steamboat navigation from Fulton and Livingston. Gibbons, who had originally been a partner with Ogden but was now his rival, was operating steamboats between New York and New Jersey by authority of a license obtained from the Federal government. Ogden, wishing to eliminate his competitor, brought suit in the courts of New York and obtained a ruling enjoining Gibbons from further operations. Whereupon, Gibbons appealed to the United States Supreme Court. In one of his most celebrated opinions, Chief Justice Marshall, speaking for the Court, ruled in favor of Gibbons. Navigation upon navigable rivers, said he, is interstate commerce. Congress had legislated

[1] See also p. 102.

[2] Whether a doctor's profession is a "trade" within the meaning of the Sherman Act was recently raised in the case of the American Medical Association *v.* United States, 317 U.S. 519 (1942), but the case was disposed of without deciding the point. The Supreme Court did say, however, that a group health cooperative was a trade or business.

[3] Gibbons *v.* Ogden, 9 Wheaton 1 (1824).

with respect to such navigation; hence all state laws in conflict with federal must give way. The case was of the utmost importance at the time, eliminating as it did the merciless commercial rivalry between the states, but its future significance derives from the broad definition of commerce contained in the words: "Commerce, undoubtedly, is traffic, but it is something more; it is intercourse. It describes the commercial intercourse between nations, and parts of nations, in all its branches, and is regulated by prescribing rules for carrying on that intercourse."

Transportation.—Transportation of persons and goods across state lines is the clearest form of interstate and foreign commerce. The method of conveyance is immaterial, whether it be people walking, cattle leisurely grazing first in one state and then in another, or travel by ship, train, canoe, airplane, pipe line, motorcar, or bicycle, it is still interstate commerce. Even logs floated down a navigable stream are interstate commerce. Though a carrier begin and end its journey within a single state, it is, nevertheless, subject to federal control if it carries passengers or goods destined for points outside the state or if it competes substantially with interstate carriers. Though a vehicle begin its journey in one state, leave the state for a considerable distance en route, and return to the state of origin, it is engaged in interstate commerce.

Communications.—At various times the contention has been put forth that only the interstate transportation of tangible things, like persons and property, constituted interstate commerce. But this idea was rejected long ago. Soon after their invention federal regulation of interstate transmission of messages by telephone and telegraph was upheld.[1] In the first case just cited, Mr. Justice Waite said:

> The powers thus granted are not confined to the instrumentalities of Commerce or the postal service known or in use when the Constitution was adopted, but they keep pace with the progress of the country, and adapt themselves to the new developments of time and circumstances. They extend from the horse with its rider to the stagecoach, from the sailing vessel to the steamboat, from the coach and the steamboat to the railroad, and from the railroad to the telegraph as these new agencies are successively brought into use to meet the demands of increasing population and wealth.

More recently, regulation of radio broadcasting and the transmission of news by wire or wireless have been held to be within the scope of the commerce power.[2]

[1] One of the earliest cases involving telegraph was Pensacola Telegraph Co. *v.* Western Union Telegraph Co., 96 U.S. 1 (1878), while early cases involving telephone were Delaware and Atlantic Telegraph and Telephone Co. *v.* Delaware, 50 Fed. 677 (1892), and Muskegee Nat. Tel. Co. *v.* Hall, 118 Fed. 382 (1902).

[2] Fisher's Blend Station, Inc. *v.* State Tax Commission, 297 U.S. 650 (1936); Associated Press *v.* National Labor Relations Board, 301 U.S. 103 (1937).

Buying and Selling.—Buying and selling of goods intended for shipment or use in other states is interstate commerce. Accordingly, Congress has made illegal all sorts of contracts that monopolize interstate commerce; it has outlawed price discrimination between buyers; it has legalized contracts whereby manufacturers may force retailers to maintain resale prices of nationally advertised products; it has regulated the buying and selling of livestock, agricultural products, and stocks and bonds; and it has outlawed unfair trade practices that may injure buyers and sellers. Moreover, Congress has fixed the rates that sellers may charge and buyers pay for interstate carriers, electric power, natural gas, and bituminous coal. A corollary of this, as will be noted more fully elsewhere, is that states cannot impose burdens upon the buying and selling of interstate products. This explains why salesmen for out-of-state concerns, such as the Fuller Brush Company and the Real Silk Hosiery Mills, who merely take and subsequently deliver orders, cannot be compelled to pay local license fees for doing business within a state.

Production and Commerce.—Transportation, buying and selling, and transmission of electricity or messages imply movement or conveyance from somewhere within one state into another. But what of the actual manufacture of a product or its extraction from the earth? Because it is ultimately bought and sold or transported across state lines, is its production a part of interstate commerce? The question became important toward the end of the last century when businesses were rapidly becoming national in size.

The Old Doctrine.—A leading case was that of United States *v.* E. C. Knight.[1] The American Sugar Refining Company had acquired control of 98 per cent of all sugar refining in the United States. Suit was brought by the Department of Justice charging the company with monopolizing interstate commerce in violation of the Sherman Act. Acknowledging that the company was of enormous size and in control of virtually all sugar refining in the country, the Court nevertheless dismissed the suit saying that the company was not engaged in interstate commerce, hence was beyond the scope of federal regulation. The Court distinguished between production and commerce, saying that the former involved merely a change in *form* while commerce involved change of *place*. The refining of sugar was antecedent to commerce but not a part of it. In other words, no matter how large a production unit became, its effect upon economic affairs in other states was so indirect and remote as to cause it to be beyond federal control under the commerce power. Subsequently, by similar reasoning, Congress was prevented from regulating not only manufacturing but also the production of oil and natural gas, mining, quarrying, and the production of electric power.

[1] 156 U.S. 1 (1895).

The Present Doctrine.—This doctrine was followed until 1937, since which time the courts have greatly expanded the scope of the commerce power. The entering wedge was driven in a case involving the constitutionality of the National Labor Relations Act.[1] The Jones and Laughlin Steel Corporation was accused of violating the act by discharging several employees in production units at its plant at Aliquippa, Pa., for union activities. The company admitted the charges but denied that the Federal government could do anything about it because the men were engaged in manufacture which was not interstate commerce. The company was the fourth largest producer of steel in the country. Though incorporated under the laws of Pennsylvania, it had nineteen subsidiaries which comprised an integrated empire. It owned or leased mines, ships, railroads, stores, mills, plants, factories, pipe lines, and refineries in several states and maintained sales offices in twenty cities and one in Canada. Approximately 75 per cent of its products were shipped out of Pennsylvania.

Admitting that the dismissed men were engaged in production, the Supreme Court went on to say that the labor practices of the employer had such an immediate and direct effect upon interstate commerce as to come within the scope of federal power. Writing for the majority, Chief Justice Hughes observed:

> In view of respondent's far-flung activities it is idle to say that the effect would be indirect or remote. It is obvious that it would be immediate and might be catastrophic. . . . When industries organize themselves on a national scale, making their relation to interstate commerce the dominant factor in their activities, how can it be maintained that their industrial labor relations constitute a forbidden field into which Congress may not enter when it is necessary to protect interstate commerce from paralyzing consequences of industrial war?

This meant that manufacturing, or any other form of productive enterprise, was interstate commerce if organized on a national scale and carried on in two or more states. This is a wide departure from the doctrine enunciated in the Knight case and subsequently followed.

Possible Reasons for the Reversal.—This decision came as a great surprise. Only 11 months before, the Court, comprised of the same nine justices, had declared the Guffey Coal Act unconstitutional, saying, among other things, that mining was not interstate commerce.[2] Many[3] confidently expected the Court to follow the same reasoning when the National Labor Relations Act came before it.

[1] National Labor Relations Board *v.* Jones and Laughlin Steel Corporation, 301 U.S. 1 (1937).

[2] Carter *v.* Carter Coal Co., 298 U.S. 238 (1936).

[3] Including an American Liberty League committee of fifty-eight prominent lawyers who publicly announced that in their view the National Labor Relations Act was un-

The decision was five to four with Chief Justice Hughes and Mr. Justice Roberts joining the "liberals" to uphold the constitutionality of the act.[1] What caused these two justices to accept the broader view must be left to conjecture. Undoubtedly the scope of the organization and operations of the steel company made a deep impression. It was also widely suspected that the reelection of President Roosevelt by large majorities in 1936, the President's attack upon the courts made in February—two months before the Jones and Laughlin decision[2]—together with the interruption of national commerce during the winter of 1936–1937 by large-scale strikes had something to do with the decision of the Court. Whatever may have been the reason, the Court has since consistently held that the productive stage of something affecting other states or foreign nations may be regulated under the commerce power.

Recent Trends.—Since the historic reversal of 1937 the commerce power has been applied to productive activities of various sorts. Though agricultural production itself remains local, considerable federal restraint has been approved through control of quantities that may be marketed.[3] In 1939 federal legislation fixing prices for bituminous coal was approved.[4] In the following year the Court upheld federal regulation of wages, hours, child labor, and working conditions for businesses engaged in the manufacture of lumber products[5] and incidentally mines and other types of enterprises considered beyond the reach of federal power prior to 1937. During the same year, comprehensive federal regulation of natural gas companies was approved,[6] and still more recently long-standing decisions have been overruled, bringing insurance within the scope of the commerce clause. Though the trend has been in the direction of applying the commerce power broadly, there is still a huge volume of economic activities that remain intrastate.

Insurance.—Although the insurance business had assumed gigantic proportions, until 1944 it was considered intrastate in character. This classification went back to Paul *v.* Virginia.[7] In that case, one named Paul, an agent for a New York insurance company, entered into a con-

---

constitutional. The opinion of the committee did much to encourage employers to ignore the act, thus helping to precipitate a crisis in industrial relations. For the opinion of the committee, see *The New York Times*, Sept. 19, 1935.

[1] See also p. 347.

[2] Cf. p. 348.

[3] Currin *v.* Wallace, 306 U.S. 1 (1939); Mulford *v.* Smith, 307 U.S. 38 (1938); Wickard *v.* Filburn, 317 U.S. 111 (1942).

[4] Sunshine Anthracite Coal Co. *v.* Adkins, 310 U.S. 381 (1940).

[5] United States *v.* Darby Lumber Co., 312 U.S. 100 (1941).

[6] Federal Power Commission *v.* National Gas Pipeline Co., 315 U.S. 590 (1941). See also Federal Power Commission *v.* Hope Natural Gas Co., 320 U.S. 591 (1943).

[7] 8 Wallace 168 (1869).

tract with a person in Virginia for fire insurance. A Virginia statute required that all insurance agents obtain licenses before selling in the state, but Paul, assuming himself to be engaged in interstate commerce and therefore beyond state control, proceeded to sell without complying with the Virginia statute. The case ultimately reached the Supreme Court, which ruled against Paul. An insurance contract, said the Court, was like any other personal contract. The policy was negotiated by a resident agent in Virginia and became binding when delivered by the insurance agent in Virginia. That the insurance company was located in New York, that the policy was sent to the home office for approval, that the funds would be handled and invested by the home office, and that benefits would be paid by an out-of-state corporation were all immaterial to the central fact that a purely personal and local contract had been entered into between Paul and his client.

This decision was followed for years afterward and reaffirmed as recently as 1935.[1] It accounts for the fact that insurance companies have been incorporated by the states and have been regulated exclusively by state commissions rather than federal.

Insurance Now Commerce.—The Paul *v.* Virginia doctrine had many critics and became increasingly difficult to reconcile with the broadening interpretation of the commerce power. Finally, a closely divided Court upset its precedents.[2] An appeal by South-Eastern Underwriters Association and its membership of nearly 200 private-stock fire-insurance companies, and 27 individuals convicted of violating the Sherman Antitrust Act brought the case before the Supreme Court. In previous cases involving insurance brought before the Court the question had been one of whether state regulation was proper; this was the first time the constitutionality of federal regulation of insurance under the commerce clause was ever reviewed. Observing that the modern insurance business held a commanding position in the trade and commerce of the nation, with assets exceeding $37 billion, annual premium receipts over $6 billion, and a labor force of over half a million, the Courts said: "Perhaps no modern commercial enterprise directly affects so many persons in all walks of life as does the insurance business. Insurance touches the home, the family, and the occupation or the business of almost every person in the United States." Accordingly, it came within the purview of the commerce clause and the conviction was upheld. This decision had immediate and far-reaching consequences, causing Congress promptly to enact a measure reaffirming the *status quo* with respect to state regulation for a period extending until June 30, 1948.[3] In the meantime, insurance companies

[1] Metropolitan Casualty Insurance Co. *v.* Brownell, 294 U.S. 580 (1935).
[2] United States *v.* South-Eastern Underwriters Association *et al.*, 322 U.S. 533 (1944).
[3] *United States Code, Annotated,* Title 15, Secs. 1011–1012.

have been adjusting their affairs to avoid future prosecutions for violating federal laws and also in anticipation of possible comprehensive federal regulation.

States Not to Burden Interstate Commerce.—Because of the close relationship between national and local commerce, the states may impose, and have imposed, many regulations upon businesses engaged in interstate commerce. From a welter of decisions three conclusions emerge: First, if Congress has already legislated on the subject, the states may not enact conflicting measures. Second, if Congress has not acted, silence does not authorize states to intervene where the subject requires uniform national control. Third, if Congress has not acted and the subject does not require national uniform control, the states may regulate provided their laws are reasonable and do not discriminate against commerce that is interstate.

Illustrations of Invalid State Laws.—In the early days of the republic, Congress legislated permitting vessels with federal licenses to operate on navigable waters. Later, the state of New York granted monopoly rights to Robert Fulton to operate steamboats on waters within the state. This, the Court held, conflicted with federal law and was therefore invalid.[1] Congress has required the enrollment and licensing of vessels; hence a state law requiring ships leaving a port within the state to file a statement at the office of the probate judge of the county setting forth the name of the vessel, name of the owners, etc., was an invalid interference with interstate and foreign commerce.[2]

In the instances just mentioned, Congress had already acted. In the following, Congress had not legislated but the subject required uniform control; hence state laws were invalid. New York and other states imposed taxes upon immigrants entering their ports, but when challenged, the Supreme Court held that immigration required uniform control; hence the state laws were unconstitutional.[3] Prior to 1886 the states imposed numerous regulations upon all railroads within their borders, but in the year mentioned the Court ruled that railroads that had become interstate required uniform control; hence state laws were invalid.[4] This forced Congress into action, which resulted in creation of the Interstate Commerce Commission. A similar situation arose around 1920 with respect to control of rates for interstate shipments of natural gas. Because uniformity was required, state laws were invalid.[5]

[1] Gibbons *v.* Ogden, 9 Wheaton 1 (1824).

[2] Sinnot *v.* Davenport, 22 Howard 287 (1859).

[3] Smith *v.* Turner (The Passenger Cases), 7 Howard 283 (1849).

[4] Wabash, St. L. & P. R. Co. *v.* Illinois, 118 U.S. 557 (1886).

[5] Public Utility Commission *v.* Landon, 249 U.S. 236 (1919); Missouri *v.* Kansas Gas Co., 265 U.S. 298 (1923).

Most numerous of all cases are those where Congress has not acted but the states have passed laws discriminating against commerce of other states. Thus, during the depression California made it illegal to bring an indigent person into the state. Many states have tried to prevent the importation of oleomargarine by taxing it heavily. Minnesota went so far as to prohibit the sale of meat products that were not produced within 100 miles of the place sold. A state law required trains to slow down or stop at all railroad crossings, thus seriously impeding their speed. Many states have tried to impose heavy license fees upon out-of-state salesmen. Southern states required interstate buses and trains to practice "Jim Crow" segregation in seating and bedding passengers. In all these instances, and many more, federal courts have held that interstate commerce had been unduly burdened.

Illustrations of Where States May Regulate.—As indicated above, states may enact local laws affecting interstate commerce where they do not conflict with federal enactments, the subject does not require uniform control, and the legislation is not unreasonable or unduly burdensome. Thus, in the interest of safety, states may prescribe rules governing railroad crossings even to the extent of requiring an interstate railroad to eliminate one or more of them. States may penalize operation of freight trains that are manned by fewer than three brakemen, or a "full crew." Limits may be placed upon the width and weight of trucks operating on state highways. Motion-picture films may be censored even though produced in other states. States may prohibit tobacco advertising on billboards and placards by resident and nonresident companies; and they may regulate the retail (but not wholesale) price of out-of-state products such as natural gas, electricity, and milk.

References

BURDICK, CHARLES K.: *The Law of the American Constitution; Its Origin and Development* (New York: Putnam, 1922).

CORWIN, EDWARD S.: *The President, Office and Powers* (New York: New York University Press, 1940).

——— *Twilight of the Supreme Court* (New Haven: Yale University Press, 1934).

——— *The Commerce Power v. States Rights* (Princeton, N.J.: Princeton University Press, 1936).

GAVIT, BERNARD C.: *The Commerce Clause of the United States Constitution* (Bloomington, Ind.: Principal Press, 1932).

HAINES, CHARLES G.: *Role of the Supreme Court in American Government and Politics, 1789–1835* (Berkeley and Los Angeles: University of California Press, 1944).

HAMILTON, WALTON H., and DOUGLASS ADAIR: *The Power to Govern* (New York: Norton, 1937).

JACKSON, ROBERT H.: *The Struggle for Judicial Supremacy* (New York: Knopf, 1941).

KALLENBACH, JOSEPH E.: *Federal Cooperation with the States under the Commerce Clause* (Ann Arbor: University of Michigan Press, 1942).

LARKIN, JOHN D.: *The President's Control over the Tariff* (Cambridge, Mass.: Harvard University Press, 1936).

RIBBLE, FREDERICK D. G.: *State and National Power over Commerce* (New York: Columbia University Press, 1937).

STORY, JOSEPH: *Commentaries on the Constitution of the United States* (Boston: Little, 4th ed., 2 vols., 1873).

UNITED STATES SENATE: *The Constitution of the United States* (annotated), Sen. Doc. 232, 74th Cong., 2d Sess. (Washington: Government Printing Office, 1938).

WARREN, CHARLES: *The Making of the Constitution* (Boston: Little, 1937).

WILLOUGHBY, WESTEL W.: *The Constitutional Law of the United States* (New York: Baker, Voorhis, 2d ed., 3 vols., 1929).

Chapter 19

FEDERAL POWERS—FOREIGN RELATIONS AND WAR

> The war power is the most dangerous one to a free government in the whole catalogue of powers. It usually is invoked in haste and excitement when calm legislative consideration of constitutional limitations is difficult. It is executed in a time of patriotic fervor that makes moderation unpopular, and is interpreted by judges under the influence of the same passions and prejudices.
>
> Justice Robert H. Jackson in
> Woods *v.* Cloyd W. Miller Co.[1]

FOREIGN RELATIONS

In no field does the Federal government have greater powers than in the field of international relations. When dealing with domestic matters the Federal government is limited to the use of delegated powers, but in the international sphere it has others that are said to be inherent. That is to say, it derives others from the fact that the United States is a sovereign nation in a world of national states that are recognized by international law as being fully competent to deal with matters pertaining to their respective interests. While some have been inclined to deny the existence of inherent powers, all doubt about the matter was removed by a recent decision of the Supreme Court[2] upholding the constitutionality of a joint resolution of Congress that authorized the President to use discretion about applying an embargo upon the sale of arms and munitions to Bolivia and Paraguay, then at war in the Chaco. Commenting upon the differences between federal powers for dealing with domestic or internal affairs and those for handling foreign affairs, the Court said, "That there are differences between them, and that these differences are fundamental, may not be doubted." The Court continued, saying:

> It results that the investment of the Federal government with the powers of external sovereignty did not depend upon the affirmative grants of the Constitution. The powers to declare and wage war, to conclude peace, to make treaties, to maintain diplomatic relations with other sovereignties, if they had never been mentioned in the Constitution, would have vested in the Federal government as necessary concomitants of nationality. . . . As a member of the family of nations,

[1] 333 U.S. 138 (1947).

[2] United States *v.* Curtiss-Wright Export Corporation, 299 U.S. 304 (1936). For a full discussion see Edward S. Corwin, *The President, Office and Powers* (New York: New York University Press, 1940), p. 202.

the right and power of the United States in that field are equal to the right and power of the other members of the international family. Otherwise, the United States is not completely sovereign.

Federal Powers Exclusive.—Moreover, federal powers in this field are not shared concurrently with the states but are exclusive. The states are not recognized in international law and the Constitution forbids them to enter into "any treaty, alliance or confederation," or, without the consent of Congress, to enter into any agreement or compact with a foreign power.[1] These prohibitions give the Federal government an unquestioned monopoly over international relations.

Conduct of Foreign Relations.—Responsibility for the conduct of foreign affairs is divided between the President, the Senate, and Congress as a whole. The President is authorized to "make treaties," to "nominate . . . and . . . appoint Ambassadors, other public ministers and consuls," and to "receive Ambassadors and other public ministers." From these brief provisions the President has become the sole instrument of communication with foreign governments; he takes the initiative in formulating foreign policies; he negotiates treaties and agreements; he decides which governments will be recognized, when diplomatic and consular relations with foreign governments will begin and terminate; and he chooses, directs, transfers, and recalls diplomats and consuls who represent the nation abroad.[2] The Senate approves treaties and confirms ambassadors, other public ministers, and consuls nominated by the President. Both the Senate and House influence the conduct of foreign relations by control of the purse, investigations and hearings, their ability to debate and enact general legislation governing the Department of State, the diplomatic and consular service, and international affairs generally.

The Treaty Power.—The President makes treaties by and with the advice and consent of two-thirds of the Senate.[3] When properly made, treaties, like statutes, become part of the "Supreme Law of the Land."[4]

The treaty power has been used to deal with a wide range of subjects. Some treaties have terminated wars. Others have acquired land, such as the Louisiana Territory from France, the Southwest Territory from Mexico, Alaska from Russia, and the Virgin Islands from Denmark. Others have secured protection, even special rights on certain occasions, for American citizens and nationals abroad. Others have provided for the exchange of consuls, extradition of fugitives, immigration, tariffs, military, naval, and air bases, rights upon the high seas and territorial waters, and a host of

[1] Article I, Section 10.

[2] See also pp. 524–525.

[3] That is, two-thirds of those present, assuming the presence of a quorum—not two-thirds of the entire membership of the Senate.

[4] Article VI.

other matters.[1] In general, treaties may deal with any subject of mutual concern to one or more nations. When concluded, some treaties, like those terminating a war or the recognition of certain rights, become effective without implemental legislation. Others, like those calling for appropriations and special administrative agencies, can have no practical effect until implemented by congressional statute. The implied-power clause gives Congress all authority necessary for making treaties effective.

Limits to the Treaty Power.—Treaties, like statutes, are subject to interpretation by the courts and can be declared unconstitutional, although to date none has been. In decisions involving treaties the Supreme Court has intimated that the treaty power extends to "all proper subjects of negotiation between this Government and those of other nations."[2] What would not be a "proper subject" has never been decided but can be imagined. A treaty, for example, by which the Federal government guaranteed all aliens the right to vote for state and local officers when state laws excluded them from exercising the franchise would doubtless deal with an improper subject, because the Constitution leaves the determination of voting qualifications to the states.

The Supreme Court has also intimated that provisions of treaties must be "consistent with our institutions" and "the distribution of powers between the General and State Governments."[3] Here, again, one can only guess at what the Court meant. Apparently, using these criteria, a treaty would be invalid if its effect were to alter any of the fundamental features of our political system—popular sovereignty, representative government, separation of powers, judicial review, etc.—discussed in another chapter;[4] or if powers reserved to the states were subverted.

Moreover, treaties must be made "under the Authority of the United States," which means that they must be made by the President with the advice and consent of the Senate and not by anyone else.

Finally, the national government cannot under the guise of a treaty do any of the things expressly forbidden by the Constitution. A treaty could not, for example, result in the diminution of equality of representation of a state in the Senate or in the imposition of tariffs on exports, both of which acts are expressly forbidden.

Treaty Power Is Broader Than Delegated Legislative Powers.—Article VI contains the statement that "This Constitution, and the Laws of the United States which shall be made in Pursuance thereof; and all Treaties made, or which shall be made, under the Authority of the United States, shall be the supreme Law of the Land. . . ." Note that laws, that is,

[1] For sources of published treaties see p. 538.
[2] Holmes *v.* Jennison, 14 Peters 540, 569 (1840).
[3] *Ibid.*
[4] Chap. 4.

acts of Congress, must be made *in pursuance of the Constitution* in order to be part of the supreme law; but treaties need be made only *under the Authority of the United States.* This raises the question of whether something might be held unconstitutional if done under a delegated power but constitutional if done by treaty. Fortunately, for purposes of illustration, this very question has been considered by the courts.

Missouri v. Holland.—In 1913 Congress enacted a law, basing it upon the commerce power, which forbade the killing of migratory birds except under strict regulation. The legislation was declared unconstitutional by the lower courts on the ground that migratory birds were property of the state, hence not interstate commerce.[1] Thereupon, in 1916, a treaty was entered into with Great Britain whereby both countries agreed to protect migratory birds. Two years later Congress passed a law forbidding the killing, capturing, or selling of birds protected by the treaty except in accordance with regulations set by the Secretary of Agriculture. Missouri brought suit against Holland,[2] a federal game warden, to restrain him from enforcing the law, contending that the measure was an unwarranted invasion of powers reserved to the states. Missouri lost. The treaty dealt with a proper subject, it was made under the authority of the United States, and the statute in question was a necessary and proper means of making the treaty effective. Accordingly, the Federal government may regulate some domestic matter in fulfillment of a treaty which it would be prevented from doing by a statute based upon an enumerated legislative power.

Possibility for Treaty Power to Be Used to Regulate Local Affairs.—Following this decision, many urged that the Federal government make treaties pledging the abolition of child labor. This could be done, it was contended, by stipulating that the contracting parties would prevent the exportation or importation of each other's goods except where they were produced or handled by businesses that did not employ children. This, it was urged, was an appropriate subject for negotiation with other nations, the treaty would be enacted under authority of the United States, and it would violate no expressed prohibition in the Constitution. Though the argument is plausible, the step was never taken. That it was seriously proposed, however, illustrates the potential scope of the treaty power. The doctrine, if carried to its logical conclusion, could be used to justify federal regulation of nearly all domestic matters. Indeed, if Congress could get other governments to cooperate to the extent of making a treaty, the distinction between delegated and reserved powers could be almost entirely obliterated.

This question has assumed new importance since the United States has joined the United Nations. Article I, Section 3, of the UN Charter, for

[1] See p. 305.

[2] Missouri *v.* Holland, 252 U.S. 416 (1920).

example, pledges the United States, along with other members, to promote and encourage ". . . respect for human rights, and fundamental freedoms for all without distinction as to race, sex, language, or religion. . . ." Until now it has been supposed that Congress lacked delegated power to impose penalties upon private parties who show disrespect for human rights and fundamental freedoms. But since Congress has ratified the Charter, does not the logic of the Missouri *v.* Holland decision suggest that Congress can now implement it with legislation that otherwise would be considered beyond the scope of federal power? If Congress should enact a law implementing the Charter and the courts should follow the Missouri *v.* Holland precedent, it would be necessary to examine the other criteria mentioned above. Are human rights and freedoms "proper subjects" for treaty making? Are the treaty provisions "consistent with our institutions" and "the distribution of powers between the General and State Governments"? Do treaty provisions transgress expressly forbidden provisions of the Constitution? Of course, no one can foretell what the Supreme Court might say, but the decision would probably hinge on whether a majority of judges thought state-reserved powers had been impaired. Apprehension over the probable attitude of the Court accounts in part for reluctance on the part of some senators to approve American adherence to such international commitments as the Convention on the Prevention and Punishment of the Crime of Genocide, and the Universal Declaration of Human Rights.

Treaties Not Superior to Statutes.—Treaties and statutes sometimes conflict, in which case the question arises as to which is to be enforced. The question was considered by the Supreme Court in the Head Money Cases, decided in 1884.[1] There Congress had imposed on vessel owners a tax of 50 cents for each alien passenger brought into the United States from foreign ports. Since this conflicted with certain treaties previously entered into, the courts were urged to declare the statute ineffective. The Supreme Court refused to do so, however, with the result that treaties are not superior to statutes; but if they conflict, the one last enacted will be enforced. This, it will be recognized, places power in the hands of Congress to repudiate a solemn treaty whenever sufficient votes can be mustered. This has, in fact, happened on a few occasions with embarrassing results.

International Executive Agreements.—Arrangements with other nations are often made by executive agreements rather than by treaties. Indeed, since 1900 executive agreements have been used more frequently than treaties.[2] They differ from treaties only in that they do not require sen-

[1] 112 U.S. 580.

[2] The following table shows the number of recent treaties and executive agreements, tabulated according to year of publication. The table to 1945 was prepared by John Bassett Moore and printed in an article by Edwin Borchard entitled "The Proposed

atorial approval. The Constitution contains no express recognition of the President's power to make international agreements without the consent of the Senate; his authority to do so must either be granted or implied from acts of Congress or previous treaties, or implied from powers clearly delegated to the President.

Most executive agreements have been made by authority of congressional statutes or treaties. Among these are innumerable postal conventions entered into by authority of legislation dating back to 1792; embargoes upon shipments of munitions to warring South American countries; the much-publicized reciprocal tariff agreements entered into by authority of the Trade Agreements Act of 1934; and agreements entered into with allies under the Lend-Lease Act of 1941.

Others have been implied from constitutional provisions conferring upon the President diplomatic powers, making him Commander in Chief of the Army and Navy and requiring that the laws be faithfully executed. Theodore Roosevelt's *modus vivendi* of 1907 whereby the American government undertook to collect customs for Santo Domingo to ensure payment of obligations owed to foreign bankers is a conspicuous illustration. The armistice of 1918, the resumption of diplomatic relations with Russia in 1933, the agreement to occupy and defend Iceland in 1941, the Atlantic

Constitutional Amendment on Treaty-making," which appeared in *The American Journal of International Law*, vol. 39 (July, 1945), p. 539. Data since 1945 were supplied by the Department of State.

Year of official printing	Treaties	Executive agreements
1930	25	11
1931	13	14
1932	11	16
1933	9	11
1934	14	16
1935	25	10
1936	8	16
1937	15	10
1938	12	24
1939	10	26
1940	12	20
1941	15	31
1942	6	52
1943	4	71
1944	1	74
1945	7	72
1946	14	106
1947	10	111
1948	4	143

Charter Agreement of 1941, the Potsdam Agreement of 1945, are other examples. These are part of the supreme law of the land whether or not later implemented by statute or treaty.[1] Their frequent use, sometimes under circumstances that suggest that the President is deliberately flouting the will of Congress, has given rise to some alarm lest Congress, especially the Senate, be stripped of one of its most cherished prerogatives.[2] Nevertheless, that the President has constitutional authority to make such agreements appears incontestable. He is limited, however, by the realization that as a practical matter public sentiment must approve his conduct and that most agreements of this type cannot be carried out without subsequent congressional approval embodied either in statutes or treaties.

WAR POWERS

Powers Granted to Federal Government.—Foreseeing the possibility that the nation might become embroiled in war, the Constitution gave the national government powers adequate for the occasion. The clear presumption of that document is that the President is to act as commander in chief but that Congress should enact the basic legislation necessary for successful defense and prosecution of wars. Accordingly, more delegated powers contained in Article I, Section 8, relate to national defense and war than to any other single subject. First, Congress is given power to tax and spend money "to provide for the common Defense." Second, Congress is authorized "To declare War, grant Letters of Marque and Reprisal, and make Rules concerning Captures on Land and Water." Third, Congress is empowered "To raise and support Armies" and "To provide and maintain a Navy." After these are created, Congress may "make Rules for the Government and Regulation of the land and naval Forces." Fourth, Congress may "provide for organizing, arming, and disciplining the Militia, and for governing such Part of them as may be employed in the Service of the United States." These are supplemented by the implied-power clause authorizing whatever is necessary and proper for carrying them into execution.

Disarming of States.—While granting broad powers to the central government, the states were forbidden to "keep Troops, or Ships of War in time of Peace" without the consent of Congress, or to "engage in War,

[1] Corwin, *op. cit.*, p. 238; but cf. John M. Mathews, "Executive Agreements," *Encyclopedia of the Social Sciences*, vol. 5, pp. 685–686.

[2] A comprehensive discussion of this subject is contained in Wallace McClure, *International Executive Agreements* (New York: Columbia University Press, 1941). A critical view is expressed by Borchard, *op. cit.*, while opposing points of view are ably argued by Green H. Hackworth and Edwin Borchard in United States Senate, Committee on Commerce, *Hearings on the Great Lakes–St. Lawrence Basin*, 78th Cong., 2d Sess. (Washington: Government Printing Office, 1945).

unless actually invaded, or in such imminent Danger as will not admit of delay." This left the states with power only to maintain a militia for the purpose of preserving order and, under remote circumstances, repelling invasion. But even their control over the militia was rendered tenuous by the provision that Congress might provide for its organization, arms, discipline, and use by the Federal government.

Declaration of War.—Only Congress can "declare" war. A declaration is a formal announcement made, usually, by a joint resolution adopted by at least a majority of both houses and signed by the President. The President may, if he wishes, veto the declaration and, in turn, Congress could pass it over the veto, although these circumstances have never occurred. Typical of declarations is the one adopted after the attack on Pearl Harbor:

PUBLIC LAW 328—77TH CONGRESS

JOINT RESOLUTION

Declaring that a state of war exists between the Imperial Government of Japan and the Government of the people of the United States and making provisions to prosecute the same.

Whereas the Imperial Government of Japan has committed unprovoked acts of war against the Government and the people of the United States of America: Therefore be it

Resolved by the Senate and House of Representatives of the United States of America in Congress assembled, That the state of war between the United States and the Imperial Government of Japan which has thus been thrust upon the United States is hereby formally declared; and the President is hereby authorized and directed to employ the entire naval and military forces of the United States and the resources of the Government to carry on war against the Imperial Government of Japan; and, to bring the conflict to a successful termination, all of the resources of the country are hereby pledged by the Congress of the United States.

Approved, Dec. 8, 1941, 4:10 P.M.[1]

Congress may declare war at any time and against anybody—other than a member state in the Union[2]—although Congress usually waits for a request from the President.

"Executive Wars."—Though only Congress can declare war, *hostilities* may be started by order of the President acting as Commander in Chief without prior congressional approval. Indeed, this has been done seventy-two times within the last 150 years. If the engagement is of a large and serious nature, the President usually asks Congress to declare war imme-

[1] Almost identical declarations were made against Germany and Italy on Dec. 11, 1941, and against Hungary, Rumania, and Bulgaria on the following day.

[2] The Prize Cases, 2 Black 635 (1863). The declaration may be made against a foreign state only. Conflict with member states is treated as insurrection if on a small scale and rebellion if on a large scale.

diately before or after the start of hostilities; but if of a limited or local nature, as when President McKinley dispatched troops to Peking during the Boxer Rebellion in 1900, or when President Wilson ordered troops into Mexico in 1913 to avenge attacks upon Americans, no declaration may be asked for. Indeed, an "executive war," if of small proportions, can be fought from beginning to end without formal declaration by Congress. Even though the President asks Congress to make declaration, circumstances have usually reached such a critical state as to leave Congress with no alternative but to comply. Not until Congress acts, however, do domestic rules and laws of war go into effect. This means that until Congress makes a formal declaration a conflict, however serious, is never legally "war" so far as our laws are concerned.[1]

Controversy Surrounding United Nations Charter.—The United Nations Charter contemplates the use of contingents of armed forces furnished by member nations for the purpose of stopping future aggression. Adherence to the charter raised the question of how far the President could be allowed to go in committing the forces furnished by the United States to participate in conflicts undertaken by the United Nations. Only Congress can declare war. If the President is henceforth to be permitted to send American troops into action in cooperation with others, has the power to declare war not been taken from Congress and given to the President? Does the Constitution not require that congressional approval be first obtained in every instance before American forces are ordered into combat?

These are difficult and serious questions. Proponents of executive discretion cite "executive wars" and other instances where arms have been used by the unilateral action of the President in support of their position.[2] Opponents insist upon the more literal interpretation of the Constitution which appears to contemplate prior congressional approval.[3] In the past the courts have recognized that the President has both the right and the duty to utilize his power as Commander in Chief and authority to see that the laws are faithfully executed, even though this has entailed the use of force, without calling upon Congress for prior approval. It is possible, therefore, that even though Congress were to enact restrictive legislation, a strong-willed President might in some future crisis assert what he deems to be his prerogatives, thus committing the nation to a course leading to

[1] So far as foreign states are concerned, international law permits them to recognize a state of war as existing prior to formal declaration by the contending parties. When this happens, the belligerents are considered to be at war and the international law of war to be applicable to them.

[2] See especially a letter to the editor of *The New York Times*, Nov. 5, 1944, by John W. Davis, *et al.;* also United States Senate, Committee on Foreign Relations, *Hearings, on Charter of United Nations*, 79th Cong., 1st Sess. (Washington: Government Printing Office, 1945), *passim*, but especially pp. 291–301.

[3] *Ibid., passim.*

war and leaving the legal issue to be settled later by the courts and historians.

Controversy Surrounding Atlantic Pact.—The question came dramatically to the fore in 1949 discussions of the North Atlantic Pact.[1] After considerable advance discussion with Senate leaders, the President proposed a treaty with Article V reading as follows:

> The Parties agree that an armed attack against one or more of them in Europe or North America shall be considered an attack against them all; and consequently they agree that, if such an armed attack occurs, each of them, in the exercise of the right of individual or collective self-defense recognized by Article 51 of the Charter of the United Nations, will assist the Party or Parties so attacked *by taking forthwith,* individually and in concert with the other Parties, such action as it deems necessary, *including the use of armed force,* to restore and maintain the security of the North Atlantic Area.[2]

Critics contended that the italicized words could be construed by the President to justify automatic use of force and thereby impair the prerogative of Congress to declare war. Ultimately, Senate approval was given but only after spokesmen for the President and Senate supporters gave repeated assurances that Article V was not to be construed as enlarging executive power or diminishing that of Congress to declare war. In spite of these assurances, a strong President might at some future time act boldly and take his chances on obtaining congressional approval of his "executive war."

Conscription of Man Power.—As noted above, Congress has the power to "raise and support armies" and "provide and maintain a navy." The Constitution also contemplates that the states will recruit and train militias according to a discipline prescribed by Congress. Nowhere does the Constitution state how man power is to be obtained, but Congress is given authority to do what is necessary and proper in order to "raise" and "provide" personnel. Obviously no constitutional difficulty arises as long as the Federal government relies upon volunteers, but serious questions emerge when it resorts to compulsory recruitment. The problem divides itself into conscription during a war or on the eve thereof and conscription for peacetime training.

Wartime Conscription.—Historically, conscription has been looked upon as alien to American ideals and institutions. It was first used during the Civil War but without too great success. It was resorted to again in 1917, after war had been declared; and it was adopted in September, 1940, more than a year before entrance into war. The principal objection on legal

[1] The issues are discussed thoroughly in United States Senate Committee on Foreign Relations: *Hearings on the North Atlantic Treaty,* 81st Cong., 1st Sess. (Washington: Government Printing Office, 3 parts, 1949).

[2] Italics supplied.

grounds has been that forcible enrollment amounted to involuntary servitude and thus violated the Thirteenth Amendment. Upon first glance this contention seems plausible, because under conscription one is compelled against one's wishes to absent oneself from home and render what may be an obnoxious service. There can be no doubt that it is "involuntary," but is it a "servitude"? In a series of cases that arose during the First World War the Supreme Court distinguished between a "servitude" and a "duty" or "fundamental obligation" and upheld the draft.[1] Although questioned several times since, there has been no serious doubt that conscription is constitutional at least during wartime or when the country faces grave danger of war.

Peacetime Conscription.—Although willing to resort to compulsion in the face of war, the thought of permanent conscription, to escape which many people who are now Americans fled from Europe, has been unpalatable. It was adopted more than a year before Pearl Harbor only after strenuous resistance and then only by narrow margins in both houses. When advocated as a permanent policy during and after the recent war, it met with unyielding opposition and its fate remains uncertain.

The principal legal question involved in peacetime is not whether the citizen's rights are violated, but whether the plans envisaged do not amount to federal usurpation of prerogatives reserved to the states. Most plans contemplate a federal draft of all men between the ages of eighteen and twenty-one for a year's training under federal military auspices.[2] But, it is argued,[3] the adult manhood of the nation constitutes the militia whose training is reserved to the states.[4] A strong case is made showing that it was the intent of those who wrote the Constitution that federal forces should be comprised of a small volunteer standing army and navy in peacetime with a citizens' militia under state control and training which could be called into federal service as occasion demanded. Assuming this to be true, the question remains whether the courts would be bound by original intention in the face of modern conditions. In any event, the power to raise and provide an army and navy, when coupled with the

[1] Selective Draft Law Cases, 245 U.S. 366 (1918). See also p. 612.

[2] See also p. 613.

[3] See the testimony of Harrop A. Freeman in United States House of Representatives, Select Committee on Postwar Military Policy, *Universal Military Training, Hearings*, 79th Cong., 1st Sess., pursuant to H. Res. 465 (Washington: Government Printing Office, 2 parts, 1945), part 1, p. 75. The opposing point of view is given in the same document at p. 83.

[4] The pertinent constitutional provision is: "Congress shall have power . . . To provide for organizing, arming, and disciplining, the Militia, and for governing such Part of them as may be employed in the Service of the United States, reserving to the States respectively, *the Appointment of the Officers, and the Authority of training the Militia* according to the discipline prescribed by Congress." Article I, Section 8. Italics supplied.

implied power, establishes a strong presumption in favor of the constitutionality of peacetime conscription as long as the system adopted does not dispossess the states of coordinate authority to officer and train militias. The peacetime conscription act of 1948 has, apparently, not been seriously contested on constitutional grounds.

Conscription of Labor.—Admitting that Congress may draft man power to serve in the Army or work for the government, can a law be enacted compelling civilian workmen to perform labor for private parties who may profit from the labor expended? Does this not amount to involuntary servitude in violation of the Thirteenth Amendment?[1] A general labor draft failed of enactment during the recent war, but severe strictures were placed upon the mobility of labor, the penalties being inability to get other jobs or the threat of reclassification and draft into military service. The War Labor Disputes Act did not make it a crime to discontinue working even in plants that had been seized by the government. Had measures been adopted making it a crime to refuse to work for government or private employers, cases challenging their constitutionality would doubtless have reached the Supreme Court, without which a definitive conclusion is impossible.

There is ample judicial precedent for legislation compelling service on behalf of government,[2] but little in support of legislation compelling workmen to serve private employers. The nearest precedent is found in the case of Robertson *v.* Baldwin.[3] There two seamen who had contracted with a private shipper deserted before completion of the trip. They were apprehended by authority of a federal law dating back to 1790, detained in prison until time for the departure of the ship, and then put back on the ship and compelled to render service until their contract had been fulfilled. The seamen challenged the federal statute, saying they had been compelled to render involuntary servitude in violation of the Thirteenth Amendment. The Supreme Court dismissed the idea that the amendment created a distinction between involuntary servitude for private persons and servitude for governmental agencies. It went on to uphold the statute, however, saying that the amendment was not meant to apply to seamen's contracts because since time immemorial these had been treated as exceptional and had always involved the surrender of a certain amount of personal liberty during the life of the contracts.[4]

[1] For a fuller discussion see United States Senate, Committee on Military Affairs, *National War Service Bill, Hearings*, 78th Cong., 2d Sess., on S. 666 (Washington: Government Printing Office, 3 parts, 1944), part 3, pp. 186*ff*.

[2] Above, p. 138.

[3] 165 U.S. 275 (1896).

[4] Justice Harlan dissented saying: "As to involuntary servitude, it may exist in the United States; but it can only exist lawfully as a punishment for crime of which the party shall have been duly convicted. . . . A condition of enforced service, even for a

According to this decision, whether workmen were forced to labor for the government or for private parties would make no difference. The test would be whether the amendment was intended to apply to the particular employments in which labor was forced. If it could not be shown that historically employment contracts in war industries had been treated as so exceptional as to permit the surrender of a certain amount of personal liberty during the course of the contracts, then a labor draft would be unconstitutional, or the precedent reviewed above would need to be reversed, or the courts would need to evolve some new basis of justification.

Conscription of Property.—If man power can be commandeered, what of property? Here the question is whether private property is taken for public use without just compensation or without due process of law. War measures adopted during the last two major wars authorized seizure of war plants and equipment under certain circumstances, always with the understanding that owners would be recompensed. The power to do so has been upheld and reaffirmed recently in the following words:

> The Constitution grants to Congress power "to raise and support Armies," "to provide and maintain a Navy," and to make all laws necessary and proper to carry these powers into execution. Under this authority Congress can draft men for battle service. . . . Its powers to draft business organizations to support the fighting men who risk their lives can be no less.[1]

Curfews.—In February, 1942, shortly after commencement of war with Japan, the President created certain military areas and zones and authorized commanding military officers to control conduct in and passage to and from the region. Shortly thereafter the entire West coast was declared such a zone and an order was issued requiring every alien German, Italian, and Japanese, and all persons of Japanese ancestry (even though natural-born American citizens) to be in their residences between the hours of 8 P.M. and 6 A.M. Congress subsequently approved these orders and provided criminal penalties for their violation. Martial law was not declared; hence civil courts remained open and available for the trial of offenses. Hirabayashi, a natural-born American citizen of Japanese ancestry, was arrested for violating the curfew and the case ultimately reached the Supreme Court.[2] The court took note of the defendant's citizenship and the obviously discriminatory character of the legislation but proceeded to sustain his conviction on the ground that the war emergency and the large number of persons of Japanese ancestry upon the West

---

limited period, *in the private business of another*, is a condition of involuntary servitude." *Ibid.*, p. 292. Italics supplied.

[1] United States *v.* Bethlehem Steel Corporation, 315 U.S. 289 (1941).

[2] Hirabayashi *v.* United States, 320 U.S. 81 (1942).

coast were sufficient cause to justify the curfew. This sets the stage for curfews applied to all citizens in future emergencies occasioned by war.

Internment of Japanese-Americans.—More drastic still were orders issued early in 1942 evacuating all persons of Japanese ancestry, whether aliens or citizens, from their homes along the West coast. Without making any test of loyalty or possible menace to national safety, all Japanese in the area (approximately 120,000) were compelled to leave, report to control stations, and thereafter live in internment camps administered by the War Relocation Authority, a civilian agency. Evacuation occasioned severe hardship, and life in the camps was anything but congenial, especially for parents accustomed to family life and children. Once in the camps, those whose loyalty was beyond question were permitted to leave as long as they did not return to the West coast area and could find employment or other means of support or educational opportunities in other parts of the country. To its victims the order made the rights of citizenship appear meaningless and called forth severe criticism from large segments of the population.

The drastic action taken during the war was never fully approved by many citizens. Remorse deepened, especially when it appeared that there was no evidence of disloyalty on the part of Japanese-Americans but, rather, countless instances of heroic patriotism. Finally, Congress, in 1948, authorized payment of reparations. Those who had suffered loss were given 18 months in which to submit claims. The Attorney General was authorized to adjudicate and pay claims amounting to $2,500 or less, while claims for larger amounts were to be settled by the Court of Claims.

The Hirabayashi case upheld the curfew without expressly passing upon the constitutionality of evacuation and detention in internment camps. In 1944 a case was brought before the Supreme Court by Korematsu, concededly a loyal American citizen, in which the evacuation program was upheld as justified at the time it was undertaken.[1] About the same time another loyal citizen challenged her detention by writ of habeas corpus.[2] She had been detained for 2 years, first at Tule Lake Relocation Center in California and then at Central Utah Relocation Center. Her citizenship and loyalty were conceded. Without altering approval given to the curfew and evacuation program given in cases previously decided, and without deciding what power the Relocation Authority might have to detain other classes of citizens, the Court ruled that it had no authority to detain loyal citizens like this for a longer period of time. This decision suggests that evacuation and detention, though justified by the war powers during periods of grave national emergency, cannot be prolonged beyond a reasonable time required for separating the loyal from probable saboteurs.

[1] Korematsu *v.* United States, 323 U.S. 214 (1944).

[2] *Ex parte* Endo, 323 U.S. 283 (1944).

Letters of Marque and Reprisal.—The Constitution expressly authorizes Congress "to grant letters of marque and reprisal" and at the same time forbids the states from doing so. When issued to private parties such letters convey authority to seize the bodies or goods of the subjects of an offending state wherever they may be found, until satisfaction is made for the injury.[1] These letters may be granted to citizens or foreigners either in time of peace or of war. They may authorize seizures on land or on water, although in recent times it has become customary to issue them to vessels only. When armed with such letters, private vessels—privateers—become ships of war and may commit acts that would normally be considered piracy.

When prizes are captured by privateers, they must be taken into some port of the country that authorized their capture for adjudication by a prize court. Prior to 1899 American law permitted prizes to be divided between the owner of the vessel making the capture, the captain, and the crew. But in the year mentioned, Congress stipulated that in the future prizes taken should become the property of the American government.

Use of Letters of Marque and Reprisal.—Letters of marque and reprisal were issued oftener in the days of small navies than in recent years. They were granted by the Continental Congress during the Revolutionary War and again during the War of 1812. They were not issued by the North during the Civil War but the Confederacy made considerable use of them. Nor were they issued during the Spanish-American and subsequent wars in which the United States has been engaged. Their use is now generally condemned by international law, although the United States retains the right to use them whenever it chooses to do so.

Armed Merchantmen and Auxiliaries Not Privateers.—Although the American government has not commissioned privateers since 1812, it has on several occasions permitted merchantmen to arm in "self-defense." As long as such weapons are used solely for defense and not for preying upon enemy ships, they do not fall within the category of privateers. The matter was explained by President Jefferson who once said:

> Though she [a merchant vessel] has arms to defend herself in time of war, in the course of her regular commerce, this no more makes her a privateer than a husbandman following his plough, in time of war, with a knife or pistol in his pocket, is thereby made a soldier.[2]

In recent years most nations have spent huge sums toward subsidizing private shipbuilding expecting that in time of war many of these vessels would become naval auxiliaries. When such private vessels are taken over

[1] Joseph Story, *Commentaries on the Constitution of the United States* (Boston: Little, 4th ed., 2 vols., 1873), vol. II, p. 89.

[2] Quoted in John B. Moore, *A Digest of International Law* (Washington: Government Printing Office, 8 vols., 1906), vol. 7, p. 536.

during wartime and used under direct command of the navy or some other department, they are not privateers. In this event, they have lost their private character, hence do not need letters of marque and reprisal.

Rules Governing Captures.—War gives the sovereign the full right to confiscate the property of the enemy wherever found.[1] But unless anarchy is to reign, someone must regulate the circumstances under which property is confiscated. For this reason Congress is empowered to "make rules concerning captures on land and waters." The captures referred to are those of property. Technically, a "capture" can be made only by those possessing letters of marque or reprisal or during war by naval and military authorities. "Seizure" is the word used to describe similar conduct on the part of civil authorities. A vessel or goods captured at sea is called "prize," while goods captured on land is called "booty." Congress has enacted a large body of rules by which captures are to be made and disposed of, but where no statutory provision exists, the rules of international law are followed. Most disputes arising from captures, of which there are many, are settled in United States district courts.

Rules for the Army and Navy.—As noted above, Congress may "make rules for the government and regulation of the land and naval forces." In addition to many general laws respecting the Army and Navy, Congress has enacted special rules by which each of the branches is to be disciplined. Those for the Army are called "Articles of War," while those for the Navy are called "Articles for the Government of the Navy."[2] These apply to all persons in or associated with the armed services and they have the same legal force that nonmilitary law has upon civilians. They make it an offense, for example, for one to desert during war or peace, for an officer to harbor a deserter, for one to be absent without leave, for one to assault and willfully disobey a superior officer, for an officer or soldier during battle to misbehave, run away, or neglect to defend his station, for one to dispose of captured or abandoned property for profit, or for one to commit such common crimes as murder, rape, larceny, and the like. The usual penalty for offenses such as these is death or confinement within a federal (but not a state) penitentiary.[3]

Administration of Rules.—Military rules are administered and enforced by the President acting through the Secretaries of Army, Navy, and Air Force, who, in turn, govern through officers, courts-martial, and courts of

[1] Brown *v.* United States, 8 Cranch 110 (1814).

[2] These may be found in *United States Code, Annotated* (Washington: Government Printing Office, 1941). Those for the Army are found in Title 10; those for the Navy in Title 34.

[3] Those whose sentence is less than a year are seldom confined in penitentiaries, but in guardhouses or barracks provided for the purpose. Those given penitentiary sentences usually serve their terms at the military prison located at Fort Leavenworth, Kans.

inquiry.[1] In the Army,[2] petty offenses may be punished by the commander in charge unless the accused demands a trial by court-martial. Minor offenses committed by most enlisted men (but not by officers, warrant officers, cadets, and other classes exempted by the President) are tried by summary court-martial presided over by one or more individuals. Serious offenses, but not those for which death is a penalty, are tried by special court-martial which may consist of any number of persons but not less than three. The most serious offenses must be tried by general court-martial consisting of not fewer than five persons, one of whom must be a "law member" to insure proper respect for and compliance with legal procedures. As noted below, since 1948 one-third of a court-martial membership may, upon request of an accused enlisted man, be comprised of enlisted men belonging to military units other than the one in which the accused is enrolled.

An attorney (called a "trial judge advocate") is appointed to prosecute every case coming before special and general courts-martial, while counsel for the defense either is appointed or the accused engages his own. Proceedings before summary courts-martial resemble those before civil justices of peace, except that records of proceedings are kept; while proceedings followed by special and general courts-martial resemble those followed in ordinary criminal courts, except that grand and petit juries are never used. The decisions of courts-martial are reviewed by representatives of the Judge Advocate General's office, and in the most serious cases by the President.

For a long time, and especially during and immediately after the last war, many complaints were heard of military justice.[3] Among these were charges that "command" influence was too great, that officers were treated more liberally than enlisted men, that review procedures were "loaded" in favor of commanding officers and courts-martial, that some penalties were excessively severe, and that there was too much opportunity for breach of due process of law. Extensive postwar investigation convinced Congress of the validity of many of these complaints, with the result that corrective legislation was passed in 1948.

Members of Armed Services Subject to Both Military and Civil Law.—Military courts have exclusive jurisdiction over violations of military

[1] Most offenses are dealt with by courts-martial, but courts of inquiry, comprised of three or more officers, may be used in exceptional cases. The procedure is much the same regardless of which method is used.

[2] The rules governing the use of courts-martial are quite similar for both the Army and Navy, although there are notable exceptions. For a detailed description see the Articles for each, cited above.

[3] For a full review see United States House of Representatives Subcommittee of the Armed Services Committee, *Hearings on H.R. 2575 to Amend the Articles of War. . . .* (Washington: Government Printing Office, 1947). See also House of Representatives Armed Service Committee Report No. 1034 on H.R. 2575.

law. Their decisions are conclusive and complete and may ordinarily not be reviewed by civil courts. However, acts committed by members of the armed forces when off duty render them liable to prosecution by both civil and military authorities. When apprehended by civil authorities for breaking the law, they may be proceeded against just as civilians may be, although the responsible commanding officer must be notified. When suspected but not apprehended while off duty, civil authorities are supposed to apply to the responsible officer who is then required to assist in every way possible.[1] Sometimes the same act is both a civil and a military offense, in which case the offender may be tried and punished by both civil and military authorities. Though tried twice for the same *act*, two *offenses* are committed—one against military and the other against civil law—hence the accused is not twice put in jeopardy of life and limb for the *same* offense in violation of the Fifth Amendment.[2]

Martial Law and Its Declaration.—Martial law is the law of necessity. It is sometimes resorted to during grave emergencies when civil authorities fail to maintain law and order. The Constitution nowhere mentions the term. Authority for its use is implied from the power to declare war; to provide for calling forth the militia to execute the laws of the Union, suppress insurrections, and repel invasions; from the President's powers to serve as commander in chief, and to see that the laws of the Union are faithfully executed; and from the obligation imposed upon the Federal government to guarantee to every state protection against domestic violence. Nor does the Constitution expressly state whether the President or Congress is to declare martial law. As matters stand, Congress has delegated broad powers to the President, authorizing him to use such force as he deems necessary to enforce the laws and preserve order. The President is to judge, therefore, when circumstances necessitate resort to this drastic remedy.

Distinction between Martial Law and Mere Use of Troops.—Martial law must be distinguished from the mere use of troops to patrol or to assist the police in maintaining order. Under martial law, a military officer is placed in complete command of a given area, the civil courts of law are closed, and military law and procedure (*i.e.*, trial by courts-martial, etc.) is substituted. But when troops are sent into conflict areas during minor and isolated disturbances, they are usually sent there to aid the civil authorities. In this event they act a role similar to that of deputy sheriffs, doing nothing on their own responsibility; and violators are apprehended in the usual manner and prosecuted before civil courts. "Military law,"

[1] In time of war accused persons are turned over to civil authorities only when the offense is a most serious one.

[2] The same situation sometimes arises when by a single act a person violates both a federal and a state law. See p. 156.

the Supreme Court said on one occasion,[1] "can never exist where the courts are open, and in the proper unobstructed exercise of their jurisdiction."

Instances of Declaration of Martial Law.—Throughout the history of the nation, martial law has never been declared during peacetime, although qualified martial law was twice declared in the period immediately following the First World War,[2] and on innumerable occasions federal troops have been used to maintain order.[3] The most conspicuous instances where martial law has been resorted to by federal authorities occurred in 1814 when, during an attack by the British, General Andrew Jackson placed New Orleans and vicinity under military rule; and again, when President Lincoln placed the Southern and border states under martial law during the Civil War. Martial law was not declared anywhere within the Union during the Mexican, Spanish-American, and First World Wars. During the Second World War, Hawaii was placed under martial law after the attack on Pearl Harbor and remained in that condition during most of the war period. This was drastic action which many thought precipitous and unwarranted,[4] and which the Supreme Court later declared illegal.[5]

Suspension of Writ of Habeas Corpus.—A declaration of martial law is usually accompanied by suspension of the writ of habeas corpus. Authority for doing so is contained in the words, "The Privilege of the Writ of Habeas Corpus shall not be suspended, unless when in Cases of Rebellion or Invasion the public Safety may require it."[6] But who is to determine when the public safety requires the suspension of the writ? The Constitution does not say. Early decisions of the Supreme Court took it for granted that the power of suspension lay with Congress, but during the Civil War Lincoln, upon the advice of his Attorney General, declared that the power lay with him and issued proclamations authorizing the suspension of the writ in places both within and without the area of active hostilities. Lincoln's action was declared illegal by Chief Justice Taney

[1] *Ex parte* Milligan, 4 Wallace 2 (1866).

[2] During a race riot that occurred in Omaha, Neb., in 1919, and during a steel strike at Gary, Ind., in the same year. For a review of these and other instances where federal troops have been used to quell disturbances, see Bennett M. Rich, *The Presidents and Civil Disorder* (Washington: Brookings, 1941).

[3] *Ibid., passim;* Robert S. Rankin, *When Civil Law Fails* (Durham, N.C.: Duke University Press, 1939).

[4] See especially John P. Frank, "Ex parte Milligan *v.* The Five Companies: Martial Law in Hawaii," *Columbia Law Review*, vol. XLIV (September, 1944), no. 5, p. 639; also W. P. Armstrong, "Martial Law in Hawaii," *American Bar Association Journal*, vol. XXIX (December, 1943), p. 698; and two articles by Robert S. Rankin, "Hawaii under Martial Law," *Journal of Politics*, vol. V (August, 1943), p. 270, and "Martial Law and the Writ of Habeas Corpus in Hawaii," *ibid.*, vol. VI (May, 1944), p. 213.

[5] Duncan *v.* Kahanamoku, 327 U.S. 304 (1945). See also p. 151.

[6] Article I, Section 9.

sitting as a circuit judge[1] on the ground that Congress alone possessed the power of suspending the operation of the writ. A short time thereafter, Congress enacted legislation authorizing suspension of the writ and proclamations issued pursuant to this legislation by President Lincoln were subsequently upheld by the Supreme Court.[2]

Thus, the question of whether the President might suspend the writ in the absence of congressional authorization was not definitely settled, nor has it been since. Writers still dispute the point, but the weight of judicial precedent appears to support the contention that the President cannot suspend the writ by virtue of his own authority but must wait for congressional authorization to do so.[3]

Whether the writ may be suspended outside zones of actual military operations is also greatly disputed, but the weight of opinion appears to dictate that the writ should be suspended only in zones of military operations and then only when the civil courts fail to function properly and successfully. Except for the instance that occurred during the Civil War and in Hawaii during the recent war, the writ has never been suspended by the Federal government.[4]

Federal Government and State Militias.—The Constitution contemplates a cooperative, joint control and use of state militias. The obvious theory is that Congress shall prescribe such general rules as are necessary to ensure a militia system with uniform arms and discipline, yet leaving to the states the details of organization, the appointment of officers, and training. Once in existence, Congress is then authorized to provide for calling the militias of the respective states into federal service when occasion demands.[5] When called into federal service, the states lose all jurisdiction. Although Congress provides for calling militias into federal service, the principle is well established that the President alone is the judge of when the call shall be made.

Purposes for Which Militias May Be Used by Federal Government.—The Constitution states that Congress may call the militia into federal service for three purposes: (1) to execute the laws of the union; (2) to suppress insurrections; and (3) to repel invasions. There has been considerable controversy over whether "to repel invasions" authorizes use outside American territory. Although the language used appears to forbid use beyond American borders, the issue is academic, because under present legislation the militia is also the National Guard which becomes a part of

[1] *Ex parte* Merryman, 17 Federal Cases, No. 9487 (1861).

[2] *Ex parte* Milligan, 71 U.S. 2 (1866).

[3] Cf. Rankin, *When Civil Law Fails*, especially pp. 185–191.

[4] For information pertaining to the use of the writ of habeas corpus by the states, see New York State Constitutional Convention Committee, *Problems Relating to Bill of Rights and General Welfare* (Albany: The Committee, 1938), Chap. 4.

[5] Additional details concerning the militia and National Guard are given in Chap. 27.

the regular Army when called into federal service. And, of course, the regular Army can be sent anywhere.

Limitation on the War Powers.—Only one restriction on the war powers is explicitly stated, but others are implied. The expressed limitation is that no appropriation of money "to raise and support armies" shall be for longer than 2 years. This was copied from the British law at the time, which, however, limited appropriations to 1 year. Note that the restriction applies to "armies" and is not repeated in the following phrase which authorizes creation of a navy. The restriction prevents the appropriation of permanent funds for the Army and gives every congressman, particularly every member of the House of Representatives whose term, it will be recalled, is for 2 years, an opportunity of scrutinizing the organization and policies of the military. By this means, the Constitution expects that the Army will be kept in complete subordination to the civil branches of government.

Implied Limitations.—The implied limitations are the same for the war powers as for others contained in the Constitution. Even in wartime Congress may not delegate its lawmaking functions to the President, the courts continue their review of acts of Congress and the President, the federal system remains, and private rights remain inviolate. This statement may seem incorrect to one who looks out upon a total war effort; but it is nevertheless true—at least from a legal point of view. The point is that the war powers, like others, are plenary and may be exercised to the full. Because those powers lie dormant much of the time, no one knows their full import until war occurs, and then what they mean must be rediscovered in the light of the intensity of an emergency. Their use doubtless has a profound impact upon society and institutions, but because of this their existence cannot be denied. Nevertheless, if the Constitution is to have any meaning at all, the war powers must be exercised within the framework of traditional political institutions. "No doctrine," said former Justice Davis, "involving more pernicious consequences, was ever invented by the wit of man than that any of its [the Constitution's] provisions can be suspended during any of the great exigencies of government. Such a doctrine leads directly to anarchy or despotism. . . ."[1]

References

BALDINGER, MILTON I.: *The Constitutionality and Operation of Certain Phases of the Selective Service System* (Washington: The Georgetown School of Law, 1941).

BERDAHL, CLARENCE A.: *The War Powers of the Executive in the United States* (Urbana: University of Illinois Press, 1921).

BINKLEY, WILFRED E.: *The Powers of the President* (New York: Doubleday, 1937).

BURDICK, CHARLES K.: *The Law of the American Constitution; Its Origin and Development* (New York: Putnam, 1922).

[1] *Ex parte* Milligan, 4 Wallace 2 (1866).

COLEGROVE, KENNETH W.: *American Senate and World Peace* (New York: Vanguard, 1944).

CORWIN, EDWARD S.: *The President's Control of Foreign Relations* (Princeton, N.J.: Princeton University Press, 1917).

——— *The President, Office and Powers* (New York: New York University Press, 1940).

——— *The Twilight of the Supreme Court* (New Haven: Yale University Press, 1934).

——— *Constitution and World Organization* (Princeton, N.J.: Princeton University Press, 1944).

FAIRMAN, CHARLES: *Mr. Justice Miller and the Supreme Court 1862–1890* (Cambridge, Mass.: Harvard University Press, 1939).

HACKWORTH, GREEN H.: *Digest of International Law* (Washington: Government Printing Office, 8 vols., 1940–1944).

LEIGHTON, ALEXANDER H.: *Governing of Men; General Principles and Recommendations Based on Experience at a Japanese Relocation Camp* (Princeton, N.J.: Princeton University Press, 1945).

LIPPMANN, WALTER: *United States Foreign Policy: Shield of the Republic* (Boston: Little, 1943).

MCCLURE, WALLACE: *International Executive Agreements* (New York: Columbia University Press, 1941).

MATHEWS, JOHN M.: *American Foreign Relations, Conduct and Policies* (New York: Appleton-Century, rev. and enl. ed., 1938).

MILTON, GEORGE F.: *The Use of Presidential Power, 1789–1943* (Boston: Little, 1944).

MOORE, JOHN BASSETT: *A Digest of International Law* (Washington: Government Printing Office, 8 vols., 1906).

RANKIN, ROBERT S.: *When Civil Law Fails* (Durham, N.C.: Duke University Press, 1939).

RICH, BENNETT M.: *The Presidents and Civil Disorder* (Washington: Brookings, 1941).

STETTINIUS, EDWARD R., JR.: *Lend-lease, Weapon for Victory* (New York: Macmillan, 1944).

STORY, JOSEPH: *Commentaries on the Constitution of the United States* (Boston: Little, 4th ed., 2 vols., 1873).

TAFT, WILLIAM H.: *Our Chief Magistrate and His Powers* (New York: Columbia University Press, 1916).

UNITED STATES SENATE: *The Constitution of the United States of America* (annotated). Sen. Doc. 232, 74th Cong., 2d Sess. (Washington: Government Printing Office, 1938).

VAN ALSTYNE, RICHARD W.: *American Diplomacy in Action* (Stanford: Stanford University Press, 1944).

WILLOUGHBY, WESTEL W.: *The Constitutional Law of the United States* (New York: Baker, Voorhis, 2d ed., 3 vols., 1929).

WRIGHT, QUINCY: *The Study of War* (Chicago: University of Chicago Press, 2 vols., 1942).

Chapter 20

FEDERAL POWERS—ADMIRALTY, POSTAL, AND OTHERS

> The power of establishing post-roads must, in every view, be a harmless power. . . .
>
> James Madison, *The Federalist*, No. 42.[1]

THE ADMIRALTY AND MARITIME POWER

Power Not Granted Directly.—Admiralty and maritime law pertains to ships upon navigable waters. Because of the close relationship of admiralty and maritime matters to international affairs generally and to interstate and foreign commerce in particular, those who wrote the Constitution gave the Federal government complete jurisdiction over the subject. Oddly enough, this authority is not enumerated among the delegated powers contained in Section 8. Instead it is derived from words found in the Judicial Article, which say:

> The judicial Power of the United States shall be vested in one supreme Court and in such inferior Courts as the Congress may from time to time ordain and establish. . . . The judicial Power shall extend . . . to all Cases of admiralty and maritime Jurisdiction. . . .

Though this is not a direct grant of power, Congress has acted as if it were. This assumption has been repeatedly approved by the courts.[2]

Scope of the Power.—To come within the scope of the admiralty power, two conditions must be met. The first is that *vessels* must be involved in one way or another. To illustrate: a collision between two houses torn loose from their foundations in a flood and floating on a river is not within the admiralty jurisdiction, but two canal boats colliding in the same waters would be. An old steamboat, stripped of its boilers, engines, and paddle wheels and used along the edge of the water as a saloon and hotel is not, the courts have held, a "vessel," hence does not come within the scope of admiralty law. A hydroplane while afloat upon waters capable of navigation has been held to be a "vessel," but a landplane that travels over the same waters would not be. Admiralty extends to ships within ports, but not to shore structures. The second condition is that waters concerned must be *navigable* or capable of being used for purposes of navigation. The

[1] (New York: Modern Library, 1941).

[2] For an excellent and comprehensive treatment of the subject, consult Gustavus H. Robinson, *Handbook of Admiralty Law in the United States* (St. Paul, Minn.: West, 1939).

size of the stream is immaterial, nor is the size of the ship a determining factor, although the power would not extend to every little stream capable of floating a casual fishing boat or hunting canoe. Rather, the waters may be said to be navigable if they are capable of common use by ships for purposes of trade.

The admiralty and maritime power grants authority to regulate virtually all sizable bodies of water within the country, territorial waters, American vessels wherever they may be, and, indeed, to prescribe rules by which foreign vessels sailing on the high seas, or for that matter, in foreign territorial waters, may adjudicate their disputes in American courts.

Admiralty and Commerce Powers Distinguished.—Care should be taken not to confuse the admiralty and maritime power with that over interstate and foreign commerce. The former extends only to vessels, officers, crew, cargo, and passengers; while the latter extends to all forms of intercourse and appurtenances thereto—radio, marine cables, travel by landplanes, shore structures such as bridges, docks, wharves, dikes, and the like. Furthermore, the admiralty power, but not the commerce, extends to all navigable waters within the United States though completely within a single state and used for carrying nothing to or from other states. Moreover, the commerce power cannot be made to apply to foreign ships on the high seas or in non-American territorial waters, while the admiralty power can. Congress can permit and prescribe rules for the settlement of disputes involving foreign vessels in such waters.

Importance of the Power.—The admiralty power has given rise to a large amount of important legislation and litigation. Congress has prescribed a large body of rules to be applied when private parties wish to settle controversies over such matters as contracts and torts arising from the ownership and operation of vessels.[1] Moreover, Congress has enacted a number of criminal statutes applicable to vessels.[2] These make it a crime, for example, for American ships to fail to register; for ships to be unseaworthy; for offenses such as murder, larceny, assault, and the like to be committed on board vessel; for ships to sail with insufficient crew and improper documents; and for shipping companies to fail to respect customs and immigration regulations. United States district courts have been made the primary courts of admiralty, having been given exclusive original jurisdiction over such matters. It is interesting to note that the bulk of all admiralty cases originates in district courts located in or about New York City.

[1] These may be consulted in *United States Code, Annotated* (Washington: Government Printing Office), particularly Title 28, following Section 723. But see index under "Admiralty" for other citations. Where no statutory provision exists the rules of international law apply.

[2] *Ibid.*

THE POSTAL POWER

Authority of Federal Government to Establish Its Own Post Offices and Roads.—The Constitution gave Congress the power "to establish Post Offices and post Roads." Immediately the question arose as to whether the Federal government could build its own offices and roads, or whether it was required to use only such buildings and roads as the states were willing to designate. As usual, the nationalists won, with the result that Congress may either use, lease, or buy such state facilities as are available, or proceed with the construction of its own.[1]

As matters have worked out, most post offices are located in buildings that are leased or rented, although an increasing number are federally owned. At the same time the mail is carried chiefly by privately owned rail, bus, water, and air lines and delivered over state, county, city, and township roads. State permission must be obtained for the use of existing roads, and the Federal government has followed the practice of doing so. Little difficulty has been encountered at this point inasmuch as the state stands to benefit greatly from it and the Federal government has generously contributed financial support for the building and maintenance of state highways.[2] Should the states refuse permission, the Federal government might buy an existing road or purchase the necessary land and build one.

Possession by Federal Government of Monopoly over Postal Service.—The power to establish post offices and roads is granted exclusively to the Federal government. Though the states have never sought to compete, private parties have from time to time, with the result that legislation has been enacted prohibiting anyone else from conveying or delivering letters (but not packages) by regular trips or at stated periods over post routes. This does not prevent institutions from establishing their own service for communicating by letter with employees in various parts of their own institutions. It would, however, prevent them from carrying letters to persons not connected with their institutions. Thus, a business firm cannot regularly either deliver "letters" itself to the homes of its customers nor can it engage anyone to do so other than United States postal employees.

Postal Power for Regulation.—The postal power, like others, may be used for purposes that are, on their face at least, incidental to their primary purpose. Congress has enacted a number of laws, the principal purpose of which is to protect the public from fraud, immorality, or something else deemed inimical to the public welfare. These, it is frequently contended,

[1] There has been much controversy over this point. For a brilliant review of the argument, see Joseph Story, *Commentaries on the Constitution of the United States* (Boston: Little, 4th ed., 2 vols., 1873), vol. II, pp. 58–77.

[2] See p. 633.

amount to usurpation of state powers in violation of the Tenth Amendment, but the courts have held otherwise. The power to establish a postal service, said the courts, also conveys authority to determine what mail would be carried and how. Accordingly, Congress excludes from the mails such things as poisons of all kinds, including poisonous animals, insects, and reptiles, explosives, inflammable materials, infernal machines, disease germs or scabs, obscene literature (including that calculated to inform persons about contraception and abortion), lotteries, and writings calculated to produce sedition or to incite to murder or arson. The theory upon which such legislation is based is that the postal power may properly be used to remedy evils spread or perpetuated by use of the mails.

Recent Use of Postal Power for Regulation.—During the depression Congress went further than ever before in using the postal power for purposes of regulation. The Securities Act of 1933, the Securities and Exchange Act of 1934, and the Public Utility Holding Company Act of 1935 were all based in part on this authority. The first two forbid the use of the mails for the purpose of selling or dealing in the securities of large corporations unless the securities are first registered by the Securities and Exchange Commission. The third forbids electric and natural-gas holding companies to use the mails except when they have registered and are conducting their affairs in accordance with the act. These are far-reaching and drastic measures, imposing a type of restraint which many supposed lay within the scope of reserved powers of the states. But their constitutionality has been upheld.[1] Here, again, the theory is that Congress may determine what is to circulate in the mails and eliminate whatever in its judgment is deceptive, fraudulent, or otherwise detrimental to the public welfare. Many oppose this doctrine, fearing that it may lead to the condition where Congress could regulate anything, regardless of how local in nature, by the mere expedient of exclusion from the mails. The tendency may have been checked by the broadened interpretation of the commerce power made since 1937.[2]

States and the Postal Service.—Whether the postal power is exclusive or concurrent has long been disputed. Had Congress failed to establish a postal service, the states might have established their own without question; but since Congress has acted, their sphere of activity is limited indeed. Such legislation as they may now enact must in no way compete or conflict with the federal service.

Because post offices and post roads are usually situated within one state or another, state legislation inevitably affects them. The point at which

[1] Jones *v.* Securities and Exchange Commission, 298 U.S. 1 (1936); Wright *v.* Securities and Exchange Commission, CCA 1940, 112 F. 2d 89; Detroit Edison Co. *v.* Securities and Exchange Commission, CCA 1941, 119 F. 2d 730.

[2] See pp. 390.

the affection is objectionable depends largely upon circumstances. States may not, for example, force drivers of postal vehicles to obtain drivers' licenses or accident insurance; they may not require mail trains to make unreasonable stops or deviations from their routes; they may not tax automobiles and essential supplies used exclusively in the postal services; they may not force a mail wagon to stop for the payment of tolls; and, although states might stop a mail carrier to serve him with a lien of execution (because to stop him is not necessarily to detain him), horses used to carry the mails could not be seized in execution of the lien.

On the other hand, states may (since 1939) tax the income of postal employees; arrest and detain a mail carrier for murder; punish a mail carrier for driving recklessly through crowded streets; require mail trains to travel at moderate speeds through city limits even though the mails may be delayed thereby. Moreover, states may pronounce criminal conduct pertaining intimately to the mails. They may, for example, convict one for highway robbery even though the person robbed the mails. Or a state might proceed against one for making intimidating threats, even though the threats may have been sent through the mail. Extortion might be punishable under state law, while the sending of an extortionate message through the mails might also be a federal crime. The question in each instance is whether, and to what extent state law unreasonably burdens or impedes operation of a federal agency or statute.

The Postal Power and Private Rights.—The rights guaranteed by the Constitution stand inviolate before the postal just as before other powers. Those most frequently involved in controversy are freedom of speech and press, and the provision in the Fourth Amendment which says that "The right of the people to be secure in their persons, houses, papers, and effects, against unreasonable searches and seizures, shall not be violated. . . ."

Freedom of Speech and Press.—Whenever federal authorities place any restrictions upon the content of mailable matter, freedom of speech and press are inhibited. And yet, as has been observed, postal authorities may exclude obscene literature, objectionable advertising, writings calculated to incite to crime, and matter advocating or urging treason, insurrection, or forcible resistance to any law of the United States. How can this be? To answer, it is necessary to recall that private rights are never absolute but must be reconciled with the exercise of powers granted by the body politic.[1] While liberty is to be presumed, this does not justify license; hence the lawmakers may proscribe what they deem injurious to the public peace and welfare. Under this formula the only hope that rights will not be emasculated lies in an alert public opinion, frequent elections, checks, and balances.

While most persons accept this understanding, many criticize the method

[1] Cf. p. 128.

by which the law is enforced.[1] Using the mails to circulate nonmailable matter is usually a crime triable before federal courts in the customary manner. But in a majority of instances criminal prosecution does not ensue; instead, objectionable mail is banned by administrative order, thereby virtually driving offenders out of business.[2] Such orders are issued by the Postmaster General after investigation. He is both judge and jury and may even issue his orders without affording a hearing. His findings of facts are final though an appeal may be taken to the courts for a review of the law and determination of sufficiency of the evidence.

Complaint is heard that the Postmaster General has been given too much power and that the procedure leads to arbitrary deprivation of freedom of speech and press. This criticism was especially pronounced during the First World War when the Postmaster General withdrew second-class privileges of a number of publications for criticisms of the war and its conduct. Among these were the *Masses*, the *Nation*, the *Milwaukee Leader*, Latzko's *Men in War*, Lenin's *Soviets at Work*, and Veblen's *Imperial Germany and the Industrial Revolution.* Despite widespread criticism, the law remains unchanged. Among the more recent actions were those banning *Esquire* and *Police Gazette* for alleged obscenity, and a pamphlet by Dr. Paul Popenoe entitled "Preparing for Marriage" for too frank discussion of sex. While the courts have upheld nearly all such orders, they occasionally call a halt, as was illustrated by the recent case involving *Esquire.* Here the Postmaster General based his action not only on alleged obscenity but also on the ground that the magazine was not of "a public character contributing to the arts, literature and sciences." For this he was strongly rebuked by a unanimous Circuit Court of Appeals, and later by the Supreme Court.

Unreasonable Searches and Seizures.—One's mail is among the "papers" and "effects" that may not be unreasonably searched and seized. Accordingly, unless the sender gives consent, no letter, publication, or package sent through the mail can be opened without a search warrant. This is never done by local postal employees. Instead, postmasters forward mail suspected of being unmailable to the dead-letter office. Thereupon, some duly authorized employee goes before a United States commissioner or district judge, describes the mail to be searched and seized, and presents

[1] The best statement of the critics is found in Zechariah Chafee, *Free Speech in the United States* (Cambridge, Mass.: Harvard University Press, 1941), *passim.*

[2] In the case of mail concerning lotteries and the like, "fraud orders" are issued, which have the effect of returning the mail to its sender or to the dead-letter office. But in the case of newspapers and magazines to which objection is made on grounds other than fraud, they are either rejected when mailed or the permit which entitles them to second-class postal rates is withdrawn. The latter is a serious penalty inasmuch as second-class rates are from eight to fifteen times lower than third-class, which they would henceforth find it necessary to pay. *Ibid.*, p. 302.

evidence to justify his suspicion. If the warrant is issued, the matter is turned over to the Post Office inspection service for further investigation, then to the solicitor, who, in turn, presents the case to the appropriate district attorney for prosecution.

STANDARDS FOR WEIGHTS AND MEASURES

Scope of the Power.[1]—Another power granted to Congress is that of fixing the "standard of weights and measures." This obviously meant that Congress might define standards of weight, length, capacity, and area; but it was not clear what else might be done. Some argued that the Federal government might "fix" standards but could not police them. Although the task of policing has been left largely to the states, there can now be no doubt but that the Federal government may do so if it wishes. Recently the question has arisen as to whether the weights-and-measures clause might also justify federal legislation fixing standards of *quality* and *identity* as well as of weight, length, capacity, and area. At present such standards are fixed only for products bought by governmental agencies for their own use and for products (mostly agricultural) entering interstate commerce.[2] Their constitutional basis is, therefore, the proprietary and commerce powers. But if the weights-and-measures clause can be stretched to include standards of identity and quality, then Congress could enact legislation requiring *all* products, whether or not used by governmental agencies or entering interstate commerce, to comply with uniform rules governing such matters as purity, quality, classification, and labeling. Since Congress has not yet gone so far, the question is largely academic, but it may someday become the subject of heated controversy.

States and Weights and Measures.—The power to fix weights and measures is a concurrent one in the sense that the states may legislate until the time Congress does and afterward they may do whatever is not inconsistent with federal law. The states assumed nearly full responsibility until 1838. Later most of them made the English and metric systems as well as the other standards specifically fixed by Congress part of state law. In addition, states have fixed standards for a number of items with which Congress has not as yet concerned itself. These may, and sometimes do, vary. For example, a ton is 2,000 pounds in some states but 2,240 pounds in others. In Wisconsin a bushel of onions is 50 pounds, but in Idaho it is 57 pounds. In Texas a bushel of sweet potatoes is 50 pounds, while in Florida it is 56 pounds. In the case of greens (mustard,

[1] See p. 638 for a full discussion of the Bureau of Standards and legislation dealing with weights and measures.

[2] See p. 639.

spinach, turnip tops, etc.), a bushel varies from 10 pounds in North Carolina to 30 pounds in Alabama.[1]

THE BANKRUPTCY POWER

A Concurrent Power.—Another power delegated to Congress is that of establishing "uniform Laws on the subject of Bankruptcies throughout the United States."[2] The clause clearly implies that the power is a concurrent one. Like other powers of this type, the states may continue their laws until such time as Congress decides to bring about uniformity. When Congress does legislate, state laws that are in conflict are suspended, but those not in conflict remain in effect. If Congress should repeal its provisions, as it did on three occasions during the nineteenth century, then the state laws could once more be enforced without reenactment. Federal law is now so complete and comprehensive that it leaves little room for state matters, although there are important instances where state insolvency laws still apply.[3]

The depression that followed 1929 brought an avalanche of business failures, causing Congress to enact liberalizing amendments including special provisions for farmers, railroads, municipalities, and certain other private corporations. Two of these ran afoul of the courts, throwing interesting light on the scope of the bankruptcy power.

Farm Mortgage Moratorium Legislation.—The first was the famed Frazier-Lemke Act, passed in the closing days of the Seventy-third Congress (June, 1934) following a filibuster conducted by Senator Huey Long of Louisiana. This measure sought to relieve farm debtors by granting an extension of time during which they might pay off farm mortgages, and by permitting farmers to obtain clear title by paying what the farm was worth during the depression rather than the face value of the mortgage. In the case of a person named Radford, a Kentucky farmer,[4] the legislation would have permitted him to settle for $4,445 rather than $9,205.09 claimed by his creditors. In a unanimous opinion, the Supreme Court ruled that the law deprived creditors of property without due process of law in violation of the Fifth Amendment.[5] Though the Court had upheld state mortgage moratorium legislation[6] and intimated that Congress might also act to stay farm foreclosures, it insisted that no legislation could act

[1] Harold D. Koontz, *Government Control of Business* (Boston: Houghton, 1941), p. 801.

[2] The clause also grants power to "establish a uniform rule of naturalization." Since this subject is discussed in Chap. 8, it is omitted here.

[3] See p. 647 for a discussion of legislation.

[4] Louisville Joint Stock Land Bank *v.* Radford, 295 U.S. 555 (1935).

[5] *Ibid.*

[6] Home Building & Loan Association *v.* Blaisdell. 290 U.S. 398 (1934).

to impair the right of mortgagors to either the full value of the mortgage or the property itself.

Following this decision, Congress without a dissenting vote adopted a new Frazier-Lemke Act,[1] designed to meet the objections of the Court. This measure permitted a district court to declare an emergency in its locality for a limited time and then to declare a 3-year mortgage moratorium. During the interim, the property was under supervision of the court, the farm debtor was obliged to pay a reasonable rental, and at the end of 3 years (or sooner at the discretion of the court) the mortgagor could either demand payment or take possession of the property. This new measure met with the unanimous approval of the Supreme Court.[2]

Reorganization of Municipal Indebtedness.—To relieve local governments suffering from tax delinquencies[3] following the collapse of 1929, Congress amended the Nelson Act by providing that municipal corporations and other political subdivisions of states might voluntarily apply to federal courts of bankruptcy to effect a readjustment of their debts.[4] Under court supervision, debts might be scaled down, compromised, or repudiated, without the surrender of any property on the part of the local government, if approved initially by creditors holding 30 per cent, and finally by those holding 66⅔ per cent of the indebtedness.

Though no objection was made to the plan of reorganization itself, a majority of the Court declared the legislation to be an unconstitutional interference on the part of the Federal government with agencies of the state.[5] If the obligations of local governments, said the court, may be subjected to revision under federal law, the states and their political subdivisions are no longer free to manage their own affairs. The minority thought this contention untenable inasmuch as local governments could proceed only when they wished to do so and then only when the state government to which they owed their creation had previously given them permission. "To hold," said Justice Cardozo, "that this purpose [reorganization of indebtedness] must be thwarted by the courts because of a supposed affront to the dignity of the state, though the state disclaims the affront and is doing all it can to keep the law alive, is to make dignity a doubtful blessing." Essentially the same provisions were reenacted in 1937 and incorporated in the Chandler Act of 1938. When tested, the

[1] This became a part of the Chandler Act of 1938, *United States Code, Annotated*, Title 11, Chap. 8.

[2] Wright *v.* Vinton Branch of the Mountain Trust Bank of Roanoke *et al.*, 300 U.S. 440 (1937).

[3] In January, 1934, 2,019 municipalities, counties, and other governmental units were known to be in default of over a billion dollars.

[4] *United States Code, Annotated*, Title 11, Chap. 9.

[5] Ashton *v.* Cameron County Water Improvement District, 298 U.S. 513 (1935). The decision was 6 to 3 with Justices Cardozo, Brandeis, and Stone dissenting.

Supreme Court,[1] whose personnel had changed in the meantime, approved the legislation,[2] thus modifying, if not reversing, its former decision. In consequence, state political subdivisions may now reorganize their indebtedness under federal bankruptcy laws.

PATENT AND COPYRIGHT POWER

An Exclusive Power.—From the seventeenth century onward it has been customary in England and the United States to grant monopolies for limited times to inventors and authors as a reward for their genius, talent, and enterprise. Borrowing from English experience, the Constitution provides that "Congress shall have Power . . . to promote the Progress of Science and useful Arts by securing for limited Times to Authors and Inventors the exclusive Right to their respective Writings and Discoveries." This power is one granted exclusively to Congress. The states were deprived of all authority over the subject in order to guarantee that inventors and authors would not be subjected to the varying laws of different states whose governments might even go so far as to discriminate deliberately in favor of their own residents.

Scope of the Power.—The phrase "to promote the progress of science and useful arts" does not convey power to do whatever Congress wishes in order to advance science and the arts. Rather, the phrase merely states the purpose for which patents and copyrights may be issued. Note also that patents and copyrights can be granted for "limited times" only. This prevents monopolies in perpetuity; although it does not prevent renewals for limited times.

Patents must be issued to "inventors" and copyrights to "authors"—not to anyone else, other than bona fide heirs and assigns. Furthermore, patents can be issued only for "discoveries" and copyrights for "writings." To be the former, it must be a new and useful creation or contrivance discovered by intellectual labor. This definition precludes obtaining a patent for merely an ingenious readjustment of existing devices; nor could one patent something found, stolen, or given to him. To be a "writing" the production must be an original, meritorious work of literature or art created by intellectual labor and published for public use. This would include books, newspapers, paintings, motion-picture films, songs, and even private letters; but it would not include prints, labels, trade-marks,[3]

[1] United States *v.* Bekins, 304 U.S. 27 (1937).

[2] The vote was 6 to 2. Justice Cardozo did not participate because of illness. Justices McReynolds and Butler were the two dissenters.

[3] The Federal government permits the registration of trade-marks for products of interstate commerce, but this is done pursuant to the commerce rather than the copyright power. See p. 645.

ideas expressed in a copyrighted book, titles of books, and songs, the news itself, or the mere publication of statutes of a state or ordinances of a city.[1]

State Authority over Patents and Copyrights.—Since the power to issue patents and copyrights is granted exclusively to the Federal government, the states have never tried to do this since the adoption of the Constitution. They have, however, imposed a number of regulations upon the use of patented and copyrighted articles. Some have been upheld, others have not. In general, the rule is that state laws are permissible if enacted pursuant to some reserved power, if they are reasonably necessary and nondiscriminatory, and if they do not impair substantive rights conveyed by the Federal government to inventors and authors. Thus, a patent right itself cannot be taxed by a state, but patented articles may be if the tax is not levied simply because the articles are patented. States may prescribe precautionary regulations as to how such things as explosives, medicines, food, and drugs, though patented, might be manufactured, transported, and sold as long as such regulations are in fact adopted to protect the public and not, for example, to discriminate against nonresident patent holders. States might prohibit the showing of a motion picture, even though copyrighted, if deemed to be obscene; or the sale of a magazine, though copyrighted, if vulgar; or the making of a contract on the part of a patent holder to dictate the resale price of a patented article, if this was deemed necessary to avoid monopoly.

THE PROPRIETARY POWER

The Proprietary Power.—The Federal government is a proprietor in the sense that it may acquire, hold, and dispose of property, enter into contracts, hire, manage, and discharge its employees, and in general, conduct its affairs. Though ample authority for the exercise of functions such as these is contained in the implied clause, additional authorization is conveyed in the words "Congress shall have Power to dispose of and make all needful Rules and Regulations respecting Territory or other Property belonging to the United States. . . ."[2] In addition to its use for general functions, Congress has recently used this power for the attainment of purposes of a highly controversial nature.

Use of Power to Justify TVA "Yardstick."—In 1935 the Tennessee Valley Authority Act was passed.[3] Its operation of Wilson Dam, at Muscle Shoals, included among other things the generation of electricity for its own use and transmission and sale of the surplus in surrounding territory. To dispose of the surplus, an energetic campaign was waged

[1] Federal legislation is discussed on p. 646.

[2] Article IV, Section 3.

[3] This legislation is fully discussed on p. 715.

to induce farmers to form cooperatives and municipalities to acquire their own distribution systems, after which electricity would be sold to them by TVA at wholesale rates thereafter to be disposed of to ultimate consumers at rates considerably lower than formerly prevailed. The purpose was not only to dispose of a surplus, but also to measure the cost of distributing electricity to farmers and residential users. Private utilities fought the program every step of the way claiming, among other things, that the Federal government lacked constitutional authority to dispose of surplus electricity in such a way as to threaten their business and bring them under federal regulation rather than state.

The controversy reached the Supreme Court in 1936.[1] The Court found[2] the building of the dam, which had been begun during the First World War, a legitimate exercise of the war power, and other operations on the river a legitimate exercise of the power over interstate commerce. As for the disposal of surplus electricity, the Court pointed out that the electricity was property of the United States constitutionally acquired and that the Constitution expressly authorized Congress "to dispose of and make all needful rules and regulations respecting . . . property belonging to the United States." The operations of TVA were, therefore, sustained. The program has since been greatly expanded in the vicinity of the Tennessee River and extended to other parts of the nation as well, with the result that Congress has discovered a highly effective weapon with which to regulate private enterprise, the affairs of which had previously been beyond its reach.

Use of Power to Justify Wage-and-hour Regulation.—The proprietary power was again used to justify the Walsh-Healy Act of 1936. This act requires that all those who contract with agencies of the Federal government for materials the value of which exceeds $10,000 shall not work employees more than 8 hours a day or 40 hours a week; that they will pay prevailing wage rates in the industry; and that they will not employ males under sixteen nor females under eighteen in the making of materials for the government. Thousands of contracts have been entered into, especially after the entrance of the United States into the Second World War, the provisions of which dictate labor regulations involving millions of employees and many employers. Though there was never much doubt about the constitutionality of this use of the proprietary power, the legislation was reviewed in 1940,[3] whereupon the Supreme Court observed that "Like private individuals and businesses, the Government enjoys the unrestricted right to produce its own supplies, to determine those with whom it will deal, and to fix the terms and conditions upon which it will

[1] Ashwander *v.* Tennessee Valley Authority *et al.*, 297 U.S. 288.

[2] The division was 8 to 1, Justice McReynolds being the lone dissenter.

[3] Perkins *v.* Lukens Steel Company, 310 U.S. 113.

make needed purchases." Since this legislation applies to all producers, whether engaged in interstate commerce or not, Congress has discovered an additional device for subjecting persons hitherto beyond its reach to federal control.

POWER TO ACQUIRE AND GOVERN TERRITORIES

The Power to Acquire Territories.—Authority to acquire territory from foreign states is implied from the war and treaty powers; authority to acquire unclaimed territory by discovery is inherent in the fact that the United States is a sovereign nation; while authority to acquire territory within existing territorial limits of the United States is both implied from the spending power and the two provisions noted below conferring power to govern territories. The Constitution assumes that where territory is acquired within the forty-eight states, it will either be ceded by the states or purchased from the states or private parties.

The Power to Govern Territories.—Authority to govern territories is expressly conferred in two sections of the Constitution. The first says Congress shall have power

> to exercise exclusive Legislation in all Cases whatever, over such District (not exceeding ten miles square) as may, by Cession of particular States, and the Acceptance of Congress, become the Seat of the Government of the United States, and to exercise like Authority over all Places purchased by the Consent of the Legislature of the State in which the Same shall be, for the Erection of Forts, Magazines, Arsenals, dock-Yards, and other needful Buildings. . . .[1]

The second provision, previously quoted, says that "Congress shall have power to dispose of and make all needful rules and regulations respecting the Territory . . . belonging to the United States."[2]

Scope of Federal Power over Its Territories.—Congress has exclusive jurisdiction over territories outside the forty-eight states, as in Alaska, Hawaii, and Puerto Rico. The same is true for the District of Columbia inasmuch as the state that formerly owned the area ceded it to the United States. But the extent of federal authority over places owned *within* the states is not so clear. The question is of considerable importance when one realizes that the Federal government owns hundreds of places such as prison camps, old soldiers' homes, army camps, shipyards, arsenals, post offices, and public lands. In every instance it becomes necessary to determine whether federal or state law applies.

The only thing said about the subject in the Constitution is contained in the provision, quoted in full above, which says that Congress shall have

[1] Article I, Section 8.
[2] Article IV, Section 3.

power "to exercise like [*i.e.*, exclusive] authority over *all places purchased by the consent of the legislature of the state in which the same shall be*, for the erection of forts, magazines, arsenals, dock-yards, and other needful buildings. . . ." In other words, federal jurisdiction is exclusive only over places purchased with the consent of the legislature of the state in which they are situated. If purchase is made without state approval, as is often the case, state law continues to control, although, since the property is owned by the Federal government, it cannot be discriminated against or unreasonably burdened.[1] The Federal government ordinarily requests state approval and the states grant it in some such language as this: "The United States, or such person or persons as may be by them authorized, shall have the right and authority to purchase the fee simple of a sufficient quantity of land in the city of Columbia on which to erect a post office and a court house; provided, that the said purchase does not exceed four acres." This would automatically convey exclusive jurisdiction over the four acres to the Federal government.[2]

This arrangement has had some interesting results. The courts have held that one who committed robbery on a road through the West Point Military Reservation could not be convicted in a state court. On the other hand, many have been tried and convicted by the Federal government for crimes committed on federal land acquired with state consent.[3] On another occasion the courts ruled that inmates of a federally owned asylum for disabled volunteer soldiers ceased to be citizens and residents of the state,[4] hence ineligible to vote, because the state had consented to federal purchase. On still another occasion the courts held that a resident on a federal reservation, purchased with the consent of the state, was not a resident of the State, hence not entitled to sue for divorce in the state court even though the Federal government had made no provision for such cases. Other illustrations similar to these can easily be imagined.

Federal Legislation.—Congress has enacted extensive legislation governing territories, much of which is discussed in a subsequent chapter.[5] Here we shall note only that the federal criminal code mentions a long list of offenses that are punishable in federal courts if committed on federal

[1] Federal land and property cannot be taxed without congressional consent, because to do so would enable a segment of the Union to place a financial burden upon the people in all the states. See p. 370.

[2] Sometimes the state reserves the right to permit its officers to serve civil and criminal processes, including the right to make arrests, on federal territory for offenses committed elsewhere. This has been upheld by the courts on the ground that it does not impair federal authority. Congress is ordinarily quite willing to grant the exception in order to prevent federal lands from becoming a refuge from criminals fleeing from state and local authorities.

[3] For an illustration see Bowen *v.* Johnson, 306 U.S. 19 (1938).

[4] But not of the United States, of course.

[5] Chap. 26.

territory within the states.[1] These include such common offenses as murder, larceny, assault, arson, rape, and robbery. As a general thing, Congress has accepted the common-law definition of such offenses, with the result that federal law on its land is not greatly different from that of the state in which the property is located.

References

CHAFEE, ZECHARIAH: *Free Speech in the United States* (Cambridge, Mass.: Harvard University Press, 1941).

FISCHER, LOUIS A.: *History of the Standard Weights and Measures of the United States*, Bureau of Standards Publication M64 (Washington: Government Printing Office, 1905).

HALLOCK, WILLIAM, and HERBERT T. WADE: *Outlines of the Evolution of Weights and Measures and the Metric System* (New York: Macmillan, 1906).

JESSUP, PHILIP C.: *The Law of Territorial Waters and Maritime Jurisdiction* (New York: Jennings, 1927).

LAVINE, A. LINCOLN: *A Hand Book on Bankruptcy* (New York: Professional Publications, 1941).

MAGRUDER, FRANK A., and GUY S. CLAIRE: *The Constitution* (New York: McGraw-Hill, 1st ed., 1933).

NATIONAL INDUSTRIAL CONFERENCE BOARD: *The Metric versus the English System of Weights and Measures*, Research Report no. 42 (New York: Century, October, 1921).

ROBINSON, GUSTAVUS H.: *Handbook of Admiralty Law in the United States* (St. Paul, Minn.: West, 1939).

ROGERS, LINDSAY: *The Postal Powers of Congress* (Baltimore: The Johns Hopkins Press, 1916).

SCHAPP, ADELBERT: *Patent Fundamentals* (New York: The Industrial Press, 1939).

STORY, JOSEPH: *Commentaries on the Constitution of the United States* (Boston: Little, 4th ed., 2 vols., 1873).

TWITTY, PETERS: *The Respective Powers of the Federal and Local Governments within Lands Owned or Occupied by the United States* (Washington: Government Printing Office, 1944).

United States Code, Annotated (Washington: Government Printing Office), Title 11.

UNITED STATES CONGRESS TEMPORARY NATIONAL ECONOMIC COMMITTEE: *Investigation of Concentration of Economic Power*, 76th Cong., 3d Sess., Monograph no. 24, "Consumer Standards" (Washington: Government Printing Office, 1941).

——— *Investigation of Concentration of Economic Power*, 76th Cong., 3d Sess., Monograph no. 31 (by Walton H. Hamilton *et al.*), "Patents and Free Enterprise" (Washington: Government Printing Office, 1941).

——— "Patents, Proposals for Changes in Law and Procedure," *Investigation of Concentration of Economic Power*, 76th Cong., 1st Sess., Hearings, part 3 (Washington: Government Printing Office, 1939).

UNITED STATES POSTMASTER GENERAL: *Postal Laws and Regulations of the United States of America* (Washington: Government Printing Office, 1940 ed., 1941).

——— *Annual Report* (Washington: Government Printing Office, 1941 and other years).

WARREN, CHARLES: *Bankruptcy in United States History* (Cambridge, Mass.: Harvard University Press, 1935).

WEINSTEIN, JACOB I.: *The Bankruptcy Law of 1938: Chandler Act; a Comparative Analysis Prepared for the National Association of Credit Men* (New York: National Association of Credit Men, 1938).

[1] That is, "places" purchased with state consent.

Chapter 21

ADMINISTRATIVE ORGANIZATION AND PROCEDURE

Organization is the arrangement of personnel for facilitating the accomplishment of some agreed purpose through the allocation of functions and responsibilities. It is the relating of efforts and capacities of individuals and groups engaged upon a common task in such a way as to secure the desired objective with the least friction and the most satisfaction to those for whom the task is done and those engaged in the enterprise.

John M. Gaus, *The Frontiers of Public Administration.*[1]

There is no more forlorn spectacle in the administrative world than an agency and a program possessed of statutory life, armed with executive orders, sustained in the courts, yet stricken with paralysis and deprived of power. An object of contempt to its enemies and of despair to its friends.

The lifeblood of administration is power.

Professor Norton E. Long, "Power and Administration."[2]

INTRODUCTORY CONSIDERATIONS

After policy has been formed, by the processes described in the first part of this book, it must be executed. The administrative process involves both policy interpretation and implementation. The initial consideration of public administration is to secure an effective machinery for carrying out the will of the policy makers—legislators, executives, judges, electorate. Certain general aspects of this question have been dealt with already in previous chapters on the executive branch. The task here is to inquire more deeply into the subject, seeking a fuller explanation of organizational theory and practice. It should be borne in mind constantly that politics is master of administration, that administration must defer to the policy makers.

Organizational Theory.—Administrative organization is not an end in itself, but a means to an end.[3] It exists to put into force, to administer the policies determined by policy formers. A well-organized and well-managed administrative unit will produce the results desired by policy makers, legislative and executive, with efficiency and speed, and with due respect for the rights of the affected parties. Under the most simple

[1] (Chicago: University of Chicago Press, 1936), pp. 66–67.

[2] *Public Administration Review,* vol. IX (Autumn, 1949), p. 257.

[3] Herman Finer, "Organization, Administrative," *Encyclopedia of the Social Sciences* (New York: Macmillan, 1930), vol. 11, p. 480.

circumstances—as in a village with a population of 100—elaborate departmental organization is unnecessary, and responsibilities may be subdivided with ease among part-time officials. A great nation, on the other hand, requires a mighty administrative leviathan with hundreds of thousands of civil servants and vast, complex administrative organization.

The great functions that government provides are usually assigned to operating departments and are called "line" functions. They provide the basic services and regulation that government is established to perform. Similar functions are usually grouped together and placed in a common department. In a small city, for example, fire and police services might be included in a department called "public safety," and all health and charitable work grouped in a "public-welfare" department. In a national state, the armed forces could be directed by a department of "national defense," and all services to business placed in a department of "trade and commerce."

In order to control and to provide specialized services for these departments, "staff" agencies are created to furnish personnel, planning, finances, or other services needed by the operating or "line" agencies. Through "staff" agencies, the administrative head can keep informed of "line" developments and may exert direction and control. The Bureau of the Budget, located in the Executive Office of the President, is an example of a staff agency.

A case often is made for the independence from direct executive or legislative control of a staff or line agency. It is argued that a business or entrepreneurial public function ought to be free of the usual governmental restrictions on finance and personnel which were designed to fit ordinary functions. Crusaders for the merit system usually demand independent status for a personnel agency in order to keep it away from the taint of spoils. Making regulatory bodies independent of regular departments is common on the ground that such agencies possess quasi-legislative and quasi-judicial powers and must therefore not be subject to external control under the separation of powers principle.

Constitutional and Statutory Provisions.—The Federal Constitution is notably silent regarding administrative structure. In Article II, Section 2, it states that the President can require an opinion in writing of the principal officer in each of the executive departments on any subject relating to the duties of his office. In the same section, Congress is given authority to vest by law the appointment of inferior officers in the President alone, in the courts, or in the heads of departments. One may infer from these provisions that the framers of the Constitution anticipated executive departments headed by individuals responsible to the President. Certainly the presumption that Congress should establish such departments, functions, and organization as necessary is justified.

Congress acted promptly, and in its first sessions (1789) created the departments of Foreign Affairs,[1] War, and Treasury. Each department was to be headed by a "secretary," appointed by the President. The first Congress also created the offices of Postmaster General and Attorney General, without the status of executive departments. For the next hundred years nearly all federal functions, as they were created, were grouped into existing or new departments.

The independent agency, responsible to no department, is largely a product of the last 60 years. Its persistence has been due primarily to the conviction that regulatory commissions must be free. The immunity from external control of the Interstate Commerce Commission, for example, is considered of high importance by the common carriers.

NATIONAL DEPARTMENTS

Organizational Confusion.—In the creation of new functions and agencies, Congress during the first hundred years under the Constitution followed the general rule that they should be placed in executive departments under presidential control. Departure from this principle began with the creation of the Civil Service Commission in 1883 and the Interstate Commerce Commission in 1887. During the Wilson administration (1913–1921), especially while the country was at war, a host of independent boards, commissions, councils, and administrations was created.[2] Some of these survived after the war. The economic depression that began in 1929 produced problems that required innovation of policies and a bewildering array of agencies was established by statute and by executive order.

Mr. Herbert Hoover, while Secretary of Commerce, in 1925 reported on the confusion of functions then existing. He found nine departments and independent agencies engaged in public works, five in conservation, six in aiding the merchant marine, four providing veterans' aid, three governing territories, three aiding education, and every one purchasing its own supplies.[3]

New Departments.—Two possible solutions are proposed for this problem. One is that new departments should be created. The other is

[1] Subsequently changed to State. See Lloyd M. Short, *The Development of National Administrative Organization in the United States* (Baltimore: The Johns Hopkins Press, 1923).

[2] A good general statement of this development is given in United States President's Committee on Administrative Management, *Report with Special Studies* (Washington: Government Printing Office, 1937), pp. 31–33.

[3] The most amusing aspect of all was the report that Alaskan bears were protected by three different departments: brown bears by Agriculture, grizzly bears by Interior, and polar bears by Commerce.

that bureaus and agencies might be reshuffled within existing departments. Most of the reports and studies of reorganization have included both features. After the First World War, the Brookings Institution recommended consolidation of the War and Navy departments into a defense department, abolition of the Department of the Interior, and creation of new Departments of Education and Science, Public Works and Public Domain, and Public Health.[1] When President Harding in 1923 sent a recommendation to Congress on reorganization, he followed the Brookings plan, except that he recommended only one new department of Education and Health. Congress took no action on this proposal.

The next scheme for additional departments was that of the President's Committee on Administrative Management in 1937. It urged the addition of two new departments, a Department of Social Welfare and a Department of Public Works, making a total of twelve departments. This was rejected by Congress, which denied the President power to create new departments in the Reorganization Act of 1939. President Roosevelt did create, however, three great new "agencies" that were like departments in all but name, and he invited the "administrators" who headed each to sit with the cabinet.

The Commission on Organization of the Executive Branch of the Government (Hoover Commission) recommended in 1949 that a new Department of Social Security and Education should be created.[2] The proposed department would include Indian Affairs but would exclude health. A strong minority report favored the establishment of a Department of Welfare, embracing health, social security, and educational functions which for a decade had been together in the Federal Security Agency. The Hoover Commission recommended the retention of the Department of the Interior, but with several responsibilities added and a few existing ones transferred elsewhere.[3] A minority called for a Department of Natural Resources, with public-works activities scattered through various departments.

Immediately after signing the Reorganization Act of 1949, President Truman sent to Congress a series of reorganization plans, of which plan 1 was to create a Department of Welfare resembling that backed by the minority of the Hoover Commission. The plan was nullified by action of the Senate. Therefore the number of full departments remains at nine, three of which have fewer employees than has the Federal Security Agency. Unquestionably the establishment of a new department in the welfare-

[1] Short, *op. cit.*, pp. 463–464.

[2] Hoover Commission, *Social Security and Education, Indian Affairs* (Washington: Government Printing Office, 1949), pp. 3–11. The minority statement appears on pp. 37–47.

[3] Hoover Commission, *Reorganization of the Department of the Interior*, pp. 7–16. The proposal for a new Department of Natural Resources, backed by a minority, appears on pp. 53–60.

education field will come up again, as it has so many times in the past. The President has already used successfully his powers to reorganize, granted under the 1949 act, to rebuild the Department of Labor, which had been greatly weakened through transfers and budget cuts.

Transfer of Bureaus.—The other solution is to reorganize bureaus and services within departments through transfers so that like functions will be brought together and duplication and overlapping of activities minimized. This process is sometimes derisively called "reshuffling" the bureaus. President Hoover asked Congress for reorganization legislation at least three times during his administration. Some reorganization was accomplished through an amendment attached to an appropriation bill in 1932.[1] It gave the President power to transfer independent agencies to departments, to move from one department to another, and to consolidate or redistribute functions. Executive orders made under the law were to lie 60 days before the two houses of Congress; either house might reject the orders by a simple resolution. In December, 1932, after his defeat by Mr. Roosevelt, President Hoover submitted to the House and Senate an extensive reorganization scheme. The House, under Democratic control, rejected the plan by resolution. The Hoover plan would have moved many public-works activities to the Department of the Interior, placing them under an assistant secretary for public works. Educational and welfare activities were sent to Interior also, to be managed by an assistant secretary for education, health, and recreation. To the Department of Commerce were transferred several agencies of a business or aid-to-business nature.

On the eve of Mr. Roosevelt's inauguration in 1933 powers of the President to effect reorganization were broadened, but it was provided that they should expire in 2 years. During that period, 1933–1935, Mr. Roosevelt made many transfers, most of them minor, but including the important grouping of agricultural credit agencies in the Farm Credit Administration. The Committee on Administrative Management recommended a revival of the presidential power to transfer and consolidate agencies, under what it called the "continuing executive responsibility for efficient organization."[2] The committee stressed the necessity of organizational flexibility, and the fact that the task of reorganization is inherently executive in nature. Behind the arguments for adapting administrative structure to changing situations lies the practical fact that Congress has not been able to reorganize. Whenever Congress undertakes to consider reworking structure, employees and pressure groups swamp it with objections, and no action results.

[1] 47 Stat. 413.

[2] United States President's Committee on Administrative Management, *op. cit.*, pp. 36–38.

The Reorganization Act of 1939 did not give the President the full authority to reorganize recommended by the committee. It did, however, permit him to make transfers, excepting seventeen agencies listed as untouchable. Authority was given for 2 years only, and executive orders could be evoked within 60 days by a concurrent resolution passed by both houses. The President promptly submitted two plans, both of which were permitted to go into effect by Congress. The first established the three "agencies," concentrating welfare and educational activities in the Federal Security Agency, construction and maintenance of public works in the Federal Works Agency, and provision of credit facilities (except farm credit) in the Federal Loan Agency. The second reshuffled bureaus among the departments, confirmed Interior as a conservation department, and made several minor changes. The powers granted by the 1939 act expired in early 1941.

After the declarations of war, the President received authority to transfer agencies and functions in the interests of the war effort in the First War Powers Act of December, 1941.[1] Agencies of the Department of Agriculture were reorganized, the National Housing Agency was created, Federal Loan Agency functions were transferred to the Department of Commerce, and other changes were made under the act.

In December, 1945, Congress adopted the Reorganization Act of 1945, which gave the President the broadest authority to reorganize within the limits prescribed, so far granted to a chief executive.[2] This measure provided that changes in administrative organization proposed by the President go into effect in 60 days unless both the Senate and House disagree. Eleven agencies were made wholly or partially exempt from presidential action; of these six were fully protected—Interstate Commerce Commission, Federal Trade Commission, Securities and Exchange Commission, National Mediation Board, National Railroad Adjustment Board, and Railroad Retirement Board. As under the 1939 act, the executive could not create or abolish departments.

The 1945 act expired at the end of March, 1948. President Truman, in a series of reorganization orders during 1946 and 1947, was able to strengthen the Federal Security Agency, to create a new Federal Housing and Home Finance Agency, and to make a number of lesser changes.

The Hoover Commission recommended strongly that Congress enact legislation giving the chief executive even more authority over reorganiza-

[1] 55 Stat. 838. It authorized the President to make such redistribution of functions as he deemed necessary. Action was limited to matters relating to the war, changes in the General Accounting Office were prohibited, and all agencies reverted to their previous status upon termination of the act. Termination was set for 6 months after the end of the war, or earlier if Congress by concurrent resolution or the President should so designate.

[2] 59 Stat. 613.

tion than was granted in the 1939 and 1945 acts.[1] Indeed, the commission declared that many of its most important proposals probably could not be put into effect unless presidential power to reorganize were revived and extended. It called for a forthright delegation, without exceptions, but subject to congressional nullification through the passage of a concurrent resolution by both houses within the prescribed time. The Eighty-first Congress enacted the necessary legislation in June, 1949, granting the President sweeping power to reorganize.[2]

The new act authorizes presidential reorganization plans affecting nearly every agency of the executive branch, except that they cannot abolish a department, increase a term of office, or extend the life of an expiring agency. The courts of the District of Columbia are exempt, as are the Comptroller General and the General Accounting Office. Reorganization plans lie before Congress for 60 days; if either house disapproves within that period, the plan is dead. Thus the act is stronger than that of 1945 in that there are fewer exemptions, but weaker in that either house can nullify, instead of action by both being required as under the earlier act.

INTERNAL DEPARTMENTAL ORGANIZATION

Departmental Management.—Federal executive departments are directed by single heads, although this is not always true of other levels of American government. It is fortunate that the first Congress established the initial departments with single heads; for that type of overhead management has great advantages over the plural or board-commission form. The unitary type concentrates responsibility for action and makes for greater speed and flexibility.

Within the department, policy is directed by the secretary, who is responsible to the President, but he must rely on various aides to keep in touch with a great department employing up to 500,000 persons. He is aided by assistant secretaries and undersecretaries, who are usually appointed for political reasons, and by administrative assistants, but there is a strong tendency to develop in most departments a group of "career" men among the top assistants who constitute the management staff. The assistant secretaries and undersecretaries may supervise a group of bureaus, or a certain type of service or function running through several bureaus in the department.[3] Professor Macmahon favors the functional type of assignment for assistants as distinguished from the subject-matter type but

[1] Hoover Commission, *General Management of the Executive Branch*, pp. ix–xii.

[2] Public Law 109, approved June 20, 1949.

[3] United States President's Committee on Administrative Management, *op. cit.*, Arthur W. Macmahon, "Departmental Management," pp. 249–270.

recognizes the difficulty of defining responsibilities in precise terms. Department heads convene assistant secretaries and bureau chiefs for "departmental cabinet" meetings, at which policy questions may be ironed out, efforts coordinated, and progress reported.

The latest thorough study of departmental management was made by the Hoover Commission.[1] First, it stressed the necessity of grouping the numerous agencies of government into departments ". . . by major purposes in order to give a coherent mission to each Department." Within each department, subsidiary bureaus and agencies should also be grouped according to major purposes. The commission further recommended that each department head should have power to organize his department as he thought best. For the typical department, the department head might have an undersecretary and the necessary number of assistant secretaries to cover the department's functions. Since all these officers would be of policy rank, the commission proposed that they should be appointed by the President with Senate confirmation.

Another type of administrative unit found within a department or an independent agency is the staff office, which performs subsidiary services for the operating agencies. These staff services are generally located near the department head. They include offices charged with providing personnel, legal, financial, research, informational, and other services. As the President keeps in touch with and controls federal line functions through his staff agencies, so the department head, within his department, contacts and manages his operating bureaus through personnel, financial, and other staff officers. The Hoover Commission urged that all major executive agencies be equipped with adequate staff assistants for legal counsel, finances, personnel, supply, management research, information, and congressional liaison.

Bureaus and Other Units.—Within each department the major subfunctions and line services are divided into "bureaus," but these major units may also be called "services" or "offices" or "administrations." The internal organization is determined by both statutes and executive orders. Many of the bureaus in the federal structure have a statutory basis, a fact that renders reorganization difficult unless the President is delegated authority to transfer units. Bureau heads generally are called "director," "commissioner," or "chief." Civil service status of the bureau head varies, but an increasingly large proportion of them are found within the classified service, and many others are appointed within the spirit of the merit system.[2]

[1] Hoover Commission, *General Management of the Executive Branch*, pp. 29–45.

[2] Arthur W. Macmahon and John D. Millett, *Federal Administrators* (New York: Columbia University Press, 1939). See also Schuyler C. Wallace, *Federal Departmentalization* (New York: Columbia University Press, 1941).

Below the bureau level terminology and organizational practice are even more variable. The title "division" is used most commonly to indicate a subdivision of a bureau, but "unit," "branch," and "section" are employed also. The lower in the administrative ladder, the less chance that form is bound by statute, and the more chance that reorganization can be achieved by executive action.

The term "agency," previously used generally to designate any administrative body, was attached in 1939 to three organizations—Federal Security, Federal Works, and Federal Loan. By this action they attained a status comparable in many respects with that of departments. Many of the bureaus of these agencies were termed "administrations," as the Social Security Administration and Public Buildings Administration. Independent establishments are sometimes divided into operating bureaus or divisions; occasionally the operating units are called "administrations" or even "departments."

The Hoover Commission proposed a standard nomenclature for agencies within a department: service, bureau, division, branch, section, and unit. The bureau would be the principal operating agency, but when several bureaus with closely related functions were operating in the same department, they would be grouped into a common "service." Bureaus would be divided further into smaller agencies as required, utilizing the names "division," "branch," "section," and "unit."

ADMINISTRATIVE PROBLEMS

Administrative Areas.—In national administration most functions are provided largely by field officers operating from offices spread over the country. About 90 per cent of federal civil employees are found in field services, and 10 per cent in Washington, D.C. Obviously, if the Department of Agriculture operated solely in the nation's capital, it would contact directly few agrarian problems and serve few farmers. It must reach out into every section and state. This spread over a wide geographic area raises grave problems of organization. Into what administrative areas shall the nation be subdivided? Shall each bureau of each department maintain branch offices in every area, reporting to the bureau in Washington? Or shall all field offices of a department clear through a central field office? Should the field services of the various federal agencies in a given locality be coordinated, or should each operate independently of the other?

The Federal government employs a bewildering variety of administrative areas. Americans were once reasonably familiar with the old nine corps areas of the Army Department (now "Army Areas"), but few realized that the country was divided on several different bases by particular services and corps of the Army. For general administrative purposes the Navy

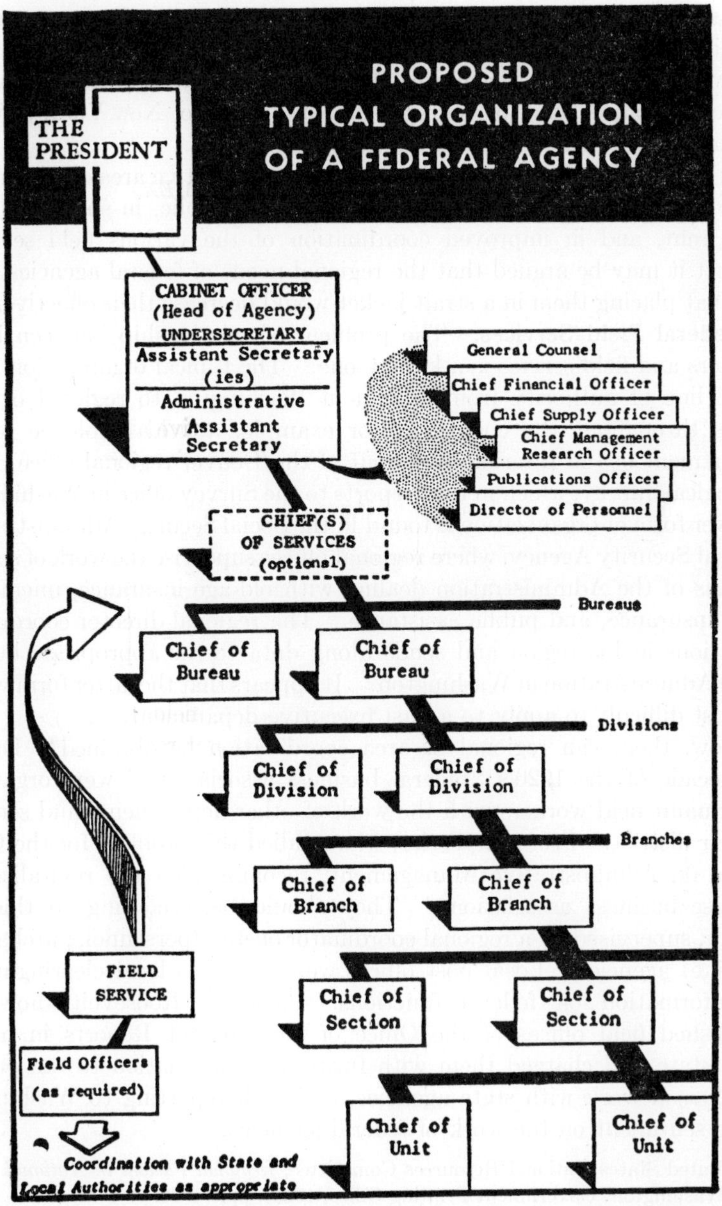

The Hoover Commission's suggestion of how a federal department ought to be organized internally is well illustrated by this diagram. The Commission held that subsidiary bureaus should be grouped by major purposes, strong staff offices ought to be at work, standard nomenclature should be employed, and—above all—the department head should have power to determine the organization within his own department. SOURCE: Hoover Commission, *General Management of the Executive Branch*, pp. 30–42.

uses seventeen naval districts, but it uses other areas for procurement, recruiting, and other purposes. Most of the federal administrative areas follow state lines. For each area there is designated a headquarters city, and federal offices tend to congregate in San Francisco, New York, Chicago, Boston, New Orleans, Denver, and Atlanta.[1]

It is sometimes proposed that federal administrative areas be standardized; this might result in simplification for the public, in some saving in office rent, and in improved coordination of the various field services. Against it may be argued that the regional needs of federal agencies vary, and that placing them in a strait jacket would decrease their effectiveness.[2]

Federal Field Services.—The problem of relationship between headquarters and field service is a knotty one. The typical organization has a direct line of authority from bureau in Washington to regional or field offices throughout the country. For example, a field employee of the Department of the Interior works out of the Denver regional office of the Geological Survey, which in turn reports to the Survey office in Washington. A newer form of organization is found in the Social Security Administration, Federal Security Agency, where regional offices supervise the work of several bureaus of the Administration dealing with old-age insurance, unemployment insurance, and public assistance. The regional director coordinates operations in his region and sends along data to the appropriate bureau of the Administration in Washington. It appears that the latter form would be most difficult to apply to a vast executive department.

How, then, can regional or area coordination be obtained? During the decade of the 1920's "federal business associations" were organized to acquaint field workers with the work of other departments and services in their district. Professor Fesler, who studied this problem for the Committee on Administrative Management, recommended the revitalization of these business associations.[3] They should be, according to this authority, supervised by a regional coordinator of staff (personnel, purchasing, and like) agencies. Local post offices were urged as local clearinghouses for information on federal functions. President Roosevelt, however, established field offices of the Office of Government Reports in nearly every state and charged them with furnishing information to the public, with liaison work with state agencies, and with reporting to Washington public sentiment on the work of federal agencies.

[1] United States National Resources Committee, *Regional Factors in National Planning* (Washington: Government Printing Office, 1935), pp. 71–73.

[2] See James W. Fesler, "Standardization of Federal Administrative Regions," *Social Forces*, vol. 15 (October, 1936), pp. 12–21; "Federal Administrative Regions," *American Political Science Review*, vol. 30 (April, 1936), pp. 257–268; and *Area and Administration* (University: University of Alabama Press, 1949).

[3] United States President's Committee on Administrative Management, *op. cit.*, "Executive Management and the Federal Field Service," pp. 275–294.

In 1943 a field service of the Bureau of the Budget was placed in operation. It was assigned four functions: (1) to advise on coordination of federal activities in the field; (2) to consult with state and local officials on federal programs related to their work; (3) to recommend improved use of supplies and equipment; and (4) to study efficiency of field operations.[1] The first four Bureau of the Budget field offices were established in Houston (now in Dallas), Chicago, Denver, and San Francisco. This development gives promise of providing more adequate regional coordination of the federal services.

The Hoover Commission gave less attention to field service problems than did the President's Committee, but it did make some pertinent criticisms and a few general suggestions. It found too many separately organized field offices representing departments, bureaus, and even divisions of bureaus. Much of the ineffectiveness of field offices, it reported, is attributable to failure to delegate authority. Lines of direction and supervision between specialized headquarters units and the field often are confused. Inadequate reporting and inspection leave central officials in the dark about field performance. Various federal field offices lack coordination of effort. Cooperation with state and local governments and with private organizations is far from adequate.[2]

Recommendations of the Hoover Commission included greater standardization of regional boundaries and headquarters, utilization of pooled administrative services (supply, motor transport, space, and other), strengthened reporting and inspection practices, and uniformity of relationships with state and local officials.

Boards and Commissions.—Although the plural form of executive has been rejected for federal departments, this is common for independent agencies. Boards and commissions have important uses under a number of circumstances. When quasi-legislative and quasi-judicial powers are assigned to an agency, the plural headship is thought to be advantageous, because independence and continuity are important to policy making and adjudication. Teachers, social workers, and others maintain that the board form is desirable for managing educational, welfare, and some other activities, because a "meeting of minds" is valuable and protection from politics is essential. In instances where the board-commission type has been employed for administrative work, confusion of responsibility and "buck passing" often have resulted.

As previously pointed out, the solution of the President's Committee on Administrative Management for the federal board-commission problems was to place substantially all of them in the executive departments. The

[1] Earl Latham, "Executive Management and the Federal Field Service," *Public Administration Review*, vol. 5 (Winter, 1945), p. 19.

[2] Hoover Commission, *General Management of the Executive Branch*, pp. 42–45.

work of regulatory commissions was to be divided, the administrative portion being handled through the appropriate department, and the legislative-administrative aspects remaining with the commission, a relatively autonomous body within the same department. Congress did not accept this solution, preferring to leave the regulatory commissions with their independent status. It is still possible, therefore, for the Federal Trade Commission to follow a policy in regard to business regulation that is out of harmony with that of the Department of Commerce.

The Hoover Commission found many faults with the independent regulatory commissions, but its proposals for change were less drastic than those of its predecessor. It recommended that all administrative responsibility of a commission be vested in its chairman. The Hoover group suggested several transfers of administrative duties from regulatory commissions to the Departments of Commerce and Interior, but rejected the proposal of its task force that a consolidated transportation commission be established. Some critics of the independent commissions regard as a backward step the Hoover recommendation that all regulatory commissioners be protected against removal by law and that the bipartisanship requirement be extended to all commissions.[1] President Truman's first plans under the Reorganization Act of 1949 included two that made the chairmen of plural bodies (Civil Service Commission and Maritime Commission) the executive officers and administrative chiefs, leaving with the full commissions rule-making and adjudicative authority.

In summary, federal boards and commissions are used for several reasons. First, the plural-headed body is established to ensure independence in the exercise of quasi-judicial and quasi-legislative powers. Examples of this are found in the Interstate Commerce Commission, the Federal Communications Commission, and other regulatory bodies. Second, the board may be used to secure interest-group representation, as on the War Production Board or the War Labor Board. Third, this form may be employed when wide discretionary or policy-forming authority is vested in an agency, as with the Civil Service Commission and the National Labor Relations Board. Finally, it is utilized, coupled with overlapping terms of office, simply to maintain continuity and prevent abrupt changes when Presidents change; this is important in justifying Tariff Commission independence. The part-time advisory board or commission, much used in state and local affairs to enlist the volunteer services of public-spirited citizens, is uncommon in national affairs due largely to the great distances to be traveled before a representative group could be assembled.

Government Corporations.—The corporate form of organization, so common in private business enterprise, has been adapted for use in publicly

[1] Hoover Commission, *The Independent Regulatory Commissions*, pp. 5–16.

owned or controlled businesses. Most governmental activities are carried on through the departmental-bureau type of organization. A few have independent status and are not directly responsible to an administrative chief, as are the regulatory boards and commissions, but are subjected to indirect control through appointments and fiscal checks of the chief executive. Even less common are the government corporations, incorporated under state or federal law, to carry out some federal function.

Several types of government corporations are possible.[1] First, the corporation may be wholly government owned, as is the Inland Waterways Corporation, now in the Department of Commerce. Second, the corporation may be owned in part by the government and in part by private investors; this type is called the "mixed enterprise" and has been widely used in Europe. Third, the corporation may be privately owned but wholly controlled by the government; this type, often called "a public-utility trust," is used by Britain in the London transport system.

The reasons for the adoption of the government corporation form are several. Independence in management is secured, freedom from dependence on annual appropriations and other fiscal controls is attained, and continuity of policy is achieved. Incorporation of federally owned corporations often takes place under the laws of some state, but the advantages of federal incorporation appear greater. Government corporations have boards of directors, sometimes composed wholly or in part of public officials acting ex officio, that determine the policies of the agencies. The directors employ a general manager, who performs functions like those of a manager in private enterprise. Employees generally do not have civil service status, for this might interfere with businesslike conduct of corporation affairs. Financial independence is considerable, with some corporations enjoying the power to borrow money on their own credit and most having authority to reinvest their own earnings. Government corporations may sue and be sued in the courts, sovereign immunity from suit being dropped under the corporate form.

Under the Government Corporation Control Act of 1945 some standard rules and practices were established.[2] No new government corporations can be created unless authorized by law; all with state incorporation were required to reincorporate under federal law by June 30, 1948. Controls

[1] An extensive literature is available. See Harold A. Van Dorn, *Government Owned Corporations* (New York: Knopf, 1926); Marshall E. Dimock, *Government Operated Enterprises in the Panama Canal Zone* (Chicago, University of Chicago Press, 1934), and *Developing America's Waterways* (Chicago: University of Chicago Press, 1935); John McDiarmid, *Government Corporations and Federal Funds* (Chicago: University of Chicago Press, 1938); John Thurston, *Government Proprietary Corporations in the English Speaking Countries* (Cambridge, Mass.: Harvard University Press, 1937).

[2] 59 Stat. 557.

over finances were set up, requiring a "business-type" budget, annual audit, and fuller fiscal reports.

The Hoover Commission made a number of recommendations designed further to increase uniformity and to curb the financial independence of government corporations.[1] Among the changes proposed were that major capital additions should require congressional approval, that boards should have advisory powers only, and that standardization should prevail in regard to borrowing powers, federal liability for corporation obligations, and budgetary presentation. The Hoover group also proposed that federal corporations should surrender to the Treasury government securities held by them and should receive in return non-interest-bearing credit; this change would reduce the total federal interest-bearing debt by some $350,000,000.

The more important examples of federal government corporations are the Panama Railway, Inland Waterways Corporation, Reconstruction Finance Corporation, Tennessee Valley Authority, Federal Deposit Insurance Corporation, Import-Export Bank, and more than 5,000 units of the Farm Credit Administration.

The Separation of Powers.—One of the cardinal principles of the American constitutional system is the separation-of-powers doctrine. All principal powers of government, according to this formula, are divided into three parts—legislative, executive, and judicial. So long as governmental problems and functions remained simple, it was possible to have the legislative branch declare public policy by law, and to confine the executive and judicial branches to interpretation and enforcement of such law. This process is found today in many activities of the various levels of American government. For example, Congress adopts and the President signs a bill forbidding counterfeiting of coins of the realm and providing for 10 years' imprisonment of all convicted of the crime. The law comes into force and is published in the *Statutes-at-large*. Secret service agents of the Treasury apprehend one Joe Luger in the act of molding lead 50-cent pieces. He is arrested, jailed, and tried in the courts. The prosecutor is the United States District Attorney for the area. On conviction Luger is sentenced to serve 10 years in Atlanta penitentiary. In this instance, the conventional methods of policy formation and law enforcement are followed, and the separation-of-powers doctrine proves suitable.

Under modern conditions, however, the problems of government have become so complex and kaleidoscopic that more flexible administration is required in many cases. When, for example, Congress decided that railroad services and rates must be regulated, it created a regulatory commission for the purpose and gave to that body extensive powers to make rules and regulations and to render decisions in cases of conflict. The

[1] Hoover Commission, *Reorganization of Federal Business Enterprises*, pp. 5–12.

alternative to this action would have been to establish rates and standards of service in the law and to make them enforceable through the judicial process. The latter scheme would have proved impossible to operate fairly, for it would have produced uneven returns for operating concerns, ranging from unreasonably large profits to severe losses. Therefore the regulatory commission was established, with powers not only to enforce law (administration), but to make rules (legislation), and to settle disputes over law and fact (adjudication).

For a time the courts stood in the way of this development, declaring it violative of the separation-of-powers doctrine.[1] Eventually it was accepted on the ground that the powers granted to administrative agencies were "quasi-legislative" and "quasi-judicial." While the power of Congress to delegate "rule-making" authority to the President has been restricted in two recent decisions, delegation of authority to regulatory bodies to legislate and to adjudicate appears well established.[2]

ADMINISTRATIVE LEGISLATION

Need for Rule-making Power.—As governmental problems have grown more complex, numerous, and changeable, Congress and the state legislatures increasingly have entrusted to administrative officers and bodies the responsibility for making detailed rules and regulations. Legislative bodies have delegated this authority for good reasons. First, the administrative officials are more expert in the technical problems to be dealt with. Second, the legislature saves time that may be used for larger problems of public policy. Third, flexibility is secured, so that rules may be adapted to changed conditions and experience.[3]

In 1937 Prof. James Hart found 115 federal agencies empowered to issue rules and regulations that affect the public.[4] Most of these authorizations have been made in the last half century; they have been exercised vigorously during war and crisis, especially in the Wilson and Franklin D. Roosevelt administrations. Administrative rule-making agencies include the President, most of the executive departments, many independent boards and commissions, and other bodies. A rule or regulation that is validly made is enforceable in the courts as law.

[1] See Charles G. Haines, "The Adaptation of Administrative Law and Procedure to Constitutional Theories and Principles," *American Political Science Review*, vol. 34, (February 1940), p. 6.

[2] Compare the Panama Refining case and the Schechter case rulings (pp. 325 and 659) with the delegation to regulatory bodies described below (p. 452).

[3] See Frederick F. Blachly and Miriam E. Oatman, *Administrative Legislation and Adjudication* (Washington: Brookings, 1934), pp. 43–53; James Hart, "The Exercise of the Rule-making Power," in United States President's Committee on Administrative Management, *op. cit.*, pp. 314–352.

[4] *Ibid*, p. 319.

Reform of Administrative Legislation.—While the necessity for administrative legislation may be established, several safeguards are required to avoid abuses of authority. Proper notice of proposed action might well be required. Opportunity to testify at a public hearing usually is made a prerequisite. After a rule or regulation has been made, it is published in usable form and circulated widely. Some over-all regulation of administrative legislation appears desirable in order to reduce inconsistencies of content and form.

Professor Hart, who made the study of rule making for the President's Committee on Administrative Management, recommended (1) the regularization of the process at the departmental level; (2) extension of prenatal procedural safeguards (due notice, hearings, group contacts, etc.); (3) postnatal publicity; (4) coordination; and (5) uniformity.[1] Some progress has been made along the lines suggested. Failure of Congress to consolidate the independent establishments into executive departments has blocked regularization at the level proposed, but individual agencies have reformed their practices. President Roosevelt by executive order implemented the Federal Register Act of 1935 with details on form for proclamations and orders.[2] The Division of the Federal Register is located in the National Archives. The *Federal Register*, issued five times a week, contains presidential proclamations and executive orders and other documents of general applicability and legal effect. An administrative committee, composed of the archivist, a Department of Justice representative, and the public printer, oversees the work of the division, which includes supervision of form and codification of administrative laws.[3] While regularization at the departmental level and the prenatal procedural safeguards have not been fully assured, the other proposals—postnatal publicity, coordination, and uniformity—have had some measure of acceptance.

A thorough study of these problems was made by the Attorney General's Committee on Administrative Procedure. Its report,[4] filed in January, 1941, and the thirteen supporting monographs,[5] constitute the chief source of data in this field. In 1946 Congress enacted and the President signed the Administrative Procedure Act. In addition to its general provisions requiring agencies to inform the public regarding organization, procedure, rules, policies, and interpretations, there are some specific requirements about rule making. (1) Notice must be published in the *Federal Register* stating the time, place, nature, and authority for the proposed rules.

[1] *Ibid.*, pp. 314–315.

[2] The law is 49 Stat. 500; the order is No. 7298, dated Feb. 18, 1936.

[3] *United States Government Manual*, Spring, 1942, p. 507.

[4] United States Attorney General's Committee on Administrative Procedure, *Administrative Procedure in Government Agencies, Report of the . . .*, 77th Cong., 1st Sess., Sen. Doc. 8 (Washington: Government Printing Office, 1941).

[5] 76th Cong., 3d Sess., Sen. Doc. 186 (Washington: Government Printing Office, 1940). There were also twenty-seven mimeographed monographs.

(2) Interested persons may participate by submitting views, data, and arguments. (3) Rules must be published at least 30 days before the effective date. (4) The right to petition for issuance, change, or repeal of a rule is guaranteed.[1]

OTHER ADMINISTRATIVE ACTION

Licensing Powers.—Another form of delegating authority to administrative officials is involved in licensing. Licensing laws customarily prohibit the practice of a profession or the operation of a business unless a permit or license has been secured in advance. The discretionary authority possessed by a licensing officer or body sometimes is very great. An application for a permit to operate a bus line in a great metropolitan area requires careful review to assure need for the service and the applicant's ability to provide it. The issuance of a retail liquor license places a grave social responsibility on both licensing officer and recipient.

Licenses of importance usually are subject to suspension or revocation for cause. A physician who performs an illegal operation may have his license to practice medicine canceled. An attorney may be disbarred or have his permit to practice suspended for unethical conduct. A radio station that violates the conditions under which its license was granted may face revocation, suspension, or failure to renew by action of the Federal Communications Commission.

State governments utilize licensing more than does the Federal government. States license those who engage in various professions and occupations, public-utility undertakings, businesses of diverse kinds, mechanical devices (such as elevators), and hunters and fishers. Municipalities, which are the creatures of the states, extend this list to include such diverse objects as dogs, restaurants, and hospitals. Federal licensing has been used from the beginning of government under the Constitution, centering largely around the commerce power.[2] The principal Federal uses of licensing are authorized in the following statutes:[3]

1916 Warehouses Act
1920 Water Power Act
1921 Packers and Stockyards Act
1922 Grain Futures Act
1927 Radio Commission Act (now Federal Communications Act of 1934)
1934 Securities Exchange Act

[1] See Foster H. Sherwood, "The Federal Administrative Procedure Act," *American Political Science Review*, vol. 41 (April, 1947), pp. 271–281.

[2] See Leonard D. White, *Introduction to the Study of Public Administration* (New York: Macmillan, 1939), Chap. 32, on "Licensing."

[3] Charles V. Koons, "Growth of Federal Licensing," *Georgetown Law Review*, vol. 24 (January, 1936), pp. 293–344.

A rather simple example of federal licensing is found in the live-poultry amendment added to the Packers and Stockyards Act of 1935.[1] Enacted to curb fraudulent practices that restrain interstate commerce at large centers of population, the act authorizes the secretary to designate which markets require regulation. All poultry handlers within a designated market must secure a license from the secretary in order to continue in business. Licenses may be denied because of a record of unfair practices within the past 2 years or inability to meet financial obligations. In administering the act, the department proceeds informally and provides much aid to applicants in filling out forms and preparing the necessary financial statement.

Administrative Orders.—Related to both rule making and adjudication is the power to issue administrative orders. Such orders usually are of two types: (1) The corrective type, which demands that alleged abuses be terminated. For example, the Food and Drug Administration issues a "cease-and-desist" order to a patent medicine company that claims its remedy will cure cancer. (2) Orders of exemption, which waive a prohibition or general rule in a particular instance. Such orders have been used by the Los Angeles County Planning Commission to secure architectural conformity on an important boulevard.[2]

The federal regulatory agencies use administrative orders as important weapons in their work of controlling great economic services. If a railroad uses equipment that falls short of safety standards, the Interstate Commerce Commission may issue a cease-and-desist order. The National Labor Relations Board has power to issue the same order if it finds an employer interfering with an employee's choice of unions. Unfair competitive practices by business interests are corrected through Federal Trade Commission cease-and-desist orders.

ADMINISTRATIVE ADJUDICATION

Adjudicative Agencies.—Administrative adjudication has been defined by Blachly and Oatman as ". . . investigation and settling of a dispute on the basis of fact and law, by an administrative agency which may or may not be organized to act solely as an administrative court."[3] So long as the administrative process remains clear of conflict, adjudication is unnecessary. When a dispute arises, however, its settlement requires adjudica-

[1] United States Attorney General's Committee on Administrative Procedure, *Monograph of the . . ., Part II, Administration of the Packers and Stockyards Act, Department of Agriculture*, Sen. Doc. 186, 76 Cong., 3d Sess. (Washington: Government Printing Office, 1940), pp. 3–4, 10–13.

[2] The neighborhood was zoned in very restrictive terms. Buildings that conformed to the architectural scheme were granted individual exemptions.

[3] Blachly and Oatman, *op. cit.*, p. 91.

tion. In instances where the decision is rendered by an administrative officer or body, the adjudication is called "administrative." Thereafter litigation continues in the courts and is called "judicial review of administrative action." Court review will be dealt with in the next subsection.

Why should administrative tribunals exist and administrative bodies be assigned quasi-judicial powers? First, because expertness is required in many technical fields of administration. Second, informal proceedings save time and expense and make possible adaptability to changed conditions. Third, decisions are rendered by officers acquainted with the social and economic philosophy underlying the function. Fourth, when government enters a new field of activity, the administrative process provides the necessary flexibility for experimentation by trial and error. The Attorney General's Committee on Administrative Procedure pointed out that the "great bulk of administrative decisions are made informally and by mutual consent."[1] This means that potential disputes are ironed out by investigation and consultation and adjustment before formal procedure is resorted to.

When formal adjudication is required, greatest care must be given to how the tribunal is constituted and what its procedure is like. Blachly and Oatman classify these adjudicative authorities into several groups, of which three are of great importance.[2] First, a few independent administrative courts exist. Examples are the Board of Tax Appeals, the Court of Claims, the Customs Court, and the Court of Customs and Patent Appeals. These tribunals operate like courts of law and are presided over by "judges." Second, several administrative tribunals are found within executive departments, as the Civil Aeronautics Board, the Patent Office, and the like. The members are specialized—but less detached than those judges of the first group. Third, the great regulatory commissions with administrative quasi-judicial and quasi-legislative powers. These include the Interstate Commerce Commission, Federal Trade Commission, Federal Communications Commission, Federal Power Commission, Securities and Exchange Commission, and others. In addition, there are executive department heads, as the Secretary of Agriculture, endowed with adjudicative powers. Also there are various licensing authorities, and the Comptroller General.

Methods of Adjudication.—The first step in formal administrative adjudication involves the filing of a complaint or a request for hearing by an interested party; the dispute may arise between conflicting private interests, or between the public agency and a private interest. Second, a "hearing officer" takes testimony and evidence upon which a fair decision may be based; in some cases the officer has power to render an initial decision in the case. Third, the board or commission or head, advised by legal

[1] *Administrative Procedure in Government Agencies*, p. 35.

[2] Blachly and Oatman, *op. cit.*, pp. 120–162.

staff, renders the ultimate decision in the case, subject to the court review prescribed by law.

After reviewing carefully the practices of the various federal agencies, the Attorney General's Committee on Administrative Procedure made several recommendations for the reform of adjudicative organization.[1] The committee proposed that hearing commissioners with fixed terms and substantial salaries be appointed for the principal agencies handling adjudication. Such officers should be appointed by the agency, subject to the approval of an Office of Federal Administrative Procedure. Some exchange of hearing officers might take place between small agencies, but most commissioners would be specialized in the work of a particular body.

The committee reported that a hearing commissioner should be empowered to preside at hearings, administer oaths, issue subpoenas, and exercise other authority over hearings. This officer, after accumulating evidence, should make findings of fact, conclusions of law, and issue orders or decisions. If within a reasonable period no appeal is taken by one of the parties from the hearing commissioner's decision, his determination should be regarded as final and binding. An agency, of course, might call up a hearing officer's determination for review of its own motion.

When the appeal is taken, the committee feels that the burden of proof should be placed upon the appellant. The agency might affirm, reverse, modify, or remand for further hearing the determination of the hearing commissioner. In instances where the agency chief is the head of a great executive department, the committee suggests that a special board of review be established and the pretense of review by the Secretary of Agriculture, Postmaster General, or other department head be dropped.

The general effect of these recommendations, if adopted, will be to separate the quasi-judicial functions from administrative functions of the various agencies concerned. This appears a proper corrective for the common complaint that in adjudicating disputes regulatory agencies often are both prosecutor and judge. The Administrative Procedure Act of 1946 does not provide for specialized hearing officers, but authorizes members of a body of examiners to function in that capacity. Prosecuting officers are barred from participating in making a decision, the recommendation for which is made by the one who receives the evidence. Detailed requirements are set down in the new law specifying due notice, fair hearing, and the like.

CONTROL OVER ADMINISTRATIVE ACTION

Judicial Review of Administrative Action.—The right to appeal decisions, rules, and orders by administrative bodies to the courts of law is widely regarded as necessary and proper. While the great majority of

[1] *Administrative Procedure in Government Agencies*, pp. 43–60.

instances of administrative action are accepted without formal dispute, as noted before, the volume of cases before administrative bodies nevertheless is large. Only a very small proportion of these cases is appealed to the ordinary courts, but such cases constitute an important share of the total litigation before the federal courts. Professor Pennock states that 23 per cent of all opinions of the Supreme Court in the 1938–1939 term involved reviewing of administrative orders.[1]

Judicial review has as its objective, according to the Attorney General's Committee on Administrative Procedure, ". . . to serve as a check on the administrative branch of government—a check against excess of power and abusive exercise of power in derogation of private right."[2] That committee stressed that the courts can review to ensure the fairness of administrative action, but that they cannot assure the correctness of such action. The volume of administrative action is too great to permit extensive review, and the court cannot match the administrative bodies in specialization and expertness. The appropriate role of the court in reviewing administrative action would appear to include examination of the propriety of the interpretation of the law, and assurance that the proceedings have not been unreasonable.

In practice these principles have been followed generally by the federal courts in reviewing administrative action. The federal courts, faced with a case involving a request for review of administrative action, first see that the Constitution has been followed, especially that there has been no deprivation of liberty or property without due process of law, either procedural or substantive.[3] Next, the court may look to the federal law under which the administrative body was created or the right of appeal was established; considerable variation exists in the right of appeal, the methods of appeal, and the degree of administrative finality. Even in cases where the Constitution is not violated and statutory requirements are met, the remedies of an aggrieved person are not exhausted. He may sue an official for damages, or seek an injunction to forbid certain acts by an administrative agency.

In general the courts have required due notice and a full and fair hearing on the procedural side. Mr. Henry A. Wallace, while Secretary of Agriculture, led a vigorous attack on a Supreme Court decision on full hearing under the Packers and Stockyards Act of 1921.[4] He criticized the courts for permitting the case to drag over 5 years, leaving dangling a pressing

[1] J. Roland Pennock, *Administration and the Rule of Law* (New York: Rinehart, 1941), p. 148.

[2] *Administrative Procedure in Government Agencies*, p. 76.

[3] See Chap. 7.

[4] The case was Morgan *v.* United States, 304 U.S. 1 (1938). The Court held that less than full hearing was had before commission agents set rates for the Kansas City stockyards.

economic problem of the farmers concerned. The court insisted that it meant only that fair play must prevail, not that excessively exhaustive procedure must be followed.

Congress has provided for appeal of administrative decisions to various court levels. Appeals from several of the regulatory commissions go directly to the Circuit Courts of Appeal. Action of other bodies is reviewable in the district courts, or before a three-judge panel in the district courts. Customs and patent appeals go to the Court of Customs and Patent Appeals.

In considering court reviewability of administrative action, one of the most important aspects concerns control over findings of fact. If the court finds that there are no facts to support the action, it holds due process lacking.[1] Beginning with the Interstate Commerce Commission, fact finding by the agency was declared in the statute to be prima facie evidence. Fact finding by several other agencies is conclusive if supported by the weight of evidence. While the courts at times have inclined to let stand administrative findings of fact unless proved insubstantial, occasionally they have intervened to the extent of reviewing facts fully and anew.

Questions of law, however, fall under the full purview of the courts. The court may set aside administrative action because of errors of law. In many cases, of course, questions of fact and law are intermingled, and the court has all necessary discretion to rule as it sees fit. Commenting on the lack of sharp distinction between questions of law and fact, John Dickinson concluded: "The knife of policy alone effects an artificial cleavage at the point where the court chooses to draw the line between public interest and private right."[2]

Reform of Court Review.—Complaints over judicial review of administrative action may be divided into two groups. One set is voiced by those who fear administrative finality and who allege that an aggrieved person has insufficient remedies. The other is presented by defenders of the administrative process, who feel the courts have interfered excessively in substituting their own findings of fact and judgment for those of the administrative body. Both sides in the controversy have agreed to the proposition that improvements in the judicial review of administrative action are possible; that procedures lack uniformity, clarity, and other attributes of a desirable appellate system.[3]

[1] See analysis of Frederick F. Blachly and Miriam E. Oatman, *Federal Regulatory Action and Control* (Washington: Brookings, 1940), pp. 119–124.

[2] John Dickinson, *Administrative Justice and the Supremacy of the Law* (Cambridge, Mass.: Harvard University Press, 1927), p. 55.

[3] See the clear exposition of proposed reforms in Arthur Harris and Robert Ward, *Administrative Decisions and Judicial Review* (Berkeley: University of California, 1941), Bureau of Public Administration, 1941 Legislative Problems, no. 7, pp. 7–23.

The Logan-Walter bill became the center of this controversy in 1939.[1] Backed by the American Bar Association, this bill passed both houses during 1940 but was vetoed by President Roosevelt. This legislation would have given the Court of Appeals for the District of Columbia jurisdiction to hear and determine, within 30 days of issuance, whether an administrative rule conflicted with law or Constitution. Decisions and orders of administrative agencies could be reviewed in Court of Appeals (D.C.) or Circuit Courts of Appeals, within 30 days, and set aside on grounds that fact findings were erroneous, due notice or fair hearing was denied, or law or Constitution violated. Appellate court decisions were to be final except where the Supreme Court called them up for review through writ of certiorari or certificate. The judicial review features of the bill were attacked vigorously as likely to lead to endless court litigation, and to render impossible proper functioning of administrative agencies.

Next came the report of the Attorney General's Committee on Administrative Procedure, a part of which was devoted to court review. This report found that in general the existing diversity in respect to which court should review administrative action is not troublesome. The committee proposed no innovations so far as judicial review is concerned but concentrated instead on adjusting procedure to minimize the necessity for appeals.[2] The hearing commissioners and the Office of Federal Administrative Procedure proposed by the Committee were to safeguard the administrative process by regular and uniform conduct. The Administrative Procedure Act of 1946 simply provides for judicial review to remedy every "legal wrong." Judicial review is authorized except when precluded by law. The new law occupies a middle ground between the Logan-Walter school, which wanted every administrative act subjected to judicial review, and some defenders of the agencies, who wished to minimize court appeals. Actually, the law will broaden somewhat court review, but the extent will be controlled by the courts themselves through their interpretations.

Legislative Control.—Administrative action is also subject to external control by legislative bodies. (1) Congress determines the statutory framework (structure, powers, duties) within which the federal administrative agencies operate. Although in recent years this control is less rigid, due to the tendency to draft legislation in general terms, supremacy of the legislature in matters of policy has been retained. (2) Congressional and state legislative control over appropriations provides a second avenue of checking administrative responsibility. The stewardship of a particular

[1] It was H.R. 6324 and S. 915 in the 76th Congress. Sections 3 and 5 related to judicial review.

[2] *Administrative Procedure in Government Agencies*, pp. 75–95 and pp. 115–120.

agency is reviewed regularly in budget hearings, and the purse strings may be tightened to indicate legislative displeasure with administrative conduct. (3) Congress and nearly all state legislatures possess power to investigate as ancillary to the power to legislate. A large proportion of the investigating committees that are established concern themselves wholly or partially with inquiring about administrative conduct. The possibility that an investigation will be made is itself an effective deterrent on administrative excesses.

The task of securing the correct amount and quality of legislative control over administration is at once intricate and colossal. Lack of vigilance by a legislative body may lead to administrative highhandedness. Overintervention in the detail of the administrative process and personnel can bring irresponsible conduct and spoils politics. The legislative branch properly determines general policy and structure and makes inquiries into administrative practices to see that legislative intent is being carried out. It should not attempt to administer, directly or indirectly, nor interfere in administration in such a manner that initiative will be curbed, flexibility made impossible, and able personnel driven from public service.[1]

References

(See also works at end of Chap. 14)

American Society for Public Administration: *Public Administration Review* (Chicago: The Society, Quarterly).

Appleby, Paul H.: *Policy and Administration* (University, Ala.: University of Alabama Press, 1949).

Blachly, Frederick F., and Miriam Oatman: *Administrative Legislation and Adjudication* (Washington: Brookings, 1934).

——— *Federal Regulatory Action and Control* (Washington: Brookings, 1940).

Caldwell, Lynton K.: *The Administrative Theories of Hamilton and Jefferson: Their Contributions to Thought on Public Administration* (Chicago: University of Chicago Press, 1944).

Committee on Public Administration of the Social Science Research Council: *Case Reports in Public Administration* (Chicago: Public Administration Service, 1940 and thereafter). Looseleaf, 100 reports.

Cushman, Robert E.: *The Independent Regulatory Commissions* (New York: Oxford, 1941).

Dickinson, John: *Administrative Justice and the Supremacy of the Law* (Cambridge, Mass.: Harvard University Press, 1927).

Dimock, Marshall E.: *Developing America's Waterways: Administration of the Inland Waterways Corporation* (Chicago: University of Chicago Press, 1935).

——— *Government-operated Enterprises in the Panama Canal Zone* (Chicago: University of Chicago Press, 1934).

[1] See the able discussion of this problem by Leonard D. White, "Congressional Control of the Public Service," *American Political Science Review*, vol. 39 (February, 1945), pp. 1–11.

DOYLE, WILSON K.: *Independent Commissions in the Federal Government* (Chapel Hill: The University of North Carolina Press, 1939).

FESLER, JAMES W.: *Area and Administration* (University, Ala.: University of Alabama Press, 1949).

FREUND, ERNST: *Administrative Powers over Persons and Property* (Chicago: University of Chicago Press, 1928).

GAUS, JOHN M.: *Reflections on Public Administration* (University, Ala.: University of Alabama Press, 1947).

——— LEONARD D. WHITE, and MARSHALL E. DIMOCK: *Frontiers of Public Administration* (Chicago: University of Chicago Press, 1936).

——— and L. O. WOLCOTT: *Public Administration and the United States Department of Agriculture* (Chicago: Public Administration Service, 1940).

GELLHORN, WALTER: *Administrative Law: Cases and Comments* (Chicago: Foundation Press, 1940).

——— *Federal Administrative Proceedings* (Baltimore: Johns Hopkins Press, 1941).

GLASER, COMSTOCK: *Administrative Procedure: a Practical Handbook for the Administrative Analyst* (Washington: American Council on Public Affairs, 1941).

GRAHAM, GEORGE, and HENRY REINING, JR. (eds.): *Regulatory Administration* (New York: Wiley, 1943).

GRAVES, W. BROOKE: *Basic Information on the Reorganization of the Executive Branch, 1912–1948*, Public Affairs Bulletin No. 66 (Washington: Library of Congress, 1949).

——— *Public Administration* (Boston: Heath, 1950).

GULICK, LUTHER: *Administrative Reflections from World War II* (University, Ala.: University of Alabama Press, 1948).

——— and LYNDALL URWICK (eds.): *Papers on the Science of Administration* (New York: Institute of Public Administration, 1937).

HART, JAMES: *An Introduction to Administrative Law, with Selected Cases* (New York: Appleton-Century-Crofts, 1940).

——— *The Ordinance-making Power of the President of the United States* (Baltimore: Johns Hopkins Press, 1925).

LANDIS, JAMES M.: *The Administrative Process* (New Haven: Yale University Press, 1938).

LATHAM, EARL, and OTHERS: *The Federal Field Service: An Analysis with Suggestions for Research* (Chicago: Public Administration Service, 1947).

LEISERSON, AVERY: *Administrative Regulation, A Study of Representation of Interests* (Chicago: University of Chicago Press, 1942).

LEPAWSKY, ALBERT: *Administration, The Art and Science of Organization and Management* (New York: Knopf, 1949).

MCDIARMID, JOHN: *Government Corporations and Federal Funds* (Chicago: University of Chicago Press, 1938).

MACMAHON, ARTHUR W., and JOHN D. MILLETT: *Federal Administrators; a Biographical Approach to the Problem of Departmental Management* (New York: Columbia University Press, 1939).

MERIAM, LEWIS, and LAURENCE F. SCHMECKEBIER: *Reorganization of the National Government, What Does It Involve?* (Washington: Brookings, 1939).

PENNOCK, J. ROLAND: *Administration and the Rule of Law* (New York: Rinehart, 1941).

PFIFFNER, JOHN M.: *Public Administration* (New York: Ronald, 2d ed., 1946).

PUBLIC AFFAIRS INSTITUTE: *The Hoover Report, Half a Loaf* (Washington: The Institute, 1949).

PRITCHETT, C. HERMAN: *The Tennessee Valley Authority: A Study in Public Administration* (Chapel Hill: The University of North Carolina Press, 1943).

SANDERS, JENNINGS B.: *Evolution of Executive Departments of the Continental Congress 1774–1789* (Chapel Hill: The University of North Carolina Press, 1935).

SECKLER-HUDSON, CATHERYN (ed.): *Processes of Organization and Management* (Washington: Public Affairs Press, 1948).

SHORT, LLOYD M.: *Development of National Administrative Organization in the United States* (Baltimore: Johns Hopkins Press, 1923).

SIMON, HERBERT A.: *Administrative Behavior: A Study of Decision-making in Administrative Organization* (New York: Macmillan, 1947).

TRUMAN, DAVID B.: *Administrative Decentralization* (Chicago: University of Chicago Press, 1940).

UNITED STATES ATTORNEY GENERAL'S COMMITTEE ON ADMINISTRATIVE PROCEDURE: *Administrative Procedure in Government Agencies, Report* . . . Sen. Doc. 8, 77th Cong., 1st Sess. (Washington: Government Printing Office, 1941).

UNITED STATES COMMISSION ON ORGANIZATION OF THE EXECUTIVE BRANCH OF THE GOVERNMENT ("HOOVER COMMISSION"): *Reports* (Washington: Government Printing Office, 19 vols., 1949).

UNITED STATES PRESIDENT'S COMMITTEE ON ADMINISTRATIVE MANAGEMENT: *Report . . . with Studies of Administrative Management in the Federal Government* (Washington: Government Printing Office, 1937).

URWICK, LYNDALL: *The Elements of Administration* (New York: Harper, 1944).

WALDO, DWIGHT: *The Administrative State; A Study of the Political Theory of American Public Administration* (New York: Ronald, 1948).

WALLACE, SCHUYLER: *Federal Departmentalization, A Critique of Theories of Organization* (New York: Columbia University Press, 1941).

WARREN, GEORGE (ed.): *The Federal Administrative Procedure Act and the Administrative Agencies* (New York: New York University School of Law, 1947).

WHITE, LEONARD D.: *Introduction to the Study of Public Administration* (New York: Macmillan, 3d ed., 1948).

——— *The Federalists: A Study in Administrative History* (New York: Macmillan, 1948).

WILLOUGHBY, WILLIAM F.: *Principles of Public Administration* (Baltimore: Johns Hopkins Press, 1927).

TEXT-FILM

The following McGraw-Hill 35mm silent filmstrip is recommended for use with Chaps. 21 and 22 of this text.

Public Administration and Civil Service. Structure and function of major governmental agencies with special emphasis on civil service.

Chapter 22

THE CIVIL SERVICE

> We must have government to live, to work, to advance, to enjoy the fruits of our labor. The success or failure of that government, and the kind of service which it renders, will rest in the last analysis upon the capacity and character of the men and women who constitute it. We must therefore maintain a governmental system under which the government attracts to the public service its share of the capacity and character of the man power of the nation.
>
> Commission of Inquiry of Public Service Personnel, *Better Government Personnel.*[1]

After administrative organization and powers, the next important prerequisite to effective administration is man power. In the days when the republic was young, few employees were necessary and the task of hiring and firing was not unlike that of a small business concern. Today, however, the administrative leviathan of the Federal government has reached enormous size, requiring careful management of every phase of personnel work. Machinery has been devised to cope with this great problem. Personnel agencies of federal, state, and municipal governments have done a fairly good job and have received much public support.

It must be remembered that civil service agencies perform functions that are essentially staff in nature. No government exists for the purpose of employing people; it is to accomplish the goals of fostering agriculture, regulating commerce, protecting life and property, that public employees are needed. If the personnel system can find and recruit the person most qualified for the job to be filled and can maintain his morale at a high level, the public interest obviously will be better served than if an ill-equipped person is given the job or if the incumbent is dissatisfied with the work. This places great emphasis on the importance of personnel work in modern governments.

DEVELOPMENT OF AMERICAN MERIT SYSTEMS

Early Personnel Policies.—The Constitution charges the President with appointing and the Senate with confirming "officers" of the United States. Authority to appoint "inferior officers" may be vested by law in the President alone, in the heads of executive departments, or in the courts. President Washington established the tradition of appointing for competency.

[1] (New York: McGraw-Hill, 1935), p. 15.

Adams showed preference for those of his own political leanings. Jefferson sought to replace Federalists with his own partisans; this turnover has been computed as involving about 25 per cent of employees under presidential control.[1] The political complexion of Madison and Monroe was in the Jeffersonian tone, minimizing the incentive to change; John Quincy Adams failed to alter the general policy of long continuance in office. Mosher and Kingsley have termed this era, 1789 to 1829, the "period of relative administrative efficiency."[2]

The Spoils System.—When Andrew Jackson took office on Mar. 4, 1829, he found many federal offices occupied by political opponents. In December of that year he gave his first annual message to Congress, in which he recommended limiting appointments to 4 years:

> There are, perhaps, a few men who can for any great length of time enjoy office and power without being more or less under the influence of feelings unfavorable to the faithful discharge of their public duties. Their integrity may be proof against improper considerations immediately addressed to themselves, but they are apt to acquire a habit of looking with indifference upon the public interests and of tolerating conduct from which an unpracticed man would revolt. . . . The duties of all public officers are, or at least admit of being made, so plain and simple that men of intelligence may readily qualify themselves for their performance; and I can not but believe that more is lost by the long continuance of men in office than is generally to be gained by their experience.[3]

The case for rotation in office was strong in Jackson's time. Governmental work was still relatively simple. Jackson's regime, representing a definite break with the past, would not be frustrated by bureaucrats held over from the John Quincy Adams administration.

Between 1829 and the close of the Civil War the spoils system flourished. To job spoils were added other types of spoils—contracts, graft, and the like. In this period of national expansion opportunities for corruption were plentiful. While the spoils system has not been wholly eliminated even today, important reforms were proposed and adopted in the two decades after the Civil War.

Civil Service Reform.—Even before the Civil War steps were taken to bring some order out of the chaos then prevailing in the personnel field. Acts of 1853 and 1855 established four classes of clerks in Washington

[1] Carl R. Fish, "Removal of Officials by the Presidents of the United States," *Annual Report of the American Historical Association for the Year 1899* (Washington: Government Printing Office, 1900), vol. I, p. 70.

[2] William E. Mosher and J. Donald Kingsley, *Public Personnel Administration* (New York: Harper, 1941), p. 16.

[3] James D. Richardson (ed.), *Messages and Papers of the Presidents* (New York: Bureau of National Literature, 20 vols., 1897–1916), vol. 3, pp. 1011–1012. Fish, *op. cit.*, p. 74, reports that Jackson removed 279 out of a total of around 610 officers.

departmental offices and set up a scale of salaries.[1] "Pass" examinations were introduced in each department, providing that an appointee must pass some departmental test before taking office. In 1871, during Grant's administration, an appropriation-bill rider authorized the President to set up regulations on appointments and to ascertain fitness of candidates for positions. Accordingly, President Grant created an Advisory Board of the Civil Service, and the first competitive examinations were given in 1872. Lacking appropriations for the purpose, Grant abandoned the experiment in 1875. Progress was made in the Hayes administration, especially in relation to federal employees in New York City.

In July, 1881, President James A. Garfield was fatally wounded by a disappointed office seeker. Public indignation over the spoils system reached a high pitch and provided an impetus for the enactment of the Pendleton Act in January, 1883. The law established a Civil Service Commission of three members and provided for open competitive examinations. Discrimination for political reasons was forbidden. Appointment continued to be a function of the President or department head, but his choice was limited to those who ranked in the top four on the eligible list prepared by the Commission. The act left to the President and Congress the extension of the "classified service," those employees coming under the protection of the formal merit system.

State and Local Adoptions.—The American states followed the Federal government in adopting civil service systems, but fewer than one-half of the states have seen fit to embrace this reform. New York and Massachusetts pioneered with their legislation of 1883 and 1885. Other states that now have state-wide merit systems are Wisconsin, Illinois, Colorado, New Jersey, Ohio, California, Connecticut, Kansas, Maryland, Michigan, Tennessee, Maine, Alabama, Rhode Island, Minnesota, Louisiana, Indiana, Virginia, Oregon, and Missouri.[2] It will be noted that all the populous states, excepting Pennsylvania and Texas, are included in the list of those with state-wide civil service systems.

A few counties have adopted civil service plans. Some have remarkably good records in the personnel field, but perhaps the majority are in the hands of spoilsmen. Less progress has been made on the county level than in any other level of government. Most of the large cities and a great many smaller municipalities have some sort of civil service systems. Policemen and firemen often are protected even where other employees are not.

[1] The growth of reform sentiment is interestingly described in United States Civil Service Commission, *History of the Federal Civil Service, 1789 to the Present* (Washington: Government Printing Office, 1941), pp. 32–52.

[2] Civil Service Assembly, *A Digest of State Civil Service Laws* (Chicago: Civil Service Assembly, 1939) and *The Book of the States, 1948–1949*, p. 201.

Townships and special districts rarely utilize civil service systems, but school districts commonly have either formal or informal merit systems. Teacher-tenure plans represent only minor variations from the general pattern of a protected personnel.

PERSONNEL AGENCIES

Types of Agencies.—The three major types of overhead organization for central public personnel agencies used in this country are: (1) commission, (2) single administrator, and (3) a combination of the two.

The commission is the most common. Normally there is an independent commission of three, appointed by the executive for terms of 3 to 6 or more years, with a bipartisan requirement. Most civil service commissions have some rule-making and adjudicative powers. This form has the advantage of providing a "council of minds" when policy is being determined or judicial decisions are being rendered; it also insulates the agency to some extent against partisan political pressures. Major disadvantages are that responsibility for administration is diffused, expertness is rarely secured from lay commissioners, and independent status deprives the chief executive of one of the main managerial "arms."[1]

The single-administrator plan has been adopted in several jurisdictions. Under this an administrator is appointed (sometimes with and sometimes without civil service standing) by the chief executive for a long term. The administrator is given approximately the same powers as are vested in a commission. Although this plan lacks the possibility of group deliberation and may be subject to political invasion, it does permit the concentration of authority in a personnel expert whose office may be coordinated with the other staff agencies near the chief executive.

A combination board-administrator has proved satisfactory and popular in recent years. It may have a number of variations, but a common form calls for a single expert administrator chosen by a personnel board which is appointed by the chief executive. The board makes rules and sits as a court in personnel cases, but administrative authority resides solely in the hands of the administrator. This would appear to combine the merits of both plans but may be criticized on the ground that, lacking much quasi-legislative and quasi-judicial work to do, the board may be tempted to interfere in administration. Such a danger emphasizes the necessity for drawing the lines of authority distinctly.

United States Civil Service Commission.—Because it was established first and because national institutions serve as models for the states, the United States Civil Service Commission deserves initial consideration.

[1] A good description of the virtues and faults of the commission type of agency is found in Mosher and Kingsley, *op. cit.*, pp. 57–73.

Established under the Pendleton Act, signed by President Arthur on Jan. 16, 1883, the Commission consists of three members appointed by the President, with Senate confirmation. No more than two might be members of the same political party. Commissioners serve for no fixed term, but at the pleasure of the President. From an original negative conception of eliminating politics in appointments, the Commission has come to play the leading role in a positive and broad personnel-improvement program. The personnel study of the President's Committee on Administrative Management computed the average length of service by commissioners at 4.7 years.[1]

The Commission is charged by the act with advising the President on civil service rules. Evidently the relationship of Commission and President rarely has been intimate. The body files an annual report, reviewing its work and making recommendations for extension of the classified service. The administrative work of the Commission under reorganization plan 5 of 1949 is the responsibility of the chairman alone. Acting through an executive director appointed by him, the chairman oversees and supervises the work of the several divisions, of which the leading ones are Examining, Investigations, Medical, Personnel Classification, Service Record, Retirement, and Training. Other divisions, performing staff-type services, are Organization and Methods, Personnel, Budget and Finance, Information, and Library.

Geographically the country is divided into fourteen civil service districts, each with a district office at a central city. The district offices publicize and conduct examinations and serve the personnel needs of the field services of the various federal agencies. In the last "normal year" before the war, 1938–1939, there were 920,310 civil employees in the executive branch of the government; of these, 622,832, or 67.7 per cent were in the competitive classified service.[2] In June, 1940, the total number of civil employees was 1,002,820, having exceeded the one-million mark for the first time in the history of the country. At that time 72.5 per cent were in the classified service.[3] During the war the number of federal employees soared, exceeding the three-million mark in 1943, 1944, and 1945. An important proportion of these employees was in Army and Navy arsenals, dockyards, and the like. In May, 1949, there were 2,120,409 federal civil employees of the executive branch.[4]

[1] Floyd W. Reeves and Paul T. David, "Personnel Administration in the Federal Service," in United States President's Committee on Administrative Management, *Report . . . with Studies . . .* (Washington: Government Printing Office, 1937), p. 74.

[2] United States Civil Service Commission, *Annual Report, 1939* (Washington: Government Printing Office, 1940), p. 56.

[3] *Ibid., 1940*, p. 34.

[4] United States Civil Service Commission, *Monthly Report of Employment Executive Branch of the Federal Government* (Washington: Government Printing Office, monthly).

Other Federal Personnel Agencies.—While the Civil Service Commission is the principal federal personnel agency, other agencies play important parts in the field. The commission is not, except for its own employees, the appointing agency; appointment is made by the department or agency in which the appointee will serve. The federal executive departments and other large agencies have directors of personnel. Such officers are placed in charge of selecting from civil service eligible lists the individuals most likely to prove suitable for particular positions, and take over many routine personnel duties of heads of departments and other agencies.

The Federal Personnel Council provides the machinery for discussion of problems common to directors of personnel and the commissioners. The Council was established by executive order in 1931. Under an executive order of 1940 it is established within the Civil Service Commission. Its present chairman was appointed by the President from outside the federal service. The Council is composed of directors of personnel in the departments and agencies and of other designated officials. Its purpose is to advise the President and the commission. It has carried out several studies on an intraagency basis that have reemphasized the value of maintaining a liaison body.

The Reorganization Act of 1939 authorized the President to appoint up to six administrative assistants. One of the first assistants appointed in 1939 was designated liaison officer for personnel management.[1] This brought the President, through his assistant's "eyes and ears," into continuous touch with the matters of personnel administration.

The personnel offices in the operating departments and agencies have emerged, since 1938, with key roles in appointing, rating, promoting, and otherwise serving federal employees. The decentralization program proposed by the Hoover Commission would place even more stress on the importance of personnel offices in operating units. For some 2 million federal civil workers, there are about 25,000 employees of personnel offices. The Hoover group criticized overstaffing in the offices of some of the agencies; in some instances it found one personnel worker for as few as thirty-eight employees. Under the reforms proposed, recruiting, examining, and selecting of employees would be conducted largely by the operating agencies, subject to the uniform employment standards and regulations determined by the Civil Service Commission.

The Loyalty Review Board was appointed by the Civil Service Commission in 1947 under the terms of an executive order creating the federal

[1] The functions of his office were defined in Executive Order No. 8248. A description of the office is given in the Report of the President's Committee on Civil Service Improvement, of which Mr. William H. McReynolds, the first incumbent, was a member. See United States President's Committee on Civil Service Improvement, *Report of* . . . House Doc. 118, 77th Cong., 1st Sess. (Washington: Government Printing Office, 1941), pp. 16–17.

employees' "loyalty check." It reviews and coordinates cases arising under executive orders and laws governing loyalty and political activities of federal employees.

The Fair Employment Board, consisting of not less than seven members appointed by the Civil Service Commission, was created in 1948. It was given advisory and coordinative responsibility for the government's antidiscrimination program, which is aimed at bias against persons because of race, color, religion, and national origin.

Proposals of President's Committee on Administrative Management.—The President's Committee on Administrative Management proposed a fairly drastic reorganization of personnel organization.[1] It recommended that the Civil Service Commission should be displaced by a Civil Service Administration, consisting of a single Civil Service Administrator and an unsalaried Civil Service Board of seven members. The administrator was to be an expert in personnel, appointed by the President with Senate confirmation, after an open competitive examination conducted under the direction of the Civil Service Board. This single administrator would succeed to the powers and duties of the present commission and should be given other powers as well.

The Civil Service Board would be almost wholly advisory. It could investigate, advise, report, study, and assist, but not administer or order. Its first function listed by the committee was to act as "watchdog of the merit system"; to continue the analogy, it could prowl and growl and bark but not bite.

In the extended hearings on reorganization bills the fear was expressed that a single administrator, serving at the pleasure of the President, would be controlled politically.[2] This point of view was taken by the National Federation of Federal Employees. The National Civil Service Reform League spokesman took a somewhat neutral stand but argued that the single administrator must be selected on the basis of merit and fitness. The League of Women Voters supported the civil service recommendations of the President's Committee.[3] The proposal for a single civil service administrator actually passed both houses but was eliminated along with some other controversial features of the bill in final efforts to get the House and Senate to agree.

The Reorganization Plans of 1949.—The problem of how to get the most effective service out of the federal personnel agency was reviewed after the

[1] A summary of its recommendations on personnel administration is available in *Administrative Management in the Government of the United States* (Washington: Government Printing Office, 1937), pp. 9–12.

[2] See testimony of Harry B. Mitchell, president of the commission, in United States Senate, Select Committee on Government Organization, *Hearings on S. 2700*, 75th Cong., 1st Sess. (Washington: Government Printing Office, 1937), p. 273.

[3] *Ibid.*, pp. 139–159.

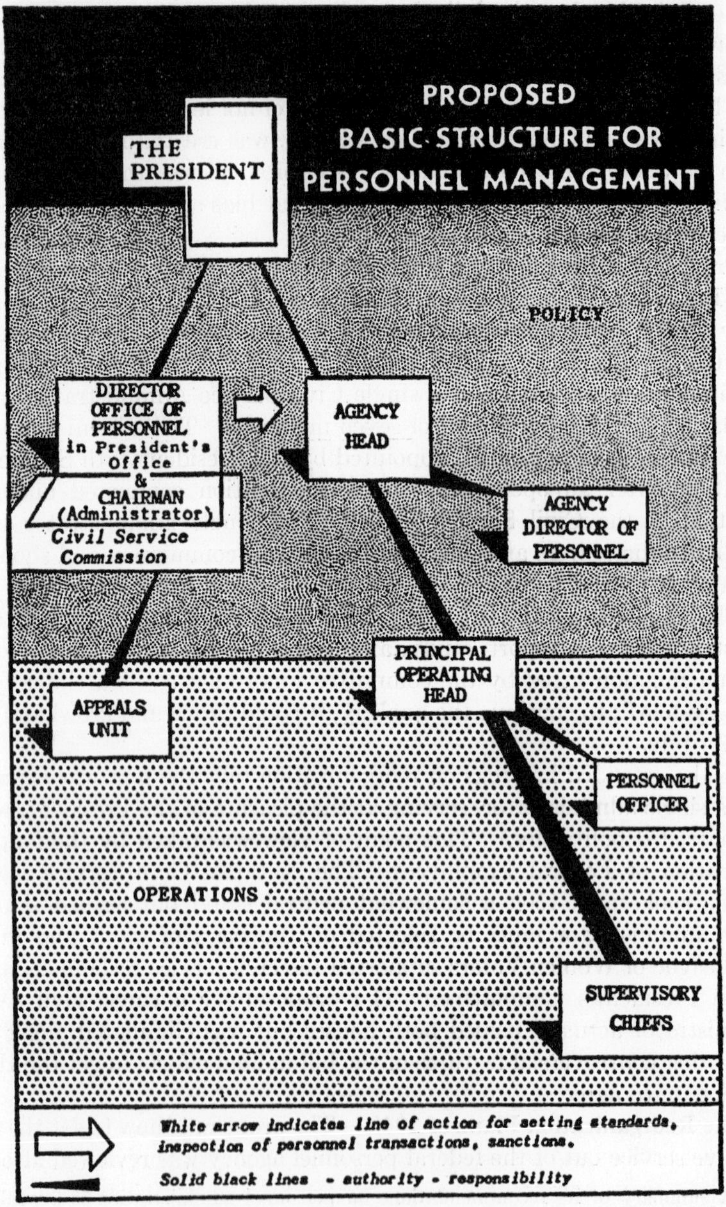

The Hoover Commission's basic recommendation in the personnel administration field, that the chairman be vested with administrative power formerly possessed by the Civil Service Commission as a body, was achieved through reorganization plan number 5 of 1949. SOURCE: Hoover Commission, *Concluding Report*, p. 38.

war by the Hoover Commission.[1] Proposed changes in the Civil Service Commission will be considered here; some of the criticisms leveled at existing personnel practices will be considered in later sections. The chairman of the Commission, under the Hoover plan, would be given responsibility for the administrative aspects of its work and would head an Office of Personnel in the President's Office. The Commission would cease to deal with the detail of personnel transactions, which would be turned over to personnel officers of the agencies. The Commission would then concentrate on setting standards, checking on personnel programs in the agencies, and hearing appeals. What the Hoover group proposed is a compromise between the commission form and the single administrator. James K. Pollock, in a statement of additional views, made a strong case for going the whole distance toward a "modern concept" of personnel management under a single personnel commissioner.

President Truman's reorganization plan 5 of 1949 effected most of the organizational changes recommended by the Hoover Commission; the chairman was vested with all administrative authority, including the functions of appointing, supervising, and directing personnel and internal organization. The Civil Service Commission as a body retains power to make rules and regulations, hear appeals, investigate, and recommend improvements. A general manager, called the executive director, is appointed by the chairman.

EXTENT OF THE PUBLIC SERVICE

Civil employment in the executive branch of the Federal government, which reached the one-million mark in 1940, rose to over 3 million during the Second World War, and dropped off to a plateau of slightly over 2 million in the first half-decade after the war.

Characteristics of Federal Personnel.—Approximately 75 per cent of all federal civil employees and in the permanent, competitive civil service; the other 25 per cent occupy exempt or temporary positions.

Geographically, the 2 million federal workers are spread throughout the world. Some 95 per cent of them is in continental United States; the heaviest concentration, as might be expected, is in Washington, where about 10 per cent is stationed.[2]

When civil employees are classified according to departments and agencies employing them, the Post Office has 514,000; the Army, 377,000; the Navy,

[1] Hoover Commission, *Personnel Management* (Washington: Government Printing Office, 1949), pp. 9–10 relates to the Civil Service Commission. Professor Pollock's case for the single administrator is on pp. 53–55.

[2] United States Civil Service Commission, *Monthly Report of Employment, Executive Branch of the Federal Government*, May, 1949.

351,000; the Veterans' Administration, 200,000; the Air Force, 167,000; the Treasury, 91,000; and Agriculture, 79,000. These seven agencies account for nearly seven-eighths of the total; all other activities of the executive branch are manned by the remaining quarter-million. During the second half of 1949 the Secretary of Defense ordered drastic cuts in the numbers of civilian employees of the armed service departments.

GOVERNMENT EMPLOYEES

UNITED STATES, 1929–1948

IN MILLIONS

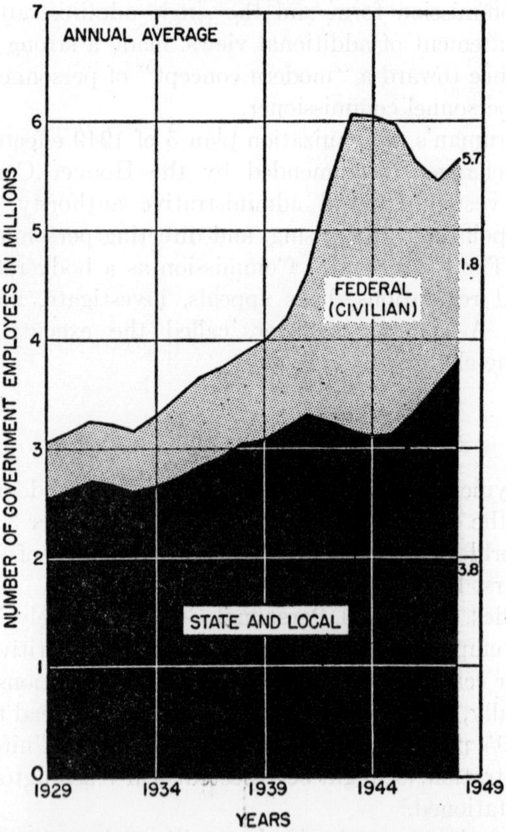

The Federal government had an average of 534,000 civilians on its pay roll in 1929. By 1941 the number had grown to 1,302,000, and by V–E Day to approximately 2,925,000. Immediately after the war there was a downward trend, but that has now been reversed. In December, 1948, the number of Federal employees was the largest since 1946. State and local government together have through the years had more employees than the Federal government, but their percentage increase since 1929 has been nowhere near so great. After a wartime decline, the state and local total has been increasing. SOURCE: United States Bureau of Labor Statistics.

Early Expansion.—The Pendleton Act provided that the "classified service" should be extended by presidential order or by act of Congress. Only 13,900 positions, or 10.5 per cent of federal executive employees, were included in the original classified status in 1883.[1] Before his term was completed, President Chester A. Arthur added around 1,650 positions to the classified service. Each President who has served since then has increased the number of positions included. Some Presidents have been motivated by a devotion to the improvement of the public service. Others have sought primarily to "blanket in" their political appointees. Until recently those holding the offices at the time of inclusion in the classified service received classified status automatically.

Recent Civil Service Extension.—When Franklin D. Roosevelt was elected President in November, 1932, the executive civil service had reached more than four-fifths classified, the highest mark in history. In meeting the problems born of the economic depression, many new agencies and services were undertaken by the Federal government. Nearly all the employees of these new agencies were exempted from the classified service. During the fiscal year of 1933 alone, the proportion of federal civil employees within the classified group declined from 80.7 per cent to 66.9 per cent; by 1936 it had declined to a low of 60.5 per cent.[2] It is fair to add that many of the new agencies were regarded as temporary and emergency, and this was one reason for not including their employees in the civil service.

During 1937, the increase of the classified service was resumed. The first great step in the New Deal era toward extending the formal merit-system coverage came with an executive order of June 24, 1938.[3] Specifically, it authorized adding to the classified service nearly all but policy-forming positions. Congress reduced the effective coverage of the order by about one-half through restrictive provisions in appropriations measures. The President delayed placing the plan into full effect by issuing another executive order on Jan. 31, 1939, in order to allow further study of certain high professional and administrative posts.[4]

Shortly afterward the President appointed a committee headed by Associate Justice Stanley Reed of the United States Supreme Court and directed it to study and recommend what should be done about the positions in question. The committee was known as the President's Committee on Civil Service Improvement. It reported in February, 1941, recommending inclusion in the classified competitive service of virtually all

[1] United States Civil Service Commission, *History of the Federal Civil Service*, p. 59.

[2] *Ibid.*, p. 123.

[3] Executive Order No. 7916.

[4] Executive Order No. 8044.

positions delayed in 1939.[1] One of its principal tasks was to examine the methods of choosing attorneys for the federal service. Alternative plans were presented: one provided for an ungraded register of eligibles from which appointments might be made; the other would have listed eligibles in the order of their examination grades. The President chose the ungraded register plan. In April, 1941, the President issued an executive order bringing the withheld positions under the classified service.

In the meantime, Congress had enacted the Ramspeck Act of 1940, which gave to the President still broader powers over extension of the classified service.[2] The President may now, with few exceptions, extend formal classified protection to all non-policy-making positions in the executive branch.

Postwar Problems.—In the postwar period the federal personnel situation approached the chaotic stage. Reduction in force by about a million employees was required. Veterans' preference set a large part of the pattern of new recruiting. The aftermath of war brought demands for able new personnel to serve in the veterans' programs and to administer overseas aid programs. High-level employment conditions in private business and low morale in the federal service combined to produce turnover, requiring a recruiting program of a magnitude unmatched in peacetime. All these major problems and a host of minor ones had to be faced with personnel machinery and practices designed in large part to curb the spoilsmen and loaded down with ". . . a maze of personnel laws, rules, and regulations."[3]

The half-million employees outside the formal classified service include two principal groups: those in exempt positions, and temporary appointees. The Hoover task force broke down the exempt category into three classes: (1) positions of a policy-determining character, (2) positions of a confidential nature, and (3) positions for which competitive examinations are impractical.[4] Both Federal Bureau of Investigation and Tennessee Valley Authority, which have independent personnel systems, are completely exempt. Many overseas employees occupy exempt posts. Collectors of customs and collectors of internal revenue remain political. Although postmasters take civil service examinations, the requirement of Senate confirmation has left their selection charged with politics.

The large number of temporary employees in the federal service is attributable in part to the ponderous method of recruiting and appointing

[1] See United States President's Committee on Civil Service Improvement, *op. cit.*, pp. 1–8.

[2] 54 Stat. 1211.

[3] Hoover Commission, *op. cit.*, p. 30.

[4] *Task Force Report on Federal Personnel*, p. 19.

(requiring 4 to 8 months) and the immediate necessity of getting someone on a job when a vacancy occurs.

Merit System Groups.—The expansion and improvement of the merit system has been made possible in large part through the interest and support of citizens and groups. Two national organizations deserve special mention in this regard. The Civil Service Assembly of the United States and Canada grew out of a conference held in Washington in 1906 on the invitation of President Theodore Roosevelt and the United States Civil Service Commission. It is the organization of civil service commissioners and personnel engaged in public personnel administration. It is not an aggressive promotional group but works mainly in the research and technical fields. Through annual conferences and periodicals—monthly *Newsletter* and quarterly *Public Personnel Review*—the assembly provides mediums for the interchange of views and the discussion of problems by personnel administrators and students.

The National Civil Service Reform League, launched in 1881, is the crusading organization in this field. It has conducted campaigns for the extension of the merit-system idea and for the expansion of the classified service after systems have been adopted.[1]

In the states there are many citizens' groups operating wholly or partially in the field of merit-system reform and defense. The League of Women Voters—national, state, and local—has been one of the most vigilant and informed of these groups.

THE SELECTION PROCESS

Recruitment.—The first task in a personnel program is to interest potential personnel in applying for positions. On the whole this work has been done poorly by American public personnel agencies. Those who knock at the gates asking for admission to the federal service often are wholly self-informed about the prospects of public employment. As a result of their passiveness, personnel agencies commonly have failed to cultivate the most promising sources of able recruits. They have contented themselves with publishing a formal announcement of forthcoming examinations and having it posted in public places. Recently there has been some improvement in recruiting practices.

The field from which recruiting is done is limited by the prerequisites stipulated for the position under consideration. Age limits are used, but ordinarily American personnel agencies are very liberal and permit a great age range for most jobs. Outside pressure is exerted to keep open maximum opportunities for public employment to persons of middle age oı

[1] For further information, see Frank M. Stewart, *The National Civil Service Reform League: History, Activities and Problems* (Austin: University of Texas Press, 1929).

after. Authorities in the personnel field favor induction of persons into the public service while they are young, making possible a long and specialized career in the government service.[1]

Closely related to age of recruiting is the question of education. In many instances the idea of giving everyone a chance has been used to justify low educational requirements or none at all. For professional posts, of course, a license to practice or a professional degree is required, but strenuous opposition develops to allegedly "undemocratic" barriers in the form of educational prerequisites. Untrained persons may be eliminated later through examinations, but the cost of giving tests to unqualified persons represents waste of public funds. Another important question in regard to education concerns the desirable type of training. Since American civil service examinations have been largely practical in nature, persons with specialized training have been favored. The experience of the British and other great civil service systems has favored the recruiting of those with general education, with specialization to follow induction.

Experience is another qualification commonly required. This varies widely with the position. Personnel agencies often stress experience to the exclusion of education, thus favoring the older applicant over the younger. Citizenship and residence almost invariably are required, although a waiver of the residence requirement is made occasionally for positions for which qualifications are rare. Sex usually is specified in a recruiting announcement; far more and better paid jobs are available for men than for women.

The public is informed of opportunities in government employment through the common formal printed announcement, inquiries in schools, use of mailing lists, newspaper advertisements and stories, and radio programs. The task of recruitment has been defined by Prof. Leonard D. White, former United States Civil Service Commissioner, in the following terms:

> It calls for special skill and in any large organization deserves separate organization. Recruitment involves more than mere announcement and passive acceptance; to meet the requirements of our present public service, it must be active, searching, selective, persistent and continuous.[2]

The Hoover Commission would make the operating agency mainly responsible for recruiting.

[1] See the report of the Commission of Inquiry on Public Service Personnel, *op. cit.*, pp. 38–45. The Hoover Commission, *Personal Management*, p. 3, declares: "Not enough time and effort are being spent on recruiting our best young men and women for junior professional, scientific, technical, and administrative posts."

[2] Leonard D. White, *Introduction to the Study of Public Administration* (New York: Macmillan, 1939), p. 316.

Application for the Job.—After he has been interested in the available position, the recruit fills out an application form. The blank should call for data necessary to establish the applicant's eligibility for the post to be filled. Spaces are provided for name, address, age, education, experience, references, and a variety of other matters. A photograph of the applicant sometimes is required. If the application is approved, the candidate for the job may take the examination. The application may be rejected if the applicant lacks some stipulated requirement, or if he has something in his record that disqualifies him.

Private industries place much stress on the application, and work over the completed form with much care. Since a formal examination is to follow directly, public personnel agencies have neglected to check up on statements entered. In cases where no formal test is to be administered, the application form is far more extensive, for it and the references provided may provide the whole basis for judgment of the applicant.

Examination.—The first civil service examinations in the United States were "pass" examinations given by examining boards of federal departments under an act of 1853.[1] They were noncompetitive and unstandardized. Competitive examinations, open to all, were experimented with in federal service as early as 1872 but were not established on a permanent basis until 1883. Today most of the positions under the federal, state, and local merit systems are filled from eligible lists made up of persons who have passed a formal written examination. From the beginning federal tests were practical in nature, related to the duties of the office sought. Practical examinations are characteristically American and are rather well suited for selecting clerical and manipulative workers. General examinations are typically British and have proved superior for the selection of persons capable of filling the higher administrative posts. Each of these two types of examinations has proved its value, and each appears to have its place in an adequate testing program. It is not enough to test technical abilities alone and leave out of consideration capacity for growth, as may be done under "practical" American tests. The general British examination would be misapplied if used as the sole test for mail sorters in the post office. The obvious conclusion is that both achievement and capacity are needed in varying degrees by public employees, and the case is rarely found where one is needed to the complete exclusion of the other.

Examinations accordingly are designed to test for these different qualities. Aptitude tests are used to measure general, social, and mechanical intelligence and capacity. Abstract or general intelligence is reported in terms of intelligence quotient (IQ), as revealed by the Army alpha test and its modern successors. Persons who fall below the level of IQ judged necessary for the occupation concerned may be eliminated from consider-

[1] United States Civil Service Commission, *History of the Federal Civil Service*, p. 28.

ation. Social intelligence may be tested through several standardized examinations, the purpose of which is to disclose adjustments and reactions to altered circumstances and different people. Mechanical intelligence tests have been experimented with recently; they are intended to test potential mechanical capacity rather than achievement.

Achievement tests measure informational and technical training—such as speed of typing, accuracy of arithmetic, knowledge of tools. These fall distinctly in the category of practical tests specified in so many American civil service laws.

Forms of Examinations.—In form, the usual examination is written rather than oral, and objective rather than essay. The oral examination has been used very satisfactorily in some places, but it is both slow and open to abuses. The interview held by the appointing officer after certification may prove sufficient for ascertaining personality, particularly when he may choose between the three highest. The short answer or objective type of examination has displaced almost entirely for the civil service the traditional essay form. The essay examination is slow to read and difficult to grade fairly, especially when a very large number of papers are involved; the essay also places a premium on literary ability and penmanship. The objective examination, on the other hand, has the assets of speedy grading and definite and standardized answers. The latest development in this field is the machine-scored test, which can be fed to a counting machine for accurate grading and lightning results. The objective tests take the usual forms—completion, true-false, multiple choice, and matching.

Tests usually are administered by employees of a personnel agency, but over one-half of recent (1947–1949) federal examinations have been given by operating departments and agencies. Under the Hoover Commission recommendations, primary responsibility would be placed upon departments and agencies, subject to commission approval of the program and inspection to assure compliance with law. Applicants generally are required to assemble at convenient locations within the jurisdiction. A few public personnel agencies charge small fees for the privilege of taking an examination, but most examinations are free to all whose applications are acceptable.

THE APPOINTING PROCESS

Preparation of Eligible List.—Applicants who receive a passing grade in the examination have their names listed on a register in the order of their scores, except that veterans are given preference. This eligible list for a particular position (as stenographer, patrolman, senior attorney) is made available to appointing officers. When the eligible list becomes exhausted or obsolete, another examination is held to renew it. Eligible lists are based upon the classification system employed by the jurisdiction. If this classification provides for thousands of minute categories, flexibility is lost; for a bookkeeper post in one agency may not be filled by a person on the eligible list for bookkeeper in another agency. The question of classification is taken up in a subsequent section of this chapter.

Veterans' Preference.—Veterans' preference constitutes one of the most hotly controversial questions in the public personnel field. The first preference law was enacted by Congress at the close of the Civil War; in 1919 preference was extended on a generous scale. Under existing law and rules, veterans and their widows are entitled to a 5 per cent preference and disabled veterans or their wives may claim an additional 5 per cent.[1] Also, veterans are favored in appointment, in retention when forces are being reduced, and in other ways. During the 20-year period, 1920–1940, 24.06 per cent of all appointed to the federal service received veterans' preference.[2]

As the Second World War drew to a close, Congress enacted the Veterans Preference Act of 1944, which virtually closes the greater part of the federal service to nonveterans for a long time to come. The act[3] provides that preference shall be given to (1) ex-service men and women with service-connected disabilities, (2) wives of disabled servicemen who are themselves unable to work, (3) unmarried widows of deceased servicemen, and (4) any ex-service person. Those in categories 1, 2, and 3 are entitled to have ten points added to examination scores; moreover, certain types of jobs, such as guards, elevator operators, messengers, and custodians, are reserved exclusively for these groups. Veterans in the fourth category receive five extra points. Persons of all categories receive generous credit for military and other experience, some waivers of age, height, weight, physical and educational requirements, and special privileges when appointments are being made.

Those who favor veterans' preference maintain that this is a proper way for a government to show its appreciation to those who risked their lives in its behalf. Opponents of preference grant the obligation of government to veterans but wish to meet it in ways that will not lower the efficiency of the public service.

The Hoover Commission sought to put veterans' preference on a defensible basis by grouping all applicants as "outstanding," "well qualified," "qualified," and "unqualified"; within each quality category, veterans would be considered ahead of nonveterans. This proposal should eliminate the appointment of veterans incapable of doing a job, yet give

[1] The most comprehensive study of this problem is John F. Miller, "Veteran Preference in the Public Service," in *Problems of the American Public Service* (New York: McGraw-Hill, 1935).

[2] United States Civil Service Commission, *Annual Report, 1940* (Washington: Government Printing Office, 1940), p. 134.

[3] 58 Stat. 387.

qualified veterans absolute advantage over nonveterans in the same quality group.

Appointment.—When the appointing officer wishes to fill a vacancy, he sends to the personnel agency for the eligible list. If he is a federal official, this process is handled by the director of personnel of his department or establishment. The request for eligibles is called a "requisition" and generally must state the title, duties, salary, and qualifications required. Federal law prescribes that the three names ranking highest on the eligible list shall be certified to the appointing officer. In the various other jurisdictions the number certified ranges from one to seven. The appointing officer is permitted to choose from among those certified to him. The arguments for allowing some latitude are strong, for personality and other factors not adequately assessed in written examinations may be judged from oral interview by the appointing officer.

Certification of eligibles by a civil service commission may be made out of regular order owing to two factors. First, veterans' preference in some jurisdictions (including the Federal government under the Preference Act of 1944) requires the disabled veteran to be certified ahead of others on the eligible list. Second, appointments to the federal positions in Washington are required to be apportioned among the states in proportion to their population. Although the latter has not been rigidly applied, it does favor those eligibles from some states and places at a disadvantage those from states the quotas of which are filled.

The usual procedure is for the appointing officer to review such information as the personnel agency has on the eligible persons. Then the one adjudged the most promising candidate is called for interview. If personal qualities and appearance are found to be satisfactory, appointment follows; if unsatisfactory, the second choice may be interviewed and appointed. Sometimes all certified persons are interviewed before a selection is made.

The Hoover Commission and its personnel task force used strong words to condemn the excessive centralization that is a barrier to getting the right person promptly into the correct job. It is impossible to break the bottleneck so long as a closed central register of eligibles must be maintained for the whole country. An active register containing thousands of names is being drawn upon constantly by appointing agencies. The letter of the law appears to require that the top three names must be certified, but in practice dozens of names may be out to different agencies simultaneously.

The appointing officer is in a difficult spot. From the "grab bag" of the active register he is certified the names of three people whose places near the top of the register may have resulted from a high score on a written examination, from veterans' preference, or from the fact that others ahead on the register had already been certified or appointed, or had declined. From personal interviews, the appointing officer may conclude that none of the eligibles has the personality or ability to do the job at hand. Under existing procedures he usually must either appoint one of the eligibles or allow the position to remain vacant and hope for a better list next time.

To correct the existing defects, the Hoover Commission recommended not only decentralization of recruiting and examining but also giving appointing officers more leeway than the "rule of three" allows.

Several abuses may be present at the appointing level. Provisional appointments sometimes are made when no eligible list is available in order to appoint some person who is qualified mainly by political services. It is possible later that provisional appointees may be blanketed into the permanent service after noncompetitive examinations. In some jurisdictions appointing officers may conspire to appoint political friends by securing "waivers" from persons higher on the eligible list by threats or promises.

Appointed at last, the new civil servant is not yet fully secure. Normally he must serve out satisfactorily a period of probation, up to 6 months in length. Within this period, or at the close of it, the probationer may be dropped from the service if he has been found unsuitable. Few civil service agencies have adequate systems for efficiency rating; the reluctance of a superior officer to dismiss except for serious deficiency is general. As a result, the probationary test period is much less meaningful than might be expected.

CLASSIFICATION AND COMPENSATION

Duties Classification.—The term "classification" is used in the personnel field in two separate ways. It is employed in a jurisdictional sense to indicate whether or not positions are within or without the "classified" or merit service. The more common use is in an occupational sense, classifying jobs on the basis of duties performed. A duties or occupational classification is necessary in order to simplify the task of personnel management and to render possible the elemental justice of equal pay, prestige, and title for equal work.

Occupational classification is accomplished through a process of job analysis. This may be done by the personnel agency or by an outside body or concern. In order to find out what work and responsibility a particular job involves, questionnaires are filled out and interviews held. When this is completed, individual positions are arranged into classes, groups, and services. Each class is assigned specifications—including title, duties, and qualifications. The plan is put into force by law or by executive order. The class is the basic unit; it is composed of a number of similar positions, as, for example, typists or clerks. Every position is then placed in a class; within each class the qualifications and scale of compensation for each position are nearly the same.

Under the Classification Act of 1949,[1] the policy of equal pay for equal work is supported by varying rates of compensation in proportion to the difficulty, responsibility, and qualifications involved. The act covers about 885,000 positions in the Federal service. A "position" consists of the work, duties, and responsibilities assignable to an officer or employee. A "class" includes those positions sufficiently similar in kind of work, level of difficulty or responsibility, and qualification requirements to warrant similar treatment. A "grade" embraces all classes sufficiently equal as to responsibility and qualifications to justify placing them within one range of rates of compensation. Each position is placed in the appropriate class and grade. The act establishes two schedules of grades and salary ranges: a "General Schedule" (GS) of eighteen grades and a "Crafts, Protective, and Custodial Schedule" (CPC) of ten grades. The new classification act is administered by the Civil Service Commission.

The movement for duties classification is of recent origin. Some state and local civil service jurisdictions pioneered in the adoption of classification plans; the Federal Classification Act became law only in 1923. This act was made to apply only to certain government positions in Washington and did not include jobs in the field service.[2] The Personnel Classification Board administered provisions of the act until 1932, when its functions were transferred to the Civil Service Commission. The Ramspeck Act of 1940, which provided the basis for great expansion of the classified service, also authorized the commission to survey the field service and recommend to the President that duties classification be extended by executive order. Some earlier appropriation acts had brought rough duties classification to the field service.

Compensation.—Once the job of classification is done, the next great task is that of fixing compensation schedules. Although it appears only elemental justice that like pay should be fixed for like work, a great range of compensation for comparable work is found in jurisdictions without adequate classification and salary standardization systems. With the installation of proper classification plans, however, the basis for salary uniformity for work of a given class and grade has been established.

The public wage scale ought to be kept in some degree of harmony with that of private employment. Wages must be high enough to attract and hold good public employees, but not so high as to make government work overly attractive. In practice, public personnel agencies constantly base

[1] 63 Stat. 782. The Classification Act of 1923 arranged classes into great services which were, at the time the 1949 act went into effect, (1) professional and scientific, (2) subprofessional, (3) clerical, administrative, and fiscal, (4) custodial, and (5) clerical-mechanical.

[2] United States Civil Service Commission, *History of the Federal Civil Service*, pp. 111–113. In 1940 about 93,000 positions in Washington were included.

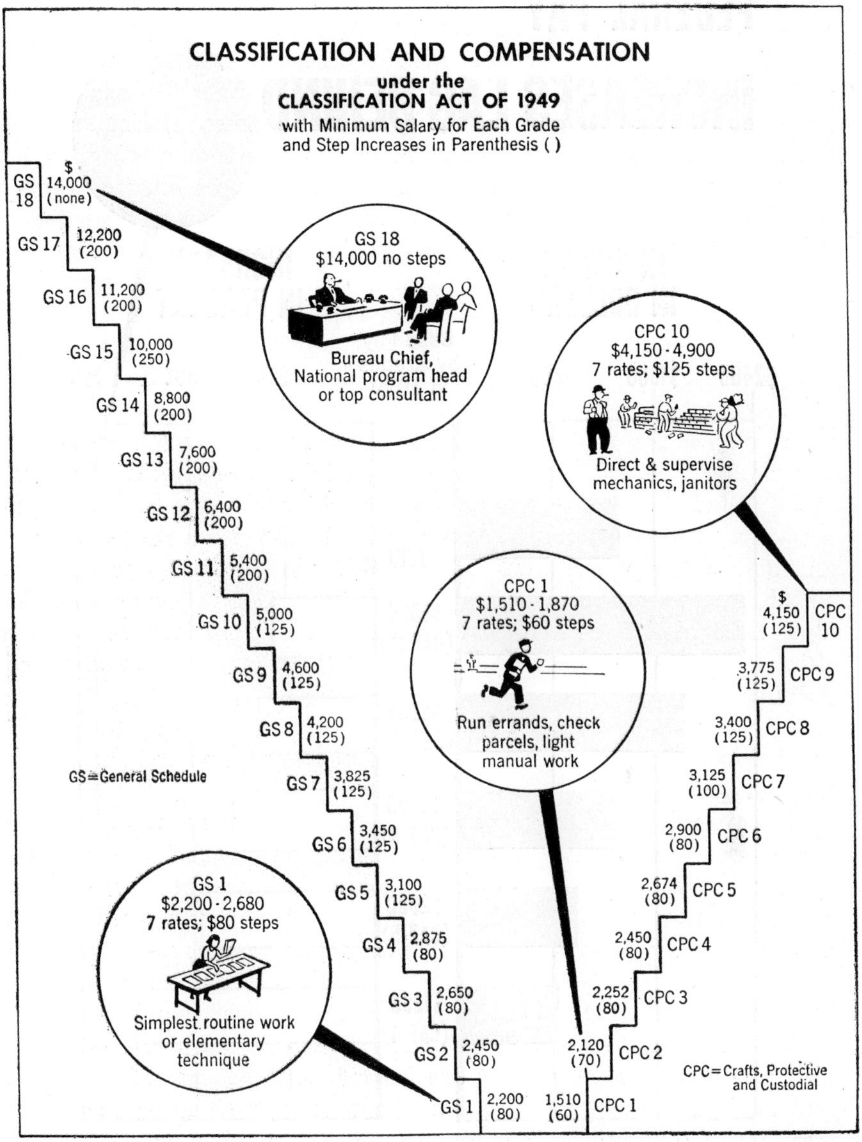

The Classification Act of 1949 reorganized the federal classified service, increased compensation, and created three new grades (16, 17, and 18) that offer added prestige and salary to higher civil servants. Step increases are normally annual if the increase is less than $200 and each year and one-half if $200 or more.

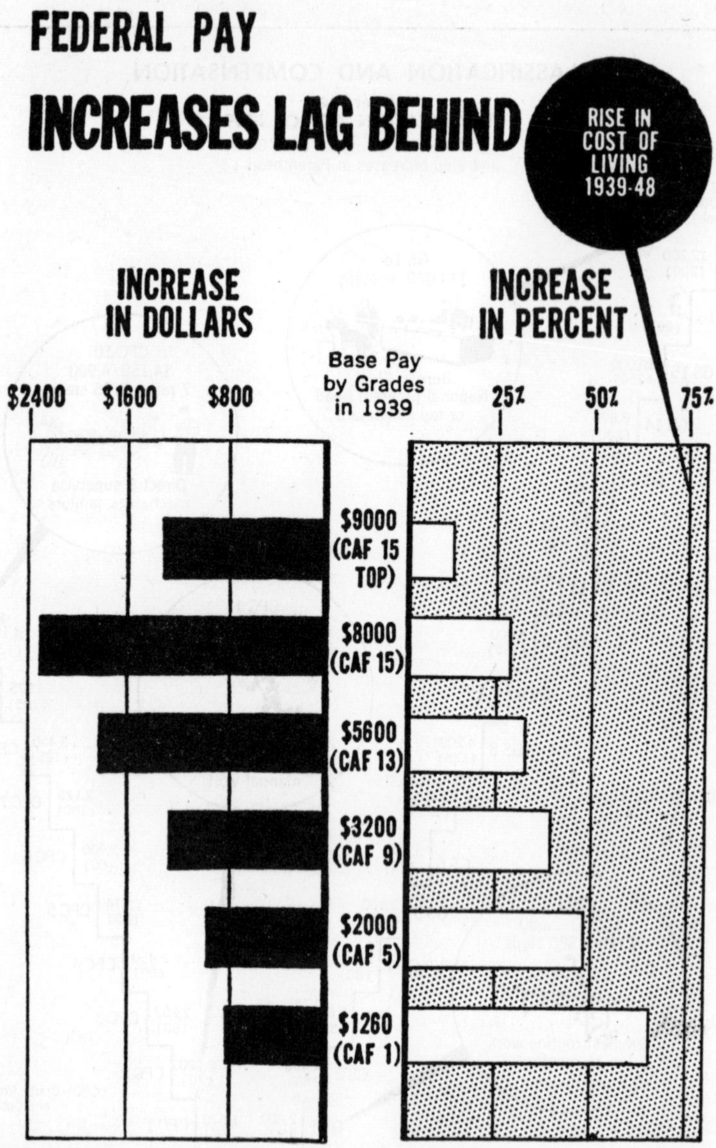

The Hoover Commission used the illustration above to show how, despite increases, federal pay has lagged behind the 75 per cent increase in cost of living between 1939 and 1948. Note how little compensation of top federal executives (CAF 15) has increased. This explains in part low morale and high turnover. SOURCE: Hoover Commission, *Concluding Report*, p. 20.

salaries upon studies of comparable positions in private employment. If the usual starting wage for a file clerk is $150 per month in private New York offices, a public agency in the same city will have to approximate that for a beginner in the same line.

Another aspect of the same problem is to provide justly for differences of education or experience required for the various posts within a public service. The occupant of a job requiring a long and expensive professional education, as a physician or attorney, will demand higher compensation than a public relations officer, who may have no educational requirement. Deference to such considerations is difficult to allow, however, and the main reliance must be placed upon competition; if naval architects are hard to find, the compensation must be raised until one is attracted.

Within each class of positions several rates of compensation will be provided, ranging from a minimum, through some intermediate categories, to a maximum. Thus a typist might enter at $2,080 per year, and advance, with two or three intermediate salaries, to a maximum of $2,600. Ordinarily a new employee starts at the minimum rate; his aspiration to move on to the next salary rank constitutes an important incentive to do well.

Sentiment is strong among public employees to make salary increases within a given position automatic, an annual or biennial increment. Such a plan produces overemphasis on time serving and seniority and fails to take into account value of services performed, as decided by superior officers, with or without formal efficiency ratings.

Standard compensation schedules may be departed from through differentials justified by some special circumstances. In the American Foreign Service, for example, a special fund is appropriated for allocation among those who serve in countries with monetary exchange unfavorable to the dollar. At certain periods it is more costly to live in one section of continental United States than in another. A construction worker on a remote Pacific island or on the Panama Canal might reasonably be paid a bonus for working under adverse climatic conditions. While adding to the difficulties of administration, some differentials would appear justified when working and living conditions vary greatly.

If public salaries are to be based upon rates for comparable private employment, consideration must be given to the fluctuations in business conditions. While public pay may not be so flexible as compensation for private employment, substantial justice may be achieved by the fact that the public salary dips less to the depths in depression periods and fails to rise as much in prosperity. The civil servant therefore may be envied in bad times and pitied in good times. If a depression is long, the public employee is likely to have a flat percentage salary cut; if cost of living increases sharply, he may lobby through an increase. A few jurisdictions have attempted to adjust salaries to a cost-of-living index formula.

Recent Pay Reforms.—The Hoover Commission had two major complaints over compensation of federal employees. The first was that the higher technical, scientific, and executive positions had inadequate salaries.

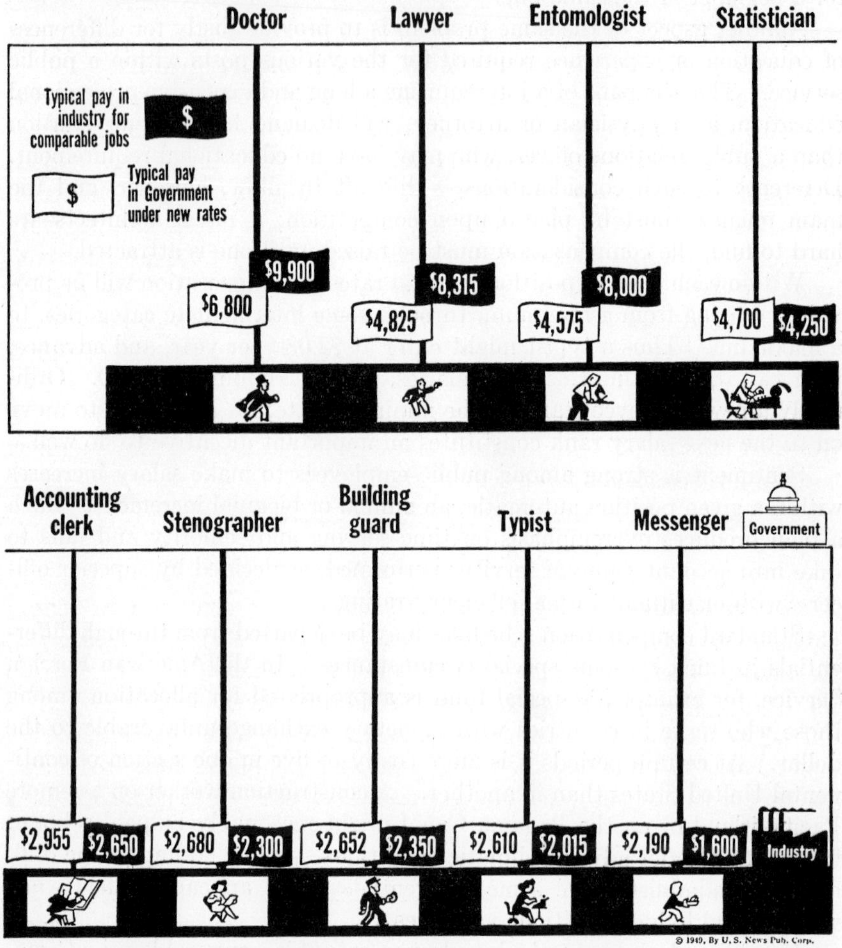

SOURCE: Reprinted from *United States News & World Report*, an independent weekly magazine on national and international affairs, published at Washington. Copyright, 1949, United States News Publishing Corporation.

With few exceptions, federal employees were limited to a maximum of $10,330 per year. For many years, but especially around the end of the war, large numbers of top administrators had been leaving the federal service for private posts that paid much higher salaries. The Eighty-first Congress in 1949 enacted legislation authorizing salaries of from $14,000 to $22,500 for 253 top officials outside the civil service. Companion legislation provided pay increases for other classes of federal workers. Three new grades were created at the top of the civil service: Grade 16, limited to 300 employees, with salaries from $11,000 to $12,000; Grade 17, limited to 75, $12,200 to $13,000; Grade 18, limited to 25, $14,000. Some 885,000 regular classified employees received increases that averaged $141 per year. The average increase for 435,000 postal workers was $120 yearly.

The other criticism relating to compensation that was made by the Hoover group concerned the "inequitable and complex" pay administrative practices. As the 1919 legislation described above illustrates, various groups of employees are dealt with, so far as pay policies are concerned, under various laws and by diverse agencies. Actually there are four main groups when arranged according to pay policies: (1) over 850,000 employees, largely of the "white collar" group, who are covered by the Classification Act of 1949; (2) some 600,000 employees, largely manual, whose wages are fixed by the agencies for which they work; (3) about 500,000 postal workers who are paid under laws limited to the Post Office; (4) the remainder, about 70,000, who have compensation fixed under several special laws. The Hoover Commission's proposal that a comprehensive pay policy be set in law has not been acted upon by Congress.

EFFICIENCY AND MORALE

Service Ratings.—How can the efficiency of public employees be tested? Civil service agencies have experimented with various systems to rate performance. Most of them have been branded as failures by authorities in the field.[1] The simplest and surest method of rating is one based upon quantity and quality of production at some routine task. Like piecework in industry, this can apply only to a limited number of jobs—as typist, machine operator, or other work capable of unit measurement. It is possible also to rate employees by examinations or tests given at regular intervals, but this method has had little development.

The formal rating schemes have had broader application. They require that the superior officer indicate on a form of some kind his evaluation of each employee under his direction. One common method is to rate by traits or level of performance, utilizing a "graphic rating scale" on which the supervisor checks the description appropriate to the employee's qualities and work.[2] Another method, called "man-to-man comparison," requires the superior officer to rank his subordinates in terms of best, average, and poorest.

[1] Mosher and Kingsley, *op. cit.*, pp. 482–483.

[2] White, *op. cit.*, pp. 376–382, gives an excellent summary of United States Civil Service Commission experience with the graphic rating scale used 1923–1934, and the simpler rating form adopted in 1935.

In recent years most attention has been given to the Probst system of service rating, developed by Mr. J. B. Probst of the St. Paul Civil Service Bureau.[1] It causes the rating officer to assess the qualities of an employee in great detail, covering principally personality traits and characteristics. The Probst system has been used in several jurisdictions and is generally looked upon more favorably than have been the graphic rating and man-to-man methods.

The basic difficulty with efficiency rating schemes lies in securing unprejudiced and frank evaluations by superior officers. In the judgment of authorities on personnel, service ratings are still in a rudimentary stage. However imperfect, they are nevertheless improving and represent an advance over the uncoordinated efforts of individual supervisors to judge performance. Certainly at the present stage of development service ratings should not be the only criteria employed in deciding on promotion but may properly be used as one of the factors to be considered.

In place of the present federal rating system, the Hoover Commission proposed an "ability and service record" rating under which the supervisor would (*a*) evaluate ability, past performance, progress, and potential usefulness on specific factors, and (*b*) discuss with the employee his strengths and weaknesses. The Hoover group urged that the rating not be used as a basis for determining salary increases, lay-offs, or dismissals.

Disciplinary Action.—It is obvious that civil servants should not be immune from disciplinary action, including removal. They are obliged to perform their duties faithfully, to obey the law, and to avoid conduct unbecoming in a public employee. Sometimes these obligations are set forth in specific detail in an administrative code; most American governments have failed to set forth employee rights and duties with clarity. The rules for the conduct of federal employees are found in laws such as the Hatch Act, and in the rules of Civil Service Commission and operating agencies.

The administrative employee of the United States may not participate in partisan political activities.[2] An employee of the classified service may be removed only for such cause "as will promote the efficiency of said service" and he must be notified in writing of the charges and given a public hearing.[3] The Civil Service Commission rules give the commission a restricted power to investigate, but the real authority over removals is in the hands of the appointing officer. Responsibility for disciplining and removal in the federal service rests almost completely with the head of the department or agency.

[1] See John B. Probst, *Service Ratings* (Chicago: Bureau of Public Personnel Administration and Civil Service Assembly, 1931).

[2] The Hatch Act of 1939 covered this aspect most fully. See 53 Stat. 1147.

[3] 37 Stat. 539.

Many forms of disciplinary action exist. A minor infraction may be dealt with by reprimand or warning. Intermediate offenses may be handled by demerits in service ratings, loss of seniority, or transfer to an undesirable location of work. Serious violations may lead to suspension, demotion, or dismissal. In the federal service, except in loyalty cases, no appeal is possible from disciplinary action approved by a department head. Proposals have been made to authorize the Civil Service Commission to review disciplinary cases, or to establish a special court to hear appeals from disciplinary action. Some civil service jurisdictions follow the existing federal scheme of permitting broad discretion on the part of the appointing officer. Others vest important disciplinary authority in the personnel commission. Still others allow appeals to the courts on a liberal basis.

Morale and Prestige.—Morale is defined as a state of mind, with reference to confidence. Leonard D. White has written:

> High morale is a state of mind in which men and women voluntarily seek to develop and apply their full powers to the task on which they are engaged by reason of the intellectual or moral satisfaction which they derive from their own self-realization, their achievements in their chosen field, and their pride in the service; it is also a social situation in which men and women are aware of the degree to which they are mutually affected by these motives and respond to this knowledge.[1]

Prestige is related to morale, but is different. It means the respect for achievement or standing of an individual or group. Both high morale and high prestige are important to the effective functioning of a public body.

Among the commonly recognized prerequisites to high morale in the public service are such factors as security from spoils politics, fairness in wages and working conditions, recognition of good work, and adequacy of retirement system. Group morale or *esprit de corps* may be heightened by an agency through attention to its employees' social life, living conditions, credit facilities, unions, and associations.

Many of the same factors that produce high morale also contribute to the prestige of an agency or of public employment generally. A worker wishes to be well thought of, to enjoy the admiration of people. The American public service has not enjoyed the prestige value of the British civil service. This low esteem may be traced to several factors, notably to spoils politics, low wages, and insecurity of tenure. Recently advances have been made on these fronts and prestige has improved. Plenty of room for further improvement remains, however, and the nation may well aspire to making employment in its service as attractive as that in any private concern.[2]

[1] White, *op. cit.*, p. 443.

[2] For further reading, see Leonard D. White, *The Prestige Value of Public Employment* (Chicago: University of Chicago Press, 1929); and *Further Contributions to the Prestige Value of Public Employment* (Chicago: University of Chicago Press, 1932).

Evidence of widespread employee dissatisfaction may be found in the high turnover rate that plagues the federal service. The Hoover Commission reported in 1949 that 500,000 persons had to be recruited each year in order to maintain a work force of 2,000,000; this means that one out of each four positions falls vacant each year.

The task force that surveyed the personnel field for the Hoover Commission secured the views of nearly 3,500 college seniors toward the public service as a career. Government employment was rated below private industry in salary, opportunities for promotion, incentives to improve efficiency, prestige and recognition, and other categories. Public service was more attractive than private only in security of job, opportunities for service, and leave, retirement, and health benefits.

Unions of Public Employees.—Until quite recent times, the question of unionization of federal employees has been highly controversial. Although postal employees organized as early as 1889, activities of the organizations were limited rigidly by departmental and presidential order. After the Lloyd–La Follette Act of 1912 legalized unions of federal employees and removed restrictions upon their activities, many new organizations were started. The worst fears that unions of public workers would lead to strikes and controlled elections have not been realized. The law of the land now requires private employers to bargain collectively with unions of their employees' choosing; it is appropriate that government should do likewise.

The early unions were craft bodies, covering only small sectors of postal employees—letter carriers, clerks, railway mail servicemen, rural letter carriers. Like the smaller craft unions in private industry, these still persist. Recently, however, unions of broader scope are increasing in power; they are of the industrial or "one big union" type. Examples of this tendency are found in the American Federation of Government Employees (AFL), the United Federal Workers (CIO), and the National Federation of Federal Employees (independent). The scattered postal workers unions still contain the majority of organized federal employees, however. The largest of these are: National Association of Letter Carriers (AFL), United National Association of Post Office Clerks (independent), National Rural Letter Carriers Association (independent), National Federation of Post Office Clerks (AFL), and Railway Mail Association (AFL). When legislation affecting the status of the public service comes before Congress, the various unions of federal employees play a large role in its disposition. The larger unions maintain staffs in Washington and employ the usual tactics of lobbyists.

Unionization is unevenly developed among state and local employees in the United States. The larger state employees associations are not affiliated with the AFL or CIO, but both groups now carry on active organizing campaigns. The largest AFL union in the local field is the International Association of Fire Fighters. The organization of the CIO is the State, County, and Municipal Workers of America.

It is almost universally agreed that unions of public employees should have restrictions on their activities that do not exist in the case of unions of private workers. The principal denial is the right to strike, but in many instances local employees have walked out. Strikes against the Federal or state governments are less probable. The theory behind this denial of the right to strike is that the state is sovereign, and that its sovereignty must not be challenged. While understandable and perhaps logical if applied to essential governmental functions, it is difficult to see why a strike by employees of a municipally owned electric utility is any more serious than one by employees of a private one.

Retirement Systems.—American governments have been slow to recognize the necessity for retirement systems for their employees as an essential feature of a sound personnel system. The national government adopted a retirement scheme for its employees only in 1920. A few states adopted superannuation plans about the same time. Several large municipalities and counties have excellent retirement programs in operation. Many school districts have provided for the retirement of superannuated employees. Since the adoption of the Social Security Act of 1935, which provides old-age insurance for private but not for public employees, public retirement plans have been widely adopted.

The motivation for establishing adequate schemes for the retirement of aged employees is only in part humanitarian. The government should be a good employer, interested in the welfare of its workers. But retirement systems are justifiable on grounds of enlightened self-interest also. Governments or private concerns without retirement systems may keep on aged employees through pity long after their usefulness has ended. This may lead to demoralization of the remainder of a staff, because opportunities for advancement must so often wait until death comes to an aged superior.

Features of public retirement systems vary considerably. Two types of funds are employed. The cash disbursement plan, used by the federal government from 1921 to 1926, involves payment of contributions into a single fund, from which annuity payments are made. The actuarial reserve scheme, adopted by Congress in 1926, requires the payment for each employee of a contribution which, with compound interest, is sufficient to secure the proper benefit when he reaches retirement age. The actuarial reserve plan is displacing the cash disbursement scheme in many jurisdictions because it spreads the burden more equitably and provides the reserves necessary to meet future contingencies.

Most American retirement plans are contributory, often requiring equal contributions by government and employee, but a few supported wholly by public appropriations exist. The age of retirement usually is set at sixty-five or seventy, but for police and firemen may be lower. The better plans provide not only for retirement at superannuation, but also pay benefits in case of disability, death, or separation from the service before retirement age. Under sound actuarial schemes, the retirement benefit is based on the number of years of service under the plan and the average annual salary over that period.[1]

Training for the Public Service.—Public-service training may be preentry or in-service. Preentry training varies greatly with the nature of positions. The regular public schools and educational institutions do the major job of training future public employees. Positions requiring special training are filled by graduates of professional and technical schools. A number of "cram" institutes have been set up in Washington and elsewhere; most of them point specifically toward certain civil service examinations. In the last 20 years many colleges and universities have established curriculums in public administration intended as preparation for the public service. There is considerable difference of opinion among personnel authorities concerning the relative value of liberal arts training and of specialized public administration training.[2]

In-service training is used to improve the employee's grasp of his job and to prepare him for advancement to a better job. Such training may be offered by the agency with which he is connected, or by an outside educational institution. The Graduate School of the United States Department of Agriculture is an example of general in-service training at its best. Many other governmental agencies provide elaborate in-service training facilities for their employees. Many universities like American (Washington), Wayne (Detroit), and New York University offer courses designed especially to accommodate those in the public service.

References

Brooks, Earl: *In-service Training of Federal Employees* (Chicago: Civil Service Assembly, 1938).

Civil Service Assembly of the United States and Canada: *A Digest of State Civil Service Laws* (Chicago: The Assembly, 1939).

——— *Public Personnel Agencies in the United States, a 1949 Census* (Chicago: The Assembly, 1949).

——— *Employee Relations in the Public Service* (Chicago: The Assembly, 1942).

——— *Employee Training in the Public Service* (Chicago: The Assembly, 1941).

——— *News Letter*, monthly, began publication 1930.

[1] See Lewis Meriam, *Principles Governing the Retirement of Public Employees* (New York: Appleton-Century, 1918).

[2] See George A. Graham, *Education for Public Administration* (Chicago: Public Administration Service, 1941).

——— *Oral Tests in Public Personnel Selection* (Chicago: The Assembly, 1943).
——— *Position-classification in the Public Service* (Chicago: The Assembly, 1941).
——— *Placement and Probation in the Public Service* (Chicago: The Assembly, 1946).
——— *Public Personnel Review*, quarterly, began publication 1940.
——— *Public Relations of Public Personnel Agencies* (Chicago: Civil Service Assembly, 1941).
——— *Recruiting Applicants for the Public Service* (Chicago: Civil Service Assembly, 1942).
COMMISSION OF INQUIRY ON PUBLIC SERVICE PERSONNEL: *Better Government Personnel* (New York: McGraw-Hill, 1935). Twelve monographs were published in 5 volumes, including those by Greer and Wilmerding listed below.
FELDMAN, HERMAN: *A Personnel Program for the Federal Civil Service*, House Doc. 773, 71st Cong., 3rd Sess. (Washington: Government Printing Office, 1931).
FIELD, OLIVER P.: *Civil Service Law* (Minneapolis: University of Minnesota Press, 1939).
GRAHAM, GEORGE A.: *Education for Public Administration* (Chicago: Public Administration Service, 1941).
GREER, SARAH A.: *Bibliography of Civil Service and Personnel Administration* (New York: McGraw-Hill, 1935).
GULICK, LUTHER (ed.): "Improved Personnel in Government Service," *Annals of the American Academy of Political and Social Science*, vol. 189 (January, 1937).
McLEAN, JOSEPH E. (ed.): *The Public Service and University Education* (Princeton, N.J.: Princeton University Press, 1949).
MERIAM, LEWIS: *Personnel Administration in the Federal Government* (Washington: Brookings, 1937).
——— *Public Personnel Problems from the Standpoint of the Operating Office* (Washington: Brookings, 1938).
——— *Principles Guiding the Retirement of Public Employees* (New York: Appleton-Century, 1918).
——— *Public Service and Special Training* (Chicago: University of Chicago Press, 1936).
MOSHER, WILLIAM E., and DONALD L. KINGSLEY: *Public Personnel Administration* (New York: Harper, 2d ed., 1941).
PROBST, JOHN B.: *Service Ratings* (Chicago: Bureau of Public Personnel Administration and the Civil Service Assembly, 1931).
SAGESER, L. B.: *First Two Decades of the Pendleton Act: a Study of Civil Service Reform* (Lincoln: University of Nebraska, 1935).
SMITH, DARRELL H.: *The United States Civil Service Commission, Its History, Activities and Organization* (Baltimore: The Johns Hopkins Press, 1928).
SPERO, STERLING D.: *The Labor Movement in a Government Industry* (New York: Doran, 1924).
——— *Government as Employer* (New York: Remsen Press, 1949).
STEWART, FRANK M.: *The National Civil Service Reform League: History, Activities and Problems* (Austin: University of Texas Press, 1929).
UNITED STATES CIVIL SERVICE COMMISSION: *Annual Report* (Washington: Government Printing Office, yearly).
——— *Federal Employment under the Merit System* (Washington: Government Printing Office, 1941).
——— *History of the Federal Service, 1789 to the Present* (Washington: Government Printing Office, 1941).
UNITED STATES COMMISSION ON ORGANIZATION OF THE EXECUTIVE BRANCH OF THE GOVERNMENT ("HOOVER COMMISSION"): *Personnel Management* (Washington: Government Printing Office, 1949).
——— *Task Force Report on Federal Personnel* (Washington: Government Printing Office, 1949).

United States Department of Agriculture, Personnel Office: *Personnel Administration, Development in the Department of Agriculture, First Fifty Years* (Washington: Department of Agriculture, 1947).

United States President's Committee on Administrative Management: *Report . . . with Studies . . .* (Washington: Government Printing Office, 1937). Study 1 is "Personnel Administration in the Federal Service," by Floyd W. Reeves and Paul T. David.

United States President's Committee on Civil Service Improvement: *Report of . . .*, House Doc. 118, 77th Cong., 1st Sess. (Washington: Government Printing Office, 1941).

——— *Documents and Reports to Accompany Report on Civil Service Improvement* (Washington: Government Printing Office, 3 vols. 1942).

White, Leonard D.: *The Prestige Value of Public Employment* (Chicago: University of Chicago Press, 1929).

——— *Further Contributions to the Prestige Value of Public Employment* (Chicago: University of Chicago Press, 1932).

Wilmerding, Lucius, Jr.: *Government by Merit* (New York: McGraw-Hill, 1935).

Ziskind, David: *One Thousand Strikes of Government Employees* (New York: Columbia University Press, 1940).

Chapter 23

PUBLIC FINANCE

> The relationship between the legislative and the executive branches largely determines the success or failure of democratic government. Hence, the budget, because it is at the same time the most important instrument of legislative control and of executive management, is at the very core of democratic government.
>
> Harold D. Smith, "The Budget as an Instrument of Legislative Control and Executive Management."[1]

Although governments are not created for the purpose of collecting and spending money, considerations of revenues and expenditures underlie virtually every governmental problem. Governmental services cost money. By managing the purse strings, executives and legislatures are able to exert both detailed and general controls over the various governmental activities. For the executive, finance is a control over administration ranking in importance with that of personnel. For the legislative body, finance looms much more important than personnel or any other form of control. The scope of the federal taxing power having been dealt with in an earlier chapter,[2] this chapter is devoted to a description and criticism of financial administration, with incidental attention to state and local practices.

FINANCIAL ADMINISTRATION

Early Federal Organization.—The Constitution places the primary responsibility for finances upon Congress. Appropriations are made by law, but the President's participation through the veto has not been particularly forceful because the executive normally is preoccupied with the necessity of securing succor for the agencies under his control. The President has used his constitutional power to recommend appropriations to the Congress, but his most effective sanction over congressional action came from his role as leader of the majority party. When his party was in control of both houses and when he was accepted as its leader, his influence often was great over fiscal and other matters. The idea of legislative supremacy in the financial field was established in Britain after centuries of controversy between King and Parliament. After the victory of Parlia-

[1] *Public Administration Review*, vol. 4 (Summer, 1944), p. 181.

[2] Chap. 17.

ment, however, responsible government developed in Britain, and the Parliament gave to the real executive, now under its own control, vast powers over money matters. In Britain today only the government (*i.e.*, the executive) may introduce legislation involving the appropriation of money.

As American Federal government developed after 1789, the financial responsibilities of Congress multiplied. The various committees of the two houses, and individual members as well, introduced and pressed for the adoption of fiscal measures raising and expending moneys. It proved difficult to fix specific responsibility for action; the trading of votes for appropriations (logrolling) and the distribution of favors among state and congressional districts (pork barrel) led to immense waste of public funds. The fidelity of financial transactions was inadequately checked, opening opportunities for corruption. Although the Secretary of the Treasury was required to provide Congress with compilations of requests for appropriations, he was given no real authority over these estimates.

The Budget and Accounting Act of 1921.—The need for reform in federal financial practices was first stated prominently by President Taft's Commission on Economy and Efficiency, the report of which was sent to Congress with presidential approval on June 27, 1912.[1] The commission recommended that the President should submit to each session of Congress a budget, containing a budgetary message, financial statements, and estimates prepared through the Secretary of the Treasury.

The important task of preparing the national budget, under the direction of the President, was assigned by the 1921 act to the Bureau of the Budget, which was created for this purpose. Originally a portion of the Treasury Department, the bureau was transferred to the Executive Office of the President by executive order in 1939. Under the terms of the law, the Bureau of the Budget has power "to assemble, correlate, revise, reduce, or increase the estimates of the several departments or establishments." President Roosevelt strengthened the bureau notably on several occasions after 1933, adding power to apportion appropriations, to require departments to set up reserves, responsibility for statistical services, and duties of research, planning, and investigation.

The Bureau of the Budget Now.—The functions of the Bureau of the Budget were enumerated in an executive order in 1939 and may be summarized as follows:[2]

[1] It was entitled "The Need for a National Budget" and was House Doc. 854, 62nd Cong., 2d Sess. This era is well covered in Frederick A. Cleveland and Arthur E. Buck, *The Budget and Responsible Government* (New York: Macmillan, 1920).

[2] Executive Order No. 8248, Sept. 8, 1939. One of the best studies of the bureau is Fritz Morstein Marx, "The Bureau of the Budget: Its Evolution and Present Role," *American Political Science Review*, vol. 39 (August, 1945), pp. 653–684, and (October, 1945) pp. 869–898.

1. To assist the President in budget and fiscal program preparation.
2. To supervise and control budget administration.
3. To conduct research on administration and to advise departments and agencies on improved organization and practices.
4. To assist the President by coordinating departmental advice on proposed legislation.
5. To plan the improvement of statistical services.
6. To keep the President informed on the work of the government.

To accomplish these ends, the bureau is organized under the director and one general assistant director into five principal divisions, each headed by an assistant director. They are the legislative reference, estimates, administrative management, statistical standards, and fiscal divisions. About 600 employees are now employed, constituting a more adequate staff than ever before. Reforms instituted in the last few years have brought the personnel and powers of the bureau near to the level urged for it by Arthur E. Buck in his able analysis made for the President's Committee on Administrative Management.[1] Each department and larger independent establishment has its own budget officer, who prepares and edits estimates and works with the Bureau of the Budget in the budget conferences and hearings that are necessary before a budget document can be submitted to Congress.

Much of the legislative reference work is nonfiscal, but it constitutes one of the great tasks of the bureau. Harold D. Smith, then director, reported that his legislative division "cleared" 4,841 bills during the Seventy-sixth Congress, and about 335 executive orders and 70 proclamations during 1940–1941.[2] The Hoover Commission noted that the Bureau, during the Eightieth Congress, advised the President or executive departments on 5,992 bills and gave the President information on 1,438 bills passed by Congress.[3] The statistical services of the bureau include the approval of forms and questionnaires used by federal agencies, in order to secure simplification and to avoid overlapping. The administrative management division, concerned with aiding departments to secure efficiency and economy, makes studies of particular agencies or problems and reports to the appropriate authorities. Its contribution, also nonfiscal in nature, is to improve the machinery of administration.

[1] United States President's Committee on Administrative Management, *Report . . . with Studies. . . .* (Washington: Government Printing Office, 1937), pp. 139–168.

[2] Harold D. Smith, "The Executive Office of the President: the Bureau of the Budget," *Public Administration Review*, vol. 1 (Winter, 1941), pp. 106–115. On the general principles of budgeting, see Smith's "The Budget as an Instrument of Legislative Control and Executive Management," pp. 181–188.

[3] Hoover Commission, *Budgeting and Accounting* (Washington: Government Printing Office, 1949), pp. 24–25.

Department of the Treasury.—Several tasks of the Treasury Department fall within the field of fiscal management. Taxes are collected mainly through the Bureau of Internal Revenue. Customs duties are collected by the Bureau of Customs.

Even more directly related to the matter of over-all financial administration, however, is the function of the Fiscal Service of the Treasury Department. Headed by a Fiscal Assistant Secretary, the Service was created by executive order in 1940 and charged with accounting, debt, and custodial functions. The Fiscal Assistant Secretary keeps in touch with the financial operations of the various departments and agencies and informs the Secretary of the Treasury. Responsible to him is the Commissioner of Accounts, who heads the Bureau of Accounts and who has the duty of supervising the accounting of the Treasury Department and of keeping the central accounts of the entire government. In addition, the Bureau of Accounts issues all Treasury warrants, makes disbursements for most of the federal agencies, and designates depositories with which government money may be placed.

Also in the Fiscal Service is the Bureau of the Public Debt, headed by the Commissioner of the Public Debt. Federal borrowing is handled by this agency. Special staffs may be created from time to time to promote bond selling, but the actual issuance and control stem from the Bureau of the Public Debt.

The final agency of importance in the Fiscal Service is the Office of Treasurer of the United States. The Treasurer receives and disburses public funds and is the custodian of public money. After Congress has appropriated funds, he credits them to the proper disbursing officer, following receipt of a warrant signed by the Secretary of the Treasury and countersigned by the Comptroller General.

If the recommendations of the President's Committee on Administrative Management had been followed by Congress, much authority now possessed by the Comptroller General would have passed to the Secretary of the Treasury and his department. Two principal powers were involved. First, the committee wished to assign to the Secretary of the Treasury authority to prescribe accounting systems, forms, and procedures.[1] Second, claims and accounts involving the Federal government should be settled by the Treasury Department. Congress did not permit such transfers, and the Comptroller General is still in effective control on both points. Creation of the Fiscal Service serves notice that the Treasury now has the machinery to take on the new responsibilities.

New criticism has now come from the Hoover Commission, which proposes a new Accountant General under the Secretary of the Treasury,

[1] United States President's Committee on Administrative Management, *op. cit.*, pp. 24–25.

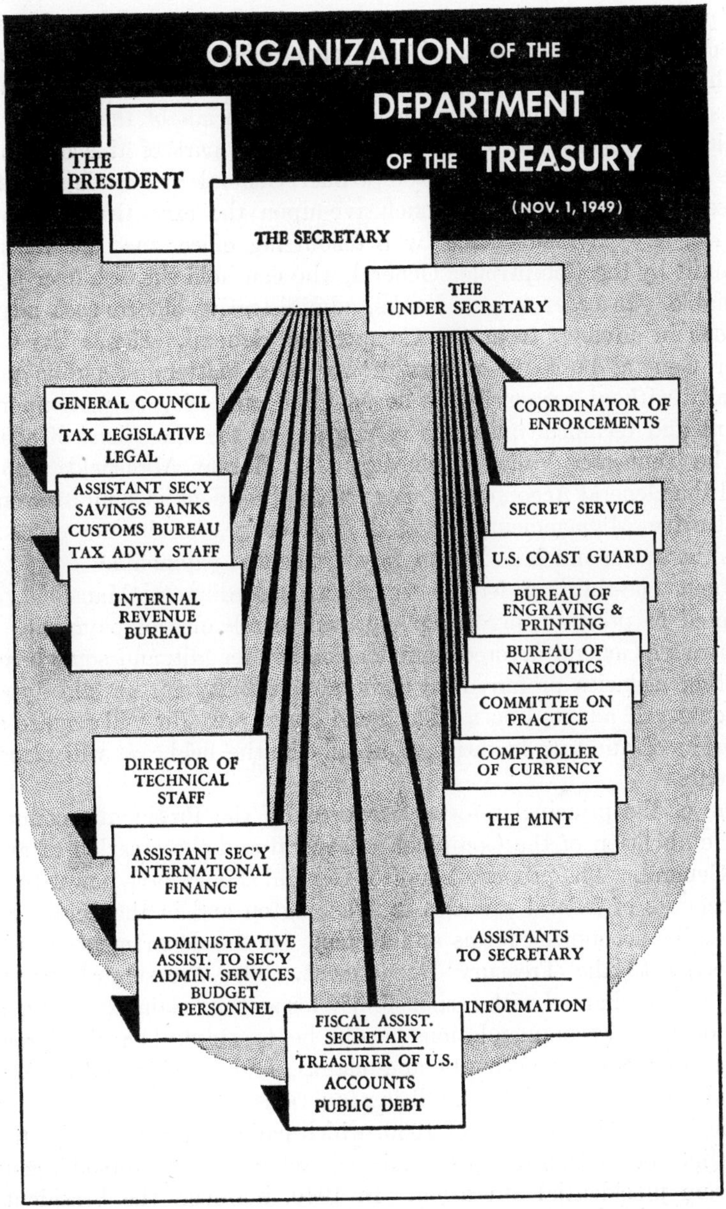

The Commission's plan called for transferring the Coast Guard and Bureau of Narcotics from the Treasury. The Treasury was to receive three independent agencies, the Reconstruction Finance Corporation, Federal Deposit Insurance Corporation, Export-Import Bank, and a new office of Accountant General: SOURCE: Drafted from information supplied by the Treasury Department.

with power to prescribe accounting methods and enforce procedures, but subject to the approval of the Comptroller General.[1]

The Comptroller General.—The Comptroller General of the United States is one of the most conspicuous fiscal officials of the country, and certainly the most controversial. The greater part of this controversy arises over the power of the Comptroller General to "settle" accounts. His settlement is final and conclusive upon the executive branch. In practice, any payment made by a disbursing officer may be denied on postaudit by the Comptroller General, who can hold the disburser personally liable. In order to avoid risks, administrative officers seek advisory opinions in advance from the Comptroller General. Hence the Comptroller General built up a great power over matters of public policy; virtually without responsibility he acquired authority to pass upon important and technical questions arising out of the operations of agencies like the Tennessee Valley Authority. Dr. Harvey Mansfield, who surveyed the General Accounting Office for the President's Committee on Administrative Management, reported such congestion in the office that postaudit was as much as 2 or more years behind payments.[2]

About one-third of federal vouchers, according to Mansfield, were subjected to preaudit, involving approval in advance of payment. The Comptroller General favored an extension of preaudit, and some heads of operating agencies preferred to shift responsibility for certain types of payments. If adopted on a widespread basis, preaudit will require great expansion of auditing facilities, especially in the field. It will also slow payments.

One of the principal reforms proposed by the President's committee was the abolition of the Comptroller General and the creation of an Auditor General. The proposed Auditor General should have power to audit the accounts of federal agencies in Washington and in the field. Power to prescribe accounting forms and systems for the departments would be transferred to the Treasury Department. The Treasury Department also would be charged with responsibility for settling claims. The general effect of these recommendations would be to strengthen the Treasury control over current accounts and claims, and to charge the Auditor General exclusively with postauditing functions.

The Reorganization Act of 1939, which embodied some of the recommendations of the President's committee, excluded the comptroller generalship from presidential alteration. In 1940, however, the President did establish the Fiscal Service of the Treasury Department, keeping central accounts, and charged it with supervising accounting forms. With the

[1] Hoover Commission, *op. cit.*, pp. 39–41.

[2] United States President's Committee on Administrative Management, *op. cit.*, p. 177.

continuing accounting control exercised under the Comptroller General this represents some duplication. While the power to settle claims still remains with the Comptroller General, the flames of controversy have died out with the passing from office of McCarl, the first incumbent. After leaving the office vacant for 3 years, President Roosevelt after 1939 had two opportunities to fill the post, and his appointees have shown less pugnacious tendencies than did McCarl.

The Hoover Commission expressed dissatisfaction with the whole picture of fiscal management, including the work of the Comptroller General. Division of responsibility between the Treasury and the Comptroller General has produced a situation in which government accounting does not show true revenues or expenses for any fiscal period. Moreover, there is no prescribed system of property or cost accounting and no positive control over assets, liabilities, and appropriations. The Hoover group was critical of the General Accounting Office practice of auditing millions of expenditure vouchers, while failing to produce the summary accounts and financial reports that are needed by the President and Congress.

The Hoover group recommended that an Accountant General be established under the Secretary of the Treasury and take over the prescribing of accounting methods and procedures, which, however, would be subject to approval by the Comptroller General. The Accountant General would combine agency accounts into summary accounts and produce financial reports for the information of those concerned. Instead of having the Comptroller General use an estimated one-half of his 10,000 employees and of his $30,000,000 per year "settling" claims represented in freight-loads of vouchers sent to Washington, spot checking would be used the country over to free the Washington office from the great volume of paper work.

In view of the fact that the Comptroller General and the General Accounting Office are exempt from presidential reorganization plans under the 1949 act, drastic change is not likely to come soon. The majority on the Hoover Commission proposed a compromise which is unacceptable both to the congressional apologists for the Comptroller General and to those who want accounting and claim settlement under the executive branch, with the Comptroller General charged with making a thorough postaudit.[1]

The General Accounting Office, which is headed by the Comptroller General is organized into five main divisions: audit, claims, postal accounts, accounting and bookkeeping, and reconciliation and clearance.

State Fiscal Organization.—By 1900 the need for reform of financial administration in the states was even more pressing than that in the

[1] Hoover Commission, *op. cit.*, pp. 35–71. Senator McClellan and Representative Manasco took the former stand in their dissents; Pollock and Rowe took the latter.

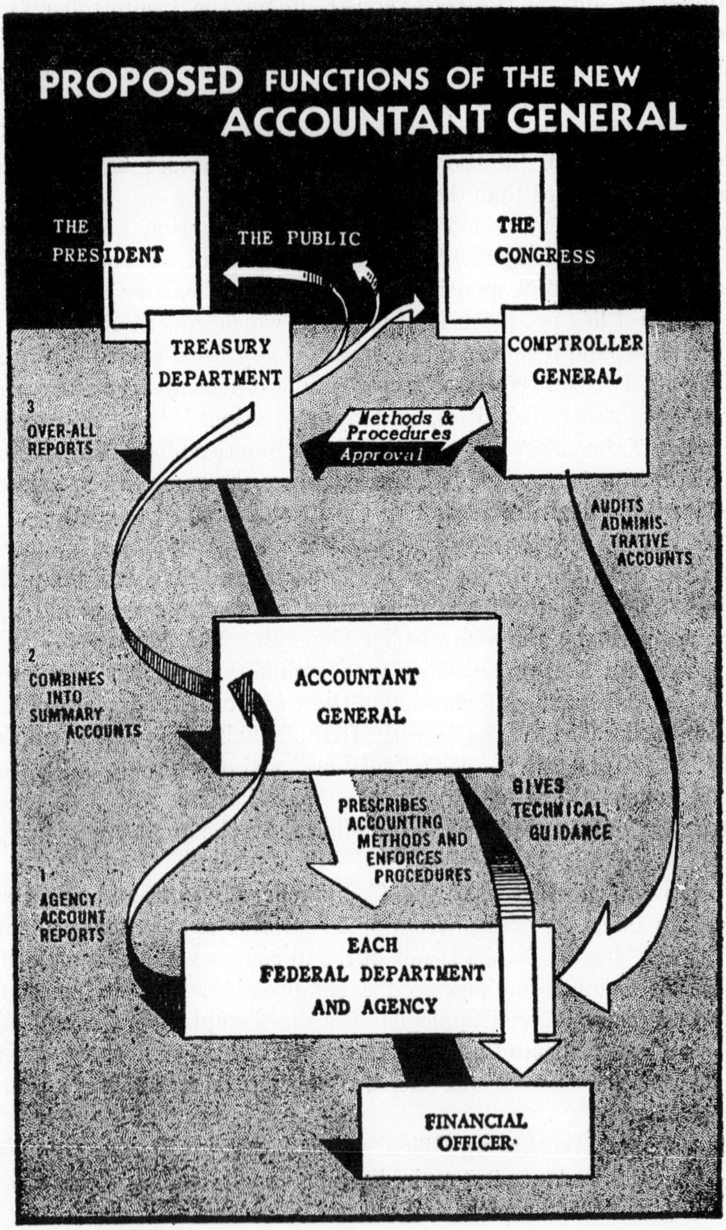

The Hoover Commission suggested adding to the Treasury Department an office of Accounting General, to be responsible for accounting and reporting. The General Accounting Office would be retained, but chiefly for auditing purposes. SOURCE: Hoover Commission, *Budgeting and Accounting*, p. 40.

national government. Legislative appropriating methods were haphazard and subject to the tug and haul of individual and partisan politics. After appropriations were made, power to make and check disbursements was divided between several officers, often elected by the people, bearing titles such as treasurer, controller, and auditor. Responsibility for tax assessment and collection was distributed among tax commissions, board of equalization, treasurer, and controller.

Following the report of the Taft Commission in 1912, the states turned their attention to budgetary reform.[1] In most cases the executive budget idea was superimposed on the existing financial organization of the state. While great improvements were made through fixing executive responsibility for preparing the budget, and some of the worst features of legislative appropriating practice were eliminated, the numerous state constitutional officers charged with fiscal powers often were retained. A good many states did establish, however, budget bureaus, departments of finance, and purchasing agencies with real powers.

Local Fiscal Organization.—Until the turn of the century local governments gave little effective attention to reforming financial administration. Since that time the reconstruction of municipal fiscal systems has been widespread, although less progress has been noted on the county front. In the commission form of city government, which started in 1901, the various fiscal agencies—collectors, treasurers, accountants, assessors—were gathered under a single commissioner of finance.[2] After 1913, the cities that turned to the city-manager plan elevated the department of finance to an even more commanding position, as an arm through which the manager kept in touch with the activities of government.

It would be a mistake to assume that all or even most municipalities have reorganized and integrated their financial structures. Some of the cities that have clung to mayor-council plans have changed nothing on the fiscal side. The older schemes still in operation usually have several relatively independent fiscal offices. The modern, reorganized municipalities bring together in one department responsible to the chief executive all offices concerned with financial matters, except that of the auditor. This often includes accounting, tax collection and assessment, purchasing, and custody of funds.

County reforms have progressed significantly during the last two decades, but fewer counties have been reorganized than have cities. A handful of counties have adopted the county-manager plan, with integrated financial administration. Some others have secured more modest

[1] A detailed presentation of early state studies and adoptions is found in Cleveland and Buck, *op. cit.*, pp. 89–330. A general survey may be found in Arthur E. Buck, *Public Budgeting* (New York: Harper, 1929), pp. 14–24.

[2] Arthur E. Buck, *Municipal Finance* (New York: Macmillan, 1926).

reforms. The great majority, however, continue to operate on the basis of the traditional elected fiscal officers.

THE BUDGETARY PROCESS

The confusion and irresponsibility that characterized early federal financial administration have been described above. A new era opened with the enactment of the Budget and Accounting Act of 1921. State reforms came both before and after the federal, spreading over a period of the last 40 years. The following analysis of the budgeting process is based primarily upon federal practice, except where otherwise noted.

Definition of a Budget.—A budget is a comprehensive financial plan, the central instrument of financial administration. The budgetary process, according to A. E. Buck, involves three elements: (1) the financial plan, (2) the procedure for formulating, authorizing, executing, and controlling the plan, and (3) some governmental authority responsible for each stage of the procedure.[1]

The budget document is the blueprint in which a government forecasts its expenditures and estimates its revenues. It is for a given fiscal period, usually for one year but sometimes (especially in state governments) for a biennium. The fiscal year of the Federal government is from July 1 to June 30. Some state and local governments use the calendar year as the fiscal year.

The second of these elements names the four stages in the budgeting process. The first is formulation, involving assembling of estimates from operating agencies and their inclusion in the financial plan. The second is authorization of the budget, through legislation adoption. The third, budget execution, consists of controlling the expenditures authorized. The fourth stage is entered when accounts are checked and transactions audited.

Responsibility for the steps in budgetary procedure is fixed upon various officers and agencies in each level of government. Increasingly, authority to prepare the budget is given to the chief executive or to some officer or bureau responsible to him. The executive needs budgeting power to strengthen his position over the administration, and, in turn, he is the official with greatest authority to enforce compliance of spending officers. Universally budgets are authorized by legislative bodies, but there is some variation in the procedure on budget bills. Execution is the responsibility of several officers and agents, including the budget preparer, accounting officer, head of operating agency, purchasing agent, personnel agency. Accountability is enforced through a postaudit, conducted by either an independent officer or agency, or one responsible to the legislative branch.

[1] Arthur E. Buck, *The Budget in Governments of Today* (New York: Macmillan, 1934), p. 46.

Budget Formulation.—Under the Budget and Accounting Act of 1921, the responsibility for budget formulation was placed upon the President, who was provided with the assistance of the Bureau of the Budget. Originally a part of the Department of the Treasury, in 1939 it was moved to the Executive Office of the President. The President determines general fiscal policy, and then delegates to his budget director power to proceed with budget formulation.

The various operating departments and agencies are called upon by the budget bureau to submit their estimates of expenditures for the forthcoming fiscal period. These preliminary estimates are analyzed by the budget agency. The chief executive is consulted on matters of policy and settles serious disagreements between budget director and operating agency. The revised estimates are then put into final form and printed. Normally the operating departments and agencies request more than they expect to receive but wish to have a safe margin that may be lost in estimate cuts.

The form and contents of budgets vary considerably. A good budget will contain several essential features. First, the executive's budget message reviews the general financial picture—anticipated revenues, business conditions, estimated expenditures, and the like. Second, financial statements compare the fiscal present with the past and with estimated future operations. Then the body of the budget contains the appropriation estimates—the executive's recommendations. The usual practice is to organize the estimates according to departments and agencies. The better budgets often have a parallel column with amounts appropriated for the last one or two fiscal periods.

In practice, the process of budget formulation involves much negotiation between budget agency and operating department, and between budget agency and chief executive. Under the federal law, the Bureau of the Budget is given power "to assemble, correlate, revise, reduce, or increase the estimates of the several departments and establishments." These estimates are subject to preliminary editing and adjustment within the operating agency by either department head or departmental budget officer. There is a natural tendency to overestimate one's needs in order to be on the safe side. Much "padding" of estimates may be eliminated by officers within a particular department and before estimates go to the budgeting agency. Sometimes the chief executive sets in advance a maximum amount allowable for each department. When this is done, the departmental adjustments of estimates loom of much greater relative importance, for the main controversies will then tend to be intradepartmental.

Next, departmental estimates are transmitted to the budgeting agency. Normally the budget bureau is saddled with the task of bringing down the expenditure estimates of operating agencies to a level stipulated by the chief executive or indicated by estimated revenues. This requires budget hearings, in which departmental officers present their cases to budget officers. The budget officer must decide, and often this decision involves a substitution of his judgment for that of the departmental officer. When a layman decides between the bomber and the carrier in Defence estimates, or for or against experimentation with sulfa drugs in those of the Public Health Service, the necessity for maturity on the part of the budgeteer is painfully obvious. Appeals to budget director or chief executive are possible, but not often politic.

Budget Authorization.—Budget or appropriation bills are drawn either by the executive budget officer or by a legislative committee. It is now recognized as proper practice for the chief executive to submit the budget and to be responsible for what is contained in it. In the Federal and in most state and local governments the legislature can decrease or increase the executive's recommendations. The existence of this power diminishes the full measure of responsibility possessed by the executive in Great Britain, where only the ministers can introduce appropriation bills and Parliament is denied the authority to increase any item.

Congress and other American legislative bodies have well-established procedures for dealing with appropriation measures. The budget bill is introduced in the manner used for other bills. In Congress and in many state legislatures revenue bills must originate in the lower house; although this restriction does not apply to appropriation measures, custom decrees that introduction in the House of Representatives is necessary. The budget goes to the legislature with the executive's budget message, detailing the fiscal picture of past, present, and future. The printed budget document shows many details not found in the appropriation bill that accompanies it. The bill may be written with considerable detail, or it may include only the principal totals and subtotals. The former is called the "segregated-item" type of appropriation measure; the latter is known as the "lump-sum" variety. The segregated-item bill is unduly restrictive and allows little administrative discretion; the lump-sum plan liberates the executive from detailed limits and permits flexibility for adjustment and economy. Federal appropriation bills are a great mixture, with some items providing for millions of dollars and some for only a few dollars.

After introduction, the budget bill is referred to the proper committee. In both the United States Senate and House of Representatives there are the "appropriations" committees. Both House and Senate have appropriations committees subcommittees for each executive department and independent agency.[1] These bodies conduct hearings and call in and

[1] The United States Senate Appropriations Committee brings in three members of certain committees with jurisdiction over the subject matter of the budget items under

question heads of operating agencies. Usually these officers are not permitted to advocate other than the estimate submitted by the chief executive. In some badly managed jurisdictions, officers violate the spirit and sometimes the letter of budget law by lobbying for the restoration of their own unrevised estimates. After hearings are completed, the committee makes its recommendation, and the house debates and acts. The same procedure or a similar one is followed in the second house.

Having been enacted by both houses, and having compromised any possible differences, the appropriation bill is sent to the executive for signature. The President is forced to approve or to reject the measure as a whole; naturally he approves almost invariably, for the agencies cannot long operate without money. Many state governors and some local executives have an item veto power, permitting them to strike out or to reduce any portion of an appropriation measure. As shown earlier, such a power in the hands of the President would strengthen materially his position in the budgetary process.

Widespread abuses still persist in the authorization of budgets by legislative bodies. Few appropriations committees have adequate staffs for dealing with the intricate problems involved in budget bills. Decisions often, perhaps inevitably, are made with considerations of "logrolling" and the "pork barrel" predominating. Most suggestions for improvement involve expansion of the role of the executive in authorization, as well as in other phases of budgeting.

Some features peculiar to federal budgetary procedure should be noted here. The President includes in his budget the appropriations requested by judicial and legislative branches of government, but he has no power to alter these estimates. In some of the best state and local jurisdictions, one single omnibus budget bill is used to cover all the appropriation items proposed by the executive. In Congress, however, a separate bill is introduced for some departments, other departments are grouped together for the purpose, and at least one bill each year is devoted to the independent establishments. The chairmen of the appropriations subcommittees of each house have charge of the bills on the floor of each house. Since the budget estimates are made up considerably in advance of the fiscal period, it is inevitable that unusual needs will arise and will require added appropriations for some purpose. These demands are handled through "deficiency" appropriation estimates and bills.

Budget Execution.—The principal agencies of financial administration of the American national government have been described already. Those with roles in budget execution include the Treasury Department, the Bureau of the Budget, the General Accounting Office, and its head, the

consideration. These three members sit with Appropriations while the budget of their special interest is being considered.

Comptroller General. Custody of funds is in the hands of the Treasury. Under current federal practice, the Treasury notifies the operating departments and agencies of the amount of money they may expend during the fiscal year. The agencies may then incur obligations. Bills are paid through disbursing officers located in various parts of the country. Most disbursing officers are in the Treasury Department, but the armed forces and Post Office still have their own disbursing agencies. Advances of funds are made available to disbursing officers through local depositaries.

The great majority of claims against the United States are settled promptly by the disbursing officers, in accordance with rules and regulations. Doubtful claims are referred to the Comptroller General for settlement, over which he has final jurisdiction.[1] During the first 4 years of the Franklin D. Roosevelt administration, vigorous attacks were made upon the arbitrary way in which the Comptroller General exercised his powers.

The Director of the Bureau of the Budget since 1933 has been empowered to apportion appropriations for each agency by periods of the fiscal year. This is one of the most important of fiscal powers, for it enables the executive to keep a quarter-by-quarter check of financial transactions of the operating establishments. Under this scheme spending agencies are given only a certain proportion of their total appropriation to spend in any given period; one common limit in state and local governments is no more than one-tenth in any one month.

Accounts are kept by the operating departments and establishments. The departmental accounting officers report monthly expenditures to the Bureau of the Budget. The Treasury also maintains a set of accounts, showing general transactions. The Fiscal Service of the Treasury, created by executive order in 1940, was directed "to establish and maintain a complete system of central accounts for the entire Government," and to prescribe standards and forms for departmental financial reports.[2] Nevertheless, the Comptroller General still possesses the power to prescribe forms, systems, and procedure for accounting to the departments and establishments. General diffusion of responsibility for accounting persists.

After the financial transaction is complete, auditing is in order. It involves the examination of the records to check on the validity of accounts and payments. In governmental circles the theory is current that a post-audit should be conducted by an officer or body independent of the executive or spending agencies. The task of checking to see whether or not expenditures have been made in accordance with law is assigned either to an independent auditor or to one responsible to the legislative branch. The Comptroller General, with 15-year term and removal only by Congress,

[1] His decisions are available in *Decisions of the Comptroller General of the United States* (Washington: Government Printing Office).

[2] See Executive Order No. 8512, Aug. 13, 1940.

was intended to be such an officer, but his powers were a strange combination that made him neither fish nor fowl.

Budget Reform.—The Hoover Commission called the federal budget "an inadequate document, poorly organized and improperly designed. . . . ."[1] Noting that the budget for 1949–1950 contained 1,625 pages with about 1,500,000 words, the commission found that it did not offer an understandable financial plan for expenditures. Some items were extremely minute; others were for huge sums. There was a great lack of uniformity, and appropriation items were ill classified.

To correct the situation, the commission proposed a "performance budget," based on functions, activities, and projects. The reformed budget would stress the work or service to be performed and the money it would cost, not merely list the salaries, supplies, and equipment needed to do the job. Using the Naval Medical Center at Bethesda, Md., as an example, it was discovered that the hospital received allotments from twelve different Navy appropriation titles; at no place in the budget was the cost of operating the Bethesda facility totaled or the work of the hospital set forth clearly. The performance budget, on the other hand, describes the significance and scope of the work, gives reasons for increases and decreases, outlines current and future programs, presents per bed and per patient costs for each hospital, and summarizes the complete cost of Navy medical care.

Other Hoover Commission recommendations call for Congress to reassess its appropriation procedures, for all agencies to separate budget estimates into current operating expenditures and capital outlays, and for full presidential power to reduce expenditures under appropriations once congressional intent is carried out.

Besides renaming the Bureau of the Budget "Office of the Budget" and strengthening it ties as a staff agency to the President, the Commission suggested several other ways to expand its effectiveness. In order to secure more consistent policies and improved management, it was suggested that in reviewing and revising departmental estimates the estimate division of the Bureau should work closely with representatives of the administrative management and fiscal divisions. Great stress was placed on the necessity of developing in the departments and agencies stronger and abler budget officers.

GOVERNMENTAL REVENUES

The scope of the federal taxing power, examined in detail in a previous chapter, is broad indeed. The Constitution provides in Article I, Section 8, that Congress shall have power

[1] Hoover Commission, *op. cit.*, p. 7.

To lay and collect Taxes, Duties, Imposts, and Excises, to pay the Debts and provide for the common Defense and general Welfare of the United States; but all Duties, Imposts, and Excises shall be uniform throughout the United States; . . .

Further limitations are found in other sections of the fundamental law. Federal direct taxes must be apportioned among the states according to population, but income taxes were exempted from apportionment by the Sixteenth Amendment. Neither Federal nor state governments may tax exports. The due-process-of-law clause of the Fifth Amendment occasionally is construed as restricting the exercise of the federal tax power. Another limitation was implied from the nature of the federal system, as forbidding federal taxation of state instrumentalities and state of federal; the field of this reciprocal immunity has been reduced greatly in recent years.

Personal and Corporate Income Taxes.—Income taxes, personal and corporate, yield a larger revenue than any other single type of federal tax. During the Civil War the Federal government adopted a personal income tax but retained it for less than a decade. In 1894 a mild income tax was applied to both personal and corporate incomes, but the Supreme Court promptly held that it was a direct tax and must therefore be apportioned among the states according to population.[1] In 1909 Congress proposed, and the necessary three-fourths of the states by 1913 ratified, the Sixteenth Amendment, specifically authorizing a federal tax on incomes. Almost at once income taxes become a principal source of federal revenues.

In 1947–1948 the personal income tax brought in $19,219,000,000 and the corporate income tax $9,681,000,000. These sums constituted 47.0 and 23.7 per cent respectively of federal revenues in that fiscal year.[2]

The personal income tax is "progressive" in that rates are higher for those with the highest incomes; in 1948 the normal tax was 3 per cent of net income, after deductions, plus a surtax which begins at 17 per cent and rises to 88 per cent, depending upon the size of income.[3] A flat deduction of $600 is allowed for the taxpayer and each of his dependents.

The corporate income tax has a much less marked progressive feature. Under the Revenue Act of 1943, the normal tax rate on corporate income varied from 15 to 24 per cent, depending upon size of earnings, plus a surtax of 6 to 14 per cent.

Death and Gift Taxes.—Like the income tax, the inheritance tax received its first important federal application during the Civil War, when every possible source of revenue had to be explored, but it was repealed

[1] Pollock *v.* Farmers' Loan & Trust Co., 157 U.S. 429, 158 U.S. 601 (1895).

[2] Unless otherwise noted, figures on revenue, expenditure, and debt are drawn from Bureau of Census series *Governmental Finances in the United States: 1948* (Washington: Government Printing Office, 1949).

[3] Revenue Act of 1948.

within a decade. After two intervening attempts, both meeting adverse court decisions, a death tax was enacted in 1916 and has been retained since that time. In recent prewar years federal revenue from death and gift taxes totaled between 300 million and 375 million dollars per year, which represented roughly 6 per cent of federal tax revenues; in 1947–1948 the two taxes yielded about 890 million dollars, but this was only about 2.2 per cent of total federal tax revenues.

The term "death taxes" includes two different forms: (1) an estate tax is levied on the total estate left by a deceased person; and (2) an inheritance tax applies to that part of a deceased person's estate passing to a particular heir or beneficiary. In order to guard against evasion by making gifts before death, the Federal government taxes such gifts. Over the years some of the other methods of evasion have been plugged up making subject to death taxes property in joint estates (like joint bank accounts), community property (jointly held by husband and wife under the laws of certain states), and certain trusts.

Federal death taxes are progressive, allowing an estate of $60,000 to pass tax free, then rising from 3 per cent on an estate above that figure to a maximum of 77 per cent. In 1924, as described previously, a federal tax offset or credit for state taxation was provided. Since 1926 states have been permitted to take as much as 80 per cent of the original or basic federal tax, but the offset feature does not apply to subsequent federal levies on estates.

Excise and Sales Taxes.—The Constitution mentions excise taxes as part of the federal taxing power, and such levies soon were made upon liquor and several other commodities and transactions. Reduced, repealed, and restored excise taxes have had a very shifting history, increasing during war and depression, declining in peace and prosperity. Viewed from the standpoint of revenue, the present excise taxes of greatest importance are on liquor and tobacco, the former yielding more than 2,255 million dollars in 1947–1948 and the latter 1,300 million dollars. After these come manufacturers' excise taxes on selective luxury and quasi-luxury items: playing cards, amusement admissions, radios, musical instruments, sporting goods, toilet preparations, and the like. Wartime taxes were added to travel and communication services: rail tickets, telephone calls, telegraph messages, and others. Some taxes, as stated in an earlier chapter, are for purposes of regulation, not revenue; these include such diverse commodities as narcotics, oleomargarine, and machine guns.

Selective sales or excise taxes, such as the Federal government employs, are not subject to the principal criticism that applies to general sales or manufacturers' taxes, as used by the states. The burden of the general sales tax falls most heavily upon the individual or family with the least capacity to pay. A family with an annual income of $1,800 must spend a large portion of it for food, clothing, and other items taxable under the general sales tax; the family with $18,000 per year in income spends a much smaller proportion on taxable commodities and therefore pays out a smaller proportion of its income in sales tax. Proposals for a general federal sales tax have often been made, but the progressive forces in Congress have been able to secure their defeat.

Customs Duties.—Throughout much of American history customs duties constituted the largest source of federal revenue. Indeed, the national treasury often was filled to the overflowing point by customs revenue. After the Civil War customs duties declined in relative importance as a source of revenue, and after the First World War tariff revenue was far outranked in size by income taxes. For the fiscal year 1948 customs receipts were just over 420 million dollars, an amount less than that returned by the corporate income tax, personal income tax, death taxes, liquor excise, tobacco excise, manufacturers' excises, and pay-roll taxes.

The tariff has been a controversial topic in American politics because of its protective aspect, not its revenue features. Young industries sought the fostering care of government while they entered fields of production previously commanded by foreign producers. Later these "infant industries" argued that differences in the cost of production as between the United States and foreign nations should be equalized through tariff duties. Since the enactment of the Trade Agreements Act of 1934, significant steps were taken toward reducing tariff barriers through reciprocal trade agreements. Revenue from customs duties has continued modest since that time. As an important source of revenue customs duties are of doubtful validity; for they add to the prices consumers must pay, providing an erratic and irresponsible subsidy system for home producers.

Pay-roll Taxes.—A newcomer of imposing size, pay-roll taxes entered the federal revenue picture only with the enactment of the Social Security Act of 1935. Since these revenues are earmarked for particular purposes, they do not affect significantly the general federal fiscal picture. The tax for old-age insurance is collected both from employee and employer; the rate started at 1 per cent on each and was increased to $1\frac{1}{2}$ only in January 1950, despite the original plan that it should increase gradually until the maximum of 3 per cent was reached in 1949. The federal tax for unemployment insurance was fixed at 3 per cent of each employer's total pay roll, but 90 per cent of this is waived if the state in which the employer operates has an unemployment-insurance system approved by the Social Security Administration. A few states require employee contributions to unemployment insurance, but most finance from employer contributions alone. Revenues derived from the small federal pay-roll tax for unemployment insurance ($\frac{1}{10}$ of 3 per cent) are allocated to the states for administrative expense incurred in their unemployment-compensation programs. During the fiscal year of 1947–1948 federal pay-roll taxes yielded a total of $2,519,000,000.

Nontax Revenues.—A great variety of nontax revenues accrue to the Federal government. Federal enterprises of a business nature—the Post Office, the Panama Canal and Panama Railroad, the Inland Waterways Corporation, the Maritime Commission—return large revenues to the Treasury, but little if any net profit is found after deducting operating expenses. Some relatively small amounts are obtained by the sale of public lands and by the rental of lands or of privileges (such as grazing or mineral extraction) on the public domain. Another source of nontax revenue is federal profit obtained through minting money. This profit represents the margin between the value of the metals used in minting (plus minting cost) and the face value of coins minted; it was nearly 40 million dollars in 1947–1948.[1] Other forms of nontax federal revenues are found in fines and penalties exacted for crimes, gifts, interest on loans, and fees.

State and Local Revenues.—The largest source of state tax revenues is state sales taxes, including general, motor-vehicle fuel, liquor, and tobacco taxes; sales taxes produced 40.3 per cent of the aggregate revenues of American states in 1948–1949.[2] In second place among state revenues is that from license and privilege taxation. Individual and corporate income taxes, property taxes, and death and gift taxes return significant state income. Revenue from federal grants-in-aid and from state proprietary enterprises, especially liquor stores, constitutes the greatest part of nontax state revenue.

Local governments are supported mainly by the traditional general property tax, which yields about 53.0 per cent of all local revenue. Sales taxes now occupy second place. Licenses and permits are third. State grants to local governments and income from municipal utility undertakings (water and electricity) occupy an important place in local nontax revenues.

Duplicating Taxation.—The traditional sources of federal revenue were customs duties and excise taxes, especially on liquor and tobacco. Adoption of the Sixteenth Amendment and the coming of the First World War brought a transformation and a diversification of the federal revenue pattern. State governments, no longer able to subsist on the revenue obtainable from the general property tax, even earlier had turned to other

[1] United States Department of the Treasury, *Annual Report . . . for the Fiscal Year Ending June 30, 1948* (Washington: Government Printing Office, 1949), p. 635.

[2] United States Department of Commerce, Bureau of the Census, *Governmental Revenue in 1948*, No. 3 in the series, "Governmental Finances in the United States: 1948" (Washington: Bureau of the Census, 1949), pp. 8–9.

forms of taxation. During the last 30 years federal and state taxes have been increasingly duplicative. This duplication may not be serious in some fields; for example, the federal tax on gasoline may be justified in view of the large federal grant-in-aid for state highways. In other fields, however, duplication is costly, awkward, and sometimes unfair; double taxation of incomes has resulted in an erratic pattern and in tax competition between the states. Federal-state duplication is found also in liquor and tobacco.

One solution for the problems arising from duplication is for the Federal government to allow credits for state taxation. The tax-offset device, as illustrated by federal death taxes, permits sharing of a source of revenue and encourages a measure of uniformity in the states. Only Nevada has no inheritance tax on its books to take advantage of the federal credit for state taxation. A similar plan might be suitable for sharing the income tax. Thirty-three states had personal income taxes in 1941; the tax paid to states is deductible from income taxable by the Federal government. Since the highest state tax rate ranges from 1 to 15 per cent, and especially because sixteen states do not tax individual incomes as such, much competition exists between states seeking to serve as the residence of wealthy persons. A tax offset, permitting credit for state taxation up to about 25 per cent of the federal tax, would regularize personal income taxation in the country and prevent unfair competition.

Another proposal is that the different levels of government should agree on a separation of sources. Usually the plan is that the states should enjoy exclusively the field of general sales taxation, while the Federal government would have wholly the taxation of personal income. Such plans can work effectively to separate state and local tax sources, for state legislative action alone often suffices to make the separation. Dividing sources between federal and state governments, however, would require unanimous consent of all forty-nine legislative bodies concerned or make a federal constitutional amendment necessary.

A more effective plan would be to enact a tax that would be federally collected, but shared with the states. This alternative would be even better than the tax-offset plan; for it would eliminate the expense and trouble of two returns on separate forms. A federally collected state-shared tax would not eliminate the possibility of duplication if any state persisted in its determination to tax the commodity or income item concerned. For income taxation this plan would have some advantages over the tax-offset plan, and decided superiority over the separation-of-sources proposal.

Reciprocal Tax Immunity.—The constitutional doctrine of reciprocal tax immunity has been traced in an earlier chapter.[1] The idea of blanket immunity of all federal transactions and instrumentalities from state tax-

[1] See pp. 370–372.

ation, and those of the state from federal taxation went far beyond the extent necessary to protect one level of government from undue burden by the other. At its height it banned state taxes on salaries of federal officials, on income from federal bonds, on sales to federal agencies; while the states enjoyed similar immunity from federal taxation. Beginning in 1938 the Supreme Court reduced considerably the scope of this immunity. The federal personal income tax is now collected from state and local government employees, and most of the states having an income tax apply it to federal employees as to anyone else. The greatest controversy arose over a Treasury proposal to eliminate tax exemption on government securities. Until recently standard practice has been that the Federal government make income from its own bond issues exempt from federal taxation, and most state governments have exempted their securities issues from their own taxes. This led to very complete immunity from taxation of most public securities issued in the country. In 1939 the Treasury Department started a campaign to secure the elimination of tax-exempt bonds. Extended hearings were held.[1] The principal opposition to the proposal came from representatives of state and local governments, who recognized that removal of tax immunity would require them to offer higher interest rates. This point was granted, but the more important question was whether or not the added interest rates might be offset by the revenue that would be derived from taxing income from public bonds. The greatest beneficiary from the old system of immunity is the person of very large income who invests heavily in tax-exempt state and local securities. Once his income reaches a point where he must pay one-half or more of the additional amount in federal income tax, the wealthy person will buy up exempt bonds, the income from which is untaxable.

Abolition of tax exemption is not an easy process. First, the Federal government has taken the lead, beginning in 1941, by making its own new bond issues subject to federal income taxation. The states might well be encouraged to take similar action in respect to their own issues. Next, the Federal government might commence taxing income from state and local governmental securities. This step has been delayed by the vehemence of state and local opposition but may be expected shortly. Finally, the states could follow the federal example and apply their taxation to federal bonds. These changes probably would apply only to future issues of securities; under the contract clause of the Federal Constitution it might be difficult to make them applicable to existing issues on which

[1] United States House of Representatives, Special Committee on Taxation of Governmental Securities and Salaries, *Hearings*, 76th Cong., 1st Sess. (Washington: Government Printing Office, 1939). See also United States House of Representatives, Committee on Ways and Means, *Hearings on Taxation of Governmental Securities*, 76th Cong., 1st Sess. (Washington: Government Printing Office, 1939).

tax exemption has been assured. If only future issues are covered, however, it will take a long time to correct the evils of the existing situation.

An Intergovernmental Fiscal Program.—During the Second World War a thorough study of intergovernmental fiscal relations was completed by a committee of experts appointed by the Secretary of the Treasury.[1] Stressing the cooperative approach, the committee proposed the establishment of a federal-state fiscal authority, which would promote joint administration of selected overlapping taxes, facilitate interstate cooperation, conduct research, and perform other services of mutual interest to Federal and state governments. This authority would be composed of three members, of which one would be appointed by the President, one by delegates of the states, and a third by the first two.

According to the committee, a number of specific taxes may be coordinated to the advantage of both Federal and state governments. For the income tax, cooperation in administration is recommended, involving joint returns, joint audits, and joint use of personnel. Death taxes need overhauling, with the Federal government extending the offset to all its levies including the gift tax, and the states improving their administration. Tobacco taxes, now levied by both levels of government, ought to be put on a federally collected, state-shared basis. To simplify payment, it was proposed that the unemployment-insurance tax offset be increased to 100 per cent, so that the taxpayer would pay solely to the state.

Tackling next the problems of tax immunities, the committee urged establishment of a standard policy for federal payments in lieu of taxes to state and local governments. To break the log jam over tax-exempt securities, the committee suggested consideration of both a federal bank for loans to states and municipalities, and a direct federal subsidy of ½ of 1 per cent on the bond issues of state and local governments.

The committee examined the results of federal grants-in-aid in the states. In many of them aided functions get the lion's share of state resources, due to the matching requirement. The need for a national minimum standard, especially in elementary education, was urged. The committee commended for use in grants-in-aid the "graduated bracket system of distribution," a sliding scale under which, for example, the United States old-age-assistance payment to the state for each aided person might be two-thirds on the first $15, one-half on $15 to $25, and one-third on $25 to $40.[2]

[1] United States Treasury Department, Committee on Intergovernmental Fiscal Relations, *Federal, State, and Local Government Fiscal Relations . . . a Report . . .*, Sen. Doc. 69, 78th Cong., 1st Sess. (Washington: Government Printing Office, 1943). Members of the committee were Harold M. Groves, Luther Gulick, and Mabel Newcomber.

[2] See also p. 764.

PUBLIC EXPENDITURES

Increasing Cost of Government.—It is commonplace to observe that the cost of governments is increasing, both absolutely and per capita. The accepted figures show that all levels of American government—national, state, and local—in 1913 expended $2,919,000,000. The same levels in 1938 spent $16,312,000,000, and in 1942 $47,327,000,000. Over the period of 25 years, 1913–1938, the cost of Federal government increased

Changing Pattern of Government Expenditures

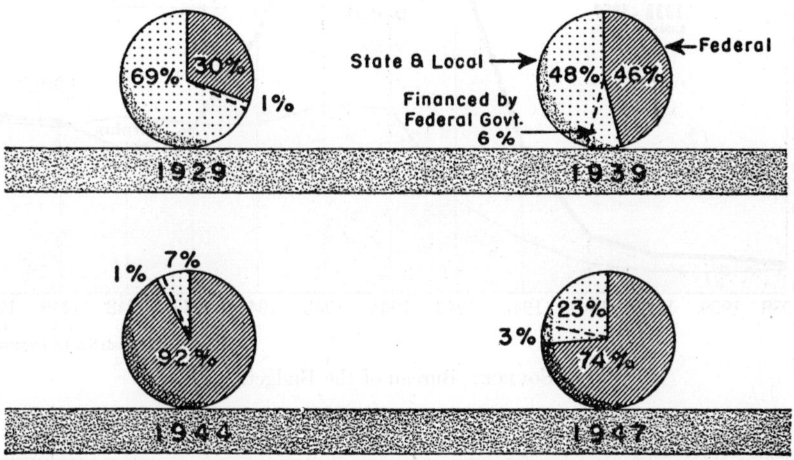

almost exactly ten times over. The cost of state government grew almost proportionately. Local governments tripled in expenditures in the quarter century. While population did increase significantly over this period, cost of government per capita quadrupled.

Comparison of governmental costs with national income is perhaps most significant. In 1913 the national income was estimated at $35,400,000,000; governmental expenditures amounted to 8.2 per cent of this amount. In 1938 national income was figured at 68 billion dollars; the cost of government was 24 per cent of the total. In 1942, when national income was 122 billion dollars, public expenses were more than 38 per cent. In 1947 national income was estimated at $202,500,000,000, and aggregate governmental expenditures were about 25 per cent of that total.

Expenditures by Functions.—Recent studies[1] show what the various functions of government cost. The totals for all governments—national,

[1] United States Department of Commerce, Bureau of the Census, *Governmental Finances in the United States, 1942* (Washington: Government Printing Office, 1945), pp. 14–15.

state, and local—in 1942 indicate the largest expenditures were for (1) public safety (including war activities), $28,331,000,000; (2) schools, $3,245,000,000; (3) public welfare, $3,120,000,000; and (4) debt service, $2,897,000,000.

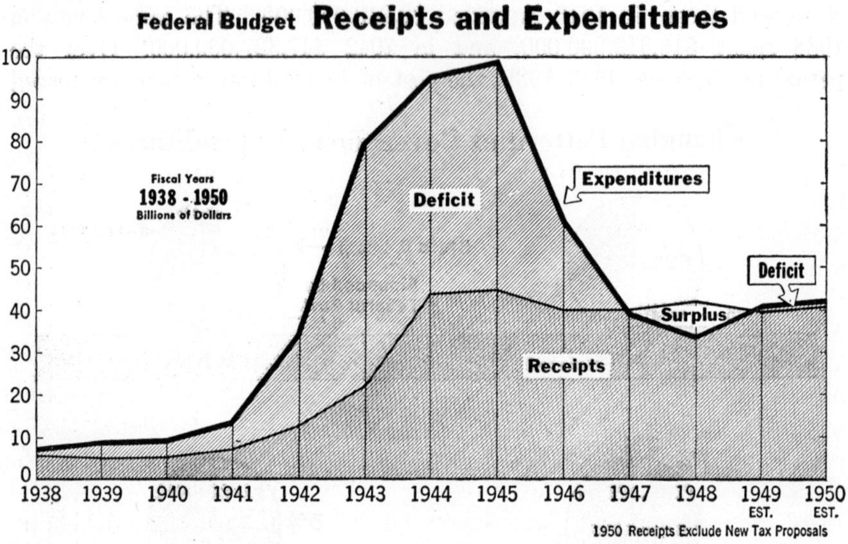

SOURCE: Bureau of the Budget.

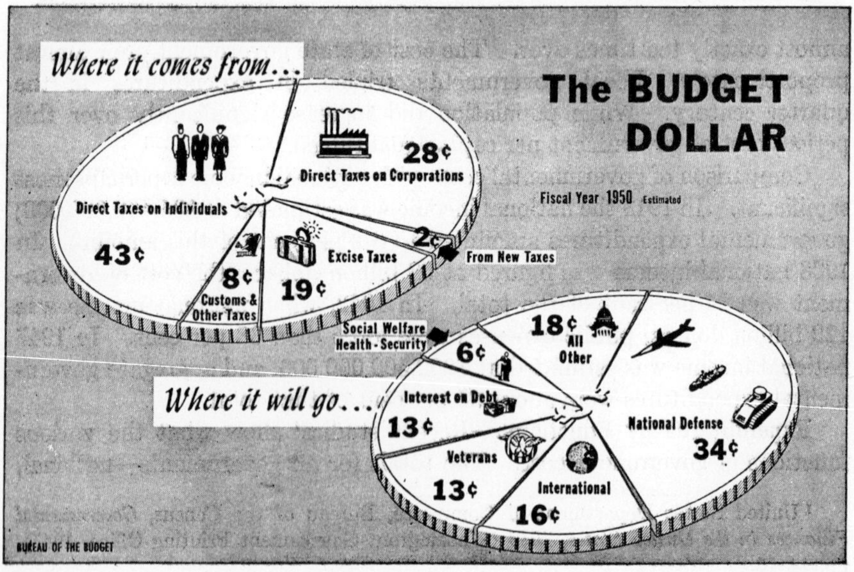

Federal expenditures in 1942 were for the following principal functions: (1) public safety (including war activities), $20,259,000,000; (2) public welfare, $1,501,000,000; (3) debt service, $1,260,000,000; and (4) natural resources (including agriculture), $1,226,000,000. In 1938, a typical prewar year, defense ran second to relief costs. Postwar expenditures will be high for debt service, veterans' care, and public works.

State expenditures for 1942 were highest for (1) highways, $1,133,000,000; (2) schools, $1,056,000,000; (3) public welfare, $908,000,000; and (4) debt service, $428,000,000. This pattern is not likely to change greatly in the immediate postwar period.

Local governmental expenditures for 1942 totaled (1) schools, $2,316,000,000; (2) debt service, $1,209,000,000; (3) public welfare, $710,000,000; and (4) highways, $689,000,000. The war affected local expenditures least.

THE PUBLIC DEBT

The Debt Problem.—Failure to keep the revenues of government in balance with the expenditures results more often in deficits than in surpluses. In depression, war, and expansion governments borrow. The resulting debt burden is enormous, both in interest charges and in repayments. Virtually every governmental unit has some power to borrow. Local governments, and some states, are restricted within certain limits. The nation and other states may borrow as much and so long as the public will approve and lenders will lend. It appears quite reasonable that governments should spend more in times of emergency and repay this in times of peace and prosperity.

During the First World War the country was saddled with a national debt of $25,500,000,000. This was reduced to $16,185,000,000 by 1930. Then depression spending intervened, and the federal debt passed the 40-billion-dollar mark during 1939. Once in war, budgets were pushed up to undreamed of heights; for fiscal year 1945, expenditures of over 100 billion dollars were made; receipts for the same period accounted for over 46½ billion dollars, leaving a deficit of about 54 billion dollars. The debt limit has been raised again and again, and is at the moment of writing set at 300 billion dollars.

From governmental borrowing practices we can learn lessons that apply to an individual's conduct too. First, do not borrow for a longer period than an improvement will last. Frequently governments will borrow for improvements but leave repayment of the loan until long after the improvement has outlived its utility. Second, do not pay ordinary operating expenses out of borrowed money. Loans sometimes are sought for ordinary operating expenses during normal times, because public bodies prefer not to levy the taxes necessary to finance them. Third, spread repayment over a period of time. Loans often are obtained for fixed periods and the whole amount falls due at a particular time, but the government makes no provision for accumulating enough funds to repay. The last abuse is corrected through issuing term bonds and setting up sinking funds to redeem them when due. Another satisfactory solution is to issue serial bonds, with redemption periods staggered over the years.

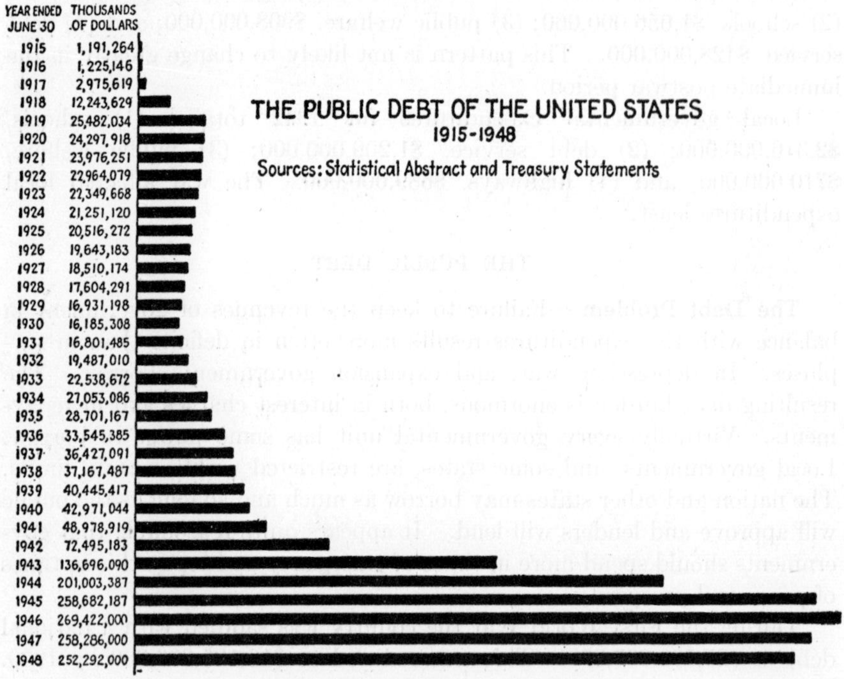

Several states have gone to considerable lengths to limit debts of local governments. Often this limitation is based upon assessed valuation. Restrictions may be avoided by increasing assessed valuation, or by forming special districts to perform certain services that require a considerable outlay, such as a water district. Debt-limitation laws have not proved very successful. The states have established central agencies to oversee local budgets and debts with varying degrees of success.

Debt Policy and Pay as You Go.—Most of us are indoctrinated with the idea that debt is unfortunate, and that a well-run family or government is one that keeps its expenditures as low as its income. The other side of the picture, however, is that few families would ever enjoy home ownership and few business ventures would ever be launched were it not for borrowed money. No sweeping verdict against all types of borrowing is in order. During war and depression, people come to accept the necessity of governmental spending beyond the possible limit of current income. In the fiscal year 1943, the Federal government alone cost about 52 per cent of the total national income; in 1944 and 1945 an even larger proportion was taken. The impossibility of taking all in taxes is obvious. Therefore, we have accepted a theory that national debt incurred in war and depression should be paid off during peace and prosperity. State and local governments may borrow for improvements, but, like businesses that expand with capital outlay, these obligations are to be paid off as quickly as possible.

In recent years, however, a new theory of national debt has developed. The public debt, primarily national, will be used as a device for controlling economic life. This national debt rose to nearly 270 billion dollars in 1945–1946. The gross federal debt outstanding as of June 30, 1948, was 252 billion dollars. Instead of paying off this debt as rapidly as possible, it might even be permitted to increase. Government would use the proceeds obtained by borrowing to prime the pump of private enterprise. Proponents of the permanent debt argue that private investment cannot take up individual savings and that government must assume this role.

MONEY AND BANKING

The National Monetary System.—Acting under the terms of its constitutional power to coin money and regulate its value, Congress has exercised far-reaching influence over the economic life of the country. The Constitution did not specify what monetary unit should be used. In 1792 Congress, on the recommendation of Secretary of the Treasury Alexander Hamilton, established the decimal system based on the dollar, which is now perhaps the most widely accepted monetary unit in the world. In departing from the traditional British pound, shilling, and pence scheme, this country liberated itself from a cumbersome plan that makes the figuring of interest or tax rates a nightmare of confusion. If an early Congress had been equally farsighted in adopting the metric system of weights and measures, the convenience of posterity would also have been served.

Manufacture of metal coins is carried out in three federal mints located in Philadelphia, Denver, and San Francisco. During the Second World War these mints also produced large quantities of coin for friendly and allied foreign nations. In recent years the mints have produced mainly 1-cent, 5-cent, 10-cent, 25-cent, and 50-cent coins. Gold coin was called in during the crisis of 1933, and production has not resumed. Silver dollars are still in circulation but are rare items in many sections of the country. Since 1943 there has been more than 1 billion dollars in coin in circulation.

Paper money has circulated in some form or other throughout American history. Although states were forbidden by the Constitution to issue paper money, state-chartered banks continued to issue until their notes were taxed out of existence during the Civil War. After 1863 banks chartered by the national government issued paper money freely. While there are many types of paper currency in circulation today, most of it consists of Federal Reserve notes, backed by commercial paper, silver certificates, backed by Treasury silver bullion, and United States notes, issued and backed by the Treasury.

At many periods of American history there has been sharp controversy over monetary standards. Gold has always been a major factor in the monetary system; over much of the period silver has also played an important role. William Jennings Bryan's great crusade of 1896 resulted in part from the demonetization of silver in 1873. Support for coinage of silver at that time was motivated largely by debtor aspirations for a cheaper money. In the last two decades the silver bloc in Congress has been interested principally in assuring a ready market and high price for silver mined in the United States. Since 1933 the United States has been legally off the gold standard but has continued to buy gold and silver at prices above the world market. The store of gold in the vaults of the federal treasury has reached over 20 billion dollars. Monetary theorists disagree over the utility of this gold, most of it stored at Fort Knox, Ky.

The Federal Reserve Plan.—The Federal Reserve System was established in 1913, replacing the national banking system created during the Civil War. The power of the Congress to charter banks had been exercised in respect to the first Bank of the United States (1791–1811) and the second Bank (1816–1836) and its constitutionality assured in McCulloch *v.* Maryland.[1] The national banking system of 1863–1864 was designed to stabilize the medium of exchange and to assist the sale of government bonds. After the paper money of state banks was taxed out of existence, the banks chartered by the national government enjoyed a monopoly over the issue of currency. In successive depressions and panics the national banking scheme was proved inadequate. Senator Carter Glass, author of the 1913 legislation, declared of the old plan: "The Siamese twins of disorder were an inelastic currency and a fictitious reserve system."[2] Inelasticity arose from the requirement that note currency might be issued by national banks only to the extent to which they were holders of government bonds. As national indebtedness was reduced, the volume of currency was reduced. The fictitiousness of the old reserve system, according to Glass, was produced by the tendency of local banks to send

[1] See p. 86.

[2] Carter Glass, *An Adventure in Constructive Finance* (New York: Doubleday, 1927), p. 60.

their surplus funds to the money centers of the great cities. There funds would be loaned for speculation, the end result of which would be panic and depression.

The Federal Reserve System of today is supervised by the Board of Governors, composed of seven members appointed by the President for 14-year terms. From its Washington headquarters, the Board determines general monetary and credit policies and oversees the twelve district Federal Reserve Banks and member private banks. The influence of the Board over credit conditions in the country is exerted mainly through its powers to alter the requirements for reserves against deposits in member banks and to change the rediscount rate, which is the rate at which Federal Reserve Banks lend money to private banks.

Actually the twelve Federal Reserve Banks are privately owned, for their stock is held by the member banks. All national banks are required to subscribe to the capital stock of their districts. State banks may become members; if they do, a similar obligation to purchase stock is required. The Federal Reserve Banks are governed by regional boards of directors. Each board has nine members, of which six are selected by member banks and three by the national Board of Governors. Reserve Banks hold on deposit reserve balances of member banks, extend credit facilities to them and other business concerns, and issue Federal Reserve notes which account for most of the money now in circulation. These notes may be backed by commercial paper, thus avoiding the inelasticity of the old national banking system, because the issue of currency can be great when demand for loans is great and less when borrowing is little.

The general utility of the Federal Reserve System has been conceded rather widely. There is still disagreement, however, over the success of the plan in decentralizing and regionalizing banking operations. Considerable sentiment exists for complete national governmental ownership of the Federal Reserve Banks.

References

Fiscal Organization and Budgets

Bartelt, Edward F.: *Accounting Procedures of the United States Government* (Chicago: Public Administration Service, 1940).

Benson, George C. S.: *Financial Control and Integration—with Special Reference to the Comptroller General* (New York: Harper, 1934).

Buck, Arthur E.: *The Budget in Governments of Today* (New York: Macmillan, 1934).

——— *Public Budgeting* (New York: Harper, 1929).

Chatters, Carl H., and Irving Tenner: *Municipal and Governmental Accounting* (New York: Prentice-Hall, 1940).

Cleveland, Frederick A., and Arthur E. Buck: *The Budget and Responsible Government* (New York: Macmillan, 1920).

Dawes, Charles G.: *The First Year of the Budget of the United States* (New York: Harper, 1923).

DEWEY, DAVIS R.: *Financial History of the United States* (New York: Longmans, rev. ed., 1934).
FAUST, MARTIN L.: *The Custody of State Funds* (New York: National Institute of Public Administration, 1925).
MANSFIELD, HARVEY C.: *The Comptroller General: a Study in the Law and Practice of Financial Administration* (New Haven: Yale University Press, 1939).
MOREY, LLOYD: *Introduction to Governmental Accounting* (New York: Wiley, 1927).
NAYLOR, ESTILL E.: *The Federal Budget System in Operation* (Washington: Haworth Co., 1941).
OAKEY, FRANCIS: *Principles of Government Accounting and Reporting* (New York: Appleton-Century, 1921).
POWELL, FRED W. (comp.): *Control of Federal Expenditures, a Documentary History, 1775–1894* (Washington: Brookings, 1939).
SELKO, DANIEL T.: *The Administration of Federal Finances* (Washington: Brookings, 1937), Pamphlet Series no. 18.
——— *The Federal Financial System* (Washington: Brookings, 1940).
SMITH, DARRELL H.: *The General Accounting Office, Its History, Activities, and Organization* (Baltimore: The Johns Hopkins Press, 1927).
UNITED STATES BUREAU OF THE BUDGET: *The Budget of the United States Government* (Washington: Government Printing Office, annual).
UNITED STATES COMMISSION ON ORGANIZATION OF THE EXECUTIVE BRANCH OF THE GOVERNMENT ("HOOVER COMMISSION"): *Budgeting and Accounting* (Washington: Government Printing Office, 1949).
——— Task Force Report on *Fiscal, Budgeting, and Accounting Activities* (Washington: Government Printing Office, 1949).
UNITED STATES COMPTROLLER GENERAL: *Annual Report* (Washington: Government Printing Office, annual).
UNITED STATES PRESIDENT'S COMMITTEE ON ADMINISTRATIVE MANAGEMENT: *Report . . . with Studies of Administration Management in the Federal Government* (Washington: Government Printing Office, 1937). Study no. 2 is "Fiscal Management in the National Government" and contains studies by Arthur E. Buck and H. C. Mansfield.
UNITED STATES SENATE, SELECT COMMITTEE TO INVESTIGATE THE EXECUTIVE AGENCIES OF THE GOVERNMENT: *Financial Administration of the Federal Government,* Sen. Doc. 5, 75th Cong., 1st Sess. (Washington: Government Printing Office, 1937).
WILLOUGHBY, WILLIAM F.: *Financial Conditions and Operations of the National Government 1921–1930* (Washington: Government Printing Office, 1931).
——— *The Movement for Budgetary Reform in the States* (New York: Appleton-Century, 1918).
——— *The National Budget System with Suggestions for Its Improvement* (Baltimore: The Johns Hopkins Press, 1927).
WILMERDING, LUCIUS, JR.: *The Spending Power: A History of the Efforts of Congress to Control Expenditures* (New Haven: Yale University Press, 1943).

REVENUE, EXPENDITURE, AND DEBT

ABBOTT, CHARLES C.: *Management of the Federal Debt* (New York: McGraw-Hill, 1946).
ALTMAN, GEORGE T.: *Introduction to Federal Taxation* (New York: Commerce Clearing House, rev. ed., 1938).
BLAKEY, ROY G., and GLADYS C. BLAKEY: *The Federal Income Tax* (New York: Longmans, 1940).
——— *Sales Taxes and Other Excises* (Chicago: Public Administration Service, 1945).

BUEHLER, ALFRED G.: *General Sales Taxation* (New York: Business Bourse, 1932).
COMMITTEE ON PUBLIC DEBT POLICY: *Our National Debt, Its History and Its Meaning Today* (New York: Harcourt Brace, 1949).
GROVES, HAROLD M.: *Financing Government* (New York: Holt, 1939).
——— *Postwar Taxation and Economic Progress* (New York: McGraw-Hill, 1946).
HAIG, ROBERT M., and OTHERS: *The Sales Tax in the American States* (New York: Columbia University Press, 1934).
HARRIS, SEYMOUR E.: *The National Debt and the New Economics* (New York: McGraw-Hill, 1947).
LUTZ, HARLEY L.: *Public Finance* (New York: Appleton-Century-Crofts, rev. ed., 1947).
MANNING, RAYMOND E.: *Federal Excise Taxes*, Public Affairs Bulletin No. 59 (Washington: Library of Congress, 1947).
PAUL, RANDOLPH: *Taxation for Prosperity* (Indianapolis: Bobbs-Merrill, 1947).
SHOUP, CARL, and OTHERS: *Facing the Tax Problem* (New York: Twentieth Century Fund, 1937).
STEWART, PAUL W., and RUFUS S. TUCKER: *The National Debt and Government Credit* (New York: Twentieth Century Fund, 1937).
STUDENSKI, PAUL: *Chapters on Public Finance* (New York: Richard R. Smith, 1935).
TAX INSTITUTE (formerly Tax Policy League): *Tax Barriers to Trade* (Philadelphia: The Institute, 1941).
——— *Tax Policy* (Philadelphia: The Institute, monthly).
——— *Tax Relations among Governmental Units* (New York: Tax Policy League, 1938).
TAX RESEARCH FOUNDATION: *Tax Systems* (Chicago: Commerce Clearing House, 9th ed., 1942). Issued at irregular intervals, annual supplements.
UNITED STATES TREASURY DEPARTMENT, COMMITTEE ON INTERGOVERNMENTAL FISCAL RELATIONS: *Federal, State, and Local Government Fiscal Relations . . . a Report . . .*, Sen. Doc. 69, 78th Cong., 1st Sess. (Washington: Government Printing Office, 1943).
VAN SANT, EDWARD R.: *The Floating Debt of the Federal Government* (Baltimore: Johns Hopkins Press, 1937).

TEXT-FILM

The following McGraw-Hill 35mm silent filmstrip is recommended for use with Chaps. 17 and 23 of this text.

Federal Finance. Taxation and monetary powers of the government. Financial administration and fiscal agencies. Analysis of governmental expenditures, revenues, and debts.

Chapter 24

THE CONDUCT OF FOREIGN RELATIONS

What, then, has democracy failed to accomplish? It has brought no nearer friendly feeling and the sense of human brotherhood among the peoples of the world towards one another. Freedom has not been a reconciler.

James Bryce, *Modern Democracies.*[1]

DEVELOPMENT OF AMERICAN FOREIGN RELATIONS

Before the Revolution, several American colonies sent agents to England (but not to other countries) to represent their individual interests, but these were not of diplomatic or consular rank. Rather, Britain managed foreign affairs for the colonies until the breach in 1776. Thereupon, the control of external affairs passed to the Continental Congress which presumed to represent the "united colonies." Its agents were nowhere received, however, except by France, who seized upon the opportunity presented to encourage dissension within the empire of her ancient enemy. Successful conclusion of the war led other states to recognize the new republic. The Netherlands was first, in 1782, then followed Spain, Portugal, and others, including Britain herself after final settlement was made in the Treaty of Paris.[2]

Origin of the Department of State.—The Department of State antedates the Constitution itself. It may be traced to the Committee on Secret Correspondence appointed by the Continental Congress in 1775 "for the sole purpose of corresponding with our friends in Great Britain, Ireland and other parts of the world." This committee has been aptly called "the embryo of an American foreign office."[3] Its name was changed to that of Committee of Foreign Affairs in 1777, but its function remained the same. Composed of a shifting membership which met intermittently, the committee proved to be a poor vehicle. Accordingly, it was superseded in January, 1781, less than 3 months before the adoption of the Articles of Confederation, by a Department of Foreign Affairs, directed by a secretary and small staff. Robert Livingston was appointed the first secre-

[1] (New York: Macmillan, 2 vols., new ed., 1924), vol. II, p. 533. Quoted by permission of the publishers.

[2] For an interesting account of the manner in which the First and Second Continental Congresses handled foreign affairs, see Edmund C. Burnett, *The Continental Congress* (New York: Macmillan, 1941), *passim.*

[3] Samuel F. Bemis, *A Diplomatic History of the United States* (New York: Holt, 1936), p. 22.

tary, serving until 1784. He was succeeded by John Jay, who held the post until the Constitution went into effect.[1] Upon organizing the new government, the first executive department to be established was a Department of Foreign Affairs, created in July, 1789. Shortly thereafter, when assigned a number of duties relating to "home affairs," its name was changed to that of Department of State, by which it has since been known.

GENERAL ASPECTS OF DIPLOMATIC AND CONSULAR PRACTICE

Diplomacy is steeped in formality and etiquette, much of which dates back to antiquity. The most important custom has to do with the ranking of diplomatic officers.

Classification of Diplomats.—All nations, except Russia, follow the classification of diplomats agreed upon by the Congress of Vienna in 1816 and supplemented from time to time. At present there are five classes: the first includes ambassadors, legates (envoys of the pope chosen from the cardinals for special assignments), and nuncios (envoys of the pope assigned to permanent posts and chosen from outside the rank of cardinals); the second, envoys extraordinary, ministers plenipotentiary, and apostolic internuncios (envoys of the pope next in rank to nuncios); the third, ministers resident; the fourth, chargés d'affaires; and the fifth, a group known as diplomatic agents.[2] Envoys rank within each class according to the date of arrival at their post, the one in the highest rank with the most seniority at a given post being known as the *doyen*, or dean of the diplomatic corps.

Envoys of the various classes perform practically the same functions and enjoy the same rights and privileges, the chief difference being a matter of prestige. Those of the first class are supposed to be the personal representatives of the sovereign, while those of the other are merely the representatives of their governments, although in modern times this has little practical significance. Those of the first class occupy embassies; those of the remaining classes, legations. Those of the first three classes are accredited to heads of states, while those of the fourth and fifth classes are accredited to ministers of foreign affairs. There is a tendency to consider chargés d'affaires as temporary officers, while diplomatic agents are as a rule assigned only to states that are not fully sovereign, such as Egypt and Morocco.

[1] Actually, a little longer. He continued unofficially to superintend the office until Jefferson entered upon his duties in March, 1790.

[2] In addition, the United States has from time to time appointed persons with the rank of commissioner. Their status is curious and must usually be assigned on the basis of the language and purport of the appointee's credentials. On the status of commissioners see Tracy H. Lay, *The Foreign Service of the United States* (New York: Prentice-Hall, 1925), p. 103.

Classification of Consuls.—Diplomats represent their country in its political relations with other governments, while consuls are commissioned to act as agents for the purpose of assisting with the administration of American laws in foreign ports, assisting American tourists, affording protection to Americans and their interests, and promoting trade. The classification of consuls in all states is almost the same, though there is much less fussing about the matter than with diplomats. Those of the United States are divided into four classes: consuls general, consuls, vice-consuls, and consular agents. Which is appointed to a particular post depends to a large extent upon the commercial and financial importance of the place so far as American interests are concerned. Some of the consuls general are given supervisory jurisdiction over all consular offices of lesser rank within a given area. Thus, the one at London has supervisory jurisdiction over all consular offices in the British Isles, except Ireland; and the one at Antwerp has supervisory authority over all of Belgium and Luxembourg.

Appointment and Reception of Diplomats.—Diplomats are invariably appointed by heads of states. In the United States chiefs of important missions are appointed by the President with senatorial confirmation. Before sending the name of a diplomat to the Senate for confirmation, the President, acting through the Department of State, usually ascertains whether the person is acceptable to the government to which he is to be accredited. The act of determining whether the envoy is *persona grata* is called *agréation* and the approval *agrément*. When confirmed by the Senate, the diplomat is given a "letter of credence" which is an official commission to be presented to the sovereign upon arrival at his post. The reverse of this procedure is followed when diplomats are sent to the United States. The President receives diplomats of higher rank, while those of lesser rank are received by the Secretary of State. Congress has nothing to do with the matter. The receptions that take place at the White House are formal and stiff, with meticulous regard for ceremony and protocol.[1] Receptions consume considerable time, inasmuch as the largest diplomatic body in the world—over 500 members—is now stationed in Washington.[2]

Appointment and Reception of Consuls.—As in the case of diplomats, consuls must be *persona grata*, although *agrément* is not usually obtained

[1] For an entertaining description of typical receptions, see Graham H. Stuart, *American Diplomatic and Consular Practice* (New York: Appleton-Century, 1936), pp. 222–223; Bertram D. Hulen, *Inside the Department of State* (New York: McGraw-Hill, 1939), pp. 187–189. For copies of remarks exchanged on such occasions, see current issues of United States Department of State, *Bulletin of the Department of State* (Washington: Government Printing Office, weekly).

[2] For a register of these see United States Department of State, *Diplomatic List* (Washington: Government Printing Office, monthly).

in advance. They are usually appointed by heads of states or by ministers of foreign affairs. In the United States those above the rank of consular agent are appointed by the President from among career Foreign Service officers,[1] while consular agents are appointed by the Secretary of State usually upon the recommendation of a superior officer located within the same country or region. Upon appointment they are given by their own government what is known as a "consular commission," which is presented to the secretary of foreign affairs upon arrival at the point of service. Though as a rule they are not received by sovereigns or heads of states, they may be, particularly if their government is without diplomatic representation in that country.[2] The receiving government issues an "exequatur" which entitles the consul to the rights and duties pertaining to his office. The reverse of this procedure is followed when foreign consuls are sent to the United States. That reception of consuls is a large task is illustrated by the fact that more than 1,000 foreign consular officers are stationed within the forty-eight states.[3]

Privileges and Immunities of Diplomats.—International law and treaties accord diplomats a number of privileges not enjoyed by ordinary persons. Among others, they are entitled to safe conduct through neutral and friendly states while their own nation is at war; they are exempt from the payment of customs duties and taxes; they may worship as they please in embassies or legations even though their particular mode of worship would otherwise be illegal, as formerly was true in Mohammedan countries; they have certain ceremonial privileges such as displaying their national flag and insignia; they are entitled to certain marks of respect, such as being addressed by appropriate title and being seated according to rank at public functions; and they are entitled to perform certain civil functions, such as notarial services.

Diplomats also enjoy certain immunities. Their person, residence, place of doing business, archives, and mails are inviolable. They cannot be arrested, though their guilt be obvious; nor can they be tried by the courts of the country in which they are stationed for crimes committed while there. Neither can they be sued or compelled to give testimony in court. These immunities extend also to members of a diplomat's family and official personnel. If diplomats misbehave, they may become *persona non grata,* whereupon their recall may be requested or they may be dismissed by the government to which they are accredited. If an offense is serious, they probably will be prosecuted in the courts of their home states.

[1] See p. 531.

[2] For illustrations see John H. Ferguson, *American Diplomacy and the Boer War* (Philadelphia: University of Pennsylvania Press, 1939), p. 115.

[3] For their names, see United States Department of State, *Foreign Consular Offices in the United States* (Washington: Government Printing Office, published periodically).

Privileges and Immunities of Consuls.—The privileges and immunities of consuls are less absolute than those of diplomatic agents inasmuch as they are based almost entirely upon treaty provisions. The treaties of most countries accord them privileges similar to those enjoyed by diplomats. Though their persons are not absolutely inviolable, they are entitled to protection and the government that fails to provide it is expected to make reparation. Their archives are inviolate, but immunity does not extend to their private papers or personal effects; nor, in the absence of treaty provisions, is the consulate free from visit and search. They are generally liable for civil suit and may be prosecuted on criminal charges unless exempted by treaty provisions.

The Removal of Diplomats and Consuls.—As noted above, diplomats and consuls must be *persona grata* at all times to the governments receiving them. Frequently when it is discovered that a foreign representative has lost favor, his own government learns of it in time to effect a transfer, or asks him to resign, before an issue arises. Where an agent can no longer be tolerated, he may be peremptorily dismissed, although the usual course is to intimate to his government that his recall is desired. Normally, before departing, diplomats and consuls pay a brief formal call to the chief of state or minister of foreign affairs, although where feeling has run high this is sometimes omitted.

ORGANIZATION OF THE DEPARTMENT OF STATE

The work of handling foreign affairs is divided between the personnel concentrated in the Department of State in Washington and members of the United States Foreign Service attached to American diplomatic and consular establishments abroad. Each will be dealt with separately.

The Secretary of State.—The Secretary of State is the chief of both the department and the Foreign Service. Next to the President himself, the Secretary is the highest ranking executive officer[1] in the Federal government. He is always the personal choice of the President; his salary is $22,500 per year; and he continues to serve as long as the President desires or until impeached. In ceremonial matters the Secretary ranks first among cabinet members, always sitting immediately to the President's right at cabinet meetings. He is the only department head who is not required to make an annual report to Congress, and when asked to furnish Congress with information affecting foreign policy, he may refuse to do so if he thinks the public interest would suffer thereby. The Secretary frequently acts as spokesman for the President, and upon the death, resignation, or removal

[1] The Vice-President, it will be recalled, is a *legislative* officer until he becomes acting President.

of the President, Vice-President, Speaker, and president pro tempore of the Senate, he becomes acting president.[1]

The Secretary is nearly always a politician—usually one of the most prominent men in the President's party. Of the men who have held the post, all but a very few have been lawyers. Only two (Bryan and Kellogg, from Nebraska and Minnesota, respectively) have come from west of the Mississippi, and to date none has been selected from the West coast area. Easterners have, therefore, dominated the office. Only comparatively few of the Secretaries had extensive previous diplomatic experience, John Hay (1898–1905) being the only one since the Civil War. Many, one may guess, neither spoke nor understood any foreign language well.

Though mostly politicians, and though lacking in certain qualifications, their caliber has, on the whole, been high. Thomas Jefferson, the first Secretary, is without a peer among American patriots, philosophers, and statesmen. An extended list of the most meritorious would doubtless include John Marshall, James Madison, James Monroe, John Quincy Adams, Henry Clay, John C. Calhoun, Daniel Webster, William H. Seward, James G. Blaine, John Hay, Elihu Root, William Jennings Bryan, Charles E. Hughes, and Cordell Hull. While some have been weak, mediocrity has been the exception rather than the rule. Indeed, as one scans the list, one is impressed by the large number whose names are indelibly associated with major events in American History.[2]

Executive Staff.—Departmental organization has fluctuated considerably in recent years. Both the department itself and the Hoover Commission made intensive study of the best way to streamline the department to meet its new responsibilities. In response to these recommendations Congress, in 1949, authorized an executive staff consisting of an undersecretary, ten assistant secretaries (two of whom may be designated deputy undersecretaries), a counselor, and a legal adviser.

Offices and Divisions.—The routine of the department is carried on by a number of offices, divisions, and boards, some of which are given on the accompanying chart. Special attention should be called to the four geographic offices. These are known as the Office of European Affairs, the office of Near Eastern and African Affairs, the Office of Far Eastern Affairs, and the Office of American Republic Affairs. These are the primary divisions through which all matters pertaining to the respective regions are channeled. It is to them that Foreign Service officers scattered throughout

[1] This is due to presidential succession acts rather than to any constitutional provision. It can, therefore, be changed at will by Congress. Thus far, no Secretary of State has ascended to the presidency in the manner provided for by Congress.

[2] Brief but reliable discussions of each of the secretaries and the major events of their administrations may be found in Samuel F. Bemis (ed.), *American Secretaries of State and Their Diplomacy* (New York: Knopf, 10 vols., 1927–1929).

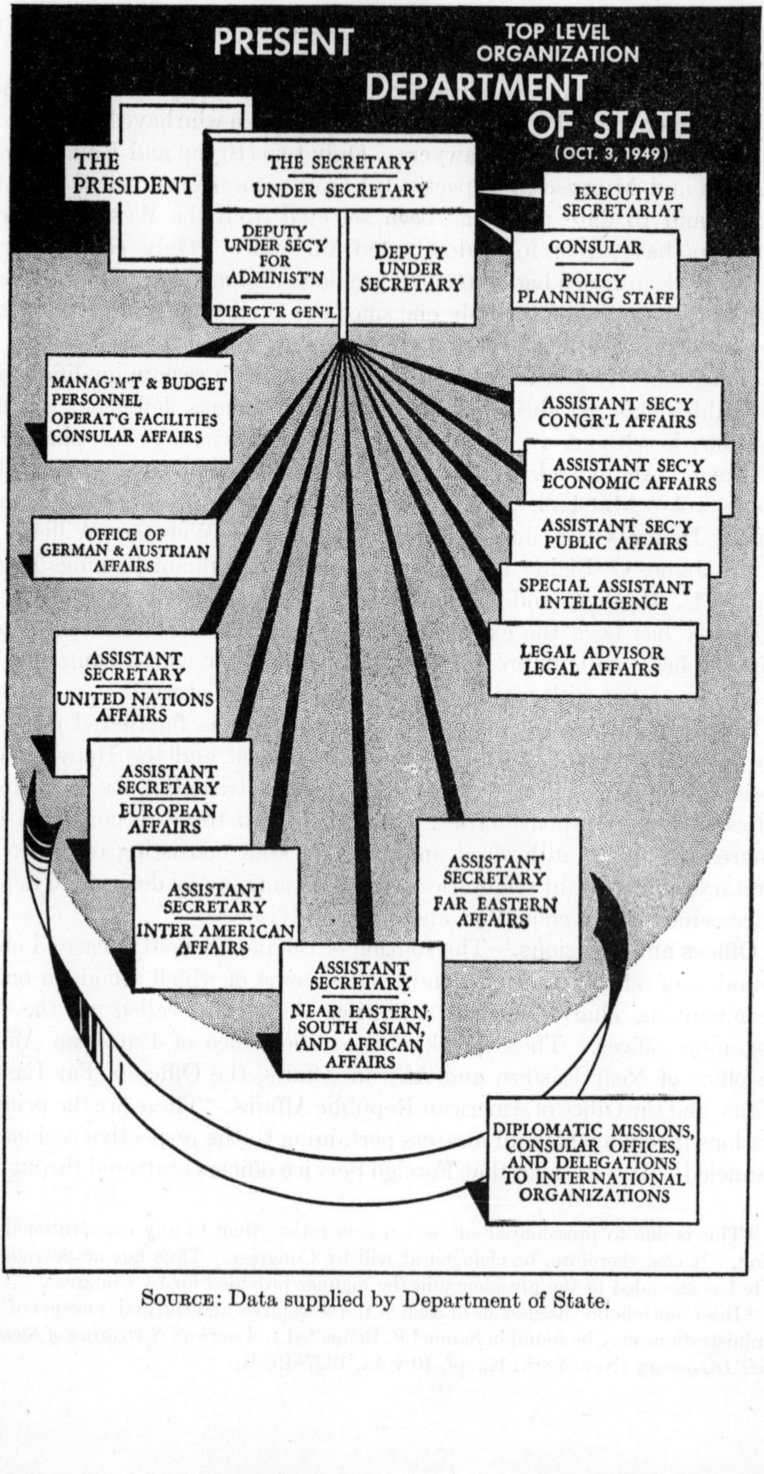
PRESENT
TOP LEVEL ORGANIZATION
DEPARTMENT OF STATE
(OCT. 3, 1949)
THE PRESIDENT
THE SECRETARY
UNDER SECRETARY
EXECUTIVE SECRETARIAT
CONSULAR
POLICY PLANNING STAFF
DEPUTY UNDER SEC'Y FOR ADMINIST'N
DIRECT'R GEN'L
DEPUTY UNDER SECRETARY
MANAG'M'T & BUDGET
PERSONNEL
OPERAT'G FACILITIES
CONSULAR AFFAIRS
ASSISTANT SEC'Y CONGR'L AFFAIRS
ASSISTANT SEC'Y ECONOMIC AFFAIRS
ASSISTANT SEC'Y PUBLIC AFFAIRS
SPECIAL ASSISTANT INTELLIGENCE
LEGAL ADVISOR LEGAL AFFAIRS
OFFICE OF GERMAN & AUSTRIAN AFFAIRS
ASSISTANT SECRETARY UNITED NATIONS AFFAIRS
ASSISTANT SECRETARY EUROPEAN AFFAIRS
ASSISTANT SECRETARY INTER AMERICAN AFFAIRS
ASSISTANT SECRETARY FAR EASTERN AFFAIRS
ASSISTANT SECRETARY NEAR EASTERN, SOUTH ASIAN, AND AFRICAN AFFAIRS
DIPLOMATIC MISSIONS, CONSULAR OFFICES, AND DELEGATIONS TO INTERNATIONAL ORGANIZATIONS

SOURCE: Data supplied by Department of State.

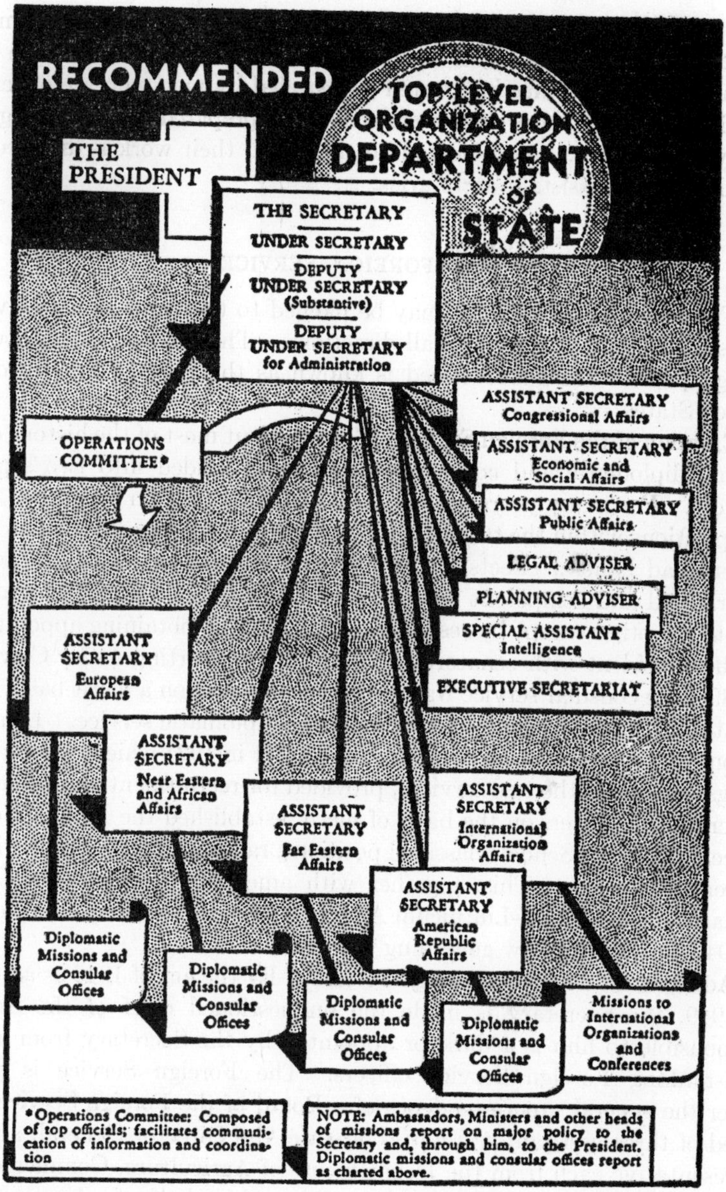

Many of the changes in administrative organization recommended by the Hoover Commission were put into effect at once in the Department of State. The Secretary's Office was strengthened by adding two assistant undersecretaries, and the various offices of the department and missions abroad were required to report through the appropriate assistant secretary. SOURCE: Hoover Commission, *Concluding Report*, p. 55.

the world address their messages and reports, and it is through them that the department sends all of its communications to officers in the field. Each division and office is directed and staffed by men who are experts in the field; hence when problems arise they are prepared to act intelligently and with dispatch. As indicated on the chart, their work is directed and coordinated by assistant secretaries.

THE FOREIGN SERVICE

The Department of State may be likened to the trunk of a tree whose limbs and branches extend in all directions. The division through which foreign policies are administered is known as the Foreign Service of the United States.

Creation of the Foreign Service.—Throughout most of the history of the nation, diplomatic and consular officers were divided into two separate services. For many years appointments to both were on a political basis, and positions within the two services were not interchangeable. The spoils system had baneful effects, while morale and efficiency suffered because experienced and competent persons in one service had no way of transferring to the other except by resigning and once more obtaining appointment by the President with senatorial confirmation. Starting under Cleveland in 1895, the consular service was gradually placed upon a merit basis, while slight improvement came to be made in the diplomatic service. Long agitation culminated in passage of the Rogers Act in 1924 which, among other things, combined the two services, provided for recruitment and promotion of permanent officers on the basis of merit, established the Foreign Service Officers' Training School, classified positions, raised salaries, and provided a retirement system. This, together with amendments added since, particularly by the Moses-Linthicum Act of 1931 and the Foreign Service Act of 1946, is the basic law governing today.

Administration of the Foreign Service.—By the act of 1946 as amended in 1949, the Secretary is made the unquestioned chief of the Service. Responsible to him is a director appointed by the Secretary from among high-ranking Foreign Service officers. The Foreign Service is placed under the general superintendence of a Board of the Foreign Service composed of three assistant secretaries of state, the Director General, and one representative each from the Departments of Agriculture, Commerce, and Labor. A Board of Examiners, not more than half of whom may be Foreign Service officers, is given the task of prescribing and supervising examinations required of candidates for appointment.

Personnel Classification and Benefits under Act of 1946.—The new law places Foreign Service personnel in six groups: (1) chiefs of missions; (2) Foreign Service officers; (3) Foreign Service Reserve officers; (4) Foreign Service staff officers and employees; (5) alien clerks and employees; and (6) consular agents. Of these, only those in the first four categories must be American citizens. Positions are carefully classified, a salary range is stated for each class, and assignments are to be made to a class and grade rather than to some particular post. Thus, the diplomatic and consular service remain united, with transfers between them frequent, as under the Rogers Act.

The law of 1946 made many other changes designed to improve the quality of those who serve the nation abroad. One of the most glaring defects of the Foreign Service had been the fact that political appointees usually held the most important diplomatic posts. While this is still possible, the new law goes far toward encouraging more frequent use of career men. Among other things, the law requires the Foreign Service Board to recommend to the President annually a list of the most meritorious senior Foreign Service officers for consideration when vacancies arise. The law also creates the position of career minister, to be held only by top Foreign Service officers. These may be appointed chiefs of missions, with senatorial approval, without jeopardizing their career status as was the case under the Rogers Act. The new law further encourages the use of career men by stipulating that the President may, without obtaining senatorial consent, assign Foreign Service officers to head missions, the chiefs of which are ministers resident, chargé d'affaires, commissioner, or diplomatic agent.

Other important changes affecting personnel were made by the 1946 law, only a few of which can be noted. Salaries were raised, more generous provision was made for travel, post, and cost-of-living allowances, officers were to be aided in returning to the United States for more frequent and extended stays in order to retain closer identification with American life, the retirement system was broadened and a disability benefit plan added, the Foreign Service Institute was created with authority to extend and improve the training of recruits and those already in service, and improvements were made in recruitment, promotion, and removal methods.

Chiefs of Missions.—Chiefs of missions[1] include the ambassadors, ministers, and other diplomats who head American embassies and legations abroad. As noted above, ambassadors, ministers, and career ministers are appointed by the President by and with the advice and consent of the Senate to serve at the pleasure of the President, but the President alone may assign Foreign Service officers to head missions of lesser rank. While it may be hoped that more important posts will be filled by career men, the fact remains that some of the incumbents have been appointed because of personal friendship, political expediency, financial or other contributions to

[1] A list of incumbent chiefs of missions and other Foreign Service personnel is published quarterly by the Department of State under the title, *Foreign Service List* (Washington: Government Printing Office).

the President's party, and a number of future appointments will doubtless be made for the same reasons.

Salaries of chiefs of missions have been low in relation to monetary demands of the office and salaries paid by other nations. Formerly, ambassadors received $17,500; ministers $10,000; but the act of 1946 raised the range to between $15,000 and $25,000 depending upon the class into which missions are placed. Allowances have also been low, with the result that only men of wealth or independent incomes could accept foreign posts, especially the more important missions like the ones at London, Paris, and Tokyo where an expense account of $50,000 a year is probably a minimum[1] for all except those like the late ambassador to Berlin, William E. Dodd, who had a congenital abhorrence of protocol and extravagance.[2] The situation should be much better since passage of the Foreign Service Act of 1946.

Foreign Service Officers.—Next to the chiefs in rank are the Foreign Service officers who constitute a permanent corps of specially recruited and trained people. These are divided into six numerical classes and a seventh known as the class of career minister. Salaries range from $3,300 for a beginner in class six to $13,500 for career minister. Entrance is by examination. Appointment of beginners is to class six but those having previously served 3 or 4 years in the Department of State, who are able to pass the examination, may enter at class five. Promotion from the lowest grade upward is based upon merit ratings. Retirement is normally at the age of sixty for all except career ministers, who serve until sixty-five. Those who reach class two and three and fail to be promoted within a reasonable period of time are retired on the principle of "promotion up or selection out" of the service.

The Examinations.—Examinations are given as often as necessary to obtain needed personnel. They are prepared by the Board of Examiners mentioned above and given in cooperation with the Civil Service Commission. In the past the examination has been both written and oral. The written usually requires 4 days and has been conducted by the Civil Service Commission in principal cities throughout the nation. The examination usually covers American history, government, and institutions since 1776; history of Europe, Latin America, and the Far East since 1776; elementary economics, including the natural, industrial, and commercial resources of the United States; political and commercial geography; elements of international, commercial, and maritime law; arithmetic as used

[1] A year in London is said to have cost Joseph Kennedy $100,000; Charles G. Dawes, $75,000; John W. Davis, between $50,000 and $60,000. Ambassador Bullitt is reported to have spent $100,000 a year in Paris.

[2] For an account of his experiences, see *Ambassador Dodd's Diary, 1933–1938*, edited by William E. Dodd, Jr., and Martha Dodd (New York: Harcourt, 1941).

in commercial statistics, tariff calculations, exchange, and simple accounting; and modern languages—French, German, or Spanish.[1] Candidates have also been rated in English, composition, grammar, spelling, and penmanship as shown in their examination.

Candidates obtaining a grade of seventy in the written examination then take an oral one sometime later. This has always been given in Washington by a board of examiners. Those making a combined grade of eighty must also pass a rigid physical examination, after which they are placed on a register from which they are chosen when needed. Those whose names ultimately reach the register may or may not receive offers of appointment, depending upon personnel needs and appropriations.[2]

Appointment and Training.—Upon appointment, the Foreign Service officer is first sent to some near-by American consulate for an internship lasting about a year. He is then brought back and enrolled in the Foreign Service Institute[3] where he combines studies with tours of various governmental agencies and services in several offices of the Department of State. After several months of this he is ready to be assigned for duty in some consular office with the rank of vice-consul or to an embassy or legation as third secretary. During his early years a Foreign Service officer may expect to be shifted from post to post about every 3 years, serving in either diplomatic or consular establishments or both. After 30 years of service, or upon attaining the age of sixty (or sixty-five if a career minister), he may retire and enjoy the benefits of a retirement fund to which both he and the government have contributed over the years.

Foreign Service Reserve.—The increase in business occasioned by the recent war led to establishment, in 1941, of an Auxiliary Foreign Service. This included presidential appointees to serve during the emergency only. Recognition of their value led to inclusion of provisions in the act of 1946 establishing the Foreign Service Reserve. This is made up of six classes corresponding to those for regular Foreign Service officers. Only citizens of 5 years' standing are eligible for appointment. The Secretary of State makes appointments on behalf of the President. Reserve officers may come from other governmental agencies, with the approval of the department head concerned, or from those not employed by the Federal govern-

[1] Knowledge of only one language has been required, although a candidate has been permitted to offer, in the oral test, any additional languages with which he was familiar.

[2] Normally, about one-third of the candidates pass the examination. See United States House of Representatives Committee on Appropriations, *Hearings . . . on the Department of State Appropriations Bill of 1943* (Washington: Government Printing Office, 1943), p. 420. Those interested in obtaining further information may write to the Department of State for its free bulletin entitled *The American Foreign Service* (Washington: Government Printing Office, rev. ed., 1942). This also includes sample written examinations.

[3] Prior to 1946, the Foreign Service Officers' Training School.

ment. Appointments may be made for as long as 4 consecutive years, but when their term has expired they cannot be reappointed until expiration of a period of time equal to the preceding tour of duty. The class to which a reserve officer is appointed depends upon his age, qualification, and experience. While on active duty he is entitled to the same salary and allowances as Foreign Service officers of like class and grade. Creation of this reserve makes possible the employment of qualified specialists for temporary periods without disturbing the independence and integrity of the Foreign Service officers' corps itself.

Foreign Service Staff Officers and Employees.—It takes a large number of staff officers, technicians, clerks, and office personnel in addition to the chief of missions and Foreign Service officers to handle foreign affairs. Their recruitment, classification, salary, promotion, removal, and retirement are, therefore, matters of great importance. The act of 1946 attempts to systematize and improve all such matters pertaining to this group. Selection is on the basis of merit. Personnel is divided into twenty-one classes with graduated salaries.

The Foreign Service Institute.—Mention has already been made of the Foreign Service Institute authorized by the act of 1946. This took over the functions of the old Officers' Training School, created by the Rogers Act, but its broadened authority is worthy of note. The Institute is headed by a director, appointed by the Secretary of State, who is a scholar and educator. The Institute has its own quarters and full or part-time staff composed either of those already employed by the government or of private scholars and specialists. The Institute is not, however, another university or college to which any qualified student might go. Rather, it is limited to government employees concerned with foreign affairs. In addition to operations in Washington, the Secretary of State may make grants of money or other gratuitous assistance to nonprofit institutions cooperating with any of the programs conducted by the Institute. The Institute may also pay the tuition and expenses of enrolled officers and employees whom it assigns to take special training and instruction at or with public or private nonprofit institutions, trade, labor, agricultural, or scientific associations or commercial firms. The Institute is trying to do for the benefit of the Foreign Service what the Army and Navy have long been permitted to do for the training of officers.

Hoover Commission Criticism.—The creation of a distinct corps of Foreign Service officers was criticized by the Hoover Commission as "a source of serious friction and increasing inefficiency."[1] One of the most serious faults is that jealousy develops between members of the elite corps and civil servants who are attached to the same department and with whom they must work. This is particularly true when civil servants do similar

[1] *Foreign Affairs* (Washington: Government Printing Office, 1949), p. 162.

work but receive smaller emoluments. It also pointed out that "such division of personnel in foreign affairs has been abandoned in all but a handful of countries. Among those in which it still exists, the United States is the only great power." The commission further observed that "the present conditions also lead to the existence of two administrative offices, one for each body of public servants, but both in the same household and dealing frequently with the same personnel questions." To cure the problem the commission recommended a consolidated Foreign Affairs Service, separate from the general Civil Service but nevertheless based upon merit. All members of the new service of the same grade would have equal status, and all would be pledged to serve at home or abroad.

SELECTED FUNCTIONS OF THE DEPARTMENT OF STATE AND FOREIGN SERVICE

The primary function of the Department of State is one of providing the President with the facts and advice necessary for determining foreign policy. Next in importance is the department's duty of executing foreign policy, of administering far-flung offices and personnel, and of enforcing laws of the United States relating to external affairs. Basic foreign policies are discussed in the next chapter; here will be mentioned only a few routine functions in order to illustrate the work done by the department and Foreign Service.

Conducting Communications.—The work of the Department of State requires endless communication not only with people in the United States, but with Americans and foreigners scattered in all parts of the globe. All mail, written, telegraphic, and even telephonic reaching or leaving the department is channeled through the Division of Communications and Records. All communications must be routed to the proper persons and filed for quick reference.

Of primary importance are communications with American diplomats and consuls in the field and representatives of foreign governments stationed in Washington. Letters to American representatives usually take the form of "instructions" while letters from the field are called "despatches." These are ordinarily forwarded in diplomatic pouches which enjoy special immunities. There is much communication by cable, and in the last few years by air-grams (brief messages dispatched by air mail and specially delivered upon arrival), and in emergencies by direct telephonic conversations. Telegrams are nearly always sent in code which must be deciphered by groups of experts in the department.[1] In addition, the department

[1] For an intriguing description of the decoding work done during and immediately following the First World War, see Herbert O. Yardley, *The American Black Chamber* (Indianapolis: Bobbs-Merrill, 1931). Though this particular institution was discontinued by Secretary Kellogg, similar work has since been done on an even larger scale.

broadcasts news reports weekly to officers in the field and keeps them up to date on international events by sending them a monthly political digest containing materials gleaned from political reports reaching the department from all parts of the world. Communications to and from the department and foreign representatives in this country usually take the form of "notes." The originals of all communications dating back to the days of the Committee of Secret Correspondence have been preserved in the department's archives. These constitute an invaluable storehouse of knowledge and one of the priceless assets of the nation. All except those of recent years may be consulted for research purposes by qualified scholars.[1]

Making Treaties.[2]—The President "makes" treaties by and with the advice and consent of two-thirds of the Senate. During the century and a half ending Apr. 30, 1939, about 800 treaties had been put into effect.[3] Some of these were bilateral, that is, between the United States and one other country; while others were multilateral, that is, between the United States and more than one other government.

Negotiation.—Usually one government or another indicates through its ambassador or minister a desire to negotiate a treaty covering certain matters. When this is done, it is customary for the government proposing the agreement to submit to the other a complete draft of its proposal. Thereafter discussions may take place in either the capital city of one of the interested nations or in any other convenient place. Those conducted in this country usually take place within the Department of State. Throughout the negotiations, representatives keep in touch with their governments and proceed according to instructions. The negotiations may be concluded within a short time or extended over months or even years, depending upon how complex, urgent, or controversial the subject matter is.

Signing the Treaty.—When the text finally suits the chief executives of both countries, a time and place are fixed for the signing of the treaty. Meanwhile, the duplicate originals of the treaty will have been prepared in what is referred to as the *alternat*—that is, with parallel columns containing the two languages side by side, the language of one of the countries being in the left-hand column of the original it is to keep but in the right-hand column of the original to be kept by the foreign government. At the appointed hour, the duly authorized plenipotentiaries appear, sign, and place their seal upon the document.

[1] A large part of this diplomatic correspondence is being published in documents known as *Papers Relating to the Foreign Relations of the United States* (Washington: Government Printing Office).

[2] For a discussion of the treaty power, see pp. 396–399.

[3] Wallace McClure, *International Executive Agreements* (New York: Columbia University Press, 1941), p. 8. In addition to the 800, 200 more intended treaties were approved by the Senate but for various reasons were never put into operation.

Obtaining Senatorial Approval.—The original kept by the American government is usually next sent to the Senate where it is given a first reading and sent to the Committee on Foreign Relations. The Senate committee considers the matter, sometimes after public or secret hearings, then reports to the Senate. After debate, the matter is put to a vote in the Senate. If two-thirds of those present (assuming the presence of a quorum) approve, the President may proceed; if not, and the signatories

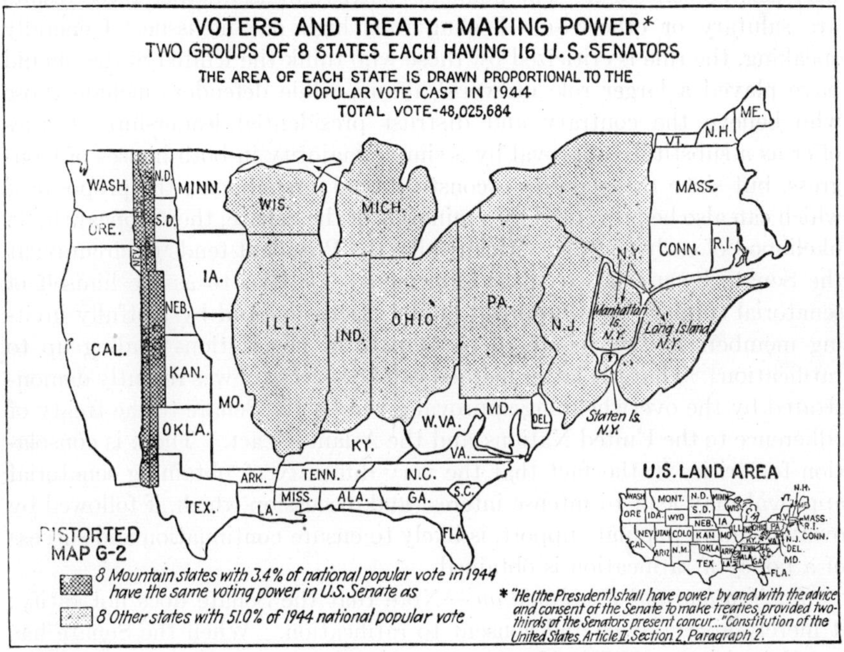

SOURCE: National Opinion Research Center.

still wish to see it adopted, it may be submitted to the Senate again when the President thinks its chances of obtaining approval are more favorable.

Much has been written and said for and against the requirement of senatorial approval.[1] The intention behind the provision was to provide the President with advice and counsel and to give the states an effective voice in the conclusion of treaties. The first intention has rarely been fulfilled, but the second has been frequently. Out of 1,000 or more treaties

[1] McClure, *ibid.*, p. 3; William S. Holt, *Treaties Defeated by the Senate* (Baltimore: The Johns Hopkins Press, 1933); George H. Haynes, *The Senate of the United States* (Boston: Houghton, 2 vols., 1938), vol. II, pp. 571–720; Royden J. Dangerfield, *In Defense of the Senate* (Norman: University of Oklahoma Press, 1933); Lindsay Rogers, *The American Senate* (New York: Knopf, 1926); Denna F. Flemming, *The Treaty Veto of the American Senate* (New York: Putnam, 1930); and Kenneth W. Colegrove, *The American Senate and World Peace* (New York: Vanguard, 1944).

submitted to the Senate more than 100 have either been rejected or were never acted upon at all.[1] While the proportion unfavorably acted upon is small, many of the treaties were of outstanding importance, as, for example, the one defeated in 1920 which would have enrolled the United States as a member of the League of Nations.

That the rule permits minority control is admitted and well illustrated on the map on page 537. That the provision also restrains the President may also be conceded. The point in controversy is whether these results are salutary or otherwise. Feeling runs high on the issue. Generally speaking, the rule is criticized by those who think the United States should have played a larger role in world affairs, while defenders include those who believe the contrary and distrust presidential leadership. Critics offer as a substitute approval by a simple majority in both houses of Congress, but since this requires a constitutional amendment, the proposal of which can also be prevented by a minority of the Senate, there appears little likelihood of early success. Meanwhile, the President tends to circumvent the Senate by use of executive agreements,[2] or tries to assure himself of senatorial support by widespread public discussion and by tactfully inviting members of the Senate to participate in negotiations leading up to ratification. That the latter method can be successful was recently demonstrated by the overwhelming approval given by the Senate to the treaty of adherence to the United Nations and the Atlantic Pact. There is consolation for critics in the fact that the very difficulty of obtaining senatorial approval may lead to intense interest and discussion which, if followed by overwhelming popular support, is likely to ensure continuation and success of a policy if ratification is obtained.

Ratification and Proclamation.—Note that the Senate does not ratify; it merely gives advice and consent to ratification. When the Senate has been heard from, the President notifies the other party, whereupon ratifications are exchanged by plenipotentiaries meeting at an appointed time and place. The treaty is then published and proclaimed, at which time it becomes legally enforceable.[3] The original is kept in the Archives of the Department of State. After proclamation, the Treaty Division must study and report on its operation and answer thousands of inquiries from people in all walks of life concerning its application.

[1] McClure, *op. cit.*

[2] See p. 400.

[3] Treaties are published in pamphlet form at the time of their proclamation in Department of State, *Treaty Series* (Washington: Government Printing Office). Those concluded prior to 1937 have been compiled and edited by William M. Malloy (ed.), *Treaties, Conventions, International Acts, Protocols and Agreements between the United States of America and Other Powers, 1776–1909* (Washington: Government Printing Office, 1910–1939). Another edition is now in preparation. See Hunter Miller, *Treaties and Other International Acts of the United States* (Washington: Government Printing Office, 1931–).

Issuing Passports.—Another important function of the State Department is that of issuing passports. The work of issuing them is headed by the Passport Division in Washington. Passports should be distinguished from visas. The former are permits granted by the American government to its citizens to *leave* the country or another country, while visas are permits to *enter* another country and must be obtained from officials of the country one is about to enter. Except in time of war, the United States does not compel its citizens to obtain passports before departing; but citizens are forced to do so by the fact that almost every country in which they wish to travel requires the showing of a passport as a condition for entry. In other words, one can get *out* of the United States in normal times without a passport, but not *into* most foreign countries.

The American government will issue passports only to those who owe it allegiance—never to aliens. Within the forty-eight states passports are issued only by the Passport Division itself; within most of the territories they are issued by the chief executives; abroad they are granted by the higher ranking consuls and in a few instances by officers attached to diplomatic posts.

Those in the United States wishing to obtain passports must make application either at the Passport Division itself, or at passport agencies located at a few principal cities, or before the clerk of any Federal or state court having authority to naturalize aliens.[1] If outside the forty-eight states but in one of the territories, application is made to the chief executives. If abroad, application is made to American consuls.

The applicant must appear in person, accompanied by a creditable witness. Members of a family may be included in one passport. The application must be supported by proof of citizenship, descriptive information, photographs of those who intend traveling on the document, and a fee of $9. An additional fee of $1 must be paid to the person who executes the application. After careful scrutiny, the passport is sent to the applicant by registered mail and is good for 2 years. It may be amended from time to time and renewed for an additional period of 2 years.

Issuing Visas.—Most aliens wishing to enter the United States must obtain visas, which are usually nothing more than the word "visa" ensconced in seal and signature on one of the blank pages of the passport. Applications must be made before American consuls. Before the entrance of the United States into the Second World War, consuls were almost the sole judges of whether the visa should be granted or refused. During the war, regulations required that applications for nearly all persons[2] be

[1] See p. 344. Of the state courts, this includes nearly all having original jurisdiction but would not, of course, include summary courts like those of justices of peace.

[2] There were many exceptions, chief of which were natives born in the Western Hemisphere and England, members of British military and naval forces who were recom-

forwarded to the Visa Division of the Department of State for an advisory opinion, which was forthcoming only after careful investigation and review by a committee comprised of representatives of the Army, Navy, Federal Bureau of Investigation, Immigration Service, and Department of State. Although this resulted in a tremendous increase of work for the Visa Division, it proved to be an almost certain method of ensuring that only eligible and desirable persons entered the country. Since the war, consular discretion has been enlarged, but provision for reviewing consuls' decisions remains in cases where applicants are suspected of being dangerous to security and welfare. Entrance visas when issued are good for 6 months and are ordinarily renewable for a second period of similar length.

Promotion of Cultural Relations.—Although the United States has long engaged in activities looking toward the interchange of culture with foreign nations, it was not until recently that it deliberately embarked upon a large-scale program. The program has been directed largely toward Latin America, partially because of a growing realization that friendliness not only is the policy consistent with religious principles and ethics but also is a better method of promoting trade than lordly, blustering methods reminiscent of the "big stick" days of Theodore Roosevelt. After 1935 the program was accelerated by a general realization of the commercial and strategic importance of Latin America in the event of a war in which the United States might become involved.

The focal points of the program are the Office of International Information and the Office of Educational Exchange in the Department of State. In addition to superior officers of the department and other offices, these offices operate under the guidance of a number of advisory committees composed of persons representing governmental and private bodies in the United States interested in education, art, research, and music.

Exchange Program.—One of the most interesting projects of the office is that of helping to effect an exchange of personnel between the United States and other countries. The exchange of persons covers three main categories: trainees in government, visiting professors and leaders, and graduate students.

Trainees are usually employees of government who come to the United States to study and observe how things are done. Some come to study agricultural economics, soil conservation, rural electrification, and related subjects under the Department of Agriculture. Others study public administration under the Bureau of the Budget. Others study civil aviation under the Civil Aeronautics Administration, and so on. In turn, American

---

mended by their superior officers, and those wishing merely to cross the Mexican and Canadian borders for brief periods. For the rules and regulations, see United States Department of State, *Laws and Regulations Affecting the Control of Persons Entering and Leaving the United States* (Washington: Government Printing Office, 1942).

trainees may be sent abroad for similar study. This program is financed by a three-way participation of the Federal government, the foreign government concerned, and the trainee.

In the case of professors and distinguished visitors, each government usually pays whatever expense is necessary. The visitors include educators (other than professors), newspapermen, doctors, scientists, directors of radio stations, officials of publishing houses, and persons who have a wide popular influence such as leaders of farm and labor groups. These people usually stay only for short periods of time.

Students (postgraduate only) desiring to participate in the program submit applications to the Institute of International Education, where a selection committee makes choices without regard to financial standing but on the basis of ability. Cooperating governments help finance travel and maintenance while various universities, both in the United States and abroad, provide scholarships.

Interpretation and Propaganda.—Interpreting American institutions and policies has become another important task of the Department of State. American diplomats and consuls have always attempted to create a favorable impression of their country, but in the modern world of conflicting ideologies this has become of paramount importance. Shortly before and during the recent war the department became the vehicle for disseminating propaganda by all types of media. Though slackened, the process continues. "The Voice of America" epitomizes the effort. This is a series of daily broadcasts, mostly over commercial stations, presented in many languages and intended to reach the radio public in foreign nations. Its programs consist of entertainment, newscasts, and interpretations intended to inform listeners and enlist their sympathy for American institutions and aims. Keeping such a program fair to all parties and interests in the United States is extremely difficult and has led to widespread criticism. Abroad the program is either welcomed or tolerated by countries whose relations with the United States are cordial but behind "iron curtains" the reception is hostile.

Not all propaganda is directed toward foreign shores. The department interprets foreign policy constantly to the American public. This is done by press conferences, press releases, publications (which are sometimes disseminated wholesale), speeches by department spokesmen, liaison officers with Congress, other government agencies, and other means. This zealousness and the expenditures it requires are often the subject of hostile comment. The department feels justified not only by the imperative importance of foreign affairs but also by the fact that it does not have an organized constituency to support its interests as the Department of Defense has in veterans' groups, the Department of Labor in unions, and the Department of Agriculture in farm groups scattered over the nation.

Domestic Functions.—Ever since its name was changed to Department of State, the department has performed a number of "home" functions in addition to those pertaining to foreign affairs. It is the custodian of the great seal, the design of which may be seen on paper currency. The seal is used only upon warrants issued by the President. The department is the agency through which official communications are exchanged with the forty-eight state governments and territories. This explains why proposed constitutional amendments are sent to the states by the department and why the Secretary of State always figures in the proclamation of amendments when notice of ratification has been received from the required number of states. This also explains why the electoral college of each state sends its report to the Secretary of State. The department is also the custodian of official acts of Congress and the President and for this reason publishes and proclaims the acts and resolutions of Congress, treaties, and executive proclamations. Formerly the department was charged with many other duties of a similar nature, but happily it is now able to devote most of its attention to foreign affairs.

REFERENCES

AMERICAN FOREIGN SERVICE ASSOCIATION: *The American Foreign Service Journal* (Washington: The Association, monthly).

BAILEY, THOMAS A.: *A Diplomatic History of the American People* (New York: Appleton-Century-Crofts, 2d ed., 1942).

BARTLETT, RUHL JACOB (ed.): *The Record of American Diplomacy, Documents and Readings. . . .* (New York: Knopf, 1947).

BEARD, CHARLES A.: *American Foreign Policy in the Making, 1932–1940; a Study in Responsibilities* (New Haven: Yale University Press, 1946).

——— *President Roosevelt and the Coming of the War, 1941; a Study in Appearances and Realities* (New Haven: Yale University Press, 1948).

BEMIS, SAMUEL F. (ed.): *American Secretaries of State and Their Diplomacy* (New York: Knopf, 10 vols., 1927–1929).

——— *A Diplomatic History of the United States* (New York: Holt, rev. ed., 1942).

——— *The Latin American Policy of the United States* (New York: Harcourt Brace, 1943).

BENDINER, ROBERT: *The Riddle of the State Department* (New York: Rinehart, 1942).

CHILDS, JAMES R.: *American Foreign Service* (New York: Holt, 1948).

COLEGROVE, KENNETH W.: *The American Senate and World Peace* (New York: Vanguard, 1944).

DENNISON, ELINORE E.: *Senate Foreign Relations Committee* (Stanford, Calif.: Stanford University Press, 1942).

FERGUSON, JOHN H.: *American Diplomacy and the Boer War* (Philadelphia: University of Pennsylvania Press, 1939).

GRAHAM, MALBONE W.: *American Diplomacy in the International Community* (Baltimore: Johns Hopkins Press, 1948).

HACKWORTH, GREEN H.: *Digest of International Law* (Washington: Government Printing Office, 8 vols., 1940–1944).

HAYNES, GEORGE H.: *The Senate of the United States, Its History and Practice* (Boston: Houghton Mifflin 2 vols., 1938).

HERSHEY, AMOS S.: *Diplomatic Agents and Immunities* (Washington: Government Printing Office, 1919).

HOLT, WILLIAM S.: *Treaties Defeated by the Senate* (Baltimore: Johns Hopkins Press, 1933).

HULEN, BERTRAND D.: *Inside the Department of State* (New York: Whittlesey, 1939).

HULL, CORDELL: *The Memoirs of Cordell Hull* (New York: Macmillan, 2 vols., 1948).

LAY, TRACY H.: *The Foreign Service of the United States* (New York: Prentice-Hall, 1925).

McCLURE, WALLACE: *International Executive Agreements* (New York: Columbia University Press, 1941).

MARKEL, LESTER, and OTHERS: *Public Opinion and Foreign Policy* (New York: Harper, 1949).

MATHEWS, JOHN M.: *American Foreign Relations, Conduct and Policies* (New York: Appleton-Century-Crofts, rev. and enl. ed., 1938).

MOWRER, EDGAR A.: *The Nightmare of American Foreign Policy* (New York: Knopf, 1948).

SCHUMAN, FREDERICK L.: *International Politics, the Destiny of the Western State System* (New York: McGraw-Hill, 4th ed., 1948).

STUART, GRAHAM H.: *American Diplomatic and Consular Practice* (New York: Macmillan, 2d ed., 1949).

THOMSON, CHARLES A. H.: *Overseas Information Service of the United States Government* (Washington: Brookings, 1949).

UNITED STATES DEPARTMENT OF STATE: *The American Foreign Service* (Washington: Government Printing Office, rev. ed., 1939).

——— *Bulletin of the Department of State* (Washington: Government Printing Office, weekly).

——— (prepared by William Gerber): *The Department of State of the United States* (Washington: Government Printing Office, rev. ed., 1942).

——— *Foreign Service List* (Washington: Government Printing Office, quarterly).

——— *Papers Relating to the Foreign Relations of the United States* (Washington: Government Printing Office, 1861–).

UNITED STATES HOUSE OF REPRESENTATIVES COMMITTEE ON APPROPRIATIONS: *Hearings . . . on the Department of State Appropriations Bill of 1950*, 81st Cong., 1st Sess. (Washington: Government Printing Office, 1949). Also hearings for other years.

WESTPHAL, ALBERT C. F.: *The House Committee on Foreign Affairs* (New York: Columbia University Press, 1942).

WHITTINGTON, WILLIAM V.: *The Making of Treaties and International Agreements and the Work of the Treaty Division of the Department of State* (Washington: Government Printing Office, 1938).

YARDLEY, HERBERT O.: *The American Black Chamber* (Indianapolis: Bobbs-Merrill, 1931).

TEXT-FILM

The following McGraw-Hill 35mm silent filmstrip is recommended for use with Chaps. 19, 24, and 25 of this text.

Foreign Relations. Principles and practices involved in foreign relations under the federal system. Department of State and Foreign Service. Traditional foreign policies and recent developments. The United States and the United Nations.

Chapter 25

FOREIGN POLICIES AND THE UNITED NATIONS

Today we are faced with the pre-eminent fact that, if civilization is to survive, we must cultivate the science of human relationships—the ability of all peoples, of all kinds, to live together and work together, in the same world, at peace. . . .

Franklin D. Roosevelt.[1]

Lake Success is, as you know, neither a lake nor, so far, a success. But we are working very hard.

Carlos P. Romulo, President of the United Nations General Assembly.[2]

No lesson has been taught more emphatically by two world wars than that of interdependence of peoples and nations. It has now become obvious to all that the political units and the people within their respective jurisdiction must learn to get along together. For years the American public has been sharply divided over the wisest course in the face of changed circumstances. To many the path of aloofness from Old World entanglements and neutrality appeared to offer the greatest hope of security and peace; but in consequence of the latest holocaust and the discovery of even more terrible weapons, most Americans have come to the conclusion that the new world interdependence demands collective action to maintain the peace.

TRADITIONAL FOREIGN POLICY

Isolation.—The American Revolution was won by the revolting colonies in alliance with France. Made in 1778, the alliance was soundly based on the self-interests of the two participants. The contracting parties agreed that they would fight until the independence of the United States was recognized. This alliance, the only formal one entered by the United States until the ratification of the North Atlantic Pact in 1949, was finally ended in 1800. From then until more than a century later the basic foreign policy of the United States was one of aloofness from involvement in the political affairs of Europe. Washington set the pace in his Farewell Address, delivered in 1796, when he said that the "detached and distant situation" of the United States made possible aloofness from Europe's controversies, and asked: "Why quit our own and stand on foreign ground?"[3]

[1] Undelivered Jefferson Day Address, April, 1945.

[2] Quoted in *The New York Times Magazine*, Dec. 18, 1949, p. 54.

[3] James D. Richardson (ed.), *Messages and Papers of the Presidents* (New York: Bureau of National Literature, 22 vols., 1897–1916), vol. 1, pp. 214–215.

As ties increased with the outside world there were few advocates of absolute isolation, but many of limited participation in world affairs. The contemporary "isolationist" would continue United States collaboration in international work along social, cultural, and technical lines, but opposes membership in a general security organization that may use American economic or military power to keep the peace.

Neutrality.—To political aloofness was coupled the belief that the best policy in time of war was to remain neutral. Indeed, during the nineteenth century the United States stood as the foremost apostle of neutrality and did much to establish and reinforce a body of rules for the protection of those who chose to remain at peace while others fought. By following the policy the United States remained free of military involvement in all wars between foreign states for a century and a quarter, except for the unfortunate conflict with Britain in 1812 which grew out of the Napoleonic Wars. More recently, the policy delayed American entrance into the First World War for 2½ years; and kept the United States out of the Sino-Japanese War, which began in 1931, for 10 years; out of the Ethiopian War altogether; and out of the recent war for more than 2 years.

Because to many this policy appeared to offer the best guarantee of noninvolvement in foreign wars, it has been stoutly defended. After 1920, studies of the factors that led the United States to become involved in the First World War, disillusionment with results of that war, and the frightful prospects of involvement in another conflict led to enactment of "neutrality" legislation in 1935 and 1937 designed to prevent a repetition of what happened between 1914 and 1917. Chief among the provisions were those authorizing the President to impose an embargo upon the sale of arms to warring powers, to restrict the travel of citizens and ships in war zones, and to require that purchasers pay cash for war materials and carry them in non-American vessels. Application of most of the provisions was not mandatory, with the result that the President applied them or not as he saw fit. In the end sentiment favoring intervention in the war against the Axis became so strong as to lead to their repeal.

The Monroe Doctrine.—An equally basic foreign policy has been the Monroe Doctrine enunciated in 1823 by President Monroe as a warning to European powers who, it was feared, were intent upon restoring Spain's authority over recently revolted Latin-American republics. The announcement first declared that, "In the wars of the European Powers in matters relating to themselves we have never taken any part, nor does it comport with our policy so to do." It then went on to say:

> We owe it, therefore, to candor and to the amicable relations existing between the United States and those powers to declare that we should consider any attempt on their part to extend their system to any portion of this hemisphere as dangerous to our peace and safety. With the existing colonies and dependencies of any

European power we have not interfered and shall not interfere. But with the Governments who have declared their independence and maintained it, and whose independence we have, on great consideration and on just principles, acknowledged, we could not view any interposition for the purpose of oppressing them, or controlling in any other manner their destiny, by any European power in any other light than as the manifestation of an unfriendly disposition toward the United States.[1]

The audacity of this statement is emphasized when it is recalled that the population of the United States had just reached 10 million. That it was possible to proclaim and enforce it was due in large measure to British assistance given because it was also to her interest to ban further European colonization in this hemisphere.

The "America for the Americans" policy of the United States has remained as it began, a proclamation of policy by the Chief Executive. It has no standing in law, yet it has been supported by Congresses and Presidents for a century and a quarter. One should note that as originally pronounced it said nothing about interrelationships between American states. As one authority put it, "The Doctrine states a case of United States *vs.* Europe, not United States *vs.* Latin America."[2]

Nevertheless, in times past, especially during the administration of Theodore Roosevelt, the doctrine served to justify a paternalistic "big stick" policy on the part of the United States. Said President Theodore Roosevelt:

If a nation shows that it knows how to act with reasonable efficiency and decency in social and political matters; if it keeps order and pays its obligations, it need fear no interference from the United States. [But] chronic wrongdoing, or an impotence which results in a general loosening of the ties of civilized society . . . may force the United States, however reluctantly, in flagrant cases of such wrongdoing or impotence, to the exercise of an international police power.[3]

Acting under assumptions such as these, the United States intervened with force on numerous occasions, to the violent displeasure of most American republics. Happily, forcible intervention has not occurred since the withdrawal of troops from Nicaragua in 1933. Meanwhile, the "good-neighbor" policy announced in 1933 has produced a friendlier relationship.

Expansion.—As noted elsewhere[4] American history is characterized by constant expansion—south to Panama, Puerto Rico, and the Virgin Islands, southwest to Mexico and later to Samoa, northwest to Alaska and the

[1] Richardson, *op. cit.*, vol. 2, p. 787.

[2] J. Reuben Clark, *Memorandum on the Monroe Doctrine* (Washington: Government Printing Office, 1930), p. 19.

[3] Message to Congress, December, 1904, *Foreign Relations of the United States*, 1904 (Washington: Government Printing Office, 1905), p. 41.

[4] Chap. 26.

western tip of the Aleutians, west to the Pacific, then to Hawaii, Guam, and the Philippines. Expansion led to friction with Britain over the Canadian boundary and rival claims in the Caribbean, with Mexico over Texas and the Southwest, with Spain over Florida, the Southeast, Cuba, and South America, with China and Japan in the Far East, and with Latin-American republics. Taking a broad view, American diplomacy has eliminated all potentially hostile competitors in the Western Hemisphere, secured title to a vast domain, and established defense bastions in the Atlantic, the Caribbean, and the Pacific. Americans prefer to call it expansion in accordance with "manifest destiny"; others call it imperialism. Be that as it may, the expansionist urge has been a constant stimulus as well as the occasion for many difficulties and considerable suspicion and ill will. From the viewpoint of the American nationalist, however, the achievement is by no means a small one.

Foreign Investments and Trade.—Before the recent war, American citizens had more than 13 billion dollars invested in foreign countries. These funds were invested in enterprises of various sorts: railroads; mines; government securities; ocean shipping; oil lands, wells, and refineries; rubber, sugar, coffee, and banana plantations; churches and mission schools, etc. Needless to say, what happens in countries where citizens' investments are large becomes of immediate concern to the investors themselves and also to their government to which they turn for protection.

Closely related to investments is foreign trade, which normally accounts for between 7 and 10 per cent of all commerce. While this appears small in proportion to the fuss that is made over it, the volume is significant, particularly for certain industries like manufacturers of textiles, processed food products, rubber and silk products, and machinery. Whether justified or not, a tremendous amount of treasure and effort has been poured into opening foreign markets and expanding foreign trade.[1]

While foreign investors and traders are normally expected to look after themselves, to abide by the laws of the countries in which they are doing business, and to obtain protection by recourse to local authorities, the American government is constantly alert to promote their interests and to protest against what it considers unfair and unjust treatment. This has frequently turned into "dollar diplomacy," a term used to refer to the use of governmental power and influence with a view to obtaining special privileges for its citizens, coupled perhaps with important economic, political, and strategic advantages for the nation itself.

Protection and promotion are usually provided through diplomats and consuls, but unfortunately many occasions have arisen when the American government has intervened with force, either alone or in concert with other nations. Illustrations from the past readily come to mind: During the

[1] Cf. p. 637.

VALUE OF AMERICAN-OWNED PROPERTY
IN FOREIGN COUNTRIES, MAY 31, 1943

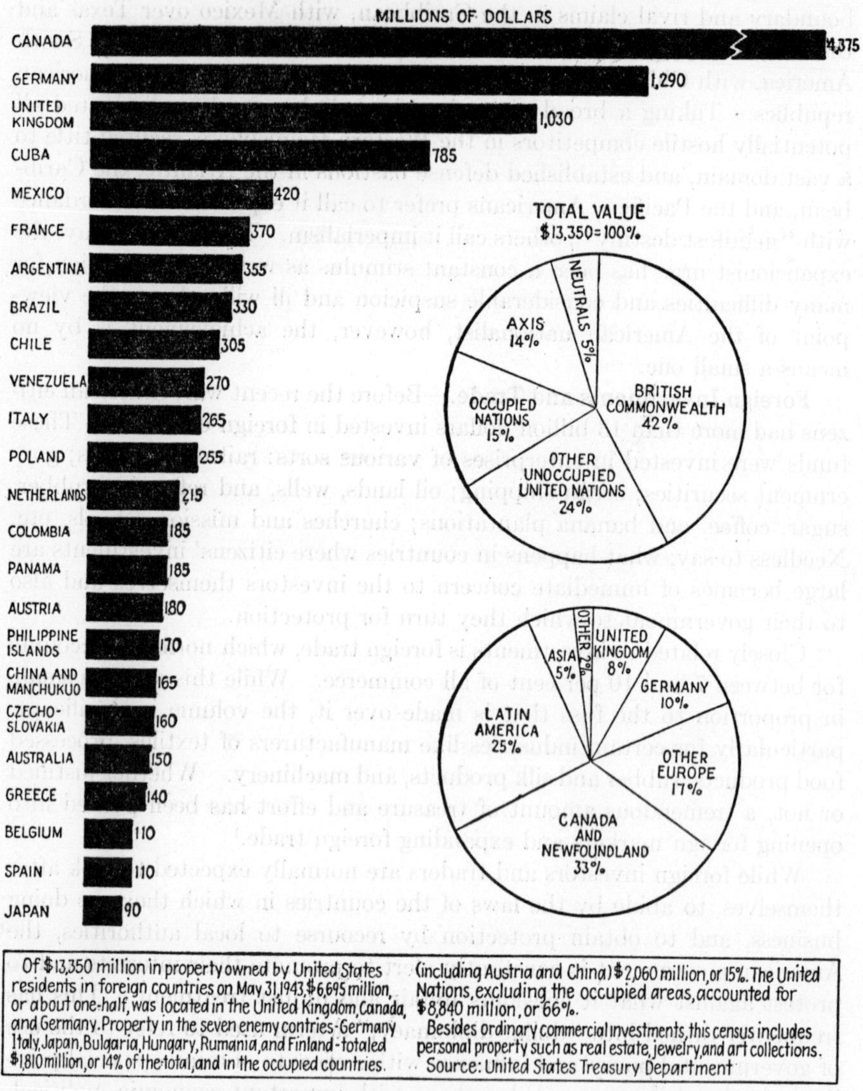

Of $13,350 million in property owned by United States residents in foreign countries on May 31, 1943, $6,695 million, or about one-half, was located in the United Kingdom, Canada, and Germany. Property in the seven enemy contries-Germany Italy, Japan, Bulgaria, Hungary, Rumania, and Finland-totaled $1,810 million, or 14% of the total, and in the occupied countries (including Austria and China) $2,060 million, or 15%. The United Nations, excluding the occupied areas, accounted for $8,840 million, or 66%.
Besides ordinary commercial investments, this census includes personal property such as real estate, jewelry, and art collections.
Source: United States Treasury Department

Source: National Industrial Conference Board, Inc., *Road Maps of Industry*, no. 436, May 5, 1944.

Boxer Rebellion in 1900 the United States, in cooperation with European powers and Japan, sent troops to China to protect lives and property; American intervention in Latin America between 1898 and 1934 occurred a number of times for the same reason. War with the Barbary States grew out of the fact that tribute had been levied on American commerce entering the Mediterranean; the war with England in 1812 arose over impressment of seamen and other interferences with commerce; in 1853 Commodore Perry threatened to bombard Japanese ports unless they were promptly opened to American commerce; after much difficulty with both the allied and central powers during the early part of the First World War the United States finally entered the war against Germany because of Germany's policy of sinking American ships; and, finally, involvement in the Second World War arose partially from attacks upon American ships.

The Open Door.—The idea of the open door is that Americans must have equal access to the markets of backward areas, especially of the Orient. It was first expressed in the middle of the last century, when China and Japan were opened to trade with the outside world. In its early twentieth century form, the open-door policy was designed to assure Americans and Britishers commercial privileges in a China that was being partitioned by foreign powers. During the First World War Japan forced China to yield many valuable concessions on the continent. Despite great power agreements reached at the Washington Conference of 1921–1922 assuring the political independence and territorial integrity of China, Japan began in 1931 a series of violations of her pledges that ended only in her defeat in the Second World War.

Enforcement of the traditional open-door doctrine, which concentrated on equality of opportunity to trade, has been difficult both for the United States and Great Britain. Until recently Asia has seemed very distant and the volume of trade with the Far East has been very small. When Japan undertook her aggressive steps in China, the American people were unprepared to run the risks involved in requiring the Japanese to respect treaties and promises. So long as Japan remained the only great power in east Asia equipped with a powerful navy and a large army, it proved impossible to curb her designs to control the greater part of the Orient both politically and economically. In the new situation brought about by the defeat of Japan and the emergence of China and Russia as strong Asiatic land powers and of the United States as the greatest sea power, the open-door policy will probably pass finally into obsolescence. The question of security has emerged so important that a purely commercial doctrine will unquestionably be subordinated.

NEW AMERICAN POLICY

Collective Security.—Having been drawn into two world wars in spite of a high resolve to remain neutral, the traditional American policy of isolation has been abandoned. It is now assumed that this ought to be one world; that no nation is likely long to enjoy peace and prosperity while others are afflicted by war and want; that in a day of atomic bombs, rockets, and long-range planes, neutrality by a major nation while others are locked in conflict is virtually impossible.

Replacing the isolationism of the past, the United States has adopted a new policy of collective security. The idea is not entirely new to Americans, for they have long recognized the validity in domestic affairs that "in unity there is strength." Having won the war through a coalition of many nations fighting the common enemy, it was logical to ask, why not peacetime unity to keep the peace? In the midst of the Second World War, the foreign ministers of the major allied powers agreed at Moscow that a general international organization would be launched at the earliest practicable time. A proposed charter was drafted at Dumbarton Oaks in the fall of 1944 by representatives of United States, Great Britain, Soviet Union, and China. The Charter of the United Nations was the product of the San Francisco Conference of April–June, 1945. Ratification of that charter by the United States Senate in August of the same year completed and formalized the abandonment of isolation and the adoption of collective security.

As provided for in the United Nations organization (UN), collective security means that the member nations stand together in opposition to aggression or threats of aggression. Primary responsibility for enforcing peace is placed on the Security Council,[1] which is given authority to settle disputes by various means, including the use of economic and armed force. A warlike or threatening act in any part of the world may receive the attention of the Security Council, which then can take appropriate action. In joining the UN, member nations pledged in advance detachments of their armed forces for use by the United Nations in carrying out its obligations, but no such forces have yet been activated.

Regional Security.—Not long after the Second World War, the victorious Allies were divided into two blocs that waged "cold war" against one another. On one side were the United States, Britain, France, and most of the countries of the Western world. On the other was the Soviet Union, her satellites of eastern Europe and the Balkans, and a China increasingly occupied by Communist forces. Although several new factors are present, this clearly represents the reemergence of the balance-of-power relationship which has been present in nearly every state system. From a Western point of view, Russia came out of the war with predominant military force on the European continent, quite capable of driving all the way to the Bay of Biscay. Moreover, the strange mixture of traditional Russian imperialism and Communist revolutionary method appeared to be a combination that would be difficult to stop.

[1] A description of the composition and functions of the UN agencies begins on p. 558.

The "Truman Doctrine," announced in March, 1947, upon the withdrawal of British forces from Greece, called for the "containment" of Communist influence. Congress responded by authorizing military, financial, and technical assistance to Greece and Turkey. Shortly thereafter, in June, 1947, the "Marshall Plan" was announced. As explained later in this chapter, it provides economic aid to countries willing to cooperate in rebuilding war-ruined economies.[1] Under Soviet pressure, eastern European nations declined to participate in the program. Both Truman Doctrine and Marshall Plan were announced and executed by the United States outside the United Nations.

The next step in redressing the balance of power was the North Atlantic Pact, which was ratified by the Senate in 1949. The decisions to negotiate and ratify this pact were among the most momentous in the history of American foreign affairs. For the first time in a century and a half the United States is bound by a peacetime alliance that will surely lead to war if one of the contracting parties is attacked. The pact is based upon the assumptions that our security is tied to that of western Europe and that our strategic frontier runs from Norwegian Lapland to the Adriatic Sea. The key provision of the pact is Article 5, which reads: "The parties agree that an armed attack against one or more of them in Europe or North America shall be considered an attack against them all. . . ." The nations that have joined are the United States, Britain, Canada, France, Belgium, Netherlands, Luxembourg, Norway, Denmark, Iceland, Portugal, and Italy. The constitutional question of congressional delegation of the power to declare war is avoided simply by not specifying what aid shall be furnished to a victim of attack.

Critics of the pact declare that, like alliances of old, this one will not prevent war but actually will encourage it, that the pact violates both the letter and spirit of the United Nations Charter, that the pact makes reconciliation more difficult between Russia and the West, that American aid must of necessity be "too little and too late" to allies that can easily be overrun by invading land forces, and that the rearmament of Europe will retard economic recovery.

Supporters of the pact claim that, since the UN security machinery has not been activated, member nations are justified under the Charter in invoking their right of individual and collective self-defense, that any intending aggressor will be deterred by the power of the combination, that economic recovery will be accelerated once security from invasion is assured, and that the chances for peace are greater if the United States declares clearly and in advance what it will do if aggression comes.

Later in 1949 Congress moved to provide arms to allies through a Military Assistance Program (MAP) involving over $1,300,000,000 outlay,

[1] The program is described on p. 553.

of which $1,000,000,000 was for pact countries and the remainder for Greece, Turkey, Iran, Korea, Philippines, and "the general area" of China.

Inter-American Unity.—Unilateral responsibility for the Monroe Doctrine accompanied by the "big stick," "manifest destiny," and "dollar diplomacy" have given way to "Pan-Americanism" and the "good-neighbor policy" in the Western Hemisphere.

United States participation in the Pan-American movement dates from 1889. Through numerous conferences held since that date, the American republics have been collaborating in technical, humanitarian, economic, and finally political and strategic matters. Once known as the International Bureau of American Republics, the common organization was named Pan-American Union in 1910. The governing board of the Union has long been composed of the ambassadors to Washington of the several Latin-American nations, with the United States Secretary of State serving as chairman. Until recently the United States has opposed Union consideration of political questions; on the other hand, the Latin Americans have been reluctant to vest much power in the Union because it was dominated by the United States.

A new spirit entered United States relations with Latin America in the late 1920's. Known during the Franklin D. Roosevelt administration (1933–1945) as the good-neighbor policy, the new plan involved a cooperative and friendly approach by the United States. Applying something like the golden rule to its relations with the other American republics, this country ceased military intervention, terminated dollar diplomacy, and ended many unequal treaties. By the time war broke out in Europe, inter-American solidarity had been proclaimed, and the nations were able to take a united stand on various issues of the crisis years. At the Mexico City Conference in 1945 a regional security arrangement was agreed upon, an economic charter adopted, and reform of the composition and powers of the Pan American Union proposed. Eventually every one of the American nations declared war on the Axis countries, and all (Argentina belatedly) took part in the San Francisco Conference and joined the United Nations organization.

At Bogotá, Colombia, in early 1948 the American republics agreed to the charter of a broader system known as "The Organization of the American States." The Pan American Union continues as the central organ and secretariat of OAS. The other organs are the Inter-American Conference, which meets each four years or so; meetings of consultation among the foreign ministers; and the Council, which is composed of one representative from each member republic with rank of ambassador. In addition there are specialized conferences and organizations, and various subsidiary councils.

The regional security arrangement outlined at Mexico City in 1945 was completed in Brazil during 1947. Known as the Treaty of Rio de Janeiro, it is a pact of mutual defense. In case of armed attack on any American state in the Western Hemisphere, all other signatories are bound to aid the victim. Nineteen nations signed the treaty and nearly all, including the United States, ratified during 1948.

Economic and Social Cooperation.—Hitherto the United States has been chiefly concerned with its own expansion, investments, commerce, and social and cultural welfare. This has resulted in high tariffs and other trade restrictions, rivalries for concessions and markets, monopolies and cartels, and other measures designed to create self-sufficiency, the cumulative effect of which has been lowered standards of living and war.

Since adoption of the reciprocal tariff program in 1934[1] the United States has been committed to a freer movement of trade between countries. More recently, at San Francisco and other wartime conferences the United Nations gave proper recognition to the long-run importance of economic and social matters in producing conditions conducive to lasting peace. One of the major agencies of the United Nations is the Economic and Social Council. Under its general direction are currency stabilization, international loan, relief and rehabilitation, food and agriculture, educational, and other functions.

While the spirit of dollar diplomacy dies hard and some foreign critics suspect ulterior motives in many aspects of American foreign aid, it is not too much to say that never before has a country helped others so much in the economic sphere. In the postwar period, beginning with the $3,750,000,000 loan to Britain in 1946, the United States has poured out vast sums in grants and loans to help revive the economies of a third of the countries of the world. Some of this foreign aid, it is true, might not have been provided had it not been for the threatening role of the Soviet Union in Europe and Asia.

The greatest foreign assistance program since the end of wartime Lend-Lease is the Economic Recovery Program (ERP), which Congress authorized in April, 1948. The 4-year program, 1948–1952, is likely to cost about 17 billion dollars; the initial appropriation was for 5.3 billion for the first 15 months. The sixteen nations of western Europe that joined the cooperative recovery effort and have received aid under it are Great Britain, France, Italy, Norway, Sweden, Belgium, Netherlands, Luxembourg, Portugal, Switzerland, Iceland, Greece, Turkey, Eire, Denmark, and Austria. Western Germany, China, and Korea have also received aid under the program. Participating nations set their own recovery goals. The program is administered by the Economic Cooperation Administrator, who is appointed by the President.

In his inaugural address of January, 1949, President Truman called for a "bold new program" to help raise the living standards of the peoples

[1] See p. 635.

(two-thirds of the world's population) who live in economically underdeveloped areas. Popularly known as the "Point Four" program, the plan proposed by the State Department called for technical assistance to other nations costing about 85 million dollars per year. Unlike the ERP,

POSTWAR FOREIGN ASSISTANCE
BY THE UNITED STATES GOVERNMENT
TOTAL, JULY 1, 1945 · JUNE 30, 1949
$26,350 MILLION = 100%

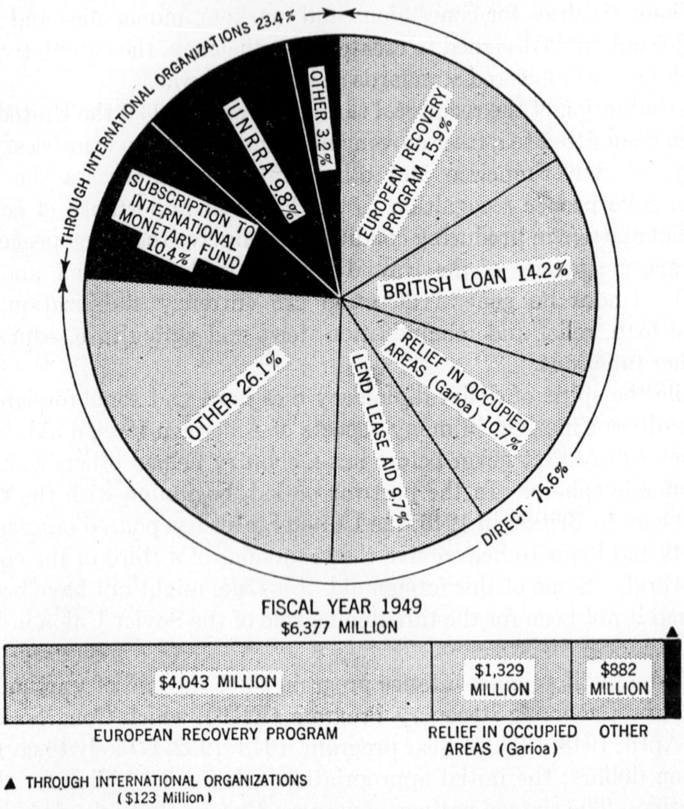

Total foreign aid includes funds going directly to countries as business loans or in other forms. Some direct aid not identified includes grants to Greece, Turkey and China, Export-Import Bank loans, property transfers through the Foreign Liquidation Commission. SOURCE: Bureau of the Budget.

the underdeveloped-areas assistance program would be operated in conjunction with the UN Economic and Social Council.

The United States is so powerful economically that its influence is exerted unconsciously in the domestic affairs of many other countries. This is a tremendous responsibility, and requires constant vigilance that economic policies adopted in this country do not spell disaster for fellow nations.

STEPS TOWARD WORLD ORGANIZATION

From Pearl Harbor to Moscow.—On Jan. 1, 1942, within a month of the Pearl Harbor disaster, the twenty-six nations at war with the Axis powers made the Declaration of the United Nations. These countries, later joined by twenty-one others, pledged their full resources in the war effort and promised not to make a separate peace with the enemy. Although this declaration did not mention world organization, it was the first general expression of unity among the allied nations, and it employed for the first time the name "United Nations."[1]

During 1942 and 1943 there was widespread discussion in the United States of the necessity for a world organization to keep the peace. In September of 1943 the Fulbright Resolution, a modest but very important expression of opinion, was adopted by the House of Representatives. This resolution declared for world machinery capable of maintaining a just and lasting peace, and favoring participation by the United States in such an organization.

On Nov. 1, 1943, at the close of the Moscow Conference of foreign ministers, the first international declaration regarding world organization was made. Representatives of United States, Soviet Union, Great Britain, and China agreed upon the "necessity of establishing at the earliest practicable date a general international organization . . . for the maintenance of international peace and security." A few days later these words were written into the Connally Resolution, which was adopted in the United States Senate. The Senate also emphasized that a treaty to join an international organization required a two-thirds vote in the Senate.

Dumbarton Oaks.—In August of 1944 the representatives of the Big Four gathered in Washington, D.C., at the historic Dumbarton Oaks estate in order to draft proposals for the general international organization mentioned in the Moscow Declaration. For 7 weeks the conference labored to produce a draft that would compromise the divergent views of the American, British, Russian, and Chinese delegates who took part. The proposals of the conference were presented to the public in the form of a draft charter on Oct. 7, 1944. One of the first reactions was that the new body would be the League of Nations under another name. In the months of discussion and debate that followed, the similarity of the proposed charter and the League was shown to be mainly superficial. The principal organs of the two were named alike, but their functions, jurisdictions, and powers were quite different. The League Assembly and Council had overlapping

[1] The documents described in this section may be found in a number of compilations including United States Department of State, *Toward the Peace Documents*, Publication 2298 (Washington: Government Printing Office, 1945), and *The United States and the Peace* (Washington: United States News, 1945), part I.

jurisdictions; the Dumbarton Oaks Assembly and Security Council had rather precisely defined functions, with the latter bearing responsibility for keeping the peace. The League had no military force with which to carry out its decisions; the United Nations was to have contingents of national land, sea, and air forces at its command.

The Dumbarton Oaks charter was incomplete. The great powers were unable to agree upon the crucial question of voting procedure in the Security Council, they had insufficient time to deal with colonial matters, and they chose to leave international judicial problems mainly for later consideration by jurists. The charter was also incomplete in that it did not contain the suggestions of the smaller nations, which had no representation at Dumbarton Oaks. As was demonstrated at San Francisco, the smaller nations had much to contribute; there they presented their views forcefully and were able to secure the adoption of many proposals.

The Big Three—Roosevelt, Churchill, and Stalin—meeting at Yalta in the Crimea in February, 1945, finally managed to reach a compromise on Security Council voting. In the Security Council, composed of eleven members, each nation should have one vote, and seven affirmative votes would be necessary to carry a proposition. In all except procedural matters, however, the affirmative votes must include those of all the permanent members of the Council—United States, Soviet Union, Great Britain, China, France. This gives the Big Five the much-controverted "veto power" over any use of economic or military force.[1] Although widely criticized by smaller nations, the Yalta voting formula was approved at San Francisco because it proved to be the only compromise all the great powers would accept. It was also at Yalta that the powers agreed to hold a conference on international organization at San Francisco beginning Apr. 25, 1945.

Public discussion of the Dumbarton Oaks proposals, already widespread, now took the form of a major educational campaign. The State Department alone distributed nearly 2 million copies of the draft charter, and many more were printed by private agencies. From public-opinion polls and other indexes, it was obvious that a very high level of public interest had been aroused.

San Francisco Conference.—Invitations to the San Francisco Conference were extended by the four sponsoring governments—United States, Soviet Union, Great Britain, and China—to forty-two other nations deemed to have participated in the war against the Axis powers. In the opening

[1] Because parties to a controversy cannot vote on questions of peaceful settlement, the direct veto is not likely to be employed at that stage. Instead the "hidden veto" may be used by a great power that is not a party to the controversy. For example, if the Security Council sought to refer a dispute between Soviet Union and Turkey to the International Court of Justice, France could veto the action.

days of the conference, the USSR won the separate admission of White Russia and the Ukraine. Argentina was admitted with United States support and over Soviet opposition. Denmark was brought in near the end of the conference. The charter was signed by representatives of fifty nations in the closing ceremonies.

Two events, the death of Franklin D. Roosevelt on Apr. 12 and the end of the war in Europe on May 8, gave occasion for the conference delegates to assess the cost of war and to rededicate themselves to the task of organizing the peace. The delegation of the United States was appointed by President Roosevelt and consisted of then Secretary of State Edward R. Stettinius, Jr., Senator Tom Connally, Senator Arthur H. Vandenberg, Representative Sol Bloom, Representative Charles A. Eaton, then Commander Harold E. Stassen, and Dean Virginia C. Gildersleeve. Three of the seven were Republicans; four were members of the Congress. The American delegation had the benefit of advice from the representatives of forty-two national organizations that were invited to send "consultants" to San Francisco[1] and many others who attended without invitations.

The early part of the conference featured plenary sessions and was highlighted by prime ministers and foreign secretaries. The inviting powers caucused repeatedly and managed to agree on most points of importance. After V–E Day the conference settled down to commission and committee study and action on the host of amendments proposed by the participating nations. The organization of the conference by commissions and committees was as follows:

Commissions	*Committees*
1. General Provisions	1. Preamble, Purposes, Principles
	2. Membership and General
2. General Assembly	1. Structure and Procedures
	2. Political and Security Functions
	3. Economic and Social Cooperation
	4. Trusteeship System
3. Security Council	1. Structure and Procedures
	2. Peaceful Settlement
	3. Enforcement Arrangements
	4. Regional Arrangements
4. Judicial Organization	1. International Court of Justice
	2. Legal Problems

[1] A list of organizations and consultants appointed by them is included in United States Department of State, *Charter of the United Nations Report to the President on the Results of the San Francisco Conference* . . . , Publication 2349 (Washington: Government Printing Office, 1945), pp. 262–266.

All amendments to the draft charter were required to be proposed by May 10, after which a catalogue of amendments was prepared.[1] Committee action was taken first, after which matters were reported to the appropriate commission for consideration.

The final phase of the conference was occupied with the reports of the commissions to the conference in plenary session, and with the signing and other closing ceremonies. The final plenary session was held on June 26, 1945, and the deliberations of the conference were closed with an address by President Truman.[2] The work of the conference ultimately will be judged by the success or failure of the permanent United Nations that it launched. By adjournment time it was obvious that the charter, while imperfect, could represent an important step toward a practical collective-security system. The participating nations had learned much about the give and take necessary in working together around the conference table. The wartime unity of the United Nations had been projected into the peacetime period. The peoples of the world had reason to hope for an eventual "more perfect union."

THE UNITED NATIONS

The Charter.—The Charter opens with an inspiring preamble which begins: "We, the peoples of the United Nations. . . ." Unique among treaties in emphasis on popular sovereignty, these words do not alter the fact that the preamble is a statement of aspirations and may not make enforceable guarantees. Advocates before the conference for a bill of human rights were appeased in part through inclusion in the preamble of a list of high purposes. The Dumbarton Oaks draft contained no preamble, but sentiment at San Francisco was strong for an idealistic declaration. As finally adopted, the preamble was largely the work of Prime Minister Jan C. Smuts of the Union of South Africa.

The body of the Charter opens with a statement of purposes. The United Nations is formed to maintain international peace and security, justice and cooperation. Among the principles enumerated are the equality of member nations, peaceful settlement of disputes, and support for United Nations actions. Membership includes the fifty nations represented at San Francisco, plus other "peace-loving" states admitted by the Assembly on recommendation of the Security Council. While there is no provision for withdrawal, the Assembly may suspend or expel if the Security Council recommends it.

[1] United Nations Conference on International Organization, *General Guide to Amendments, Comments and Proposals Concerning the Dumbarton Oaks Proposals for a General International Organization*, Doc. 288 (English), G/38 (May 14, 1945).

[2] The text of plenary proceedings is available in United States Department of State, *The United States and the Peace*, part II.

The Charter creates six "principal" organs of the United Nations—General Assembly, Security Council, Economic and Social Council, Trusteeship Council, International Court of Justice, and Secretariat. Each of the first five will be described in subsequent sections. The secretariat consists of the secretary general and staff. The secretary general, chief administrative officer of the United Nations, is selected by the General Assembly on recommendation of the Security Council. This high office was first filled in January, 1946, with the election of Trygve Lie of Norway.

Under the heading of "miscellaneous provisions" the Charter requires member nations to file all treaties into which they enter with the secretariat for publication by it. The Charter is made supreme over all other international obligation entered into by member nations. The UN and its officials and delegates are given the privileges and immunities in each member nation necessary to exercise their functions.

Provision for amendment and ratification is made in final chapters of the Charter. Amendments require a two-thirds vote in General Assembly and ratification by their own constitutional processes of two-thirds of the member nations including all of the Big Five. A conference to review the charter, similar to a constitutional convention, may be convened by a two-thirds vote of the Assembly and seven affirmative votes in the Security Council; ratification of any amendments proposed is accomplished through the same two-thirds vote of member nations but must include all of the Big Five.

The San Francisco Charter was to be put into effect, when ratified according to their own constitutional processes, by the United States, Soviet Union, Great Britain, France, and China, and a majority of the other signatory states. Ratifications were deposited with the United States. The United States ratified through Senate action in early August, 1945, by a vote of 89 to 2, and the American ratification was the first deposited. Other nations filed during August, September, and October. The Charter came into force on Oct. 24, 1945, on receipt of the ratification of the Union of Soviet Socialist Republics, the twenty-ninth nation to ratify and the fifth and last of the great powers. By the time the first Assembly session opened in London in early 1946, every one of the fifty signatory states plus Poland had ratified.[1]

[1] In addition to ratification of the Charter, Congress also provided for United States membership by enacting the United Nations Participation Act, 59 Stat. 619, which became law on Dec. 20, 1945. It provides for appointment of a chief delegate by the President, with Senate approval. This representative has the status of an ambassador and is United States representative on the Security Council. Other representatives were authorized. The President was empowered to provide for United States participation in economic and communications sanctions. He was also given power to negotiate with the Security Council, subject to approval of Congress by act or joint resolution, concerning the military forces and facilities that the United States will furnish.

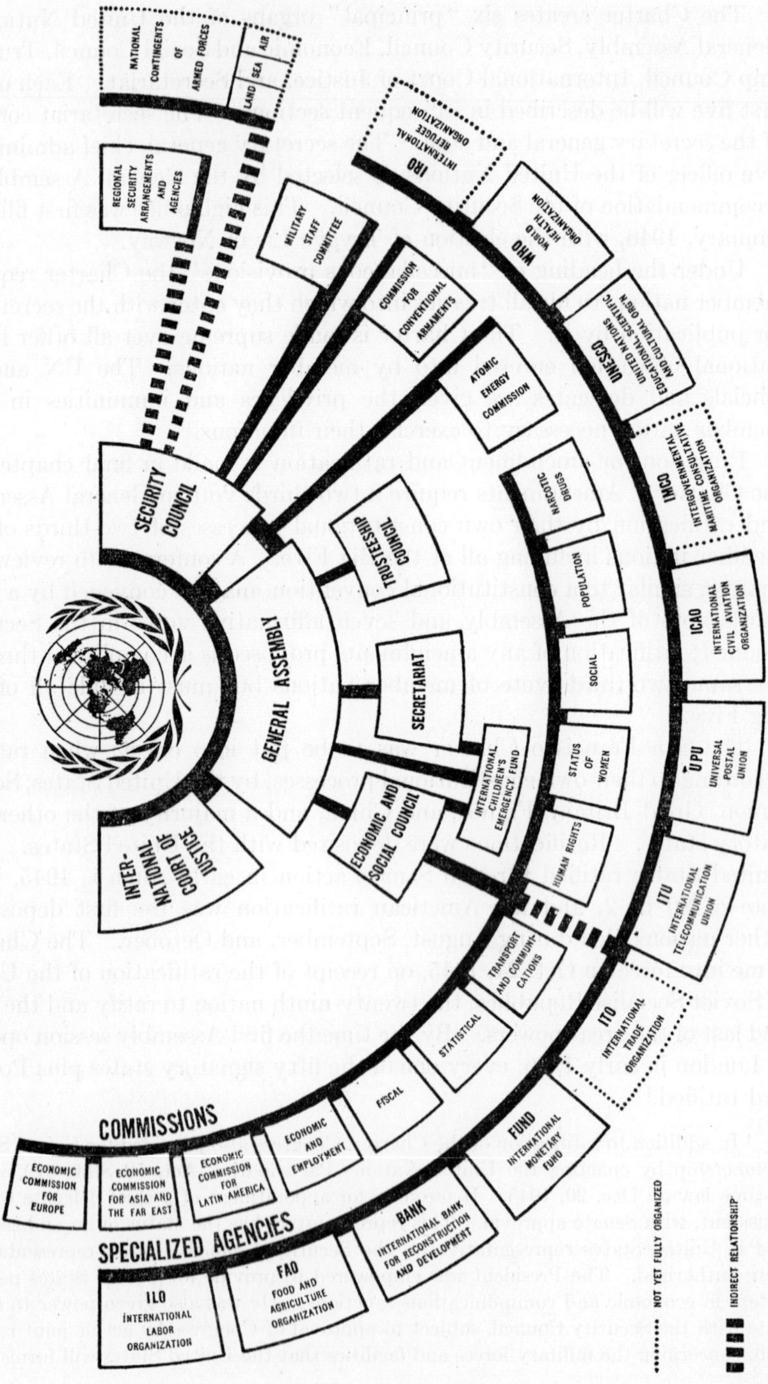
NATIONAL CONTINGENTS OF ARMED FORCES
LAND
SEA
AIR
REGIONAL SECURITY ARRANGEMENTS AND AGENCIES
IRO
INTERNATIONAL REFUGEE ORGANIZATION
MILITARY STAFF COMMITTEE
WHO
WORLD HEALTH ORGANIZATION
COMMISSION FOR CONVENTIONAL ARMAMENTS
UNESCO
UNITED NATIONS EDUCATIONAL SCIENTIFIC AND CULTURAL ORG'N
ATOMIC ENERGY COMMISSION
SECURITY COUNCIL
IMCO
INTERGOVERNMENTAL MARITIME CONSULTATIVE ORGANIZATION
NARCOTIC DRUGS
TRUSTEESHIP COUNCIL
POPULATION
ICAO
INTERNATIONAL CIVIL AVIATION ORGANIZATION
GENERAL ASSEMBLY
SECRETARIAT
SOCIAL
UPU
UNIVERSAL POSTAL UNION
STATUS OF WOMEN
INTERNATIONAL CHILDREN'S EMERGENCY FUND
ECONOMIC AND SOCIAL COUNCIL
INTER-NATIONAL COURT OF JUSTICE
HUMAN RIGHTS
ITU
INTERNATIONAL TELECOMMUNICATION UNION
TRANSPORT AND COMMUNI-CATIONS
STATISTICAL
ITO
INTERNATIONAL TRADE ORGANIZATION
FISCAL
FUND
INTERNATIONAL MONETARY FUND
COMMISSIONS
ECONOMIC AND EMPLOYMENT
ECONOMIC COMMISSION FOR EUROPE
ECONOMIC COMMISSION FOR ASIA AND THE FAR EAST
ECONOMIC COMMISSION FOR LATIN AMERICA
BANK
INTERNATIONAL BANK FOR RECONSTRUCTION AND DEVELOPMENT
SPECIALIZED AGENCIES
FAO
FOOD AND AGRICULTURE ORGANIZATION
ILO
INTERNATIONAL LABOR ORGANIZATION
NOT YET FULLY ORGANIZED
INDIRECT RELATIONSHIP

THE UNITED NATIONS

The General Assembly.—The General Assembly consists of delegates from all the member nations, and each nation casts one vote. The functions of the Assembly are to deliberate, to administer, to elect, to approve budgets, to initiate amendments. Senator Vandenberg called it a "town meeting of the world." It has general authority to discuss any matter within the scope of the Charter and may make recommendations except on disputes being considered by the Security Council. The latter limitation was deemed necessary to prevent the confusion of jurisdiction that existed in the League. The General Assembly oversees the work of all organs of the United Nations and is assigned special responsibilities over the Economic and Social Council and the Trusteeship Council. The Assembly's power to elect is considerable, extending to the nonpermanent seats on the Security Council, the judgeships on the International Court of Justice, the Economic and Social Council, and part of the Trusteeship Council. Funds for the UN are secured by the General Assembly, which is given power to apportion expenses among member nations.

The voting procedure in the General Assembly is relatively simple. Each nation has one vote. Decisions on important questions like elections, suspension, expulsion, budgets, and trusteeship must be made by two-thirds vote. Decisions on less important matters are made by an ordinary majority.

Meeting in London in January, 1946, the first Assembly made a creditable record. It proceeded to fill the offices of the various UN agencies. The voting on important issues and elections disclosed a tendency of nations to group into blocs such as the United States and the Latin American nations, and the Soviet Union and the eastern European countries. Despite this, the smaller nations were gratified to see that the great powers did not present a united front on every issue.

The hopes that had been placed in the Security Council having been frustrated in part by Russian use of the veto, world opinion has centered new hopes on the General Assembly. Step by step, Assembly deliberations have contributed to an emerging conscience of the world. One of the most hopeful agencies created since the UN got under way is the Interim Committee of the General Assembly, popularly known as the "Little Assembly." Created in 1947, it was assigned the task of doing spadework between General Assembly sessions. All member nations are entitled to representation on the Little Assembly, but it was boycotted from the start by the Soviet bloc. It has studied the veto power carefully, and has recommended its abolition in regard to membership applications and peaceful settlement but its retention on matters of enforcement action. The interim group also voted in favor of calling a general conference to revise the UN Charter.

Obviously the General Assembly is not a full-blown "parliament of mankind." Its powers are modest indeed, and they include nothing like the lawmaking authority of a national parliament or congress. Among the many barriers to prompt development of the Assembly along the line of a statute lawmaker are (1) great power, especially Russian, concern over retention of position and sovereignty, and (2) the unrepresentative composition of the Assembly which gives the same voting power to a nation of 2 million people as it gives to another with 200 million. Great changes in attitudes will be required before the first obstacle can be surmounted, while drastic reform of the basis of representation will be necessary to solve the second difficulty. When the nations and their peoples are ready for a more perfect union, then the General Assembly probably will be the key instrument through which they will work.

Security Council.—For the present and near future, the Security Council is the major agency on which must rest the hopes of the world for an enforced peace. The Council is composed of eleven member nations, of which five—United States, Soviet Union, Great Britain, China, and France—hold permanent seats and six are elected to nonpermanent seats for 2-year terms by the General Assembly. The Charter mentions as standards in election to nonpermanent seats the ability to contribute to maintenance of peace and security and equitable geographic representation.

Assigned the primary responsibility for keeping peace and security, the Council is given powers to settle disputes ranging from negotiation, conciliation, arbitration, and judicial decision to interruption of communications, severance of diplomatic relations, economic sanctions, and military action. All members of the UN are required to pledge in advance units of their armed forces available for use by the Security Council. Under the Yalta voting formula, a decision to use force requires the concurrence of all permanent members of the Security Council. The Charter also requires seven affirmative votes out of the eleven. A provision added to the Charter at San Francisco on the insistence of the smaller powers makes it possible for a UN member nation without a seat on the Security Council to participate in decisions regarding the use of that member's armed forces. The great-power veto makes extremely unlikely the use of force against one of the Big Five.

Plans for the employment of armed force are supposed to be made by a military staff committee under the Security Council. The committee is composed of chiefs of staff of the five great powers. Representatives of other UN member nations may be invited to participate in the work of the committee. The committee has been so deadlocked from the beginning that no progress has been made.

The Security Council is also given power to oversee regional security arrangements, which are permitted providing they are consistent with the UN Charter. Enforcement action under a regional pact may not be undertaken without the approval of the Security Council. For example, if the

American nations desired to curb an aggressor under the terms of the Treaty of Rio de Janeiro and the Treaty of Rio, they would have to obtain the consent of the Security Council. The Latin-American nations fought long and hard at San Francisco for recognition of regional security arrangements, but succeeded in obtaining provision only for a system subordinate to the general security scheme. Another article exempts from this limitation, however, regional pacts made during the Second World War and directed against revival of aggression by an enemy state. This exemption retains the validity of the Franco-Soviet mutual assistance pact.

Much of the criticism of the UN stems from the predominant position assigned to the major nations in the Security Council. Although some provisions, such as the veto power, are indefensible on their merits and acceptable only as an alternative to no security organization at all, there is much to be said for putting the major responsibility for peace keeping on the shoulders of the strong. In industrial potential, fighting power, and population the Big Five are so great that the major task of fighting a world war inevitably will fall to them. Small nations have their uses and can make distinctive contributions to the UN in social, economic, and humanitarian lines; but the responsibility of policing the world against aggression must be assigned primarily to the great powers.

For the United States one of the most crucial decisions respecting UN membership was the pledging in advance of contingents of armed forces for use in the service of the United Nations. A portion of the opposition was deflated by the decision at Yalta on voting; for under the scheme the United States could veto any use of military force proposed. Objection still remained to the use of military forces of the United States without a formal declaration of war. This objection was met to the satisfaction of many, but not all, through a review of American history. In 1945 a former assistant secretary of state reported at least one hundred instances in which the President, without a declaration of war, used the armed forces of the United States against other countries.[1] The plain fact is that, with the weapons of modern war, no nation can afford to wait until it is attacked or until it has time to debate and pass a declaration of war. Modern wars come with alarming suddenness. Therefore the Security Council is a continuous body, constantly on the job and alert to every potential threat to the peace. As a corollary, the armed forces of member nations were to be held in readiness for use by the UN.

Framed before the world-shaking initial use of the atomic bomb, the Charter did not take into consideration the new conditions created by the

[1] James Grafton Rogers, *World Policing and the Constitution, an Inquiry into the Powers of the President and Congress, Nine Wars and a Hundred Military Operations*, 1789–1945 (Boston: World Peace Foundation, 1945) See p. 402 for a discussion of the constitutional issue.

event. Some critics declared that the UN was rendered obsolete before it was put into effect. Proponents stressed that world organization was even more necessary than before. Early in 1946 the General Assembly created a new UN body, the Atomic Energy Commission. It is composed of the eleven member nations of the Security Council plus Canada. This development is watched with greatest interest, for a UN monopoly over the use of atomic energy for military purposes would be the strongest sanction ever devised.

East-West differences over the control of atomic weapons led to deadlock in that important field. All except the Soviet bloc agreed to a powerful international agency with a monopoly over source materials and dangerous operations, licensing power over other atomic activities, and authority to inspect in all nations to prevent secret projects. The atomic armament race continued unabated.

Looking back over the first half-decade of the Security Council, one must exert himself to find achievements to balance the disappointments. The basic cause of the meager record in security matters has been the deep East-West split. The extent of this cleavage was not anticipated by the founding fathers at San Francisco, who counted on continuance of the kind of cooperation that characterized joint efforts in wartime. Obviously the UN, based on a one-world principle, cannot fulfill the expectations of its founders so long as the nations of the world are grouped into two hostile armed camps.

Despite the "iron curtain" and the suspicions entertained by those on both sides of it, substantial progress has been made in peaceful settlement of international disputes. Nearly all the major postwar problems among nations have been brought before the UN. Although handicapped by the frequent use of the veto power by Russia, the Security Council has been able to act effectively in most cases. The greatest achievements are the settlements in Palestine and Indonesia, where fighting wars were stopped through UN mediation and intervention. Armed only with the moral power of the world organization, UN representatives negotiated truces and peaceful settlements. Overcoming the handicap of the veto, the Security Council provided facilities for the airing of all sides, for investigation, and for mediation. Each settlement has contributed to the formulation of patterns of good conduct.

Economic and Social Council.—To get at some of the basic causes of war through improved standards of living, social and economic progress, the United Nations created the Economic and Social Council and its cooperating agencies. The council is composed of eighteen members, elected by the Assembly for 3-year terms.

While the field of operation of the Economic and Social Council is broad, its actual coercive powers are meager. It can study, report, recommend, prepare agreements, and call conferences. Although the Charter does not provide specifically for their subordination to the council, several United Nations agencies are supervised by the council.

The oldest of these is the International Labor Organization (ILO), the only major agency of the League of Nations to which the United States belonged. According to Herman Finer, the principal problems that have concerned the ILO are labor standards, migration of workers, full employment, public works, workers' health, and welfare of colonial peoples.[1] The ILO functions through its conference, which meets at least once a year and is composed of delegates representing government, labor, and employers of each member country. An executive body, called the "governing body," manages the affairs of the ILO between conferences. The secretariat, headed by the director, is termed the International Labor Office. After the outbreak of war in Europe, the ILO transferred its headquarters from Geneva, Switzerland, to Montreal, Canada. In the past the ILO has operated mainly through the framing of international conventions regarding the conditions of labor.

The Food and Agriculture Organization (FAO) was launched in interim form at the close of the conference held at Hot Springs, Va., in May and June, 1943. It has been called the "first permanent United Nations agency." The FAO hopes to stimulate increased food production and improved nutrition. Its methods are mainly research and informational—the collection of statistics, the exchange of expert personnel, the dissemination of information.

The International Monetary Fund was one of two agencies established under the Bretton Woods agreements of July, 1944. Its purpose is to encourage world trade and prosperity through stabilizing the value of currencies of participating nations.

The International Bank for Reconstruction and Development is the second of the Bretton Woods agencies. Carrying on from where UNRRA left off, it tries to guarantee or make direct loans to countries in need of capital for rebuilding after the devastation of war or for developing new productive facilities.

The United Nations Educational, Scientific, and Cultural Organization (UNESCO) was born in London in November, 1945. UNESCO is designed to be the agency through which member nations are encouraged to exchange information and ideas through all the diverse mediums of communication.

The International Civil Aviation Organization (ICAO) developed from the Chicago conference of November–December, 1944. Although it was established as an interim organization limited to 3 years, subsequent agree-

[1] Herman Finer, *The United Nations Economic and Social Council* (Boston: World Peace Foundation, 1946), pp. 26–33.

ments are expected to make the body permanent. Its powers are largely technical and advisory, but ICAO may later become a highly important regulatory body for world civil aeronautics.

Trusteeship Council.—The San Francisco Conference had to start from scratch in preparing sections of the Charter on dependent areas. The Dumbarton Oaks conference had not touched this important field, and the great powers had been unable to meet together before the San Francisco convening date. The Charter, in three chapters on trusteeship, establishes general policy to govern all dependent areas, sets forth the rules governing territories placed under United Nations "trust," and establishes the Trusteeship Council to supervise the system.

In the Atlantic Charter, signed by President Roosevelt and Prime Minister Churchill at sea in August, 1941, Great Britain and the United States declared that they sought no territorial aggrandizement. At San Francisco many compromises were necessary. First, the American State Department view had to be reconciled with that of the Army and Navy. Then, the United States and British drafts had to be brought into agreement. Finally, there ensued a spectacular fight over whether the goal of colonial peoples should be self-government or independence.

As finally adopted, the general provisions regarding trusteeship admonish nations with dependent areas to ensure their political, economic, social, and educational advancement, to develop self-government, to report on progress in their colonies to the UN, and to adopt an attitude of good-neighborliness.

The international trusteeship system had no specific territories assigned to it by the Charter. Trust territories were to come later from the following sources: (1) old League mandates, (2) conquered Axis colonies, and (3) other colonies voluntarily placed under the trusteeship plan. All the mandates except Southwest Africa, which may be annexed by the Union of South Africa, promptly were transferred to the trusteeship system by action of the mandatory powers. The United States accepted trusteeship over the former Japanese mandates of the Pacific—the Marshalls, the Carolines, and the Marianas. Former Italian colonies in North Africa were later placed under direct UN administration while Italy was given a trusteeship over Italian Somaliland. No important colonial power has yet indicated willingness to place its colonies under trust.

The Trusteeship Council was made a principal organ of the UN. It consists of member nations administering trust territories, other members of the Big Five, and enough other nations to make an equal number of state-administering and not-administering trust territories. The council has modest powers of accepting petitions, considering reports, and visiting trust areas. It supervises all ordinary trust territories. Trust areas of strategic importance are supervised by the Security Council and, as the

United States Army and Navy demanded, the trust power has a free hand to maintain bases. Although the new system does not contain striking new departures, it does obligate all nations with colonies to treat them decently and to report on their stewardship to the UN.

International Court of Justice.—In early April, 1945, just on the eve of the San Francisco Conference, a committee of jurists representing many naionst met in Washington to consider the form and organization of the judicial organ of the United Nations. Like the question of dependent areas, judicial matters were little considered at Dumbarton Oaks. The work of the committee of jurists was put before the conference at San Francisco. The principal controversy over judicial organization at the conference was over the continuation of the old Permanent Court of International Justice. The statute of the League court was reasonably satisfactory, and forty-five nations had accepted the principle of compulsory jurisdiction over disputes arising from treaties. On the other hand, several nations that were not members of the United Nations adhered to the World Court. It finally proved advisable to adopt a new statute creating a new International Court of Justice. Charter provisions regarding the court are very brief; the statute of the court is annexed to the Charter.

The court consists of fifteen judges, no two of whom may be nationals of the same state. The term of office is 9 years. Judges are elected by the General Assembly and the Security Council, each proceeding independently to elect from a list of nominees proposed by national groups. Membership in the court is automatic for all members of the UN. The statute made the new court successor to existing treaty provisions which named the old court as arbiter in disputes.

In view of the great tension of the era, it is not surprising that the International Court of Justice has heard few cases. Most of the serious disputes between nations have been of a "political" nature and have not been submitted to adjudication. In the first 3 years the court decided one case and rendered several advisory opinions.

THE UNITED STATES IN ONE WORLD

Can UN Keep the Peace?—Only a fool or a seer will attempt a final answer to this all-important question. A start has been made toward building a collective security system. The machinery appears reasonably well suited to the task. Although sharp disagreements marked the initial sessions of both General Assembly and Security Council, some consolation may be derived from the thought that differences were openly discussed and the world knew how they were resolved.

Only a part of the job of building lasting peace can be done through formal organization. Beyond that is required mutual understanding by peoples. International understanding demands a high degree of tolerance for the institutions, culture, and practices of other nations. Actual contact with the people of another country helps greatly an individual's ability to appreciate its virtues and shortcomings. Since travel abroad is not possible for the great masses of people, it is necessary to rely upon the indirect modes of contact through literature, music, history, and the great channels of communication like the radio, motion picture, and printed page. Lacking some firm knowledge of other countries, an individual often draws a ridiculous conclusion based upon distorted press reports of a single episode. A motion picture depicting nationals of a country as bandits may lead to formation of attitudes that lead to future distrust.

Fundamental to the understanding that is prerequisite to durable peace is tolerance. The bigot who regards every foreigner with suspicion makes a contribution to unrest. Concerned over the new might of Russia, many an American has allowed his own lack of information about that country to work him up into a frenzy of fear.

The peace is not likely to be kept if nations adopt policies that undermine the economic life of others. A high-tariff policy by the United States can catapult the whole world into depression. From economic suffering may come the dread diseases of militarism and absolutism.

Freely predicting the Third World War, the prophets of doom see in every disagreement in the UN its imminent failure. The war so recently ended was so devastating that no would-be aggressor is likely to be able to fight a large-scale war within 5 or 10 years. Perhaps the last best hope of the world is that this interval may provide sufficient time in which to perfect the UN and to achieve a high level of international understanding.

Toward World Government.—Strong criticism of the UN is voiced by two principal schools of thought in the United States. Some people, despite the great changes in the world that render their position less and less tenable, persist in isolationist leanings. A considerable number of people, without much knowledge of other countries and lacking clearly formulated views on these matters, are thrown into the isolationist-imperialist camp by their despair over the bad news of international rivalries that so often comes from UN sessions.

On the other extreme, sometimes equally lacking in faith in the UN, are the advocates of world federation or world government. The disagreement of this group with supporters of the UN is mainly over tactics, not policy. Many UN backers hope ultimately for its development into a stronger union, but they stress the necessity of taking one step at a time, as was done in early American history in the transition from Continental Congress to Articles of Confederation, to Constitution. The world federalist, however, argues that the way to start is to form a federation of those nations willing or fit to join, and to allow other nations to enter after they are converted.

As a practical matter, this approach would leave Russia and her neighbors out of the international union. It might lead to a situation in which the world was divided into two armed camps, with war between them a fairly certain prospect for the future.

After the destruction of Hiroshima and Nagasaki by atomic bombs, the world-government school received much vigorous support from many scientists who had worked on atomic energy or who were in a position to know its destructive force. It is easy to understand the reaction of those who helped create this modern Frankenstein; having intimate knowledge of its power, they became Paul Reveres riding to warn of impending danger. The testimony of leading scientists is nearly unanimous that no effective defense is yet conceivable against the atomic bomb, and that other nations may be able to perfect the bomb in a few years. Six weeks after the San Francisco Conference adjourned, and one week after the United States Senate voted ratification of the UN Charter, the cloud of smoke above Hiroshima on Aug. 5, 1945, signaled the birth of a new era of insecurity. The end of the Second World War came 9 days later, but the peace was an uneasy one.

To most Americans the mirage of world government is nearly as remote a possibility as the old illusion of isolation. It is visionary to suppose that all nations will now relinquish their sovereignty in order that the new world state may be born. A federation of democracies, which is nearer the realm of possibility, certainly would provoke the nations left out of the union to challenge its peace and prosperity. Since the peace is indivisible, only a universal organization can be counted on to keep down aggression. Those who advocate world federation or government must realize that a perfectionist attitude may undermine confidence in the UN to such an extent that the steppingstone to world order may be destroyed. Perhaps the San Francisco Charter is to the United Nations what the Articles of Confederation was to the United States, a device to preserve unity of diverse states until the necessity for more perfect union was clear to all.

References

American Association for the United Nations: *Changing World* (New York: The Association, monthly).

Armstrong, Hamilton F.: *The Calculated Risk* (New York: Macmillan, 1947).

Bailey, Thomas A.: *A Diplomatic History of the American People* (New York: Appleton-Century-Crofts, 2d ed., 1942).

——— *The Man in the Street; The Impact of American Public Opinion on Foreign Policy* (New York: Macmillan, 1948).

Bartlett, Ruhl J.: *The Record of American Diplomacy; Documents and Readings* . . . (New York: Knopf, 1947).

Bemis, Samuel F.: *The Latin American Policy of the United States* (New York: Harcourt Brace, 1943).

Bisson, Thomas A.: *America's Far Eastern Policy* (New York: Institute of Pacific Relations, 1945).

Boyd, Andrew: *The United Nations Organization Handbook* (New York: Pilot Press, 1946).

Brinton, Crane: *From Many, One; The Process of Political Integration; the Problem of World Government* (Cambridge, Mass.: Harvard University Press, 1948).

Brookings Institution: *Major Problems of United States Foreign Policy, 1947; a Study Guide* (Washington: Brookings, 1947). Similar volumes have been issued for 1948 and 1949.

Campbell, John C., and Others: *The United States in World Affairs, 1945–1947* (New York: Harper, 1947). A similar volume has been issued for 1947–1948.

Chamberlain, Lawrence H., and Richard C. Snyder (eds.): *American Foreign Policy* (New York: Rinehart, 1948).

Culbertson, Ely: *Total Peace, What Makes Wars and How to Organize Peace* (New York: Doubleday, 1943).

Dean, Vera Micheles: *The United States and Russia* (Cambridge, Mass.: Harvard University Press, 1948).

Dolivet, Louis: *The United Nations; a Handbook on the New World Organization* (New York: Farrar, Straus, 1946).

Ehrmann, Howard M. (ed.): "Foreign Policies and Relations of the United States," *Annals of the American Academy of Political and Social Science*, vol. 255 (January, 1948).

Evatt, Herbert V.: *The United Nations* (Cambridge, Mass.: Harvard University Press, 1948).

Ferguson, John H.: *American Diplomacy and the Boer War* (Philadelphia: University of Pennsylvania Press, 1939).

Fox, William T. R.: *The Super-powers; The United States, Britain and the Soviet Union—Their Responsibility for Peace* (New York: Harcourt Brace, 1944).

Goodrich, Leland M., and Edvard Hambro: *The Charter of the United Nations, Commentary and Documents* (Boston: World Peace Foundation, 1946).

Graham, Malbone W.: *American Diplomacy in the International Community* (Baltimore: Johns Hopkins Press, 1948).

Griswold, A. Whitney: *The Far Eastern Policy of the United States* (New York: Harcourt Brace, 1938).

Harley, J. Eugene: *Documentary Textbook on the United Nations* (Los Angeles: Center for International Understanding, 1947).

Harris, Seymour E.: *The European Recovery Program* (Cambridge, Mass.: Harvard University Press, 1948).

Hoskins, Halford L.: *The Atlantic Pact*, Public Affairs Bulletin No. 69 (Washington: Library of Congress, Legislative Reference Service, 1949).

Kalijarvi, Thorsten V. (ed.): "Peace Settlements of World War II," *Annals of the American Academy of Political and Social Science*, vol. 257 (May, 1948).

Markel, Lester, and Others: *Public Opinion and Foreign Policy* (New York: Harper, 1949).

Mowrer, Edgar A.: *The Nightmare of American Foreign Policy* (New York: Knopf, 1948).

Pan American Union: *Annals of the Organization of American States* (Washington: The Union, quarterly). Commenced 1949.

Patterson, Ernest M. (ed.): "Looking toward One World," *Annals of the American Academy of Political and Social Science*, vol. 258 (July, 1948).

Perkins, Dexter: *The Evolution of American Foreign Policy* (New York: Oxford, 1948).

——— *Hands Off: a History of the Monroe Doctrine* (Boston: Little, Brown, 1941).

SCHUMAN, FREDERICK L.: *International Politics; The Destiny of the Western State System* (New York: McGraw-Hill, 4th ed., 1948).

STREIT, CLARENCE: *Union Now* (Washington: Federal Union, Inc., 1943).

STUART, GRAHAM H.: *Latin America and the United States* (New York: Appleton-Century-Crofts, 3d ed., 1949).

THOMSON, CHARLES A. H.: *Overseas Information Service of the United States Government* (Washington: Brookings, 1949).

UNITED NATIONS CONFERENCE ON INTERNATIONAL ORGANIZATION: *Documents of the . . .* (New York: UN Information Organizations, 15 vols., 1945).

UNITED NATIONS DEPARTMENT OF PUBLIC INFORMATION: *United Nations Bulletin* (Lake Success: United Nations, monthly).

UNITED NATIONS INTERNATIONAL COURT OF JUSTICE: *Conditions of Admission of a State to Membership in the United Nations* (New York: Columbia University Press, 1948).

——— *Yearbook, 1947–1948* (New York: Columbia University Press, 1948).

UNITED STATES DEPARTMENT OF STATE: *Papers Relating to the Foreign Relations of the United States* (Washington: Government Printing Office, 1861–19—).

——— *Peace and War; United States Foreign Policy, 1931–1941*, Publication 1853 (Washington: Government Printing Office, 1942).

VAN ALSTYNE, RICHARD W.: *American Diplomacy in Action* (Stanford University, Calif.: Stanford University Press, rev. ed., 1947).

WELLES, SUMNER: *We Need Not Fail* (Boston: Houghton Mifflin, 1948).

WORLD PEACE FOUNDATION: *Documents on American Foreign Relations* (Princeton, N. J.: Princeton University Press; recent vols. cover two years or less).

WRIGHT, QUINCY (ed.): *A Foreign Policy for the United States* (Chicago: University of Chicago Press, 1947).

——— *A Study of War* (Chicago: University of Chicago Press, 2 vols., 1942).

Chapter 26

TERRITORIES, THE DISTRICT OF COLUMBIA, AND OCCUPIED AREAS

An ambition to win the mastery of the Pacific and control its rich commerce runs persistently through the entire history of the United States. It was a powerful motivating force in every acquisition of territory on the Pacific from Oregon and California to Hawaii and the Philippines.

Foster H. Dulles, *America in the Pacific, a Century of Expansion.*[1]

In 1790 the territory of the United States consisted of a comparatively small strip of land commencing with Maine on the north, ending with Georgia on the south, and extending beyond the Appalachians to poorly defined limits. By 1850 the southern boundary had been extended to Florida Keys, the northwest to the 49th parallel, the west to the Pacific Ocean, and the southwest to the Rio Grande. The next three-quarters of a century witnessed the building of an overseas empire. From a land area of 888,811 square miles in 1790 the United States had more than quadrupled its domain by 1940 to include a total of 3,735,209 square miles. It is a portentous fact, perhaps ominous so far as other nations are concerned, that during the same period no other nation successfully extended and maintained its sovereignty over an area of equal size. More recently, the fortunes of the Second World War left a legacy of additional territory and responsibility.

Methods Used to Acquire Territory.—Looking over the American territories and possessions, five methods of acquisition can be observed. A minor proportion was acquired by discovery and occupation. Another negligible proportion has been obtained by lease. A somewhat larger proportion was obtained by voluntary cession and annexation. A considerably larger amount was acquired by conquest or directly in consequence thereof. The largest proportion was acquired by purchase. How particular territories were acquired, together with other pertinent information, is shown on the chart given on pages 582–583.

Types of Territories.—When territory is acquired, sovereignty changes, with the result that the new sovereign must provide some method whereby its will is recognized and executed. Sometimes a territory is left "unorganized," again it is "organized." In the latter event a local legislature is created with considerable authority over matters of local concern.

[1] (Boston: Houghton, 1932), p. 1.

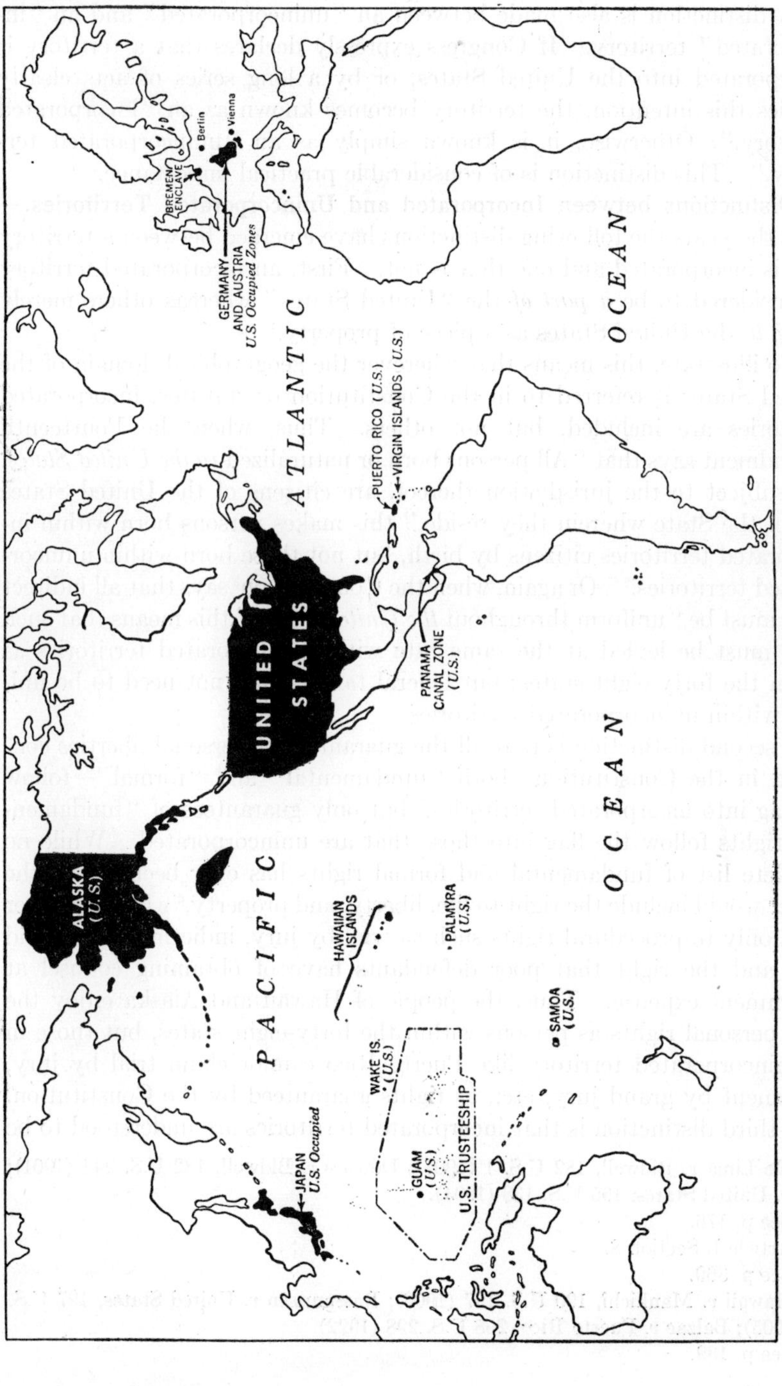

The American Empire

A distinction is also made between an "unincorporated" and an "incorporated" territory. If Congress expressly declares that a territory is incorporated into the United States, or by a long series of acts clearly implies this intention, the territory becomes known as an "incorporated territory." Otherwise, it is known simply as an "unincorporated territory." This distinction is of considerable practical importance.

Distinctions between Incorporated and Unincorporated Territories.—Over the years the following distinctions have emerged between a territory that is incorporated and one that is not. First, an incorporated territory is considered to be *a part of* the "United States" whereas others merely *belong to* the United States as a piece of property.[1]

To illustrate, this means that wherever the geographical domain of the United States is referred to in the Constitution or statutes, incorporated territories are included, but not others. Thus, when the Fourteenth Amendment says that "All persons born or naturalized *in the United States*, and subject to the jurisdiction thereof, are citizens of the United States and of the State wherein they reside," this makes persons born within incorporated territories citizens by birth, but not those born within unincorporated territories.[2] Or again, when the Constitution[3] says that all indirect taxes must be "uniform throughout *the United States*," this means that such taxes must be levied at the same rate within incorporated territories as within the forty-eight states; but federal taxes would not need to be uniform within unincorporated territories.[4]

A second distinction is that all the guarantees of personal liberties contained in the Constitution—both "fundamental" and "formal"—follow the flag into incorporated territories,[5] but only guarantees of "fundamental" rights follow the flag into those that are unincorporated. While no complete list of fundamental and formal rights has ever been made, the former would include the right to life, liberty, and property,[6] while the latter refers only to procedural rights such as trial by jury, indictment by grand jury, and the right that poor defendants have of obtaining counsel at government expense. Thus, the people of Hawaii and Alaska enjoy the same personal rights as persons within the forty-eight states, but those in an unincorporated territory like Puerto Rico cannot claim trial by jury, indictment by grand jury, etc., as rights guaranteed by the Constitution.

A third distinction is that incorporated territories are understood to be

[1] De Lima *v.* Bidwell, 182 U.S. 1 (1901); Downes *v.* Bidwell, 182 U.S. 244 (1901); Dorr *v.* United States, 195 U.S. 138 (1904).

[2] See p. 176.

[3] Article I, Section 8.

[4] See p. 369.

[5] Hawaii *v.* Mankichi, 190 U.S. 197 (1903); Rassmussen *v.* United States, 197 U.S. 516 (1905); Balzac *v.* Puerto Rico, 258 U.S. 298 (1922).

[6] See p. 139.

in a stage preparatory to statehood, whereas others are not. Though this implication is made, Congress is the sole judge as to when the territory should be admitted as a state.[1]

Territorial Governments Subordinate to the National Government.—Congress has complete dominion over every aspect of territorial affairs. This means that it may legislate not only concerning external affairs of the territory but also concerning every subject upon which the legislature of one of the forty-eight states might legislate. Thus, Congress possesses not only all its delegated powers, but also reserved powers for use within territories whenever it thinks necessary. To state it otherwise, the relationship between the government at Washington and its territories is like that within a unitary state rather than a federal state. Though Congress may legislate directly with respect to such local matters as schools, roads, garbage collection, sewage disposal, and water supply, it usually transfers its responsibility to a territorial government. After doing so, the territorial government, like cities within a state, has only such powers as are granted to it. Congress may authorize the President to oversee administration within the territories or veto colonial legislation; Congress itself may amend or abrogate the acts of colonial legislatures; and the United States courts may declare void any action of a territorial government that is not in harmony with acts of Congress or the Constitution.

Administrative Supervision of Territories.—For years administrative responsibility for American territories has been divided among three departments—War, Navy, and Interior. This is still the case, but to a lesser extent than previously. As a consequence of executive orders beginning in 1934, the Army has been divested of all except the Panama Canal Zone; the Navy of all but Samoa, Guam, several small Pacific islands,[2] and the recently acquired trust territories; while the Division of Territories and Island Possessions of the Department of Interior, has been given supervisory jurisdiction over the remainder. As a result, those with fairly large native populations, such as Alaska, Puerto Rico, and Hawaii, are now under a civilian branch. This, many hoped, would lead to greater democracy within the territories and more solicitude on the part of the American people for the welfare of the natives.

Beside the departments mentioned, there are others directly or indirectly interested in territorial problems. In Alaska alone there were fifty-two different federal agencies at work in 1939. The Soil Conservation Service, Post Office Department, Rural Electrification Administration, Census Bureau, Civil Aeronautics Authority, FBI, Immigration and Naturalization Service, Housing Agency, Social Security Administration, Army, and Navy were only a few of the agencies. For the most part today,

[1] See p. 90.

[2] Midway, Wake, Johnston, and Kingman Reef.

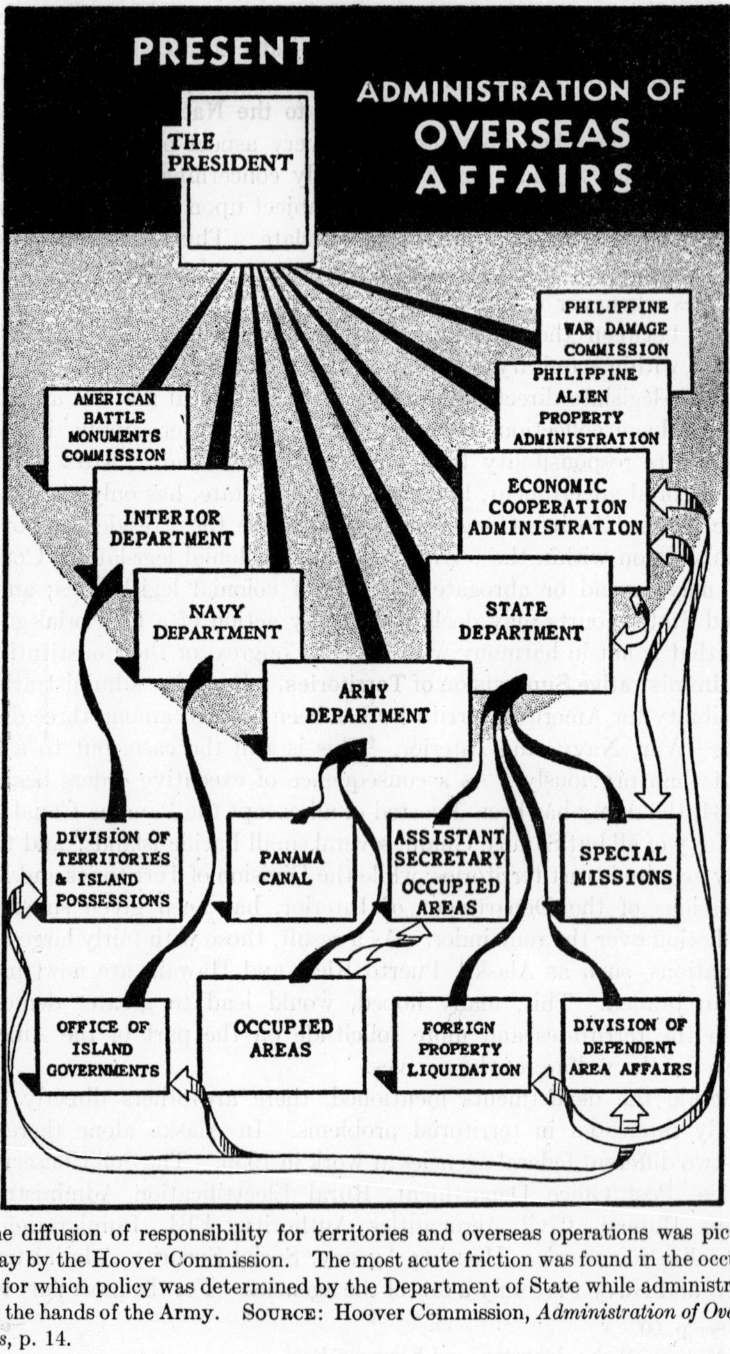

The diffusion of responsibility for territories and overseas operations was pictured this way by the Hoover Commission. The most acute friction was found in the occupied areas, for which policy was determined by the Department of State while administration was in the hands of the Army. SOURCE: Hoover Commission, *Administration of Overseas Affairs*, p. 14.

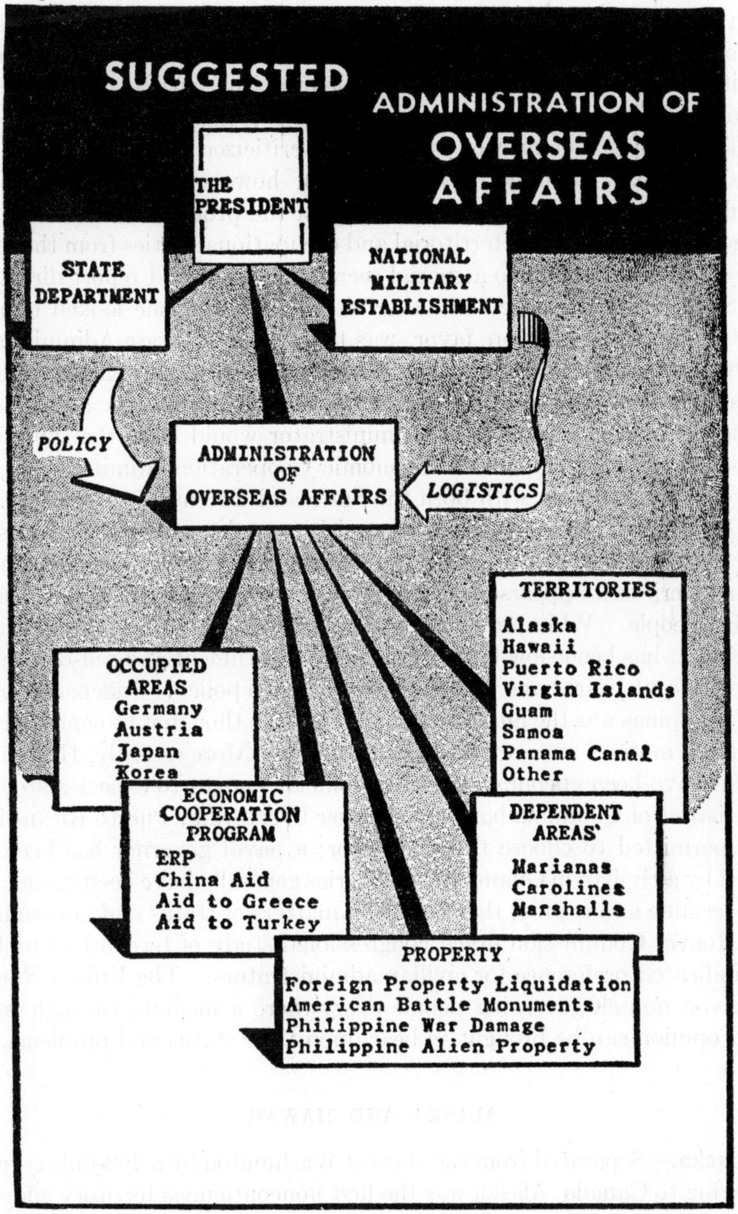

The Hoover Commission did not make a positive recommendation for reform of overseas affairs administration, but instead suggested alternative approaches to be studied by Congress. The plan pictured above secured the most favorable comment from the Commission, and was urged for adoption by Commissioners Hoover, Pollock, and Mead. SOURCE: Hoover Commission, *Administration of Overseas Affairs*, p. 15.

each goes its own way, as in the forty-eight states, without clearing through either any central agency in Washington or the governor's office in the territories. This has led to considerable criticism, particularly on the part of some of the territorial governments.

The Hoover Commission studied and criticized management of territorial affairs.[1] Its only recommendation, however, was that Congress should undertake a comprehensive study of the problem. One alternative suggested was to take all territorial and occupational duties from the armed forces and assign them to a special secretary who would report directly to the Secretary of Defense. Another alternative, and one looked upon by the Commission with more favor, was to create a separate Administration of Overseas Affairs and give it jurisdiction over all territorial and occupational activities abroad except State Department diplomatic and consular services. Under this plan the Administrator would have the same independent status as that of the Economic Cooperation Administrator, but he would work closely with both the State and Defense Departments.

Democratic Trends.—American acquisition and control of territories and their peoples has always been seriously criticized at home as well as abroad. To many critics it appears contradictory for a democracy to hold and control subject people. While American policy has been paternalistic and usually humane, it has been slow to encourage self-government and self-determination. Recent years have witnessed some shift in policy. Independence for the Philippines was the most dramatic step, even though it be conceded that American motives were not entirely altruistic. More recently, Hawaii and Alaska have been encouraged by high official sources to expect statehood; the District of Columbia has moved closer to self-rule; Puerto Ricans have been permitted to choose their governor; a naval governor has been displaced by a civilian in Guam; and territories generally have been encouraged to determine and express themselves on matters of status and government. The Hoover Commission urged congressional study of territorial problems and indicated preference for civilian administrators. The United Nations has given nonself-governing people everywhere a medium through which world opinion can be brought to bear upon their status and problems.

ALASKA AND HAWAII

Alaska.—Separated from the state of Washington by a 400-mile corridor belonging to Canada, Alaska was the first noncontiguous territory added to the American empire. Its vast sprawling territory encompasses 586,400 square miles—an area more than twice as large as Texas, thirteen times as large as Pennsylvania, and three and one-half times as large as California.

[1] *Administration of Overseas Affairs* (Washington: Government Printing Office, 1949), pp. 3–10.

Shortly after its purchase from Russia in 1867, Alaska was made an incorporated territory, but it remained unorganized until 1884. Since it is incorporated, both fundamental and formal rights are protected by the Constitution. At the same time, all general laws of Congress apply unless they specifically state otherwise. The residents have no vote in presidential elections, while their only representative in Congress is a delegate elected every 2 years, who has a seat without vote in the House of Representatives.

The treaty with Russia provided that those inhabitants who wished to retain their allegiance to Russia should depart within 3 years. All others, except "uncivilized" native tribes, were collectively naturalized, while their children subsequently born within the territory became citizens by birth. Members of the "uncivilized" tribes are considered wards of the Federal government, although they were collectively naturalized in 1924 along with tribal Indians in the states. Accordingly, nearly everyone now born within the territory is an American citizen.

Hawaii.—Twenty-four hundred miles south and west from San Francisco lie the Hawaiian Islands, "Uncle Sam's capital of the American Pacific." Though twenty in number, there are eight principal islands. Beginning with Hawaii at the southeastern end of the series, these extend 390 miles in a northwesterly direction in the following order: Hawaii, Kahoolawe, Maui, Lanai, Molokai, Oahu, Kauai, and Niihau. The total area, including the small outlying islands, is about twice the combined size of Delaware and Rhode Island. "Scenic" Hawaii is the largest; the "Valley Island" of Maui, second; "Glorious" Oahu, the site of Honolulu and Pearl Harbor, third; while the "Garden Island" of Kauai is fourth.

Before annexation in 1898, Hawaii was an independent republic with a long tradition of monarchical rule. Like Alaska, it is now an incorporated territory, becoming so by the Organic Act of 1900. Though citizens, the people have no vote in presidential elections, and their only representative in Congress is a delegate chosen by the voters every 2 years who has a nonvoting seat in the House of Representatives. General laws of Congress apply to the territory unless exception is expressly made. Residents enjoy the guarantees of both fundamental and formal rights contained in the Constitution.

The act of 1900 collectively naturalized all within the territory who previously owned allegiance to the Hawaiian government. Since then, those born within the territory have become American citizens by birth. Many aliens in the territory at the time of annexation and many immigrants who have since arrived have become naturalized, but due to the fact that American laws have barred Chinese, Japanese, Filipinos, and other Orientals from becoming American citizens, about 20 per cent of the total population remain aliens.

In addition to the many aliens, there are a considerable number who possess dual nationality. This arises from the fact that children born there are citizens by the rule of *jus soli* and yet because of the former allegiance of their parents they are also considered citizens by another state that follows the rule of *jus sanguinis.* Though the vast majority of the children are undoubtedly loyal Americans, their dual citizenship has tended to make them suspect. This is especially true of some 50,000 Japanese who have never taken steps permitted by Japanese law to expatriate themselves and in consequence owe allegiance to both the United States and Japan. The situation could and should be remedied by treaty, as it has been with a number of other countries, as soon as circumstances permit.[1]

Governments.—Alaska and Hawaii have governments that are similar, except that the latter has been given greater autonomy. Both have for chief executives governors appointed by the President with the consent of the Senate for 4-year terms. Hawaii has been the only American territory where the governor is chosen from among local residents, but the custom was instituted for Puerto Rico in 1946 for the first time. Except for a secretary who is appointed by the President to assist with administration, other executive and administrative officers are appointed by the governors.

The legislatures of both territories are bicameral and elected by the voters. They resemble American state legislatures both in organization and by the way they proceed. With a few exceptions, the legislatures have authority to deal with all matters of local concern. Their enactments must be sent to Washington where Congress may disapprove them, but this rarely happens.

The judicial systems of the two territories are somewhat different. In Alaska there are no local territorial courts. Instead, a United States district court is divided into four divisions to enforce and interpret both federal and territorial laws. Judges are appointed by the President to serve for terms of good behavior. Summary cases are handled by United States commissioners appointed by the judge of each judicial district. The commissioners are at once justice of peace, probate judge, coroner, town clerk, recorder, jailer, and guardian of minors and the insane. Their formal education may be sketchy and they may know little law. Indeed, it is reported that commissioners have been known to issue a divorce decree by the simple expedient of tearing up the marriage license and refunding the fee.[2]

In Hawaii there is a dual system of courts: federal and territorial. The federal consists of a district court, manned by judges who are appointed by the President from among citizens and residents of Hawaii for terms of 6 years. Territorial courts consist of a supreme court, five circuit courts which resemble county courts in the states, and thirty-five district

[1] For further discussion see Joseph Barber, *Hawaii: Restless Rampart* (Indianapolis: Bobbs-Merrill, 1941), pp. 141–142.

[2] Merle E. Colby (American Guide Series), *A Guide to Alaska, Last American Frontier* (New York: Macmillan, 1939), p. 54.

courts corresponding to those of justices of peace. Territorial courts have jurisdiction over all nonfederal cases arising within the territory. Decisions of the territorial supreme court are final but may be reviewed by the United States Supreme Court when the matter concerns an act of Congress or provisions of the Constitution. Decisions of the federal district court in both Alaska and Hawaii may be appealed to the Ninth Circuit Court of Appeals with headquarters in San Francisco.

Local governments exist in both territories. In Alaska there are a few incorporated towns and a large number of unincorporated towns and villages. There are no counties. Local governments in Hawaii consist of five counties, two cities (Honolulu and Hilo), and a number of unincorporated towns and villages.

Campaigns for Statehood.—Agitation for admission to statehood has been incessant in Hawaii. It is argued that historically territories have been admitted after a period of tutelage; that as American citizens they are entitled to equal rights and participation in government; that continued territorial status is contrary to the ideal of democracy over which Americans have been so effusive; that they are discriminated against by acts of Congress, particularly those appropriating funds for public improvements; that they are controlled by a Congress in which they have no vote, by a President whom they may not help elect, and by a Constitution that they may not help to amend; that they pay the same federal taxes as do citizens on the mainland; that their sons are conscripted; and that they are qualified by character, education, and experience to assume the full obligations that would arise from statehood.

The long campaign for Hawaiian statehood culminated in a plebiscite held in 1940, at which time the electorate voted on the question "Do you favor statehood for Hawaii?" Out of a total registration of approximately 84,000 voters, 45,344 voted for statehood, while 22,240 voted against it—a 2-to-1 victory for the proponents of admission to the Union. Congress has held several hearings (the last in 1948) and the subject has been widely debated, but citizens on the mainland remain either hostile or indifferent. Meanwhile, in 1946, Alaskans voted 3 to 2 for statehood.

The chief objections of those who voice opinions are that the process of Americanization has not gone far enough, especially in Hawaii where there are many of oriental ancestry, and that it is unfair to give newly admitted territories equality of voting power in the Senate with existing large states; in times past, the Army and Navy have objected because they thought statehood would subject their handling of bases and installations to more civilian controls. Statehood for both territories has been strongly urged by recent Presidents, Secretaries of Interior, Republican and Democratic party platforms, and the Annual Conference of State Governors. Bills to admit both territories have been pushed vigorously in recent congresses and passed the House early in 1950.

PRINCIPAL AMERICAN

Territory	Date acquired	Status before acquisition	How acquired	Incorporated or unincorporated
District of Columbia	1790	Part of Maryland	Donated by Maryland	Incorporated
Alaska	1868	Possession of Russia	Purchase by treaty	Incorporated
Hawaii	1898	Independent republic	Mutual agreement	Incorporated
Puerto Rico	1898	Spanish colony	War and treaty with Spain	Unincorporated
Guam	1898	Spanish colony	War and treaty with Spain	Unincorporated
Panama Canal Zone	1902	Territory of Panama	Perpetual lease and annual payment	Unincorporated
Samoan Islands	1904	Independent	Treaty with native chiefs	Unincorporated
Virgin Islands	1917	Danish colony	Purchase by treaty	Unincorporated
Trust territory of the Pacific islands	1947	Japanese mandates	Conquest	Unincorporated

TERRITORIES

Citizenship of natives	Legislature	Executive
U.S. Citizens	U.S. Congress	3 commissioners appointed by President for 3-year terms
U.S. Citizens	Senate elected for 4-year terms House elected for 2-year terms	Governor appointed by U.S. President for 4-year terms
U.S. Citizens	Senate elected for 4-year terms House elected for 2-year terms	Governor appointed by U.S. President for 4-year terms
U.S. Citizens by collective naturalization, 1917	Senate elected for 4-year terms House elected for 2-year terms	Governor elected by voters (since 1946)
Not U.S. Citizens	Elected advisory Council	Civilian Governor appointed by Secretary of Navy (Interior after July 1, 1950)
Not U.S. Citizens	None	Governor appointed by Secretary of Army
Not U.S. Citizens	None	Commandant appointed by Secretary of Navy
U.S. Citizens by collective naturalization, 1927	Unicameral. Composed of municipal council of 7 members from islands of St. Thomas and St. John, and municipal council of 9 members from St. Croix Island	Governor appointed by U.S. President for an indefinite term
Not U.S. Citizens	None	High Commissioner appointed by Secretary of Navy

PUERTO RICO AND THE VIRGIN ISLANDS

Puerto Rico.—Puerto Rico, where Columbus first set foot in the new world, lies in almost a direct line southeast from Florida through Cuba, then Haiti, and then Santo Domingo. Situated between the Greater and Lesser Antilles, the island guards the approaches to Central and northern South America—hence its name "Key to the Caribbean." The island itself is 95 miles long from east to west and 35 miles wide. Its land area, including adjacent islands, is 3,435 square miles.

Acquired from Spain in 1898, Puerto Rico became an organized territory by the Foraker Act of 1900. Later, in 1917, on the eve of the entrance of America into the First World War, in what looked like a bid for greater loyalty, the Jones Act reorganized the government of the Island, giving it greater autonomy. The same measure made Puerto Ricans citizens of the United States. From this it was contended that the territory had been incorporated, but the Supreme Court held otherwise.[1]

The Virgin Islands.—The Virgin Islands lie 40 miles east of Puerto Rico and 1,400 miles southeast of New York. They consist of fifty islands and cays, only three of which are inhabited or of any considerable size. Nearest to Puerto Rico is St. Thomas, 14 miles long and 2 miles wide. Three miles to the east lies another island of about the same size called St. John. Forty miles southward lies St. Croix, largest of the three. The total area of these three is only 140 square miles, St. Croix having nearly two-thirds of it all. Although of little economic importance, the islands have much of historic and scientific interest, while their strategic location and the excellent harbor at Charlotte Amalie (St. Thomas) makes them of prime value to any power wishing to control the Caribbean.

The islands have been an organized unincorporated territory since shortly after their purchase from Denmark in 1917. Legislation enacted in 1927 made all natives citizens who lived in the islands on Jan. 17, 1917, while an act of June 28, 1932, extended citizenship to all inhabitants regardless of their place of residence in 1917.

Governments.—The government of Puerto Rico is very similar to that of Hawaii and Alaska. It has a governor, elected, since 1946, by the voters; a bicameral legislature elected by the voters; and both federal and territorial courts. For purposes of local government, the island, and those near by, are divided into municipal districts. The principal town in each district is its administrative center and is governed by an elected mayor and municipal assembly.

The Virgin Islands has a governor appointed by the President, usually from among nonresidents, and both federal and territorial courts. Otherwise the government is peculiar, due to the fact that the population dwells

[1] Balzac *v.* Puerto Rico, 258 U.S. 298 (1922).

on three separate islands and the basic organization was developed by the Danes. By the Organic Act of 1936, two municipalities were created: one of St. Croix and the other of St. Thomas and St. John. These are not municipalities in the American sense but, rather, miniature states, almost completely independent of each other for purposes of local government and yet tied together for the purpose of handling matters of mutual concern. Each has a single-house legislature called a "municipal council" which is elected by the voters. Sitting separately, the councils deal with local matters within their respective jurisdictions, but once a year, or oftener at the call of the governor, the two meet jointly in St. Thomas to constitute the "Legislative Assembly of the Virgin Islands." As such they have practically the same powers as legislatures in other unincorporated territories. In 1949 the electorate voted, in what was their first referendum, against proposals to unite the two municipal councils into one, to create one treasury, and to elect the governor by popular vote.

Puerto Rico is represented in Washington by a resident commissioner elected by the voters every 4 years. He is accredited to the executive branch and has a nonvoting seat in the House of Representatives. The Virgin Islands have no representation in Congress.

Puerto Rico is desperately poor and overpopulated. Conditions have been such as to lead to incessant demand for reform, especially for greater local autonomy. A few go so far as to demand complete independence after some such manner as that worked out for the Philippines, while others demand admission to statehood.

SAMOA AND GUAM

American Samoa.—Samoa lies south of the equator, 4,160 miles south of San Francisco and 2,263 miles beyond Hawaii. The Samoan archipelago stretches almost directly east and west and comprises innumerable islands, most of which are very small and uninhabited. The two largest, Savai'i and Upolu, together with a few smaller islands are known as Western Samoa. These belonged to Germany until seized by New Zealand during the First World War and afterward made a mandate under supervision of New Zealand. Eastern, or American Samoa, is made up of the island of Tutuila, a small outlier called Aunuu, and a group of three small islands known collectively as Manua, Rose, and Swains. Altogether, the American islands comprise only 76 square miles. The chief interest of the United States in the islands is its naval base at the Tutuilian harbor of Pago Pago, one of the finest in the South Seas.

Germany, England, and the United States each had claims upon the islands until 1899 when a tripartite arrangement left Eastern Samoa to the Americans. A year later the native chiefs ceded Tutuila and Aunuu to the United States and 4 years later ceded the Manuan and Rose Islands. In 1925 Swains, which had long belonged to American citizens, was annexed. Though an executive order promptly placed the newly acquired islands under command of the Navy, Congress steadfastly refused to accept the islands formally until 1929. The islands must now be classified as an unorganized and unincorporated territory.

Guam.—Guam is the largest and southernmost of the Mariana Islands. It lies 4,000 miles west of Hawaii and only 1,300 miles directly south of Japan among fourteen other tiny islands to which the Japanese fell heir for their participation in the First World War. The island is 30 miles long by 4 to 8½ miles wide, comprising a total of 225 square miles.

Guam was a trophy of the war with Spain. Immediately after its cession to the United States, the whole island was declared a naval station and such it has remained except for the brief interlude when conquered and occupied by the Japanese. Guam may be classified as an unorganized and unincorporated territory. Its people are designated as "citizens of Guam," but they have never been made citizens of the United States. They remain, therefore, merely nationals.

Governments.—In Samoa authority is concentrated in a naval officer, designated by the Secretary of the Navy, who is both governor and commandant of the naval station. The commandant has absolute power, subject to the rules and regulations of the Navy Department and the acts of Congress. The natives are allowed to participate in handling local affairs. Justice is administered by courts manned by naval officers, although natives frequently preside over district and village courts. Appeals may not be taken to courts in the United States; the naval governor's word is final on matters of law.

In Guam, the situation has been much the same. The chief difference has been that a locally elected bicameral legislature has existed for the purpose of advising the governor. An important change occurred in September, 1949, when an executive order set July 1, 1950, as the change-over date from naval to civilian rule under supervision of the Secretary of Interior. In the interim the Navy appointed as civil governor an official proposed by the Interior Department.

In both territories American rule has been paternalistic and despotic, although benevolently so. In response to incessant agitation and disturbances in Samoa, a congressional commission visited the islands in 1930 and later unanimously recommended the substitution of civil government for naval. The same report recommended that the inhabitants be made American citizens.[1] Legislation incorporating these suggestions passed

[1] United States American Samoan Commission, *Report*, Sen. Doc. 249, 71st Cong., 3d Sess. (Washington: Government Printing Office, 1931). See also *Hearings* by the same commission, 71st Cong., 2d Sess. (Washington; Government Printing Office, 1931).

the Senate but was rejected by the House in 1933. In consequence, the Navy still rules and the inhabitants are nationals but not citizens. The islanders have no representation in Washington. In spite of satisfaction on the part of the Navy Department, there is still agitation and strong justification for civil rule. A change similar to that made for Guam is probable in the near future.

THE PANAMA CANAL ZONE

The Panama Canal Zone is a strip of territory leased in perpetuity from the Republic of Panama in 1903. For it the United States agreed to pay an original sum of 10 million dollars and an annual rental of 250 thousand dollars (after 1936, $430,000). The Zone extends 5 miles on each side of the historic canal and includes certain other territory, including islands in the Bay of Panama on the Pacific side. All economic activity centers around the canal, defense establishments, and auxiliary services.

Every resident in the Zone must be an employee of one of the government agencies. Virtually all the inhabitants are white officials and their families from the States, Negroes, or those who are part Negro from the Caribbean region. The population is concentrated at both ends of the canal; however, more (roughly three-fifths) live in the Balboa district nearest the Pacific Ocean than in the Cristobal district nearest the Caribbean.

The Canal Zone is a government reservation administered by an organization known as the Panama Canal. When thought of as a territory it must be classed as one that is unorganized and unincorporated. People born there are nationals but not citizens by the rule of *jus soli*. However, if born of American parents who have previously lived in the United States the requisite period of time,[1] children are citizens. Residents vote for no officer of the United States, unless they do so by mail or return home, and no delegate is sent to Washington.

Government.—There is no legislature in the Zone; all laws must be passed by Congress. Indeed, there is not a single elected official in the entire area. The chief officer is a governor appointed by the President and confirmed by the Senate for a 4-year term.[2] The governor is usually an Army engineer who has previously held the next highest office, that of Engineer of Maintenance. The governor functions under the direction and supervision of the Secretary of Army who acts on behalf of the Presi-

[1] See p. 177.

[2] In time of war or other national emergency, civil government may be displaced by military, in which case the territory is placed under a commanding general. This happened in 1917 and again in 1939.

dent. Past governors have not been political appointees, as has been the case in many of the territories, and this, coupled with the fact that they have had previous training and experience, has resulted in unusually efficient and competent administration.[1]

The civil government is headed by the governor and the engineer of maintenance, who are assisted by a number of administrators, some of whom are Army officers and some civilians. The various military reservations are independent of the civil government and are governed by military and naval officers. The various business enterprises are the property of two agencies—the Panama Canal and the Panama Railroad Company—the capital of which is owned exclusively by the United States. The Panama Canal is an administrative unit directly subject to the President (acting through the Secretary of Army) and Congress, whereas the Panama Railroad Company is a corporation having its own board of directors and being subject to only indirect control from Washington. Both, however, are under the immediate supervision of the governor.[2] Early in 1950 the President took steps to reorganize the two business agencies along lines suggested by the Hoover Commission. Among his suggestions to Congress was one calling for merger of the Panama Canal and the Panama Railroad Company under a corporation to be named the Panama Canal Company. The President did not, however, do as the Hoover Commission suggested and ask for transfer of Canal Zone operations from the Army to Department of Commerce.

The principal court in the Canal Zone is a United States district court divided into two divisions: one for the Balboa district, the other for the Cristobal district. One judge, appointed by the President for a term of 8 years, heads the court and serves both divisions. Minor civil and criminal cases are handled by magistrate courts existing in each town and whose officers are appointed by the governor. Appeals may be taken from the district court to the Fifth Circuit Court of Appeals with headquarters at New Orleans, thence to the Supreme Court.

Local subdivisions, called towns, and rural divisions have been created for administrative purposes. They differ from those usually found in the United States in that they have no local legislature nor executive but only administrators and judicial officers appointed by the governor to perform under supervision of one of the central administrative departments.

[1] Marshall E. Dimock, *Government-operated Enterprises in the Panama Canal Zone* (Chicago: University of Chicago Press, 1934), pp. 18–19; Norman J. Padelford, *The Panama Canal in Peace and War* (New York: Macmillan, 1942), pp. 197–198. See also Hoover Commission: *Federal Business Enterprises* and the Commission's Task Force Report on *Revolving Funds and Business Enterprises of the Government* (Washington: Government Printing Office, 1949).

[2] For a discussion of the functions of these two agencies, see p. 701.

GUANO ISLANDS

Before Chile became a large-scale producer of nitrates, the small islands in the Pacific Ocean were important sources of guano, the accumulated excrement of sea birds. Being of considerable commercial value, shipping companies of various countries engaged in extensive explorations for possession of guano islands around 1841. Their activities led the United States to enact the Guano Island Act of 1856, which provided that whenever an American citizen discovered and occupied an island with guano deposits that did not belong to another country, the President might consider the island as belonging to the United States. The discoverer, meantime, was to be allowed the exclusive right to exploit the guano deposits under the protection of American naval vessels. By authority of this legislation, the United States now lays claim to a number of Pacific islands, but in several instances its claims are disputed by other powers, especially Great Britain and Colombia.[1]

Though title to some of the islands remains in doubt, the United States has fairly clear title to seven—Midway, Wake, Kingman Reef, Johnston, Howland, Baker, and Jarvis. A *status quo* arrangement was entered into in 1928 with Colombia respecting several tiny atolls useful as lighthouse stations, while an agreement was entered into with Great Britain in 1937 whereby both parties agreed to joint use of Canton and Enderbury, leaving the determination of sovereignty until a future date.

Four of the islands just mentioned—Midway, Wake, Kingman Reef, and Johnston—are naval reservations governed by the Navy. These are all uninhabited except for naval personnel who are stationed ashore. The others—Jarvis, Baker, Howland, Canton, and Enderbury—are under the jurisdiction of the Division of Territories and Island Possessions in the Department of the Interior. Actual contact is made by a field representative, located in Honolulu. Though normally uninhabited, groups of four Hawaiians were settled on Jarvis, Baker, and Howland in 1935, while a number of officers and employees of the national government and transpacific air transportation companies are now stationed on Canton and Enderbury. Justice for those not under the Navy is administered by the United States district court in Hawaii, all trials taking place in Honolulu.

TRUST TERRITORIES

The mandate system established by the League of Nations ended when the United Nations came into being in 1945. At the close of the First

[1] For an excellent review of the basis of American claims, see Beatrice Orent and Pauline Reinsch, "Sovereignty over Islands of the Pacific," *The American Journal of International Law*, vol. 35 (July, 1941), pp. 443–461.

World War the United States refused to accept responsibility for mandated territory, but a quarter of a century later sentiment had changed. The Marshall, Caroline, and Mariana Islands had been mandated to Japan as a reward for her contribution during the First World War. Wresting them from the Japanese in the recent conflict proved to be a costly and bloody ordeal. Having done so the United States had the option of annexing and governing the islands as ordinary territories or of accepting trusteeship under the United Nations. Decision did not need to await a peace treaty with Japan, because technically ownership lay with the League of Nations and its successor. The strategic value of the islands could not be gainsaid. A battle royal developed between those in the defense departments who wanted to retain exclusive jurisdiction and those in the Department of State and elsewhere who thought the United States should abstain from what appeared to be territorial aggrandizement. The fact that trust territories might be either strategic or nonstrategic provided a solution. By November, 1946, the decision was reached in favor of strategic trusteeship, and this arrangement was subsequently approved by the United Nations.

The territory includes ninety-eight islands and island clusters, with a total land mass of 846 square miles and a total population of 48,000 native inhabitants. Under the present arrangement the islands are referred to as "trust territory" with the United States designated administering authority. Congress legislates for the islands; the Navy Department governs through a resident commandant in collaboration with native leaders and institutions. Reports must be made to the United Nations; visits, petitions, and questionnaires must be permitted. The United States pledges itself to use the islands to further international peace and security. It also agrees to promote the welfare of the people. It obliges itself to

> promote the development of the inhabitants of the trust territory toward self-government, or independence as may be appropriate to the particular circumstances of the trust territory and its peoples and the freely expressed wishes of the people concerned.[1]

The islands may be fortified. Basic freedoms are guaranteed "subject only to the requirements of public order and security." Citizenship status may be decided by Congress. Members of the United Nations must not be discriminated against. Changes in the trust agreement cannot be "altered, amended or terminated without the consent of the administering authority."[2]

[1] Trusteeship Agreement for the Japanese Mandated Islands, Article 6.

[2] *Ibid.*, Article 15.

United States Trust Territories and Possessions in the Northeast Pacific.

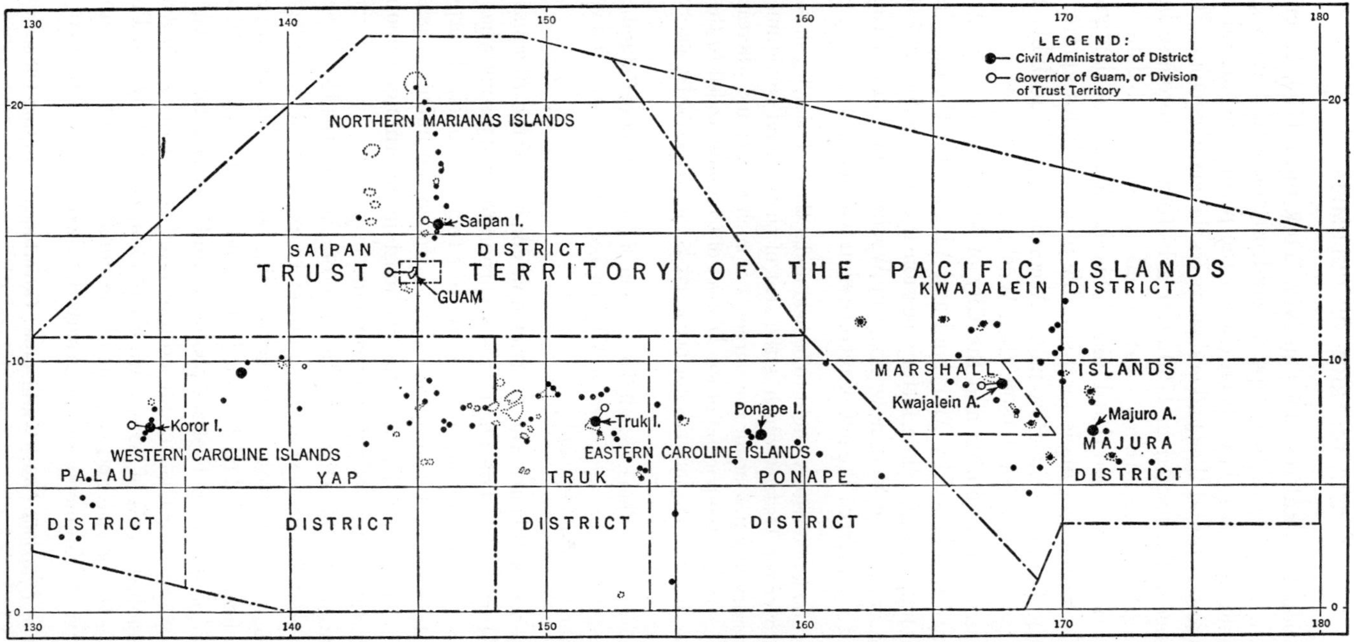

In addition to its prewar possession of Guam, the United States now administers the Marianas, Caroline, and Marshall islands, under a trust agreement with the United Nations.

THE DISTRICT OF COLUMBIA

The national capital remained in New York until 1790, except for a brief sojourn in Trenton to escape an epidemic of scarlet fever. Philadelphia would doubtless have been chosen the permanent capital had the Southern planters found the Quakers' views on slavery congenial. Instead, the Residence Bill, enacted in 1790 after a historic compromise in which the North agreed to a southerly location and the South to federal assumption of state debts, provided that Philadelphia should become the temporary capital while search was made for a suitable plot "10 miles square" somewhere on the banks of the Potomac. Accordingly, Philadelphia became the seat of government until 1800, then Washington.

The District of Columbia and the City of Washington.—An area "10 miles square" was ceded by Maryland and Virginia for the establishment of the national capital. The latter's cession was retroceded in 1846. In view of the congestion that now exists in Washington and environs, it is interesting to read from the act of retrocession which says:

> Whereas no more territory ought to be held under the exclusive legislation given to Congress over the District which is the seat of the General Government than may be necessary and proper for the purposes of such a seat; and whereas experience hath shown that the portion of the District of Columbia ceded to the United States by the State of Virginia has not been, nor is ever likely to be, necessary for that purpose . . . Therefore,
>
> Be it enacted . . . That . . . all that portion of the District of Columbia, ceded to the United States by the State of Virginia be ceded . . . and forever relinquished to the State of Virginia.[1]

In consequence of this act, the District now consists of the 70 square miles ceded by Maryland. The District is a corporate entity somewhat analogous to a county, while within the same territory a municipal corporation known as the City of Washington exists. Hence the name: Washington, District of Columbia. Though the two exist in coterminous boundaries, they are controlled by a single government.

Government of the District.—In view of the constitutional provision which says that *Congress* shall have power to exercise exclusive legislation over the District, Congress is the lawmaking body for the area. A committee has been established by the House and another by the Senate for the purpose of studying District problems and recommending legislation. Laws enacted for the District are administered by a three-member Board of Commissioners, two of whom are civilians appointed by the President by and with the advice and consent of the Senate. The third is an officer of the Corps of Engineers of the Army detailed by the President for an

[1] *District of Columbia Code* (Washington: Government Printing Office, 1940 ed.), vol. I, p. XLVI.

indefinite term, lasting usually about 4 years. The two civilians must be residents of the District; their term is for 3 years, or until replaced. In addition to the commissioners, there are boards, officers, and employees such as one usually finds in any large city. The judiciary consists of a circuit court of appeals, a district court, a municipal court, a juvenile court, and a police court. Judges are all appointed by the President by and with the advice and consent of the Senate. The government of the District is financed in part by an annual lump-sum appropriation made by Congress, and in part from taxes levied by Congress, usually upon the recommendation of the Board of Commissioners.

Disfranchisement of the Residents of the District.—Until 1871 the District was governed by a mayor and legislative council chosen by the people, and between the year mentioned and 1874 the District was represented in the House of Representatives by a delegate chosen by the voters. In spite of having the appearance of being democratic, the locally elected officials were without effective power due to the constitutional provision which says that Congress shall have power to exercise exclusive legislation over the District. After considerable experimentation, the present form of government was created in 1874, whereby residents of the District elect none of the officials who run the government under which they live.

Neither are residents of the District permitted to vote for presidential and vice-presidential electors, or members of Congress. This is because the Constitution requires that "states" appoint electors, that representatives be apportioned among the "states" on the basis of population, and that "states" shall be represented in the Senate. Since the District is not a state, it could obtain representation only by the adoption of a constitutional amendment. A Citizens' Joint Committee on National Representation for the District of Columbia, with affiliated organizations throughout the United States, has worked strenuously to arouse sentiment in favor of a constitutional amendment, but outside a few circles, the American public has shown little interest in the matter.

Meanwhile, residents of the District have worked strenuously for at least the right to choose local officials. This requires no constitutional amendment but merely an act of Congress. Not only does this request appear reasonable, fair, and consistent with democratic theory and practice, but it would also help to relieve a sorely pressed and overburdened Congress. The La Follette-Monroney report of 1946 on the reorganization of Congress[1] proposed self-government as a means of lightening the burden on Congress, but the suggestion was omitted in the act which finally passed. Since then the issue has been before Congress constantly. In 1949 the Senate passed a "home-rule" bill, but the measure remained stymied by a House committee.

[1] P. 286.

Though residents have no vote in the District, a large percentage are able to maintain voting residences in their home states, and both major political parties have influential local organizations in the District which send delegates to the national party conventions. In addition, it should be said that local residents are capable of obtaining a measure of personal representation by having constant access to congressmen from their home states or districts and, of course, the House and Senate committees hold frequent sessions at which interested residents and organizations may appear.

OCCUPIED AREAS

All wars in which the United States has been engaged have involved the government of occupied areas. Although usually for brief periods, the task has been exceptionally difficult and fraught with serious consequences. Some of those responsible for planning operations of the Second World War foresaw the need and set to work planning for military government in occupied territory. Training personnel took place chiefly at the University of Virginia, Columbia University, Fort Custer, Mich., and Civil Affairs Training Schools (CATS) located on various university campuses.[1] Both the Army and Navy trained large numbers of men who later helped organize, direct, and administer military government in North Africa, Italy, Central Europe, the Far East, and Pacific islands. Their work continues in some of these sectors.

Military Law and Administration.—Congress has enacted general and special statutes providing the basic framework and authority of military government. Added to these are the orders of the President, as Commander in Chief, and his duly authorized subordinates. These are supplemented by, and are supposed to be consistent with, the rules of international law and established customs of war.

In Washington, responsibility has centered in the War and Navy Departments, now Defense. Having the military govern civilian populations runs counter to American traditions, and it is generally agreed that the training and experience of military personnel poorly equips them to cope with the many social, economic, and political problems arising during occupation. Accordingly, the assumption has been that as soon as possible civilian personnel will replace military in all phases except possibly helping maintain order. This was strongly recommended by the Hoover Commission.[2]

[1] Harold Zink has written of this experience as well as other aspects of military government in Germany in *American Military Government in Germany* (New York: Macmillan, 1947).

[2] *Report on Overseas Administration*, p. 4–5.

Within occupied territory itself the military commander, sometimes called "governor" or "civil affairs administrator," bears full responsibility. Within limits of military law he has supreme legislative, executive, and judicial authority, although much of this is delegated to subordinates. Military law and orders are enforced through courts-martial. Local sovereignty is suspended, and governments formerly in control exist and function at the discretion of the commander. Control is as strict and extensive as is deemed necessary to achieve the objectives of the occupying power. Generally speaking, the Bill of Rights does not extend to the inhabitants of occupied territory.

Military Government in Europe.—Military government operated in North Africa for many months after invasion in 1942–1943. Later, Italy became the most important theater; still later, Austria and parts of Germany. Usually responsibility was shared with one or more allies. The over-all objective declared by the United States and allies is one of establishing peaceful and responsible communities which never again will constitute a threat to the peace of the world. More particularly, occupation duties consist of maintaining order, trying war criminals, purging those responsible for the war, supplying the necessities of life, coordinating the area with allied policies, commencing rehabilitation, and reestablishing indigenous governments. By the end of 1949 full responsibility had been restored to national governments of formerly occupied territories in Africa and Italy, but not in Germany and Austria. In the latter, the Austrian Central Government had been given considerable authority, but pending conclusion of a peace treaty a four-power council retained limited jurisdiction.

At the Yalta Conference, held in 1945, victorious allied powers established the plan by which Germany has since been governed. A four-power council of foreign ministers was created, with authority to negotiate and oversee. Berlin was placed under jurisdiction of an allied control council upon which each of the four powers was to be represented. The remainder of Germany was divided into four zones. The Soviet Union was made responsible for an eastern zone, Britain for an area in the north and west, France for the area near her border, and the United States for the central and southern area. Until the middle of 1949 the American member of the allied control council for Berlin was also the military governor of the American zone.

Control within the American zone, as in the others, has extended to nearly every phase of life. Meanwhile, experts have devoted themselves to the reestablishment of stable governments to which full responsibility will some day be passed. Quarrels between the occupying powers, particularly between those of the West and the Soviet Union, have seriously retarded efforts. Within the American zone local and state (*Land*) governments were promptly organized along democratic lines[1] and about the middle of 1946 were given considerable authority over matters primarily of local and areal concern. Continued impasse between the occupying powers led the three Western nations to decide in 1948 to establish a central government for their combined zones, leaving Berlin under four-power control until more harmonious relations prevailed between the West and East. A constituent assembly met at Bonn in September, 1948, and drafted a constitution for Western Germany which was later ratified by state (*Land*) legislatures—not by referendum as was seriously proposed. A new state was proclaimed in May, 1949. The new constitution provided for a federal republic, a president chosen by national convention but with little power, a chancellor (or premier) chosen by parliament, bicameral legislature, elaborate bill of rights, independent judiciary, and popular elections. The constitution outlaws "aggressive war" but, unlike the Japanese charter, does not renounce all war. Establishment of the new state led the United States to substitute a civilian high commissioner for military governor and begin transition to complete civilian rule and ultimate withdrawal. Full departure awaits agreement between the major powers and conclusion of a peace treaty with a reconstituted government for the whole of Germany.

Military Government in the Far East.—Events similar to those taking place in Central Europe have been happening in the Far East. The Army is charged with responsibility for military government in Japan and the Ryukyu Islands which stretch in southwesterly direction from the lower part of Japan proper. The Navy now operates military governments in former Japanese islands in the Bonin and Volcano groups. It did likewise for the former Japanese Mandated Islands (the Marshalls, Marianas, and Carolines) until 1946 but since then has governed them as trust territories under the United Nations. As has been noted, it also continues administrative supervision over several American-owned Pacific islands. Today, Japan is the major Far Eastern area under American military government.

The plan of control for Japan was established in conferences between representatives of allied powers. This called for a Far Eastern Commission (FEC) on which powers which have important interests in the area were represented; an Allied Council for Japan (ACJ) with one representative from the United States, one from the Soviet Union, one from China, and one representing jointly the United Kingdom, Australia, New Zealand, and India; and a Supreme Commander of the Allied Powers (SCAP).

The FEC was established to set standards for, and review, Japan's fulfillment of terms of surrender; to review, on request of any member, directives issued by the Supreme Commander; and to consider other matters

[1] A brief review of this experience together with copies of *Land* constitutions may be found in Civil Administration Division, Office of Military Government (US), *Constitutions of the German Laender* (Washington: Office of Military Government, 1947).

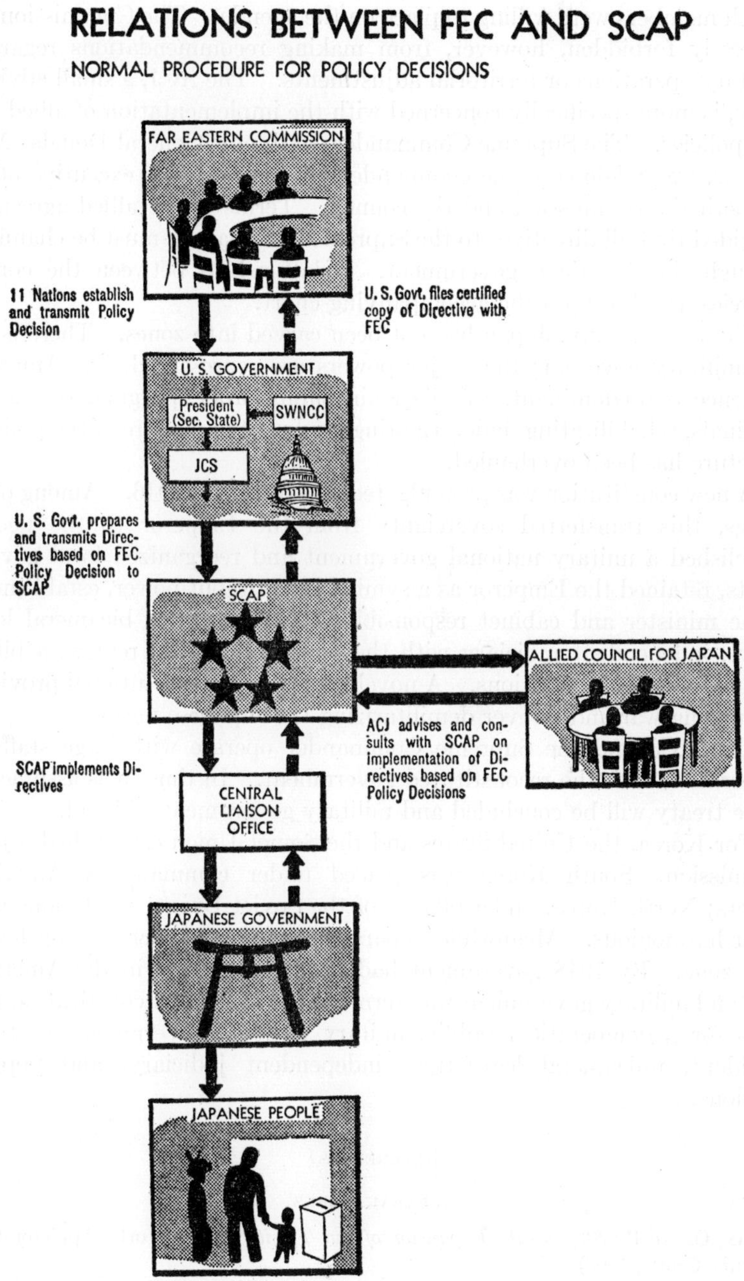

SOURCE: Secretary General FEC, *Activities of the Far Eastern Commission* (Washington: Government Printing Office, 1947).

which members were willing to place on the agenda. The Commission was expressly forbidden, however, from making recommendations regarding military operations or territorial adjustments. The ACJ, a small advisory body, is more specifically concerned with the implementation of allied control policies. The Supreme Commander, until now General Douglas MacArthur, was made supreme commander for the area and executive officer for both the commission and the council. Terms of the allied agreement provided that all directives to the Supreme Commander must be channeled through the American government. Relationships between the control agencies are shown on the accompanying chart.

Unlike Germany, Japan has not been carved into zones. There is but one military governor; the major powers are represented, but American influence is predominant. While maintaining order, purging, trying war criminals, rehabilitating, indoctrinating, and relieving distress, the political structure has been overhauled.

A new constitution was promulgated in November, 1946. Among other things, this transferred sovereignty from the Emperor to the people, established a unitary national government and reorganized local governments, retained the Emperor as a symbol but without power, established a prime minister and cabinet responsible to parliament, a bicameral legislature, independent judiciary with the power of judicial review, a bill of rights, and popular elections. A novel feature is a constitutional provision renouncing war and forever demilitarizing the Japanese nation.

The ACJ and the Supreme Commander operate with large staffs in cooperation with the reconstituted government. In time, it is assumed, a peace treaty will be concluded and military government will end.

For Korea, the United States and the Soviet Union established a joint commission. South Korea was placed under command of American officers; North Korea, under officers of the Soviet Union. Relations were never harmonious. Meanwhile, separate governments were established in each zone. By 1948 government had been reorganized in the American zone and military government was terminated. The new constitution provides for a democratic republic, unitary national government, a strong president, unicameral legislature, independent judiciary, and popular elections.

References[1]

GENERAL WORKS

Austin, Oscar P.: *Steps in the Expansion of Our Territory* (New York: Appleton-Century-Crofts, 1903).

Blanchard, Paul: *Democracy and Empire in the Caribbean; A Contemporary Review* (New York: Macmillan, 1947).

[1] Consult also innumerable government documents pertaining to particular areas.

DULLES, FOSTER H.: *America in the Pacific, a Century of Expansion* (Boston: Houghton, 1932).

FARRAND, MAX: *The Legislation of Congress for the Government of the Organized Territories of the United States 1789–1895* (Newark: Baker, 1896).

HAAS, WILLIAM (ed.): *The American Empire* (Chicago: The University of Chicago Press, 1940).

HALL, H. DUNCAN: *Mandates, Dependencies, and Trusteeships* (Washington, D.C.: Carnegie Endowment, 1949).

REID, CHARLES F.: *Overseas America, Our Territorial Outposts* (New York: Foreign Policy Association, 1942).

REMINGTON, WOODBERN E.: *Cross Winds of Empire* (New York: Day, 1941).

UNITED STATES DEPARTMENT OF COMMERCE, BUREAU OF THE CENSUS, *Fifteenth Census of the United States—1930—Outlying Territories and Possessions* (Washington: Government Printing Office, 1932).

UNITED STATES DEPARTMENT OF INTERIOR, Annual reports of governors of the respective territories (Washington: Government Printing Office).

——— General information regarding each of the territories (Washington: Government Printing Office).

WEINBERG, ALBERT K.: *Manifest Destiny, a Study of Nationalist Expansionism in American History* (Baltimore: The Johns Hopkins Press, 1935).

ALASKA

ALASKA PLANNING COUNCIL: *Alaska Development Plan* (Juneau, Alaska: Planning Council, January, 1941).

——— *General Information Regarding Alaska* (Juneau, Alaska: Planning Council, 1941).

ANDERSON, H. DEWEY, and WALTER C. EELLS: *Alaska Natives. A Survey of Their Sociological and Educational Status* (Stanford: Stanford University Press, 1935).

COLBY, MERLE E. (American Guide Series): *A Guide to Alaska, Last American Frontier* (New York: Macmillan, 1939).

PILGRIM, MARIETTA S.: *Alaska, Its History, Resources, Geography, and Government* (Caldwell, Idaho: Caxton Printers, Ltd., 1939).

SPICER, GEORGE W.: *The Constitutional Status and Government of Alaska* (Baltimore: The Johns Hopkins Press, 1927).

UNITED STATES NATIONAL RESOURCES COMMITTEE: *Regional Planning—Alaska, Its Resources and Development* (Washington: Government Printing Office, 1937).

HAWAII

BARBER, JOSEPH, JR.: *Hawaii: Restless Rampart* (Indianapolis: Bobbs-Merrill, 1941).

CHAMBERS, HENRY: *Constitutional History of Hawaii* (Baltimore: The Johns Hopkins Press, 1896).

CLARK, THOMAS B.: *Hawaii, the Forty-ninth State* (New York: Doubleday, 1947).

FERGUSSON, ERNA: *Our Hawaii* (New York: Knopf, 1942).

PRATT, JULIUS W.: *Expansionists of 1898; the Acquisition of Hawaii and the Spanish Islands* (Baltimore: The Johns Hopkins Press, 1936).

PUERTO RICO

DIFFIE, BAILEY W., and JUSTINE W. DIFFIE: *Puerto Rico: A Broken Pledge* (New York: Vanguard, 1931).

FEDERAL WRITERS' PROJECT (American Guide Series): *Puerto Rico: A Guide to the Island of Boriquen* (New York: The University Society, Inc., 1940).

PAGAN, BOLIVAR: *Puerto Rico: The Next State* (Washington, D.C.: Privately printed, 1942).

PETRULLO, VINCENZO: *Puerto Rican Paradox* (Philadelphia: University of Pennsylvania Press, 1947).

TUGWELL, REXFORD G.: *The Stricken Land: the Story of Puerto Rico* (New York: Doubleday, 1947).

VAN DEUSEN, RICHARD J., and ELIZABETH K. VAN DEUSEN: *Puerto Rico: A Caribbean Isle* (New York: Holt, 1931).

THE VIRGIN ISLANDS

TANSILL, CHARLES C.: *The Purchase of the Danish West Indies* (Baltimore: The Johns Hopkins Press, 1932).

THE PANAMA CANAL ZONE

DIMOCK, MARSHALL E.: *Government-operated Enterprises in the Panama Canal Zone* (Chicago: University of Chicago Press, 1934).

PADELFORD, NORMAN J.: *The Panama Canal in Peace and War* (New York: Macmillan, 1942).

SMITH, DARRELL H.: *The Panama Canal, Its History, Activities, and Organization* (Baltimore: The Johns Hopkins Press, 1927).

SAMOA, GUAM, AND OTHER PACIFIC ISLES

KEESING, FELIX M.: *Modern Samoa* (Stanford University, Calif.: Stanford University Press, 1934).

——— *The South Seas in the Modern World* (New York: Day, 1941).

LEFF, DAVID N.: *Uncle Sam's Pacific Islets* (Stanford University, Calif.: Stanford University Press, 1940).

RYDEN, GEORGE H.: *The Foreign Policy of the United States in Relation to Samoa* (New Haven: Yale University Press, 1933).

THOMPSON, LAURA: *Guam and Its People; A Study of Cultural Change and Colonial Education* (San Francisco: American Council, Institute of Pacific Relations, 1941).

UNITED STATES NAVY: *Handbook on the Trust Territory of the Pacific Isles* (Washington: Government Printing Office, 1948).

——— *Trust Territory of the Pacific Islands* (Washington: Navy Department, 1948).

WASHINGTON, D.C.

CAEMMERER, HANS P.: *A Manual on the Origin and Development of Washington* (Washington: Government Printing Office, 1939).

——— *Washington: The National Capital* (Washington: Government Printing Office, 1932).

FEDERAL WRITERS' PROJECT (American Guide Series): *Washington: City and Capital* (Washington: Government Printing Office, 1937).

OCCUPIED AREAS

FRIEDRICH, CARL J.: *American Experiences in Military Government in World War II* (New York: Rinehart, 1948).

MOULTON, HAROLD G., and LOUIS MARLIO: *The Control of Germany and Japan* (Washington: Brookings, 1944).

UTLEY, FREDA: *The High Cost of Vengeance* (Chicago: Regnery, 1949).

YANAGA, CHITOSHI: *Japan since Perry* (New York: McGraw-Hill, 1949).

ZINK, HAROLD: *American Military Government in Germany* (New York: Macmillan, 1947).

Chapter 27

NATIONAL DEFENSE AND WAR MEASURES

What, then, is the source of our strength? That source is our ethical and moral standards of precepts, and our democratic faith in man. This faith is the chief armament of our democracy. It is the most potent weapon ever devised. Compared with it, the atomic bomb is a firecracker.

David E. Lilienthal, Chairman, Atomic Energy Commission.[1]

War is an ancient institution. Its causes are many. Throughout history it has been used by social groups both as an instrument of defense and as a method of trying to advance group interests. Modern wars have become extremely devastating and costly, in terms of both wealth and human resources, with the result that the primary problem of modern times is one of devising means whereby peoples of the world can live together in peace and harmony.

The Problem of Security.—Where the issues are so important, it is natural that opinions differ sharply. Some insist that human nature is so cussed as to make war inevitable. To them the fact that there have always been wars is positive proof that they will recur in the future. Those of this opinion are usually skeptical of peace programs but advocate instead a program of unilateral national preparedness as the method most likely to minimize the possibility of war and ensure victory if it should come. To them preparedness is a form of national insurance against inevitable wars.

Others insist that man is naturally a cooperative, social creature, capable of evolving a social system in which wars are minimized or entirely eliminated. This group is generally skeptical of obtaining security through a program of national preparedness. They deny the appropriateness of calling preparedness insurance. The latter provides security against such things as accidents, fires, floods, sickness, and death, whereas national defenses are directed at other people or communities. Insurance does not create in others fear and suspicion leading to counter defensive plans, but national armaments do. Thus, this group believes that instead of contributing to peace and security, armaments actually sow the seeds of war. Accordingly, those of this persuasion urge reduction of armaments, the broadening of understanding among races, the gradual transfer of loyalty from national states to larger legal and political units, and the erection of international machinery through which disputes among nations

[1] *The New York Times Magazine*, Mar. 6, 1949, p. 11.

can be settled by amicable or legal procedures rather than by recourse to international violence.

The average American finds himself groping somewhere in between these two schools of thought. While his hopes and reason subscribe to the second, he is nevertheless inclined to be dubious of the practicability of world-peace plans, and unwilling to dispense with armaments. Discovery of such instruments of wholesale death as the atom bomb has only intensified the confusion. But, on the whole, there is an increasing tendency to agree that nations must now cooperate or perish.

Meaning of "Adequate" Defense.—Almost every speaker on the subject pledges support for "adequate" defense. But what is adequate? The term is obviously relative. No defenses at all are adequate along the 3,000 mile Canadian border. Virtually no navy and a small army were adequate before 1900. What might be adequate for the defense of continental United States would be insufficient to carry the attack to another continent. What might be adequate for a small agrarian nation might not be for a large imperialist power. What would be adequate with allies would not be without them. What was adequate before the atom bomb is less so now. Obviously, the concept of adequacy is variable. It depends upon geography, the amount of good will that exists, the strength of allies and potential enemies, technological developments, and foreign and domestic policies followed by various countries of the world. All this suggests that national defense programs cannot be static but must be adapted to changing conditions. It also suggests that in the long run the best defense is a program designed to minimize world tensions.

DEPARTMENTAL FEDERATION AND UNIFICATION

From Separate to Federated Departments.—With postwar expenditures for national defense reaching staggering sums and accounting for a third or more of all federal expenditures, attention was naturally drawn to ways and means of ensuring maximum returns. Until 1947 the War and Navy Departments were organically separate, and each had its own nearly autonomous air force. Coordination was obtained through liaison officers, joint meetings of chiefs of staff, committees, boards, cabinet officers, and conferences with the President. Over the years many complained of this separation, alleging that it prevented integrated planning, that it led to rivalries for public and congressional favor, that it encouraged competition in recruitment and procurement, and that it led to duplication, inefficiency, and confusion. The experience of both world wars indicated the necessity for a unified command, which was achieved only after expensive delays, while the disaster at Pearl Harbor was attributed in large measure to the division of responsibility between the Army and the Navy. Unification, with a single supreme command over both departments, resting in one person directly responsible to the President, was urged. Opponents resisted, saying that a single chief would inevitably show preference for one branch or another; that a single head would become so powerful as to dominate other branches of the government; and that greater efficiency, economy, and striking power would not result. They pointed with pride to the long record of achievements under separate departments.

Those favoring unification launched a vigorous campaign shortly after the recent war closed. President Truman, the Army, and their partisans favored change; the Navy and its friends opposed. Extensive hearings were held and various proposals were widely debated both in and out of Congress. Washington has seldom, if ever, witnessed a more bitter and intransigent struggle. A partial solution was provided in the National Security Act of 1947. While this represented a victory for proponents of change, it was never fully satisfactory to them, nor did it end interservice feuding. Instead of outright unification it achieved more nearly what has been called departmental federation.

The National Security Act.—The act of 1947 authorized a National Military Establishment within which were three departments—Army, Navy, and Air Force. The first was to be headed by a Secretary of Defense appointed by the President with Senate approval. Each of the three subordinate departments was also given a secretary appointed similarly. All four secretaries were to be civilians. Only the Secretary of Defense was made a member of the President's cabinet. Of him, the law said he "shall be the principal assistant to the President on all matters relating to national security."

The Secretary of Defense was given general direction of the three departments and allied agencies; he was required to take appropriate steps to eliminate unnecessary duplication and overlapping; he was charged with supervising and coordinating budget preparation and execution. Nevertheless, the law expressly stated that the three departments "shall be administered as individual executive departments by their respective Secretaries and all powers and duties relating to such departments not specifically conferred upon the Secretary of Defense by this Act shall be retained by each of their respective Secretaries." It also provided that each department chief might, after informing the Secretary of Defense, make reports and recommendations directly to the President and Director of the Budget.

The act established three additional agencies for defense planning and coordination. The first was a National Security Council whose membership, the statute prescribed, should consist of the President, Secretary of State, Secretary of Defense and his three subdepartment chiefs, Chairman of the National Security Resources Board, and other officers to be designated by the President with Senate approval. The Council's primary purpose was to be that of advising the President and Congress on ways and means of integrating domestic, foreign, and military policies relating to national security. A General Intelligence Agency was the second authorized. Its function was to be one of reviewing, coordinating, and evaluating existing intelligence agencies and their data bearing upon national security. It was not, the statute declared, to have "police, subpoena, law-enforcement, or internal security functions," nor was it to displace or duplicate the work of existing intelligence bodies. A National Security Resources Board was the third agency authorized. Membership should consist of a civilian chairman and representatives of other departments and agencies designated by the President. The Board's function was to be one of developing plans for military, industrial, and civilian mobilization. In addition to these three agencies, the act authorized several more within the National Military Establishment itself for purposes of collaboration and joint action. Among these were a War Council, Joint Chiefs of Staff, Joint Staff, Munitions Board, and Research and Development Board.

Criticisms of the National Security Organization.—As indicated above, the 1947 legislation was not fully satisfactory to many advocates of unification. The President and Secretary of Defense were both outspokenly in favor of further changes.

The Hoover Commission was especially critical.[1] After stressing that the three essentials of good government management are efficiency, economy, and clear accountability to Congress and the people, the commission went on to say, "The National Military Establishment as set up under the act of 1947 is perilously close to the weakest type of department." The Commission reported continued disharmony and lack of unified planning, extravagance in military budgets and waste in expenditure, interservice rivalries, and lack of close working relationship among important segments of the defense structure. It supported the contention that the President and Secretary of Defense had too little authority, and it insisted that, as the department was then constituted, civilian control was in jeopardy.

To correct these shortcomings the Commission made numerous detailed recommendations that cannot be fully recited here. Their essence was that full responsibility for policy formulation and administration be centered in the Secretary of Defense, subject only to the President and Congress. To this end they suggested that all statutory authority then vested in the service departments, or their subordinate units, be granted directly to the Secretary of Defense. To indicate subordinacy of service secre-

[1] *The National Security Organization* (Washington: Government Printing Office, 1949).

taries, the Commission suggested their titles be changed to "undersecretary." Adoption of these and other recommendations, the Commission reported, would change departmental federation to real unification.

1949 Unification.—In Congress, prompt consideration was given to this sector of the Hoover Commission report and some of its recommendations were adopted in July, 1949. The National Military Establishment was changed to Defense Department with rank next below State. The Army, Navy, and Air Force Departments were retained with "military" but not "cabinet" status. Heads of the military departments retained the title of "secretary." The Defense Secretary was given "authority, direction, and control" over all three services, but under a compromise worked out in conference committee, the secretary is required to report to the House and Senate Armed Services Committees before giving any order "substantially" affecting the statutory functions of the military departments. The Defense Secretary was required to report twice yearly to Congress rather than once like other departments, while the military departments were authorized to bring any problem and make recommendations to Congress independently of the Defense Secretary. The post of Deputy Undersecretary replaced that of Defense Undersecretary, and three Assistant Defense Secretaries (not to be confused with secretaries of the military establishments) were authorized. A Joint Chiefs of Staff chairman was established, who is to be the principal adviser to the President and Defense Secretary but who has no vote at Joint Chiefs of Staff meetings. The President was authorized to appoint any cabinet members to the National Secretary Council provided these nominations were confirmed by the Senate. Finally, fiscal and budgetary reorganization was ordered, with the performance-type budget made mandatory. These provisions, it will be observed, incorporate some important recommendations of the Hoover Commission but leave vestiges of privileges formerly enjoyed by the military departments.

Present Defense Organization.—In the Executive office of the President are several interdepartmental planning and coordinating agencies, among them the National Security Council, National Resources Board, and the Central Intelligence Agency. The latter agency operates with the greatest secrecy. Unlike most, it is not required to publish or disclose its organization, functions, names, official titles, salaries, or even the numbers of personnel employed. The Budget Bureau is forbidden to make reports disclosing the agency's operations, and funds may be spent without regard for the usual laws and regulations. As noted elsewhere,[1] the Agency may, with approval of the Attorney General and Commissioner of Immigration, admit alien informers and their immediate families for permanent residence without regard for quotas or other immigration restrictions.

[1] P. 168.

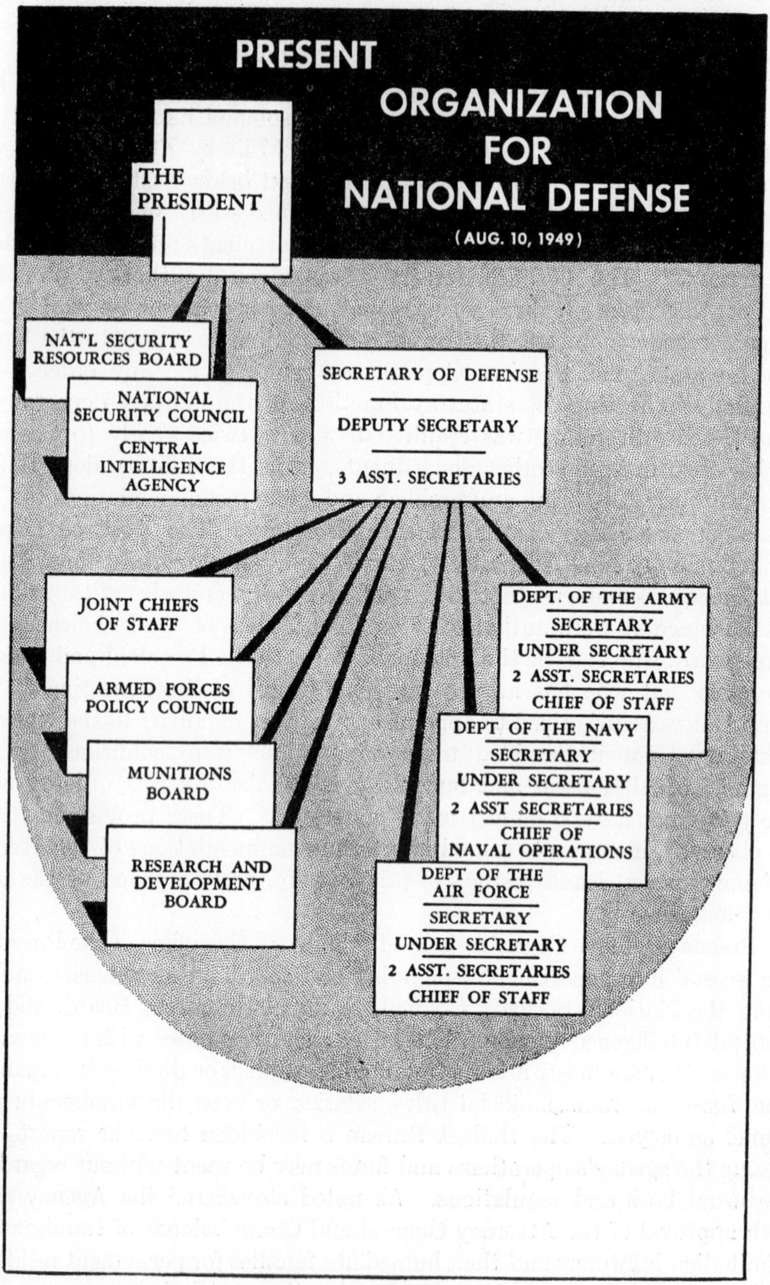
PRESENT
ORGANIZATION
FOR
NATIONAL DEFENSE
(AUG. 10, 1949)
THE PRESIDENT
NAT'L SECURITY RESOURCES BOARD
NATIONAL SECURITY COUNCIL
CENTRAL INTELLIGENCE AGENCY
SECRETARY OF DEFENSE
DEPUTY SECRETARY
3 ASST. SECRETARIES
JOINT CHIEFS OF STAFF
ARMED FORCES POLICY COUNCIL
MUNITIONS BOARD
RESEARCH AND DEVELOPMENT BOARD
DEPT. OF THE ARMY
SECRETARY
UNDER SECRETARY
2 ASST. SECRETARIES
CHIEF OF STAFF
DEPT OF THE NAVY
SECRETARY
UNDER SECRETARY
2 ASST SECRETARIES
CHIEF OF NAVAL OPERATIONS
DEPT OF THE AIR FORCE
SECRETARY
UNDER SECRETARY
2 ASST. SECRETARIES
CHIEF OF STAFF

SOURCE: Data supplied by United States Defense Department.

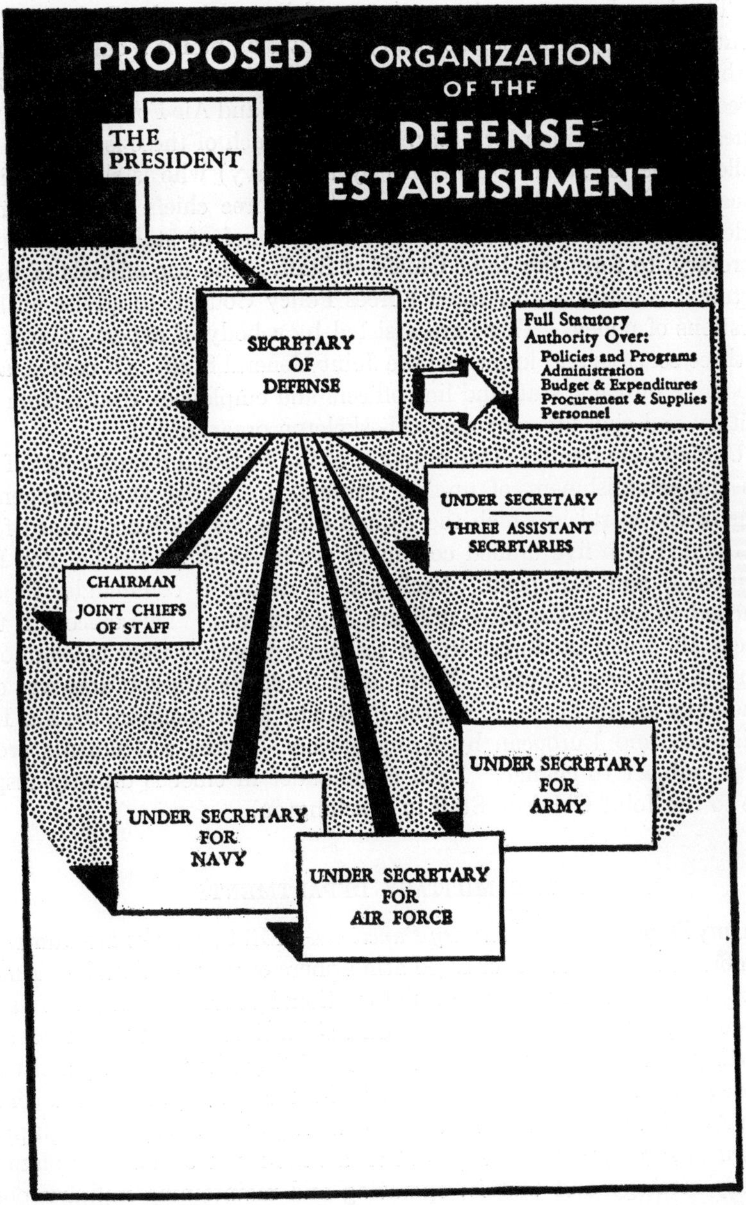

The National Security Act amendments adopted by the Eighty-first Congress, First session, fell short of the proposals of the Hoover Commission. The civilian heads of the three armed services were not reduced to undersecretaries, but the Secretary of Defense got more help and was given power to appoint the chairman of the Joint Chiefs of Staff. SOURCE: Hoover Commission, *Concluding Report*, p. 58.

The interdepartmental agencies are followed by the Defense Department, headed by a civilian secretary. Advising him is a chief of staff who is the nation's top military officer. Within the Defense Department are three subordinate departments (Army, Navy, and Air Force) each of which is headed by a civilian secretary. Advising each of these is a chief of staff (called Chief of Naval Operations by the Navy) who is the top military officer in his particular department. The three chiefs of staff combine, under the nonvoting chairmanship of the chief of staff to the Defense Secretary, to form the Joint Chiefs of Staff. The top officials of the department constitute an Armed Forces Policy Council to advise on broad questions of policy. These are assisted by a body of experts drawn from all three services and known as the Joint General Staff. Of course, a host of boards, bureaus, staff and line officers and employees, drawn from both military and civil life, surround this skeleton organization.

Unified Commands.—One outcome of the National Security Act of 1947 was the establishment of unified commands. Under this arrangement, areas of the world in which the United States has stationed armed forces are divided into five unified command areas: Alaskan, Pacific, Far East, Caribbean, and European. Each area is under a commander in chief attached to one of the three military departments. This officer, in turn, directs all American forces in his territory, whether they belong to the Army, Navy, or Air Force. Thus, as of 1948, the Alaskan area was commanded by an Air Force officer; the Pacific by a Navy officer; the Far East, Caribbean, and European by Army officers. These assignments are, of course, subject to change. Each commander in chief is directly responsible to the Joint Chiefs of Staff in Washington.

THE MILITARY DEPARTMENTS

Army Department. *Military Functions.*—Military tasks are numerous, the more so because of the charged atmosphere of the past decade. Among others, they include helping formulate national policies on matters relating to security; collaboration with the United Nations on security measures; operating or assisting government in occupied areas; providing assistance to special overseas missions like those in Greece, Turkey, Iran, and certain Latin American countries; recruiting, training, disciplining, and equipping the armed forces; fostering research on a wide range of matters; planning military strategy and tactics; operating and maintaining military posts, vessels, and establishments; keeping informed about military plans and resources of other nations; collaborating with National Guard units; and helping maintain order when ordered to do so by the President.

Civilian Functions.—In addition to military functions, the Army Department has been given numerous duties of a civil nature. It governs the

Panama Canal and business operations within the Zone.[1] The Corps of Engineers helps the Federal Power Commission investigate water-power sites; it develops and executes plans for improvement of harbors and rivers, flood control, and the generation of hydroelectric power and irrigation.[2] The department makes surveys of the Great Lakes and international water boundaries. It constructs national monuments and memorials; assists communities stricken with disaster; preserves the American Niagara Falls; establishes harbor lines; approves plans and issues permits for bridges and other construction on navigable waters; removes wrecks from, and regulates the use of, navigable waters. Imposing as this list appears, the major proportion of the funds and personnel of the department are devoted to military matters.

Service Areas and Commands.—Headquarters for the Army are, of course, in Washington. But throughout the country numerous matters are handled by area offices. Six areas exist, each with a headquarters and commanding officer. Abroad, similar functions are performed by the five commands mentioned above.

Components of the Army.—The Army of the United States consists of the Regular Army, the National Guard while in the service of the federal government, and the Organized Reserves, including the Officers' Reserve Corps and the Enlisted Reserve Corps.

The Regular Army is a permanent, professional force made up of officers and soldiers who have chosen the Army as a career or who may have been drafted. It consists also, since 1948, of a Women's Army Corps (WAC).

The National Guard consists of two parts: one, for the District of Columbia and territories like Hawaii and Alaska, is under the exclusive control of the Regular Army; the other is, during normal times, a state organization. Although largely financed by the Federal government and trained in accordance with discipline prescribed by the Regular Army, state Guard units are officered and trained by state appointees. This duality of responsibility helps explain the constant undertone of hostility and friction that exists between officers of the Regular Army and those of the state Guards. The officers and men of the Guard are volunteers who take regular training at armories near home or at special encampments. During wartime or national emergencies the Guard may be called into federal service, during which it loses its state character and becomes an indistinguishable part of the federal army.[3]

The Organized Reserve is made up of volunteer officers, men, and (since 1948) women. This is a federal reserve entirely unrelated to the National

[1] These are discussed on pp. 701–703.

[2] See also p. 715.

[3] See also p. 414.

Guard. Older members are generally those who have served in previous wars; younger ones usually receive their training in college Reserve Officer Training Corps (ROTC) units or in special Citizens' Military Training Camps. Members generally remain on an inactive status without pay, although they may be occasionally ordered to spend short periods in active duty. During wartime or national emergencies they may, of course, be called into active service.

Navy Department. *Functions.*—The duties of the Navy Department are numerous, varied, and far-flung. Its staff also helps formulate national policies and plans for war. It helps promote research designed to improve naval operations. It designs ships, operates a number of yards for shipbuilding, and oversees construction by private companies. It maintains and deploys the fleet. It governs several Pacific islands and supports American forces in occupied areas.[1] It recruits, trains, and disciplines personnel. It aids the development and building of bases, ports, and harbor facilities at home and at many places abroad. It operates a number of naval hospitals and a home in Philadelphia for aged servicemen. It operates a radio system for communication with vessels. It sends officers to advise friendly foreign governments, and it frequently dispatches ships to strategic areas to support foreign policy. It handles leases of enormous oil reserves in Alaska and western United States. It manufactures numerous supplies and equipment needed for naval operation and maintenance.

Components of the Navy.—The Navy consists of the Regular Navy, Marine Corps, Coast Guard, Naval Reserve, Naval Air Reserve, and Marine Corps Reserve. The Regular Navy is a permanent professional force of male and female officers and enlisted personnel. The Marine Corps comprises the Navy's personnel who are especially trained and equipped for landing operations, land fighting, and occupation. The Coast Guard is a part of the Navy at all times, although it operates under the Treasury Department in peacetime. It serves as the seaboard police for the nation and as an auxiliary to the Navy and merchant marine. The various reserves exist to provide a force of qualified officers and enlisted men available for immediate mobilization.

The Fleet.—The fleet consists of all fighting ships and auxiliary vessels assigned to the Navy Department. It is divided into "capital" ships, meaning battleships, which are huge, heavily armed carriers of destruction; cruisers, which are smaller, faster, and more lightly armed; aircraft carriers; destroyers, which are especially designed and armed for pursuit and convoy duty; submarines; and auxiliary craft. In 1948–1949 about a third of the total fleet was in active duty; the remainder was in "moth balls" at "berthing areas" along the American coast.

Most naval vessels in active service are divided about equally between

[1] See p. 575.

two major fleets, the Atlantic and Pacific. For operational purposes the two major fleets are organized into task fleets and forces and subdivisions thereof.

Air Force Department. *Reasons for a Separate Air Force.*—Air power first demonstrated its military importance during the First World War. Ever since, there have been sharp differences of opinion over the future potential of air power and the best methods of development and use. Before 1947 the War and Navy Departments each had an air force of its own. This was justified on the ground that forces could best be developed and directed by the departments whose land or naval operations they were intended to assist. Thus, the Navy could best train and direct pilots and planes used to supply and support naval operations; the Army could best train and direct pilots and planes used to supply and support land operations. When cooperation was desired it was assumed this could be achieved through joint conferences, committees, and the President.

Although it was obvious to all that the separate air forces played an important role in the Second World War, many thought a better job could have been done if responsibility had not been as divided as it was. Many also believed that if left under the Army and Navy the air force would be neglected by departmental officers whose chief interests lay with other phases of defense. Foreseeing future wars when air power would be even more decisive, champions insisted upon an autonomous air force equipped with sufficient money and man power to keep abreast of the rapid technological changes that lay ahead. As indicated above, passage of the National Security Act of 1947 authorized a separate Department of Air Force with rank equal to those of the Army and Navy. Today, the Army and Navy have relatively few aircraft, and these are used chiefly for local supporting operations.

Air Force Department Functions.—Being new, the Air Force Department has not been saddled with functions unrelated to its major objectives. Like the other military departments, one of its primary duties is that of helping formulate national policies on matters related to security. The department must collaborate intimately with other agencies, particularly those concerned chiefly with defense, in order to secure maximum coordination and economy. In no field is scientific research more decisive; accordingly, a large part of the department's attention is devoted to such matters. The department also keeps informed about the air power of other nations. For this purpose, it maintains attachés in other nations and collaborates with United States intelligence agencies. It also supports government in occupied areas and special missions to friendly countries. Recruiting, training, and disciplining personnel is a primary task, for which the 1948 draft law has not been used. Planning home defenses is an important assignment, made more so by the omnipresent threat of "push-button" warfare with rockets, disease germs, and atomic weapons. Procuring equipment and supplies and planning for industrial mobilization are also important tasks.

Components of the Air Force.—The Air Force consists of a body of professional officers and enlisted personnel. Since 1948 women may enlist and become officers. Civilians may enroll in the Air National Guard, the Air Force Reserve, the Air Reserve Officer Training Corps (Air ROTC), Civil Air Patrol, or Air Scouts. The first three are similar to their counterparts in other branches of the service. The Air Patrol is a legal auxiliary of a semimilitary character. Its purpose is to enroll, train, and equip air-minded citizens to meet local and national emergencies and to generally promote the advancement of aviation. Air Scouts are given nonmilitary training in aeronautics, communications, and navigation. A limited number of Senior Scouts attend summer encampments, and a few are taken for short flights as passengers.

Training Schools.—Officers are trained for all branches of the service in existing civilian institutions and those especially provided for the purpose. For the Army, the United States Military Academy located at West Point, on the Hudson River north of New York City, is the principal training center for officers. The United States Naval Academy located at Annapolis, Md., a short distance east of Washington, D. C., plays a similar role for the Navy. The Coast Guard maintains an academy at New London, Conn. The Air Force does not have a similar institution, but in the past it has drawn heavily from West Point graduates. If unification succeeds, the Air Force may draw equally from both institutions; otherwise, it may press for a separate academy. For postgraduate or in-service officers' training, three schools are held jointly by the military departments. The National War College emphasizes the broad aspects of national policy with emphasis upon foreign policy, international relations and law, and logistics. The Industrial War College stresses the economic problems of mobilization and war. The Armed Forces Staff College deals especially with problems of administration. In addition, selected officers are assigned for special study to civilian educational institutions, and a number of specialized schools are conducted by each of the three military departments. Interestingly, the Air Force Department has what it calls the Air University consisting of the Air Tactical School, the Air Command and Staff School, and the Air War College.

VOLUNTEERS OR CONSCRIPTS?

Past Use of Conscription.—Throughout most of our history military and naval personnel have been obtained by volunteer enlistment, the exceptions occurring during the Civil War, First World War, the last war, and since.

Although conscription worked badly during the Civil War, it worked smoothly during the First World War and the same pattern has been followed since. The first instance of peacetime conscription occurred with the adoption of the Selective Training and Service Act in September, 1940—more than a year before Pearl Harbor but at a time when it was obvious that the United States was becoming increasingly involved in the war. Conscription was continued throughout the war and for several months after V-J Day. When the act expired in May, 1946, it was first extended for only 6 weeks and then renewed on a much restricted basis until the following Mar. 31. Then it expired.

Campaign for a Permanent Draft.—Almost a year before the war ended, a campaign was launched to obtain enactment of a peacetime conscription statute. Those favoring an immediate decision argued that with the matter settled the military departments would know how many officers, facilities, and pieces of equipment should be kept for the purpose. They also contended that a decision at that time would serve notice to friend and foe of intention to keep strongly armed after the war. Most advocates also frankly admitted that they had long favored a draft and thought it would be easier to obtain its enactment during wartime than after the nation had returned to peacetime habits. This campaign was strongly resisted both by those who objected as a matter of principle and by those who thought it unwise and unfair to adopt such a far-reaching proposal under wartime circumstances and at a time when thousands of servicemen who would be seriously affected were prevented from participating in the decision. The campaign failed of its immediate objective. But when war ended, and especially as the wartime draft neared termination, the drive was intensified.

Spearheading the campaign were President Truman, his defense advisers, major veterans' groups, the United States Chamber of Commerce, some important newspapers and periodicals (notably *The New York Times* and the Hearst press), and scattered individual educators. Some wanted Universal Military Training (UMT), which would require young men to spend a year or two training in the Army. Others wanted a plan whereby young men would take part of their training in the Army, the remainder in the National Guard, ROTC, or special encampments. Under both plans emphasis was to be placed upon *training* rather than actual *service* in the armed forces. Others preferred outright federal draft for training and service similar to wartime practices.[1] Under these plans it was variously

[1] Various plans are outlined and defended in United States House of Representatives, Select Committee in Postwar Military Policy, *Universal Military Training, Hearings* 79th Cong., 1st Sess., pursuant to H. Res. 465 (Washington: Government Printing Office, 2 parts, 1945). General Marshall's views are set forth in his *Biennial Report of the Chief of Staff of the United States Army . . . to the Secretary of War* (Washington:

estimated that approximately a million youths would be drafted annually, about 175,000 officers would be required for instructional purposes, and the cost would amount to two or three billion dollars annually.[1]

Arguments Favoring Universal Training.—Advocates of conscription argue that there is nothing in the present situation to justify the expectation that there will not be another war; hence the United States must remain "fully prepared." A choice must be made between a large standing army with a small trained reserve, or a small standing army and a huge citizen reserve comprised largely of those who have had at least one year of training. The latter is preferred because a large standing army is contrary to American tradition, all citizens need to be trained to fight a total war which may come unexpectedly and quickly, and it would prove cheaper in the long run. Adoption of this plan, it is argued, would not arouse fear and suspicion in other nations but rather would serve notice of intention to back up commitments made under the United Nations Charter. It is further suggested that this show of determination and force would increase national bargaining strength at the conference table, especially with Russia. Finally, it is urged that the training would improve the patriotism, health, morals, religion, skills, and minds of those who take the training.

Arguments against Peacetime Training.—Opposed to the proposals are virtually all important religious, educational, liberal, farm, and labor organizations. They insist that such a plan is alien to American life; countries that have had conscription often have been dictatorial and warlike; countries like France, that have long had conscription in peacetime, were not necessarily better prepared when war came because of it; it will lead to military domination of civilian life; the training of all youths will be wasteful because most of them will never see combat or if war does come they will need to be retrained, especially since the character of warfare is rapidly changing; the billions of dollars spent on a program of this type could be better spent on scientific research, public health, and education; if adopted it would encourage other nations to do likewise, thus leading to an armament race, especially with Russia; its adoption would be an evidence of lack of faith in world cooperation and collective security; and that patriotism, health, religion, morals, knowledge and skills can be better taught as traditionally by the home, school, and church.

Special Handling of Conscientious Objectors.—During the Civil War religious objectors who were members of "historic peace churches" were allowed by the Union government to perform noncombatant service in

---

Government Printing Office, 1945), pp. 117–123; President Truman's views were given in a public address on Oct. 23, 1945, a copy of which may be found in *The New York Times* for the following day.

[1] Constitutionality is discussed on p. 405.

hospitals or in the care of freedmen; and, like other citizens, they had the privilege of purchasing exemption for $300, the money going to care for the sick and wounded. In the South there was no provision for noncombatant service but exemption could be bought for $500. In both sections, however, many felt that they could not conscientiously buy special privileges and suffered for their convictions.

Legislation adopted during the First World War provided exemption only for members of recognized peace churches like those of the Brethren, the Society of Friends (Quakers), and the Mennonites.[1] But even for these there was exemption from combatant service only.[2]

With this background of experience, the Selective Training and Service Act broadened the exemption to include not only members of "historic peace churches" but anyone who "by reason of religious training and belief, is conscientiously opposed to participation in war in any form."[3] Objectors were required to register like others, although some went to prison rather than do so. Following registration they were processed in the same general manner as others, the local draft boards deciding (subject to appeal) whether exemption was justified. Those willing to perform noncombatant service were placed in Class I–A–O and, if physically qualified, were given the same basic military training as others, except training in the use of weapons. Later they were put to work in the medical corps of either the Army or Navy where they were entitled to the same treatment and emoluments as ordinary soldiers. Those who thought noncombatant service too directly connected with the war were placed in Class IV–E and if physically qualified and inducted were assigned to "work of national importance under civilian direction." Most of this work was done under supervision of the National Park Service, Forestry Service, and Soil Conservation Service, although many of the objectors ("assignees") did such things

[1] In practice the law was broadly interpreted to cover not only all religious objectors, but also those whose objections were primarily philosophic or economic, although there was considerable variation among local boards.

[2] Ultimately certain nonmilitary forms of alternative service were approved, but all drafted men were considered to be members of the Army until finally discharged. Many were confined to the guardhouse, imprisoned, and maltreated in consequence of their refusal to take the oath, wear the uniform, or otherwise follow the orders of Army officers. See especially Norman M. Thomas, *The Conscientious Objector in America* (New York: Viking, 1923); Walter G. Kellogg, *The Conscientious Objector* (New York: Boni & Liveright, 1919); and S. Hartzler, *Mennonites in the World War; or, Nonresistance under Test* (Scotdale, Pa.: Mennonite Publishing House, 1922).

[3] Note that objections must have been based upon religious grounds, not economic and political, although in practice the term "religious" was frequently interpreted broadly. A considerable number, however, went to prison while others gave up and entered the Army because draft boards deemed their objections to be based upon grounds other than religion. In spite of the fact that the law was more liberal, more objectors went to prison than during the First World War.

as serve as attendants in publicly operated mental hospitals and correctional institutions, dairy-cattle testers, or as "guinea pigs" for the advancement of scientific and medical knowledge. Assignees remained civilians throughout; they received no compensation,[1] dependency allowances, compensation for accidents or death, benefits of the GI Bill of Rights, or other emoluments. While drafted they were subject to rules relating to furlough, leave, etc., similar to those of the Army. Although treatment may have been more liberal than during previous wars, the denial of pay and benefits as well as the manner of administration has been the subject of much concern and criticism.[2]

In the 1948 conscription law, religious objectors are accorded more liberal treatment. Those who "by reason of religious training and belief" are "conscientiously opposed to participation in war in any form" are given the choice of noncombatant service or complete exemption. "Religious training and belief" is carefully defined to require "belief in a relation to a Supreme Being involving duties superior to those arising from any human relation, but does not include essentially political, sociological, or philosophical views or a merely personal code."

1948 Conscription.—While the debate over UMT raged, Congress adopted a draft-for-service law to run for 2 years, or until June 23, 1950. The law is administered by the Selective Service System with headquarters in Washington and state capitals. Regional boards are set up to handle appeals while local draft boards of three or more civilians handle details. The law sets the maximum authorized strength for the Army, Navy, Marine Corps, and Air Force, then permits as many to be drafted as necessary to meet these quotas. After more than a year's operation only the Army had resorted to the draft, the other branches filling their needs by enlistment. Spurred by this law and by added emoluments, enlistments increased to a point where the Army also soon discontinued using the draft. Until the law expires or is repealed any of the services may, of course, resort to draft if enlistments should lag.

The first step in the draft process is registration. This is required of all men between the ages of eighteen and twenty-six. Then follow questionnaires by which additional information is secured. Those most likely to be drafted may then be ordered to take a physical examination. Thereupon, the local draft board may place each man in one of the following classes:

[1] Some, like the dairy testers, worked for private agencies which were required to pay the prevailing wage. Only $15 of this, however, went to assignees as an allowance for clothing, medical care, etc., the remainder being paid into the United States Treasury to be disposed of after the war as Congress saw fit.

[2] See especially, Julien Cornell, *The Conscientious Objector and the Law* (New York: John Day, 1943); American Friends Service Committee, *The Experience . . . in Civilian Public Service* (Philadelphia: The Committee, 1945).

Class I

I–A. Available for military service.

I–A–O. Conscientious objector available for noncombatant service only.

I–C. Member of the Armed Forces of the United States, the Coast Guard, the Coast and Geodetic Survey, or the Public Health Service.

I–D. Member of a reserve component or student taking military training.

Class II

II–A. Deferred because of civilian employment (except agriculture).

II–C. Deferred because of employment in agriculture.

Class III

III–A. Deferred because of dependents.

Class IV

IV–A. Registrant who has completed service; sole surviving son.

IV–B. Official deferred by law.

IV–D. Minister of religion or divinity student.

IV–E. Conscientious objector opposed to both combatant and noncombatant military service.

IV–F. Physically, mentally, or morally unfit.

Class V

V–A. Registrant over the age of liability for military service.

Only those in Class I are liable for draft, but those placed in other classes may later be shifted to Class I and thereby become eligible. Men are not chosen by national lottery, as during the war, but rather by birthday sequence. Men in the twenty-five-year-old bracket are taken first, then others from the older to younger. Deferments may be granted by local boards to permit high school students to continue their courses, if their record is satisfactory, until graduation or age twenty-one, whichever is first. College students may be deferred until the end of the academic year. Appeals from local boards may be made to appeal boards, thence to state and national headquarters.

The period of service for men eighteen through twenty-five is 21 months, plus 5 years in a reserve after discharge. Men eighteen years old may, if the quota permits, enlist for 1 year with the understanding that at the end of that period they must serve 6 years in a reserve, during which time they may be called for training periods of 30 days' duration annually.

PLANNING FOR MOBILIZATION

Industrial Mobilization for the Second World War.—Modern wars require mobilization[1] of all resources and productive facilities. Looking toward this end, an Industrial Mobilization Plan was developed following the First World War which the War and Navy Departments tried hard, but in vain, to induce Congress to adopt before war recurred.[2] Even without it, the coming of war in 1941 found the United States equipped with an unrivaled industrial plant, a reservoir of natural resources, a transportation and communication system second to none, and millions of trained workmen. On the eve of war both the President and Congress took steps to stimulate and convert the economy to production of sufficient goods to meet war needs and yet cause as few dislocations as possible and provide adequately for civilian needs. In addition to the Selective Training and Service Act, discussed above, the major statutes were the Lend-Lease Act, the First War Power Act of 1941, the Emergency Price Control Act of 1942, and the Second War Powers Act of 1942.

Office of Emergency Management.—The principal administrative organization especially established for the purpose of mobilization was the Office of Emergency Management, created in June, 1940. This office was set up outside the executive departments and made directly responsible to the President. Later, numerous subsidiary units were created to handle various phases of the war program. Among these was the War Production Board, whose task it was to stimulate production, assist with and help finance plant expansion, and establish priorities whereby existing materials were made available to those contributing most to the war effort. Another was the War Manpower Commission, whose task was to help keep workmen from leaving vital jobs in search of others and also helping to provide sufficient man power where it was most needed. Another was the Office of Defense Transportation, whose function was that of coordinating transportation policies and facilities, limiting unessential travel, and otherwise securing the greatest amount of transportation facilities and ensuring their most efficient use. Another was the Board of Economic Warfare, whose duty it was to control exports, secure needed products from abroad, block economic activities of enemy countries, and otherwise promote the "economic defense" of the nation. Still others were the National War Labor Board,[3] the Office of Price Administration,[4] the Office of Lend-Lease Admin-

[1] But not necessarily conscription or confiscation of industry and man power for civilian purposes, because it frequently turns out that compulsion brings with it so much resistance, regimentation, and red tape that its primary purpose is defeated.

[2] This plan is discussed in detail by Harold J. Tobin and Percy W. Bidwell in *Mobilizing Civilian America* (New York: Council on Foreign Relations, 2d printing, 1940).

[3] Discussed on p. 742.

[4] See p. 666.

istration, the Office of Civilian Defense, and numerous other agencies that played important roles.[1]

Planning Industrial Mobilization for the Third World War.—Since the last war, Congress has legalized no specific and comprehensive plan for mobilization, but much planning has taken place. The agency chiefly responsible for the task is the National Security Resources Board, attached to the Executive Office of the President. Since total mobilization is the objective, it is impossible to detail the activities in progress. They include stockpiling essential resources and materials; drafting detailed plans for meeting military and civilian man power needs, for rationing, price, wage, and rent control; planning with representatives of industry, agriculture, and labor for prompt expansion of productive facilities; anticipating housing, health, and educational needs; and planning for defense against bombing, bacterial warfare, and sabotage. Some experts think these plans should be promptly formalized and embodied in legislation in order to ensure their fulfillment. Others believe it is better to keep them fluid until near war and then call upon Congress for action. Those of this persuasion argue that formalized plans are likely to be outdated when an emergency arrives, that too much attention to detailed planning now may lead to regimentation of the American economy and people, and that optimum preparedness is both an expensive and a dangerous illusion.

Civilian Defense.—While defense of the homeland is primarily the function of the armed forces, state militias, and local police, modern wars require civilian participation. Recognizing this, the Office of Civilian Defense was established in May, 1941. Regional offices were established whose areas of operation were coterminous with the former Army corps area, later called "service commands." Both the national and regional offices worked through state and local defense councils composed largely of volunteers. Through this machinery an elaborate air-raid defense system was established which in certain regions entailed constant surveillance of the air by volunteer watchers, practice air raids, and blackouts. Emergency first-aid and fire-fighting training were also given in hundreds of communities. The defense councils also provided a medium for bringing information to the public on matters pertaining to health, hygiene, dietetics, conservation, and other community needs. At home, these plans were never seriously put to the test, while abroad even the best that could be devised could not prevent serious suffering and losses among civilians.

The abandonment of neutrality by the United States, its rise to a position of dominance in world affairs, and the revolutionary changes in weapons and tactics endanger the American homeland more than ever

[1] For a complete list and description of the war agencies consult *United States Manual* or *Congressional Directory* (both published by the Government Printing Office, Washington, D.C.) for any or all of the war years.

before. Realizing this, many defense agencies are currently devoting attention to civilian security. One of the basic questions is the extent to which cities and industries should be and can be decentralized to meet the threat of modern weapons. Thus far a decision on this thorny question has been avoided. Instead, the basic pattern appears to be similar to that followed at home and abroad during the past war. Although better than nothing, this can give little comfort to those who contemplate the consequences to civilians of atomic bombs and rays, bacterial warfare, and perhaps even more diabolic weapons.

COLLECTIVE SECURITY

The United States helped form, and joined, the United Nations primarily for the purpose of obtaining security collectively rather than by individual effort or by temporary alliances. The Charter recognizes that there is a long-range task to be done of changing attitudes and reducing the underlying causes of war, but it also recognizes the immediate need of settling disputes and stopping aggressors.

Dispute Settlement.—In case of serious dispute the Charter first contemplates settlement by "pacific" means; that is, settlement without using force. Briefly, this calls for investigation, hearing all sides of the question, discussion, calling on third parties to mediate, referring the matter to a board of arbitrators for decision, referring legal questions to the World Court, and other peaceful steps that may be agreed upon at the time. If these measures should fail, more forceful ones may be taken. In that event, the Security Council may do the following: (1) call upon member nations to break off economic and diplomatic relations; (2) interrupt communications with an aggressor; and (3) use armed forces to do battle with an aggressor.

With a view to this third possibility, the Charter provides that the United Nations is to have forces ready for call at all times. It also pledges every member to cooperate to the fullest extent. Thus far the United Nations has been unable to agree sufficiently to provide the international police force contemplated by the Charter. A small corps of guards, with distinctive uniforms and insignia, has been established, but that is all. If and when the Charter provisions are put into effect, the world police force would consist of "contingents" of soldiers, naval vessels, and air forces which the respective nations had agreed in advance to keep in readiness for immediate use when asked for by the Security Council. How many each would contribute is to be agreed upon in advance. Details are to be worked out by the Security Council with the advice of a Military Staff Committee, which would also direct whatever military operations might be undertaken. Thus far, none of the great powers has shown much disposition to see the

United Nations adequately equipped with military forces. A committee appointed to work on the matter has been in stalemate almost from the start.

The Goal of Disarmament.—Assuming that collective security would be attained through the United Nations, its architects envisaged disarmament or at least a reduction in the armed forces of member nations. A United Nations Commission has labored with the problem but with little success in view of postwar tensions. If and when disarmament can be attained, the resources and energy now devoted to huge military establishments can be directed to constructive uses that will enrich lives and raise standards of living which for millions of people are distressingly low.[1]

THE ATOMIC BOMB

When the atomic bomb was unexpectedly dropped on Hiroshima and Nagasaki shortly before the war with Japan ended, a new issue of momentous import was thrown into the hopper of national and world politics. The military and political implications were incalculable. Henceforth, new assumptions were required of all those charged with responsibility for American security.

Secrecy or Cooperation?—Everyone admitted the necessity of control, but opinions differed over the form it should take. The basic question was whether an attempt should be made to confine knowledge of the manufacturing processes to the United States, Great Britain, and Canada, the latter two having participated in the experiments, or demonstrate a willingness to share it with other nations. In general, those who believe in unilateral preparedness argue that, having developed the bomb, it should be kept and used for bargaining purposes and as a threat to recently conquered enemies and potential foes. They also insist that since no effective agency for international control exists, the weapon might fall into the hands of irresponsible persons. Others, including most of the scientists of the nation, counter by saying knowledge of the secrets of the bomb cannot be kept secret, that, having joined the United Nations, to insist on national control would demonstrate a lack of confidence in collective security, and that failure to share the bomb would provoke an armament race that would be certain to end in war.

Soon after atomic bombs were first used, President Truman proposed legislation looking toward domestic control. A short time later, after consulting with leaders of Great Britain and Canada, he announced willingness to share atomic secrets as soon as effective and enforceable safeguards against their use for destructive purposes could be devised. There-

[1] For further discussion of military and other obligations assumed under the United Nations Charter see p. 558.

upon, the United Nations created an Atomic Energy Commission to wrestle with the problem, but opinion promptly split over proposals made on behalf of the United States by Bernard Baruch and other proposals made by the Russian delegate on the Security Council. Stalemate has continued since.

The Atomic Energy Commission.—Meanwhile, a heated debate was going on throughout the country over whether atomic energy should be

The Vast U.S. Network for Production of Atomic Energy

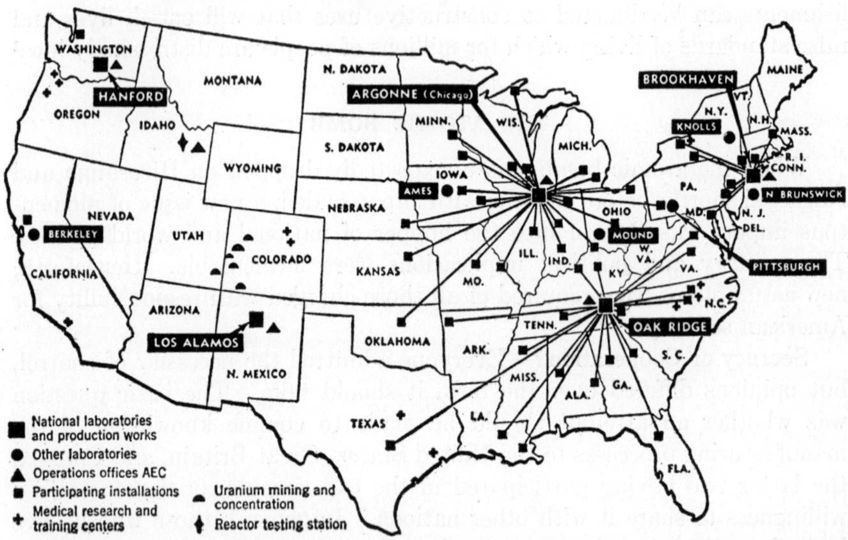

There are 1,272 separate atomic facilities under AEC direction. Most are in the United States; a few are in Canada and the Marshall Islands. The major installations in the United States are shown here. Oak Ridge, Los Alamos, Hanford, Argonne, and Brookhaven are key production and laboratory centers. The lines radiating from Oak Ridge, Argonne, and Brookhaven designate laboratories in universities under contract to major research centers. Other laboratories are under AEC contract for research in special fields. SOURCE: *The New York Times*, Sept. 25, 1949.

placed under military or civilian control in the United States. In August, 1946, Congress passed an atomic-energy control law which, while placing civilians in control, provides for constant liaison with the Army and Navy Departments.

The act creates a commission of five members to be appointed from civilian life by the President with senatorial approval. Terms are for 5 years, terms overlap, and salaries are $15,000 for all except the chairman who receives $17,500. A general manager was provided to handle administration. Four divisions were created—research, production, engineering, and military application—with the stipulation that the chief of the last-mentioned division shall be a member of the armed forces. This superstructure is supposed to operate under the constant scrutiny of three committees: a general advisory committee of nine members appointed by the President for 6-year terms; a military liaison committee appointed by the Secretaries of War and Navy; and a joint committee of Congress composed of nine from each house. The legislation then gives the United States government a monopoly of fissionable material and gives the commission broad authority over research, production, and utilization. The commission is even given authority to limit the dissemination of "restricted data," in other words, to keep secret certain data and prosecute those who disclose it.

So far as international aspects are concerned, the law anticipates control by saying that its provisions are to be superseded by conflicting treaties or agreements later to be entered into. It further states, however, that American secrets are not to be made known to the rest of the world until "effective and enforceable international safeguards against the use of atomic energy for destructive purposes have been established." Some distrust of the President is evinced by provisions that only Congress is to determine when it is safe to relinquish unilateral knowledge and control. Meanwhile, American manufacture of bombs continues, scientists the world over are engaged in a mad race to learn more about atomic energy, while military experts are trying to discover what atomic energy means to traditional concepts and weapons.

In addition to headquarters in Washington, the Commission operates through five operating managers located at New York City, Chicago, Oak Ridge, Hanford, and Los Alamos. Actual operations are carried on largely through contractual arrangements with industrial firms, colleges and universities, and government agencies. Fewer than 10 per cent of the total number of employees working on the atomic-energy program have been direct employees of the federal government. The production and improvement of atomic weapons has received the major attention of the Commission. The center for this part of the program is the Los Alamos Scientific Laboratory operated under contract with the University of California. In its report for 1948[1] the Commission said, "New designs of weapons have been tested and found to be successful, and further developments are now in progress." It also reported that a total of eight atomic weapons had been detonated: one in the test at Alamogordo in July, 1945; two at Hiroshima and Nagasaki in August, 1945; two in the tests at Bikini in July, 1946; and three in the tests at Eniwetok in April and May, 1948.

[1] P. 40.

References

AGETON, ARTHUR A.: *The Naval Officer's Guide* (New York: McGraw-Hill, 1943).

BALDWIN, HANSON W.: *Navy at War* (New York: Morrow, 1943).

——— *The Price of Power* (New York: Harper, 1947).

BOUTWELL, WILLIAM D., *et al.*: *America Prepares for Tomorrow; the Story of Our Total Defense Effort* (New York: Harper, 1941).

CORNELL, JULIEN: *The Conscientious Objector and the Law* (New York: John Day, 1942).

ELIOT, GEORGE FIELDING: *The Strength We Need; A Military Program for America Pending Peace* (New York: Viking, 1946).

FENNELL, MARGARET: *Acts of Congress Applicable in Time of Emergency*, Public Affairs Bulletin No. 35 (Washington: Library of Congress Legislative Reference Service, 1945).

FITZPATRICK, EDWARD A.: *Universal Military Training* (New York: McGraw-Hill, 1945).

FRENCH, PAUL C.: *We Won't Murder* (New York: Hastings House, 1940).

GANOE, WILLIAM A.: *A History of the United States Army* (New York: Appleton-Century-Crofts, rev. ed., 1942).

GLENN, GARRARD, and ARTHUR A. SCHILLER: *The Army and the Law* (New York: Columbia University Press, 1943).

KERWIN, JEROME G.: *Civil-Military Relationships in American Life* (Chicago: University of Chicago Press, 1948).

KNOX, DUDLEY W.: *A History of the United States Navy* (New York: Putnam, 1936).

MARION, GEORGE: *Bases and Empire* (New York: Fairplay Publications, 1948).

MILITARY SERVICE PUBLISHING CO.: *The Officer's Guide* (Harrisburg, Pa.: The Telegraph Press, 10th ed., 1944).

MOCK, JAMES R., and EVANGELINE W. THURBER: *Report on Demobilization* (Norman, Okla.: University of Oklahoma Press, 1944).

NELSON, DONALD M.: *Arsenal of democracy—The Story of American War Production* (New York: Harcourt Brace, 1946).

NEWMAN, JAMES R., and BYRON S. MILLER: *The Control of Atomic Energy: A Study of Its Social, Economic, and Political Implications* (New York: McGraw-Hill, 1948).

PALMER, JOHN M.: *America in Arms; the Experience of the United States with Military Organization* (New Haven: Yale University Press, 1941).

SPAULDING, OLIVER L.: *The United States Army in War and Peace* (New York: Putnam, 1937).

STIMSON, HENRY L., and MCGEORGE BUNDY: *On Active Service in Peace and War* (New York: Harper, 1948).

THOMAS, NORMAN M.: *The Conscientious Objector in America* (New York: Viking, 1923).

TOBIN, HAROLD J., and PERCY W. BIDWELL: *Mobilizing Civilian America* (New York: Council on Foreign Relations, 2d printing, 1940).

VILLARD, OSWALD G.: *Our Military Chaos* (New York: Knopf, 1939).

WELLER, GEORGE: *Bases Overseas; An American Trusteeship in Power* (New York: Harcourt Brace, 1944).

WRIGHT, QUINCY: *A Study of War* (Chicago: University of Chicago Press, 2 vols., 1942).

Chapter 28

AIDS TO GENERAL BUSINESS

Contrary to wide-spread belief, *laissez-faire* was never more than a theory imperfectly applied. The happy, imagined time when government did not interfere in the freedom of the individual by meddling in business never in fact existed.

Carl Becker, *Modern Democracy*.[1]

Types of Business.—For present purposes businesses may be divided into four categories: general businesses, financial institutions, public utilities, and public enterprises. The first includes private manufactures, construction, mining and quarrying, wholesale, retail, and service establishments. Among these competition is usually an important factor. The second includes private banks, credit institutions, insurance companies, real estate speculators and brokers.[2] The third includes privately owned businesses having such an important and vital relationship to community welfare as to be designated "public utilities" by state legislatures or Congress.[3] Among these are railroads and other common carriers; electric, gas, water, telephone, and sewage systems. The fourth group comprises those that are publicly—*i.e.*, governmentally—owned and operated.[4] Among these are the postal system, the Tennessee Valley Authority, and many others. This chapter deals primarily with those agencies and activities of the Federal government related to the group we have called "general businesses," although it is obvious that many of the services described affect the entire national economy.

Changing Character of Business Enterprise.—The industrial revolution which occurred during the middle of the last century has completely changed the character of the American economy. Until then agriculture with its auxiliary services was dominant. Farms were owned and operated by families;[5] businesses were comparatively small and operated by those who owned them. Now, well over half the population lives in urban centers,[6] 42 per cent of the farms are operated by tenants, and a considerable number of farms are commercially operated by corporations. Most of the nation's business is no longer conducted by small proprietors who own

[1] (New Haven: Yale University Press, 1941), p. 70.

[2] See Chap. 29.

[3] See Chap. 30.

[4] See Chap. 31.

[5] With the help of slaves in the South.

[6] See p. 163.

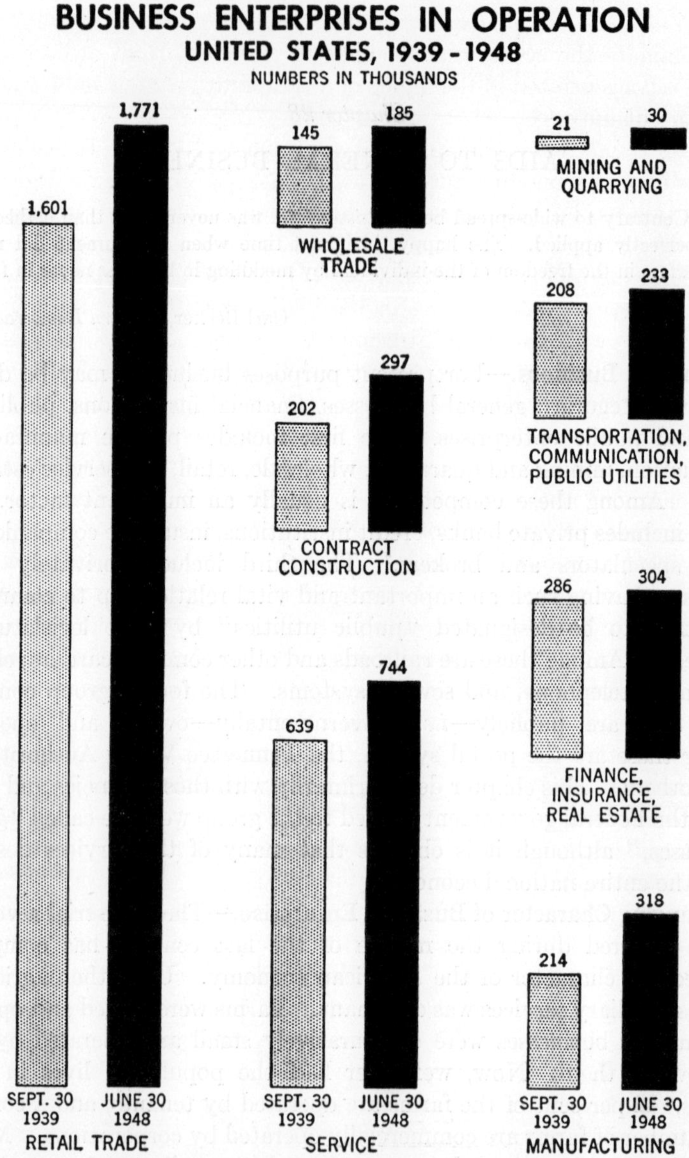

The number of business enterprises declined during the war, jumped sharply in the two years following V–J Day, and since September, 1947, has grown at a slower rate. An all-time peak of 3,882,000 was reached in June, 1948; but the gain during the preceding nine months was only 65,000. The leveling off in the business "birth rate" was most evident in manufacturing and in finance, insurance, and real estate, although all major sectors of the company were affected. SOURCE: *Road Maps of Industry,* Jan. 7, 1949. Copyright by National Industrial Conference Board, Inc., New York, 1949.

their enterprises and manage them personally; rather, giant corporations now dominate the scene, management is separated from ownership, and control is concentrated in the hands of a comparatively few industrial managers and financiers.[1]

These trends have had and will continue to have far-reaching consequences both in economics and politics. Concepts of property, legal rights, competition, social values, and the human equation have changed. The word "democracy" has taken on a different meaning. The entire economy has become increasingly interdependent. Producers, wholesalers, retailers, and labor have become highly organized to exert unified pressure on public opinion and government. Governments have been called upon to assist, regulate, and promote almost every economic and social interest. Corporate bigness requires big government, which, in turn, enhances the role of professional government managers and bureaucrats. Meanwhile, new techniques of government have been and must continue to be found.

Department of Commerce.—The Department of Commerce is to businessmen what the Department of Agriculture is to farmers and the Department of Labor is to workingmen. Created in 1903, it was known as the Department of Commerce and Labor until Labor was set off in a separate department in 1913. The department occupies one of the largest buildings in Washington, a structure built during the Coolidge and Hoover administrations when business interests tended to predominate in national politics.

At the head of the department is a Secretary who is also a member of the President's cabinet. The Secretary is nearly always a politician who has supported the President's party and usually reflects the attitude of the Administration toward business. The Secretary's principal assistants and the internal organization of the department are shown on the chart on page 628. Activities of the department throughout the nation are directed and coordinated through field offices located in principal cities.

The Hoover Commission proposed several important changes in departmental organization.[2] In addition to its general recommendations for improving administration, the commission suggested that the department's focus should be on (1) nonregulatory transportation activities, and (2) industrial and commercial services. To the first should be added the nonregulatory functions now performed by such agencies as the Interstate Commerce Commission, Maritime Commission, and Civil

[1] For a classic portrayal and analysis of this transition, see Adolph A. Berle and Gardner C. Means, *The Modern Corporation and Private Property* (New York: Macmillan, 1933). See also United States Congress, Temporary National Economic Committee, *Investigation of Concentration of Economic Power*, Monograph No. 11, entitled "Bureaucracy and Trusteeship in Larger Corporations" (Washington: Government Printing Office, 1940); National Resources Committee, *The Structure of the American Economy*, part 1 (Washington: Government Printing Office, 1939).

[2] *Department of Commerce* (Washington: Government Printing Office, 1949), pp. 1–7.

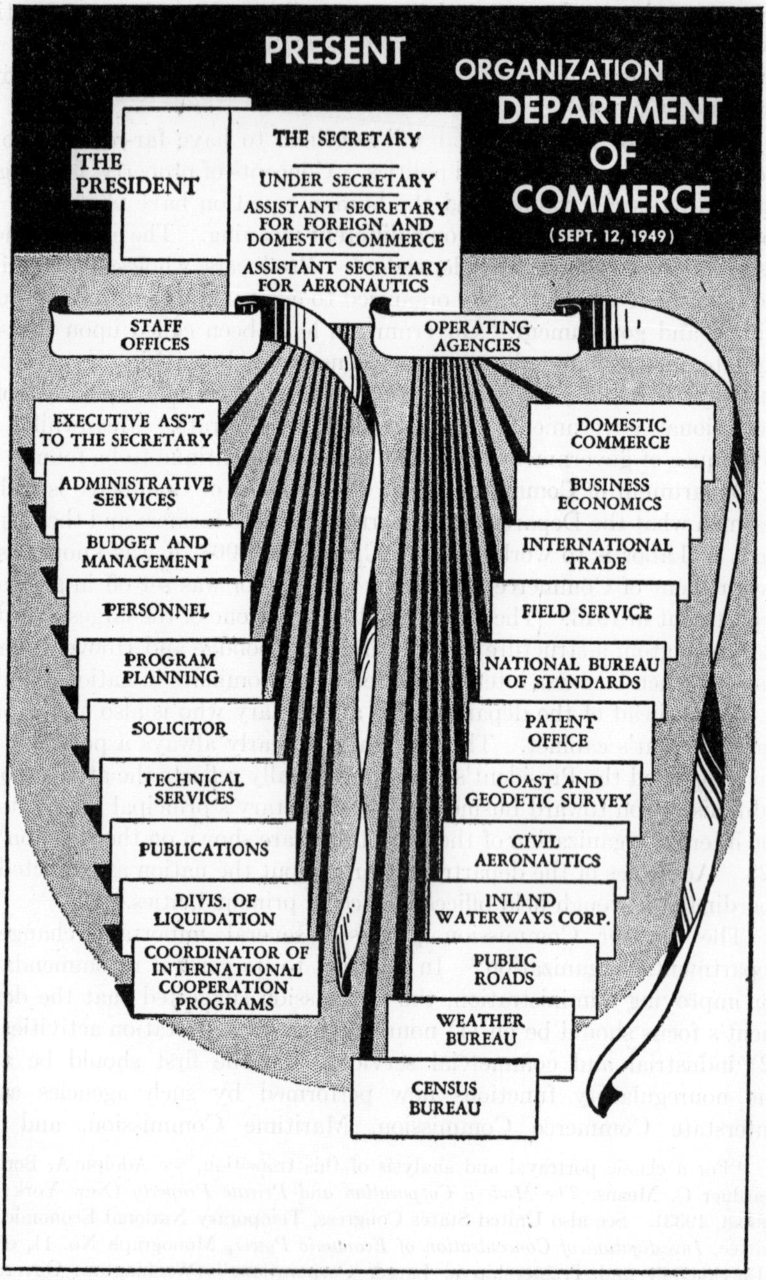

SOURCE: Prepared from data supplied by the United States Department of Commerce.

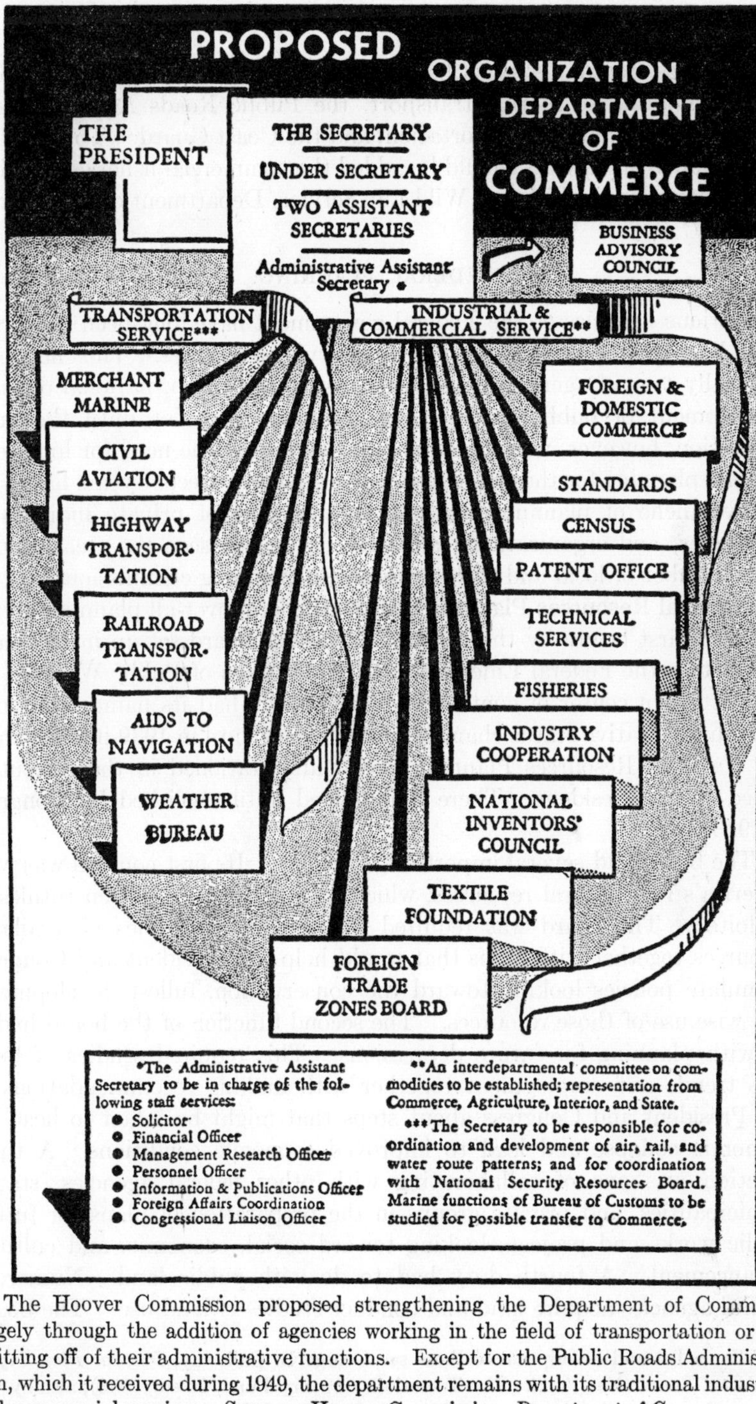

The Hoover Commission proposed strengthening the Department of Commerce largely through the addition of agencies working in the field of transportation or the splitting off of their administrative functions. Except for the Public Roads Administration, which it received during 1949, the department remains with its traditional industrial and commercial services. SOURCE: Hoover Commission, *Department of Commerce.*

Aeronautics Board. Also to be added were the services of the Customs Bureau relating to marine transport, the Public Roads Administration, the Office of Defense Transportation, and the Coast Guard. To industrial and commercial services should be added the commercial fisheries activities then centered in the Fish and Wild Life Service, Department of the Interior.

FEDERAL PLANNING

Various agencies of the Federal government have long been concerned with long-term planning for their particular activities. This has been especially true of agencies concerned with conservation, national defense, development of public roads, rivers, and harbors. Not until the great depression, however, was there much concern over the need for long-term over-all planning for the entire national economy. Recent years have seen an avalanche of planning activities on the part of private individuals, businesses, and organizations; and they have also seen the creation of a large number of local and state government-planning commissions.[1]

National Resources Planning Board.—Federal over-all planning activities were first begun by the National Planning Board set up in 1934 as a unit within the Federal Emergency Administration of Public Works. Always a storm center of controversy, the agency had its name, functions, and administrative status changed several times until in 1939 it was named the National Resources Planning Board and stationed in the Executive Office of the President. There it remained until abolished by Congress in 1943.

The board had several important functions. Its first concern was with America's rich natural resources, which have all too often been ruthlessly exploited. The board was required to prepare inventories of available resources together with plans that would help the President and Congress formulate policies looking toward the conservation, fullest development, and wise use of those resources. The second function of the board had to do with planning for future depressions. This required studies of business trends and employment together with making recommendations to the President and Congress about steps that might be taken to head off economic collapse and lead to improved economic conditions. A third function was one of collaborating with other federal agencies, states, municipalities, and private groups in the preparation of plans for future public works and projects looking toward social, economic, and cultural advancement. A fourth duty had to do with public land. Numerous federal agencies acquire land and conduct studies of land use. The board

[1] For a list and description of these see George B. Galloway, *Postwar Planning in the United States* (New York: The Twentieth Century Fund, 2d ed., 1943); also by the same author, *Planning for America* (New York: Holt, 1941).

was given the task of recording all acquisitions and studies, not only to provide a central reservoir of information but also to enable its staff to advise various agencies with respect to future acquisitions and utilization. In carrying out its duties, the board established several regional offices through which it worked closely with existing public and private agencies and stimulated the creation of many new ones. The latter was probably its most important contribution.

As indicated above, the board was abolished in 1943. It was never popular, due in part to congressional opposition to some of the persons who comprised its membership, but also to other reasons. Many congressmen thought planning a legislative function rather than something that should be done by the executive. Many came to oppose it because its advice to the President and the Bureau of the Budget acted as a brake on expenditures for rivers, harbors, etc., in which individual congressmen were interested. Further objections arose from the fact that some administrative agencies disliked having their activities coordinated, while others feared that too much federal planning would lead to undesirable interference with and regimentation of business and economic life. In spite of criticisms such as these, abolition of the board was viewed as a grave mistake by many.

Although the board may not have been properly staffed and administered, there is urgent need for some agency within the Federal government charged with responsibility for planning programs for the future while at the same time stimulating and coordinating similar activities by state and local governments and private parties. Adoption of the Employment Act of 1946 may ultimately fill the need.

Planning for Full Employment.—When the war ended, thoughts turned to problems of reconversion and employment. Fears arose of another depression with all that would mean in terms of unemployment, suffering, and social upheaval. To be prepared for such eventualities, legislation was introduced in Congress which emerged as the Employment Act of 1946.

The stated policy of the act is for the Federal government in cooperation with industry, agriculture, labor, state, and local governments to develop, coordinate, and utilize plans to provide useful employment opportunities for those able, willing, and seeking to work and to promote maximum employment, production, and purchasing power. This is an ambitious resolve which will require careful planning and courageous action. The planning is to be done by a three-man Council of Economic Advisers and a staff of experts attached to the Executive Office of the President. With the advice and assistance of the council and staff, the President is required to prepare and submit an "Economic Report" to Congress annually at the beginning of each regular session. The report is to project and interpret economic trends and include plans and recommendations for meeting anticipated problems.

To facilitate consideration in Congress, the act establishes a Joint Committee on the Economic Report comprised of fourteen members from the House and Senate. This committee, which is provided with a small staff, is to make continuous studies of matters relating to the Economic Report and, not later then May 1 of each year, file a report with the House and Senate containing findings and recommendations. With these at hand, bills embodying the recommendations will be introduced, referred to regular standing committees, and thereafter travel the route of other measures.

This is a conservative, considerably "watered down" measure as compared with proposals originally introduced. The Council of Economic Advisers is without power to coordinate the planning activities of other federal agencies or to work extensively with planning agencies throughout the country. One should also note that the council cannot of itself move to create a single job. Its functions are limited to those of conducting studies and analyses, preparing plans, making recommendations, and advising the President. Nevertheless, the legislation does recognize the need for federal planning, it establishes an agency that may be able to demonstrate the desirability of having a planning body with broader powers, and it sets up a procedure which, it may be hoped, will help to anticipate and forestall economic booms and depressions.

Planning Public Works.—Public works consist of those activities that entail construction by, or on behalf of, governmental agencies. While a large volume of construction cannot be postponed, some of it can be put off until prices are favorable or the economy lags. The omnipresent threat of depression makes it imperative that governments and private concerns maintain portfolios of carefully planned projects, the construction of which can be timed to economic conditions. Recognition of this truth has led to the expenditure of much time, energy, and money, especially in recent years.

The Federal Works Agency, transferred in July, 1949, to the General Service Administration, has been the focal point of public-works planning, although it must be remembered that each agency does most of its project planning itself. Most current planning activities center around federal buildings, public roads, public works in the Virgin Islands, and aid to the states. Immediately after the war, aid given to the states by the Federal Works Agency was directed principally toward two objectives: expanding educational facilities for returning veterans and providing technical assistance, loans, and grants for designing a backlog of public works intended to relieve anticipated unemployment. Later the emphasis was on helping states and local governments design and construct sewage disposal works. 1949 legislation empowers the General Services Administrator to make interest-free loans to states and their subdivisions for public-works planning, other than housing. Loans are made with the understanding that Congress is in no way obligated to help finance construction. Moreover, loans are made only for projects that conform to over-all plans approved by competent state, local, or regional authorities. Loans are to be repaid when the public works are started or after 3 years have elapsed.

Public Roads.—Normally, roads constitute the bulk of all public works. Even though the Constitution had not said that Congress shall have power to "establish post offices and post roads," the Federal government doubtless could build roads, or subsidize their building, under its authority to regulate commerce, its power to spend money for the common defense and general welfare, or its proprietary power.[1] Be that as it may, the Federal government has played a leading part in honeycombing the nation with ribbons of concrete and asphalt.

In the beginning road building was purely a local function. First the county, then the state, then the Federal government intervened. The first federal road construction was undertaken in 1806 when Congress appropriated funds for improving the National Pike, but the modern era of federal action began in 1893 in response to demands for better roads from farmers and bicycle riders. After that date federal activity increased until the great depression, when it expanded by leaps and bounds. During the recent war all road construction not required for the war effort was discontinued, but when the war ended well-laid plans immediately went into operation.

Classification of Roads.—For administrative purposes roads are classified into three groups: state systems, county and local roads, and city streets. The first includes the primary intercity and intercounty routes and connecting links through cities. Among these, principal interstate arteries are marked with the familiar United States highway number sign. County and local roads include most of the lightly traveled rural roads and are for the most part under the jurisdiction of counties and other local units. City streets are those within municipalities.

Bureau of Public Roads.—As mentioned above, federal activity is supervised by the Bureau of Public Roads. The Federal government assumes full responsibility for building and maintaining roads on federal areas such as national parks and Indian reservations. Otherwise, federal assistance is confined to research, planning, financing, and supervising the construction and maintenance of highways, bridges, and grade-crossing elimination done under the direction of state highway departments. Normally, most federal aid goes to state systems, but during the recent

[1] See p. 427.

depression large sums were spent through the Public Works Administration and Works Progress Administration on county and local roads and city streets.

The basic plan of federal action was established by the Federal Highway Act of 1921. This offered aid divided among the states on the basis of area, population, and rural post mileage, usually with the proviso that federal grants be matched by equal amounts of state funds.[1] Federal-aid funds are confined to construction, and grants are contingent upon the maintenance of improvements to federal standards.

TARIFFS AND SUBSIDIES

Protective Tariffs.—Tariffs are levies upon imported goods. The Constitution, it will be remembered, gives Congress the power to lay and collect "duties" and "imposts," meaning tariffs.[2] Every American tariff law, including the first adopted in 1789, has had two purposes: one, to raise revenue; the other, to "protect" domestic industries, at least certain of them. The intent of a "protective" tariff is to keep foreign products out in order to give American-made products a competitive advantage in the home market. The advantage results from the fact that by restricting foreign selling, competition is eased, causing domestic prices to remain higher than they otherwise would. By this process a tax is levied upon American consumers, the proceeds of which are paid as a subsidy to the makers of American goods.

Whether this is a wise or an unwise policy cannot concern us here. Whether for good or ill, many American businesses ("infant industries") have been built behind tariff walls and, without such assistance, probably would never have been "born" or would have fallen by the wayside. Tariffs not only play a large role in deciding what kind of goods shall enter the country, but they also determine, to a considerable extent, the volume of exports, since countries will not readily buy here unless they can also sell. Indeed, tariffs affect the entire economy and an unwise tariff policy may have devastating effects not only upon the United States but upon the entire world.[3] The intense interest of businessmen in tariff policy accounts

[1] Grade-crossing funds are outright grants to states and are apportioned one-half on the basis of population, one-fourth on railroad mileage, and one-fourth on federal-aid highway mileage.

[2] For a full discussion of this power see p. 364.

[3] American economists are almost unanimous in saying, for example, that the Smoot-Hawley Tariff law of 1930 intensified the world-wide depression and seriously retarded recovery. It is also generally agreed that the international commercial warfare, of which tariffs were the principal weapon, which characterized the 1930's, contributed to the rise of dictatorships and the Second World War. See especially Joseph M. Jones, Jr., *Tariff Retaliation, Repercussions of the Hawley-Smoot Bill* (Philadelphia: University

for the fact that tariff making has provided more controversy in Congress than almost any other issue.

Tariff Schedules.—Tariff laws include many schedules, or classifications of commodities, wherein each product is listed together with the amount of the tax, if any. Tariffs are either "specific," *i.e.*, so much per unit, or ad valorem, *i.e.*, a stated percentage of the value of the commodity. Before goods leave foreign ports for the United States invoices must be certified by American consular officers, and upon arrival they must be appraised by officers attached to the Customs Bureau of the Treasury Department. Decisions of the customs officers may be reviewed by the United States Custom Court, and further appeal may be taken on questions of law to the Court of Customs and Patent Appeals.[1]

The Tariff Commission.—Making tariffs is an exceedingly complicated and technical task for which Congressional committees seldom have either the time or training. Hence, in 1916, a bipartisan commission was created with twelve members appointed by the President with the advice and consent of the Senate. In 1930 the membership was reduced to six, who serve for terms of 6 years. The commission is not a quasi-legislative or quasi-judicial body, nor does it exercise administrative powers. It is an investigational and advisory agent whose primary duty is that of conducting research and furnishing information to Congress and the President on matters relating to American and foreign tariffs.

"Flexible" Tariffs.—Formerly when Congress fixed tariff rates, they remained unalterable until changed by Congress. Not only did this produce rigidity, but it invited incessant agitation and lobbying on the part of special interests to secure favorable changes. The McKinley Tariff of 1890 empowered the President to levy special rates upon certain imports in retaliation for "unjust and unreasonable" charges levied by foreign nations upon American products. Since 1922 tariff rates have been based upon the cost-of-production theory, *i.e.*, the duty fixed is supposed to be determined by the difference between the cost of production at home and abroad. When the Tariff Commission finds a difference between foreign and American costs, a report is made to the President, who may raise or lower the tariff to the advantage of the American producer. Maximum and minimum rates are stated in the law, and the President is forbidden to raise or lower any existing tariff by more than 50 per cent. Articles covered by a reciprocal tariff agreement, described below, are exempt from these provisions.

Reciprocal Tariffs.—Still greater flexibility was provided in the Reciprocal Tariff Act of 1934. This sought to regain vanishing American export

---

of Pennsylvania Press, 1934); Leverett S. Lyon and Victor Abramson *et al.*, *Government and Economic Life* (Washington: Brookings, 2 vols., 1940), vol. II, pp. 592–595.

[1] Cf. p. 343.

markets by authorizing the President to negotiate tariff agreements with countries willing to make satisfactory concessions. Negotiations are conducted under direction of an Interdepartmental Committee on Trade Agreements, of which the Secretary of State is chairman.

The Tariff Commission has always been relied upon for information, but amendments added in 1948 by a critical Congress gave it a special role. These changes required the President to obtain a full factual report from the Tariff Commission that gave special attention to the effect of proposed changes on similar products produced in the United States. Among other things, this report was to include a "peril point" for each product beyond which a tariff reduction would adversely affect similar American products. The commission was given 120 days in which to investigate and report, during which time the President was estopped from putting an agreement into effect. At the end of the time indicated, two reports were supposed to reach Congress: one from the President, giving his proposals with justification, and the other from the Tariff Commission. The assumption behind this procedure was that with this data at hand Congress would be in a position to investigate and air opposition views. Supporters of the agreement program heatedly opposed these concess ons, and the matter was made an issue in the 1948 presidential campaign. The following Congress succeeded in repealing these restrictive provisions, thus restoring the pre-1948 procedures.

Although the tariff agreements resemble treaties, they are not considered to be such, and they do not require Senate approval. The President is not unlimited in his power, however: (1) no rates may be raised or lowered by more than 50 per cent; (2) articles on the dutiable list may not be transferred to the free list, nor vice versa; and (3) no agreement to reduce the indebtedness of a foreign government may be made. The agreements have generally, but not drastically, lowered tariffs and stimulated trade. Whether there have been instances where particular industries have been adversely affected is a matter of controversy; the Department of State thinks not, but others violently disagree. Agreements can be suspended by the President if in his opinion the other party is discriminating against American commerce or otherwise following policies that will defeat the purposes of the act.

The act has a 3-year time limit,[1] hence becomes the subject of periodic congressional review. The discussion has always been heated, if not acrimonious. Principal critics are usually high-tariff advocates, industries that think they have been injured or fear they might be, and those who claim that they are opposed in principle to the broad grant of discretion given to the President. Most of these refrain from advocating outright repeal but urge some sort of congressional review before agreements go into effect.

[1] Except for the period from 1943 to 1945, when the time was shortened to 2 years.

Subsidies.—In addition to tariffs, the list of direct and indirect subsidies made to business groups is a long one. Only a few will be suggested here. Generous land grants were made to railroads during the last century. Federal grants for rivers and harbors have been a boon to many localities, businessmen, and shippers. Appropriations for public roads have been an important direct and indirect subsidy to the construction industry, the makers of automobiles, carriers by bus and truck, as well as an invaluable service to the general public. Generous payments have been made to rail, water, and air carriers for carrying the mail; while mail has been carried for below-cost rates, or free of charge, for the benefit of special groups as well as the public.[1] The construction of air lines and airports has been an important stimulus to the aircraft industry. Several federally owned utilities, like the Inland Waterways Corporation and the Alaskan Railroad[2] have subsidized certain groups and areas by below-cost operations. Shipbuilders and the merchant marine have been generously assisted.[3] During the depression the Federal government deliberately spent huge sums to stimulate business activity;[4] while throughout the war federal funds were lavishly spent to encourage the production of war materials and hold prices in line. While other groups in the country—farmers, workmen, unemployed, veterans, consumers, etc.—have also received financial assistance on innumerable occasions, the business community has without doubt done well by itself.

PROMOTION OF FOREIGN TRADE

As noted in a previous chapter dealing with foreign relations,[5] citizens of the United States have billions of dollars invested abroad and trade interests in all parts of the world. In addition to the Department of State, the chief centers of trade promotion are the Office of International Trade in the Bureau of Foreign and Domestic Commerce and the Export-Import Bank.

Foreign Trade Services.—The Office of International Trade uses its influence to rid world trade of restrictions, instabilities, discrimination, and bilateral limitations. Its aim is a "balanced, multilateral trade." To this end it has worked with other agencies and the United Nations trying to form an acceptable International Trade Organization. It also helped launch the Economic Recovery Administration (Marshall Plan), and it helps formulate reciprocal tariff agreements. Export licenses, now required of about 50 per cent of all exports from the United States, are issued by this office. Moreover, the office helps administer Foreign Trade

[1] See p. 700.
[2] P. 703.
[3] P. 649.
[4] Cf. p. 649.
[5] P. 548.

Zones—port areas designated by Congress where foreign goods may stop temporarily, without tariffs, for repacking and reshipment. A constant stream of economic data from all parts of the world makes this office an invaluable source of information and advice for both private and governmental agencies.

The Export-Import Bank.—This corporation dates back to 1934. After being a part of several agencies it is now a permanent independent establishment. It is organized under the laws of the District of Columbia and governed by a board of directors consisting of the Secretary of State ex officio and four full-time members. Its capital stock is owned entirely by the Federal government, most of it by the Reconstruction Finance Corporation with which there is close cooperation. The bank was originally intended to help finance trade with Russia; it later proved more helpful in the Latin American theater; and it is now aiding trade with countries in war-torn areas. The bank has two primary functions: one to lend money to exporters and importers who cannot obtain desired funds from private banks, to help them take advantage of foreign business opportunities; the other, to make loans to foreign governments to help them develop their resources, stabilize their economies, market products in an orderly manner, and recover from the war.

Loans to foreign governments have been largely of four types: one for improving their monetary and exchange situation; the second for developing internal improvements and production facilities; the third for developing strategic materials for use during the war emergency; the fourth for financing relief and reconstruction. Brazil has been the largest borrower in the Western Hemisphere, many of the credits having been used for highways, railroads, ore mines, and steel mills. Mexico has borrowed large sums for the purchase of capital equipment. Cuba has also borrowed heavily for such things as highways, irrigation, warehouses, agricultural implements, and telegraph equipment. China, in the Orient, and France, in Europe, have borrowed heavily. Loans are rarely made in lump sums; rather they usually result in establishing a line of credit. The borrower uses only as much as he needs and pays no interest on the remainder authorized. Most of the loans have led directly to purchases of American goods for export.

RESEARCH, STANDARDS, AND STATISTICS

Of inestimable value to business are governmental research, standards, and statistics. While this is an important function of many agencies in Washington,[1] only the work of those in the Department of Commerce will be discussed at this point.

[1] In 1941 there were at least forty-six federal agencies engaged in research, inspection, and other activities connected with the establishment and maintenance of standards

National Bureau of Standards.—This bureau is the principal agency of the federal government engaged in physical research. In addition to its large plant in Washington, the bureau has small branch laboratories, proving grounds, and testing and field stations located in and around the United States. Working at the bureau are its own highly skilled staff, research associates assigned by private organizations, and scientists and engineers of foreign countries who work as guests.

In an earlier chapter[1] it was pointed out that Congress has authority to fix standards of weights and measures. It was also observed that Congress has legalized both the British system of weights and measures and the metric system. It was emphasized that, with a few exceptions, federal law does not make conformity to standards mandatory but depends for enforcement upon voluntary compliance and upon state and local governments.

Standards.—Although recommended by President Washington and the subject of exhaustive reports, few standards were fixed by the Federal government prior to 1838. Meanwhile,[2] the country operated under state standards that had been inherited from the colonial period. To bring about greater uniformity, Congress, in the year mentioned, legalized the English system (foot, inch, gallon, quart, pound, ounce, etc.), with which everyone is familiar. Later, in 1866, the metric system (meter, liter, gram, etc.) commonly used in Europe, was also legalized.[3] Ever since, both systems have been legal, although use of the metric system is confined largely to laboratories, technical institutions, and to a few manufacturers for export. Federal law, except in a few instances, compels no one to follow either system, although the federal courts assume that all legal transactions are based upon one or the other.

Since enacting these basic measures, specific standards have been fixed for measuring sheet and plate iron and steel, electricity, barrels, baskets and

---

for things bought by federal, state, and local governmental agencies and for products entering interstate commerce. This included fixing a "score" for butter, grades for meat, fruits, vegetables, wool, cosmetics, and many more articles. For a comprehensive review of the work of the agencies referred to, see Temporary National Economic Committee, *op. cit.* Monograph No. 24, "Consumer Standards."

[1] See p. 423.

[2] For a history of weights and measures, see William Hallock and Herbert T. Wade, *Outlines of the Evolution of Weights and Measures and the Metric System* (New York: Macmillan, 1906). Consult also National Industrial Conference Board, *The Metric versus the English System of Weights and Measures*, Research Report No. 42 (New York: Century, October, 1921); and, by the same authors, *Weights and Measures in the United States, Arguments for and against a Change*, Special Report No. 34 (New York: National Industrial Conference Board, Inc., 1926). See also Louis A. Fischer, *History of the Standard Weights and Measures of the United States*, Bureau of Standards Publication M 64, 1905 (Washington: Government Printing Office, 1905).

[3] The exact measures and weights with their equivalents are given in *United States Code, Annotated*, Title 15, Section 205.

hampers for vegetables and fruit, and time. Although copies of these are sent to the states, who may also adopt and enforce them, federal law makes compliance with them mandatory.[1]

Over a period of years the bureau has not only established basic standards for common weights and measures, but for many other items as well. The more permanent of these are called "American Standards" and are fixed in accordance with procedures established in cooperation with the American Standards Association, a private organization. Others are called "Commercial Standards." The chief difference lies in the fact that the former are established by a more deliberate process, hence enjoy greater prestige, at least in the eyes of some. Copies may be found in *Handbooks*, a series entitled *Commercial Standards*, and circulars, published by the bureau.

A standard is fixed after extensive research and consultation with representatives of state and local governments, scientific societies, producers, distributors, and consumers. Businessmen who agree to comply with standards are certified and may refer to this in their advertising. A list of commercial standards includes such common items as mopsticks, pipe nipples, clinical thermometers, fuel oils, dress patterns, men's pajamas, wallpaper, mirrors, hosiery lengths and sizes, Venetian blinds, and many others.

Research.—Performance of its duties requires research into nearly all branches of the physical sciences. Some of the fields are electricity (including radio), weights and measures, heat and power, optics, chemistry, atomic and molecular physics, metallurgy, clay and silicate products, trade standards, and building materials and structures. Results are published monthly in the *Journal of Research* and in separate articles entitled *Research Papers*. Progress of work in the laboratories and other activities can be followed in the *Technical News Bulletin*, published monthly.

Testing and Consulting.—Testing and calibrating to ascertain whether items, especially those purchased by governmental agencies, conform to standards is also an important function of the bureau. This service is free to agencies of the Federal and state governments, but a fee is charged for private tests. During a year thousands of tests are made of objects varying from sugar and light bulbs to clinical thermometers and varnish. In its testing the bureau cooperates closely with the American Society for Testing Materials, a national technical society devoted to the promotion of the knowledge of engineering and the standardization of specifications and methods of testing.

Simplified Practices.—Of special interest to businessmen are the efforts of the bureau to diminish waste in industry by eliminating unnecessary

[1] In the case of time, only common carriers engaged in interstate commerce and officials of the Federal government are obliged to follow whatever time is legally declared standard. Failure on the part of any person to adhere to the standards prescribed for barrels, baskets, and hampers is declared a crime and punishable in federal courts.

variety of products. Upon request of an industry, the Division of Simplified Practice makes a survey of the size, variety, and trade demand for a particular type of product. It may find, as it has, that production costs are unnecessarily high due to the fact that a large variety is produced in order to cater to the demands of a few. It found, for example, that it took only 70 styles and colors of a certain product to satisfy 90 per cent of the purchasers but 3,614 additional styles and colors to satisfy the other 10 per cent. This disclosure led manufacturers to reduce and simplify their styles and colors, with resultant savings to all concerned. Over the years the bureau has helped to simplify the number and variety of hundreds of items, including such as bolts and nuts, paper boxes, grocers' paper bags, shovels, spades and telegraph spoons, pocketknives, wheelbarrows, carbonated beverage bottles, cans for fruits and vegetables. This service has been of incalculable value to businessmen and the general public.

The Bureau of the Census.—This bureau was originally created to count the people for purposes of apportioning members of Congress and direct taxes. Nearly everyone is familiar with the fact that censuses are taken, but few realize what becomes of the data. Nor is it commonly realized that the bureau does more than take a census every 10 years. It is the principal statistical agency of the Federal government. It is concerned not only with gathering and compiling data but also with improving statistical methods.

The sixteenth decennial census was taken in 1940, requiring the services of more than 100,000 persons. The data collected, and now published,[1] relate to population, occupations, unemployment, housing, agriculture, irrigation, drainage, manufactures, business, and mineral industries. Here is a mint of information! More is to come after the 1950 census.

In addition to this over-all enumeration, the bureau takes a special census of religious bodies and of agriculture every 10 years, a 5-year census of electric and other utilities and of manufactures, and numerous other special censuses. Also assembled and published are life tables and statistics of natality and mortality, statistics of state and local governments, prison and reform institutions, crimes, business trends, and many others. Businessmen find it profitable to consult the *Statistical Abstract of the United States,* published about every 2 years, *Foreign Commerce and Navigation of the United States,* published annually, and special reports bearing upon their particular interests.

Bureau of Foreign and Domestic Commerce.—In addition to services rendered to foreign traders, this bureau is engaged extensively in economic and business research. Information is gleaned constantly through consular reports and intimate contacts of field agents stationed in various parts of the

[1] United States Department of Commerce, *Sixteenth Census of the United States: 1940* (Washington: Government Printing Office, 1942).

country. This is made available to other government agencies and to the public in *Survey of Current Business* and *Domestic Commerce*, both of which are published monthly, the *Foreign Commerce Weekly*, and special publications. The bureau attempts to cooperate with collegiate schools of business and departments of economics in the promotion of research, and it encourages local communities to study and improve their economic welfare. It has been especially concerned with the removal of interstate and foreign trade barriers.

Weather Bureau.—The Weather Bureau was transferred from the Department of Agriculture to that of Commerce in 1940. Weather observations are made at thousands of places throughout the country. Its airway stations make observations and telegraph reports at scheduled times throughout the day, while others make observations daily and report as required. Summary reports are exchanged with meteorological centers of other nations. Observations comprise all surface weather conditions, river and flood stages, and upper-air conditions. In addition, the bureau sponsors a number of research projects seeking fuller knowledge of meteorology. Its results provide the basis for weather maps and reports which appear in the daily press and which are broadcast over the radio. Special warnings are given of storms, hurricanes, cold waves, frosts, forest fires, and floods; while specialized daily forecasts are issued for aeronautics, agriculture, engineering, and navigation. Here is a basic and invaluable service to businessmen and the general public.

Coast and Geodetic Survey.—This bureau is one of the oldest, dating back to 1807 when it was authorized to make an authentic survey of the coast. Its work has followed the expansion of the country in all directions.

Besides the main office in Washington, there are field stations and observatories scattered throughout the United States and its territories. The agency's surveys, charts, maps, and reports are of special value to those interested and engaged in navigation, fishing, engineering, aeronautics, building, and radio industries. While its work is basic to the American nation and economy, it is seldom dramatized. The average citizen hears of it only at times of earthquakes.

PATENTS, TRADE-MARKS, AND COPYRIGHTS

Patents.[1]—Present patent laws were enacted in 1870. They are administered by the United States Patent Office, a unit of the Department of Commerce. Their provisions have had a profound effect upon the entire American economy. Nearly 25,000 patents were issued during the fiscal year of 1948. One should not assume that all these are granted to obscure geniuses whose laboratory is attic or cellar; rather, well over half are issued

[1] The patent power is discussed on p. 426.

to corporations, a good number of which are foreign. Distribution over a period of 17 prewar years is shown in the following charts.

Patent Applications.—Applications for patents are sent to the Patent Office in Washington. Upon receipt of notice that the application has been filed, use of the familiar "patent pending" is permissible. Prior to 1870 each applicant had to file a model together with a drawing and

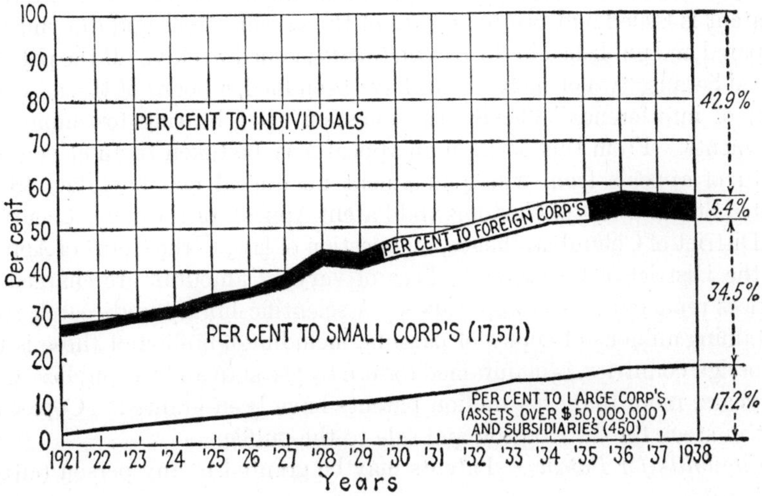

SOURCE: U.S. Patent Office.

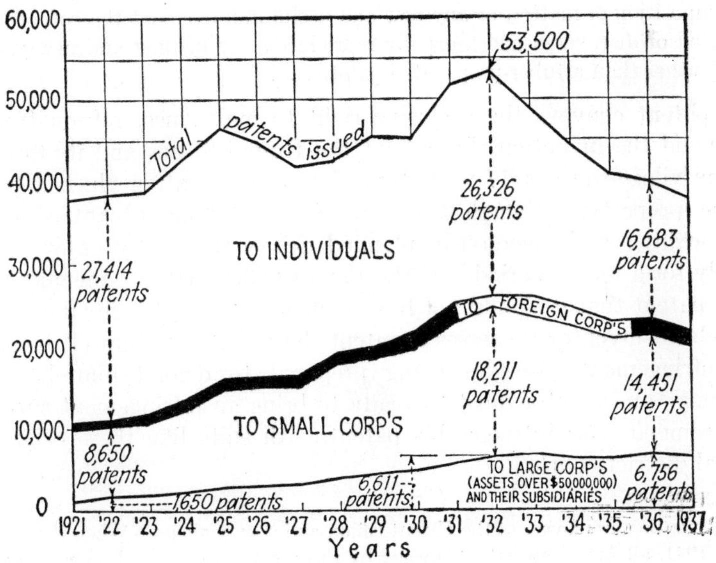

SOURCE: U.S. Patent Office.

description of his invention; now models are required only where an examiner thinks it necessary or useful. Upon receipt of an application it is checked to see if it is in the proper form; then it goes to one of a number of examining divisions, where it is looked over to see whether the invention is fully and clearly disclosed. Then a search is made through domestic and foreign patents and literature to ascertain whether a prior invention has been patented. If the office is satisfied that the inventor's claims are valid, a patent is issued and printed copies of the specifications and drawings are prepared and published in the *Official Gazette*, issued weekly. If the patent is denied because two or more claims have been filed, a board of three "examiners of interference" decides the question after hearing testimony and arguments. From this decision an appeal may be taken to an eleven-man board of appeals from whose judgment an appeal can be taken to the United States Court of Customs and Patent Appeals or the district court for the District of Columbia, thence, on question of law, to the Court of Appeals for the District of Columbia.[1] Fees of varying amounts are charged for services rendered patent applicants. A scientific library and search room containing millions of copies of patents, including 6 million of those issued by foreign countries, is maintained for use by the staff and the public. Over the years, more than 2⅓ million patents have been granted. Copies are kept in stock for distribution and sale to the public.

Eligibility for Patents.—Patents may be granted to any person (citizen or alien)[2]

> Who has invented or discovered any new and useful art, machine, manufacture, or composition of matter, or any new and useful improvement thereof, or who has invented or discovered and asexually reproduced any distinct and new variety of plant, other than a tuber-propagated plant. . . .

The patent conveys the exclusive right to make, use, refrain from use, and vend the invention throughout the United States and its territories. The privilege runs for 17 years from date of issue, after which it becomes public property, although the patentee by taking advantage of legal technicalities and ingeniously planned delays frequently enjoys his monopoly for a longer period. If the Patent Office makes a mistake in issuing a patent that it should not have issued, the patent is invalid. Hence, though an inventor possesses a patent, he might find himself being sued for infringement. Besides being prepared to defend himself in such instances, an inventor must be ready to bring an infringement suit whenever someone else infringes his patent. All suits like these originate in federal district courts.

[1] Cf. p. 343.

[2] Excepting employees of the Patent Office, and enemy aliens. When the war broke out in 1941, all American patents owned by the enemy or enemy aliens were seized by the Alien Property Custodian.

Criticisms of Patent Laws.—Patent laws, which have been virtually unchanged since 1870, recently have been the subject of much investigation and criticism.[1] The chief complaint is that large corporations, to whom many patents are issued, abuse their patent monopolies by entering into agreements of various sorts with others for the purpose of diminishing competition and restraining trade. It is also complained that patented inventions are "suppressed," which means that inventors are given patent monopolies and then do not use them but, rather, hold on to them for 17 years simply to keep someone else from patenting and marketing the invention. By this means, a large corporation holding several key patents might prevent the use of some new process or product for many years. Other complaints are that "patents-pending" privileges are abused; that the big intimidate the weak by threats of infringement suits; that there is too much litigation and expense connected with obtaining patents; and that the judges who handle court disputes lack technical training necessary to ensure uniformity and justice. Many suggestions for reform have been made and though bills have been introduced, Congress has, at this writing,[2] taken no action.

Trade-marks.—Trade-marks are governed by Congress under its power to regulate interstate and foreign commerce. The latest legislation[3] is the Lanham Trade-mark Act of 1946—a measure long striven for by interested parties. This law generally codifies, revises, and simplifies common and federal statutory law on the subject.

Under the new legislation not only trade-marks may be registered but also service marks, collective marks, and certification marks. A trade-mark is a word, name, symbol, or device, or any combination of them, which identifies and distinguishes goods. Examples are "Kodak" for cameras and "Philco" for radios. A service mark is one which identifies and distinguishes a service, for example "Greyhound" for bus transportation and "Amos 'n' Andy" for entertainment. A collective mark is one used by a group or association to identify or distinguish goods or services of members, for example "Indian River" for oranges, "Mohawk Valley" for apples, the pine tree for Rochdale cooperatives, and the Boy Scout emblem. A certification mark is one used for goods and services of any person other than owners to certify regional origin, quality, accuracy, mode of manufacture, and the like. Examples are various seals, like the

[1] See especially: Temporary National Economic Committee, *Investigation of Concentration of Economic Power*, Monograph No. 31, by Walton Hamilton *et al.*, "Patents and Free Enterprise," and Temporary National Economic Committee, *Investigation of Concentration of Economic Power*, *Hearings*, part 3, "Patents, Proposals for Changes in Law and Procedure."

[2] Fall, 1949.

[3] For an excellent historical commentary and analysis see *United States Code, Annotated*, Title 15, Chap. 22.

"Good Housekeeping Seal of Approval" and the labor union symbol used to indicate that work was done by organized labor under collective bargaining.

Marks of all types are registered with the Patent Office. The procedure is much the same as that explained above for patents. Among marks not to be registered are those showing a flag or symbol of any American or foreign government; those that are immoral, deceptive, or scandalous; those which may suggest a connection with or likeness to persons living or dead, institutions, beliefs, or national symbols; or those that closely resemble marks already registered. Marks of all types are good for 20 years provided that after 5 years registrants file affidavits showing that their marks are still in use or that nonuse is due to special circumstances. After the first 20 years registrations may be renewed for subsequent periods of similar length. As in the case of patents and copyrights, registrants must protect their own rights by resort, if need be, to the courts.

Copyrights.—Unlike the agencies described above, this office is not in the Department of Commerce, but rather is a part of the Library of Congress. Copyrights may be obtained only *after* writings are published. To secure them two copies must be sent to the Copyright Office with an appropriate fee. When received, the work is registered and the author is duly notified. Henceforth he enjoys the exclusive right to "print, reprint, publish, copy and vend" the work. The privilege extends for a period of 28 years and is renewable for a second, but not a third, period of the same duration. Notice of copyright must be printed somewhere near the front of the publication; if it is not, others may copy or reproduce the work in any way they please. As compared with the issuance of patents, the procedure is simple and brief. As in the case of patents, the Copyright Office does not guarantee the originality of the writing, nor will it protect the author from infringement. Such protection must be obtained by resort to the United States district court.

At present one may copyright the following:

1. Books, including composite and encyclopedic work directories, gazetteers, and other compilations
2. Periodicals, including newspapers
3. Lectures, sermons, addresses (prepared for oral delivery)
4. Dramatic and dramatico-musical compositions
5. Musical compositions
6. Maps
7. Works of art, models or designs for works of art
8. Reproductions of a work of art
9. Drawings or plastic works of a scientific or technical character
10. Photographs
11. Prints and pictorial illustrations

12. Motion-picture photoplays
13. Motion pictures other than photoplays

There is a fundamental difference between patents and copyrights. The former protects the subject matter for which patents are granted even against a bona fide inventor who may independently make the same invention. A copyright, on the other hand, protects only against actual copying. One may write a book, for example, describing Niagara Falls, and secure a copyright thereon; this does not prevent someone else from writing a book on the same subject, as long as he does not copy from the former. One may take a photograph and have it copyrighted, but this would not prevent someone else from taking a picture of the same scene. Several authors may write textbooks about the same subject; their books will necessarily be similar, but their copyrights will not be infringed unless one actually copies from another.

DEBT RELIEF AND FINANCIAL AIDS

Bankruptcy.—Because many businessmen fail, provision for their orderly liquidation is an important contribution to business enterprises and the public.[1] No agency of the executive branch has been set up by Congress to administer laws relative to insolvent businesses. Instead, administration is left largely to the courts. Bankruptcy cases originate as equity proceedings before United States district courts. With a few exceptions, they may be started either by the debtor himself or by his creditors. After a debtor has been declared a bankrupt, settlement of the estate usually takes place under the supervision of a referee appointed by the court and one or more trustees chosen by the creditors. Appeal may, as usual, be taken to the Circuit and Supreme Courts.

Federal Bankruptcy Legislation.—Except for three brief periods, all of which followed major and minor depressions,[2] Congress left the field entirely to the states prior to the enactment of the Nelson Act in 1898. Following discovery of numerous bankruptcy frauds and widespread criticism of the Nelson Act, President Hoover, in 1931, caused a nation-wide survey of the results of the law. The disclosures of this report, coupled with widespread economic distress, led to a number of amendments. Finally, in 1938, the Chandler Act was passed, which, while retaining the framework

[1] The power upon which bankruptcy legislation is based is discussed on p. 424.

[2] The first bankruptcy act, Apr. 4, 1800, followed the minor depression of 1798. It was repealed in 1803. The second, Aug. 18, 1841, followed the severe depression of 1837 and was repealed in 1843. The third, Mar. 3, 1867, followed the financial disturbances incident to the Civil War, and was repealed in 1878. Subsequent legislation has also been born of depression. The Nelson Act of July 1, 1898, followed the depression of 1893, while the revisions that culminated in the Chandler Act of 1938 grew out of the great depression.

of the Nelson Act, embodied many amendments and codified existing law on the subject. The changes included special provisions for farmers, railroads, municipalities, and certain other types of private corporations.[1]

Business Credit.—In normal times private financial institutions, with the aid of the Federal Reserve System and only incidental assistance from the Treasury Department, have been able to meet the credit needs of the business community. The First World War brought unusual demands, causing Congress to create the War Finance Corporation to lend directly, when funds from private sources were unavailable, to industries whose operations were "necessary or contributory to the prosecution of the war," and also to banking institutions and building and loan associations. In 1919 the same corporation was authorized to help finance the railroads, then under governmental operation, and American exporters. During the 1920's these activities were terminated, but the depression caused a resumption of federal lending on an unprecedented scale. During the Second World War most of these activities were continued and even greatly expanded. In this field two wars and a major depression have wrought a revolution, the Federal government now assuming responsibility for directly or indirectly underwriting the credit needs of the national economy.

The Reconstruction Finance Corporation (RFC).—Of all federal lending agencies the Reconstruction Finance Corporation is the largest and the one most directly concerned with general business. This gigantic institution was started under the Hoover administration in 1932. It was given corporate form in order to afford greater freedom and flexibility of action, with a life span of 10 years which has since been extended through June 30, 1956. Prior to 1945 it was part of the Department of Commerce. Its transfer to the Federal Loan Agency occurred in February, 1945, when President Roosevelt removed the chairman, Jesse Jones of Texas, and nominated former Vice-President Henry A. Wallace, who was thought by a coalition of conservative Democrats and Republicans to be too radical to be placed in charge of such a mammoth financial institution. In 1947 the Federal Loan Agency was abolished and all its functions turned over to the RFC, which has subsequently been an independent establishment. The corporation has a capital stock of 100 million dollars, all of which is owned by the Federal government. Management is vested in a three-man board of directors. The Corporation functions through a principal office in Washington, a representative in Honolulu, and loan agencies located in thirty-one principal cities. Federal Reserve Banks act as depositories and fiscal agents for the corporation. Established to help finance industry through the depression, it has now become one of the largest financial institutions in the Western world.

[1] For a discussion of the controversy over the constitutionality of some of these provisions, see pp. 424–426.

Functions of the RFC.—During the depression the RFC came to the aid of many businessmen and many state and local governments. As the war approached, RFC funds were used to finance expansion of war industries, and later its resources were devoted almost entirely to this purpose. After the war it helped finance reconversion. During the war period the RFC went into business itself on a large scale. Indeed, as of January, 1945, it and its subsidiaries were operating 125 plants, among them steel mills, aircraft factories, munitions plants, and the like. The RFC has also helped finance some of the other federal agencies, including the Federal Deposit Insurance Corporation, the Export-Import Bank, and the Federal Home Loan Banks.

Presently, the RFC is liquidating many outstanding loans, lending to private businessmen when funds may be unavailable from other sources, lending to state and local governments for public works, continuing to help finance other federal agencies, lending money where necessary because of floods or other catastrophes, liquidating some of its war-started productive facilities, and continuing to operate some of its enterprises. Among the latter are a tin metal works in Texas, a sisal plantation in Hawaii, abaca plantations in Central America, and a press for forging light metals at Worcester, Mass.

Federal Emergency Spending.—During the depression years, besides making credit available on easy terms, the Federal government followed a deliberate policy of spending public funds to alleviate distress and create purchasing power which it hoped would "prime the pump" and restore business to normal levels. Ordinary expenditures increased from 3 billion dollars in 1931 to more than 4½ billion in 1938, while nonrepayable expenditures for relief and recovery amounted to a total of nearly 15 billions for the years 1932–1938. The principal emergency spending agencies were the Public Works Administration and the Works Progress Administration, whose activities are discussed in a later chapter.

Government spending during depressions for "public works" is nothing new. What occasioned extraordinary controversy during the 1930's was the fact that the Federal government for the first time stepped boldly into the field; the unprecedented extent to which the program was carried; fear lest the activities become permanent; and apprehension lest this become the first stage of eventual transition to state socialism. Federal lending and spending undoubtedly eased the lot of many farms, homes, financial and business institutions, provided many useful public buildings and social improvements, and generally helped sustain morale throughout a distressed world. Critics insist, however, that permanent recovery would have come quicker had policies been adopted which looked more toward the restoration of confidence in private enterprise.

Spending for armaments and eventual war began in earnest in 1939.

During the period between 1939 and 1944 a total of more than 194 billion dollars was spent for preparedness and war alone. Needless to say, this "primed the pump" with a vengeance! Almost overnight traditions of individualism and fears of socialism disappeared and the national economy became a collective giant with almost every segment under government control. Both the short- and long-run consequences for business are incalculable.

After the war, inflation at home acted as a restraint on federal spending for economic reasons, but large-scale outlays for military purposes and overseas relief and rehabilitation had a stimulating effect on the economy. Steps proposed to be taken to rearm signatories of the North Atlantic Pact and to help undeveloped regions to prosper are likely to have the same effect. With every dip in the business cycle the clamor increases for more government spending. In consequence, politics and economics have become increasingly intermingled, with the Federal government at the center striving to plan, serve, control, and "save" the economy and those most likely to get hurt. Whether this is wise policy, or whether the Federal government can accomplish what is proposed, will provoke an argument in almost any quarter and at any time.

References

Bailey, Stephen K.: *Congress Makes a Law; The Story behind the Employment Act of 1946* (New York: Columbia University Press, 1949).

Beckett, Grace L.: *Reciprocal Trade Agreements Program* (New York: Columbia University Press, 1941).

Berle, Adolph A., and Gardner C. Means: *The Modern Corporation and Private Property* (New York: Macmillan, 1933).

Blinken, Donald M.: *Wool Tariffs and American Policy* (Washington: Public Affairs Press, 1948).

Chase, Stuart: *The Road We Are Traveling 1914–1942* (New York: Twentieth Century Fund, 1942).

Currie, Brainerd (ed.): "The Patent System," *Law and Contemporary Problems*, vol. XII, No. 4 (Durham, N.C.: Duke University School of Law, 1947).

Fainsod, Merle, and Lincoln Gordon: *Government and the American Economy* (New York: Norton, 2d ed., 1949).

Fischer, Louis A.: *History of the Standard Weights and Measures of the United States*, Bureau of Standards Publication M 64, 1905 (Washington: Government Printing Office, 1905).

Fuller, Douglas R.: *Government Financing of Private Enterprise* (Stanford University, Calif.: Stanford University Press, 1948).

Gordon, Robert A.: *Business Leadership in the Large Corporation* (Washington: Brookings, 1945).

Hallock, William, and Herbert T. Wade: *Outlines of the Evolution of Weights and Measures and the Metric System* (New York: Macmillan, 1906).

Kimmel, Lewis H.: *Postwar Tax Policy and Business Expansion* (Washington: Brookings, 1943).

KOONTZ, HAROLD A.: *Government Control of Business* (Boston: Houghton Mifflin, 1941).
LETICHE, JOHN M.: *Reciprocal Trade Agreements in the World Economy* (New York: King's Crown Press, 1948).
LYON, LEVERETT S., VICTOR ABRAMSON, *et al.*: *Government and Economic Life* (Washington: Brookings, 2 vols., 1940).
MOULTON, HAROLD G.: *Controlling Factors in Economic Development* (Washington: Brookings, 1949).
RICHBERG, DONALD: *Government and Business Tomorrow: A Public Relations Program* (New York: Harper, 1943).
ROHLFING, CHARLES C. *et al.*: *Government and Business* (Chicago: Foundation Press, 5th ed., 1949).
RUML, BEARDSLEY: *Government, Business, and Values* (New York: Harper, 1943).
SCHAPP, ADELBERT: *Patent Fundamentals* (New York: The Industrial Press, 1939).
SCHATTSCHNEIDER, ELMER E.: *Politics, Pressures and the Tariff* (New York: Farrar, 1942).
TASCA, HENRY J.: *Reciprocal Trade Policy of the United States; A Study in Trade Philosophy* (Philadelphia: University of Pennsylvania Press, 1938).
TOULMIN, HARRY A.: *Patents and the Public Interest* (New York: Harper, 1939).
TWENTIETH CENTURY FUND, INC.: *Big Business: Its Growth and Place* (New York: The Twentieth Century Fund, 1937).
UNITED STATES BOARD OF INVESTIGATION AND RESEARCH: *Public Aids to Domestic Transportation*, House Doc. 159, 79th Cong., 1st Sess. (Washington: Government Printing Office, 1945).
UNITED STATES DEPARTMENT OF COMMERCE, BUREAU OF THE CENSUS: *Sixteenth Census of the United States:* 1940 (Washington: Government Printing Office, 1942).
UNITED STATES NATIONAL RESOURCES COMMITTEE: *The Structure of the American Economy* (Washington: Government Printing Office, 1939).
WEINSTEIN, JACOB I.: *The Bankruptcy Law of* 1938: *Chandler Act; A Comparative Analysis Prepared for the National Association of Credit Men* (New York: National Association of Credit Men, 1938).

Chapter 29

GENERAL BUSINESS REGULATION, CONSUMERS' SERVICES, AND HOUSING

It is a matter of common knowledge that corporations are not natural persons. They are artificial persons. They are creatures of the government. Only on the authorization of government can they come into existence. Only with the sanction of government can they perform any acts, good or bad. The corporate abuses which have occurred, the concentration of wealth which has come about under their operations, all can be laid directly and immediately at the door of government. There is no escape from this responsibility.

Charles A. Beard.[1]

REGULATION OF SECURITIES

Need for Regulation.—When corporations organize, their securities—stocks, bonds, debentures, certificates, etc.—are sold to the public, generally through "stock markets" or "security exchanges." Corporate securities are owned by millions of persons, many of whom own only a few shares. Without governmental regulation, poorly informed investors may easily be misled, even by reliable brokers, while many will fall prey to unscrupulous promoters.

The states have attempted to protect the investing public by "blue-sky laws" aimed primarily at fraudulent sales, and by statutes requiring the registration of securities with some state agency. While of value, these provided inadequate protection and the states hesitated to enact drastic laws fearing exchanges would move to some more accommodating state. Moreover, the interstate character of corporate financing made effective state control virtually impossible.

Securities and Exchange Legislation.—The stock-market crash of 1929 and subsequent disclosures clearly revealed the necessity for federal control. Congress responded by enacting the Federal Securities Act in 1933 and the Securities Exchange Act in 1934. These laws are administered by a Securities and Exchange Commission, created in 1934 and composed of five members appointed for terms of 5 years.

The Federal Securities Act seeks to provide the public with accurate information about corporate securities, while the Securities Exchange Act provides for the regulation of buying and selling of stocks and bonds

[1] United States Senate, Committee on the Judiciary, *Federal Licensing of Corporations, Hearings*, 75th Cong., 1st Sess., on S. 10 (Washington: Government Printing Office, 1937), part 1, p. 72.

on security exchanges throughout the country. Their purpose is not to guarantee the investments of individuals but to provide them with essential information by which to judge the securities they buy, and to protect them from misrepresentation. More specifically, the basic requirement is that corporations issuing securities to the public, security exchanges, and persons dealing in securities outside the exchanges ("over-the-counter" sales) must register with the Securities and Exchange Commission. Before offering securities for sale, corporations must file with the commission a statement containing essential information about the business upon which the value of their securities depends. Exchanges, brokers, and dealers are required to keep accounts in accordance with methods prescribed by the commission, and make periodic reports. In addition, the law makes illegal certain unfair competitive practices such as "washed sales" and "matched orders."[1] As a means of further controlling speculative booms, the Federal Reserve Board is empowered to fix "margins," *i.e.*, fix the amount of credit that may be extended to those who buy securities.

It is now generally agreed that legislation such as this was long overdue and will be retained regardless of which party is in office, although there are some who believe the regulations should be relaxed to help "restore confidence" in business.

COMPETITION AND TRADE PRACTICES

Capitalist theory assumes that private business should and will compete freely. Experience demonstrates, however, that there is a difference between theory and practice resulting in combinations of one sort or another with tendencies to monopolize the market. Such control as was deemed necessary was left to the states until near the end of the last century, but the emergence of large-scale trusts in oil, sugar, meat, steel, and other basic industries led to the passage of the Sherman Antitrust Act of 1890. This is still the basic law on the subject. At the same time many states have retained their statutes with respect to intrastate commerce.

Antitrust Legislation.—Provisions that proscribe monopolies and monopolistic practices in interstate and foreign commerce are found in five principal statutes: the Sherman Act of 1890, the Clayton Act of 1914, the Federal Trade Commission Act of 1914, the Robinson-Patman Act of 1936, and the Wheeler-Lea Act of 1938.

[1] The former is an arrangement whereby one speculator agrees to sell at a point higher than that commanded by a security on the market at a given time and another agrees to buy for the purpose of creating the impression that the security is commanding buyers. "Matched orders" are those in which a party hires two brokers unknown to each other, one to offer for sale and the other to buy, in order to create the impression of an active market to attract buyers.

The Sherman Act forbids the following:

Every contract, combination, in the form of trust or otherwise, or conspiracy in the restraint of trade or commerce among the several states, or with foreign nations. . . .

It says further:

Every person who shall monopolize, or attempt to monopolize, or combine or conspire with any person or persons, to monopolize any part of the trade or commerce among the several states, or with foreign nations, shall be deemed guilty of a misdemeanor. . . .

The Clayton Act supplements these provisions by outlawing three specific evils: price discrimination, exclusive agreements, and interlocking directorates among large competing companies. The Federal Trade Commission Act condemns "unfair methods of competition" among those engaged in interstate and foreign commerce; the Wheeler-Lea Act of 1938 amends the Federal Trade Commission Act to prohibit also "unfair or deceptive acts or practices in commerce"; while the Robinson-Patman Act amends the Clayton Act in order to outlaw transactions through which chain stores received the benefit of prices that did not always correctly reflect all legitimate costs. It outlaws discrimination in prices for goods of "like grade and quality" where the effect is substantially to lessen competition or where it tends to create a monopoly and also where the effect is to "injure, destroy or prevent competition which any person who either grants or knowingly receives the benefit of such discrimination or with customers of either of them."

Exemptions from Antitrust Laws.—Although the law is broadly stated, there are many exemptions from its provisions. After a long and bitter contest, labor organizations are finally immune, except possibly where they combine with nonlabor forces in activities that restrain trade.[1] The Webb-Pomerene Act of 1918 permits cooperative arrangements among those engaged in export trade as long as their agreements are registered with the Federal Trade Commission. The Transportation Act of 1920 permits railroad consolidations that are approved by the Interstate Commerce Commission. The Agricultural Exemption Act of 1922 and later amendments permit farmers, planters, dairymen, and others engaged in agriculture to form associations for the more effective marketing of products. The National Industrial Recovery Act, now invalid, and later the Guffey Coal Acts, now expired, exempted codified industries from the antitrust laws under the theory that the public was sufficiently protected by code and public authorities. The Merchant Marine Act of 1936 permits agreements among shipping lines if approved by the Maritime Commission;

[1] See p. 734.

while mergers and combinations are permitted among gas and electric holding companies, interstate motor carriers, interstate electric-power and natural-gas companies, and to a limited extent telephone, telegraph, and cable companies if approved by the regulatory commissions having jurisdiction over them. The Miller-Tydings Act of 1937 legalized resale price maintenance agreements between manufacturers and distributors in those states where such agreements are not illegal so far as local commerce is concerned. Finally, the Reed-Bulwinkle Act of 1948 permits common carriers of particular classes to agree among themselves on rates and charges provided approval of the Interstate Commerce Commission is first obtained.

Enforcement.—Alleged violations of the antitrust laws may be dealt with in four ways: by criminal prosecution, the penalties for conviction being fine or imprisonment, or both, and confiscation of property; by injunctions, which may be obtained from courts by either agents of the government or injured parties; by civil suits brought by either the government or private individuals; or, in some instances, by administrative adjudication by the Federal Trade Commission. Prosecutions are handled by the Department of Justice, which has created a special division for the purpose, although the Federal Trade Commission frequently participates in investigating and assembling the factual data.

Enforcement has been one of the most difficult assignments imaginable and there are many who have criticized, even ridiculed, the attempt. Investigations into the corporate structures and activities of such industrial giants as the Aluminum Company of America, the Standard Oil Company, the Pullman Car Company, and the United States Steel Corporation require a reservoir of determination—too often dissipated by time and political processes—statutes whose meanings are clear and concise, and a large, competent staff. A combination of all three has seldom if ever existed.

Findings and Recommendations of the TNEC.—After extended study by a staff of outstanding specialists and extensive hearings, the Temporary National Economic Committee[1] made a number of recommendations. Concerning antitrust laws the committee was unanimous in recommending that enforcement be strengthened. "No hope," said the committee, "of preventing the increase of evils directly attributable to monopoly is possible, no prospect of enforcing and maintaining a free economic system

[1] This was a committee made up of twelve members, with equal representation from the House, Senate, and the executive branch, appointed pursuant to a congressional resolution (Public Resolution No. 113, 65th Cong.). Senator Joseph C. O'Mahoney, of Wyoming, was chairman. The hearings of the committee have been published in thirty-one parts, while forty-three monographs prepared by outstanding specialists have also been published. These contain materials that are indispensable to an understanding of the American economy and current problems.

under democratic auspices is in view, unless our efforts are redoubled to cope with the gigantic aggregations of capital which have become so dominant in our economic life."[1]

More specifically it recommended that the patent laws be seriously overhauled; that trade associations be required to register with an agency of the Federal government and publicize their activities; that the Federal Trade Commission be given authority to approve mergers of large corporations; that fines be increased from the present maximum of $5,000 to $50,000; that the Federal Trade Commission be authorized to act as master in chancery and thereby be enabled to hear evidence and make findings of fact and conclusions in law in any pending antitrust proceeding (these findings would be advisory to the federal courts, thus providing the latter with the benefit of more expert advice than is now possible); and, finally, that the Federal government enact legislation designed to strengthen state control over insurance companies.[2]

Unfair Methods of Competition.—Among other duties, the Federal Trade Commission is charged with responsibility for preventing "unfair methods of competition" and "unfair or deceptive acts or practices" on the part of those engaged in interstate and foreign commerce. Unfair methods are all attempts to achieve business gains through wrongdoing or undue restraints that injure competitors or the public.[3] The list of methods declared to be illegal, unfair, and deceptive is long, but they fall into two classes: unfair methods that are opposed to good morals; and unfair methods that tend unduly to hinder competition and effect trade restraints and monopoly. Only a few illustrations can be mentioned.

Methods Inconsistent with Good Morals.—Some which fall in this class are:

1. The use of false or misleading advertising concerning, and the misbranding of, commodities.
2. Representing products to have been made in the United States when the mechanism or movements, in whole or in important part, are of foreign origin.
3. Selling rebuilt, secondhand, renovated, or old products by representing them as new or failing to indicate that they are not made of new materials.
4. Using merchandising schemes based on lot or chance, or on a pretended contest of skill.

[1] United States Congress, Temporary National Economic Committee, *Investigation of Concentration of Economic Power, Final Report and Recommendations*, Sen. Doc. 35, 77th Cong., 1st Sess. (Washington: Government Printing Office, 1941), p. 35.

[2] *Ibid.*, pp. 35–43.

[3] John H. Norwood, *Trade Practice and Price Law—Federal* (New York: Commerce Clearing House, Inc., 1938), p. 33.

5. Schemes to create the impression that the customer is being offered an opportunity to make purchases under unusually favorable conditions when such is not the case (as, the use of the "free goods" or service device to create the impression that something is actually being thrown in without charge, when it is fully covered by the amount exacted in the transaction as a whole, or by services to be rendered by the recipient).

6. Using deceptive containers.

7. Giving products misleading names so as to give them a value that they would not otherwise possess (*e.g.*, saying a coat made of rabbit fur is made of "Baltic fox" or "beaver"; or falsely suggesting that a product has been approved by some well-known medical, dental, or other professional organization).

8. Simulation of competitors' trade names, labels, dress of goods, or counter-display catalogues (*e.g.*, using such words as "Importing," "Manufacturing Co." or "Foundry" when the firms involved were merely processors or dealers; using the name "Westinghouse Union Company" in simulation of "Westinghouse Electric Co.," or using the title "Who's Who and Why" in competition with the well-known "Who's Who in America").

Methods Tending to Restraints and Monopoly.—A few of these are:

1. Conspiring to maintain uniform selling prices, terms, and conditions of sale through the use of a patent-licensing system.

2. Trade boycotts or combinations of traders to prevent certain wholesale and retail dealers from procuring goods at the same terms accorded to the boycotters or conspirators.

3. Buying up supplies for the purpose of hampering competitors and stifling or eliminating competition.

4. Using concealed subsidiaries, ostensibly independent, to obtain competitive business otherwise unavailable.

5. Combinations or agreements of competitors to fix, enhance, or depress prices, maintain prices, bring about substantial uniformity in prices, or divide territory or business, to cut off or interfere with competitors' source of supply, or to close markets to competitors.

6. Intimidation or coercion of a producer or distributor to cause him to organize, join, or contribute to, or to prevent him from organizing, joining, or contributing to, a producers' cooperative association, or other association, advertising agency, or publisher.

7. Harassing competitors (*e.g.*, by bribing or hiring their employees, by threatening needless and vexatious lawsuits, and by making false and misleading statements about competitors and their products).

8. Selling below cost or giving products without charge, with the intent of hindering or suppressing competition.

9. Coercing and forcing uneconomic and monopolistic reciprocal dealing.

False and Misleading Advertising.—Prior to 1938 the Federal Trade Commission had no specific authorization to deal with advertising affecting commerce but had to proceed on the basis that false and misleading advertising was an unfair and deceptive trade practice. This is still the basis for action with respect to most commodities, but an amendment in 1938 grants specific authority to suppress false and misleading advertising of foods, drugs, devices, and cosmetics.[1] The amendment also grants authority for the commission to intercede not merely when competitors are injured but when the public is also.

Reports of the Trade Commission are filled with illustrations of false and misleading advertising, of which only a few can be mentioned. A firm in Los Angeles was stopped from advertising that its fingernail polish "Nailife" provided a "perfect nail food" which "will transform irregular broken nails into well formed symmetrical ones" and "make your nails strong and healthy." A physical culture firm was ordered to discontinue advertising that its course of study would "make muscles grow like magic" or "start new inches of massive power pushing out your chest" or "put regular mountains of muscles under your biceps" or "banish constipation, poor digestion, pimples, skin blotches, and similar conditions that rob you of the good things of life." Another firm was stopped from advertising coffee under the trade name "Rico Café" when it was not a Puerto Rican coffee or blend thereof.

Federal Trade Commission Procedure.—The Trade Commission has evolved a procedure for handling violations that has received wide acclaim and provided a model for several regulatory agencies more recently established. First, it should be noted that the function of the commission is primarily remedial, not punitive. Although it has power to impose penalties, its principal object is to protect the public, not to punish the offender.

Violations are suspected either as a result of complaints that reach the commission or through investigations conducted by the commission's own accountants, economists, and attorneys. When a questionable practice is being followed by several in the same trade, a trade-practice conference is called at which codes of fair competition may be agreed upon whereby members of the trade agree to discontinue the obnoxious practice. Where particular individuals are involved, a thorough investigation is made, following which the case may be dismissed for lack of merit or the suspected party may enter into what is known as a "stipulation" whereby the charges are admitted and the respondent stipulates that he will mend

[1] This work of the Federal Trade Commission should not be confused with that of the Food and Drug Administration which is discussed on p. 663. The Trade Commission polices trade practices and advertising while the Food and Drug Administration checks the misbranding and adulteration of foods, drugs, devices, and cosmetics.

his ways.[1] Unless the charges are withdrawn or a stipulation is issued, the commission issues a formal complaint. Thereupon, a hearing is held before a trial examiner, testimony is taken, and a report is made to the commission by the examiner. If the commission finds the respondent guilty, it issues a "cease and desist" order. Appeals may be taken to the United States Circuit Courts but the commission's findings of facts, if supported by sufficient evidence, are final. Prior to 1938 the commission lacked power to impose penalties but was required to rely upon the courts for enforcement. In the year mentioned, however, it was authorized to impose penalties of not more than $5,000 for disobedience to final orders.

The National Industrial Recovery Act.—This measure was enacted on June 16, 1933, as an attempt to stem the deflation and restore prosperity. Producers were urged to form "codes of fair competition" which, when approved by a majority of the producers and the President, became the law for the entire trade. Some 700 codes were approved. All of them were required to contain provisions forbidding monopolistic practices, the employment of children, and recognizing the rights of employees to organize and bargain collectively through representatives of their own choosing. While forbidding monopoly, the antitrust laws were nevertheless suspended in codified industries. Furthermore, the codes fixed minimum wages, maximum hours, trade practices, and sometimes prices. When approved by the President, *all* producers in codified industries were obliged to comply with code provisions or be subject to fine and imprisonment. Primary responsibility for enforcement was delegated to the National Recovery Administration in cooperation with code authorities set up within each industry. After nearly 2 years of operation, the act was declared unconstitutional,[2] but it stands as an interesting landmark of an attempt on the part of government and business jointly to control industry and bring about economic recovery.

Although the NRA collapsed, many of its objectives have been attained, at least partially, through other legislation. Child labor was outlawed, and minimum wages and maximum hours were fixed for businesses engaged in interstate commerce by the Walsh-Healy Public Contracts Act, adopted in 1936, and the Fair Labor Standards Act, adopted in 1938.[3] The rights guaranteed to labor by the NRA received even greater protection under the National Labor Relations Act, enacted in 1935.[4] For only one nonutility industry, however, the bituminous coal, were the price-fixing provisions

[1] Stipulations are not permitted where intent to mislead or defraud is discovered; nor in cases involving false advertisement of food, drugs, devices, or cosmetics that may be injurious to health; nor in other instances involving more serious violations.

[2] Schechter Poultry Corp. *v.* United States, 295 U.S. 495 (1935); for further discussion of the constitutional aspects of this case see p. 382.

[3] For a fuller discussion of these measures see p. 741.

[4] See p. 735.

reenacted; antitrust provisions were never subsequently suspended;[1] and while trade associations are used for consultative purposes, no subsequent attempt has been made to utilize them as official agencies for the administration and enforcement of law.

Bituminous Coal Acts.—One disadvantage of the democratic-capitalist system is that government control of competitive industries is often unobtainable until business in general or particular industries find themselves in the doldrums. This has been especially true of the coal industry, which between the two world wars was one of the sickest of all ailing industries.

Following the collapse of NRA, Congress promptly enacted similar legislation governing the bituminous coal industry. Little action resulted, however, chiefly because of doubts over constitutionality—doubts that were soon to be confirmed by the Supreme Court.[2]

Following this judicial rebuff, Congress reenacted those sections of the earlier law which provided for fixing minimum and maximum coal prices. Several other changes were made, the most important of which were that commission membership was increased from five to seven and a tax was levied amounting to 20 per cent of the sale price at the mine, less 19½ per cent for those producers who joined the code.

While the constitutionality of this measure was never seriously doubted,[3] many administrative difficulties were encountered. Because of these and patronage squabbles among members of the commission, the commission was abolished in 1939 and made a division in the Department of the Interior. Even there progress was slow and the act was finally permitted to expire in 1943. At that time the coal industry was booming because of the war, but if it again becomes depressed, attempts will doubtless be made to reenact something similar to the coal acts.

LIQUOR AND NARCOTICS

Legal Results of Repeal.—From a legal point of view, the much-controverted Eighteenth (prohibition) Amendment was due in part to court decisions which made it difficult if not impossible for dry states to control the interstate aspects of the liquor traffic.[4] The Eighteenth Amendment abolished both interstate and intrastate manufacture, transportation, and sale of alcoholic beverages and gave the Federal and state governments concurrent jurisdiction to enforce these provisions. Although the Twenty-

[1] Except temporarily during the war, when enforcement would have disrupted economic activities essential to winning the war, and for railroad under the Reed-Bulwinkle Act mentioned above.

[2] Carter *v.* Carter Coal Co., 298 U.S. 238 (1936). See also p. 389.

[3] It was upheld in Sunshine Anthracite Coal Co. *v.* Adkins, 310 U.S. 381 (1940). See also p. 390.

[4] For a fuller discussion see p. 381.

first Amendment completely repealed the Eighteenth, it did not return legal matters entirely to where they were before prohibition. Rather, the Twenty-first contains this significant sentence: "The transportation or importation into any State, Territory, or possession of the United States for delivery or use therein of intoxicating liquors, in violation of the laws thereof, is hereby prohibited." Thus federal law completely surrounds a dry state, helping with enforcement. Note that this does not prevent the transportation of liquors *across* dry states; it simply forbids transportation or importation *for delivery* or *use* therein.

Methods of State Control.—Control of the traffic in liquor and its use has long been a concern of governments everywhere. The states have primary responsibility since the problem so intimately affects the health, safety, and morals of the community. The states follow a variety of plans. Two states (Mississippi and Oklahoma) have retained prohibition. Twenty-eight states and the District of Columbia depend upon a licensing system whereby all activities incident to the manufacture, distribution, and sale of liquor are handled by individuals licensed by the states. In Wyoming state stores monopolize all wholesale transactions, while sixteen states monopolize retail outlets. In both situations other aspects of the industry are controlled through licensing.

Federal Legislation.—In addition to aiding dry states, federal legislation has had three objectives: The first has been to protect American producers from foreign competition. The second has been to obtain revenue. The third has been to apply controls with respect to competition, unfair trade practices, adulteration, misbranding, advertising, wages, hours, and working conditions similar to those applied to other industries. The latter was first done under NRA codes, but when these were declared unconstitutional similar provisions were reenacted which have since remained in effect. As a means to this end, federal permits are required of all importers, distillers, rectifiers, and wholesalers, but not brewers and retail distributors.

Much to the consternation of those who feel strongly about the evils of the liquor traffic, the Federal government, like most of the states, has not sponsored temperance instruction nor has it deliberately sought to diminish consumption by other means. Except for the fact that alcoholic beverages are luxury items and as such are heavily taxed, the Federal government has considered the liquor industry to be legitimate and entitled to the same rights as other businesses.

Administration of Liquor Controls.—Tariffs are collected by the Customs Bureau; excise taxes by the Bureau of Internal Revenue. Criminal violations of revenue provisions and laws aimed at protecting the states are enforced by the Department of Justice. Labor provisions are handled by agencies dealing with those matters for other businesses. Under the

NRA, the Federal Alcohol Control Administration administered the code, but upon its demise, a long struggle, still unended, ensued over whether a separate independent agency should be established or whether regulation should become the permanent responsibility of the Treasury Department. The proponents of Treasury administration won at first with the creation of the Federal Alcohol Administration in 1935 as a division. A year later the FAA was separated from the Treasury and made an independent establishment, governed by a three-man board. In April, 1940, an executive order sent the FAA back into the Treasury Department where its functions were consolidated with the Bureau of Internal Revenue. Today, therefore, the Bureau of Internal Revenue is responsible for both tax collection and economic regulation of the interstate and foreign aspects of the liquor industry.

Control of Narcotics.—Effective control of narcotics is an international, national, and local problem. The United States is a large user of narcotics for medicinal purposes and it has its share of addicts in both the states and territories. The United States is signatory to the Hague Convention of 1912 wherein a number of nations agree upon certain control measures. The League of Nations tried valiantly to get world cooperation and, although not a member of the League, this country participated in some of its conferences looking toward more effective control. However, when it came to signing the Geneva Treaty of 1925, which was a great advance over the Hague Convention, the American government refused. In spite of many efforts, international control has been neither comprehensive nor effective. Within the country, all the states have legislation designed to control narcotic drugs and deal with addiction, but without federal assistance they are powerless to protect themselves from traffic originating outside their borders. Although the Federal government has intervened, there remains a large volume of illicit traffic within the nation. Effective control, therefore, remains an unsolved problem.

Federal Narcotic Legislation.—Federal legislation is contained in three principal acts: the Harrison Act of 1914; the Jones-Miller Act of 1922; and the Marihuana Tax Act of 1937. Among other things, these require licenses of all those who produce (grow in the case of marihuana), transport, sell, or dispense opium, marihuana, and certain other narcotic drugs. Evidence of these provisions may be seen in any drugstore or physician's office. Exports and imports are regulated by permits and imports are further restricted by a system of quotas and allocations designed to secure proper distribution for medical needs. Penalties include fine, imprisonment, and confiscation of both the products and vehicles wherein they are transported.

Administration of Narcotic Controls.—Administration and enforcement are done by the Bureau of Narcotics, a unit of the Treasury Department, in cooperation with the states, Department of Justice, and the Public Health Service. There is always a considerable volume of business. In 1944 there were 337,799 persons licensed to handle narcotics and marihuana and even a considerable number of these were involved in violations. The same period saw 1,711 arrests for violations of the narcotic laws and 918 arrests for violations of marihuana laws. Interestingly, among penalties imposed for the latter were the eradication of 150 acres of wild marihuana growth and confiscation of 21,484 marihuana cigarettes. In the end, the federal hospitals for narcotics, mentioned elsewhere,[1] get many addicts for treatment.

CONSUMERS' SERVICES

Nature of Consumer Interest.—The relationship between government and consumers is difficult to discuss. Not because government does nothing for consumers, but because it is difficult to segregate people's interests as consumers and their interests as producers. The two are more often than not inextricably intermingled. In helping farmers produce better corn, for example, the government may improve their position as consumers. Likewise, in helping workmen organize for purposes of collective bargaining the government may also be rendering assistance that will enable them to purchase more in the market place. Because people are both producers and consumers, it appears to many that there is no separate consumer interest.

Many disagree, however, and their views have had increasing influence. This group points out that while everyone may be a producer and seller, he is also a purchaser of consumers' goods for himself and his dependents and as such is desirous of buying as much, both in terms of quantity and quality, for as little as must be paid. This, then, is the consumer interest. As yet the consumers' movement is weak as compared with other organized functional groups, with the result that consumers' interests are likely to be lost sight of in the mad scramble among those for whom profit making is the primary consideration.

No Single Consumer Agency.—A survey made in 1941 disclosed twenty-six federal "consumer" agencies scattered through seven departments and four independent establishments. Some of these have been discontinued while others have been added, but they still remain scattered, much to the disgust of those active in the consumers' movement. Defenders of the existing situation insist that the consumer will be better served by the regulatory agencies in the several fields that are supposed to look after their interests than by one or more special consumer agencies.

Food and Drug Regulation.—Federal intervention to protect consumers from impure foods and drugs began in 1906 as a result of a wave of public

[1] See p. 759.

indignation following publication of Upton Sinclair's sensational novel, *The Jungle,* dramatizing the unspeakable circumstances under which meats were handled in Chicago packing plants. Today three federal agencies concern themselves with the subject: the Food and Drug Administration (Security Agency), the Federal Trade Commission, and the Bureau of Animal Industry (Department of Agriculture). The Food and Drug Administration prevents the misbranding or adulteration of foods, drugs, devices, and cosmetics entering interstate and foreign commerce; the Federal Trade Commission is responsible for preventing the false and misleading advertising of the same products; while the Bureau of Animal Industry enforces laws relating to the inspection and purity of meats. The contest for powers adequate to deal with clever and powerful food and drug interests has been a long and difficult one. Continuous gains have been made, however. The most recent occurred in 1948 when Congress granted statutory authority for regulating goods and devices being held *after* interstate shipment.

The term "food" includes articles used for food or drink by man or other animals, chewing gum, and articles used for components of any such articles. A "drug" is (1) any article recognized as such by the *United States Pharmacopoeia, Homeopathic Pharmacopoeia,* or *National Formulary;* (2) articles intended for use in the diagnosis, cure, mitigation, treatment, or prevention of disease in man or other animals; (3) articles, other than food, intended to affect the structure of any function of the body of man or other animals; and (4) articles intended for use as a component for any of those specified above. "Devices" are instruments, apparatus, and contrivances, including their parts and accessories, intended (1) for use in the diagnosis, cure, mitigation, treatment, or prevention of disease in man or other animals; or (2) to affect the structure or any function of the body of man or other animals. Cosmetics, being neither foods nor drugs, were not regulated until 1938. They are now defined as articles, other than soap, intended to be rubbed, poured, sprinkled, or sprayed on, introduced into, or otherwise applied to the human body for purposes of cleansing, beautifying, promoting attractiveness, or altering its appearance.

In general, foods are adulterated if they contain poisonous, deleterious, filthy, putrid, or decomposed substances, if produced under unsanitary conditions, if produced from diseased animals, or if their containers are composed of substances injurious to health. Similar standards exist for drugs, cosmetics, and devices although there are variations due to differences in the products. Misbranding is also carefully defined, but in general labeling, packaging, etc. in such a manner as to deceive the buyer is forbidden. False and misleading advertising, also forbidden, includes practices of all sorts intended to create impressions of products that are untruthful.[1]

The Food and Drugs Administration and the Bureau of Animal Industry have agents in all parts of the country who inspect places of manufacture and storage and examine countless articles in transit. Violators may be fined or imprisoned, and substandard products may be seized and later sold or destroyed. Violations are detected constantly. During the fiscal year 1944, 2,143 seizures were made of adulterated or misbranded products. Among other items, this included about 2 million pounds of flour; a lot of stored split green peas which inspectors found infested with rats; a consignment of granulated sugar completely ruined by rodent feces and urine and by filth dragged in by rodents; cheese containing nests of baby rats; over a million cases of imported liquor, most of which contained slivers of glass; a hair dressing colored with coal-tar color that is known to produce cancer; 5,000 tons of imported figs contaminated by shipment near copra; and a large shipment of cheese from the Argentine wrapped in lead foil and thus contaminated with lead poisoning. At the same time the Bureau of Animal Industry seized quantities of impure and decomposed meats.

Nutritional Research and Education.—The Bureau of Human Nutrition and Home Economics was established in the Department of Agriculture in 1923 in order to find new uses for agricultural products. Over a period of years no federal agency has more completely identified itself with consumers' interests than this one. Its functions are primarily those of research, consultation, and education through its own laboratories and in conjunction with university and private laboratories. Though chiefly concerned with foods and nutrition, its inquiries extend to textiles and clothing; housing and household furnishings; and family economics. Its findings are distributed through a constant stream of bulletins and contacts maintained with home economists, consumer's research organizations like *Consumers Union* and *Consumer's Research,* cooperatives, the extension services of land-grant colleges, and others.

Consumers' Counsels.—In order to rectify the fact that the "public" and consumers may be poorly represented in conflict situations where interest groups are vying for all they can get, the practice of appointing special agents to represent their interests has had some acceptance. The practice was first followed by some of the state public-utility commissions and a partial counterpart is found in the public defenders that many municipalities have created to defend the legal rights of those who may be too poor to look after themselves. The idea was first tried by the Federal government under the NRA when a Consumers' Advisory Board, which later became a Consumers' Division, was authorized to sit with repre-

[1] See also p. 658.

sentatives of labor, industry, and government in drafting and administering the codes. Later a Consumers' Counsel was established in the Department of Agriculture; still later another was created by authority of the Bituminous Coal Acts,[1] which ultimately became an independent agency in the Department of the Interior. While each of these did much to stimulate the consumers' movement and publish materials for discerning buyers, they all felt a sense of frustration in their attempts to battle with more powerfully organized groups. In the end, their activities were either discontinued completely or absorbed by defense and war agencies. This experience suggests that the plan of appointing special counsels to protect consumers' interests cannot fully succeed until there exists a much larger and better organized consumers' movement.

Consumer Protection during the War.—When the Office of Emergency Management was created in May, 1940, the President anticipated that the defense effort would adversely affect consumers. Accordingly, an Adviser on Consumer Protection was included in the National Defense Advisory Commission. After several intermediate changes in administrative status, the Division of Consumer Protection became part of the Office of Price Administration. The first task of the Consumers' Division was that of discovering "consumer" agencies for the purpose of forming a central clearinghouse of information. With these data at hand, its function was to speak for consumers' interests at every point where they were seriously affected.

Like most offices in Washington, the Consumers' Division soon realized that it would be necessary to have offices throughout the nation that would be in direct contact with consumers. Accordingly, a campaign was carried on to secure the appointment of consumers' committees on state and local defense councils. All the states and hundreds of communities established such committees. These provided mediums at the local level for propaganda, education, and action in support of price control, rationing, conservation of waste products, war-bond drives, and anti-inflation programs generally.

Office of Price Administration (OPA).—Probably no war agency was better known, more talked about, and more controversial than the OPA, as it was popularly known. It dated back to the prewar defense effort when it was first established by executive order in April, 1941, as part of the Office of Emergency Management. It was given statutory status in January, 1942, by the Emergency Price Control Act but remained in the Office of Emergency Management and directly responsible to the President. The legislation continued into the postwar period, but when it was about to expire on July 1, 1946, Congress approved a weakened bill that President Truman vetoed. This left the nation with no price control but with con-

[1] See p. 660.

troversy raging between those who favored a "strong" law and those who favored a "weak" one or none at all. Toward the end of July, Congress passed a somewhat strengthened measure that the President signed reluctantly, thinking it better than nothing. In December, 1946, the OPA was transferred to the Office of Temporary Controls where wartime functions have since been liquidated.

At the head of the agency was an Administrator who was assisted by the usual administrative, technical, and clerical staff, many of whom were stationed at regional offices. Under the law as revised in 1946, responsibility for deciding which products should be controlled and which should not was divided between the Administrator, a three-man Decontrol Board, and the Secretary of Agriculture. The Administrator, however, was the one chiefly responsible for law enforcement. Locally, the OPA functioned through price and ration boards in cooperation with the consumers' councils mentioned above. Members of the boards served on a volunteer basis, but the OPA paid clerical salaries, rent, and other necessary operating expenses. The OPA had two principal functions: one, to fix and maintain ceiling prices for commodities and rents; the other, to ration scarce commodities.

Price Control.—While there is probably no way by which prices can be kept from rising during and following a modern war, the brakes can be kept on. Unless they are, the pent-up demand arising from full employment and widespread shortages creates an inflationary spiral that is easily one of the most costly and dangerous domestic consequences of war. To prevent this from happening, the OPA was empowered to fix ceiling prices, *i.e.*, upper limits beyond which it was illegal to charge. The law authorized fixing of ceilings at every stage of the distributive process—from producers through wholesalers, commission men, brokers, and retailers to the consuming public. The usual procedure was to establish a base date period when prices were not unduly inflated and either declare prices existing during that period to be the legal maximums, or make adjustments upward from them as circumstances suggested. At one time 8 million different prices were under control, involving fully 90 per cent of all items sold. Violations were punishable by fine or imprisonment and also by civil suit on the part of overcharged customers. While the general price level rose and there was considerable black-market activity, the situation was much better than during and after the First World War. As a result, consumers and governmental agencies were spared billions of dollars.

Wartime price controls ended in a storm of controversy. Opponents claimed that increased black-marketing was inevitable and could not be prevented without resort to police-state methods. They also argued that removal of controls would so stimulate production that the general price level would not rise, but rather stabilize or even fall. Those favoring price control insisted the remedy lay in larger appropriations for enforcement personnel and operations. In spite of their warnings, most price controls were removed in 1946 with serious inflationary consequences. President Truman several times urged reenactment of price control legislation to check inflation, but Congress would not comply.

Rent Control.—Rent ceilings were applied for the same reason that other prices were controlled. Unlike most commodities, however, rents have not been controlled everywhere. Rather, rents have been fixed only for areas in which the President found critical housing shortages, which usually have been areas of great war activity. Like other prices, rents have been fixed at a base-period level and adjusted upward as circumstances have warranted. Although there have been evasions and some upward trends, rents generally remained stable and by doing so resulted in savings to consumers estimated at over a billion dollars annually.

As soon as war ended, strong pressure was exerted, chiefly by real-estate interests and landlords, to obtain removal of rent controls. While succeeding in obtaining more liberal treatment, they have failed to obtain complete repeal. The Housing and Rent Act of 1949 retained the basic plan of control but made important concessions to critics. Federal rent legislation is administered by the Housing Expediter in cooperation with five-member local advisory boards appointed by the Expediter from names submitted by state governors. The Expediter is required by the 1949 law to revise rents in such manner as to yield landlords a "fair net operating income." This is a complicated formula that makes administration exceptionally difficult, and its operation has resulted in general rent increases.

Another concession contained in the 1949 law has to do with decontrol. Champions of tenants' interests preferred a strictly federal law, while critics demanded a large measure of "home rule" for state and local governments. The latter won. The 1949 law provides that rents shall be decontrolled (1) when a state governor advises the Housing Expediter that the legislation of his state "adequately" provides for rent control, or the governor specifically expresses the intent that state rent control shall be in lieu of federal; (2) when any state law declares federal rent control is no longer necessary; and (3) when the governing body of any city or other local government petitions the Housing Expediter for decontrol and such petition is approved by the state governor. There has been no rush to decontrol rents. The question was seriously raised in the courts of whether the decontrol provisions just summarized did not amount to unconstitutional delegation of federal power to the states, but the Supreme Court declared they did not.

Rationing.—Rationing is a method of equitably distributing among consumers a limited supply of goods. During the recent war, rationing began first for tires, then spread to hundreds of items including meats, shoes, canned food, sugar, gasoline, and many more. Textiles, clothing, coal, electricity, transportation, and housing were among the important items that remained unrationed throughout the war period. When critical shortages appeared likely, the usual method was to declare certain unit or point values for the scarce items, then issue to consumers ration books containing coupons which would permit them to buy only limited amounts. Ration books were issued through local price and ration boards, frequently with the assistance of schoolteachers and other volunteers. Though the rationing program occasioned inconveniences and at times serious criticisms by both dealers and customers, it was generally accepted as an essentially fair method of distribution and an inevitable companion of modern total war.

HOUSING

While housing has always been a necessity, "adequate" housing has only recently become so, and even yet millions still live in dwellings that are scarcely fit for human occupancy. All important cities have their "slums" or "blighted areas" and many rural sections are covered with dwellings that are equally bad, if not worse. Not only are there many substandard dwellings, but there is also an over-all shortage of houses, as anyone who has tried moving during recent years can attest. Social workers and others have called attention to this situation for nearly a generation, but it was not until recently that the public became sufficiently aroused to support vigorous action by the Federal government.

Except for the building done in Washington and other critical areas during the First World War, federal housing activities stemmed from the great depression. An act creating a system of Federal Home Loan Banks in 1932 was the first venture. Then followed other legislation aimed at helping distressed mortgagees refinance their obligations, making credit more easily available for home renovation and building, clearing slums and providing low-cost housing for low-income groups, and, later, providing housing in critical areas for defense and war workers, returning veterans, and others.

Housing Agencies.—At one time housing activities were carried on by seventeen different agencies. In 1942 these were consolidated into the National Housing Agency and in 1947 most of them, together with housing credit agencies, were brought together in the Housing and Home Finance Agency. In 1945, to meet postwar emergency housing demands, the position of Housing Expediter was established in the Executive Office of the President. Under present legislation, this office is to continue until July 1, 1950, during which time it is principally concerned with rent control and veterans' housing affairs. The Hoover Commission[1] reported con-

[1] *Federal Business Enterprises* (Washington: Government Printing Office, 1949), p. 250.

siderable overlapping between the two separate housing agencies and recommended consolidation under a single administrator. The principal operational divisions within the Housing and Home Finance Agency are the Home Loan Bank Board, the Federal Housing Administration, and the Public Housing Administration.

Home Loans.—Under the Home Loan Bank Board are three subordinate units engaged, now or in the past, in helping finance homes. One of these is the Federal Home Loan Bank System, another is the Federal Savings and Loan Insurance Corporation, and the third is the Home Owners Loan Corporation.

Home Loan Bank System.—This is comprised of eleven banks located in principal cities.[1] Each bank has twelve directors, four appointed by the Board and eight elected by member institutions. These banks do not deal directly with individuals who desire to borrow. Rather, they are banks for building and loan associations, saving and loan associations, cooperative banks, homestead associations, insurance companies, or savings banks which in turn lend directly to borrowing home builders. The great bulk of member institutions are of the savings and loan type. Loans are made to member, and nonmember institutions in some instances, primarily on the basis of first-mortgage collateral. By so doing they supply funds with which member institutions can meet the home-financing needs of their communities and the withdrawal demands of savers and investors.

Savings and Loan Associations.—Rather than deposit their savings in the local bank many people prefer to place them with savings and loan associations either as an investment or with the expectation of later financing a home. These were all organized under state laws until 1933 but since then they may organize under federal auspices. These can be organized anywhere in the United States or its territories upon the application of a responsible group of citizens to the nearest Federal Home Loan Bank. When approved and established, each one automatically becomes a member of the Federal Home Loan Bank System and must insure its deposits with a federal corporation provided for the purpose.[2] As of June 30, 1944, there were 1,465 such institutions in operation. Their primary function is one of financing home building within the vicinity of their home office.

Home Owners Loan Corporation.—The depression put many home owners in a situation where they could neither continue payments on their mortgages nor borrow more for that purpose. To help such people the Home Owners Loan Corporation was established in 1933. In cases where

[1] Boston, New York, Pittsburgh, Winston-Salem, Cincinnati, Indianapolis, Chicago, Des Moines, Little Rock, Topeka, and San Francisco.

[2] This is the Federal Savings and Loan Insurance Corporation. Its plan is similar to that conducted by the Federal Deposit Insurance Company for ordinary commercial banks.

home owners could not procure financing elsewhere, the corporation took over the mortgage, giving its own bonds in exchange. Thereupon with the mortgage as collateral, the corporation made loans to the home owner which were repayable in 15 years or less. After making 1,017,821 loans involving over 3 billion dollars, lending activities were terminated in June, 1936, since which time the corporation has been liquidating its obligations. The corporation has since found it necessary to foreclose on many properties because of defaults, but doubtless decidedly fewer borrowers lost their homes than otherwise would have.

Federal Housing Administration (FHA).—During the depression the banks and credit agencies, including the newly created Home Loan Banks and Federal Building and Loan Associations, generally had plenty of money, but they were timid about lending it on long-term real-estate mortgages. Or when they were willing to lend, they were inclined to require such a large down payment as to discourage home building. To meet this situation, the Federal Housing Administration was established in 1934, and it is still in business.

The FHA is primarily an insurance agency. Its goal is one of encouraging the improvement of existing housing facilities, the building of new small homes and apartment dwellings, and the manufacture of housing by industrial methods. The administration does not lend directly to home builders and manufacturers. Instead, it lets local financial institutions lend the money while it guarantees payment of the mortgage, thus removing virtually all risk of nonpayment to the money lender. A premium is charged the financial institution for this service, the income from which is expected to pay the cost of operation. The amount of the loan depends upon the size and cost of the project. On some as much as 90 per cent of the cost may be financed by the FHA. Not more than a stipulated rate of interest may be charged on insured loans, the projects must be executed in accordance with approved specifications, and payments must be made periodically until the obligation is fully retired. Thus far, many mortgages have been insured with few defaults.

Subsidized Low-cost Housing.—The housing agencies described above exist to help finance private parties whose credit is good. The role of the Federal Public Housing Authority (FPHA) is very different. Here is a government corporation whose primary purpose is to clear slums and provide low-cost housing. It does not do so directly, however. Rather, it enters into contracts with municipal, county, and state authorities, where state laws permit, to get the job done. The procedure is for a local authority to frame plans for slum clearance and new construction, then submit them to FPHA for approval. If the plans are approved, a contract is entered into whereby the federal agency agrees (1) to lend a large part of the cost of the project at prevailing rates of interest plus a small charge for administrative costs, the principal to be repaid over a long period of years; and (2) to make annual contributions over a period of years as a subsidy for low rents.

Tenants must be citizens and in the low-income category; none may be admitted whose aggregate income exceeds fixed amounts. If, after occupancy, the size of the family or income increases beyond what the regulations permit, different quarters must be found. While rents vary considerably, those fixed by a typical authority[1] in 1942 began with a minimum of $13 a month for a three-room apartment and went to a maximum of $46 a month for a 6½-room apartment, both figures including water, gas, heat, light, and refrigeration. During the war the FPHA revised its contracts with many local authorities to permit projects originally intended for low-cost housing to be made available to war workers, but with the return of peace these projects have been reverting to their original purpose.

1949 Legislation.—Over intense opposition, the 1949 Housing Act provided for a vastly expanded federal program. Loans and grants were made available for helping local housing agencies finance redevelopment of project areas. A broad program of research was authorized for the purpose of cheapening housing costs, improving design, and stimulating construction. Moreover, the law authorized a farm home program. The latter permits the Secretary of Agriculture, through the Farmer's Home Administration, to make long-term loans for building or renovating farm dwellings, and it permits either loans or grants to poor farmers willing and able to use the funds for housing improvements or additions. Technical assistance is offered and even moratoriums on mortgage payments are authorized if necessary. The farm home plan is administered in cooperation with local farm committees.

References

ADAMS, JAMES T.: *Big Business in a Democracy* (New York: Scribner, 1946).

ARNOLD, THURMAN: *The Bottlenecks of Business* (New York: Reynal & Hitchcock, 1940).

BAKER, RALPH H.: *National Bituminous Coal Commission 1937–1941* (Baltimore: Johns Hopkins Press, 1942).

BERLE, ADOLPH A., and GARDNER C. MEANS: *The Modern Corporation and Private Property* (New York: Macmillan, 1933).

CLARK, JOHN M.: *Alternative to Serfdom* (New York: Knopf, 1947).

COPELAND, DOUGLAS B.: *The Road to High Employment: Administrative Controls in a Free Society* (Cambridge, Mass.: Harvard University Press, 1945).

DIMOCK, MARSHALL E.: *Business and Government* (New York: Holt, 1949).

[1] That of Pittsburgh, Pa. An interesting story is told of this authority by Dr. M. Nelson McGeary in *The Pittsburgh Housing Authority* (State College, Pa.: The Pennsylvania State College, 1943).

FAINSOD, MERLE, and LINCOLN GORDON: *Government and the American Economy* (New York: Norton, 2d ed., 1949).

FULLER, DOUGLAS R.: *Government Financing of Private Enterprise* (Stanford University, Calif.: Stanford University Press, 1948).

GRAHAM, GEORGE A., and HENRY REINING, JR.: *Regulatory Administration* (New York: Wiley, 1943).

HARRIS, SEYMOUR E.: *Price and Related Controls in the United States* (New York: McGraw-Hill, 1945).

——— *Saving American Capitalism; A Liberal Economic Program* (New York: Knopf, 1948).

HARRISON, LEONARD V., and ELIZABETH LAINE: *After Repeal; a Study of Liquor Control Administration* (New York: Harper, 1936).

KOBBE, HERMAN: *Housing and Regional Planning* (New York: Dutton, 1941).

LAMB, RUTH DE F.: *American Chamber of Horrors: The Truth about Food and Drugs* (New York: Grossett & Dunlap, Inc., 1938).

LERNER, ABBA P., and FRANK GRAHAM: *Planning and Paying for Full Employment* (Princeton, N.J.: Princeton University Press, 1946).

LYON, LEVERETT S., VICTOR ABRAMSON, *et al.*: *Government and Economic Life* (Washington: Brookings, 2 vols., 1940).

MCGEARY, M. NELSON: *The Pittsburgh Housing Authority* (State College, Pa.: The Pennsylvania State College, 1943).

NORWOOD, JOHN W.: *Trade Practice and Price Law—Federal* (New York: Commerce Clearing House, Inc., 1938).

PEARCE, CHARLES A.: *NRA Trade Practice Programs* (New York: Columbia University Press, 1939).

PEGRUM, DUDLEY F.: *Regulation of Industry* (Chicago: Irwin, 1949).

ROHLFING, CHARLES C., *et al.*: *Business and Government* (Chicago: Foundation Press, 5th ed., 1949).

ROSTOW, EUGENE V.: *A National Policy for the Oil Industry* (New Haven: Yale University Press, 1948).

SIMONS, HENRY C.: *Economic Policy for a Free Society* (Chicago: University of Chicago Press, 1947).

STEIN, EMANUEL: *Government and the Investor* (New York: Rinehart, 1941).

STOCKING, GEORGE W., and MYRON W. WATKINS: *Cartels or Competition?* (New York: Twentieth Century Fund, 1948).

TOULMIN, HARRY A.: *Treatise on the Law of Food, Drugs, and Cosmetics* (Cincinnati, Ohio: Anderson, 1942).

TWENTIETH CENTURY FUND, HOUSING COMMITTEE: *American Housing* (New York: Twentieth Century Fund, 1944).

UNITED STATES COMMISSION ON ORGANIZATION OF THE EXECUTIVE BRANCH OF THE GOVERNMENT ("HOOVER COMMISSION"): *Department of Commerce* (Washington: Government Printing Office, 1949).

——— *Regulatory Commissions* (Washington: Government Printing Office, 1949).

UNITED STATES CONGRESS TEMPORARY NATIONAL ECONOMIC COMMITTEE: *Investigation of Concentration of Economic Power, Final Report and Recommendations*, Sen. Doc. No. 35, 77th Cong., 1st Sess., pursuant to Pub. Res. No. 113 (Washington: Government Printing Office, 1941). The *Hearings* were published in 31 parts; there were 43 monographs.

UNITED STATES DEPARTMENT OF COMMERCE: *Annual Report* (Washington: Government Printing Office, annual).

WILSON, STEPHEN: *Food and Drug Regulation* (New York: American Council on Public Affairs, 1942).

Chapter 30

REGULATION OF UTILITIES

If regulation does not keep pace with the operations of the vast enterprises, the people of the country may unexpectedly find that the utilities which, according to law, tradition, and reason, should be the servants in the house, have become its masters.

William E. Mosher and Finla G. Crawford.[1]

Public Utility Defined.—A public utility is a private business that renders an indispensable service to the community under circumstances that require continuous public regulation. Examples are railways, waterways, ferries and bridges, buses, wharves, grain elevators, gas, water, telephone, and electricity. Such businesses are sufficiently clothed with public interest to warrant regulation that would be considered unconstitutional if applied to businesses of the usual, competitive type. Whether an enterprise may be classified as a public utility depends upon a number of factors, including whether monopoly is present, geographic location, character of service, immediacy of patrons' needs, the amount of capital invested, the scale of operations, and whether it has been considered a public enterprise in times past. Congress and state legislatures make the classification subject to court approval. While the list of businesses that may be considered utilities tends to become longer, the Supreme Court has ruled that ice plants,[2] theater-ticket brokerages,[3] gasoline stations,[4] and meat-packing industries[5] may not be classed and regulated as utilities. Milk and coal productive and distributive agencies lack some of the essentials usually possessed by utilities, yet they are sufficiently affected with a public interest to permit at least fixing their prices.[6]

Types of Carriers.—Running through discussions of public utilities are references to three types of carriers: common, contract, and self-servers. Common carriers are those that hold out their facilities and service for "common" or general use to all comers. Contract carriers are those that perform services only under terms of specific contracts entered into with customers. A bus, for example, that operates regularly over a given

[1] *Public Utility Regulation* (New York: Harper, 1933), p. xvii.

[2] New State Ice Co. *v.* Liebmann, 285 U.S. 262 (1932).

[3] Ribnick *v.* McBride, 277 U.S. 350 (1928).

[4] Williams *v.* Standard Oil Company of Louisiana, 278 U.S. 235 (1929).

[5] Wolff Packing Company *v.* Court of Industrial Relations of Kansas, 262 U.S. 522 (1923).

[6] Nebbia *v.* New York, 291 U.S. 502 (1934). For coal see p. 660.

route stopping for all who wish to ride would be a common carrier; but a bus that had to be chartered every time an individual or group wished to use it would be a contract carrier. Then there are self-servers—those that provide service for themselves. A large industry, for example, may own its own railroad for carrying its own products, or its own power plant, water system, or buses. In framing legislation, provisions must be varied to account for differences between these three types of carriers.

Federal and State Spheres of Operation.—Most utilities are local enterprises, hence remain under control of state and local governments. Public-utility commissions exist in the District of Columbia and all the states. As business and communications have grown and the sense of community has broadened, the Federal government has intervened, relying for the most part upon the power to regulate foreign and interstate commerce. Like the states, the Federal government regulates utilities by various means—general laws, actual or threatened government competition, taxation, etc. Unlike most of the states, however, regulation of a large variety of enterprises has not been concentrated in the hands of a single commission, but rather, several of them, each dealing with a particular functional group. Federal and state activities touch and overlap at innumerable points, requiring constant collaboration and cooperation between the officials involved.

Regulatory Procedure.—The national Constitution forbids both Federal and state governments from depriving persons of life, liberty, or property without due process of law.[1] Governmental agencies must, therefore, follow procedures that allow ample notice, opportunity for a full and fair hearing, and appeal to the courts.

Entry into Service.—The pattern of control differs for each industry and regulatory body, but there are many similarities. First of all, utility regulation requires authority to make investigations. Having this, regulatory bodies usually are given control over entry into service. Accordingly, parties wishing to do business must file applications. The regulatory body may follow a policy of allowing an unlimited number of competitors to enter the field, but more often than not it follows a policy of allowing limited monopoly. Thus, in the case of a railroad application the Interstate Commerce Commission would probably forbid a competitor to enter the business unless it could be clearly demonstrated that another railroad was necessary to serve the public interest. Authorizations usually take the form of "certificates of public convenience and necessity," licenses, or permits.

Security Issues, Rates, Service, etc.—Regulation also usually implies control over security issues and intercorporate relationships. Once operations have started, utilities are generally required to submit budgets,

[1] See p. 139.

reports, and proposed rate schedules. In doing so they are required to follow a uniform system of accounts to ensure that each entry has the same meaning to all concerned. The regulatory body may approve the schedule of rates proposed or, after investigation and hearing, insist upon changes. Rate control involves property valuations to determine the fair value of the service rendered, and this, in turn, usually involves extensive engineering surveys of the total plant. As all this is being done, the regulatory body must hear and adjust complaints, see that proper safety practices are followed, and otherwise make sure the law and regulations are obeyed. Finally, if utilities wish to extend their facilities or services, go out of business, or sell or abandon some of their facilities, approval must be obtained.

The Problem of Rate Making.—Rate fixing is the most difficult and controversial aspect of utility regulation. As a rule the law requires that rates be fixed high enough to earn a "fair return" on the "fair value" of the property used and useful in rendering a public service. What is a "fair return" is usually not hard to determine; the law is generally satisfied if it is in the vicinity of from 5 to 8 per cent of "fair value." Far more difficult is the task of coming to a decision about what is "fair value," or the "rate base." If the figure is set too low investors will lose money, in which case the matter will probably be taken to court, where it could be held illegal on the ground that property was being taken without due process of law. If, on the other hand, "fair value" is set too high, the public will be gouged.

Theories of Valuation.—The crux of effective utility rate control boils down to the theories and methods followed in determining "fair value," or the "rate base." Several methods may be followed: one might take the total value of the securities of a company; or, one might take the original cost (sometimes referred to as "historical cost") and subtract depreciation; or, one might settle for reproduction cost new less depreciation; or, finally, one might follow the "prudent-investment" theory whereby an attempt is made to ascertain what a prudent or wise investor would have invested in the enterprise. There are difficulties with each of these. The economic difficulties are little short of appalling and they have been aggravated by court decisions.

Smyth v. Ames.[1]—The basic case on the subject of valuations is Smyth *v.* Ames, decided in 1898. There the Supreme Court had before it a case arising from rates fixed for a number of railroads by the Board of Transportation for the state of Nebraska. The state board had based its rates chiefly upon the reproduction-cost-new-less-depreciation theory but the railroads involved in the case had been constructed in a period of high prices, hence contended for a valuation based upon original cost less de-

[1] 169 U.S. 466 (1898).

preciation. The Court, however, refused to accept either theory to the exclusion of the other. Instead, it said that in determining fair value, consideration must be given to a number of factors including

> The original cost of construction, the amount expended in permanent improvements, the amount and market value of its bonds and stocks, the present as compared with the original cost of construction, the probable earning capacity of the property under particular rates prescribed by statutes, and the sum required to meet operating expenses. . . .

The difficulty with this is not only that the procedure entails extensive investigation, with resultant costly delays, but also that the Court said nothing about how much weight should be given to each of the factors mentioned. It sometimes happens that an original cost estimate differs from one of the same company based upon the reproduction-cost-new-less-depreciation estimate by millions of dollars. In such an event, what figure represents "fair value"? Faced with this situation, regulatory bodies follow their personal predilections, meanwhile trying to guess what the courts might have to say and finally ending with a compromise favorable to the utilities.

In a recent case before the Supreme Court[1] Justice Frankfurter, with the concurrence of Justice Black, objected to relying upon Smyth *v.* Ames which he said had been "widely rejected by the great weight of economic opinion, by authoritative legislative investigations, by utility commissions throughout the country, and by impressive judicial dissents."[2] Nevertheless, the Supreme Court refused to reopen the issue in the case cited.

More recently, however, the Court has not only reopened the matter but has seriously modified its historic position. This occurred in a series of cases dealing with the fixing of "just and reasonable" rates under the Natural Gas Act.[3] As matters now stand, regulatory commissions are not bound to follow any single formula (like reproduction-cost-new), or combination of formulas (like that required by Smyth *v.* Ames), in determining rates. Rather, commissions are free to take a pragmatic approach. If rates that they establish enable a company to operate successfully, to attract capital, and to compensate investors for the risks assumed, the courts may now sustain them regardless of the theory or formula followed by the regulatory body. Needless to say, this gives those responsible for regulation a freer hand in determining fair value than in the past.

[1] Driscoll *v.* Edison Light and Power Co., 307 U.S. 104 (1939).

[2] One of the best analyses of this controversy is found in Irston R. Barnes, *The Economics of Public Utility Regulation* (New York: Crofts, 1942), Chaps. 11 to 17, inclusive.

[3] See especially Federal Power Commission *et al.* *v.* Hope Natural Gas Co., 320 U.S. 591 (1943).

REGULATION OF TRANSPORTATION

Department of Transportation Proposed.—As noted elsewhere,[1] transportation services and regulation have been the responsibility of several federal agencies, chiefly the Department of Commerce and the independent commissions mentioned below. The Hoover Commission and its task forces devoted much attention to the problem of obtaining maximum coordination and integration.[2] A minority argued for a cabinet department of transportation,[3] but the majority was unwilling to go this far. Instead, they recommended transferring all nonregulatory transportation functions to the Department of Commerce but leaving regulatory functions where they then were.[4]

Interstate Commerce Commission (ICC).—The ICC is the oldest of all federal regulatory commissions. It was established in 1887 after the breakdown of attempts on the part of state governments to control satisfactorily systems that had become interstate in character. There are now eleven members on the commission appointed by the President for staggered terms of 7 years. Not more than six may be from the same political party. From its membership the commission selects its own chairman. The commissioners appoint, in accordance with civil service regulations, a secretary, chief counsel, directors of bureaus (other than the Bureau of Locomotive Inspection, who is appointed by the President) and other personnel. The commission may make decisions as a body or, and this is unique among agencies of this sort, it may create divisions of not less than three members and a decision of a division has the same force and effect as one made by the entire commission. Cases decided in this manner may, however, be reheard by the entire commission if it thinks it desirable. The commission is now organized into five divisions plus a number of sections and bureaus. Since the adoption of the Hepburn Act in 1906, the orders of the commission have had the force of law. Fines and penalties may be imposed by the commission itself, while serious violations are turned over to the Department of Justice for prosecution.

Jurisdiction of the ICC.—In addition to nearly all railroads in the country, the ICC has been given jurisdiction over the following: motor carriers engaged in interstate and foreign commerce; water carriers operating coastwise, intercoastal, and upon inland waters of the United States;

[1] P. 627.

[2] See its report entitled *Regulatory Commissions* and its *Task Force Report on Regulatory Commissions* (Washington: Government Printing Office, 1949).

[3] This is also the plea of Charles L. Deering and Wilfred Owen, *National Transportation Policy* (Washington: Brookings, 1949).

[4] For the Hoover Commission's recommendations for bringing about improved administration by the independent establishments, see p. 444.

FEDERAL UTILITY REGULATORY COMMISSIONS

Agency	Date established	Number of members	Terms, years	Utility jurisdiction
Interstate Commerce Commission.........	1887	11	7	Railroads; motor carriers; shipping by coastwise, intercoastal, and inland waters; pipe lines (except natural gas and water); express companies; carriers using rail-and-water routes; sleeping-car companies
Federal Power Comission................	1920	5	5	Water-power sites, electric power, natural-gas pipe lines
Securities and Exchange Commission.........	1934	5	5	Electric and natural-gas holding companies
Federal Communications Commission....	1934	7	7	Radio, telephone, telegraph, cables
United States Maritime Commission.........	1936	5	6	Shipping in foreign commerce
Civil Aeronautics Authority..........	1938	Board, 5 Administration, 1 administrator	6	Air lines, airways, and airports

pipe lines, except those for water and gas;[1] express companies; carriers using through rail-and-water routes; and sleeping-car companies. The ICC also determines mail transportation rates and, interestingly enough, fixes standard time zones for continental United States and Alaska.

Regulation of Railroads.—In 1947 there were approximately 227,000 miles of railroads in the United States—many times more than any other country in the world. Unlike those in most countries, virtually all railroads in the United States are privately owned and operated. They provide the backbone of the American transport system.

[1] Gas pipe lines are now regulated by the Federal Power Commission, while no federal agency regulates water pipe lines. See p. 688.

Basic transport policy is contained in the Transportation Act of 1920, which, among other things, reversed the traditional attitude toward the railway industry. Prior to that enactment federal law looked with disfavor upon consolidations, mergers, and close cooperation among the roads on the theory that these tended toward the diminution of competition with resultant monopoly and inefficiency. With the breakdown of private management during the First World War freshly in mind, and the existence of a commission powerful enough to protect the public interest, Congress in the Transportation Act of 1920 instructed the ICC to act affirmatively in helping to develop and maintain an adequate national transportation service, even though this might result in the elimination of some of the weaker roads.

Since 1920, except for legislation affecting employer-employee relationships,[1] most legislation has been of an emergency nature designed to help the railroads overcome the results of general economic depression, overcapitalization and expansion, excessive competition among themselves, and competition from newer forms of transportation, especially motor carriers but more recently airways. During the recent war there was close coordination and supervision of all forms of transportation both by permanent agencies like the ICC and by the Office of Defense Transportation.[2] In 1948 Congress passed the Reed-Bulwinkle Act permitting, with ICC approval, common carriers of particular classes to agree among themselves on rates and charges.

ICC Controls.—In its relations with the railways, the ICC is constantly engaged in applying the utility controls described above with respect to rates, accounts, security issues, etc. It also considers questions of basic policy and makes recommendations to the President and Congress. Moreover, it applies and enforces many special laws and regulations. These, among others, forbid railroads to transport products made by enterprises in which they own or control an interest; forbid railroads to own or control any competing water carriers unless the ICC finds that it is in the public interest to do so and will not reduce competition; prevent charging more for short than long hauls over the same route; require the installation and use of safety devices; require the use of uniform bills of lading; forbid price discrimination and other monopolistic practices; and prescribe methods of transporting explosives and other dangerous articles. The ICC must also investigate railway accidents, inspect locomotives, check and limit the hours of service for railroad employees, and determine fair and reasonable rates for mail transportation by railway carriers, urban and interurban electric carriers.

For purposes of control the railroads are grouped in three classes on the

[1] See p. 730.

[2] See also p. 742.

basis of total operating revenues. Class I roads, which include those whose annual operating revenues exceed 1 billion dollars, do the bulk of the business. The ICC also divides railroads geographically into three districts and eight subsidiary regions. Each railroad is treated as a unit and placed wholly in some one district or region. Broadly speaking, the eastern district includes territory east of Chicago and north of the Ohio and Potomac rivers; southern district, territory east of the Mississippi River and south of the Ohio and Potomac rivers; and western district, the remainder of the country.

Regulation of Motor Carriers.—State regulation of motor carriers began in Pennsylvania in 1914. Other states soon followed and had the field to themselves until 1935 when Congress adopted the Motor Carrier Act. Prior to that time, the Federal government had confined its efforts to investigating the industry, granting subsidies for road building, and maintaining standards for road construction.

Carriers Brought under Control.—Motor carriers, like others, group themselves into common, contract, and private carriers. In addition to the carriers themselves, transportation brokers and forwarders are of considerable importance to the industry. Brokers are intermediaries who undertake to bring users and carriers together, while forwarders are persons, other than carriers, who offer to serve the public by assembling or consolidating property with a view to reshipment by rail, water, or other carriers. All these were brought under regulation by the Motor Carrier Act and amendments, although some more than others.

Exemption of Carriers from Federal Control.—As all motorists know, the Motor Carrier Act does not apply to them. But even a large number of those engaged in carrying passengers and commodities are exempt. These include school and hotel buses; taxicabs; buses operated in the national parks under the control of the Secretary of the Interior; motor vehicles owned and operated by farmers, cooperative associations, and newspapers; motor trucks used exclusively for the carriage of fish and agricultural products; trolley buses operated by electrical power from fixed overhead wires; casual, occasional, or reciprocal transportation of persons or property; and buses or trucks operating within a metropolitan area even though engaged in interstate or foreign commerce unless the ICC finds regulations necessary.

The Grandfather Clause.—When the Motor Carrier Act went into effect, thousands of carriers were then in existence. Obviously it was necessary to require them to come under the new law, and yet it would have been difficult, if not an unconstitutional deprivation of property, to deny existing companies permits to operate. The dilemma was met by the inclusion of a "grandfather" clause. This provides that common carriers operating on and since June 1, 1935, and contract carriers on and since July 1, 1935, automatically be given certificates and permits. While this was doubtless an expedient solution, it nevertheless robs the ICC of much of its power to control the character and supply of motor transportation service.

Imposition of Controls by the ICC.—Common carriers, which include most interstate bus and freight trucking companies, are required to obtain certificates of public convenience and necessity and are otherwise regulated to about the same extent as railroads. This includes control over inter-company relationships, accounts, rates, and service.

Contract motor carriers are not, strictly speaking, public utilities; at least the courts have to date refused states permission to regulate them as completely as if they were "affected with a public interest."[1] Federal law requires them to obtain permits from the ICC before commencing operations, and these are to be granted if the applicant is considered "fit, willing, and able" to perform the service and conform with rules and regulations, and if the proposed operation is "consistent with the public interest and the policy" set forth in the law. Carriers of this type must adhere to the same rules as common carriers with respect to hours of service of employees, standards of equipment, and safety of operation. Rate schedules must be filed with the ICC, carriers may not charge less than these rates, and the commission has authority to prescribe minimum rates. The ICC also has authority to require periodic reports, prescribe accounts, approve consolidations, mergers, and other combinations, and approve the issuance of securities above specified amounts.

Brokers and transportation forwarders must respect the same rules as carriers with respect to hours of service of employees, standards of equipment, and safety. Brokers must obtain licenses before operating and in doing so they must post bond to ensure adequate financial responsibility. They are also subject to accounting regulations and other rules for the protection of travelers and shippers. There must be no price discrimination, but the ICC lacks authority to prescribe tariffs. Forwarders must also establish financial reliability and file reports and tariffs, but, as with brokers, the ICC lacks authority to fix rates. It will be noted that neither brokers nor forwarders are subjected to such complete control and supervision as is the case of carriers.

Regulation of Water Carriers.[2]—Water carriers may be divided into four groups: inland, coastal, intercoastal, and foreign. Inland carriers include those operating on inland rivers, canals, connecting channels, and lakes.[3] Coastal, or coastwise, carriers are those that operate along the

[1] Michigan P.U. Commission *v* Duke, 266 U.S. 570 (1925); Frost *v.* R. R. Commission of California, 271 U.S. 583 (1926).

[2] Other aspects of the American Merchant Marine are discussed on p. 704.

[3] Because the Great Lakes are not completely within the United States but are shared by Canada, carriers upon them are often discussed separately, but for present purposes they will be considered inland carriers.

various coasts of the United States but not through the Panama Canal. Intercoastal are those operating through the Panama Canal between Atlantic and Pacific ports. All of these, with exceptions noted below, were placed under the ICC by the Transportation Act of 1940. Foreign carriers are those engaged in commerce with foreign ports. These are regulated by the United States Maritime Commission.

Exemption of Water Carriers from Federal Control.—From what was just said, one must not conclude that all water carriers have been brought under federal supervision; a very substantial proportion have not, except with respect to safety. This is due to a number of exemptions written into statutes. Exemptions include operators in intrastate commerce and even local and small operators engaged in interstate commerce; contract carriers that do not compete "actually and substantially" with other types of carriers; private carriers of all types; common carriers that transport goods in bulk in cargo space used for not more than three commodities; and tank vessels, even though common carriers, that transport liquid cargoes in bulk. This accounts for a formidable volume of traffic. Being unregulated, these enjoy a favored competitive position which has brought many complaints, especially from railways.

General Provisions.—Water navigation is an ancient industry that has been of vital concern to the American people since they first sailed to these shores. Billions of dollars have been spent for river and harbor improvement, dredging canals, and subsidizing shipping lines and ship construction. Meanwhile, state and local governments have imposed regulations, although because of the interstate and foreign character of most water carriers these have been indifferently enforced.

At the same time, the Federal government has enacted general laws of a wide variety. Of primary importance are requirements for identification and documentation. As soon as a vessel is launched, she acquires a personality of her own. She becomes competent to contract, is individually liable for her obligation, and may sue in the name of her owner and be sued in her own name; she may become a quasi-bankrupt and even commit suicide. Accordingly, she must be officially recorded, measured, and named. Smaller craft engaged in fishing, pleasure pursuits, and commerce in inland and coastal waters are "licensed." Those of 20 tons or more plying the same waters must be "enrolled," while vessels engaged in foreign trade must be "registered." Only citizens may so record ships of any class.

Many federal regulations pertain to safety: Vessels must not be overloaded, they must carry specified numbers of lifeboats and life belts, ships must be equipped with fire signals and protective devices, etc. Other regulations pertain to officers and personnel: There must be satisfactory accommodations for officers and crews; licensed officers must be American citizens; all employees must be citizens on American cargo vessels whose building or operations have been subsidized by the Maritime Commission; 75 per cent of the crew on any ship entering American ports must be able to understand any order given by a ship's officer; the minimum number of employees, their qualifications, wages, hours, food, clothing, and treatment are all covered by federal law. Other regulations relate to areas of operations: Only American vessels may engage in coastal, inland, and intercoastal commerce; routes and channels are specified as well as rules governing entrance from abroad into American waters, harbors, and ports. Other regulations relate to the care and treatment of passengers, rates, entrance into war zones, financial responsibility, insurance, and, in fact, almost every aspect of shipping.

Administration of Water-carrier Controls.—Until recently, many of the general provisions just mentioned were the responsibility of the Bureau of Marine Inspection and Navigation, of the Department of Commerce. Among their agents were shipping commissioners, stationed at the various ports, and numerous inspectors. The bureau's enforcement of safety regulations has at times been notoriously lax, with the result that until recent years American ships were rapidly acquiring the distinction of being the most dangerous on the ocean. A number of marine disasters, including the burning of the *Morro Castle* in 1934 and the sinking of the *Mohawk* during the following year, focused public attention upon the inadequacy of safety devices and the incompetence of officers, crews, and the inspection service. An aroused public opinion resulted in the enactment of legislation in 1935 and 1936 which brought about some improvement. As a war measure, the functions of the bureau were transferred in 1942 to the Commissioner of Customs and the Coast Guard.

While the two agencies just mentioned continue their work, two other federal bodies, the ICC and the United States Maritime Commission, concern themselves with other aspects of water commerce. The former was given jurisdiction of inland, coastal, and intercoastal shipping by the Transportation Act of 1940; and the latter was given authority to regulate foreign shipping in 1936.

Inland, Coastal, and Intercoastal Carriers.—Common carriers are required to obtain certificates of public convenience and necessity from the ICC. In granting these, the commission must keep in mind the declared national policy of providing the public with adequate, coordinated transportation of high quality at reasonable prices. Rates, routes, accounts, and service are regulated to about the same extent as railroads. Contract carriers must obtain permits and submit to about the same regulations as contract motor carriers. Private carriers are all exempt from ICC control, as mentioned above.

Foreign Commerce Carriers.—Virtually all ships engaged in the foreign trade, except tramp vessels, are common carriers. Although they might be, these have not been subjected to the same degree of regulation as railroads and other common carriers. The Maritime Commission does not have control over entrance into service, except for ships that it owns or has subsidized. This being the case, the door is wide open for extensive competition and for the most part jungle law prevails. All American ships must, however, be registered, but this is handled by the Customs Bureau. Nor does the commission have authority to regulate security issues and intercorporate relationships. Its authority over rates is limited to seeing that tariffs are filed and that they are nondiscriminatory, although in the case of charges for wharfage and dockage it may prescribe minimums. The commission does have authority to designate and approve routes; to hear and adjust complaints; to subsidize shipbuilding and operations; to handle matters pertaining to wages, hours, and working conditions of seamen; to prescribe accounts and require reports; and, in general, to collaborate with the industry for its protection and promotion.

An interesting feature of foreign shipping regulation is the degree of cooperation permitted among shipping companies. Those who wish to may join a "conference," which resembles a domestic trade association, for the purpose of pooling information and entering into agreements regarding such matters as rates, allotment of traffic, pooling of earnings, and methods to be employed in meeting competition from nonconference members. If filed with the Maritime Commission and approved, these agreements are immune from antitrust laws.

Regulation of Air Commerce.—Air commerce among the states and with foreign nations is regulated by the Civil Aeronautics Authority established in 1938. The Authority consists of two parts: the Civil Aeronautics Board and the Civil Aeronautics Administration. The board is a five-member body appointed by the President for staggered terms of 6 years. Not more than three members may be of the same political party, and the chairman is designated annually by the President. The board is an independent agency, although it is within the Department of Commerce for administrative housekeeping purposes.

In contrast with this arrangement, the Civil Aeronautics Administration is a staff unit under the direct supervision of the Secretary of Commerce. The administration is headed by an administrator who is appointed by the President. While both agencies are charged with responsibility for the promotion and development of civil aeronautics and air commerce, the board is a quasi-legislative and judicial body concerned with fact finding, rule making, and the adjudication of disputes; while the administration is in charge of the administration and enforcement of rules and regulations. The Authority itself performs no functions, it should be noted: rather, the work is all done by either the board or the administration.

Jurisdiction of the Civil Aeronautics Authority.—The Authority has power to prescribe air routes and rules governing safety for all aircraft, including military, naval, private, and those engaged in local commerce.[1] Other controls apply only to common and contract carriers engaged in interstate and foreign commerce. The administration is charged with the planning, construction, maintenance, and operation of an up-to-date federal airways system. It also administers and directs all federally sponsored civil pilot programs. It builds federally owned airports and cooperates with the states and local governments in developing others. Upon the request of the Army and Navy it establishes and operates airport control towers. It also operates the Washington National Airport located across the Potomac from the capital city.

Air Commerce Regulations.—All planes must be registered; all pilots must be examined and rated in accordance with qualifications for flight service; and all planes must follow prescribed air-traffic rules.

Planes that are engaged in interstate and foreign commerce must not only comply with the above-mentioned rules but must also obtain ratings as to airworthiness and have periodic inspection by certified mechanics. Common carriers must obtain certificates of convenience and public necessity; they must furnish safe and adequate facilities and service; they may not discriminate in price or service; they must charge only fair and reasonable rates which have been filed and approved by the Civil Aeronautics Board; they must follow prescribed accounting procedures and make reports. Combinations of all kinds must be approved, and routes may not be abandoned without board approval. There is no control over the issuance of securities, however, other than that of a general nature done by the Securities and Exchange Commission.[2]

Regulation of Pipe Lines.—Pipe lines are used for the transportation of various liquids and gases, but their predominating use in the United States is for the transportation of crude petroleum, gasoline, and natural gas. In rich petroleum centers the earth may be honeycombed with pipes. In the Pittsburgh area, for example, there is literally one pipe on top of another and they crisscross and parallel each other in a most confusing manner.

The recent war saw rapid expansion and renovation of pipe lines for the transportation of petroleum. The most important and dramatic project was the construction of the "Big Inch"—a 24-inch line from east Texas to Philadelphia and New York, the longest and largest pipe line ever installed for transporting petroleum. The job was done by the Federal

[1] While the Supreme Court has not yet passed upon this assertion of authority over local commerce, a lower court has approved it [Neismonger *v.* Goodyear Tire and Rubber Co., 35 F. (2d) 761 (1929)], and both railway experience and logic support it.

[2] See p. 652.

government; oil began moving through it in February, 1943; and by August of the same year through connections had been made to the East coast.

Federal Controls.—Federal control of interstate pipe lines began in 1906 when the Interstate Commerce Commission was given jurisdiction over all except those for transporting water, natural, and manufactured gas. The latter were brought under control in 1938, along with other aspects of the industry,[1] but responsibility for administration was placed in the hands of the Federal Power Commission. It must also be remembered that the Holding Company Act of 1935 applied to natural-gas companies,[2] many of whom own or control interstate pipe lines. Thus, as matters now stand, the Interstate Commerce Commission regulates pipe lines transporting crude oil, gasoline, and miscellaneous products; the Federal Power Commission deals with those conveying natural gas; while the Securities and Exchange Commission is engaged in reorganizing the holding-company structures for companies engaged in the production, transportation, and wholesale distribution of natural gas. The pipeline companies are all declared to be common carriers and are regulated to about the same extent as are railroads.

REGULATION OF ELECTRIC POWER AND NATURAL GAS

The Federal Power Commission.—Advent of the power age brought with it recognition that if the public interest was to be protected federal legislation was needed to supplement state control. A desire to conserve resources, threatened by the quest on the part of electric-power companies for sites along rivers and lakes, occasioned the first federal legislation in 1920. The Water Power Act of that year created the Federal Power Commission for the primary purpose of surveying the water resources of the nation and determining who would be permitted to establish hydroelectric projects along navigable waters and on public lands. Since then the powers of the commission over the interstate operations of electric utilities have been extended, and in 1938 it was given jurisdiction over the interstate transportation and sale of natural gas.

The commission now consists of five members appointed for 5-year terms. The commissioners choose their own chairman. It is an independent establishment organized in about the same manner as other agencies of this character.

Regulation of Electric Utilities.—Electric service divides itself naturally into three parts: generation, transmission, and distribution. Generation involves the manufacture of electric energy; transmission, its transportation from the generating station to the locality where consumed; and dis-

[1] For a discussion of the regulation of these see p. 688.

[2] See p. 689.

tribution, the retail sale and delivery of energy to the consumers. Generation is usually highly localized and the same is true of distribution. In most instances they are, therefore, controlled by state and local agencies. The Federal government interests itself with generation only at the point of approving water-power sites along navigable waters and on public lands; and it is directly concerned with distribution only at the point of regulating the wholesale prices charged distributors who purchase electricity shipped from out of state. It is with transmission that the Federal government is primarily concerned because this is frequently not localized and may be interstate in character.

Power-commission Controls.—As indicated above, the commission must approve all hydroelectric power projects on navigable waters or public lands. Pending final decision, preliminary permits, which are valid for 3 years, are often given, thus ensuring priority over other applicants. If licenses are issued later, they may run for as long as 50 years, although the law expressly reserves the right for either the Federal or state government to reacquire the site at any time. The commission lacks authority to require a showing of public necessity and convenience before electric companies extend their lines across state boundaries (this would be a matter reserved to the states), but it can encourage voluntary interconnections to be made under certain circumstances. To help accomplish this purpose, the commission has divided the country into regional districts. When it comes to transmission of electric energy to points outside the United States, however, the commission must approve every instance.

The commission also has complete jurisdiction over long-term security issues made by electric utilities under its jurisdiction. So far as short-term issues are concerned, it may scrutinize only those issued by companies organized and operating in states that do not provide for the regulation of security issues. Service must be adequate, although in obtaining such the commission must cooperate with state agencies. Rates (always wholesale, otherwise state utility commissions have jurisdiction) must be just, reasonable, and nonpreferential. Uniform accounts must be kept and reports filed. Interlocking relationships must also be approved.

Regulation of Natural Gas.—Very little *manufactured* gas is transported across state lines; hence its regulation is left to the states. With *natural* gas the situation is different. Most of this originates in the wells of a few states and is transported, principally by pipe lines, to others. Several states attempted regulation, but in a series of decisions[1] the Supreme Court ruled that neither the state in which the gas was produced nor the one in which it was distributed to the ultimate consumer could regulate the interstate rate. These decisions, together with the disclosures made in the

[1] For a review of this history with appropriate citations, see Federal Power Commission *et al. v.* Hope Natural Gas Co., 320 U.S. 591 (1943).

Federal Trade Commission's sweeping survey of holding-company structures and practices, led Congress to pass the Natural Gas Act of 1938.

The controls given to the Federal Power Commission over natural gas are nearly the same as for interstate electric utilities. An amendment adopted in 1942 looks toward the establishment of areas of operations for the various natural-gas companies. To accomplish this end, companies are required to apply to the commission for certificates of public convenience and necessity before undertaking new constructions or acquisitions of extensions, or abandonment of facilities. However, after their areas are assigned, natural-gas companies may enlarge or extend their facilities for the purpose of supplying increased market demands in the areas without further authorization. This, coupled with provisions of the Holding Company Act, should go far toward stabilizing the industry.

Regulation of Electric and Gas Holding Companies.—A holding company is one organized to "hold" securities of operating companies, supposedly for the purpose of profiting from their reinvestment. Illegal at common law, they were legalized by state statutes, beginning with New Jersey in 1888. By this device, securities of competing companies were brought together under single management, often with monopolistic results. This was especially true in the electric-power field. By 1932, thirteen large holding companies controlled 75 per cent of the entire privately owned electric-utility industry, with more than 40 per cent concentrated in the hands of the three largest groups—United Corporation, Electric Bond and Share Company, and Insull. Even these three systems were not totally independent. A report made in January, 1935, by the Federal Trade Commission disclosed a maze of unsound financial structures, widespread lobbying and propaganda activities intended to disparage government regulation and ownership, and extensive intercompany dealings which saddled operating companies, and ultimately consumers, with exorbitant expenditures.

The Holding Company Act.—After one of the most sensational legislative contests in recent years, the Holding Company Act relating to electric and gas utility holding companies was approved on Aug. 26, 1935. Some of its provisions are:

1. Electric and gas holding companies register with the Securities and Exchange Commission.

2. Commission approval is necessary before new securities are issued or an interest is acquired in any other utility.

3. All holding companies above the second must be abolished, unless excepted by the commission, and their operations confined to integrated regional systems.

4. Intercompany loans and interlocking directorates with banking institutions were made illegal.

5. Holding companies might not, without commission approval, sell goods, perform services, or undertake construction work for any associated utility.

6. Holding companies might not contribute to political parties or candidates for public office, nor lobby without disclosing the object sought and expenditures.

7. Holding companies must use uniform accounts, make reports to the commission, and otherwise follow rules and regulations established by the commission.

Results of the "Death Sentence."—During the legislative battle over the Holding Company Act, much was heard about the so-called "death sentence" provisions contained in Section 11 and referred to under No. 3 in the above list. This section makes it the duty of the Securities and Exchange Commission to simplify holding-company structures by confining them to integrated regional systems and eliminating all beyond the second degree. Thus the holding companies that were pyramided several stories high and spread all over continental United States must be completely revamped. They can exist only up to and including the second degree; which means that there may be an operating company, a holding company controlling the operating company, and a holding company controlling the first holding company—but no more. Moreover, the properties must be regrouped and confined to regional systems. A large number of separate electric, gas, and nonutility properties have been removed from the control of registered holding companies; while many of the complicated holding-company structures have been dissolved or liquidated. Although the legislation has been on the books for over a decade, more time is required before reorganizations are completed.

REGULATION OF COMMUNICATIONS

Federal Communications Commission.—Prior to 1934, radio and wire communications were partially regulated by several agencies, chiefly the Interstate Commerce Commission, the Postmaster General, and the recently created Federal Radio Commission. The laws were consolidated and broadened in the Communications Act of 1934. At the same time, their administration was placed in the hands of one agency, the Federal Communications Commission. This agency consists of seven members appointed by the President for staggered terms of 7 years. It is an independent establishment and not more than four of its members may be of the same political party. Its jurisdiction extends to all interstate and foreign radio, telephone, telegraph, and cable service, stations, and operators.

Regulation of Telephone, Telegraph, and Cable Service.—Congress has charged the commission with ensuring "a rapid, efficient, nation-wide and world-wide wire and radio communication service with adequate facilities at reasonable charges." So far as wire communications are concerned, ownership and control rest largely in the hands of three companies: the Bell Telephone Company, Western Union, and International Telephone and Telegraph Corporation. Until recently, competition aided in regulating telegraph service, but with the merger of Western Union and Postal Telegraph in 1943, a single company dominates the field. Of the three types of wire communications, telegraph service has probably been the most deficient. Although considerably speeded up in recent years, it still fails to meet the highest standards. Although telephone service in metropolitan areas is generally satisfactory, rural service is woefully inadequate.

Federal Controls.—Federal control of wire and cable communications was weak and comparatively ineffective prior to 1934. Although strengthened by the Communications Act of that year, regulation is still less comprehensive than for railroads. Companies are required to provide reasonably adequate service when asked to do so. Certificates of public convenience and necessity must be obtained before new lines can be built or old ones extended. The commission has power to order the establishment of physical connection between carriers and for through routes. It may also order the extension of common carrier lines when the public interest would be served thereby, provided the extension does not involve too much expense. A recent amendment requires commission approval of service curtailments. Undue or unreasonable discrimination in service is prohibited. With respect to rates, tariffs must be filed with the commission where they are scrutinized to ascertain whether they are just and reasonable; where they are not, tariffs may be suspended until such time as a complete investigation is made. In so doing, the commission may make valuations, although here is an area where considerable dependence is placed upon the valuation figures obtained by state utility commissions. Telegraph and cable rates have remained about the same in recent years, but since 1935 interstate telephone rates have been revised progressively downward. Accounting is carefully controlled and reports must be filed.

In spite of these broad powers, the authority of the commission is incomplete. It has no jurisdiction over the issuance of securities; it can investigate but not control transactions between operating and affiliated companies—an area where such scandalous abuses were discovered among electric and gas operating and holding companies;[1] and the commission lacks authority to control fully telephone, telegraph, and cable consolidations and combinations, although legislation is pending which would authorize the commission to supervise the merging of existing international communications carriers.

[1] See p. 689.

Regulation of Radio.—Radio broadcasting is regulated *exclusively* by the Federal government. The first legislation on the subject was in 1910 when Congress enacted a statute requiring steam vessels to have radio equipment for emergency use. A second act was passed in 1912 wherein the Secretary of Commerce was authorized to require and issue licenses for radio transmission, but it failed to make clear whether he had authority to determine the frequency, station, power, or the hours of transmission. In 1926 a Chicago station "jumped" its frequency bands and broadcast at hours not permitted by its license. When prosecuted, a United States district court[1] held that the Secretary was without power to enforce his order. Anarchy reigned on the ether, compelling Congress to provide more effective control. The Federal Radio Act of 1927 was the result. By this the Federal Radio Commission was created and the basic rules by which radio is regulated were laid down. The Radio Commission was abolished in 1934 and its functions were transferred to the Communications Commission.

Licenses.—Whoever broadcasts by radio from any point in the United States must obtain a license in order to operate legally. Among other things, this assigns the band and frequencies of operation. Licenses for standard broadcasts may be issued for a period not to exceed 3 years, while those for broadcasts of other types may run for 5 years. Until 1939 standard broadcast licenses were issued for only 6 months; since then for 1 year; while licenses for other than standard broadcasts run for 2 years. Issuing these is an exceedingly difficult task, because there are many applicants and relatively few frequencies to be divided among them.

The criteria established in the law for the guidance of the commission in issuing licenses are very general. The principal ones are: licenses may not be issued to aliens, foreign governments, or foreign interests; the commission must be convinced that the public interest, convenience, and necessity will be served; and licenses must be distributed among the states in such a way as to "provide a fair, efficient, and equitable distribution of radio service."

The power of the commission to grant or deny licenses is one of the most powerful weapons possessed by any regulatory agency. During the time when licenses had to be renewed every 6 months, broadcasting companies were kept in constant uncertainty over their prospects of obtaining renewals. While this doubtless had a potent corrective influence upon the industry, it led to charges of abuse and favoritism. Adoption of a longer period during which licenses are valid has diminished criticism but the possibility of abuse remains. Indeed, it is certain to remain as long as there is commission control of a privately owned industry like this.

Regulations.—The Communications Act expressly states that radio broadcasting stations are not common carriers. Accordingly, the com-

[1] United States *v.* Zenith Radio Co., 12 F. 2d 614 (1926).

mission lacks direct authority to regulate rates charged of advertisers, services, discrimination, security issues, and intercorporate relationships. Nor does it have the power of censorship. Such control as it has over these and other matters stems largely from its power to grant, renew, and revoke licenses.

The rules of the commission require all standard stations to keep daily logs of programs and incidents. No profanity or obscenity is permitted. All legally qualified candidates for particular political offices must be given equal opportunity to present their views,[1] and to this end a record must be kept of all requests for political broadcasts. Typical of other regulations are those requiring that schedules of tariffs and charges be filed with the commission; that extensions be approved; that stations be tested and inspected; and that stations clearly identify themselves and the sponsors of broadcasts.

References

Barnes, Irston R.: *Public Utility Regulation* (New York: Appleton-Century-Crofts, 1938).

Bauer, John: *The Public Utility Franchise: Its Functions and Terms under State Regulation* (Chicago: Public Administration Service, 1946).

Baum, Robert D.: *Federal Power Commission and State Utility Regulation* (New York: American Council on Public Affairs, 1943).

Beard, William: *Regulation of Pipe Lines as Common Carriers* (New York: Columbia University Press, 1941).

Bonbright, James C.: *Public Utilities and the National Power Policies* (New York: Columbia University Press, 1940).

——— *The Valuation of Property* (New York: McGraw-Hill, 2 vols., 1937).

Chamberlain, Joseph P., and Others: *Judicial Functions in Federal Administrative Agencies* (New York: Commonwealth Fund, 1942).

Cushman, Robert E.: *The Independent Regulatory Commission* (New York: Oxford, 1941).

Dearing, Charles L., and Wilfred Owen: *National Transportation Policy* (Washington: Brookings, 1949).

Dimock, Marshall E.: *Business and Government* (New York: Holt, 1949).

Elsbree, Hugh L.: *Interstate Transmission of Electric Power* (Cambridge, Mass.: Harvard University Press, 1931).

Fainsod, Merle, and Lincoln Gordon: *Government and the American Economy* (New York: Norton, 2d ed., 1949).

[1] Section 315 of the Communications Act reads: "If any licensee shall permit any person who is a legally qualified candidate for any public office to use a broadcasting station, he shall afford equal opportunity to all other such candidates for that office in the use of such broadcasting station, and the Commission shall make rules and regulations to carry this provision into effect: *Provided*, That such licensee shall have no power of censorship over the material broadcast under the provision of this section. No obligation is hereby imposed upon any licensee to allow the use of its station by any such candidate." Note that broadcasting stations are not required to allow candidates to speak, but if they do permit one to do so, they must afford all others running for the same office to have as nearly identical time as possible.

GOODMAN, GILBERT: *Government Policy toward Commercial Aviation; Competition and the Regulation of Rates* (New York: King's Crown Press, 1944).

HALL, FORD P.: *Concept of a Business Affected with a Public Interest* (Bloomington, Ind.: Principia, 1940).

HERRING, JAMES M., and GERALD C. GROSS: *Telecommunications, Economics and Regulation* (New York: McGraw-Hill, 1936).

JOHNSON, EMORY E., *et al.*: *Transportation: Economic Principles and Practices* (New York: Appleton-Century-Crofts, 1940).

——— *Transportation by Water* (New York: Appleton-Century-Crofts, 1935).

MOSHER, WILLIAM E., and FINLA G. CRAWFORD: *Public Utility Regulation* (New York: Harper, 1933).

MOULTON, HAROLD G., *et al.*: *The American Transportation Problem* (Washington: Brookings, 1933).

PUSEY, MERLO J.: *Big Government: Can We Control It?* (New York: Harper, 1945).

RADIUS, WALTER A.: *United States Shipping in Transpacific Trade*, 1922–1938 (Stanford University: Stanford University Press, 1944).

ROHLFING, CHARLES C.: *National Regulation of Aeronautics* (Philadelphia: University of Pennsylvania Press, 1931).

RUGGLES, CHARLES O.: *Aspects of the Organization, Functions and Financing of State Public Utility Commissions* (Cambridge, Mass.: Harvard University Press, 1937).

SHARFMAN, ISAIAH L.: *The Interstate Commerce Commission* (New York: Commonwealth Fund, 5 vols., 1931–1937).

SOCOLOW, A. WALTER: *Law of Radio Broadcasting* (New York: Baker, Voorhis, 1939).

THOMPSON, C. WOODY, and WENDELL SMITH: *Public Utility Economics* (New York: McGraw-Hill, 1941).

UNITED STATES COMMISSION ON ORGANIZATION OF THE EXECUTIVE BRANCH OF THE GOVERNMENT ("HOOVER COMMISSION"): *Regulatory Commissions* (Washington: Government Printing Office, 1949).

UNITED STATES FEDERAL TRADE COMMISSION: *Economic, Financial and Corporate Phases of Holding and Operating Companies of Electric and Gas Utilities*, Sen. Doc. 92, Pt. 72B, 70th Cong., 1st Sess. (Washington: Government Printing Office, 1936).

——— *Economic, Corporate, and Financial Phases of the Natural-gas-producing, Pipeline and Utility Industries*, Sen. Doc. 92, Pt. 73A, 70th Cong., 1st Sess. (Washington: Government Printing Office, 1936).

——— *Investigation of the Telephone Industry in the United States*, House Doc. 340. 76th Cong., 1st Sess. (Washington: Government Printing Office, 1939).

UNITED STATES NATIONAL RESOURCES PLANNING BOARD: *Transportation and National Policy* (Washington: Government Printing Office, 1942).

VAN ZANDT, JOHN P.: *Civil Aviation and Peace* (Washington: Brookings, 1944).

WILSON, G. LLOYD, *et al.*: *Public Utility Industries* (New York: McGraw-Hill, 1936).

——— (ed.): "Transportation: War and Postwar," *The Annals of the American Academy*, vol. 230 (November, 1943).

ZEISS, PAUL M.: *American Shipping Policy* (Princeton, N.J.: Princeton University Press, 1938).

Chapter 31

FEDERAL ENTERPRISES

> The New Deal . . . does not wish to run or manage any part of the economic machine which private enterprise can run and keep running. That should be left to individuals, to corporations, to any other form of private management, with profit for those who manage well. But when an abuse interferes with the ability of private enterprise to keep the national conveyor belt moving, government has a responsibility to eliminate that abuse.
>
> Franklin D. Roosevelt.[1]

> Even if the government conduct of business could give us the maximum of efficiency instead of least efficiency, it would be purchased at the cost of freedom.
>
> Herbert Hoover.[2]

THE PROBLEM OF GOVERNMENT OWNERSHIP

Whether government should engage in enterprises customarily owned and operated by private parties is one of the most controverted questions of public policy. The individualist would keep the number of government enterprises at an absolute minimum; the socialist seeks public ownership and operation of the major instruments of production and distribution. Most Americans occupy a middle ground; little moved by theoretical considerations, they take the pragmatic approach and grope for what seems best under prevailing conditions. One often finds, for example, that communities of rock-ribbed conservatives will nevertheless stanchly defend municipal ownership of their local waterworks, electric systems, and other utilities. As noted in the introductory chapter, the general direction of our time is toward collectivism, but no one can say how far it will go.

Reasons for Government Participation in Business.—Government entrance into the business field takes place for a variety of reasons. In some instances private ownership of some essential enterprise fails and the public takes over. This was the case with the Panama Canal, the Alaskan Railroad, and innumerable local utilities. Again, government may intervene to provide a basic universal service like the postal system and coinage of money. Frequently considerations of health, safety, and morals are the primary consideration, as in the case with water systems or government-owned liquor monopolies. Sometimes the government intervenes for

[1] *The Public Papers and Addresses of Franklin D. Roosevelt* (New York: Random House, Inc.), 1938 vol., p. 588.

[2] *The Challenge to Liberty* (New York: Scribner, 1934), p. 203.

reasons of national defense. This was the case with railroad, telephone, and telegraph systems during the First World War. This was also the reason why during the recent war the government took over the railroads, coal mines, Montgomery Ward, and many other war plants either to avert work stoppages or to get operations resumed. This also explains government ownership and operation of atomic-energy industries. Again, government may commence operations in an attempt to conserve and obtain more effective utilization of natural resources. This explains government ownership and operation of forests, public lands, the reclamation projects described later, and regional projects like the Tennessee Valley Authority and those along the Columbia River. Again, the government may enter business as a competitor in order to regulate more effectively those engaged in the industry. This was an important consideration behind the electric power operations of the TVA and other recent federal power projects. Another reason is one of convenience. The Federal government finds, for example, that it is more convenient to print and publish its own documents than to bother with letting bids and dealing with private publishers. Still another reason is that public ownership may be highly profitable, with the proceeds going toward tax reduction. This has been an important consideration so far as local water and electric utilities are concerned. It also helps to explain public enthusiasm for state liquor monopolies.

Sometimes, of course, ideological considerations are paramount; that is to say, those who favor government ownership as a matter of principle may force the decision. This has doubtless been at least a subjective factor in many of the instances cited above.

Evaluation of Arguments and Experience.—For the above and additional reasons, government ownership at both federal and state levels has steadily increased in spite of strenuous opposition. Critics usually assert that government ownership and operation are unfair in that enterprises may be tax free and their prices do not reflect all legitimate costs because of subsidies collected from the public in the form of taxes. It is also alleged that government ownership involves an excessive amount of bureaucracy and red tape. The issue is finally disposed of with the assertion that because of the absence of personal risk, competitive factors, and the lure of profit, government-owned enterprises are lacking in incentive, imagination, and initiative. Many illustrations can be found to prove one or all of these assertions, and it must be admitted that there are dangers in public ownership as well as private. Like most generalizations, however, they claim too much.

Fortunately, the subject is no longer academic; there has now been enough experience with government-owned corporations to suggest that they can be so organized and managed as to avoid the evils suggested above, bear all legitimate costs, and compete successfully with private competitors both as to quality and price. This is not to advocate the wholesale extension of government ownership; it is merely to suggest that a wise person will bring to the solution of issues as they arise an awareness of the advantages, disadvantages, and pitfalls of both private and public ownership.

As the following discussion of government enterprises develops, it will be noted that some of them aim at operating within a framework of costs and prices that will provide a net profit to the public treasury. This is true of the electric-power aspects of the Tennessee Valley Authority, Hoover Dam, and the Bonneville Administration. Other enterprises are less concerned with costs, prices, and profit than with providing an essential service. This is the case with the Postal Service, reclamation projects, the Panama Canal, the Maritime Commission, Inland Waterways Corporation, the Alaskan Railroad, and others. Whether the following examples of federal ownership are "profitable," therefore, depends upon the criteria used in making a judgment. If the enterprise is set up for the sole purpose of providing a service at a profit, experience proves that it can be done with costs and prices that compare favorably with those of competing private enterprises. When, however, the government-owned agency is set up, as most of them are, for the purpose not only of providing a service but also of conserving natural resources, or providing a direct or indirect subsidy to some of the users, or something else, one cannot look merely at costs, prices, profits or losses and conclude that government ownership is necessarily less "efficient" than private. Whether under private or governmental operation, the important thing from the point of view of the public is not monetary profit or loss but whether high-quality service has been provided at a minimum cost as measured both in terms of money and the utilization of material and human resources.

Variety of Federal Undertakings.—A list of business undertakings in which the Federal government is engaged is surprisingly large. These include the production of motion pictures for educational and propaganda purposes; operation of farms by federal penal, correctional, educational, and experimental agencies; manufacture of mailboxes, mailbags, and mail keys; shipbuilding by the Maritime Commission and the Navy; manufacture of guns, ammunition, binoculars, rope, varnish, paint, furniture, mattresses, and other supplies for national defense; manufacture of clothing for the Army and Navy; manufacture of ink, stamps, gum for stamps and envelopes; providing musical concerts by military bands; operating pipe lines, railroads, air and shipping lines; printing and binding; manufacturing and selling electric power and fertilizers.[1] The list is inflated due to the

[1] For others, together with discussion, see United States House of Representatives, Special Committee to Investigate Government Competition with Private Enterprise, *Government Competition with Private Enterprise, Report. . . .* House Rep. No. 1985, 72d Cong., 2d Sess. (Washington: Government Printing Office, 1933). See also Hoover

war, and the next few years are likely to see a decline. Space prevents a discussion of all governmental undertakings; hence consideration is given only to the older and more permanent ones.

THE POSTAL SERVICE

Until 1774 postal service in the colonies had been under the control of Great Britain, although the control was more nominal than real. Benjamin Franklin was the last Postmaster General appointed by Britain, but his appointment was canceled when the colonies declared independence. He was immediately reappointed, however, and to him belongs the credit for laying the foundations of our modern postal system. The constitutional basis is found in the brief phrase, "Congress shall have power . . . to establish Post Offices and Post Roads."[1] Today the Postmaster General boasts that his is "the largest business in the world."[2] Whether all would agree with this or not, it is true that the service has grown to startling proportions.

The Post Office Department.—The head of the department, unlike most chiefs of executive departments who are called "secretaries," is called Postmaster General. Though one of the earliest officers to be appointed in the young republic, he was not accorded cabinet status until Jackson's time, in 1829, and his office was not given separate departmental status until 1872. During all that time his office was considered a unit within the Treasury Department, although the Postmaster General himself was directly responsible to the President. The Postmaster General is nearly always a politician. Indeed, it has long been customary for him to be none other than the chairman of the President's political party.[3] Associated with him is the usual staff and administrative personnel who operate within the framework of a number of offices, bureaus, and divisions.

Auxiliary Services.—Besides handling the mail, the Post Office Department operates a parcel-post service; a system of registry and insurance for mail; a money-order system;[4] a postal-savings business for small depositors;

Commission, *Federal Business Enterprises* and *Task Force Report on Revolving Funds and Business Enterprises of the Government* (Washington: Government Printing Office, 1949).

[1] Article I, Section 8. See also p. 419.

[2] *United States Government Manual*, 1st ed., 1945 (Washington: Government Printing Office, 1945), p. 277.

[3] See also p. 219.

[4] For many years the money-order system was operated at a loss. Moreover, it entailed considerable time and inconvenience and fees were increased gradually throughout the years, with the result that many persons made remittances in the forms of stamps and cash rather than bother to pay the required fees. To meet this problem the Post Office Department offered for sale early in 1945 postal notes in amounts up

a collection of cash-on-delivery service; and a special-delivery service. Moreover, it handles the sale of small-denomination government bonds and stamps and collects several types of taxes. In addition, it provides local headquarters for a number of federal agencies, especially the Civil Service Commission, Department of Justice, and Bureau of Internal Revenue. Incidentally, through its far-flung activities, offices in almost every city and hamlet, and rural carriers, it has been the principal post through which the Administration in power has observed current trends and sentiment. It has also been an important instrument for influencing local opinion and elections by the handling of federal patronage. As noted elsewhere,[1] the Post Office Department owns some of its nearly 45,000 post offices, but leases most of them. It operates shops for manufacturing and repairing mailbags, mailboxes, mail keys, etc. but purchases a huge quantity of its equipment and materials from other agencies, both governmental and private. Except for some of its local delivery facilities, it contracts with railways and other carriers for the transportation of mail and parcels.

Postal Profits and Losses.—For the first quarter of a century, the postal service was operated along lines followed by private business and a profit was shown practically every year. After 1814, especially during and after the presidency of Andrew Jackson, three factors influenced the course of management: one, the spoils system; another, legislation providing for the extension of the postal service to all parts of the country, especially the developing West, even though uneconomic; and the third, legislation granting subsidies to special groups either in the form of higher prices paid to the railways and other carriers for mail transportation, free postage, or reduced rates. It is obvious that the terms "profits" and "losses" lose their usual meaning when considerations such as these must be reckoned with.

The situation today is somewhat the same, albeit on the road to improvement, one may at least hope.[2] Among its many employees are many political appointees, with the result that management is less efficient than it otherwise might be. Uneconomic expansion is a factor of diminishing importance since the service now pretty well covers the country. It is still true that rates paid to water, motor, and air carriers for transporting mail carry hidden subsidies and are therefore higher than need be. Preferred

---

to and including $10; there is also one for amounts less than $1. Odd amounts are arranged for by affixing of special postal-note stamps. The postal note requires no written application and may be issued in approximately half the time required for money orders.

[1] See p. 419.

[2] See p. 470 for a discussion of the application of civil service regulations to postal employees.

treatment is still given special groups.[1] From the study of financial reports it is also clear that the rates for mail of all classes, except possibly the first, are too low to pay expenses assignable to them.

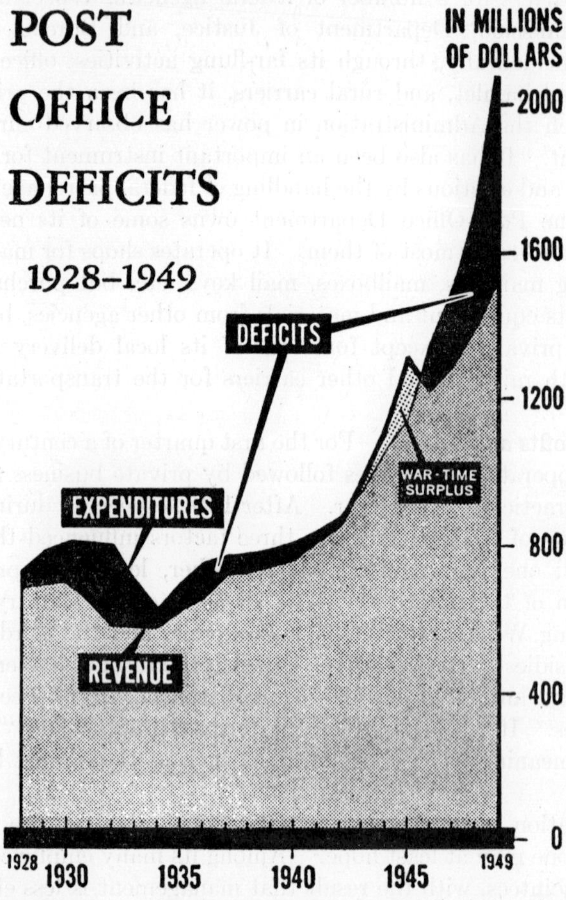

SOURCE: Bureau of the Budget. 1948, unaudited; 1949, estimated.

Recommendations of the Hoover Commission.—The Hoover Commission was particularly critical of the Post Office Department. Among its suggestions for improvement were the following: (1) discontinuance of the practice of appointing the chairman of the President's political party as

[1] Mail that may be sent free includes official mail of members of Congress and officers of other branches of the government; letters, including V-mail, sent by personnel of the armed forces; reports, bulletins, and correspondence relating to agriculture sent by state agricultural colleges and experiment stations; matter for the blind; mail sent by widows of former presidents under their franks; newspapers and other publications of the second class sent by publishers to subscribers within the county of publication.

Postmaster General; (2) appointment of an experienced executive, preferably from the service, to be the operating head of the postal service; (3) decentralization of the postal service into fifteen regions under regional directors and district superintendents; (4) appointment of an unpaid advisory board of laymen representative of different elements of the public; (5) placing all employees on a merit basis and, to this end, discontinuance of Senate confirmation of all postmasters; (6) adoption of the performance-type budget with auditing done by the Comptroller General; (7) simplification of departmental organization to provide greater flexibility; (8) final determination of rates by Congress on a basis that will cause all classes of mail and services to pay their way; and, finally, (9) payment of carrier subsidies, where Congress thinks wise, from tax funds rather than from postal revenues. Until some of these changes are made, one must assume that the public is less concerned with financial "profit" and efficiency than with the services and other values it is buying.

PANAMA CANAL ZONE OPERATIONS[1]

Although the plan of life in the Canal Zone was not conceived by socialists, it is organized completely along socialist lines. The Federal government holds title to all land in the Zone, the famous canal itself, the Panama Railroad which parallels the canal, a steamship line which operates between New York and the Zone, hotels, bakeries, manufacturing plants, the electric, telephone, and telegraph systems, coaling plants, stores, farms, and other businesses. Indeed, no one owns his own house, and all houses are rented furnished.

Panama Canal and Panama Railroad Company.—The various business enterprises are the property of two agencies: the Panama Canal and the Panama Railroad Company, the capital of which is owned exclusively by the Federal government. The two are easily confused. The Panama Canal is an administrative unit directly subject to Congress and the President, via the War Department and the immediate supervision of the governor. In addition to operating the canal, it operates a number of businesses including the electric system, water supply system, hospitals, postal system, local press, and the rental of land. The Panama Railroad Company is an independent corporation having its own board of directors and being subject only to indirect control from Washington. Besides the railroad and steamship lines mentioned above, it manages the coal plants, telephone system, hotels, commissaries, dairy farms, and many other businesses.

It is impossible to analyze each of these here; all that can be done is to state the conclusions of careful observers. The best over-all survey was

[1] The general aspects of government in the Canal Zone are discussed in the chapter dealing with territories. See p. 587.

made by Prof. Marshall E. Dimock and published in 1934.[1] He reported that from an administrative point of view the "Canal Zone compares favorably with the best examples of British colonial administration . . . and that it is easily the most successful government enterprise under the American flag outside the continental United States."[2] Continuing, he said, "The general results of business management in the Canal Zone supply additional confidence in the ability of government to conduct economic services satisfactorily, judged by any standards of comparison."[3] From a financial point of view, he concluded that "The Isthmian undertaking has been a satisfactory financial investment for the United States government."[4]

This judgment as to financial results was confirmed in 1940 by Mr. Joseph B. Eastman, Federal Coordinator of Transportation, in his exhaustive study of transport problems when he said: "It is reasonable to conclude, therefore, that the Canal operations proper, the so-called 'business properties,' and, in the aggregate, the operations of the Panama Railroad have made a creditable showing."[5] Criticism has been directed chiefly at the steamship line because of its competition with private carriers. This, it must be admitted, is among the least profitable of the undertakings of the Canal Zone.

A committee of the House of Representatives made an extensive tour of the Panama Canal Zone and reported in July, 1947.[6] The report was generally favorable; adverse comment was confined to what appeared to be an excessive number on the pay rolls of the Panama Canal and Panama Railroad Company. The committee's only recommendation was that substantial force reductions be made at once.

The Hoover Commission made no general assessment of the quality of Canal Zone administration but it did suggest several changes,[7] some of which President Truman, early in 1950, took steps to implement. These included consolidation of the Panama Canal and the Panama Railroad Company into a new agency called the Panama Canal Company and the revision of fiscal and accounting practices. The President did not at this

[1] *Government-operated Enterprises in the Panama Canal Zone* (Chicago: University of Chicago Press, 1934).

[2] *Ibid.*, p. 212.

[3] *Ibid.*

[4] *Ibid.*, p. 215.

[5] United States Federal Coordinator of Transportation, *Public Aids to Transportation* (Washington: Government Printing Office, 4 vols., 1940), vol. I, p. 24.

[6] Report No. 781, Union Calendar No. 400, 80th Cong., 1st. Sess. (Washington: Government Printing Office, 1947).

[7] *Federal Business Enterprises*, pp. 5–12, and *Task Force Report on Revolving Funds and Business Enterprises of the Government*, pp. 126–134 (Washington: Government Printing Office, 1949).

time follow the Hoover Commission suggestion of urging transfer of administrative responsibility from the Army to the Department of Commerce.

THE ALASKAN RAILROAD

The Alaskan Railroad is a federally owned corporation under the direction of the Division of Territories and Island Possessions of the Department of the Interior. Federal ownership was authorized in 1914 after private companies had proved unprofitable and had been unable to extend service into the interior of the territory. Commercial operations began in 1923 and now extend over 500 miles, reaching from Seward to Fairbanks. In addition, the company owns and operates telephone and terminal facilities along the line, river boats on the Yukon, and some auxiliary ocean-going and coastwise vessels; promotes Alaskan agricultural and industrial development; investigates minerals and other resources; operates hotels at Curry and Mt. McKinley Park; and maintains a hospital and medical staff. Operations are under the direction of a business manager appointed by the Secretary of the Interior.

Here is another federally owned multiple-purpose agency whose success cannot be measured solely in terms of monetary profits. From a strictly economic point of view, the railroad has usually operated at a loss; nor has it been conspicuously successful in stimulating the economic development of the country. It is possible that as a result of new interest in the territory caused by the war, the Alcan Highway, and the development of air commerce the future picture will be brighter. In spite of these shortcomings, there is little disposition to abandon the enterprise. Private capital might be interested in acquiring the lucrative parts of the program though probably not all; but to sell those would leave the government holding the most unprofitable segments, thus incurring even larger deficits. It is likely, therefore, that the American taxpayers will continue helping to subsidize transportation for the area if for no other reason than to promote the economic, social, and cultural development of the territory.

INLAND WATERWAYS CORPORATION

To meet the acute transportation shortage which developed during the First World War, the United States Shipping Administration undertook the operation of a barge line principally upon the New York State Barge Canal, Mississippi and Warrior Rivers. Large losses were incurred, forcing Congress to consider continuance under improved management, sale to private interests, or outright abandonment. In 1921 operations were discontinued on the New York Barge Canal and intracoastal routes while the remainder was turned over to the War Department for operation. Regulations of the War Department proved unduly burdensome and earnings disappointing, leading to reconsideration of the problem in 1924 when an independent government corporation was established. From then until now it was hoped that the corporation could operate so successfully as to demonstrate the practicability of private operation, but the corporation still remains in government hands.

Although within the Department of Commerce for administrative reasons, the corporation is independently managed. The capital stock is owned by the Federal government; policy is determined by an advisory board; and the enterprise is managed by the president of the advisory board.

The corporation is the largest barge-line operator in the United States. Its fleets ply the Missouri, Mississippi, Illinois, and Warrior Rivers, and the Gulf of Mexico between New Orleans and Mobile. The corporation also owns a short (18.12 miles) railroad between Birmingport and Ensley, Alabama.

Results of Operations.—From a financial point of view, transportation economists are generally agreed that the corporation has not been a success. On the other hand, it has helped develop and improve navigation facilities along its routes; competition that it offers has helped lower rail and other transportation rates in the area; and its added facilities came in handy during the war. In spite of these advantages, the weight of informed opinion gives rise to doubt as to the advisability of continued operation. The Hoover Commission recommended its prompt liquidation. Railroad managements would have the lines abandoned completely. If any change is made, which would be surprising, a more probable disposition is likely to be abandonment of the least profitable routes and continuation of the rest either under government or private ownership. The present law permits lease or sale to anyone except railroad interests, with the proviso that the Mississippi River facilities must continue to be operated as a unit, the Warrior River facilities must be operated as a unit, and assurances must be given that the "facilities would be continued in the common carrier service in a manner substantially similar to the service rendered by the Corporation."

THE MERCHANT MARINE

The American Merchant Marine consists of all merchant ships plying under the registry of the United States. There appears to be something gratifying to patriotic impulses for nations to have ships plying the seas and stopping at the world's ports. At the same time, shipping interests the world over have enjoyed either natural economic advantages or governmental subsidies, making it difficult for American shippers and shipbuilders to compete successfully. This has led to the formation of powerful lobbies

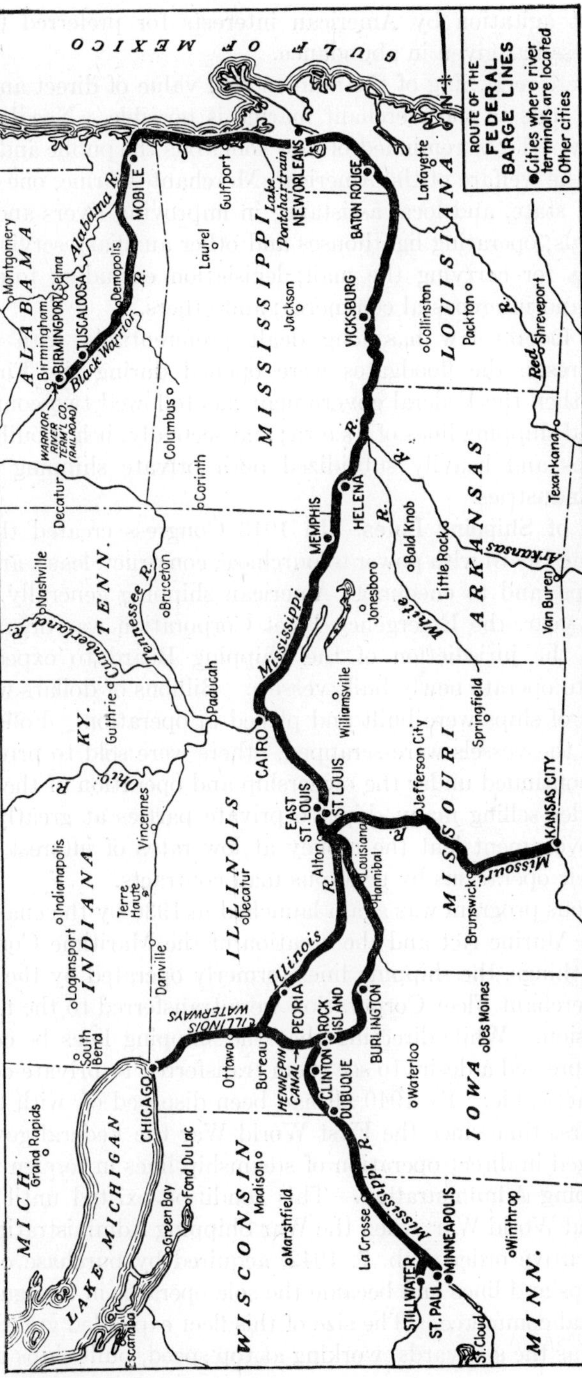

SOURCE: The Inland Waterways Corporation.

and incessant agitation by American interests for preferred treatment, which Congress has given in abundance.

No complete reckoning of the number and value of direct and indirect governmental aids to the merchant marine is possible. Needless to say, they are many. To be reminded of how solicitous the public and Congress has been for the welfare of the American Merchant Marine, one need only recall federal, state, and local assistance in improving rivers and harbors; dredging canals; operating lighthouses and other auxiliary services; profitable contracts for carrying the mail; legislation excluding foreign ships from coastal and intercoastal commerce; and others.

Although federal law has long dealt preferentially with American shipping interests, the floodgates were opened during the First World War. Since then the Federal government has followed two courses: first, it has operated shipping lines of its own; and secondly, it has built, bought, and sold ships and heavily subsidized both private shipping lines and shipbuilding industries.

Operation of Shipping Lines.—In 1916 Congress created the United States Shipping Board with power to purchase, construct, lease, and operate merchant ships, and to encourage American shipping generally. During the following year, the Emergency Fleet Corporation was organized and placed under the jurisdiction of the Shipping Board to expedite shipbuilding and to operate newly built vessels. Billions of dollars were spent and hundreds of ships were built and placed in operation. Following the war, many of the vessels were scrapped, others were sold to private lines, while others continued under the ownership and operation of the Shipping Board. Besides selling many ships to private parties at greatly reduced prices, the government lent the money at low rates of interest and then subsidized their operations by generous mail contracts.

An ambitious program was again launched in 1936 by the enactment of the Merchant Marine Act and the creation of the Maritime Commission. Among other things, the shipping lines formerly operated by the Shipping Board and Merchant Fleet Corporation were transferred to the new Maritime Commission. While directing that the shipping lines be continued, the statute expressed a desire to see them transferred to private companies as soon as practicable. By 1940 all had been disposed of, with the result that for the first time since the First World War the Federal government was not engaged in direct operation of steamship lines in foreign trade.

War Shipping Administration.—This condition existed until entrance into the Second World War, when the War Shipping Administration, established by executive order, Feb. 7, 1942, acquired by purchase or charter all private ships and lines and became the sole operator in foreign, coastal, and intercoastal commerce. The size of this fleet expanded greatly during the war years as the shipyards, working at top speed, built ships in greater number and in less time than ever before. Although the War Shipping Administration acquired this merchant fleet, it did not operate any of the vessels. Instead, the ships were assigned or allocated by charter to some company to operate in a way that would contribute most to war operations. Not infrequently a steamship company would receive back from the War Shipping Administration one of its own vessels, but more frequently this was not the case. The end of the war left the government with more than 50 million dead-weight tons of shipping to be returned to private operators, sold, kept in reserve, scrapped, or operated.

Shipbuilding, Buying, and Selling.—The First World War activities were mentioned above. Since 1936 the Maritime Commission has been the largest merchant-ship broker in the country. Between the inception of the program in 1937 and June 30, 1944, the commission supervised the construction of 4,910 vessels costing over 8 billion dollars and on the last date mentioned had 1,855 under construction or contract. Prior to 1940 some of these were built for operation by the commission itself in foreign trade, but later most of these were sold. Others were built on order for private shipping interests or built directly for the commission and sold to private parties. After the War Shipping Administration came into existence in 1942, the commission built exclusively for it. In addition to building new ships, the commission bought, reconditioned, and sold many used ones. For its building and repairing operations shipyards belonging to the Navy or private companies were used, although the commission frequently helped finance expansion and improvement of these facilities.

Subsidies to Shippers and Shipbuilders.—What concerns us here are the direct subsidies now given to shippers and indirectly to the shipbuilding industry, because these are so closely related to the proprietary activities of the United States Maritime Commission.

Since 1936, the Maritime Commission has offered two principal types of subsidies: one to shipbuilders, called a "construction differential," and the other to ship operators, called an "operating differential." The first works this way: at the request of a private citizen wishing to engage in foreign shipping, the Maritime Commission may contract to have a vessel built in an American shipyard, pay the construction cost, and then sell the vessel to the applicant for an amount equal to the estimated cost of constructing the vessel if it had been built in a foreign shipyard. In no case may the differential be more than 50 per cent of the cost of making the vessel. The applicant is required to post a bond to insure good faith pending completion of the vessel and is required to pay part of the purchase price in cash and the remainder plus interest over a period of years.

The operating differential works similarly. When a citizen operating a vessel used in an essential service, route, or line in foreign commerce (but not inland, coastal, or intercoastal) finds in his operating expenses items that place him at a competitive disadvantage with foreign operators, the Maritime Commission will pay him a differential high enough to equalize the cost of operation.

The commission may also aid citizens in the construction of new vessels to be operated in the foreign, coastal, or intercoastal trade when no construction differential is granted. Here the commission will pay the cost of approved national-defense features and lend a large part of the cost of the vessel which is repayable, with interest, over a period of years. If the operator makes more than a 10 per cent profit over a 10-year period the government may recapture half of the excess, up to the full amount of the subsidy paid.

Mortgage Insurance.—Under terms of the Merchant Marine Act of 1936, the Maritime Commission is authorized to insure the payment of mortgages that secure loans aiding construction of vessels in domestic, North American, and near-by island trades. By thus lessening risks of nonpayment, banking institutions are readier to advance the large sums of money required for building ships. For this service premiums are collected from the mortgagor just as in other insurance plans.

Conclusions.—From an economic point of view, federal operation of shipping lines as described above has never been profitable, but rather it has been extremely expensive. The same must be said of most of the aids and subsidies. What the nation has paid for is not economical transportation but national defense, international prestige, gratification of patriotic impulses, and assistance to important industries. Whether results justify the expenditures must remain a matter of opinion. Few will doubt, however, that the Maritime Commission has performed its work well and that in time of war it is essential to have the ships and shipyards.

FEDERAL POWER PROJECTS

Agencies and Scope of Operations.—Several federal agencies are deeply involved in electric power operations. Many of them generate and transmit electric energy, but comparatively few distribute to ultimate consumers. The customary pattern is for federal agencies to generate and transmit electric energy to a given point at which it is sold at wholesale to states, municipalities, other public bodies, and nonprofit cooperatives. These, in turn, handle distribution. After meeting the demands of preferred customers, sales are often made to private utilities and industrial concerns.

Operations have reached gigantic proportions. The Hoover Commission[1] reported that as of June 30, 1947, 47 hydroelectric and 10 steam power plants had been built or purchased, 37 additional plants were under construction, and 79 more had been authorized by Congress. This, according

[1] *Federal Business Enterprises*, pp. 51–129.

MAJOR HYDROELECTRIC POWER DEVELOPMENTS RECENTLY COMPLETED, NOW UNDER CONSTRUCTION, OR AUTHORIZED FOR POSTWAR CONSTRUCTION

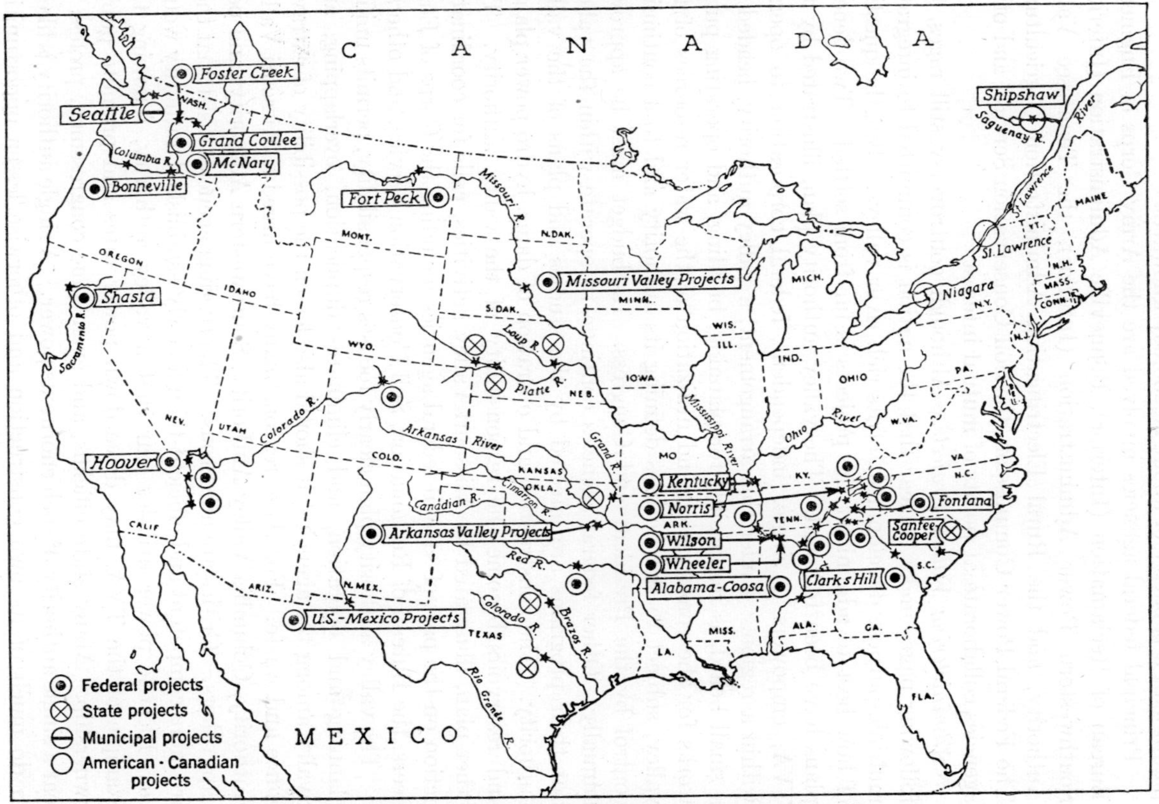

SOURCE: Power Authority of the State of New York, 1947.

to the commission, would give the nation by about 1960 a total of 172 plants with a capacity of about 20,233,637 kilowatts.

Principal federal agencies involved are the Army Corps of Engineers, Bureau of Reclamation (Interior), Bonneville Administration (Interior), Southwestern Power Administration (Interior), the Tennessee Valley Authority, and the Rural Electrification Administration (Agriculture). The Federal Power Commission, the Soil Conservation Service, and other agencies collaborate at points of mutual interest.

Administering Valley Projects.—Although controversy still rages, the following pages make it clear that the nation is committed to integrated multiple-purpose development of its rich river valleys. But the question of how best to administer the projects is far from settled. Two general plans have been followed. The valley authority plan, illustrated by the TVA, empowers a single, independent, federal corporation to operate within a region. Under this arrangement, a valley authority, headed by a small board, is responsible for planning, building, and operating public works for the conservation and utilization of the water resources of the valley, subject to the statutes defining its authority and to a continuing control by the President and Congress. Its budget must be approved annually. Other federal agencies continue to operate within the valley, but their programs are affected by the studies and plans of the valley authority. The construction and operation of dams, hydro power plants, and reservoirs become the responsibility of the valley authority. The other plan, illustrated by Missouri Valley activities, calls for coordinated action on the part of several federal agencies including the Corps of Engineers, the Bureau of Reclamation, Soil Conservation Service, and others.

The valley authority plan clearly focuses responsibility, permits unified planning and operation, and eliminates duplication, overlapping, and rivalry among the agencies; it should also lessen the possibility of extravagance and waste. For these reasons many have urged a Missouri Valley Authority, Columbia Valley Authority, Southwestern Authority, and perhaps others. Critics are numerous. The rivaling agencies insist that they are more competent and efficient than a newly established authority would be. Electric power utilities fear that a valley authority, following the example of the TVA, may drive down power rates and promote public ownership. Many state officials, and even some congressmen, profess to fear a single authority of such enormous power. A single authority is likely to do much of its own construction and otherwise lessen opportunities for contractors, realtors, and other private interests. These, and other reasons, evoke sympathy from States'-rights advocates, champions of free enterprise, and opponents of such federal projects generally. Thus far, opposition has been strong enough to keep valley authorities to one, the TVA, but what the future holds cannot be foretold. The Hoover Com-

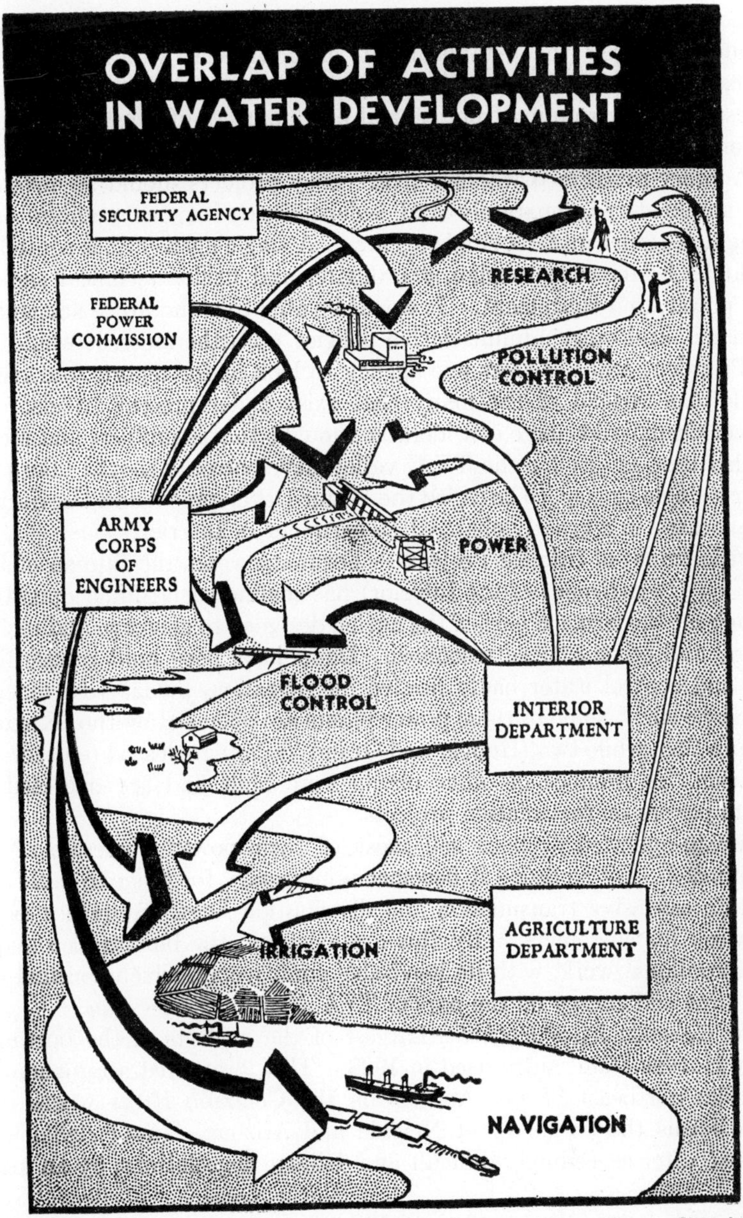

The Hoover Commission effectively called public attention to the conflicts in jurisdiction in water development and stream control. One of the boldest and most controversial proposals of the Commission was to transfer the river and harbors and flood control activities of the Army Corps of Engineers to the Department of the Interior. SOURCE: Hoover Commission, *Reorganization of the Department of the Interior*, pp. 24–35. This illustration is from *Concluding Report*, p. 28.

mission, while strongly condemning present interagency jealousy and overlapping, opposed the establishment of additional valley authorities.[1] Instead, it expressed preference for agency consolidation, with direct lines of responsibility running from central headquarters in Washington to the various river valleys.

Another problem is whether river valley projects should be developed and administered separately and independently of one another or be brought together under a single agency. A single agency, it is contended, would be better able to plan, coordinate, and utilize technical services, man power, and equipment. It would be able to standardize accounting, personnel, and other administrative policies. Furthermore, it would give the President and Congress one agency to look to for reports and recommendations instead of the many that exist under present trends. The Hoover Commission gave considerable thought to this problem and recommended that except for the TVA, valley developments should take place under a single agency, to be called the Water Development and Use Service, to be located in a greatly changed Department of Interior.[2]

Department of Interior Projects.—For many years the Bureau of Reclamation (Department of the Interior) has conducted far-flung operations throughout the western part of the nation designed to conserve and reclaim the soil and other natural resources. Dams have been built primarily to store and control water badly needed for irrigation, but also to generate electric power. Some of these power plants are operated by the Bureau of Reclamation, while two (Hoover and Grand Valley) are leased to others for operation. A number of other plants were built and are operated by private parties on reclamation projects.

Bureau-operated stations sell most of their power wholesale at the switchboard. By so doing it becomes unnecessary for them to build and maintain extensive transmission and distribution lines, but rather leaves that work for customers.[3] By this arrangement, the bureau also avoids the promotional work, with its inevitable controversy, which consumes so much time and energy on the part of TVA.

The Colorado River Project.—Largest of the projects of the bureau is one at Hoover Dam, authorized in 1928. This is situated approximately 250 miles northeast of Los Angeles on the Colorado River where that stream forms the boundary of Nevada and Arizona. River rights were obtained, after exceedingly difficult and delicate negotiations, by an inter-

[1] *Department of the Interior.* See also the task force report entitled *Natural Resources,* pp. 16–39.

[2] *Department of Interior,* p. 14.

[3] In the case of the Grand Coulee project, electricity generated by the Bureau of Reclamation is transferred to the Bonneville Administration for disposition. See below, p. 720.

state agreement with the seven states concerned known as the Colorado River Compact.[1] When completed, the dam was the highest in the world; it created the world's largest reservoir; and it made possible the world's largest power plant; but in every respect except height it has since been superseded by the Grand Coulee Dam on the Columbia River. The project was built to do four things: help control floods, store water and provide sufficient water for irrigation, control silt in the river, and generate electric power. Operations are under the direction of a manager appointed by the Secretary of the Interior.

While there was plenty of opposition from private utilities at the time the project was authorized, this has become a fading echo by comparison with the controversy surrounding the Tennessee Valley Authority and Columbia River projects. This is partly due to the difference in methods used in disposing of electric energy. Instead of operating the plant and marketing the energy itself, generating facilities at Hoover Dam are leased to others. At present two parties hold the leases: the Los Angeles department of water and power and the Southern California Edison Company, the former a municipal and the latter a private concern. Another difference that lessens controversy is that Hoover Dam does not prescribe the resale rates at which its lessees may dispose of their energy.

This is another illustration of a multiple-purpose, joint-cost enterprise. Whether the purchasers of electric power enjoy a subsidy depends upon whether costs have been properly allocated to power operations, and also whether all legitimate overhead and operating costs have been considered in fixing wholesale rates. While there are still skeptics, the weight of informed opinion tends to the conclusion that Hoover Dam power operations are both economically sound and well managed.

The Missouri Valley Project.—Another Department of Interior project of great magnitude is the Missouri Basin Plan, better known as the Pick-Sloan plan because of the men who pioneered the project. The area to be served stretches from Three Forks, Mont., in the Northwest, to the Mississippi at St. Louis. It encompasses 7 million people, one-sixth of the United States, and all or parts of ten states. Authorized by the flood control act of 1944, the Bureau of Reclamation and the Corps of Engineers are developing a coordinated plan for the entire region which calls for more than 100 dams and reservoirs and twenty new power plants. The purposes are the same as those of other valley projects. Parts of the plan are completed, others are in progress, while others are in preliminary stages. Under present plans, the Corps of Engineers will operate the power plants while the Bureau of Reclamation will market the energy, giving preference to states, municipalities, other public bodies, and cooperatives. Net revenues are to be applied toward repayment of the cost of construction.

[1] Cf. p. 103.

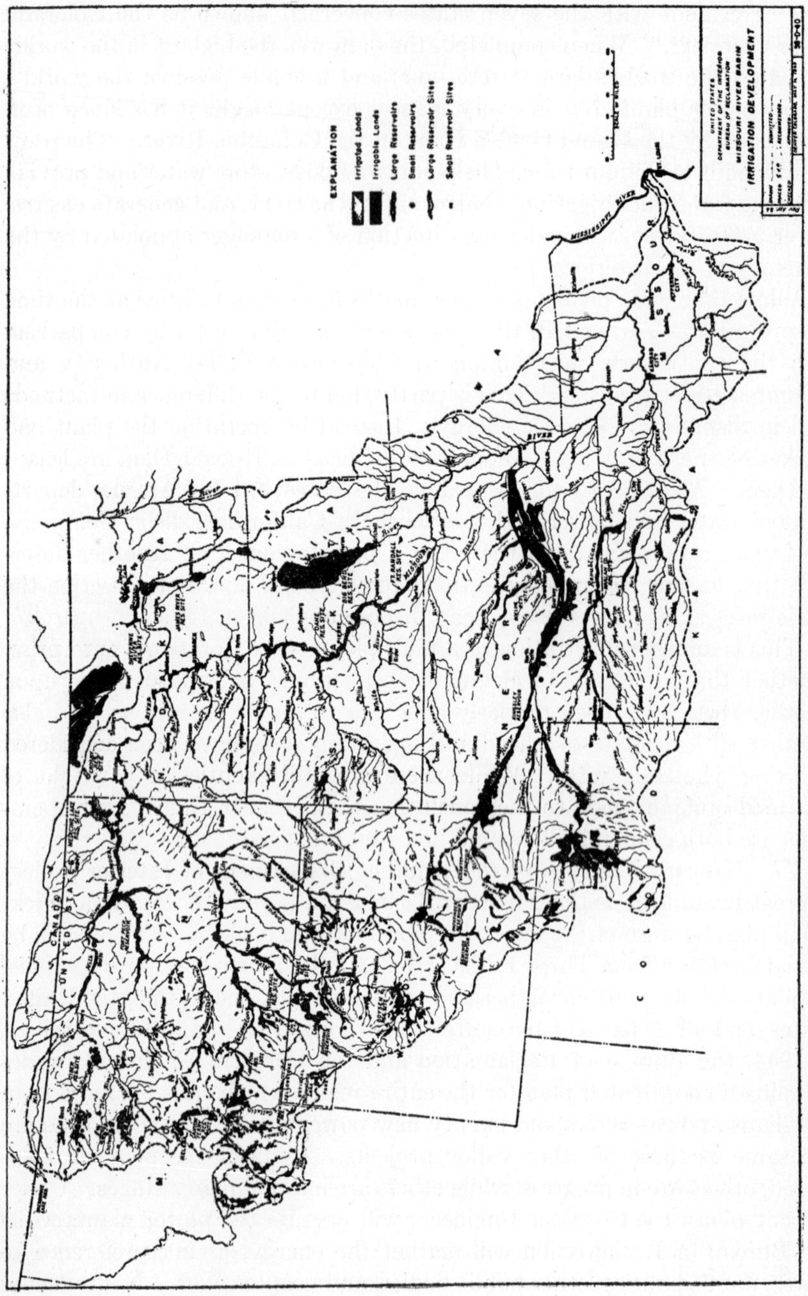

Missouri River Basin irrigation development. SOURCE: United States Department of the Interior Bureau of Reclamation.

War Department Projects.—The Army Engineer Corps has long been charged with responsibility for devising means of controlling floods. This has, among other things, entailed the construction of dams and other facilities looking toward the integrated development and control of river basins. Some of these dams have been equipped with hydroelectric generating facilities and are operated by the Engineer Corps. In general the tendency has been to avoid involving Army personnel in permanent electric-power operations, with the result that the Engineer Corps now operates

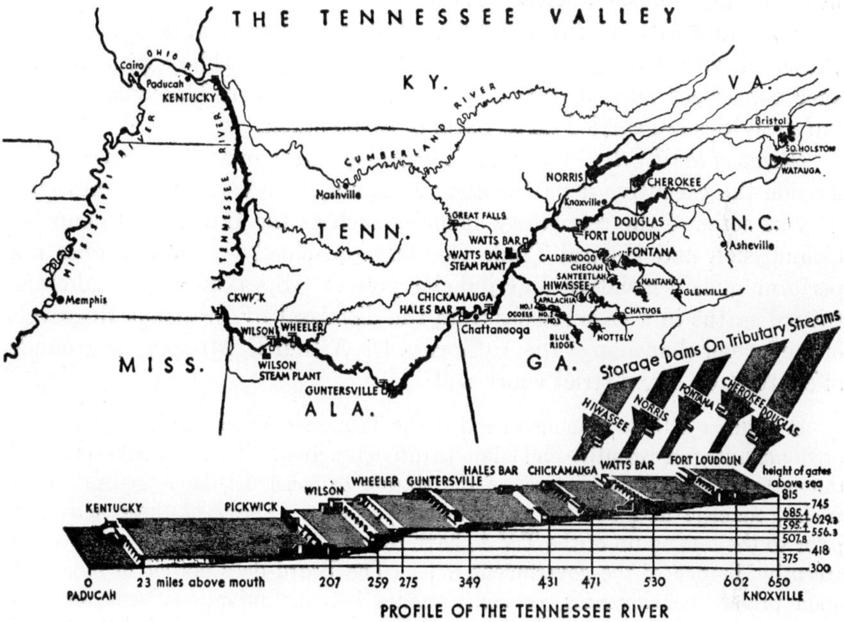

SOURCE: The Tennessee Valley Authority.

only a few plants and in no instance does it engage in retail marketing of energy. Power generated at Bonneville is marketed by the Bonneville Administration; that produced at Fort Peck is marketed by the Bureau of Reclamation; that produced at Denison and Norfolk is turned over to the Southwestern Power Administration; and the small amount produced at Dalecarlia is sold exclusively to the Washington Aqueduct Water Supply System of the District of Columbia.

The Tennessee Valley Authority (TVA).[1]—The TVA stems from operations begun during the First World War. At that time the government started building Wilson Dam at Muscle Shoals, Ala., for the purpose of providing power with which to transform into munitions rich deposits of nitrate found there. The war ended before plans were completed, leaving

[1] For a discussion of the constitutionality of TVA see p. 427.

the government with a large investment on its hands. Strong sentiment developed in favor of selling to private bidders, chief of whom was Henry Ford. These attempts were blocked by a small group of "insurgent" senators led by the late Senator George W. Norris, of Nebraska, who later became popularly known as the "father of TVA" and for whom one of the largest dams and the near-by community of Norris, Tenn., is named. Senator Norris and others envisaged a large-scale regional program designed to bring about coordinated development and utilization of natural resources in the entire Tennessee River Valley.

The Authority is directed by a three-man board appointed by the President with Senate concurrence for 9-year terms,[1] while a general manager supervises administration. Its chief office is at Knoxville, Tenn., but activities are carried on in parts of seven states.

Status of the TVA.—The TVA is organized as a government corporation outside the executive departments. It is not, however, in the same category as some of the regulatory agencies such as the Interstate Commerce Commission and Federal Trade Commission, chiefly because it does not perform quasi-legislative and judicial powers. Speaking of its administrative status in a case arising from the dismissal by President Roosevelt of the former chairman of the Authority, Dr. Arthur E. Morgan, on grounds of contumacy, the district court said[2]

> It requires little to demonstrate that the Tennessee Valley Authority exercises predominantly an executive and administrative function. To it has been entrusted the carrying out of the dictates of the statute to construct dams, generate electricity, manage and develop government property. Many of these activities, prior to the setting up of the T.V.A. have rested with the several divisions of the executive branch of the government. . . . The Board does not sit in judgment upon private controversies, or controversies between private citizens and the government, and there is no judicial review of its decision, except as it may sue or be sued. . . . It is not to be aligned with the Federal Trade Commission, the Interstate Commerce Commission, or other administrative bodies mainly exercising clearly quasi-legislative or quasi-judicial functions—it is predominantly an administrative arm of the executive department. . . .

Although independent of the executive departments, the Authority is, therefore, subject to presidential direction, including a larger measure of control than the chief executive has over most of the "independent establishments."[3]

Purposes and Functions.—The primary purpose of TVA is that of fostering the "orderly and proper physical, economic, and social development" of the area. Its first concern must be navigation and flood control. Beyond that it is directed to produce nitrate and phosphate products for

[1] The term was 5 years for those first appointed.
[2] Morgan *v.* Tennessee Valley Authority, 115 F 2d 990 (1940).
[3] See p. 318 for a fuller discussion of the President's power of removal.

use as fertilizers in peacetime and munitions in time of war, operate electric plants for its own use and sale of the surplus, foster afforestation, soil conservation, and diversification of industry. A valuable by-product of its activities is improved recreational opportunities which include some of the best fishing, camping, swimming, and boating to be found.

Ranging up and down the Tennessee River are nine dams; on its tributaries are seventeen dams; and on tributaries of the Cumberland River are two dams. Behind these are impounded enormous lakes of water forming a total water line longer than the salt-water boundary of the entire continental United States.[1] Each of the main river dams has a spillway section, a navigation lock, and a powerhouse. The series of nine dams provides a navigation channel of 9-foot minimum depth for the entire 650-mile length of the Tennessee River. Tributary dams are essentially storage dams; none has a navigation lock, but all but two have, or will have when completed, hydroelectric generating plants. The Authority also directs the operation of five Aluminum Company of America dams on tributaries of the Tennessee, thereby assuring more efficient control and utilization of water power. In addition to its hydroelectric plants, the Authority has four major and eleven small plants at which power may be generated by fuel instead of water. It maintains a network of transmission lines, a switchyard at each hydro or steam plant to put the power on the lines, and substations throughout the power-service area for taking power from the lines. The Authority also owns and operates chemical plants for manufacturing nitrate and phosphate products.

Electric Power Operations.—Most controvery has centered around the sale by the Authority of surplus electric power. The act of 1933 permits

Year	Average annual use of electric power, kilowatt-hours		Average cost per kilowatt-hour, cents		Average annual bill	
	TVA area	United States	TVA area	United States	TVA area	United States
1945	1,754	1,186	1.85	3.47	$32.45	$41.15
1946	1,902	1,290	1.79	3.31	33.96	42.70
1947	2,197	1,385	1.66	3.14	36.51	43.49
1948	2,520	1,505	1.57	3.03	39.67	45.60
Change, 1945–1948, per cent	43.7	26.9	− 15.1	− 12.7	22.2	10.8

SOURCE: Tennessee Valley Authority, *Annual Report*, 1948 (Washington: Government Printing Office, 1948), p. 94.

[1] David E. Lilienthal, *TVA; Democracy on the March* (New York: Harper, 2d ed., 1944), p. 13.

the sale either at the generating stations or elsewhere. It also requires that in selecting customers preference be given to cooperative associations and municipalities. It has contracts for sale of power with municipalities, cooperatives, a number of privately owned utility companies, government plants, and large industrial concerns, the largest being the Aluminum Company of America. All contracts with municipalities and cooperatives stipulate not only the rates to be paid TVA but also the rates at which the energy will be resold. In the beginning those rates were from 40 to 60 per cent lower than those previously charged by private utilities in the area, although now most private utilities in the area have lowered rates to nearer the TVA level.[1] The statistics in the table on previous page show comparative trends.[2]

Opposition and Criticism.—Opposition to TVA came chiefly from private utilities, coal and railway interests, local groups who feared their land would be taken or other interests adversely affected, banking and financial groups, States'-rights advocates, manufacturers of fertilizers, and others opposed to the principle of government ownership or increased federal control. The entire controversy cannot be reviewed here; all that can be done is to consider the question of fairness of the rate policies of TVA and mention a few general conclusions.

Two criticisms have been made of the rate policies of the Authority: first, that its wholesale rates do not accurately reflect all the cost of generating power; second, that the retail rates charged by cooperatives and municipalities, but dictated by TVA, do not reflect all proper costs. If either allegation is correct, clearly the users of TVA electricity enjoy a subsidy from the taxpayers of the entire country. At the same time, if either is true, TVA rates are an improper measurement ("yardstick") of what it should cost private utilities to render the same service.

Findings of Investigating Bodies.—The nearest to an early impartial study available is the report of an investigation made by a joint committee of Congress in 1939, but even this is not entirely convincing because members of the committee were divided sharply along political lines. In general, a majority of the committee concurred with the Authority's allocation of costs between navigation, flood control, electric power, and other phases of the program. The majority also concluded that the

[1] In 1945 TVA basic residential rates were as follows: first 50 kilowatt-hours per month, 3 cents per kilowatt-hour; next 150 kilowatt-hours per month, 2 cents per kilowatt-hour; next 200 kilowatt-hours per month, 1 cent per kilowatt-hour; next 1,000 kilowatt-hours per month, 0.4 cent per kilowatt-hour; excess over 1,400 kilowatt-hours per month, 0.75 cent per kilowatt-hour. While these are basic rates, a few municipalities charge less.

[2] United States Congress, Joint Committee to Investigate the TVA, *Investigation of the Tennessee Valley Authority, Report* . . . Sen. Doc. 56, 76th Cong., 1st Sess. (Washington: Government Printing Office, 1939).

Authority's wholesale rates were high enough to cover all costs attributable to power, including interest, amortization, depreciation, and taxes, and still leave, when the system was fully developed, a balance to pay part of the costs of the navigation and flood-control programs. The majority found also that TVA wholesale rates were about the same as similar rates charged by private utilities in the area; hence even though they were subsidized, they would not be unfair in the sense that users of TVA power enjoyed a competitive advantage. As for retail rates, the majority concluded that the municipalities and cooperatives were charging their accounts with all proper costs including interest; taxes including federal and state plus the equivalent of taxes that private utilities would pay if they were serving the vicinity; depreciation; etc. The majority report, therefore, supported the Authority's contentions so far as rates were concerned, although, as noted above, there was vigorous dissent from three Republican members of the committee.

The Hoover Commission paid considerable attention to the TVA but ended by making no judgment about merits of the rate controversy. Its task force did, however, make the following observations:[1] (1) It noted, without confirmation or disapproval, that the General Accounting Office in 1949 had concluded that the TVA had allocated to power an insufficient share of the cost of multiple-use facilities. (2) On the basis of this allocation, "power revenues are well in excess of those required to repay over 50-year periods the cost of facilities allocated to power, even when construction interest is charged at 3 per cent on the unpaid debt balance." (3) TVA made payments to states and counties in lieu of taxes at rates gradually decreasing from 10 per cent to 5 per cent (beginning July 1, 1948) of gross revenue from power sales. By comparison, Class A and B electric utilities paid in taxes for 1946 an average of 19 per cent of gross revenues.[2] (4) TVA annual reports were found to be comprehensive and to present clearly the financial condition of the authority and the results of operation. The task force noted, again without comment, that the General Accounting Office had said in 1945 of TVA accounts that they "generally were well conceived, supervised, and maintained, and the Authority is to be commended as one of the foremost Government corporations in the use of accounting management, comparing quite favorably in this respect with well-managed private corporations."

[1] *Revolving Funds and Business Enterprises of the Government*, pp. 88–97.

[2] This comparison may be unfair to the TVA, as one member of the Hoover Commission pointed out (*ibid.*, pp. 116–117). Private utilities paid in taxes 19 per cent of gross revenues derived from all phases of their electric activities, including generation, transmission, and distribution. TVA activities, however, are confined largely to generation, transmission, and disposal at wholesale. If taxes paid by distributors of TVA power and value of free services be added to payments made by TVA in lieu of taxes, the comparison is decidedly favorable to the TVA.

General Observations.—Regardless of the merits of the rate issue, several things about the Authority and its operations are clear. All informed neutral observers agree that the corporation has been well run from an administrative point of view; it has been ruthlessly correct in abstention from political favoritism; from an engineering point of view dams and other structures were soundly and beautifully built; public ownership has been encouraged in the area; electric rates have been lowered generally throughout the area; low rates have greatly increased the use of electric

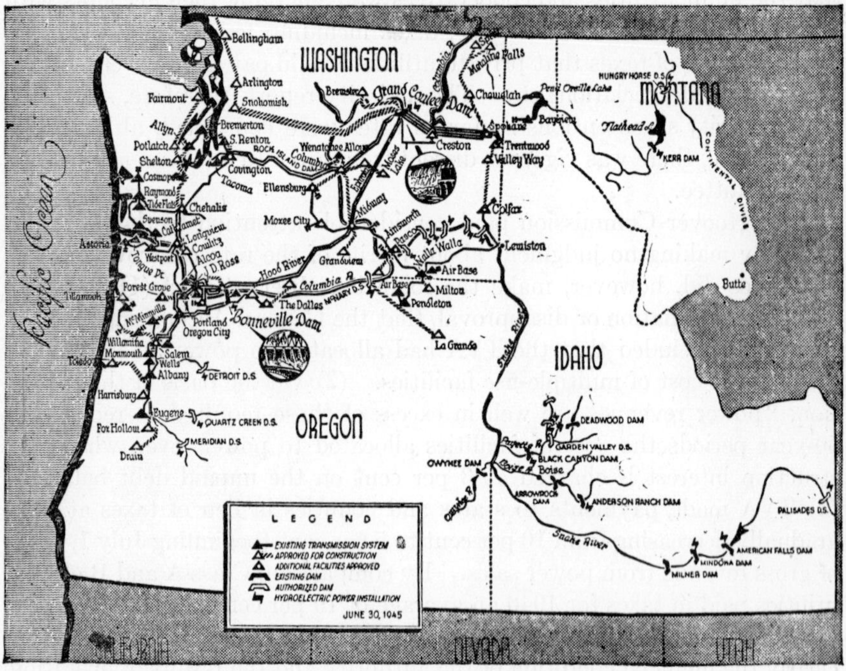

SOURCE: The Bonneville Administration.

energy, tended to stabilize population, diversify industry, and attract new capital; great strides have been made in controlling flood waters, conserving soil, and improving navigation; manufacture of nitrates and phosphates has helped to lower fertilizer prices and otherwise encourage its use; and the Authority has been unusually considerate in its handling of personnel and the social and cultural problems, of which there are many.

The Bonneville Administration.—As early as 1925 Congress authorized a survey of the Columbia River basin with a view to its development for navigation, irrigation, flood control, and power production. Plans proposed in 1932 for the construction of ten dams have grown to contemplate approximately thirty on the Columbia and its tributaries. Of the dams proposed several have been completed, chief of which are Bonneville, nearest the Pacific Ocean and about 40 miles east of Portland, Ore., and Grand Coulee, highest on the Columbia and near the Canadian border.

Ultimately a single administration of all projects in the area is contemplated. Meanwhile, construction, maintenance, and operation of the dams is done by three parties: the Secretary of Army and Chief of Army Corps of Engineers (as at Bonneville); the Bureau of Reclamation, Department of the Interior (as at Grand Coulee); and private interests (as at Rock Island). For the purpose of marketing electric power, however, the Bonneville Power Administration was created in 1937. This is directed by an administrator appointed by the Secretary of the Interior. The administrator obtains power from existing plants and transmits and sells electric energy throughout the area. Sales may be made to both private and public bodies but, as with most federal projects, preference must be given to cooperatives and municipalities. Since 1940 the administrator has had authority also to prescribe the retail rates that public bodies charge their customers.

The Columbia River projects follow the TVA pattern, although when completed they will represent a much larger investment and productive capacity. As with other multiple-purpose projects, an attempt has been made properly to allocate costs to various phases of the project, pay legitimate operating expenses, and ultimately return to the government the full investment allocated to power as well as some, if not all, of its investment in the entire project. Rates have been comparatively low and the administrator has vigorously pushed the sale and use of energy throughout the area.

Southwestern Power Administration.—In 1944, as part of a flood-control program, multiple-purpose dams built by the Army Engineers Corps were completed at Denison, Tex., on the Red River, and at Norfolk, Ark., on the White River. Meanwhile, the state of Oklahoma, with the help of WPA funds, had undertaken a similar project on the Grand River, which is a large contributor to the Arkansas basin floods. Still unfinished, this was taken over by the Federal government in 1941 by authority of the Federal Power Act and brought to completion in the years following, first by the Federal Works Agency and later by the Southwestern Power Administration. Ultimately, more than two dozen dams will dot the region. Although the Engineer Corps operates the generating stations at Denison, Norfolk, and the Grand River projects, the three market and distribute their electricity through a single agency—the Southwestern Power Administration, established in 1943 as an agency within the Interior Department. Thus far, operations have been on an experimental basis, but a permanent policy is evolving that is similar to the plan followed by the Bonneville Administration.

The St. Lawrence Waterway and Power Project.—Both the United States and Canada have long been interested in the feasibility of developing the St. Lawrence River. Numerous studies have been made and projects proposed,[1] in consequence of which a series of canals has been constructed enabling ships to sail from interior Great Lakes ports to Ogdensburg, N.Y., and Prescott, Ont. Unfortunately, from the points mentioned

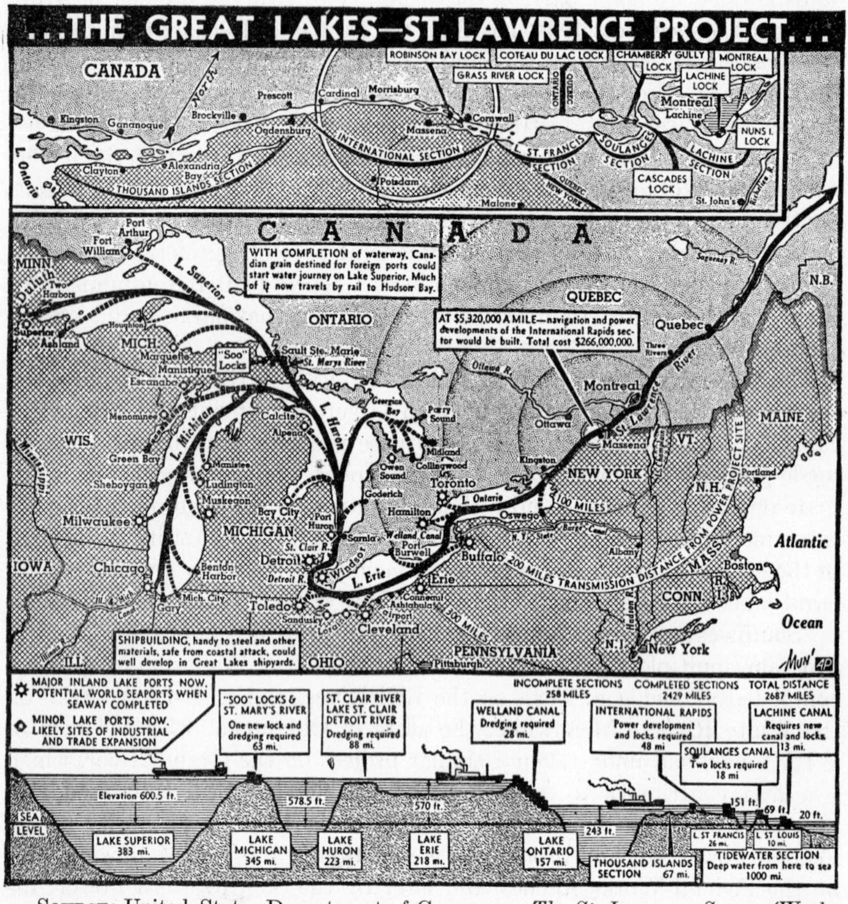

SOURCE: United States Department of Commerce, *The St. Lawrence Survey* (Washington: Government Printing Office, 1941), Part 7, p. 12.

to Montreal on the Atlantic, a distance of 119 miles, the St. Lawrence channel is obstructed. Removal of the obstructions would open an uninterrupted course for ocean-going vessels to travel from as far interior as Duluth, Minn., to the Atlantic and thence to coastal and world ports.

The St. Lawrence project contemplates removal of the impediments; construction of dams and locks; dredging canals; and the building of

[1] See especially, United States Department of Commerce, *The St. Lawrence Survey* (Washington: Government Printing Office, 7 parts, 1941).

hydroelectric facilities at a dam to be erected on the International Rapids near Massena, N.Y. The annual average output of electricity would exceed 13 billion kilowatt-hours, to be divided equally between New York state and the province of Ontario. After completion, plans contemplate that electric facilities will be transferred to the New York Power Authority for operation and sale of energy. Total cost is estimated at $429,474,515, to be shared by the United States, New York, and Canada.

All presidents since Woodrow Wilson have advocated completion of the project and both major parties have recorded approval. Canada has indicated willingness and has already completed the Welland Canal, an essential feature in the project. A treaty embodying the proposal was submitted to the Senate but rejected in 1934.[1] In 1941 the proposal was embodied in an executive agreement between Canada and the United States which, though not requiring ratification by two-thirds of the Senate, did require the assent of both houses of Congress as well as the Canadian parliament. Handling the matter by executive agreement rather than by treaty evoked considerable criticism.[2] At the same time stiff opposition has been encountered from numerous sources, chief of which are rail, power, and coal interests, and Atlantic seaboard cities who fear diminished use of their ports. As a result, action is still pending.

Electric Cooperatives for Farmers.—In 1935 only 754,954 American farms, or less than 11 per cent, were receiving central station electric service. By 1949 this number had increased to 4,582,954, or over 78 per cent of all farms reported in the latest farm census. More than half of the increase in electrified farms was due to the Rural Electrification Administration (REA), established by executive order in 1935 and by statute the following year. The REA is a Department of Agriculture agency with funds and authority for aiding farmers who are not served by existing central station facilities.

The plan is simple. When enough farmers with sufficient income and stability are willing to proceed, a cooperative is formed. The REA supplies advice, consults on legal and engineering matters, and may lend up to 100 per cent of installation cost. The cooperative may install generating facilities or merely a transmission and distribution system for the purpose of conveying energy bought at wholesale from other utilities, private or public. A board of officers, elected by participating farmers, handles business affairs and employs whatever technical personnel may be required. Rates charged farmers are supposed to be fixed high enough to

[1] The vote was forty-six yeas and forty-two nays, considerably short of the required two-thirds majority required.

[2] For one of the best debates in print on this subject, see the testimony of Green H. Hackworth and Dr. Edwin Borchard in United States Senate, Committee on Commerce, *Hearings on Great Lakes—St. Lawrence Basin*, 78th Cong., 2d Sess. (Washington: Government Printing Office, 1945).

pay operating costs and amortize indebtedness over a period of 25 to 35 years. The REA is also authorized to finance the wiring of farmsteads and the purchase and installation of electrical appliances and plumbing. These loans are made to suppliers, not to consumers, and are usually repayable within 5 years.

Although bitterly fought by private utilities and hampered by restrictive state legislation and utility commission rulings, the REA appears to have weathered the storm. It has been aided considerably by the availability of electric power from federal, and in some instances state, public power projects.

Satisfied with results in the field of electricity, Congress, in 1948, authorized the REA to embark on a program of expanding telephone (but not telegraph or radio broadcasting) facilities in rural areas. The REA may lend money to existing cooperatives, nonprofit, limited-dividend, or mutual associations, and in the future it may help finance new ones. Under this legislation, a rural area includes most places with fewer than 1,500 people.

References

Bird, Frederick L.: *The Management of Small Municipal Electric Plants* (New York: Municipal Administration Service, 1932).

——— *A Study of the Port of New York Authority; Its Purpose—Its Accomplishments—Its Plans for the Future* (New York: Dun & Bradstreet, 1949).

Burns and McDonnell Engineering Co.: *Results of Municipal Lighting Plants* (Kansas City: Burns and McDonnell Co., published annually).

Chase, Stuart: *Government in Business* (New York: Macmillan, 1935).

Costigan, Edward P.: *Public Ownership of Government* (New York: Vanguard, 1940).

Dearing, Charles L., and Wilfred Owen: *National Transportation Policy* (Washington: Brookings, 1949).

Dimock, Marshall E.: *Developing America's Waterways: Administration of the Inland Waterways Corporation* (Chicago: University of Chicago Press, 1935).

——— *Business and Government* (New York: Holt, 1949).

——— *Government-operated Enterprises in the Panama Canal Zone* (Chicago: University of Chicago Press, 1934).

——— *Modern Politics and Administration; A Study of the Creative State* (New York: American Book, 1937).

Eldridge, Seba, and Associates: *Development of Collective Enterprise* (Lawrence: University of Kansas Press, 1943).

Ferguson, John H., and Charles Lee Decker: *Municipally Owned Waterworks in Pennsylvania* (State College: Pennsylvania Municipal Publications Service, 1948).

Hodgson, James G.: *Government Ownership of Public Utilities* (New York: H. W. Wilson, 1934).

Koontz, Harold A.: *Government Control of Business* (Boston: Houghton Mifflin, 1941).

Lilienthal, David E.: *TVA: Democracy on the March* (New York: Harper, 1944).

Lyon, Leverett S., Victor Abramson, *et al.*: *Government and Economic Life* (Washington: Brookings, 2 vols., 1940).

McDiarmid, John: *Government Corporations and Federal Funds* (Chicago: University of Chicago Press, 1938).

McGeary, M. Nelson: *Pennsylvania and the Liquor Business* (State College, Pa.: Penns Valley Publishers, 1948).

Merritt, LeRoy C.: *United States Government as Publisher* (Chicago: University of Chicago Press, 1943).

O'Brien, Terence H.: *British Experiments in Public Ownership and Control* . . . (New York: Norton, 1937).

Padelford, Norman J.: *The Panama Canal in Peace and War* (New York: Macmillan, 1942).

Prichett, C. Herman: *The Tennessee Valley Authority; A Study in Public Administration* (Chapel Hill: The University of North Carolina Press, 1943).

United States Board of Investigation and Research: *Public Aids to Domestic Transportation*, House Doc. 159 (Washington: Government Printing Office, 1945).

United States Commission on Organization of the Executive Branch of the Government ("Hoover Commission"): *Federal Business Enterprises; Task Force Report on Revolving Funds and Business Enterprises of the Government; Task Force Report on Natural Resources; Regulatory Commissions; Department of Interior.* (All published: Washington: Government Printing Office, 1949.)

United States Congress, Joint Committee on the Investigation of TVA: *Investigation of the Tennessee Valley Authority Report* . . . Sen. Doc. 56, 76th Cong., 1st Sess., pursuant to Pub. Res. No. 83 (Washington: Government Printing Office, 1939).

United States Federal Coordinator of Transportation (Joseph B. Eastman): *Public Aids to Transportation* (Washington: Government Printing Office, 4 vols., 1940).

——— *Report on Regulation of Transportation*, Sen. Doc. 152, 73d Cong., 2d Sess. (Washington: Government Printing Office, 1934).

United States House of Representatives, Special Committee to Investigate Government Competition with Private Enterprise: *Government Competition with Private Enterprise, Report,* . . . House Rep. No. 1985, 72d Cong., 2d Sess. (Washington: Government Printing Office, 1933).

Wilcox, Delos F.: *The Administration of Municipally Owned Utilities* (New York: Municipal Administration Service, 1931).

Chapter 32

LABOR

Generally speaking, the nineteenth century doubted the existence of Man. Men it knew, and nations, but not Man. Man in General was not often inquired after. Friends of the Human Race were barely to be found. Humanity was commonly abandoned to its own devices.

Carl Becker, *The Declaration of Independence.*[1]

While American society was chiefly agrarian there was little need for laws relating to wages, hours, industrial accidents, housing, old-age pensions, and the like. To be sure, there were the destitute, insane, and indigent aged, but they were left either to shift for themselves or to be provided for by relatives or by religious and philanthropic agencies. Local governments lent assistance through poor boards, poor houses, asylums, while relations between capital and labor were governed by public opinion and the common law. The industrial revolution divorced millions from the land, made them dependent upon machines, urbanized more than half the population, and set in motion the forces that necessitated governmental intervention in increasing amounts. Little labor and social legislation was enacted prior to the Civil War and the bulk of it has come in this country since 1910. The substance of it is discussed in this and the following chapter.

The Labor Department.—A Bureau of Labor was first established in 1884, under the Interior Department. Soon thereafter the bureau was made independent as a Department of Labor, but without executive rank, and in 1903 it became a bureau in the Department of Commerce and Labor. Ten years later it was organized as a separate department with rank equal to that of the nine other departments. At its head is a Secretary who, like others of similar rank, is a member of the President's cabinet and directly responsible to him. This office has the distinction of being the only one in the cabinet ever held by a woman.[2] Normally the Secretary is a member of the President's party who is closely identified with the ranks of organized labor. Associated with the Secretary are the usual administrative assistants and clerical staff.

Reflecting the antagonism between management and workers, the Department of Labor has often been a storm center. Congressional

[1] (New York: Harcourt, 1922), p. 279.

[2] Frances Perkins, of New York State, held the office from Mar. 4, 1933, until early in 1945.

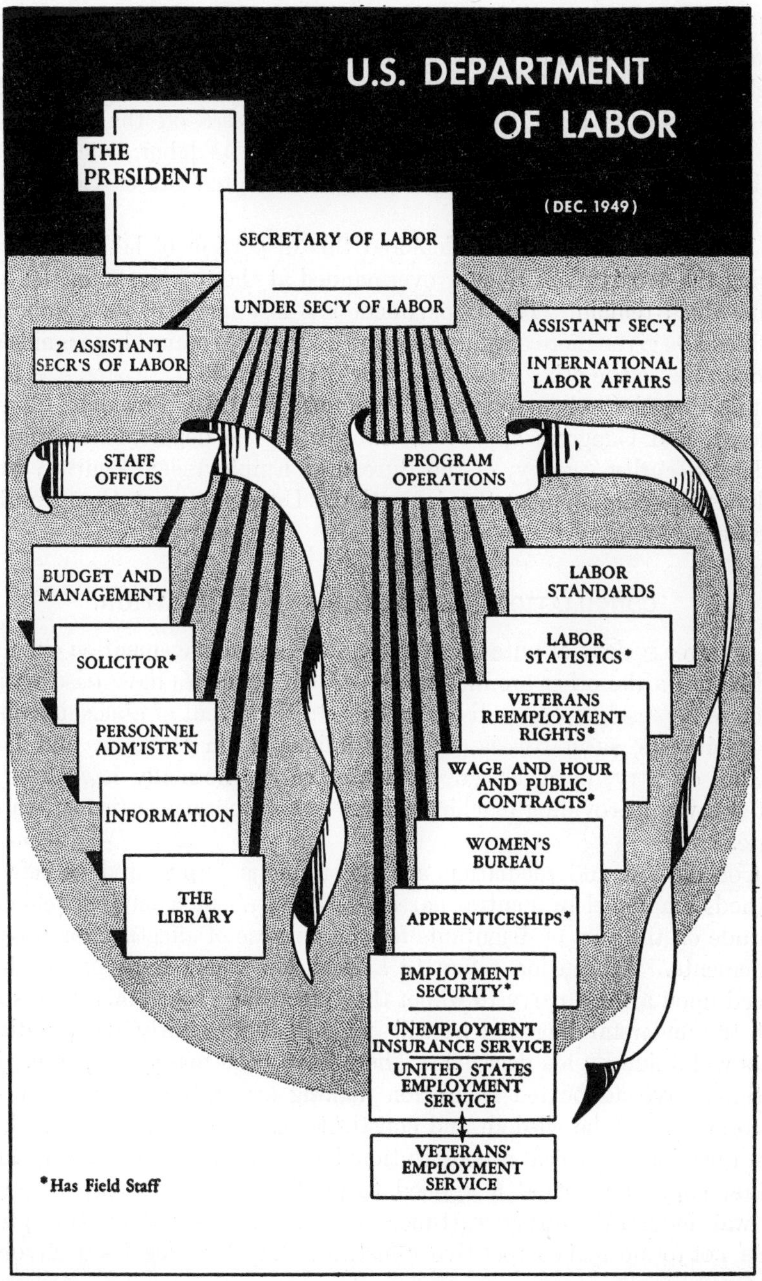

The Hoover Commission noted that the Department of Labor had "been steadily denuded of functions at one time established within it." During 1949, reorganization plan no. 2 brought the Bureau of Employment Security (unemployment compensation and employment service) from the Federal Security Agency to Labor. Several lesser agencies may be added latter. SOURCE: Data furnished by Department of Labor.

critics have thought the department too prolabor and have at times given to other agencies certain functions to which it was properly entitled. The Eightieth Congress (January, 1947–January, 1949), the first controlled by the Republicans after 1932, was especially severe on the department, transferring the Children's Bureau (except for its labor functions), the United States Conciliation Service, and the United States Employment service to other departments.

The Hoover Commission deplored this dispersion of labor activities,[1] saying the department "is now overmanned at the top levels for the functions which remain. The Department has lost much of its significance. It should be given more essential work to do if it is to maintain a significance comparable to the other great executive departments." A step was taken in this direction when, during the summer of 1949, President Truman ordered, and Congress approved, transfer to the department, from the Federal Security Agency, of the Bureau of Employment Security, which includes the Employment Service and the Unemployment Compensation Service.

CONCILIATION, MEDIATION, AND ARBITRATION

In a free society disputes between capital and management on one hand and labor on the other are inevitable. Other countries have tried various schemes for resolving such disputes, even to the extent of abolishing either the capitalists, as in Russia, or labor unions, as in Germany and Italy. In this country, however, governmental efforts normally have been directed toward providing machinery by which voluntary settlement can be made.

Conciliation and mediation are synonymous terms used to refer to methods employed by neutral parties to bring about a more conciliatory attitude on the part of disputants for the purpose of affecting compromise settlements. Arbitration refers to a situation where both parties have agreed upon a third party to whom they are willing to submit the dispute with the understanding that he will judge the issues fairly and the disputants will abide by his decision. There have been many who, from time to time, have advocated legislation making arbitration compulsory but up to now both the wisdom and constitutionality of such proposals have been questioned. From a constitutional point of view, compulsory arbitration might be upheld if applied to public-utility industries or essential war industries during wartime,[2] but, on the basis of existing precedents, not for normal competitive industries. The basic legal issue involved

[1] *Department of Labor* (Washington: Government Printing Office, 1949).

[2] The leading Supreme Court decision on this question is Wolff Packing Co. *v.* Court of Industrial Relations, 262 U.S. 522 (1923).

in such proposals is whether life, liberty, and property are taken without due process of law.

The Mediation and Conciliation Service.—Normally federal law provides only for voluntary conciliation, mediation, and arbitration. The principal agencies involved are the Federal Mediation and Conciliation Service and the National Mediation Board, although employees of other labor agencies, especially the National Labor Relations Board, effect a great many compromises in controversies that might otherwise flare into major disputes.

As already indicated, the Federal Mediation and Conciliation Service was transferred from the Department of Labor and made an independent establishment in 1947. The motive alleged for this action was the desire for greater objectivity on the part of the Service. Whether this treatment was deserved or wise from an administrative point of view is highly controverted.

The Service tries to prevent disputes from arising by trying to improve human relations in industrial life. It also seeks to create an atmosphere congenial to collective bargaining and use of its personnel. In doing these things it works closely with state conciliation agencies. The Taft-Hartley Act of 1947 requires employers and unions to file with the Service notice of every dispute affecting commerce not settled within 30 days after one or the other party to a collective agreement gives notice of intention to terminate or modify an existing contract. When given this information, the Service proffers its assistance.

The procedure followed by the Conciliation Service varies somewhat depending upon the nature of the case. The Conciliation Service keeps constantly informed about industrial conditions and special situations affecting interstate and foreign commerce which might become disturbed. If major disputes arise, the Secretary of Labor or someone in the Conciliation Service may take the initiative and propose that its services be used to mediate; or parties to the dispute may indicate that assistance is desired. Where both parties are willing, commissioners of conciliation intervene seeking to provide data pertinent to the argument and ascertain, in confidence, the most that one party will give and the least that the other will take without starting a lockout or a strike. While many agreements are effected in this way, agents of the Conciliation Service are powerless if either party is unwilling to cooperate or accept proffered proposals.

Occasionally both parties display enough confidence in a particular agent or panel of neutrals to submit the dispute to them for arbitration, but even where this is done there are no criminal penalties that can be imposed upon the parties if they should refuse to abide by the award.[1]

[1] There may be penalties provided for, however, in the basic agreement to arbitrate which would be enforceable in civil suits under state laws governing contracts.

National Railroad Adjustment Board.—By the Railway Labor Act of 1926, as amended in 1934, a National Railroad Adjustment Board of thirty-six members was established, on which employers and employees are equally represented, for the purpose of settling minor grievances arising from interpretation of agreements respecting wages, hours, and working conditions. The headquarters of the board are in Chicago. It operates through four divisions, whose findings of facts are conclusive. After investigating and considering cases, the divisions report to the entire board which, while accepting the facts as reported, reviews the cases and makes awards. In the event of deadlock, the National Mediation Board may appoint a referee to break the tie. Awards are enforceable in the federal courts. Here is an instance of compulsory settlement of particular types of disputes, namely, those arising from interpretations of agreements and involving major public utilities. As the name implies, the Railroad Adjustment Board deals only with railway disputes.

National Mediation Board.—Railway labor disputes unrelated to interpretation of existing agreements and commerical-air-line labor disputes are handled by the National Mediation Board, established in 1934. This agency is an independent establishment headed by three members who are appointed by the President with Senate approval. The board is assisted by a staff of conciliators as well as the usual administrative and clerical employees.

When a dispute occurs, neither management may lock out nor labor strike until steps prescribed by law are taken. First the National Mediation Board attempts to mediate; if unsuccessful, an attempt is made to induce the disputants to submit the matter to arbitration; if arbitration is refused, a strike vote must be taken and approved by a majority at least 30 days before work stoppages may start, during which time the President may appoint an emergency board to investigate and report. If, after all these steps have been taken, a settlement has still not been reached, the parties may lock out or strike. Although disputes have traveled this entire route several times, a general work stoppage has occurred only once—for 2 days in May, 1946—but was promptly terminated following threats of drastic action made by President Truman and many members of Congress. Another strike was narrowly averted during the recent war only by the government's taking over the railroads and operating them pending final settlement.

Fact-finding Boards for Other Industries.—Experience with railway legislation led President Truman to propose, during December, 1945, adoption of similar measures for other businesses engaged in interstate and foreign commerce. The recommendation asked for a law requiring a 30-day "cooling-off" period before commencing a lockout or strike, during which time a fact-finding board might be appointed by the President with power to investigate and make recommendations.[1] The proposal did not provide for compulsory arbitration; *i.e.*, it was not suggested that the law should try to compel disputants to accept recommendations made by the fact-finding boards. Rather, it contemplated that after the "cooling-off" period management would be free to lock out and labor to strike. The expectation was that by full disclosures of facts, the government, supported by public opinion, would be better able to effect adjustments without serious work stoppages. The President's proposal encountered such strenuous opposition from both management and labor as to result in its defeat.

In the meantime, however, the President appointed several boards to investigate and report on important disputes, chief of which was one between General Motors Corporation and the United Automobile Workers and one between the steel companies and their employees (1949). Boards like these operate under the handicap of being unable to compel the appearance of witnesses and the submission of evidence. Moreover, since legislation is needed to keep industries operating during a "cooling-off" period, they often find it necessary to function after work stoppages have commenced. Nevertheless, the disclosures and recommendations of the boards do help to clear the atmosphere and frequently establish bases for settlements.

A modified version of President Truman's fact-finding board proposal was included in the Taft-Hartley Act for work stoppages involving "national emergencies." According to these provisions the President may, when a national-emergency work stoppage is threatened, appoint a board of inquiry with power to compel attendance of witnesses and production of pertinent materials. The board's report, the law states, is to set forth the facts and contentions "but shall not contain any recommendations." When the report is received, the President is required to file a copy with the Mediation and Conciliation Service and make its contents public. Thereupon, the President may direct the Attorney General to go to court for an 80-day injunction restraining the threatened stoppage. During the 80-day "cooling-off" period the Service is required to do its best, and the board of inquiry is to be reconvened for study and to make a report that includes the employer's "best offer." This report is to be made public, and the National Labor Relations Board is directed to hold an election to determine whether a majority of workers wishes to accept or reject the best offer.

If at the expiration of 80 days the dispute remains unsettled, the injunction terminates, the President reports to Congress, and the work stoppage may take place unless Congress by that time decides upon more drastic

[1] The recommendation, legislative bill, and hearings may be found in United States Senate, Committee on Education and Labor, *Hearings on Labor Fact-finding Boards Act*, 79th Cong., 1st and 2d Sess. (Washington: Government Printing Office, 2 parts, 1946).

action. Although this procedure has been used a few times, authorities are divided over its success and wisdom. Aside from the fact that it restrains the freedom of parties involved and is therefore naturally disliked by them, the principal objection to the procedure is that it merely postpones the date of showdown and thereby removes some of the incentives for bargaining. Instead of weakening collective bargaining, critics suggest that more be done to ensure its success.

PROTECTING RIGHTS OF EMPLOYERS AND EMPLOYEES

The Right to Organize and Bargain Collectively.—At common law all combinations, whether of entrepreneurs or workmen, were long considered illegal conspiracies in restraint of trade. Early in the nineteenth century, merchants and other capitalists were granted the legal right to combine for business purposes, but it was not until later that combinations of workingmen were looked upon with favor by the courts. The turning point came when the Supreme Court of Massachusetts[1] recognized the legality of labor unions. The right is now recognized by all the states and the national government, but the conspiracy doctrine continues to influence the courts when they have to consider the legality of strikes, boycotts, and certain other union activities.

The primary purpose of labor organization is to enhance the bargaining ability of employees by enabling them to do it collectively. The desire for joint action grows out of the fact that in an unorganized market labor is extremely competitive, with those having labor for sale in a much weaker bargaining position than employers. The situation was well explained by the United States Supreme Court in 1921:[2]

> They [labor unions] were organized out of the necessity of the situation. A single employee was helpless in dealing with an employer. He was dependent ordinarily on his daily wage for the maintenance of himself and family. If the employer refused to pay him the wages that he thought fair, he was nevertheless unable to leave the employ and to resist arbitrary and unfair treatment. Union was essential to give laborers opportunity to deal on equality with their employer.

While the legal right to organize and bargain collectively has been recognized for nearly a century, employers were free to use economic weapons to prevent labor from doing so. For years many employers tried to suppress unionization by the use of industrial spies, black lists, yellow-dog contracts, lockouts, company unions, and sometimes strong-arm methods. Moreover, employers were at liberty to fire or discriminate against employees who dared to participate in union activities.

[1] Commonwealth *v.* Hunt, 45 Mass. 111 (1842).

[2] American Steel Foundries Co. *v.* Tri-city Central Trades Council, 257 U.S. 184 (1921).

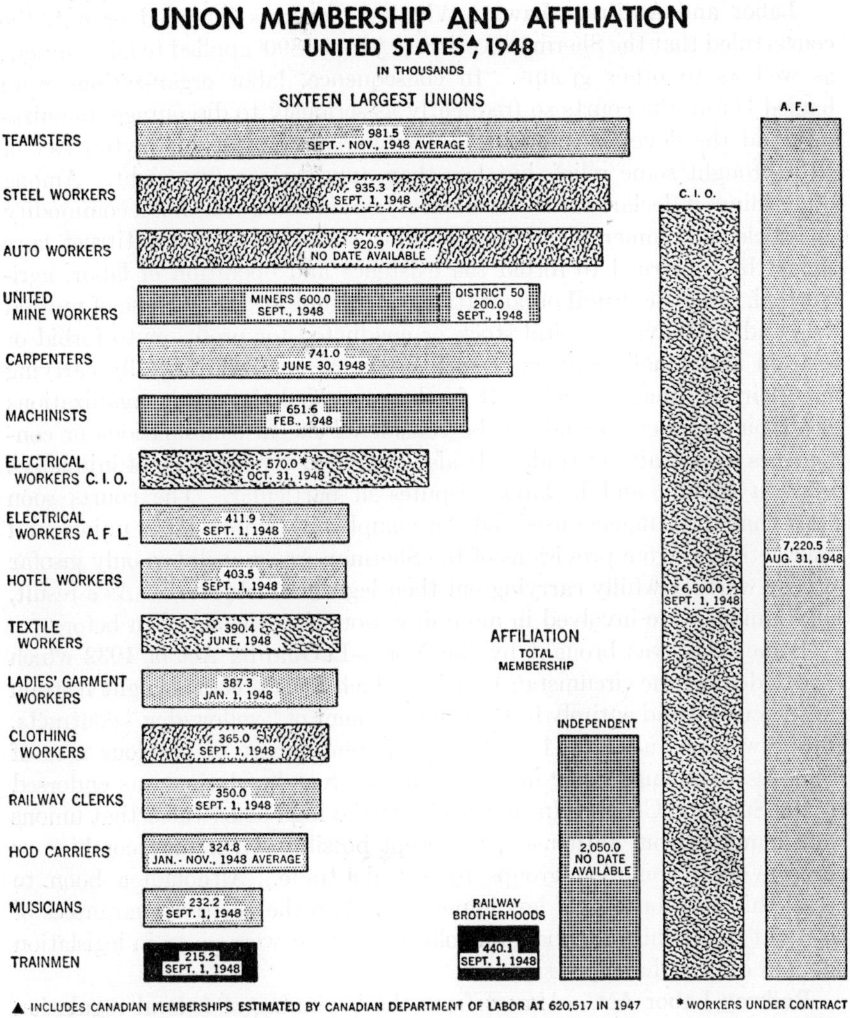

Unions with headquarters in the United States claimed membership of approximately 16,210,000 in 1948. The figure includes Canadian membership of international unions, estimated at 620,517 in 1947, and leaves United States membership at approximately 15.6 million. The sixteen largest unions account for approximately 8,680,000 members, or more than half of total union strength. (All figures, except for UAW–CIO, were supplied by unions to the National Industrial Conference Board.) SOURCES: The Conference Board: Bureau of Labor Statistics; Canadian Department of Labor. Road Maps of Industry, Weekly Chart Service, Jan. 14, 1949, No. 681. Copyright, 1949, by National Industrial Conference Board.

Labor and Antitrust Laws.—Whether Congress intended or not, the courts ruled that the Sherman Antitrust Act of 1890[1] applied to labor unions as well as to other groups. In consequence, labor organizations were hauled before the courts so frequently as seriously to discourage unionization and the development of collective bargaining. The Clayton Act of 1914 brought some relief, but less than appeared on first sight. Among other things it declared that the labor of human beings was not a commodity or article of commerce and that nothing contained in the antitrust laws should be construed to forbid the existence and operation of labor, agricultural, or horticultural organizations instituted for the purpose of mutual help and not having capital stock or conducted for profit, or to forbid or restrain individual members of such organizations from lawfully carrying out their legitimate objects. It further provided that such organizations and their members should not be considered illegal combinations or conspiracies in restraint of trade. It also restricted the granting of injunctive relief in general and in labor disputes in particular. The courts soon ruled that the language used did not completely remove labor unions and their activities from provisions of the Sherman Act, but did so only insofar as they were "lawfully carrying out their legitimate objects." As a result, labor unions were involved in more litigation after the act than before.

Some relief was brought by the Norris-LaGuardia Act of 1932 which clearly defined the circumstances under which federal courts might restrain union activity and entirely forbade enforcement of "yellow-dog" contracts. But it was not until 1941 that the apparent intent of previous acts of Congress to exempt labor unions from antitrust legislation was endorsed by the Supreme Court. In that decision[2] the high court ruled that unions were immune from antitrust laws except possibly when they combine or conspire with nonunion groups to restrain trade. Although a boon to labor, this decision was of less importance than the positive guarantees of the right to organize and bargain collectively that were given in legislation adopted during the depression.

Railway Labor Act.—Almost from the beginning of federal regulation of railroads, Congress has legislated to encourage settlement of management-labor disputes by conciliation and arbitration. Moreover, from an early date Congress has recognized the need for restraining some of the worst forms of employer interference with the rights of employees to form unions and bargain collectively. Its first step in this direction was a provision in the Erdman Act of 1898 prohibiting "yellow-dog" contracts, but this provision was later declared an unconstitutional abridgment of the right

[1] See p. 653.

[2] United States *v.* Hutcheson, 312 U.S. 219 (1940). For a recent instance of where a labor union was declared guilty of violating the antitrust laws because of conspiracy with business organizations, see Allen Bradley Co. *v.* Union, 325 U.S. 797 (1944).

of contract.[1] The following years brought trials and errors which culminated in the Railway Labor Act of 1926 and subsequent amendments.

In addition to providing the conciliation and arbitration machinery described above, the Railway Labor Act guaranteed the right to organize and bargain collectively through unions of workers' choice, authorized the National Mediation Board to hold elections to determine appropriate bargaining units when unions disagreed over which represented a majority, required both management and labor to bargain in good faith, and outlawed certain unfair labor practices, including "yellow-dog" contracts, when committed by employers. Unlike legislation discussed below, however, unfair labor practices were made enjoinable by courts rather than by an administrative board. These provisions of the Railway Labor Act apply to interstate railroads and airways. This legislation has been declared constitutional.[2]

National Labor Relations Act of 1935.—Section 7A of the National Industrial Recovery Act guaranteed the right of labor to organize and bargain collectively, free from employer interference, and also authorized the establishment of administrative machinery for the protection of those rights. Following the collapse of this measure in 1935, similar provisions were incorporated in the National Labor Relations Act. This measure was administered by a National Labor Relations Board composed of three men appointed by the President with Senate concurrence for terms of 5 years. The board had jurisdiction over all nongovernmental employees and employers engaged in interstate and foreign commerce except those in the railway and airway industries, which are handled by the National Mediation Board.

The board had two principal functions: one, to ascertain by conducting elections which union represented a majority within a plant or industry;[3] the other, to prevent employers from committing certain unfair labor practices. The law stated that it was an unfair labor practice for an employer to (1) interfere with, restrain, or coerce employees in the exercise of their right to organize, participate in union activity, and bargain collectively through representatives of their own choosing; (2) dominate or interfere with the formation or administration of any labor organization or contribute financial or other support to it; (3) discriminate in regard to hire or tenure of employment or any term or condition of employment as a method of encouraging or discouraging membership in labor unions; (4) discharge or otherwise discriminate against an employee because he has filed charges or

[1] Adair *v.* United States, 208 U.S. 161 (1908).

[2] Virginian Railway Co. *v.* System Federation No. 40 *et al.*, 300 U.S. 515 (1937); Texas & New Orleans R.R. *v.* Brotherhood of Ry. Clerks, 218 U.S. 548 (1930).

[3] During the war it was also required to conduct elections before strikes could be called in war plants.

given testimony under the act; and (5) refuse to bargain collectively with representatives of his employees.

The National Labor Relations Act of 1935 was designed to extend to all workers the right to organize, bargain collectively, and to choose their own union or bargaining agent to represent them. The National Labor Relations Board created by the Act was not established to settle labor disputes but only to protect workers in their right to organize into unions and to bargain collectively. The Act was "one-sided" in that it restrained employers from interfering with the formation of unions or engaging in discriminatory practices against union members, but placed no restraints on unfair practices by labor unions against employers. The reason given for this was that employers, being stronger, were able to look after themselves; the evil to be cured was employer interference with the rights of economically and socially weaker workers. This legislation was a boon to organized labor, and to them it became the most essential of federal statutes. Employers, understandably, vehemently objected and relentlessly fought its enforcement. Objection was made to its assumptions, purposes, controls, and methods of administration. Aided by postwar inflation and a series of nation-wide strikes, sufficient sentiment developed to elect a Congress that would tackle revision of the act. In 1947 Congress adopted, over the President's veto, the Labor Management Act of 1947, better known as the Taft-Hartley Act. This, in turn, incurred the uncompromising opposition of organized labor, and the feud continues.

The Taft-Hartley Act.—This act was in the form of an amendment to the National Labor Relations Act. It first changed membership of the board from three to five and circumscribed its role. Reflecting accusations that the board had been rule maker, prosecutor, judge, and jury, the board was given responsibility for general administration and adjudication, but the office of General Counsel was established to investigate charges, issue complaints, and prosecute. To this end, the General Counsel was empowered to supervise all board attorneys (except trial examiners and legal assistants to board members) and other officers and employees in regional offices.

Other provisions were numerous; only a few can be mentioned here. Union officers, but not employers, were required to file non-Communist affidavits or be denied board facilities and other benefits of the law. The closed shop was outlawed, but the union shop was permitted if approved by at least 70 per cent of the employees. (A closed shop employs only union members, while a union shop may employ persons who are not union members, provided they join within a specified time.) Supervisors, including foremen, were denied benefits of the law. Employers were granted greater freedom of speech about plant and contract matters. The "checkoff" was permitted but only for employees who gave advance consent in writing. Employer contributions to union health and welfare funds were permitted under certain conditions, one of which was that employers and employees be equally represented in the administration of the fund. Hiring through union halls was forbidden. Excessive and discriminatory union initiation fees were outlawed. Union and company contributions to political campaigns were forbidden. Thirty-day notice was required of intention to modify or terminate contracts. Suits by employers and unions were authorized for alleged violations of collective-bargaining contracts. The board, but not employers, was authorized to obtain injunctions to prevent certain union conduct. Unions were forbidden to commit unfair labor practices including: refusal to bargain collectively with an employer, restraint or coercion of other employees in the exercise of their rights, discrimination against employees, engaging in secondary boycotts and jurisdictional strikes, charging excessive or discriminatory initiation fees, and forcing employers to pay or deliver things of value for services not performed or to be performed. Finally, "national emergency" strikes were forbidden except under the circumstances noted above.

As matters stand, the NLRB and its agents have three principal functions: the first requires them to file materials required by the law, such as non-Communist affidavits and union financial reports; the second involves stopping by injunction or orders unfair labor practices when committed by employers or unions; the third requires the holding of elections to determine union shop authorizations and appropriate bargaining units when unions disagree over which one of them commands a majority. Most complaint cases, *i.e.*, those in which unfair labor practices are alleged, are settled informally, but a few go through a formal process resembling a trial without jury on criminal charges. In such cases, the board lacks authority to enforce its own decisions but may appeal to United States Circuit Courts to do so.

The effects of the Act will not be known definitely until it has been interpreted by the courts in cases litigated before them, which will take years. It has been strenuously opposed by organized labor because of the restrictions which it places upon union activities and the fact that it strengthens the bargaining position of employers. Although the Democratic party was pledged to its repeal, the first session of the Eighty-first Congress was unable to agree on a substitute measure, and the Taft-Hartley Act continues as the subject of controversy.

CHILD-LABOR LEGISLATION

Legal Contest over Child-labor Legislation.—Since children are looked upon as special wards of the state, there has never been any question about the constitutionality of state laws regulating, or even prohibiting, their employment in industry. About the middle of the last century the movement began to forbid the employment of children, but states, fearing competition with other states, were reluctant to act. Ultimately it became clear that only by a uniform national law could the problem be met. Accordingly, in 1916, Congress enacted the Keating-Owen Act forbidding the transportation in interstate commerce of products made in factories in which children under fourteen were employed, or in which children between fourteen and sixteen had worked more than 8 hours a day or 6 days a week, or at night. Similar prohibitions applied to products of mines in which children under sixteen were employed. Two years later this legislation was declared unconstitutional because it applied to productive facilities like factories or mines, which province the Supreme Court then considered reserved to the states.[1]

Undismayed, Congress turned to the power to tax to provide for the general welfare and included within the general Revenue Act of Feb. 24, 1919, a tax of 10 per cent upon the annual net profits of concerns violating certain standards, chief of which was the employment of children under fourteen. This also was declared an unconstitutional invasion of state powers.[2]

Following these two unsuccessful attempts, Congress mustered enough votes to propose a constitutional amendment giving the Federal government the desired authority.[3] To date the proposal has been ratified by twenty-eight states—eight fewer than the required number.

While the amendment was before the states, Congress again tried to abolish child labor by statute; this time by means of the National Industrial Recovery Act of 1933. All the NRA codes stipulated that the employment of children under sixteen was illegal and these provisions were generally obeyed until the act was declared unconstitutional in May, 1935.[4]

Still undeterred, Congress incorporated a provision in the Public Contracts Act of 1936[5] prohibiting persons awarded government contracts involving sums in excess of $10,000 from employing male persons under sixteen and female persons under eighteen. This was an exercise of the proprietary power[6] and doubtless constitutional, but it applied to only a comparatively few employers.

Finally, resorting to the commerce power again, more sweeping provisions were incorporated in the Fair Labor Standards Act of 1938. These received Supreme Court approval in 1941,[7] a decision that expressly reversed

[1] Hammer *v.* Dagenhart, 247 U.S. 251 (1918). For a fuller discussion of the constitutional issue see p. 388.

[2] Bailey *v.* Drexel Furniture Company, 259 U.S. 20 (1922). See also p. 367.

[3] The full text of the proposed amendment is given on p. 831.

[4] Schechter Poultry Corporation *v.* United States, 295 U.S. 495 (1935).

[5] Often referred to as the Walsh-Healy Act.

[6] See p. 427.

[7] United States *v.* Darby Lumber Co., 312 U.S. 100 (1941).

Hammer *v.* Dagenhart decided 23 years earlier. While this law applies only to interstate and foreign commerce, hence does not have the coverage which would be possible if the proposed child-labor amendment were finally ratified, it does cover the major industries and probably puts an end to attempts to get additional states to ratify the amendment.

Existing Child-labor Legislation.—Child labor is now, therefore, governed by two federal statutes: the Public Contracts Act of 1936 and the Fair Labor Standards Act of 1938. Enforcement is handled by the Children's Bureau, now a unit of the Federal Security Agency, in cooperation with the Department of Labor.

In cooperation with state governments, certificates of age are issued to minors fourteen through nineteen years of age who wish to be employed in controlled occupations.[1] The Public Contracts Act forbids those working on government contracts involving more than $10,000 from employing anyone under nineteen without a certificate. It then prohibits employment of boys under sixteen and girls under eighteen.[2] Exceptions may be granted by the Secretary of Labor.

The Fair Labor Standards Act is more flexible. Under it, employments are divided into three categories: those that are completely exempt; those that are nonpermissible for fourteen- and fifteen-year-olds; and those that are too hazardous for those between sixteen and eighteen years old. Those that are completely exempt include retailing, personal service, street trades, motion pictures, children employed in agriculture at a time when they are not required to attend school, and children working for their parents, except in manufacturing and mining. The list of nonpermissible employments for children of fourteen and fifteen excludes most school children from interstate mining, manufacturing, processing occupations that take them into rooms where manufacturing is going on, work on power-driven machinery and hoisting apparatus, operation of motor vehicles or service as helpers, and public messenger service.[3] The third category, which includes hazardous occupations forbidden to those between sixteen and eighteen years old, prevents youths of the ages mentioned from working in explosive plants, as motor-vehicle driver and helper, coal mines, logging and sawmilling, operating metalworking and woodworking machines, and occupations involving exposure to radioactive substances.

Inspections are made by employees of the Wage and Hour and Public

[1] Inquiry about any town or city, especially at public schools, will usually lead to discovery of a near-by point where certificates are issued.

[2] There was some relaxation of the provisions during the war, especially for sixteen- and seventeen-year-old girls.

[3] The war saw some relaxation of regulations for this group also. The principal instance was to permit after-school employment of fourteen- and fifteen-year-olds to head and peel shrimp for shipment as fresh raw or fresh frozen shrimp, and also to pick turkeys.

Contracts Division as they get around over the country checking up on other labor standards. Violations are also frequently reported by state officials, especially by state departments of labor and education. Legal responsibility for obeying the law rests with the employer rather than with youths or their parents. Each year sees a number of violations and the number increased greatly during the war. Many of the minors are very young; some are as young as eight years. The canning and packing industry is a conspicuous offender.

REGULATION OF HOURS AND WAGES

Legislation regulating hours and wages are filled with distinctions between children, women, and men. There has never been much question about whether states and the Federal government, within their respective jurisdictions, might regulate the employment of children. For women there was more doubt, and for men still more.

Constitutionality of Hour Laws.—The basic constitutional question has been whether hour laws deprived liberty and property without due process of law.[1] Because of woman's nature and the vital role she plays in society, the courts finally, albeit reluctantly, admitted that states might reasonably limit hours as a means of promoting the health, safety, and morals of the community.[2] Now nearly all states have such laws which, while they vary, tend in the direction of an 8-hour day and 44-hour week with special restrictions upon night work and employment in certain types of business, such as barrooms and restaurants.

Men were considered by the courts to be more rugged and less in need of legislative protection. At first state laws were declared unconstitutional;[3] then legislation limiting employment in hazardous occupations was approved;[4] and finally, the courts permitted hour laws for men in general occupations.[5] Now most states have such laws, but the coverage is less general than for women. The same doubts have enshrouded federal hour laws but all these disappeared in 1941 when the Supreme Court upheld the Fair Labor Standards Act.[6]

Constitutionality of Wage Laws.—The courts have been even more unwilling to uphold state and federal fixation of minimum wages. Massachusetts enacted the first minimum-wage law for women in 1912 and other

[1] Cf. p. 139.

[2] See especially John R. Commons and John B. Andrews, *Principles of Labor Legislation* (New York: Harper, 1936 ed.), pp. 113–116. The two early leading Supreme Court decisions upholding state hour laws for women are Holden *v.* Hardy, 169 U.S. 366 (1898) and Muller *v.* Oregon, 208 U.S. 412 (1908).

[3] Commons and Andrews, *op. cit.*, p. 132.

[4] Holden *v.* Hardy, 169 U.S. 366 (1898).

[5] Bunting *v.* Oregon, 243 U.S. 246 (1917).

[6] United States *v.* Darby Lumber Co., 312 U.S. 100 (1941).

states followed. Constitutionality was challenged promptly but the outcome remained doubtful until 1923 when a federal wage law for women in the District of Columbia came before the Supreme Court. In that case[1] the law was declared an unconstitutional deprivation of liberty and property. During the next few years the states tried to devise laws that would circumvent the ruling of the court. Formerly the statutes based minimum wages upon the cost of living of an entirely self-supporting woman; after the Adkins decision, they tried to base them upon the value of services rendered. One of these, that of New York state, came before the Supreme Court in 1935, but a majority of five of the Court's membership refused to see any essential difference between this and the legislation declared unconstitutional in Adkins *v.* Children's Hospital.[2] A year later, however, the court reversed itself in another five-to-four decision, this time upholding a statute of the state of Washington.[3] This decision opened the door not only for state but also for federal minimum-wage legislation for women. An entering wedge having been driven, it was only a short time until the Supreme Court upheld federal, and incidentally state, wage control for men also.[4]

Fair Labor Standards Act.—Federal wage and hour laws relate first of all to the government's own employees, whose wages are, of course, prescribed and whose hours are normally restricted to an 8-hour day and 40-hour week. Separate statutes limit the hours of seamen and longshoremen, employees of railway, motor, and air carriers. The first federal wage and hour legislation providing coverage for general occupations was the National Industrial Recovery Act, but this was short-lived. Then followed the Public Contracts Act of 1936 regulating hours and minimum wages for employees working on government contracts, and finally the Fair Labor Standards Act in 1938 and subsequent amendments.

The wage-and-hour provisions of this legislation apply to all employees, including both men and women, in non-exempt businesses engaged in interstate commerce or in the production of goods for interstate commerce. If even a small part of the goods he works on is moved in interstate commerce an employee is covered if the employer has reason to believe, at the time of production, that the goods will move in interstate commerce or will become a part of such goods (*e.g.*, putting buttons on shirts). Employees within the District of Columbia, territories, and possessions are also included.

[1] Adkins *v.* Children's Hospital, 261 U.S. 525 (1923).

[2] Morehead *v.* New York ex rel. Tipaldo, 298 U.S. 587 (1936).

[3] West Coast Hotel Co. *v.* Parrish, 300 U.S. 379 (1937). Within the year the Court's membership had not changed but Justice Owen J. Roberts had changed his mind. By doing so, legislation became valid which for 14 years had been considered unconstitutional. For a discussion of the composition of the Supreme Court at that time and the controversy surrounding it, see p. 347.

[4] United States *v.* Darby Lumber Company, cited above.

A number of groups are exempt, however. Among these are executives, administrative and professional workers, outside salesmen, and persons engaged in local retail selling; employees of retail or service establishments, the greater part of whose business is intrastate; employees of air lines, railways,[1] and local transportation agencies; switchboard operators of small telephone exchanges; employees of small weekly or semiweekly county newspapers; fishermen, seamen, and agricultural workers, and those engaged in processing agricultural products within the area of production.

The act provided two ways by which minimum wages were to be fixed. First, the statute itself placed a "floor" under wages, saying that until Oct. 24, 1945, the minimum would be 30 cents an hour and after that date 40 cents. After much agitation and discussion Congress finally, in 1949, raised the minimum to 75 cents. Second, minimum wages were fixed by administrative order. As a means of raising the general minimum to 40 cents by October, 1945, the administrator was authorized to appoint industry committees composed of equal representation of employers, employees, and the public. Upon their recommendation the administrator might fix the minimum anywhere between 30 and 40 cents. By July, 1944, seventy industry committees had been appointed, many of whose recommendations were put into effect, thus making the transition to 40 cents easier than otherwise would have been the case.

The act provides no absolute limitation upon the number of hours that employees might work. It merely requires that time and a half be paid for all time worked beyond 40 hours a week. Nor is there any limitation on the number of hours that may be worked in any one day.

These wage and hour provisions are administered and enforced by the Wage and Hour Division of the Department of Labor. Violators may be fined up to $10,000 or, in the case of a second conviction, imprisonment up to 6 months, or both. In addition, workers may collect in court double the back wages due them plus attorneys' fees and court costs. Inspections are made by a large force of officers working in and out of field offices located in principal cities.

Wage and Hour Control during the War.—The basic provision respecting wages and hours remained the same throughout the war period, but because of full employment and labor shortages the problem changed from one of controlling minimum wages to one of putting ceilings upon them in order to help stabilize prices. This task fell largely to the National War Labor Board established in 1942. Under this legislation, board approval of all general wage and salary increases had to be obtained. Shortly after

[1] So far as employees of interstate motor carriers are concerned, they are all subject to the wage provisions, but drivers, drivers' helpers, mechanics, and loaders are exempt from the hour provisions. Hours for these employees are governed by the Motor Carrier Act and regulated by the Interstate Commerce Commission.

its creation the board, in ruling upon a request for higher wages on behalf of workers in the steel industry, announced the much-controverted "Little Steel Formula" which became the basis for subsequent decisions with respect to wage increases. According to this formula, wage increases would not be permitted in excess of 15 per cent of what they were on Jan. 1, 1941. Failure to respect the board's decision carried with it the penalty of government confiscation of the business and made work stoppages subsequent to seizures illegal. Provisions relating to hours remained the same: time and a half for all hours worked above 40 a week.

EMPLOYMENT OFFICES

Employers who need workmen and men who need jobs must get together somehow. The usual method is for the employer to hang out a "Help Wanted" sign or advertise in newspapers, while the employee walks the streets, dropping in where there are signs, or answering advertisements. The procedure is haphazard, inefficient, and destructive of morale. Numerous fee-charging private employment agencies came into existence to help meet the need and as time has gone on philanthropic organizations and local, state, and federal governments have entered the scene.

Regulation of Private Employment Agencies.—An employee in need of a job is peculiarly susceptible to exploitation and many fee-charging agencies have taken advantage of their opportunity. Various states have attempted regulation, but it is the almost unanimous testimony of investigators and public officials that state regulation has not succeeded in stamping out the abuses.[1] This experience led to attempts on the part of the states to outlaw private fee-charging agencies. This was stopped by the United States Supreme Court which ruled that such legislation was denial of liberty and property without due process of law and a denial of the equal protection under the law required by the Fourteenth Amendment.[2] Later, New Jersey declared employment services businesses affected with a public interest[3] and provided for regulation similar to that applied to public utilities, including limitations upon fees. This, too, was disapproved by the Supreme Court for similar reasons.[4] Finally, in 1941, the Supreme Court reversed its precedents by upholding comprehensive state regulation[5] and inferentially federal.

Public Employment Services.—The Federal government has not yet undertaken to regulate private employment offices, but it has taken the

[1] Commons and Andrews, *op. cit.*, p. 9.
[2] Adams *v.* Tanner, 244 U.S. 590 (1917).
[3] Cf. p. 674.
[4] Ribnik *v.* McBride, 279 U.S. 350 (1928).
[5] Olsen *v.* Nebraska, 313 U.S. 236 (1941).

lead in providing a nation-wide, coordinated system of public employment offices. This was done in the Wagner-Peyser Act of 1933. This established the United States Employment Service as a bureau in the Department of Labor. Since then the Service has had a stormy career. In 1939 its functions were consolidated with those pertaining to unemployment compensation and transferred to the Federal Security Agency. In 1942 employment services were transferred to the War Manpower Commission. They were returned to Labor in 1945, given back to the Federal Security Agency in 1948, and in 1949 returned to Labor.

The original plan called for federal grants to states on a matching basis, with the understanding that the states would administer their own programs but in accordance with federal standards. In January, 1942, as an aid to the war effort, all state services were taken over by the Federal government. Immediately after the war, sentiment arose demanding return to the states. This was authorized by Congress in 1946 over strong protest from President Truman, labor groups, and others who prefer an integrated national system to forty-eight federated plans.

Whether under direct federal operation or as originally conceived, the employment services provide a ready source of assistance to both employers and employees. Offices exist in the principal towns of every state, and in smaller places representatives call at regular intervals to receive applications for jobs and to put employers in touch with suitable workers. Because they are coordinated, the offices maintain a nation-wide clearance system, so that workers who cannot be placed at home can be referred to jobs in other areas. These offices are also integral parts of the social-security system; all payments for unemployment compensation are made through them.

References

American Association for Labor Legislation: *American Labor Legislation Review* (New York: Published quarterly).

Berman, Edward: *Labor Disputes and the President of the United States* (New York: Columbia University Press, 1924).

——— *Labor and the Sherman Act* (New York: Harper, 1930).

Bowman, Dean O.: *Public Control of Labor Relations; A Study of the National Labor Relations Board* (New York: Macmillan, 1942).

Breen, Vincent I.: *United States Conciliation Service* (Washington: Catholic University of America, 1943).

Brooks, Robert R. R.: *When Labor Organizes* (New Haven: Yale University Press, 1937).

——— *Unions of Their Own Choosing, an Account of the National Labor Relations Board and Its Work* (New Haven: Yale University Press, 1939).

Bureau of National Affairs: *Wartime Wage Control and Dispute Settlement* (Washington: Bureau of National Affairs, 1945).

Commons, John R., and John B. Andrews: *Principles of Labor Legislation* (New York: Harper, 4th ed., 1936).

Eby, Herbert O.: *Labor Relations Act in the Courts . . .* (New York: Harper, 1943).

Fainsod, Merle, and Lincoln Gordon: *Government and the American Economy* (New York: Norton, 2d ed., 1949).

Frankfurter, Felix, and Nathan Greene: *The Labor Injunction* (New York: Macmillan, 1930).

Gregory, Charles O.: *Labor and the Law* (New York: Norton, 1946).

Keller, Frances: *American Arbitration* (New York: Harper, 1948).

Killingsworth, Charles C.: *State Labor Relations Acts; A Study in Public Policy* (Chicago: University of Chicago Press, 1948).

Koontz, Harold A.: *Government Control of Business* (New York: Harper, 1943).

Lombardi, John: *Labor's Voice in the Cabinet; A History of the Development of Labor from Its Origin to 1921* (New York: Columbia University Press, 1942).

Lyon, Leverett S., Victor Abramson, *et al.*: *Government and Economic Life* (Washington: Brookings, 2 vols., 1940).

Mariano, John H.: *Wartime Labor Relations* (New York: National Public and Labor Relations Service, 1944).

Mason, Alpheus T.: *Organized Labor and the Law; With Special Reference to the Sherman and Clayton Acts* (Durham, N.C.: Duke University Press, 1925).

Metz, Harold W.: *Labor Policy of the Federal Government* (Washington: Brookings, 1945).

Reed, George L.: *Law of Labor Relations* (Newark, N.J.: Soney and Sage, 1942).

Reede, Arthur H.: *Adequacy of Workmen's Compensation* (Cambridge, Mass.: Harvard University Press, 1947).

Schlotterbeck, Karl T.: *Postwar Re-employment, The Magnitude of the Problem* (Washington: Brookings, 1943).

Seidman, Joel I.: *The Yellow-dog Contract* (Baltimore: Johns Hopkins Press, 1932).

Teller, Ludwig: *Law Governing Labor Disputes and Collective Bargaining* (New York: Baker, Voorhis, 1940).

Twentieth Century Fund, Inc.: *Labor and the Government; an Investigation of the Role of the Government in Labor Relations* (New York: Twentieth Century Fund, 1935).

United States Commission on Organization of the Executive Branch of the Government ("Hoover Commission"): *Department of Labor* (Washington: Government Printing Office, 1949).

Witte, Edwin M.: *The Government in Labor Disputes* (New York: McGraw-Hill, 1932).

Chapter 33

SOCIAL INSURANCE, EDUCATION, AND WELFARE

In all truth, one of the most significant facts of this age is the continuous unemployment of millions of good people. Out of this is bound to come pressure which will either destroy the old world, or create a new world, or do both.

Henry A. Wallace, *New Frontiers*.[1]

Among the varied and numerous activities of government, there is none closer guarded from excessive Federal control than education. . . .

Hoover Commission, *Task Force Report on Public Welfare*.[2]

The term "general welfare" appears twice in the Constitution: once in the preamble and again in the tax clause. As noted earlier,[3] neither of these is a grant of power to Congress for doing whatever it thinks necessary to promote the general welfare. Rather, the first is merely a declaration of purpose, while the second states one of the objectives for which Congress might tax and spend. Nevertheless, through the latter provision and other grants of power from which Congress has implied authority, much legislation has been enacted intended to enhance the welfare of particular groups or of the populace as a whole.

Federal Security Agency.—Federal social insurance, education, and welfare activities are scattered among numerous agencies, but in recent years the desirability of consolidation has been widely recognized. As noted elsewhere,[4] both the Hoover Commission and President Truman have strongly urged establishment of a new department in the welfare-education field, but to date sufficient congressional support has been lacking. Accordingly, the Federal Security Agency remains the administrative center of many, but by no means all, social insurance, education, and welfare services. This is an agency directly responsible to the President. It was established by executive order in April, 1939. At present it consists of the following units: Bureau of Employees' Compensation, Employees' Compensation Appeals Board, Food and Drug Administration, Office of Education, Office of Vocational Rehabilitation, Public Health Service, Social Security Administration, and St. Elizabeths Hospital. It also discharges certain duties in connection with the American Printing House for the Blind, Columbia Institution for the Deaf, and Howard University. At the head of the

[1] (New York: Reynal & Hitchcock, 1934), p. 5.

[2] (Washington: Government Printing Office, 1949), p. 277.

[3] P. 361.

[4] P. 435.

agency is the Federal Security Administrator, whose term and manner of appointment are similar to those of department heads.

FEDERAL AIDS TO EDUCATION

Who teaches the youth of the country, what and how they are taught, are among the most vital of public issues. Generally speaking, the American people have viewed with alarm proposals looking toward diminution of local control, with the result that today primary responsibility rests in more than 125,000 local popularly elected school boards and numerous private institutions scattered throughout the land. Centralizing influences have been at work, however, in this field as in most others. First the county, then the state, and finally the Federal government have taken an interest, although hostility to federal intervention has been so strong as to limit its role severely.

Nevertheless, an inventory of federal educational activities is long.[1] Merely to mention schools for Indians, the GI Bill of Rights, military and naval academies, the Foreign Service Institute, UNESCO, land-grant colleges, the Library of Congress, low postal rates for books and periodicals, student and faculty exchange with foreign nations, agricultural extension services, Bureau of Standards and Atomic Energy scholarships, and school lunches is to suggest the wide scope of federal interest. On the whole, however, federal aid has been for special purposes stipulated in statutes rather than for general education.

United States Office of Education.—Most federal activities in aid of education are centered in the Office of Education, which dates back to 1867. It was created "for the purpose of collecting such statistics and facts as shall show the condition and progress of education in the several States and Territories, and of diffusing such information respecting the organization and management of schools and school systems, and methods of teaching, as shall aid the people of the United States in the establishment and maintenance of efficient school systems, and otherwise promote the cause of education throughout the country." At its head is a commissioner who is appointed by the President with Senate approval. The office is one of the smaller agencies. Among its duties are those related to research, cooperation with school authorities, administration of federal laws relating to colleges, vocational education and rehabilitation, the blind, and, during the war, training of workers for war employments.

Land-grant Colleges.—Passage of the Morrill Act in 1862 marks the beginning of federal grants in aid of education. That measure and supplementary legislation donated 11,367,832 acres of land to the states with the stipulation that it, or the proceeds from the sale thereof, be used for educa-

[1] For a rather complete list see Hoover Commission, *op. cit.*, p. 553.

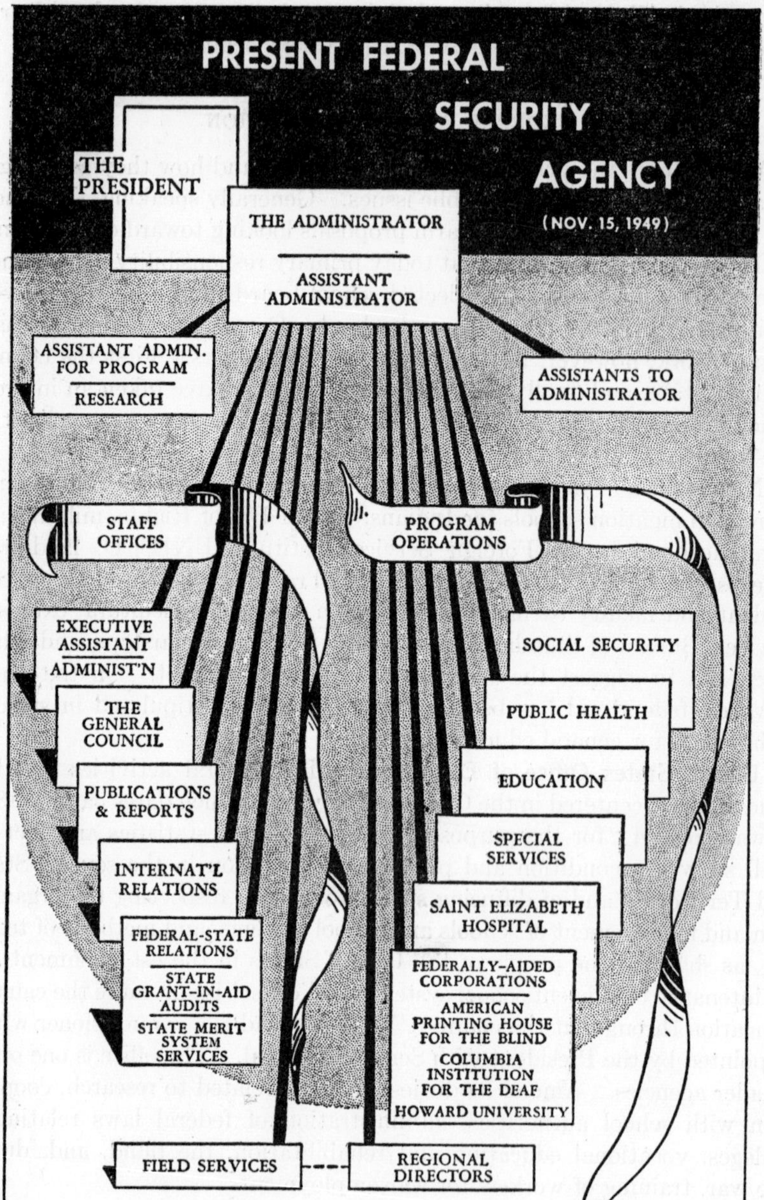
PRESENT FEDERAL
SECURITY
AGENCY
(NOV. 15, 1949)
THE PRESIDENT
THE ADMINISTRATOR
ASSISTANT ADMINISTRATOR
ASSISTANT ADMIN. FOR PROGRAM
RESEARCH
ASSISTANTS TO ADMINISTRATOR
STAFF OFFICES
PROGRAM OPERATIONS
EXECUTIVE ASSISTANT
ADMINIST'N
THE GENERAL COUNCIL
PUBLICATIONS & REPORTS
INTERNAT'L RELATIONS
FEDERAL-STATE RELATIONS
STATE GRANT-IN-AID AUDITS
STATE MERIT SYSTEM SERVICES
SOCIAL SECURITY
PUBLIC HEALTH
EDUCATION
SPECIAL SERVICES
SAINT ELIZABETH HOSPITAL
FEDERALLY-AIDED CORPORATIONS
AMERICAN PRINTING HOUSE FOR THE BLIND
COLUMBIA INSTITUTION FOR THE DEAF
HOWARD UNIVERSITY
FIELD SERVICES
REGIONAL DIRECTORS

Source: Data supplied by Federal Security Agency.

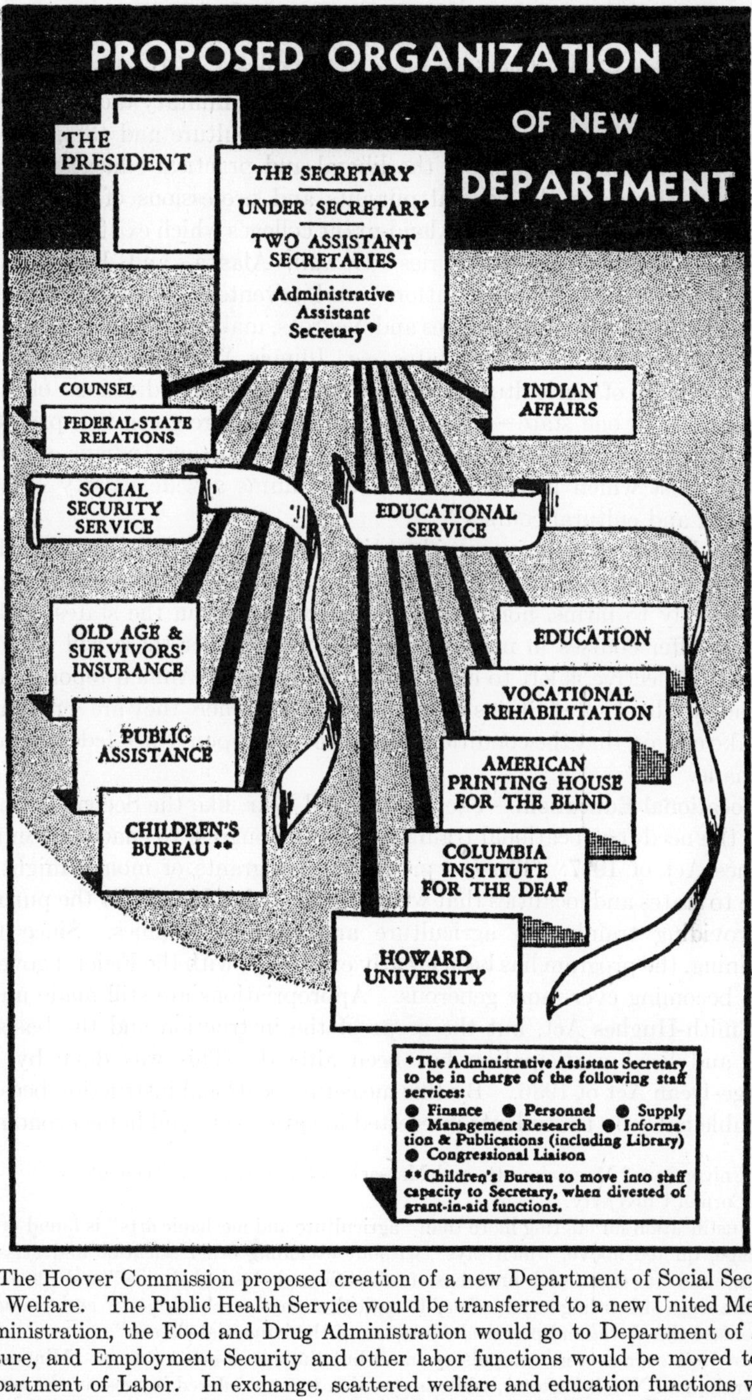

The Hoover Commission proposed creation of a new Department of Social Security and Welfare. The Public Health Service would be transferred to a new United Medical Administration, the Food and Drug Administration would go to Department of Agriculture, and Employment Security and other labor functions would be moved to the Department of Labor. In exchange, scattered welfare and education functions would be brought into the new Department of Social Security and Welfare. SOURCE: Hoover Commission, *Social Security, Education, Indian Affairs.*

tional purposes. The "leading object," says the act, is "without excluding other scientific and classical studies, and including military tactics, to teach such branches of learning as are related to agriculture and the mechanic arts, . . . in order to promote the liberal and practical education of the industrial classes in the several pursuits and professions of life." This legislation provides the basis for land-grant colleges which exist in the forty-eight states and three territories—Hawaii, Alaska, and Puerto Rico. Massachusetts has two institutions[1] and seventeen states divide their income between schools for whites and Negroes, making a total of sixty-nine land-grant colleges. In some states, *e.g.*, Illinois, Wisconsin, and Pennsylvania, schools of agriculture and mechanical arts are divisions of state universities; in one state—New York—the grants are given to a privately controlled institution;[2] in others, *e.g.*, Iowa, Michigan, and Indiana, separate colleges exist which include in their curriculums a wide variety of both technical and cultural courses.[3]

In addition to offering resident institution, each land-grant college maintains an experiment station and extension service which takes instruction directly to farms, homes, and communities within the states. Most of them offer courses in military science, but whether these will be compulsory or elective is left to each college to decide.[4] Annual reports must be made to the United States Office of Education where they are scrutinized to make certain that the conditions have been met upon which federal grants are made.

Vocational Education.—The First World War, like the Second, emphasized the need for vocational training and led Congress to enact the Smith-Hughes Act of 1917. The act provided that grants of money might be made to states and localities that would match federal funds for the purpose of providing training in agriculture and home economics. Since this beginning, the program has been greatly expanded, with the Federal government becoming ever more generous. Appropriations are still made under the Smith-Hughes Act, but the scope of the instruction and the basis of state and local participation has been altered. This was done by the George-Dean Act of 1936. By this measure vocational instruction became available not only to students interested in agriculture and home economics

[1] University of Massachusetts and Massachusetts Institute of Technology.

[2] Cornell University.

[3] Justification for offering more than "agriculture and mechanic arts" is found in the language, quoted above, which says "without excluding other scientific and classical studies" and "to teach such branches of scientific and classical studies" and "to teach such branches of learning as are *related* to agriculture and mechanic arts," and "in order to promote the *liberal* and practical education of the industrial classes."

[4] In 1941 courses were compulsory in all but three land-grant colleges (Minnesota, Wisconsin, and North Dakota), while instruction was not offered in most of the seventeen Negro schools.

but also to those interested in trade and industry. Funds were also made available for the training of teachers and supervisors, and the direction of distributive occupations, agricultural, trade and industrial, and home-economic subjects. In order to induce state participation on an expanded scale, the act stipulates that the states and territories must match only 50 per cent of the federal grant for the first 5 years, this percentage being increased by 10 per cent annually thereafter until it reaches 100 per cent beginning July 1, 1946. Thus, since the middle of 1946, states have been required to match federal funds dollar for dollar. Virtually all the states are participating in the programs just described.

This program was supervised by the Office of Education with the advice of an unsalaried Federal Board of Vocational Education until 1946, when the board was abolished. It is administered in participating states by departments of education in cooperation with schools and colleges.

Research, Consultative, and Advisory Educational Services.—Ever since its creation the United States Office of Education has collected data of all sorts that show the condition and progress of education in the United States and its territories. It has also made extensive surveys of state and local school systems, provided advisory services to other government agencies, school officials, and educational associations. It publishes a bi-weekly magazine entitled *School Life*, which is available to subscribers, as well as other pamphlets and bulletins.

Proposals for the Extension of Federal Aid to Education.—Surveys of state educational systems indicate that there are many areas where educational facilities are entirely lacking or woefully inadequate. This may be due to a number of factors, one of which frequently is the lack of sufficient wealth from which to obtain needed funds. A number of the states have tried to equalize opportunities within their limits by subsidizing poor areas more heavily than others, and while this helps it provides no solution for entire states whose resources are comparatively poorer than those of other areas. To meet this situation many strenuously urge the enactment of federal legislation that will subsidize public-school education, especially in poorer states.[1] While these proposals have the backing of such groups as the Farm Bureau Federation, National Education Association, and organized labor, they are also opposed by formidable bodies, chief of which are the National Catholic Welfare Conference, the Association of American Colleges, and the National Conference of Church-related Colleges.

Opponents stress the danger of federal domination. If federal funds are taken, they argue, sooner or later federal control will result. This, they insist, is likely to lead to thought control by the national government and

[1] See especially Senate Bill 1305, 76th Cong., 1st Sess. Also United States Senate, Committee on Education and Labor, *Federal Aid to Education Act, Hearings*, 76th Cong., 1st Sess. (Washington: Government Printing Office, 1939)

diminution of a sense of responsibility at state and local levels. State and local governments can meet the need, opponents continue, if and when they realize the importance of the task. To meet these objections, all bills in Congress specifically state that federal assistance must be confined to the granting of money, with only such accounting and reporting as will ensure honest use of funds for educational purposes. Still, many critics remain dubious.

Particularly thorny is the problem of what to do about private schools, many of which are church related. Everyone recognizes their great contribution to American education and also the fact they are doing a job that would otherwise need to be done and paid for by taxpayers. To grant federal aid to public schools and not to private ones adds an additional burden on those who prefer the latter and perhaps also makes it more difficult for private schools to compete for students and faculty. But to give them aid, it is contended, is contrary to the American doctrine of separation of church and state. Many spokesmen for private schools do not want federal aid either for themselves or public schools; others do not mind federal aid for public schools but want none of it for themselves; still others, especially spokesmen for the Catholic Church, want federal aid for all, with assistance for private schools confined to incidentals like textbooks, transportation, and school lunches. Such assistance is now given by a number of states without running afoul of Supreme Court interpretations of the appropriate role of church and state.[1]

Other proposals seriously advocated by responsible groups are federal participation in a state-operated plan of adult and workers education along lines similar to those followed by the extension services of the land-grant colleges and the vocational educational plans described above.[2] Proponents stress the need for an alert and well-informed citizenry in a democracy and point out that in spite of our vaunted educational system the educational level remains astonishingly low. They also stress the need for constant stimulation, discussion, and refresher training in a technological era when citizens are supposed to keep informed on a multiplicity of important issues. They also ask why educational services should be provided at federal expense for farmers, rural folk generally, and certain occupational groups, but not for industrial workers and other adults. Here, again, opposition stems largely from fear of federal intrusion. There has been less public discussion of this proposal than the one mentioned in the previous paragraph; hence opinions have not crystallized so firmly. The chief backers of the plan are prolabor forces and the land-grant colleges.

Vocational Rehabilitation.—In an industrial society there are always numbers of individuals who have been so injured that they need help in

[1] See p. 143 for a discussion of the constitutional issue.

[2] *Ibid.;* also Senate Bill 1669, 78th Cong., 2d Sess.

retraining and rehabilitating themselves. Unless governmental assistance is given, many of these will be a heavy burden upon their relatives and ultimately may find themselves begging on public streets or inhabiting penal, mental, or other public institutions. Not only is it considered humane for assistance to be provided at opportune moments, but it is also generally considered sound public policy, even from a financial point of view.

Federal assistance was first provided by the Vocational Rehabilitation Act of 1920 but has been expanded since, especially by amendments adopted in 1943. The federal program is administered by the Office of Vocational Rehabilitation in the Federal Security Agency. "Vocational rehabilitation" and "vocational rehabilitation services" are defined as any services necessary to render a disabled individual fit to engage in a remunerative occupation. Funds are granted to the states on the basis of needs and their ability to match federal funds, although the Federal government will bear the entire cost of administering state programs and the full cost of guidance and placement of handicapped persons. Where war-disabled civilians[1] and the blind are involved, the Federal government will pay the full cost. In addition to training and guidance, federal grants may be used for physical restoration services, necessary hospitalization, transportation, occupational licenses, and necessary occupational tools and equipment, prosthetic devices essential to obtaining or retaining employment, and maintenance not exceeding the estimated cost of subsistence during training. More physical defects are of an orthopedic nature than any other, but many result from poliomyelitis, hernia, tuberculosis, defective vision and hearing, and mental illness.

Howard University.—Howard University, located in the District of Columbia, was originally chartered by Congress in 1867 for the purpose of providing higher education for Negro students. Most of its funds come from the Federal government and it is governed by a self-perpetuating twenty-four-member board of trustees of whom approximately half are colored and half white. Its students come from every state in the Union, a goodly number come from the Caribbean area, and occasionally students come from Africa and other parts of the world. Although intended primarily for Negroes, whites may attend and a few do. The faculty includes Negroes and whites. Howard University is doubtless the leading educational institution for Negroes in the world.

Schools for Indians.—Most Indians in the United States live on reservations. Some of their children attend near-by public schools, others attend mission schools; but for others the Office of Indian Affairs (Department of the Interior) maintains a system of elementary and secondary schools. These are similar to ordinary public schools except that many of them are boarding schools. No special facilities are provided for college or pro-

[1] That is, those disabled in civilian defense activities and the merchant marine.

fessional study, although federal loans are available. Those who are interested and able must seek enrollment in the same colleges and universities as other Americans. Schools for Indians are taught by teachers selected by the Office of Indian Affairs in accordance with civil service regulations. In addition to the usual subjects, emphasis is placed upon instruction in agriculture, home economics, mechanical arts, the values inherent in native culture, arts, and crafts. Considerable attention is also given to adult education. Commendable as this program is, educational opportunities are admittedly inadequate and inferior to those for white children.[1]

WELFARE PROGRAMS

Aid to Veterans.—Nearly one-third of the population consists of veterans, their dependents, and their beneficiaries.[2] Although various government agencies administer laws providing veterans' preference, the principal one is the Veterans' Administration created in 1930. This is an independent establishment headed by an Administrator and the usual staff. A special Board of Appeals exists for holding hearings and considering final appeals on matters relating to veterans' claims. In addition to the central office in Washington, the Administration maintains a number of regional, insular, and area offices. The Hoover Commission recommended merging the Veterans' Administration and other important agencies concerned with health and hospitalization into a new United Medical Administration.

Veterans' Hospitals.—Veterans suffering from wounds, injuries, and illnesses resulting from military service are entitled to free hospitalization, care, and treatment. For this purpose the Veterans' Administration operates numerous hospitals. Of its thousands of patients, a large majority require neuropsychiatric care. Others are treated in clinics or public and private hospitals which serve under contract for the Administration. The handling of patients under care of the Veterans' Administration has often been the subject of considerable criticism, including charges of brutality, neglect, unhygienic conditions, etc. A sweeping investigation, made in 1945 by a House committee, substantiated some of these charges and stimulated correction of some of the unfortunate conditions which were found to exist.[3]

[1] For an important critical survey, see United States House of Representatives, Committee on Indian Affairs, House Rep. 2091, 78th Cong., 2d Sess. (Washington: Government Printing Office, 1944). See also current publication of the Office of Indian Affairs.

[2] Until 1944 the Federal government was still paying a pension to the aged daughter of a private who served in the War of 1812.

[3] United States House of Representatives, Committee on World War Veterans' Legislation, *Investigation of the Veterans' Administration . . .*, *Hearings*, 79th Cong., 1st Sess., pursuant to H. Res. 192 (Washington: Government Printing Office, 6 vols., 1945).

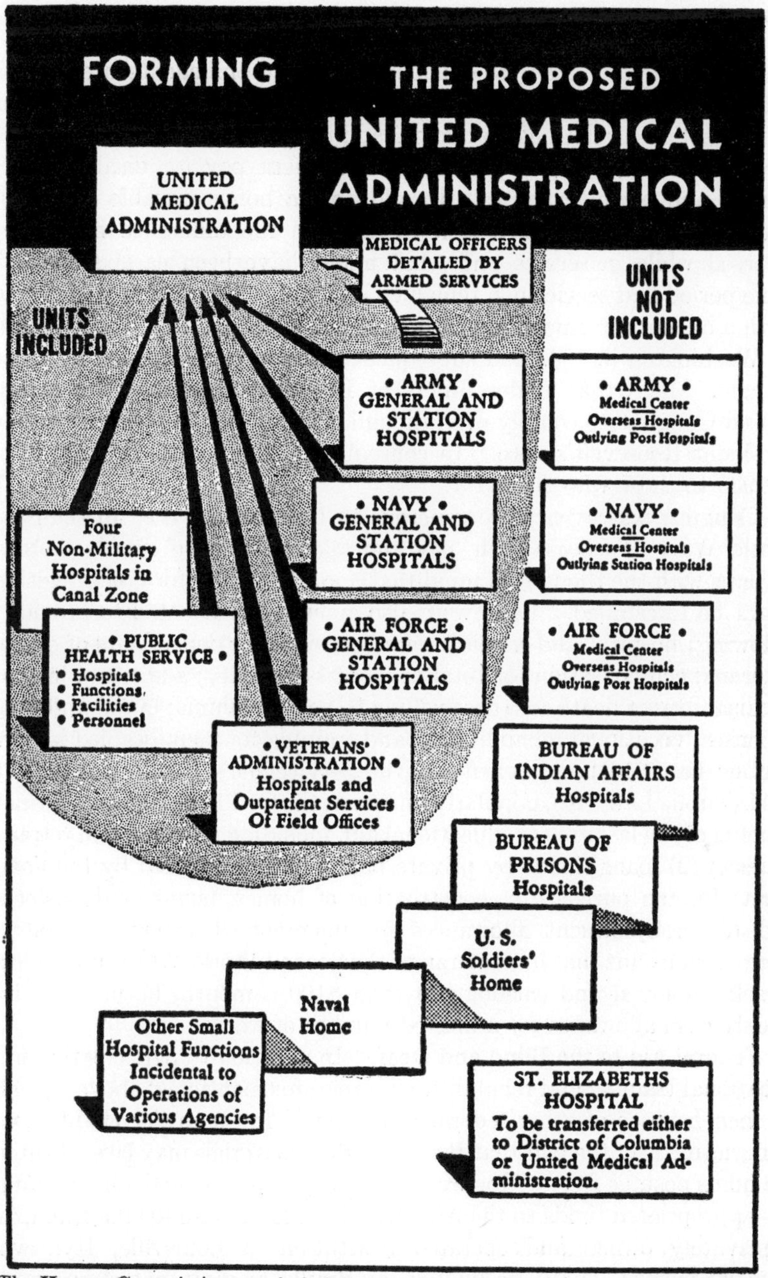

The Hoover Commission concluded that "only the creation of a new United Medical Administration can remedy the weaknesses of the present organization and give the leadership, direction and planning urgently needed." The new Administration would report directly to the President and include the Public Health Service and other agencies concerned chiefly with medical care and hospitalization. SOURCE: Hoover Commission, *Medical Activities.*

Other Veterans' Benefits.—Topping the list of benefits are pensions.[1] Liberal provisions were made for the First World War veterans, providing compensation for disability or death, additional life and disability insurance for those willing to pay premiums, retirement pay for disabled officers, funeral and burial expenses. In addition, a bonus payable in 1945 was authorized which was intended to equalize the difference between pay received while in service and what might have been earned during the same period had servicemen remained civilians. Depression years brought forth a clamor for immediate cash payment which led to a "bonus march" on Washington in 1932 and subsequent eviction by troops led by General Douglas MacArthur under orders of President Hoover. The agitation caused Congress to comply even though it meant passing the measure over President Roosevelt's veto. In consequence, the bonus was paid in cash in 1935 to those who desired it.

Congress was even more generous to those who served in the Second World War. To begin with, pay and allotments were greatly increased, perhaps with the thought in mind that another clamor for bonus legislation might be forestalled. Laws were also amended or enacted to provide the following: hospital and medical care; pensions for dependents of deceased veterans; compensation for total or partial disability; additional insurance for disability or death for those willing to pay premiums; burial and funeral expenses; vocational rehabilitation and training for men disabled in service (Public Law 316); and benefits of the Servicemen's Readjustment Act of 1944 (Public Law 346), popularly known as the GI Bill of Rights. Principal benefits of the last are (1) educational aid, including refresher and retraining courses; (2) loans (made by private banks but guaranteed by the government) for the purchase or construction of homes, farms, and businesses; and (3) readjustment allowances for unemployed veterans. The last-mentioned means that if a veteran of the Second World War is unemployed, or self-employed and earning less than $100 a month, he may receive a weekly cash allowance for a limited number of weeks.

Federal Aid to the Blind and Deaf.—In addition to participation in the vocational training and rehabilitation programs mentioned above, the blind are beneficiaries of other federal legislation. In an earlier chapter[2] mention was made of the fact that Braille reading materials may be sent through the mails postage free. Moreover, for many years the Federal government has appropriated funds to the American Printing House for the Blind, Inc., a privately owned and operated institution in Louisville, Ky., whose primary purpose is the production of Braille reading materials for state schools for the blind. Established in 1858, this is the oldest national institution for the blind in the United States and the largest printing house of its kind in the world.

[1] Generally spoken of as "compensation" since the First World War.

[2] See p. 700.

Further assistance was provided by the Randolph-Sheppard Act of 1936 whereby the blind were permitted to operate stands in federal buildings and the Office of Education was authorized to conduct surveys and otherwise try to find jobs for the blind. Direct financial assistance was provided

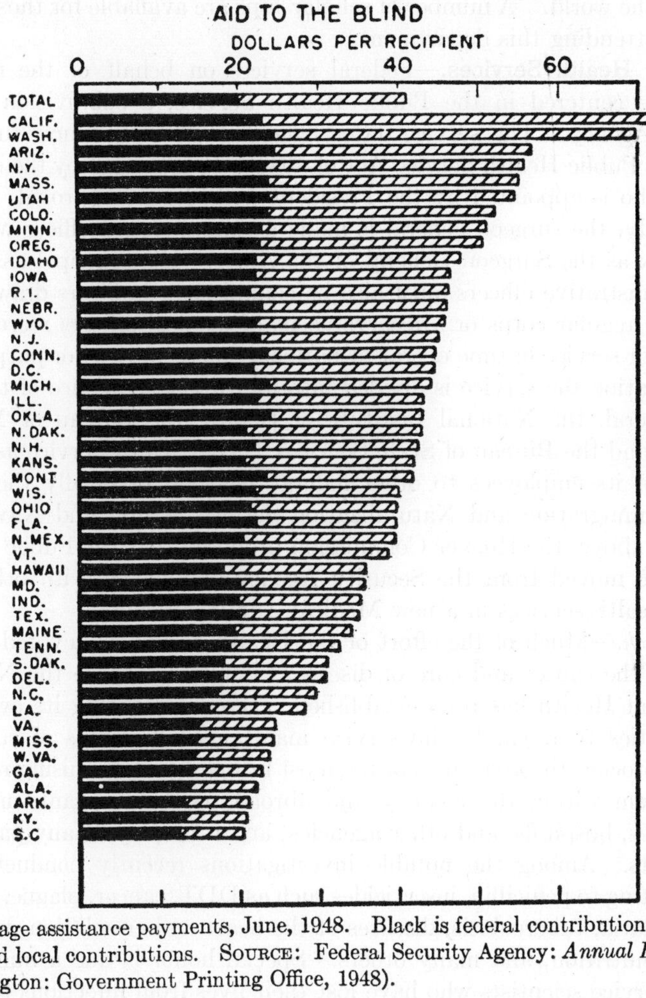

Average assistance payments, June, 1948. Black is federal contribution; hatched is state and local contributions. SOURCE: Federal Security Agency: *Annual Report, 1948* (Washington: Government Printing Office, 1948).

by the Social Security Act of 1935. This permits the Social Security Administration to help finance approved state plans for providing old-age pensions for the needy blind. Under this arrangement the Federal government will match state funds up to a total federal-state monthly grant of $50 for eligible blind persons sixty-five years of age or more who are not in public institutions and not receiving old-age assistance.

Deaf people may participate in the vocational rehabilitation programs. In addition, since 1857, the Federal government has operated the Columbia

Institution of the Deaf, located in the District of Columbia, for the instruction of the deaf and dumb. All white[1] mutes living in the District are admitted without charge. The advanced department, known as Gallaudet College, offers the only advanced course especially for the deaf given anywhere in the world. A number of scholarships are available for those interested in attending this department.

Public Health Services.—Federal services on behalf of the nation's health are centered in the Public Health Service, a subdivision of the Security Agency. The service dates back to 1798 but it now functions under the Public Health Service Act of 1944. It is headed by the surgeon general who is appointed by the President with Senate approval. If not one already, the surgeon general is made a commissioned officer with the same rank as the Surgeon General of the Army. His principal assistants and administrative officers must also be commissioned officers drawn from either the regular corps or a reserve corps of medical officers recruited or enrolled for service in time of war or national emergency. For purposes of administration the service is divided into four divisions: Office of the Surgeon General, the National Institute of Health, the Bureau of Medical Services, and the Bureau of State Services. The Health Service assigns a number of its employees to other federal agencies, especially the Coast Guard, Immigration and Naturalization Service, Army, and Navy. As indicated above, the Hoover Commission proposed that the Public Health Service be moved from the Security Agency and joined with other important health services in a new Medical Administration.

Research.—Much of the effort of the Health Service is devoted to discovery of the causes and cure of disease. For this purpose the National Institute of Health has been established. Besides devoting its own staff and facilities to research, the service maintains fellowships of sufficient value to procure the assistance of the most brilliant and promising research fellows from within the country and abroad; it makes grants-in-aid to universities, hospitals, and other agencies; and it employs many part-time consultants. Among the notable investigations recently conducted are those relating to penicillin, insecticides such as DDT, cancer, plague, typhus fever, malaria, tuberculosis, diseases of the heart and circulation, venereal diseases, nutrition, and many others. Special honor is due a number of Health Service scientists who have lost their lives from infections received while conducting research.

Cooperation with the States.—Federal-state cooperation on matters pertaining to public health is of the utmost importance. The law requires that the surgeon general call an annual conference of state health authorities. It also stipulates that upon the request of five or more states, the surgeon

[1] Colored mutes are cared for at the Maryland School for the Blind at Overlea, Md., near Baltimore.

general must call special conferences of all state and territorial health authorities joining in the request. At such conferences each state is entitled to one vote.

Recently the Federal government has launched an ambitious program looking toward eventual establishment of a coordinated nation-wide system of public-health facilities and activities. To attain this goal, grants-in-aid are made available to states willing to cooperate. Grants are now made for the training of personnel, the establishment of health services and clinics, and the control of venereal diseases and tuberculosis. To be eligible, states need not necessarily match federal funds; rather, grants are made on the basis of population, the extent of venereal diseases, tuberculosis, and other health problems, and the financial needs of the states. All the states are now cooperating, although of the 3,050 counties a considerable number still lack full-time health organizations. As this program expands, treatment and instruction are becoming accessible to many who have hitherto been unable to afford such services. Of special importance are the quick-treatment clinics which have sprung up for the treatment of venereal diseases. With these and the discovery of new drugs, the surgeon general was able to say in 1944 that within 5 years syphilis and gonorrhea need no longer be major public-health problems.

Hospitals.—The Federal government has many civilian beneficiaries for whom it is legally responsible. Most of these are covered by federal workmen's compensation laws.[1] Of those so covered, the most numerous are members of the Coast Guard, longshoremen and harbor workers, and government employees. Where possible it is mandatory that hospital and medical care be provided by federal medical officers, hospitals, and dispensaries; otherwise, the best arrangements possible are made. For this purpose the Public Health Service maintains a number of marine hospitals and hospital dispensaries at principal ports. For the care of legal beneficiaries in Washington, D.C., dispensaries are provided.

The Federal government operates two civilian hospitals in the District of Columbia: Freedman's hospital, a general hospital for Negroes, and St. Elizabeths, for mental patients. Freedman's hospital accommodates people from all over the country but must always allot 90 per cent of its facilities to residents of the Washington metropolitan district. Most of the patrons are charity patients, although there are a few who pay. In addition to providing regular hospital service, it offers instruction for nurses, physicians, and medical students; it spreads health information through out-patient clinics; and it sponsors medical research. It has always served as the training center for students of Howard University College of Medicine. Through this relationship and other activities, Freedman's hospital has become the most important center in the world for training Negro physicians

[1] See p. 772.

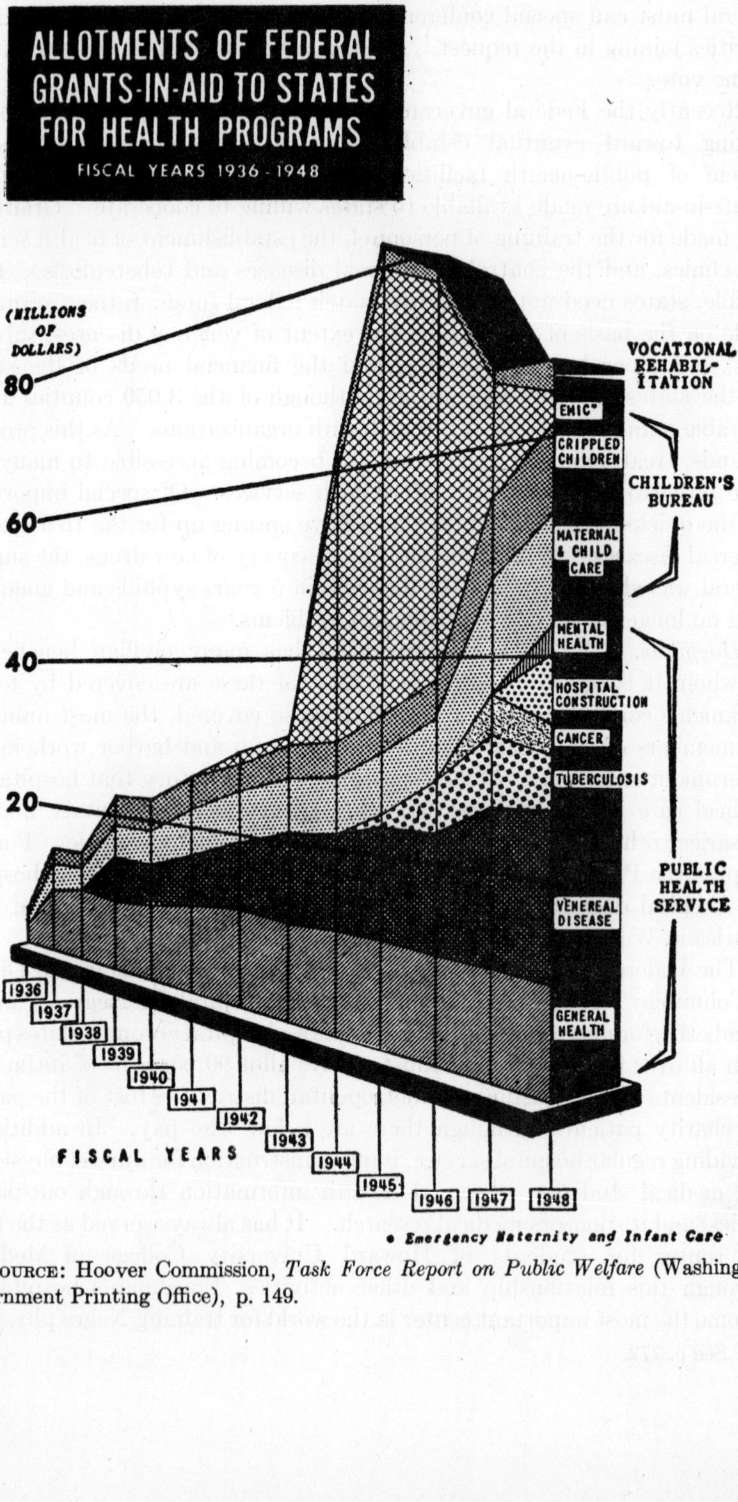

SOURCE: Hoover Commission, *Task Force Report on Public Welfare* (Washington: Government Printing Office), p. 149.

and is indeed in some respects the only center for advanced training of Negro physicians and surgeons.

St. Elizabeths is a large institution whose patients number nearly 7,000. Most patients are residents of the District of Columbia. A number from the Navy, Coast Guard, and Marine Corps on active-duty status were also

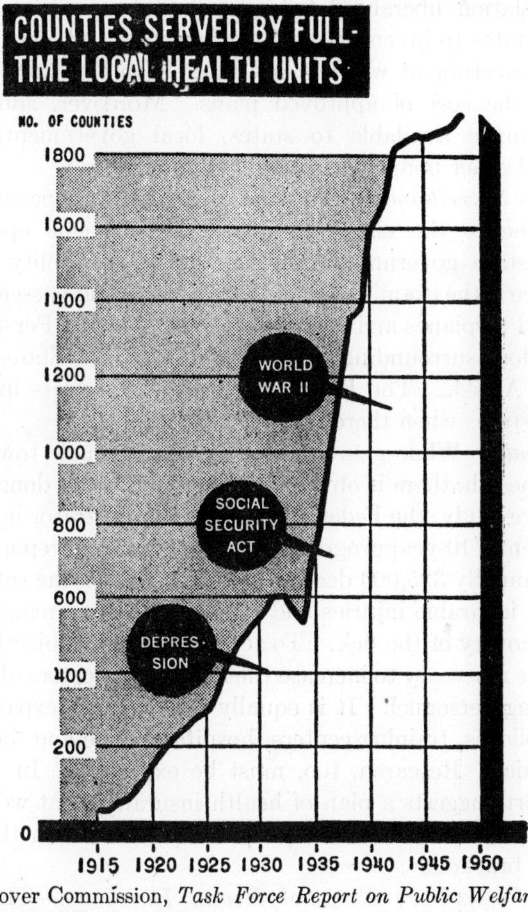

SOURCE: Hoover Commission, *Task Force Report on Public Welfare* (Washington: Government Printing Office), p. 161.

cared for here until 1946. In addition to caring for patients, the hospital carries on an ambitious training program. Both Freedman's and St. Elizabeths are administrated by the Public Health Service.

The Public Health Service also operates the National Leprosarium—a hospital for lepers—located at Carville, La., and two hospitals for the care and cure of drug addicts. The two hospitals for drug addicts are located at Fort Worth, Tex., and Lexington, Ky. While most of these patients are either legal beneficiaries or those held in custody, interestingly enough some are addicts who voluntarily seek admission in order to obtain treatment. During the war a number of psychotic patients and servicemen were treated at these hospitals rather than at St. Elizabeths, due to overcrowded conditions at the latter. The Public Health Service also supervises medical and psychiatric service in federal penal and correctional institutions.[1]

1949 legislation liberalized federal aid to hospitals. As a means of stimulating states to inventory existing hospitals and construct new ones, the Federal government will pay not more than two-thirds nor less than one-third of the cost of approved plans. Moreover, additional federal funds were made available to states, local governments, universities, hospitals, and other nonprofit institutions for research.

Quarantine Surveillance.—Bugs and germs are no respecters of territorial boundaries; hence the elaborate quarantine systems operated by the federal and state governments. A special responsibility of the Public Health Service is the examination of immigrants,[2] and passengers and crews of vessels and airplanes arriving from foreign ports. For this purpose it operates stations surrounding the continental United States, Puerto Rico, Hawaii, and Alaska. The Health Service also inspects interstate traffic between the states when there is special danger.

Health Goals.—While great strides have been made toward improving the nation's health, there is obviously much more to be done. Following a comprehensive study, the Federal Security Administrator in 1948 proposed to the President a 10-year program. According to this report,[3] it is possible to prevent annually 325,000 deaths, greatly diminish the suffering of those afflicted with incurable injuries and ailments, prevent many illnesses, and hasten the recovery of the sick. To accomplish these objectives, the report continues, it is necessary to increase the number of doctors, dentists, nurses, and supporting personnel. It is equally necessary to expand the number of medical colleges, training centers, hospitals, state and local health centers, and clinics. Research, too, must be expanded. In addition to all this, the report suggests a plan of health insurance that would bring adequate medical care to all families, especially to those in the middle- and lower-income brackets.

Proposed Compulsory National Health Insurance.—The proposal to launch a national health insurance plan ran immediately into a storm of controversy.[4] Briefly, the proposal calls for a federal-state plan under which insured workers and their families would be entitled to receive

[1] A list of these is given on p. 355.

[2] See also p. 170.

[3] Oscar R. Ewing, *The Nation's Health, a Ten Year Program* (Washington: Government Printing Office, 1948).

[4] The plan is briefly outlined in *ibid.*, pp. 62–114. For the pros and cons, see Congressional hearings on the subject, especially, *Hearings before a Subcommittee of the Committee on Labor and Public Welfare, United States Senate*, 80th Cong., 2d Sess. (Washing-

medical service from doctors of their own choice, the cost to be borne by a fund derived from a tax on payrolls and incomes. For the plan, it is argued that the state of the nation's health demands a bold attack;

GAPS IN OUR HEALTH SERVICES
Feasible goals for 1960

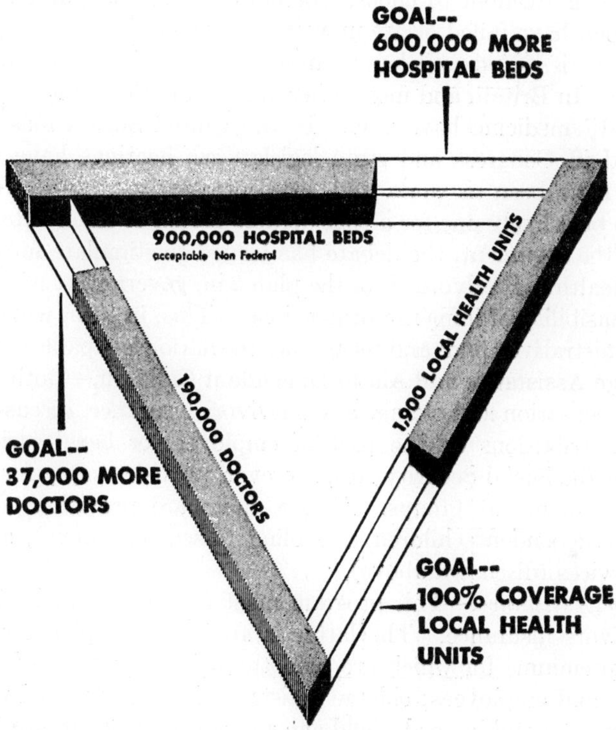

SOURCE: Oscar R. Ewing, *The Nation's Health, a Ten Year Program* (Washington: Government Printing Office, 1948).

that millions cannot now afford adequate medical care; that national coverage will reduce the per capita cost; that present facilities are inadequate and cannot be sufficiently improved by voluntary efforts; and that the proposed plan is not revolutionary, modeled as it is after present social-security programs. The chief spokesman for the opposition is the American Medical Association, backed by "conservative" interests generally. These

ton: Government Printing Office, 5 parts, 1948). For a critical study, see George W. Bachman and Lewis Merriam, *The Issue of Compulsory Health Insurance* (Washington: Brookings, 1948). See also publications of the American Medical Association.

contend that the nation's health is generally good and steadily improving; that the present voluntary medical insurance systems provide superior medical practitioners and service; that additional low-cost medical care can better be obtained through individual and voluntary cooperative efforts; that national insurance will result in a huge government administrative bureaucracy; that medical practitioners will inevitably shift from their present status to employees of federal and state governments; that patients will lose their freedom to choose doctors of preference; and that similar plans abroad have failed or are unworthy of emulation.

The issue is joined as it has been at times past in many other parts of the world. In Britain and most other Western nations, the proponents of "socialized" medicine have won. In the United States, bills have been introduced in Congress and state legislatures, hearings have been held, lobbyists have been at work, and people are taking sides. The issue is certain to be a lively one for a considerable period of time. Regardless of merits of the argument, the debate has helped to stimulate interest in the nation's health. If advocates of the plan win, government will be given a new responsibility of immense proportions. This, in turn, will call for the best administrative minds and techniques the nation is capable of producing.

Old-age Assistance and Aid to Dependent Children.—Both unemployment compensation and old age and survivors insurance, discussed below,[1] require contributions on the part of employers or beneficiaries. Other sections of the Social Security Act, however, provide simply for assistance to certain important groups. Among these are provisions for old-age assistance, dependent children, the blind (discussed above), and public-health services (discussed above).

Old-age Assistance.—This program must not be confused with old age and survivors insurance. The latter is an insurance plan for employed workers, premiums for which are paid through taxes assessed upon both employers and employees; old-age assistance is given to aged people who are unemployed and in need. Old age and survivors insurance is administered solely by the Federal government, while old-age assistance is provided by a joint federal-state arrangement.

For old age assistance the Federal government matches state appropriations, dollar for dollar, up to a federal-state total of $50 a month for each needy individual over 65, and adds 5 per cent to help defray administrative cost. The states frame and administer their own laws within general limits and standards prescribed by federal law and the Social Security Board. While the Federal government is willing to pay $15 of the first $20 per recipient and one-half of the balance up to a federal-state total of $50, the average pension during June, 1949 was only $43.60; twelve states exceeded $50.

To be eligible for a "pension," as grants are popularly known, an indi-

[1] See pp. 763–776.

vidual must be at least sixty-five, not an inmate of a public institution, a resident of the state for certain periods of time, a citizen (in most states), and in need. What constitutes need is a ticklish subject. Most states

OLD-AGE AVERAGE ASSISTANCE PAYMENTS

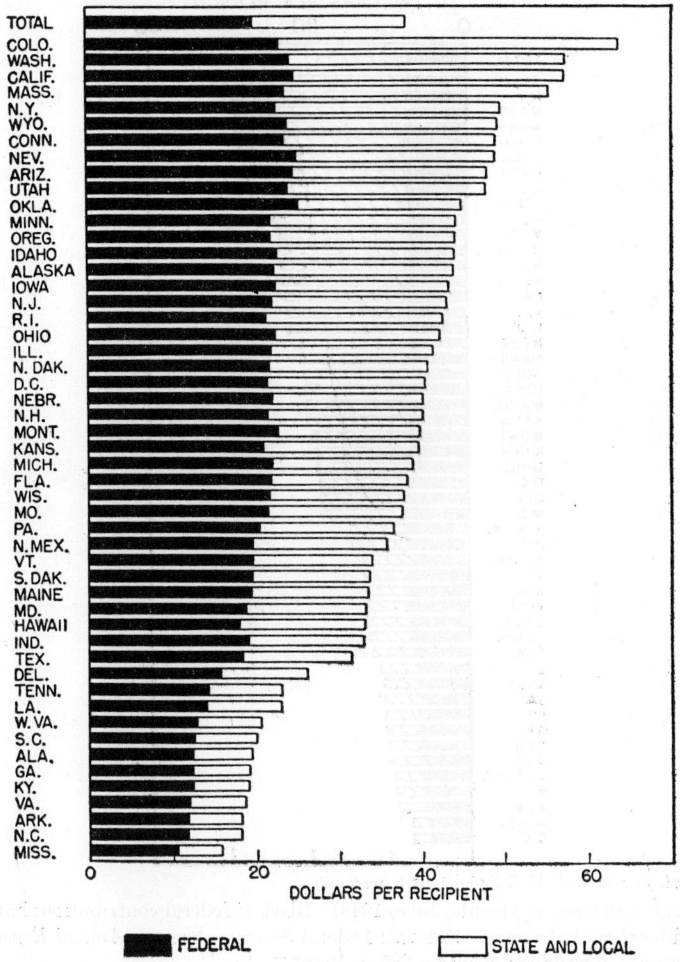

Average annual assistance payments, June, 1948. SOURCE: Federal Security Agency, *Annual Report, 1948* (Washington, Government Printing Office, 1948).

require applicants for aid to disclose their resources, assets, and income (if any), after which grants may be made that are sufficient, at least in the eyes of the administrators, to meet a minimum budget. Most states allow payments to more than one eligible person in a family if need warrants. On the whole, the states have taken a defensive, miserly attitude in setting up their plans, with the result that complaints are widespread. The most frequent criticisms are that the grants are too low to provide security, that in many instances the states require applicants to be or become destitute before granting assistance, and that administration permits too much

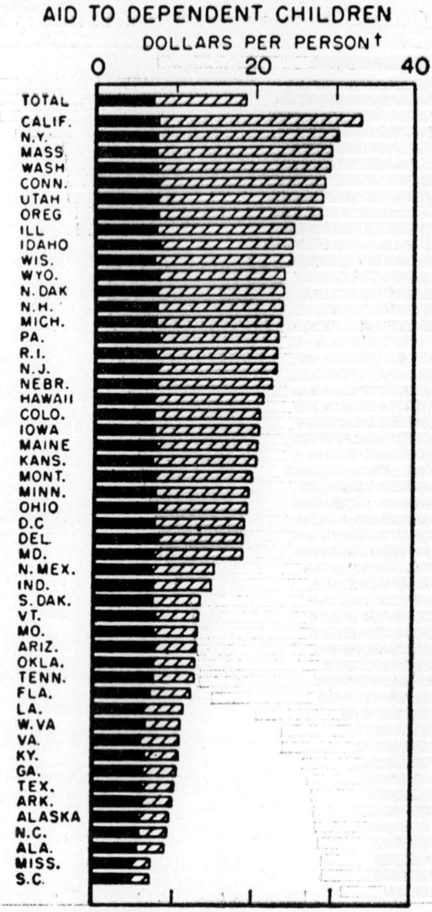

† Recipients represent children plus 1 adult per family.

Average assistance payments, June, 1948. Black is federal contribution; hatched is state and local contributions. SOURCE: Federal Security Agency, *Annual Report, 1948* (Washington: Government Printing Office, 1948).

opportunity for snooping into personal and family affairs. These complaints partially explain the sustained support given by many to more extreme proposals like the Townsend and "Ham and Eggs" plans which are well known, especially along the West Coast.

Aid to Dependent Children.—The Social Security Board also helps finance approved state plans aiding dependent children. A dependent child is defined as a needy child under the age of sixteen, or eighteen if regularly attending school, who has been deprived of parental support or care by reason of the death, continued absence from home, or physical or mental incapacity of a parent, and who is living and making his home with his father, mother, grandfather, grandmother, or other near relatives. The Federal government will match state funds up to a total federal-state grant of $27 a month for the first child and $18 for each additional child. Applications are made to state headquarters, and payments are made on the basis of need. Seldom is the maximum grant paid, and the amounts vary considerably among the states. Thus, at the close of the 1948 fiscal year, state averages ranged from about $32 a month for a child in the state of California to about $7.50 in South Carolina and Mississippi.

General Relief.—The great depression found the Federal government with no legislation providing for general and work relief. Before that the assumption had been that the relief of needy people was entirely the function of local governments and charitable agencies, but even they were caught unprepared for the avalanche. In most instances state legislation, generally known as "poor laws," dated back to Colonial times. Assistance was meager and seldom in the form of cash, while recipients were treated as paupers and frequently deprived of many of the privileges of citizenship. This system, even with the aid of private agencies, was incapable of coping with the unprecedented needs arising during the early 1930's. In consequence, first the state governments, then the federal, were called upon to assist. The states, however, could provide only limited amounts because they, too, were experiencing serious financial difficulties; nor could many of them borrow sufficient funds, partly because of constitutional limitations upon the issuance of bonds.

Federal Intervention.—The first federal intervention came in 1930 when President Hoover appointed the President's Emergency Committee for Employment. For the next 2 years federal action was directed principally to urging industry to spread employment, encouraging state and local public works, suggesting methods of meeting the relief problem on state and local levels, and stimulating contributions to private charities. In 1932 the Federal Farm Board gave huge quantities of surplus wheat and cotton to the Red Cross for processing and distribution. During the same year the Emergency Relief and Construction Act was passed authorizing the Reconstruction Finance Corporation to lend money to states for public assistance with the understanding that the funds would be repaid in full with 3 per cent interest and that relief would be dispensed by state and local agencies.[1] In spite of these efforts, unemployment reached an unprecedented peak in March, 1933, which proved to be the highest point of the depression period. This, coupled with the unavailability of state and

[1] Legislation adopted in 1934 canceled most of the obligations incurred by the states under this arrangement with the result that only a small proportion was ever repaid.

private funds, the defeat of the Republicans, and the inauguration of the Democrats in 1933, brought about federal intervention on a huge and unprecedented scale.

The Federal Emergency Relief Administration (FERA).—The Federal Emergency Relief Act, adopted in May, 1933, provided for the first direct financial grants in aid of the unemployed. This legislation established the Federal Emergency Relief Administration which continued to be the principal federal agency for handling assistance during the years 1933, 1934, and 1935. It did not make payments directly to the needy but rather extended grants-in-aid to the states which in turn dispensed assistance through state and local relief administrations. The FERA continued to function in this manner until December, 1935, by which time the Federal government had begun withdrawing from extending aid for general relief in favor of a more permanent program of work relief for "employables" and assistance to special groups.

Work Relief and Special Assistance Programs.—Final grants for general relief were made by FERA in November and December, 1935.[1] Meanwhile, the PWA and WPA, described below,[2] had gotten under way. The Social Security Act went into effect toward the end of 1935 providing assistance for the aged, dependent children, vocational rehabilitation, public-health services, and a plan for unemployment and old-age insurance.[3] Added to these were a number of programs first begun as emergency stopgaps and now made more or less permanent, among which were those conducted by the Civilian Conservation Corps, National Youth Administration, Surplus Marketing Administration,[4] and the Farm Security Administration.[5]

The Civilian Conservation Corps (CCC).— The CCC program originated in 1933 by an executive order based upon the Emergency Conservation Act of that year. During its early years the CCC was operated under the Department of the Interior; in 1939 it was transferred to the Federal Security Agency; and in 1942 it was entirely discontinued. Although primary administrative responsibility rested in either the Department of the Interior or the Security Agency, the camps were administered by the War Department and work projects were directed by technical agencies such as the National Park Service and the Forestry Service.

[1] Except for small grants made during the first half of 1936 to meet commitments made before the beginning of that year. Not all federal general relief was terminated with FERA, however, as is indicated on the chart found on page 769. This was dispensed to farmers through the Farm Resettlement Administration and its successor the Farm Security Administration (see p. 790), and the Surplus Commodity Corporation and its successor the Surplus Marketing Administration (see below, p. 785).

[2] Pp. 770–771.

[3] Pp. 773*ff*.

[4] P. 785.

[5] P. 790.

Enrollees were young men who volunteered, chiefly from families on relief or work-relief projects. They worked a 40-hour week and were paid maintenance and $30 a month, of which at least $15 had to be turned over to dependents. Camps consisted of approximately 200 men each. They were scattered in isolated places over the country and engaged in such work as forestry, fire suppression, soil conservation, flood control, and maintenance and improvement of national parks. At the peak of the

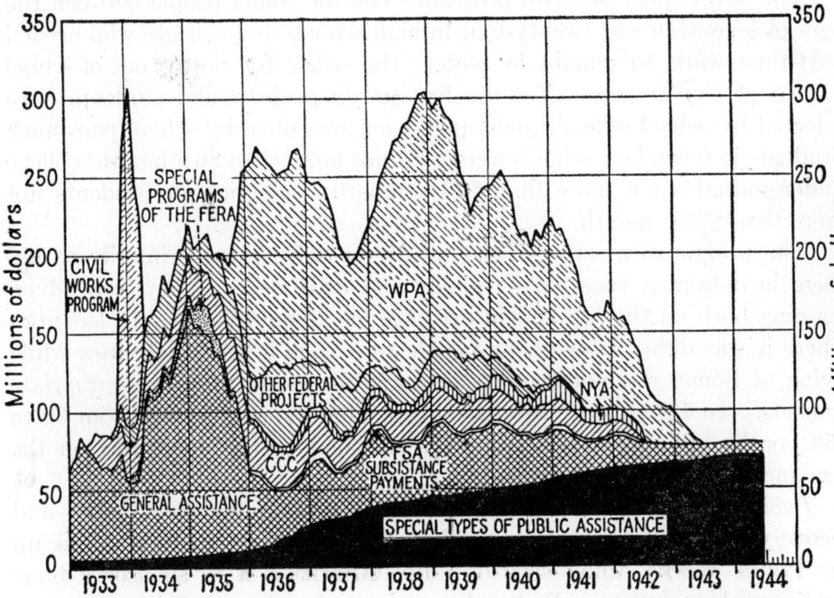

SOURCE: Social Security Board, *Annual Report*, 1944 (Washington: Government Printing Office, 1944), p. 4.

program there were 900 camps. Though the War Department was responsible for camp administration, as distinguished from that of the project, enrollees remained civilians throughout.[1] Many desirable projects were undertaken, the camp experience proved beneficial to most of the enrollees, and the system provided a convenient method of assisting families on relief. On the other hand, the work output was comparatively low, many projects were overmanned, funds and equipment were carelessly used, and the extracurricular educational program was primitive and generally inadequate.

National Youth Administration (NYA).—The NYA was launched in 1935 by an executive order based upon the Emergency Relief Appropriation

[1] However, camps were directed by uniformed military officers who organized and administered the camps after the familiar military pattern. After 1941 emphasis was placed upon training for national defense and close-order drill without weapons was instituted.

Act of that year. It functioned within the Works Progress Administration until 1939, then within the Security Agency, and in 1942 it was entirely discontinued. The national office determined basic policy with the advice of an advisory committee comprised of representatives of education, business, labor, agriculture, racial minorities, and other groups. Policies were executed through state youth administrations who, in turn, were advised by voluntary state and local committees.

The NYA sponsored two programs: one for young people between the ages of seventeen and twenty-four in high schools and colleges who needed part-time work to remain in school; the other for needy out-of-school youths of similar ages. For the first group projects and students were selected by school officials and supervision was done by school personnel. Students in secondary schools were paid not more than $6 a month; college undergraduates not more than $20 a month; and graduate students not more than $30 a month.

The program for out-of-school youths was intended primarily to aid them in obtaining vocational training and experience. They were given training both on the job and in existing vocational schools. In localities where it was difficult for young people to engage in work activities while living at home, resident centers were established to provide appropriate projects. In 1942 there were 535 such centers ranging in size from 20 to 450 youths. Wages varied from $17 to $30 monthly depending on the size and location of the community.

Public Works Administration (*PWA*).—Among the early relief and recovery measures adopted during the great depression was one setting up the Public Works Administration and authorizing it to sponsor a huge public works program. Reduced to essentials, the administration was given authority to make grants and loans to state and local governmental bodies, for the purpose of providing needed public structures, immediate employment, and purchasing power which it was hoped would stem the tide of deflation. Primary responsibility for sponsoring plans and projects rested with local and state governments. If plans were approved, PWA gave grants up to a maximum of 45 per cent, leaving the balance to be financed by the sponsor with the help of PWA if desired.

Illustrative of the types of projects so financed are school buildings, waterworks, sewer and power systems, hospitals, city halls, auditoriums, jails and other penal buildings, streets and highways, bridges, and tunnels. Contracts for construction were usually let by the sponsor to private contractors who were free to employ whomever they pleased, whether on relief or not. Both the sponsor and PWA were responsible for seeing that the contract was satisfactorily fulfilled. This program, with variations, extended from 1933 until 1939, after which the agency devoted itself entirely to seeing that old projects were completed and liquidated.

Works Progress Administration (*WPA*).—Those on relief rolls in 1939 could be divided into two groups: those incapable of working because of age, health, or other reasons; and those who were employable. The Federal Emergency Relief Act of 1933 provided direct relief for the former[1] and work relief for the latter. Work relief was first administered by the Federal Emergency Relief Administration in cooperation with state and local relief administrations. The Civil Works Administration took over most of the task during the winter of 1933–1934, but when abolished in March, 1934, the FERA continued the program. Finally, in May, 1935, the Works Progress Administration was created for the purpose.

It is easy to confuse PWA and WPA. As noted above, the former was authorized in 1933; the latter began in 1935. PWA aimed at stimulating the capital-goods industries by helping build permanent structures. Under its program contractors could employ personnel not on relief. WPA, on the other hand, was set up primarily to provide useful work to those on relief rolls. Its projects usually included less investment of capital and sometimes very little, if any.

The procedures followed in starting and administering projects were similar for both agencies. Under the WPA program, state and local public bodies proposed and sponsored projects. If approved, the sponsors paid not less than 25 per cent of the costs in funds, materials, equipment, and supervision; while WPA paid labor costs. Ninety-five per cent of all labor used had to come from the ranks of those on relief. Although a matter of extreme controversy, wages paid were usually comparable to prevailing wages paid for like work in the same area. State and local bodies tried hard, albeit often with little imagination, to discover projects that were both useful and suited to the needs of those on relief. How extensive the program was is shown on the chart on page 769. Although often the subject of popular derision, many of the projects were both of temporary and long-term value in themselves and they did much to sustain morale and consumer purchasing power during a most distressing period.

SOCIAL INSURANCE

Workmen's Compensation.—Until recent years employers generally assumed that they had no responsibility toward workmen injured during the course of employment. At common law, an injured workman's only recourse was a civil suit for damages, which he usually could ill afford. Besides being expensive and long drawn out, it was almost impossible for a workman to win because he was required to prove (1) that the employer had been negligent; (2) that negligence on his (the worker's) part in no way contributed to the accident; (3) that the accident was not due to the

[1] See p. 768.

negligence of a fellow workman; and (4) that the accident was not the result of a risk he had assumed by consenting to work in the occupation.

Since 1902 all states have enacted statutes designed to give greater protection to workmen, and the Federal government has done likewise for certain types of workmen within its jurisdiction. Such legislation is based upon the theory that compensation for industrial accidents should be included in the cost of production and borne partially by the producers and the general public rather than entirely by injured workmen and their families.

Insurance for Government Employees.—Most employees of the Federal government are insured against injuries received during the course of employment. For this purpose no insurance fund is established but, rather, Congress appropriates funds annually to the Federal Security Agency which, in turn, makes payments directly to injured workmen. The amount paid is usually proportionate to seriousness of the injury and the amount of time lost from work. After a brief waiting period, and within minimums and maximums, payments are made for partial, permanent partial, and total disability. Payments may also be made for medical, surgical, and hospital service, death, and even burial in the case of death from accident received during the course of employment. Administration involves considerable investigation, hearings, etc., which are handled by employees of the Bureau of Employees' Compensation. Since 1946, appeals may be taken to a three-man Employees' Compensation Appeals Board and to federal courts if constitutional issues are involved.

Insurance for District of Columbia, Longshoremen, and Harbor Workers.—Federal law also compels private employers in the District of Columbia and employers of longshoremen and harbor workers to insure against accidents. Employers may either set up their own insurance funds or insure with a private company approved by the Federal Security Administrator. A schedule of benefits is provided for various types of disability and death while payments are also prescribed for medical, surgical, hospital, and burial service. The cost of insurance is borne by employers but administrative costs are paid by the Federal government. These provisions are administered by the Bureau of Employees' Compensation which functions with the aid of regional districts, in charge of deputy commissioners, set up chiefly for the convenience of longshoremen and harbor workers. Appeals are not heard by an administrative board but by federal district courts.

Provisions for Railway Workers and Seamen.—Because these employees are engaged in interstate and foreign commerce, they are immune from state workmen's compensation laws. Nor has the Federal government made provision for them, although this has often been proposed. For their protection, therefore, injured workmen must resort to civil suits in state or federal courts. Their lot is not so unfortunate as might appear, however, because federal laws have modified the common-law assumptions referred to above. This occurred for railway employees by the Employers' Liability Act of 1908, and for seamen by the Jones Act of 1920.

The changes made by these acts were first, the fellow-servant rule was eliminated, placing the entire responsibility for negligence either upon the employer or the employee; second, the contributory-negligence rule was modified to permit recovery of damages even though an employee may have been partly to blame, with the provision that a jury might reduce the amount of damages in proportion to the amount of the employee's negligence, and with the further provision that an employee was absolved from all negligence if the carrier had violated a safety statute; third, the rule of assumption of risks was eliminated. As a result of these changes, an injured workman can always collect damages if an employer violated a safety statute or if the accident occurred because of negligence on the part of an employer. Even though both the company and he were negligent, he can also collect although a jury might reduce the amount of damages in proportion to the employee's share of the blame. While this legislation is of considerable help, it still involves an injured employee in more litigation, expense, uncertainty, and insecurity than if he were covered by compensation insurance statutes.

Unemployment Compensation.—Unemployment is without doubt the most serious domestic problem facing modern nations. There is always a certain amount of unemployment among willing workers, even in so-called "normal" times, and the volume rises sharply during depressions. The large and prolonged unemployment which followed the collapse of 1929 hastened enactment of a plan that would provide an income to workmen during periods of unemployment.

Provisions of Social Security Act.—This system is provided for in Title III of the Social Security Act of 1935 and administered by the Department of Labor, through its Bureau of Employment Security, in cooperation with the states. The act requires employers of eight or more employees to pay a tax of 3 per cent of their pay rolls, exclusive of amounts in excess of $3,000 paid to one employee in 1 year. It goes on to stipulate that a credit of 90 per cent of the amount collected will be allowed those employers situated in states that enact laws fitting the federal pattern.[1] This was such a heavy penalty upon employers in noncooperating states that it forced early enactment of state plans. Now all the states, the District of Columbia, Alaska, and Hawaii have unemployment insurance systems. The state laws vary considerably, but they must meet federal standards

[1] Critics contended that this was an unconstitutional use of the federal taxing power, but the legislation was sustained by the Supreme Court when the first case came before it. For further discussion of the constitutional issue, see pp. 366*ff*.

or else see their employers lose the 90 per cent tax credit and also forfeit the right to certain financial grants made in payment of the costs of administration.

State Plans.—Nearly all the states impose a pay-roll tax upon employers and a few impose a similar levy upon employees. The money is deposited in an Unemployment Compensation Fund maintained in the United States Treasury. From this each state pays workmen benefits as they become unemployed and make application at near-by federal-state employment offices. The amount paid varies among the states. A typical plan provides that after a waiting period of 2 weeks, during which time the employee must be physically able and available for work, he will receive weekly payments for a period of 15 weeks of not less than $5 nor more than $20, the exact amount depending upon the workman's average earnings over a base period. The average weekly payment for the whole country during 1947–1948 was about $18. Further statistics are shown on the opposite chart.

Unemployment Compensation for Railway Workers.—Although railway employees are exempt from provisions of Title III of the Social Security Act, they are covered by separate legislation enacted in 1938. The plan is administered by the Railroad Retirement Board. It is financed by a payroll tax paid by employers. In other respects the plan operates much like the general one explained on the opposite page.

Old-age and Survivors Insurance (OASI).—Title II of the Social Security Act instituted a nation-wide plan of insurance intended to guarantee a minimum income to most wage earners and low-salaried workers after they reached the age of sixty-five and ceased working. Unlike the unemployment compensation features, this system is operated entirely by the Federal government. It is administered by the Social Security Administration through the Bureau of Old Age and Survivors Insurance.

The Federal Plan.—All employers and employees, other than those in exempted occupations,[1] are required to participate. Employers must pay a tax on pay rolls and employees must pay an identical amount on their income, the total being collected from the employer. The amount each was to pay began at 1 per cent and was to be gradually stepped up until by 1949 both would pay 3 per cent, or a total of 6 per cent, but levies have been maintained at 1 per cent since 1939. The money is deposited in an Old Age and Survivors Trust Fund in the United States Treasury where it is invested in interest-bearing obligations of the Federal government or obligations whose interest and principal are guaranteed by the Federal government.

[1] These include agricultural labor; domestic servants in private homes; casual labor; officers and seamen on American and foreign vessels; national, state, and local government employees; and persons employed by religious, charitable, scientific, or educational institutions.

UNEMPLOYMENT INSURANCE 1946–1948

(Selected data on benefits, claims, employment, and finance, by state, for specified periods; corrected to Aug. 10, 1948)

State	Beneficiaries, fiscal year	Total amount, thousands	Average weekly benefit for total unemployment	State	Beneficiaries, fiscal year	Total amount, thousands	Average weekly benefit for total unemployment
1945–46	5,303,295	$1,091,062	$18.76	Miss.	18,144	$2,151	$12.44
1946–47	4,057,500	833,718	18.05	Mo.	84,686	14,426	16.16
1947–48	3,820,774	752,537	18.19	Mont. . . .	7,766	1,275	16.03
Ala.	41,304	7,683	14.77	Nebr. . . .	6,588	959	15.00
Alaska . .	5,243	1,095	23.26	Nev.	4,991	1,133	19.83
Ariz.	9,246	1,420	18.29	N.H.	19,876	3,035	15.35
Ark.	33,891	3,552	15.44	N.J.	224,257	52,142	19.62
Calif. . . .	506,686	128,395	19.81	N. Mex. .	4,041	580	16.03
Colo.	8,465	1,118	15.31	N.Y.	684,414	169,884	19.03
Conn. . . .	66,007	11,472	19.64	N.C.	51,868	5,832	11.10
Del.	6,250	872	15.19	N. Dak. .	1,717	342	17.96
D.C.	13,015	2,986	16.69	Ohio	101,036	19,753	17.47
Fla.	46,709	6,351	13.64	Okla. . . .	26,952	4,600	16.25
Ga.	37,380	5,675	13.44	Oreg. . . .	48,317	7,618	16.85
Hawaii. .	4,366	768	20.37	Pa.	274,644	49,519	17.24
Idaho . . .	8,018	1,398	18.12	R.I.	56,174	12,348	20.75
Ill.	275,822	47,641	18.31	S.C.	21,508	3,186	14.40
Ind.	54,164	8,830	17.32	S. Dak. .	2,055	259	15.90
Iowa. . . .	15,547	2,415	15.56	Tenn. . . .	63,094	10,614	13.30
Kans. . . .	19,461	3,020	15.13	Tex. . . .	42,338	5,477	13.70
Ky.	31,107	4,365	11.21	Utah. . . .	11,831	2,436	22.82
La.	35,290	5,965	14.15	Vt.	7,229	1,233	16.88
Maine . .	33,815	4,630	14.15	Va.	42,258	4,250	12.72
Md.	76,665	9,842	18.32	Wash. . . .	93,211	18,472	18.07
Mass. . . .	223,669	50,624	22.13	W. Va. . .	41,468	5,302	15.31
Mich. . . .	259,979	35,928	20.08	Wis.	35,263	4,127	17.28
Minn. . . .	30,528	5,189	15.08	Wyo. . . .	2,421	352	18.51

SOURCE: Federal Security Agency: *Annual Report, 1948* (Washington: Government Printing Office, 1948).

Annuities are paid monthly to those who retire at the age of sixty-five and are continued until death. Sums paid may not be less than $10 nor more than $85 a month, the exact amount depending upon previous earnings and the number of years contributions have been made. Payments are stopped if the insured or his dependents recommence working at a job covered by the law that pays $15 a month or more. If the insured is married and living with his wife, who is also over sixty-five, he receives an additional sum equal to one-half the primary benefit. He is also entitled to a like sum for each unmarried dependent child under sixteen years of age, or eighteen if regularly attending school. If the insured dies before reaching the age of sixty-five, proportionate payments are made monthly to his survivors. Provision is also made for a lump-sum payment upon death of the insured for funeral expenses.

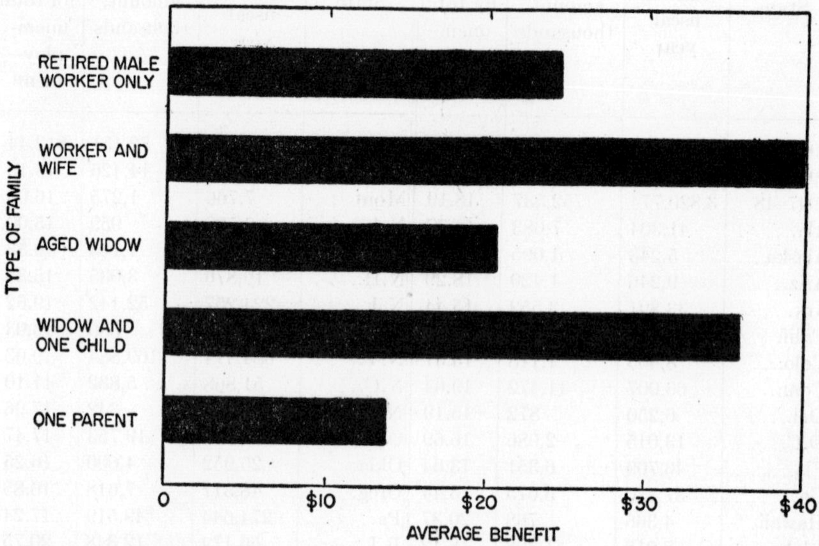

SOURCE: Federal Security Agency: *Annual Report, 1948* (Washington: Government Printing Office, 1948).

Note that from common knowledge of living costs it is clear that even maximum OASI benefits would scarcely suffice to meet the entire cost of living. Note also that an old couple with OASI benefits receives less than the maximum old-age assistance payable under many state laws.

Retirement Plans for Government and Railroad Workers.—Neither employees of the Federal government nor those of railroads are covered by the retirement features of the Social Security Act. Government employees, however, have had a retirement plan of their own since 1920 which is similar to the general one just explained. This is administered by the Retirement Division of the Civil Service Commission.

A similar plan was adopted for railway workers in 1935 which is administered by the Railroad Retirement Board, an independent three-member agency. Provisions of this plan were liberalized considerably by legislation enacted in 1946.

References

Adams, Grace K.: *Workers on Relief* (New Haven: Yale University Press, 1939).

Brown, Josephine Chapin: *Public Relief 1929–1939* (New York: Holt, 1940).

Burns, Eveline M.: *Toward Social Security; An Explanation of the Social Security Act and a Survey of Larger Issues* (New York: McGraw-Hill, 1936).

Chase, Stuart: *Goals for America* (New York: The Twentieth Century Fund, 1942).

Commons, John R., and John B. Andrews: *Principles of Labor Legislation* (New York: Harper, 4th ed., 1943).

Douglas, Paul H.: *Social Security in the United States; An Analysis and Appraisal of the Social Security Act* (New York: Random House, 1936).

Epstein, Abraham: *Insecurity—A Challenge to America; a Study of Social Insurance in the United States and Abroad* (New York: Random House, 1936).

Ewing, Oscar R.: *The Nation's Health, a Ten Year Program* (Washington: Government Printing Office, 1948).

Falk, Isador S.: *Security against Sickness; A Study of Health Insurance* (New York: Doubleday, 1936).

Federal Works Agency: *Final Statistical Report of the Federal Emergency Relief Administration* (Washington: Government Printing Office, 1942).

Howard, Donald S.: *WPA and Federal Relief Policy* (New York: Russell Sage Foundation, 1943).

Hutchins, Robert M.: *The Higher Learning in America* (New Haven: Yale University Press, 1936).

Kramer, Victor H.: *National Institute of Health; A Study in Public Administration* (Washington: S. P. Kramer, 1937).

MacMahon, Arthur W., and Others: *Administration of Federal Work Relief* (Chicago: Public Administration Service, 1941).

Millis, Harry A., and Royal E. Montgomery: *Labor's Risks and Social Insurance* (New York: McGraw-Hill, 1939).

Mustard, Harry S.: *Government in Public Health* (New York: Commonwealth Fund, 1945).

Reed, Louis S.: *Health Insurance: The Next Step in Social Security* (New York: Harper, 1937).

Rubinow, Isaac M.: *The Quest for Security* (New York: Holt, 1934).

Smillie, Wilson G.: *Public Health Administration in the United States* (New York: Macmillan, 1935).

Tobey, James A.: *Public Health Law* (New York: Commonwealth Fund, 1939).

United States Advisory Committee on Education: *Report of the Committee* (Washington: Government Printing Office, 1938).

United States Commission on Organization of the Executive Branch of the Government ("Hoover Commission"): *Social Security, Education, Indian Affairs; Task Force Report on Public Welfare* (Washington: Government Printing Office, 1949).

United States President's Commission on Higher Education: *Higher Education for American Democracy* (Washington: Government Printing Office, 6 vols., 1947).

Wallace, Henry A.: *New Frontiers* (New York: Reynal & Hitchcock, 1934).

Williams, Edward A.: *Federal Aids for Relief* (New York: Columbia University Press, 1939).

Williams, J. Kerwin: *Grants-in-Aid under the Public Works Administration* (New York: Columbia University Press, 1939).

Chapter 34

AGRICULTURE

> Our thoughts may ordinarily be concentrated upon the cities and the hives of industry . . . but it is from the quiet interspaces of the open valleys and the free hillsides that we draw the sources of life and prosperity, from the farm and the ranch, from the forest and the mine. Without these every street would be silent, every office deserted, every factory fallen into disrepair.
>
> President Woodrow Wilson, "First Annual Address," delivered Dec. 2, 1913.[1]

Agriculture is America's basic industry, producing the foods and raw materials upon which our population and manufactures largely depend. Yet the process of urbanization has steadily reduced the proportion of the population gainfully employed in agriculture from 26.3 per cent of the total gainfully employed in 1920, to 18.5 per cent in 1940.[2] Agriculture's share of the national income decreased markedly too; in 1850 agriculture contributed 34 per cent, but this was reduced to only 8.7 per cent in 1930, and to 6.8 per cent in 1940 but was restored to 9.5 per cent by 1947.[3] No matter what standard of comparison is used between rural and urban dweller—income available for living, literacy, medical care, conveniences—the average farm family appears at a disadvantage, and its city cousin has the advantages.[4] This disadvantageous position has caused government to provide not only the usual services that might be expected for an important enterprise of the people, but also extraordinary aid and relief designed to restore agriculture to a position of parity with industry.

The Department of Agriculture.—In many ways the federal Department of Agriculture constitutes a model in departmental organization. Frequently reorganized to improve its services to the American farmer, the department has placed great stress on management and personnel techniques. For so vast an organization, the department has long been admirably administered by first-rate personnel with high morale. Report-

[1] James D. Richardson (ed.), *Messages and Papers of the Presidents* (New York: Bureau of National Literature, 20 vols., 1897–1916), vol. 18, p. 7908.

[2] United States Department of Commerce, Bureau of the Census, *Statistical Abstract of the United States, 1942* (Washington: Government Printing Office, 1943), pp. 66–67; Bureau of Foreign and Domestic Commerce, *Statistical Abstract of the United States, 1931* (Washington: Government Printing Office, 1931), p. 56.

[3] United States Department of Agriculture, Agricultural Adjustment Administration, *Agriculture's Share in the National Income*, October, 1935, p. 7, and *Statistical Abstract.*

[4] See Donald C. Blaisdell, Jr., *Government and Agriculture* (New York: Rinehart, 1940), pp. 2–12.

ing directly to the secretary, the undersecretary, and one assistant secretary, are the various staff offices—bureaus of agricultural economics, personnel, information, finance, foreign agricultural relations, plant and operation, library. They provide the department with coordinating and housekeeping services that both assist the operating units and provide the departmental management with effective controls over the administrative leviathan.

The line functions of the department are divided into eleven units, each of which is headed by a chief responsible to the Secretary. These groups are as follows:

Agricultural Research Administration
Commodity Credit Corporation
Commodity Exchange Authority
Federal Crop Insurance Corporation
Extension Service
Farm Credit Administration
Farmers' Home Administration
Forest Service
Production and Marketing Administration
Rural Electrification Administration
Soil Conservation Service

AGRICULTURAL RESEARCH

The earliest services performed by the national government for agriculture were of the research nature, designed to improve production. These services have continued, lighting the torch of scientific agriculture to be carried to the farmer through bulletins, extension services, demonstrations, and the like. It may appear contradictory to show farmers how to increase production through improved seed or stock, disease control, and fertilization, and on the other hand to encourage reduction of production. The answer is that no one can expect agriculture to retreat from its scientific advances, and that production restriction is a stopgap measure, aimed at securing a measure of justice until a more adequate solution is devised.

Livestock and Meat.—Since 1884 the Bureau of Animal Industry, Department of Agriculture, has carried out extensive investigations in the diseases, feeding, breeding, and utilization of farm animals and poultry. The bureau also has law-enforcement functions: it conducts meat inspection, supervises interstate transportation of animals, and imposes quarantines on diseased animals. Its meat-inspection service provides the consumer with protection in regard to both purity and quality. The best grades of beef and veal are stamped "U.S. Prime" and "U.S. Choice"; intermediate is labeled "U.S. Good"; lower grades are marked "U.S.

Commercial" and "U.S. Utility." The wise meat buyer will look for the official purple stamp. Comparable agencies in state departments of agriculture do similar work.

Dairying.—Both Federal and state governments devote much attention to the dairying industry, which yields about one-half of total income from farm products in some states. The federal agency concerned with it is the Bureau of Dairy Industry, Department of Agriculture. Until 1924 dairying work was handled by a division of the Bureau of Animal Industry.[1] The bureau is engaged almost exclusively in research work. It investigates the feeding, breeding, and management of dairy cattle, studies the handling of milk products, and other problems.

Much more has been done for dairying by the states and by local governments. They make the inspections necessary to assure cleanliness in milk production. They determine the grades and standards under which milk and milk products may be sold. The marketing of milk has been regulated in great detail in some states. After the favorable decision in Nebbia *v.* New York in 1934,[2] upholding milk price fixing, many states enacted comprehensive legislation embodying price fixing. Although milk was not held to be a public utility, the police power of the state might properly be exercised to set prices on so important a commodity.

Plant Life.—Crop farming is served by the Bureau of Plant Industry, Soils, and Agricultural Engineering of the federal Department of Agriculture and by comparable state agencies. Soil studies begin with classification of soil types and continue through the search for the appropriate fertilizers, cultivation, and crops for each type. New plants are imported, propagated, and introduced to American agriculture. The control of diseases is experimented with, and the results of investigations are made known to farmers.

The crop farmer is also furnished with information and protection through the federal department's Bureau of Entomology and Plant Quarantine. Entomology is the branch of zoology that deals with insects. The federal bureau studies insects, seeking methods of control for harmful ones, and ways of propagation of helpful ones. The plant quarantine work of the bureau falls more in the field of law enforcement. It involves inspection of plant life entering the United States, cooperation with the states in controlling insects and diseases attacking plants, and control of interstate shipments of plants.

All over this country federal and state officers stand guard and do battle against insect pests and plant diseases. They constitute bulwarks against

[1] A. P. Chew, *The United States Department of Agriculture, Its Structure and Functions*, United States Department of Agriculture, Miscellaneous Publication No. 88 (Washington: Government Printing Office, 1940), p. 95.

[2] 291 U.S. 502 (1934).

the enemies of man and his crops—the boll weevil, the Mediterranean fruit fly, the Japanese beetle, the mosquito, the tick, and others.[1]

Agricultural Chemistry.—Chemical research work has long constituted one of the main activities of state and federal agricultural departments. The science of chemistry is put to work on agricultural products, to develop new uses, improve processing, establish nutritional values, test fertilizers. The federal agency in this field is the Bureau of Agriculture and Industrial Chemistry and Engineering. Its engineering aspect includes investigations of mechanical farm equipment, of farm structure, of processing machines, of rural electrification, and the like. State agencies and experiment stations carry out chemical and engineering projects that relate to the peculiar needs of the state.

Home Economics.—The frontiers of research on the problems of the home—food, clothing, and shelter—are tackled by the Bureau of Human Nutrition and Home Economics, Department of Agriculture. From the standpoint of the farm producer its work is important because it finds new and expanded uses for farm products. For the consumer it provides standards and buying aids. For the processor and manufacturer it makes available the latest information for product improvement.

Farm Economics.—Among the most practical of the services provided by the Department of Agriculture are those relating to farm economics. The Bureau of Agricultural Economics is its agency on this front. In departmental organization in 1938 it was attached to the Secretary's office as a staff service in order that the department head may have direct access to the economic facts upon which the general departmental program may be based. Nevertheless, this must not be allowed to obscure the many services of the bureau in the research field. Its research includes farm management, ownership and tenancy, marketing, transportation, and rural sociology.

Getting Research Results to the Farmer.—The channels of information through which the story of research results flow to the farmer are many. One is the experiment stations located in each state and financed jointly by state and federal funds. The stations carry on their own research work and publish the results in bulletins and circulars which are distributed free to farmers. The stations are supervised by the Office of Experiment Stations of the federal department.

The federal department itself disseminates the results of research through the Office of Information, which handles its publications, and arranges for press and radio releases. The department's Extension Service cooperates with state colleges in the maintenance of a nation-wide system of extension work. These, in turn, cooperate with the well-known county agent. These joint federal-state missionaries of better agriculture establish

[1] See Chew, *op. cit.*, pp. 103–115.

contact with the farmer through direct services, demonstrations, exhibits, and organizational associations.

AGRICULTURAL CREDIT

Another front on which American farmers needed help was credit; to buy land and to equip a farm it becomes necessary for the average agriculturist to go into debt. If the farmer is to succeed, this credit must be available at low interest rates and be repayable over a long period of time. Private capital is available for farm financing in most sections of the country, but where the risk is great the interest charges tend to be high. A small-town bank with heavy investments in farm mortgages may be wiped out by a series of bad crop years. After crop failures the farmers who owe the bank lose their farms through foreclosures.

Under these conditions, it is not surprising that pressure should have been exerted upon the government to assume responsibilities for farm financing. The Federal government has provided nearly all of the direct loans to agriculture. During the last 30 years federal farm-financing facilities have expanded enormously.

Early Farm Loans.—The first step in the federal program of farm loans came in 1916, when Congress created the Federal Farm Loan Board. The country was divided into twelve districts, in each of which a federal land bank was established to raise money through bond issues, and to lend money through farm loan associations. Short-term credit needs of farmers were provided for in 1923 by the creation of intermediate credit banks in the same districts.

Long-term Farm Loans.—Federal land bank loans are still made through local farm loan associations. They are long-term borrowings secured by first mortgages upon farms. Interest rates are low, currently at 4.0 and 4.5 per cent. While these loans primarily are for the purchase of farm land, the money is available also for improvements of mortgaged farms. If young John Perkins, just home from a civilian war job, wants to settle down as a farmer near Sioux City, he first locates a piece of land that is suitable and for sale. He goes to the offices of the Woodbury County National Farm Loan Association and files application for a loan. If he is judged a good risk and the farm a good buy, the association will advance him up to one-half the value of the land, taking a first mortgage as security. In this case, the loan amounts to $5,000. Perkins must agree to repay in 20 to 30 years by annual or semiannual installments, and must buy some shares of stock in the land bank or local association. When the loan is paid off, the stock is redeemed.

Short-term Farm Credit.—In order to finance the operations of producing, harvesting, and marketing of crops, farmers need loans for short periods. Credit is obtained for buying seed, feed, machinery, livestock, and many other purposes. The length of time of a short-term loan depends upon the crop season, ranging from 2 to 9 months; loans on livestock may be for longer periods. These loans are available from local production-credit associations, which, like the local farm loan associations, are cooperative organizations of farmers. The local association obtains the money it lends largely from the Federal Intermediate Credit Bank of the farm loan district, and from the regional production credit corporations. The latter agencies were added in 1933 to assist with short-term loan facilities. The overhead financing operations are even more complicated than those connected with long-term farm loans. Farmer Sam Barnard, who needs cash for sugar-beet seed in order to plant his next crop, travels to near-by Lamar, Col., and applies to the Prowers County Production Credit Association for a $300 loan for 6 months' duration. If the loan is made, Barnard is required to acquire a share in the association; he becomes thereby a voting member of the cooperative.

Credit for Farm Cooperatives.—Special provision is made for financing farmers' cooperatives. Since 1933 cooperative credit needs have been served by the Central Bank for Cooperatives and the twelve district banks for cooperatives in the farm credit districts. Farmers' cooperatives are organized for marketing of products, purchasing agricultural supplies, or for other purposes. The loans are of three types. Commodity loans, for which the interest rate is lowest, are used to finance the handling or processing of farm products. Operating capital loans, at middle interest, provide funds to supplement a cooperative's own capital during peak activities. Facility loans, bearing the highest interest, are used to finance land, buildings, and equipment needed for the cooperative. The cooperatives that borrow are required to buy 5 per cent of their loan in bank-for-cooperatives stock.

Commodity Credit.—As a means of stabilizing prices, loans are made to farmers to enable them to keep commodities off the market in periods of low prices. The Commodity Credit Corporation, which functions in this field, also has several other major responsibilities. Working closely with the Production and Marketing Administration, the CCC plays a leading role in the price-support program. It makes "nonrecourse" loans (either directly or through lending agencies) at support prices; if the price goes up, the farmer may pay off his loan plus interest and sell his commodity on the market; if it goes down, he may deliver the commodity to the CCC and his obligation is discharged in full. During the war and immediate postwar period, this scheme succeeded in keeping farm prices above parity. Parity meant a level necessary to provide the farmer with purchasing power equal to that which he enjoyed during 1910–1914. The CCC also serves as procurement agent for the government in buying farm commodities for such purposes as the European Recovery Program and other foreign aid. Another aspect of its work is the purchasing abroad of commodities needed by the United States for domestic consumption or for foreign assistance.

Farm Credit Administration.—The Federal agency that coordinates most of the diverse agricultural loan activities is the Farm Credit Administration. Created by executive order in 1933, it was given jurisdiction over both the previously existing farm credit agencies and those created in the same year. From 1933 to 1939 the agency was independent of departmental control and the governor of the Farm Credit Administration was responsible to the President directly. President Roosevelt transferred it to the Department of Agriculture in his reorganization plan No. 1 of 1939, settling a sharp controversy over the proper administrative relationship to other agencies. Secretary of Agriculture Wallace won, and the previous governor resigned and was replaced.[1] While the Administration was looked upon as "semiautonomous" within the department at first, its policies are believed now fully under the control of the Secretary of Agriculture. Even granting merit to the argument for independence on grounds of fiscal operations, the advantages of concentrating responsibility for services to farmers appear to predominate.

The Hoover Commission found that the services and policies of the several farm credit agencies overlap and should be reorganized.

MARKETING SERVICES

From its beginning the United States Department of Agriculture concerned itself with the problems of increasing agricultural productivity. By the time of the First World War it was apparent that the American farmer no longer commanded European markets without serious competition. During the war new marginal areas were brought into production, adding to the complexities of postwar farm readjustments. Overproduction reached a serious level, and farmers sought aid in marketing and in planning for future crops. At first reliable information on markets was demanded and obtained. Later special devices for handling surpluses were explored. During the last decade both marketing and production control have been resorted to in attempting to secure a measure of prosperity for the American farmer.

Crop Reporting.—One essential in deciding what to plant is data on what has been produced in the past and is likely to be produced in the future. This information is supplied through the Crop Reporting Service, which is conducted jointly by federal and state officials. Estimates are

[1] The public statements are available in John M. Gaus and Leon O. Wolcott, *Public Administration and the United States Department of Agriculture* (Chicago: Public Administration Service, 1940), pp. 254–261.

made of acreage, yields, sales, prices, and other facts concerning the various crops. Regular market news service is maintained by the federal department, giving farmers the benefit of the latest information on prices, demand, and market conditions generally.

Standards and Grades.—The creation of distinct standards and grades for farm products is of benefit to both farmer and consumer. If adequate standards are defined and enforced, the farmer is assured a price based upon actual quality of his product. The consumer, if he is alert and informed, may rely upon the uniform grade as assurance of actual quality of the product being bought. The standards so established are nationwide, but their application is largely voluntary. The consumer has a particularly great stake in pressing Congress to make grading and labeling of foods, both processed and unprocessed, compulsory. Standardization of containers has been accomplished through use of the federal power over weights and measures. Mandatory grading of products according to quality probably must rely upon federal power over interstate and foreign commerce.

Commodity Exchanges.—Farmers also have a great concern in future transactions involving farm products. Traders and speculators have long been wont to buy and sell agricultural commodities long in advance of their availability. It is argued that such futures trading serves a useful purpose by establishing a price level on a given commodity at a date sufficiently in advance to create a measure of stability in the market. The first attempt of Congress to regulate futures transactions came in 1921 and was based on the taxing power; this was declared invalid by the Supreme Court. A modest grain futures act was enacted in 1922; subsequent additions have brought the list of commodities under control to include wheat, cotton, corn, oats, rye, barley, flaxseed, grain sorghums, millfeeds, rice, butter, eggs, Irish potatoes, wool tops, fats and oils, cottonseed meal, cottonseed, peanuts, soybeans, and soybean meal.

Regulation is carried out by the Commodity Exchange Authority, which has power to designate which exchanges may engage in futures trading, to register commission merchants and brokers, to limit the size of transactions, and to forbid manipulative and fraudulent practices.

Surplus Marketing.—In the depth of the depression the existence of large surpluses of farm products, as well as millions of unemployed and hungry people, led to efforts to correct this situation. In 1933 an agency was created to remove surpluses from the market by purchasing them and then diverting them to needy families, school lunches, by-product uses, and export. Distribution to families was handled through regular retail outlets by the use of food stamps which could be presented as payment for surplus commodities.

The postwar diversion program places heaviest emphasis on the national school-lunch program, which was placed on a regular basis by legislation in 1946. Schools that cooperate receive both federal funds and surplus commodities. During 1947–1948, 70 million dollars was spent on federal aid for school lunches, and an additional 20 million dollars to buy surplus foods for schools. Some surplus foods still go to charitable institutions and to families on relief.

Funds for a portion of the diversion program come from customs receipts, 30 per cent of which by law are available to the Secretary of Agriculture for encouraging export or domestic use of surpluses.

Marketing Agreements.—The "orderly marketing" of farm products is encouraged further by agreements between growers and handlers and the Secretary of Agriculture governing the marketing program of a particular commodity. Such agreements were first authorized in 1933, but the law has been amended several times since. Usually the request for such an agreement comes from the producers and handlers. After being petitioned for an agreement, the Department of Agriculture conducts a hearing. An agreement may then be drawn up for the commodity. It becomes effective when signed by handlers of one-half the commodity by volume; if an order is involved, a two-thirds vote of producers on referendum is required. The usual agreement order involving fruits or vegetables covers both quantity and quality control; the volume of the product flowing on the market is regulated, as is the size or grade. Milk marketing agreements, in 1939 found constitutional,[1] govern minimum prices to producers and modes of payment.

PRODUCTION CONTROL

Ideally it would appear reasonable for the farmer to cease the wasteful practice of producing more than can be marketed. Some urban critics of American agriculture appear to feel that the fault is due to the farmer's lack of determination. This overlooks the multiform difficulties involved. Producers number in the millions; they grow crops under conditions ever made uncertain by weather and insects; they sell many products in a world-wide market. The problems are so complex that rather few proposals for production control have been made. During the 1920's and early 1930's farm prices declined seriously. After efforts to bolster prices through government purchasing failed, even that historic individualist, the American farmer, was prepared to resort to the controversial expedient of production control. The famed McNary-Haugen bill, passed by Congress and vetoed by President Coolidge in both 1927 and 1928, provided export subsidies, financed by fees on domestic sales, but no production control. The Republican party having rejected the McNary-Haugen bill in its 1928 convention, President Hoover supported hopefully a makeshift measure—

[1] United States *v.* Rock Royal Cooperative, 307 U.S. 533 (1939).

the Agricultural Marketing Act of 1929, emphasizing loans to cooperatives and the purchase and holding of farm commodities during critical times. Prices continued to fall, however, and the Federal Farm Board was left with a large accumulation of wheat and cotton.

Agricultural Adjustment of 1933.—After his election in 1932, President Roosevelt made clear that he would push such farm legislation as the major farm groups could agree upon. The resulting Agricultural Adjustment Act of 1933 was one of the most far-reaching laws in the history of the country.[1] It represented a departure in farm legislation through its production-control features; farm mortgage relief and devaluation of the dollar were appended. The act applied to cotton, wheat, tobacco, corn, hogs, rice, milk, and milk products; later it was applied to other commodities. Several methods were employed by the AAA to bring supply and demand into adjustment. Contracts were offered to farmers who wished to cooperate; if the grower would agree to reduce his production, the government would pay him cash benefits. This money was raised by a tax collected at the processing stage, and the incidence fell upon the consumer except where demand was inelastic. The tax was figured at the difference between the market price and "parity," which was defined as the price necessary to give farm commodities a purchasing power with respect to what farmers buy equal to that existing in 1909–1914. Some commodity loans were made to encourage withholding from the market. A penalty tax was imposed on excess production of cotton and tobacco.

The AAA of 1933 was declared unconstitutional in January, 1936.[2] Constitutional issues that were involved have been dealt with in an earlier chapter. Briefly restated, the Court ruled by a six-to-three vote that the Congress had exceeded its power in controlling production, and that the earmarked tax was discriminatory and invalid. The decision was a shock to farm leaders, many of whom attributed the revival of agriculture after 1933 largely to the AAA program.

Soil Conservation and Domestic Allotment.—A transitional period of 2 years followed the invalidation of some of the main features of the AAA program. The Soil Conservation and Domestic Allotment Act of 1936[3] initiated this period. In place of direct production control, a system was developed to induce farmers to plant soil-conserving crops in place of soil-depleting ones. The incentive offered was a "soil conservation payment," drawn from the general funds of the Treasury and not to exceed 500 million dollars annually. The general goal of adjusting supply to demand and of securing parity for farmers remained. Soil conservation has been dealt with in the following chapter. It should be noted here, however, how it

[1] 48 Stat. 31.

[2] United States *v.* Butler, 297 U.S. 1 (1935). See p. 373.

[3] 49 Stat. 1148.

was used in the interim, 1936 to 1938, to fill the gap left by the invalidation of the production control features of the AAA of 1933.

The Ever-normal Granary.—The Agricultural Adjustment Act of 1938[1] brought back to life much of the voided program of 1933 and represented an important step toward Henry A. Wallace's aspirations for an ever-normal granary. The latter is the idea that surplus crops from good years should be stored for use in poor years, thus regularizing the supply of staple farm products and protecting both farmer and consumer from excessive price fluctuations. The additional goal of soil conservation was continued. So was the long-term objective of securing for the farmer an equitable share of the national income.[2]

The 1938 AAA program employed three methods of achieving adjustment. First, payments were made to farmers who cooperated by reducing acreage of soil-depleting crops and increasing that of soil-restoring crops; each farmer who cooperated was paid for "soil conservation" and for "parity." Second, producers of cotton, corn, wheat, rice, tobacco, and peanuts might, by a two-thirds vote in a referendum, establish acreage allotments and marketing quotas; such quotas might be enforced through tax penalties on sales over the quotas. Third, loans were made on many agricultural commodities to help farmers to keep their crops off the market in years of overproduction, and to market them when supply was less and process higher. The Commodity Credit Corporation, which handled loans for this purpose, is described with other farm credit services.

AAA Operation.—The first two features of the existing AAA program—conservation payments, and acreage allotments—required an extensive field organization. This administrative machinery was dovetailed into and superimposed upon the existing local agricultural structure. The county agents and extension officials assisted both in launching and continuing the AAA, but local administration was directed by committees of farmers elected for the purpose. Farmers that cooperated in the program were members of county agricultural-conservation associations; community committees of three members were elected by each association, and it was upon these committees that the task of recommending acreage allotments and checking compliance fell. The county committee, elected by delegates from the local associations, made the actual acreage allotments among the individual farmers and performed other administrative work. The county agent often was elected as secretary of the county committee, the added expenses incurred by the county agent's office being met in whole or in part by transfer of AAA funds to the state extension services for the purposes.[3]

[1] 52 Stat. 31.

[2] The constitutionality of the 1938 act was upheld in Mulford *v.* Smith, 307 U.S. 38 (1939).

[3] Gladys Baker, *The County Agent* (Chicago: University of Chicago Press, 1939), pp. 79–83. Dr. Baker estimates that 50 per cent of the county secretaries in the ten

Crop Insurance.—Crop insurance against loss has been started by the Federal government, beginning with the wheat crop of 1939 and the cotton crop of 1942. It was authorized by the Agricultural Adjustment Act of 1938 and covers all unavoidable hazards such as hail, flood, drought, wind, disease, and insect damage. The farmer pays a premium computed from the loss history of the farm and other pertinent facts; in case of loss he receives from 50 to 75 per cent of the average yield, payments being made in commodities and not in cash. The program is carried out by the Federal Crop Insurance Corporation, which is within the Department of Agriculture. Crop insurance appears a practical and essential step toward building a security for the farmer roughly comparable to that provided by unemployment insurance for the wage earner. Crop insurance under existing legislation may cover wheat, cotton, flax, corn, tobacco, and other commodities in a limited number of counties.

FARM SECURITY

Rural Poverty.—The varied and extensive services provided for American agriculture, as described above, have affected comparatively little the status or prospects of the depressed or very poor farmer. In 1935 there were 1,700,000 farm families, representing nearly 8,000,000 people, with incomes of $500 per year and less, including value of products used.[1] Such figures do much to dispel the stereotyped idea of the self-sufficient and prosperous farmer. The one-third of farmers ill-fed, ill-clothed, and ill-housed are not in a position to apply the lessons taught by agricultural science. The illiterate cannot read; the uneducated understand only with difficulty; the bankrupt lack security for a loan. For those who live in rural poverty, a special program is needed if agricultural advancements are to be made.

The causes of rural poverty are as varied as those of urban poverty. A recent listing of the more significant ones has been given as follows:[2]

1. The price of land
2. The closed frontier
3. Technology on the farm
4. Poor tenure system
5. Unemployment on the land
6. The growth of rural population
7. Adverse prices and low income
8. Single cropping for cash
9. Soil erosion
10. Natural catastrophes

Since 1935 the Federal government has sought to attack the problem of rural poverty both by providing relief and by attempting to correct the causes.

---

leading corn-hog states were the county agents. The county agent was an ex officio member of the county committee in any case. *Ibid.*, p. 72.

[1] Joseph Gaer, *Toward Farm Security* (Washington: Government Printing Office, 1941), p. 7.

[2] *Ibid.*, p. 10.

One of the most dramatic episodes of the 1930's was the mass migration of hundreds of thousands of impoverished American farm people. They left home farms after suffering from depression, dust storm, and drought and wandered over the face of the country seeking livelihoods. These people needed food, and the Farm Security Administration (FSA) provided the necessary cash. They needed shelter, and the FSA built migratory labor camps for them. While the relief and camp program was concentrated in the West, where the problem was greatest, it was extended to nearly all parts of the country. Fifty-nine camps in all were established; here the migrant family could find shelter for a small payment and the friendly hand and reliable information needed to send it along hopefully to jobs if any existed.

Even earlier the FSA inherited from a predecessor, the Resettlement Administration, the responsibility for constructing and managing homestead projects. Many, but not all, were subsistence homestead projects, designed for impoverished rural and urban families who were stranded in an area of little promise and who needed removal and rehousing for a fresh start. Usually stress was placed upon large garden plots from which the family could obtain subsistence, with the possibility of working for wages part time in neighboring industries or farms.

After the war, with farm income up and close to full employment achieved, the aspect of the program related to relief for victims of rural poverty was curtailed. Since 1946 the Farmers Home Administration[1] has concentrated largely on loans of various types to farmers who cannot elsewhere get the credit they need on reasonable terms. Money may be borrowed for farm operations (such as livestock, equipment, seed, feed, and the like), farm ownership, water facilities, and a few other purposes. Interest rates are similar to those charged by the various lending institutions under the Farm Credit Administration.

If depression comes again the Farmers Home Administration may have added to its loan operations a vast problem of rural relief like the one so capably handled by its predecessor, the FSA.

Wartime Price Supports.—From 1942 to 1948 the Steagall amendment set the basic pattern in farm prices. For the duration of the war plus two years, price supports were made mandatory on the basic commodities at 90 per cent of parity. Other commodities could be included if an increase in production of them were called for by the Secretary of Agriculture; some twenty commodities so qualified.[2] The purpose of the price support pro-

[1] Walter W. Wilcox, *Alternative Policies for American Agriculture,* Public Affairs Bulletin No. 67 (Washington: Library of Congress, 1949), p. 9.

[2] Previously this work was done by the Farm Security Administration. The Farmers Home Administration Act of 1946, 60 Stat. 72, abolished the FSA and defined the present program.

gram—to stimulate production—certainly was achieved. In nearly all commodities the prices received by farmers were above support prices, but the guarantee gave them the confidence necessary to expand production. The wartime support legislation expired at the end of 1948.

Aiken Act of 1948.—Instead of allowing a resumption of the 1938 act, Congress enacted the Agricultural Act of 1948, which extended supports (largely ranging from 60 to 90 per cent of parity) on some nineteen commodities.[1] In 1950 and after, the Aiken Act provided that prices would be supported on a sliding scale depending on the supply of a particular commodity. If supply were abnormally large, support would be set at 60 per cent; if normal, at 75; if below normal, at 90.

The 1948 legislation, popularly known as the "Aiken Act," did not satisfy a large portion of the farmers, and many blamed the Republicans, who had a majority in both houses during the Eightieth Congress. In the 1948 presidential election, state after state with large farm populations and Republican traditions—Ohio, Iowa, Minnesota, Illinois—went for Truman and his advocacy of 90 per cent support prices and a more favorable parity base. By the time the Eighty-first Congress convened it was obvious that some upward revision would alter the Aiken Act if only the various farm groups could agree upon a plan.

Upward Revision of Supports.—The Eighty-first Congress had before it many proposals for changes in the price-support program. The large deficits incurred in supporting the prices of potatoes, peanuts, poultry, and eggs, and the large surpluses on hand of these commodities, resulted in much criticism of price supports. Chief interest centered around the "Brannan plan," sponsored by the Secretary of Agriculture. This plan would permit farm prices to find their "natural" levels through the operation of supply and demand, thus giving the consumer the benefit of any fall in the farm commodity market. The farmer would be assisted and protected by direct subsidy payment of an amount representing the deficiency difference between the price received and the parity price. The Senate, in the first session of the Eighty-first Congress, refused to permit even a "trial run" of the Brannan plan.

The House adopted the Gore bill, which extended something like the wartime arrangement, including a fixed 90 per cent support for basic commodities that are under production control or marketing quotas. The Senate passed the Anderson bill, which provided for a flexible support at 75 to 90 per cent of parity. In conference committee, Administration spokesmen successfully pressed for the more rigid and higher guarantee.

Although the 1949 legislation will govern the next crop year, the Brannan

[1] United States Department of Agriculture, Production and Marketing Administration, *Price Programs of the United States Department of Agriculture, 1949*, Misc. Pub. 683 (Washington: Government Printing Office, 1949).

plan doubtless will be revived in another session of Congress. It may yet prove to be the means through which farmers secure income stabilization, and consumers receive the benefits of "natural" prices, the balance being paid out of federal revenues.

Proponents of the Brannan Plan claim it will do away with induced scarcity and put in its place a program of expanding consumption and farm income. Farmers would be encouraged to shift from overproduced commodities, like wheat and cotton, to products in shorter supply, such as dairy products, meat, fruits, and vegetables. This change-over would be induced by providing firm and favorable price supports on livestock and perishables. Since these commodities cannot easily be stored and held over from season to season, the Brannan Plan calls for direct subsidies to compensate the farmer for the difference between the market price and the supported price. These subsidies would encourage farmers to grow more of the needed crops and provide valuable foods to the consumer at lower prices, thus increasing consumption.

References

Ackerman, Joseph, and Marshall Harris (eds.): *Family Farm Policy* (Chicago: University of Chicago Press, 1947).

Baker, Gladys: *The County Agent* (Chicago: University of Chicago Press, 1939).

Ball, Carleton R.: *Federal, State, and Local Interrelationships in Agriculture* (Berkeley and Los Angeles: University of California Press, 2 vols., 1938).

Benedict, Murray R.: *Farm People and the Land after the War*, Planning Pamphlet No. 28 (Washington: National Planning Association, 1943).

Black, John D.: *Agricultural Reform in the United States* (New York: McGraw-Hill, 1929).

——— *Parity, Parity, Parity* (Cambridge, Mass.: Harvard University Press, 1942).

Blaisdell, Donald C., Jr.: *Government and Agriculture* (New York: Rinehart, 1940).

Clark, William H.: *Farms and Farmers: The Story of American Agriculture* (Boston: L. C. Page & Company, 1945).

Davis, Joseph S.: *On Agricultural Policy* (New York: Food Research Institute, 1939).

Deering, Ferdie: *USDA, Manager of American Agriculture* (Norman, Okla.: University of Oklahoma Press, 1945).

Fainsod, Merle, and Lincoln Gordon: *Government and the American Economy* (New York: Norton, 1941).

Gaus, John M., and Leon O. Wolcott: *Public Administration and the United States Department of Agriculture* (Chicago: Public Administration Service, 1940).

Gee, Wilson: *The Social Economics of Agriculture* (New York: Norton, 1932).

Lyon, Leveret S., and Others: *Government and Economic Life* (Washington: Brookings, 2 vols., 1939–1940).

Rightmire, George W.: *Federal Aid and Regulation of Agriculture and Private Industrial Enterprise in the United States* (Columbus, Ohio: The Ohio State University Press, 1944).

Sparks, Earl S.: *History and Theory of Agricultural Credit in the United States* (New York: Crowell, 1932).

Taylor, Paul S.: *Adrift on the Land*, Public Affairs Pamphlet No. 42 (New York: Public Affairs Committee, 1940).

TRUMAN, DAVID B.: *Administrative Decentralization: a Study of the Chicago Field Office of the United States Department of Agriculture* (Chicago: University of Chicago Press, 1940).

UNITED STATES COMMISSION ON ORGANIZATION OF THE EXECUTIVE BRANCH OF THE GOVERNMENT ("HOOVER COMMISSION"): *Department of Agriculture* (Washington: Government Printing Office, 1949).

——— *Task Force Report on Agriculture Activities* (Washington: Government Printing Office, 1949).

UNITED STATES DEPARTMENT OF AGRICULTURE: *Yearbook* (Washington: Government Printing Office, annual).

WILCOX, WALTER W.: *Alternative Policies for American Agriculture,* Public Affairs Bulletin No. 67 (Washington: Library of Congress, 1949).

——— *The Farmer in the Second World War* (Ames: Iowa State College, 1947).

Chapter 35

CONSERVATION OF NATURAL RESOURCES

> The two billion acres of land within the United States; the rain and snow that fall on this land; the rivers, waterfalls, and lakes; the coal, oil, gold, and silver, and other mineral deposits that lie on and beneath the land; the people that live here and their multitude of talents, skills, and activities form our natural resources. The wealth of the nation is measured in the way we conserve, use, and develop these resources.
>
> National Resources Committee,
> *National Resources Planning Facts.*[1]

Nature provided America bounteously with great riches, living and inanimate. The story of man's use of them and of what he has done to preserve them for posterity is of greatest importance. The natural wealth of the United States makes possible a high standard of living if these resources are used wisely. But if our forests, soil, waters, minerals, fish, animals, and birds are exploited and wasted, future generations may be condemned to live in barren poverty.

The fact is that the natural resources of the United States already have been devastated and severed to a serious extent. Experts estimate that one-third of the nation's farm land has been ruined or impoverished by soil erosion. The inroads of wind and water are made because our people have overgrazed the grasslands, have farmed land that never should have been ploughed, have cleared land that should have remained in forest. After man removed the protective covering of trees, shrubs, and grasses, erosion began to take away the fertile topsoil, leaving waste lands. The removal of vegetation, together with the added numbers of hunters and fishers, brought death and destruction to wild life as well.

Below the surface men tap mineral resources to serve a growing population. An obvious ugliness often accompanies severance of subsoil deposits. Even more serious, however, is the likelihood of exhaustion of essential mineral resources like oil, copper, zinc, and lead. At the present rate of severance, these deposits will soon be gone, and this will necessitate vast changes in the economic life of the country.

THE RISE OF CONSERVATION

The Coming of Conservation.—One of the first observations made by the student of nature is that a sort of balance exists. In the primeval forest a delicate adjustment developed naturally. Trees and grasses held

[1] (Washington: Government Printing Office, 1939), p. 1.

and enriched the soil, and provided food and protection for birds and animals. Waters irrigated vegetation and harbored fish and fowl. Each animal appeared to have its natural enemy or rival, and one form of life rarely triumphed completely and permanently over another. The Indian disturbed the way of nature but little. He fished and hunted and tilled the soil, but always in moderation. The fine balance of nature remained until the coming of the white man.

The white man took what he wanted of nature's gifts. He chopped down trees for his houses, he cleared land for his fields, he killed off animals for food and for sport. For 300 years the North American continent was exploited with little consideration for the morrow. After the coming of industrialization the waste became even more obvious. Mineral deposits were tapped and exhausted, and the surface was littered with ugly debris. Mechanical tractors were used to plough up the prairie grasses that sustained life and held down the soil. Industrial plants and cities poured out their waste, polluting streams and rendering them unable to sustain fish or impossible for human consumption. Forests were ground up into pulp to feed the mills for paper, rayon, and a hundred other uses. Fabulous wealth was made from petroleum—black gold—but the American people have suffered the depletion of their oil resources and the loss of natural gases burned as waste.

The white man has not yet fully reformed; the spoiler is still around. But increasingly citizens have recognized that the balance of nature must be restored, that the power of the government must be utilized to save what is left and to rebuild the resources that have been exploited. Those who have taken part in this work are called "conservationists," and the total program is called the "conservation movement."

The Conservation Movement.—The original white American conservationist has not been found. Perhaps he was a pilgrim farmer who alternated his crops, or the frontiersman who was careful with his fire and who killed only such game as he could eat, or perhaps it was William Penn, who in 1681 required that one acre out of every five should not be cleared but left in trees. In any case, not all of our forefathers were wasters: many recognized that a devastated farm was no heritage for their sons, and therefore did what they could to preserve the land and forests and waters.

Much more is known about the beginnings of organized attempts to save natural resources in the second half of the nineteenth century. One of the first organizations to commence work in this field was the American Forestry Association, which was launched in 1875.[1] Soon Congress author-

[1] Wallace W. Atwood, "The Conservation Movement in America," in Almon E. Parkins and Joe R. Whitaker (eds.), *Our Natural Resources and Their Conservation* (New York: Wiley, 2d ed., 1939), p. 3.

ized a forestry agent in the Department of Agriculture and established the first national forest reserve in 1891. Attention was given even earlier to protection of fisheries; the post of Federal Commissioner of Fish and Fisheries was created in 1871. Two aspects of conservation developed from sections of the Geological Survey: an irrigation division was established in 1888 and it began federal reclamation work; the attention given to mining in the survey led to the development of the many services of the Bureau of Mines.[1]

Great impetus was given to the conservation movement during the Theodore Roosevelt administration (1901–1909). The national forests, previously under the Department of the Interior, were transferred in 1905 to the Department of Agriculture, Bureau of Forestry. Roosevelt withdrew millions of acres from the public domain and placed them in national forests. In 1908 President Roosevelt assembled a distinguished company of federal officials, governors of states, and conservationists for a "White House Conference" on conservation.[2] He followed this with the appointment of a National Conservation Commission, which was headed by Chief Forester Gifford Pinchot of Pennsylvania. Its task was to inventory natural resources of the country and to report on the possibility of their exhaustion. By the close of Roosevelt's full term great progress had been made toward saving the public lands and their resources from selfish exploitation, and an auspicious beginning had been made in the modern conservation movement.

By 1950 the conservation movement sparked by Theodore Roosevelt had run its course. Great champions like Roosevelt and Pinchot were gone, and public interest in natural resources waned. The public agencies that had been created, the citizens' associations that had been formed, the policies that had been written on the statute books—all these might hold the line against those who would overexploit resources *if* the people took an intelligent interest. Much evidence exists to indicate that the spoilers again constitute an acute threat to the nation's natural heritage. Only rarely is the issue black versus white, good against bad. Cattle and sheep graze on public lands under permits issued by federal agencies. Admittedly the livestock industry produces valuable foodstuffs for the American consumer. When, however, the stockman's urge to produce more leads him to overgraze the range, the results may be floods, erosion, destruction of wildlife, and ruin to grasslands.

The attack on conservation is made on many fronts. The Forest Service may be rendered less effective by reducing its appropriations below the level necessary for efficient operation. The public lands may be sold

[1] F. G. Tryon, "Conservation," *Encyclopedia of the Social Sciences*, vol. 4, pp. 227–229.

[2] Atwood, *op. cit.*, pp. 6–7.

to private interests and thereby taken out of strict regulation. The housing shortage can be used as justification for relaxed standards in logging and reforestation rules. A high tariff can be used to exclude foreign petroleum, thus stimulating the further depletion of domestic reserves. Reclamation laws may be amended to allow big interests to swallow up small ones. So far the line has been held on most fronts. It remains to be seen whether leadership can be found again to stimulate public interest in conservation as did Roosevelt and Pinchot just after the turn of the century.[1]

Federal Conservation Agencies.—Most of the federal agencies concerned primarily with conservation are located in the Department of the Interior. It is a vast department that spreads out like a tent to cover many diverse services. The Secretary has one undersecretary and two assistant secretaries. The Hoover Commission proposed one additional assistant secretary. The major operating agencies of the department which are concerned directly or incidentally with natural resources are the Bureau of Land Management, Bureau of Reclamation, Fish and Wildlife Service, Geological Survey, and National Park Service.

In the Department of Agriculture both the soil conservation service and the forest service are conservation activities. During the depression of the thirties many of the relief and rehabilitation programs instituted by the Federal and state governments did much to aid the cause of conservation. The most important of these to conservation was the Civilian Conservation Corps (CCC) which took young men into the countryside to work on natural resource development.

SOIL AND WATER

Soil Conservation.—The soil is the No. 1 natural resource. Waste of it has been spread over such a long period, however, that one has difficulty dramatizing the need for its conservation. When lands on the Eastern seaboard declined in fertility, settlers moved on west to new lands. So long as new lands were still available in the West, farmers were able to avoid the consequences of wasteful cropping. After all good lands were taken up, the problem of taking proper care of the soil could no longer be avoided. Much more than restoring fertility to the soil was involved; certainly some restoration is accomplished through fertilization. The problem is one of restoring nature's balance or something akin to it.

In the first place, the early settlers removed the natural cover from the ground. The grasses, shrubs, and trees protected the soil from wind and water, conditioned it by adding humus—which made it porous, and restored

[1] An able exponent of the conservation revival is Bernard DeVoto, who writes the "Easy Chair" for *Harper's Magazine*. See his article, "Sacred Cows and Public Lands," *ibid.*, vol. 197 (July, 1948), pp. 44–55.

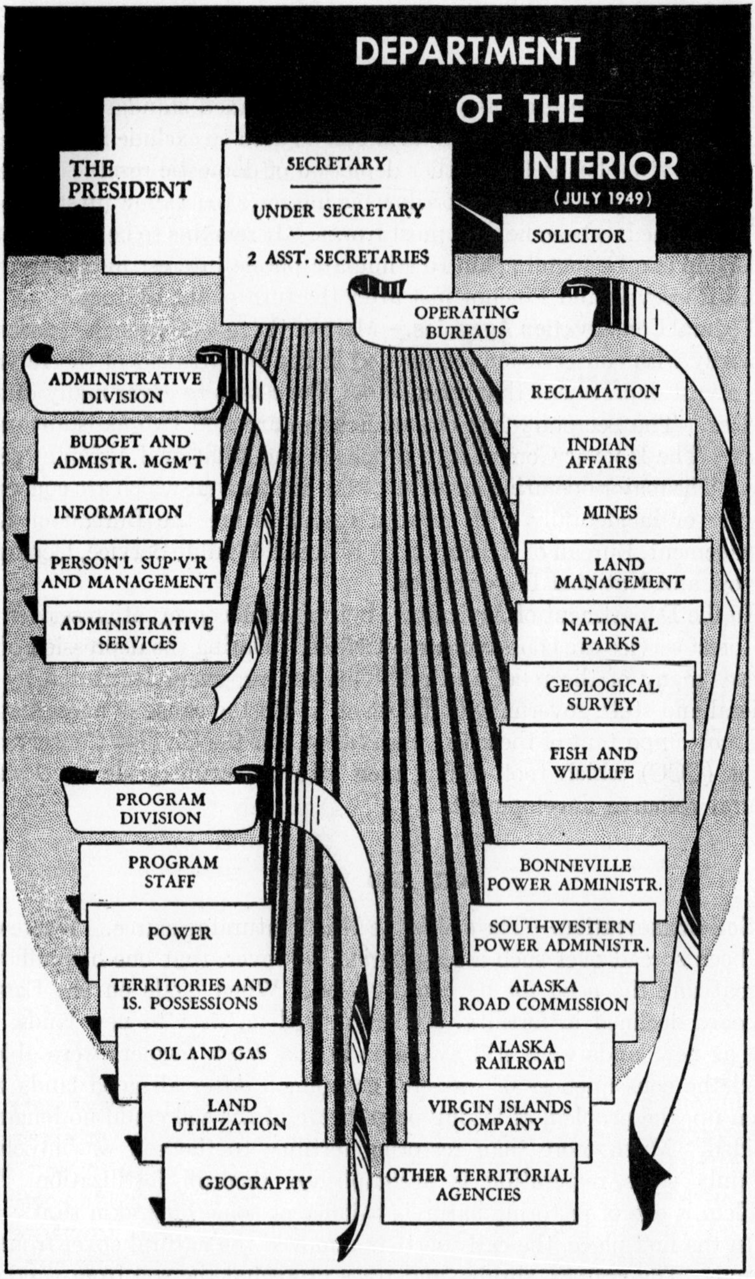

The extensive transfers to and from the Department of Interior, proposed by the Hoover Commission, were not put into effect during 1949. The Department retains Indian Affairs, Land Management, and commercial fisheries—all suggested for transfer to other departments. It has not acquired the flood control and rivers and harbors duties of the Army Engineers, as recommended by the Hoover group. SOURCE: Prepared from data in *United States Government Manual*, 1949, p. 586.

minerals used in plant growth. Man ploughed and planted, and reaped the harvest. The most obvious destruction that followed came through water erosion. Hilly lands, stripped of the binding power of roots of natural vegetation, gullied and the soil washed down to the lowlands, perhaps to the sea. In many areas the whole layer of topsoil washed away. Moreover, the capacity of the soil to retain moisture was impaired seriously; for few farmers made provision for restoring vegetable matter to the land.

Federal lands, under the control of different agencies, yet intermingled and adjacent, are commonly found in the western states. The major conflict is between the Forest Service of the Department of Agriculture and the Bureau of Land Management of the Department of the Interior. The Hoover Commission recommended that they be consolidated in Agriculture. SOURCE: Hoover Commission, *Department of Agriculture*, pp. 23–26. This diagram is from *Concluding Report*, p. 30.

The burning strawstack after the harvest often was a symbol of wastefulness and ignorance. After the water erosion came wind erosion: sweeping over cultivated land in the Middle West, winds have been known to carry great quantities of earth for a thousand miles and more across half a continent.

The first approach of the American government to soil conservation was to encourage farmers to adopt soil-saving practices through educational work. The United States Department of Agriculture has long carried out investigations in soil building, and so have the experiment stations maintained by each of the states. The information is sent to farmers through publications, demonstrations, and the field work of farm-adviser or county agent extension services. Among practices advocated through the years have been crop rotation, contour ploughing, check dams, reforestation, cover cropping, and the like.

In 1933 a soil-erosion service was established in the federal Department of the Interior; in 1935 it was transferred to the Department of Agriculture and assigned the name Soil Conservation Service.[1] The service seeks to spread the use of soil-erosion-control practices through (1) demonstrations in selected areas, and (2) assistance of soil-conservation districts organized under state laws. By 1949 there were over 2,000 soil-conservation districts, embracing nearly 4½ million farms. The service aids these farmer-managed districts with technical advice, materials, and equipment.

Water Conservation.—When angry flood waters swirl seaward, taking with them a toll in life and property, people may think of water as a demon. In ordinary times, however, water properly is regarded as life-giver. Enormous quantities of water are required to support plant and animal life. If you take a globe and whirl it around, the light blue color predominates; for roughly three-quarters of the surface of the earth is covered with water. Nature's process, of course, involves the taking up of moisture through evaporation, and returning it to the earth's surface through rain, snow, or other precipitation. Man has not interfered with this cycle seriously, but he has altered the power of the soil to hold moisture and the flow and purity of streams.

When settling in a new section of the country, one of the first considerations of the pioneer was to secure an adequate supply of water. If springs or lakes or streams were not available or were inadequate, wells were dug to tap subsurface waters. As consumption increased, water levels fell and deeper wells were required. Large cities in semiarid districts bring water great distances; Los Angeles is served from behind the Sierra Nevada Mountains and from the Colorado River, distances of 170 and 270 miles, respectively. Great areas of the West have rich land but insufficient rainfall to support agriculture; vast reclamation projects of the Federal government have made the irrigated deserts bloom.

Government has played a major role in getting water to the people and to the land. Domestic water supply is furnished over much of the country by municipally owned projects. Water for irrigation often is supplied through public irrigation districts. The Bureau of Reclamation of the Department of the Interior has constructed and operates some huge dam projects in western United States. These projects generally are multipurpose. They serve to make water available for irrigation, to generate hydroelectric power, and to aid in flood control. Sometimes they improve navigation, provide recreational facilities, and control salt water encroachment as well. Some of the most important reclamation projects of recent

[1] See Hugh H. Bennett, "Soil Erosion and Its Prevention," in Parkins and Whitaker, *op. cit.*, pp. 85–93.

years have been Hoover Dam on the Colorado River, the Central Valley Project in California, the Grand Coulee and the Bonneville Dams on the Columbia River.[1]

Protection of the flow and purity of streams has been approached from several angles. Dams constructed for power, flood control, or domestic and irrigation purposes may serve also to regularize stream flow, which in turn permits fish propagation and recreational uses. Pollution is controlled primarily by state law, prohibiting dumping of industrial waste or raw sewage into rivers. Where a stream flows through several states, interstate action may prove necessary. Such is the case with the Delaware River, which is controlled by the Interstate Commission on the Delaware River Basin (Incodel), an agency of Delaware, New Jersey, New York, and Pennsylvania. Since 1936 this commission has provided the machinery through which joint state action can be planned for the orderly development of the basin and the correction of pollution.

FORESTS AND WILD LIFE

Forest Conservation.—In its virgin state, at the beginning of white settlement in North America, the land area that is now the United States was about 43 per cent forested.[2] These forests have been seriously depleted: some of the timber has been used for construction, fuel, and industry; the remainder has been wasted and destroyed. The many uses of wood in modern life are well known. About one-half of forest cut, according to Guise, is used for lumber; one-fourth goes into fuel; the remainder into miscellaneous industrial products.

It has already been shown that forests provide a natural cover for soil and for animal and bird life. When forests are cleared, soil is exposed to erosion, game is left without protective cover, and streams are filled with silt. Trees also act as windbreaks, reducing wind erosion of the soil. It also appears that forests have a moderating influence on climate, reducing heat in summer, protecting against cold winds in winter, providing moisture for crops and comfort. The recreational value of forests has been recognized by national, state, and local governments in the parks, forests, and resorts that have been provided for public use and enjoyment.

All this is not to be taken as argument against any severance of the timber in American forests. The usual way of life could scarcely continue without utilization of timber resources. The point is that our remaining forest resources should be used wisely, in order that future generations

[1] See p. 712.

[2] Cedric H. Guise, "Conservation of Forests, Parks, and Grazing Lands," in Axel F. Gustafson and Others, *Conservation in the United States* (Ithaca: Comstock Publishing Company, Inc., 1939), p. 162.

may have an adequate supply for use and enjoyment. In evaluating the prospects for forest conservation, the ownership pattern of forest lands looms of great importance. A report filed with Congress in 1933 shows that there were 614,558,000 acres of forest lands.[1] Of this acreage 484,898,000 were classed as commercial and 119,660,000 as noncommercial. Twenty per cent of the commercial forest land was owned by governments, primarily the Federal government. The four-fifths under private ownership is divided into 55 per cent owned by lumber companies and other industries, and 25 per cent included in farm wood lots. Since governments hold their forests for purposes other than profit, they can be trusted to resist exploitation of their holdings. In general, logging operations are permitted only on a selective basis, with public foresters marking the trees that may be felled, and enforcing rigid specifications for protection of young growth. The more the public ownership of forest lands spreads, the greater the assurance that this natural resource will be available for posterity. Farm wood-lot trees are relatively safe from wholesale devastation; for the farmer commonly regards trees as a crop and recognizes the necessity of replanting.

Private Ownership.—The great problem is regulating the industrial owner of commercial forest lands. He is in the business of cutting and marketing timber products, and his primary motivation often is immediate profit. Mechanized logging operations take not only mature trees but destroy young growth and leave debris that constitutes a serious fire hazard. The more progressive lumbering concerns have cooperated with the Forest Service of the Department of Agriculture in fire prevention and reforestation work, but the great majority have devastated the forests with little thought of the morrow. Governments can encourage wise use of timber by a tax policy that does not penalize the owner for keeping growing trees to full maturity; some states have done this by exempting forests from ordinary real-property taxes, and collecting instead a severance tax at the time the trees are felled. States can do more than they have to require reforestation by laws, based on the state police power, forcing a replanting program upon concerns or individuals who engage in lumbering operations.

The geographical distribution of forest lands is worthy of attention. The South has nearly one-third of all forest acreage, but the Pacific coast has by far the greatest quantity of saw timber, capable of use as lumber. An important development in the South during recent years has been the establishment of pulp mills to utilize southern pine. Most of the publicly owned forest lands are in the West; one-half or more of commercial forest

[1] United States Department of Agriculture, Forest Service, *A National Plan for American Forestry*, Sen. Doc. 12, 73d Cong., 1st Sess. (Washington: Government Printing Office, 2 vols., 1933), vol. 2, p. 122.

areas of the Rocky Mountain and Pacific coast regions are owned by governments. The ownership pattern in all other sections is predominantly private, with all the attendant problems of control. Guise points out that no one can estimate when our forest resources will be exhausted; for the trees are growing constantly and demand for lumber is inconstant. Virgin forests of large and slow-growing trees are likely to be exhausted rather soon, for their severance exceeds the rate of growth. By constant care and wise management, it is altogether possible that an adequate supply of forest products will be available for generations.

The United States Forest Service.—The Forest Service, Department of Agriculture, is by far the most influential of government agencies working in the field of forest conservation. Custody of the 160 national forests is entrusted to the service. It provides fire protection, disease control, recreational facilities, and regulation of grazing and timber harvesting. In addition, the Forest Service conducts an extensive research program on every aspect of forest management and utilization. The service cooperates with the states in the development of state forests and works with private forest interests in conservation work.

National forests, excluding Alaskan and Puerto Rican forests, occupy 159 million acres, one-twelfth of the nation's land area. Of this vast area, 123 million acres are actually forested lands. The Federal government began withdrawing forest lands from the public domain in 1891, but it was not until 1911 that the purchase of lands was authorized by law. Most of the national forest lands are remote and inaccessible, a fact that has handicapped the Forest Service in administering them. Many of the federally owned areas are poorly consolidated, being fragmentized by plots under private ownership. Until the Second World War, the Forest Service held most of the national forest timber on a stand-by basis, for use after private holdings were exploited. Despite heavy drains on national forests during and after the war, however, by 1948 they contained one-third of the nation's saw-timber resources.

The general principles that guide the management of the national forests were stated recently by the Forest Service as follows:[1] (1) to serve the greatest public good in the long run; (2) to build up and perpetuate forests through wise care and use; (3) to provide maximum public benefits through multiple use; and (4) to work closely with state, local, and regional agencies and to adapt to local conditions.

Other Public Forests.—In addition to the vast holdings of the Forest Service, other federal agencies have jurisdiction over nearly 55 million acres of forest lands, of which over 15 million are commercial. The great-

[1] United States Department of Agriculture, Forest Service, *Forests and National Prosperity*, Miscellaneous Publication No. 668 (Washington: Government Printing Office, 1948), p. 88.

est block of this is under the Bureau of Land Management, Department of the Interior, which controls grazing lands, public domain, and certain other lands rich in timber resources. The Indian Service, Department of the Interior, also manages a vast area of forest lands. The National and other agencies account for the balance of federally owned forest lands.

The extent of state and local ownership of forest lands is approximately 38 million acres, the largest share of which is located in Northern states.

In recent years there has been much controversy over the continuation and expansion of publicly owned lands. Private grazing, lumbering, and other interests complain over the alleged severity of restrictions imposed upon users of federal lands. State and local governments are concerned over the large amounts of tax-exempt land within their territorial jurisdictions. The Forest Service lists six categories for which it regards public ownership of forest lands as best: (1) where soil, climate, species, or other factors make for slow growth or poor quality; (2) where large investment and long waiting will be required because of depletion of timber-growing stock; (3) where private management is inadequate and a threat to stable supplies and dependent communities; (4) where public ownership is vital to control and use of water; (5) where area has high value for recreation, wild life propagation, and the like; and (6) where lands are so intermingled with public forests that they hamper proper management of the public.[1]

Applying such principles as these, and given fair dealing with affected private interests and generous payments in lieu of taxation to other governments, surely satisfactory ways can be found to manage public forests and other lands.

The National Park Service.—Our national park system, containing some of the great natural wonders of the world, is administered by the National Park Service, Department of the Interior. These beautiful park areas are preserved, maintained, and developed for the enjoyment of the people. The brash commercialization that has spoiled some Eastern works of nature is prevented from entering Yellowstone, Yosemite, Sequoia, Grand Canyon, Smoky Mountain, and the other national parks. The primary purpose of the service is to preserve and to develop natural beauty spots and historical monuments for the recreation and enjoyment of the people. Hundreds of thousands of visitors each year visit the national parks, which provide a guarantee that the wonders included in them will never be despoiled by man.

Fish and Wild Life Conservation.—Since 1940 the fish and wild life conservation work of the Federal government has been performed by a consolidated Fish and Wild Life Service, Department of the Interior. Previously, two agencies—the Bureau of Fisheries and the Bureau of Biological Survey, both of the Department of the Interior—performed the work in

[1] *Ibid.*, p. 91.

their separate fields. The state has extensive fish and game functions, and much of the primary work of conservation in this field is done through state and local agencies and laws.

Fish represents an important food for man. Many thousands of people have an economic stake in the fishing industry, as fishermen, handlers, or canners. Many more are sportsmen, who fish for recreation and enjoyment. The last factor, especially, has given much impetus to the fish-conservation movement; some of the commercial fishing interests have shown intelligent interest in protecting the supply of fish.

The research investigations that disclose the principles upon which a fish-conservation program shall be based are conducted both by the Federal Fish and Wild Life Service and by the state fish and game agencies. Both levels of government operate hatcheries for the propagation of fishes; the young stock is then planted in suitable waters. State and federal agencies assist and regulate commercial fishermen; state authority is most extensive, but federal jurisdiction extends to the highly important Alaskan seal and salmon industry and permits patrol activities on the high seas under some treaty arrangements. Basic protection is obtained for the fish supply through the enforcement of seasonal limits and quantitative restrictions, mostly imposed by state law. Although at one time certain species of fish almost wholly disappeared, careful management and propagation have restored them.

Native animals and birds provided an important part of the foodstuffs consumed by the pioneers of this country. They are less important today as food but remain valuable for their furs, service to agriculture, and recreational incentive. Many types of wild life have been reduced to extinction or near extinction. The buffalo, once numbering perhaps 60 million in North America, is now only a few thousand.[1] The beautiful passenger pigeon is fully extinct; wild ducks and geese have been depleted to a fraction of their former numbers; antelope, elk, and moose have become rare. Wild life has been decimated by excessive hunting and trapping, the destruction of natural haunts, lack of food, and other reasons. Some reduction of wild life would have seemed inevitable as settlement spread across the country: predatory animals were killed off for good reason; fenced farms reduced the feeding areas of animals.

The Federal Fish and Wild Life Service forms the spearhead of the nation's bird and animal conservation work. It conducts research both of its own and in cooperation with state agencies. The service administers federal grants to states for wild-life restoration. One of its most important duties is to protect migratory birds covered by treaty; it licenses hunters and limits their kill of protected birds. Some 251 wild-life refuges

[1] William J. Hamilton, "Conservation of Wildlife," in Gustafson and Others, *op. cit.*, pp. 298–301.

have been created and maintained by the service. In the states well-developed fish and game agencies enforce the game laws, license hunters, and provide refuges and propagation facilities.

MINERALS AND LAND

Mineral Resources.—After the Japanese invasion of Malaya and Netherlands East Indies in 1942, great interest was shown in the loss to this country of its principal source of tin. The needs of modern war for aluminum emphasized our deficiencies in another mineral. The war brought out as nothing ever has the importance of having an adequate supply of the essential mineral resources. The United States was blessed by nature with a greater abundance of mineral deposits than those found in any other country. The chief deficiencies of this country in metals are in chromite, manganese, nickel and tin.[1] Our iron supply comes primarily from the deposits around Lake Superior; while these may be exhausted in the next generation, adequate quantities of lower grade ore are available for posterity. Copper comes largely from the Western states; while the United States appears to have about one-third of the copper deposits of the world, it is using them at a fairly rapid rate and may someday suffer. Bauxite, the mineral from which aluminum is extracted, is found in Arkansas, but great quantities are imported also from British and Netherlands Guiana. Lead is a major product of Missouri, but the deposits are being mined so rapidly that a serious shortage may result. Zinc is highly important for galvanizing iron to prevent rust; American deposits are mainly in Oklahoma and New Jersey and are sufficiently limited to cause concern over future supply. Gold and silver are found in considerable quantities in the United States. The country is short on both chromium and manganese, which are so essential in steel production. Nickel is available in Canada.

Prof. H. Ries has pointed out several methods by which mineral resources may be conserved: (1) improved mining methods can reduce waste; (2) better processes of mineral separation to avoid loss; (3) more economical use of finished products; (4) extensive use of scrap materials; (5) federal and state measures of conservation to promote saving.[2] The Federal and state governments are working on each of the fronts suggested. The Bureau of Mines, Department of the Interior, carries on research programs touching upon the first four points mentioned above. It carries out a safety program directed toward saving life and property from loss in

[1] See Charles K. Leith and D. M. Liddell, *The Mineral Resources of the United States and Its Capacity for Production* (Washington: Government Printing Office, 1936). A National Resources Board study.

[2] Heinrich Ries, "Conservation of Mineral Resources," in Gustafson and Others, *op. cit.*, pp. 354.

mining accidents. It produces helium gas for use by the Army and Navy. The bureau has extensive responsibilities for carrying out investigations of strategic minerals.

Still broad is the work of the Geological Survey, Department of the Interior, which investigates mineral and water resources, classifies public lands, prepares topographic maps. The Survey is in a commanding position over government lands, in its role of supervisor of oil, gas, and mining operations under leases. It also investigates water supplies. During the war it was given crucial tasks in finding new sources of strategic minerals.

Coal Conservation.—Coal is one of the most valuable nonmetal mineral resources. It is plentiful in the United States, with reserves adequate to care almost indefinitely for the needs of a great population. The distribution over the country is rather well known. Anthracite, or hard coal, is found only in the eastern half of Pennsylvania. Bituminous, soft coal, is found in a belt stretching from Pennsylvania to Alabama, on both sides of the Mississippi River, and in the southern Rocky Mountains. The lower grades of coal, lignite and subbituminous, are scattered through the South and West. New England and the Pacific coast are almost wholly without usable coal deposits.

The Bureau of Mines devotes much attention to coal production and utilization. Because the demand for coal slumped after the First World War, especially in the 1930's, special arrangements were made to care for the sick industry. The first remedial legislation was the Bituminous Coal Conservation Act of 1935, known as the Guffey Act, declared unconstitutional in Carter *v.* Carter Coal Co.[1] In 1937 Congress enacted the more modest Bituminous Coal Act. President Roosevelt abolished the commission created under the act in a reorganization of 1939 and vested its functions in the Bituminous Coal Division, Department of the Interior. The conservation aspects of its work were meager, for it existed primarily to enforce a code that covered fair trade practices, minimum prices, and the like. State governments and universities provide many services to coal miners and coal users.

Federal Land Policy.—The greater portion of the country's land has, at one time or another, belonged to the Federal government. Had the government kept title to these lands, the tasks of planning and conservation might be much simpler today. On the other hand, the inducement of lands in the West drove men to seek their fortunes on the frontier. Of the total public lands of 1,800 million acres, over 1 billion were turned over to state and private owners.[2] These included homesteads, sales, grants to states, and grants to railroads. The acreage remaining under federal title

[1] 298 U.S. 238 (1936). See also p. 660.

[2] Stephen S. Visher, "The Public Domain and Its Disposal," in Parkins and Whitaker, *op. cit.*, pp. 21–23.

included national forests and parks, grazing districts, Indian reservations, and other lands withdrawn from entry.

The Bureau of Land Management, Department of the Interior, is the agency with general custody of public lands. It handles the survey, management, and disposition of the public domain. Virtually all government lands suitable for agriculture have long since been granted or sold. The office issues permits and leases for grazing, mining, and other uses of the lands under its jurisdiction.

The Grazing Service of the Department of the Interior had jurisdiction over 142 million acres of range lands in the West until 1946, when it became part of the newly created Bureau of Land Management. The bureau leases lands to stock owners under a policy that requires close supervision to prevent overgrazing, with attendant losses through erosion and flood.

References

American Forestry Association: *American Forests* (Washington: The Association, monthly).

Bateman, Allan M.: *Economic Mineral Deposits* (New York: Wiley, 1942).

Bennett, Hugh H.: *Soil Conservation* (New York: McGraw-Hill, 1939).

Chase, Stuart: *Rich Land, Poor Land* (New York: McGraw-Hill, 1936).

De Roos, Robert W.: *The Thirsty Land: The Story of the Central Valley Project* (Stanford University, Calif.: Stanford University Press, 1948).

Dewhurst, J. Frederic, and Others: *America's Needs and Resources* (New York: Twentieth Century Fund, 1947).

Du Puy, William A.: *The Nation's Forests* (New York: Macmillan, 1938).

Finch, Vernor C., Glenn T. Trewartha, and M. H. Shearer: *The Earth and Its Resources* (New York: McGraw-Hill, 2d ed., 1948).

Flynn, Harry E., and Floyd E. Perkins: *Conservation of the Nation's Resources* (New York: Macmillan, 1941).

Gabrielson, Ira: *Wildlife Conservation* (New York: Macmillan, 1941).

Glover, Katherine: *America Begins Again* (New York: McGraw-Hill, 1939).

Gustafson, Axel F., and Others: *Conservation in the United States* (Ithaca: Comstock Publishing Company, Inc., 2d ed., 1944).

Holbrook, Stewart H.: *Burning an Empire, The Story of American Forest Fires* (New York: Macmillan, 1943).

Ise, John: *United States Forest Policy* (New Haven: Yale University Press, 1920).

——— *United States Oil Policy* (New Haven: Yale University Press, 1926).

Jacks, Graham V., and R. O. White: *Vanishing Lands* (New York: Doubleday, 1939).

Leith, Charles K.: *World Minerals and World Peace* (Washington: Brookings, 1943).

National Parks Association: *National Parks Magazine* (Washington: The Association, quarterly).

Neuberger, Richard L.: *Our Promised Land* (New York: Macmillan, 1939).

Parkins, Almon E., and Joe R. Whitaker (eds.): *Our National Resources and Their Conservation* (New York: Wiley, 2d ed., 1939).

Renner, George T.: *Conservation of Natural Resources, An Educational Approach to the Problem* (New York: Wiley, 1942).

Robbins, Roy M.: *Our Landed Heritage, the Public Domain, 1776–1936* (Princeton, N.J.: Princeton University Press, 1942).

Royal Institute of International Affairs: *World Production of Raw Materials*, Information Department Papers, No. 18B (London: Oxford, 1941).

United States Commission on Organization of the Executive Branch of the Government ("Hoover Commission"): *Reorganization of the Department of the Interior* (Washington: Government Printing Office, 1949).

——— *Task Force Report on Natural Resources* (Washington: Government Printing Office, 1949).

United States Department of Agriculture, Forest Service: *A National Plan for American Forestry*, Sen. Doc. 12, 74th Cong., 1st Sess. (Washington: Government Printing Office, 2 vols., 1933).

——— *Forests and National Prosperity*, Misc. Publication No. 668 (Washington: Government Printing Office, 1948).

United States Department of the Interior, Bureau of Reclamation: *The Reclamation Era* (Washington: Government Printing Office, monthly).

United States Department of the Interior, Fish and Wild Life Service: *Fishery Resources of the United States*, House Doc. 51, 78th Cong. 1st Sess. (Washington: Government Printing Office, 1945).

Appendix I

THE DECLARATION OF INDEPENDENCE

In Congress, July 4, 1776

THE UNANIMOUS DECLARATION OF THE THIRTEEN UNITED STATES OF AMERICA

When in the Course of human events, it becomes necessary for one people to dissolve the political bands which have connected them with another, and to assume among the Powers of the earth, the separate and equal station to which the Laws of Nature and of Nature's God entitle them, a decent respect to the opinions of mankind requires that they should declare the causes which impel them to the separation.

We hold these truths to be self-evident, that all men are created equal, that they are endowed by their Creator with certain unalienable Rights, that among these are Life, Liberty and the pursuit of Happiness. That to secure these rights, Governments are instituted among Men, deriving their just powers from the consent of the governed, That whenever any Form of Government becomes destructive of these ends, it is the Right of the People to alter or to abolish it, and to institute new Government, laying its foundation on such principles and organizing its powers in such form, as to them shall seem most likely to effect their Safety and Happiness. Prudence, indeed, will dictate that Governments long established should not be changed for light and transient causes; and accordingly all experience hath shown, that mankind are more disposed to suffer, while evils are sufferable, than to right themselves by abolishing the forms to which they are accustomed. But when a long train of abuses and usurpations, pursuing invariably the same Object evinces a design to reduce them under absolute Despotism, it is their right, it is their duty, to throw off such Government, and to provide new Guards for their future security. — Such has been the patient sufferance of these Colonies; and such is now the necessity which constrains them to alter their former Systems of Government. The history of the present King of Great Britain is a history of repeated injuries and usurpations, all having in direct object the establishment of an absolute Tyranny over these States. To prove this, let Facts be submitted to a candid world.

He has refused his Assent to Laws, the most wholesome and necessary for the public good.

He has forbidden his Governors to pass Laws of immediate and pressing importance, unless suspended in their operation till his Assent should be obtained; and when so suspended, he has utterly neglected to attend to them.

He has refused to pass other Laws for the accommodation of large districts of people, unless those people would relinquish the right of Representation in the Legislature, a right inestimable to them and formidable to tyrants only

He has called together legislative bodies at places unusual, uncomfortable, and distant from the depository of their Public Records, for the sole purpose of fatiguing them into compliance with his measures.

He has dissolved Representative Houses repeatedly, for opposing with manly firmness his invasions on the rights of the people.

He has refused for a long time, after such dissolutions, to cause others to be elected; whereby the Legislative Powers, incapable of Annihilation, have returned to the People at large for their exercise; the State remaining in the mean time exposed to all the dangers of invasion from without, and convulsions within.

He has endeavoured to prevent the population of these States; for that purpose obstructing the Laws of Naturalization of Foreigners; refusing to pass others to encourage their migration hither, and raising the conditions of new Appropriations of Lands.

He has obstructed the Administration of Justice, by refusing his Assent to Laws for establishing Judiciary Powers.

He has made Judges dependent on his Will alone, for the tenure of their offices, and the amount and payment of their salaries.

He has erected a multitude of New Offices, and sent hither swarms of Officers to harass our People, and eat out their substance.

He has kept among us, in times of peace, Standing Armies without the Consent of our legislature.

He has affected to render the Military independent of and superior to the Civil Power.

He has combined with others to subject us to a jurisdiction foreign to our constitution, and unacknowledged by our laws giving his Assent to their acts of pretended legislation:

For quartering large bodies of armed troops among us:

For protecting them, by a mock Trial, from Punishment for any Murders which they should commit on the Inhabitants of these States:

For cutting off our Trade with all parts of the world:

For imposing taxes on us without our Consent:

For depriving us in many cases, of the benefits of Trial by jury:

For transporting us beyond Seas to be tried for pretended offences:

For abolishing the free System of English Laws in a neighboring Province, establishing therein an Arbitrary government, and enlarging its Boundaries so as to render it at once an example and fit instrument for introducing the same absolute rule into these Colonies:

For taking away our Charters, abolishing our most valuable Laws, and altering fundamentally the Forms of our Governments:

For suspending our own Legislature, and declaring themselves invested with Power to legislate for us in all cases whatsoever.

He has abdicated Government here, by declaring us out of his Protection and waging War against us.

He has plundered our seas, ravaged our Coasts, burnt our towns, and destroyed the lives of our people.

He is at this time transporting large armies of foreign mercenaries to compleat the works of death, desolation and tyranny, already begun with circumstances of Cruelty & perfidy scarcely paralleled in the most barbarous ages, and totally unworthy the Head of a civilized nation.

He has constrained our fellow Citizens taken Captive on the high Seas to bear Arms against their Country, to become the executioners of their friends and Brethren, or to fall themselves by their Hands.

He has excited domestic insurrections amongst us, and has endeavoured to bring on the inhabitants of our frontiers, the merciless Indian Savages, whose known rule of warfare, is an undistinguished destruction of all ages, sexes and conditions.

In every stage of these Oppressions We have Petitioned for Redress in the most humble terms: Our repeated Petitions have been answered only by repeated injury. A

Prince, whose character is thus marked by every act which may define a Tyrant, is unfit to be the ruler of a free People.

Nor have We been wanting in attention to our British brethren. We have warned them from time to time of attempts by their legislature to extend an unwarrantable jurisdiction over us. We have reminded them of the circumstances of our emigration and settlement here. We have appealed to their native justice and magnanimity, and we have conjured them by the ties of our common kindred to disavow these usurpations, which, would inevitably interrupt our connections and correspondence. They too have been deaf to the voice of justice and of consanguinity. We must, therefore, acquiesce in the necessity, which denounces our Separation, and hold them, as we hold the rest of mankind, Enemies in War, in Peace Friends.

We, therefore, the Representatives of the united States of America, in General Congress, Assembled, appealing to the Supreme Judge of the world for the rectitude of our intentions, do, in the Name, and by Authority of the good People of these Colonies, solemnly publish and declare, That these United Colonies are, and of Right ought to be Free and Independent States; that they are Absolved from all Allegiance to the British Crown, and that all political connection between them and the State of Great Britain, is and ought to be totally dissolved; and that as Free and Independent States, they have full Power to levy War, conclude Peace, contract Alliances, establish Commerce, and to do all other Acts and Things which Independent States may of right do. And for the support of this Declaration, with a firm reliance on the Protection of Divine Providence, we mutually pledge to each other our Lives, our Fortunes and our sacred Honor.

JOHN HANCOCK [1]

[1] The remaining signatures are omitted.

Appendix II

ARTICLES OF CONFEDERATION

ARTICLES OF CONFEDERATION AND PERPETUAL UNION BETWEEN THE STATES OF NEW-HAMSHIRE, MASSACHUSETTS-BAY, RHODEISLAND AND PROVIDENCE PLANTATIONS, CONNECTICUT, NEW-YORK, NEW-JERSEY, PENNSYLVANIA, DELAWARE, MARYLAND, VIRGINIA, NORTH-CAROLINA, SOUTH-CAROLINA AND GEORGIA

Article I. The stile of this confederacy shall be "The United States of America."

Article II. Each State retains its sovereignty, freedom and independence, and every power, jurisdiction and right, which is not by this confederation expressly delegated to the United States, in Congress assembled.

Article III. The said States hereby severally enter into a firm league of friendship with each other, for their common defence, the security of their liberties, and their mutual and general welfare, binding themselves to assist each other, against all force offered to, or attacks made upon them, or any of them, on account of religion, sovereignty, trade, or any other pretence whatever.

Article IV. The better to secure and perpetuate mutual friendship and intercourse among the people of the different States in this Union, the free inhabitants of each of these States, paupers, vagabonds and fugitives from justice excepted, shall be entitled to all privileges and immunities of free citizens in the several States; and the people of each State shall have free ingress and regress to and from any other State, and shall enjoy therein all the privileges of trade and commerce, subject to the same duties, impositions and restrictions as the inhabitants thereof respectively, provided that such restrictions shall not extend so far as to prevent the removal of property imported into any State, to any other state of which the owner is an inhabitant; provided also that no imposition, duties, or restriction shall be laid by any State, on the property of the United States, or either of them.

If any Person guilty of, or charged with treason, felony, or other high misdemeanor in any State, shall flee from justice, and be found in any of the United States, he shall upon demand of the Governor or Executive power, of the State from which he fled, be delivered up and removed to the State having jurisdiction of his offence.

Full faith and credit shall be given in each of these States to the records, acts and judicial proceedings of the courts and magistrates of every other State.

Article V. For the more convenient management of the general interest of the United States, delegates shall be annually appointed in such manner as the legislature of each State shall direct, to meet in Congress on the first Monday in November, in every year, with a power reserved to each State, to recall its delegates, or any of them, at any time within the year, and to send others in their stead, for the remainder of the year.

No State shall be represented in Congress by less than two, nor by more than seven members; and no person shall be capable of being a delegate for more than three years in any term of six years; nor shall any person, being a delegate, be capable of holding any office under the United States, for which he, or another for his benefit receives any salary, fees or emolument of any kind.

Each State shall maintain its own delegates in a meeting of the States, and while they act as members of the committee of the States.

In determining questions in the United States, in Congress assembled, each State shall have one vote.

Freedom of speech and debate in Congress shall not be impeached or questioned in any court, or place out of Congress, and the members of Congress shall be protected in their persons from arrests and imprisonments, during the time of their going to and from, and attendance on Congress, except for treason, felony, or breach of the peace.

Article VI. No State without the consent of the United States in Congress assembled, shall send any embassy to, or receive any embassy from, or enter into any conference, agreement, alliance or treaty with any king, prince or state; nor shall any person holding any office of profit or trust under the United States, or any of them, accept of any present, emolument, office or title of any kind whatever from any king, prince, or foreign state; nor shall the United States in Congress assembled, or any of them, grant any title of nobility.

No two or more States shall enter into any treaty, confederation or alliance whatever between them, without the consent of the United States in Congress assembled, specifying accurately the purposes for which the same is to be entered into, and how long it shall continue.

No State shall lay any imposts or duties, which may interfere with any stipulations in treaties, entered into by the United States in Congress assembled, with any king, prince or state, in pursuance of any treaties already proposed by Congress, to the courts of France and Spain.

No vessels of war shall be kept up in time of peace by any State, except such number only, as shall be deemed necessary by the United States in Congress assembled, for the defence of such State, or its trade; nor shall any body of forces be kept up by any State, in time of peace, except such number only, as in the judgment of the United States, in Congress assembled, shall be deemed requisite to garrison the forts necessary for the defence of such State; but every State shall always keep up a well regulated and disciplined militia, sufficiently armed and accoutered, and shall provide and constantly have ready for use, in public stores, a due number of field pieces and tents, and a proper quantity of arms, ammunition and camp equipage.

No State shall engage in any war without the consent of the United States in Congress assembled, unless such State be actually invaded by enemies, or shall have received certain advice of a resolution being formed by some nation of Indians to invade such State, and the danger is so imminent as not to admit of a delay, till the United States in Congress assembled can be consulted; nor shall any State grant commissions to any ships or vessels of war, nor letters of marque or reprisal, except it be after a declaration of war by the United States in Congress assembled, and then only against the kingdom or state and the subjects thereof, against which war has been so declared, and under such regulations as shall be established by the United States in Congress assembled, unless such State be infested by pirates, in which case vessels of war may be fitted out for that occasion, and kept so long as the danger shall continue, or until the United States in Congress assembled shall determine otherwise.

Article VII. When land-forces are raised by any State for the common defence, all officers of or under the rank of colonel, shall be appointed by the Legislature of each State respectively by whom such forces shall be raised, or in such manner as such State shall direct, and all vacancies shall be filled up by the State which first made the appointment.

Article VIII. All charges of war, and all other expenses that shall be incurred for the common defence or general welfare, and allowed by the United States in Congress assembled, shall be defrayed out of a common treasury, which shall be supplied by the several States, in proportion to the value of all land within each State, granted to or surveyed for any person, as such land and the buildings and improvements thereon shall be estimated according to such mode as the United States in Congress assembled, shall from time to time direct and appoint.

The taxes for paying that proportion shall be laid and levied by the authority and direction of the Legislatures of the several States within the time agreed upon by the United States in Congress assembled.

Article IX. The United States in Congress assembled, shall have the sole and exclusive right and power of determining on peace and war, except in the cases mentioned in the sixth article—of sending and receiving ambassadors—entering into treaties and alliances, provided that no treaty of commerce shall be made whereby the legislative power of the respective States shall be restrained from imposing such imposts and duties on foreigners, as their own people are subjected to, or from prohibiting the exportation or importation of any species of goods or commodities whatsoever—of establishing rules for deciding in all cases, what captures on land or water shall be legal, and in what manner prizes taken by land or naval forces in the service of the United States shall be divided or appropriated—of granting letters of marque and reprisal in times of peace—appointing courts for the trial of piracies and felonies committed on the high seas and establishing courts for receiving and determining finally appeals in all cases of captures, provided that no member of Congress shall be appointed a judge of any of the said courts.

The United States in Congress assembled shall also be the last resort on appeal in all disputes and differences now subsisting or that hereafter may arise between two or more States concerning boundary, jurisdiction or any other cause whatever; which authority shall always be exercised in the manner following. Whenever the legislative or executive authority or lawful agent of any State in controversy with another shall present a petition to Congress, stating the matter in question and praying for a hearing, notice thereof shall be given by order of Congress to the legislative or executive authority of the other State in controversy, and a day assigned for the appearance of the parties by their lawful agents, who shall then be directed to appoint by joint consent, commissioners, or judges to constitute a court for hearing and determining the matter in question: but if they cannot agree, Congress shall name three persons out of each of the United States, and from the list of such persons each party shall alternately strike out one, the petitioners beginning, until the number shall be reduced to thirteen; and from that number not less than seven, nor more than nine names as Congress shall direct, shall in the presence of Congress be drawn out by lot, and the persons whose names shall be so drawn or any five of them, shall be commissioners or judges, to hear and finally determine the controversy, so always as a major part of the judges who shall hear the cause shall agree in the determination; and if either party shall neglect to attend at the day appointed, without showing reasons, which Congress shall judge sufficient, or being present shall refuse to strike, the Congress shall proceed to nominate three persons out of each State, and the Secretary of Congress shall strike in behalf of such party absent or refusing; and the judgment and sentence of the court to be appointed, in the manner before prescribed, shall be final and conclusive; and if any of the parties shall refuse to submit to the authority of such court, or to appear or defend their claim or cause, the court shall nevertheless proceed to pronounce sentence, or judgment, which shall in like manner be final and decisive, the judgment or sentence and other proceedings being in either case transmitted to Congress, and lodged among the acts of Congress for the security of the parties concerned: provided that every commissioner, before he sits in judgment, shall take an oath to be administered by one of the judges of the supreme or superior court of the State, where the cause shall be tried, "well and truly to hear and determine the matter in question, according to the best of his judgment, without favour, affection or hope of reward:" provided also that no State shall be deprived of territory for the benefit of the United States.

All controversies concerning the private right of soil claimed under different grants of two or more States, whose jurisdiction as they may respect such lands, and the States which passed such grants are adjusted; the said grants or either of them being at the same time claimed to have originated antecedent to such settlement of jurisdiction, shall on the petition of either party to the Congress of the United States, be finally determined as near as may be in the same manner as is before prescribed for deciding disputes respecting territorial jurisdiction between different states.

The United States in Congress assembled shall also have the sole and exclusive right and power of regulating the alloy and value of coin struck by their own authority, or by that of the respective States—fixing the standard of weights and measures throughout the United States—regulating the trade and managing all affairs with the Indians, not members of any of the States, provided that the legislative right of any State within its own limits be not infringed or violated—establishing and regulating post-offices from one State to another, throughout all the United States, and exacting such postage on the papers passing thro' the same as may be requisite to defray the expenses of the said office—appointing all officers of the land forces, in the service of the United States, excepting regimental officers—appointing all the officers of the naval forces, and commissioning all officers whatever in the service of the United States—making rules for the government and regulation of the said land and naval forces, and directing their operations.

The United States in Congress assembled shall have authority to appoint a committee, to sit in the recess of Congress, to be denominated "a Committee of the States," and to consist of one delegate from each State; and to appoint such other committees and civil officers as may be necessary for manageing the general affairs of the United States under their direction—to appoint one of their number to preside, provided that no person be allowed to serve in the office of president more than one year in any term of three years; to ascertain the necessary sums of money to be raised for the service of the United States, and to appropriate and apply the same for defraying the public expenses—to borrow money, or emit bills on the credit of the United States, transmitting every half year to the respective States an account of the sums of money so borrowed or emitted,—to build and equip a navy—to agree upon the number of land forces, and to make requisitions from each State for its quota, in proportion to the number of white inhabitants in such State; which requisition shall be binding, and thereupon the Legislature of each State shall appoint the regimental officers, raise the men and cloath, arm and equip them in a soldier like manner, at the expense of the United States; and the officers and men so cloathed, armed and equipped shall march to the place appointed, and within the time agreed on by the United States in Congress assembled; but, if the United States in Congress assembled shall, on consideration of circumstances judge proper that any State should not raise men, or should raise a smaller number than its quota, and that any other State should raise a greater number of men than the quota thereof, such extra number shall be raised, officered, cloathed, armed and equipped in the same manner as the quota of such State, unless the legislature of such State shall judge that such extra number cannot be safely spared out of the same, in which case they shall raise, officer, cloath, arm and equip as many of such extra number as they judge can be safely spared. And the officers and men so cloathed, armed and equipped, shall march to the place appointed, and within the time agreed on by the United States in Congress assembled.

The United States in Congress assembled shall never engage in a war, nor grant letters of marque and reprisal in time of peace, nor enter into any treaties or alliances, nor coin money, nor regulate the value thereof, nor ascertain the sums and expenses necessary for the defence and welfare of the United States, or any of them, nor emit bills, nor borrow money on the credit of the United States, nor appropriate money, nor agree upon the number of vessels of war, to be built or purchased, or the number of land or sea forces to be raised, nor appoint a commander in chief of the army or navy, unless nine States assent to the same: nor shall a question on any other point, except for adjourning from day to day be determined, unless by the votes of a majority of the United States in Congress assembled.

The Congress of the United States shall have power to adjourn to any time within the year, and to place within the United States, so that no period of adjournment be for a longer duration than the space of six months, and shall publish the journal of their proceedings monthly, except such parts thereof relating to treaties, alliances or military operations, as in their judgment require secresy; and the yeas and nays of the delegates of each State on any question shall be entered on the journal, when it is desired by any delegate; and the delegates of a State, or any of them, at his or their request shall be furnished with a transcript of the said journal, except such parts as are above excepted, to lay before the Legislatures of the several States.

Article X. The committee of the States, or any nine of them, shall be authorized to execute, in the recess of Congress, such of the powers of Congress as the United States in Congress assembled, by the consent of nine States, shall from time to time think expedient to vest with them; provided that no power be delegated to the said committee, for the exercise of which, by the articles of confederation, the voice of nine States in the Congress of the United States assembled is requisite.

Article XI. Canada acceding to this confederation, and joining in the measures of the United States, shall be admitted into, and entitled to all the advantages of this Union; but no other colony shall be admitted into the same, unless such admission be agreed to by nine States.

Article XII. All bills of credit emitted, monies borrowed and debts contracted by, or under the authority of Congress, before the assembling of the United States, in pursuance of the present confederation, shall be deemed and considered as a charge against the United States, for payment and satisfaction whereof the said United States, and the public faith are hereby solemnly pledged.

Article XIII. Every State shall abide by the determinations of the United States in Congress assembled, on all questions which by this confederation are submitted to them. And the articles of this confederation shall be inviolably observed by every State, and the Union shall be perpetual; nor shall any alteration at any time hereafter be made in any of them; unless such alteration be agreed to in a Congress of the United States, and be afterwards confirmed by the Legislatures of every State.

Appendix III

CONSTITUTION OF THE UNITED STATES OF AMERICA

We, the people of the United States, in order to form a more perfect union, establish justice, insure domestic tranquility, provide for the common defence, promote the general welfare, and secure the blessings of liberty to ourselves and our posterity, do ordain and establish this Constitution for the United States of America.

ARTICLE I

Section 1. All legislative powers herein granted shall be vested in a Congress of the United States, which shall consist of a Senate and House of Representatives.

Section 2. (1) The House of Representatives shall be composed of members chosen every second year by the people of the several States, and the electors in each State shall have the qualifications requisite for electors of the most numerous branch of the State legislature.

(2) No person shall be a Representative who shall not have attained to the age of twenty-five years, and been seven years a citizen of the United States, and who shall not, when elected, be an inhabitant of that State in which he shall be chosen.

(3) Representatives and direct taxes shall be apportioned among the several States which may be included within this Union, according to their respective numbers, [which shall be determined by adding to the whole number of free persons,] [1] including those bound to service for a term of years, and excluding Indians not taxed, [three fifth for all other persons].[2] The actual enumeration shall be made within three years after the first meeting of the Congress of the United States, and within every subsequent term of ten years, in such manner as they shall by law direct. The number of Representatives shall not exceed one for every thirty thousand, but each State shall have at least one Representative; [and until such enumeration shall be made, the State of New Hampshire shall be entitled to choose three, Massachusetts eight, Rhode Island and Providence Plantations one, Connecticut five, New York six, New Jersey four, Pennsylvania eight, Delaware one, Maryland six, Virginia ten, North Carolina five, South Carolina five, and Georgia three.] [3]

(4) When vacancies happen in the representation from any State, the executive authority thereof shall issue writs of election to fill such vacancies.

(5) The House of Representatives shall choose their Speaker and other officers; and shall have the sole power of impeachment.

Section 3. [(1) The Senate of the United States shall be composed of two Senators from each State, chosen by the legislature thereof, for six years; and each Senator shall have one vote.] [4]

(2) Immediately after they shall be assembled in consequence of the first election, they shall be divided as equally as may be into three classes. The seats of the Senators of the first class shall be vacated at the expiration of the second year, of the second class

[1] Modified by Fourteenth Amendment.
[2] Superseded by Fourteenth Amendment.
[3] Temporary provision.
[4] Superseded by Seventeenth Amendment.

at the expiration of the fourth year, and of the third class at the expiration of the sixth year, so that one third may be chosen every second year; [and if vacancies happen by resignation, or otherwise, during the recess of the legislature of any State, the executive thereof may make temporary appointments until the next meeting of the legislature, which shall then fill such vacancies.] [1]

(3) No person shall be a Senator who shall not have attained to the age of thirty years, and been nine years a citizen of the United States, and who shall not, when elected, be an inhabitant of that State for which he shall be chosen.

(4) The Vice President of the United States shall be president of the Senate, but shall have no vote, unless they be equally divided.

(5) The Senate shall choose their other officers, and also a president pro tempore, in the absence of the Vice President, or when he shall exercise the office of President of the United States.

(6) The Senate shall have the sole power to try all impeachments. When sitting for that purpose, they shall be on oath or affirmation. When the President of the United States is tried, the Chief Justice shall preside: and no person shall be convicted without the concurrence of two thirds of the members present.

(7) Judgment in cases of impeachment shall not extend further than to removal from office, and disqualification to hold and enjoy any office of honor, trust, or profit under the United States: but the party convicted shall nevertheless be liable and subject to indictment, trial, judgment, and punishment, according to law.

Section 4. (1) The times, places, and manner of holding elections for Senators and Representatives shall be prescribed in each State by the legislature thereof; but the Congress may at any time by law make or alter such regulations, except as to the places of choosing Senators.

[(2) The Congress shall assemble at least once in every year, and such meeting shall be on the first Monday in December, unless they shall by law appoint a different day.] [2]

Section 5. (1) Each House shall be the judge of the elections, returns, and qualifications of its own members, and a majority of each shall constitute a quorum to do business; but a smaller number may adjourn from day to day, and may be authorized to compel the attendance of absent members, in such manner, and under such penalties, as each House may provide.

(2) Each House may determine the rules of its proceedings, punish its members for disorderly behavior, and, with the concurrence of two thirds, expel a member.

(3) Each House shall keep a journal of its proceedings, and from time to time publish the same, excepting such parts as may in their judgment require secrecy; and the yeas and nays of the members of either House on any question shall, at the desire of one fifth of those present, be entered on the journal.

(4) Neither House, during the session of Congress, shall, without the consent of the other, adjourn for more than three days, nor to any other place than that in which the two Houses shall be sitting.

Section 6. (1) The Senators and Representatives shall receive a compensation for their services, to be ascertained by law, and paid out of the Treasury of the United States. They shall in all cases, except treason, felony, and breach of the peace, be privileged from arrest during their attendance at the session of their respective Houses, and in going to and returning from the same; and for any speech or debate in either House, they shall not be questioned in any other place.

(2) No Senator or Representative shall, during the time for which he was elected, be appointed to any civil office under the authority of the United States, which shall have been created, or the emoluments whereof shall have been increased, during such

[1] Modified by Seventeenth Amendment.

[2] Superseded by Twentieth Amendment.

time; and no person holding any office under the United States shall be a member of either House during his continuance in office.

Section 7. (1) All bills for raising revenue shall originate in the House of Representatives; but the Senate may propose or concur with amendments as on other bills.

(2) Every bill which shall have passed the House of Representatives and the Senate, shall, before it become a law, be presented to the President of the United States; if he approve he shall sign it, but if not he shall return it, with his objections, to that House in which it shall have originated, who shall enter the objections at large on their journal, and proceed to reconsider it. If after such reconsideration two thirds of that House shall agree to pass the bill, it shall be sent, together with the objections, to the other House, by which it shall likewise be reconsidered, and if approved by two thirds of that House, it shall become a law. But in all such cases the votes of both Houses shall be determined by yeas and nays, and the names of the persons voting for and against the bill shall be entered on the journal of each House respectively. If any bill shall not be returned by the President within ten days (Sundays excepted) after it shall have been presented to him, the same shall be a law, in like manner as if he had signed it, unless the Congress by their adjournment prevent its return, in which case it shall not be a law.

(3) Every order, resolution, or vote to which the concurrence of the Senate and House of Representatives may be necessary (except on a question of adjournment) shall be presented to the President of the United States; and before the same shall take effect, shall be approved by him, or being disapproved by him, shall be repassed by two thirds of the Senate and House of Representatives, according to the rules and limitations prescribed in the case of a bill.

Section 8. (1) The Congress shall have power to lay and collect taxes, duties, imposts, and excises, to pay the debts and provide for the common defense and general welfare of the United States; but all duties, imposts, and excises shall be uniform throughout the United States;

(2) To borrow money on the credit of the United States;

(3) To regulate commerce with foreign nations, and among the several States, and with the Indian tribes;

(4) To establish an uniform rule of naturalization, and uniform laws on the subject of bankruptcies throughout the United States;

(5) To coin money, regulate the value thereof, and of foreign coin, and fix the standard of weights and measures;

(6) To provide for the punishment of counterfeiting the securities and current coin of the United States;

(7) To establish post offices and post roads;

(8) To promote the progress of science and useful arts, by securing for limited times to authors and inventors the exclusive right to their respective writings and discoveries;

(9) To constitute tribunals inferior to the Supreme Court;

(10) To define and punish piracies and felonies committed on the high seas, and offenses against the law of nations;

(11) To declare war, grant letters of marque and reprisal, and make rules concerning captures on land and water;

(12) To raise and support armies, but no appropriation of money to that use shall be for a longer term than two years;

(13) To provide and maintain a navy;

(14) To make rules for the government and regulation of the land and naval forces;

(15) To provide for calling forth the militia to execute the laws of the Union, suppress insurrections, and repel invasions;

(16) To provide for organizing, arming, and disciplining the militia, and for govern-

ing such part of them as may be employed in the service of the United States, reserving to the States respectively the appointment of the officers, and the authority of training the militia according to the discipline prescribed by Congress;

(17) To exercise exclusive legislation in all cases whatsoever, over such district (not exceeding ten miles square) as may, by cession of particular States, and the acceptance of Congress, become the seat of the government of the United States, and to exercise like authority over all places purchased by the consent of the legislature of the State in which the same shall be, for the erection of forts, magazines, arsenals, dock-yards, and other needful buildings; and

(18) To make all laws which shall be necessary and proper for carrying into execution the foregoing powers, and all other powers vested by this Constitution in the government of the United States, or in any department or officer thereof.

Section 9. [(1) The migration or importation of such persons as any of the States now existing shall think proper to admit, shall not be prohibited by the Congress prior to the year one thousand eight hundred and eight, but a tax or duty may be imposed on such importation, not exceeding ten dollars for each person.] [1]

(2) The privilege of the writ of habeas corpus shall not be suspended, unless when in cases of rebellion or invasion the public safety may require it.

(3) No bill of attainder or ex post facto law shall be passed.

[(4) No capitation, or other direct, tax shall be laid, unless in proportion to the census or enumeration hereinbefore directed to be taken.] [2]

(5) No tax or duty shall be laid on articles exported from any State.

(6) No preference shall be given by any regulation of commerce or revenue to the ports of one State over those of another: nor shall vessels bound to, or from, one State, be obliged to enter, clear, or pay duties in another.

(7) No money shall be drawn from the Treasury, but in consequence of appropriations made by law; and a regular statement and account of the receipts and expenditures of all public money shall be published from time to time.

(8) No title of nobility shall be granted by the United States: and no person holding any office of profit or trust under them, shall, without the consent of the Congress, accept of any present, emolument, office, or title, of any kind whatever, from any king, prince, or foreign State.

Section 10. (1) No State shall enter into any treaty, alliance, or confederation; grant letters of marque and reprisal; coin money; emit bills of credit; make anything but gold and silver coin a tender in payment of debts; pass any bill of attainder, ex post facto law, or law impairing the obligation of contracts, or grant any title of nobility.

(2) No State shall, without the consent of the Congress, lay any imposts or duties on imports or exports, except what may be absolutely necessary for executing its inspection laws: and the net produce of all duties and imposts, laid by any State on imports or exports, shall be for the use of the treasury of the United States; and all such laws shall be subject to the revision and control of the Congress.

(3) No State shall, without the consent of Congress, lay any duty of tonnage, keep troops, or ships of war in time of peace, enter into any agreement or compact with another State, or with a foreign power, or engage in war, unless actually invaded, or in such imminent danger as will not admit of delay.

ARTICLE II

Section 1. (1) The executive power shall be vested in a President of the United States of America. He shall hold his office during the term of four years, and, together with the Vice President, chosen for the same term, be elected, as follows:

[1] Temporary provision.

[2] Modified by Sixteenth Amendment.

(2) Each State shall appoint, in such manner as the legislature thereof may direct, a number of electors, equal to the whole number of Senators and Representatives to which the State may be entitled in the Congress: but no Senator or Representative, or person holding an office of trust or profit under the United States, shall be appointed an elector.

[The electors shall meet in their respective States, and vote by ballot for two persons, of whom one at least shall not be an inhabitant of the same State with themselves. And they shall make a list of all the persons voted for, and of the number of votes for each; which list they shall sign and certify, and transmit sealed to the seat of the government of the United States, directed to the president of the Senate. The president of the Senate shall, in the presence of the Senate and House of Representatives, open all the certificates, and the votes shall then be counted. The person having the greatest number of votes shall be the President, if such number be a majority of the whole number of electors appointed; and if there be more than one who have such majority, and have an equal number of votes, then the House of Representatives shall immediately choose by ballot one of them for President; and if no person have a majority, then from the five highest on the list the said House shall in like manner choose the President. But in choosing the President, the votes shall be taken by States, the representation from each State having one vote; a quorum for this purpose shall consist of a member or members from two thirds of the States, and a majority of all the States shall be necessary to a choice. In every case, after the choice of the President, the person having the greatest number of votes of the electors shall be the Vice President. But if there should remain two or more who have equal votes, the Senate shall choose from them by ballot the Vice President.] [1]

(3) The Congress may determine the time of choosing the electors, and the day on which they shall give their votes; which day shall be the same throughout the United States.

(4) No person except a natural-born citizen, or a citizen of the United States, at the time of the adoption of this Constitution, shall be eligible to the office of President; neither shall any person be eligible to that office who shall not have attained to the age of thirty-five years, and been fourteen years a resident within the United States.

(5) In case of the removal of the President from office, or of his death, resignation, or inability to discharge the powers and duties of the said office, the same shall devolve on the Vice President, and the Congress may by law provide for the case of removal, death, resignation, or inability, both of the President and Vice President, declaring what officer shall then act as President, and such officer shall act accordingly, until the disability be removed, or a President shall be elected.

(6) The President shall, at stated times, receive for his services a compensation, which shall neither be increased nor diminished during the period for which he shall have been elected, and he shall not receive within that period any other emolument from the United States, or any of them.

(7) Before he enter on the execution of his office, he shall take the following oath or affirmation: "I do solemnly swear (or affirm) that I will faithfully execute the office of President of the United States, and will, to the best of my ability, preserve, protect, and defend the Constitution of the United States."

Section 2. (1) The President shall be commander in chief of the army and navy of the United States, and of the militia of the several States, when called into the actual service of the United States; he may require the opinion, in writing, of the principal officer in each of the executive departments, upon any subject relating to the duties of

[1] This paragraph superseded by Twelfth Amendment, which, in turn, is modified by the Twentieth Amendment.

their respective offices, and he shall have power to grant reprieves and pardons for offenses against the United States, except in cases of impeachment.

(2) He shall have power, by and with the advice and consent of the Senate, to make treaties, provided two thirds of the Senators present concur; and he shall nominate, and by and with the advice and consent of the Senate, shall appoint ambassadors, other public ministers and consuls, judges of the Supreme Court, and all other officers of the United States, whose appointments are not herein otherwise provided for, and which shall be established by law: but the Congress may by law vest the appointment of such inferior officers, as they think proper, in the President alone, in the courts of law, or in the heads of departments.

(3) The President shall have power to fill up all vacancies that may happen during the recess of the Senate, by granting commissions which shall expire at the end of their next session.

Section 3. He shall from time to time give to the Congress information of the state of the Union, and recommend to their consideration such measures as he shall judge necessary and expedient; he may, on extraordinary occasions, convene both Houses, or either of them, and in case of disagreement between them, with respect to the time of adjournment, he may adjourn them to such time as he shall think proper; he shall receive ambassadors and other public ministers; he shall take care that the laws be faithfully executed, and shall commission all the officers of the United States.

Section 4. The President, Vice President, and all civil officers of the United States, shall be removed from office on impeachment for, and conviction of, treason, bribery, or other high crimes and misdemeanors.

ARTICLE III

Section 1. The judicial power of the United States shall be vested in one Supreme Court, and in such inferior courts as the Congress may from time to time ordain and establish. The judges, both of the Supreme and inferior courts, shall hold their offices during good behavior, and shall, at stated times, receive for their services a compensation, which shall not be diminished during their continuance in office.

Section 2. (1) The judicial power shall extend to all cases, in law and equity, arising under this Constitution, the laws of the United States, and treaties made, or which shall be made, under their authority;—to all cases affecting ambassadors, other public ministers, and consuls;—to all cases of admiralty and maritime jurisdiction;—to controversies to which the United States shall be a party;—to controversies between two or more States; [—between a State and citizens of another State;] [1]—between citizens of different States;—between citizens of the same State claiming lands under grants of different States, and between a State, or the citizens thereof, and foreign States, citizens, or subjects.

(2) In all cases affecting ambassadors, other public ministers, and consuls, and those in which a State shall be party, the Supreme Court shall have original jurisdiction. In all the other cases before mentioned, the Supreme Court shall have appellate jurisdiction, both as to law and fact, with such exceptions, and under such regulations, as the Congress shall make.

(3) The trial of all crimes, except in cases of impeachment, shall be by jury; and such trial shall be held in the State where the said crimes shall have been committed; but when not committed within any State, the trial shall be at such place or places as the Congress may by law have directed.

Section 3. (1) Treason against the United States shall consist only in levying war

[1] Limited by Eleventh Amendment.

against them, or in adhering to their enemies, giving them aid and comfort. No person shall be convicted of treason unless on the testimony of two witnesses to the same overt act, or on confession in open court.

(2) The Congress shall have power to declare the punishment of treason, but no attainder of treason shall work corruption of blood, or forfeiture except during the life of the person attainted.

ARTICLE IV

Section 1. Full faith and credit shall be given in each State to the public acts, records, and judicial proceedings of every other State. And the Congress may by general laws prescribe the manner in which such acts, records, and proceedings shall be proved, and the effect thereof.

Section 2. (1) The citizens of each State shall be entitled to all privileges and immunities of citizens in the several States.

(2) A person charged in any State with treason, felony, or other crime, who shall flee from justice, and be found in another State, shall, on demand of the executive authority of the State from which he fled, be delivered up, to be removed to the State having jurisdiction of the crime.

[(3) No person held to service or labor in one State, under the laws thereof, escaping into another, shall, in consequence of any law or regulation therein, be discharged from such service or labor, but shall be delivered up on claim of the party to whom such service or labor may be due.] [1]

Section 3. (1) New States may be admitted by the Congress into this Union; but no new State shall be formed or erected within the jurisdiction of any other State; nor any State be formed by the junction of two or more States, or parts of States, without the consent of the legislatures of the States concerned as well as of the Congress.

(2) The Congress shall have power to dispose of and make all needful rules and regulations respecting the territory or other property belonging to the United States; and nothing in this Constitution shall be so construed as to prejudice any claims of the United States, or of any particular State.

Section 4. The United States shall guarantee to every State in this Union a republican form of government, and shall protect each of them against invasion; and, on application of the legislature, or of the executive (when the legislature cannot be convened), against domestic violence.

ARTICLE V

The Congress, whenever two thirds of both Houses shall deem it necessary, shall propose amendments to this Constitution, or, on the application of the legislatures of two thirds of the several States, shall call a convention for proposing amendments which, in either case, shall be valid to all intents and purposes, as part of this Constitution, when ratified by the legislatures of three fourths of the several States, or by conventions in three fourths thereof, as the one or the other mode of ratification may be proposed by the Congress; provided [that no amendment which may be made prior to the year one thousand eight hundred and eight shall in any manner affect the first and fourth clauses in the ninth section of the first article; and] [2] that no State, without its consent, shall be deprived of its equal suffrage in the Senate.

[1] Superseded by Thirteenth Amendment so far as it relates to slaves.

[2] Temporary provision.

ARTICLE VI

(1) All debts contracted and engagements entered into, before the adoption of this Constitution, shall be as valid against the United States under this Constitution, as under the Confederation.

(2) This Constitution, and the laws of the United States which shall be made in pursuance thereof; and all treaties made, or which shall be made, under the authority of the United States, shall be the supreme law of the land; and the judges in every State shall be bound thereby, anything in the constitution or laws of any State to the contrary notwithstanding.

(3) The Senators and Representatives before mentioned, and the members of the several State legislatures, and all executive and judicial officers, both of the United States and of the several States, shall be bound by oath or affirmation to support this Constitution; but no religious test shall ever be required as a qualification to any office or public trust under the United States.

ARTICLE VII

The ratification of the conventions of nine States shall be sufficient for the establishment of this Constitution between the States so ratifying the same.

Done in convention by the unanimous consent of the States present the seventeenth day of September in the year of our Lord one thousand seven hundred and eighty-seven, and of the independence of the United States of America the twelfth. In witness whereof, we have hereunto subscribed our names.

AMENDMENTS

Article I

Congress shall make no law respecting an establishment of religion, or prohibiting the free exercise thereof; or abridging the freedom of speech, or of the press; or the right of the people peaceably to assemble, and to petition the government for a redress of grievances.

Article II

A well regulated militia, being necessary to the security of a free State, the right of the people to keep and bear arms shall not be infringed.

Article III

No soldier shall, in time of peace, be quartered in any house, without the consent of the owner, nor in time of war, but in a manner to be prescribed by law.

Article IV

The right of the people to be secure in their persons, houses, papers, and effects, against unreasonable searches and seizures, shall not be violated, and no warrants shall issue, but upon probable cause, supported by oath or affirmation, and particularly describing the place to be searched, and the persons or things to be seized.

Article V

No person shall be held to answer for a capital or otherwise infamous crime, unless on a presentment or indictment of a grand jury, except in cases arising in the land or naval forces, or in the militia, when in actual service in time of war or public danger; nor shall any person be subject for the same offence to be twice put in jeopardy of life or limb; nor shall be compelled in any criminal case to be a witness against himself, nor be deprived of life, liberty, or property, without due process of law; nor shall private property be taken for public use, without just compensation.

Article VI

In all criminal prosecutions the accused shall enjoy the right to a speedy and public trial, by an impartial jury of the State and district wherein the crime shall have been committed, which district shall have been previously ascertained by law, and to be informed of the nature and cause of the accusation; to be confronted with the witnesses against him; to have compulsory process for obtaining witnesses in his favor, and to have the assistance of counsel for his defense.

Article VII

In suits at common law, where the value in controversy shall exceed twenty dollars, the right of trial by jury shall be preserved, and no fact tried by a jury shall be otherwise re-examined in any court of the United States than according to the rules of the common law.

Article VIII

Excessive bail shall not be required, nor excessive fines imposed, nor cruel and unusual punishments inflicted.

Article IX

The enumeration in the Constitution of certain rights shall not be construed to deny or disparage others retained by the people.

Article X

The powers not delegated to the United States by the Constitution, nor prohibited by it to the States, are reserved to the States respectively, or to the people.[1]

Article XI [2]

The judicial power of the United States shall not be construed to extend to any suit in law or equity, commenced or prosecuted against one of the United States by citizens of another State, or by citizens or subjects of any foreign State.

Article XII [3]

The electors shall meet in their respective States, and vote by ballot for President and Vice President, one of whom, at least, shall not be an inhabitant of the same State with themselves; they shall name in their ballots the persons voted for as President, and in distinct ballots the persons voted for as Vice President, and they shall make distinct lists of all persons voted for as President, and of all persons voted for as Vice President, and of the number of votes for each, which lists they shall sign and certify, and transmit sealed to the seat of the government of the United States, directed to the president of the Senate;—the president of the Senate shall, in the presence of the Senate and House of Representatives, open all the certificates, and the votes shall then be counted;—the person having the greatest number of votes for President, shall be the

[1] The first ten amendments appear to have been in force from November 3, 1791.
[2] Proclaimed January 8, 1798.
[3] Proclaimed September 25, 1804.

President, if such number be a majority of the whole number of electors appointed; and if no person have such majority, then from the persons having the highest numbers not exceeding three on the list of those voted for as President, the House of Representatives shall choose immediately, by ballot, the President. But in choosing the President, the votes shall be taken by States, the representation from each State having one vote; a quorum for this purpose shall consist of a member or members from two thirds of the States, and a majority of all the States shall be necessary to a choice. And if the House of Representatives shall not choose a President whenever the right of choice shall devolve upon them, before the fourth day of March next following, then the Vice President shall act as President, as in the case of the death or other constitutional disability of the President.—The person having the greatest number of votes as Vice President, shall be the Vice President, if such number be a majority of the whole number of electors appointed, and if no person have a majority, then from the two highest numbers on the list, the Senate shall choose the Vice President; a quorum for the purpose shall consist of two thirds of the whole number of Senators, and a majority of the whole number shall be necessary to a choice. But no person constitutionally ineligible to the office of President shall be eligible to that of Vice President of the United States.[1]

Article XIII [2]

Section 1. Neither slavery nor involuntary servitude, except as a punishment for crime whereof the party shall have been duly convicted, shall exist within the United States, or any place subject to their jurisdiction.

Section 2. Congress shall have power to enforce this article by appropriate legislation.

Article XIV [3]

Section 1. All persons born or naturalized in the United States, and subject to the jurisdiction thereof, are citizens of the United States and of the State wherein they reside. No State shall make or enforce any law which shall abridge the privileges or immunities of citizens of the United States; nor shall any State deprive any person of life, liberty, or property, without due process of law; nor deny to any person within its jurisdiction the equal protection of the laws.

Section 2. Representatives shall be apportioned among the several States according to their respective numbers, counting the whole number of persons in each State, excluding Indians not taxed. But when the right to vote at any election for the choice of electors for President and Vice President of the United States, Representatives in Congress, the executive and judicial officers of a State, or the members of the legislature thereof, is denied to any of the male inhabitants of such State, being twenty-one years of age, and citizens of the United States, or in any way abridged, except for participation in rebellion, or other crime, the basis of representation therein shall be reduced in the proportion which the number of such male citizens shall bear to the whole number of male citizens twenty-one years of age in such State.

Section 3. No person shall be a Senator or Representative in Congress, or elector of President and Vice President, or hold any office, civil or military, under the United States, or under any State, who, having previously taken an oath, as a member of Congress, or as an officer of the United States, or as a member of any State legislature,

[1] This amendment modified by the Twentieth.
[2] Proclaimed December 18, 1865.
[3] Proclaimed July 28, 1868.

or as an executive or judicial officer of any State, to support the Constitution of the United States, shall have engaged in insurrection or rebellion against the same, or given aid or comfort to the enemies thereof. But Congress may by a vote of two thirds of each House, remove such disability.

Section 4. The validity of the public debt of the United States, authorized by law, including debts incurred for payment of pensions and bounties for services in suppressing insurrection or rebellion, shall not be questioned. But neither the United States nor any State shall assume or pay any debt or obligation incurred in aid of insurrection or rebellion against the United States, or any claim for the loss or emancipation of any slave; but all such debts, obligations, and claims shall be held illegal and void.

Section 5. The Congress shall have power to enforce, by appropriate legislation, the provisions of this article.

Article XV [1]

Section 1. The right of citizens of the United States to vote shall not be denied or abridged by the United States or by any State on account of race, color, or previous condition of servitude.

Section 2. The Congress shall have power to enforce this article by appropriate legislation.

Article XVI [2]

The Congress shall have power to lay and collect taxes on incomes, from whatever source derived, without apportionment among the several States, and without regard to any census or enumeration.

Article XVII [3]

The Senate of the United States shall be composed of two Senators from each State, elected by the people thereof, for six years; and each Senator shall have one vote. The electors in each State shall have the qualifications requisite for electors of the most numerous branch of the State legislature.

When vacancies happen in the representation of any State in the Senate, the executive authority of such State shall issue writs of election to fill such vacancies: *Provided,* That the legislature of any State may empower the executive thereof to make temporary appointments until the people fill the vacancies by election as the legislature may direct.

This amendment shall not be so construed as to affect the election or term of any Senator chosen before it becomes valid as part of the Constitution.

Article XVIII [4]

Section 1. After one year from the ratification of this article the manufacture, sale, or transportation of intoxicating liquors within, the importation thereof into, or the exportation thereof from the United States and all territory subject to the jurisdiction thereof for beverage purposes is hereby prohibited.

[1] Proclaimed March 30, 1870.

[2] Passed July, 1909; proclaimed February 25, 1913.

[3] Passed May, 1912, in lieu of Article I, Section 3, Clause I, of the Constitution and so much of clause 2 of the same Section as relates to the filling of vacancies; proclaimed May 31, 1913.

[4] Passed December 3, 1917; proclaimed January 29, 1919. Repealed by the Twenty-first Amendment.

Section 2. The Congress and the several States shall have concurrent power to enforce this article by appropriate legislation.

Section 3. This article shall be inoperative unless it shall have been ratified as an amendment to the Constitution by the legislatures of the several States, as provided in the Constitution, within seven years from the date of the submission hereof to the States by the Congress.

ARTICLE XIX [1]

(1) The right of citizens of the United States to vote shall not be denied or abridged by the United States or by any State on account of sex.

(2) Congress shall have power, by appropriate legislation, to enforce the provisions of this article.

ARTICLE XX [2]

Section 1. The terms of the President and Vice President shall end at noon on the 20th day of January, and the terms of Senators and Representatives at noon on the 3rd day of January, of the years in which such terms would have ended if this article had not been ratified; and the terms of their successors shall then begin.

Section 2. The Congress shall assemble at least once in every year, and such meeting shall begin at noon on the 3rd day of January, unless they shall by law appoint a different day.

Section 3. If, at the time fixed for the beginning of the term of the President, the President elect shall have died, the Vice President elect shall become President. If a President shall not have been chosen before the time fixed for the beginning of his term, or if the President elect shall have failed to qualify, then the Vice President elect shall act as President until a President shall have qualified; and the Congress may by law provide for the case wherein neither a President elect nor a Vice President elect shall have qualified, declaring who shall then act as President, or the manner in which one who is to act shall be selected, and such person shall act accordingly until a President or Vice President shall have qualified.

Section 4. The Congress may by law provide for the case of the death of any of the persons from whom the House of Representatives may choose a President whenever the right of choice shall have devolved upon them, and for the case of the death of any of the persons from whom the Senate may choose a Vice President whenever the right of choice shall have devolved upon them.

Section 5. Sections 1 and 2 shall take effect on the 15th day of October following the ratification of this article.

Section 6. This article shall be inoperative unless it shall have been ratified as an amendment to the Constitution by the legislatures of three fourths of the several States within seven years from the date of its submission.

ARTICLE XXI [3]

Section 1. The eighteenth article of amendment to the Constitution of the United States is hereby repealed.

Section 2. The transportation or importation into any State, Territory, or possession of the United States for delivery or use therein of intoxicating liquors, in violation of the laws thereof, is hereby prohibited.

[1] Proclaimed August 26, 1920.
[2] Proclaimed February 6, 1933.
[3] Proclaimed December 5, 1933. This amendment was ratified by state conventions.

Section 3. This article shall be inoperative unless it shall have been ratified as an amendment to the Constitution by conventions in the several States, as provided in the Constitution, within seven years from the date of submission hereof to the States by the Congress.[1]

[1] Six amendments have been proposed but not ratified. The first and second were proposed on Sept. 25, 1789, along with ten others which became the Bill of Rights. The first of these dealt with the apportionment of members of the House of Representatives. It was ratified by ten states, eleven being the necessary three-fourths. The second provided that "No law, varying the compensation for the services of the Senators and Representatives, shall take effect, until an election of Representatives shall have intervened." It was ratified by six states, eleven being necessary. A third was proposed on May 1, 1810, which would have abrogated the citizenship of any persons accepting foreign titles or honors. It was ratified by twelve states, fourteen being necessary. A fourth was proposed on Mar. 4, 1861, which prohibited the adoption of any amendment "to abolish or interfere, within any state, with the domestic institutions thereof, including that of persons held to labor or service by the laws of that state." This was approved by three states. The fifth, the proposed child-labor amendment, was proposed on June 2, 1924. It provides:

Section 1—The Congress shall have power to limit, regulate, and prohibit the labor of persons under eighteen years of age.

Section 2—The power of the several States is unimpaired by this article except that the operation of State laws shall be suspended to the extent necessary to give effect to legislation enacted by Congress.

This has been ratified by twenty-eight states and rejected in eleven. The approval of thirty-six states is necessary to complete ratification. A sixth, intended to limit the President to two terms, was proposed in March, 1947. It reads:

Section 1—No person shall be elected to the office of the President more than twice, and no person who has held the office of President, or acted as President, for more than two years of a term to which some other person was elected President shall be elected to the office of the President more than once. But this Article shall not apply to any person holding the office of President when this Article was proposed by the Congress, and shall not prevent any person who may be holding the office of President, or acting as President, during the term within which this Article becomes operative from holding the office of President, or acting as President during the remainder of such term.

Section 2—This Article shall be inoperative unless it shall have been ratified as an amendment to the Constitution by the legislatures of three-fourths of the several States within seven years from the date of its submission to the States by the Congress.

As of January 21, 1949, twenty-two states had ratified, thirty-six being required.

Appendix IV

CHARTER OF THE UNITED NATIONS

We the peoples of the United Nations determined to save succeeding generations from the scourge of war, which twice in our lifetime has brought untold sorrow to mankind, and to reaffirm faith in fundamental human rights, in the dignity and worth of the human person, in the equal rights of men and women and of nations large and small, and to establish conditions under which justice and respect for the obligations arising from treaties and other sources of international law can be maintained, and to promote social progress and better standards of life in larger freedom, *and for these ends* to practice tolerance and live together in peace with one another as good neighbors, and to unite our strength to maintain international peace and security, and to ensure, by the acceptance of principles and the institution of methods, that armed force shall not be used, save in the common interest, and to employ international machinery for the promotion of the economic and social advancement of all peoples, *have resolved to combine our efforts to accomplish these aims.*

Accordingly, our respective Governments, through representatives assembled in the city of San Francisco, who have exhibited their full powers found to be in good and due form, have agreed to the present Charter of the United Nations and do hereby establish an international organization to be known as the United Nations.

CHAPTER I

PURPOSES AND PRINCIPLES

Article 1

The Purposes of the United Nations are:

1. To maintain international peace and security, and to that end: to take effective collective measures for the prevention and removal of threats to the peace, and for the suppression of acts of aggression or other breaches of the peace, and to bring about by peaceful means, and in conformity with the principles of justice and international law, adjustment or settlement of international disputes or situations which might lead to breach of the peace;

2. To develop friendly relations among nations based on respect for the principle of equal rights and self-determination of peoples, and to take other appropriate measures to strengthen universal peace;

3. To achieve international cooperation in solving international problems of an economic, social, cultural, or humanitarian character, and in promoting and encouraging respect for human rights and for fundamental freedoms for all without distinction as to race, sex, language, or religion; and

4. To be a center for harmonizing the actions of nations in the attainment of these common ends.

Article 2

The Organization and its Members, in pursuit of the Purposes stated in Article 1, shall act in accordance with the following Principles.

1. The Organization is based on the principle of the sovereign equality of all its Members.

2. All Members, in order to ensure to all of them the rights and benefits resulting from membership, shall fulfil in good faith the obligations assumed by them in accordance with the present Charter.

3. All Members shall settle their international disputes by peaceful means in such a manner that international peace and security, and justice, are not endangered.

4. All Members shall refrain in their international relations from the threat or use of force against the territorial integrity or political independence or any state, or in any other manner inconsistent with the Purposes of the United Nations.

5. All Members shall give the United Nations every assistance in any action it takes in accordance with the present Charter, and shall refrain from giving assistance to any state against which the United Nations is taking preventive or enforcement action.

6. The Organization shall ensure that states which are not Members of the United Nations act in accordance with these Principles so far as may be necessary for the maintenance of international peace and security.

7. Nothing contained in the present Charter shall authorize the United Nations to intervene in matters which are essentially within the domestic jurisdiction of any state or shall require the Members to submit such matters to settlement under the present Charter; but this principle shall not prejudice the application of enforcement measures under Chapter VII.

CHAPTER II

MEMBERSHIP

Article 3

The original Members of the United Nations shall be the states which, having participated in the United Nations Conference on International Organization at San Francisco, or having previously signed the Declaration by United Nations of January 1, 1942, sign the present Charter and ratify it in accordance with Article 110.

Article 4

1. Membership in the United Nations is open to all other peace-loving states which accept the obligations contained in the present Charter and, in the judgment of the Organization, are able and willing to carry out these obligations.

2. The admission of any such state to membership in the United Nations will be effected by a decision of the General Assembly upon the recommendation of the Security Council.

Article 5

A Member of the United Nations against which preventive or enforcement action has been taken by the Security Council may be suspended from the exercise of the rights and privileges of membership by the General Assembly upon the recommendation of the Security Council. The exercise of these rights and privileges may be restored by the Security Council.

Article 6

A Member of the United Nations which has persistently violated the Principles contained in the present Charter may be expelled from the Organization by the General Assembly upon the recommendation of the Security Council.

CHAPTER III

ORGANS

Article 7

1. There are established as the principal organs of the United Nations: a General Assembly, a Security Council, an Economic and Social Council, a Trusteeship Council, an International Court of Justice, and a Secretariat.
2. Such subsidiary organs as may be found necessary may be established in accordance with the present Charter.

Article 8

The United Nations shall place no restrictions on the eligibility of men and women to participate in any capacity and under conditions of equality in its principal and subsidiary organs.

CHAPTER IV

THE GENERAL ASSEMBLY

Composition

Article 9

1. The General Assembly shall consist of all the Members of the United Nations.
2. Each Member shall have not more than five representatives in the General Assembly.

Functions and Powers

Article 10

The General Assembly may discuss any questions or any matters within the scope of the present Charter or relating to the powers and functions of any organs provided for in the present Charter, and, except as provided in Article 12, may make recommendations to the Members of the United Nations or to the Security Council or to both on any such questions or matters.

Article 11

1. The General Assembly may consider the general principles of cooperation in the maintenance of international peace and security, including the principles governing disarmament and the regulation of armaments, and may make recommendations with regard to such principles to the Members or to the Security Council or to both.
2. The General Assembly may discuss any questions relating to the maintenance of international peace and security brought before it by any Member of the United Nations, or by the Security Council, or by a state which is not a Member of the United Nations in accordance with Article 35, paragraph 2, and, except as provided in Article

12, may make recommendations with regard to any such questions to the state or states concerned or to the Security Council or to both. Any such question on which action is necessary shall be referred to the Security Council by the General Assembly either before or after discussion.

3. The General Assembly may call the attention of the Security Council to situations which are likely to endanger international peace and security.

4. The powers of the General Assembly set forth in this Article shall not limit the general scope of Article 10.

Article 12

1. While the Security Council is exercising in respect of any dispute or situation the functions assigned to it in the present Charter, the General Assembly shall not make any recommendation with regard to that dispute or situation unless the Security Council so requests.

2. The Secretary-General, with the consent of the Security Council, shall notify the General Assembly at each session of any matters relative to the maintenance of international peace and security which are being dealt with by the Security Council and shall similarly notify the General Assembly, or the Members of the United Nations if the General Assembly is not in session, immediately the Security Council ceases to deal with such matters.

Article 13

1. The General Assembly shall initiate studies and make recommendations for the purpose of:

a. promoting international cooperation in the political field and encouraging the progressive development of international law and its codification;

b. promoting international cooperation in the economic, social, cultural, educational, and health fields, and assisting in the realization of human rights and fundamental freedoms for all without distinction as to race, sex, language, or religion.

2. The further responsibilities, functions, and powers of the General Assembly with respect to matters mentioned in paragraph 1 (b) above are set forth in Chapters IX and X.

Article 14

Subject to the provisions of Article 12, the General Assembly may recommend measures for the peaceful adjustment of any situation, regardless of origin, which it deems likely to impair the general welfare or friendly relations among nations, including situations resulting from a violation of the provisions of the present Charter setting forth the Purposes and Principles of the United Nations.

Article 15

1. The General Assembly shall receive and consider annual and special reports from the Security Council; these reports shall include an account of the measures that the Security Council has decided upon or taken to maintain international peace and security.

2. The General Assembly shall receive and consider reports from the other organs of the United Nations.

Article 16

The General Assembly shall perform such functions with respect to the international trusteeship system as are assigned to it under Chapters XII and XIII, including the approval of the trusteeship agreements for areas not designated as strategic.

Article 17

1. The General Assembly shall consider and approve the budget of the Organization.

2. The expenses of the Organization shall be borne by the Members as apportioned by the General Assembly.

3. The General Assembly shall consider and approve any financial and budgetary arrangements with specialized agencies referred to in Article 57 and shall examine the administrative budgets of such specialized agencies with a view to making recommendations to the agencies concerned.

Voting

Article 18

1. Each member of the General Assembly shall have one vote.

2. Decisions of the General Assembly on important questions shall be made by a two-thirds majority of the members present and voting. These questions shall include: recommendations with respect to the maintenance of international peace and security, the election of the non-permanent members of the Security Council, the election of the members of the Economic and Social Council, the election of members of the Trusteeship Council in accordance with paragraph 1 (c) of Article 86, the admission of new Members to the United Nations, the suspension of the rights and privileges of membership, the expulsion of Members, questions relating to the operation of the trusteeship system, and budgetary questions.

3. Decisions on other questions, including the determination of additional categories of questions to be decided by a two-thirds majority, shall be made by a majority of the members present and voting.

Article 19

A Member of the United Nations which is in arrears in the payment of its financial contributions to the Organization shall have no vote in the General Assembly if the amount of its arrears equals or exceeds the amount of the contributions due from it for the preceding two full years. The General Assembly may, nevertheless, permit such a Member to vote if it is satisfied that the failure to pay is due to conditions beyond the control of the Member.

Procedure

Article 20

The General Assembly shall meet in regular annual sessions and in such special sessions as occasion may require. Special sessions shall be convoked by the Secretary-General at the request of the Security Council or of a majority of the Members of the United Nations.

Article 21

The General Assembly shall adopt its own rules of procedure. It shall elect its President for each session.

Article 22

The General Assembly may establish such subsidiary organs as it deems necessary for the performance of its functions.

CHAPTER V

THE SECURITY COUNCIL

Composition

Article 23

1. The Security Council shall consist of eleven Members of the United Nations. The Republic of China, France, the Union of Soviet Socialist Republics, the United Kingdom of Great Britain and Northern Ireland, and the United States of America shall be permanent members of the Security Council. The General Assembly shall elect six other Members of the United Nations to be non-permanent members of the Security Council, due regard being specially paid, in the first instance to the contribution of Members of the United Nations to the maintenance of international peace and security and to the other purposes of the Organization, and also to equitable geographical distribution.

2. The non-permanent members of the Security Council shall be elected for a term of two years. In the first election of the non-permanent members, however, three shall be chosen for a term of one year. A retiring member shall not be eligible for immediate re-election.

3. Each member of the Security Council shall have one representative.

Functions and Powers

Article 24

1. In order to ensure prompt and effective action by the United Nations, its Members confer on the Security Council primary responsibility for the maintenance of international peace and security, and agree that in carrying out its duties under this responsibility the Security Council acts on their behalf.

2. In discharging these duties the Security Council shall act in accordance with the Purposes and Principles of the United Nations. The Specific powers granted to the Security Council for the discharge of these duties are laid down in Chapters VI, VII, VIII, and XII.

3. The Security Council shall submit annual and, when necessary, special reports to the General Assembly for its consideration.

Article 25

The Members of the United Nations agree to accept and carry out the decisions of the Security Council in accordance with the present Charter.

Article 26

In order to promote the establishment and maintenance of international peace and security with the least diversion for armaments of the world's human and economic resources, the Security Council shall be responsible for formulating, with the assistance of the Military Staff Committee referred to in Article 47, plans to be submitted to the Members of the United Nations for the establishment of a system for the regulation of armaments.

VOTING

Article 27

1. Each member of the Security Council shall have one vote.

2. Decisions of the Security Council on procedural matters shall be made by an affirmative vote of seven members.

3. Decisions of the Security Council on all other matters shall be made by an affirmative vote of seven members including the concurring votes of the permanent members; provided that, in decisions under Chapter VI, and under paragraph 3 of Article 52, a party to a dispute shall abstain from voting.

PROCEDURE

Article 28

1. The Security Council shall be so organized as to be able to function continuously. Each member of the Security Council shall for this purpose be represented at all times at the seat of the Organization.

2. The Security Council shall hold periodic meetings at which each of its members may, if it so desires, be represented by a member of the government or by some other specially designated representative.

3. The Security Council may hold meetings at such places other than the seat of the Organization as in its judgment will best facilitate its work.

Article 29

The Security Council may establish such subsidiary organs as it deems necessary for the performance of its functions.

Article 30

The Security Council shall adopt its own rules of procedure, including the method of selecting its President.

Article 31

Any Member of the United Nations which is not a member of the Security Council may participate, without vote, in the discussion of any question brought before the Security Council whenever the latter considers that the interests of that Member are specially affected.

Article 32

Any Member of the United Nations which is not a member of the Security Council or any state which is not a Member of the United Nations, if it is a party to a dispute under consideration by the Security Council, shall be invited to participate, without vote, in the discussion relating to the dispute. The Security Council shall lay down such conditions as it deems just for the participation of a state which is not a Member of the United Nations.

CHAPTER VI

PACIFIC SETTLEMENT OF DISPUTES

Article 33

1. The parties to any dispute, the continuance of which is likely to endanger the maintenance of international peace and security, shali, first of all, seek a solution by

negotiation, enquiry, mediation, conciliation, arbitration, judicial settlement, resort to regional agencies or arrangements, or other peaceful means of their own choice.

2. The Security Council shall, when it deems necessary, call upon the parties to settle their dispute by such means.

Article 34

The Security Council may investigate any dispute, or any situation which might lead to international friction or give rise to a dispute, in order to determine whether the continuance of the dispute or situation is likely to endanger the maintenance of international peace and security.

Article 35

1. Any Member of the United Nations may bring any dispute, or any situation of the nature referred to in Article 34, to the attention of the Security Council or of the General Assembly.

2. A state which is not a member of the United Nations may bring to the attention of the Security Council or of the General Assembly any dispute to which it is a party if it accepts in advance, for the purposes of the dispute, the obligations of pacific settlement provided in the present Charter.

3. The proceedings of the General Assembly in respect of matters brought to its attention under this Article will be subject to the provisions of Articles 11 and 12.

Article 36

1. The Security Council may, at any stage of a dispute of the nature referred to in Article 33 or of a situation of like nature, recommend appropriate procedures or methods of adjustment.

2. The Security Council should take into consideration any procedures for the settlement of the dispute which have already been adopted by the parties.

3. In making recommendations under this Article the Security Council should also take into consideration that legal disputes should as a general rule be referred by the parties to the International Court of Justice in accordance with the provisions of the Statute of the Court.

Article 37

1. Should the parties to a dispute of the nature referred to in Article 33 fail to settle it by the means indicated in that Article, they shall refer it to the Security Council.

2. If the Security Council deems that the continuance of the dispute is in fact likely to endanger the maintenance of international peace and security, it shall decide whether to take action under Article 36 or to recommend such terms of settlement as it may consider appropriate.

Article 38

Without prejudice to the provisions of Articles 33 to 37, the Security Council may, if all the parties to any dispute so request, make recommendations to the parties with a view to a pacific settlement of the dispute.

CHAPTER VII

ACTION WITH RESPECT TO THREATS TO THE PEACE, BREACHES OF THE PEACE, AND ACTS OF AGGRESSION

Article 39

The Security Council shall determine the existence of any threat to the peace, breach of the peace, or act of aggression and shall make recommendations, or decide what measures shall be taken in accordance with Articles 41 and 42, to maintain or restore international peace and security.

Article 40

In order to prevent an aggravation of the situation, the Security Council may, before making the recommendations or deciding upon the measures provided for in Article 39, call upon the parties concerned to comply with such provisional measures as it deems necessary or desirable. Such provisional measures shall be without prejudice to the rights, claims, or position of the parties concerned. The Security Council shall duly take account of failure to comply with such provisional measures.

Article 41

The Security Council may decide what measures not involving the use of armed force are to be employed to give effect to its decisions, and it may call upon the Members of the United Nations to apply such measures. These may include complete or partial interruption of economic relations and of rail, sea, air, postal, telegraphic, radio, and other means of communication, and the severance of diplomatic relations.

Article 42

Should the Security Council consider that measures provided for in Article 41 would be inadequate or have proved to be inadequate, it may take such action by air, sea, or land forces as may be necessary to maintain or restore international peace and security. Such action may include demonstrations, blockade, and other operations by air, sea, or land forces of Members of the United Nations.

Article 43

1. All Members of the United Nations, in order to contribute to the maintenance of international peace and security, undertake to make available to the Security Council, on its call and in accordance with a special agreement or agreements, armed forces, assistance, and facilities, including rights of passage, necessary for the purpose of maintaining international peace and security.

2. Such agreement or agreements shall govern the numbers and types of forces, their degree of readiness and general location, and the nature of the facilities and assistance to be provided.

3. The agreement or agreements shall be negotiated as soon as possible on the initiative of the Security Council. They shall be concluded between the Security Council and Members or between the Security Council and groups of Members and shall be subject to ratification by the signatory states in accordance with their respective constitutional processes.

Article 44

When the Security Council has decided to use force it shall, before calling upon a Member not represented on it to provide armed forces in fulfillment of the obligations assumed under Article 43, invite that Member, if the Member so desires, to participate in the decisions of the Security Council concerning the employment of contingents of that Member's armed forces.

Article 45

In order to enable the United Nations to take urgent military measures, Members shall hold immediately available national air-force contingents for combined international enforcement action. The strength and degree of readiness of these contingents and plans for their combined action shall be determined, within the limits laid down in the special agreement or agreements referred to in Article 43, by the Security Council with the assistance of the Military Staff Committee.

Article 46

Plans for the application of armed force shall be made by the Security Council with the assistance of the Military Staff Committee.

Article 47

1. There shall be established a Military Staff Committee to advise and assist the Security Council on all questions relating to the Security Council's military requirements for the maintenance of international peace and security, the employment and command of forces placed at its disposal, the regulation of armaments, and possible disarmament.
2. The Military Staff Committee shall consist of the Chiefs of Staff of the permanent members of the Security Council or their representatives. Any Member of the United Nations not permanently represented on the Committee shall be invited by the Committee to be associated with it when the efficient discharge of the Committee's responsibilities requires the participation of that Member in its work.
3. The Military Staff Committee shall be responsible under the Security Council for the strategic direction of any armed forces placed at the disposal of the Security Council. Questions relating to the command of such forces shall be worked out subsequently.
4. The Military Staff Committee, with the authorization of the Security Council and after consultation with appropriate regional agencies, may establish regional subcommittees.

Article 48

1. The action required to carry out the decisions of the Security Council for the maintenance of international peace and security shall be taken by all the Members of the United Nations or by some of them, as the Security Council may determine.
2. Such decisions shall be carried out by the Members of the United Nations directly and through their action in the appropriate international agencies of which they are members.

Article 49

The Members of the United Nations shall join in affording mutual assistance in carrying out the measures decided upon by the Security Council.

Article 50

If preventive or enforcement measures against any state are taken by the Security Council, any other state, whether a Member of the United Nations or not, which finds itself confronted with special economic problems arising from the carrying out of those measures shall have the right to consult the Security Council with regard to a solution of those problems.

Article 51

Nothing in the present Charter shall impair the inherent right of individual or collective self-defense if an armed attack occurs against a Member of the United Nations, until the Security Council has taken the measures necessary to maintain international peace and security. Measures taken by Members in the exercise of this right of self-defense shall be immediately reported to the Security Council and shall not in any way affect the authority and responsibility of the Security Council under the present Charter to take at any time such action as it deems necessary in order to maintain or restore international peace and security.

CHAPTER VIII

REGIONAL ARRANGEMENTS

Article 52

1. Nothing in the present Charter precludes the existence of regional arrangements or agencies for dealing with such matters relating to the maintenance of international peace and security as are appropriate for regional action, provided that such arrangements or agencies and their activities are consistent with the Purposes and Principles of the United Nations.
2. The Members of the United Nations entering into such arrangements or constituting such agencies shall make every effort to achieve pacific settlement of local disputes through such regional arrangements or by such regional agencies before referring them to the Security Council.
3. The Security Council shall encourage the development of pacific settlement of local disputes through such regional arrangements or by such regional agencies either on the initiative of the states concerned or by reference from the Security Council.
4. This Article in no way impairs the application of Articles 34 and 35.

Article 53

1. The Security Council shall, where appropriate, utilize such regional arrangements or agencies for enforcement action under its authority. But no enforcement action shall be taken under regional arrangements or by regional agencies without the authorization of the Security Council, with the exception of measures against any enemy state, as defined in paragraph 2 of this Article, provided for pursuant to Article 107 or in regional arrangements directed against renewal of aggressive policy on the part of any such state, until such time as the Organization may, on request of the Governments concerned, be charged with the responsibility for preventing further aggression by such a state.
2. The term enemy state as used in paragraph 1 of this Article applies to any state which during the Second World War has been an enemy of any signatory of the present Charter.

Article 54

The Security Council shall at all times be kept fully informed of activities undertaken or in contemplation under regional arrangements or by regional agencies for the maintenance of international peace and security.

CHAPTER IX

INTERNATIONAL ECONOMIC AND SOCIAL COOPERATION

Article 55

With a view to the creation of conditions of stability and well-being which are necessary for peaceful and friendly relations among nations based on respect for the principle of equal rights and self-determination of peoples, the United Nations shall promote:

a. higher standards of living, full employment, and conditions of economic and social progress and development;

b. solutions of international economic, social, health, and related problems; and international cultural and educational cooperation; and

c. universal respect for, and observance of, human rights and fundamental freedoms for all without distinction as to race, sex, language, or religion.

Article 56

All Members pledge themselves to take joint and separate action in cooperation with the Organization for the achievement of the purposes set forth in Article 55.

Article 57

1. The various specialized agencies, established by intergovernmental agreement and having wide international responsibilities, as defined in their basic instruments, in economic, social, cultural, educational, health, and related fields, shall be brought into relationship with the United Nations in accordance with the provisions of Article 63.

2. Such agencies thus brought into relationship with the United Nations are hereinafter referred to as specialized agencies.

Article 58

The Organization shall make recommendations for the coordination of the policies and activities of the specialized agencies.

Article 59

The Organization shall, where appropriate, initiate negotiations among the states concerned for the creation of any new specialized agencies required for the accomplishment of the purposes set forth in Article 55.

Article 60

Responsibility for the discharge of the functions of the Organization set forth in this Chapter shall be vested in the General Assembly and, under the authority of the General Assembly, in the Economic and Social Council, which shall have for this purpose the powers set forth in Chapter X.

CHAPTER X

THE ECONOMIC AND SOCIAL COUNCIL

COMPOSITION

Article 61

1. The Economic and Social Council shall consist of eighteen Members of the United Nations elected by the General Assembly.

2. Subject to the provisions of paragraph 3, six members of the Economic and Social Council shall be elected each year for a term of three years. A retiring member shall be eligible for immediate re-election.

3. At the first election, eighteen members of the Economic and Social Council shall be chosen. The term of office of six members so chosen shall expire at the end of one year, and of six other members at the end of two years, in accordance with arrangements made by the General Assembly.

4. Each member of the Economic and Social Council shall have one representative.

Functions and Powers

Article 62

1. The Economic and Social Council may make or initiate studies and reports with respect to international economic, social, cultural, educational, health, and related matters and may make recommendations with respect to any such matters to the General Assembly, to the Members of the United Nations, and to the specialized agencies concerned.

2. It may make recommendations for the purpose of promoting respect for, and observance of, human rights and fundamental freedoms for all.

3. It may prepare draft conventions for submission to the General Assembly, with respect to matters falling within its competence.

4. It may call, in accordance with the rules prescribed by the United Nations, international conferences on matters falling within its competence.

Article 63

1. The Economic and Social Council may enter into agreements with any of the agencies referred to in Article 57, defining the terms on which the agency concerned shall be brought into relationship with the United Nations. Such agreements shall be subject to approval by the General Assembly.

2. It may coordinate the activities of the specialized agencies through consultation with and recommendations to such agencies and through recommendations to the General Assembly and to the Members of the United Nations.

Article 64

1. The Economic and Social Council may take appropriate steps to obtain regular reports from the specialized agencies. It may make arrangements with the Members of the United Nations and with the specialized agencies to obtain reports on the steps taken to give effect to its own recommendations and to recommendations on matters falling within its competence made by the General Assembly.

2. It may communicate its observations on these reports to the General Assembly.

Article 65

The Economic and Social Council may furnish information to the Security Council and shall assist the Security Council upon its request.

Article 66

1. The Economic and Social Council shall perform such functions as fall within its competence in connection with the carrying out of the recommendations of the General Assembly.

2. It may, with the approval of the General Assembly, perform services at the request of Members of the United Nations and at the request of specialized agencies.

3. It shall perform such other functions as are specified elsewhere in the present Charter or as may be assigned to it by the General Assembly.

VOTING

Article 67

1. Each member of the Economic and Social Council shall have one vote.

2. Decisions of the Economic and Social Council shall be made by a majority of the members present and voting.

PROCEDURE

Article 68

The Economic and Social Council shall set up commissions in economic and social fields and for the promotion of human rights, and such other commissions as may be required for the performance of its functions.

Article 69

The Economic and Social Council shall invite any Member of the United Nations to participate, without vote, in its deliberations on any matter of particular concern to that Member.

Article 70

The Economic and Social Council may make arrangements for representatives of the specialized agencies to participate, without vote, in its deliberations and in those of the commissions established by it, and for its representatives to participate in the deliberations of the specialized agencies.

Article 71

The Economic and Social Council may make suitable arrangements for consultation with non-governmental organizations which are concerned with matters within its competence. Such arrangements may be made with international organizations and, where appropriate, with national organizations after consultation with the Member of the United Nations concerned.

Article 72

1. The Economic and Social Council shall adopt its own rules of procedure, including the method of selecting its President.

2. The Economic and Social Council shall meet as required in accordance with its rules, which shall include provision for the convening of meetings on the request of a majority of its members.

CHAPTER XI

DECLARATION REGARDING NON-SELF-GOVERNING TERRITORIES

Article 73

Members of the United Nations which have or assume responsibilities for the administration of territories whose peoples have not yet attained a full measure of self-government recognize the principle that the interests of the inhabitants of these territories are paramount, and accept as a sacred trust the obligation to promote to the utmost, within the system of international peace and security established by the present Charter, the well-being of the inhabitants of these territories, and, to this end:

a. to ensure, with due respect for the culture of the peoples concerned, their political, economic, social, and educational advancement, their just treatment, and their protection against abuses;

b. to develop self-government, to take due account of the political aspirations of the peoples, and to assist them in the progressive development of their free political institutions, according to the particular circumstances of each territory and its peoples and their varying stages of advancement;

c. to further international peace and security;

d. to promote constructive measures of development, to encourage research, and to cooperate with one another and, when and where appropriate, with specialized international bodies with a view to the practical achievement of the social, economic, and scientific purposes set forth in this Article; and

e. to transmit regularly to the Secretary-General for information purposes, subject to such limitation as security and constitutional considerations may require, statistical and other information of a technical nature relating to economic, social, and educational conditions in the territories for which they are respectively responsible other than those territories to which Chapters XII and XIII apply.

Article 74

Members of the United Nations also agree that their policy in respect of the territories to which this Chapter applies, no less than in respect of their metropolitan areas, must be based on the general principle of good-neighborliness, due account being taken of the interests and well-being of the rest of the world, in social, economic, and commercial matters.

CHAPTER XII

INTERNATIONAL TRUSTEESHIP SYSTEM

Article 75

The United Nations shall establish under its authority an international trusteeship system for the administration and supervision of such territories as may be placed thereunder by subsequent individual agreements. These territories are hereinafter referred to as trust territories.

Article 76

The basic objectives of the trusteeship system, in accordance with the Purposes of the United Nations aid down in Article 1 of the present Charter, shall be:

a. to further international peace and security;

b. to promote the political, economic, social, and educational advancement of the inhabitants of the trust territories, and their progressive development towards self-government or independence as may be appropriate to the particular circumstances of each territory and its peoples and the freely expressed wishes of the peoples concerned, and as may be provided by the terms of each trusteeship agreement;

c. to encourage respect for human rights and for fundamental freedoms for all without distinction as to race, sex, language, or religion, and to encourage recognition of the interdependence of the peoples of the world; and

d. to ensure equal treatment in social, economic, and commercial matters for all Members of the United Nations and their nationals, and also equal treatment for the latter in the administration of justice, without prejudice to the attainment of the foregoing objectives and subject to the provisions of Article 80.

Article 77

1. The trusteeship system shall apply to such territories in the following categories as may be placed thereunder by means of trusteeship agreements:

a. territories now held under mandate;

b. territories which may be detached from enemy states as a result of the Second World War; and

c. territories voluntarily placed under the system by states responsible for their administration.

2. It will be a matter for subsequent agreement as to which territories in the foregoing categories will be brought under the trusteeship system and upon what terms.

Article 78

The trusteeship system shall not apply to territories which have become Members of the United Nations, relationship among which shall be based on respect for the principle of sovereign equality.

Article 79

The terms of trusteeship for each territory to be placed under the trusteeship system, including any alteration or amendment, shall be agreed upon by the states directly concerned, including the mandatory power in the case of territories held under mandate by a Member of the United Nations, and shall be approved as provided for in Articles 83 and 85.

Article 80

1. Except as may be agreed upon in individual trusteeship agreements, made under Articles 77, 79, and 81, placing each territory under the trusteeship system, and until such agreements have been concluded, nothing in this Chapter shall be construed in or of itself to alter in any manner the rights whatsoever of any states or any peoples or the terms of existing international instruments to which Members of the United Nations may respectively be parties.

2. Paragraph 1 of this Article shall not be interpreted as giving grounds for delay or postponement of the negotiation and conclusion of agreements for placing mandated and other territories under the trusteeship system as provided for in Article 77.

Article 81

The trusteeship agreement shall in each case include the terms under which the trust territory will be administered and designate the authority which will exercise the administration of the trust territory. Such authority, hereinafter called the administering authority, may be one or more states or the Organization itself.

Article 82

There may be designated, in any trusteeship agreement, a strategic area or areas which may include part or all of the trust territory to which the agreement applies, without prejudice to any special agreement or agreements made under Article 43.

Article 83

1. All functions of the United Nations relating to strategic areas, including the approval of the terms of the trusteeship agreements and of their alteration or amendment, shall be exercised by the Security Council.

2. The basic objectives set forth in Article 76 shall be applicable to the people of each strategic area.

3. The Security Council shall, subject to the provisions of the trusteeship agreements and without prejudice to security considerations, avail itself of the assistance of the Trusteeship Council to perform those functions of the United Nations under the trusteeship system relating to political, economic, social, and educational matters in the strategic areas.

Article 84

It shall be the duty of the administering authority to ensure that the trust territory shall play its part in the maintenance of international peace and security. To this end the administering authority may make use of volunteer forces, facilities, and assistance from the trust territory in carrying out the obligations towards the Security Council undertaken in this regard by the administering authority, as well as for local defense and the maintenance of law and order within the trust territory.

Article 85

1. The functions of the United Nations with regard to trusteeship agreements for all areas not designated as strategic, including the approval of the terms of the trusteeship agreements and of their alteration or amendment, shall be exercised by the General Assembly.

2. The Trusteeship Council, operating under the authority of the General Assembly, shall assist the General Assembly in carrying out these functions.

CHAPTER XIII

THE TRUSTEESHIP COUNCIL

Composition

Article 86

1. The Trusteeship Council shall consist of the following Members of the United Nations:

a. those Members administering trust territories;

b. such of those Members mentioned by name in Article 23 as are not administering trust territories; and

c. as many other Members elected for three-year terms by the General Assembly as may be necessary to ensure that the total number of members of the Trusteeship Council is equally divided between those Members of the United Nations which administer trust territories and those which do not.

2. Each member of the Trusteeship Council shall designate one specially qualified person to represent it therein.

Functions and Powers

Article 87

The General Assembly and, under its authority, the Trusteeship Council, in carrying out their functions, may:

a. consider reports submitted by the administering authority;

b. accept petitions and examine them in consultation with the administering authority;

c. provide for periodic visits to the respective trust territories at times agreed upon with the administering authority; and

d. take these and other actions in conformity with the terms of the trusteeship agreements.

Article 88

The Trusteeship Council shall formulate a questionnaire on the political, economic, social, and educational advancement of the inhabitants of each trust territory, and the administering authority for each trust territory within the competence of the General Assembly shall make an annual report to the General Assembly upon the basis of such questionnaire.

Voting

Article 89

1. Each member of the Trusteeship Council shall have one vote.
2. Decisions of the Trusteeship Council shall be made by a majority of the members present and voting.

Procedure

Article 90

1. The Trusteeship Council shall adopt its own rules of procedure, including the method of selecting its President.
2. The Trusteeship Council shall meet as required in accordance with its rules, which shall include provision for the convening of meetings on the request of a majority of its members.

Article 91

The Trusteeship Council shall, when appropriate, avail itself of the assistance of the Economic and Social Council and of the specialized agencies in regard to matters with which they are respectively concerned.

CHAPTER XIV

THE INTERNATIONAL COURT OF JUSTICE

Article 92

The International Court of Justice shall be the principal judicial organ of the United Nations. It shall function in accordance with the annexed Statute, which is based upon the Statute of the Permanent Court of International Justice and forms an integral part of the present Charter.

Article 93

1. All Members of the United Nations are *ipso facto* parties to the Statute of the International Court of Justice.

2. A state which is not a Member of the United Nations may become a party to the Statute of the International Court of Justice on conditions to be determined in each case by the General Assembly upon the recommendation of the Security Council.

Article 94

1. Each Member of the United Nations undertakes to comply with the decision of the International Court of Justice in any case to which it is a party.

2. If any party to a case fails to perform the obligations incumbent upon it under a judgment rendered by the Court, the other party may have recourse to the Security Council, which may, if it deems necessary, make recommendations or decide upon measures to be taken to give effect to the judgment.

Article 95

Nothing in the present Charter shall prevent Members of the United Nations from entrusting the solution of their differences to other tribunals by virtue of agreements already in existence or which may be concluded in the future.

Article 96

1. The General Assembly or the Security Council may request the International Court of Justice to give an advisory opinion on any legal question.

2. Other organs of the United Nations and specialized agencies, which may at any time be so authorized by the General Assembly, may also request advisory opinions of the Court on legal questions arising within the scope of their activities.

CHAPTER XV

THE SECRETARIAT

Article 97

The Secretariat shall comprise a Secretary-General and such staff as the Organization may require. The Secretary-General shall be appointed by the General Assembly upon the recommendation of the Security Council. He shall be the chief administrative officer of the Organization.

Article 98

The Secretary-General shall act in that capacity in all meetings of the General Assembly, of the Security Council, of the Economic and Social Council, and of the Trusteeship Council, and shall perform such other functions as are entrusted to him by these organs. The Secretary-General shall make an annual report to the General Assembly on the work of the Organization.

Article 99

The Secretary-General may bring to the attention of the Security Council any matter which in his opinion may threaten the maintenance of international peace and security.

Article 100

1. In the performance of their duties the Secretary-General and the staff shall not seek or receive instructions from any government or from any other authority external to the Organization. They shall refrain from any action which might reflect on their position as international officials responsible only to the Organization.

2. Each Member of the United Nations undertakes to respect the exclusively international character of the responsibilities of the Secretary-General and the staff and not to seek to influence them in the discharge of their responsibilities.

Article 101

1. The staff shall be appointed by the Secretary-General under regulations established by the General Assembly.

2. Appropriate staffs shall be permanently assigned to the Economic and Social Council, the Trusteeship Council, and, as required, to other organs of the United Nations. These staffs shall form a part of the Secretariat.

3. The paramount consideration in the employment of the staff and in the determination of the conditions of service shall be the necessity of securing the highest standards of efficiency, competence, and integrity. Due regard shall be paid to the importance of recruiting the staff on as wide a geographical basis as possible.

CHAPTER XVI

MISCELLANEOUS PROVISIONS

Article 102

1. Every treaty and every international agreement entered into by any Member of the United Nations after the present Charter comes into force shall as soon as possible be registered with the Secretariat and published by it.

2. No party to any such treaty or international agreement which has not been registered in accordance with the provisions of paragraph 1 of this Article may invoke that treaty or agreement before any organ of the United Nations.

Article 103

In the event of a conflict between the obligations of the Members of the United Nations under the present Charter and their obligations under any other international agreement, their obligations under the present Charter shall prevail.

Article 104

The Organization shall enjoy in the territory of each of its Members such legal capacity as may be necessary for the exercise of its functions and the fulfillment of its purposes.

Article 105

1. The Organization shall enjoy in the territory of each of its Members such privileges and immunities as are necessary for the fulfillment of its purposes.

2. Representatives of the Members of the United Nations and officials of the Organization shall similarly enjoy such privileges and immunities as are necessary for the independent exercise of their functions in connection with the Organization.

3. The General Assembly may make recommendations with a view to determining the details of the application of paragraphs 1 and 2 of this Article or may propose conventions to the Members of the United Nations for this purpose.

CHAPTER XVII

TRANSITIONAL SECURITY ARRANGEMENTS

Article 106

Pending the coming into force of such special agreements referred to in Article 43 as in the opinion of the Security Council enable it to begin the exercise of its responsibilities under Article 42, the parties to the Four-Nation Declaration, signed at Moscow, October 30, 1943, and France, shall, in accordance with the provisions of paragraph 5 of that Declaration, consult with one another and as occasion requires with other Members of the United Nations with a view to such joint action on behalf of the Organization as may be necessary for the purpose of maintaining international peace and security.

Article 107

Nothing in the present Charter shall invalidate or preclude action, in relation to any state which during the Second World War has been an enemy of any signatory to the present Charter, taken or authorized as a result of that war by the Governments having responsibility for such action.

CHAPTER XVIII

AMENDMENTS

Article 108

Amendments to the present Charter shall come into force for all Members of the United Nations when they have been adopted by a vote of two thirds of the members of the General Assembly and ratified in accordance with their respective constitutional processes by two thirds of the Members of the United Nations, including all the permanent members of the Security Council.

Article 109

1. A General Conference of the Members of the United Nations for the purpose of reviewing the present Charter may be held at a date and place to be fixed by a two-thirds vote of the members of the General Assembly and by a vote of any seven members of the Security Council. Each Member of the United Nations shall have one vote in the conference.

2. Any alteration of the present Charter recommended by a two-thirds vote of the conference shall take effect when ratified in accordance with their respective constitutional processes by two thirds of the Members of the United Nations including all the permanent members of the Security Council.

3. If such a conference has not been held before the tenth annual session of the General Assembly following the coming into force of the present Charter, the proposal to call such a conference shall be placed on the agenda of that session of the General Assembly, and the conference shall be held if so decided by a majority vote of the members of the General Assembly and by a vote of any seven members of the Security Council.

CHAPTER XIX

RATIFICATION AND SIGNATURE

Article 110

1. The present Charter shall be ratified by the signatory states in accordance with their respective constitutional processes.

2. The ratifications shall be deposited with the Government of the United States of America, which shall notify all the signatory states of each deposit as well as the Secretary-General of the Organization when he has been appointed.

3. The present Charter shall come into force upon the deposit of ratifications by the Republic of China, France, the Union of Soviet Socialist Republics, the United Kingdom of Great Britain and Northern Ireland, and the United States of America, and by a majority of the other signatory states. A protocol of the ratifications deposited shall thereupon be drawn up by the Government of the United States of America which shall communicate copies thereof to all the signatory states.

4. The states signatory to the present Charter which ratify it after it has come into force will become original Members of the United Nations on the date of the deposit of their respective ratifications.

Article 111

The present Charter, of which the Chinese, French, Russian, English, and Spanish texts are equally authentic, shall remain deposited in the archives of the Government of the United States of America. Duly certified copies thereof shall be transmitted by that Government to the Governments of the other signatory states.

In faith whereof the representatives of the Governments of the United Nations have signed the present Charter.

Done at the city of San Francisco the twenty-sixth day of June, one thousand nine hundred and forty-five.

Appendix V

LIST OF VISUAL MATERIALS

The following list of visual materials may be used to supplement some of the material in this book. This list, although subdivided by chapters, is comprehensive rather than selective. Therefore, we would suggest that each film be previewed before using, since some may contain information that is too advanced while others may contain information that is too elementary.

These films can be obtained from the producer or distributor listed with each title. (The addresses are given at the end of the bibliography.) In many cases these films can be obtained from your local film library or local film distributor; also, many universities have large film libraries from which films may be borrowed.

The running time (min) and whether it is silent (si) or sound (sd) are listed with each title. All the motion pictures are 16mm black and white films unless otherwise stated.

Each film has been listed once in connection with the chapter to which it is most applicable. However, in many cases the film might be used advantageously in other chapters.

CHAPTER 1—GOVERNMENT AND MODERN SOCIETY

The Meaning of Feudalism (Coronet 10min sd). Presents physical elements and recreates flavor and spirit of feudal times.

Interdependence (Howard 30min si). Shows the dependence of individuals, communities, and nations upon one another.

Man the Enigma (Pictorial 30min sd). Democracy as a way of life.

Democracy (EBF 11min sd). Presents nature and meaning of democracy with emphasis upon the economic and social conditions required to make it succeed.

Despotism (EBF 11min sd). Portrays characteristics of despotic governments with emphasis upon underlying economic and social phenomena.

CHAPTER 2—COLONIZATION, INDEPENDENCE, AND CONFEDERATION

Colonial Expansion (EBF 11min sd). North America, 1492–1763, showing conflicts among French, English, Dutch, and Spanish.

Discovery and Exploration (EBF 11min sd). North America, 1492–1700, showing paths of explorers and early trade routes.

Courageous Mr. Penn (Allied 84min sd). Struggle for liberty in England under Charles II; Penn's part in founding a free commonwealth in Pennsylvania.

Early Settlers of New England (EBF 11min sd). Shows people of Salem about 1626, their mode of life, the beginnings of American democracy.

Eighteenth Century Life in Williamsburg, Virginia (Eastman 44min sd color). A chronicle of early colonial history illustrated by the restoration of Williamsburg, the capital of colonial Virginia.

A Planter of Colonial Virginia (EBF 12min sd). Representative phases of colonial life, 1740–1785.

Give Me Liberty (TFC 20min sd). Virginia in 1765, featuring Patrick Henry's famous speech.

Sons of Liberty (TFC 20min sd color). Story of Haym Solomon, who raised a fortune to finance American revolution.

Jefferson of Monticello (VaStDeptEd 18min sd color). Portrays Jefferson's role in history, including drafting the Declaration of Independence.

Our Declaration of Independence (Post 20min sd). Shows characters and events that resulted in adoption of the Declaration of Independence.

Declaration of Independence (TFC 20min sd color). Depicts preliminary drafting and signing of Declaration of Independence.

Life in the Colonies (Still Films 50 frames FS).

Old New York (Still Films 50 frames FS). Covers 1675–1775.

Period Following Revolution—Adoption of Constitution (Still Films 50 frames FS).

Declaration of Independence (Still Films 50 frames FS).

CHAPTER 3—FRAMING AND ADOPTING THE CONSTITUTION

Servant of the People (TFC 20min sd). Shows the background and making of the Constitution.

Benjamin Franklin (EBF 20min sd). Events in the life of the great American statesman, concluding with the Constitutional Convention.

Seed of the Constitution (Nu-Art 9min sd). Dramatizes Benjamin Franklin's plan for a union of the colonies under the British Crown.

CHAPTER 4—CONSTITUTIONAL PRINCIPLES AND METHODS OF CHANGE

Our Living Constitution (Coronet 10min sd color). Shows how basis of our government changes and how it grows to meet needs of the times while holding to the original principles of thought.

Meet Your Federal Government (YA 15min sd). Explains power and function of Federal government and its three main branches.

Our National Government (Knowledge 11min sd). Gives a graphic analysis of the national government in all its branches.

CHAPTER 5—THE FEDERAL SYSTEM

Westward Movement (EBF 12min sd). Territorial expansion and admission of new states, 1790–1890.

Toward Better Schools for All Children through Federal Aid (NEA FS). Supports proposed grants-in-aid for general education.

CHAPTER 7—INDIVIDUAL RIGHTS

Glass Bell (AFFilms 11min sd). Story of the average man in France under a life of tyranny and threat to all men who are indifferent to democratic process.

Universal Declaration of Human Rights (UnFlmDiv FS). Describes human rights of all mankind and gives specific examples of violation.

Crossroads for America (Research Inst. 35min sd). The other side of the film "Deadline for Action" (listed under Chapter 9). Shows what Communists are after and how they work.

Bill of Rights (TFC 20min sd color). Shows struggle to incorporate Bill in the Federal Constitution.

World We Want to Live In (NCCJ 11min sd). Emphasizes the importance of religious liberty and tolerance.

Americans All (MOT 20min sd). A study of how to prevent religious and racial intolerance.

CHAPTER 8—POPULATION, IMMIGRATION, ALIENS, AND CITIZENSHIP

Immigration (EBF 11min sd). Describes immigration to United States and naturalization and induction to citizenship.

Procedures of the United States for Ships and Passengers Entering the United States (Frith 15min si). An authentic description of the procedure.

Swedes in America (Castle 20min sd). Emphasizes the contribution of Americans of Swedish descent.

Greenie (TFC 10min sd). A story of a Polish immigrant child learning about America.

Sing a Song of Friendship (Anti-D.L. 30min sd). Through animation and music makes strong case for tolerance of all Americans, regardless of national origins.

CHAPTER 9—PUBLIC OPINION AND PRESSURE GROUPS

Gallup Poll (TFC 11min sd). Shows how this popular poll is conducted.

Public Opinion (EBF 11min sd). A realistic analysis of public opinion, what it is, and how it is formed.

Does It Matter What You Think? (BIS 15min sd). Depicts formation of opinions and their importance.

Deadline for Action (UE 40min sd). Demonstrates political action in influencing Congress.

Discussion in a Democracy (Coronet 10min sd color). How students tackled the problem of fire losses in their community.

CHAPTER 10—POLITICAL PARTIES

You, the People (TFC 20min sd). Shows the operations of a corrupt political machine.

Political Parties (Coronet 10min sd). Depicts organization and functioning of political parties.

People's Convention (Union 15min sd). Story of the founding of the Progressive Party at Philadelphia.

CHAPTER 11—SUFFRAGE, NOMINATIONS, AND ELECTIONS

Hell Bent for Election (Brandon 20min sd). Animated cartoon political propaganda for the reelection of Franklin D. Roosevelt in 1944.

Tuesday in November (UWF 20min sd). Explains election process and significance of secret ballot.

A President Is Elected (NYTimes FS). The story of the 1948 election.

The Old Way and the New (Film Classic 15min si). A campaign film, made in 1916, in support of Woodrow Wilson for President.

CHAPTERS 12-13—CONGRESS

Nation's Capital (MOT 11min sd). Portrays the various branches of government, the city, and the buildings.

The Congress (MOT 13min sd). Shows the functions of the two houses of Congress.

Inside the Capitol (TFC 11min sd). Shows various parts of the capitol with commentary pertaining to its historical background.

Washington—Shrine of American Patriotism (B&O 30min sd). A sight-seeing tour of the nation's capital.

How a Bill Becomes a Law (Pictorial 20min sd). Simple explanation of how a law is made, where it originates, and procedures it must go through.

CHAPTERS 14-15—THE PRESIDENT

Inside the White House (TFC 11min sd). Gives an intimate view of the White House, executive offices, cabinet members, etc.

The White House (MOT 15min sd). The house and its traditions.

Mr. President (Official 10min sd). Highlights from careers of presidents from McKinley to Franklin D. Roosevelt.

Great American Presidents (Handy FS). Series of four strips on Washington, Jefferson, Jackson, and Lincoln.

Johnson and Reconstruction (TFC 33min sd). An abridged version of the feature film *Tennessee Johnson*, including impeachment trial.

Roosevelt Story (Brandon 80min sd). A "film biography" of the life and times of Franklin D. Roosevelt. Covers over 40 years of American history.

The Presidency (MOT 10min sd). Traces present position of presidency from Constitutional beginning of office through development of implied powers to status of presidency today.

Franklin D. Roosevelt (Official 11min sd). His wartime activities, at training camps and conferences abroad, UNRRA speech, fourth inaugural address, and death.

Teddy the Rough Rider (TFC 20min sd). Theodore Roosevelt, 1898–1914, covering Spanish-American War, New York governorship, vice-presidency, and presidency.

Lincoln in the White House (TFC 20min sd). Covers his life and events from inauguration to Gettysburg address.

The Perfect Tribute (TFC 20min sd). President Lincoln at Gettysburg and subsequent episode.

Old Hickory (TFC 20min sd). Biography of Andrew Jackson, including his years as President.

CHAPTER 16—FEDERAL COURTS AND LAW ENFORCEMENT

The Supreme Court (Coronet 10min sd). Depicts function and operation of Supreme Court.

Basic Court Procedures (Coronet 15min sd). Points out function of courts and how our laws operate. The place of a judicial system in a democracy.

The Supreme Court (MOT 10min sd). How the court works, progress of a case to and through the court.

CHAPTER 18—FEDERAL POWERS: INTERSTATE COMMERCE

Along Our Shores (USCoastGd 15min sd). Depicts various activities and functions of United States Coast Guard.

CHAPTER 20—FEDERAL POWERS: ADMIRALTY, POSTAL, AND OTHERS

Federal Taxation (Coronet 10min sd). Documents entire United States Federal system of taxation.

CHAPTER 22—THE CIVIL SERVICE

Politics and Civil Service (MOT 6min sd). Spoils system in the United States and efforts to eliminate patronage.

Merit System Advancing (NYCCSC 28min sd). Kinds of examinations, types of jobs, and methods of promotion.

CHAPTER 23—PUBLIC FINANCE

The Mint (TFC 11min sd). The inside story of the newest United States mint at San Francisco.

Federal Taxation (Nu-Art 10min sd). National revenues.

Uncle Sam's Budget (LeagueWVs FS). Relation of federal budget to a stable economy.

The U. S. Customs Safeguards Our Foreign Trade (Firth 15min sd color).

CHAPTERS 24-25—FOREIGN RELATIONS

Monroe Doctrine (TFC 20min sd). Shows the circumstances that surrounded announcement of the policy.

Americans All (Castle 20min sd). Shows the interdependence of peoples in the Western Hemisphere.

Expanding World Relationships (Castle 11min sd color). Shows development of economic and social interdependence from Jefferson's time to present, emphasizing need for nations to work out ways of settling their differences peacefully.

Watchtower over Tomorrow (TFC 10min sd). Discussion film; shows need for international organization to avoid future wars; Dumbarton Oaks and San Francisco conferences.

Pattern for Peace—Charter of the United Nations (BIS 15min sd). Depicts structure and purposes of United Nations.

People's Charter (FON 17min sd). Shows how and why idea of United Nations was born and how it was organized.

Now the Peace (Brandon 20min sd). Clarifies basic aspects of the organization and program of the United Nations. Contrasts the League of Nations with United Nations.

Defense of the Peace (UnFlmDiv 12min sd). Describes over-all organization and functions of the various branches of the United Nations.

Men of Good Will (UnFlmDiv 10min sd). Story of "international civil servants" working at United Nations Headquarters and how they work together in international cooperation for peace.

We, the People of the United Nations (YA 11min sd). Shows the purposes and functions of the United Nations.

Uncle Sam, the Good Neighbor (MOT 20min sd). Portrays the roles of Department of State and duties of Foreign Service personnel.

We, the Peoples, Unit 1, The Needs and Purposes of the Charter (YA 40 frames FS).

We, the Peoples, Unit 2, The Charter's Organization (YA 40 frames FS).

United Nations Charter (FilmPub FS). Explains provisions of the Charter.

Searchlight on the Nations (Nu-Art 20min sd). How the United Nations is working to break down barriers to understanding between peoples.

Where Will You Hide? (TFC 20min sd color). If a third world war comes.

UN Report (UnFlmDiv FS). A review of four years of United Nations history.

The Marshall Plan (NYTimes FS). The ECA idea in action.

Foreign Trade (FilmPub FS). Shows nature, extent, and importance of foreign trade in modern society.

Round Trip (IFB 20min sd). Relationship of world trade to American life.

CHAPTER 26—TERRITORIES AND THE DISTRICT OF COLUMBIA

Territorial Possessions of the United States (IntGeog 22min sd). Story of American expansion with photographs of territorial possessions.

Our Louisiana Purchase (Post 20min sd). Depicts the background and purchase of this territory from France.

Alaska—Reservoir of Resources (EBF 11min sd). Describes the territory, its products, and people.

Alaska—A Modern Frontier (Coronet 10min sd). Our northern territory and potential state.

People of Hawaii (EBF 11min sd). Describes setting of the islands, their native people, and economy.

Democracy at Work in Puerto Rico (USDA 20min sd). The people of Puerto Rico, their farms, crafts, and home industries.

The Philippine Republic (MOT 16min sd). Reviews past and current history of Philippine Islands and presents present problems.

Panama—Crossroads of the Western World (Coronet 10min sd). Presents summary and appraisal of influences determining culture and economy.

Washington, D.C. (TFC 11min sd). Describes the seat of government.

Puerto Rico and Possessions of United States (StillFilm 50 frames FS).

Guam (StillFilm 50 frames FS).

CHAPTER 27—NATIONAL DEFENSE AND WAR MEASURES

United States Military Academy—West Point (TFC 11min sd). Shows life and activities at the academy.

West Point (RKORadio 17min sd). Story of United States Military Academy.

This Is Worth Working For (VA 20min sd). Gives comprehensive picture of Veterans' Administration.

Annapolis (RKORadio 16min sd). Story of United States Naval Academy.

Coast Guard Academy (USCG 20min sd). Shows student life at the New London, Connecticut, academy.

Serving the Merchant Marine (USCG 30min sd). Shows the wide range of duties performed by the Coast Guard.

The United States Navy (StillFilm 50 frames FS).

The Atomic Bomb (Visual Sciences 60 frames FS).

Atomic Energy—Problems of International Control (UnFlmDiv FS). The formation of the United Nations Atomic Energy Commission; its proposals.

Air Power Is Peace Power (Eastern Air 30min sd color). Presents progress of aviation, showing Captain Rickenbacker asking for powerful air forces to repel aggressor nations.

Air Power (USAirForce 18min sd). Shows tactical role Air Force played during First World War and its development to important strategic force in Second World War.

CHAPTERS 29-30—GOVERNMENT AND BUSINESS

Black Marketing (Castle 11min sd). A case history in the problem of price administration.

Bob Marshall Comes Home (Castle 22min sd). Story of Rural Electrification Administration activities.

Two Way Street (U.S.Rubber 13min sd). Government experts discuss many aspects of world trade.

Great Swindle (Union 35min sd). Presents labor's view of causes of inflation and high prices resulting from removal of controls after war.

Development of Transportation (EBF 12min sd). Transportation in the United States during the last 150 years.

Machine, Master or Slave (NYU 14min sd). Problems of management in approach to human and financial factors in technological progress.

Rural Electrification (ACE 44 frames FS). Shows importance of electric power to rural district.

CHAPTER 31—FEDERAL ENTERPRISES

Library of Congress (Castle 11min sd). Describes organization and operation of Library of Congress.

Your Postal Service (MOT 18min sd). Shows inner workings of United States Post Office.

TVA (TVA 20min sd). Presents work and accomplishments of this government project.

Miracle of Hydro (TFC 11min sd). A descriptive presentation of the significance of the Bonneville and Grand Coulee Dams.

Guardians of Our Nation's Health (Frith 15min sd color). Quarantine and inspection at ports of entry.

CHAPTERS 32-33—LABOR, WELFARE, PUBLIC WORKS, AND HOUSING

People's Program (Pictures 23min sd). Story of labor's program on cost of living, housing, Taft-Hartley law, civil liberties, and independent political action.

Within the Gates (USDL 20min sd). Shows development of the factory system; makes an appeal for improved working conditions, especially for women workers.

What's in a Dress? (USDL 11min sd). Portrays labor problems in the dress industry.

Men and Dust (Brandon 16min sd). Depicts hazards of employment in a lead mine and need for regulation of working conditions.

Millions of Us (Brandon 20min sd). Portrays problems of unemployment and role of unions.

Roads and Erosion (USSCS 20min sd). Shows highways and typical erosion problems.

Place to Live (Brandon 20min sd). Depicts housing conditions in large cities using Philadelphia as an example.

No Place Like Home (RKORadio 16min sd). Depicts the current housing problem and the many factors involved in it.

New Towns for Old (BIS 11min sd). An English film demonstrating need of community planning in rebuilding towns.

The City (MMA 30min sd). Shows need for city planning and housing. Contrasts slums with modern housing developments.

Housing in Our Times (FPHA 20min sd). Shows operation of the housing authority and current housing activities.

City Within a City (ACE 41 frames FS). A modern housing project.

Clearing the Slums (ACE 43 frames FS). Slum areas and the public housing projects that have replaced them.

Capital Story (Castle 20min sd). Depicts functions and activities of Public Health Service.

Industry's Disinherited (Union 20min sd). Deals with problems of workers' pensions and old age benefits.

Life with Grandpa (MOT 17min sd). Discusses physical and economic problems of old age and suggests various remedies.

Old Age and Family Security (SSB 11min sd). Gives a description of federal old-age and survivors insurance and its operation.

Social Security (TFC 11min sd). Interprets operation of Social Security Act from the time of its passage through its various steps to the final payment of beneficiaries.

The Work of the United States Public Health Service (Bray 70min sd). Story of the Service from simple beginnings in 1798, its duties, and accomplishments.

CHAPTERS 34-35—AGRICULTURE AND CONSERVATION

The Land (MMA 40min sd). Tells the story of erosion, which in a century has destroyed one-seventh of our land.

Decision for Bill (Castle 25min sd). Depicts activities of United States Department of Agriculture.

The Plow That Broke the Plains (MMA 30min sd). Depicts the mishandling of the land drained by the Mississippi, the causes and effects of erosion.

The River (TVA 30min sd). A dramatization of the Mississippi River down to recent floods and erosion disasters.

Heritage We Guard (USSCS 30min sd). Traces early exploitation of land and wild life with resulting denudation, erosion, and dust storms.

Conservation of Natural Resources (EBF 12min sd). Shows steps being taken to conserve water power, forests, and farm lands, effects of wind and water erosion and unwise farming, and efforts to check these abuses.

Seeds of Destruction (EBF 10min sd). The urgency and need for conservation.

Reclamation of the Arid West (BR 11min sd). Shows the reclamation of deserts resulting from the building of such dams as Boulder and Grand Coulee.

America the Beautiful (USTreas. 20min sd color). Portrays the land, people, and resources of America, including vistas of the national parks.

Water Power (EBF 14min sd). Development of water power in United States from early days to modern projects of Niagara, Boulder, and TVA.

Tree of Life (Castle 19min sd). Depicts story of our use of forest resources, replanting, and fire protection.

The South Grows Green (USSCS 20min sd). Portrays the results of changing from one crop system to diversified farming.

Sign of Dependable Credit (USDA 20min sd). Shows how cooperative credit system meets farmers' needs.

Here Is Tomorrow (Coöp League 27min sd). The story of cooperatives.

Ten Years of Coöp Credit (Castle 20min sd). Describes farm credit system.

Kids Must Eat (Castle 15min sd). Discusses Federal school lunch program.

Harnessing Rivers (ACE 39 frames FS). Control of a large river system through dams with resultant flood control, electric power, and soil conservation.

Soil Conservation (ACE 51 frames FS). Major factors in conservation program; flood and erosion control, tree planting, crop rotation, contour plowing, etc.

Forests of the United States (ACE 48 frames FS). The story of forests and the use of their products.

National Parks of the United States (ACE 46 frames FS). Scenes from Mt. Rainier, Mt. McKinley, Glacier, Yellowstone, Great Smoky, and International Peace Parks.

Indians of the Southwest (ACE 47 frames FS). A general picture of Indian tribes from time of Spaniards to present.

Forest Conservation (EBF 11 min sd color). Points out how the forests have been depleted, shows what is and must be done to save them.

SOURCES OF FILMS LISTED ABOVE

ACE—American Council on Education, 744 Jackson Place, Washington, D.C.

AFFilms—A. F. Films, Inc., Room 1001, 1600 Broadway, New York 19.

Allied—Allied 16mm Distributors Corp., 1560 Broadway, New York 16.

Anti-D.L.—Anti-defamation League, 212 Fifth Ave., New York 10.

B&O—Baltimore & Ohio Railroad Company, Director of Public Relations, Baltimore, Maryland.

BIS—British Information Services, 30 Rockefeller Plaza, New York 20.

BR—Bureau of Reclamation, Department of the Interior, Washington, D.C.

Brandon—Brandon Films, Inc., 1700 Broadway, New York 19.

Bray—Bray Studios, Inc., 729 Seventh Ave., New York 19.

Castle—Castle Films Division United World Films, Inc., Russ Building, San Francisco 4, California.

Coöp League—Cooperative League, 167 W. 12 St., New York 11.

Coronet—Coronet Instructional Films, 65 E. South Water St., Chicago 1, Illinois.

Eastern Air—Eastern Airlines, 10 Rockefeller Plaza, New York 20.

Eastman—Eastman Kodak Company, Informational Films Division, 343 State St., Rochester 4, New York.

EBF—Encyclopaedia Britannica Films, Inc., 1150 Wilmette Ave., Wilmette, Illinois.

FPHA—Federal Public Housing Authority, Washington, D.C.

Film Classic—Film Classic Exchange, 1645 N. La Brea Ave., Hollywood 28, California.

FilmPub—Film Publishers, Inc., 25 Broad St., New York 4.
FON—Films of the Nations, Inc., 55 W. 45 St., New York 19.
FPI—Federal Prisons Industries, Department of Justice, Washington, D.C.
Frith—Frith Films, 840 Seward St., Hollywood 38, California.
Handy—Jam Handy Organization, 2821 E. Grand Blvd., Detroit 11, Michigan.
Howard—Howard University, Washington, D.C.
IFB—International Film Bureau, Suite 1500, 6 N. Michigan Ave., Chicago 2, Illinois.
IntGeog—International Geographic Pictures, 1776 Broadway, New York 19.
Knowledge—Knowledge Builders, 625 Madison Ave., New York 22.
LeagueWVs—League of Women Voters, 726 Jackson Pl., Washington 6, D.C.
MMA—Museum of Modern Art Film Library, 11 W. 53 St., New York 19.
MOT—March of Time Forum Films, 369 Lexington Ave., New York 17.
NCCJ—National Conference of Christians and Jews, 381 Fourth Ave., New York 16.
NEA—National Education Association, 1201 16 St. N.W., Washington 6, D.C.
Nu-Art—Nu-Art Films, Inc., 145 W. 45 St., New York 19.
NYCCSC—New York City Civil Service Commission, 299 Broadway, New York 7.
NYTimes—New York Times School Service Department, New York 18.
NYU—New York University Film Library, 26 Washington Pl., New York 3.
Official—Official Films, Inc., 25 W. 45 St., New York 19.
Pictorial—Pictorial Films, Inc., 625 Madison Ave., New York 22.
Pictures—Pictures, Ltd., 141 N. Orange Dr., Hollywood 36, California.
Post—Post Pictures Corp., 115 W. 45 St., New York 19.
Research Inst.—Research Institute of America, Inc., 292 Madison Ave., New York 17.
RKORadio—RKO Radio Pictures, Inc., 1270 Sixth Ave., New York 20.
SSB—Social Security Board, Washington, D.C.
Still Films—Still Films, Inc., 8443 Melrose Ave., Hollywood 46, California.
TFC—Teaching Film Custodians, Inc., 25 W. 43 St., New York 18.
TVA—Tennessee Valley Authority, Film Services, Knoxville, Tennessee.
UE—United Electrical, Radio, and Machine Workers of America, 11 E. 51 St., New York 22.
UnFlmDiv—United Nations, Film Division, Lake Success, New York.
Union—Union Films, 111 W. 88 St., New York 24.

USAirForce—United States Department of the Air Force, Directorate of Public Relations, Washington 25, D.C.
USCG—United States Coast Guard Headquarters, Chief, Public Information Division, Washington 25, D.C.
USCoastGd—See USCG.
USDA—United States Department of Agriculture, Motion Picture Service, Office of Information, Washington 25, D.C.
USDL—United States Department of Labor, Motion Picture Division, Washington, D.C.
U.S.Rubber—United States Rubber Co., Advertising Department, 1230 Sixth Ave., New York 20.
USTreas.—United States Treasury Department, United States Savings Bonds Division, Washington 25, D.C.
UWF—United World Films, Inc., 1445 Park Ave., New York 29.
VA—Veterans' Administration, Visual Aids Service, Office of Public Relations, Washington 25, D.C.
VaStDeptEd—Virginia State Department of Education, Film Production Service, Richmond 16, Virginia.
Visual Sciences—Visual Sciences, Suffern, New York.
YA—Young America Films, Inc., 18 E. 41 St., New York 17.

INDEX

F

J

K

L

T

U

V

W

Y